Law for Business

Law for Business

Bruce D. Fisher, J.D.
University of Tennessee

Marianne Moody Jennings, J.D.
Arizona State University

West Publishing Company
St. Paul New York Los Angeles San Francisco

A STUDENT STUDY GUIDE

A study guide has been developed to assist students in mastering the concepts presented in this text. It reinforces chapter material presenting it in a concise format with review questions. An examination copy is available to instructors by contacting West Publishing Company. Students can purchase the study guide from the local bookstore under the title *Study Guide to Accompany Law for Business* prepared by James Miles.

Copyediting: Editing, Design, and Production, Inc.
Composition: Parkwood Composition Service, Inc.

Printed in the United States of America

Library of Congress Cataloging in Publication Data

Fisher, Bruce D.
Law for business.

Includes index.
1. Commercial law—United States. I. Jennings, Marianne. II. Title.
KP889.F49 1986 346.73'07 85-20207
ISBN: 0-314-93178-3 347.3067

To our students

Contents

Chapter 9
Government Regulation: How Regulations Are Made 103

Chapter 10
Government Regulation: Enforcement and Adjudication of a Regulation 125

Chapter 11
Consumer Protection 133

Chapter 12
Environmental Law: Particular Federal Statutes 145

Chapter 31
Obligations and Performance 373

Chapter 32
Remedies Under Article II 385

PART FIVE
AGENCY AND EMPLOYMENT 395

Chapter 33
Creation of the Agency Relationship 397

Chapter 43

Management of Corporations 511

Chapter 44

Rights and Responsibilities of Shareholders 521

PART SEVEN
PROPERTY 531

Chapter 45
Personal Property 533

Chapter 46
Bailments 543

Chapter 47
Real Property Interests and Regulation 553

Chapter 48
Real Property Transfers 567

Chapter 49
Landlord-Tenant Relationships 579

Chapter 50
Wills, Estates, and Trusts 593

PART EIGHT
COMMERCIAL PAPER 607

Chapter 51
Commercial Paper: The Basic Concepts 609

Chapter 56
Introduction to Secured Credit Transactions 675

Chapter 57
Priorities of Creditors in Secured Credit Transactions 685

Chapter 58
Enforcement and Collection of Credit Transactions 697

Chapter 59
Bankruptcy 709

Chapter 60
Insurance 727

Table of Cases

Preface

The teaching of law to undergraduates is changing. In many schools there is a need for a "plain English" treatment of legal environment topics and an even more compressed treatment of traditional business law topics from a business person's point of view. *Law for Business* aims to fill these needs. In effect, this text is every person's guide to the legal system. *Law for Business* covers virtually all environmental and traditional law subjects; it aims to fill the needs of schools wanting a summary treatment of law. The need for business students to study some law as it relates to business is reflected in the American Assembly of Collegiate Schools of Business' (AACSB) accreditation standards which state that business students should be exposed to the legal environment of business.

The coverage of "environmental topics" (business and government) in *Law for Business* includes unique contemporary chapters on the regulation-making process and regulation enforcement, which tell how business people in both large and small firms can contribute to the regulation-making process.

The environmental approach stresses areas of *public law;* that is, law applicable to large social and economic problems—a macro approach to law. Examples of legal topics covered are legal ethics, administrative law (government regulation), antitrust law, employer-employee relations, consumer protection, and environmental law—areas currently of interest to business. At present, however, many existing business law texts do not address legal environment issues adequately; their focus is on traditional business law, with less attention to public law topics. This text covers both areas.

Law for Business has three main advantages over existing texts: *more contemporary coverage, newer cases,* and *stronger pedagogy.* The text addresses the legal issues which are important in today's business world. The cases in *Law for Business* are briefed cases (summary statements of recent significant or factually provocative cases) written in "plain English."

A major strength of *Law for Business* is its pedagogy. The book presents the material in an appealing format with many student learning aids:

1. Stories presenting scenarios with unanswered legal problems based on cases the students will encounter later in the chapter are found at the start of each chapter.
2. Technical and legal terms used in the text are placed in boldface type and are defined in the glossary.
3. Discussion questions based on actual cases are at the end of each chapter.
4. Subtle use of the SQ3R (study, question, read, recite, review) learning technique is part of the chapter structure: The introductory story giving the students an

idea of what they can expect later in the chapter, followed by the chapter containing answers to legal questions raised by the introductory story, concluded by discussion questions at the chapter's end that review the chapter.

5. A visual orientation for today's students; charts and diagrams illustrate principles.
6. Many examples of principles in the text.
7. A "plain English" conversational tone is used to enhance the student's understanding of the material; "legalese" is all but absent from the writing.

An instructor's manual complete with a test bank and transparency masters has been prepared to accompany the text. A student study guide is also available.

Acknowledgments

We wish to acknowledge the reviewers of this text who provided invaluable comments and suggestions.

John Balek
Morton College

Francis Ballard
Florida Junior College

Stanley Berkowitz
Northeastern University

Jones Davis
Florida Junior College

Patricia DeFrain
Glendale College

James Dolan
Valencia Community College

Frank Hood
Mississippi College

James Miles
Anoka Ramsey College

Douglas Pettis
Community College of Rhode Island

Felicenne Ramey
California State University-Sacramento

Susan Schoettler
Central Piedmont Community College

John Sherry
Cornell University

David Steenstra
Davenport College

Charles R. B. Stowe
Sam Houston State University

Kim Tyler
Shasta College

We would like to thank the following people for their help and support: Kenneth Zeigler, Phyllis Mueller, Gary Woodruff, Jane Gregg, Kristi Shuey, Gwyn Williams, Brian House, Brenda Henderson, Cherri Miller, Mr. Terry Jennings, Mr. & Mrs. James L. Moody, and Sarah.

Bruce D. Fisher
Marianne Moody Jennings

Note to Students

This book is unique. This is a book conceived, written, and designed for students. The language is not "legalese"; it is "plain English." Although the language is simple, the purpose of having you understand the law and how it will affect you personally and in your business career is still accomplished. This book will reduce the law to realistic and applicable terms for you. It was designed for business people; it is practical and helpful.

Several features in the text can help you learn the material more easily:

Chapter Previews

At the beginning of each chapter, you will find a list of the concepts and ideas the chapter will cover. You can look over this list before you read the chapter to help alert you to key ideas as you read, and you can use the list after you have read the chapter to help you review what you've already read.

Chapter Headings and Subheadings

All of the chapters are broken down into small parts through the use of headings and subheadings. Each page has at least one heading or subheading to keep legal concepts organized. In fact, each chapter can be outlined simply by using the headings and subheadings as divisions in the outline.

Cases

There are briefed cases (summary statements of cases) in all chapters that illustrate principles of law discussed in the text. The cases are colorful to help you remember the application of the law. A "Legal Tip" follows each case. These Legal Tips give you practical, legal advice based on what the parties in the case did wrong, and illustrates how you could avoid these mistakes.

Charts and Diagrams

Throughout the book there are charts and diagrams to help you visualize difficult concepts. Thinking of the chart will help you remember the material and more easily apply it to chapter problems and the "real life" problems you encounter later in your careers and personal lives.

Key Terms

At the end of each chapter is a list of key terms. These terms are bold-faced in the chapter and defined in the glossary. Studying the key terms in the lists at the end of the chapter will help you organize what you should learn in each chapter.

Chapter Problems

Each chapter has 10 problems to help you review the material covered. Those problems noted with an asterisk (*) in the margin are problems that are not covered directly in the text. These are thought problems that require you to do some extra thinking to reach a conclusion. These problems help show you that the law sometimes has new questions and, as yet, no answers.

Our hope is that we have made not only enjoyable and colorful reading, but have left you with an impression of the importance of understanding business law in order to maximize your business success.

Law for Business

Part One

Introduction to Law

> *"Jurisprudence is the principal and . . . perfect branch of ethics."*
>
> Blackstone

Chapter 1

Law and Legal Ethics

CHAPTER PREVIEW

- Definition of law
- Values (ethics) law promotes
- Reasons for studying law
- Classifications of law
- Overview of law
- Law cases

George Geary stared out the window wondering if justice still existed. Until a few minutes ago, he had been a salesman with United States Steel Corporation but had just been fired. What troubled him was the reason for his dismissal: He had pointed out a probable defect in one of the company's products that could have endangered lives and property. He had told his immediate supervisor about the problem, but nothing had happened. Knowing the seriousness of the problem and the fact that the company might be sued for millions of dollars when it injured purchasers, George went over his boss's head to a company vice president. A while later, the company withdrew the product from the market. Then George was fired. George decided to sue his employer for wrongful dismissal. The case went all the way to the Pennsylvania Supreme Court. What is the result?

On July 25, 1884, three seamen and a young boy drifted in a small, open boat. They had been floating for twenty days after their yacht had been wrecked in an ocean storm. They were about 1000 miles off southern Africa. They had no fresh water. They had not eaten for 8 days, and there were no reasonable signs of relief. For several days, two of the seamen tried to convince the third to kill and eat the boy. Two of the 3 seamen killed the boy, ate his flesh, survived four more days when they were rescued. Then the two seamen who killed the boy were charged with murder. They defended themselves on the grounds of necessity. Did they win?

The preceding stories trouble us because they contain many conflicting ideas about law. That is, we feel the cases could have been decided either way. Both sides to the case have strong arguments. Which side is right? Which one is better?

Such questions are part of an area of study called *jurisprudence.* **Jurisprudence** tries to define law. Putting it another way, jurisprudence tries to establish what values or moral principles (ethics) law contains.

This chapter first defines law and then examines five ethics, or values, which the law promotes. The chapter then looks at reasons for studying law, some legal classifications, and an overview of law. Finally, we conclude by seeing what law cases are.

WHAT IS LAW?

When most people use the word ***law,*** they are referring to "positive law." Basically, positive law is a rule made by a government with some sort of punishment or sanction if someone breaks it.

Examples of Positive Law

Statutes (laws passed by legislatures), common law (law that judges make), and ordinances (laws that city councils enact) are all positive laws because they are government-made rules.

What Is Not Positive Law

Some things are called *law* that really are not law. Law as we will discuss it here is positive law. For example, the "law" of gravity is not law but a scientific principle. The "law" of supply and demand is not law but an economic truth. An IBM company rule requiring salespeople to wear white shirts is not positive law since IBM is not a governmental rulemaker.

LEGAL ETHICS

Ethics are values or moral principles. **Positive law** (or *law* as we commonly call it) promotes many ethics. This section examines the ethics of justice, stability, freedom, decency, and utility.

Freedom

Laws appear to rob us of freedom because they stop us from doing what we might want. However, laws can actually *give* people freedom.

If we had no law, we would have complete freedom in theory but not in practice. For example, people could be in danger whenever they went outside their homes since murder, assault, and battery would be legal! People might be afraid to cross the street since there would be no speed limits or stop lights. Business might come to a halt because no one would want to make contracts that could be broken without having to pay damages. Law gives people practical freedom by making it generally safe to go outside and possibly profitable to enter contracts.

Justice

One way to define justice is to use the word *fairness.* The idea that positive law should be fair is called **natural law.**

Most positive laws try to promote justice. An example would be federal laws providing loans so students can attend college. Such laws give many lower-income students a chance to realize their ambitions. Giving lower-income people opportunities otherwise unavailable to them is fair.

The justice ethic appeals to us since we generally support the concept of what is "right." But one problem of justice is that the concept has a different meaning for each of us. This is called the "**multiple conscience problem.**" For example, we might all agree that murder is wrong but disagree about what punishment is "right."

The *Ott v. Midland-Ross Corporation* case illustrates the justice ethic. The case mentions a "statute of limitations," which is a law requiring a person to sue another within a certain time after the harm occurs. If this requirement is not met, the person loses the case. Now read *Ott v. Midland-Ross* for an example of the justice ethic.

OTT v. MIDLAND-ROSS CORPORATION

U.S. Court of Appeals (6th Cir.).
523 F.2d 1367 (1975).

FACTS Ott was a sixty-year-old employee dismissed on January 4, 1971. He filed a private suit and a complaint with the Equal Employment Opportunity Commission (EEOC), alleging a violation of the Age Discrimination in Employment Act. The EEOC notified Ott that it had reached a settlement in the case, which required Midland-Ross (MR) to rehire Ott.

While Ott awaited a job assignment, MR talked him out of his private lawsuit. In return, MR agreed to make Ott a consultant for ten days each month. Ott would have made more money under this arrangement than as an employee. He agreed to it, took early retirement, and let the statute of limitations expire on his private lawsuit. Then MR refused to make him a consultant as it had promised. Ott sued MR for violating the Age Discrimination in Employment Act. MR defended on grounds that the statute of limitations had expired.

ISSUE Could Ott recover even though the statute of limitations had expired?

DECISION The United States Court of Appeals decided that the statute of limitations had expired but refused to let MR use it as a defense. The court relied on the estoppel idea, which stops a person from taking advantage of its own wrong (here, misleading Ott into foregoing his suit in promise of a job and then breaking the promise).

Utility

Utility (and the **utilitarian ethic**) means promoting the greatest good for the greatest number of people. In other words, being economical increases utility. The rule forbidding people from trying a lawsuit more than once (called *res judicata*) helps achieve economy in running the court system. Lawsuits would be much more expensive if we could retry them because we thought of better legal arguments, found a better lawyer, or got a more sympathetic judge and jury. The antitrust laws also promote utility by forbidding price-fixing, monopolizing, and other restraints of trade that distort market values.

Stability

Stability refers to a **custom,** or any longstanding conduct that is performed year after year. People are more comfortable and secure doing what they have always done.

Positive law follows custom. Custom is called the "historic theory of law." There are many examples of the way custom influences and stabilizes the law. Consider wills, the documents used to transfer property when people die. Wills take effect only when a person dies. By then the testator[1] is no longer with us. In effect, a dead person is telling the living what to do with such resources as money and

[1]A "testator" (or "testatrix" if a woman) is a person who makes a will.

other property left by the dead person. Transferring property by will is a long-standing custom that is recognized by positive law.

Owning private property (the idea that one person can own a house or car) is another long-standing custom recognized by positive law. The definition of private property occasionally changes. At one time, for example, slaves were property that could be bought and sold at slave exchanges; perhaps one day planets will be considered property that can be owned.

Contracts are a third example of how the legal ethic of custom can affect positive law. Contracts have long been enforceable in the United States. Contracts are agreements voluntarily entered into between private persons or groups and enforceable in court. A graduating student who agrees to work for IBM for $20,000 per year has made a contract. A person can change his or her life by entering a contract. (For example, some important questions are: Which job offer should one accept? Should one buy a house or raw land that might have oil under it?) An example of a longstanding custom that has found its way into positive law is that an employer may fire an employee any time for any reason in an "at-will" employment relationship. The *Geary v. U.S. Steel Corporation* case discusses this issue.

GEARY v. U.S. STEEL CORPORATION

Supreme Court of Pennsylvania.
319 A.2d 174 (1974).

FACTS George B. Geary, was continuously employed by United States Steel Corporation (hereinafter "company"), from 1953 until July 13, 1967, when he was dismissed from his position. Geary's duties involved the sale of tubular products to the oil and gas industry. Geary alleges that he believed a tubular casing designed for use under high pressure had not been adequately tested and constituted a serious danger to anyone who used it. He voiced his concerns to his superiors and was ordered to "follow directions." He continued to express his reservations, taking his case to a vice president in charge of selling the product. As a result of Geary's efforts, the product was reevaluated and withdrawn from the market. At all times he performed his duties to the best of his ability and always acted with the best interests of the company and the general public in mind. Because of these events he was summarily discharged without notice. Geary asserts that the company's conduct in so acting was "wrongful, malicious and abusive," resulting in injury to his reputation in the industry, mental anguish, and direct financial harm, for which he seeks damages . . . .

ISSUE Did the employer have the right to dismiss Geary even though he pointed out a defect in a company product.

DECISION The Supreme Court of Pennsylvania said that Geary was not wrongfully dismissed by his employer. Geary recovered nothing from his former employer.

Up to the time of this case, no court in Pennsylvania has ever recognized a non-statutory cause of action for an employer's termination of an at-will employee.

The praiseworthiness of Geary's motives does not eliminate the company's legitimate interest in preserving its normal operational procedures from disruption.

Decency

Decency, or civilized actions, influence positive law. The psychoanalyst Sigmund Freud said that law shows the ethic of decency and frustrates, or tries to stop, our bad instincts.

Law helps us to act decently by telling us what is acceptable behavior. For example, we may not misrepresent the mileage on our car when we sell it, since this dishonesty could involve fraud. We may not cheat our business partner, since cheating violates our fiduciary duty, or duty of loyalty. We may not dump untreated chemicals into a stream, because this would violate the Clean Water Act. In addition, we may not drive our car above the speed limit, nor may we fail to turn over part of our income to the government as taxes, or discriminate in employment based on age for persons forty to seventy years of age. These and other laws can frustrate our base instincts. However, laws do not totally restrict us, since humans do enjoy some activities that do not arise from their base instincts (for example, working, studying, and helping others).

The cannibalism case of *Regina v. Dudley and Stephens* illustrates the civilization ethic.

REGINA v. DUDLEY AND STEPHENS
L.R., Q.B. 61 (1884).

FACTS On July 25, 1884, three seamen and a young boy drifted in a small boat in the ocean. They were 1000 miles off the African coast. They had no fresh water and had not eaten for eight days. There were no signs that they would be rescued. They had been floating for twenty days after their yacht had been wrecked in a storm. The three men argued quietly among themselves about killing one of them for food so the others would be saved. The three knew they meant the boy would be the one killed. They said nothing to the boy. On the nineteenth day, two of the three men wanted to draw lots to decide who would die so the others could eat. One man refused to draw. On the twentieth day, one man with one other's consent (the third man disagreed) went to the boy, told him what was going to happen, put a knife to the boy's throat, and killed him. The boy did not agree to be murdered. All three men ate the boy and survived four more days. Then they were rescued.

The two men agreeing to kill the boy were later tried in England for murder. They raised the defense of necessity.

ISSUE Is the deliberate killing of an unoffending and unresisting boy murder if the killing is necessary to permit others to survive?

DECISION The English court did not allow necessity as a defense. The court said that morality and law are not always the same. But law and morality should be the same as often as possible. Separating law from morality would be a mistake; and this separation would occur if necessity were a defense to murder.

Dudley and Stephens were convicted of murder. The death sentence was commuted to six months' imprisonment.

REASONS FOR STUDYING LAW

Law governs almost everything we do. Today there are more laws in effect in the United States than at any time in our history. Over 210 one-inch thick (or thicker) books contain the United States statutes. There are over 180 books containing federal regulations. There are over 1000 books containing federal cases (judge-made law). But that is not all. Every state has a constitution, statutes, case law, and regulations; every city and town has ordinances, or laws. There are literally thousands and thousands of laws. Some of these rules tell us if children can make contracts, if an oral lease is valid, if our boss can fire us even if we are doing a good job, and if we can get an engagement ring back if the wedding is called off.

Know and Obey

We should study law so we will know the rules. No one wants to pay a fine or go to prison for committing a crime. It is important to know what the rules are. Did you know that it is illegal to dump cow manure or anything into a stream without a permit? Who would think a seemingly innocent act could be a crime? But it is!

Preventive Law[2]

Citizens generally, and businesspeople in particular, want to keep down the cost and paperwork of regulation. They can do this by taking part in making laws and regulations. **Preventive law** points out weaknesses and paperwork burdens in proposed laws *before* they are formalized.

Legal Careers

Many people who went on to become lawyers and judges did in fact first study law *before* they attended law school. Some knowledge of law is useful for court personnel (clerks, reporters, and stenographers). The demand for paralegals, who investigate, interview, and do basic research, is presently increasing.

This book is one way to "get your feet wet," in the area of legal study. However, do not decide that you are or are not suited for law by this exposure. Nonetheless, this book will provide you with information about law and help you to determine your interest in the subject.

FORMS OF LAW

Law comes in many forms. It can be in constitutions, statutes, administrative regulations, or municipal ordinances, to name some of its most common forms. The diagram in Figure 1-1 indicates some forms that law assumes.

Constitutions

A **constitution** is the skeleton for a legal system that sets out the form and basic principles by which the government will operate. A constitution covers matters such as the number of branches of government and the powers given each. Since constitutions are enduring statements of principle, they are designed so that changing them is difficult.

Statutes

Statutes are enactments by national and state legislatures. Laws passed by *city* governments are referred to as **ordinances,** not as statutes, even though they represent efforts by city councils, which are legislative bodies. States and the national government are separate sovereigns according to the dual-sovereignty notion that is the basis for federalism. However, cities, being mere creations of the state in which they are located, are not on the same level politically with either national or state governments.

CLASSIFICATIONS OF LAW

Law can be classified in a number of ways. Two of the main classifications are substantive-procedural and civil-criminal.

Substantive and Procedural Law

Substantive law refers to rules that govern people's relations with one another in their daily lives. Some examples are a rule of contract law that an acceptance takes effect when sent, the rule of environmental law that a person must have an NPDES[3] permit to discharge into United States waters, and the consumer law rule that lets homeowners escape contracts with door-to-door salespersons three days after the contract is made. Such rules determine what people can do in society.

[2]The authors acknowledge Toby Montgomery, Esquire, of Stanford, California, for suggesting this term.

[3]National Pollutant Discharge Elimination System

Figure 1-1 **Diagram of the Forms of Law**

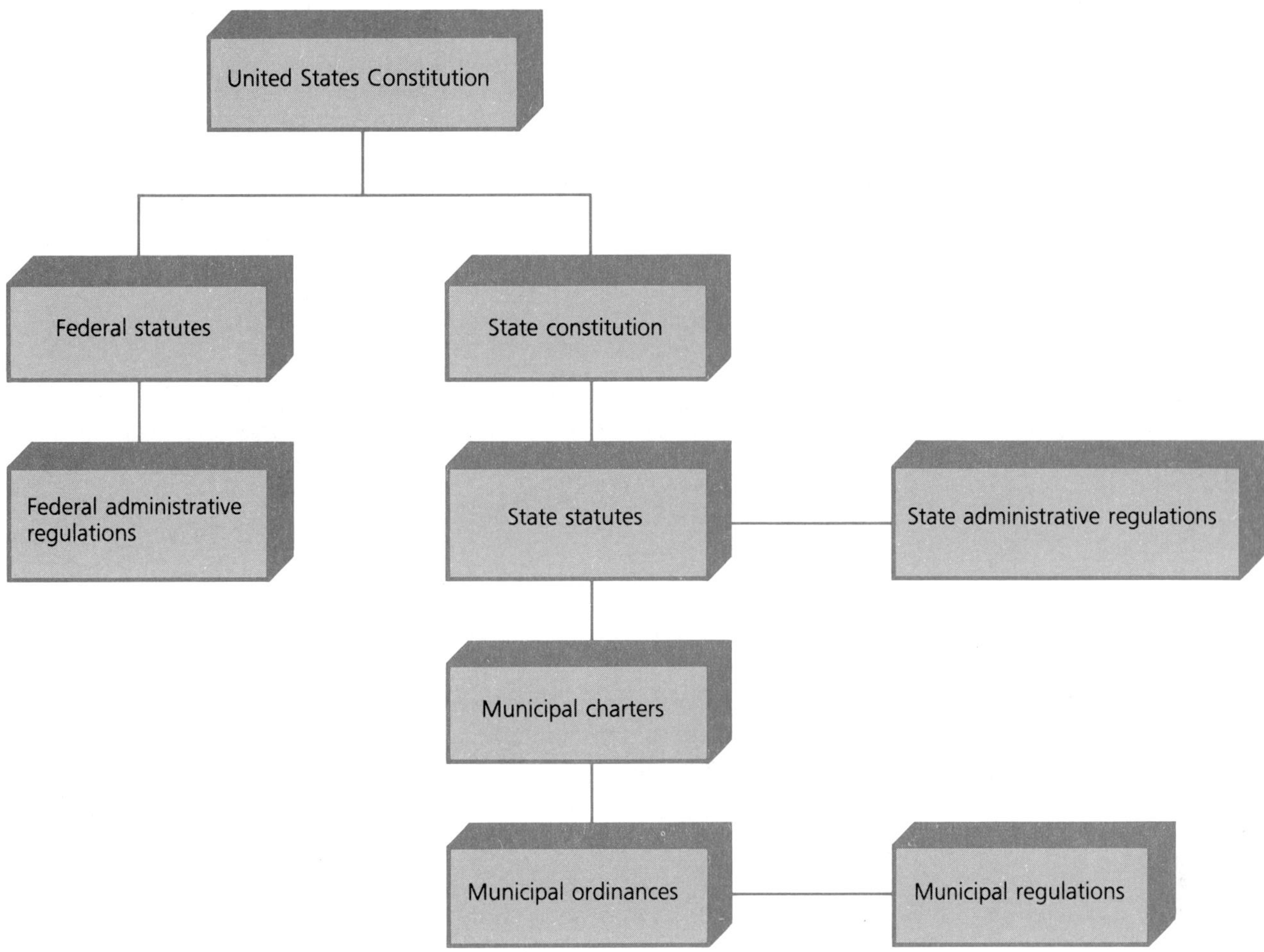

Contrast substantive law with **procedural law.** Procedural laws are rules of legal administration. Statutes of limitations, for instance, are usually procedural laws that tell us we must file suit against someone who harms us within a specified time period. The rule setting the number of persons on a jury is procedural, because it deals with an administrative matter. Unlike substantive law, it does not tell us how to act in our everyday lives.

Civil and Criminal Law

Law can be divided into two parts: civil and criminal law. Figures 1-2 and 1-3 show civil and criminal law with some subparts of each type. **Civil law** refers to several things. Here, the term principally means rules determining rights and duties between and among *private* individuals. **Criminal law** refers to rules designed to protect and vindicate *society's* interest with respect to individuals. For example, in a murder, even though only one member of society is killed, society is deemed to be harmed, or at least threatened; such outrageous, anti-social conduct threatens the silent bond of restraint distinguishing civilization from the jungle.

Differences Between Civil and Criminal Law

Several differences exist between civil and criminal law. First, each has a different *objective.* Civil law is generally compensatory, whereas criminal law is generally punitive. For example, when one person sues another for breaking a contract, the

Figure 1-2 **Traditional Business Law**

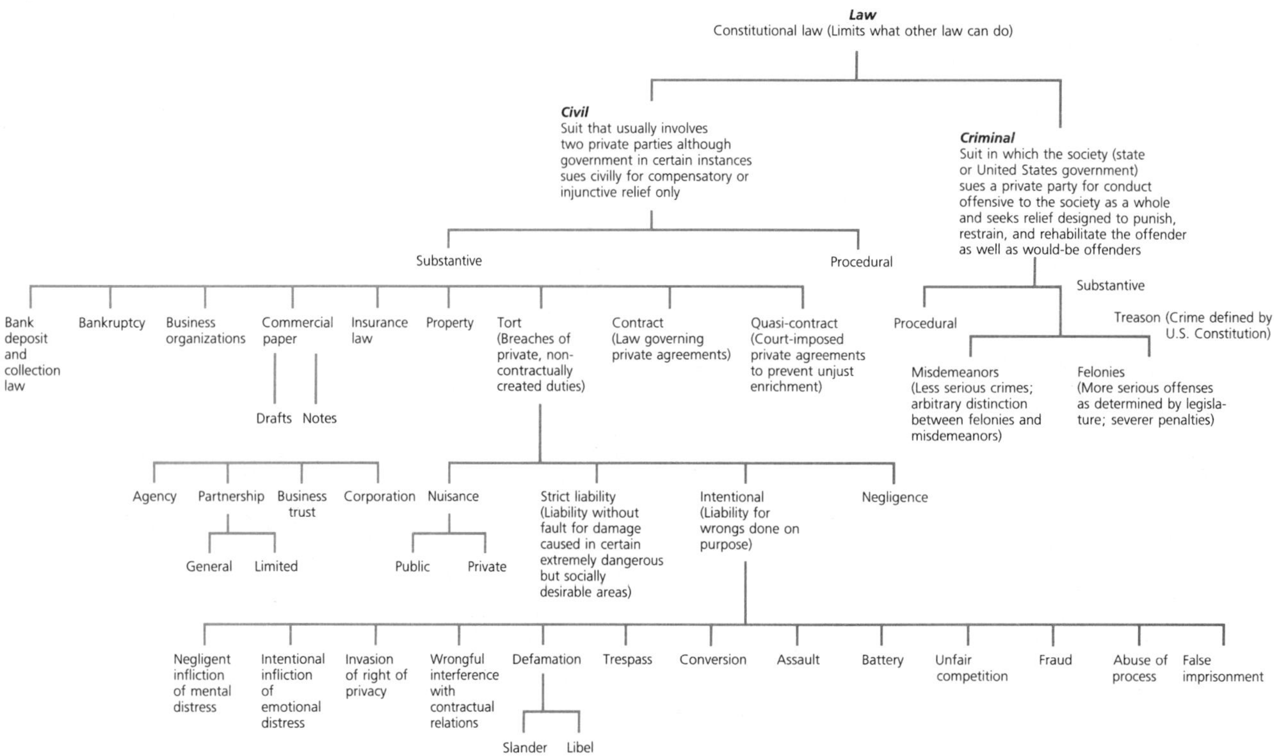

Note: The above definitions do not purport to be complete but are merely indications of the nature of the various areas of the law.

party suing (or the plaintiff) hopes to recover damages that he or she has sustained as a result of the other person's (or the defendant's) breach of contract. Even though the damage recovery is taken from the defendant and turned over to the plaintiff, this compensation is not considered punishment of the defendant. After all, the reasoning goes, all the defendant is doing is paying for harm that he or she caused.

Now we turn our attention briefly to the criminal law's objectives. One of the most frequently mentioned is punishment of those who break society's criminal laws, sometimes referred to as retribution, which occurs by imprisonment, fines, or a combination of the two.

The punitive aspect of criminal law is but one of four ends of that branch of the law. Others frequently mentioned include restraint, deterrence, and rehabilitation. Restraint occurs when people are convicted and imprisoned so that they cannot repeat, at least not immediately, the sort of antisocial activity that landed them in prison. Deterrence occurs when one person's punishment by the criminal law system serves to inhibit or stop other would-be criminals from committing crimes. This justification is commonly given for the death penalty. The rehabilitative objective of criminal law is usually more a hope than a reality. Too often it is "achieved" by sending a person to prison for several years, where after being counseled by various prison officials, he or she emerges several years later as a hardened criminal.

Aside from the objectives, other differences exist between civil and criminal law. The plaintiff in criminal cases is always a government. The plaintiff in a civil

Figure 1-3 Legal Environment of Business

- ***Law*** — Constitutional law (Limits what other law can do)
  - ***Civil*** — Suit that usually involves two private parties although government in certain instances sues civilly for compensatory or injunctive relief only
    - Substantive
      - Antitrust
        - Sherman Act
        - Clayton Act
        - Robinson-Patman Act
        - Federal Trade Commission Act
      - Business organizations (formation)
        - Sole proprietorship
        - Partnership
          - General
          - Limited
        - Business trust
        - Corporation
      - Consumer law
        - Common law
        - Statutes
          - Administrative regulations
      - Employment law
        - Common law
        - Statutes
      - Environmental law
        - Common law
        - Statutes
      - Labor law
      - Securities regulation
      - Product liability
        - Tort
          - Misrepresentation
            - Fraud
            - Innocent
          - Negligence
          - Strict liability
        - Contract
          - Express warranty
          - Implied warranty
          - Magnuson-Moss Warranty Act
    - Procedural
      - Civil procedure (Rules governing conduct of lawsuit)
      - Administrative law
        - Laws governing administrative agencies' operations
          - Federal Register Act
          - Administrative Procedure Act (federal)
            - Sunshine Act
            - Privacy Act
            - Freedom of Information Act
  - ***Criminal*** — Suit in which the society (state or United States government) sues a private party for conduct offensive to the society as a whole and seeks relief designed to punish, restrain, and rehabilitate the offender as well as deter would-be offenders
    - Procedural
    - Substantive
      - Treason (crime defined by United States Constitution)
      - Misdemeanors (Less serious crimes, with arbitrary distinction between felonies and misdemeanors)
      - Felonies (More serious offenses as determined by legislature, with severer penalties)

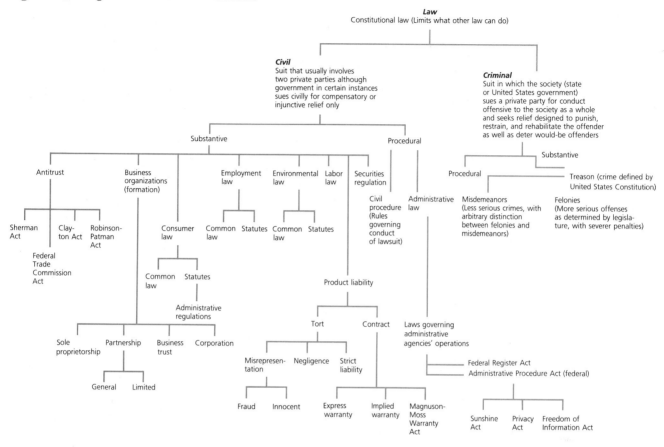

case is usually a private (non-government) person. However, governments can also sue civilly.

One final distinction between civil and criminal law lies in the different burdens of proof that plaintiffs have to satisfy in each type of case. In a civil case, a plaintiff generally must prove his or her case by a preponderance of the evidence. In a criminal case, the government (the plaintiff) must prove its case beyond a reasonable doubt, a heavier burden than what the civil plaintiff must satisfy.

Possible Overlap of Civil and Criminal Law

There is a possible overlap in civil and criminal law in the following sense: a fact situation could give rise to both a criminal lawsuit and a civil lawsuit. For example, if a person gets drunk and drives a car carelessly, killing another person, the prosecutor could sue the drunk driver for manslaughter (a crime), and the surviving family of the person killed could sue the drunk driver for wrongful death (a civil lawsuit). In other words, two lawsuits arose from the same basic fact pattern.

Diagrams of Civil and Criminal Law

Figures 1-2 and 1-3 are diagrams of civil and criminal law. Figure 1-2 is a traditional way of looking at law. The two broad categories of civil and criminal law are broken down into substantive and procedural rules. There are civil procedural laws (such as a statute of limitations for breach of contract) and criminal procedural laws (such as a statute of limitations for the crime of federal income tax evasion). There are *civil* substantive laws (such as tort law, which deals with broad classes of breaches of noncontractual duties that do not arise by contract; specific examples of torts are fraud and negligence). There are criminal substantive laws (such as the law forbidding arson). Figure 1-2 looks detailed but is by no means complete; many legal theories are not shown here.

Figure 1-3 is a modern way of classifying law, the focus of which is on *problems* or *situations*. First, a problem is recognized; then the rules available for solving problems or coping with situations are examined. For example, product liability is listed in Figure 1-3 and deals with products that do not work. The figure groups together legal theories that help people recover if a defective product injures them, their property, or someone else or someone else's property. Another example is environmental law, which tries to maintain and improve the quality of the human environment.

Constitutional law is shown in Figures 1-2 and 1-3. Such law belongs *above* all four general areas (civil substantive law, civil procedural law, criminal substantive law, and criminal procedural law) in both figures because constitutional law limits what the rules in these areas can do.

The remainder of this book looks in detail at all the areas diagramed in both Figures 1-2 and 1-3.

What Are Cases?

This book has cases in every chapter. A **law case** is a judge's written opinion which decides a legal dispute. The opinion will state the dispute's facts, the legal argument each party made, the decision, and the reasons for the decision.

Cases arise when one person sues another. Many people think that all legal matters involve lawsuits. This is not true. Most legal matters *never* involve lawsuits. For example, if you buy a house, a lawyer will do a title search and write up the contract. This title search involves legal work but it does not require going to court. It is not a case.

Even if a legal matter involves a lawsuit, most lawsuits are "settled;" settlements mean that the persons suing agree on a solution before the judge decides the matter. If a case goes to trial and the judge decides it, there may not be a written judicial opinion. Most trial court judges do not write opinions in cases they decide; they do not have to. Traffic court judges, probate judges, juvenile court judges, small claims judges, and judges in most state trial courts do not write opinions. They are excused from doing so largely because of the need for fast decision-making and a lack of enough judges to write opinions.

Some judges do write opinions. Federal district court judges, federal court of appeals judges, United States Supreme Court justices, and judges on state courts of appeal and courts of last resort (usually called "supreme courts") all write opinions. These written opinions are the source of the cases in this book.

Parts of a case Figure 1-4 diagrams the parts of a case: the style (name of person suing and being sued), the cite, the date the case was decided, the name (or names) of the judges (called "justices" if they sit on the state's highest court or the United States Supreme Court), the name of the court making the decision,

Figure 1-4 **Case Parts Illustrated**

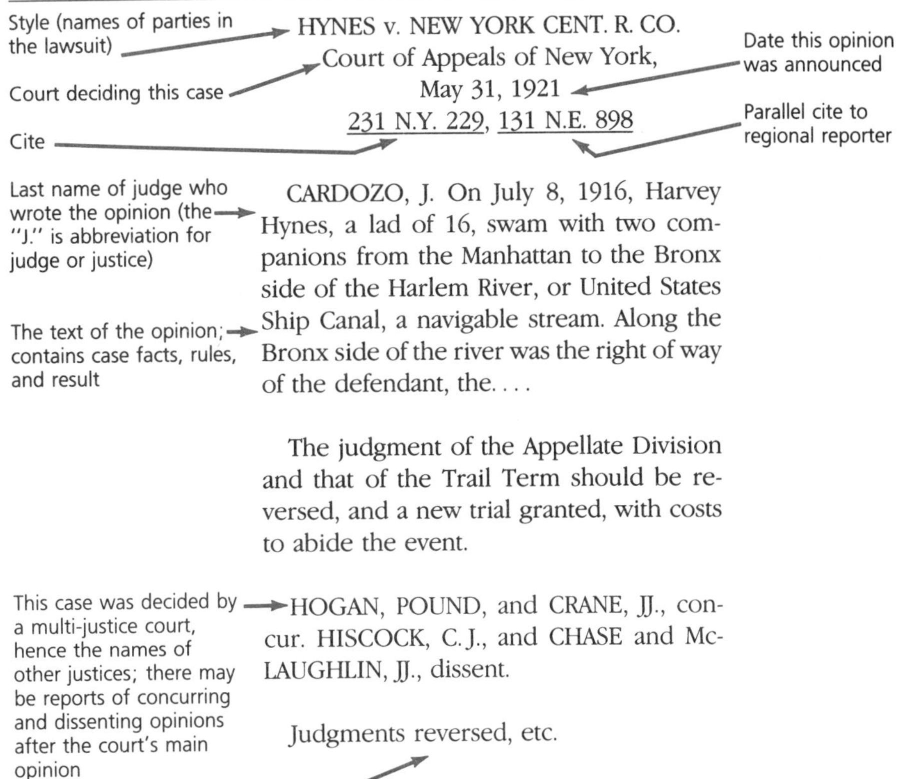

and the opinion. The actual opinion could be short (one or two pages) or long (twenty or more pages). The length depends on how complex the case is. Cases in this text are rewritten to shorten them.

Style (names of parties in the lawsuit)
HYNES v. NEW YORK CENT. R. CO.
Court of Appeals of New York,
May 31, 1921
231 N.Y. 229, 131 N.E. 898
Court deciding this case
Date this opinion was announced
Cite
Parallel cite to regional reporter
Last name of judge who wrote the opinion (the "J." is abbreviation for judge or justice)
CARDOZO, J. On July 8, 1916, Harvey Hynes, a lad of 16, swam with two companions from the Manhattan to the Bronx side of the Harlem River, or United States Ship Canal, a navigable stream. Along the Bronx side of the river was the right of way of the defendant, the. . . .
The text of the opinion; contains case facts, rules, and result
The judgment of the Appellate Division and that of the Trail Term should be reversed, and a new trial granted, with costs to abide the event.
This case was decided by a multi-justice court, hence the names of other justices; there may be reports of concurring and dissenting opinions after the court's main opinion
HOGAN, POUND, and CRANE, JJ., concur. HISCOCK, C.J., and CHASE and McLAUGHLIN, JJ., dissent.
Judgments reversed, etc.
The case result. Here the lower court's judgment was reversed; if it had been affirmed, the appellate court would have agreed with the lower court's decision. Reversal means the appellate court disagreed with the lower court's decision.

The **case cite** helps us find the case in the law library. The cite is different for each case. For the case in the diagram, the cite is 231 N.Y. 229. Those funny looking numbers and letters mean the following: "231" refers to the book number in a particular set of books (called a "reporter") containing cases of a particular court or courts. The middle letters tell what reporter the case is in. Here, "N.Y." tells us the reporter is the "New York Reports." The "229" to the right of the reporter's abbreviation is the page number in book 231 of the reporter. In other words, this opinion *starts* on page 229 of volume 231 of the New York Reports.

KEY TERMS

Law
Ethics
Jurisprudence
Positive law
Natural law
Utilitarian ethic
Custom
Preventive law

Constitution
Statutes
Ordinances
Substantive law
Procedural law
Civil law
Criminal law
Law case
Case cite
Case style

CHAPTER PROBLEMS

1. Recall the *Geary* case earlier in this chapter. In this case, a judge said that an employer can fire an employee even though the employee did nothing wrong. Courts in over twenty other states limit an employer's right to fire employees. What ethics or values in this chapter explain why many courts do not let employers fire employees for no reason at all?
2. The United States Supreme Court decides a case. Is this positive law? Why?
3. In Nazi Germany there were laws saying that Jews could not hold certain jobs. What legal ethics discussed in this chapter would disagree with such laws?
4. Do judges write opinions in all cases? In which cases are there no written opinions?
5. Is contract law civil substantive law or criminal substantive law? Refer to the diagram in this chapter to answer this question.
6. Why might a person be interested in studying law?
7. What part of the case is the "style"?
8. Explain the paradox, or contradiction, that law both takes away *and* gives us freedom.

"As citizens of this democracy, you are the rulers and the ruled."
Adlai Stevenson

Chapter 2

Sources of Law: Courts and Legislatures

CHAPTER PREVIEW

- Legal institutions that make law
- Number of court systems in the United States
- The court where lawsuits start in the state court system
- Courts of record
- State courts that are not courts of record
- Difference between law and equity courts
- Ways to correct judges' mistakes
- Federal courts
- Locations of federal courts of appeals

"It's having to buy justice!" shouted Robert Steinpreis. Portage County, Wisconsin sued Steinpreis for unpaid ambulance services provided by the county. Steinpreis said he did not owe anything. The case was brought in small claims court. Acting as his own attorney, Steinpreis asked for a jury trial; he was told that such a request required payment of $43 in jury fees before trial. Steinpreis argued that this prepayment was unconstitutional because plaintiffs in courts other than small claims did not have to prepay jury fees before trial. Steinpreis claimed that he was having to "buy justice." Was he right?

It was a dark night. Harry Tompkins walked on the Erie Railroad's right-of-way parallel to its tracks. A passing freight train whizzed by. A train door negligently left open struck Tompkins, knocking him under the train. As a result, his right arm was cut off at the shoulder. He saw a lawyer about suing the Erie Railroad. The lawyer analyzed the problem as follows: The accident occurred in Pennsylvania; Tompkins was a Pennsylvanian; and the railroad was a New York corporation. Since there was diversity of citizenship jurisdiction, Tompkins could sue the railroad in federal court in New York or Pennsylvania, and he could sue in state court in New York or Pennsylvania. The lawyer recommended against suing in Pennsylvania, because Pennsylvania law could be applied, causing Tompkins to lose. Instead, the lawyer recommended suing in a federal district court in the state of New York. The lawyer thought the judge there would apply the Swift v. Tyson *Rule, which would let the federal judge apply a federal common-law rule more favorable to Tompkins' case. Tompkins could not believe this attempt would work. Did it?*

In Chapter 1 we explored the general subject of law and legal ethics. This chapter looks at sources of law in the United States and considers courts and legislatures.

INSTITUTIONAL SOURCES OF LAW: COURTS AND LEGISLATURES

Institutional sources of law refer to governmental bodies with the power to make law. The average person will probably name courts and legislatures when asked where law comes from, which is partly correct. But note that the major governmental and institutional source of rules in our society today is the administrative agency. An administrative agency is any nonlegislative, nonjudicial, governmental lawmaker. Later chapters discuss these lawmakers in detail.

Courts and Court Systems

Courts (meaning judges) are a major source of law in the United States. Judge-made law is called **common law.** The United States has two major court systems: the federal court system and the state court system.

Why two court systems exist in the United States There are several reasons for having two **court systems in the United States,** when one would seem to be enough. First, we have dual sovereigns (that is, the federal and state governments), and each sovereign, or government, wants its own court system. When the United States Constitution was set up, many resisted a federal court system. They argued that federal courts unnecessarily duplicated state courts. Also, they feared a strong national government. Others, realizing how provincial the individual states and their citizens were saw a need for a more neutral court when people from other states were sued. Thus, federal courts, with judges appointed for life, were felt to be more neutral than state courts, which have elected judges. Many also felt that federal judges would know more about national law than would state courts.

State Courts

Each state has set up its own court system. Actually, the United States has fifty-one separate court systems (the fifty separate state court systems, plus one federal court system.)

Most lawsuits in the United States take place in state courts. Figure 2-1 diagrams the typical state court system. Keep in mind, however, that the fifty states' court structures do differ.

Types of state courts The first item to note in Figure 2-1 is that there are eight types of courts. A court where a case starts is called a **court of original jurisdiction.** A case that deals with juvenile delinquency or divorce, for example, starts in a **domestic relations court.** Or, if someone's father dies and leaves a will disposing of his property, that person (or representative lawyer) would take the will to a **probate court** (called a **surrogate's court** or **orphan's court** in some states). Probate courts deal with estate administration, which involves collecting a dead person's assets, paying off his or her debts, and distributing any remaining assets according to a legislatively drafted will, which is called a "statute of descent." County courts hear cases involving relatively small civil matters (such as a homeowner's breaking a contract with a painter) or criminal matters (such as a bank teller's embezzling $1500). Such courts are also called **common pleas courts,**

Figure 2-1 **State Judicial System**

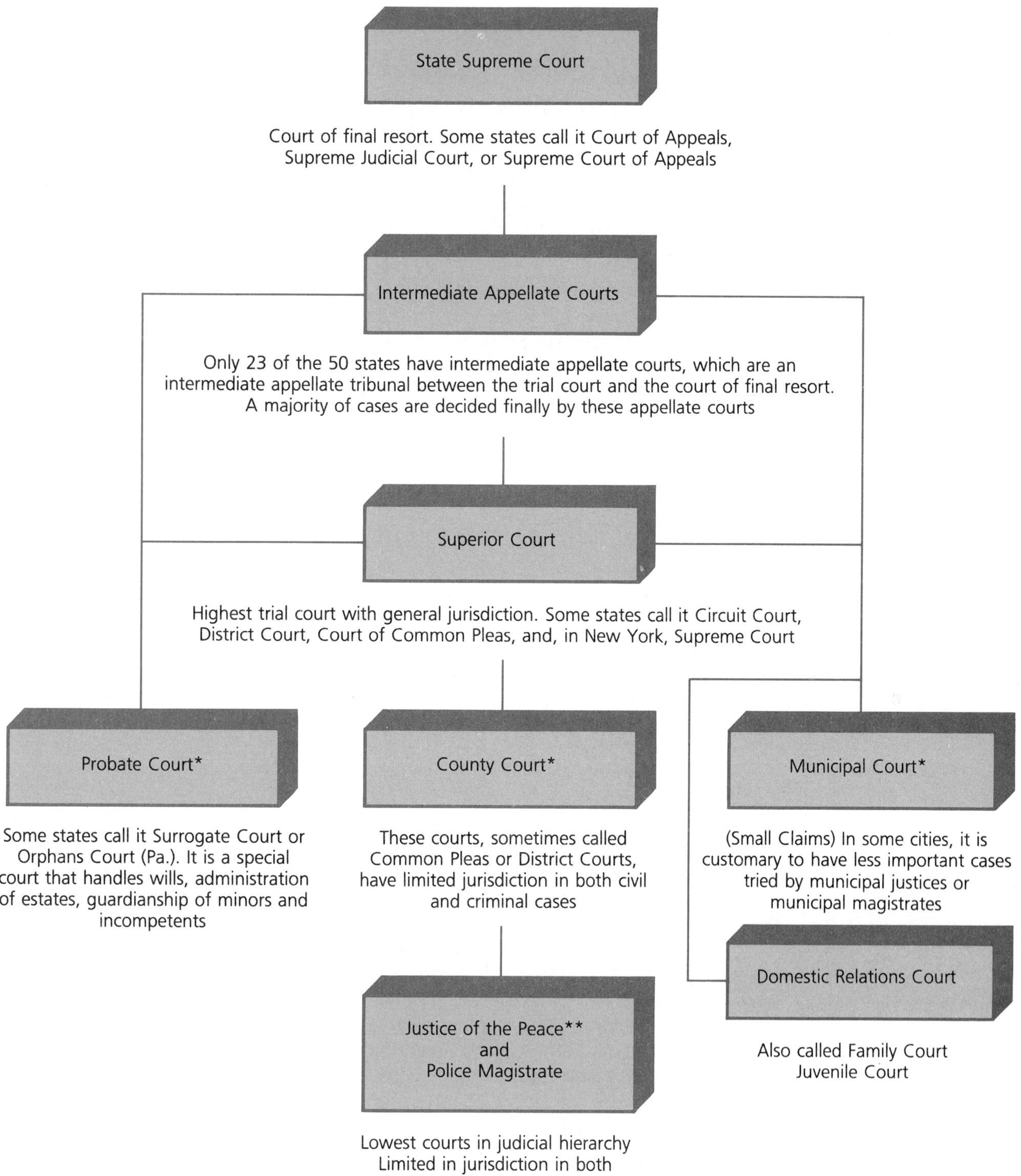
State Supreme Court
Court of final resort. Some states call it Court of Appeals, Supreme Judicial Court, or Supreme Court of Appeals
Intermediate Appellate Courts
Only 23 of the 50 states have intermediate appellate courts, which are an intermediate appellate tribunal between the trial court and the court of final resort. A majority of cases are decided finally by these appellate courts
Superior Court
Highest trial court with general jurisdiction. Some states call it Circuit Court, District Court, Court of Common Pleas, and, in New York, Supreme Court
Probate Court*
Some states call it Surrogate Court or Orphans Court (Pa.). It is a special court that handles wills, administration of estates, guardianship of minors and incompetents
County Court*
These courts, sometimes called Common Pleas or District Courts, have limited jurisdiction in both civil and criminal cases
Municipal Court*
(Small Claims) In some cities, it is customary to have less important cases tried by municipal justices or municipal magistrates
Domestic Relations Court
Also called Family Court Juvenile Court
Justice of the Peace** and Police Magistrate
Lowest courts in judicial hierarchy Limited in jurisdiction in both civil and criminal cases

Note: The names of courts are illustrative. Others are used.

* Courts of special jurisdiction, such as Probate, Family, or Juvenile, and the so-called inferior courts, such as Common Pleas or Municipal courts, may be separate courts or may be part of the trial court of general jurisdiction.

**Not all states have Justices of the Peace. Their jurisdictions vary greatly from state to state where they do exist.

or district courts, in a number of states. County courts typically have jurisdiction up to a certain dollar amount (such as $3000).

Some, but not all, states have **justice of the peace (JP) courts.** These, along with police magistrates, deal with very minor legal violations (traffic offenses, for example) of both a civil and criminal nature. (The basic difference between civil and criminal law is the party protected: society in criminal law and the individual in civil law. Chapter 3 explains the difference in greater detail.)

In a number of states, the municipal courts also deal with minor civil and criminal offenses. You may be wondering why so many types of low-level courts have **concurrent jurisdiction.** Sometimes this overlapping is justified on the basis of specializing to create judicial expertise. In less populous areas, one court (such as the county court) may do the job of several different types of low-level state courts (such as domestic relations, JP courts, and municipal courts).

The courts in the state court diagram in Figure 2-1 that are lower than the **superior courts** (those already described) are not courts of record. This means that no court stenographer makes a record of the proceedings, which saves society money. If a litigant in such a court wishes to appeal the result to the superior court, the case is retried from beginning to end. Retrial occurs because there is no lower court record of witnesses' testimony to review. Economy is also promoted by not having juries in courts below the superior court level. The judge in such courts fills the jury's fact-finder role as well as presides over the proceedings and rules on legal issues.

State trial courts of record The basic trial level courts are called **superior** or circuit **courts.** (In New York state they are called **state supreme courts.**) These are courts of record, where a court stenographer records the proceedings so that if the matter is appealed, all comments made by witnesses, attorneys, or the judge will be available for the appellate court to consider. The presence of the stenographer recording the proceedings tends to make all persons in the courtroom—including the judge—more careful about their remarks. Juries are available if requested for most types of cases. Superior courts can usually hear civil or criminal cases. In larger cities, superior courts are sometimes separated into civil and criminal courts.

Law and equity courts Occasionally, one hears the terms **law courts** and **equity courts.** (Recall that we discussed these terms in Chapter 1 under the topic of legal ethic of justice.) The distinction between law and equity results from the United States' patterning its legal system after England's.

Equity courts are also called **chancery courts.** The "judge" in chancery courts is called a chancellor. Equity courts are civil—not criminal. No right to a jury exists in equity courts. Sometimes chancellors appoint advisory juries in equity cases. Early settlers in the United States brought the English law and equity courts with them. By the mid-twentieth century, the law and equity court functions had been combined in most states (as well as in the federal courts).

Mistakes by judges What happens if a state judge makes a mistake in a case? The person who thinks that an error has occurred may appeal to a higher court (a court above any other shown in Figure 2-1). Generally, cases described by a lower court can be appealed to the next higher court in the diagram. For example, a matter decided by a probate court can be appealed to superior courts and from there to intermediate state **appellate courts.** If a person is still not satisfied, the case can be appealed to the state supreme court. If the case involves a federal constitutional, federal statutory, or federal treaty issue, it is possible that the United States Supreme Court will hear the case.

Features of appellate courts A few points should be noted about state intermediate appellate and supreme courts. First, no juries or witnesses appear in these courts; only lawyers, who argue law and not usually facts appear in appellate courts. Generally, the facts in a dispute are decided by the trial court. Appellate courts accept the trial court facts unless they are clearly erroneous. Second, every state has at least one appellate court level. Many have two levels of appellate courts (such as in the state court diagram in Figure 2-1). All states have a highest level appellate court called the state supreme court (except in New York where it is called the court of appeals). Third, appellate courts above the superior court level have several judges (called "justices" at the highest level). The idea here is that several heads are better than one. This idea is particularly true if the legal issue is complex or politically sensitive.

Wrong court The state court system is complex. What happens if a person takes his or her case to the wrong court? First, a person should hire an attorney to prevent this problem from occurring. However, if a layperson insists on acting pro se, or as his or her own attorney, and starts the case in the wrong court, it will be thrown out without a trial. The *County of Portage v. Steinpreis* case is an example of a person acting pro se.

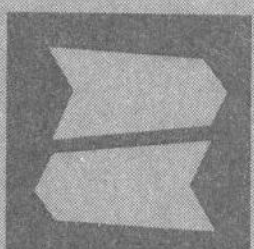

COUNTY OF PORTAGE v. STEINPREIS

Supreme Court of Wisconsin.
104 Wis.2d 466, 312 N.W.2d 731 (1981).

FACTS Portage County Wisconsin sued Robert Steinpreis in a Wisconsin Small Claims Court. The County claimed that Steinpreis owed for ambulance service, which the County provided. Steinpreis, representing himself, denied the claim and asked for a jury trial. The clerk of the court told Steinpreis that a Wisconsin statute required his paying a fee of $24 before getting a jury trial. Steinpreis challenged the state statute claiming that it was unconstitutional because persons asking for jury trials in regular Wisconsin trial courts did not have to prepay a jury fee before trial. The trial court rejected Steinpreis' argument. He appealed to the Wisconsin Court of Appeals, which reversed the trial court decision and agreed with Steinpreis. The original plaintiff, Portage County, appealed to the Wisconsin Supreme Court.

ISSUE Was it constitutional for the Wisconsin statute to require persons asking for jury trials in small claims courts to prepay a jury fee?

DECISION Yes. The Wisconsin Supreme Court said the $24 jury fee was reasonable. The court noted that the purpose of a small claims court was to give a cheap, fast way to dispose of minor lawsuits. People who ask for jury trials in such cases defeat this objective. Requiring the person who requests a jury to pay a jury fee "up front" insures the sincerity of the jury demand. Also, the court said that other trial courts handling larger claims have different fees. The court concluded that different treatment of persons suing in various state courts with different purposes was constitutional. The prepaid jury fee was not having to "buy justice."

Federal Courts

Federal district courts The **federal district courts** are those courts where most lawsuits begin in the federal court system. The federal court system is diagramed in Figure 2-2. Each state has at least one federal district court. The federal district judge performs the function of a law court judge and equity court chancellor. He or she also has subject matter jurisdiction to hear either civil or

Figure 2-2 **Federal Judicial System**

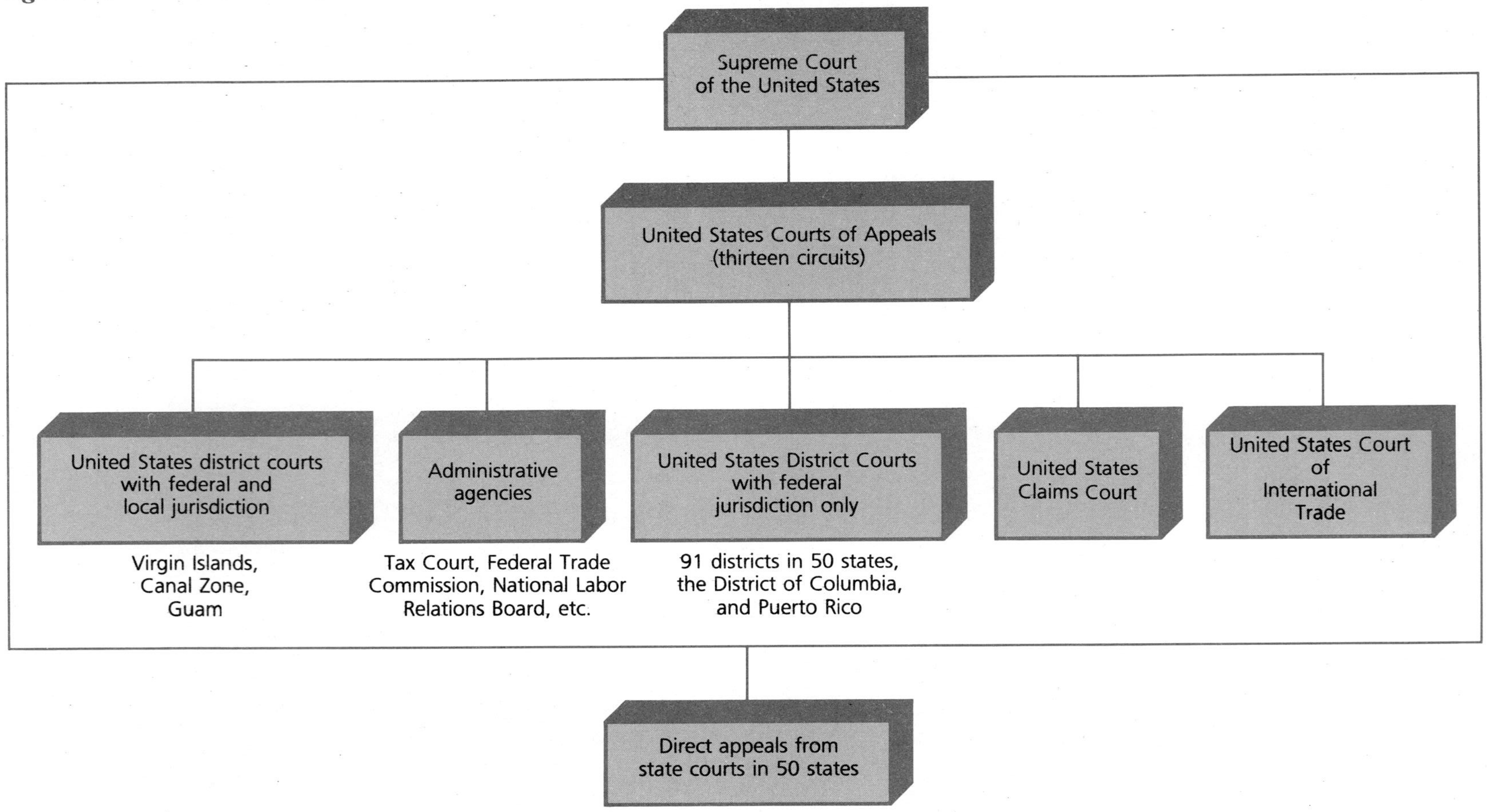

Supreme Court
of the United States

United States Courts of Appeals
(thirteen circuits)

United States district courts
with federal and
local jurisdiction

Virgin Islands,
Canal Zone,
Guam

Administrative
agencies

Tax Court, Federal Trade
Commission, National Labor
Relations Board, etc.

United States District Courts
with federal
jurisdiction only

91 districts in 50 states,
the District of Columbia,
and Puerto Rico

United States
Claims Court

United States Court
of
International
Trade

Direct appeals from
state courts in 50 states

Note: Used with permission, the American Bar Association

criminal cases. However, federal courts are courts of limited jurisdiction. That is, not all civil or criminal lawsuits may be heard there. Basically, two types of civil cases may be brought into federal district courts: **diversity of citizenship cases,** which involve lawsuits where a person from one state sues a person from a different state, and **federal question cases,** which involve lawsuits where a federal constitutional or statutory right is at issue. There is also a $10,000 jurisdictional limit in diversity cases that is designed to keep out small disputes, which are better handled in state courts. Such a limit no longer exists in federal question cases.

Administrative, or federal, agencies The administrative agencies refer to nonjudicial, nonlegislative government entities that have rule-making authority. These agencies are not even courts. Their rules and adjudications may often be appealed directly to the federal courts of appeals that bypass the trial-level federal district courts.

United States Court of International Trade The United States Court of International Trade (formerly called the Customs Court) is a federal court having exclusive power to decide cases arising under the United States tariff laws (covering such matters as appraised value or classification of imported goods). It tries cases without juries and has appellate authority from customs officers under the Anti-Dumping Act of 1921.

United States Claims Court The **United States Claims Court** came into existence on October 1, 1982. This court decides matters such as federal income tax refund claims, suits concerning supply or construction contracts with the federal government, and back-pay claims for government employees.

United States Courts of Appeals Most **United States Courts of Appeals** (formerly called the United States Circuit Courts of Appeals) were established in 1891 to ease the burden on the Supreme Court. Generally, appeals from federal trial level courts must go to one of the thirteen United States Courts of Appeals before they can be considered by the United States Supreme Court.

The United States has thirteen Courts of Appeals including the recently created Court of Appeals for the Federal Circuit in the District of Columbia (refer to Figure 2-2). Cases do not start in United States Courts of Appeals. There are no witnesses, juries, or evidence in these courts. Instead, lawyers argue before judges. Cases in Courts of Appeals come from one of the courts or administrative agencies shown in the boxes directly below the United States Courts of Appeals. Each Court of Appeals usually hears cases in panels made up of three judges. Their purpose is to correct mistakes made in lower courts.

Figure 2-3 is a diagram showing the states contained in each of the thirteen federal judicial circuits covering the fifty states and territories, plus the District of Columbia and federal circuits there.

United States Supreme Court The **United States Supreme Court** was formed on February 2, 1790. The Court now consists of a chief justice and eight associate justices. Supreme Court justices take office after presidential nomination and United States Senate confirmation.

The Supreme Court has the power to hear cases dealing with criminal and civil law, admiralty, treaties, United States Constitutional matters, and federal statutes.

Figure 2-3 **The Thirteen Federal Judicial Circuits**

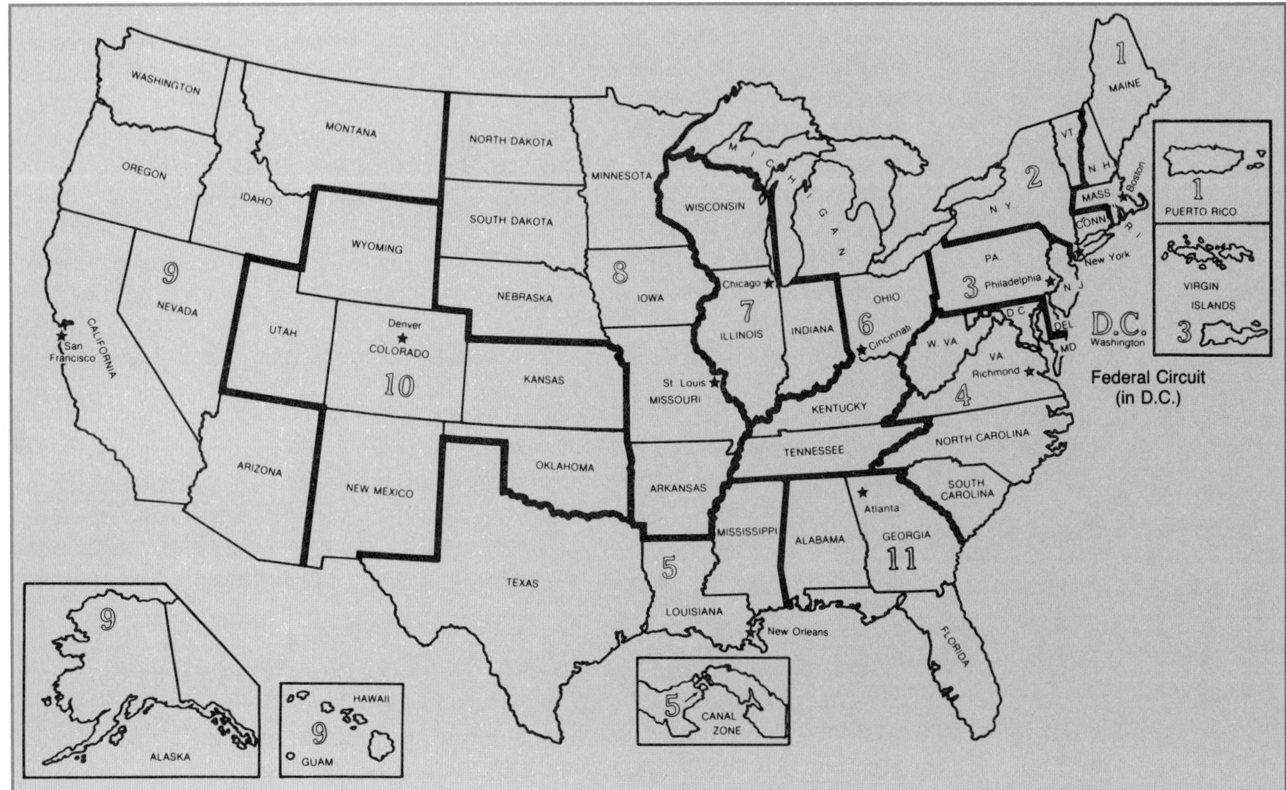

Note: The names of courts are illustrative. Others are used.
* Courts of special jurisdiction, such as Probate, Family, or Juvenile, and the so-called inferior courts, such as Common Pleas or Municipal courts, may be separate courts or may be part of the trial court of general jurisdiction.
**Not all states have Justices of the Peace. Their jurisdictions vary greatly from state to state where they do exist.

Which Court System?

There is a state court system and a federal court system. Which court system should a person sue in? The plaintiff, or person suing, decides whether the state or federal courts will be used.

The defendant, or person sued, can move a case from state to federal court in two cases: First, if there is diversity of citizenship (for example, a plaintiff and defendant live in different states) and the matter sued about is $10,000 or more; or, second, if there is a federal question that involves interpretation of the United States Constitution, a treaty, a federal statute, or a regulation).

If a plaintiff starts a case in federal court, a defendant may not usually move it to state court.

Selecting a court system Recall the story about Harry Tompkins at the start of this chapter. A person like Tompkins can start his case in either the federal district court or state superior court. Which court should he choose?

When a federal court hears a diversity case, it acts as a state court, but presumably without the local prejudice of a state court judge. But is there any limit on a federal judge's lawmaking authority when he or she rules in a diversity case? What if the state court had made a rule one way on an issue? Could the federal court in another, later case involving similar facts in the same state make a contrary rule? Harry Tompkins lost an arm and learned in the *Erie Railroad Co. v. Tompkins*

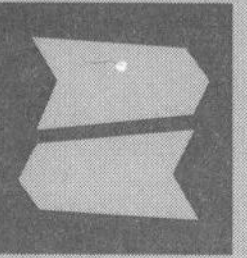

ERIE RAILROAD CO. v. TOMPKINS

Supreme Court of the United States. 304 U.S. 64 (1938).

FACTS Tompkins, a citizen of Pennsylvania, was injured on a dark night by a passing freight train of the Erie Railroad Company. This occurred along Erie's right of way at Hughestown in that state. He claimed that the accident happened through negligence in the operation of the railroad. The Erie Railroad Company was a New York citizen since it was incorporated in New York. Tompkins sued Erie in a federal district court in New York instead of Pennsylvania because Pennsylvania law was unfavorable. The federal judge in New York disregarded Pennsylvania law and decided the case in favor of Tompkins. Erie appealed.

ISSUE May a federal judge make a rule of law in a diversity case different from the state law governing the matter?

DECISION No. The United States Supreme Court decided the case in favor of the railroad. Tompkins lost. The Supreme Court said that federal courts deciding a diversity case must apply state substantive law. In this case, rules dealing with landowners' liability to persons on their land is an area falling into the states' area of lawmaking, not the federal area of lawmaking. Thus, in this case, the New York federal district court should have applied the Pennsylvania rule, which would have denied Tompkins' recovery because he was a trespasser on railroad property.

case that federal judges have no power to make common law in areas reserved to the states by the United States Constitution. Federal judges must follow state law when they decide diversity cases, which involve a reserved power matter (most property, contract, and torts—such as slander and negligence—covered by state law; that is, areas reserved for state lawmaking).

Legislatures and Legislative Forms

Legislatures are public bodies of elected officials who make law by passing statutes. The national legislature is called the Congress of the United States, which comprises the House and Senate. Each state also has a legislature. This section focuses on how a bill becomes a statute, some ways to influence legislation, and differences between courts and legislatures. The work of the United States Congress starts with a proposal taking one of the following four forms; a bill, a joint resolution, a concurrent resolution, or a simple resolution.

Bills Most federal legislation takes the form of a **bill** when proposed. A bil becomes an act or session law when it is passed by both Houses of Congress and is signed by the president, when two-thirds of each House overrides a presidential veto, or when the president fails to return it with his objections to the originating House within ten days while Congress is in session. Federal bills can start in either the House or Senate, except for revenue raising or general appropriation bills (tax bills), which must originate in the House of Representatives (HR). A bill originating in the House is designated HR, followed by a number (such as HR 2070), which it keeps during its parliamentary stages. Senate bills are similarly designated S (for Senate) followed by a number (such as S 7).

Figure 2-4 indicates some major steps by which a bill becomes a statute. A proposed statute introduced by a member of Congress is called a bill. If the bill survives and becomes law, it is called an act, statute, or session law. Acts can be private acts (a law passed to deal with nonrecurring, private matters, such as a law to pay a farmer when a military jet crashes into and destroys the farmer's barn) or public acts (laws having general social impact).

Figure 2-4 **Steps on How a Bill Becomes an Act of Congress**

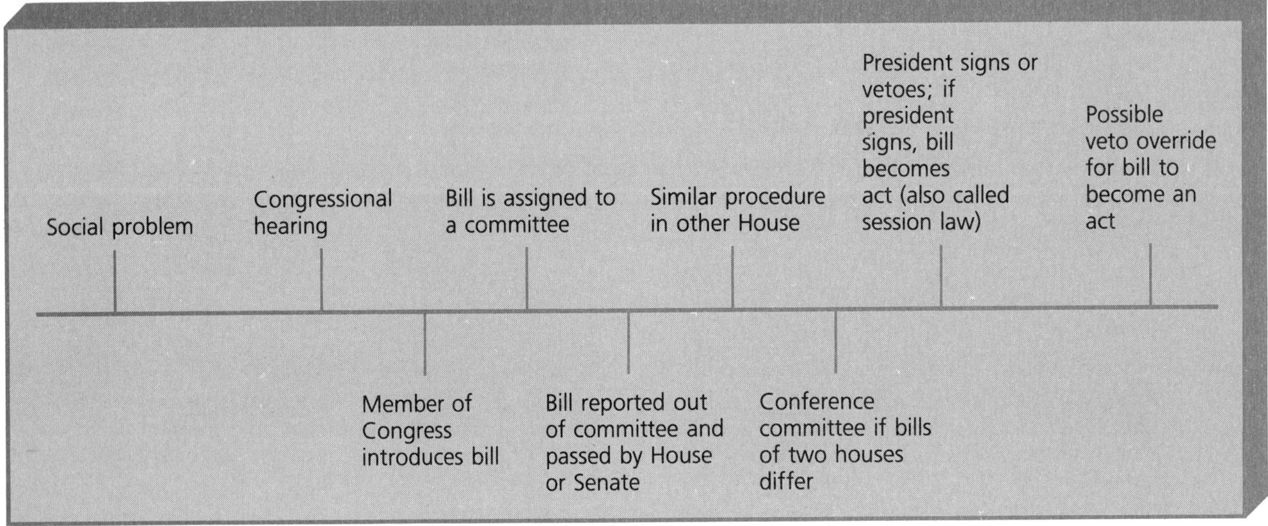

Relation Between Legislative and Court Law

As we have seen, both courts and legislatures make law. Courts (federal and state) may make law in any area subject to constitutional limits. What if a statute rules one way and a case the opposite? The statute wins if it is constitutional.

If a legislature passes a vague statute, the courts are allowed to clarify the vagueness. For example, the Sherman Antitrust Act makes some contracts restraining trade illegal. The legislature left it to the courts to decide *which* contracts restrain trade illegally.

Courts also can strike down statutes that violate the constitution. For example, the Supreme Court said that the statute preventing people from giving more than $1000 to a candidate running for public office breaks the constitution.

KEY TERMS

Common law
Court systems in the United States
Court of original jurisdiction
Domestic relations court
Probate court
Surrogate's court
Orphan's court
Common pleas court
Justice of the peace (JP) courts
Concurrent jurisdiction
Superior courts
Circuit courts
State supreme courts
Law courts
Equity courts
Chancery courts
Appellate courts
Federal district courts
Diversity of citizenship cases
Federal question cases
United States Claims Court
United States Courts of Appeals
United States Supreme Court
Bill

CHAPTER PROBLEMS

1. What are some institutional sources of law?
2. How many court systems are there in the United States?
3. Name four kinds of state courts.
4. Explain what is meant by a "court of record."
5. What can be done if a judge makes a mistake in a case?
6. How do appellate courts differ from trial courts?
7. What is the basic trial level court in the federal court system?

*8. Does a country have to have courts? The Appellate Division of the New York Supreme Court said, "It is a fundamental obligation of every civilized government to provide a system of impartial courts which can fairly adjudicate disputes involving its citizens." The case involved a suit by the country of Iran against the former Empress of Iran for alleged wrongs she committed against the people of Iran while in Iran. *Islamic Republic of Iran v. Pahlavi,* 464 N.Y.S.2d 487 (1983).

9. In some larger cities, there are several criminal court judges. It is thought that some judges are "tougher" than other judges on criminal defendants. The criminal court clerk decides what judge tries a case. Must the clerk make "blind assignments" to prevent unfairness to the defendant? *Hobbs v. State,* 451 N.E.2d 356 (Ind.App. 1st Dist.)(1983).

*10. In 1854, the Ohio Supreme Court created the sovereign immunity doctrine for Ohio. This doctrine specified that if state or municipal governments in Ohio committed torts (certain private wrongs such as negligence or slander) against citizens, the citizen could not sue the government for damages. In 1983, a case challenged this longstanding rule. If judges create a law, are they allowed to invalidate it? *Enghauser Mfg. Co. v. Ericksson Engineering,* 451 N.E.2d 228 (1983).

"Lawsuit: A machine you go into as a pig and come out as a sausage."

Ambrose Bierce
The Devil's Dictionary

Chapter 3

Ways to Settle Disputes

CHAPTER PREVIEW

- Ways administrative agencies settle disputes
- Definition of compromise of claims
- Pro se litigants
- Mediation
- Difference between arbitration and mediation
- Ways lawyers can help business people avoid lawsuits
- Steps in civil lawsuits

Elena De Zavala did not really understand all that was happening. She was nine years old. She and her grandfather were in federal court in Knoxville, Tennessee. She knew her father had been killed in a head-on car accident in Tennessee while returning home to Iowa. Her grandfather had told her that they were suing the Tennessee woman and her husband for $1.2 million. That sounded like a lot of money to Elena. Suddenly, the courtroom became quiet. The jury had returned with its verdict. Did Elena win? And if so, how much money was recovered?

It was late October 1977. Earl Johnson of Knoxville, Tennessee, was in Atlanta, Georgia. He visited Atlanta's fabulous Lenox Square Shopping Mall. He wanted to purchase a stereo as a Christmas present for his parents, who had retired to Sun City, Arizona. He walked into the Frank Music Company's store in Lenox Square. After some bargaining with the salesperson, Earl fully paid $418 for the stereo receiver, two speakers, and delivery charges to Sun City. Earl impressed upon the salesperson that he wanted immediate delivery. The salesperson assured him that the stereo would be shipped the following week.

Earl sent his parents a letter the next week telling them a stereo was on its way. November came and went. Earl called his parents to ask how they liked the stereo. They reported that it hadn't arrived. Earl called Frank Music's Lenox Square store to ask about delivery. The salesperson assured him that the stereo had been sent. When it didn't arrive the next week, Earl's mother called Frank Music's Lenox store. She spoke to a person who identified himself as the manager. He assured her the matter would be taken care of.

Two weeks later, on December 20, Earl flew to Phoenix to celebrate Christmas with his parents. The stereo still hadn't arrived. Earl again called Frank Music's Lenox Square store in Atlanta. The salesperson assured him that the stereo had been shipped. Earl said that he'd heard that line before. The salesperson told him it was true. Earl hung up the telephone and wondered what to do. Suing was not practical because an attorney and court costs would be at least $250, not to mention the time and trouble of finding an attorney in Georgia and possibly having to make several trips there to settle the matter. Such an effort to recover the $418 seemed foolish. It irritated him to think that a business could sell an item, be paid for it, and then not deliver it.

Earl wondered if the State of Georgia had a consumer protection agency. He called Atlanta Information and was given a telephone number. He called it, *told his story to a staff attorney, and within one-half hour received another call from Frank Music. This time the salesperson apologized for the "mixup," confessed that the stereo hadn't been sent, and said that it would be shipped that day. Ten days later on December 30, 1977, the day Earl was to fly back to Tennessee, a freight company called to tell him a stereo had arrived in Phoenix and would be delivered the next day. Since his father had heart disease and was unable to assemble the stereo, Earl suggested driving into Phoenix and picking up the stereo so that he could set it up before leaving. Upon arrival at the freight depot, Earl was handed a freight bill for $35.82. He informed the shipper that he had paid the seller for freight when he bought the stereo. The freight agent said that all he knew was that the freight had not been paid and refused to turn over the stereo until he was paid.*

Earl called Frank Music's Lenox store. He yelled at the salesperson who'd sold him the stereo, saying that he'd paid for the stereo and freight over two months ago. The salesperson was of no help. Earl's father, a heart patient, couldn't stand the excitement. He quietly paid the $35.82 freight bill. Earl set up the stereo and flew back to Knoxville. He sent a copy of Frank Music's October 27, 1977, invoice showing payment for the freight to the Georgia consumer protection agency along with a $35.82 receipt for his father's payment for the same freight. On February 5, 1978, Earl's father received a check for $35.82 for the twice-paid freight. The Frank Music salesperson had written an accompanying note saying: "I apologize for the inconvenience and hope that you do not hold this occurrence as a reflection of the quality of sales assistance in the Frank Music Company." (Names have been changed to protect the parties' privacy. The story is otherwise true.)

This chapter helps businesspeople avoid lawsuits and settle disputes. We believe that people should try to settle their own disputes first. But lawyers can help! We want to emphasize that seeing a lawyer can help *avoid* lawsuits.

ALTERNATIVES TO LAWSUITS

Administrative Agencies

Administrative agencies are government lawmakers that are *not* legislatures or judges. An example is the Federal Trade Commission or the State Health Department.

How administrative agencies settle disputes Administrative agencies can include consumer protection agencies. Consumer protection agencies, for example, have the power to make regulations and enforce them by suing. The Earl Johnson story at the start of this chapter is an example. This subject will be elaborated upon in Chapter 11.

Saving people the time and expense of suing are advantages of using administrative agencies to settle disputes. Disadvantages include the lack of administrative agencies to solve all problems and their cost to taxpayers.

Compromising Claims

Compromising claims refers to people in a dispute settling their claims by themselves; each party "gives up" a little, or compromises. An example would occur in the Earl Johnson case (chapter-opening story) if Earl had gotten his money back instead of the stereo.

Compromising saves time and lawyer's fees. The disadvantage is that one often gets less than one originally bargained for. Earl Johnson, for example, might not have been able to buy as good a stereo for $418 elsewhere.

Mediation

Mediation is a way to settle a dispute without going to court. The parties bring in a neutral third party (called a *mediator*) to listen to all sides of a dispute. The mediator analyzes the parties' arguments and talks with each party. This discussion helps settle the matter. A mediator's decision does not bind the parties; rather, the mediator tries to find grounds for compromise leading to a settlement.

Mediation is used in business and other matters. For example, during the major league baseball strike of 1981, the parties to the dispute (players and team owners) brought in a federal mediator to help settle the contract dispute. In international affairs, Pope John Paul II has helped mediate a boundary line dispute between two South American countries.

Virtually anyone acceptable to the parties involved can serve as a mediator. Mediators need not be lawyers, although they often are.

Arbitration

Arbitration involves turning over a dispute to a nonjudicial third person for a binding decision. "Formal" arbitration means that arbitration is done by contract or statute (usually the former). The contract often is made before the dispute arises; but an agreement to arbitrate can be made any time—even after the dispute arises. Labor, consumer, and international disputes—in fact, virtually any commercial matter—can be submitted for arbitration.

The third person (or someone not associated with either party involved in the dispute) whom the disputants turn the matter over to for decision is called an **arbitrator.** Sometimes more than one arbitrator is used. In effect, an arbitrator is a private judge. Arbitrators do not have to be lawyers, although many are. The social advantages of using arbitrators include speed and economy. Arbitrators help reduce legal costs and time spent in court, which, in turn, decongests the courts.

Arbitrators follow their own procedural and evidentiary rules. They may also make up their own rules of substantive law within limits. An arbitrator's decision is called an **award.** An arbitrator's decision binds persons who agree to arbitrate. Courts will enforce an arbitrator's decision just as though it were a court's judgment. This enforcement occurs even when the arbitrator did not use rules of law followed by courts. Arbitrators do not have to give reasons for their opinions, although they usually do.

LAWSUITS

Being Your Own Lawyer (The Perils of Pro Se)

A person may legally be his or her own lawyer in almost any legal matter. This person is called a **pro se** litigant (pro se means "through oneself").

Generally it is unwise to act as your own attorney. People lack objectivity and legal know-how. An exception occurs in small claims courts where people speak for themselves without lawyers. The idea is to keep legal costs low since claims in these courts are small. The *Dioguardi v. Durning* case shows the perils, or risks, of pro se.

How Lawyers Can Help People Avoid Lawsuits

When people think of **lawyers,** they imagine courtrooms and lawsuits. Lawyers actually try to avoid lawsuits. They do this in several ways:

1. By giving their clients regular legal "checkups," just as medical doctors regularly examine patients.

DIOGUARDI v. DURNING

U.S. Court of Appeals, Second Circuit.
139 F.2d 774 (1944).

FACTS Dioguardi, an Italian American, could not speak or write English well. He acted as his own attorney and sued the collector of customs in Federal District Court in New York City. The dispute apparently involved some tonics Dioguardi was importing from Italy and a question arose concerning who was supposed to pay duty for them. After reading Dioguardi's complaint, the trial judge was unable to understand what the facts were in Dioguardi's case. The trial judge dismissed Dioguardi's complaint but let him rewrite and submit it again. Dioguardi did so but his rewritten complaint was no clearer than his first attempt. Dioguardi never got a jury trial. The judge again dismissed Dioguardi's complaint because he could not determine what Dioguardi's suit was about. Dioguardi appealed.

ISSUE Should a pro se plaintiff's complaint be dismissed with prejudice (meaning that it cannot be rewritten and resubmitted) if the trial judge has given a plaintiff one chance to rewrite it?

DECISION No. The United States Court of Appeals thought Dioguardi stated a claim. It felt that Dioguardi satisfied the statute requiring a short and plain statement of the claim, showing that the pleader was entitled to relief.

LEGAL TIP
In complicated cases, hire a lawyer. Do not act as your own attorney.

2. By writing out business agreements so misunderstandings and forgetful memories will not create disputes.
3. By doing income tax planning to minimize tax and comply with the law (for example, certain taxpayers can legally reduce their federal income taxes if they buy insulating window curtains).
4. By doing insurance planning so people have enough coverage (for example, checking to see if your homeowner's insurance covers you if your golf ball hits someone on the golf course or seeing if your car insurance covers you if someone recovers a whopping $1,000,000 judgment resulting from your carelessness).
5. By doing estate planning to get maximum property (and low estate tax) and to get that property to loved ones quickly when a person dies.
6. By writing letters to people with whom one has legal disputes and by negotiating settlements before matters go to court.

Suing Through a Lawyer

Suppose that none of the ways to settle a dispute already mentioned works. Suppose also that you do not want to pro se your case (act as your own attorney). Then you should see an attorney about suing (which this chapter discusses later).

Just because you see (and hire) an attorney does not necessarily mean that you will sue anyone. The attorney might decide that no one has legally harmed you. Also, the wrongdoer may have a good defense to your suit (for example, the statute of limitations indicates that you waited too long before *starting* suit), or you may not have evidence to prove your claim in court. Remember that the burden of proof is usually on the one suing and evidence is easily lost. For example, a consumer often throws away a sales slip proving who sold a defective oven.

Figure 3-1 **Steps in a Civil Lawsuit**

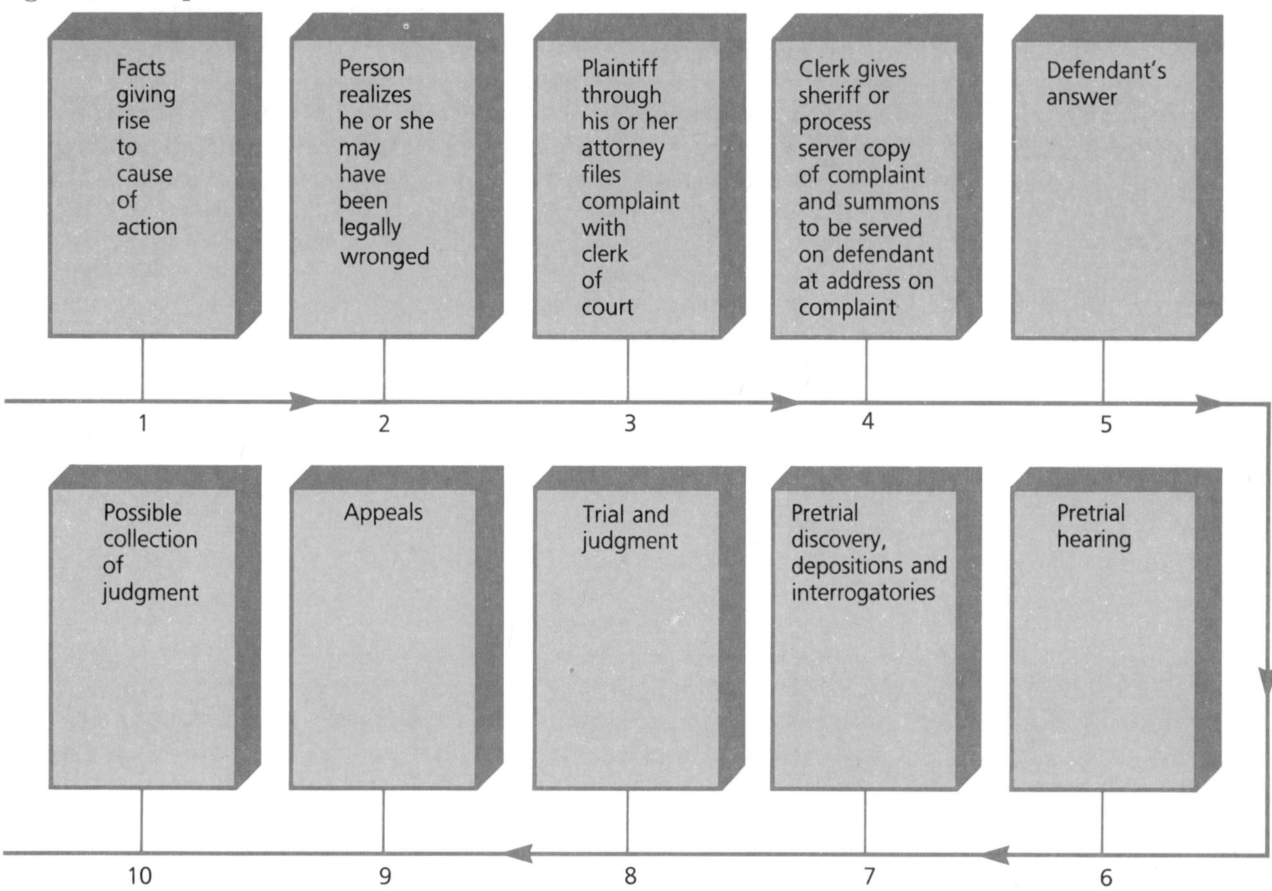

Perhaps your attorney says that you should sue. What are the steps in a court suit? How long will it take? The next section gives *some* answers. Figure 3-1 is a road map of possible steps in a civil lawsuit.

Parties to the Dispute

The party who is complaining about his or her rights being broken is called the plaintiff. The defendant is the alleged "bad actor" in the scenario, who had supposedly violated the plaintiff's rights.

Jurisdiction

Jurisdiction means power or authority over something. When used in reference to courts, this term refers to the power to hear and try a case. Jurisdiction has personal and subject matter aspects.

Subject matter jurisdiction refers to a court's having power to deal with a particular type of case. A number of courts have jurisdiction over only a limited sort of case. For example, probate courts deal only with determining the validity of wills. Thus, a murder case could not be brought in a probate court, because it has no subject matter jurisdiction over criminal matters. Subject matter jurisdiction is in part a result of history and in part recognition of the large case load that no single court could bear.

In personam jurisdiction refers to a court's power over people. State courts generally have in personam jurisdiction over persons physically within their borders who are "served with process," which refers to delivering a summons and complaint to the defendant personally or to the defendant's residence. **Long-arm statutes** let a state get in personam jurisdiction over out-of-staters for certain wrongs occurring within the state (usually such incidents as auto accidents). For example, if an Oregonian injured a Californian in San Francisco and hurried back to Oregon before process could be served on him or her, had California a long-arm statute covering auto accidents, the Californian could get in personam jurisdiction over the Oregonian in California. Mechanically, the Californian sends the process to a state official (usually the state's secretary of state), who sends it to the Oregonian. If the Oregonian does not answer, the plaintiff wins a default judgment for the amount sued for. This judgment can then be taken to the defendant's home state and enforced against the defendant just as if the case had been tried there.

Facts Giving Rise to a Cause of Action

The term **cause of action** has a special legal meaning. It refers to facts that indicate that someone has been legally wronged by someone else and is entitled to have a court give relief (or a remedy).

Just because someone is injured by another person does not necessarily mean the injured victim has a cause of action. The person injuring the victim might have legal defenses. Any legal defense usually completely stops a victim from getting legal relief. For example, the complaint in Figure 3-2 indicates that the injured victim (the little girl suing through her grandfather) tries to state a cause of action. Note paragraph VI of the complaint. The plaintiff points out several laws that she claims the defendants violated when Betty Hobbs killed the plaintiff's father.

The defendants in their answer (the document in the text after the complaint) admit certain factors (for instance, diversity jurisdiction in paragraph 2) and set up certain defenses (in paragraphs 5 through 8). Note that in paragraph 6, the defendants claim that the plaintiff's father died instantly. If this is true, it would mean that the plaintiff's father sustained no pain and suffering. (Note paragraph 5 of the complaint: ". . . plaintiff's intestate (her father) was crushed and mangled in a horrible manner . . . after suffering a large amount of pain and mental anguish . . ." Pain and suffering can sometimes be recovered.)

Starting Lawsuits: The Complaint

A person does not start a lawsuit (see Figure 3-2) by walking into the courthouse, finding the nearest judge, and stating the problem to the judge. All sorts of rules protect the defendant who often does not yet know that he or she is about to be sued.

Assume that the plaintiff does not act pro se but instead hires an attorney. The plaintiff's attorney drafts a complaint (see Figure 3-2). The complaint tells the defendant that he or she is being sued and what he or she is being sued for—breach of contract or slanderous remarks, for example.

The complaint and two copies are taken to the clerk of the court, who puts a stamp on the complaint indicating the time and date that the complaint is filed. (The sample complaint has a time stamp in the right-hand center of the first page.) The complaint is put in a file folder that the clerk starts for that case, a copy is given to the plaintiff, and another copy is given along with a summons to an official

Figure 3-2 **The Complaint**

IN THE UNITED STATES DISTRICT COURT
FOR THE EASTERN DISTRICT OF TENNESSEE,
NORTHERN DIVISION

ELENA DeZAVALA a minor who sues by next friend and grandfather, LOUIS B. DeZAVALA, citizens and residents of Linn County, Iowa, and of no other place, PLAINTIFFS

vs.

BETTY J. HOBBS and JAMES B. HOBBS, 126 South Purdue Avenue, Oak Ridge, Anderson County, Tennessee, DEFENDENTS

No. 3-75-125

COMPLAINT

The plaintiff, Elena DeZavala, is a minor, nine years of age, who sues by next friend and grandfather, Louis B. DeZavala, both of whom are citizens and residents of Linn County, Iowa, and of no other place, and further aver that said plaintiff, Elena DeZavala, is the sole surviving child and lineal descendant and next of kin of Louis Victor DeZavala who died in Sullivan County, Tennessee on May 2, 1975. Said plaintiffs complain of the defendants, Betty J. Hobbs and James B. Hobbs, of 126 South Purdue Avenue, Oak Ridge, Tennessee, who are citizens and residents of Anderson County, Tennessee, and of no other place and State.

Said plaintiff, Elena DeZavala, brings this suit by her grandfather and next friend, Louis B. DeZavala, by reason of the wrongful death of her father, Louis Victor DeZavala, who was divorced from the mother of the plaintiff, said mother having remarried.

I

Plaintiff avers that the amount in controversy exceeds the sum of Ten Thousand Dollars ($10,000) exclusive of interest and costs, and that a complete diversity of citizenship exists between the plaintiff and the defendents, and jurisdiction of this Honorable Court is based on Title 28 U. S. Code Section 1332(a).

II

Plaintiff avers that on May 2, 1975, at approximately 11:00 a.m., that the plaintiff's intestate-father was operating his vehicle in a southwardly direction along Interstate Highway 81, approximately one mile south of the intersection of said Interstate 81 with Tennessee Highway 137. Plaintiff avers that said vehicle of Louis Victor DeZavala was being operated in a southwardly direction in a proper and lawful manner upon its right hand side of said Interstate which at that point was a two lane two-way highway.

Figure 3-2 Continued

III

Plaintiff avers that said highway was plainly marked every thousand feet as a two-way highway for more than six miles in each direction from the location aforedescribed.

IV

Plaintiff avers that at said time and place as plaintiff's intestate and deceased father, Louis Victor DeZavala, was operating his said vehicle in a southwardly direction along said highway in a proper and lawful manner and upon its right hand side of the highway in broad daylight, that the defendant, Betty J. Hobbs, operating a vehicle within the purview of the Family Purpose Doctrine, which said vehicle was the property of her husband, James B. Hobbs, in a northwardly direction along said highway, meeting the automobile of the plaintiff's intestate father. That the said defendant, Betty J. Hobbs, while operating her automobile at a high, reckless, wrongful and negligent rate of speed, and without keeping her said vehicle under control, and without keeping a lookout ahead, undertook to overtake and pass a truck traveling northwardly along said highway, and drove her said vehicle from its right hand or proper side of the highway to its left hand or improper side of the highway in an effort to overtake and pass said tractor-trailer traveling in the same direction in which she was traveling and drove her said vehicle in the manner and under the conditions aforedescribed into a violent head-on collision with the vehicle operated by the plaintiff's intestate and father.

V

Plaintiff avers that as the direct and proximate result of the negligence of the defendent as aforedescribed, operating her vehicle upon the highway upon the business of the defendant, James B. Hobbs, and within the purview of the Family Purpose Doctrine, that the plaintiff's intestate was crushed and mangled in a horrible manner sustaining such comprehensive, mangling and horrible injuries that as a direct and proximate result thereof after suffering a large amount of pain and mental anguish, that said plaintiff's intestate died, as a result of said injuries and as a proximate result of the negligence of the defendants as aforedescribed.

VI

Plaintiff avers that the defendants by the negligence as aforedescribed violated the following sections of the 1956 Tennessee Code Annotated, and that such violations on their part were the proximate contributing cause to the collision heretofore described and the death of plaintiff's intestate and the destruction of the automobile belonging to him at the time and place complained of:

Section 59-815
Driving on right side of roadway.

Figure 3-2 Continued

Section 59-819
Limitations on overtaking on the left.

Section 59-820
Further limitations on driving to the left of center of roadway.(1)

Section 59-821
No passing zones.

Section 59-823
Driving on roadways laned for traffic (a).

Section 59-852
Speed limit (a).

Section 59-858
Reckless driving (a).

VII

Plaintiff avers that the death of plaintiff's intestate[4] resulted solely from the negligence of the defendants as aforedescribed and that the plaintiff's intestate was a young and healthy man, 30 years of age. Plaintiff was the intestate's only child. Plaintiff has further been put to the expense of the funeral bills and medical expenses, and the destruction of the automobile being occupied by the plaintiff's intestate at the time and place complained of.

WHEREFORE, plaintiff respectfully prays judgment against the defendants and each of them in the sum of Six Hundred Thousand Dollars ($600,000) and respectfully demand a jury to try the issues joined.

KENNERLY, MONTGOMERY, HOWARD & FINLEY

By ______________________
George D. Montgomery,
Attorneys for Plaintiff
12th Floor
Bank of Knoxville Building
Post Office Box 442
Knoxville, Tennessee 37901

COST BOND

We do hereby acknowledge ourselves as surely for the costs in this cause in an amount not to exceed Two Hundred Fifty Dollars (250.00).

KENNERLY, MONTGOMERY,
HOWARD & FINLEY

By ______________________

4. An intestate is someone who dies without a will.

process server (such as a deputy sheriff or some other person employed to perform this task). The summons directs the defendant to appear in court to answer the complaint. The process server takes a copy of the complaint and the summons to the address the plaintiff put on the complaint and hands them to the defendant or leaves them at the address indicated if the defendant is not there.

Defendant's Response: The Answer

Upon receiving the complaint, the defendant will realize that he or she has just been sued, maybe for more money than he or she has. Once defendants recover from this shock, they will probably hire an attorney to draft an answer (see Figure 3-3). The answer is a piece of paper that the defendant must file with the clerk of court where the plaintiff sued. The answer must be filed within a short time after defendant has received a copy of the complaint—usually within thirty days. The answer will give the defendant's version of the facts. It may also state defenses to escape liability. If the defendant does not file an answer, the plaintiff wins without even having to go to trial, barring unusual circumstances excusing an answer. This result is called a **default judgment.** Figure 3-3 shows the answer that was filed in response to the sample complaint. The complaint and answer together are referred to as the "pleadings."

Pretrial Discovery and Pretrial Conferences

Pretrial discovery permits a party to find out what sort of evidence the other party has that relates to the suit at hand. Certain privileged matters are not subject to discovery. Depositions (or sworn statements on a matter concerning the lawsuit, such as a witness's reactions) are taken. Depositions record testimony of persons who are unavailable for the trial or save a witness's reaction while it is fresh in his or her mind.

Pretrial conferences are simply meetings where opposing lawyers get together with the judge before trial. The lawyers tell the judge the heart of their case and how they intend to prove it. This conference, along with pretrial discovery reduces trial time, and helps speed up settlement.

The Trial, Verdict, and Judgment

A trial tries to settle disputes without violence. It gives a litigant an opportunity to have his or her day in court to present publicly his or her evidence and legal theories of recovery. Aside from the litigants and their attorneys, the judge and jury are the principal "actors" in a trial. The judge insures that only proper evidence and legal arguments are presented for the fact trier's consideration. When a case reaches trial, there is usually some conflict in what the parties claim are the facts. It is the jury's job to resolve fact disputes. If a jury trial is waived (given up), the judge is the fact finder.

Once each party's case has been presented, the fact trier decides who is telling the truth by announcing its verdict. The judge usually then pronounces judgment in accordance with the jury's verdict. The **judgment** is a court decree that a defendant is or is not obligated in some way to a plaintiff. See Figure 3-4. A court's judgment does not have to follow what the jury has decreed as its verdict. If, for example, the jury has returned a verdict completely at odds with the evidence (motivated, for instance, by sympathy for one of the parties), the other party can ask the court for **judgment notwithstanding the verdict.** This is a jury control device and is a reduction of the power that the jury otherwise has. Much the same is true of the **directed verdict,** which is a motion that a party's counsel makes during the actual trial, asking, in effect, that the judge stop the trial and direct, or order, the verdict. This motion is made on the premise that the evidence up to that point destroys the other party's case so that no later evidence can change the result.

Figure 3-3 **The Answer**

IN THE UNITED STATES DISTRICT COURT
FOR THE EASTERN DISTRICT OF TENNESSEE,
NORTHERN DIVISION

FILED JUN 18 1975

ELENA DeZAVALA b/n/f
LOUIS B. DeZAVALA, PLAINTIFFS
VS.
BETTY J. HOBBS
and
JAMES B. HOBBS, DEFENDENTS

NO. 3-75-125

ANSWER

The defendents, Betty J. Hobbs and James B. Hobbs, for answer to the complaint filed against them in this cause, say as follows:

1. They admit that they are citizens of Tennessee and that Louis Victor DeZavala died in Sullivan County, Tennessee, on May 2, 1975, but they have no knowledge as to the other allegations in the first and second paragraphs of the complaint so they neither admit nor deny such allegations and demand strict proof thereof.

2. They admit that this Court has jurisdiction of this action, provided there is diversity of citizenship, as alleged.

3. They admit that the defendant, Betty J. Hobbs, was driving the automobile which collided with the automobile driven by the deceased, Louis Victor DeZavala at or about the time and place alleged.

4. They admit that the defendant, James B. Hobbs, was the owner of the automobile being driven by his wife, Betty J. Hobbs, at the time of this accident, and that the family purpose doctrine is applicable.

5. They deny all allegations of negligence and statutory violations on the part of the defendant, Betty J. Hobbs.

6. They admit that the deceased, Louis Victor DeZavala, died as a result of injuries in this accident, but they aver that his death was instantaneous.

7. For lack of knowledge, they neither admit nor deny the allegations in paragraph VII of the complaint, and demand strict proof thereof.

8. They plead proximate or remote contributory negligence on the part of the deceased.

AND NOW HAVING ANSWERED, the defendants pray to be hence dismissed with their costs and demand a jury to try this cause.

Fred H. Cagle, Jr.
P. O. Box 39
Knoxville, Tennessee 37901

Attorney for Defendants
FRANTZ, McCONNELL & SEYMOUR

CERTIFICATE OF SERVICE

I certify that an exact copy of the foregoing document has been served upon counsel for all parties to the litigation to which it pertains, either by hand delivery of a copy thereof to the offices of said counsel, or by mailing a copy to said counsel in a properly addressed and stamped envelope regularly deposited in the United States Mail.

This 17 day of Jun, 1975.

For FRANTZ, McCONNELL & SEYMOUR

Figure 3-4 **Example of a Judgment**

United States District Court

FOR THE

EASTERN DISTRCT OF TENNESSEE, NORTHERN DIVISION

ELENA DeZAVALA, b/n/f/
and grandfather
LOUIS B. DeZAVALA

VS.

BETTY J. HOBBS &
JAMES HOBBS

CIVIL ACTION FILE NO. 3-75-125

JUDGMENT

This action came on trial before the Court and a jury, Honorable Robert L. Taylor , United States District Judge, presiding, and the issues having been duly tried and the jury having duly rendered its verdict;

It is Ordered and Adjudged that the Plaintiffs, Elena DeZavala, b/n/f and grandfather, Louis B. DeZavala, recover of the defendents Betty J. Hobbs and James Hobbs, the sum of Twenty-Five Thousand ($25,000) Dollars, plus property damage in the amount of Three Hundred ($300) Dollars, with interest thereon at the rate of six percent as provided by law, and their costs of action.

Dated at Knoxville, Tennessee , this 25th day of August, 1975.

Filed 25 day of Aug 1975
Ent'd ___ Order Book 71, p. 326
KARL D. SAULPAW, JR., CLERK
by [signature] Dep. Clerk

KARL D. SAULPAW, JR.
Clerk of Court
By [signature]

"This daily metamorphosis never fails to amaze me. Around the house, I'm a perfect idiot. I come to court, put on a black robe, and, by God, I'm it!"

Res Judicata Rule

Parties in a lawsuit have a right to have their case tried only once under normal circumstances. This right is known as the **res judicata rule.** The idea is to settle disputes, not let them be retried over and over.

Appeals

The goal of the res judicata rule is to end a dispute, except in the case of an appeal. A party dissatisfied with the trial court's disposition of the case may appeal to a higher court on the theory that the trial court made a mistake at some point. The appellate court's main job is to insure that the proper legal rules were recognized and correctly applied in disposing of the case in the lower court. If an error in law or a serious fact determination affecting the outcome was made, the appellate court returns the case in the lower court and directs a retrial to apply the correct principles.

Collecting a Judgment

Suppose a civil lawsuit and all appeals have ended in the defendant's favor. Assuming no counterclaim was filed by the defendant in the case, the matter would end with no order of payment of money from the defendant to the plaintiff.

If, on the other hand, the plaintiff has won the lawsuit, won any appeals, and been awarded a money judgment, with the result that the defendant has been ordered to pay the plaintiff a sum of money, the plaintiff becomes a **judgment creditor.** The losing defendant becomes a **judgment debtor** in such a case. If the world were perfect from the judgment creditor's standpoint, the judgment debtor would pull out his or her wallet, peel off cash in the amount of the judgment, and turn it over to the judgment creditor. Then the dispute would end. Successful plaintiffs in civil lawsuits seldom see this happen. Often, of course, defendant/judgment debtor's liability insurance pays the judgment in full, which ends the matter. Other times, the defendant proves to be "judgment-proof," meaning that he or she is so poor that any attempt to collect would be futile. However, judgments last for a number of years and can be renewed. Therefore, a judgment creditor may have a number of years to collect from a judgment debtor. Thus, one should not quickly give up hope of collecting the judgment. Also, a judgment that has not been paid by the judgment debtor can be sold by the judgment creditor (for a fraction of the judgment's face amount) to a third party.

Judgment debtor's property Assume that the judgment creditor tries to collect the judgment from the judgment debtor's assets. The first question that arises concerns what property is available to pay the creditor's claims? The general rule is that all of the debtor's property presently owned or possibly acquired at some future date may be seized by the judgment creditor unless it is exempt. For example, the debtor's car, house, personal belongings, club memberships (to the extent they have commercial value), stocks, bonds, notes receivable from third parties, and proprietary interests in a sole proprietorship or partnership business may all be seized and sold to pay amounts owed to a judgment creditor unless they are exempt.

Exempt property **Exempt property** results from state and federal laws designed to protect the debtor's ability to survive by letting him or her keep bare necessities—those items required to survive. The theory of state exemption laws is that while a debtor should pay his or her debts, the debtor should not be cast naked and penniless on welfare with no place to live or without clothes or basic household goods.

Items covered by exemption laws What specific items a person owns fall into the category of exempt property that may not be seized to pay his or her debts? The answer is complex, since exemption laws are both state and federal; there is also variance among the states as to what items are exempted. Most states give a debtor a **homestead exemption,** which, as the name suggests, refers to the house where the debtor lives. This exemption is often limited to a low dollar figure, which may be enough to protect debtor's home equity. All states exempt life insurance policies to some extent. The earnings or wages of the debtor are generally not exempt under exemption laws, but state and federal garnishment limitations, discussed below, *do* limit a creditor's ability to take a debtor's wages. It would seem incredible to allow a judgment creditor to seize a debtor's welfare payments, given the live-and-let-live philosophy of exemption laws; yet about half of the states do not exempt welfare payments. Generally, amounts of money that debtors receive from retirement programs—both public and private—are exempt from creditors' claims, although some private plans are exempt only up to a specific dollar amount. Usually alimony and child support payments are not exempt—another peculiarity. Certain household and personal items, such as furniture, stoves, refrigerators, beds, and televisions, are exempt, along with miscellaneous property that includes wedding rings, bibles, family pictures, books, guns, historical and scientific collections, and cemetery lots.

Exemption waivers Two final points about exemptions. **Exemptions** may be waived, or voluntarily given up, and certain debts may be collected even from exempt property.

Writs of execution and garnishment As the above discussion illustrates, much potential property of the judgment debtor is available to pay off a judgment obtained by the successful plaintiff. The next inquiry is: What legal devices are available to enable the judgment creditor to obtain such property? Generally speaking, a judgment creditor may not simply walk onto a judgment debtor's property and take whatever property can be found that appears valuable enough to pay off the judgment debt. Rather, the judgment creditor must again return to the legal system and in another hearing try to collect the judgment. After-judgment legal devices the judgment creditor may use to obtain the judgment debtor's property include writs of execution and garnishment, which are state law remedies and, thus, vary in detail from state to state.

A **writ of execution** is a form the judgment creditor gets from the clerk of the court telling a court official (such as the sheriff) to go onto the judgment debtor's property and take nonexempt assets. After the official seizes the property, he or she conducts a public auction to sell the property and turns over the money received to the judgment creditor. Any amount greater than the judgment debt is returned to the judgment debtor. If the amount received is insufficient to pay the judgment, more nonexempt property of the judgment debtor may be seized and sold in like manner.

If the writ of execution results in the seizure and sale of all the debtor's nonexempt property and this money is still not enough to pay off the judgment debt, **garnishment** is another legal method available to the judgment creditor to obtain payment of his or her judgment. One could well ask what value garnishment

Figure 3-5 **How to Find a Lawyer**

We are all consumers. For transportation we "know" whether we need a new or used pickup truck, four-door sedan, station wagon, or rental car.

When it comes to legal services, how can we as consumers find the "right" lawyer? ("Attorney-at-law" and "lawyer" are synonymous.) We probably know generally what our legal problem is. For example, mom, a widow, just died and left a house, a car, and insurance. She had no will. How do we decide who gets the property?

The "right" lawyer is the one who will give competent, fast, and reasonably priced service *for your particular problem.* (You do not neet an antitrust lawyer to handle a traffic ticket.)

Here are a few tips on finding a lawyer for your problem (this list is by no means complete):

1. Call the local bar association, which is the lawyers' professional organization. Such organizations are usually listed in the telephone book's yellow pages. When you call, generally describe your problem and ask for names of attorneys who could help you. Ask if there is any charge for talking to the lawyer the first time (an "initial consultation fee") and ask how much the fee is if there is one.
2. Ask friends, who have had similar legal problems, for the names of their lawyers. If they were satisfied, you probably will be too.
3. Look at the telephone book's yellow pages, at newspaper ads, and at television and radio ads for attorneys' advertisements, which often indicate the fees for routine legal services.

has if the writ of execution has already resulted in the sale of all of the debtor's nonexempt property. The answer is that writs of execution are used only to take property directly from the judgment debtor. However, many times other people (called "garnishees" if a creditor goes after the debtor's property in their hands) owe the judgment debtor money. An employer, for example, could owe the judgment debtor salary or wages. Also, the debtor may own property that is not in his or her possession. A writ of execution cannot reach such property. The garnishment order may be obtained from the clerk of court to reach assets of the sorts described. However, it usually may not be obtained until after a writ of execution fails to produce enough property to satisfy the judgment.

KEY TERMS

Administrative agencies
Compromising claims
Mediation
Arbitration
Arbitrator
Award
Pro se
Lawyers
Subject matter jurisdiction
In personam jurisdiction
Long-arm statutes
Cause of action
Default judgment
Judgment
Judgment notwithstanding the verdict
Directed verdict
Res judicata rule
Judgment creditor
Judgment debtor
Exempt property
Homestead exemption
Exemption
Writ of execution
Garnishment

CHAPTER PROBLEMS

1. Can a state prevent attorneys from advertising?
2. What is the difference between arbitration and mediation?
3. What is an administrative agency? How does it help settle disputes?
4. Who benefits from a default judgment?
5. What is a pro se litigant?
6. What items are protected from creditor seizure under exemption laws?
7. Name three steps in civil lawsuits.

*8. Juror misconduct is one reason an appellate court will thow out, or overturn, a lower court's judgment based on a jury's verdict. Jurors are only supposed to consider relevant evidence in deciding if and how much damage someone suffers. Whether a defendant has liability insurance to pay a plaintiff's injuries is irrelevant. William Lightfoot sued his dentist, J. J. Tucker for negligently performing an overdenture procedure. The procedure resulted in great pain, pus discharge, and embarrassment from "Bugs Bunny" false teeth, which the dentist sold Lightfoot. During the trial, one juror casually remarked to another juror that dentists usually carry liability insurance. Was this juror misconduct that would cause the appellate court to overturn the lower court's $77,500 judgment for Lightfoot? *Tucker v. Lightfoot*, 653 S.W.2d 587 (1983).

9. In one case Goldfarb hunted for an attorney to do a title search. No attorney would perform such legal services for less than the minimum fee set by the bar association. Goldfarb then sued the bar association claiming that it violated the antitrust laws by price fixing. Was Goldfarb right? *Goldfarb v. Virginia State Bar*, 355 F.Supp. 491.

*10. Alan Keel was at Green's Disco. The bartenders at Green's switch on red lights on their cash registers when they need a crowd controller (or "bouncer"). One evening, a bartender summoned a bouncer and told him that two shot glasses and a bottle of Southern Comfort bourbon had disappeared. One bouncer noticed Alan Keel a few feet from the bar with a shot glass in one hand. Two bouncers "escorted" Keel from the bar allegedly with some violence. Green's assistant manager signed an affidavit claiming that Keel had stolen the shot glass. Keel was arrested, booked, and jailed. His parents bailed him out the next morning. At a hearing, a magistrate dismissed charges against Keel. Keel then sued Green's Disco for malicious prosecution, false imprisonment, and assault. A jury awarded him $45,000. Green's Disco appealed. May an appellate court set aside a jury verdict as excessive if the verdict was *not* due to prejudice or corrupt influence on the jury? *Medoc Corp. v. Keel,* 305 S.E.2d 134 (1983).

". . . make the punishment fit the crime."

Gilbert and Sullivan
The Mikado

Chapter 4

Business Crimes

CHAPTER PREVIEW

- General parts of a crime
- Four classic objectives of criminal law
- Superior protection of criminal over civil procedure
- Distinction between felony and misdemeanor
- Definition of embezzlement
- Discussion of obtaining property under false pretenses
- Six general defenses to criminal charges
- Definition of larceny
- Extortion example

"All I did was return the car late to the used car lot," said Ms. DeWall. "Now they're charging me with embezzlement." She had taken a used car out on a test drive at 4 PM and when she returned, the car lot was closed. She then drove the car 300 miles into a neighboring state and returned the car to the lot early the next morning. Was this embezzlement?

This chapter defines "crime" and states the objectives of criminal law. It presents defenses to crimes and also surveys the business crimes of embezzlement, credit card fraud, "bad check" statutes, obtaining property under false pretenses, and the Racketeer Influenced and Corrupt Organizations Act (RICO).

OBJECTIVES OF CRIMINAL LAW

There are four classic objectives of criminal law:

1. *Restraining* persons convicted of crimes.
2. *Deterring* would-be violators.
3. *Avenging* the wrong to society.
4. *Rehabilitating* the convicted wrongdoer.

These objectives protect both society and the accused.

Criminal Law Enforcers

The district attorney, attorney general, or **prosecutor** is the person who represents society and prosecutes, or sues, the defendant. Private persons may not prosecute others criminally.

State and Federal Criminal Law

Each state has its own set of criminal laws. In addition, the national, or federal, government has its own criminal laws.

Criminal Procedures Protect the Accused

Criminal procedures, which are governing the mechanics of trying criminal cases, protect the accused in several ways. First, the accused is presumed innocent. Second, the government must prove its case beyond a reasonable doubt, or a "heavy burden." Third, the defendant is entitled to an open, speedy jury trial. Fourth, the state must tell defendants about the charges brought against them. Fifth, the government must not conduct illegal searches and seizures to get evidence. Sixth, defendants do not have to testify against themselves.

Definition of a Crime

A **crime** has two parts: a prohibited act, or **"actus reus,"** and criminal intent or **"mens rea."** In general, the two elements must be present simultaneously to satisfy the definition of "crime." In some cases, legislatures eliminate the intent element and create strict liability crimes; in these cases, doing the act is a crime, no matter what the intent. A crime that doesn't require intent is the Rivers and Harbors Act, which makes it illegal to dump refuse into navigable waters. No intent is required.

Types of Crimes

There are three general types of crimes: treason, felonies, and misdemeanors. **Treason** is the one and only crime that the United States Constitution defines. This definition states that treason consists of levying war against the United States or giving aid and comfort to their enemies.

Either the states or federal government can create felonies and misdemeanors. In theory, **felonies** are serious crimes while **misdemeanors** are small offenses. The difference between felonies and misdemeanors at the federal level is the possible punishment. Felonies are punishable by death or imprisonment for over one year; misdemeanors are punishable by fines or imprisonment of one year or less. States make similar distinctions between felonies and misdemeanors.

Defenses to Criminal Charges

There are many criminal defenses including:

1. Failure of prosecution to prove an element of the crime.
2. Failure of prosecution to prove its case beyond a reasonable doubt.
3. Insanity (there are several insanity tests).
4. Mistake of fact (if it negates the crime's mental element).
5. Mistake of law (if it negates the crime's mental element; however, ignorance of the law is no defense).
6. Minority.
7. Entrapment.
8. The statute of limitations (for some crimes).
9. Drunkenness (if it negates the crime's mental element).

Obtaining Property Under False Pretenses ("Swindling")

Obtaining property under **false pretenses** is a statutory crime; the definition varies slightly in each jurisdiction since state laws are involved.

Definition The definition of false pretenses in most states includes five elements: 1. *False representation* of a material past or present fact; 2. *causing* the victim; 3. to *pass title;* 4. to his or her *property* to the wrongdoer; 5. who *knows* that his or her representation is false and intends to use it to defraud the victim.

Defenses The following are defenses used in false pretense cases:

1. If the defendant makes a true statement but mistakenly believes that it is false, there are no false pretenses.
2. An opinion, such as one speculating about the "worth" of a building or land, is "seller's talk" and *not* fact—even if exaggerated. Sometimes courts hold defendants liable for false opinions where the matter is peculiarly within the speaker's knowledge. In one case, a defendant knew realty was worth $330 at most but sold it for $7700; the defendant had represented to the victim that the property was worth $11,000. The defendant was convicted of false pretenses.
3. There is "no reliance" if the defendant's false representations cause the victim to transfer property to defendant. The defendant is not guilty of false pretenses if the victim does not believe defendant.

The *Harwei, Inc. v. State* case illustrates this type of situation.

Embezzlement

Embezzlement is the fraudulent conversion of another's property by someone who lawfully possesses it. In other words, the wrongdoer lawfully has someone else's property but converts it to his or her own use. "Convert" here means that the wrongdoer seriously interferes with the owner's rights. The act of embezzlement must be intentional, and not mistaken or negligent.

Embezzlement is a statutory crime. It differs from false pretenses because the wrongdoer in embezzlement legally has possession of another's property and *then*

HARWEI, INC. v. STATE
Indiana Appellate Ct. (2nd Dist.).
459 N.E.2d 52 (1984).

FACTS The Marion County prosecutor's office was conducting an operation known as "Transcam." Their objective was to identify and convict transmission repair shops doing unnecessary auto repairs. On March 31, 1982, Wilson, an employee in the prosecutor's office, drove a 1979 Olds Cutlass to the Precision transmission shop. She told Harris, who was president of Harwei, Inc., and doing business as Precision Transmission, that the car would only go thirty miles per hour, seemed to be in the same gear all the time, and used excessive amounts of gasoline. About three hours later Harris told her that the clutch and some of the transmission gears were ruined and needed replacing. The next day she picked up the repaired car and paid a $194.04 bill. It covered replacing the valve body and governor ($101.00) as well as removing and replacing the transmission ($89.00 plus tax). Dailey, a police detective, had a 1979 Olds towed to Precision. He told Harris that the car was overheated and locked the torque converter to the front of the pump. Harris told Dailey that the transmission was beyond repair. Dailey told Harris to replace it, and paid the $502.92 bill. Before either Wilson's or Dailey's cars were taken to Precision, a Purdue University mechanical engineering professor had inspected each car to insure that they were in good condition. Under his direction, mechanics put a defective governor gear in each car, which can be easily replaced without removing the transmission. In all other respects, the transmissions were perfect. The prosecutor charged Harwei, Inc. (Precision) and Harris each with a statutory crime of theft by false impression (substantially the same as obtaining property by false pretenses). Defendants argued that since Wilson and Dailey were "in on" the prosecutor's scheme, they knew that Harris' representations were untrue; therefore, Harris gave no false impression (or pretense) and hence could not have defrauded them.

ISSUE Is it necessary that the intended victim actually be tricked to prove that property was obtained under false impression (pretense)?

DECISION Yes. Charges of theft by false impression were thrown out. However, Harris and Harwei, Inc. were guilty of *attempting* to obtain property by false pretenses. It is not necessary for an intended victim to be defrauded or tricked in a crime of attempt.

LEGAL TIP

Businesses should be aware that knowingly performing unnecessary work for customers can make them criminally liable for obtaining property under false pretenses.

converts it. In a case involving false pretenses, the wrongdoer does something illegal to get possession of another's property.

Defenses A person cannot convert his or her own property. One also cannot embezzle labor, or another's services, since it is not "property." Other defenses include mistake of fact or law if they cancel the intent to defraud. Infancy and insanity are additional defenses.

Replacement no defense It is no defense for the wrongdoer to misuse the entrusted property and then replace it. For example, a banker who converts bank money for weekend gambling in Atlantic City, makes money, and replaces the amount converted before anyone notices, is an embezzler. However, replacement would probably reduce the punishment if the wrongdoer were caught. The *State v. DeWall* case is an example of embezzlement.

Bad Check Statutes

Virtually all states have passed **bad check statutes.** These laws differ from state to state. Generally these statutes require giving a "bad" check (one where insufficient funds are in the account drawn on) and a "bad state of mind" (wording varies from state to state).

STATE v. DEWALL

**Supreme Court of South Dakota.
343 N.W.2d 790 (S.D. 1984).**

FACTS At 4:00 PM one afternoon, DeWall and her cousin looked over some used cars on Russ Devine's car lot in Watertown, South Dakota. They asked if they could test drive a 1980 Citation. DeVine gave them permission to drive the car to a local motel where DeWall's mother worked. DeWall and her cousin drove by the motel and stopped at some other local businesses. When they returned to DeVine's car lot, it was closed. After filling up with gas, DeWall and her cousin took a 300-mile drive through South Dakota and Minnesota. When they arrived back in Watertown in the early morning, DeWall had her cousin return the car to DeVine's lot and lock the keys in it. DeWall was tried and convicted for embezzling property that she received in trust. DeWall claimed she did receive property (the car) in trust but that did not intend to deprive DeVine of it permanently.

ISSUE Does "embezzlement" under South Dakota law require that a defendant intend to deprive the victim of his or her property *permanently?*

DECISION No. DeWall's embezzlement conviction was upheld. The South Dakota embezzlement statute requires proof of "intent to defraud" in appropriating property to a use outside the defendant's trust. The embezzlement statute does not require "intent to deprive" another of his or her property permanently. This is how embezzlement differs from theft, where there is a requirement that the wrongdoer "intend to deprive" the owners of their property permanently.

LEGAL TIP

A bailee, or person borrowing someone else's property, who uses property beyond the scope of the trust commits embezzlement.

Property from the victim Most bad check laws do *not* require that the passer get anything from the victim, although bad check passers usually *do* get something.

Passer's state of mind Many bad check statutes require that bad check passers *know* that they lack money in the account and *intend* to defraud. Some statutes merely require the check passer to *know* that the account lacks sufficient funds to cover the check.

If the bank dishonors the check and the passer does not pay within ten days after notice, statutes often say that this establishes prima facie the passer's "bad" state of mind. *People v. Kunzelman* is an example of a "bad check" case.

Mail Fraud

It is a federal felony to use the mails in furtherance of a scheme to defraud. Thus the elements of **mail fraud** are:

1. A scheme to defraud.
2. Mailing a letter (or anything) to execute the scheme.

The scheme need not actually defraud anyone (unlike false pretenses where the victim must be defrauded). In other words, there does not have to be direct, tangible economic loss to the victim.

Reckless indifference for the truth can be fraudulent under the mail fraud statute. The *United States v. Uhrig* case illustrates mail fraud.

PEOPLE v. KUNZELMAN

Colorado Court of Appeals.
649 P.2d 340 (1982).

FACTS On November 16, 1977, Wallace, a car salesman, arranged for a customer, Kunzelman, to buy tires at a dealer discount store. Wallace gave the tire dealer one of his employer's purchase order numbers. Kunzelman then picked up twelve studded snow tires. Kunzelman did not pay for the tires when he picked them up, so the discounter charged $1039.93 to Wallace's account. Wallace promptly paid. Several days later Wallace went to Kunzelman's home to get the tires he had paid for. Kunzelman offered Wallace a check for a full purchase price. Wallace accepted it and let Kunzelman keep the tires. When Kunzelman wrote the check, his account was already overdrawn by $39.84. His check to Wallace was returned to the bank twice because of insufficient funds. Kunzelman was convicted of check fraud under a Colorado "bad check" statute. He argued that his conviction was improper because he already had the tires when he gave Wallace the check and had therefore not received a "thing of value," as required by the bad check statute. In effect, he argued, he was paying on a pre-existing debt.

ISSUE Had Kunzelman received anything of value when he gave Wallace his bad check?

DECISION Yes. The Colorado bad check statute required that a "thing of value" be given for the bad check. The Colorado Supreme Court, in a prior case, had held that giving a bad check for a *pre-existing debt* did not amount to receiving a "thing of value" for the check (since the debt already existed when the check was given). In this case, Wallace—not Kunzelman—owned the tires. Therefore, Wallace had the right to possess the tires when he went to Kunzelman's to pick them up. Wallace gave up his ownership and right to possession when Kunzelman gave him the check. Since Kunzelman did get something for the bad check, his conviction for check fraud was upheld.

LEGAL TIP

Before finding that there is check fraud, some courts rely on bad check statutes which require the person giving a "bad" check to receive something of value.

Extortion, or "Blackmail"

The essence of extortion, or **blackmail,** is making a threat with the intent to cause a victim to give up his or her property.

Extortion makes it a crime for public officials to receive a fee that they are not entitled to under "color of public office." Basically, the official "sells" his or her

UNITED STATES v. UHRIG

U.S. Court of Appeals (7th Cir.).
443 F.2d 239, certiorari denied
404 U.S. 832 (1971).

FACTS Uhrig, a "highly articulate and persuasive former minister," ran an executive placement business. He sent promotional material through the mails saying that his business was placing applicants "on an almost daily basis." The mailings also claimed that Uhrig's firm dealt with 25,000 companies at the top level. In fact, the business placed only 5 applicants during its existence and only dealt with companies through standard business directories. Uhrig's firm would send resumes and call company executives listed in them. Uhrig was convicted of federal mail fraud. He argued that his mailings were merely "puffing."

ISSUE Were the statements in Uhrig's promotional mailings made with the knowledge that they were false?

DECISION Yes. Given what the defendant knew about the operation of the new business he had started up, he must have known that the statements mailed in the promotional material were false.

LEGAL TIP

To avoid mail fraud, do not exaggerate in mailed advertising.

office a bit at a time by committing extortion. Extortion used to be a common law misdemeanor; now, however, extortion statutes outlaw threats by *anyone* made with intent to cause a victim to part with his or her property. Some statutes require that the victim actually give up the property.

How is extortion made? Extortion threats can be either oral or written.

What threats are used in extortion? Extortion threats can involve harming the victim or the victim's property or family; exposing disgraceful defects (even if true); or accusing one of criminal conduct (even if true). The threat can involve the victim or his or her family and can be a present or future threat.

United States v. Kelly is an extortion case under the federal Hobbs Act.

UNITED STATES v. KELLY
U.S. Court of Appeals (1st Cir.).
722 F.2d 873 (1983).

FACTS Mr. Kelly was a Massachusetts State Senator. He served on the state Ways and Means Committee. He was indicted for extortion for accepting money, travel, and equipment from Masiello and Associates (architects). In exchange, Kelly allegedly directed state building contracts to Masiello. Trial testimony indicated that Kelly threatened the Masiello firm or caused them to fear retaliatory action "under color of official right." For example, Masiello testified that "[someone] asked . . . if Senator Kelly could . . . have our contracts cancelled in Massachusetts . . . and I said, There isn't any question about it." Federal prosecutors charged Kelly with extortion under the Hobbs Act. The Hobbs Act defines "extortion" as "the obtaining of property from another, with his consent, induced by wrongful use of actual or threatened force, violence, or fear, *or* under color of official right." Kelly argued that Masiello's statements about fearing Kelly were not proof of extortion under color of official right. Rather, the statements showed that taking property by actual or threatened force provoked violence or fear. Kelly was not charged with the second type of extortion, just the first.

ISSUE Had Kelly, the state senator, committed extortion by obtaining property under color of official right?

DECISION Yes. Kelly argued that the Hobbs Act created extortion in two ways: 1) taking property by wrongful use of actual or threatened force, violence, or fear; or 2) "taking property under color of official right." Kelly argued that he was charged under #1 but convicted under #2; this violates his procedural rights. The accepted interpretation of the "under color of official right" allows proof of threats inherent in public office. The use of public office with the authority to grant or withhold benefits, takes the place of pressure or threats. So therefore, it did not prejudice Kelly to be charged under one "prong" of the extortion definition and convicted under another "prong." Kelly knew what the alleged wrongs were and had a chance to defend against them.

LEGAL TIP
A public official who demands "favors" for doing what he or she has a public duty to do could be committing extortion.

Credit Card Statutes

Credit card use today often involves three parties: the consumer-user, the card issuer, and the creditor (or the business where the consumer shops). Usually the issuer pays the creditor the amount of the user charges minus a fee. The consumer-user then pays the issuer, who risks misuse of the card.

Most states have **credit card statutes.** These make it either a felony or misdemeanor to get property or services by use of stolen, revoked, cancelled, or forged credit cards. Such laws also prohibit other unauthorized credit card use. *People v. Ford* is an example of unauthorized credit card use.

PEOPLE v. FORD

Supreme Court of Michigan.
331 N.W.2d 878 (Mich. 1982).

FACTS On July 22, 1978, Mr. Ford presented a Clark Oil credit card to a Battle Creek, Michigan, gas station. The card had been issued to the Calhoun County Action Agency in the name of Al Johnson. Ford signed Al Johnson's name on the credit card sales slip and got $21.30 cash from the attendant. Johnson had not authorized Ford to use the card. Ford admitted that he presented the card to defraud the attendant. Ford was charged and convicted of uttering and publishing a false instrument or writing under a Michigan statute. He received a four- to fourteen-year sentence. Michigan also had a more specific statute prohibiting credit card misuse. It had a four-year maximum penalty. Ford argued that when two statutes cover the same subject matter, one statute being general and the other specific, the specific controls.

ISSUE Is it proper to prosecute a defendant under a general "uttering false instruments" statute for credit card fraud when a specific credit card statute also covers the offense?

DECISION Yes. There was no exclusivity provision in the credit card statute. Therefore, the credit card misuse statute did not expressly prohibit prosecutions under the more general, false instruments statute. Clearly, each statute covered the offense here. Since the specific credit card statute did not necessarily involve the same elements as the more general statute, the specific statute does not prohibit prosecution and conviction under the more general statute.

LEGAL TIP

Persons using credit cards without authorization often can be prosecuted criminally under more than one statute.

Racketeer Influenced and Corrupt Organizations Act (RICO)

The Racketeer Influenced and Corrupt Organizations Act (**RICO**) is a federal statute passed in 1970. It is a federal attack on complex criminal activity.

Basically RICO makes it illegal for people to commit two or more specified crimes during a ten-year period. The two crimes must be related to an "enterprise," which is broadly defined. Enterprise covers legitimate organizations (such as governors' offices, police departments, corporations, partnerships, individuals or groups of individuals, and unions) and illegitimate organizations (such as the "mafia").

Racketeering pattern prohibited RICO prohibits a "pattern of racketeering." As stated above, a "racketeering pattern" occurs when someone takes part in two or more "racketeering acts related to an enterprise during a ten-year period.

Racketeering acts RICO defines specific racketeering acts. These acts include federal crimes and eight state felonies. Therefore, if a person commits any two of these thirty-two acts during a ten-year period and they relate to an enterprise, the individual *also* violates RICO.

Examples of some of the twenty-four federal crimes, which RICO defines as racketeering acts, include: sports bribery, counterfeiting, embezzlement of welfare and pension funds, mail fraud, extortionate credit, certain gambling and drug offenses, interstate prostitution, interstate shipment of stolen property, embezzlement of union funds, and fraud in the sale of securities. However, federal antitrust and federal income tax violations are *not* RICO racketeering acts.

Punishment RICO's criminal sanctions include fines up to $25,000, up to twenty years of imprisonment, and forfeiture of assets obtained illegally. These penalties are added to those given for committing the racketeering acts (which are separate crimes). *United States v. LeRoy* is a case illustrating RICO.

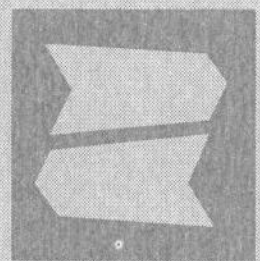

UNITED STATES v. LEROY

U.S. Court of Appeals (2nd Cir.).
687 F.2d 610 (1982); certiorari denied 103 S.Ct. 823 (1983).

FACTS Kevin V. LeRoy was vice president of a local union from June 1975 until May 1978. The union's business manager assigned LeRoy to a brewery construction job employing union laborers. LeRoy was job steward as well as a laborer on the construction site. The construction contracting company gave LeRoy time off for union business. LeRoy, in fact, never did any physical labor on this job. Nonetheless, the general contractor paid him $4430 in wages. The contractor admitted that he put LeRoy on the payroll to assure that there would be no serious labor disputes. LeRoy was similarly on several subcontractors' payrolls at the same time. In 1978 the union elected LeRoy business manager at a $38,000 annual salary plus expenses for union business. In 1979 he had car brake repairs at Barillo's AAA for $250.27 and paid for them. The union reimbursed him for this. Then he got another $212.24 check from the union payable to Barillo's . He took it to Barillos, told them it was for a bill he had already paid, and asked them to cash it and give him the money so he could be paid. Barillo's did so, unaware of his scheme. LeRoy also would have the union pay gas credit card bills as well as issue checks to himself for the purchases. Thus, the union paid for LeRoy's gas twice. Embezzling labor union funds is a racketeering act under the Racketeer Influenced and Corrupt Organizations Act (RICO). Since LeRoy embezzled union funds more than once in ten years, he engaged in a pattern of racketeering that was outlawed by RICO. LeRoy was convicted of violating RICO, sentenced to three concurrent three-year prison terms, and fined $5000. LeRoy appealed, agreeing that the government proved the enterprise, or union, affecting interstate commerce as well as his union association. However, LeRoy argued that his embezzlement was in furtherance of his own personal affairs and not those of the union (the enterprise).

ISSUE Were LeRoy's illegal activities in furtherance of the enterprise (as required by RICO) or in furtherance of his personal interest?

DECISION In furtherance of an enterprise (in this case, the union), RICO makes it unlawful "for any person . . . associated with any enterprise engaged . . . in interstate commerce . . . to participate . . . in the conduct of such enterprise's affairs through a pattern of racketeering activity." The racketeering does not have to be in *furtherance* of the enterprise. It is enough that the racketeering take place in conducting the union (the enterprise). Racketeering acts must be *related to* the enterprise to satisfy RICO's requirement that "one conduct the activities of an enterprise through a patter of racketeering."

LEGAL TIP

Not all federal crimes are RICO racketeering acts.

Forgery

Forgery aims to protect documents' genuineness. State laws create the crime of forgery and, therefore, differ somewhat. One case defined forgery as making or passing a false instrument with the intent to defraud. Some cases say that the false writing must have apparent legal significance. Thus, if an unknown artist uses a famous one's signature on a picture, forgery has not occurred since a picture is not a legally significant document (unlike a check or deed). Also, state laws do not require a victim to suffer a loss for forgery to exist.

KEY TERMS

Prosecutor
Criminal procedure
Crime
Actus reus
Mens rea
Treason
Felonies
Misdemeanors
False pretenses
Embezzlement
Bad check statutes
Mail fraud
Blackmail
Credit card statutes
RICO
Forgery

CHAPTER PROBLEMS

1. Give the four objectives of criminal law.
2. Whom does criminal procedure protect?
3. Define a crime.
4. What are three general types of crimes?
5. Name some defenses to criminal charges.
6. Is replacing the embezzled property a defense to an embezzlement charge?

*7. "Hanging paper," or issuing bad checks, is unfortunately standard operating procedure for some people. Lloyd was convicted of feloniously issuing bad checks. The judge took into account Lloyd's past record, including grand larceny by check, and sentenced Lloyd to five years in prison. Was this sentence an abuse of discretion? *State v. Lloyd,* 676 P.2d 229 (Mont. 1984).

*8. Has a buyer obtained property under false pretenses if he or she charges goods to a credit card, knowing that contractual payments are impossible? *Matter of Borah,* 36 B.R. 535 (Bkrtcy. Fla. 1983).

*9. Bobby Graham gave his friend, Ronnie Johnson, permission to charge long-distance telephone calls to Graham's number. Both lived in Alabama. After Johnson refused to repay Graham about $67 in calls, Graham told Johnson not to charge any more calls to that number. However, Johnson did telephone his girlfriend in Kansas and charged $300 more to Graham. Did Johnson commit a theft of services crime, which is an offense under Alabama statutes (roughly the same as unauthorized use of a credit card by a third party)? *Johnson v. State,* 421 So.2d 1307 (Ala. Cr. App. 1982).

*10. In criminal law, more than one statute frequently prohibits the same act. For example, general statutes outlaw obtaining property under false pretenses. These are often felony statutes carrying long prison terms and large fines. Michigan has such a law as well as an odometer tampering statute, which makes it a misdemeanor to set back odometers on cars, trucks, and similar vehicles. Violating this statute carries a maximum $100 fine and up to ninety days of imprisonment. Employees of Harvey Cadillac in Grand Rapids turned back the odometer on a 1977 Cadillac from 30,000 to 14,275 miles. The State of Michigan prosecuted them under the tougher (10-year maximum prison term) false pretenses statute. The defendants argued that they had to be prosecuted only under the more specific and lenient odometer statute. Were they right? *People v. Houseman,* 339 N.W.2d 666 (Mich. App. 1983).

"Tort law is a legal laboratory."
Prosser and Keeton
Torts, 5th Edition

Chapter 5

Negligence and Strict Liability

CHAPTER PREVIEW

- Definition of a tort
- Parts of the tort of negligence
- Two defenses to negligence
- Negligence per se
- Meaning of res ipsa loquitur
- Example of negligent infliction of mental distress
- Situations where strict liability applies
- Defenses to strict liability

"How could my car dealership have caused this customer's death?" asked Bob Haygood. A mechanic had negligently installed a wheel on a new car. The wheel came off on Interstate 85 just after Hariston, the customer, had taken delivery of the new car at Haygood's dealership. Hariston managed to stop the car in the interstate's right-hand lane. Another motorist in a van stopped immediately behind Hariston to help. Hariston got out of his car, went to his trunk, and stood between the two parked vehicles. Both vehicles had their flashers on. Within ninety seconds, a third person negligently drove a flatbed truck into the rear of the van knocking it into the rear of Hariston's new Continental. Hariston stood between the two parked vehicles during the collision and was killed. His widow sued Haygood's dealership for negligently causing her husband's death. Was Haygood's negligent installation of the wheel the proximate *cause of Hariston's death?*

WHAT IS A TORT?

The word "tort" comes from the French word meaning "to twist." In other words torts are "wrongs," or actions that are not "straight" (twisted). A **tort** is a breach of a noncontractual civil duty.

Look at the parts of the tort definition for a minute. As we have already said, torts are "civil wrongs." For example slander, libel negligence, and fraud are "civil wrongs." "Civil wrongs." mean wrongs individuals do to other individuals (as opposed to society as a whole, which are criminal—not civil—wrongs).

PLACING TORTS IN GENERAL BUSINESS LAW

Figure 1-2 is a diagram of traditional business law. The negligence, strict liability, and intentional tort areas shows the placement of these torts. As you can see, such torts are *civil* (not criminal), substantive law.

Tort Law Is Mainly State Law

Tort law is mainly state law. However, there is a Federal Tort Claims Act, which lets persons sue the United States Government for **torts** that its agents commit.

There are fifty states plus the District of Columbia and the territories. This means two things: First, it is possible that something could be a tort, or a wrong, in one state but not another. Second, even if a particular tort (such as slander) exists in all states, each state could define it differently.

Actually there is not much variation from state to state in what torts exist and how they are defined. Some states (such as California and New York) often recognize new legal wrongs (torts) sooner than others.

Tort Law Is Generally Judge Made Law

The common law tradition is that judges make most tort law. That is, judges decide what is a "wrong," or a tort, and thereby determine community standards of "right and wrong."

Torts Compared with Crimes

Overlap Torts and crimes have differences and similarities, and *could* overlap. One similarity is that both try to stop wrongful conduct. An area of overlap is that, some acts, such as slugging another in anger, could be *both* a tort (battery) and a crime (criminal battery).

To whom is duty owed? Torts differ from crimes in several ways. First, a person owes tort duties to another *person.* A person owes a duty to *society* not to commit crimes. This distinction, however, is not completely satisfactory since one owes tort duties to all individuals, which in a sense is society.

Enforcers Another difference between torts and crimes is who enforces them. It is society's representative—such as the district attorney—who enforces criminal law, whereas the injured victim enforces tort law. Of course government (society) can sue a person in tort for damages to government property.

Objectives Still another difference between tort and criminal law is their *objectives.* One of the objectives of criminal law is to punish. Tort law is usually compensatory—designed to restore the victim to the position that he or she was in before the tort. Occasionally, tort remedies include punitive damages designed to punish the person committing the tort.

Tort Law Is a Legal Laboratory

Tort law has been called a legal laboratory because courts' (judges') ideas change about what a tort is. For example, at one time there was no tort for invasion of privacy, but today there is one. Also, certain torts apply to more situations now than they once did. For instance, strict liability first applied to water leaking onto another's property causing damage. Today it also arises regarding defective products, handling wild animals, flying airplanes, and other situations.

Tort law has been a growing trend. In other words, there is a tendency on the part of courts to recognize new kinds of wrongs.

Tort Classifications

Type of victim: Property/person Torts can be classified in several ways. One classification—property torts and torts against the person—focuses on the victim. Property torts include trespass and conversion, while torts against persons include assault and battery. In a way, all torts are against people since they own property and sue if it is damaged.

Type of wrong Another tort classification looks at the *type* of wrong. For example, there are *intentional* torts, torts involving carelessness (negligence), and torts involving ultrahazardous activities (strict liability).

This chapter discusses negligence and strict liability. Chapter 6 examines intentional torts.

Negligence

Negligence involves carelessness that injures others. It is a tort that can occur almost anywhere—while driving a car, doing an audit, or supervising one's children.

There are four parts to negligence: (1) duty; (2) a breaking of the standard of care; (3) that proximately causes; (4) damages. All four parts must exist for negligence to occur.

Duty The "duty" part of negligence usually arises by "operation of law," meaning that a court or legislature says a person owes a duty of care to others. People do not have to pay each other $2 per month to create these duties. In other words, the duty to drive carefully (as in most activities) arises automatically because a lawmaker says so.

Standard of care People have duties to be careful in everything they do. But how careful? The degree is indicated by the "standard of care." The exact standard of care is what the ordinary, reasonable, prudent person (ORP person) would do in the same situation. It is an objective and not a subjective standard. Therefore, "reasonable" is determined by an ORP person and *not* by the person accused of negligence. An ORP person is just like each of us except that he or she is *always* reasonable and prudent. Occasionally we are not. When we are not, we have broken the standard of care that we owe others; breaking this standard is being legally "careless."

The standard of care is objective, but it takes many factors into account. For example, if a driver has a car accident, the amount of traffic, visibility, weather conditions, and much else determine how careful the driver should be (the standard of care). The driver's conduct is compared with these conditions to see if it meets the standard of care. The *Davenport v. Nixon* case discusses this issue.

DAVENPORT v. NIXON

Court of Appeal of Louisiana
(1st Cir.).
434 S.2d 1203 (1983).

FACTS Mr. Davenport was a 48-year-old man partially paralyzed from two previous strokes. He arrived at 2:45 AM to check in at the Admiral Hotel on Airline Highway in Baton Rouge. While walking to the check-in window, a stranger approached and asked Davenport to join him in his room for a drink. Davenport declined, and the stranger left. Davenport rang the night bell at the late-night check-in window. Mrs. Pearl Nixon, one of the owners, answered. She recognized Davenport, and due to his partially paralyzed hand, helped him with his money and filled in his registration card. Davenport asked to come inside to pay because he told her he carried a large sum of money. He also claimed to have told her about the stranger and his fear about showing money if he was still around. Mrs. Nixon said it was against her policy to admit people to the office after 10 PM Davenport paid and returned to his truck. The stranger reappeared and demanded Davenport's money. The stranger pulled a knife and began slashing at Davenport's chest. He reached into Davenport's pocket, took all the money, and cut Davenport's throat twice before Davenport broke off the blade. The man fled. Davenport was bleeding but managed to reach the check-in window to ring for help. Mrs. Nixon called an ambulance but did not help him further. Davenport sat on the curb bleeding until the ambulance took him to the hospital. He recovered and sued the Nixons for negligence in not protecting him from the stranger's criminal acts. The Nixons argued that businesses have no duty to protect customers against unforeseeable and unanticipated criminal acts of independent third persons.

ISSUE Did the owner or manager of the business here have a duty to protect the customer against an independent third person's criminal acts?

DECISION Yes. The general rule is that a business does *not* have a duty to protect customers against unforeseeable or unanticipated criminal acts of independent third persons. Here, however, the stranger's criminal acts were foreseeable. The attacker was another hotel guest, Fraser. Mrs. Nixon, an owner, had been aware of Fraser's suspicious activity around the hotel where he had been a guest for a week. This, coupled with Davenport's request for protection against a specific threat, could have led Mrs. Nixon to safeguard Davenport to his room. For example she could have watched him until he got to his room (she did not). She could have turned on a loud siren from inside the office upon seeing the attack (she did not).

LEGAL TIP

Businesses generally have no duty to protect customers from unforeseeable criminal attacks by independent third parties.

Many states recognize the *negligence per se* doctrine. It helps plaintiffs prove defendants were careless. This rule says that a defendant conclusively breaks a duty of care by not obeying a statute (or regulation) setting a level of care (for example, speed limit laws) and the statute is intended to protect the plaintiff and prevent the type of loss plaintiff suffers. The *Munford, Inc. v. Peterson* case illustrates negligence per se.

Res ipsa loquitur is Latin. This phrase means that "the thing speaks for itself." It is another legal idea helping a negligence plaintiff prove that the defendant was careless (broke the standard of care). Courts apply this idea where three facts occur: first, only the defendant controls what caused the harm; and second, the loss would not usually have happened unless there had been negligence; and third, the event must not have been due to any voluntary action or contribution by the plaintiff. If these three facts occur, res ipsa loquitur allows an *inference of negligence,* meaning that a plaintiff has negligence unless a defendant has some defense. *Brown v. Racquet Club of Bricktown* is a case example.

MUNFORD, INC. v. PETERSON

Supreme Court of Mississippi.
368 So.2d 213 (1979).

FACTS A Mississippi statute prohibited the sale of beer to any person under 18 years old. After baseball practice 5 boys (3 aged 14, one aged 13, and one aged 15) went to the Magic Market and bought some orange juice. They drank it with vodka one of the boys had. They then returned to the Magic Market where a fourteen year old bought a six pack of fourteen-ounce cans of beer. The woman operator asked if he was eighteen. The boy said, "Yes," and she did not request proof of age. The boys drank the beer at David Black's house. Four of the boys left David. They returned to the Magic Market and bought a six pack of beer two more *different* times that night. No inquiry was made about the buyer's age either time. The four boys drank the beer and began to drive around. About 4 AM Tommy Blankenship, one of the four boys was driving. He lost control of the car. It hit a seawall, flew fifty-seven feet, rolled over five times, killing one of the boys, Scott Peterson. Scott's parents sued Munford Inc., owner of Magic Market for damages resulting from negligently selling beer in violation of the state statute.

ISSUE Was it negligence per se for a store to sell beer to minors in violation of a state statute?

DECISION Yes. When a person violates a statute, that person breaks the negligence standard of care. If this breach of the standard of care causes or contributes to another's injury, the injured person is entitled to recover. The way to determine a minor's age is for the seller of alcohol to make that assessment. The liquor seller has the responsibility to see that the law is not broken. The parents did state a cause of action based on negligence.

LEGAL TIP

Liquor sellers must check ages. Selling to minors is **negligence per se.**

BROWN v. RACQUET CLUB OF BRICKTOWN

Supreme Court of New Jersey.
471 A.2d 25 (1984).

FACTS The Ocean Tennis Association was a non-profit group of tennis players. It had tennis courts and a two-story clubhouse. Inside, wood stairs led from the first to the second floor. A fashion show and luncheon were held on the second floor on April 17, 1977, eleven months after issuance of the certificate of occupancy. Margaret Piscal and Jerilyn Brown attended the event. They were on the stairway when suddenly it pulled away from the wall and collapsed. Both were injured and sued the club. They tried to prove negligence by using res ipsa loquitur. Their argument was that the stairs were under the club's exclusive control when they collapsed. They also claimed that falling stairs raise an inference of negligence on the part of the party controlling them when they collapse. The defendant argued that it did not own or control the building when it and the stairs were built. Therefore, it should not be liable for someone else's negligence. The defendant also said that the defect was hidden and not easily discoverable.

ISSUE Does res ipsa loquitur apply when part of a building collapses and the present owner did not control the building during construction?

DECISION Yes. Res ipsa loquitur allows an inference that defendants break the standard of care in the following situations: first, the occurrence itself ordinarily suggests negligence; second, the cause of injury was within defendants' exclusive control; third, there is no indication in the circumstances that the injury resulted from plaintiffs' neglect. In this particular case the stairs collapsed partly because the defendant failed to inspect them and such inspection would have revealed the defect. The defendant came into control of the recently built clubhouse, intending to invite the public to enjoy it. The defendant occupied the building for eleven months without reasonably inspecting the stairs. These circumstances allowed the jury to infer the defendant's lack of due care contributed to the stairs' collapse. Res ipsa loquitur applied here to help plaintiff prove that the defendant did not use due care.

LEGAL TIP

It is sometimes possible for a plaintiff to prove that a defendant lacked due care by using res ipsa loquitur.

Damages If a defendant owes a duty of care to a plaintiff and breaks that duty, this act alone does not let plaintiff recover. The breach of the duty must *damage* plaintiff, meaning that a defendant must have damaged plaintiff's person or property.

Proximate cause A plaintiff must prove that a defendant proximately caused a plaintiff's injuries. Proximate cause means that a defendant's carelessness *in fact caused* a plaintiff's damage; that is, "but for" a defendant's carelessness, a plaintiff would not have been injured. A defendant's carelessness also must be close in time and space to justify holding a defendant liable. Courts use different words such as "foreseeable" to decide the proximate cause issue. Proximate cause in effect says that a defendant is not liable for all injuries that he or she causes. For example, a defendant's negligence results in his factory's burning down, and the flames spread from building to building until the entire town burns. Proximate cause says that a defendant is liable for the first building's burning but *not* the whole town's destruction. Factors such as wind conditions and the efficiency of the fire department could counteract a defendant's carelessness. Also, public policy favors limiting people's negligence liability.

One proximate cause problem involves intervening causes. This happens when a defendant's negligence starts a series of events, but some other "intervening factor" directly harms plaintiff. For example, a defendant incorrectly installs a wheel

HARISTON v. ALEXANDER TANK & EQUIPMENT CO.

Supreme Court of North Carolina. 311 S.E.2d 559 (1984).

FACTS On Friday April 14, 1978, John O. Hariston took delivery of a new Lincoln Continental from Haygood Lincoln Mercury, Inc. The car had standard wheels, but since Hariston had paid for spoke wheels, he insisted that they be replaced with spokes, which a mechanic did. The service manager did not check the work. The left rear wheel bolts were loose. Hariston drove the car on Interstate 85. After 3.5 miles, the left rear wheel came off. Hariston stopped the car in the right lane after the wheel hub left a 208-foot gouge mark. Whitby, another motorist, stopped to help. He parked his van 20 feet behind Hariston's Continental. Both vehicles had their emergency flashers on. Hariston stood between the two parked vehicles trying to open his trunk. Within 90 seconds, Alexander negligently drove his GMC flatbed truck into the rear of the van, which caused the van to ram the Continental. Hariston, standing between the van and Continental during the collision, was crushed to death. Hariston's widow sued Haygood Lincoln Mercury, Inc., claiming its negligent wheel installation was the proximate cause of her husband's death. The dealership argued that the intervening negligence of a third party resulted in the dealership's not being the proximate cause of Hariston's death.

ISSUE Was Haygood's breach of its duty of care to install the wheel properly the proximate cause of Hariston's death?

DECISION Yes. Proximate cause means defendant's carelessness must be the *close* cause of plaintiff's loss. Proximate cause is a cause which, in a natural and continuous sequence unbroken by any new and independent cause, produces plaintiff's damages. To be a *proximate* cause, the harm must be *foreseeable* to a person of ordinary prudence. However, it is not necessary that the defendant foresee a plaintiff's exact loss. The defendant must foresee that *some* injury would happen based on his or her carelessness. Here the dealer could foresee that its failure to put the wheel on properly could harm Hariston. The damage happened merely six minutes and 3.5 miles after Hariston took delivery of the new car from the dealer. Therefore, the dealer's carelessness was *proximate* to plaintiff's loss.

LEGAL TIP

Proximate cause refers to foreseeable harms that a plaintiff suffers because of a defendant's carelessness.

on plaintiff's car. The wheel comes off on the interstate highway. The plaintiff stops, gets out of the car, and another car negligently strikes him. Did defendant's careless wheel installation proximately cause plaintiff's injury? Courts generally say that if the intervening cause is *independent* or highly unusual, it is not foreseeable. This determination results in excusing the original defendant's carelessness since the intervening cause was the *proximate* cause of plaintiff's injuries. *Hariston v. Alexander Tank & Equipment Co.* is an intervening cause case.

Defenses to negligence Even if a plaintiff proves the four parts of negligence, a defendant can raise affirmative defenses. If defendant can prove any one affirmative defense, this defeats plaintiff's negligence claim. Two affirmative defenses are contributory negligence and assumption of risk.

Contributory negligence Contributory negligence means that a plaintiff's own carelessness partly caused his or her loss. Contributory negligence generally prevents a plaintiff from recovering anything. This rule is harsh, since a plaintiff could be only 5% contributorily negligent and yet recover nothing. To reduce this harshness, some states have comparative fault. Comparative fault schemes vary among the states, but ordinarily a contributorily negligent plaintiff recovers damages reduced by the amount of his or her contributing fault. For example if a plaintiff's damages are $10,000 and a plaintiff is 10% contributorily negligent, the plaintiff gets $9,000. *Kuntz v. Windjammer "Barefoot" Cruises, Ltd.* is an example of negligence and contributory negligence.

KUNTZ v. WINDJAMMER "BAREFOOT" CRUISES, LTD.

U.S. District Court (Pa.).
573 F.Supp. 1277 (1983).

FACTS Christine Ann Kuntz, a twenty-one year old, drowned while scuba diving in the Bahamas. The death occurred on April 14, 1978, while she was on a Windjammer Cruise. Ms. Kuntz could swim but was a novice diver. She attended a scuba-diving lecture and made a shallow dive supervised by a Windjammer employee, Tom Miller, before her fatal dive. On the evening before her fatal dive, she smoked two to three marijuana cigarettes between 7 PM and 9 PM. She also drank alcoholic beverages so that she had to be helped to her cabin. Just prior to drinking, she had consumed at least one amphetamine capsule. She was drunk at midnight on the day of her fatal dive. On April 14, 1978, Ms. Kuntz took part in an open water, deep dive with others under Miller's direction. Miller failed to set up a "buddy system," had no surface support station, and failed to remain present during the deep dive. Instead, Miller went spear fishing even though he knew or should have known that Ms. Kuntz was a "problem student." It was during this open water deep dive that she drowned. Her estate sued Miller and his employer, Windjammer.

ISSUES Was Tom Miller negligent in supervising Ms. Kuntz on the dive? Was Ms. Kuntz contributorily negligent?

DECISION Yes to both questions. Miller was negligent in the following ways:

1. By failing to set up a "buddy system."
2. By not directly supervising the deep dive.
3. By failing to set up a surface system.
4. By leaving the area of the dive to spear fish.
5. By not helping Ms. Kuntz with her mask.

However, the court also found Ms. Kuntz's drinking and drug use the night before was contributory negligence. A *comparative negligence statute* controlled. The court decided that her contributory negligence was 50% to blame for her death. Therefore, her estate's total recovery was half the actual damages (in this case, recovery was $118,369).

LEGAL TIP

Instructional employees need to stay with students. Novices impose great liability on their teachers.

Damage apportionment Some states refine comparative fault by asking two questions: First, how much did plaintiff's fault contribute to the accident; courts reduce plaintiff's recovery by this percentage. Second, how much did plaintiff's contributory negligence contribute to his or her *damages;* courts reduce plaintiff's recovery *again* by this percentage. For example, a motorcyclist's failure to wear a protective helmet might contribute little to an auto collision. However, it might greatly increase his or her injuries. The *Halvorson v. Voeller* case is an example of this type of situation.

HALVORSON v. VOELLER

Supreme Court of North Dakota.
336 N.W.2d 118 (1983).

FACTS Kevin Halvorson was eighteen years old. He was riding a motorcycle into an intersection when Neil Voeller's car pulled out in front of him from a stop sign. Kevin collided with the driver's side of Voeller's car and was thrown from the motorcycle. Kevin sustained severe brain damage. A jury awarded him $2,767,324.61 damages. The state of North Dakota had a statute requiring anyone *under* eighteen years old to wear protective headgear while operating or riding a motorcycle. The defendant tried to show that Kevin's damages would not have been so severe if he had been wearing a helmet. The trial court refused to admit evidence of nonuse of the helmet to determine the amount of the damages.

ISSUE Is evidence of a person's failure to wear a protective helmet while motorcycle riding admissible to reduce damages?

DECISION Yes. Usually, nonuse of a helmet would not cause the accident. However not using a helmet may contribute to the injuries. Therefore, such nonuse is relevant to the damage issue. Comment C of Section 465 of 2 *Restatement of Torts 2d* allows damage apportionment in certain cases. Specifically, the *Restatement* allows damage apportionment when a plaintiff's negligence did not contribute in any way to the original accident or injury but was a substantial contributing factor in increasing the harm (or damages). The court also noted that just because the state helmet law did *not* require those eighteen years old or older to wear helmets, did not mean that they were necessarily living up to the ordinary, reasonable, prudent person standard of care by *not* wearing helmets. The State Supreme Court sent the case back to the trial court for a new trial on the damage issue.

LEGAL TIP
Failure to use a protective device can reduce a plaintiff's damage recovery.

Negligent Infliction of Mental Distress

Courts are hesitant to give damages for **mental distress.** They fear false claims. On the other hand, when a plaintiff sustains physical injury, courts routinely give damages for mental suffering. This is called the "parasitic damage rule" (mental damages are parasitic to, or given only if, physical injuries exist). Physical injury shows that a plaintiff probably is not "faking" mental harm. Also, the ***kind*** of physical injury tells jurors how serious the mental harm is. Another rule, the Impact Rule, allows recovery for mental distress when a defendant touches a plaintiff in any way. The idea behind the Parasitic Damage Rule and the Impact Rule is to make plaintiff's claim of mental distress believable.

Recently, courts have awarded damages when a defendant negligently caused a plaintiff mental suffering where there was no physical injury or touching of any kind. False claims are possible in such cases. Courts usually limit awards for negligent infliction of mental distress without physical injury or contact to facts

MOLIEN v. KAISER FOUNDATION HOSPITALS

Supreme Court of California.
616 P.2d 813 (1980).

FACTS Plaintiff and his wife, Valerie, are members of the Kaiser Health Plan. Mrs. Molien went to Kaiser for a routine physical exam. Dr. Kilbridge, a staff physician, negligently examined and tested her. He told her that she had an infectious type of syphilis, when, in fact, she did not. Nonetheless, she underwent treatment for the disease. She also told her husband that she had syphilis. He was required to undergo blood tests himself to see if he had the disease and if he had infected his wife. The tests showed that he did not have the disease. As a result of the incorrect diagnosis, the plaintiff's wife became upset and suspicious that he had engaged in extramarital sex. Tension and hostility arose between the two, causing a breakup of their marriage and the start of dissolution proceedings. Plaintiff sued Kaiser and Dr. Kilbridge for negligent infliction of mental distress. Defendants argued that there was no impact or physical damage to the plaintiff, so no liability existed for mere negligent infliction of mental distress.

ISSUE May a plaintiff recover for negligent infliction of mental distress, where plaintiff has no physical injuries?

DECISION Yes. A cause of action may exist for negligent infliction of extreme emotional distress. The unqualified requirement of physical injury is no longer justifiable when a plaintiff seeks damages for mental distress. The line between physical and mental harm is unclear. Basically, a plaintiff's claim for mental suffering should be genuine. This is a proof problem for the fact trier. Jurors should draw on their experience to decide if and to what extent a defendant's conduct caused plaintiff's mental distress. The negligent examination of Mrs. Molien and the conduct flowing therefrom are objectively verifiable. They foreseeably caused plaintiff's serious emotional distress, which helps decide if plaintiff's claim is real. Also, in this case, the false claim of syphilis is slander per se (damages are presumed due to the seriousness of the charge). The plaintiff stated a cause of action for negligent infliction of mental distress.

LEGAL TIP

Persons can be liable if they negligently cause serious mental suffering even if the victim has no physical damage.

strongly supporting mental suffering. The *Molien v. Kaiser Foundation Hospitals* case is an example involving mental distress.

Strict Liability

Strict liability means that a person is liable for harm proximately caused, even though no fault is shown. The defendant merely did or failed to do something that is close enough to a plaintiff's damages to justifiably hold the defendant liable.

Examples There are many situations where strict liability can occur. Persons engaged in ultrahazardous activities are strictly liable to persons whom they proximately injure. Examples of ultrahazardous activities include dynamiting, fumigation, flying airplanes, and keeping wild animals. Courts also apply strict liability to defective consumer goods. Chapter 27 below discusses this issue.

Why allow ultrahazardous activities Since ultrahazardous activities are so risky, why allow them? The reason is that their social value outweighs prohibiting them. But those in ultrahazardous activities are liable for any harm that they proximately cause no matter how careful they are. Strict liability encourages people in ultrahazardous activities to be careful.

Defenses Assumption of risk can be a defense to strict liability. However, contributory negligence is generally not a defense in strict liability cases. *Indiana Harbor Belt Railroad v. American Cyanamid Co.* is a case example of strict liability.

INDIANA HARBOR BELT RAILROAD v. AMERICAN CYANAMID CO.

U.S. District Court.
517 F.Supp. 314 (1981).

FACTS American Cyanamid Company (Cyanamid) manufactured and shipped acrylonitrile, a hazardous, flammable, toxic substance. Cyanamid arranged for Missouri Pacific to transport acrylonitrile to Indiana Harbor Belt Railway's (Indiana Harbor) freight yard in Illinois. There the railroad car containing the substance was to be turned over to Conrail for delivery to Cyanamid in New Jersey. Upon arrival at Indiana Harbor's freight yard, substantial amounts of acrylonitrile leaked from the freight car. Indiana Harbor claims extensive damage to property, equipment, and the water supply over a 2-mile area. The spill resulted in the evacuation of 3000 people from their homes. There was also extensive interference with railroad operations for a substantial time. Indiana Harbor spent much to fix its property. Indiana Harbor sued Cyanamid for its damages based on a strict liability theory. Cyanamid argued that even though acrylonitrile is a hazardous substance, strict liability only applies to ultrahazardous activities. Cyanamid claimed that common sense tells us that *transporting* a hazardous substance is not ultrahazardous or inherently dangerous.

ISSUE Does strict liability apply to transporting a hazardous substance?

DECISION Yes. This case is similar to blasting cases, where strict liability applies. If an activity is inherently dangerous and harm naturally and probably results from it despite exercising utmost care, strict liability results. Shipping acrylonitrile is inherently dangerous both because of the type of chemical and the equipment that it was shipped in. The natural and probable consequences of loading and shipping acrylonitrile in a defective tank car is property damage and personal injury. The defendant here acted for its own purposes and profit by putting this peril into the community. This case is similar to another one where a court held a shipper of gasoline strictly liable when gas spilled over a highway, caught fire, and incinerated a motorist.

LEGAL TIP

Shippers of hazardous chemicals will likely be held strictly liable for damages such activities proximately cause. Insure against this risk.

KEY TERMS

Tort
Negligence
Negligence per se
Res ipsa loquitur
Negligent infliction of mental distress
Strict liability

CHAPTER PROBLEMS

1. What is a tort?
2. Explain the difference between torts and crimes.
3. What does it mean to say that tort law is a legal laboratory?
4. List the four parts of the negligence definition.
5. How is the ORP person different from each of us?
6. Name two defenses to negligence.

*7. A motorcyclist was in an accident with a postal service jeep. The motorcyclist proved damages for injuries, medical expenses, pain and suffering, and disability and impairment amounted to $12,346.15. His negligence was 50% of the cause of the accident. The government showed that it sustained $589.67 in damages. The jurisdiction follows a comparative negligence scheme. What did each party recover? *Wright v. United States,* 574 F.Supp. 160 (1983).

*8. Someone kidnapped a nine-day old infant from Jamaica Hospital. The parents sued the hospital for negligent infliction of mental distress. The hospital defended by citing the general requirement that physical harm must occur before mental suffering is recoverable. What is the result? *Johnson v. Jamaica Hospital,* 467 N.Y.S.2d 634 (1983).

*9. Hector and Ricardo Castillo were doing Christmas shopping in the Laredo, Texas Sears store. The store was in a shopping mall. Rodolfo and Andres Torres approached the Castillos while they were in Sears. The Torres threatened the Castillo brothers and told them to step outside. The Castillos did so. Immediately outside Sears, the Torres broke Hector's jaw and stabbed Ricardo. The Castillos sued Sears and the mall for negligently failing to provide security forces, which resulted in the plaintiffs' injuries. What is the result? *Castillo v. Sears, Roebuck & Co.,* 663 S.W.2d 60 (Tex. App. 4th Dist. 1983).

*10. Does strict liability apply to hold liable the owner of a gasoline trailer for a motorist's death? The motorist died when her car encountered a pool of spilled gasoline at night on the highway. The gasoline exploded and incinerated the motorist. The gasoline trailer had broken away from defendant's truck had rolled down a hill onto a highway used by the motorist, and had leaked gas. *Siegler v. Kuhlman,* 502 P.2d 1181 (S. Ct. Wash. 1973).

"A wrong is always wrongest in Kentucky."
James Hilary Mulligan

Chapter 6

Intentional Torts

CHAPTER PREVIEW

- The difference between intentional torts and torts of negligence
- Possible remedies available for victims of intentional torts
- Similarities and differences between torts and crimes
- Similarities and differences between torts and contracts
- Elements of fraud
- Four "wrongs" covered by the right of privacy
- Elements of false imprisonment
- Elements of conversion
- Some defenses against defamation
- Definition of "abuse of process"

"It's only competition," Cassius Buck told Ed Tuttle. Cassius hated Ed, who was the village barber. Cassius was a rich banker, who hired a barber and set up a competing barber shop for the sole reason of driving Ed out of business. After this goal was accomplished, Cassius planned to close his new barber shop. Ed thought this kind of competition was wrong. Was it?

This chapter examines intentional torts and compares them with other torts and crimes. This chapter also explores possible remedies for victims of intentional torts. A few intentional torts in business situations are discussed in this chapter, including fraud, invasion of the right of privacy, intentional infliction of mental distress, false imprisonment, abuse of process, conversion, defamation, wrongful interference with contractual relations, and a general intentional "wrong."

INTENTIONAL TORTS

Intentional Torts Compared with Crimes

Intentional torts are similar to *and* different from crimes.

Similarities Both crimes and intentional torts are wrongs that usually involve some kind of intent; however, there are a few strict liability crimes that do not involve intent. Since both crimes and intentional torts are intentional wrongs, there is justification for punishing the wrongdoer. Also, the same act (assault and battery, for example) can be both an intentional tort *and* a crime.

Differences The victims of intentional torts are individuals. Crimes, of course, have individual victims (the person robbed, for example). Since crimes are acts against general society, the punishment can be much greater, such as death or imprisonment. Society never sentences a person to prison or death for committing an intentional tort.

Intentional Torts Compared with Negligence

Intentional torts are different from and similar to the tort of **negligence.** The main difference is that the "wrong" in negligence is *carelessness,* and the "wrong" in intentional torts concerns some kind of *intent.* Also, punitive damages are possible for intentional torts but *not* for negligence.

There are several similarities between intentional torts and negligence. First, both are torts, which are *civil* wrongs. The victims are *individuals* not society in general. Second, victims can recover both nominal and compensatory damages for negligence and intentional torts.

Intentional Torts Compared with Contracts

Contracts and intentional torts have both similarities and differences.

Similarities First, contracts and intentional torts are areas of civil law; neither is a crime. Second, a person injured by either a breach of contract or an intentional tort can possibly recover both nominal and compensatory damages.

Differences There must be a broken contract before a person can recover contract damages. There does *not* have to be an agreement that is broken to recover for an intentional tort. Also, intentional tort victims can recover punitive damages, which is not possible for victims of broken contracts.

Remedies for Intentional Torts

There are basically two types of remedies for tort victims: legal and equitable.

Legal remedies Legal remedies include various kinds of damages, which refer to money. There are nominal, compensatory, and punitive damages.

Nominal damages are a small amount of money (6¢ or a dollar), which a victim receives when his or her right is broken but no substantial harm occurs. For example, Norman could spit on Bruce (a battery), but what real harm does Bruce suffer? Nominal damages are proper since no real harm was suffered.

Compensatory damages refer to money needed to "make a victim whole." In other words, the victim has a physical or financial loss of some sort. For example, if Arthur slanders Tom's accounting book (by saying that it has too many errors when it really does not), sales of Tom's book could fall. Therefore, Tom can receive compensatory damage.

Punitive damages punish wrongdoers when their conduct is particularly outrageous. For example, when Norman spits on Bruce, it is proper to make Norman pay Bruce punitive damages.

Equitable remedies Equitable remedies include injunctions, specific performance, and accountings. Plaintiffs can only recover these remedies when their legal remedies are inadequate.

Injunctions are court orders to do or not do something. For example, a court might order a defendant not to trespass on a plaintiff's property.

Specific performance is basically a contract remedy, which orders a person breaking a contract to perform an obligation. This remedy is available only when legal remedies, such as money, are inadequate.

Accountings refer to court orders that direct someone, such as an agent, to present income and expense records to someone else. For example, if a former employee uses a former employer's trade secrets without authorization, the employee will have to account for (and turn over) any profits made.

Fraud

Fraud is: a misrepresentation of a material fact, which the defrauding person knows about; the defrauding person intends to defraud, and the victim is damaged as a result of reasonably relying on the misrepresentations.

Fraud is one of the most frequently committed business torts and often occurs to persuade others to enter contracts. For example, if someone wants to sell a car, what better way to sell it than by lying about, or understating, its true mileage? However, lying in this situation may involve fraud, and the victim can set aside or escape the contract and recover damages.

Elements of fraud Since fraud is so common, a few other points should be noted:

First, the person misrepresenting must *intend* to defraud. If someone mistakenly misrepresents something, innocent misrepresentation—*not* fraud—occurs. The contract can be "undone," but generally no damages can be recovered.

Second, either a buyer or seller (or both) can commit fraud in one contract.

Third, seller's talk, puffing, and opinions are different from misrepresentations of facts. Facts are objective, definite, or observable. For example, Jerry says his car will get twenty miles per gallon. This statement is a representation of fact because any person can determine its truth. If the statement is false, then it is a misrepresentation of fact. Puffing, opinions, or seller's talk *are not* misrepresentations of fact; they are subjective. For example, statements such as "This house is wonderful;" "That car is the most stylish;" or "That picture is beautiful" are subjective. Words such as "wonderful," "most stylish," and "beautiful" are opinion, not fact, and are unlike objective descriptions such as "three feet" or "one carat." It is necessary that a misrepresentation of fact (not a misrepresentation of opinion) be made for fraud to exist.

Fourth, fraud can occur by **concealment.** That is, if a seller "keeps his or her mouth shut" instead of disclosing a material fact not easily discoverable by the other party, fraud can occur. In one case, a homeowner offered his house for sale. The other party bought the house but discovered later that the water was only available between 7 AM and 7 PM. The seller had said that the buyer could have "all the water he wanted" and did not specify to the buyer that water would be available for "only half of the day." The court said this case involved fraud by concealment. The seller had a duty to disclose material facts not readily ascertainable.

Kinsey v. Scott is a case showing fraud.

KINSEY v. SCOTT

Appellate Court of Illinois.
463 N.E.2d 1359 (1984).

FACTS William Scott owned an apartment building. Originally it had four apartments. Scott later modified the building, without getting a building permit, by adding a fifth apartment.

In 1973 Scott offered the building for sale. He said it had five rental apartments and indicated the rent for each unit.

Helen Kinsey looked at the building, intending to buy it. She asked Scott if it complied with the city's building codes. He said that it did. Helen did not check with the city as to whether the building actually did conform with the building code. She bought the building from Scott in 1973.

In 1981 the city of Waukegan "red tagged" the fifth basement apartment in her building. The city claimed that the apartment was uninhabitable because it was not in compliance with the city health and housing code. Helen stopped renting the fifth apartment.

She then sued Scott for fraud, arguing that he misrepresented the building as being in compliance with the city code when it was not. Scott defended by claiming that Helen was not reasonable in relying on his representation since the codes are matters of public record.

ISSUE Is a buyer reasonable in relying on a seller's representation that his building complies with the city's building and health code?

DECISION Yes. Even though the city code is a public record (which the buyer could check), the buyer was not experienced in real estate transactions or city housing and building codes. It would be unreasonable for a buyer to investigate if the building complied with the city codes when there was nothing to warn or arouse the buyer's suspicion of noncompliance.

LEGAL TIP

Real estate sellers should fully inform prospective buyers about compliance with city codes. Buyers should check city codes.

Remedies Persons falsely imprisoned can recover *nominal damages* (a very small amount of money)—such as 6¢ or $1.00. *Actual or compensatory damages* (money to cover real losses or injuries) are also available. Finally, the victim can recover punitive damages where the wrongdoer had a bad intent or recklessly disregarded a plaintiff's interests. However, a plaintiff receives no punitive damages when a defendant made a good-faith error.

False Imprisonment

False imprisonment occurs when one person totally restrains another for an "appreciable period of time," such as even a few minutes. The person restrained need not be physically harmed since the confinement, or restraint, itself is the harm. Most cases say that the victim must be aware of the confinement *when it happens* before he or she can be falsely imprisoned. The confinement need not be in a room, although it often is.

Defenses to false imprisonment One of the main defenses to false imprisonment is the "shopkeeper's privilege." Basically, this privilege allows a merchant with reasonable cause to detain a customer suspected of shoplifting for investigation, which must be conducted in a reasonable manner and time.

Gortarez v. Smitty's Super Valu, Inc. is a false imprisonment case involving the shopkeeper's privilege.

GORTAREZ v. SMITTY'S SUPER VALU, INC.

Supreme Court of Arizona.
680 P.2d 807 (1984).

FACTS Ernest Gortarez, age sixteen, and his cousin, Albert Hernandez, age eighteen, went to Smitty's store around 8 PM. They visited the automotive department. Hernandez bought and paid $22 for a power booster. During this time, Gortarez picked up a 59¢ vaporizer used to freshen air in cars. He asked if he could pay for it in the front of the store when he finished shopping. The clerk said, "Yes" but decided the request was suspicious. The clerk thought Gortarez would try to leave without paying for the vaporizer. He followed the two boys to the front of the store, where they exited through an unattended check-out aisle. Since the clerk did not see Gortarez pay for or put down the vaporizer, he concluded that Gortarez stole the item.

The clerk told Miller, Smitty's assistant manager, and Gibson, Smitty's security guard, that "those two guys ripped us off." Gibson, Miller, and two other store employees ran out of the store to catch Gortarez and Hernandez. The two boys were about to get in their car. Miller went for Gortarez and Gibson for Hernandez. Gibson said he was an officer and showed his badge. (He was an off-duty policeman "moonlighting.") Gibson told Hernandez, "I believe you have something that you did not pay for." Gibson seized Hernandez, put his arms on the car, and began searching him. Hernandez did not resist. Gibson searched Hernandez, who kept repeating that he did not steal anything.

Gortarez was outraged at Gibson's searching and shoving Hernandez. He yelled at Gibson to leave his cousin alone. Gortarez told Miller and Gibson that the vaporizer was in the store. Gortarez ran around the car to push Gibson away from Hernandez. Gibson grabbed Gortarez and put a choke hold on him until he stopped struggling. A carry-out boy then told Gibson and Miller the vaporizer was in a basket at the check-out stand. Gibson and Miller released the boys. Gortarez needed medical treatment from the choke-hold injuries.

Both boys sued Smitty's store for false imprisonment. Smitty's argued that it merely exercised the shopkeeper's privilege of temporary detention for investigation.

ISSUE Was the detention of the suspected shoplifters carried out in a reasonable way?

DECISION No. Smitty's went beyond the shopkeeper's privilege. There was reasonable cause to detain and investigate because the one boy had the vaporizer and was not seen paying for it before leaving the store.

However, the detention itself was unreasonable. There was no request that the two boys remain. No one asked if Hernandez had the vaporizer. Hernandez did not resist or attempt to escape. The theft of a 59¢ item did not suggest the boys were armed and dangerous. Gibson could have asked Hernandez to remain before searching him. There was no evidence that such a request to Hernandez would have been futile.

LEGAL TIP

Store owners should instruct their security people about the shopkeeper's privilege to detain and investigate suspected shoplifters.

Invasion of Privacy

The intentional tort of **invasion of privacy** covers four loosely related but separate wrongs. They are:

1. Intrusion upon a plaintiff's seclusion or into his or her private affairs.
2. Public disclosure of private facts.
3. Unauthorized appropriation of a person's name or likeness.
4. Unreasonable intrusion upon a person's solitude or seclusion.

In other words, if someone does any one of these four wrongs above, he or she commits the tort of invasion of privacy.

False light Holding up a person in a **false light** in the public eye can arise in many situations. For instance, Ralph's illegitimate use of Michael Jackson's name to suggest Michael's connection with Ralph's product, book, or company is a "false light" case.

One famous false light case involved a defendant's unauthorized use of plaintiff's name on a telegram to the governor. The telegram asked the governor to act in a certain way on a pending law. The plaintiff actually did not agree with the telegram. Therefore, the telegram held the plaintiff up in a false light.

Unauthorized appropriation The **unauthorized appropriation** of a plaintiff's name or likeness for a defendant's benefit frequently occurs in business cases. For example, Mace's Department Store advertises its dishes using Nancy Shurtz's name as a satisfied customer. The fact that Nancy uses Mace's dishes is no defense, because Nancy's privacy is the protected interest.

Intrusion upon solitude or seclusion **Intrusion upon solitude or seclusion** is a third invasion of privacy. This invasion can occur if defendant sets up telescopes, listening devices, or "snoops" into a plaintiff's private life in a way that would be objectionable to a "reasonable person."

Unauthorized wiretapping of a plaintiff's private conversation has been held as an intrusion upon a plaintiff's solitude and seclusion. An unauthorized photo of Herman using toilet paper for its intended purpose would usually invade his solitude or seclusion.

Public disclosure of private facts Public disclosure of private facts is a fourth type of invasion of privacy. The facts disclosed must be private. Courts have said that a person's personal finances and details about a personal part of the human body are private. Matters of public record (such as the amount of property taxes a homeowner pays) are *not* private facts.

Defenses to invasion of privacy No right of privacy exists:

1. When the matter published is of public or general interest.
2. When the matter is *privileged* under libel and slander laws.
3. When the individual claiming privacy consents to publication.

Harkey v. Abate is an invasion of privacy case, showing intrusion upon a person's solitude or seclusion.

Conversion

Conversion is the unauthorized and unjustified interference with the dominion and control of another's personal property. Personal property is anything movable. That is, things other than land and buildings can be converted.

Conversion is a wrong commonly called "stealing." Conversion is not a crime however, but an intentional tort.

Interfering with another's personal property *must* be intentional. The intent does not have to be to harm—just interfere.

HARKEY v. ABATE

Michigan Court of Appeals.
346 N.W.2d 74 (1983).

FACTS Mrs. Harkey and her daughter were at "The Rink, Inc.," a roller-skating rink managed by Mr. Abate. While at The Rink, the Harkeys used the women's restroom provided for customers. Mrs. Harkey later discovered that Abate had installed see-through ceiling panels in the restroom, which allowed secret observation of the entire restroom from above.

Mrs. Harkey claimed that Abate had personally viewed her and her daughter. However, she could not prove that Abate had actually watched them in the restroom.

Mrs. Harkey sued Mr. Abate for invasion of privacy by wrongful intrusion into their seclusion and solitude. Abate defended by claiming that he never looked at the Harkeys through the see-through ceiling.

ISSUE Does a defendant intrude into the plaintiff's seclusion and solitude by merely installing a secret viewing device in a public restroom when there is no proof of its use?

DECISION Yes. The mere installation of hidden viewing devices is an interference with Mrs. Harkey's right of privacy. A reasonable person would find the intrusion here highly offensive. The lack of proof that the defendant used the devices could reduce the damages but does not destroy Mrs. Harkey's claim.

LEGAL TIP

Businesses desiring to "police" their public restrooms should remember customers' right of privacy.

What can be converted? Any tangible personal property (such as a horse, car, or diamond ring, for example) can be converted. Modern courts say that intangible personal property can be converted. This conversion is particularly true when there is a tangible symbol of an intangible right (such as a stock certificate representing a share of stock, an insurance policy representing insurance, or a savings bank book representing a savings account).

Land and buildings *cannot* be converted. Neither can gravel, trees, or crops. Once severed from the land, gravel, trees, and crops can be converted.

Examples of conversion A person who steals personal property commits conversion. However, there are subtler forms of conversion. A person buying *or* selling stolen goods is considered a converter, even if *unaware* that the goods are stolen.

A person who rightfully gets possession of goods but who refuses to give them to the owner is a converter. The *Gross v. Kouf* case illustrates conversion.

Abuse of Process

The essential parts of **abuse of process** are: an ulterior purpose and the wilful act in the use of the process not proper in the regular conduct of the proceeding.

"Process" refers to civil or criminal legal procedures. "Arrest warrants" and "service of a summons and complaint" in civil cases are examples of process.

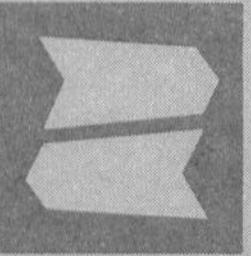

GROSS v. KOUF

Supreme Court of South Dakota.
349 N.W.2d 652 (1984).

FACTS Bill Gross owned a damaged 1976 Chevy. Gross hired Terry Durham, who ran a body shop in a building leased from Roger Kouf, to repair it.

In July 1980 Durham vacated Kouf's building and left Gross' car there. Kouf removed Gross' car from the building and took it to his auto salvage business in Watertown, South Dakota.

In August 1980 Kouf sent Gross a letter saying that Gross' car was in Kouf's possession. Kouf demanded that Gross pay towing and storage charges. Kouf said if payment was not made in thirty days, the car would be disposed. Gross refused to pay and demanded the return of his car. Kouf refused to return the car, dismantled it, and stored it at his salvage yard.

Gross sued Kouf for conversion of the car. A trial court jury awarded Gross $2200 actual damages and $6600 in punitive damages. Kouf appealed, arguing that he was an involuntary depository of the car and as such could not be liable for conversion.

ISSUE Is a person liable for conversion if he or she takes possession of the place where the bailed property is kept as well as the bailed property, and if he or she sells or disposes of the property without authorization?

DECISION Yes. It is ordinarily the duty of a person who has another's personal property to deliver it to the owner on demand. Failure to do so is conversion. (There was no mention of any lien or other claim the building owner might have to the car involuntarily coming into his possession.)

LEGAL TIP
Building owners should check state laws to see if they legally can keep another's goods before refusing to return them.

When process is used properly, there is no tort; however, the intentional tort of abuse of process occurs when a person misuses process. That is, process justified for one purpose is used for an improper purpose.

Generally malice is not required for abuse of process. The case or matter also does not have to end in a plaintiff's favor. The crux of abuse of process is *improper use*.

Palmer Ford, Inc. v. Wood is a case example that deals with abuse of process. Note that a creditor used the criminal process to force a debtor to pay a bill.

Wrongful Interference with Business

In the United States, the free market and the right to compete for business are a "way of life." Economic competition means that one person tries to take customers away from another. This attempt could injure the seller losing the business but is usually *not* an intentional tort. We allow such injury because one competitor is trying to help itself even though it also hurts someone else.

Can trying to take business away from someone else *ever* be a tort? The *Tuttle v. Buck* case says "Yes" when one competitor tries to attract another's customers *solely* to injure another maliciously. If injury occurs, **wrongful interference with business** has occurred.

Wrongful Interference with Contractual Relations

The elements of **wrongful interference with contractual relations,** are:

1. a valid, enforceable contract exists between B and C.
2. D, a third person, must know that the contract between B and C exists.
3. D must intentionally induce B or C to break the contract between B and C.

PALMER FORD, INC. v. WOOD

Court of Appeals of Maryland.
471 A.2d 297 (1984).

FACTS Frank Wood was a 20-year-old, part-time college student. He worked full-time in the evening. His parents were divorced and he lived with his mother. He also was the attentive owner of a 1970 Mustang convertible, which needed major repairs.

Wood took the car to Palmer Ford (Palmer). Palmer gave Wood a $400 written estimate for the repair work. Wood authorized the work because his father had given him $400 for that purpose. As work progressed, Palmer convinced Wood that the car needed another $150 or $200 (at the most) of work. Palmer gave Wood no written estimate for this.

Palmer finished the work and gave Wood a $924 bill. Wood was shocked and outraged at the amount. He was unable to pay and get the car back. That evening an unidentified telephone caller (suspected to be a Palmer employee) told Wood that if he put $400 under a trash can in Palmer's men's room, he would find there a $924 bill marked "paid" along with his car keys. Wood followed these instructions and got his car back.

Palmer later discovered that it had no record of receiving $924 from Wood. Kirby, the comptroller from Palmer had a meeting with Wood. Kirby told Wood that Palmer was not interested in prosecuting and only wanted to be paid. Kirby said if Wood "told everything," Palmer would arrange some kind of payment schedule. Wood told the "entire story," and Kirby said he was unsure if Palmer would deduct $400 from Wood's bill. The next day, Kirby told Wood that the entire $924 would have to be paid. Kirby spoke to Wood's mother about the bill on April 26, 1977. He said the bill would have to be paid or her son would go to jail. Mrs. Wood said that she did not want her son to go to jail and that she would borrow money from her credit union to pay the bill.

On April 28, 1977, Palmer had Wood arrested for embezzlement. It brought no charges against employee Jones, who was suspected of calling Wood and putting the bill marked "paid" under the trash can. On May 3, 1977, Mrs. Wood gave Palmer a check for the entire $924. She said that she assumed "this arrest business is over"; Kirby said, "Yes."

Criminal charges against Wood were *not* dropped. The trial was postponed several times. In October 1977 a hearing was held and Wood was recharged. Finally in February 1978 charges against Wood were dropped.

Wood then sued Palmer for, among other things, abuse of process. A jury verdict for Wood of $100,000 compensatory and $400,000 punitive damages was reduced to $25,000 compensatory and $100,000 punitive damages. The award was for both malicious prosecution and abuse of process.

ISSUE Had Palmer committed abuse of process against Wood?

DECISION Yes. Palmer was using the criminal proceedings to collect a debt, which is not the purpose of the arrest process. Palmer was not using the arrest process to bring a suspected embezzler or larcener to justice but was using the process to get paid. This effort was an abuse of process, and the case was remanded for further proceedings.

LEGAL TIP

Creditors must avoid using the criminal process as a debt collection technique.

The intentional tort of wrongful interference with contractual relations makes contracts stable. This tort makes it wrong for a third person to upset an existing contract between two parties.

Note that the defendant *need not have* either *malice* or *bad faith.*

Defenses Defenses to wrongful interference include lack of a part of the definition (of this tort) or *justification.* Justifications include moral, social, or economic pressures lawful in and of themselves. For example, if D's ads are so effective they cause B to break a contract with C, this is economic justification.

The *Walsh v. Fanslow* case illustrates the tort of wrongful interference with contractual relations.

TUTTLE v. BUCK

Supreme Court of Minnesota.
119 N.W. 946 (1909).

FACTS Ed Tuttle was a barber in the village of Howard Lake, Minnesota. Cassius Buck was a banker, a man of wealth and influence in Howard Lake.

Tuttle claimed that Buck willfully, wrongfully, and maliciously tried to destroy Tuttle's barbershop business. Buck allegedly did this in several ways. First, Buck made false and malicious claims about Tuttle to Tuttle's customers. Buck, through threats of personal displeasure, induced people not to do business with Tuttle. Furthermore, Buck was not interested in barbering. Yet he set up a competing barbershop in the village. He could not get a barber to rent the shop so he paid two successive barbers a salary to run the shop. Buck's salaried barber paid no rent for the use of Buck's barber shop, and all income went to Buck.

Tuttle argued that Buck set up the competing shop *solely* to injure Tuttle. Tuttle was, in fact, damaged and claimed that Buck had no legitimate profit interest in setting up the shop. Tuttle sued Buck for intentionally injuring his business with no justification.

ISSUE Is it an intentional tort for a person to enter business in competition with another if the *only purpose* for doing so is to harm that person?

DECISION Yes. Competing economically with another person is usually *not* a wrong, even if economic competition harms the other person financially. Economic competition is usually allowed since taking business from a rival serves a person's justifiable need to survive and make a profit.

But when a person goes into business not to make a profit but only to drive a competitor out of business (and intends to retire when this goal is accomplished), that person commits an intentional tort. In other words, economic competition is not always legal.

LEGAL TIP

When you compete, be sure you do so to benefit yourself and not just to injure someone else.

WALSH v. FANSLOW

Court of Appeals of Illinois.
462 N.E.2d 965 (1984).

FACTS James Walsh was a realtor who made an oral contract with Fanslow. According to the contract, Walsh would receive a 10% commission (less the mortgage) for finding a buyer for two buildings that Fanslow owned in Morton Grove, Illinois.

In January 1977 Walsh gave Robinson information concerning the property. Robinson knew then that Walsh was a realtor hired to sell the property.

Robinson bought the property from Fanslow for over $2 million without using Walsh. To hide the purchase, Robinson transferred the property to a partnership he belonged to.

Walsh sued Robinson for wrongful interference with his contractual relation with Fanslow. Robinson argued that the contract Walsh had with Fanslow was unenforceable since it was oral.

ISSUE Did Walsh show facts to state a claim against Robinson for wrongful interference with contractual relations?

DECISION Yes. No particular form of words is needed to hire a realtor in Illinois. All that is required is the property owner's consent, which can be oral. There was a binding contract between Fanslow and Walsh. Robinson knew of the contract and interfered with it by dealing directly with Fanslow.

LEGAL TIP

Realtors as a matter of good business practice should get their brokerage contracts in writing.

Intentional Infliction of Mental Distress

The tort **intentional infliction of mental distress** places liability on a person for intentionally causing severe emotional distress in situations where the actor's conduct goes beyond reasonable decency.

Intentional infliction of mental distress tries to protect people's peace of mind by allowing recovery if another person causes a plaintiff serious mental distress by an extremely outrageous act (or acts). An example would be wrapping a bloody dead rat in a loaf of bread and giving it to a sensitive person to open. The *Duty v. General Finance Co.* is an example of intentional infliction of mental distress.

DUTY v. GENERAL FINANCE CO.

Supreme Court of Texas. 273 S.W.2d 64 (1964).

FACTS Mr. and Mrs. Duty owed money to several creditors. The debts were past due. The creditors did several things to collect. They made lengthy telephone calls to the Dutys every day. Creditors threatened to blacklist the Dutys with the Merchants' Retail Credit Association. Creditors also accused the Dutys of being deadbeats; talked to the Dutys in a harsh, loud voice, and told the Dutys' neighbors and employers that the Dutys were unreliable. These creditors were asking Mrs. Duty what she was doing with her money; accusing her of spending money in other ways than in payments on the loan transaction; threatening to cause both plaintiffs to lose their jobs unless they made the payments demanded; and calling each of the plaintiffs at their employment several times daily. They were also threatening to garnish their wages; berating the plaintiffs to their fellow employees; requesting that their employers require them to pay the debt; and flooding them with a barrage of demand letters, dun cards, special delivery letters, and telegrams both at their homes and their places of work. Other tactics included sending the Dutys cards bearing the opening statement: "Dear Customer: We made you a loan because we thought that you were honest;" sending telegrams and special delivery letters at approximately midnight to awaken them; calling a neighbor in the disguise of a sick brother of one of the plaintiffs, and on another occasion as a stepson; leaving red cards with insulting notes and thinly veiled threats in their door; calling Mr. Duty's mother at her place of employment in Wichita Falls collect as well as Mr. Duty's brother in Albuquerque, New Mexico, to harangue them about the alleged balance owed by the plaintiffs.

It was further alleged that all of the above acts were willful and committed with knowledge that they could cause the plaintiffs mental injury, would render them less capable of performing their work, and would cause them to suffer physical illness.

It was alleged that the foregoing course of conduct caused the plaintiffs to suffer, among others, the following injuries: Both plaintiffs developed a state of high nervousness, irritability, and inability to perform their work as well as they had previously performed it; they each developed severe headaches; Mrs. Duty's stomach was upset with nervous indigestion; they lost numerous hours of sleep; Mrs. Duty was discharged from her work at a cafe as a result of the excessive harrassing attacks, which decreased her ability to work; their credit rating was destroyed; Mrs. Duty became unable to do her housework; and she lost weight that she could not afford to lose.

ISSUE Did the creditors intentionally inflict mental distress on the Dutys?

DECISION Yes. The creditors committed this tort if the Dutys prove that the creditors did everything their complaint claims.

No ethical business or professional person would ever do the outrageous things which the creditors allegedly did here to the Dutys. This case does not outline how far creditors may go to collect overdue bills. Using every cruel device that a creditor can think of to collect money with the intention of causing the debtor great mental anguish, which results in physical injury and the loss of the debtor's job makes the creditor liable for damages.

LEGAL TIP

Debtors owing past due amounts *have rights.* Creditors should review their debt collection practices to make sure that they do not violate debtors' rights.

Some pointers Intentional infliction of mental distress is a fairly new tort. Courts have for a long time given persons with physical injuries money for mental suffering "parasitic" (added on) to physical harm. The idea was that the victim was unlikely to be "faking" mental suffering if he or she had physical injuries.

There are problems with allowing recovery for mental injury when there is no physical harm. First, mental suffering can be faked, allowing recovery for false claims. Second, this tort could flood the courts with lawsuits since today's stressful society produces much mental suffering. Third, this tort could encourage people to become "cry babies" who cannot stand the stress of modern life. Fourth, this tort could be a way for angry employees to "get even" with a boss who has properly disciplined them.

Defamation

There are several key elements in **defamation.** First, there must be a *statement* made by someone about another person. Second, the statement must hold the person about whom the statement is made up to ridicule, contempt, or scorn. Generally, favorable statements (such as "she is an intelligent person") are not defamatory because they fail to satisfy the "holding up to ridicule, contempt, or scorn" requirement. Third, the statement must be published. "Publication" for defamation purposes merely means that the statement is heard (if oral) or seen (if written) by at least one other person. Publication does not mean published in book form.

Defamation is an intentional tort designed to protect a person's relations with other people. This tort tries to make a person liable who says or writes untrue statements about another that hold the person spoken about up to ridicule, contempt, or scorn in the minds of others.

Defenses There are several defenses to defamation including:

1. Truth.
2. Lack of an element of the definition.
3. Privilege (absolute or qualified).

Truth can be used as a defense, if, for example, Sally says something ***true*** to Maggie that makes Irene look ridiculous, contemptuous, or scorned. Most states say that this type of statement is *not* defamation.

Privilege means that even though a defendant has uttered or written statements that would otherwise be defamatory, a defendant is not liable because of some superior public policy of free expression. There are two types of privileges: absolute and qualified. Absolute privilege means that a person may make the defamatory remark maliciously or without necessity. Qualified privilege is a right to make defamatory statements limited by motive and manner in which the remarks were made. Some examples of absolutely privileged comments include remarks made on the floor of legislatures or at legislative hearings, executive communications, court or judicial hearings, husband-wife communications, and in publications consented to by the plaintiff.

Types of defamation There are two types of defamation: libel and slander. Libel is written and slander is oral, although there are some difficult "in-between" areas. For example, are defamatory remarks spoken on television or radio slander or libel? Some courts have said that such remarks are libelous.

The Harmonica Man, Inc. v. Godfrey is a case showing that a corporation and its products can be defamed.

THE HARMONICA MAN, INC. v. GODFREY

Supreme Court of New York (N.Y. County).
102 N.Y.Supp.2d 251 (1951).

FACTS The Harmonica Man, Inc. (HMI), sells a $2.99 ukulele and advertises the ukulele widely. Arthur Godfrey is a radio and television personality. On an April 11, 1950, television show, Godfrey, who often played the ukulele, showed three brands of ukulele. The first sold for about $11; Godfrey called it a "good instrument." The second sold for about $5.50; Godfrey said it was suited for beginners. The third was made by HMI; Godfrey said it was unsuited for either study or performance. He pointed out this last ukulele lacked frets and merely had a painted line to show where the frets should be. He played it to show that the tone was poor and concluded that it might not be against the law to sell such ukuleles, but people who did so should be jailed. He added that no one should be tricked into buying this ukulele. He did not actually mention the manufacturer's name.

HMI sued Godfrey for defamation.

ISSUE Is it possible to slander a product manufacturer? Is it possible to slander a product?

DECISION Yes, to both questions.

It is possible to slander a product manufacturer. Slander of a person (including a corporation) in his or her trade, business, or profession is **slander per se.** Damages are presumed and need not be proven.

It is also possible to slander a product, which is **slander per quod.** Here, damages (such as lost sales and lost profits) must be proven before there is any recovery.

LEGAL TIP

Manufacturers should watch the media (newspapers, television, and radio) to see if commentators defame either their companies or products.

KEY TERMS

Torts
Intentional torts
Negligence
Fraud
Concealment
False imprisonment
Equitable remedies
Invasion of privacy
False light
Unauthorized appropriation
Intrusion on solitude or seclusion
Public disclosure of private facts
Conversion
Abuse of process
Wrongful interference with business
Wrongful interference with contractual relations
Intentional infliction of mental distress
Defamation
Privilege
Slander per se
Slander per quod

CHAPTER PROBLEMS

1. What is the difference between intentional torts and crimes?
2. Is tort law generally state or federal law?
3. Compare intentional torts with negligence.
4. Explain the similarities between contracts and intentional torts.
5. What kind of remedies are available for intentional torts?
6. Define fraud.

*7. A landlord had secretly installed a listening device in his tenants' bedroom. This device enabled him to monitor and record voices and sounds in the bedroom. The tenants did *not* claim that the landlord actually used the listening device. Did the tenants have a good claim for invasion of their right of privacy? *Hamberger v. Eastman,* 206 A.2d 239 (N.H. 1964).

*8. Hallmark Builders, Inc. sued a local television station for defamation. The local television newscast reported on problems encountered by new home buyers, including defects in construction. Did a close-up camera-shot of hairline masonry cracks in the house accurately represent the cracks or was this defamatory? *Hallmark Builders, Inc. v. Gaylord Broadcasting Co.,* 733 F.2d 1461 (11th Cir. 1984).

*9. A manufacturer's regional sales manager criticized a particular salesperson's job performance to the company president. The remarks related solely to the sales work for the company. Were these remarks privileged? *Humphrey v. National Semiconductor Corp.,* 463 N.E.2d 1197 (Mass. App. 1984).

*10. Is a newspaper's accurate publication of an inaccurate arrest report of a famous pro football player (the person arrested was an imposter) defamatory or privileged? *Bell v. Associated Press,* 584 F.Supp. 128 (D.C.D.C. 1984).

Part Two

Business and Government

". . . the Constitution is what the judges say it is. . . ."

Charles Evans Hughes, 1907, (later Chief Justice, United States Supreme Court)

Chapter 7

The Constitution and Business

CHAPTER PREVIEW

- Definition of a constitution
- Two central purposes of a constitution
- Federalism
- Constitutional power giving the United States government almost unlimited power to regulate
- Area where the United States Constitution authorizes state lawmaking
- Three limits on state and federal lawmaking
- Due process
- Degree of discrimination that the equal protection clause allows

Fred Darby wondered who was running his business. He was a Georgia manufacturer. He set wages and hours at what he considered were "fair" levels. Workers had a job, and Darby made money. Then Congress used the Constitution's commerce clause to pass the Fair Labor Standards Act (FLSA). This law set minimum hourly wages and maximum hours employees could work weekly. Darby remembered from his Legal Environment course at State College that Congress could only regulate interstate *business under the commerce clause. Since his factory was in Georgia, Darby thought the FLSA was unconstitutional and would not regulate his business. Was he right?*

This chapter surveys constitutional law and discusses three main topics: First, we will examine what a constitution is and the purpose it serves. Second, we will look at the major parts of the constitution regulating business, and third, we will see some limits the constitution puts on lawmaking and regulation.

WHAT IS A CONSTITUTION?

A **constitution** is the most important law of a country. It sets out a country's basic legal ideas. If any other law in the country conflicts with the constitution, the other law is invalid, or unconstitutional.

Constitution's Purposes

Constitutions in western, non-communist countries have two main purposes. First, a constitution sets out the structure of government. That is, it tells who makes the laws, who enforces the laws, and who interprets the laws.

Second, a constitution *limits* the government's powers to make laws. One way is by giving persons basic rights (such as freedom of speech and freedom of religion).

The Elements of the United States Constitution

The United States Constitution is made up of seven parts, called "articles," plus twenty-six amendments.

Separation of power The national government has three parts: the legislature (legally created by Article I), the chief executive or president (legally created by Article II), and the Supreme Court (legally created by Article III). The idea that there are three branches or parts of government is called **separation of powers.** The purpose behind separation of powers is to discourage concentrated power in any one branch of government. There is distrust of concentrated power.

Federalism **Federalism** means dual sovereigns, two supreme lawmakers. How can there be *two* supreme lawmakers? Who are they?

Two supreme lawmakers exist by giving each sovereign a lawmaking area where it is supreme. The two sovereigns are the national, or federal, government and state governments.

The United States Constitution (through Article I) gives lawmaking power to the national government (more specifically, Congress). Congress has the power to make laws in the enumerated areas, that is, areas listed in the Constitution. Congress can also pass laws in areas needed to carry out **enumerated powers,** which are also called implied powers.

Example of a federal enumerated power: Commerce clause Article I, Section 8 of the Constitution gives Congress the power to make laws dealing with interstate commerce. The **commerce clause** gives the national government great power to regulate business. The *United States v. Darby* case shows this power.

States' police power The United States Constitution's Tenth Amendment gives states the power to make law; this power is called "reserved power." Examples of areas reserved for state lawmaking include property law, tort law, contract law,

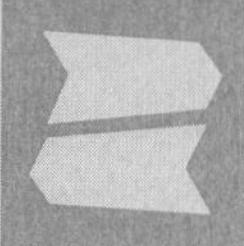

UNITED STATES v. DARBY
U.S. Supreme Court.
312 U.S. 100 (1941).

FACTS Darby manufactured lumber goods in Georgia. Congress passed the Fair Labor Standards Act (FLSA). As originally passed, the FLSA set a 25¢ per hour minimum wage. This Act also set a forty-four-hour maximum working week before overtime pay rates applied. The FLSA prohibited interstate shipment of goods made in violation of the Act. FLSA violations were crimes.

Darby paid less than 25¢ per hour. His employees worked more than forty four hours per week without overtime. The United States government prosecuted Darby for violating the FLSA. He defended himself by arguing that the FLSA was unconstitutional. He reasoned that Congress used the Constitution's commerce power to pass the Act. However, the commerce clause only gave Congress the power to pass laws regulating *inter*state commerce. Darby only made lumber products in Georgia. This was *intra*state commerce. Therefore, he argued, Congress lacked the power under the commerce clause to regulate his business.

ISSUE Did the Constitution's commerce clause give Congress the power to pass the FLSA?

DECISION Yes. Congress has the power under the commerce clause to prohibit the interstate shipment of goods produced for substandard wages and hours. Congress' motive and purpose in passing the FLSA are matters for legislative judgment. The Constitution does not limit what Congress thinks is proper to regulate under the commerce clause. The power to regulate interstate commerce includes the power to pass laws regulating things which affect interstate commerce. Even if commerce is local (intrastate), such as manufacturing, it can affect interstate commerce. Darby lost.

LEGAL TIP
Congress' power to pass laws regulating business under the commerce clause is practically unlimited.

and police power. "Police power" means making laws that promote "health, safety, morals, and general welfare." *Hawaii Housing Authority v. Midkiff* is a recent case example involving a **state's police power.**

SOME LIMITS ON GOVERNMENTAL LAWMAKING

We just saw two examples of governmental lawmaking. One (the *Darby* case) was under a federal enumerated power, the commerce clause. The other (the *Hawaiian Housing Authority* case) showed state lawmaking power under the police power. Judging by what happened in those cases, you know that government has much lawmaking power at all levels.

However, the United States Constitution does limit lawmaking in several ways:

1. By limiting lawmaking of the United States Government to only those areas listed (enumerated) in the United States Constitution (and areas reasonably implied therefrom).
2. By adhering to the United States Constitution's Bill of Rights (first ten Amendments).
3. By applying the Fourteenth Amendment's due process clause.
4. By implementing the Fourteenth Amendment's equal protection clause.

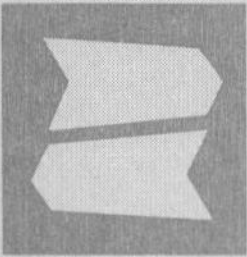

HAWAII HOUSING AUTHORITY v. MIDKIFF

U.S. Supreme Court.
52 L.W. 4673 (1984).

FACTS In the 1960's the Hawaii legislature discovered that the State and Federal Governments owned almost 49% of Hawaii's land. Also, only seventy-two private landowners owned 47% of the state's land. (This concentrated land ownership resulted from a feudal land tenure system set up by an ancient Polynesian high chief, ali'i nui, who owned all the land. He in turn *assigned* it to sub-chiefs and sub-sub chiefs. The modern owners traced their ownership from this arrangement.) In effect, most modern Hawaiian "homeowners" were not owners at all; instead, they were tenants leasing their homes from the seventy-two private landowners.

The Hawaii legislature concluded that the concentrated land ownership was responsible for inflating land prices and injuring the public tranquility and welfare. To correct this problem, the state legislature decided to force large landowners to break up their estates and passed the Land Reform Act of 1967. This Act created the Hawaiian Housing Authority (HHA) to condemn the land and sell it to existing single family residential tenants. (The condemnation reduced adverse tax effects on landowners forced to sell.)

The landowners fought this condemnation. They said the Land Reform Act violated the Fifth Amendment's Public Use Clause, which limited the states' takings of property, because it was read into the Fourteenth Amendment's Due Process Clause. The landowners said Hawaii's law took their privately owned land and turned it over (by sale) to other private persons. The existing tenants were preferred, but the HHA could also sell to other private persons under certain circumstances.

ISSUE Was the Hawaiian Land Reform Act a valid exercise of the State's police power or did it violate the Fifth and Fourteenth Amendments?

DECISION The state statute was a valid exercise of the state's police power. The Fifth Amendment says "private property (shall not) be taken for *public* use without just compensation." The landowners argued that the taking was for a *private* use (for the existing tenants, who wanted to *own* rather than *lease* their single family residences).

The Supreme Court does not substitute its judgment for a state legislature's as to what is a "public use" unless the use is without foundation. Using the eminent domain power rationally relates to a conceivable public *purpose;* a "taking" that the government pays for is not stopped by the Fifth Amendment's Public Use Clause. Correcting the evils of concentrated land ownership is rational. "Public use" means public purpose.

LEGAL TIP

The government (federal, state, or local) can take a person's land, pay for it, and turn it over to other private persons if a rational public purpose is served.

First Amendment: Free Speech and Business

The Constitution's **First Amendment** protects a speaker's right to free speech as well as a listener's right to hear ideas. Justice Holmes said, "The best test of truth is the power of the thought to get itself accepted in the competition of the market."

Commercial speech **Commercial speech** is advertising. In 1942, the United States Supreme Court said that the First Amendment's protection of free speech did not apply to advertising. This result meant that government could regulate, or limit, advertising much more than other speech; however, this regulation changed in the 1970's.

Today, the First Amendment's free speech gives some protection to advertising. If government wants to limit advertising it must show that:

1. Some substantial interest justifies limiting the advertising.
2. The restriction directly promotes the other interest.
3. No other way exists to limit the ads as well with fewer restrictions.

Examples of valid limits on advertising Government can stop fraudulent, or untrue, ads as well as ones dealing with illegal activity. For example, one case outlawed sex-based want-ads. Time, place, and manner regulations not limiting what ads say are legal. For example, 10 PM curfews on door-to-door salespeople probably are valid (people dislike answering doorbells at 3 AM).

Political speech Corporations have full, free **political speech** under the First Amendment. This means government *cannot* stop corporations from making statements about public issues even if the corporation's business is *not involved* with the issue. For example, a state cannot stop an auto manufacturer from buying time on television to talk about prayer in the schools. The Supreme Court case allowing this type of action was *First National Bank of Boston v. Bellotti,* which was decided in 1978.

Due Process: Another Limit on Lawmaking

Due process means that the government owes something to the people (something is "due"). Government owes *fair procedures* (called "procedural due process") and *fair substance* (called "substantive due process") in its laws.

Due process is basically a natural law requirement that positive law must meet. The Fifth Amendment's due process clause limits the United States Government. The Fourteenth Amendment's due process clause limits states and municipalities.

Procedural due process **Procedural due process** means that the law must give *notice* and *fair hearing.* A vague law violates procedural due process's notice requirement. Laws forbidding "loitering" are vague and often violate procedural due process. The reason for this violation is that people are unsure about what constitutes "loitering." If a law is too vague, it violates procedural due process and is invalid.

The "fair hearing" part of procedural due process means a trial in a court case. In an administrative case it means a "hearing." Usually "hearing" means:

1. The right to a neutral, third-party judge.
2. The right to know the charges.
3. The right to confront and cross-examine witnesses.
4. The right to present evidence.
5. The right to have decisions based on evidence presented at the hearing.
6. The right to a jury in certain trials.
7. The right to have a lawyer represent a person.

The amount of due process depends on what rights are affected. For example, the Supreme Court requires hearings in public school disciplinary matters involving suspensions. The Supreme Court does not require matters where students question their course grade.

Substantive due process **Substantive due process** means legislatures must pass "fair" laws. This requirement sounds good, but who is to judge whether a law is fair? If judges do, they take over the legislature's job. The idea of substantive due process is seldom used today to invalidate laws.

Equal Protection: Another Limit on Lawmaking

The United States Constitution's Fourteenth Amendment says that states cannot deny anyone **equal protection** of the laws. This idea also limits the United States Government because the Supreme Court has said that the Fifth Amendment's "due process" words include the equal protection idea.

Equal protection is important because it says that laws should treat people equally. This idea is appealing since the law should not "play favorites."

Some laws do treat people differently and the Supreme Court allows them even though the equal protection clause exists. The Supreme Court allows discriminatory laws if they meet certain tests. The tests are **rational basis** and **strict scrutiny.**

The rational basis test lets lawmakers treat people differently if there is a *reason* for the different treatment. This test applies to most laws. *Minnesota v. Clover Leaf Creamery Co.* is a case example.

MINNESOTA v. CLOVER LEAF CREAMERY CO.

U.S. Supreme Court.
101 S.Ct. 715 (1981).

FACTS In 1977, the Minnesota legislature passed a law stopping the sale of milk in plastic, nonreturnable, nonrefillable containers. The law allowed paperboard milk cartons even if they were nonreturnable and nonrefillable. The purpose of the statute was to control garbage, promote energy conservation, and stop natural resource depletion.

The makers of plastic milk cartons sued the State of Minnesota, arguing that the statute discriminated against them. Therefore, they argued, the law violated the equal protection clause.

ISSUE Did the Minnesota statute prohibiting some (but not all) milk containers violate the equal protection clause?

DECISION No. The statute was valid. The statute had valid objectives. By treating various milk containers differently, the state could attack the garbage and energy problems with less disruption than if it suddenly outlawed *all* nonreturnable milk containers. States can deal with a problem on a piecemeal basis. The legislature's wisdom is not at issue if the law's purpose is rational.

LEGAL TIP

Legislatures can treat businesses differently if there is a reason.

Strict scrutiny Courts allow legislatures to discriminate less in certain matters. For example, when laws discriminate and affect **fundamental rights** or **suspect categories,** courts apply the strict scrutiny test.

Basically, this test says that legislatures should very seldom discriminate in certain areas. One such area is *fundamental rights.* Rights such as voting, having children, traveling interstate, and having a fair criminal proceeding are fundamental.

Courts also apply the strict scrutiny test when judging laws that discriminate in *suspect categories.* For example, sex, race, national origin, illegitimacy, and alien status are all suspect categories. Therefore, a state real estate licensing law that forbids persons of Japanese ancestry from being realtors would be judged according to the strict scrutiny test.

The strict scrutiny test makes it hard, but not impossible, to justify discriminatory laws.

KEY TERMS

Constitution
Separation of powers
Federalism
Enumerated power
Commerce clause
States' police power
First Amendment
Commercial speech
Political speech
Due process
Procedural due process
Substantive due process
Equal protection
Rational basis
Strict scrutiny
Fundamental rights
Suspect categories

CHAPTER PROBLEMS

1. Does the First Amendment protect advertising?
2. How does due process protect people?
3. Give an example of a law that Congress could pass because of the United States Constitution's commerce clause.
4. Do corporations have any rights to free speech under the First Amendment?
5. What is procedural due process?
6. Define federalism.
7. What two purposes do constitutions in non-communist countries try to achieve?
8. How many amendments does the United States Constitution have?

*9. The University of California-Davis Medical School set an express racial quota for admission. What constitutional problem(s) does this quota raise? *Regents of the University of California v. Bakke,* 438 U.S. 265 (1978).

*10. An Alabama statute required that ex-husbands but not ex-wives pay alimony after divorce. Should the rational basis or strict scrutiny test be used to judge this law when challenged under the equal protection clause? *Orr v. Orr,* 99 S.Ct. 1102 (1979).

"The rise of administrative bodies probably has been the most significant legal trend of the last century . . ."

Justice Jackson dissenting in *FTC v. Ruberoid Co.*, 343 U.S. 470 (1952)

Chapter 8

Government Regulation: An Overview

CHAPTER PREVIEW

- Definition of an administrative agency
- Reasons administrative agencies exist
- Definition of a regulation
- Three parts of the Federal Register System
- Function of enabling statutes
- Purpose of the Administrative Procedure Act
- Agencies that the Federal Privacy Act applies to
- Requirements of the Sunshine Law
- Four ways to control regulators

A farmer in Booneville County, Idaho, went to a local United States Government office to buy federal crop insurance. The federal employee checked the crop insurance regulations and told the farmer that all of his crop was insurable. Relying on this information, the farmer bought the insurance. Later that season the farmer's crop was destroyed. The farmer tried to collect on his federal insurance policy but was told that his crops were not protected. The farmer pointed out that the federal agent had told him that the crops were covered when he bought the insurance. The federal agency replied that federal regulations clearly indicated that the farmer's crop was not insured and that the local agent's negligently misinforming the farmer was no excuse, since the federal crop insurance regulations in the Federal Register *provided sufficient notice. The farmer sued the federal agency for the lost crop, claiming that he bought federal agency insurance covering them. Did he recover damages?*

This chapter presents a survey of administrative law consisting of several parts. First, we present some basic definitions. Then we examine why administrative agencies exist, look at the structure of a typical administrative agency, and examine a diagram of a number of federal agencies. Finally, we discuss controls on administrative agencies. Chapters 9 and 10 discuss the three basic functions of administrative agencies: to make regulations, to adjudicate (decide cases like courts), and to enforce their statutes and regulations.

DEFINITION OF ADMINISTRATIVE LAW

Administrative law is a phrase with more than one meaning. Broadly defined, it is all law concerning administrative agencies (including statutes, rules, regulations, and court and agency interpretations). Narrowly defined, it means court review of administrative agencies' performance. The broad definition is described in the following subsection.

Definition of an Administrative Agency

An **administrative agency** is any nonlegislative, nonjudicial governmental lawmaker. This definition excludes rules made by private business corporations. An administrative agency could be a person or an institution possessing governmental authority. This person or institution has no single official name and need not include the word *"agency."* Titles could be the "Environmental Protection Agency," the "Federal Trade Commission," the "Police Department of Portland, Maine," or the "Department of Public Health of the State of Tennessee." As these names suggest, administrative agencies exist at the federal, state, and municipal levels of government.

Organic act Agencies are usually created by a statute called the agency's **organic act.** In an agency's organic act, the legislature recognizes that a problem exists, creates an agency to deal with the problem, and delegates legislative authority to the agency to make appropriate regulations to cope with the problems. The organic act also gives judicial authority to the agency for hearing cases that deal with the agency's subject matter. Finally, the organic act confers executive authority, which allows the agency to investigate and administer its subject matter.

The number of administrative agencies The number of administrative agencies at the federal level undoubtedly runs into the hundreds. Acronyms such as SEC (Securities and Exchange Commission), ICC (Interstate Commerce Commission), FDA (Food and Drug Administration), EPA (Environmental Protection Agency), and OMB (Office of Management and Budget) all identify different federal agencies. Figure 8-1 dramatizes the nature and extent of federal agencies. The figure distinguishes between executive departments and independent agencies. This difference is based on the fact that executive agencies are within the executive branch of the government; independent agencies are not. Because of this distinction, the president has more control over executive than independent agencies.

Reasons Administrative Agencies Exist

Expertise There are several reasons why administrative agencies exist. First, legislatures and courts do not have the technical expertise to deal with the many complicated problems that the nation faces today. For example, the technical problems associated with licensing limited radio frequencies require the skills of specialists, not courts or legislatures.

Protection against social harm Second, there is a need to oversee activities when there is a small impact on each individual but tremendous overall social consequences for individuals. For example, the harm from air pollution on a single person is small, but over time such pollution could cause skin cancer, destroy crops, and cause other damage.

Protection for the weak Another reason for the rise of administrative agencies is to help the weak and poor fight corporate giants. For example, farmers in the Midwest in the late 1800's were victims of discriminatory railroad rates. They took their case against the railroads to Congress and the Interstate Commerce Commission (ICC) was created to, among other things, regulate railroad rates. Actually, the ICC has since been "captured" by the powerful, organized interests that it was originally designed to regulate.

Speed and economy The rise of administrative agencies also occurred because of the need for speed and economy in running the government. For example, it wastes time and money to have court proceedings merely to license a barber.

Class struggle Finally, some people see administrative agencies as sources for solving social roadblocks put up by judges. In the late nineteenth century, workers who tried to form labor unions were brought before courts and tried for criminal conspiracy. Judges at that time often saw unions as threats to a person's right to manage his or her own business. Labor leaders, on the other hand, viewed the labor factor as part of the production process. They tried to get the judges to legalize unions. In the short run they failed. Later, a combination of events—including the removal of much federal court jurisdiction to stop union activity and the establishment of a federal administrative agency, the National Labor Relations Board (NLRB), to deal with labor matters such as union recognition—legalized the labor union. The NLRB is probably the most prominent example of an administrative agency created to get around the judiciary. This agency made one political group (organized labor) stronger than another (business).

The Source of Administrative Agencies

The United States Constitution does not create administrative agencies; instead, federal statutes usually create federal agencies. As such, they can legally be eliminated by Congress. For instance, Congress could eliminate all statutorily created federal administrative agencies merely by passing another law. This outcome will probably never occur but shows some Congressional power over federal agencies. Executive orders can also create administrative agencies.

Legislative Delegations to Agencies: Enabling Acts

A statute is a law passed by a federal or state legislature. Statutes are important in administrative law because agencies have the power to make legally binding regulations only if the legislature gives them this power. The way legislatures give

Figure 8-1 Number of Federal Agency Employees

ORGANIZATION	EMPLOYEES IN UNITED STATES	PERSONNEL OUTSIDE UNITED STATES	TOTAL PAID EMPLOYEES JAN. 1, 1985	JAN. 1, 1984	JAN. 1, 1975	JAN. 1, 1965
Executive Office of the President	**1,618**		**1,618**	**1,624**	**2,845**	**1,924**
Executive Departments	**1,648,650**	**[1]118,764**	**1,767,414**	**1,731,871**	**1,697,206**	**2,085,046**
1. Department of Agriculture	118,301	1,462	119,763	114,077	103,326	98,162
2. Department of Commerce	34,225	759	34,984	35,104	35,114	55,901
3. Department of Defense	963,624	98,212	1,061,836	1,036,627	1,035,270	1,019,382
Office of the Secretary of Defense	76,204	12,468	88,672	84,118	74,332	39,855
Department of the Air Force	232,715	16,041	248,756	246,328	269,349	291,183
Department of the Army	338,304	44,723	383,027	370,991	369,454	361,691
Department of the Navy	316,401	24,980	341,381	335,190	322,135	326,653
4. Department of Education	5,140		5,140	5,152		
5. Department of Energy	16,699		16,699	17,256		
6. Department of Health and Human Services	141,948		141,948	145,948	[2]143,202	[2]83,417
7. Department of Housing and Urban Development	12,108		12,108	12,633	16,825	
8. Department of the Interior	73,855	370	74,225	74,470	74,202	61,616
9. Department of Justice	61,320	538	61,858	59,358	51,054	32,439
10. Department of Labor	19,137		19,137	19,662	13,739	9,043
11. Department of State	8,977	15,860	24,837	24,016	32,157	41,328
12. Department of Transportation	62,695	541	63,236	63,281	72,342	
13. Department of the Treasury	130,621	1,022	131,643	124,287	119,975	85,524
Independent Agencies	**1,103,551**	**[3]21,980**	**1,125,531**	**[4]1,099,427**	**[5]1,112,166**	**[6]386,383**
1. ACTION	507		507	526	1,956	
2. Administrative Conference of the United States	21		21	21	40	
3. Advisory Commission on Intergovernmental Relations	38		38	45	47	32
4. American Battle Monuments Commission	11	393	404	404	403	423
5. Appalachian Regional Council	7		7	7	10	
6. Board for International Broadcasting	18		18	18		
7. Commission of Fine Arts	7		7	7	7	6
8. Commodity Futures Trading Commission	538		538	479		
9. Consumer Product Safety Commission	567		567	595	828	
10. Delaware River Basin Commission	2		2	2	2	
11. Environmental Protection Agency	12,650		12,650	11,444	10,764	
12. Equal Employment Opportunity Commission	3,231		3,231	3,142	2,255	
13. Export-Import Bank of the United States	367		367	339	429	297
14. Farm Credit Administration	311		311	330	215	230
15. Federal Communications Commission	1,999		1,999	1,945	1,977	1,529
16. Federal Deposit Insurance Corporation	4,965	111	5,076	3,847	2,755	1,387
17. Federal Election Commission	251		251	218		
18. Federal Emergency Management Agency	2,766		2,766	2,701		
19. Federal Home Loan Bank Board	1,533		1,533	1,570	1,427	1,248
20. Federal Labor Relations Authority	321		321	306		
21. Federal Maritime Commission	231		231	246	290	238
22. Federal Mediation and Conciliation Service	356		356	358	491	437
23. Federal Mine Safety and Health Review Commission	50		50	60		
24. Federal Reserve System (Board of Governors)	1,591		1,591	1,589	1,372	
25. Federal Trade Commission	1,433		1,433	1,426	1,621	1,150
26. General Services Administration	29,667	11	29,678	30,252	38,414	34,821
27. Inter-American Foundation	67		67	65	68	
28. International Development Cooperation Agency	2,309	2,832	[7]5,141	5,246		
29. Interstate Commerce Commission	1,025		1,025	1,224	1,983	2,398
30. Merit Systems Protection Board	450		450	492		
31. National Aeronautics and Space Administration	21,866	10	21,876	22,435	25,525	33,503
32. National Capital Planning Commission	50		50	51	64	51
33. National Credit Union Administration	600		600	622	575	
34. National Foundation on the Arts and Humanities	587		587	586	1,882	
35. National Labor Relations Board	2,646		2,646	2,761	2,465	2,136
36. National Mediation Board	55		55	57	101	127
37. National Science Foundation	1,889	1	1,890	2,007	2,390	1,426
38. National Transportation Safety Board	336		336	322	279	
39. Nuclear Regulatory Commission	3,578		3,578	3,469		
40. Occupational Safety and Health Review Commission	86		86	94	171	
41. Office of Personnel Management	6,570	18	6,588	6,424		
42. Overseas Private Investment Corporation	156		156	153	132	
43. Panama Canal Commission	14	8,056	8,070	8,359	[8]15,680	[8]15,112
44. Peace Corps	666	463	1,129	1,054		
45. Pennsylvania Avenue Development Corporation	35		35	37		
46. Postal Rate Commission	64		64	62	81	
47. Railroad Retirement Board	1,577		1,577	1,607	1,730	1,769

Figure 8-1 Continued

ORGANIZATION	EMPLOYEES IN UNITED STATES	PERSONNEL OUTSIDE UNITED STATES				
48. Securities and Exchange Commission	2,040		2,040	1,860	1,888	1,384
49. Selective Service System	308		308	298	2,599	7,442
50. Small Business Administration	4,980	103	5,083	4,978	4,612	3,518
51. Susquehanna River Basin Commission	26		26	2	2	
52. Tennessee Valley Authority	32,824		32,824	34,830	25,841	16,500
53. U.S. Arms Control and Disarmament Agency	241		241	226	263	234
54. U.S. Commission on Civil Rights	254		254	220	257	102
55. U.S. Information Agency	3,941	4,428	8,369	8,029	8,952	11,798
56. U.S. International Trade Commission	444		444	417	359	[9]281
57. U.S. Postal Service	710,995	3,059	714,054	688,377	714,436	[10]598,234
58. Veterans Administration	239,434	2,495	241,929	240,757	209,434	171,560
Total, Executive Branch (966 WOC)	**2,753,819**	**140,744**	**[11]2,894,563**	**[11]2,832,922**	**[11]2,812,217**	**[11]2,473,353**
Total, Legislative Branch			**[12]38,598**	**[12]38,989**	**[13]35,083**	**[14]25,471**
Total, Judicial Branch			**17,171**	**16,528**	**9,789**	**5,862**
Total			**2,950,332**	**2,888,439**	**2,857,089**	**2,504,686**

[1]Total American citizens: 67,479; nationals of other countries: 51,285.
[2]Listed as Department of Health, Education, and Welfare in 1965 and 1975 charts.
[3]Total American citizens: 9,671; nationals of other countries: 12,309.
[4]Reflects total employees of all independent agencies existing as of January 1, 1984.
[5]Reflects total employees of all independent agencies existing as of January 1, 1975.
[6]Reflects total employees of all independent agencies existing as of January 1, 1965.
[7]Includes AID: 5,130 employees—2,832 outside U.S. of whom 1,530 are American citizens and 1,302 are foreign nationals.
[8]Listed as Panama Canal Company on 1965 and 1975 charts.
[9]Listed as U.S. Tariff Commission on 1965 chart.
[10]Listed as Post Office Department on 1965 chart.
[11]Does not include the Central Intelligence Agency.
[12]Includes Congress, Architect of the Capitol, U.S. Botanic Garden, Congressional Budget Office, Copyright Royalty Tribunal, General Accounting Office, Government Printing Office, Library of Congress, Office of Technology Assessment, and United States Tax Court.
[13]Includes the Congress, General Accounting Office, Library of Congress, Government Printing Office, Architect of the Capitol, United States Tax Court, Cost Accounting Standards Board, National Study Commission, and U.S. Botanic Garden.
[14]Includes the Congress, General Accounting Office, Government Printing Office, Library of Congress, and the Architect of the Capitol.

agencies power is called "legislative delegation." Statutes delegating legislative power to make rules are called "enabling statutes."

Definition of a Regulation

Administrative agencies have the power to make laws, called regulations (regs) or rules.[1] There are two general types of regulations: *interpretative* and *substantive* (sometimes called legislative). Substantive regulations are given the force and effect of law by courts since they are legally binding. They must be made through rulemaking (or regulation-making) procedures. The Federal Administrative Procedure Act (APA) sets out the guidelines for rulemaking.

Interpretative rules, general agency policy statements, or rules of agency procedure, practice, or organization are not given the effect of law by courts. Interpretative rules are generally effective as soon as the federal agency announces their existence.

[1]The words rules and regulations (regs) are used interchangeably here. Professor Kenneth Culp Davis considers them synonymous, although some authorities do not.

OVERVIEW OF SOME IMPORTANT FEDERAL ADMINISTRATIVE STATUTES

The Federal Register Act

One of the least known and most important federal laws is the Federal Register Act, which was passed in 1935. This Act provides a way to get up-to-the-minute information about an agency and its regulations. This function is done by the Federal Register System, created by the Federal Register Act.

The Federal Register System The **Federal Register System** has three parts: the federal *Government Manual* (formerly called the *Government Organization Manual*), the *Federal Register,* and the *Code of Federal Regulations.*

Government Manual The ***Government Manual*** lists the names and addresses of all United States Government agencies (plus much more information about each agency). A new edition of this book is published each year. You can buy this book from the United States Government Printing Office for a small amount of money.

Federal Register The ***Federal Register*** is like a small newspaper published by the federal government every business day, Monday through Friday. Some of the more important things that the *Register* contains are presidential proclamations, notices of federal agency public meetings, proposed federal regulations, and promulgated federal regulations. A federal agency's substantive regulation is usually not the law unless it is promulgated in the *Federal Register.* The function of the *Federal Register* is to give public notice of federal agencies' official acts. You can find the *Federal Register* in most large libraries.

Code of Federal Regulations The *Code of Federal Regulations* (CFR) is the third part of the Federal Register System. This register arranges all currently effective federal agency regulations by agency. When regulations are promulgated in the *Federal Register,* they are not arranged by agency. A regulation simply appears when the agency delivers a regulation to the Federal Register office. Thus, we needed a way to get all of a particular agency's regulations together in one place. The CFR organizes this information in a multi-volumed set of paperbound books. Each book usually contains practically all of the agency's current regulations.

***Need to read the* Federal Register** Is the average citizen bound by what appears in *Federal Register* daily editions and the CFRs? An Idaho farmer learned the hard way about his duty to read the *Federal Register* in the *Federal Crop Ins. Corp. v. Merrill* case.

Administrative Procedure Act

Even though the 1930's saw the creation of many new administrative agencies at the federal level, the **Administrative Procedure Act** (APA) was not passed until 1946. It was enacted because of widespread concern with the lack of regularized procedures for agency actions. For example, before the APA was created, some federal agencies would decide cases after hearing only one side's (the government's) evidence.

FEDERAL CROP INS. CORP. v. MERRILL

U.S. Supreme Court.
332 U.S. 380 (1947).

FACTS Merrill applied for crop insurance with the Federal Crop Insurance Agency to insure a wheat crop in Idaho. Part of the crop was reseeded. He asked the government employee if his crop was insurable. The government official said, "Yes." Merrill bought crop insurance. Later his crops were destroyed by drought. He filed a claim under his crop insurance. The government agency refused to pay because a regulation said reseeded crops were not insurable. Merrill said that he did not know of the regulation. He also said that the agency official said his crop was insurable.

The trial jury and judge said that Merrill could recover. The Idaho Supreme Court agreed.

The Federal Crop Insurance Corporation appealed to the United States Supreme Court.

ISSUE If a government employee inaccurately tells a citizen that a regulation allows crops to be insured (when actually the regulation says such crops are *not* insurable), can the citizen recover on the insurance from the government insurer?

DECISION No. All members of the public are held accountable for government regulations because the government is not a private insurer, and regulations are public and available to everyone.

LEGAL TIP

You are bound by regulations in the *Federal Register.* Businesses should belong to a trade association that reads these rules and tells them about regulatory matters.

Administrative agencies make rules. They decide cases by applying agency rules. The APA sets the requirements, or structure, for conducting rulemakings and adjudications.

The APA has been amended several times since its original passage in 1946. Among the more important APA amendments are the Freedom of Information Act, the Privacy Act of 1974, and the Government in the Sunshine Act.

Freedom of Information Act

The **Freedom of Information Act** (FOIA) was passed in 1966. The main purpose of this Act is disclosure of information that federal (*not* state) agencies have in their possession. The information might include photos, studies, files, letters, and many other tangible bits of information.

Making an FOIA request How does a person make an FOIA request from an agency? No particular form is required. A simple letter directed to the particular agency's FOIA office is usually sufficient. An FOIA request must have a reasonable description of the records that one wants. This description helps the agency to locate the information being sought (for example, a request for all information that the Federal Trade Commission has about price discrimination is too broad; but a request for the FTC study of the life insurance industry in the late 1970's would probably be specific enough). The request must have been made in accordance with an agency's rules about the time, place, fees, and procedures to be followed. An agency must make records promptly available after an FOIA request has been made. Usually an agency has ten business days to decide whether to honor an FOIA request.

Exemptions The federal FOIA has nine exemptions, meaning that certain types of information falling within any one of the nine exemptions do not have to be disclosed even after public requests. However, the *FOIA exemptions* do not allow agencies to withhold information from Congress. The nine FOIA exemptions involve:

1. National defense or foreign policy matters.
2. Internal personnel rules and practices of an agency.
3. Other statutes specifically allowing nondisclosure.
4. Privileged or confidential trade secrets and commercial or financial information obtained from a person.
5. Interagency or intraagency memoranda or letters.
6. Personnel, medical, and similar files the disclosure of which would clearly involve an unwarranted invasion of personal privacy.
7. Investigatory records compiled for law-enforcement purposes.
8. Material in reports of agencies responsible for regulating or supervising financial institutions (such as bank examiners' reports).
9. Geological or geophysical information and data (including maps) concerning wells.

Federal Privacy Act of 1974

Purpose Congress passed the **Federal Privacy Act of 1974** (FPA) to protect individual privacy resulting from misuse of federal agency information. The alleged misuse of information took many forms and involved both government and private sources. Social Security cards were used for identification purposes (check cashing, for example) even though the card face says on it that it cannot be used for identification.

Conflict Federal agency use and assembly of information involves an inherent conflict of values. Agencies need accurate, complete information to perform efficiently. However, the United States was established to promote individual freedom (which includes the right of privacy) and to have a limited government. The FPA tries to strike a proper compromise between efficient government management and individual privacy.

Main provision The main provision of the FPA stops an agency from disclosing any record in a system of records by any means of communication to any person or agency without the prior *written* consent of the individual the record is about. This provision has several key points and many qualifications. The FPA is generally limited to federal agencies (although it also applies to federal contractors, including states or businesses receiving federal contracts, unless otherwise exempt.

One final point about the FPA: An individual's name and address may not be sold or rented by a federal agency unless specifically authorized by another law.

Government in the Sunshine Act

The **Government in the Sunshine Act** (Sunshine Act) became federal law in 1976. It is sometimes called an *open meeting law.* The main objective of this Act is to open up the official decision-making processes of the federal government. The Sunshine Act requires that an agency headed by a collegial body must not conduct or dispose of agency business unless every portion of the business meeting is open to the public. A collegial body is two or more individuals heading an agency, a majority of whom are presidential appointees confirmed by the United States Senate. Thus, the Sunshine Act would apply to the Federal Trade Commission, since it is headed by five presidentially appointed, Senate-confirmed commissioners. The Sunshine Act would not apply to the United States Environmental Protection Agency, since only one person, the administrator, heads this agency.

Controlling Administrative Agencies

The growth of administrative agencies over the past fifty years has been tremendous. Even though some functions that they perform are essential and many more are desirable, society has limited resources and wants limited intrusion into its members' lives. Thus, ways have been developed to legally and economically control administrative agencies at all levels of government. The sections below discuss such controls.

The Courts

Administrative agency actions are reviewable by courts, which are the major legal control over administrative agencies. Generally, state courts review state administrative agency actions, and federal courts review federal agency actions. There are exceptions to this rule. Judicial review of agency action is established by the APA at the federal level, and by APAs and common law at the state level. Courts can overturn agency actions for the following reasons.

1. The agency violated the United States Constitution.
2. The agency acted ultra vires (beyond its statutory authority).
3. The agency action was arbitrary, capricious, or an abuse of discretion; or the action broke some other law.
4. The agency did not follow legal procedures.
5. The agency adjudication was unsupported by substantial evidence.

Amount of evidence to support agency action The concept of limited judicial review of administrative action permits courts to review questions of law. It lets agencies decide the facts. Agency fact decisions must be supported by evidence. Courts use two separate tests to judge whether there is enough evidence to support administrative agency actions: substantial evidence and arbitrary, capricious, and unreasonable evidence. The **substantial evidence test** is used to review adjudications (agency orders resulting from hearings) and formal and **hybrid rulemakings.**[2] The **arbitrary, capricious, and unreasonable test** is usually used to judge informal rulemakings unless a statute requires the stricter substantial evidence rule.

Arbitrary, capricious, and unreasonable The arbitrary, capricious, and unreasonable test comes from the federal Administrative Procedure Act. This test is not so strict as the substantial evidence test. In other words, the federal agency does not have to produce as much evidence to justify its actions under the arbitrary, capricious, and unreasonable rule as it does under the substantial evidence test.

Sunset Laws

The so-called **sunset laws** have been enacted at different levels of government. They terminate administrative agencies in one of several ways: by cutting off the agency's budget, revoking the law that creates the agency, or requiring periodic

[2]"Hybrid rulemakings" refer to a process that an agency uses to make regulations that "adds to" the notice and comment procedures agencies follow in "informal rulemaking." "Added procedures" could include public hearings.

renewal of the law creating the agency. For example, every time an agency's budget is up for renewal, the sun could set on all or part of that agency's operations. Other laws have the same objective but are called by other names. Budgets (via appropriations bills) could be sunset laws for an agency or its programs.

Ombudspersons

Ombudspersons are agency employees who check to see that the agency is operating properly. In other words, an agency polices itself when it uses ombudspersons. Universities, cities, states, and various federal departments have ombudspersons. Sometimes they are known by other names, such as "inspectors general." The jurisdiction of ombudspersons may be broad or narrow. For example, some university ombudspersons may investigate student but not faculty complaints.

Federal Civil Rights Suits

Federal civil rights suits refer to lawsuits based on Sections 1981, 1982, and 1983 of Title 42 of the United States Code (USC). These sections allow persons whose federal civil rights are denied by private persons or by state (or municipal) officials to sue the wrongdoer in federal court. These laws can be used to hold state (or municipal) agency employees liable for abusing their power and violating people's civil rights.

Examples of federal civil rights violations subjecting state or municipal officials to liability include the following:

1. A refusal of a municipality to license a public coffee house run by "hippies," solely because the officials do not like these people.
2. Denying a radical (right- or left-wing) student group access to a state-owned auditorium when such access is routinely granted to other public groups (assuming no other basis for the denial exists).
3. Refusal of state welfare administrators to conform to federal welfare standards that require a hearing before ending welfare payments.

Possible remedies available for federal civil rights violations include injunctions, actual damages, and punitive damages.

Legislative Vetoes

A legislative veto is either the United States House or Senate or both saying to a regulator, "We invalidate your regulation." Since Congress created most administrative agencies, some argue that it should have the power to veto particular agency regulations it does not like.

The **legislative veto** is controversial for several reasons. First, it interferes with the orderly rulemaking process (described in Chapters 9 and 10). Second, Congress arguably takes an inconsistent position when it vetoes a regulation, since by passing an enabling statute it gave the agency the power to make the regulation.

Supporters of the legislative veto first point to it as a way to get government off the people's backs, thereby helping to increase productivity.

In the *I.N.S. v. Chadha* case, the United States Supreme Court invalidated the legislative veto.

Federal Tort Claims Act

Sovereign immunity The federal government and its agencies are protected from lawsuits by the **sovereign immunity** doctrine. As a result, the Defense Department is not liable to soldiers injured when poor battle plans cause high casualties. Also, federal employees are protected as individuals from suit based on their official acts. For example, if a mail carrier puts a Social Security check in the

I.N.S. v. CHADHA

U.S. Supreme Court.
103 S.Ct. 2764 (1983).

FACTS Congress passed a law called the Immigration and Nationality Act (Act). This Act authorizes the United States Attorney General to let particular deportable aliens stay in the United States. (The U.S. Attorney General is an administrative agency in this matter.) In the Act, Congress also authorized either the United States Senate or House to veto (invalidate) the Attorney General's decision to let a deportable alien stay here.

Chadha was a foreign student who came into the United States on a nonimmigrant student visa. He stayed in the United States after his visa had expired. The Immigration and Naturalization Service (I.N.S.) ordered Chadha to show why he should not be deported. Chadha then tried to get his deportation suspended. An I.N.S. administrative law judge (after a trial) suspended Chadha's deportation. This suspension let Chadha stay in the United States.

Then the United States House of Representatives passed a resolution vetoing the suspension, which would result in Chadha's having to leave the United States. The deportation started up again, and the I.N.S. ordered Chadha deported.

Chadha appealed to the courts, arguing that the legislative veto was unconstitutional.

ISSUE Was the legislative veto unconstitutional?

DECISION Yes. The United States Supreme Court reasoned that the legislative veto violates the United States Constitution. Specifically, the legislative veto violates the bicameralism idea (requiring that both houses of Congress—the House and Senate—have the power and right to be involved in lawmaking). Similarly, the Supreme Court said that the legislative veto violates the United States Constitution's presentment clause. This part of the Constitution requires that the president be given a chance to sign (approve) or veto (reject) any proposed law. When the Congress legislatively vetoes a regulation, this procedure is basically the same thing as passing a law (statute). Therefore, the same Constitutional steps must be followed in legislative vetoes as in passing a statute.

LEGAL TIP

Businesses and others can no longer rely on the legislative veto to get rid of unwanted federal regulations.

wrong mailbox, causing a retiree to miss a car payment and resulting in the repossession of the car, the carrier is not liable.

Waiver The federal government is liable for damages, injuries, property loss, or death if it has waived (given up) its sovereign immunity (and the claimant otherwise establishes a theory of recovery). One of the most important instances where the federal government has waived its sovereign immunity is in the **Federal Tort Claims Act.** By virtue of this Act, the federal government allows suit against itself, its agencies, and employees for torts that they commit. If, for example, an Internal Revenue Service (IRS) agent trespasses onto a person's business property to obtain evidence, the federal government and the employee as an individual would be liable (assuming no valid defense is available).

Limits Several important limits have been placed on this liability of federal agencies and their employees. First, the law of the state where the alleged wrong occurred defines whether the behavior causing the suit is a legal wrong. For example, if the alleged wrong was an invasion of privacy and had occurred in Alabama, but Alabama did not recognize invasion of privacy as a civil wrong, no basis would exist for suit under the Federal Tort Claims Act. Second, the alleged wrong must occur within the scope of the federal employee's official duties. Third, recoveries under this act include damages and injunctions. Punitive damages are not available. Finally, the Federal Tort Claims Act does not give up (waive) sovereign immunity for certain types of claims.

KEY TERMS

Administrative law
Administrative agency
Organic act
Federal Register System
Government Manual
Federal Register
Code of Federal Regulations
Administrative Procedure Act
Freedom of Information Act
Federal Privacy Act of 1974
Government in the Sunshine Act
Substantial evidence test
Arbitrary, capricious, and unreasonable test
Sunset laws
Ombudspersons
Hybrid rulemakings
Legislative vetoes
Sovereign immunity
Federal Tort Claims Act

CHAPTER PROBLEMS

1. What is an administrative agency?
2. What are some of the reasons that administrative agencies exist? Which of these reasons are the most persuasive today?
3. What are the controls on administrative agencies?
4. What is the FOIA?
5. Explain what an agency's organic act is.
6. What is the difference between a "sunshine" and a "sunset" law?
7. What is the main provision of the Federal Privacy Act?

*8. The Federal Tort Claims Act lets people sue and recover damages from the United States Government for torts (noncontractual civil wrongs), which federal employees commit. The Act does not, however, let a person recover punitive damages against the United States Government. In one case a government employee negligently drove a federal car and caused permanent brain damage to an innocent victim. The victim's relatives sued and recovered $2,201,013.80 for the victim (permanently in a coma). Was this jury award "punitive" and therefore not allowed by the Federal Tort Claims Act? *Flannery v. United States,* 718 F.2d 108 (4th Cir. 1983).

*9. Is the Texas Parole Board an "agency" covered by the *federal* Administrative Procedure Act? *Johnson v. Wells,* 566 F.2d 1016 (1978).

*10. Congress and Congressional committees have much valuable information about the Central Intelligence Agency. Can the public get this information by bringing a Freedom of Information suit against Congress? *Paisley v. C.I.A.,* 712 F.2d 686 (1983).

"Unlike sausage making, where it is better not to know how the product was produced, more people should be aware of what goes into regulations so that they can contribute to and improve what comes out at the end."

Anonymous

Chapter 9

Government Regulation: How Regulations Are Made

CHAPTER PREVIEW

- Three kinds of rulemakings
- Steps in informal rulemakings
- Federal agency's notice of proposed regulations
- Effect of an improper notice of a proposed regulation
- Comments to a proposed rule
- Impact of public comments on a proposed regulation
- Length of time public has to comment on a proposed regulation
- Reasons people can use to invalidate a regulation
- Recent changes in regulation-making that help small business

"We've got them now," shouted Mary Smith. Mary ran a travel agency. A federal regulator, the Interstate Commerce Commission (ICC), proposed a regulation that would add costs to Mary's business. Mary remembered something from her Legal Environment course at City College: regulators have to give public notice of a proposed regulation in the Federal Register *before the regulation becomes "law." Mary went to the public library and looked up the* Federal Register. *She found the regulation in its final form, which told her the page where it first appeared in the* Federal Register. *Mary turned to that page and discovered that the notice was incorrect because it did not say anything about a regulation. Mary went to her lawyer, and they sued the regulator. She argued that the regulation was invalid and should be thrown out. Was she right?*

WHAT AGENCIES (REGULATORS) DO

Figure 9-1 sets out the major steps that could be involved in the life of a federal regulation. This figure shows the executive, adjudicatory, and legislative jobs of the typical agency.

Executive

Executive functions basically involve law enforcement and administration. This process involves investigating and enforcing regulations and doing the scores of mundane things that make any organization run—such as hiring, firing, and issuing licenses.

Adjudications

Agency **adjudication** refers to hearings before administrative law judges (ALJs) who are legally independent from agency prosecutors, investigators, and rulemakers. ALJs make rulings on admissibility of evidence (the rules of evidence here are usually more lenient than in courts) and control the conduct of the hearing.

Legislative

The legislative function of an administrative agency refers to rulemaking.

The remainder of this chapter begins to look at the possible steps in the life of a federal regulation. Not every step will occur in every regulation's life, although it could. Chapter 10 continues the discussion of regulations.

Figure 9-1 **Major Steps in the Life of a Federal Regulation**

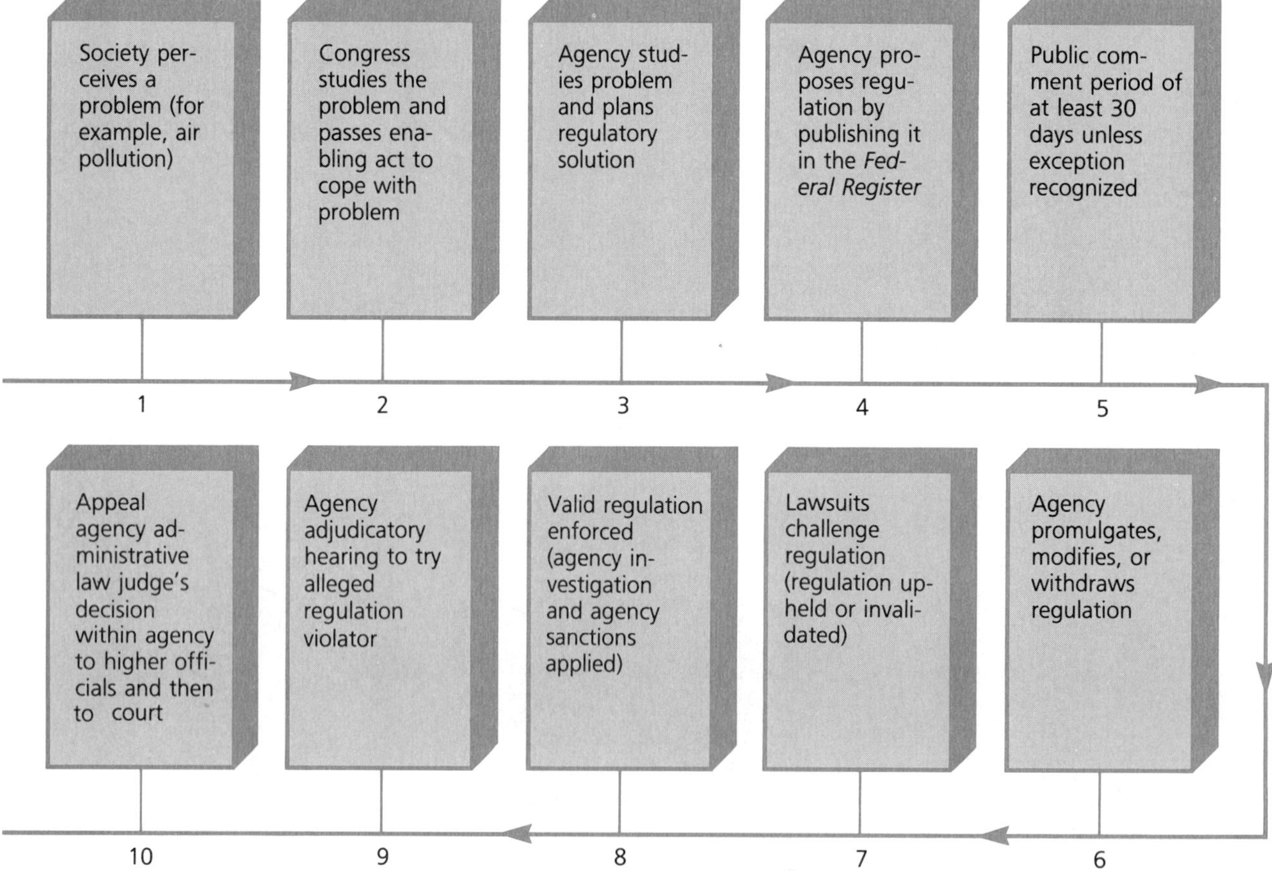

CATEGORIES OF RULEMAKINGS

There are three kinds of **rulemakings:** informal, formal, and hybrid.

Informal Rulemaking

Informal rulemaking refers to regulation-making using the "notice-and-comment process," which is usually the way agencies make regulations. Essentially, this process involves a federal agency's placing a notice of a **proposed rulemaking** in the *Federal Register,* receiving comments from interested persons on the proposed regulation, making any changes, and promulgating the regulation. No trials or hearings are held, and no face-to-face contact is made between the regulator and the public. Regulation-making done this way is "on paper." If a court challenge is offered to an informal rule, the arbitrary, capricious, and unreasonable evidentiary standard of evidence is used to review the rule.

Formal Rulemaking

Formal rulemaking occurs when a statute requires rulemaking on the record. A notice of the proposed rulemaking takes place, and a hearing follows. Witnesses give testimony under oath, transcripts of testimony are made, cross-examination of witnesses occurs, and rules of evidence apply (though not as strictly as in courts). At the end of the hearing, the agency makes written, formal findings; the agency then promulgates a regulation based on the evidence at the hearing. Courts use the substantial evidence test (discussed in Chapter 8) to decide if the agency has enough evidence to justify the regulation's existence.

Formal rulemakings are extremely expensive and can be slow to take effect. The classic example occurred when the Food and Drug Administration spent approximately ten years to promulgate a regulation setting the appropriate peanut content of peanut butter.[1] The 7700-plus-page transcript is an example of unwieldy formal rulemaking and excessive free speech. It shows the impracticality of formal rulemakings despite some redeeming qualities, such as cross-examination. Formal rulemaking is rarely required by statutes today.

Hybrid Rulemaking

Hybrid rulemaking is a cross between formal and informal rulemaking. The notice and comment aspects of informal rulemaking are combined with the requirement of a public hearing. Also, the substantial evidence test is used to judge sufficiency of agency evidence to support the regulation.

Society Sees a Problem (Step One)

Society often sees problems before the legislatures do. Individuals may bring problems to the attention of the legislature by writing letters, forming citizens groups, hiring lobbyists, and making campaign contributions.

Congress then must study the problem to understand its exact nature. Members of Congress do not personally study all problems brought to their attention; no one has that much time. Instead, each member of Congress has a sizeable staff, often exceeding 100 people. In addition, the congressional committees (and often subcommittees) have large staffs. These staffs are generally responsible for studying problems.

Congress Passes an Enabling Act (Step Two)

People sometimes point their fingers at administrative agencies for causing the oversupply of regulations. This response is similar to blaming an optometrist for

[1] The content was set at 90% peanuts. The decision was made in the case *Corn. Prod. Co. v. FDA,* 427 F.2d 511 (3rd Cir. 1970), *cert. denied sub. nom. Derby Foods, Inc. v. FDA,* 400 U.S. 957 (1970).

bad eyesight, since the doctor is only doing what the patient asks. Similarly, the legislature tells agencies what to do when enabling acts are passed.

Enabling acts **Enabling acts** are the legislatures telling agencies to make regulations. Agency regulations are valid only if the legislature (Congress at the federal level) gives the agency the necessary power. Agencies have no inherent power to make legally binding regulations; they may do only what the legislature allows in enabling acts. Remember that these are **legislative**—sometimes called "substantive" rules—**regulations** and not **interpretative regulations.**

Examples of enabling acts The following section of a federal statute (the Magnusen-Moss Warranty–Federal Trade Commission Improvement Act), which gives a federal agency the power to make regulations, is an example of an enabling act. The enabling statute gives the exact words the legislature (or Congress) used to tell an agency (or the Federal Trade Commission) to make a regulation:

> (b) The Commission shall initiate within one year after January 4, 1975, a rulemaking proceeding dealing with warranties and warranty practices in connection with the sale of used motor vehicles; and, to the extent necessary to supplement the protections offered the consumer by this chapter, shall prescribe rules dealing with such warranties and practices. In prescribing rules under this subsection, the Commission may exercise any authority it may have under this chapter, or other law, and in addition it may require disclosure that a used motor vehicle is sold without any warranty and specify the form and content of such disclosure. Publ. L. 93-637, Title I, Paragraph 109, January 4, 1975, 88 Stat. 2183.

Agency Studies a Problem (Step Three)

When the legislature passes an enabling statute, it has implicitly said society has a problem. The enabling statute tells an agency to do something about the problem and gives it some guidelines or policies to make regulations to solve the problem.

Before an agency can propose or promulgate a regulation, it must conduct a study, which can be done by an in-house group (the agency's own employees) or be contracted out to a consulting firm. The study is the key to the regulation because it is the scientific or factual justification for the regulation. For example, the FTC can promulgate a regulation forcing used-car dealers to put window stickers on cars telling consumers about the car's condition. Used-car dealers may question this regulation, and in response, the FTC will refer to the Magnusen Moss–FTC Improvement Act, which is the law telling the FTC to make the used-car industry fairer for consumers.

Think of the cost that such a regulation imposes on the used-car industry: This industry might have to spend hundreds of millions—perhaps even billions—of dollars to comply with the regulation. (Of course, defective used cars are a serious consumer problem causing great damage to people.) Therefore, the study behind a regulation must be excellent in purpose, design, and execution and logical in its conclusions.

Agency Proposes a Regulation (Step Four)

After the agency concludes its study, it drafts a regulation based on the study's conclusions. Different agency offices or personnel examine the draft regulation (such as the Office of General Counsel, the agency's lawyers, economists, and scientists) to try to find problems with it.

Once the agency's draft regulation has been reviewed within the agency, the heads of the agency sign it and send it over to the Federal Register Office in the National Archives and Records Service. There, the draft regulation is published in a daily edition of the *Federal Register.*

The law governing federal agencies' regulation-making The federal law governing regulation-making comes from the Administrative Procedure Act (APA). It governs most federal agencies. The APA's regulation-making rules do not apply to United States military or foreign affairs functions; to matters relating to agency management and personnel; or to public property, loans, grants, benefits, or contracts. Also state and municipal regulation-making is not covered by the federal APA. (Remember that many states have "little APAs," which govern state administrative agencies.) In addition to the APA, sometimes special statutes (such as the Occupational Safety and Health Act) place other requirements on agency rule-makings.

***The notice in the* Federal Register** When an agency proposes a regulation, general notice of the proposed regulation must be published in the *Federal Register,* with two exceptions: when persons subject to the regulation are named and either are personally served or otherwise have actual notice.

Contents of notice These items must be in the notice of the proposed rule-making published in the *Federal Register:*

1. The time, place, and nature of public regulation-making in general.
2. Agency laws giving authority to make the proposed rule.
3. Provisions of the proposed rule or a description of the subjects and issues involved. (In other words, the rule itself does not have to be published when it is proposed.)

What regulations need not be published The following regulations do not have to be published: interpretative regulations, general policy statements, or rules of agency organization, procedure, or practice. These rules do not have to be published because they are too general or trivial and because courts do not treat such items (interpretative regulations, etc.) as law.

When notice of proposed regulation is excused One other instance excuses an agency from giving notice of a proposed substantive regulation. When an agency for good cause finds that notice and public procedures are impracticable, unnecessary, or contrary to public interest, *Federal Register* notice is not required (of even a substantive regulation). Does the *Northwest Airlines, Inc. v. Goldschmidt* case give an example of a "good cause" excusing *Federal Register* notice?

Problems in finding the notice In the vast majority of cases, the publication in the *Federal Register* is the only official notice the public gets before a regulation takes effect. The average person has never seen the *Federal Register,* let alone read a proposed regulation. Figure 9-2 shows two pages of a proposed regulation lim-

Figure 9-2 **The Proposed Regulation***

FEDERAL TRADE COMMISSION

[16 CFR Part 455]

SALE OF USED MOTOR VEHICLES

Disclosure and Other Regulations

Notice of proceeding, proposed trade regulation rules, statement of reason for proposed rules, invitation to propose disputed issues of fact for consideration in public hearings, and invitation to comment on proposed rules.

Notice is hereby given that the Federal Trade Commission, pursuant to the Federal Trade Commission Act, as amended, 15 U.S.C. 41, et seq., the Magnuson-Moss Warranty-Federal Trade Commission Improvement Act, 15 U.S.C. 2301, et seq., the provisions of Part 1, Subpart B of the Commission's procedures and rules of practice, 16 CFR 1.7, et seq., and section 553 of Subchapter II, Chapter 5, Title 5, U.S. Code (Administrative Procedure), has initiated a proceeding for the promulgation of Trade Regulation Rules concerning the disclosure of certain material information and other regulations concerning used motor vehicles offered for sale.

Accordingly, the Commission proposes the following Trade Regulation Rules and would amend Subchapter D, Trade Regulation Rules, Chapter 1 of CFR by adding a new Part 445 as follows:

PART 455—DISCLOSURE AND OTHER REGULATIONS CONCERNING THE SALE OF USED MOTOR VEHICLES

AUTHORITY: 38 Stat. 717, as amended, 15 U.S.C. 41, et seq.

§ 455.1 Definitions.

For the purpose of this Part, the following terms and definitions shall apply:

(a) "Person" means any individual, partnership or corporation.

(b) "Used motor vehicle dealer" means any person, partnership, or corporation, or any employee or agent thereof, engaged in the business of offering for sale, sale or distribution of any used motor vehicle to the general public.

(c) "Motor vehicle" means an automobile, truck, recreational vehicle or other motorized vehicle designed to transport not more than fifteen (15) individuals upon the public roads, streets and highways.

(d) "Used motor vehicle" means a motor vehicle which is offered for sale after:

(1) A prior sale to a person who purchased the motor vehicle in good faith for a purpose other than resale; or

(2) Use of the motor vehicle as a rental, driver education, or demonstration motor vehicle, or for the personal or business transportation of the manufacturer and/or dealer or any of their employees or for any use other than the limited use necessary in moving or road testing a vehicle prior to delivery to a customer.

(e) "Warranty" means:

(1) Any written or oral affirmation of fact or promise made in connection with the sale or any used motor vehicle, which relates to nature of the material or workmanship of such used motor vehicle and affirms or promises that such material or workmanship is free of any mechanical defect or will meet any specified level of performance over any specified period of time, or

(2) Any written or oral undertaking made in connection with the sale of any used motor vehicle, to the effect that any person will refund, repair, replace or take other remedial action with respect to such used motor vehicle in the event said use motor vehicle fails to meet the specifications set forth in the undertaking, which written or oral affirmation, promise, or undertaking becomes part of the basis of the bargain between a used motor vehicle dealer and a buyer for purpose other than resale of such used motor vehicle.

(f) "Service contract" means a contract to perform, over any period of time or for any specified mileage, services relating to the maintenance or repair (or both) of any used motor vehicle.

(g) "Mechanical defect" means any defective or damaged part of the mechanical, electrical, or hydraulic system of any used motor vehicle including, but not limited to, the motor and transmission, and any defective or damaged part of the body, chassis, suspension or other part of said used motor vehicle.

(h) "Potential purchaser" means any person other than a used motor vehicle dealer, who expresses an interest or intention to purchase a used motor vehicle. Such person shall be of at least minimum legal driving age, possess sufficient credit worthiness to purchase the used motor vehicle under consideration and have no infirmities which would bar consummation of the sales transaction.

§ 455.2 Vehicle Information Disclosure.

In connection with the offering for sale, sale or distribution of any used motor vehicle to the public, in or affecting commerce as "commerce" is defined in the Federal Trade Commission Act, as amended, it is an unfair or deceptive act or practice for any used motor vehicle dealer to fail to affix to the right rear window of any used motor vehicle offered for sale a disclosure statement containing the following information in the order it appears below and in a clear, and conspicuous manner:

(a) The name, address, and chief executive officer of the used motor vehicle dealer.

(b) The make, model and year of manufacture of the used motor vehicle.

(c) The approximate odometer reading reflecting the amount of mileage the used motor vehicle has been driven.

(d) If known to the used motor vehicle dealer, the identity of any commercial or governmental entity which previously used, owned or leased the used motor vehicle and the nature of the principal prior use of such vehicle including but not limited to rental, lease, driver education, taxi and police vehicles.

(e) A description of any work (including reconditioning) performed by, or on behalf of the

Figure 9-2 Continued

used motor vehicle dealer or otherwise known to such dealer and relating to any damaged or defective component (including bent frame) or condition (including flooding) of the used motor vehicle which may affect the performance or useful life of the vehicle or which exceeded one hundred dollars ($100.00) in dealer costs.

(f) A description of the extent of component coverage, allocation of costs and duration of any warranty or service contract provided with the used motor vehicle and a statement that the potential purchaser may obtain a copy of any warranty or service contract offered from the used motor vehicle dealer.

(g) If the used motor vehicle is sold without a warranty and the seller attempts to disclaim any implied warranty, the following statements shall appear:

This vehicle is sold *without* any *warranty*. The purchaser will bear the *entire expense* of repairing or correcting any defects that presently exist and/or may occur in the vehicle unless the salesperson promises *in writing* to correct such defects." [Rule 1]

§ 455.3 "As is" disclosure.

In connection with the offering for sale, sale or distribution of any used motor vehicle to the public, other than to used motor vehicle dealers, in or affecting commerce as commerce is defined in the Federal Trade Commission Act, as amended, it is an unfair or deceptive act or practice for any used motor vehicle dealer to fail to disclose, in any sales contract, or any other writing used to evidence the sale of any used motor vehicle for which no warranty, either expressed or implied, is given, the following information in a clear, concise and conspicuous manner on the face of such document:

'*AS IS*

THIS USED MOTOR VEHICLE IS SOLD AS IS *WITHOUT* ANY *WARRANTY*, EITHER EXPRESSED OR IMPLIED. THE PURCHASER WILL BEAR THE *ENTIRE EXPENSE* OF REPAIRING OR CORRECTING ANY DEFECTS THAT PRESENTLY EXIST OR THAT MAY OCCUR IN THE VEHICLE.' " [Rule 2]

§ 455.4 Prohibition of contrary oral statements.

In connection with the offering for sale, sale, or distribution of any used motor vehicle in or affecting commerce as 'commerce' is defined in the Federal Trade Commission Act, as amended, it is an unfair or deceptive act or practice for any used motor vehicle dealer:

(a) To make any statements or claims, written or oral, or engage in any practices which directly or by implication contradict, mitigate, disparage or detract from any printed disclosure required by §§ 455.2 and 455.3; or

(b) To make any false, misleading or deceptive representation, directly or by implication, of the quality, performance, reliability or lack of mechanical defects of any used motor vehicle offered for sale.

(c) To make any representation, directly or by implication, of the quality, performance, reliability or lack of mechanical defects of any used motor vehicle offered for sale without possessing at the time of such representation a reasonable basis. [Rule 3]

§ 455.5 Retention of Documents.

To assure compliance with the provisions of this part, it is an unfair practice for all used motor vehicle dealers subject to such provisions to fail to retain and make available for inspection by officials of the Federal Trade Commission, upon request, true and correct copies of the written disclosures required by § 455.2 for at least three (3) years after the date on which the used motor vehicle subject to the disclosure was sold, and a copy of any sales contract, or other agreement used to consummate the sale of a used motor vehicle containing the disclosure required by § 455.3 for at least three (3) years from the date the used motor vehicle subject to the disclosure was sold." [Rule 4]

STATEMENT OF REASON FOR THE PROPOSED RULE

It is the Commission's purpose, in issuing this statement, to set forth its reasons for proposing this Trade Regulation Rule with sufficient particularity to allow informed comment. The precise format of such statements may vary from rule to rule depending on the complexity of the issues involved. In this proceeding the Commission has determined that meaningful comment by the public will be facilitated by presenting (1) a statement describing the basic factual and legal premises underlying the Commission's determination to propose the Rule, and (2) a series of questions designed to draw to the public's attention matters which the Commission deems particularly pertinent and on which comment is especially solicited.

The Commission emphasizes that neither the statement of factual and legal premises nor the questions set out in the materials accompanying the proposed Rule should be interpreted as a designation of disputed issues of fact. Such designations shall be made by the Commission or its duly authorized presiding official pursuant to the Commission's procedures and rules of practice.

STATEMENT

The Commission has reason to believe that a substantial number of used motor vehicles, as that term is defined in the proposed rule, are offered for sale or sold to the general public with mechanical defects which affect the performance or reliability of the vehicles. Potential purchasers are not in a position to determine the mechanical condition of the used motor vehicles under consideration and dealers, who know or should know of the defects do not inform the prospective purchaser of such defects. In addition, some dealers misrepresent the mechanical performance and reliability of the vehicles they offer for sale.

The Commission also has reason to believe that used motor vehicle dealers frequently recondition the appearance of the vehicles they offer for sale. Such reconditioning, which includes body work, painting and cleaning eliminates signs of the vehicle's previous use and normal wear and tear. Because of reconditioning, consumers often make erroneous assumptions concerning the prior use and care and of the mechanical performance and reliability of the used vehicles which are offered for sale.

NORTHWEST AIRLINES, INC. v. GOLDSCHMIDT

U.S. Court of Appeals (8th Cir.).
645 F.2d 1309 (1981).

FACTS In the late 1960's many United States airports had too many planes taking off and landing. In 1968 the Federal Aviation Administration promulgated a regulation to reduce take-off and landing delays at five crowded airports (Kennedy, LaGuardia, O'Hare, Newark, and National). Basically this rule limited the number of landing and take-off "slots" to sixty per hour at Washington's National Airport. The rule gave forty of the sixty slots to commercial planes; the five commercial airlines always wanted more than the forty slots. Until October 1980, they voluntarily allocated the forty slots among themselves. In 1980 a new airline, New York Air, wanted some of the limited Washington, D.C., "slots." Attempts to get the existing airlines to give up slots failed. The Thanksgiving-Christmas holiday season was near, and the Secretary of Transportation (a federal agency) proposed a regulation allocating the forty slots to avoid "chaos in the skies" during the upcoming holidays. The notice of proposed rulemaking was made on October 16, 1980; however, it was not published in the *Federal Register* until October 20, 1980. The comment period was seven days starting on October 16, 1980. The airlines and other persons submitted thirty-seven comments to the proposed regulation. Northwest Airlines sued the Secretary of Transportation, arguing the Administrative Procedure Act (APA) required a minimum of thirty days for the public to comment on proposed regulations. The Secretary argued that the APA allowed shortening the comment period "for good cause."

ISSUE Was the regulation allocating airport slots invalid because the agency proposing the regulation only gave the public seven days to comment on it?

DECISION No. The regulation was valid. The Administrative Procedure Act (APA) usually requires at least a thirty-day public comment period. The purpose of this period is to let the public praise, criticize, or suggest changes in the proposed regulation.

The APA, however, lets the proposing agency shorten the comment period or even eliminate it if there is a "good cause." The "good cause" must be discussed when the agency publishes (promulgates or puts into effect) the rule. The "good cause" here was to avoid disrupting airline service during the holiday season.

LEGAL TIP

Businesspeople should be aware that federal regulations can suddenly and immediately take effect if the promulgating agency has good cause. Usually, the public has thirty days (or more) to comment on proposed regulations.

iting used-car dealers.[2] Perhaps after examining this proposal, you will understand why the *Federal Register* will never make the best seller list.

Items to watch for The material in Figure 9-2 is reproduced from proposed regulations. These proposed regulations are published to implement the enabling statute quoted earlier in the chapter. Note several points:

1. The proposed regulations were published on pages 1089 and 1090 on January 6, 1976. The numbering starts at page one each calendar year. From this system, one gets some idea how many items—such as presidential proclamations, notices of federal agency meetings, proposed regulations, and promulgated regulations—are published each year. (There were already over 1000 pages in the *Federal Register* 6 days into the new year.)

[2]This chapter focuses on informal (notice-and-comment) rulemaking. Technically, the FTC used-car warranty rule set out here is a product of hybrid rulemaking. It contains the basic notice-and-comment format of informal rulemaking but adds other procedures (such as public hearings) to the format. Also, there were several rounds of notices and comments between 1976 (the time of the first notice) and 1984 (when the rule was ultimately promulgated). The authors use this rulemaking as an example because of its interesting subject matter.

2. Often some introductory remarks are made before the proposed regulation. (The note on *Federal Register* page 1089 contains remarks about the proposed regulations. The introductory remarks on *Federal Register* page 1089 identify the proposing agency, tell what the enabling statutes are, and indicate where in the *Code of Federal Regulations* the agency plans to put the proposed regulations once they are promulgated.)
3. The proposed regulations do not go into the *Code of Federal Regulations.*
4. When the regulations are later promulgated, the introductory remarks tell us that the regulations *when promulgated* will go into 16 C.F.R. Part 455. The "16" indicates the book number in the *Code of Federal Regulations* where the promulgated regulations will go, and "Part 455" indicates the specific section of that book.

Inadequate notice Suppose a federal agency publishes a notice in the *Federal Register* asking the public what changes it would like to see in a statute the agency enforces. (Assume the agency plans to turn these suggestions over to Congress, hoping it will pass amendments to the act the agency enforces.) But after the agency starts receiving the public's suggestions, the agency instead promulgates a regulation dealing with the matter, which saves the agency from going to Congress to get a statute passed.

One problem that could occur in this situation concerns *notice.* Examine Figure 9-1 at the beginning of this chapter. Remember, also, the APA notice requirements for *proposed* regulations: A federal agency must first give notice by publishing either the regulation in draft form or information about it in the *Federal Register.* The *National Tour Brokers Ass'n v. United States* case illustrates how a

NATIONAL TOUR BROKERS ASS'N. v. UNITED STATES

U.S. Court of Appeals (D.C. Circuit).
591 F.2d 896 (1978).

FACTS The National Tour Brokers Association (NTBA) was a group of travel agents, who sued the United States Interstate Commerce Commission (ICC). The ICC had promulgated regulations putting new, expensive duties on travel agents. The NTBA argued that the ICC did not first *propose* its regulations in the *Federal Register,* which the Administrative Procedure Act requires. The ICC did publish a *Federal Register* notice, but the notice did not mention any proposed regulation applying to tour brokers. The ICC argued that it did all it had to by publishing a very general notice asking for the public's ideas on how to limit tour brokers.

ISSUE Was the ICC regulation limiting tour brokers invalid because the ICC put no proposed regulation in the *Federal Register?*

DECISION Yes. The ICC's failure to put the proposed regulation in the *Federal Register* violated the Administrative Procedure Act. This law sets out the steps federal agencies must follow when they make regulations. The ICC should have put the proposed regulations in the *Federal Register* to give the public notice. "Notice" lets the public have an idea of *what* and *how* a regulator wants to regulate *before* regulation occurs. This notice also helps the public file comments on proposed regulations. Comments are letters the public sends to the regulator. Usually, the public's letters criticize proposed regulations, and an agency can benefit from these ideas and change the regulations *before* they are promulgated. The ICC deprived itself of public comments by not publishing the proposed regulations in the *Federal Register.* The court therefore invalidated the ICC's regulations.

LEGAL TIP

Watch the *Federal Register* for notice of proposed agency regulations. If an agency tries to regulate without first publishing proposed regulations, usually the regulations are invalid.

regulation promulgated without a prior notice (usually allowing at least thirty days for public comment) is invalid.

Public Comment Period (Step Five)

The **comment period,** which is step five in Figure 9-1, is one of the most crucial from the public's standpoint. During this time *anyone*— (such as a private business, a teenager, a state government official, or another federal official)—may submit comments to the agency proposing the regulation.

Time to comment A federal agency must usually give the public at least thirty days to comment on a proposed regulation before its effective date. As a practical matter, federal agencies often give the public much longer—sometimes months—between a proposal and the end of the comment period.

Form for comment Comments do not have to follow any particular form; a simple letter directed to the proposing agency is sufficient. Comments are usually critical of agency proposed regulations but can present other ideas as well. Consider the comment letters submitted by the Virginia Independent Automobile Dealers Association and the Classic Car Club of America (Figures 9-3 and 9-4) in response to the FTC's proposed regulation in Figure 9-2. Note that both comments are critical but in different ways. The car club comment believes the proposed regulation should exempt them. The used-car dealers (who will bear the regulation's burden) think the proposed regulation is *too* tough.

What agencies must do with comments After the comment period, the Administrative Procedure Act (APA) directs the agency to "consider the relevant material presented." This direction could lead the agency to: promulgate the rules as they were proposed or modify the proposed regulations in view of the comments.

Why comment? The principal importance of commenting lies in the fact that the public can suggest changes in proposed regulations *before* they become law. In effect, the public is helping the agency write its regulations.

As a practical matter, an agency need do nothing with public comments. The APA tells agencies to *consider* comments. Agencies do read, consider, and sometimes modify—or even totally withdraw—proposed regulations in response to comments. An example of this last possibility occurred when the Securities and Exchange Commission withdrew[3] its proposed regulation that would have encouraged earnings projections in financial statements. Public comments do influence regulations.

Agency Promulgates, Modifies, or Withdraws the Regulation (Step Six)

After the public comment period closes, the APA tells the federal agency proposing the regulation to consider the comments. The APA does not require that the agency write letters to all the commenters with the agency's reaction to the comments. Nor does the APA require that the agency promulgate the regulation.

An agency has three basic choices after a public comment period ends: promulgate the regulation, modify the regulation and either promulgate it as modified

[3] 41 Fed. Reg. 19,982 (1976).

or repropose it for another round of public comments with an eye toward eventual promulgation; or withdraw the regulation. Let us examine each of these alternatives.

Promulgate now If the agency makes a regulation on a topic that is noncontroversial or the agency is knowledgeable about the matter to be regulated, there are no staffing, budgetary, or other problems in the agency, the **promulgated regulation** will probably be put into effect as proposed (after the comment period ends). Figure 9-5 is an example of a promulgated regulation.

Modify and repropose Suppose the agency does not have a full understanding of the problem, or that the subject matter is controversial. In such a case, the public comments could educate agency personnel by pointing out flaws in the proposed regulations—a great help to federal agencies that can prevent ineffective or overly burdensome proposed regulations from ever being promulgated. Public comments, which do not cost much, may be the greatest service a business or member of the public could provide in the entire regulatory process. Furthermore, the number and nature of public comments indicate the extent of interest in a problem. Numerous pro *or* con public comments signal the likelihood of a regulatory program's future success.

Withdraw Sometimes comments to an agency's proposed regulation indicate overwhelming criticism. In this situation, an agency may withdraw and "kill" the proposed regulation.

Possible Court Challenges to Promulgated Regulations (Step Seven)

After an agency promulgates a regulation, it has the practical effect of law. However, there are legal ways of challenging a regulation after promulgation. According to the APA, such challenges can occur if the regulation does any of the following:

1. Violates the United States Constitution.
2. Is arbitrary, capricious, unreasonable, an abuse of discretion, or otherwise not in accordance with law.
3. Is beyond the authority (ultra vires) of the enabling act.

Violates the U.S. Constitution

A regulation that violates the United States Constitution is invalid. A regulation is presumed valid until a court decides otherwise. This rule applies whether a federal, state, or municipal regulation is involved. Examples of unconstitutional regulations are:

1. At the federal level, the Internal Revenue Service (IRS) promulgates a regulation that allows IRS agents to secretly enter private businesses without the owner's approval. This regulation would violate the Fourth Amendment's unreasonable search-and-seizure prohibition.
2. At the state level, the state real estate licensing board promulgates a regulation prohibiting persons of Japanese ancestry from sitting for the state real estate licensing exam. This regulation would violate the Fourteenth Amendment's equal protection clause.

Arbitrary, capricious, or unreasonable The description "arbitrary, capricious, an abuse of discretion, or otherwise not in accordance with law" refers to

Figure 9-3 Public Comment to Proposed Rule

March 19, 1976

Ms. Joan Z. Bernstein
Acting Director
Bureau of Consumer Protection
Federal Trade Commission
Washington, D.C. 20580

Dear Ms. Bernstein:

I have just finished reading and absorbing the contents of the proposed TRR concerning the Used Car Industry prepared by Mr. Edward Steinman and his staff. To say I feel chagrin would be the gross understatement of the century. I could hardly believe the proposal or the pseudo authority upon which it was reportedly based.

I attended a meeting chaired by Mr. Steinman and his associate Mr. Bernard J. Phillips in Washington recently. All of the proposals contained in this report for a proposed TRR were presented at that meeting. All of the proposals were met with valid well-thought-out reasons based on the experience the several members of the Used Car Industry at that meeting possessed to the effect the proposals were not workable.

All during the meeting which lasted the better part of the day Mr. Steinman kept referring back to his own personal experience concerning the purchase of a new automobile whereby he was forced to stand in line, which stretched around the block, several times before he was able to get service on his complaints. He intimated he was able to obtain satisfaction only after getting face to face with the dealer. After reading his proposed report for the TRR and recognizing the total absence of any of the substantial evidence he was given at our meeting concerning the lack of workability of the proposals convinces me he is still more irritated at the automotive industry for causing him personal inconvenience than he is as a Staff Head in unbiasly garnering enough information so the FTC can equitably and justly extend its obligation to the United States Congress who mandated that it take appropriate action concerning the proper verbiage to be used in a car warranty; making certain that a warranty was not mandatory, and finally interpreting the language to be used to appraise the prospective purchaser of any vehicle purchased in an "as is" condition.

To indicate how vindictive the proposal was, I would like to point out some of the information and proposals made by Mr. Steinman and his staff:

1) He insisted this action was necessary because Mr. Hartke, the Senator for Indiana, had attempted to get his Used Car Warranty Bill passed but he did not state this Bill was defeated by Mr. Hartke's constituents who represented all areas of the United States nor did he establish Mr. Hartke's motivation for presenting the bill other than "headline seeking", by virtue of the fact Mr. Hartke, according to this report, went on a mail campaign to try to stir interest in his effort. The thing that leaves me a bit astounded is the fact the public never went to Mr. Hartke asking for help in this area; to the contrary, the complete opposite was the case.

Figure 9-3 Continued

2) Mr. Steinman tried to build up the fact the "Hartke Amendment" to the Magnuson-Moss Act was approved by a large margin. He failed to sufficiently bring out that after this amendment was passed by the Senate it was then turned over to conferrees who watered it down considerably in the interest of trying to maintain "a free market place" with a minimum of "Government intervention or red tape."

The Legislators and the President are telling us they will help to eliminate some of the Federal paperwork which is suffocating the small business community in the United States and at the same time would entertain a proposal such as this which could triple his paper work and I'm afraid in some cases absolutely cripple the Used Car Dealers' effort to maintain his place under the "American Free Enterprise System."

3) Mr. Steinman's proposal prefers to eliminate the intent of Congress with this mandate by dwelling not on what Congress ordered but on the small print which would enable the FTC to gain more control over the Used Car Industry by <u>ordering</u> any number of TRR's designed to stiffle these businessmen's efforts to survive; by stating the Commission could utilize any statuatory authority in prescribing Paragraph 109B of the rules.

4) All through this proposal Mr. Steinman repeatedly refers to an article entitled "The Used Car Game" written by Joy Browne. Who is Joy Browne? By what stretch of the imagination does she qualify as an expert in the Used Car Industry? He also repeatedly refers to various newspaper articles written by innumerable reporters as a basis for the Commission to go along with this proposal. Again I ask by what authority do the authors of these various articles qualify as an "expert" in the Used Motor Vehicle Industry?

5) Mr. Steinman's bent is further evidenced by his attack on the appearance reconditioning of motor vehicles which all dealers practice as a service to themselves and their customers. He could see nothing but evil intent on the part of the dealer for making certain the interior of the vehicles was thoroughly cleansed and sanitized for the customer's benefit. He thought it was done to mislead the customer. He could see no worth in cleaning and waxing the surface of an automobile so a customer and the dealer could both appraise its "real" condition. Again, he saw this as an effort to mislead the consumer.

6) The most chilling aspect of Mr. Steinman's proposal was the feeling I got that although Congress wanted this thing done in a simple and just manner he felt his proposal should include all future areas the Federal Trade Commission might want to control so by some "quirk of rules" he or the Commission would not have to go through this type of action in order to get them passed. IS THIS THE INTENT OF THE COMMISSION?

In closing I would like to go on record as stating the Virginia Independent Automobile Dealers Association has in the past and is still ready and willing to aid the FTC in the proper evaluation of this problem so a speedy and just conclusion can be drawn.

We would like to be informed as to when and where additional hearings will be held by the Commission so we may be present to further state our views.

Sincerely,

W.H. Wilcox

W.H. Wilcox
Executive Director
WHW/lfk

CC: Dr. G. Williams Whitehurst, Congressman Second Congressional District of Virginia

Figure 9-4 **Public Comment to Proposed Rule**

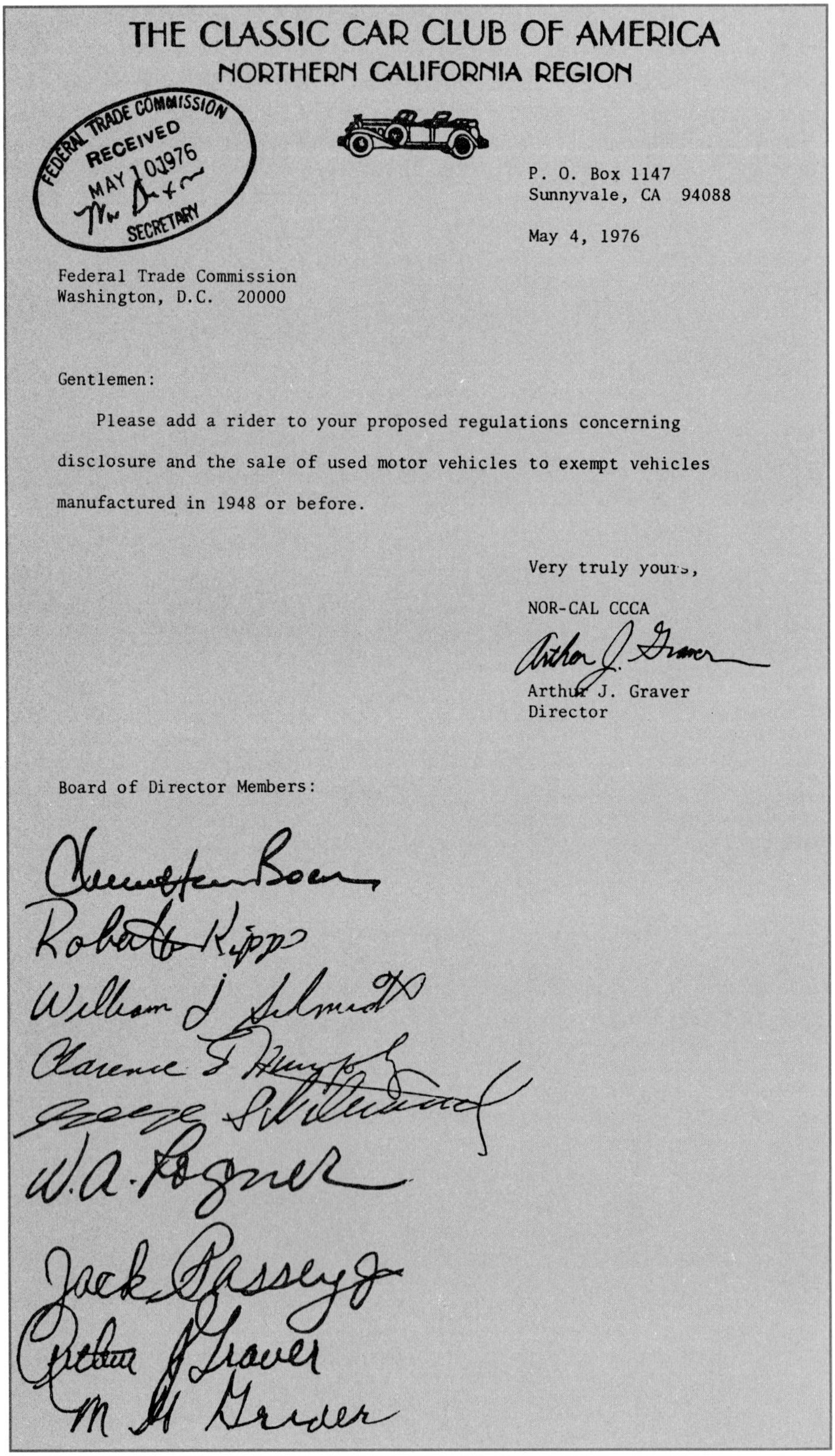

THE CLASSIC CAR CLUB OF AMERICA
NORTHERN CALIFORNIA REGION

P. O. Box 1147
Sunnyvale, CA 94088

May 4, 1976

Federal Trade Commission
Washington, D.C. 20000

Gentlemen:

Please add a rider to your proposed regulations concerning disclosure and the sale of used motor vehicles to exempt vehicles manufactured in 1948 or before.

Very truly yours,

NOR-CAL CCCA

Arthur J. Graver
Director

Board of Director Members:

Figure 9-5 **A Promulgated Regulation 16 CFR § 455 et seq. (1985)**

PART 455—USED MOTOR VEHICLE TRADE REGULATION RULE

Sec.

AUTHORITY: 88 Stat. 2180, 15 U.S.C. 2309; 38 Stat. 717, as amended 15 U.S.C. 41 et. seq.

SOURCE: 49 FR 45725, Nov. 19, 1984, unless otherwise noted.

EFFECTIVE DATE NOTE: At 49 FR 45725, Nov. 19, 1984, Part 455 was added, effective May 9, 1985.

§ 455.1 General duties of a used vehicle dealer; definitions.

(a) It is a deceptive act or practice for any used vehicle dealer, when that dealer sells or offers for sale a used vehicle in or affecting commerce as "commerce" is defined in the Federal Trade Commission Act:

(1) To misrepresent the mechanical condition of a used vehicle;

(2) To misrepresent the terms of any warranty offered in connection with the sale of a used vehicle; and

(3) To represent that a used vehicle is sold with a warranty when the vehicle is sold without any warranty.

(b) It is an unfair act or practice for any used vehicle dealer, when that dealer sells or offers for sale a used vehicle in or affecting commerce as "commerce" is defined in the Federal Trade Commission Act:

(a) To fail to disclose, prior to sale, that a used vehicle is sold without any warranty; and

(2) To fail to make available, prior to sale, the terms of any written warranty offered in connection with the sale of a used vehicle.

(c) The Commission has adopted this Rule in order to prevent the unfair and deceptive acts or practices defined in paragraphs (a) and (b). It is a violation of this Rule for any used vehicle dealer to fail to comply with the requirements set forth in §§ 455.2 through 455.5 of this part. If a used vehicle dealer complies with the requirements of §§ 455.2 through 455.5 of this part, the dealer does not violate this Rule. (d) The following definitions shall apply for purposes of this part:

(1) "Vehicle" means any notorized vehicle, other than a motorcycle with a gross vehicle weight rating (GVWR) of less than 8500 lbs., a curb weight of less than 6,000 lbs., and a frontal area of less than 46 sq. ft.

(2) "Used vehicle" means any vehicle driven more than the limited use necessary in moving or road testing a new vehicle prior to delivery to a consumer, but does not include any vehicle sold only for scrap or parts (title documents surrendered to the state and a salvage certificate issued).

(3) "Dealer" means any person or business which sells or offers for sale a used vehicle after selling or offering for sale five (5) or more used vehicles in the previous twelve months, but does not include a bank or financial institution, a business selling a used vehicle to an employee of that business, or a lessor selling a leased vehicle by or to that vehicle's lessee or to an employee of the lessee.

(4) "Consumer" means any person who is not a used vehicle dealer.

(5) "Warranty" means any undertaking in writing, in connection with the sale by a dealer of a used vehicle, to refund, repair, replace, maintain or take other action with respect to such used vehicle and provided at no extra charge beyond the price of the used vehicle.

(6) "Implied warranty" means an implied warranty arising uder state law (as modified by the Magnuson-Moss Act) in connection with the sale by a dealer of a used vehicle.

(7) "Service contract" means a contract in writing for any period of time or any specific mileage to refund, repair, replace, or maintain a used vehicle and provided at an extra charge beyond the price of the used vehicle, provided that such contract is not regulated in your state as the business of insurance.

Figure 9-5 Continued

(8) "You" means any dealer, or any agent or employee of a dealer, except where the term appears on the window form required by § 455.2(a).

§ 455.2 Consumer sales—window form.

(a) *General duty.* Before you offer a used vehicle for sale to a consumer, you must prepare, fill in as applicable and display on that vehicle a "Buyers Guide" as required by this Rule.

(1) Use a side window to display the form so both sides of the form can be read, with the title "Buyers Guide" facing to the outside. You may remove a form temporarily from the window during any test drive, but you must return it as soon as the test drive is over.

(2) The capitalization, punctuation and wording of all items, headings, and text on the form must be exactly as required by this Rule. The entire form must be printed in 100% black ink on a white stock no smaller than 11 inches high by 7¼ inches wide in the type styles, sizes and format indicated. When filling out the form, follow the directions in (b) through (e) of this section and § 455.4 of this part.

(b) *Warranties—*(1) *No Implied Warranty—"As Is"/No Warranty.* (i) If you offer the vehicle without any implied warranty, i.e., "as is," mark the box provided. If you offer the vehicle with implied warranties only, substitute the disclosure specified below, and mark the box provided. If you first offer the vehicle "as is" or with implied warranties only but then sell it with a warranty, cross out the "As Is—No Warranty" or "Implied Warranties Only" disclosure, and fill in the warranty terms in accordance with paragraph (b)(2) of this section.

(ii) If your state law limits or prohibits "as is" sales of vehicles, that state law overrides this part and this rule does not give you the right to sell "as is." In such states, the heading "As Is—No Warranty" and the paragraph immediately accompanying that phrase must be deleted from the form, and the following heading and paragraph must be substituted. If you sell vehicles in states that permit "as is" sales, but you choose to offer implied warranties only, you must also use the following disclosure instead of "As Is—No Warranty":

Implied Warranties Only

This means that the dealer does not make any specific promises to fix things that need repair when you buy the vehicle or after the time of sale. But, state law "implied warranties" may give you some rights to have the dealer take care of serious problems that were not apparent when you bought the vehicle.

(2) Full/Limited Warranty. If you offer the vehicle with a warranty, briefly describe the warranty terms in the space provided. This description must include the following warranty information:

(i) Whether the warranty offered is "Full" or "Limited."[2] Mark the box next to the appropriate designation.

(ii) Which of the specific systems are covered (for example, engine, transmission, differential"). You cannot use shorthand, such as "drive train" or "power train" for covered systems.

(iii) The duration (for example, "30 days or 1,000 miles, whichever occurs first").

(iv) The percentage of the repair cost paid by you (for example, "The dealer will pay 100% of the labor and 100% of the parts."

(v) If the vehicle is still under the manufacturer's original warranty, you may add the following paragraph below the "Full/Limited Warranty" disclosure: MANUFACTURER'S WARRANTY STILL APPLIES. The manufacturer's original warranty has not expired on the vehicle. Consult the manufacturer's warranty booklet for details as to warranty coverage, service location, etc. If, following negotiations, you and the buyer agree to changes in the warranty coverage, mark the changes on the form, as appropriate. If you first offer the vehicle with a warranty, but then sell it without one, cross out the offered warranty and mark either the "As Is—No Warranty" box or the "Implied Warranties Only" box, as appropriate.

(3) *Service contracts.* If you make a service contract (other than a contract that is regulated in your state as the business of insurance) available on the vehicle, you must

Figure 9-5 Continued

add the following heading and paragraph below the "Full/Limited Warranty" disclosure and make the box provided.[3]

☐ Service Contract

A service contract is available at an extra charge on this vehicle. If you buy a service contract within 90 days of the time of sale, state law "implied warranties" may give you additional rights.

(c) *Name and Address.* Put the name and address of your dealership in the space provided. If you do not have a dealership, use the name and address of your place of business (for example, your service station) or your own name and home address.

(d) *Make, Model, Model Year, VIN.* Put the vehicle's name (for example, "Chevrolet"), model (for example, "Vega"), model year, and Vehicle Identification Number (VIN) in the spaces provided. You may write the dealer stock number in the space provided or you may leave this space blank.

(e) *Complaints.* In the space provided, put the name and telephone number of the person who should be contacted if any complaints arise after sale.

§455.3 Window form.

(a) *Form given to buyer.* Give the buyer of a used vehicle sold by you the window form displayed under § 455.2 containing all of the disclosures required by the Rule and reflecting the warranty coverage agreed upon. If you prefer, you may give the buyer a copy of the original, so long as that copy accurately reflects all of the disclosures required by the Rule and the warranty coverage agreed upon.

(b) Incorporated into contract. The information on the final version of the window form is incorporated into the contract of sale for each used vehicle you sell to a consumer. Information on the window form overrides any contrary provisions in the contract of sale. To inform the consumer of these facts, include the following language conspicuously in each consumer contract of sale:

The information you see on the window form for this vehicle is part of this contract. Information on the window form overrides any contrary provisions in the contract of sale.

§455.4 Contrary statements.

You may not make any statements, oral or written, or take other actions which alter or contradict the disclosures required by §§ 455.2 and 455.3. You may negotiate over warranty coverage, as provided in § 455.2(b) of this part, as long as the final warranty terms are identified in the contract of sale and summarized on the copy of the window form you give to the buyer.

§ 455.5 Spanish language sales.

If you conduct a sale in Spanish, the window form required by § 455.2 and the contract disclosures required by § 455.3 must be in that language. You may display on a vehicle both an English language window form and a Spanish language translation of that form. Use the following translation and layout for Spanish language sales:[4]

§ 455.6 State exemptions.

(a) If, upon application to the Commission by an appropriate state agency, the Commission determines, that—

(1) There is a state requirement in effect which applies to any transaction to which this rule applies; and

(2) That state requirement affords an overall level of protection to consumers which is as great as, or greater than, the protection afforded by this Rule; then the Commission's Rule will not be in effect in that state to the extent specified by the Commission in its determination, for as long as the State administers and enforces effectively the state requirement.

(b) Applications for exemption under Subsection (a) should be directed to the Secretary of the Commission. When appropriate, proceedings will be commenced in order to make a determination described in paragraph (a) of this section, and will be conducted in accordance with Subpart C of Part 1 of the Commission's Rules of Practice.

§ 455.7 Severability.

The provisions of this part are separate and severable from one another. If any provision is determined to be invalid, it is the Commission's intention that the remaining provisions shall continue in effect.

Figure 9-5 Continued

BUYERS GUIDE

IMPORTANT: Spoken promises are difficult to enforce. Ask the dealer to put all promises in writing. Keep this form.

vehicle name ________ model ________ year ________ ________

Dealer Stock Number (optional) ________

WARRANTIES FOR THIS VEHICLE:

☐ AS IS - NO WARRANTY

YOU WILL PAY ALL COSTS FOR ANY REPAIRS. The dealer assumes no responsibility for any repairs regardless of any oral statements about the vehicle.

☐ WARRANTY

☐ FULL ☐ LIMITED WARRANTY. The dealer will pay ____% of the labor and ____% of the parts for the covered systems that fail during the warranty period. Ask the dealer for a copy of the warranty document for a full explanation of warranty coverage, exclusions, and the dealer's repair obligations. Under state law, "Implied warranties" may give you even more rights.

SYSTEMS COVERED: DURATION:

☐ SERVICE CONTRACT. A service contract is available at an extra charge on this vehicle. Ask for details as to coverage, deductable, price, and exclusions. If you buy a service contract within 90 days of the time of sale, state law "implied warranties" may give you additional rights.

PRE PURCHASE INSPECTION: ASK THE DEALER IF YOU MAY HAVE THIS VEHICLE INSPECTED BY YOUR MECHANIC EITHER ON OR OFF THE LOT.

SEE THE BACK OF THIS FORM for important additional information, including a list of some major defects that may occur in used motor vehicles.

Below is a list of some major defects that may occur in used motor vehicles.

Frame & Body
- Frame cracks, corrective welds, or rusted through
- Dogtracks—bent or twisted frame

Engine
- Oil leakage, excluding normal seepage
- Cracked block or head
- Bolts missing or inoperable
- Kocks or misses related to camshaft lifters and push rods
- Abnormal exhaust discharge

Transmission & Drive Shaft
- Improper fluid level or leakage excluding normal seepage
- Cracked or damaged case which is visible
- Abnormal noise or vibration caused by faulty transmission or drive shaft
- Improper shifting or functioning in any gear
- Manual clutch slips or chatters

Differential
- Improper fluid level or leakage excluding normal seepage
- Cracked or damaged housing which is visible
- Abnormal noise or vibration caused by faulty differential

Cooling System
- Leakage including radiator
- Improperly functioning water pump

Electrical System
- Battery leakage
- Improperly functioning alternator, generator, battery, or starter

Fuel System
- Visible leakage

Inoperable Accessories
- Gauges or warning devices
- Air conditioner
- Heater & Defroster

Figure 9-5 **Continued**

Brake System
- Failure warning light broken
- Pedal not firm under pressure (DOT spec.)
- Not enough pedal reserve (DOT spec.)
- Does not stop vehicle in straight (DOT spec.)
- Hoses damaged
- Drum or rotor top thin (Mfg. Specs.)
- Lining or pad thickness less than 1/32 inch
- Power unit not operating or leaking
- Structural or mechanical parts damaged

Steering System
- Too much free play of steering wheel (DOT specs.)
- Free play in linkage more than 1/4 inch
- Steering gear bangs or jams
- Front wheels aligned improperly (DOT specs.)
- Power unit belts cracked or slipping
- Power unit fluid level improper

Suspension System
- Ball joint seals damaged
- Structural parts bent or damaged
- Stabilizer bar disconnected
- Spring broken
- Shock absorber mounting loose
- Rubber bushings damaged or missing
- Radius rod damaged or missing
- Shock absorber leaking or functioning improperly

Tires
- Tread depth less than 2/32 inch
- Sizes mismatched
- Visible damage

Wheels
- Viusible cracks, damage or repairs
- Mounting bolts loose or missing

Exhaust Systm
- Leakage

DEALER

ADDRESS

SEE FOR COMPLAINTS

IMPORTANT: The information on this form is part of any contract to buy this vehicle. Removal of this label before consumer purchase (except for purpose of test-driving) is a violation of federal law (16C.F.R.455)

several reasons agency regulations could be invalid; evidence must exist to support agency regulations. Courts use two tests to determine if the studies and data that agencies use to justify regulations are sufficient: (1) arbitrary, capricious, or an abuse of discretion and (2) substantial evidence.

The arbitrary, capricious, and unreasonable standard controls informal rulemaking. This standard is more lenient than the substantial evidence test since it allows agencies to make rules with less data, studies, and evidence than the substantial evidence standard.

The substantial evidence test is used for hybrid and formal rulemaking as well as any other rulemaking where a statute specifically requires it.

The *Motor Vehicle Mfgrs. Ass'n. v. State Farm Mutual* case illustrates that the arbitrary, capricious, and unreasonable test applies when agencies rescind (or eliminate) regulations.

MOTOR VEHICLE MFGRS. ASS'N. v. STATE FARM MUTUAL

U.S. Supreme Court.
103 S.Ct. 2856 (1983).

FACTS A federal statute (the National Traffic and Motor Vehicle Safety Act of 1966) tells the secretary of transportation to make car safety regulations. The Act requires the secretary to consider "relevant motor vehicle safety data" in making the regulations. In 1977, the secretary promulgated a car safety regulation. The regulation required new motor vehicles produced after September 1982 to have passive restraints (either continuous spool automatic seat belts or airbags). The choice of which type of passive restraint to use was left to the manufacturers. The car manufacturers geared up to comply with the passive restraint regulation. In February 1981 new Secretary of Transportation Drew Lewis reopened the subject of this rulemaking for discussion due to a changed economy and problems in the auto industry. Two months later the secretary proposed rescinding the passive restraint regulation. The public then submitted comments to the proposed rescission. The secretary held a public hearing on the matter. On October 29, 1981, the Secretary rescinded the passive restraint regulation. An auto insurer (State Farm) sued, claiming that the secretary's action was arbitrary, capricious, and unreasonable. State Farm argued that the secretary had not adequately explained the rescission.

ISSUE Was the secretary of transportation's rescission of the passive restraint arbitrary, capricious, and unreasonable and therefore invalid?

DECISION Yes. The United States Supreme Court reasoned that the arbitrary, capricious, and unreasonable standard is used to judge if a regulator's withdrawal of a promulgated regulation is proper. Here, the secretary had seen that manufacturers planned to put continuous spool automatic seat belts in about 99% of the cars. Since such seat belts could easily be detached and left that way permanently, the secretary thought the passive restraint regulation would not be effective. However, the Supreme Court said that the secretary should have considered requiring airbags only. The regulation allowed either airbags or continuous spool seat belts; since such seat belts would not work, the possibility of using airbags should have been explored. The secretary's failure to consider an airbags-only regulation before rescinding the seat-belt or airbag regulation was arbitrary, capricious, and unreasonable. Therefore, the secretary's rescission of its regulation was invalid.

LEGAL TIP

Regulators must have facts to justify withdrawing regulations in effect. Withdrawals must not be arbitrary, capricious, or unreasonable.

Beyond the authority of the enabling act Recall that an administrative agency may make a regulation only if the legislature gives it the power. Administrative agencies have no inherent power to make substantive regulations. A valid enabling act transferring regulation-making power from the legislature to the agency must exist.

An administrative agency acts **ultra vires** when it either makes regulations beyond the authority that the enabling act grants or makes regulations when no enabling act exists at all. When an agency acts ultra vires, the courts discipline the agency by invalidating the regulation.

The *Ernst & Ernst v. Hochfelder* case provides such an example. The enabling act in this case is the Securities Exchange Act of 1934. An important part of that act is Section 10b, which lets the Securities and Exchange Commission (SEC) make regulations covering fraud (which involves "scienter" or intent). However, Section 10b of the Act does not empower the SEC to make regulations covering negligent misrepresentations. In the *Hochfelder* case, the United States Supreme Court was asked whether SEC Rule 10b-5 was ultra vires, or outside the power granted by Section 10b of the Securities Exchange Act of 1934.

ERNST & ERNST v. HOCHFELDER

96 S.Ct. 1375 (1976).
U.S. Supreme Court.

FACTS Ernst & Ernst is an independent public accounting firm, which audited a stockbroker. The stockbroker sold fraudulent securities to several investors, who lost money on the securities. The investors sued the accounting firm under Section 10b of the Securities and Exchange Act and Rule 10b-5 for negligently auditing the stockbroker. The investors claimed that if the accounting firm had audited the stockbroker properly, they would have uncovered the fraud. Rule 10b-5 made accountants liable for negligent audits. The accountants argued that the enabling act (the SEC Act) only prohibited fraud, not negligence. Therefore, the accountants said that Rule 10b-5 was ultra vires, or beyond the authority of the enabling act. As a result, they argued the rule was invalid when it tried to cover negligence.

ISSUE Was the SEC Rule 10b-5 covering negligence invalid?

DECISION Rule 10b-5 was partly invalid. Specifically, the part of the rule covering negligent acts was invalid because a regulation must be *within* the authority of the enabling act. Here, the enabling act was the Securities and Exchange Act of 1934, which let the SEC make rules covering fraud. The enabling act did not let the SEC make regulations covering negligence. Therefore, when Rule 10b-5 covered negligence, it went beyond the enabling act and was invalid.

LEGAL TIP

If regulations exceed the authority of the enabling act, they are invalid.

Recent Changes in Rulemaking

In 1980, Congress amended the APA to improve informal, notice-and-comment rulemaking by passing the **Regulatory Flexibility Act** (RF Act). This Act strengthens the APA's notice requirements. As a practical matter, most small businesspeople (and the public in general) do not know that a publication called the *Federal Register* exists; furthermore, many do not read it even when they are aware of its existence. Congress knew about this problem when it enacted the *Regulatory Flexibility Act.* One of the Act's provisions encourages federal agencies to publish proposed rules having a substantial impact on small entities (such as small hospitals, municipal governments, and small businesses) in journals likely to be obtained by those entities (in addition to the *Federal Register*). Whether affected persons will read the proposed regulations and take the initiative by sending critical comments to the proposing agency is uncertain; but at least the RF Act is a step in the right direction.

Concluding Points About Regulation-Making

No right to a hearing When a federal agency engages in informal, notice-and-comment rulemaking, the due process clause of the United States Constitution's Fifth Amendment does not require the agency to hold an evidentiary hearing. A practical effect of this clause is that a business never has a chance to hear evidence presented by the government's experts, which contributes to the agency's regulations. The agency's "experts" are never cross-examined by business lawyers who could point out weaknesses in the agency's regulations. Most trial lawyers will agree that one of the most important parts of a trial is the right to cross-examine the opposition's witnesses.

A warning While there is no Fifth Amendment right to a hearing when an agency engages in informal rulemaking to make substantive regulations, specific agency statutes might require such hearings. However, there usually is no right to cross-examine opposing viewpoints in this type of hearing. Also, at least one United States Court of Appeals interprets the Administrative Procedure Act as allowing cross-examination on crucial administrative issues.

KEY TERMS

Adjudication
Rulemakings
Informal rulemaking
Proposed regulation
Formal rulemaking
Hybrid rulemaking
Enabling acts
Legislative regulations
Interpretative regulations
Comment period
Promulgated regulation
Ultra vires
Regulatory Flexibility Act

CHAPTER PROBLEMS

1. What is a proposed regulation?
2. Is a proposed regulation binding as "law"?
3. What is a promulgated regulation?
4. Define informal rulemaking.
5. Give a disadvantage that exists for small businesspeople when a federal agency makes rules.
6. What is the purpose of the comment period during a rulemaking?
7. Explain "hybrid" rulemaking.

*8. Recall the case involving the Secretary of Transportation's airport slot regulation. In the same case, Northwest Airlines, Inc. also challenged that regulation because the notice of proposed rulemaking did not indicate exactly what the promulgated regulation would look like. Must the regulation itself be published in the *Federal Register* when the agency proposes it? *Northwest Airlines, Inc. v. Goldschmidt,* 645 F.2d 1309 (1981).

*9. The EPA proposed regulations setting air pollution standards for new or modified cement plants. The EPA did not make available test results and methodology used (in part) as the basis for these regulations until after promulgation. The Portland Cement Association sued the EPA, claiming that Portland had a right to see the data, which partially contributed to formation of the regulations, *before* filing comments to the proposed regulations. Was Portland right? *Portland Cement Association v. Ruckelshaus,* 486 F.2d 375 (1973).

*10. Figure 9-5 is the FTC's final, promulgated used-car window sticker regulation. An early proposed version of this regulation is presented in Figure 9-2, and the public's comments on this regulation are provided in Figures 9-3 and 9-4.

"Men must turn square corners when they deal with the government."

Justice Frankfurter in *Federal Crop Ins. Corp v. Merrill*, 332 U.S. 380 (1947)

Chapter 10

Government Regulation: Enforcement and Adjudication of a Regulation

CHAPTER PREVIEW

- Major functions of a government regulator
- Executive functions of an agency
- Administrative search and regulators' need for a warrant
- Regulators' lack of power to punish a person criminally
- Regulators' power to impose civil penalties on a person
- Federal government's power to force those disobeying regulations to report on themselves
- Description of an administrative hearing
- Legal barriers to overcome when appealing an administrative agency's decision
- Court remedies for regulators' mistakes

A plumbing and heating business in Pocatello, Idaho, hardly seemed like the place for a national constitutional case. However, on the morning of September 11, 1975, an inspector from Occupational Safety and Health Administration (OSHA) entered the customer service area of Barlow's, Inc. The president and general manager, Ferrol G. "Bill" Barlow was on hand. The OSHA inspector, after showing his credentials, informed Mr. Barlow that he wished to search the working areas of the business. Mr. Barlow asked if any complaint had been received about his company. The inspector answered, "No", but Barlow's, In had simply turned up in the agency's selection process. The inspector again asked to enter the nonpublic area of the business. Mr. Barlow asked if the inspector had a search warrant. The inspector had none, but pointed out that the Occupational Safety and Health Act allows inspection of businesses without a warrant. Mr. Barlow still refused to admit the inspector, and the case went all the way to the United States Supreme Court. Who was right?

This chapter continues the discussion of federal regulations. We will view regulatory enforcement (investigation and prosecution) and look at adjudicative hearings (where accused regulation violators are tried).

Chapter 9 examined the formation of a regulation, and this chapter continues that explanation by covering steps not discussed in the preceding chapter.

EXECUTIVE FUNCTION

Investigation, Prosecution, and Administration (Step Eight)

General functions An administrative agency's executive job includes issuing permits and licenses. This function often involves testing competency of practitioners (such as realtors, engineers, or accountants). An administrative agency also prosecutes violators of its statutes and regulations.

Permits and licenses Not all agencies issue permits or licenses; however, administering many agency statutes and regulations often does involve permits. For example, the Clean Water Act requires that anyone placing an object or substance into United States waters have a permit. In other words, much of the almost 100-page Clean Water Act boils down to getting a permit.

Prosecuting If a person, business, or other entity violates a permit or an administrative statute or regulation, the agency enforcing the act or regulation must generally prove the violation. In other words, persons are innocent of administrative violations until proven guilty. Prosecutorial discretion applies here: namely, the agency may prosecute whomever it chooses, subject only to its judgment about the strength of each case, staff resources, and other factors known only to prosecutors.

Searches and investigations: Police and FBI Agencies must gather evidence to prove regulatory or statutory violations. Many times, alleged regulatory violations occur on private property such as in a factory, home, or store. The Fourth Amendment to the United States Constitution says that **warrantless searches** by government officials are illegal. However, in certain exceptional cases, warrantless searches by law enforcement officials are allowed.

Administrative searches today Do administrative officials (not police or the FBI) need search warrants to do **administrative searches?** In two cases, *Camara*[1] and *See*,[2] the Supreme Court decided that administrative officials must have search warrants to do health and other administrative searches of homes *(Camara)* and businesses *(See)*. This regulation is true unless the owner consents or there is an emergency. The Supreme Court modified its "administrators need a search warrant" rule in the later cases of *Colonnade*[3] and *Biswell*.[4] In these cases, the court said that when a business' merchandise is pervasively regulated (for example, liquor in *Colonnade* and firearms in *Biswell*), the business expects no privacy. So the Fourth Amendment's rule against warrantless searches does not apply. In other

[1]*Camara v. Mun. Ct.*, 387 U.S. 523 (1967).
[2]*See v. City of Seattle*, 387 U.S 541 (1967).
[3]*Colonnade Catering Corp. v. United States*, 397 U.S. 72 (1970).
[4]*United States v. Biswell*, 406 U.S. 311 (1972).

words, warrantless searches of pervasively regulated businesses are legal. Then came the *Barlow's*[5] case in 1978.

In this case, Bill Barlow demanded a search warrant before he would let the Occupational Safety and Health Administration (OSHA) inspector onto his premises. The OSHA statute expressly allowed inspectors to enter private property without search warrants to see if OSHA regulations were being obeyed. Was the OSHA statutory right-of-entry provision for inspectors valid or invalid? The United States Supreme Court answered in the *Marshall v. Barlow's* case.

MARSHALL v. BARLOW's

U.S. Supreme Court.
436 U.S. 307 (1978).

FACTS The Occupational Safety and Health Act (OSHA) lets government inspectors search nonpublic work areas of businesses for OSHA violations. An OSHA inspector went to Barlow's, an electrical and plumbing business, in Pocatello, Idaho. The inspector asked Bill Barlow (the president and manager) for permission to enter and inspect the business' work areas. Barlow asked the inspector if there were any complaints; he learned that none existed and that the inspector did not have a search warrant. Since Barlow would not let the inspector enter, the government sued for and got an admission order. However, Barlow went to court to prevent the inspector from entering. The court enjoined (stopped) the OSHA inspector's entry, saying that the United States Constitution's Fourth Amendment requires a warrant for this kind of search. The court held OSHA's warrantless search provision unconstitutional. The government (represented by secretary of labor) appealed to the United States Supreme Court.

ISSUE Are OSHA warrantless searches of a business's nonpublic work areas constitutional?

DECISION No. The United States Constitution's Fourth Amendment forbids unreasonable searches and seizures, protecting commercial buildings as well as private homes. OSHA searches of nonpublic work areas are unreasonable unless the owner consents or the inspector has a warrant. OSHA must show a magistrate, a low-level judge, probable cause that a particular business is violating OSHA to get a search warrant. The probable cause to get an OSHA search warrant is less than that needed in criminal cases.

LEGAL TIP

If a government inspector asks to search your business, you have the right to ask for a search warrant if your business is not highly regulated.

The general rule The *Barlow's* case sets out the general rule that search warrants are required before government inspectors can enter commercial facilities. But the *Colonnade* case (recognized in *Barlow's*) held that search warrants are not required in industries where there is a long history of pervasive regulation. Thus, in 1981, the United States Supreme Court held that federal mine safety inspectors did not need a search warrant to inspect stone quarries. That case asked whether there was a long history of government inspection in the industry. The U.S. Supreme Court said that there was. As a result of this decision, managers must consider whether their particular business is subject to the general rule of *Barlow's* (meaning that managers can demand a search warrant before allowing inspection of work areas). If not, the *Colonnade* exception may apply (meaning that government inspectors may enter *without* a warrant when the industry has a long history of pervasive government regulation).

[5]*Marshall v. Barlow's,* 436 U.S. 307 (1978).

Practical tip As a practical matter, many business managers and other individuals admit government inspectors into their factories, farms, and homes without a warrant. Sometimes entry is granted based on the belief that a cooperative attitude will induce inspectors to be forgiving as well as reasonable. A cooperative attitude also suggests that there is nothing to hide or cause suspicion. Some agencies (such as OSHA), will perform "courtesy inspections" before official ones to point out areas for safety and health improvement. Courtesy inspections help businesses comply with OSHA regulations and avoid fines.

Administrative sanctions A final part of agency enforcement is punishing persons who violate its regulations or statutes. Agencies do not have the power to punish someone *criminally,* since agency procedures do not give defendants (called "respondents") all of the constitutional protections that courts provide (such as the right to jury trial). However, many regulatory statutes have criminal sanctions. Agencies such as the Federal Trade Commission must therefore ask the United States Justice Department to bring criminal charges when such statutes are violated. In these situations, the Justice Department has prosecutorial discretion—the power to bring or not bring criminal charges.

Civil penalties Many statutes also give administrative agencies the power to assess **civil penalties.** They enable agencies to punish while avoiding the delay caused by all of the procedural protections given to criminal defendants.

The United States Supreme Court upheld the idea that federal administrative agencies can assess civil penalties in *United States v. Ward* case.

UNITED STATES v. WARD

U.S. Supreme Court.
448 U.S. 242 (1980).

FACTS The Clean Water Act prohibits the discharge of oil or hazardous substances into navigable United States waters. Violations can be punished with civil penalties up to $5000 per offense. The Clean Water Act also requires violators to report their violations to the United States Coast Guard (which sets the civil penalty for violators). Ward had an oil retention pit at a drilling site near Enid, Oklahoma. Oil escaped into Boggie Creek, and Ward notified the Coast Guard of his violation. The Coast Guard (a federal agency in the Department of Transportation) imposed a civil penalty of $500 on Ward. Ward sued to stop collection of the penalty, claiming that the Coast Guard violated his protection against self-incrimination under the United States Constitution's Fifth Amendment.

ISSUE Did the Clean Water Act *break* the protection against self-incrimination by requiring violators to file reports on themselves?

DECISION No. The Constitution's Fifth Amendment protection against self-incrimination *only* applies to *criminal* punishments. Since the Clean Water Act here only had a civil penalty, it did not violate the Fifth Amendment.

LEGAL TIP
Some regulatory statutes can require you to report on yourself. These laws do not violate protections against self-incrimination if they only impose civil—not criminal—penalties.

JUDICIAL FUNCTION

Adjudicatory Hearings (Step Nine)

In addition to forming and executing regulations, administrative agencies also hold hearings, which are similar to courtroom trials. This process is called **adjudica-**

tion. The federal Administrative Procedure Act provides basic rules for agency hearings.

The hearing To visualize an agency hearing, think of an ordinary courtroom trial and eliminate the jury. There is no jury or right to a jury trial in an **administrative hearing.** There will, of course, be two parties: the agency (or "moving party") and the prosecutor, where someone is accused of breaking agency regulations. A private person, often a business, is the defendant ("respondent"). A private party can be the moving party under certain circumstances. Notice of agency adjudicatory hearings must include the time, place, and subject matter of the hearing.

Administrative law judge The presiding official at an adjudicatory hearing is an administrative law judge (formerly called "hearing examiner"). Technically, this person is independent of the agency personnel prosecuting the case, keeping the administrative law judge off the agency's prosecutorial team.

Parties Parties to an agency adjudication may introduce evidence, witnesses, and arguments to support their position. Settlement offers are allowed. In setting the time and place of a hearing, the convenience and necessity of the parties involved are considered.

Possible Appeal of Administrative Law: Judge's Decision (Step Ten)

Referring to Figure 9-1, one sees that an appeal can be made after an administrative law judge makes a decision.

Standing The "standing doctrine" says that only the person injured may sue to correct a wrong. The standing doctrine applies to actions by administrative agencies. Therefore, a farmer whose land will be flooded by the Tennessee Valley Authority (a federal agency) "has standing" to sue.

Exhaustion The **exhaustion doctrine** says that a person must generally go through an agency's decision-making structure before taking an agency action to court. The purpose of this doctrine is to give an agency a chance to correct its own mistakes by having an appeal process *within the agency itself.* This process saves the time and expense of suing in court. Consider a simple example: Mildred Smith retires at age 65 and files for Social Security benefits. The Social Security office mistakenly confuses her with another Mildred Smith and declares her ineligible. Mildred appeals to a higher level *within* the Social Security administration, which corrects the mistake. Mildred soon receives her Social Security checks—*without* ever suing in court.

Exceptions to the exhaustion doctrine There are times when the exhaustion doctrine does not apply. If agency action would cause irreparable injury, exhaustion is excused. A person also does not have to exhaust administrative remedies when agency actions are beyond its jurisdiction or when the use of agency channels would be a futile effort.

Appeals to the court A person suffering a legal wrong by agency action may take the matter to court. For example, if the state real estate commission suspends a realtor's license after an adjudicatory hearing, he or she may appeal this action in court.

Appealable agency action Generally, only an agency's final action may be appealed to a court. This rule gives an agency the opportunity to correct itself before the courts do.

Proper court Once a federal agency takes final action, the action may be appealed to a federal district court unless a special statute provides for appeal to another court, such as the United States Court of Appeals. Very often, federal agency actions are directly taken to the United States Court of Appeals. For example, Securities and Exchange Commission and Federal Trade Commission adjudications are appealed to the United States Court of Appeals.

Courts of appeals are not trial courts. They have no juries, hear no witnesses, and accept the evidence developed at the agency adjudicatory hearing. Instead, federal district courts are trial courts. They have juries, hear witnesses, and evidence is presented. Thus, an agency case that comes to a federal district court is usually entirely retried, a process called de novo review. In effect, de novo review insults an administrative agency by implicitly saying, "What you (the agency) have done has to be repeated since your hearing was not good enough."

When the facts developed at agency adjudications are accepted by United States Courts of Appeals, stature is given to agencies, saving everyone's time and resources by not having to retry cases.

Ripeness **Ripeness** refers to an administrative agency's action being sufficiently developed for a court to "get a handle on it." In other words, the agency must have *actually* acted officially rather than simply sending up trial balloons. Courts will not review an agency's action unless it is "ripe"—that is, the agency's actions must be complete enough for a court to determine its legality. Ripeness is therefore an argument made by one who does not want the agency action challenged. Often, this party is the agency itself.

An example of ripeness in an administrative agency action is as follows: The Securities and Exchange Commission (SEC) *proposes* a regulation requiring that securities salespersons have a college degree in finance. The National Association of Securities Dealers (NASD) immediately sues the SEC to invalidate the proposed regulation. The SEC would argue the matter is not yet ripe, since the regulation is only proposed—not promulgated. The SEC would win based on the ripeness doctrine, since the SEC has not taken any definite, concrete, or final action. On the other hand, the ripeness defense would be weaker if NASD were to sue *after* the SEC promulgates the regulation. Promulgation involves a definite, concrete, or final agency action.

Court remedies for agency wrongdoings A reviewing court will declare agency action illegal and either force or stop agency action. Court remedies are proper when:

1. An agency acts arbitrarily, capriciously, or unreasonably—abusing discretion or otherwise not acting in accordance with the law.
2. An agency acts contrarily to constitutional right, power, privilege, or immunity.
3. An agency acts beyond its statutory authority.
4. An agency acts without observing legal procedures.
5. An agency acts without substantial, supportive evidence.

WASSON v. SECURITIES AND EXCHANGE COMMISSION

U.S. Court of Appeals (8th Cir.)
558 F.2d 879 (1977).

FACTS The Securities and Exchange Commission (SEC) suspended Wasson's broker's license for 45 days. This suspension occurred after an SEC adjudicatory hearing. Wasson acted pro se at the SEC hearing, and an administrative law judge presided at the hearing, concluding that Wasson sold unregistered stock. Wasson appealed to the United States Court of Appeals, saying he was denied his right to confront and cross-examine witnesses at the hearing since the administrative law judge did not tell Wasson of this right. The complaint also said that he sold 23,000 shares of unregistered stock when he actually sold a block of 30,000 unregistered shares. This misidentification of shares, he argued, misled him in preparing his case. He also argued that he did not act willfully, and that the SEC had not produced substantial evidence of his violation.

ISSUE Was the SEC hearing run properly?

DECISION Yes. The Court of Appeals said that the SEC's incorrect identification of stock did not deprive Wasson of notice. Wasson's hearing testimony and letters to the SEC showed he knew what stock was in question. The Court of Appeals said that the administrative law judge should have told Wasson he had a right to cross-examine witnesses against him. However, this was a harmless error. The Court of Appeals concluded there was substantial evidence supporting two of the three charges against Wasson. The Court of Appeals dismissed the third charge for lack of substantial evidence.

LEGAL TIP

Agency hearings must satisfy the Administrative Procedure Act. However, small errors do not make hearing actions invalid.

In the *Wasson v. Securities and Exchange Commission (SEC)* case, a securities broker whose license was temporarily suspended as a result of an SEC adjudication appealed the matter to the United States Circuit Court of Appeals. His basic arguments were that APA (Administrative Procedure Act) adjudicatory hearing requirements were not satisfied. He tried his adjudicatory hearing *pro se,* meaning that he had only himself as an attorney. This approach is possible but not advisable in agency adjudications.

Agency hearings thus must satisfy different rules (constitutions, statutes, and even regulations).

KEY TERMS

Warrantless searches
Administrative searches
Civil penalties
Adjudication
Exhaustion doctrine
Administrative hearing
Ripeness

CHAPTER PROBLEMS

1. What is the exhaustion doctrine?
2. Give the purpose of the exhaustion doctrine.
3. Is the executive or judicial function of an agency involved when a regulator issues a license?
4. Can a regulator ever search a business without a search warrant?
5. Describe an agency adjudicatory hearing. What is the one main difference between such a hearing and a jury trial in a superior court?

6. What court generally hears appeals from administrative agencies?
7. Can a regulator impose a civil and/or criminal penalty?

*8. Section 103(a) of the Federal Mine Safety and Health Act of 1977 requires federal mine inspectors to check underground mines at least four times a year and surface mines at least twice a year. This inspection is to insure compliance with health and safety standards and to make follow-up inspections to determine whether previously discovered violations have been corrected. Section 103(a) also grants inspectors the right to enter any coal or other mine and provides that no advance notice of an inspection need be given. For example, if a mine operator refuses to allow a warrantless inspection under Section 103(a), the Secretary of Labor is authorized to bring a civil action for injunctive or other relief. In an actual case *Donovan v. Dewey,* 101 S.Ct. 2534 (1981), a federal inspector attempted a follow-up inspection of a company's stone quarries, and a company officer refused to allow the inspection. The company relied on the *Marshall v. Barlow's Inc.* case (cited in this chapter), as authority for denying the inspector admission to company property without a search warrant. What is the result?

*9. A veteran brought a constitutional challenge to a federal law limiting lawyers' fees to $10 for representing veterans before the Veterans Administration. The law dates to the 1860's when it was passed to protect Civil War vets from exploitation. The lower federal court upheld the law. The veteran appealed to the United States Supreme Court. What is the result? *Walters v. National Association of Radiation Survivors,* 53 U.S.L.W. 4947 (1985).

*10. Immigration and Naturalization Service (INS) officials often conduct surprise raids on factories looking for illegal aliens. In one case, officials entered a factory after getting either the owner's permission or a search warrant. Some officials stood at the doors while others went through the factory asking workers about their immigration status. Workers who could not answer the INS officials satisfactorily or produce immigration papers were arrested. These arrests often involved half of the workers in certain California factories. The United States Court of Appeals for the Ninth Circuit held that these searches were unconstitutional, reasoning that the surprise raids were unconstitutional seizures of the entire factory's workforce. This court also said that INS officials could not question workers individually unless officials had a reasonable suspicion that a worker was an illegal alien. The INS appealed to the Supreme Court. Were the surprise raids unconstitutional? *I.N.S. v. Delgado,* 104 S.Ct. 1758 (1984).

"There's a sucker born every minute."
P. T. Barnum

Chapter 11

Consumer Protection

CHAPTER PREVIEW

- How consumer protection helps business
- Sources of consumer protection law
- Eight common law rules protecting consumers
- The Federal Trade Commission—the federal agency protecting consumers
- The FTC's thirty-day mail-order regulation
- The FTC's door-to-door sales regulation

When Bob Martin opened his monthly credit card bill, his eyes almost fell out; the amount owing was $5300. Martin had loaned his American Express credit card to a business associate, E. L. McBride. Martin had orally told McBride he could charge up to $500. Martin also had sent a letter to American Express before turning over the card to McBride. In the letter, he had asked American Express not to allow charges on his account to exceed $1000. Before Martin received the $5300 monthly bill, McBride returned the credit card and then disappeared. Martin refused to pay American Express. The federal Truth-in-Lending Act has a provision limiting credit-card holders' losses for unauthorized use to $50. Martin claimed that this provision limited his liability to $50. Did it?

Consumer purchases for food, clothing, personal care, housing, household operation, and recreation amounted to $2.155 trillion in 1983 according to the 1985 *U.S. Statistical Abstract.* Most purchases result in satisfied customers. Some purchases, however, produce consumer agony. This chapter focuses upon problem cases.

WHO IS A CONSUMER?

A consumer is any person who buys goods or services for his or her personal consumption. For example, a widow who buys aluminum siding for her house and a five-year-old child who buys an ice cream cone are both consumers.

Why Protect Consumers?

Arguments against consumer protection Many reasons exist for not protecting consumers. First, of course, is the cost. Consumer protection can raise the price of goods and services if merchants pass the price increase along to their buyers. How would consumer protection raise prices? One way is by requiring businesses to test products more thoroughly before selling them which costs money. Another way is by increasing the extent to which a business is liable if a product is defective. There used to be (and still is, to some degree) something called the "privity rule." This rule says a seller is liable only to the person with whom it deals directly (usually the person buying the product). Privity of contract means "in a contractual relation with someone." The privity rule has been modified, and businesses are now liable to parties other than immediate buyers.

Another reason for not protecting consumers is suggested by the old **caveat emptor** doctrine, which allows consumers to protect themselves. The theory states that since most people are mature and self-reliant, they surely can watch out for their own financial interests.

Arguments for consumer protection Natural law is based on basic notions of fairness and suggests that we should equalize economic power. The law has traditionally protected the weak from the strong. According to this view, consumers are small, defenseless people (such as widows and orphans) who are pitted against industrial giants (such as Exxon and General Motors) and, therefore, deserve protection.

Another reason for protecting consumers is to protect *honest* businesses. For example, if a consumer buys inferior goods or is cheated by one business, sales could be diverted from a more ethical merchant. By establishing standards, consumer protection helps honest merchants who offer value to consumers in the following two ways. First, it makes life difficult for scoundrels. Second, it encourages people to buy more with less hesitation. This is because consumers know that if their purchases are unsatisfactory, a remedy is available.

Sources of Consumer Protection Law

Consumer protection rules are made by courts, legislatures, and administrative agencies. Furthermore, consumer protection occurs at federal, state, and municipal levels.

The many sources of these laws make consumer protection complex. For example, it is possible to have fifty different state statutes governing a consumer's right to revoke acceptance of a contract with a door-to-door salesperson. This possibility complicates life for a national magazine publisher who sells subscriptions door to door.

Common Law Protection of Consumers

Common law is judge-made law. Courts have always had the power to make rules when deciding cases. Eight common law rules that protect consumers are *consideration, undue influence, duress, fraud, innocent misrepresentation, contracts contrary to public policy, illegal contracts,* and *unconscionability.*

Consideration

Consideration is a requirement for making a contract. A contract is an agreement supported by consideration between competent parties (not insane people) and enforceable in a court. Consideration is the voluntary, bargained-for giving up of a right in exchange for someone else's right. For a contract to be enforceable, each party to the contract must give consideration to the other.

For example, if Dugald Huddy promises to buy Gail Heckman's house for $50,000 and Gail agrees to sell the house for that amount, consideration is exchanged. The consideration Gail gives to Dugald is the promise to sell her house. The consideration Dugald gives to Gail is the promise to buy the house.

Adequacy of the consideration Usually courts do not examine the **adequacy of the consideration.** For example, a judge *will not* say to Dugald, "You didn't promise Gail enough money for her house. Give her more money, or I won't enforce your contract." Gail has no recourse if she decides *after making the contract* that Dugald did not promise her enough money. A court will not force Dugald to give Gail more money. After all, Gail *herself* determined that $50,000 was adequate compensation when she made the contract. Adequacy of consideration is fancy legal wording for the following: Are you getting enough for what you are giving up? If you are getting enough, the consideration is adequate. If you are not getting enough, the consideration is inadequate. The persons who make a contract must examine consideration's adequacy. Their self-interest is usually the best consumer protection that a person could have.

Exceptions to adequacy rule There are exceptions to the rule that courts will not examine the adequacy of the consideration. For example, an unequal exchange of money is inadequate (assuming no antique or foreign money is involved) because duress is presumed, since no person would voluntarily exchange $5 for $10. This exception is based on the idea of consumer protection.

Undue Influence

If two people enter a contract, the courts presume that the parties involved protect their own best interests. Sometimes a person makes a contract with a close relative, family doctor, lawyer, or business associate, relying on the relationship of trust and judgment of the other party as protection. Usually, this trust is justified, and a "fair deal" results. Occasionally, however, the family doctor, lawyer, relative, or business associate double-crosses a person and makes an unfair bargain, which is called **undue influence.** If, for example, a woman sells her farm to her favorite nephew (relying on his trust and assurance that the farm is worthless) for an amount way under market value, the nephew is using undue influence. Courts will set aside contracts that they find are the result of undue influence—another court-devised consumer protection idea.

Duress

Duress is another judge-made rule that protects people from being forced into unwanted contracts. For example, if Robert Borley points a gun at Lee Mead's head and says, "Sign this contract to sell your house for $40,000 or I'll pull the trigger," Mead will sign the contract. But does Mead have to sell his house to Borley? No.

Courts have developed the duress rule, which says: If one person commits a wrongful act that forces another against his or her will to agree to a contract, the contract is *voidable* (can be set aside by a court). Duress is based on the natural law concept that it is unfair to force people into contracts they do not want to enter. Contract formation should be voluntary.

Fraud

Fraud is a type of tort, or private wrong, that protects consumers from being lied to in order to get them to enter contracts. There are six parts to fraud:

1. Misrepresentation.
2. Material fact.
3. Knowledge of misrepresentation.
4. Intent to deceive.
5. Reasonable reliance on misrepresentation.
6. Damages resulting from misrepresentation.

Some of these elements rest with the victim. For example, the fraud victim must have suffered damages from reasonable reliance on a misrepresented fact. The fraud defendant (or the party allegedly committing the fraud), on the other hand, must have misrepresented a fact that is material to the victim's decision to purchase (or sell), must have the knowledge that the fact is misrepresented, and must have intent to defraud.

Since fraud is such a common wrong, further analysis is in order. First, a buyer, seller, or both can commit fraud in a single transaction. Second, fraud can be committed when realty, services, or goods are sold. Third, seller's talk, opinions, or "puffing" should not be confused with facts. Representations of facts are events that have occurred or are definite, concrete, or objective. For example, stating that a car gets twenty miles per gallon is a representation of fact, which can be objectively determined.

Puffing **Puffing,** seller's talk, or opinions are to be distinguished from facts. As previously noted, facts are objectively ascertainable, whereas opinions, puffing, or seller's talk are not. The following are examples of puffing, opinions, or seller's talk: "This dress is beautiful." "That boat is fast." Each of these statements is puffing, because they are not definite, concrete, or objectively quantifiable facts. "Beautiful" and "fast" are subjective, not objective terms. These descriptions depend on the personal judgment of each individual rather than common terms such as "three feet" or "one carat." A misrepresentation of fact, not seller's talk, must be made if fraud is to be proven.

Affirmative fraud and fraud by concealment Fraud usually occurs in an affirmative form when someone says something is true when it is not. **Fraud by concealment** can occur when a person fails to disclose a material fact not discoverable by ordinary inspection. Common law fraud gives limited consumer protection because it is hard to prove the knowledge and intent elements of the person misrepresenting.

Innocent Misrepresentation

Innocent misrepresentation is similar to fraud, except that the one misrepresenting lacks *knowledge* and *intent.* Beyond this difference, all other elements of the fraud definition apply.

For example, Richard May has a piece of cut glass that looks like a diamond. He believes that the cut glass is a diamond and tells Bill Steward about it. May offers the cut glass to Steward for $1000. Steward accepts but later learns the truth. Can Steward escape the contract? Yes, because May committed innocent misrepresentation.

A usual remedy for innocent misrepresentation is *rescission,* which cuts off the bargain, and *restitution,* which requires each party to return what it got from the other. In the example above, May would return the $1000 to Steward, and Steward would return the piece of glass to May.

Contracts Contrary to Public Policy

"Public policy" is a loosely defined term that generally refers to desirable social goals or conduct. Sometimes courts will refuse to enforce a contract because it is contrary to public policy.

Contracts contrary to public policy include certain **exculpatory clauses,** which excuse or limit someone's liability. For example, roller coaster tickets might indicate that "Anyone injured in any way while riding the roller coaster agrees to hold the management harmless." But if the tower holding the roller coaster collapses and injures a customer, a court would undoubtedly refuse to honor the exculpatory clause because it is contrary to public policy.

Illegal Contracts

Illegal contracts are void, meaning that they are "nothing," (a nullity). **Void contracts** involve agreements that are legally nothing. Even if a piece of paper has the word "contract" written at the top, is signed at the bottom, and is witnessed (which does not have to be done to execute a contract), if it is an illegal contract, it is void. It is not a contract and cannot be enforced in court. It is simply a piece of paper with writing on it.

For example, a contract is illegal if it involves either an illegal subject matter or commission of an illegal act; it is thus void. An example of a contract with an illegal subject matter is an agreement to buy fifty pounds of marijuana. A contract to commit murder is also illegal because it requires commission of an illegal act. Other examples of illegal contracts are agreements to commit crimes or torts (civil wrongs such as assault) or contracts contrary to public policy.

The rule that illegal contracts are void protects honest, but not dishonest, consumers. The law will not protect persons ***in pari delicto*** (both are equally guilty). For example, when a drug addict purchases illegal drugs, judges refuse to protect the consumers. Consumers cannot recover their money from a drug dealer if they have paid for diluted or contaminated drugs.

Unconscionability

Unconscionability deals with contracts that are extremely favorable to one party and extremely unfavorable to the other. This judge-created idea is based on natural law (meaning fairness, rightness, and justice). Unconscionability protects the weak from the strong. If an entire contract or part of a contract is unconscionable, courts refuse to enforce the unconscionable portion(s).

Unconscionability focuses on the parties, the bargain, and the effect of the bargain. No one of these three factors is necessarily more important in all cases. The factors must be considered on a case-by-case basis. Specifically, a great difference in the knowledge, intelligence, business sophistication, and bargaining power of the parties suggests that the contract could be unconscionable. However, the contract itself has to be examined: Is it lopsided? Do its terms unreasonably favor the much more capable, sophisticated, economically powerful party? If so, the case is stronger for applying unconscionability. Finally, when the contract is performed, if its effect is oppressive and grossly unfair to the unsophisticated, weaker party, then a proper case exists for applying unconscionability.

For example, a welfare mother, with seven children and no husband, whose sole means of support was $218 per month from the government bought a $514 stereo on an installment basis. The seller, an appliance dealer in Washington, DC, knew the buyer's background and financial situation when the sale was made. The seller had previously sold the buyer items that were paid for in part. The installment contract for the stereo had an equity-leveling provision, which resulted in lowering the buyer's equity in prior purchases from this seller when an unpaid balance existed. The equity was raised on the last purchase so that all items with an unpaid balance (no matter when they were purchased) had the same buyer's equity. The contract gave the seller a claim on all prior purchases having an unpaid balance as security for the last item purchased. The seller also had the right to repossess all items on which an unpaid balance existed if there was a default in an installment payment on any one item. Thus, if the buyer defaulted on the last item purchased, the seller could repossess all of the welfare mother's purchases on which an unpaid balance existed. The welfare mother did default on a stereo payment, and the seller, under his contract rights, repossessed the stereo and all her prior purchases that had an unpaid balance. These facts are from the case *Williams v. Walker-Thomas* (1965), which the United States Circuit Court of Appeals for the District of Columbia sent back to trial court on the issue of unconscionability.

Weakness in Common Law for Consumers

There is one main weakness with common law as consumer protection: The *consumer* must sue the business that does not live up to its obligations, which often results in *damnum absque injuria*—meaning a harm without a legal remedy. This situation occurs because people often lack the time, money, or desire to take the trouble to sue. Particularly when a relatively small amount is at stake, consumers often shrug at being "fleeced" and chalk it up to experience. Consumer despair ("Why bother—it will cost more to sue than what I lost") has resulted in both federal and state legislatures passing statutes to increase consumer protection.

FEDERAL TRADE COMMISSION (FTC)

Background

There is no federal consumer protection agency called a "consumer protection agency." However, because one of the Federal Trade Commission's (FTC's) main functions is consumer protection, practically speaking, there *is* a federal consumer protection agency.

FTC Consumer Protection Regulations

Since the FTC consumer protection laws are discussed extensively in another chapter, only four FTC consumer protection regulations are discussed here. The FTC has authority under the Federal Trade Commission Act to make regulations preventing unfair competition and unfair or deceptive acts and practices. The FTC has made many consumer protection regulations. Four regulations discussed here are the bait-and-switch regulation, the regulation modifying the holder-in-due-course rule, the mail-order merchandise regulation, and the three-day cooling-off regulation for door-to-door sales.

Bait-and-switch regulation The following example involves the **bait-and-switch regulation:** Robert Berry sat dejectedly in his appliance store. He had fifty expensive color console televisions to sell, which were difficult to finance through a local bank. Richard May, one of Berry's hot-shot salespeople, suggested that Berry aggressively advertise new, black-and-white, portable televisions for $10 each. May told Berry to do one of three things when a customer came in: say that he had just sold the last $10 set, say that he could not find the $10 sets, or bad-mouth the $10 sets and direct the customer to the expensive color consoles. Should Berry approve May's idea?

May's idea violates the FTC regulation, "Guides on Bait Advertising." Bait advertising occurs when a business advertises goods or services at a very low price to attract buyers into the seller's business. The seller then switches the buyer to more expensive products or services. The FTC regulations prohibit salespeople from refusing to show the low-priced, bait item; indicating that the bait item will not be available for a long time; having an inadequate supply of the bait item; or telling employees to sell items other than the bait item when a customer seeks it.

Modification of the holder-in-due-course rule The following example involves **modification of the holder-in-due-course rule:** Bill Vanderpuddle was excited. He had just bought a new microwave oven from E-Z Appliance Company. Vanderpuddle did not have the full $500 purchase price, but E-Z had him sign a *negotiable note* for $400 plus interest and pay $100 down. Vanderpuddle took the oven home, used it a couple of times, but discovered that the oven took ten times longer to cook food as it was supposed to.

Vanderpuddle returned the oven to E-Z but got the runaround. When the manager said: "It will take a month to get the parts and another two weeks to get it repaired," Vanderpuddle told him that he would stop making installment payments on the oven unless he received better service. The E-Z manager told Vanderpuddle that his signed, negotiable note had been sold to City Bank, and that since the bank was a *holder in due course,* it was not subject to Vanderpuddle's claims against E-Z. A holder in due course is a good-faith purchaser for value without notice of any personal defenses (such as breach of warranty, which Vanderpuddle might have against E-Z.) The E-Z manager told Vanderpuddle that his claims (such as Vanderpuddle's warranty claim that the oven did not work) were personal (between Vanderpuddle and E-Z only) and could not be asserted by Vanderpuddle when the bank tried to collect monthly payments on the installment note.

Vanderpuddle was angry. He had bought a defective oven and had lost his bargaining power to stop monthly payments, since the seller had sold the negotiable note, which Bill used to buy the oven, to a holder in due course. It did not seem fair to Vanderpuddle.

This type of situation occurred daily before the FTC promulgated its regulation changing the holder-in-due course (HIDC) rule. The HIDC rule is of common-law origin and was later codified (or made part of a lengthy commercial law statute) in the Uniform Commercial Code (UCC). The part of the UCC having the HIDC rule is the law in the District of Columbia and in every state except Louisiana. The purpose of the HIDC rule is to encourage people to buy "negotiable instruments" which are commercial *promissory notes* and other *commercial paper* having a certain form. The HIDC rule encourages buying commercial paper because it is a "courier without luggage"—someone or something that is not weighted down by personal defenses between the person issuing the commercial paper and the one originally accepting it as payment). The idea is to make commercial paper the same thing as money.

The HIDC rule made commercial paper equivalent to money at the expense of consumers such as Bill Vanderpuddle in the example above. To correct this injustice, the FTC promulgated a regulation in 1976 that modified the HIDC rule. Banks and consumer finance companies who buy commercial paper on consumer installment contracts and who would otherwise have been holders in due course now are subject to consumer claims and defenses against the seller. Now Bill Vanderpuddle (from the example) would have a claim against the bank (probably breach of warranty), which would justify stopping payments until the oven was fixed.

Several points need to be made about the FTC regulation modifying the HIDC rule. First, the regulation applies *only* to individual consumers, not to businesses that buy goods or services. Second, it applies to *consumer* purchases or leases of either goods or services. Third, it does not apply to credit-card issuers. Therefore, if Vanderpuddle buys an oven at K-Mart with a Visa credit card and the oven doesn't work, he must still pay Visa for the oven. Vanderpuddle has lost his bargaining power with K-Mart, since the oven has been paid for by Visa.

Thirty-day mail-order merchandise rule The following example involves the **thirty-day mail-order merchandise rule:** Carl Johnson had always wanted to win the Lake St. Helen annual fishing contest. He received his spring copy of the famous *L. L. Toadstool Sporting Goods Catalog,* which advertised a set of dry flies for $15.95, a fly rod for $60, and fishing tackle for $20. Johnson sent in his order on April 1, which was received by L. L. Toadstool on April 5. L. L. Toadstool knew on April 10 that it would be unable to fill Johnson's order until June 1 due to a run on fishing equipment. L. L. Toadstool did not notify Johnson, who still had not received his fishing gear on May 15. The Lake St. Helen's contest was almost over. What rights (if any) does Johnson have against L. L. Toadstool?

The Federal Trade Commission Act outlaws unfair methods of competition and unfair or deceptive acts and practices. This act gives the FTC power to promulgate regulations declaring that certain specific acts are unfair methods of competition and unfair or deceptive practices. Thus, the FTC has made a thirty-day mail-order a merchandise rule. The rule makes it an unfair method of competition and an unfair or deceptive act and practice for a *seller* to solicit orders for merchandise from the buyer through the mails unless the seller reasonably expects to be able to ship the goods within thirty days (or less if promised) after getting a properly completed order. In other words, mail-order companies cannot entice buyers to order and send money, and then sit on the orders. Sellers must ship promptly, meaning within thirty days.

If sellers cannot ship mail-ordered merchandise within a thirty-day period, they must notify buyers of their rights to either cancel their orders and receive a prompt refund or get delayed shipment. After realizing that a delay is likely, sellers must tell buyers about delays within a reasonable time.

What happens if sellers break this FTC thirty-day rule? The FTC can issue a formal or informal complaint against the alleged regulation breaker. An FTC administrative hearing possibly followed by an appeal to the federal Courts of Appeals is then possible. Only the courts have the power to punish violators of FTC regulations. The FTC can issue a cease-and-desist (C & D) order against regulation breakers. Court-ordered *civil* penalties up to $10,000 per violation of FTC C & D orders are possible.

The FTC thirty-day mail-order rule does *not* cover:

1. Subscriptions (including ones for a magazine) ordered for serial delivery, after the first shipment complies with this regulation.
2. Orders of seeds and growing plants.
3. Cash-on-delivery orders (delay is tolerated because the consumer has not sent in any money).

The FTC's thirty-day mail-order rule does not preempt state or municipal laws agreeing with it or putting equal or greater burdens on mail-order sellers. However, the FTC rule *does* replace state or municipal rules putting *lesser* duties on mail-order sellers.

Cooling-off periods for door-to-door sales The following example involves the **rule on cooling-off periods for door-to-door sales:** The doorbell rings, and the homeowner answers the door to a smiling aluminum-siding salesperson. Many of these sales people hypnotize consumers with talk; before consumer-homeowners know it, they have signed contracts to have aluminum siding installed for $1000—agreeing to pay five days later (after installation). As consumers lie in bed on the night of the purchase, they realize that they could have had a carpenter friend do the same job for half the cost. Is there anything these consumers can do?

Here are three suggestions: First, they should ask the seller to release them from the contract. Unperformed contracts can be ended by the parties' agreement any time before both finish performing (a possible but unlikely solution). Second, many state statutes provide three-day cooling-off periods for contracts entered into with door-to-door salespersons. (In other words, consumers do not have three days to escape contracts that they make in stores.) A third suggestion involves a regulation that makes it an unfair and deceptive act or practice for any door-to-door seller not to furnish a buyer with a fully completed receipt or contract copy including the following notice:

> You, the buyer, may cancel this transaction at any time prior to midnight of the third business day after the date of this transaction. See the attached notice-of-cancellation form for an explanation of this right.

The completed receipt or contract copy must also contain a completed notice-of-cancellation form, which helps the buyer cancel any contract made with a door-to-door salesperson. The cancellation right must be exercised within three business days after making the contract. The contract, receipt, and notice-of-cancellation form must all be in the *same language* (all in Spanish, for example, for Spanish-speaking people).

This FTC rule applies to the sale, lease, or rental of consumer goods or services with a purchase price of $25 or more.

The following sales are *not* covered by this FTC rule:

1. Sales made by prior negotiations when a buyer visited a seller's permanent showroom.
2. Sales wherein a buyer has the right to rescind the transaction under the Consumer Credit Protection Act or its regulations.
3. Sales wherein a buyer first contacted a seller, and the goods or services are needed for the buyer's personal emergency. In these cases, the buyer gives the seller a separate, signed statement in the buyer's handwriting, which describes the situation and waives the right to cancel within three business days.
4. Sales made and completed entirely by telephone or mail, without any other contract between a buyer and seller's agents before delivery or performance.
5. Sales of realty, insurance, or securities or commodities from a broker registered with the Securities and Exchange Commission.
6. Sales wherein the buyer first contacted the seller and asked the seller to visit the buyer's home for repair or maintenance purposes of the item purchased.

Door-to-door sellers who do not give a receipt or contract with the notice-of-cancellation form, as required by FTC regulation, risk possible court-imposed civil penalties up to $10,000.

KEY TERMS

Caveat emptor
Consideration
Adequacy of consideration
Undue influence
Duress
Fraud
Puffing
Fraud by concealment
Innocent misrepresentation
Contracts contrary to public policy
Exculpatory clauses
Illegal contracts
Void contract
In pari delicto
Unconscionability
Bait-and-switch regulation
Modification of the holder-in-due-course rule
Thirty-day mail-order merchandise rule
Rule on cooling-off periods for door-to-door sales

CHAPTER PROBLEMS

1. Explain the concept that "business benefits from consumer protection."
2. What is the problem with using common law for consumer protection?
3. Give three defenses to fraud.
4. Who benefits from the caveat emptor rule?
5. Define duress.
6. Give an example of "puffing."

7. What does the FTC thirty-day mail-order rule require of sellers?
8. How many days does a consumer have to cool off under the FTC door-to-door salesperson rule?

*9. A jewelry store owner orally told a customer the value of a bracelet. Was this a misrepresentation of an existing fact? *Hall v. T. L. Kemp Jewelry, Inc.*, 322 S.E.2d 7 (N.C. App. 1984).

*10. Is it against public policy to permit a builder to disclaim warranty protection to a home buyer for the effects of latent (hidden) defects? About two years after the Nastris had bought a home, cracks appeared throughout the structure. A crack in the kitchen floor was 12 inches × 20 feet, which resulted in a difference in the height of the kitchen floor on the two sides of the crack. The roof also buckled over two bedrooms. The builder selling the house had put an exculpatory clause in the contract, excusing the builder from liability for latent defects that actually caused cracking in the house. Was the exculpatory clause disclaiming warranty protection valid? *Nastri v. Wood Brothers Homes, Inc.*, 690 P.2d 158 (Ariz. App. 1984).

"A river is more than an amenity, it is a treasure."

Justice Oliver Wendell Holmes, Jr. in *New Jersey v. New York*, 283 U.S. 336 (1931)

Chapter 12

Environmental Law: Particular Federal Statutes

CHAPTER PREVIEW

- Three functions of the National Environmental Policy Act (NEPA)
- The importance of a National Pollutant Discharge Elimination System (NPDES) permit in controlling water pollution
- Ways that primary and secondary air-quality standards control air pollution
- Problems that caused Congress to pass the Solid Waste Disposal Act and the Resource Conservation and Recovery Act
- How the Toxic Substances Control Act controls poisons

Guido and James Frezzo owned and operated a mushroom farm in Avondale, Pennsylvania. They mixed horse manure and water together as a growing base for the mushrooms. They dumped manure into their storm water runoff system, which ran into a creek. Federal law requires that persons discharging anything into a stream, lake, or river have a permit to do so. The Frezzos had no permit and had not even applied for one. Law enforcement officials caught the Frezzos, who argued that government officials should first have sued them civilly before bringing a criminal suit for something as harmless as discharging water and horse manure into a creek. Government officials pointed to the fact that the law had been in effect several years, and the Frezzos had not even applied for a permit. Were the Frezzos fined, put in jail and fined, or was their case dismissed?

This chapter looks at the National Environmental Policy Act and federal statutes addressing specific environmental problems such as water, air, and noise pollution; land disruption from surface mining; waste disposal; and extinction of life forms.

THE NATIONAL ENVIRONMENTAL POLICY ACT (NEPA)

The **National Environmental Policy Act (NEPA)** of 1969 was signed into law on January 1, 1970, by President Nixon. The Act's name is misleading since the title suggests a law correcting all sorts of environmental harm. However, NEPA is actually responsible for the following:

1. It established the Council on Environmental Quality (CEQ).
2. It requires federal agencies to take environmental concerns into account when they take certain actions.
3. It requires federal agencies to prepare detailed environmental statements (popularly called "environmental impact statements") in certain situations.

Environmental Rights

The NEPA does *not* give persons any national right to a healthy environment. For example, if polluted air causes lung cancer or carcinogenic water causes bladder cancer, NEPA is *not* violated. The NEPA merely says that each person should enjoy (not *will* enjoy or have a right to enjoy) a healthful environment. In reality, the NEPA is not a potent statute.

Environmental Impact Statements

NEPA requires all federal agencies to prepare **environmental impact statements** (EIS's) in two cases: when the agency sends a proposed law to Congress and whenever the agency proposes major federal action significantly affecting the quality of the human environment. NEPA requires that five items be contained in an EIS:

1. The environmental impact of the proposed action.
2. Any adverse environmental effects of the proposed action.
3. Alternatives to the proposed action.
4. The relation between short-term uses of the environment and the maintenance and enhancement of long-term productivity.
5. Any irreversible and irretrievable resource commitments involved in an agency action about to be implemented.

Most lawsuits dealing with NEPA have concerned EIS's. The EIS requirement is the core, or "action-forcing" part, of NEPA since it forces federal agencies to prepare an EIS. The *Calvert Cliffs' Coordinating Committee, Inc. v. U.S. Atomic Energy Commission* case examines this issue.

THE CLEAN WATER ACT

The Act's Goals

EPA tries to control water pollution by keeping unwanted matter out of the rivers, lakes, and streams in the United States. The **Clean Water Act** (formerly called the

CALVERT CLIFFS' COORDINATING COMMITTEE, INC. v. U.S. ATOMIC ENERGY COMMISSION

U.S. Court of Appeals (D.C. Cir.).
449 F.2d 1109 (1971).

FACTS An environmental group (Calvert Cliffs' Coordinating Committee, Inc.) sued the Atomic Energy Commission (AEC) claiming that the AEC had not followed NEPA when writing its regulations. The AEC claimed that it had followed NEPA. The AEC said that it took environmental matters into account when drafting its regulations and writing its EIS.

ISSUE Had the AEC taken environmental matters enough into account when writing its regulations and EIS?

DECISION No. The United States Court of Appeals required compliance with NEPA "to the fullest extent possible." Congress did not want agencies to follow NEPA only as much as they desired. NEPA requires federal agencies to disclose fully (in the EIS) how a proposed project will affect the environment.

LEGAL TIP

If a federal agency does not fully disclose a project's environmental impacts (in an EIS), the project can be stopped.

Federal Water Pollution Control Act, or FWPCA) first set goals in stages: to have swimmable, fishable waters by 1983 and zero discharge of pollutants by 1985.

How the Act Works

The Act basically tries to stop water pollution by making it illegal to discharge pollutants from **point sources** into water of the United States unless one has a **National Pollutant Discharge Elimination System (NPDES) permit.** Every direct point-source discharger into United States waters (including municipalities, businesses, farms, and all other point-source dischargers) must have an NPDES permit. Many industries discharge into municipal sewers. Such dischargers have to **pretreat** their sewage before putting it into municipal sewers, since municipal treatment plants were not equipped to filter out heavy metals and other toxic substances common in industrial discharge.

Some things are not point sources and do *not* need NPDES permits. For instance, general runoff from a farmer's field at no particular point does not need an NPDES permit. Pollutants from general land run-off are treated by **area-wide waste treatment programs** under the Clean Water Act. An example of such a program is a buffer zone of grass or vegetation next to a stream filtering the run-off before it goes into the water.

What is a pollutant? A **pollutant** could be anything foreign to water in its natural state (such as heat, sewage, or any chemical). "Waters of the United States" is so broad a term that a person pouring Scotch into water (technically speaking) needs an NPDES permit to do so. Recall from an earlier chapter that the federal government may regulate almost anything *affecting* interstate commerce. Therefore, since all water in some way affects interstate commerce, anytime anyone puts a pollutant into water, one may need an NPDES permit to do so. This explanation is called a commerce clause definition of water.

NPDES permits What is an NPDES permit? It is a piece of paper that every discharger from a point source (a discrete point such as a pipe or outlet as opposed to general run-off) needs to legally discharge a pollutant into *any* lake, river, or stream in the United States (even on one's own land). Such a permit first must be obtained from the EPA, which limits what the permit holder can put into the water.

How does the EPA decide what amounts of a pollutant can be put into the water? Since the Clean Water Act is an enabling act, it directs the EPA to conduct studies to identify dangerous pollutants. From these studies, the EPA proposes and promulgates regulations limiting harmful amounts of pollutants.

Enforcement

The Clean Water Act has both civil and criminal sanctions, meaning that either private parties or governmental bodies (EPA, the United States Justice Department, or a state government if it has assumed administration of the NPDES permit program) can enforce the Act. The governmental units may bring either civil suits (for example, to enjoin or stop dumping of pollutants into streams) or criminal suits.

Violators of the Clean Water Act are liable for damages, civil penalties, clean-up costs, fines (up to $25,000 per day), and prison terms of up to one year. The *U.S. v. Frezzo Brothers, Inc.* case illustrates that the courts will put businesspeople in jail and slap them with stiff fines if they dump pollutants into streams without having an NPDES permit to do so.

U.S. v. FREZZO BROS., INC.

U.S. Court of Appeals (3rd Cir.)
602 F.2d 1123 (1979); *cert. denied,*
444 U.S. 1974 (1980).

FACTS Frezzo Brothers, Inc., was in the mushroom farming business. The business was family run by James and Guido Frezzo. Part of raising mushrooms involves mixing hay, horse manure, and water, which ferments outside on wharves. The Frezzo brothers as individuals and their corporation were criminally charged with willfully discharging manure into the East Branch of White Clay Creek. A jury convicted the Frezzos and their corporation. The court fined the corporation $50,000 and the two Frezzos $50,000. Additionally, James and Guido each received a 30-day jail sentence. The Frezzos appealed on grounds that the government should have first sued them *civilly* before prosecuting them *criminally* for violating the Clean Water Act.

ISSUE May the United States Government prosecute persons criminally for violating the Clean Water Act without first suing them civilly?

DECISION Yes. The Clean Water Act does not require the United States to first sue a water polluter civilly before prosecuting them criminally. The Frezzos had no NPDES permit as required by the Clean Water Act. Therefore, they could not legally discharge any pollutant into United States waters.

LEGAL TIP

Anyone, including businesspeople, must have an NPDES permit before they can legally discharge any pollutant *directly* into United States waters (such as lakes, streams, or rivers).

THE CLEAN AIR ACT[1]

Pre-Federal Air Pollution Control

The first statutory attempts to control air pollution were made by the states. Uneven standards and enforcement were common. Various common-law doctrines, such as nuisance, were also available to private party plaintiffs, but these were inadequate for broad pollution-control efforts.

[1] The authors acknowledge reliance on government documents in preparing this segment.

Federal Air Pollution Control

In 1955, for the first time, a federal statute dealt with air pollution. It merely authorized research and federal technical and financial assistance. In 1963, Congress passed the **Clean Air Act,** the first federal attempt to regulate pollution. The statute had two main flaws: It did not define air pollution, merely saying that it was designed to prevent and control air pollution; and enforcement was hampered by a requirement that courts were to give consideration to the practicability and physical and economic feasibility of stopping pollution.

The 1965 Amendments

The 1965 Amendments to the Clean Air Act attacked the problem of air pollution caused by automobiles and trucks by authorizing emission standards for mobile sources. The United States Public Health Service was to set the numbers. Again, however, economic and technical feasibility conditions affecting the development of such standards weakened emission controls.

The 1967 Amendments

The Clean Air Act was again amended in 1967. The theory behind these amendments was that air clean-up requires a national effort, but that states should keep the primary authority for doing so. The 1967 Amendments required that states establish ambient air-quality standards for air-quality control regions (or regions that are state and federally determined). After the air-quality standards were determined, states were required to establish state implementation plans to achieve ambient air-quality standards.

From the environmental viewpoint, weaknesses of the Clean Air Act after the 1967 Amendments included the continued failure to define air pollution, the economic and technical feasibility conditions to the standards, the absence of private suit provisions, the lack of citizen surveillance, the excessive discretion in the Act's administration.

The 1970 Amendments

The 1970 Amendments to the Clean Air Act provided a definition of air pollution and eliminated the economic and technical feasibility loophole that previously existed. Three objectives of the 1970 Amendments were to establish the nondeterioration principle, primary air-quality standards, and secondary air-quality standards. Primary air-quality standards are ambient or general environmental standards that outdoor air must meet to protect the public health. The time set for achieving primary air-quality standards was 1975. The secondary standards are designed to protect public welfare, including the avoidance of any adverse effects on any human-made or aesthetic aspects of the environment. These standards were to be achieved within a "reasonable" time after 1975.

Pollutants Covered

Only six pollutants are covered by the ambient air-quality standards: hydrocarbons, carbon monoxide, sulfur dioxide, nitrogen oxides, particulates, and photochemical oxidants. Actually, more than six substances are now covered because hydrocarbons, particulates, and photochemical oxidants are generic, embracing more than one element. The Clean Air Act allows expansion of the list of air pollutants. Additionally, the 1970 Amendments further authorize the administrator to establish **direct emission standards** for any stationary source emitting substances designated by the administrator as hazardous (meaning that these sources may cause or contribute to mortality or irreversible or incapacitating illness). Vinyl chloride, asbestos, beryllium, mercury, and benzene have thus far been designated as hazardous pollutants. Finally, the 1970 Amendments give the Administrator authority to set **standards of performance** for new sources that contribute significantly to air pollution or endanger the public health or welfare.

The heart of the federal air pollution control program is the **state implementation plan (SIP).** This plan requires each state to submit to the EPA administrator's decisions in order to achieve the federally set primary and secondary air-quality standards. **Nondeterioration standards** were made a mandatory part of the SIP after the Sierra Club successfully sued the EPA Administrator to force such an inclusion. States were given until January 31, 1972, to submit proposed SIPs to the EPA for approval. EPA could either approve or disapprove all or part of the SIP. If the EPA approved a SIP, it became part of federal law. The EPA may amend a SIP to conform to federal ambient air criteria.

The SIPs contain a compilation of state air pollution statutes, regulations, municipal ordinances, emission limits, schedules and timetables for compliance, land use controls, and transportation control plans.

Enforcement

Violations of the Clean Air Act can lead to civil penalties or criminal sanctions. The latter includes fines up to $25,000 per day and up to one year in prison (making the violation a misdemeanor). There is also authority for citizen suits against any person (including the United States government) allegedly in violation of the Clean Air Act. This provision is the basis for a number of environmental group suits against EPA to force promulgation of regulations. EPA has on a number of occasions failed to meet *statutory* deadlines for promulgation of regulations or has promulgated weak regulations.

EPA has emergency power to go to court to shut down any source or combination of sources that presents imminent, substantial danger to the public's general health. This power was used in 1971 in Birmingham, Alabama, to close, among other things, steel mills.

Mobile sources account for slightly over 50% of the air pollution in the United States. EPA has emission standard authority for two general moving sources: all new vehicles and engines in vehicles used on streets, as well as aircraft engines. Additionally, the EPA has the authority to regulate vehicular fuel, since it affects vehicular emissions.

Emission off-sets The 1977 Amendments adopted the proposed EPA emission off-set policy in modified form by allowing new sources in dirty air areas "only if they attain the lowest achievable emission rates" and if other sources in the state under the same ownership or control are in compliance with relevant emission control provisions. The state must reduce emissions in the dirty air area each year and make progress toward meeting the 1982 or 1987 deadline for these **emission standards.**

Noncompliance penalties Improving Clean Air Act compliance and enforcement is another major area tackled by the 1977 Amendments. In an unusual attempt to gain industry's compliance with air pollution control regulations, the Amendments establish a scheme that sets an economic penalty equal to the economic benefit of being out of compliance. The *Duquesne Light Co. v. E.P.A.* case examines the noncompliance penalty.

Solid Waste

In general, garbage disposal in the United States is primitive. Our consumption-oriented society yields over 154 million tons of municipal waste, not counting sewage, each year. (Sewage and agricultural run-off are not considered solid waste here.) Even though technology in many areas has improved, we still commonly use a trash disposal method known for over 100 years—open dumping.

DUQUESNE LIGHT CO. v. EPA

U.S. Ct. App. D.C.
698 F.2d 456 (1983).

FACTS One section of the Clean Air Act authorizes the EPA to penalize those not meeting Clean Air Act emission limits. The amount of the noncompliance penalty is supposed to equal the benefit that the air polluter received from not meeting air pollution requirements. The EPA used industry-wide rather than company-specific data in calculating the penalty. Duquesne Light Company was assessed a penalty for not meeting Clean Air Act requirements. Duquesne argued that the benefits it received from not meeting such requirements were less than benefits other utilities would enjoy by not complying.

ISSUE May EPA use average industry benefits from noncomplying utilities to calculate how much to penalize a particular company?

DECISION Yes. The EPA was faced with calculating noncompliance benefits for each company individual *or* using industry-wide averages. The EPA chose the industry-average benefit since they can be checked much more easily. Also, past performance for a particular firm may have been influenced by nonrecurring factors (or one-time oddities).

LEGAL TIP

The EPA has the power to use industry averages in determining how much a particular business benefits by being out of compliance with the Clean Air Act.

Solid waste disposal was considered a state and local government concern before 1965. In 1965, Congress passed the Solid Waste Disposal Act. This Act was the first federal statute to deal with dumping's effect on the environment. Basically, this Act gave federal money to states and municipalities for waste disposal research. However, garbage was still viewed as mainly a state and municipal matter.

Congress amended the Solid Waste Disposal Act when it passed the Resource Recovery Act of 1970. This federal law recognized the economic benefits of recycling (recovering and reusing resources from waste) and gave federal money to urban areas with severe solid waste problems.

In the early 1970's, the federal role in solid waste was limited, consisting of several elements:

1. Construction of waste management and resource recovery demonstration projects.
2. Technical and financial aid to state agencies' recycling waste management programs.
3. National research and development on collection, recovery, recycling, and safe disposal of nonrecoverable waste.
4. Federal guidelines (which included nonbinding suggestions on the proper way to collect, transport, separate, recover, and dispose of solid waste).
5. Occupational training grants.

However, solid waste disposal continued to be viewed as primarily a state and municipal matter. The federal role was limited.

Then the roof fell in. In the mid-1970's, the following disclosures were made:

1. There was massive PCB (toxic oil) contamination of the Hudson River.
2. Love Canal in Buffalo, New York, was filled with discarded chemicals that threatened the health of hundreds of families living nearby.

3. Kepone (a pesticide), which was dumped into the James River in Hopewell, Virginia, had caused serious human health damage as well as harm to fisheries in the James River and Chesapeake Bay.

These disclosures merely hinted at the secret dumping and disposal of hazardous wastes nationwide that threatened groundwater, surface water, and public health. People would build houses on top of buried radioactive waste simply because they were unaware of the presence of hazardous material.

Congress enacted the Toxic Substances Control Act (discussed later in this chapter) and the Resource Conservation and Recovery Act (RCRA) to deal with these problems.

RESOURCE CONSERVATION AND RECOVERY ACT OF 1976

The **Resource Conservation and Recovery Act (RCRA)** is a federal statute that deals with solid waste problems on a national basis. RCRA tries to control solid waste management practices that pose a danger to public health. This Act also regulates hazardous and nonhazardous solid wastes. RCRA defines solid wastes to include waste solids, sludges, liquids, and contained gases. Solid and dissolved sewage, irrigation return flows, industrial discharge covered by NPDES permits, and some radioactive wastes are *not* covered. RCRA defines a *hazardous waste* as one that may cause or significantly contribute to serious illness or death or that poses a substantial threat to human health of the environment if managed improperly.

Goals

RCRA has two main goals: to control management of solid waste that would endanger public health or the environment and to encourage resource conservation and recovery.

Implementation

RCRA tries to accomplish its goals in several ways. First, the federal government provides money and know-how (technical advice) to state and municipal governments for developing programs to deal with land disposal of solid wastes. Second, there is "cradle-to-grave" regulation of hazardous wastes, which monitors the substance from creation to disposal. Third, the Act provides for resource recovery and conservation (such as salvaging metal beer cans and reusing the metal). Fourth, EPA establishes (by regulation) federal standards and a permit program for controlling hazardous wastes. States meeting these standards may run their own hazardous waste control programs. If they do not meet federal standards, EPA runs the program.

Manifest system The heart of the **hazardous waste control programs** is a **manifest system,** which is similar to a permit system. All persons (including businesses) generating hazardous wastes must get a permit (manifest) to manage them on their property or to ship them to an EPA-approved treatment, storage, or disposal facility. The idea of the manifest system is that a piece of paper (a manifest) accompanies each hazardous waste substance from creation to disposal. This procedure keeps society informed about the location of hazardous wastes so people will not unwittingly be building houses on them or do anything else with them unknowingly.

Note that the manifest system applies only to *hazardous* wastes. The manifest system has caused a great deal of controversy. A former EPA official estimated that 750,000 hazardous materials are generated in the United States. There is much paperwork and expense for persons generating hazardous wastes (mainly the chemical industry), given the "paper trail" of the manifest system. On the other hand, we must remember that hazardous wastes may cause or significantly contribute to serious illness or death or pose a substantial threat to the environment if improperly managed.

Sanctions

RCRA has criminal and civil penalties for hazardous waste violations. Civil penalties can be as much as $25,000 per day per violation; criminal penalties include up to one year in prison and as much as $25,000 per day per offense, or both. One question has been whether the EPA will receive enough money to implement RCRA.

TOXIC SUBSTANCES CONTROL ACT (TOSCA)

The **Toxic Substances Control Act (TOSCA)** is a federal law passed in 1976. It is an enabling act. As such, it is a conferral of authority from Congress to an administrative agency to regulate the manufacture, use, and disposal of toxic substances. The reason TOSCA became law was so that the public could learn more about chemicals' possible adverse effects on humans and on our air, water, and natural resources.

TOSCA expressly recognizes that disposing of many human-made chemicals involves unreasonable risks to both natural resources (such as groundwater, where we get much of our drinking water) and humans. TOSCA gives EPA power to make cradle-to-grave regulations controlling disposal of all toxic organic chemicals now found in groundwater supplies. EPA has been slow (and is behind) in implementing the waste regulations.

Control of Toxic Chemicals

Recall that TOSCA gives EPA the power to regulate chemicals over their entire life cycle (from development through manufacture to disposal). TOSCA orders EPA to inventory the approximately 55,000 chemicals in interstate commerce. TOSCA then requires chemical manufacturers to notify EPA of all new chemical substances *before* they are made. This is called the **premanufacture notice (PMN)** requirement. TOSCA also lets EPA make record-keeping, testing, and reporting requirements at all stages of toxic chemicals' life cycles (again, the cradle-to-grave part of TOSCA).

Stopping manufacture Once EPA has all of the information about toxic chemicals, TOSCA authorizes it to stop the manufacture of new chemicals that present an unreasonable risk to people or the environment (due only after EPA studies the data submitted by industry). This authority involves great regulatory power over the chemical industry. However, the risks are great, since we are talking only about *toxic* chemicals. EPA also has the power under TOSCA to issue temporary limits on chemicals if EPA has insufficient information to decide that a chemical presents unreasonable risks.

TOSCA *limits* EPA's regulatory power over the chemical industry in one very important way: EPA has the burden of proof to show that a new chemical presents an unreasonable risk to people. In other words, chemicals are presumed safe and nontoxic until EPA proves otherwise.

Criticisms of TOSCA

There have been a number of criticisms of TOSCA coming from both environmental (pro-regulatory) and chemical (anti-regulatory) industry groups. The chemical industry complains about the red tape, cost, and possible loss of trade secrets because of TOSCA's reporting requirements. Environmental groups complain that EPA has been slow to regulate. Since TOSCA's passage in 1976, only *five* chemical classes have been regulated at all (PCBs, chloroflourocarbons, phthalate esters, chlorinated benzenes, and chloromethane).

Even the EPA has complaints about TOSCA, which are based on the issue of delayed regulation. EPA officials worry about the staff shortage, a concern that delays putting TOSCA into effect. Also, the EPA complains about industry foot-dragging in supplying information that the EPA needs to study the possible toxic effects of chemicals. This problem is particularly troublesome, since the burden of showing that chemicals are toxic is on the EPA. If toxins are creeping into the water, air, and food chain (through fertilizers and insecticides, for example), they could pose serious long-term, perhaps irreversible, threats to humans and the environment.

KEY TERMS

National Environmental Policy Act (NEPA)
Environmental impact statements (EIS's)
Clean Water Act
Point sources
National Pollutant Discharge Elimination System (NPDES) permit
Pretreat
Area-wide waste treatment programs
Pollutant
Clean Air Act
Direct emission standards
Standards of performance
State implementation plan (SIP)
Nondeterioration standards
Mobile sources
Emission standards
Resource Conservation and Recovery Act of 1976 (RCRA)
Hazardous waste control program
Manifest system
Toxic Substances Control Act (TOSCA)
Premanufacture notice (PMN)

CHAPTER PROBLEMS

1. What is an "EIS"?
2. What sort of permit must a person have who discharges pollutants directly into United States waters?
3. Describe the manifest system under the Resource Conservation and Recovery Act (RCRA).
4. Are chemicals presumed safe (nontoxic) or unsafe (toxic) under the Toxic Substances Control Act (TOSCA)?
5. What pollutants does the Clean Air Act cover?
6. What type of pollution do SIP's try to control?

*7. The Clean Air Act says, "Stop polluting or close down." In response, industry has raised the defense of technical and economic infeasibility ("it cannot be done" or "it is too expensive to do"). In one case, an electric utility made this argument. What is the result? *Union Elec. Co. v. E.P.A.,* 96 S.Ct. 2518 (1976).

*8. What does "nearby" mean? This question arose when Congress passed a Clean Air Act amendment allowing the EPA to set emission limits from smokestacks "nearby." *Sierra Club v. EPA,* 719 F.2d 436 (D.C. Cir. 1983).

*9. The Clean Air Act limits air pollution from stationary sources (such as buildings). The Act sets stricter air pollution limits for new buildings than for buildings existing before the Clean Air Act became law. A Rhode Island asphalt concrete plant was substantially remodeled, which did not materially increase plant capacity or air pollution. Was this a "new source" subject to stricter air pollution limits or could it be treated as an "old source"? *U.S. v. Narragansett Imp. Co.,* 517 F.Supp. 688 (D.C. R.I. 1983).

*10. The Clean Water Act requires business to install expensive water pollution control equipment. Are the regulations legal if EPA's pretreatment regulations would close down many metal finishing businesses? *National Ass'n. of Metal Finishers v. EPA,* 719 F.2d 624 (3rd Cir. 1983).

"From this country's beginning, there has been an abiding and widespread fear of the evils that flow from monopoly—that is, concentration of economic power in the hands of a few."
Justice Black in *U.S. v. Von's Grocery Co.*, 384 U.S. 270 (1966)

Chapter 13

Antitrust Law: The Sherman Act

CHAPTER PREVIEW

- General objective of the federal antitrust laws
- Areas exempt from the federal antitrust laws
- Pleas an antitrust defendant can make
- Reason why the "rule of reason" exists
- Definition of an antitrust *per se* offense
- Conduct outlawed by Section 2 of the Sherman Act

Jim Wheeler knew that his problems had just begun. He had recently been elected president of the Corrugated Container Corporation; his firm and all the others in the industry faced declining profits. Price cutting to keep customers was common. Wheeler went to a meeting of his trade association, the Corrugated Box Manufacturers. After listening to complaints, Jim said: "One cardboard box is just like all the rest. Customers will continue to play us off against one another unless we do something. I propose that we exchange information on prices that we charge particular customers. Then, if we see costs going up, we can adjust prices accordingly. This plan will end needless price competition, and every member of our association can start making money again." Association members followed Wheeler's advice, and all made a profit. The United States Justice Department learned of the exchange of price information and sued Wheeler and his competitors for violating the Sherman Act. Wheeler claimed that the Sherman Act outlawed contracts, combinations, and conspiracies in restraint of trade but not the exchange of information about specific prices and customers. Was he right?

Maintaining competition is the chief objective of the antitrust laws. To accomplish this goal, certain business conduct is prohibited. This chapter examines those laws in detail.

The word **antitrust** comes from the early business practice of several corporate competitors' putting their stock into a **trust.**[1] The trustee would manage the businesses to minimize competition among the former competitors. When attempts were made to control anticompetitive business trust arrangements, the term *antitrust* was coined. By now, antitrust means virtually any anticompetitive business practice involving abuse of economic power.

RESTRAINTS OF TRADE

For hundreds of years, business people have tried to restrain trade to increase profits. In 1711, the English case of *Mitchel v. Reynolds* laid down the rule that not all agreements restraining trade were illegal—just the unreasonable ones. This became known as the **rule of reason.** According to this rule, an agreement to restrain trade might be legal or illegal.

The rule of reason announced in the *Mitchel v. Reynolds* case continues today in United States antitrust cases. This rule lets a court determine the validity of some trade restraints by looking at their object and effect. But, as we shall see, *some* trade restraints in the United States today are illegal per se. This means that once their existence is proven, they are conclusively presumed to be unreasonable and illegal. The court will not examine their reasonableness.

EARLY ANTITRUST LAWS IN THE UNITED STATES

The United States followed an economic policy of laissez-faire during much of the nineteenth century. **Laissez-faire** means business is given much freedom to conduct its affairs with little government interference and few rules curbing business practices.

The common law in the United States in the nineteenth century did forbid some anticompetitive practices, such as monopolies. The enforcers (or private parties) and jurisdictional limits (since we are talking about state, not federal, common law) prevented common law from being an effective means of controlling anticompetitive conduct. Today, many states have antitrust statutes, but since their scope, enforcement, and effectiveness vary widely, they are not discussed here.

The formulation of large corporations and industrial firms that began in the mid-nineteenth century led to many economic abuses. Some of the worst came from the railroads. They engaged in many undesirable practices, such as charging customers with no economic power high rates and powerful shippers low rates, often by giving secret rebates. Such abuses led to passage of the Interstate Commerce Act of 1887, which established the Interstate Commerce Commission to regulate railroads. Elimination of unfair and unreasonable rail rates was one of the Act's price goals.

[1]A trust is a way to own property. There are two owners to trust property: the trustee, who owns the legal title, and the beneficiary, who owns the beneficial or equitable title.

The increasing economic concentration (a few large firms in an industry rather than many small or medium-sized firms) and the predatory tactics used by business trusts to force small firms to sell out were among the factors leading to passage of the Sherman Act in 1890.

Summary of Federal Antitrust Laws

Figure 13-1 shows the major federal antitrust laws and their important provisions. Chapters 13 through 15 examine each of these laws.

Areas Exempt from the Antitrust Laws

Before examining some Sherman Act cases, it is important to note that certain activities are not covered by any of the federal antitrust laws—meaning that even if exempted businesses do something that antitrust laws prohibit, they are not liable. The reasons that these areas are exempt run the gamut from pure political power to policy reasons. One of the latter is enabling United States businesses to compete with foreign businesses, which are often subsidized by their governments or are themselves monopolies. The following subsections indicate some of the exempt areas.

Most labor union activities Labor unions were exempted only after long legal battles took place to equalize the bargaining power of workers and their employers in Congress and the courts. The policy of national labor law is to *eliminate* competition in the labor market, while antitrust law is designed to *promote* competition in the product market. Sometimes even today, labor unions can lose their antitrust immunity if they join with employer groups to restrain competition.

Intrastate industries having no effect on interstate commerce The federal antitrust laws are based on the national government's enumerated power to regulate interstate commerce. If a business is not in or does not affect interstate commerce, the national government has no power to regulate it. Since most businesses located in one state affect interstate commerce in some way, they would be covered by federal antitrust laws unless some other exemption applied.

Farmer and fisherman organizations The Capper-Volstead Act permits farmers to organize and fix prices, control output, and engage in activities otherwise violating the antitrust laws. The Fisheries Cooperative Marketing Act of 1934 lets fishermen do roughly the same things. These exemptions can be lost if fishermen's or farmers' organizations produce prices that are excessive.

Export associations United States firms can form associations to make them more competitive with foreign competitors, which are often monopolies subsidized by their governments. This exemption applies so long as export associations do not try to influence the price and quantity of goods within the United States.

Baseball Baseball, besides being a national pastime, is the only professional sport exempt from federal antitrust regulation. This exemption was made by court decision and is an historic oddity.

Figure 13-1 **Summary of Federal Antitrust Laws**

ACT	REQUIREMENTS
Sherman Act	
Section 1	Declares illegal every contract, combination, or conspiracy in restraint of trade; federal felony offense punishable by fine not over $1 million dollars for corporations or not over $100,000 for any other person. Persons other than corporations may be imprisoned for as much as three years, fined, or both. Two or more persons need to violate this provision.
Section 2	Outlaws monopolizing or attempts to monopolize; penalties same as Section 1. One or more persons or businesses may violate this section.
Clayton Act (covered in Chapter 14)	
Section 2 (includes amendments by the Robinson-Patman Act of 1936)	Declares it unlawful for any person to discriminate in price between different purchasers of goods of like grade and quality where the effect may be to lessen competition; create a monopoly in any line of commerce; or injure, destroy, or prevent competition with the seller, the buyer, or either's customers.
Section 3	Makes it unlawful to sell or lease goods on the condition that the buyer or lessee shall not use or deal in goods sold or leased by the seller's or lessor's competitor, where the effect of such agreement may be substantially to lessen competition or tend to create a monopoly. In effect, this section outlaws exclusive dealing and tie-in arrangements.
Section 7	Forbids corporate asset or stock mergers where the effect may be substantially to lessen competition or to tend to create a monopoly.
Section 8	Forbids persons from serving on boards of directors of competing corporations.
Federal Trade Commission Act (covered in Chapter 15)	
Section 5	Declares unlawful unfair methods of competition in or affecting commerce and unfair or deceptive acts or practices in commerce.

Regulated industries Regulated industries (such as insurance companies) already controlled by governmental agencies do not need the control that competition brings. Thus, they usually are not covered by the federal antitrust laws. Sometimes, though, even regulated industries (banks, for example) are subject to antitrust laws to stop anticompetitive conduct, such as mergers.

Small businesses The Small Business Act of 1953 permits small businesses to commit certain acts that otherwise would violate the antitrust laws.

Right to petition (the "Noerr doctrine") The First Amendment to the United States Constitution gives the people the right to petition the government. This right is known as the **Noerr doctrine.** In the *Eastern R. R. President's Conference v. Noerr Motor Freight* case (1961), the United States Supreme Court said that competing businesses may join together to petition the government to pass laws harmful to competitors. Limits are placed on this right of joint petition by competing businesses.

Business and professional activities covered by the "state action" doctrine State governments are immune from the federal antitrust laws for federalism reasons. The theory is that one sovereign, the national government, should not regulate another sovereign, the state government. This exemption extends to many businesses and professions regulated by the states. In the case *Parker v. Brown* (1943), the Supreme Court held that a state anticompetitive marketing program is exempt from the federal antitrust laws because it "derived its authority and efficacy from the legislative command of the state." The gist of the **Parker doctrine** is that if there is enough state involvement in a business or profession, then that business or profession gets the state's antitrust immunity. In the *California Retail Liquor Dealers Ass'n v. Midcal Aluminum, Inc.* case, there was not enough state involvement in the resale price maintenance scheme to qualify the wine-pricing program for the state antitrust exemption. As you read the case, watch for examples of state-regulated business activities that have and have not qualified for the state government exemption.

CALIFORNIA RETAIL LIQUOR DEALERS ASS'N v. MIDCAL ALUMINUM, INC.

U.S. Supreme Court.
100 S.Ct. 937 (1980).

FACTS A California statute required resale price maintenance and price posting for the wholesale wine trade. Midcal Aluminum, Inc. was a California wine distributor charged with violating the aforementioned law. Midcal defended by arguing the state's wine pricing system violated the Sherman Act. California's resale price maintenance statute for wines was defended on grounds that it was exempt (not covered) by the Sherman Act under the *Parker v. Brown* doctrine. This doctrine says that "state action" is exempt from the Sherman Act.

ISSUE Did the California price posting and resale price maintenance statute exempt the wholesale wine trade under the "state action" doctrine?

DECISION No. *Parker v. Brown* did make the rule that "state action" (or state government activities) can be exempt from the Sherman Act. There are two tests for antitrust immunity under *Parker v. Brown.* First, the challenged restraint must be one clearly articulated and affirmatively expressed as state policy. Secondly, the policy must be "actively supervised" by the state. The California system for wine pricing satisfies the first standard. However, the second test was not met because California simply authorizes price fixing and enforces the prices set by private parties. The state neither sets the prices nor reviews their reasonableness. There was not enough state involvement in the resale price maintenance here to justify exempting it from the Sherman Act.

LEGAL TIP

If business or professional groups can get state government to fix prices and actively review and supervise prices, this is probably *legal* price fixing.

THE SHERMAN ACT

The **Sherman Act** of 1890 has two short but important provisions, Section 1 and Section 2.

The big difference between Sections 1 and 2 of the Sherman Act is that only one person (which includes businesses) is needed to violate Section 2, while at least two people are necessary to violate Section 1. The reason is that only one person is needed to monopolize business (Section 2), while at least two are required to combine, contract, or conspire (as prohibited by Section 1). Section 2 looks at the structure of an industry. If monopoly power exists, predatory business practices are likely to be illegal. However, it is possible for conduct to violate both Sections 1 and 2 of the Sherman Act. An example is an agreement between competitors to merge, with the resulting company having monopoly power.

Who Can Sue and Where to Sue

If Section 1 or 2 of the Sherman Act is violated, the United States Justice Department can sue. Also, any private person whose business was injured when the Sherman violation occurred can sue. Private parties have an incentive to sue under the Sherman and Clayton Acts, since **treble damages** are awarded if the case is not settled and the injured party wins. Sherman Act cases are usually brought in federal district courts in the district where the alleged, wrongful conduct occurs.

Penalties and Recoveries

The Sherman Act is both criminal and civil. Therefore, a defendant convicted of violating the Act can be punished criminally and could possibly be sued civilly for damages and other remedies as well. Corporations, partnerships, and individuals can violate the Sherman Act. A Sherman Act violation is a federal felony. The criminal penalties for individual violators are up to 3 years in prison, fines up to $100,000, or both. When a corporation is criminally convicted, it can be fined up to $1 million, but the corporation itself obviously is never imprisoned. Also, in civil suits by the government, the defendants can be enjoined from committing such conduct in the future. Another civil remedy could result in the defendant firm's being broken up into smaller firms (called **"dissolution"**). Finally, part of the firm could be ordered sold (called **"divestiture"**). One sanction that is possible but infrequently used is seizure of goods shipped interstate in violation of the Sherman Act.

The Sherman Act also allows civil suits, permitting a private person or business injured by a Sherman Act violation to sue the wrongdoer to get damages or injunctive relief (to stop the defendant from future violations). The Sherman Act encourages private-party enforcement by letting private parties recover *three times* the damages that they actually sustain (called "treble damages"). Reasonable attorney fees are also available to successful plaintiffs in civil antitrust cases.

Pleas in a Sherman Act Criminal Case

A Sherman Act criminal defendant can make three pleas: guilty, not guilty, or **nolo contendere.** (A criminal defendant could also stand mute, in which case a not-guilty plea is usually entered.) The advantage to the defendant in making a nolo contendere plea is that the criminal judgment may not be used as evidence in a later treble damage suit brought by a private party. This result makes it harder, but not impossible, for a later civil plaintiff to win treble damages from defendant.

THE RULE OF REASON

Section 1 of the Sherman Act says that every contract, combination, or conspiracy in restraint of trade is illegal. Yet, almost all contracts are themselves restraints of trade since one is required to perform a duty under a contract that cannot be done elsewhere. For example, if James agrees to be Dwight's cook for $200 per week, he cannot do so for Elmer. James's ability to sell his services is restrained by this contract with Dwight. Yet we usually do not want to stop people from entering contracts.

With these considerations, the United States Supreme Court announced the rule of reason in the Standard Oil case. The rule of reason has been applied to Section 1 of the Sherman Act. This rule tolerates restraints of trade so long as they are not unreasonable; later cases affirm this position. "Unreasonable" is determined on a case-by-case basis. Thus, when a business is charged with violating the Sherman Act, it tries to use the rule of reason, which lets defendants show that an action which possibly violates the Act is not illegal because economic benefits outweigh economic costs. One problem with this rule is the uncertainty involved: businesspeople can never be certain that conduct is legal until a court or other official body says that it is.

Per Se Offenses

The fact that the rule of reason exists does not mean that this rule can justify *every* trade restraint justified by this rule. In fact, the courts have held that some trade restraints are so obviously harmful that they are per se offenses. A **per se offense** is one whose harm is presumed so that proof that the act has occurred establishes illegality. No defenses or justifications are allowed for such offenses. As the Supreme Court stated in the *Northern Pacific R. Co. v. United States* case (1958):

> There are certain agreements or practices which because of their pernicious effect on competition and lack of any redeeming virtue are conclusively presumed to be unreasonable and therefore illegal without elaborate inquiry as to the precise harm they have caused or the business excuse for their use.

However, while proof of the act provides sufficient evidence of liability if the government sues, a private party must still show damages to recover if a per se offense occurs.

Several types of competitive activities have been declared per se offenses: horizontal market division, horizontal price fixing, vertical price fixing, group boycotts, and certain tying contracts. Each of these agreements is illegal regardless of whether it is express or implied. As we have seen, proof of conscious parallel business behavior does not conclusively establish an agreement to violate the Sherman Act. But business behavior (for example, one firm's consistently raising its price after a competitor does) is admissible circumstantial evidence that lets a jury infer that an agreement exists.

Horizontal market division **Horizontal market division** refers to agreements among or between competitors at the same level of business (such as manufacturers, wholesalers, or retailers) to divide the geographic market. For example, two nationally competing beer manufacturers, one in Wisconsin, the other in Michigan, might decide that one can sell in Illinois and the other in Indiana, when in a competitive situation both would have sold in Illinois and

Indiana. The vice of such market divisions is the detrimental effect that it can have on **interbrand competition.** Horizontal market divisions can involve more than two competitors. Even if a horizontal market division actually *promotes* rather than harms competition, courts have held that the practice is illegal.

Horizontal price fixing **Horizontal price fixing** is an agreement among competitors at the same level to fix prices. The practice is similar to horizontal market division, since the parties to the agreement are at the same level and both are per se offenses. The agreement can be either express or implied. At least part of the perceived evil of horizontal price fixing is that it eliminates the main form competition takes—price. (In fact, classic economic theory views price as the *only* way firms compete.) No matter how prices are fixed—high, low, or at reasonable levels—such action is illegal.

Sometimes the facts of a case indicate that although competitors are exchanging price information, they have not expressly agreed to fix prices. The *United States v. Container Corp.* case indicates that such conduct violates Section 1 of the Sherman Act but is less clear on whether it is a per se violation. In other words, is the competitors' voluntary exchange of price information in and of itself illegal, or must an effect on prices be shown? Read the *United States v. Container Corp.* case to see if you think it is a per se case.

UNITED STATES v. CONTAINER CORP.

U.S. Supreme Court.
393 U.S. 333 (1969).

FACTS The United States Government sued Container Corporation (Container) civilly for price fixing in violation of the Sherman Act. Container did not expressly agree with competitors to fix prices. Instead, Container exchanged price information with competitors. The price information exchanged was of specific sales to identified customers (not average prices where no one was identified). Container and its competitors would furnish each other, on request, with the most recent price charged or quoted. Such price exchanges among competitors were on an irregular and infrequent basis. The product sold was standardized, corrugated containers.

ISSUE Did competitors' exchange of price information without any express agreement to fix prices violate Section 1 of the Sherman Act?

DECISION Yes. The government's complaint stated a cause of action. The court was unclear, however, on whether this situation involved a per se offense. The result of the reciprocal price exchange was to stabilize prices downward. Knowing a competitor's price usually meant matching it. The fact that such exchanges took place only occasionally did not make such exchanges legal under Section 1 of the Sherman Act. The corrugated container market is dominated by a few sellers. The product is standardized. Demand for the product is constant no matter what the price. The exchange of price information tends toward price uniformity. Stabilizing prices as well as raising them is banned by Section 1 of the Sherman Act. Price is too critical a control to let it be used even informally to restrain competition.

LEGAL TIP

Competitors should not exchange specific price information. Exchanging such information could violate Section 1 of the Sherman Act.

Vertical price fixing **Vertical price fixing** involves price fixing between a buyer and seller at different levels of the manufacturing and distribution process. The most usual form of vertical price fixing occurs when a manufacturer refuses to sell to a retailer unless the retailer agrees to maintain a minimum retail price.

This is often called **resale price maintenance.** The vice of such acts is their possible detrimental effect on **intrabrand competition.**

The legality of resale price maintenance has fluctuated. Before 1937, it was a per se violation of the Sherman Act. Then, in 1937 the **Miller-Tydings Act** excluded resale price maintenance from Sherman Act coverage and let individual states pass fair trade laws, which legalized such vertical price fixing. Thus, if a state had a fair trade law, a manufacturer could, for example, force a retailer to sell goods at a particular price.

Then the policy regarding resale price maintenance changed, in large part because of the consumer movement and its demand for low prices. Congress repealed the Miller-Tydings Act as of March 13, 1976, making resale price maintenance once again a per se Sherman Act violation. No longer could a manufacturer decide who would be a distributor of its products based on the distributor's agreement to maintain prices.

Group boycotts **Group boycotts** are per se violations of the Sherman Act that usually involve several sellers (often manufacturers) jointly refusing to sell to a certain type of distributor (often a discounter). Such joint conduct usually provides sufficient legal taint to violate the Sherman Act, since the idea of competition is that each competitor operates independently of the others.

One competitor may refuse to deal with a particular buyer or a class of buyers without violating the Sherman Act. The seller might refuse to sell to a discounter because its credit is bad or because it provides no service department for customer warranty claims. One reason some discounters are able to offer buyers such low rates results from their elimination of full service—including salespeople, who will point out product features and give instructions in operating the product, or well-trained service personnel should the product not work. Full-service product sellers, bound by agreement to service their manufacturer's products no matter where the customer bought them, become annoyed when buyers from a discounter demand service from them. The customer wants the advantages but not the disadvantages of the discounter and the full-service dealer.

To deal with the discounter problem, a single manufacturer might join with some of its full-service dealers and boycott the discounter. The *United States v. General Motors Corp.* case tells us if such a boycott between a manufacturer and its distributors is a per se violation of Section 1 of the Sherman Act.

Tying arrangements Certain tying arrangements have on occasion been called Sherman Act per se offenses by the United States Supreme Court. A **tying arrangement** is one in which a seller requires the buyer to purchase one item, called the **tied product** or service, as a condition of purchasing another item, called the **tying product** or service. An example is a record store's requiring the purchase of Beethoven's nine symphonies as a condition to buying an autographed Michael Jackson album. Although nearly everyone in a certain age group might want the autographed Jackson album, not many in that same group would want the Beethoven set.

The seller's goal in a tying arrangement is to extend a market from a desirable item (the tying item) to include a less desirable item (the tied item) that could be purchased from anyone else or not at all. In doing so, the seller restrains trade in the tied item, which is a negative aspect of tying arrangements.

UNITED STATES v. GENERAL MOTORS CORP.

U.S. Supreme Court.
381 U.S. 127 (1966).

FACTS General Motors (GM) manufactures Chevrolets (Chevys). GM sells Chevys through franchised dealers. The GM-Chevy dealers franchise agreement does not limit who the dealer may sell to. However, the franchise agreement did have a "location clause," prohibiting dealers from moving to a different location or opening a branch office unless GM approved. In the late 1950's, discount houses in Los Angeles began to sell new Chevys to the public as low as $85 over the dealer's cost. Discounters got new Chevys from a few regular Chevy dealers. Customers would buy new Chevys from discounters and then go to regular Chevy dealers for warranty work and service. (The customer in warranty cases does not pay the dealer, but any Chevy dealer must service a Chevy wherever it was bought.) Chevy dealers in the Los Angeles area who did not sell to discounters complained to GM; they wanted GM to stop some dealers from selling to discounters. Chevy's regional sales manager told the "misbehaving" dealers to stop selling to discounters or he would "knock their teeth down their throats." The offending dealers agreed, and the complaining dealers policed the agreement. The United States Justice Department sued GM and its complaining dealers (who did not sell to discounters), alleging that their conduct violated Section 1 of the Sherman Act.

ISSUE Did GM and several Los Angeles Chevy dealers have a conspiracy to restrain trade when they stopped other Chevy dealers from selling to discounters?

DECISION Yes. The conduct of GM and its "complaining" dealers violated Section 1 of the Sherman Act in a "classic" conspiracy in restraint of trade. GM and the complaining dealers tried to get rid of a class of competitors who wanted to sell to discounters. When businesspeople concert their actions to deprive others of access to goods they want to sell, they commit a per se violation of Section 1 of the Sherman Act.

LEGAL TIP

Group boycotts are per se violations of Section 1 of the Sherman Act.

Points about tying arrangements First, tying arrangements for either goods or services can be attacked under the Sherman Act. Second, tying arrangements involving goods (but not services) may be attacked under the Clayton Act (discussed in Chapter 14). Third, the amount of economic power that the seller has over the tying item strongly influences the Supreme Court's willingness to call the tying arrangement a per se offense under the Sherman Act. For example, patented or otherwise unique tying items (such as land) are more likely to confer market power on the seller than unpatented tying items and, hence, lead a court to declare them a per se offense. Fourth, it is confusing to say that a situation sometimes is a per se offense and that sometimes is it not. Yet, this is what the United States Supreme Court has done with respect to tying arrangements. Some are per se offenses and others are subject to the rule of reason. However, point three must be remembered: a tying arrangement involving a patented tying product (or land) is more likely to be a per se offense than a tying arrangement involving an unpatented tying product.

From Per Se to Rule of Reason

Business defendants under the Sherman Act would rather have their conduct tested under the rule of reason than under the per se rule. Conduct is more likely to be legal under the rule of reason than under a per se test.

On the other hand, per se rules are "bright lines." Since they clearly tell a business that certain conduct is or is not legal. Contrast the clarity of legality under per se with the clarity of legality under the rule of reason. One really never knows if conduct is illegal under the rule of reason until after a court has examined the particular conduct in the particular case and weighed its relative economic benefits and costs. By then it is too late to avoid illegality (except in the future). However, one other point should be made: If conduct is not illegal per se, that conduct could still be illegal; the rule of reason could find the conduct either justified or not justified (and, hence, illegal).

The *Continental T.V., Inc. v. GTE Sylvania, Inc.* case deals with vertical nonprice restraints that manufacturers put on retailers to reduce intrabrand competition.

CONTINENTAL T.V. INC. v. GTE SYLVANIA, INC.

U.S. Supreme Court.
433 U.S. 36 (1977).

FACTS GTE Sylvania, Inc. (Sylvania) makes and sells televisions. Sylvania stopped selling through wholesalers and started selling directly to a smaller, more select group of franchised retailers. Sylvania limited the number of franchises it had in any geographic area. Sylvania also required each franchised retailers to sell televisions only from that location. Sylvania could add retailers in an area if it desired. The idea behind this marketing strategy was to reduce intrabrand (Sylvania v. Sylvania) competition so that Sylvania dealers could increase interbrand (Sylvania versus other makers of televisions) competition. A former distributor under the "old wholesaler" marketing network (cut out by the new marketing plan) sued Sylvania, claiming Sylvania's new location restrictions violated Section 1 of the Sherman Act. (A former United States Supreme Court decision in the *Schwinn* case held that vertical location restrictions were per se illegal.)

ISSUE Does the per se rule or rule of reason determine whether vertical, location restraints are legal?

DECISION The rule of reason is the proper test for judging vertical location restrictions because such restrictions are not necessarily anticompetitive. The rule of reason considers all factors to decide if a restraint is illegal under Section 1 of the Sherman Act. In other words, restraints could be both competitive and anticompetitive since courts decide under the rule of reason whether pro-competitive effects outweigh anti-competitive effects. Sylvania's vertical location restrictions should be judged under the rule of reason.

LEGAL TIP
Vertical location restrictions are not per se illegal.

Section 2 of the Sherman Act

Section 2 of the Sherman Act tries to stop a business from having monopoly power (the power to control prices or to keep out competition). A single firm can violate this section. Two firms could also violate this section if, for example, their merger resulted in a firm that has monopoly power. Nor does it matter if defendants are in the product or service market, since Section 2 outlaws monopolizing in either product or service markets.

What is illegal under Section 2 Section 2 does not outlaw all monopolies. Instead, this section outlaws monopolizing or *attempts* to monopolize, which requires both monopoly power and the intent to monopolize. In other words, it is possible that a monopoly might not violate Section 2 if it lacks the *intent* to monopolize.

Relevant market To violate Section 2 of the Sherman Act, intent to monopolize and monopoly power must exist. What is monopoly power? A firm that is the only one in the industry is an example of a monopoly. But the question is: What is "the industry"? Or stating the question another way: What is the "relevant market"?

These questions lead to the subject of substitute or competing products. For example, a business can convince a court that many functional equivalents for the product exist, the court is likely to enlarge the market and therefore reduce the possibility of monopolizing. Business defendants usually want broad market definitions, while government plaintiffs usually want narrow market definitions. In the *United States v. Du Pont Co.* case the government challenged Du Pont with monopolizing the cellophane market (a Sherman Act, Section 2 violation). Du Pont argued that the relevant market was not just cellophane but all flexible packaging materials. What was the market definition of "cellophane" or "flexible packaging materials"?

To learn the United States Supreme Court's answer, read the *Du Pont* case.

UNITED STATES v. DU PONT CO.

U.S. Supreme Court.
351 U.S. 377 (1955).

FACTS The United States Government sued the Du Pont Company under Section 2 of the Sherman Act. The United States claimed that Du Pont was monopolizing the cellophane market. Du Pont argued that the relevant market was not just cellophane but rather all types of flexible wrappings such as aluminum foil, Saran wrap, and polyethylene. The lower court said that the relevant product market was flexible packaging materials and decided that Du Pont did not monopolize that market. The United States appealed the decision to the Supreme Court.

ISSUE Was the relevant product market here cellophane or all flexible packaging? Did Du Pont have monopoly power in that market?

DECISION The relevant market was flexible packaging material, not just cellophane. Du Pont did *not* have monopoly power, or power to control price or exclude competition in the relevant market. There were competing products that were functionally interchangeable.

LEGAL TIP

One way to define the relevant product market to decide if there is monopoly power is to see if substitute products exist.

KEY TERMS

Antitrust
Trust
Rule of reason
Laissez faire
Noerr doctrine
Parker doctrine
Sherman Act
Treble damages
Dissolution
Divestiture
Nolo contendere
Per se offense
Horizontal market division
Interbrand competition
Horizontal price fixing
Vertical price fixing
Intrabrand competition
Resale price maintenance
Miller-Tydings Act
Group boycotts
Tying arrangement
Tying product
Tied product

CHAPTER PROBLEMS

1. Where does the word "antitrust" come from?
2. Explain the rule of reason.
3. Name three areas exempt from federal antitrust laws.
4. How many people does it take to violate Section 1 of the Sherman Act?
5. If a Sherman Act victim has $100,000 in damages, how much may the victim recover?
6. Give five examples of per se offenses under the Sherman Act.
7. Very briefly, what does Section 2 of the Sherman Act outlaw?

*8. Are employee agreements not to compete or interfere with their employer's business after they leave that company decided under the per se rule or the Rule of Reason? *Aydin Corp. v. Loral Corp.*, 718 F.2d 897 (9th Cir. 1983).

*9. Chambless, a veteran seaman and former labor union member, claimed that pension plan regulations restrained union members' ability to work for different employers. The pension regulations called for reduction of retirement from $920 to $470 in Chambless' case. Further, employees working even 1 day for *other* employers could not retire before 65 (it is a common practice for seamen to retire earlier) and draw benefits. Did these pension provisions violate Section 1 or 2 of the Sherman Act? *Chambless v. Masters, Mates, & Pilots Pension Plan,* 571 F.Supp. 1430 D. NY (1983).

*10. Spray-Rite Service Corporation was a wholesaler of Monsanto's agricultural herbicides in Illinois. Spray-Rite sold Monsanto's products below Monsanto's suggested resale prices. Other Monsanto distributors complained to Monsanto about Spray-Rite's price cutting. Monsanto warned Spray-Rite to sell only at suggested prices. Spray-Rite continued to price cut; Monsanto then cut Spray-Rite off as a supplier. Spray-Rite sued Monsanto for conspiring with its distributors to vertically price fix in violation of Section 1 of the Sherman Act. Monsanto defended on grounds that there was not enough evidence of an illegal price-fixing conspiracy. The Court of Appeals held that it was possible to find a price-fixing conspiracy when competitors complained to the manufacturer, who then stopped selling to the price cutter. Monsanto appealed to the United States Supreme Court. What type of evidence is needed to prove a price-fixing conspiracy between a distributor and manufacturer? *Monsanto v. Spray-Rite,* 52 U.S.L.W. 4341 (1984).

"While the law (of competition) may be sometimes hard for the individual, it is best for the race, because it insures the survival of the fittest in every department."
Andrew Carnegie

Chapter 14

Antitrust Law: The Clayton and Robinson-Patman Acts

CHAPTER PREVIEW

- Price discrimination outlawed by Section 2 of the Clayton Act
- Tying arrangements
- Exclusive dealing
- Requirements contracts
- Civil remedies available under all federal antitrust laws
- Mergers outlawed by Section 7 of the Clayton Act
- Three elements necessary to violate Section 8 of the Clayton Act

Bob had worked long and hard to make it happen. It seemed to be good business. "It" was a merger. Bob Von Horn's Grocery Company chain was going to buy another supermarket chain, Shopping Bag Food Stores. Both were retail supermarket chains in the Los Angeles area. Before the merger, Bob asked his attorney if the merger might be illegal. His lawyer looked at him and said, "Bob, will you stop worrying? We have only 7.5% of the Los Angeles grocery market after *the merger. The United States Government would never challenge such a merger." Who was right, Bob or his lawyer?*

This chapter continues surveying the federal antitrust laws. The Clayton Act and the Robinson-Patman Act, which try to stop certain anticompetitive practices that the Sherman Act did not outlaw, are examined in the following pages.

THE CLAYTON ACT

As originally passed, the **Clayton Act** had a number of provisions. The five provisions focused on here are Sections 2, 3, 4, 7, and 8. In general, Section 2 forbids a seller from discriminating in price between and among different purchasers of the same commodity. Section 3 aims to deal with three problems: requirements contracts, tying arrangements, and exclusive dealing. Section 4 covers remedies. Section 7 tries to prevent mergers that may tend to substantially lessen competition in any line of commerce in any section of the country. Section 8 prevents certain interlocking directorates, people who serve on boards of directors of competing companies.

Enforcers

Clayton Act enforcers include the federal government (Justice Department and Federal Trade Commission), private parties (who may obtain treble damages), the Federal Communications Commission (for the broadcasting industry only), and the Federal Reserve Board (for banks only).

Reasons for Passing the Clayton Act

The Clayton Act is a federal antitrust law enacted in 1914. The Act was passed because of certain problems with the Sherman Act, which proved inadequate to stop monopolizing and certain specific abuses of economic power at an early age. Also, the Sherman Act did not outlaw directors' serving on the boards of competitors. Labor unions were unhappy with the application of the Sherman Act to them and wanted an exemption. Finally, the Sherman Act was vague. Businesses and others wanted clearer definitions of legal and illegal practices under the antitrust laws. In response to these concerns, the Clayton Act of 1914, the Robinson-Patman Act of 1936, and the Celler-Kefauver Amendments of 1950 were introduced and passed.

Price Discrimination Under Section 2 of the Clayton Act: The Robinson-Patman Act

Section 2 of the Clayton Act prohibits a seller from discriminating in price between different buyers of goods (but not services) of like grade and quality. The goods must be sold for use, consumption, or resale within the United States. Also, the effect of such discrimination may be to substantially lessen competition or tend to create a monopoly in any line of commerce. The **Robinson-Patman Act** of 1936 amended Section 2 of the original Clayton Act. The general objective of Section 2 is to stop large firms from exerting excessive economic power to drive out small competitors in local markets.

Primary-line injury A Robinson-Patman Act violation can occur at several levels of competition. Price discrimination can cause injury at the primary level. **Primary-line injury** occurs when one seller's price discrimination injures a competing seller. Figure 14-1 illustrates this problem. Note that seller A sells in both Kentucky and Tennessee. Seller A reduces its price only in the Kentucky markets to drive seller B out of Kentucky, where A and B both compete. If A has enough market power to threaten injury to B, the Robinson-Patman Act has been violated.

Figure 14-1 **Primary-line Injury**

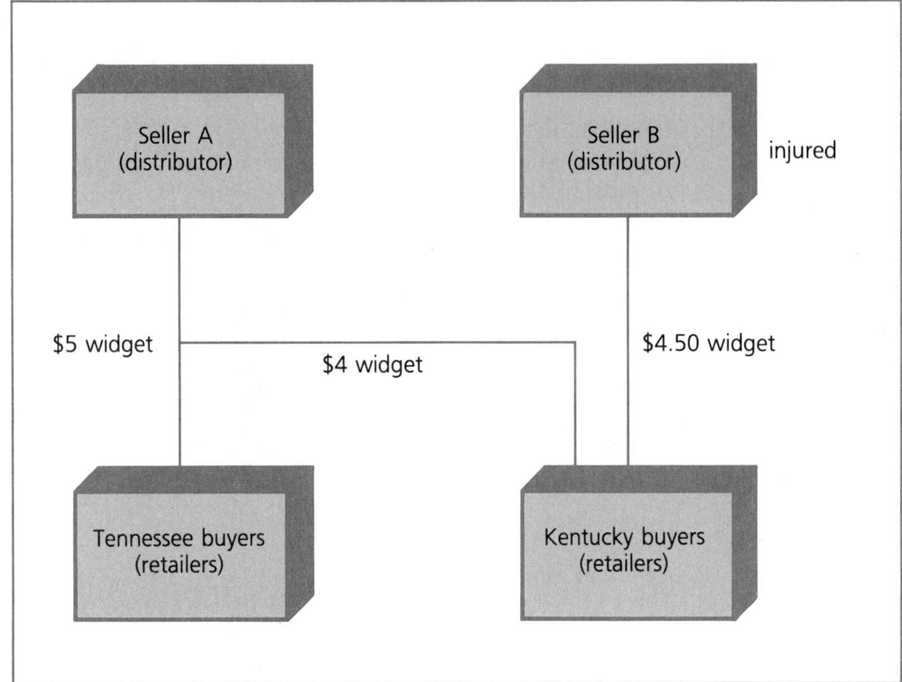

In the above example, seller A discriminated in the prices it charged consumers in different states to hurt A's competitors. This type of competitive injury was the original focus of Section 2 of the Clayton Act.

Problems with the original Section 2 However, it became apparent that large *buyers* might also use this economic power to injure competition by requesting and getting lower prices than other buyers. The original Section 2 of the Clayton Act did not prohibit this kind of price discrimination.

Robinson-Patman Act The Robinson-Patman Act was passed during the Great Depression largely in response to demands by "mom-and-pop" grocery stores. These small operations asked Congress to prevent large retailers from getting quantity discounts, which drove small competitors out of business. Congress amended Section 2 of the Clayton Act by prohibiting price discrimination injuring competition *between buyers*. Figure 14-2 illustrates second-line injury, which is defined in the next subsection.

Secondary-line injury **Secondary-line injury** from price discrimination happens when a seller discriminates in price between competing buyers, B_1 and B_2. The injury here is to B_2, who has to pay S higher prices that B_1 has to pay. Figure 14-2 illustrates secondary-line injury.

Figure 14-2 **Secondary-line Injury**

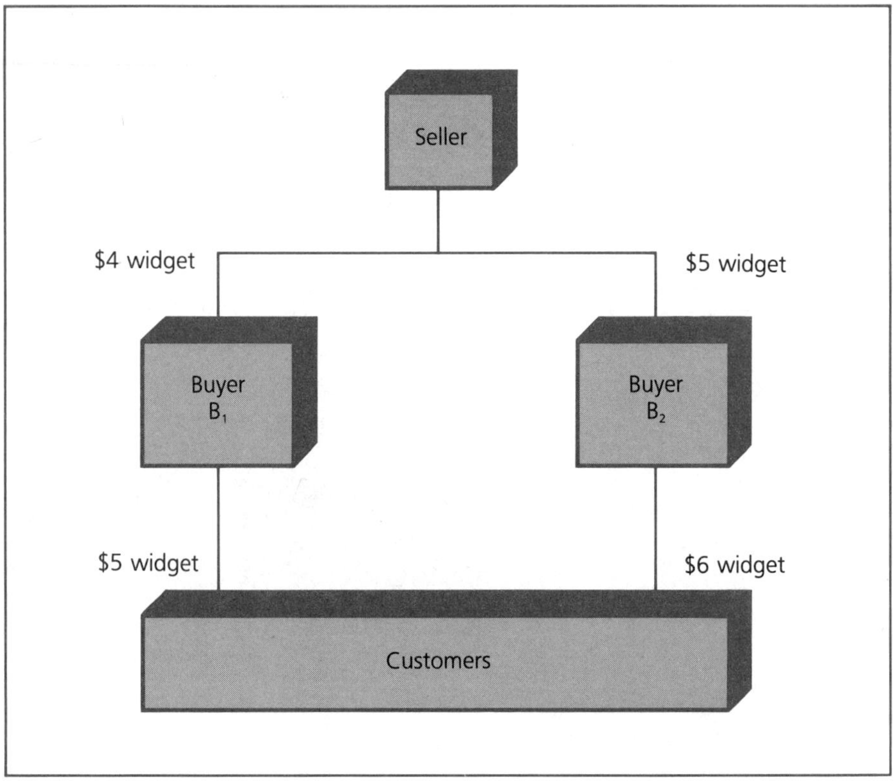

Seller

$4 widget

$5 widget

Buyer B$_1$

Buyer B$_2$

$5 widget

$6 widget

Customers

Establishing a Robinson-Patman Act Violation

The elements required to violate the Robinson-Patman Act are as follows:

1. A sale (not a lease or refusal to deal) must take place.
2. The sale must be of goods (not of services or other intangibles).
3. The goods must be of like grade and quality.
4. The goods must sell at a different price (included in price is aid such as marketing assistance to sell the goods).
5. The sale must injure competition (not necessarily a particular competitor).
6. The sale must be in interstate commerce (meaning that at least one of the sales must actually be in another state—the goods in at least one of the sales must actually go to another state).

Once these elements are proven, the Robinson-Patman violation is sufficiently established to get the case to a jury.

Robinson-Patman Act Defenses

A Robinson-Patman Act charge includes several defenses:

1. *Cost justification.* If a plaintiff otherwise proves his or her case, the defendant may still escape liability by showing that giving the buyer a lower price actually

saved the defendant money. Merely giving a quantity discount, however, does not automatically prove a cost savings.

2. *Meeting a competitor's equally low price.* A seller may discriminate among its buyers to meet, but not beat, a competitor's equally low price made to one or more of the seller's buyers.
3. *Selling perishables.* A seller of perishables may discriminate among buyers when goods are about to rot if not sold at once.
4. *"Goods" that are not goods.* The "goods" are services or intangibles (for example, custodial service).
5. *Interstate contact.* Unlike the Sherman Act and some other parts of the Clayton Act, the interstate commerce requirement of the Robinson-Patman Act has been narrowly construed so that at least one of the sales involved must pass into another state.
6. *Goods of different grade or quality.* The difference must be more than mere superficialities, such as different decals.
7. *No injury to competition.* This defense is difficult to establish, because all the Act requires is that the effect of the price discrimination may be to substantially lessen competition or to *tend* to create a monopoly.

The *Utah Pie Co. v. Continental Baking Co.* case illustrates how courts can disagree as to whether sufficient injury to competition exists to prove a Robinson-Patman Act violation.

UTAH PIE CO. v. CONTINENTAL BAKING CO.

U.S. Supreme Court.
87 S.Ct. 1326 (1967).

FACTS Utah Pie Company was a small firm located in Utah, where the company made and sold frozen pies since 1957. The frozen pie market expanded in Salt Lake City between 1958 and 1961; Utah Pie's market share dropped from 66.5% in 1958 to 45.3% in 1961, but the company continued to make money despite this decrease. One competitor, Continental Baking Company, sold pies in Utah that were manufactured in California. Continental and several other out-of-state pie makers sold cheaper in Utah than in California to compete in Salt Lake City. Price was the major form of competition for frozen pies. As Utah Pie lost market share and profits dropped due to intense price competition, it discovered Continental and other out-of-state competitors' practice of selling their pies at lower prices in Utah than in other markets closer to their plants. Utah Pie sued Continental and other out-of-state manufacturers, alleging that their price discrimination violated the Robinson-Patman Act.

ISSUE Did Continental's selling pies at different prices in different markets (California and Utah) violate Section 2 of the Clayton Act, as amended by the Robinson-Patman Act?

DECISION Possibly yes. There was enough evidence to show that competition was injured. The Supreme Court sent the case to a lower court for further proceedings. In other words, the evidence was strong enough to find that Continental and the other defendants discriminated in price to different buyers in different markets (Utah and California). The effect was likely to injure Utah Pie. Even though the total pie sales in Salt Lake City increased, this result does not mean Utah Pie was not injured. The Supreme Court noted that the downward pressure on prices was anticompetitive.

LEGAL TIP

If a business sells goods at different prices in different markets and injures competition, it breaks the Robinson-Patman Act (unless it establishes a defense).

Section 3 of the Clayton Act: Tying Arrangements, Exclusive Dealing, and Requirements Contracts

Section 3 regulates three practices: tying arrangements, exclusive dealing, and requirements contracts. Section 3 does not establish a per se rule. Therefore, not all tying arrangements, exclusive dealing, and requirements contracts are illegal, just certain ones. First, only those contracts dealing with goods are covered (services are not covered by Section 3). Second, the required effect of the prohibited practices must be present: they must substantially lessen competition or tend to create a monopoly. Third, Section 3 applies to the lease or sale of goods but not **consignments.** A consignment arises when the owner of goods puts them in the possession of someone else, who then tries to sell them for the owner.

We have been using the terms *tying arrangements, exclusive dealing,* and *requirements contracts.* Let us examine these terms more closely.

Tying arrangements A **tying arrangement** requires a buyer of goods to purchase another good from the seller—called the **tied product**—as a condition to purchasing what the buyer wants—called the **tying product.** Tying arrangements are considered bad because they restrain trade in the tied product; the buyer probably would not buy the tied product from the seller if he or she did not have an intense need for the tying product.

An example of an illegal tying arrangement under Section 3 of the Clayton Act would involve a data processing machine manufacturer who required consumers to purchase data cards as a condition for buying the data processing machines. Why let the data processing manufacturer extend the advantage of its unique data processing equipment to another market (data cards), where it otherwise has no advantage? Section 3 of the Clayton Act does not allow this to occur if the seller has significant economic power in the tying product and if sales of the tied product are "not insubstantial" (for example, $500,000).

Tying arrangements may also violate Section 1 of the Sherman Act. Remember that this Act imposes criminal sanctions but the Clayton Act does not. Also, the Sherman Act applies to the sale of services, while Section 3 of the Clayton Act does not.

Exclusive Dealing An **exclusive dealing** arrangement is an agreement in which the sale of a product is contingent on the buyer's agreement to deal only in that product or not to deal in a competitor's goods. This arrangement requires that a business sell *only* one brand of a particular item. For example, a drug manufacturer might require that a drugstore carry only its line of drugs as a condition to the manufacturer's selling to that particular druggist.

Not all exclusive dealing arrangements are illegal, just those that involve sales or leases of goods that may substantially lessen competition or tend to create a monopoly.

Requirements contracts **Requirements contracts** force one person (usually a business) to buy all of its needs of some commodity from a particular buyer. Requirements contracts violate Section 3 of the Clayton Act if they involve sales or leases of goods that may substantially lessen competition or tend to create a monopoly in any line of commerce.

Section 4 of the Clayton Act

Section 4 of the Clayton Act sets out civil remedies available under *all* federal antitrust laws. In other words, these remedies apply to the Sherman Act as well as to the Clayton Act (including Robinson-Patman).

Who may sue? Any person injured in his or her business or property in a way forbidden by the antitrust laws may sue. The suit may be brought in any United States District Court wherein the defendant resides or has an agent. The usual $10,000 minimum amount for a federal claim does not apply. Thus, claims smaller than $10,000 are permitted. However, antitrust claims are usually for larger amounts of money.

Amount of recovery The person injured by an antitrust violation may recover *three times the amount of the injury* (treble damages) to his or her business or property. **Treble damages** serve two purposes: they deter antitrust violations and create a private police force by encouraging private parties to enforce the antitrust laws.

The injured party may recover, in addition to treble damages, the cost of the suit, including reasonable attorney fees. One case involving attorney fees for 28 attorneys in a private antitrust case was settled for $67,640,000 and resulted in attorney fees (for the 28 attorneys) of $9,252,599.

Section 7 of the Clayton Act

Section 7, one of the most important sections of the Clayton Act, outlaws certain mergers.

What is a merger? In general, a merger occurs when one corporation buys enough of another corporation's stock or assets to give the buying corporation control over the company bought. Actually, the combination of firms can take several forms. The combining of two or more corporations to form a new corporation not previously existing is a consolidation. A merger technically occurs when two or more corporations combine, but one of the combining firms stays in existence, and the other becomes a part of (merges into) the survivor.

Accountants know an important fact about corporations: corporations consist of assets and equity claims (stock) on those assets, both of which can be bought. This fact was overlooked when the original Clayton Act, Section 7, was passed in 1914, since it outlawed only **stock mergers** but did not stop **asset mergers.** This loophole was corrected 36 years later (in 1950) by the Celler-Kefauver Amendment to the Clayton Act, which brought asset mergers within the scope of the Clayton Act.

Keys to Section 7 The Clayton Act, Section 7, does not make all mergers illegal; this just makes them illegal "where in any line of commerce in any section of the country the effect of such acquisition may be substantially to lessen competition or to tend to create a monopoly." There are several keys to understanding when Section 7 makes mergers illegal.

First key First, Section 7 tries to stop certain mergers in their incipiency (or before they start). Section 2 of the Sherman Act tolerated mergers too much. Section 7 of the Clayton Act introduced the incipiency idea to stop competitively harmful mergers at an early stage. The language in Section 7 that says "may be substantially to lessen competition or to tend to create a monopoly" shows the incipiency idea. Thus, Section 7 might stop a merger when there is no proven reduction in competition, but a decrease *tends* to occur.

Second key A second key to the Clayton Act, Section 7, is that mergers can be illegal even if not nationwide. Mergers "in any section of the country" can be illegal. Even a merger between corporations both located in one state can be illegal if a substantial effect on interstate commerce occurs.

Third key A third key to the Clayton Act, Section 7, is that it has been applied to horizontal, vertical, and conglomerate mergers. Again, not all are illegal, but any type of merger *might* be illegal. **Horizontal mergers** are between firms dealing with the same product on the same level (for example, two manufacturers or two retailers). **Vertical mergers** occur when corporations at different levels of business combine (for example, a manufacturer and a retail chain). Pure **conglomerate mergers** are between corporations in unrelated businesses (for example, an airplane manufacturer and a bank).

Fourth key A fourth key to Section 7 of the Clayton Act is that it does not make mergers illegal per se.

Defenses to Section 7 Charges

If one is charged with violating the **antimerger provision** of the Clayton Act, several defenses are available.

Merger not interstate commerce First, one could argue that the merger has no substantial effect on interstate commerce. Since the constitutional basis for the federal antitrust laws is the national government's power to regulate interstate commerce, no constitutional power exists to regulate purely intrastate (or local) matters.

Merger involves a failing company The **failing company defense** is another argument against a Clayton Act, Section 7 charge. If the acquired corporation was about to go out of business, its merger only makes inevitable what was about to happen anyway. Hence, one corporation's merger with a failing company does not violate Section 7.

Merger does not lessen competition A defense still available to Clayton Act Section 7 defendants is that the merger does not substantially lessen competition or tend to create a monopoly in any line of commerce, in any section of the country. Essentially, this defense says that the merger is not significant enough to be prohibited by Section 7. *United States* v. *Von's Grocery Co.,* the leading case on this subject, discusses how significant a merger must be before Section 7 will invalidate it.

Conglomerate Mergers

A conglomerate merger occurs when two (or more) corporations in different product markets combine into one corporation. An example is Swift & Co.'s acquisition of the Wilson Sporting Goods Company. Swift & Co. is a meat-packing firm.

Conglomerates present problems for the antitrust laws. First, because most conglomerates arose in the 1960's long *after* the Clayton Act was passed, the antitrust laws were not written to address them. Many conglomerates present no legal problems under Section 7 of the Clayton Act because they involve small or medium-sized firms. They pose no threat to competition "in any line of commerce in any section of the country."

UNITED STATES v. VON'S GROCERY CO.

U.S. Supreme Court.
384 U.S. 270 (1966).

FACTS In 1960 the United States sued Von's Grocery Company (Von's) under Section 7 of the Clayton Act. Von's, a large Los Angeles (LA) retail supermarket chain, merged with Shopping Bag Food Stores, another LA chain. The relevant market was the retail grocery market. Before the merger, Von's ranked third in area retail sales, and Shopping Bag ranked sixth. After the merger their combined market share was 7.5% of the total $2.5 billion dollar market in annual sales. Both Von's and Shopping Bag were highly successful, aggressive competitors *before* the merger. *After* the merger, they were the second largest grocery chain in LA. The District Court found the merger did not violate Section 7 of the Clayton Act. The United States appealed to the Supreme Court.

ISSUE Does the merger of two retail chains, resulting in a firm with a 7.5% market share, "tend substantially to lessen competition" and therefore violate Section 7 of the Clayton Act?

DECISION Yes. The merger was illegal. There was a long-term trend toward concentration in the Los Angeles grocery market. Neither of the merging companies was failing. Both were successful, aggressive competitors before the merger, and Section 7 of the Clayton Act tries to stop monopolies in their incipiency. This merger was part of "exactly the sort of trend which Congress . . . declared must be arrested."

LEGAL TIP

Section 7 of the Clayton Act can stop mergers between businesses even if they are both in one section of the country.

Prohibition of Interlocking Corporate Directorates

Section 8 of the Clayton Act prohibits persons from being directors of competing corporations. Specifically, to violate Section 8 three elements must exist: First, one of the corporations must have a net worth of at least $1 million. Second, the corporations must be competitors (have a horizontal market relationship). Third, the relationship between the competing corporations must be such that eliminating competition by agreement between them would violate any federal antitrust law.

From these tests, it is clear that not all **interlocking directorates** are illegal under Section 8. For example, if the corporations do not compete, one person can be a director of both. If both corporations are small (neither has a net worth of $1 million), one person could be on the board of each. Section 8 was intended to be preventive. It is therefore not necessary that a violation of any antitrust law actually occur during the period of simultaneous service.

KEY TERMS

Clayton Act
Robinson-Patman Act
Primary-line injury
Secondary-line injury
Consignments
Tying arrangements
Tied product
Tying product
Exclusive dealing
Requirements contracts
Treble damages
Stock mergers
Asset mergers
Horizontal mergers
Vertical mergers
Conglomerate mergers
Antimerger provision
Failing company defense
Interlocking directorates

CHAPTER PROBLEMS

1. Who enforces the Clayton Act?
2. Does Section 2 of the Clayton Act (also called the Robinson-Patman Act) prevent price fixing of services?
3. If a seller gives different prices to two competing buyers, is this primary-line or secondary-line price discrimination?
4. Name the six elements of a Robinson-Patman Act violation.
5. Give four defenses against a Robinson-Patman Act charge.
6. What three practices does Section 3 of the Clayton Act prohibit?
7. Seller B offers buyer C a case of beer for $2 if C will also agree to buy four jars of mustard for $1 each. Identify the tied and tying products.
8. What does Section 7 of the Clayton Act prohibit?

*9. Is photographic work a service and therefore not covered by the Robinson-Patman Act? *Burge v. Bryant Public School Dist. of Saline County,* 658 F.2d 611 (8th Cir., Ark. 1981).

*10. If two Dallas, Texas area garbage collection companies merge and have 48.8% of the Dallas market after the merger, does this violate Section 7 of the Clayton Act? *United States v. Waste Management, Inc.,* 743 F.2d 976 (2nd Cir. 1984).

"The careless and the unscrupulous must rise to the standards of the scrupulous and diligent. The FTC was not organized to drag standards down."

Justice Cardozo in *FTC v. Algoma Lumber* 291 U.S. 67 (1934)

Chapter 15

The Federal Trade Commission

CHAPTER PREVIEW

- Two main purposes of the Federal Trade Commission (FTC)
- The number of FTC commissioners and how they get their jobs
- Laws that the FTC enforces
- Section 5 of the FTC Act
- Corrective advertising
- Information funeral homes must give to consumers
- Testimonial advertising and FTC limitations

Harold Bryant was angry. He owned a funeral home and "unit priced" funerals so people would not have to worry about details during a time of grief. Bryant never gave out price information over the phone since there were different "grades" of funerals. It was easier to show customers the differences in caskets and services than explain them over the telephone. Bryant learned that the Federal Trade Commission (FTC) had made a rule concerning these practices. Harold sued the FTC, claiming that it lacked evidence of funeral abuses to justify changing the way all funeral directors had to act. He also claimed that the FTC's funeral home regulation violated his free speech. Was Bryant right?

Listerine Antiseptic Mouthwash has been sold since 1879. Listerine's formula has never been changed and has always had a reputation for helping consumers cope with colds, cold symptoms, and sore throats. Warner-Lambert, the manufacturer, began advertising Listerine's cold and other curative qualities to consumers in 1921. In 1972, following a hearing, the FTC ordered Warner-Lambert to cease and desist advertising that Listerine prevents, cures, or alleviates the common cold. The FTC also ordered the following corrective statement in future Listerine ads: "Contrary to prior advertising, Listerine will not help prevent colds or sore throats or lessen their severity." The Warner-Lambert executives thought that the FTC corrective advertising order was illegal. Was it?

THE FEDERAL TRADE COMMISSION

Purposes The **Federal Trade Commission** (FTC) was created in 1914. The FTC has two main functions: consumer protection and maintenance of economic competition. In other words, the FTC tries to encourage free and fair business competition.

What is the FTC? The FTC is a federal *independent* administrative agency. The FTC is not part of the executive, legislative, or judicial branches of the federal government. It stands alone. The FTC's "independent" label may be misleading, since this agency gets money from Congress, and the five FTC commissioners are presidential appointees confirmed by the United States Senate. Thus, the FTC is *legally* independent but *economically* dependent on Congress. Also, the president and Congress could simply pass a law at any time to eliminate the FTC or sharply reduce its functions. In 1980, this result almost occurred when the FTC's consumer protection duties were viewed as extreme.

The FTC Commissioners

Job appointments There are five FTC commissioners appointed by the president. The FTC Commissioners are appointed for seven-year staggered terms and must be confirmed by the Senate before taking office. Only three of the commissioners may be from the same political party. One of the commissioners is designated by the president as chairperson.

FTC employees The five FTC commissioners have help in carrying out the FTC's duties. The FTC had an annual budget of $70 million and 1274 employees in fiscal year 1982. It has offices both in and outside of Washington, DC.

Figure 15-1 is an FTC organizational chart. The cities at the bottom of the chart indicate locations of FTC regional offices. These offices are the usual starting point of the average business or consumer who wants to contact the FTC.

Laws the FTC Enforces: An Overview

To accomplish its general duties of consumer protection and maintenance of economic competition, the FTC administers many statutes.

1. *The Federal Trade Commission Act.* The Federal Trade Commission Act, among other things, authorizes the FTC to stop unfair acts or practices and unfair methods of competition in interstate commerce.
2. *The Wheeler-Lea Act.* This act amended the Federal Trade Commission Act allowing the FTC to stop unfair competition even if a competitor were not shown to be harmed by a business practice. It is enough to violate Section 5 of the FTC Act after the Wheeler-Lea Act was passed if a *consumer* is injured by deceptive acts or practices.
3. *The Clayton Act.* The Clayton Act was described in Chapter 14. The FTC has concurrent jurisdiction with the Justice Department and private parties to enforce this Act.
4. *The Robinson-Patman Act.* The Robinson-Patman Act, like the Clayton Act, was described in Chapter 14. The FTC has concurrent jurisdiction with the Justice Department and private parites to enforce this Act.

Figure 15-1 **Federal Trade Commission**

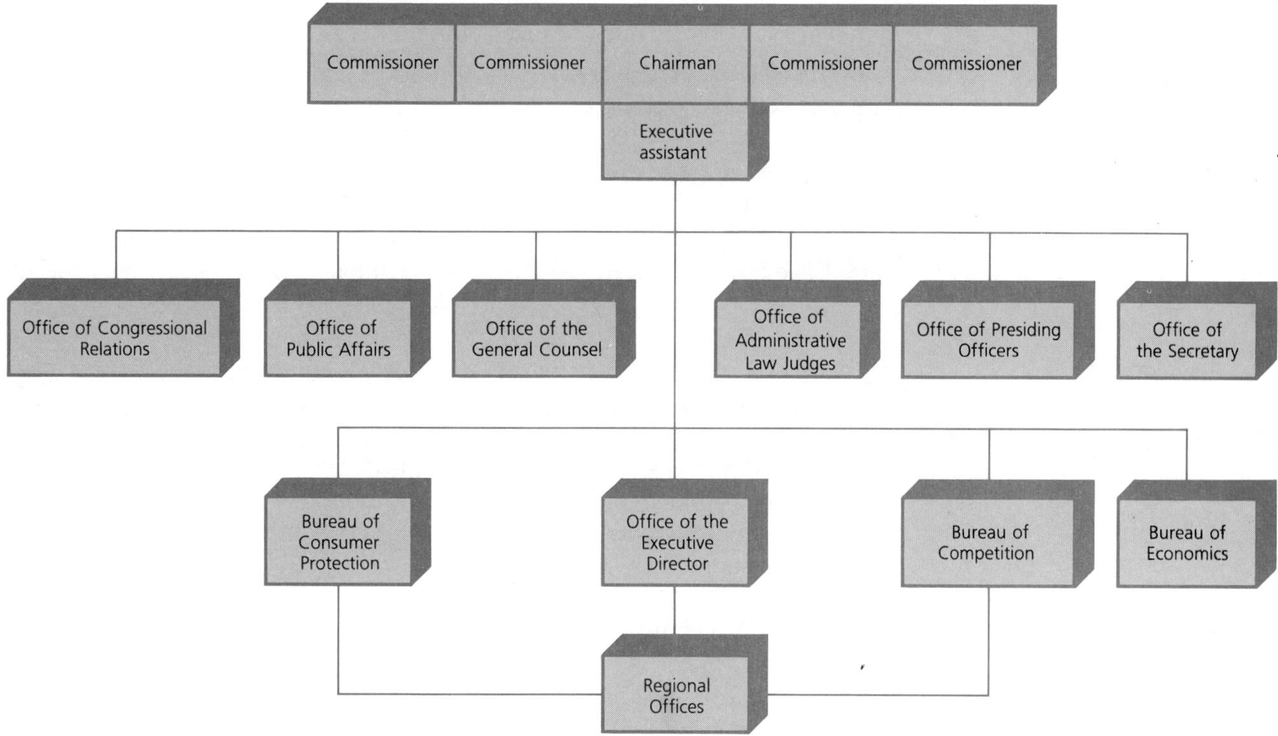

5. *The Magnuson-Moss Warranty/FTC Improvement Act.* This act modifies the Holder-in-Due-Course Rule in certain cases where consumer goods are bought on credit.
6. *The Lanham Trade-Mark Act.* This statute provides for the federal registration and protection of trademarks.
7. *The Truth-in-Lending Acts.* These laws require disclosure of all interest and other finance charges. They also put some limits on garnishments and limit credit-card liability to $50 if another person uses the card without authorization.
8. *The Fair Credit Reporting Act.* This law protects consumers against the circulation of inaccurate or obsolete credit reports and controls consumer reporting agencies.
9. *The Export Trade Act.* The FTC supervises registration and operation of associations of American exporters as a result of this law.
10. *The Wool Products Labeling Act, the Fur Products Labeling Act, and the Textile Fiber Products Identification Act.* These three laws deal with truthful labeling of textile and fur products.
11. *The Fair Packaging and Labeling Act.* This law's goal is regulating packaging and labeling of certain consumer commodities to facilitate consumer comparisons and stop consumer deception.

Three FTC Functions

The FTC has three major functions:

1. It legislates (makes rules or regulations).
2. It executes (enforces) its rules.
3. It gives hearings (like trials) to persons accused of violating rules, or regulations.

Legislating **Legislating** means that the FTC makes regulations. In other words, the Commission refers to the steps that a regulator must follow in making a regulation. Basically, this is the notice of proposed rulemaking, a public comment period, and promulgation of the regulation. Chapter 9 covers this process in detail.

An Example of an FTC Rule: Regulation of Funeral Costs

On January 1, 1984, and April 30, 1984, two parts of an FTC rule regulating the funeral industry took effect. Before the rule took effect, certain funeral homes sometimes engaged in deceptive sales techniques. For example, many funeral homes would not indicate the cost of individual funeral goods and services (such as caskets, embalmment, cremation, and use of the funeral home). Many funeral homes also would not give information over the telephone.

Here are some of the FTC funeral home regulations now in effect:

1. Funeral homes must give consumers an itemized list of services and materials which they offer.
2. Funeral homes must give this itemized list *before* a person agrees to any arrangements.
3. Funeral homes must give price information over the telephone if consumers call and ask for it.
4. Funeral homes may not misrepresent state laws dealing with embalmment, which is usually required only when a certain contagious disease (such as diptheria or tuberculosis) causes death. No state law requires embalmment.

Case challenging FTC funeral regulations The FTC funeral regulations are controversial. These rules were challenged but upheld in the *Harry and Bryant Co. v. FTC* case.

Executive function The **executive function** of the FTC involves investigating and prosecuting violations of statutes and regulations. The executive function also involves issuing advisory opinions.

Judging The FTC also holds hearings for persons accused of violating FTC rules. Technically one of three persons (or groups of persons) may run the hearing: the five FTC commissioners, one or more FTC commissioners, or an administrative law judge (ALJ). The results of FTC hearings may be appealed to the court system. The FTC does not have the power to fine or imprison anyone.

The Federal Trade Commission Act: Section 5

The Federal Trade Commission Act of 1914 created the FTC. Section 5 of that law empowered the FTC to prevent "unfair methods of competition." Today the FTC can challenge business practices under Section 5 if they injure either competitors *or* consumers.

HARRY AND BRYANT CO. v. FTC

U.S. Court of Appeals (4th Cir.).
726 F.2d 993 (1984).

FACTS Persons buying funeral goods and services complained to the FTC. Consumers said that they could not learn the price of purchasing a casket or using a funeral parlor; therefore, many consumers were forced to have their loved one's body embalmed when state law did not require it. In 1972 the FTC began investigating funeral homes across the United States. As a result, the FTC started to regulate the funeral industry. The FTC published a proposed rule in the *Federal Register* and gave reasons for this proposal. The FTC asked for public comments on the proposed rule and held hearings in six cities across the United States in 1976. At the hearings, the presiding officer let a limited number of witnesses testify about the proposed rule. He let equal numbers of pro-rule (generally consumers) and anti-rule witnesses (generally funeral home owners) testify about the proposed rule, even though more anti-rule witnesses had applied. The presiding officer also refused to let the anti-rule persons cross-examine consumers whose written complaints became part of the record. Mr. Bryant owned a funeral home and claimed that the FTC lacked substantial evidence to support the proposed funeral home rule. Despite this claim, the FTC passed the funeral home rule. Mr. Bryant and other funeral home owners sued the FTC, raising the objections mentioned above.

ISSUE Did the FTC conduct the funeral home rulemaking properly? Did the FTC have substantial evidence to support the funeral home rule?

DECISION Yes to both issues. The United States Court of Appeals said that Mr. Bryant and other anti-rule persons had no right under the FTC Improvements Act to cross-examine consumers. The court said that when the FTC made the funeral home rule, it was a rulemaking and not a trial, or a judicial proceeding. At trials there are more rights to cross-examine and testify. Limiting the number of persons testifying in favor of and against the rule was within the FTC's discretion and helped the Commission run an orderly hearing. The court examined consumer complaints against funeral home practices (such as unit pricing) and concluded that there was substantial evidence to justify the funeral home rule.

LEGAL TIP

When the FTC makes a rule, people do not have as many rights as they do in jury trials to cross-examine and present witnesses.

Consumer authority to enforce Section 5 Consumers have no authority to enforce Section 5 of the FTC Act. Consumers must rely on FTC enforcement.

How broad is Section 5? Different views are held about the power to stop unfair methods of competition, acts, or practices. Regulators at the FTC and many others favor this broad language, which enables them to attack novel forms of unfair competition or deceptive practices that were not thought of when the FTC Act was passed.

On the other hand, business people who might be subject to overly enthusiastic FTC regulators question the fairness of vague language that might prohibit unspecified business conduct. For instance, how is a business to know whether a planned marketing campaign is legal or subject to FTC attack as unfair or deceptive competition, acts, or practices? After all, the United States Constitution requires that procedural due process by given, meaning that laws must give notice of what they prohibit and must not be vague. (An answer to this problem is provided by the FTC's **advisory opinion,** a device, which allows the FTC to tell business in advance if a proposed business practice violates Section 5. The United States Supreme Court explained why Section 5 of the FTC Act is vague in the *FTC v. Sperry & Hutchinson Co.* case.

FTC v. SPERRY & HUTCHINSON CO.

U.S. Supreme Court.
405 U.S. 233 (1972).

FACTS Sperry and Hutchinson Co. (S & H) sold trading stamps to retailers such as supermarkets and gas stations. The stamps encouraged consumers to buy from retailers issuing the stamps since consumers could turn in books of stamps for "free" merchandise at S & H redemption centers. To overcome the competitive advantage of merchants giving green stamps, those who did not devised a scheme to sell their goods at lower prices if consumers *gave the merchant* green stamps. This plan reduced the incentive for consumers to buy from retailers offering green stamps. Professional trading stamp exchanges were also developed, where consumers with unused S & H stamps could either trade them for other types of stamps (such as gold or yellow) or sell them to the exchange. S & H tired to kill unauthorized stamp exchanges by suing and obtaining 43 injunctions (court orders to stop a business from operating) against unauthorized stamp exchanges between 1957 and 1965. S & H also threatened to sue 140 other unauthorized exchanges, which usually forced unauthorized exchanges to stop allowing consumers to trade stamps. To maintain the element of fair business, the FTC ordered S & H to stop suppressing competition in stamp exchanges. S & H appealed to the United States Court of Appeals, arguing that the FTC could not stop them from suing and threatening to sue unauthorized trading stamp exchanges and redemption centers. S & H said that the FTC only could stop a competitive practice as "unfair" (under Section 5 of the FTC Act) if the action violated the federal antitrust laws. The Court of Appeals agreed with S & H and reversed the FTC's order. The FTC appealed to the United States Supreme Court.

ISSUE Was S & H's practice of suing and threatening to sue unauthorized stamp exchanges and redemption centers "unfair" under Section 5 of the FTC Act, even though S & H broke no other antitrust law?

DECISION Yes. The Supreme Court reversed the decision made by the Court of Appeals, deciding that S & H had violated Section 5 of the FTC Act by suing and threatening to sue competitors for merely competing with S & H. Section 5 protects consumers—not just competitors. (In this case, the unauthorized stamp exchanges and redemption centers *helped* consumers.) Therefore, a competitor can violate Section 5 even though that conduct does not break the Sherman Act, Clayton Act, or Robinson-Patman Act. This decision helps the FTC stop more unfair practices than just those that the other antitrust laws stop. The vagueness of Section 5 helps the FTC stop new kinds of unfair competition.

LEGAL TIP

The FTC can attack many anticompetitive practices under Section 5 of the FTC Act. Business practices may be legal under other federal antitrust laws and still break Section 5 of the FTC Act as "unfair competition."

Corrective Advertising

Corrective advertising is business advertising that admits in some way that the product does not do or have some characteristic that it appears to.

Justification A justification for corrective advertising is to correct mistaken consumer beliefs about a product, which may be the result of past advertising claims. Suppose, for example, that a business advertises a mouthwash as curing or preventing colds and sore throats. Since the mouthwash does not in fact cure or prevent colds and sore throats, the manufacturer may stop these claims; however, consumers might still believe the previous claims, based on false advertising from the past. To correct the consumers' mistaken present beliefs based on the prior false ads, future corrective ads are required.

The Listerine case The mouthwash case itself, informally known as the "Listerine case" and formally as the *Warner-Lambert Co. v. FTC* case, was decided in 1977. Read the case to see how the FTC forced Warner-Lambert to incorporate corrective advertising in their next $10 million of advertising.

WARNER-LAMBERT CO. v. FTC

U.S. Court of Appeals (D.C. Cir.).
562 F.2d 749 (1977).

FACTS Warner-Lambert Company (W-L) made and sold Listerine mouthwash since 1879. The formula had never changed. Since 1879 the seller claimed that Listerine was beneficial in helping to cure colds, cold symptoms, and sore throats. Direct advertising of Listerine to consumers began in 1921. In 1972 the FTC issued a complaint charging W-L with violating Section 5 of the FTC Act. The FTC claimed W-L misrepresented Listerine's effectiveness against common colds. An ALJ (administrative law judge) hearing concluded there was no proof that Listerine helped stop, prevent, or cure colds. The FTC affirmed the ALJ's decision, ordering W-L to stop advertising that Listerine would cure, prevent, or stop colds and sore throats. The FTC also ordered W-L to put the following statement in Listerine's next $10 million of ads: "Contrary to prior advertising, Listerine will not help prevent colds or sore throats or lessen their severity." W-L appealed this order to the United States Court of Appeals. W-L argued that there was no substantial evidence for the FTC order. W-L also argued the FTC had no power to order corrective advertising.

ISSUE Was the FTC's order supported by substantial evidence? Did the FTC have the power to order corrective advertising?

DECISION The United States Court of Appeals said that substantial evidence existed, showing that Listerine did not live up to claims made by prior advertising. The court also upheld the FTC's power to order corrective advertising, saying that the FTC has the power to "shape" remedies. However, Congress did not tell the FTC what remedies it could impose if someone violated Section 5 of the FTC Act. Congress wanted the FTC to have broad discretion when considering remedies. The FTC's corrective advertising order helped information reach the public, which corrected past Listerine ads.

LEGAL TIP

Businesspeople should only advertise product features they can prove. The FTC has the power to force advertisers to correct past incorrect ads.

Use of Testimonials and Endorsements in Ads

The FTC has promulgated guides for advertising **testimonials** and **endorsements.** The Commission treats the two similarly. Businesses must follow FTC rules when advertising "in commerce" (that is, when an ad affects interstate commerce.)

An endorsement or testimonial encourages consumers to think that the advertised message is the *honest* belief, opinion, experience, or finding of someone *other than* the sponsoring advertiser. These statements may not contain representations unsupported by facts.

For example, a newspaper ad includes a quote and signature line from a film critic's review that says: "This movie is the best picture of the year; *John Adams, critic.*" The review is an endorsement because the critic gives his *own* opinion—not the film producer's or exhibitor's. Therefore, any quote not fairly representing the review's general opinion violates FTC standards.

KEY TERMS

Federal Trade Commission
Legislating
Executive function
Advisory opinion
Corrective advertising
Testimonials
Endorsements

CHAPTER PROBLEMS

1. What are the two purposes of the FTC?
2. How many FTC commissioners are there?
3. How many people work for the FTC?
4. Where would the average consumer file a complaint with the FTC?
5. Evelyn Cherry could not stop crying; her brother had suddenly died. Evelyn's sister-in-law was upset and asked Evelyn to handle the funeral arrangements. Evelyn phoned three local funeral homes, which all refused to give prices over the telephone. Evelyn then visited the funeral homes. One owner said that state law required embalmment in all deaths. (Evelyn later learned that this was untrue.) Another owner said he priced funerals as a unit and did not give prices on individual items or services. What rights does Evelyn have?
6. Who can enforce Section 5 of the FTC Act?
7. Are all businesses, honest businesses, consumers, FTC employees, or someone else helped by the FTC?
8. Can the FTC order a firm to correct past claims in future advertising?

*9. May consumers and competitors sue alleged wrongdoers under Section 5 of the FTC Act? The answer is "No". Only the FTC may sue. Private litigants continue to raise such claims hoping that a court will allow them. In one case, tobacco had been water-damaged while being shipped from England to the United States. The tobacco belonged to Alfred Dunhill Limited, a high-quality manufacturer, which used tobacco tins with Dunhill's trademark. Dunhill collected from its insurer for the damaged tobacco. The insurer salvaged the tobacco, which was bought by Interstate Cigar Company, Inc. (Interstate). No conditions were placed on Interstate when the company bought the salvaged tobacco, even though the tobacco still was in the Dunhill tins. Dunhill learned of the sale to Interstate and demanded that Interstate mark the tins as salvaged tobacco or stop selling them. Evidence showed that retailers sold the tobacco in the Dunhill tins at very low prices but did not label it as salvaged. Dunhill sued Interstate under Section 5 of the FTC Act, claiming that such sales involved unfair competition. What was the result? *Alfred Dunhill Limited v. Interstate Cigar Company, Inc.*, 499 F.2d 232 (1974).

*10. A television advertisement for golf balls shows a prominent and well-recognized pro golfer hitting golf balls. Would this advertisement be an endorsement by the golfer, even if he says nothing? 16 CFR 2550, example 5 (1985).

"*Ticker tape ain't spaghetti.*"
Fiorello La Guardia

Chapter 16

Securities Regulation

CHAPTER PREVIEW

- Federal definition of "security," covers many types of investments
- The Howey test for defining a security
- The objective of the Securities Act of 1933
- The Securities Act of 1933
- Meaning of "registration"
- Exempt transactions
- Exempt securities
- Elements of a Section 11 case under the Securities Act of 1933
- Provisions of the Securities Exchange Act of 1934
- "Insiders" under Rule 16(b)

"How could this happen?" Mort Zaretsky screamed to his wife, Betty. The Zaretskys had put their entire life savings of $25,000 in the hands of a stockbroker. They had told him to invest the money conservatively to help in their retirement. After 15 months, their broker had made 147 separate sales and purchases for their account. The Zaretskys owed $24,664.24 for commissions, fees, taxes, and margin interest. Did they have to pay this?

Federal securities laws are controversial, and investors' thoughts on the subject vary. Some say, "These laws are great because they give me information and protection if something goes wrong." Other investors are ignorant about protections that such laws provide.

Businesses subject to federal securities laws also have mixed feelings about such rules. Some firms see such laws as evidence of the heavy hand of government regulation and claim that the laws add compliance costs and slow securities marketing. Some firms also say that such laws give the average investor more information than he or she needs to make an investment decision. Other businesses accept securities regulations as a fact of life; they see these laws as necessary protection against scoundrels. If this result is achieved, the public does not lose confidence in the many reputable securities businesses.

OVERVIEW OF THE FEDERAL SECURITIES LAWS

Federal securities laws refer to six federal laws passed between 1933 and 1940, two enacted in the 1970's, and one passed in 1984.

1. The Securities Act of 1933.
2. The Securities Exchange Act of 1934.
3. The Public Utility Holding Company Act of 1935.
4. The Trust Indenture Act of 1939.
5. The Investment Company Act of 1940.
6. The Investment Advisers Act of 1940.
7. The Securities Investor Protection Act of 1970.
8. The Foreign Corrupt Practices Act of 1977.
9. The Insider Trading Sanctions Act of 1984.

We shall look at each of these briefly and then examine in depth the Securities Act of 1933, the Securities Exchange Act of 1934, and the Foreign Corrupt Practices Act of 1977 (an amendment to the 1934 Act).

Securities Act of 1933 The **Securities Act of 1933** (SA) sets out the rules for selling securities to the investing public. This Act basically deals with the primary market, or the sale of "new" or "just issued" securities. The main requirement is that securities be registered with the federal Securities and Exchange Commission before they are offered or sold.

Securities Exchange Act of 1934 Regulating all of the *old* securities bought and sold daily in the *secondary markets* is a job of the **Securities Exchange Act of 1934** (SEA). The SEA also created the Securities and Exchange Commission (SEC) to administer and enforce the federal securities laws.

Public Utility Holding Company Act of 1935 The Public Utility Holding Company Act of 1935 (PUHCA), administered by the SEC, aims to stop abuses in the financing and operations of gas and electric public utility holding companies.

Trust Indenture Act of 1937 The Trust Indenture Act of 1937 (TIA) regulates the sale of debt securities (such as bonds) to the public. The law requires debt securities registered under the SA to satisfy TIA's requirements as well. The TIA requires that the debt contract (trust indenture) contain certain provisions (which the SA does not require) to protect investors. Some debt arrangements have a trustee who is supposed to look out for the lenders' (creditors') interests. The TIA requires that the trustee be independent of obligations other than those of the investors that the trustee is supposed to represent.

Investment Company Act of 1940 The Investment Company Act of 1940 (ICA) lets the SEC regulate publicly owned companies that invest and trade in securities. Selection of managers, managers' salaries, size of sales charges, investment strategies, and other related matters are controlled by ICA authority.

Investment Advisers Act of 1940 The Investment Advisers Act of 1940 (IAA) gives the SEC the authority to regulate investment advisors, who are people advising others about financial investments.

Securities Investor Protection Act of 1970 The Securities Investor Protection Act of 1970 (SIPA) set up a federal corporation (called the Securities Investor Protection Corporation, or SIPC) to administer the liquidation of brokerage firms with financial problems. For example, an investor whose stockbroker is forced out of business by financial problems would present his or her claims to SIPC for payment.

Foreign Corrupt Practices Act of 1977 The Foreign Corrupt Practices Act of 1977 (FCPA) grew out of revelations in the 1970's that United States business would sometimes have to bribe foreign government officials, political parties, or political candidates to get business. The FCPA prohibits certain bribes to foreign officials and requires that certain businesses set up systems of internal control, enabling responsible managers to be aware of such activity. Greater discussion of this important law follows in the chapter on international law. (Chapter 61)

Insider Trading Sanctions Act of 1984 In recent years, scandals have occurred involving corporate insider trading. This problem undermines public confidence in the securities markets. To increase the risk for trading on inside information, Congress enacted the Insider Trading Sanctions Act of 1984, which significantly increased possible punishment for such activity.

Definition of a Security

A basic inquiry of this chapter is: What is a security? "Security" might have different definitions in various statutes. To be safe, one should see if and how security is defined for a particular statute.

Substance, not form **Securities** usually includes shares of stock. In one case, however, the United States Supreme Court said that shares of stock in a cooperative housing corporation were not securities, reasoning that the incentive for buying was solely to get low-cost housing and not to invest for a profit. The Supreme Court emphasized that form should be disregarded for substance and that economic reality should be stressed. Thus, the fact that something is called stock does not conclusively mean that it is a security for purposes of a particular federal securities statute. Security is not limited to equity (ownership) interests.

Howey test One problem area in defining "security" is investment contracts. Often no piece of paper called a "security" or "stock" is involved. Yet courts have often said that investment contracts are securities. In *SEC v. Howey* [328 U.S. 293 (1946)], the United States Supreme Court said that an investment contract is a security if "the person invests his money in a common enterprise and is led to expect profits solely from the efforts of the promoter or a third party." This principle is known as the **Howey test.**

The *SEC v. Howey* case held that separate rows of orange trees accompanied by contracts to cultivate, pick, and sell the oranges were securities under the Securities Act of 1933. Other investment contracts that have been declared securities in given situations include whiskey warehouse receipts, merchandise marketing programs, oil drilling investment programs, farm lands and animals, and condominiums.

Recent cutback on securities protection In recent years, the changed composition of the United States Supreme Court has led to a narrower definition of *security*. The *International Brotherhood of Teamsters v. Daniel* case is evidence of this trend. In this case, the United States Supreme Court decided that a non-

INTERNATIONAL BROTHERHOOD OF TEAMSTERS v. DANIEL

U.S. Supreme Court.
99 S.Ct. 790 (1979).

FACTS Daniel had worked as a truck driver for twenty years. His employer had entered a collective bargaining agreement with several trucking firms. Part of that agreement was an employee pension plan, which required all *employers* to pay into the plan for employees. Individual *employees* made no contribution but they all had to join the plan. To be eligible for a pension, an employee had to have twenty years of continuous service. When Daniel applied for his pension, it was denied on grounds that Daniel had had a break in service and therefore had not worked twenty *continuous* years for his employer. Daniel was shocked and sued the union and pension fund trustee on grounds that they had omitted material facts on the value of the employee's interest in the pension plan. Daniel alleged that his interest in the pension was a security under Section 10(b) of the Securities Exchange Act of 1934. He further argued that the omissions in the pension plan were fraud under Section 10(b) of the Securities Exchange Act of 1934. He further argued that the omissions in the pension plan were fraud under Section 10(b) of the Securities Exchange Act of 1934 and Rule 10b-5. The Federal District Court and United States Court of Appeals both held that Daniel's interest in the pension fund was a security. The union appealed to the United States Supreme Court.

ISSUE Was the employee's interest in the non-contributory, compulsory pension plan a "security" under the Securities Exchange Act of 1934 and the Securities Act of 1933? (Daniel also brought a claim under the Securities Act of 1933.)

DECISION No. An employee's interest in a non-contributory, compulsory pension plan was not a "security" under the Securities Exchange Act of 1934 and the Securities Act of 1933. The pension plan was not an "investment contract." The definition of "investment contract" is a scheme involving investment of money in a common enterprise with profits to come solely from others' efforts. In this case, the Supreme Court said that an employee's participation in a non-contributory, compulsory pension plan did not agree with the commonly held idea of investment contract. Regarding the "investing money" part of the definition of "security," the investment here is a relatively insignificant part of the total and indivisible employee pay package. The employee is really selling his or her labor to make a living, not making a future investment. Regarding the "profit expectation" part of the definition, the employee has too small of a chance of taking part in the pension fund's earnings to call it a "profit expectation." Therefore, the federal securities laws did not help this retired truck driver get his pension.

LEGAL TIP

An employee who does not get his or her pension because of "fine print" in the pension contract will get little help from federal securities laws.

contributory compulsory pension plan was not a security for purposes of either the Securities Act of 1933 or the Securities Exchange Act of 1934.

Securities Act of 1933

Objective The main objective of the Securities Act of 1933 (SA) is to provide the public with full and fair disclosure about new securities offered for sale.

Main requirement Issuers of new securities must register them with the SEC before offering them to the public. Registration takes place when the SEC files a submitted registration statement. It is *illegal* to offer or sell securities in interstate commerce or through the mails *unless* one first registers them.

A registration statement consists of two parts: a **prospectus** and Part II. A copy of the prospectus must be given to the security buyer before or when the purchase occurs. The prospectus contains detailed information about the issuer, the business, its officers, directors, assets, and liabilities. As a practical matter, many buyers never ask for or read the prospectus before placing an order with their broker, which throws away a large part of the SA's protection. Undoubtedly, many investors do not want to wade through the details in a prospectus. Instead, they rely on their broker's judgments and the implied threat of withholding future business if the broker makes a mistake. Part II of the registration statement (containing various exhibits) need not ever be given to the investor. This statement is available for public inspection at the SEC.

Registering securities under the Securities Act An issuer files information with the SEC in a proposed registration statement. Many professionals (such as accountants, lawyers, underwriters, engineers, and possibly geologists) might contribute to a particular registration statement. An issuer may not offer a security for sale until the registration statement becomes effective. This process automatically occurs twenty days after the issuer files the proposed registration statement with the SEC. (This twenty-day period is called the "waiting period.") However, the SEC may accelerate or delay the registration statement's effective date. Delays occur because the SEC believes that the registration statement misleads, omits, or falsely states information that investors need to evaluate the security.

What registration means The SEC does not judge a security's merits as an investment (that is, the SEC does not stamp a security "a good buy" or "fool's gold"). Instead, the SEC merely determines if the registration statement gives prospective investors full and fair disclosure of facts pertinent to making an investment decision. It cannot be stressed too strongly that a security registered with the SEC does *not* signify that the SEC thinks the security is a good investment.

Exemptions Persons thinking about selling securities should check the **exemptions.** There are exempt securities as well as exempt transactions. Basically, exemptions mean that the security does not have to be registered, which saves the security seller time and money. The security buyer could also save money, too, if the seller's saving is passed on to the buyer. Exemptions also reduce investor protection.

Civil Liability Under the Securities Act of 1933

People can be civilly liable under the Securities Act of 1933 (SA) if they offer or sell unregistered securities (a violation of Section 5 of SA) or if the registration statement has material omissions or misstatements (a violation of Section 11 of SA). Section 11 violations deal *only* with securities registered under the SA. Section 12 of the SA puts civil liability on those committing fraud in the sale or offer of *any* security even if not registered under the SA. The remainder of this section deals with Section 11, (material omissions or misstatements in the registration statements), violations.

Section 11 claims Section 11 of the SA allows those acquiring a security covered by a registration statement to recover damages if they show the following:

1. They acquired the security.
2. A registration statement covers the security.
3. The registration statement has a material misstatement or omission.
4. They lost money on the security.

Note that the investors need not show that they relied on the registration statement.

Section 11 defendants The following individuals can be sued in a Section 11 claim:

1. Signers of the security's registration statement (the issuer, the issuer's chief executive, financial and accounting officers, and a majority of the board *all must* sign the registration statement; they all may therefore be sued).
2. All directors.
3. All persons who agree to be directors.
4. Experts agreeing to be named as having prepared all or part of the registration statement (which might include, among others, geologists, lawyers, accountants, and engineers).
5. All underwriters.

Extent of liability Not only may all of the above individuals be sued on a Section 11 claim, but each is jointly and severally liable for the claim. This means that if an investor lost $100,000 and a director signed the registration statement, that individual director could be forced to pay the entire $100,000. (Assuming the director paid the entire claim, he or she would have a right of contribution from others liable for their proportionate share of the loss.) Experts are liable *only* for the material omissions or misstatements in the *part* of the registration statement with which they were involved.

Defenses to Section 11 Given the great liabilities facing a wide variety of persons under Section 11, the following defenses are available:

1. *Due diligence.* Most defendants can raise the due diligence defense. However, the issuer may not, since he or she is liable in virtually all cases for material omissions or misstatements. Due diligence means that the individuals sued satisfied the standard of care regarding the accuracy and completeness of information in their part of the registration statement. If an expert (such as a lawyer) is involved, he or she has to meet the due diligence of his or her profession.

2. *Immateriality.* An omission or misstatement in the registration statement that is immaterial (a matter that the average, prudent investor ought not to know about before buying the security) is a defense. This defense is part of the plaintiff security buyer's case to show that the omission or misstatement was material. However, the defendant can rebut this defense.
3. *Purchaser knowledge.* The defendant's ability to show that the purchaser knew of the omission or misstatement when the security was brought is a defense.
4. *Other causes of damages.* A defendant can escape liability under Section 11 by showing that the plaintiff's loss was from causes *other than* the material omission or misstatement. For example, a general economic recession could account for a decline of the stock of all firms in an industry, significantly apart from omissions or misstatements in the registration statements.
5. *No reliance.* A Section 11 plaintiff need not prove reliance on the material error or omission. A defendant may, however, escape liability by proving that the plaintiff did not rely on the error or omission, which is almost impossible. However, if a plaintiff bought the security after the issuer released an income statement covering a period of a year or more *after* the registration statement took effect, the *plaintiff must show reliance* on the omission or misstatement.
6. *Statute of limitations.* A peculiar one-year-three-year statute of limitations exists for SA civil violations. Suits must be started one year after discovering the violation but in no case later than three years after the violation.

The leading interpretation of Section 11 of the Securities Act of 1933 is the *Escott v. BarChris Construction Corp.* case.

Criminal Punishment Under the Securities Act of 1933

The Securities Act of 1933 (SA) has criminal sanctions. It is a crime to commit fraud in the sale of securities, whether they are exempt or nonexempt, *or* to willfully violate the SA. Possible punishment is up to five years in prison, up to a $10,000 fine, or both.

SECURITIES EXCHANGE ACT OF 1934

The Securities Exchange Act of 1934 (SEA) covers many different securities areas, unlike the Securities Act of 1933, which basically requires registration of new issues. The SEA concentrates on the secondary, or used, securities and their markets. Matters covered in the SEA include establishing the Securities and Exchange Commission and regulating the securities exchanges, dealers, and brokers as well as publicly held companies.

Purposes

The purposes of the Securities Exchange Act of 1934 include the following:

1. Regulating securities markets.
2. Regulating securities traded in securities markets.

ESCOTT v. BARCHRIS CONSTRUCTION CORP.

Federal District Court (S.D. N.Y.). 283 F.Supp. 643 (1968).

FACTS Some investors bought bonds that BarChris Construction Corporation (BarChris) issued. BarChris' executives, attorneys, accountants, and underwriters prepared and filed a registration statement for the bonds. On May 16, 1961, the registration statement took effect. BarChris sold the bonds in May 1961 and used the money in its business. BarChris built bowling alleys. However, by 1962 it was obvious that there were too many bowling alleys. In October 1962, BarChris filed for bankruptcy and defaulted on bonds it had sold just a year earlier. Bond investors lost their money and pointed out the following errors in the bond registration statement:

Summary

For convenience, the various falsities and omissions are summarized here.

1. *1960 Earnings*
   (a) *Sales*
   Per prospectus $9,165,320
   Correct Figure 8,511,420
   Overstatement $ 653,900
   (b) *Net Operating Income*
   Per prospectus $1,742,801
   Correct figure 1,496,196
   Overstatement $ 246,605
   (c) *Earnings per Share* . . . . . $ .75
   Correct figure 65
   Overstatement $ .10
2. *1960 Balance Sheet Current Assets*
   Per prospectus $4,524,021
   Correct figure 3,914,332
   Overstatement $ 609,689
3. *Contingent Liabilities as of December 31, 1960, on Alternative Method of Financing*
   Per prospectus . . . . . $ 750,000
   Correct figure 1,125,795
   Understatement $ 375,795
   Capitol Lanes should have been shown as a direct liability $ 325,000
4. *Contingent Liabilities as of April 30, 1961*
   Per prospectus . . . . . $ 825,000
   Correct figure 1,443,853
   Understatement $ 618,853
   Capitol Lanes should have been shown as a direct liability $ 314,166
5. *Earnings Figures for Quarter Ending March 31, 1961*
   (a) *Sales*
   Per prospectus $2,138,455
   Correct figure 1,618,645
   Overstatement $ 519,810
   (b) *Gross Profit*
   Per prospectus $483,121
   Correct figure 252,366
   Overstatement $ 230,755
6. *Backlog as of March 31, 1961*
   Per prospectus $6,905,000
   Correct figure 2,415,000
   Overstatement $4,490,000
7. *Failure to Disclose Officers' Loans Outstanding and Unpaid on May 16, 1961* $ 386,615
8. *Failure to Disclose Use of Proceeds in Manner Not Revealed in Prospectus*
   Approximately $1,160,000
9. *Failure to Disclose Customers' Delinquencies in May 1961 and BarChris's Potential Liability with Respect Thereto*
   Over $1,350,000
10. *Failure to Disclose the Fact That BarChris Was Already Engaged and Was About to be More Heavily Engaged in the Operation of Bowling Alleys*

Investors who bought BarChris bonds and lost money sued the following:

1. BarChris' directors.
2. BarChris' executive officers.
3. BarChris' controller.
4. BarChris' attorney.
5. All persons who signed BarChris' registration statement for the bonds.
6. The bond underwriters.
7. Independent auditors who prepared financial statements, which became part of the registration statement.

Investors based their claim on Section 11 of the Securities Act of 1933. Section 11 allows buyers of securities covered by a registration statement to recover damages if they show that:

1. They bought the security.
2. A registration statement covers the security.
3. The registration statement has a material misstatement or omission.
4. They lost money on the security.

ISSUES Who is liable for the errors and omissions in BarChris' registration statement? Were the errors and omissions material? Is the due diligence defense available?

DECISION The federal district court said that officers, directors (old and new), signers of the registration statement, underwriters, and accountants were liable under Section 11 of the Securities Act. The errors and omissions in the registration statement were material. The due diligence defense was claimed by the defendants, who argued that they should not be liable for errors and omissions in the registration statement. The court rejected this defense in most instances because due diligence requires proof that the job was done carefully.

LEGAL TIP

A single person who signs a registration statement for a new security registered under the Securities Act of 1933 could be liable for all investor losses caused by registration statement errors and omissions.

3. Registering and regulating broker-dealers, municipal securities dealers, securities, information processors, clearing agencies, and transfer agents.
4. Regulating publicly held companies.
5. Requiring public disclosure.

Main Provisions

The main provisions of the SEA are as follows:

1. Creation of the Securities and Exchange Commission.
2. Registration requirements.
3. Reporting requirements.
4. Proxy solicitation rules.
5. Regulation of credit in securities markets.
6. Anti-fraud provisions.
7. Insider trading limitations.
8. Tender offer limits.

The Securities and Exchange Commission (SEC)

The Securities and Exchange Commission (SEC) is the leading enforcer of the federal securities laws. The SEC enforces the Securities Act of 1933, the Securities Exchange Act of 1934, the Public Utility Holding Company Act of 1935, the Investment Company Act of 1940, the Investment Adviser Act of 1940, and the Trust Indenture Act of 1939. Interestingly, the SEC was established in 1934 by the Securities Exchange Act of 1934—one year *after* the Securities Act of 1933, the *first* major federal act regulating securities, became law. The Federal Trade Commission enforced the 1933 Act during its first year. This responsibility was transferred from the FTC to the SEC upon the SEC's establishment.

Basically, the SEC promulgates rules and regulations, enforces them, and adjudicates cases where rules and regulations are allegedly violated. The SEC is a federal administrative agency and performs most of the functions described in earlier chapters.

SEA Registration Requirements

To achieve the SEA's purposes of regulating securities and the securities markets, the SEA imposes registration requirements. Securities exchanges, security broker-dealers, municipal securities dealers, and certain securities must be registered with the SEC.

Securities Registration

The SEA requires that certain securities be registered with the SEC. Any security (bonds or equity security) traded on any national securities exchange must be registered unless exempt. Also, any company with 500 or more shareholders ***and*** over $3 million in assets must register its equity (***not debt***) securities if they are traded in interstate commerce. Thus, securities traded over the counter, and not on an exchange, must be registered if the issuer has over $3 million in assets and 500 or more shareholders. It cannot be emphasized too strongly that SEA registration is ***in addition to*** registration under the Securities Act of 1933, which was discussed earlier.

Exempt securities Some securities are exempt from registration under the SEA, including federal, state, or municipal obligations (notes or bonds) and obligations guaranteed by such governments. A broker or dealer who trades municipal securities must register such securities, which are not exempt.

SEA Proxy Restrictions

A proxy is a person who acts for another. In a corporation, it is common practice for shareholders to give the right to vote their shares to incumbent management or a challenging group. When someone solicits proxies of shares registered under the SEA, the SEA and its rules and regulations impose certain requirements.

Short-Swing Profit Rule

Insiders An officer, director, or large shareholder (holder or beneficial owner of more than 10% of an equity class) is an insider for Section 16(b). Insiders often know a great deal more about the issuer than the market does. They could profit from this knowledge by trading in the issuer's securities. At one time, this privilege was thought to be a "fringe" benefit of being an insider. Then Congress enacted Section 16(b) of the Securities Exchange Act of 1934, its short-swing profits rule.

Section 16(b) **Section 16(b)** says that an insider must return to the issuer any profit from any sale and purchase or purchase and sale of the issuer's equity securities occurring within a six-month period. The intent of the insider is irrelevant. In other words, if the prohibited acts occurred within the six-month period, the insider is presumed to have used inside information to make the gain even if the insider actually had no inside information unknown to the market. The idea behind the rule is to put all investors on the same footing and to eliminate insiders' special advantages.

Section 10b and Rule 10b-5

Purpose **Rule 10b-5** is aimed at preventing fraud in buying and selling securities. The rule's language clearly says that it applies to "any person," meaning corporate insiders ***and*** outsiders. Hence, in this way it is broader than Section 16(b). On the other hand, it is similar to Section 16(b), because it can stop profit-taking in the firm's securities by corporate insiders who have inside information not available to the general public.

Examples of Rule 10b-5 violations Some specific fraudulent acts include knowingly spreading false rumors about securities issuers to affect the issuer's securities prices; matching buy-and-sell orders from different people (such as two brokers from the same firm); a broker's "churning" a customer's account (see the *Zaretsky v. E. F. Hutton & Co.* case for an explanation.); or one person's simultaneously buying and selling the same security (wash sales) to give the appearance of market activity in the stock.

ZARETSKY v. E. F. HUTTON & CO.

U.S. District Court (S.D. N.Y.).
509 F.Supp. 68 (1981).

FACTS On February 14, 1977, Betty and Mort Zaretsky opened a brokerage account with E. F. Hutton & Co. (Hutton); their account executive was Tom Hanlon. The Zaretskys told Hanlon they were placing their entire $25,000 life's savings in his care. They told him they wanted conservative investments to help in their retirement. On May 12, 1978, the Zaretskys shifted their account to Advest, Inc., to follow Hanlon, who had changed firms. They continued to trade through Hanlon until November 1978. By then Hanlon had made 147 separate purchases and sales for their account. They owed or had paid $24,664.24 for commissions, fees, taxes, and margin interest ($15,715.18 allegedly was incurred for commissions and other brokerage charges at Hutton, and $8,949.06 was allegedly incurred for similar charges at Advest). The account had made an $11,755.10 profit while at Hutton. The Zaretskys sued Hutton, alleging that Hanlon had "churned" their account while there.

ISSUE Did the Zaretskys state a good claim for "churning?"

DECISION Yes. Section 10(b) and Rule 10b-5 of the Securities Exchange Act of 1934 view "churning" as a fraudulent act. "Churning" occurs when the broker trades excessively despite the type of account, and the broker effectively controls the account. Factors relevant to the control element of the account include the discretion given the broker-dealer, the age, education, intelligence, and business and investing experience of the client, the relationship between client and broker, and the customer's reliance on the broker. The court said that the plaintiffs' allegation was supported when they told Hanlon they were placing their entire life's savings of $25,000 into his care for conservative investment to generate some extra retirement income. The plaintiffs also claimed that Hanlon promised that they would "make good money on option," that Hanlon said he would make money for them, and that Hanlon claimed he was the "best in the business." The court said these remarks supported the plaintiffs' claim that Hanlon controlled the account.

LEGAL TIP

If brokerage commissions are high, check to see if there is churning (an excessive amount of trading in your brokerage account). Churning is illegal.

Rule 10b-5 applies to all securities Virtually any fraud in connection with the sale or purchase of *any* security where the mails or instrumentality or interstate commerce is involved is covered by Rule 10b-5. This rule even applies to securities that are otherwise exempt (such as government bonds) or ones that do not have to be registered under the SEA (because, for instance, the issuer has fewer than 500 stockholders). Unlike Section 16b, only a sale *or* purchase (not both) of securities is required to violate Rule 10b-5.

Criminal Violations of SEA

It is possible to violate the SEA or its rules and regulations, although violations must be willful to be crimes. Section 32 of the SEA makes criminal the willful and knowing making of a statement in a required report, application, or document that is false or misleading in any material respect. An example of a Section 32 violation is an accountant's signing a corporation's financial statements as being fair representations of the firm's financial status when the accountant knows that they are not. Accountants have been convicted for committing this federal felony.

Penalties Punishment can be up to 5 years in prison, up to a $100,000 fine, or both for SEA criminal violations. Conviction for a criminal violation prevents certain benefits under the securities laws (for example, use of the small issue exemption under the SA of 1933 or association with a registered investment company).

KEY TERMS

Securities Act of 1933
Securities Exchange Act of 1934
Security
Howey test
Primary market
Secondary market
Registration statement
Prospectus
Exemptions
Section 16b
Rule 10b-5

CHAPTER PROBLEMS

1. Can something be a security for purposes of the federal securities laws even if it is not a stock or bond?
2. What is the basic idea behind requiring registration of securities?
3. If a security is exempt from registration under the federal securities laws, who is helped? Who could be hurt?
4. If there is a material omission or error in a registration statement, who could be liable?
5. What are some defenses to Section 11 claims?
6. Name some of the purposes of the Securities Exchange Act of 1934.
7. What is the short-swing profit rule?
8. What does Rule 10b-5 try to prevent?

*9. Securities brokers get commissions whenever a customer buys or sells a security (even if the customer loses money). This tempts brokers to urge customers to buy and sell securities frequently even if such sales or purchases are not in the customer's best interests. Such frequent broker-encouraged trading is called "churning." Is it a violation of the Securities Exchange Act of 1934 (that is, is it considered a fraud in connection with the purchase and sale of securities)? *Costello v. Oppenheimer & Co., Inc.*, 711 F.2d 1361 (8th Cir. 1983).

*10. Are punitive damages recoverable under a Rule 10b-5 claim? *Meyers v. Moody,* 693 F.2d 1196, *reh'g. denied* 701 F.2d 173 (5th Cir. 1982).

Part Three

Contracts

Freedom to Choose
Milton Friedman

Chapter 17

Nature, Definition, and Classification of Contracts

CHAPTER PREVIEW

- The *Restatement, Second, Contracts* definition of a contract
- Different contract definitions
- Contract law and the market economy
- Unilateral and bilateral contracts
- Express and implied contracts
- Valid, voidable, void, and unenforceable contracts
- Contracts implied in fact and implied in law (quasi-contracts)

Paul Campbell had just received the news. "Gertrude's estate rejected our claim," said Paul to his wife LaVon. "You cooked her meals, did her laundry, cleaned her house. I repaired her roof and carted her to the doctor for the five years before she died. I think charging her estate $60 per week or $5000 total for this work is reasonable." Paul and LaVon Campbell had taken care of Gertrude Milburn, a neighbor, for five years before she had died. The Campbells now wanted payment for their services. Milburn's estate argued that she and the Campbells had no contract covering their services. Did the Campbells recover anything?

With this chapter we begin a section of chapters covering contracts. In this chapter, we shall define contracts, discuss how contracts fit into the United States legal system, and examine basic contract classifications.

HOW CONTRACTS FIT INTO THE MARKET ECONOMY

In introductory economics courses, you learned about the market economy and the intersection of supply-and-demand curves (which set the price of goods and services). It is important to note that these supply-and-demand curves summarize not one but millions of **contracts,** which are agreements between buyers and sellers of all goods and services.

In other words, contracts are the basis for the market economy. When people trade either for money or for barter (exchanging goods for goods) they make contracts.

Trends in Contract Law

Hundreds of years ago in the Middle Ages, people were born serfs or nobility. With a few exceptions, they kept their status of prince or serf for their entire lives. Serfs essentially were slaves with few rights; they had no freedom to enter contracts to work where they wanted in order to improve their economic and social status.

In the nineteenth and early twentieth centuries, the market economy thrived, and individual freedom increased. People were free to work where they wanted and could own property in their own names. People could change their status by working and contracting. This is also possible today.

In the mid and late twentieth century there have been two trends in contract law. First, there has been a trend toward long-term contracts. For example, a utility company may enter a ten- or twenty-year contract to buy coal. Second, since the late 1970's there has been a definite trend toward monopolies, which concentrate economic power. This second trend is largely caused by the merger "mania" of the early 1980's. Since monopolies reduce the number of competitors, a few large businesses have great power to set contract terms. These terms include price, warranty, and quality standards.

Philosophies Found in Contract Law

Several philosophies, or beliefs, are found in contracts. First is the *libertarian* idea that people have freedom of choice. For example, people can contract for a particular job, buy or rent a house, buy a Ford or a Cadillac, and spent or save all or part of their paychecks. Since individuals are free to choose and shape their lives, they answer these questions on an individual basis.

Another philosophy found in contracts is the *utilitarian* concept of the greatest good for the greatest number. Again, each individual determines the "greatest good" for him or herself. For example, a person contracts to go to school to learn to be an insurance broker; he or she *thinks* spending money on education is more valuable than spending it on a car or vacation. Another person might do the opposite.

Finally, contracts are *not* positive law using John Austin's definition of positive law (a command of government with sanctions if it is broken). Instead, private people (*not* governments) make their own contracts. If a person breaks a contract, damages—but not punishment—usually result.

Law Governing Contracts

The law governing contracts is generally state law, including state statutes or common law (judge-made rules). Every state except Louisiana has passed the Uniform Commercial Code's (UCC) Article II. Article II sets the rules for contracts dealing with goods. (See Chapter 27 for more detail.) Real estate, services, and insurance contracts are controlled by common law and other state statutes.

Contract Definitions

Various legal scholars and authorities give us contract definitions. The American Law Institute (ALI) is a nongovernmental group of legal scholars, including professors and practicing lawyers. The ALI members read many cases and try to restate them in an easy-to-understand way. The ALI does this for contracts in a set of books called the *Restatement, Second, Contracts.*

Restatement's *contract definition* After reading thousands of cases, ALI scholars define a contract as follows: "A contract is a promise or a set of promises for the breach of which the law gives a remedy, or the performance of which the law in some way recognizes as a duty."

Basically, this definition means that *if* a judge would make someone keep a promise, it is a contract. A problem with this definition is that a person has to sue to get a judge's decision.

Another contract definition Another contract definition is: "an agreement between competent parties enforceable in court."

An "agreement" involves an offer and acceptance. The next chapter discusses offers and acceptances in detail. The offer and acceptance must be "bargained for," which Chapter 19 discusses.

"Competent parties" refers to the idea that minority, insanity, and drunkenness on the part of one or more persons will result in an agreement that is void or voidable. Chapter 21 on Capacity deals with this subject.

The "enforceable in court" part of the contract definition refers to several points. First, not all agreements are legally enforceable contracts. Social agreements (or "dates") are not contracts. For example, if Fred breaks a date with Marsha, Marsha will *not* get a judge to award her a remedy for breach of contract. Second, excited utterances (such as "I'll give a billion dollars to anyone who saves my drowning child," yelled by a mother to a crowd as she watches her child pulled under by an ocean current) do not give rise to contracts. Therefore, the hero who saves the woman's child is not entitled to a billion dollars given her excitement when she made the offer. Third, there are other problems (such as fraud, mistake, innocent misrepresentation, duress, unconscionability, lack of a written contract where required) that could make a contract unenforceable. Later chapters in the contracts section (Part 3) of this book explain these and other problems (including illegality and remedies).

The objective theory of contracts The **objective theory of contracts** means that contracts are determined by what people *appear to have done* (which is "objective"), *not* what they *think* they have done (which is "subjective"). This theory of contracts forces judges to point to evidence people can see (such as a signed contract) to decide if a contract exists.

For example, Jim thinks he is playing a joke on Sarah. He pretends to offer his \$20,000 Cadillac to her for \$15,000 and signs a contract saying so. He does not actually intend to follow through on such an offer. However, based on appearances, any reasonable person would say Jim made an offer. Therefore, the objective theory of contracts says Jim and Sarah have a contract (even if Jim does not want one).

CONTRACT CLASSIFICATIONS

We shall now examine five different contract classifications:

1. Bilateral and unilateral.
2. Express and implied.
3. Valid, voidable, void, and unenforceable.
4. Executed and executory.
5. Quasi-contracts.

Bilateral and Unilateral Contracts

The basis for the unilateral and bilateral contract classification is the number of promises.

Bilateral contracts When two people exchange promises—one promise for another—they make a **bilateral contract.** For example, Irving says to Herman "Promise to paint my house, and I'll promise to pay you $500." If Herman promises to do so, he has made a bilateral contract with Irving.

Note the difference between bilateral and unilateral contracts: In a situation involving a unilateral contract, the offeror asks for a return act ("paint my house")—*not* a promise. However, if an offeror asks for a return *promise,* he or she wants to enter a bilateral contract. Only a return promise (not an act) will form the contract in a bilateral case.

One other point: a person does *not* have to use the word "promise" to make a promise. Any words showing you promise (such as "OK" "I agree") will do.

Unilateral contracts A **unilateral contract** consists of a promise and an act. A person makes a promise and also asks for an act in return.

One example is: "I'll pay you $500 (the promise) if you paint my house (the requested act). The promise is the offer, and the offeree's performance of the requested act is the acceptance. Only when the requested act is complete is there a contract.

The *Davis v. Jacoby* case examines the distinction between unilateral and bilateral contracts.

Express and Implied Contracts

Express contracts **Express contracts** are those having the terms completely stated in words. Such contracts can be either oral or written. A contract between a homeowner and a buyer covering many details is an example of an express written contract. Calling the local pizza shop and ordering a 14-inch pizza with mushrooms and sausage to be delivered to your dorm room is an example of an express oral contract.

Implied contracts **Implied contracts** can also be determined from the parties' conduct even though *nothing is said.* Such contracts are implied in fact (meaning the facts justify assuming that the parties intend a contract). A later section discusses contracts implied in law.

DAVIS v. JACOBY

Supreme Court of California.
34 P.2d 1026 (1934).

FACTS Caro Davis was the niece of Blanche and Rupert Whitehead, who were childless. The Whiteheads were very fond of Caro, who lived with them in California for a while. Then Caro married Frank Davis and moved to Canada.

When Mr. Whitehead became ill, he wrote to Caro and Frank. In the letter, he asked them to come to California and care for the Whiteheads until they died. In return for doing so, Mr. Whitehead promised to give Caro everything in his will, (estimated at $150,000 in 1931) to Caro. Frank Davis sent a return letter saying he and Caro accepted Mr. Whitehead's offer. The Davises prepared to leave Canada but before leaving, they received word that Mr. Whitehead had committed suicide.

The Davises went to California to care for Mrs. Whitehead until she died. Soon after, they learned that Mr. Whitehead's will did not give them anything. The estate argued Mr. Whitehead's letter was an offer requesting an act (an offer for a unilateral contract). Since the act (going to California and caring for the Whiteheads) was not done *before* Whitehead died, the estate executor argued there was no contract.

The Davises argued that Mr. Whitehead had asked for a *return promise* (not a return act). The Davises had made a return promise *before* Whitehead died.

ISSUE Had Mr. Whitehead tried to form a unilateral or bilateral contract?

DECISION Mr. Whitehead had tried to form a bilateral contract. In this type of case, the *offeror's* language determines which type of contract is desired. The offeror here was Mr. Whitehead. His language was not clear in indicating whether he wanted a return act or promise. When there is a doubt which contract the offerer requests, legal authorities generally favor bilateral contracts. The reason is that a bilateral contract immediately and fully protects both parties. (The requested act must be complete before there is a unilateral contract.)

Also, Mr. Whitehead asked the Davises to care for both him and Mrs. Whitehead. If he had died first, Mr. Whitehead would have relied on the Davises' present *promise* to care for his wife.

LEGAL TIP

If you are offering to form a contract, be sure to say whether you want a return act or a return promise. Which one you ask for controls whether you are bound in a contract.

The following example involves an implied-in-fact contract: A student is in a bookstore, picks out a book, takes it to the cashier, and puts down the necessary money. The clerk makes change and bags the book. Nothing is said, yet the parties' conduct shows they intended to make a contract. This is a contract *implied in fact.*

Valid, Voidable, Void, and Unenforceable Contracts

Valid contracts A contract is valid if it has no legal flaws. A valid contract is enforceable under virtually all circumstances.

Voidable contracts Contracts are voidable when they have certain defects which could, but not necessarily will, make the contract unenforceable. At least one of the parties may escape voidable contracts by noting the defect. Defects making contracts voidable include fraud, innocent misrepresentation, and lack of contractual capacity (such as minority). For example, if a ten-year-old signs a contract to buy a Cadillac, he or she can avoid the contract because he or she is a minor.

Void contracts Sometimes contracts have such serious flaws that they are called legally void. Legally void means that there was no contract at all—ever. A contract can be void even though a piece of paper exists saying that it is a contract.

Factors which make an attempted contract void include illegality of the subject matter (such as contracts to commit murder), contracts against public policy, and attempts by persons adjudged legally insane to contract.

Unenforceable contracts Unenforceable contracts are those failing to meet a procedural or formal requirement which makes them unenforceable.

A *procedural* flaw would be not suing within the statute of limitations period. A *formal* error would involve making an oral contract when the statute of frauds requires a written one.

Executed and Executory Contracts

We can also classify contracts according to the degree that they have been performed. Contracts partly performed or totally unperformed are **executory contracts.** Contracts fully performed by both parties are **executed contracts.**

It is possible for a contract to be fully performed (an executed contract) by one party and unperformed or partly performed (an executory contract) by the other party. For example, Claude Teagarden pays Bill Haymaker $10 to mow his lawn. Teagarden has fully executed his part of the contract, but Haymaker's part is executory until he finishes mowing.

Quasi-contracts

Quasi-contracts are not contracts but a legal idea that lets judges force a contract on parties *even though they did not have one.* The term "quasi-contract" means "like a contract." Quasi-contracts are also known as contracts implied-in-law meaning a judge creates them.

Why does quasi-contract exist? Quasi-contract exists to prevent unjust enrichment. It applies in situations where one person confers benefits on another when it is reasonable to believe payment is expected, no gift is intended, and where no contract exists. A judge will tell the person receiving the benefits to pay the reasonable value (the judge sets this) of the benefits received.

Example of a quasi-contract The following example involves a quasi-contract: Charles Walker calls Ace Painting Company (Ace) and tells them to paint his building. Ace mistakenly drives up in front of Bill Eshee's building and starts painting. Eshee sees the Ace truck and realizes they should be painting Walker's building next door. Eshee says nothing, hoping for a free paint job. When Ace finishes the job, Mr. Ace says to Eshee: "Well Mr. Walker, how do you like the paint job?" Eshee replies, "It's great. But I'm Eshee. Walker's building is next door."

To allow Eshee to get a free paint job when he had reason to know pay was expected would be unjust enrichment. Ace has no contract with Eshee. However, Ace can ask a judge to apply the quasi-contract idea to let Ace recover the reasonable value of the benefits Eshee got.

Limits on quasi-contracts There are times when a judge will not allow a person to use the quasi-contract concept. If the person receiving benefits does not have a reasonable opportunity to reject the benefits *before* getting them, judges will not allow quasi-contract recovery. For example, suppose Ace Painting Company had painted Eshee's building, and Eshee had not known about the job until completion. Eshee would not have to pay on the basis of a quasi-contract since he had no reasonable opportunity to reject the benefits.

A quasi-contract also does not apply when parties have a valid contract covering the matter. For example, suppose Ace Paint Company has a contract to paint Walker's building for $1000. Mr. Ace does the job but discovers that the job costs are $2000. He cannot use the quasi-contract concept to recover $2,000 since his contract for $1000 controls.

The *Matter of Estate of Milborn* case gives an example of a quasi-contract.

MATTER OF ESTATE OF MILBORN

Illinois Appellate Court.
461 N.E.2d 1075 (1984).

FACTS When Gertrude Milborn died, Paul and LaVon Campbell filed claims against Milborn's estate for $5000. These claims were for services they performed for Milborn during the five years before her death. They based their claims on an implied contract.

The services performed included making all of Milborn's meals during the period, doing her housekeeping, laundry, mowing her lawn, and patching her roof. Mr. Campbell also took Milborn to see out-of-town doctors and managed her financial affairs under a power of attorney.

The executor of Milborn's estate defended by arguing that the Campbells never proved that Milborn requested and expected to pay for the Campbells' services.

ISSUE Was there an implied in fact or implied in law contract between Milborn and the Campbells concerning their services?

DECISION There was no contract implied in fact because there were no acts, conduct, or circumstances permitting a judge to infer a promise or intent to be bound. There was *no mutual understanding* between Milborn and the Campbells on the terms of an agreement.

There was, however, a contract implied-in-law, quasi-contract, which prevents one person's enrichment at another's expense.

When services are rendered by one person to another and are knowingly and voluntarily accepted, the law presumes such services were given and received in expectation of payment. The law implies a promise to pay a reasonable value for the services. In this case, there is no requirement to prove Milborn requested the services since no one meddlesomely "forced" unwanted services on Milborn.

The Campbells also did not make a gift of their services to Milborn. When persons live together as a family (even if not blood relatives), giving services to each other does *not* lead the law to say there is an implied promise to pay for the services. Services given among family members are presumed to be a gift. Since the Campbells did not live with Milborn as part of her family, their services were not presumed to be a gift. The Campbells recovered $60 per week ($5000) based on a contract implied in law.

LEGAL TIP

If a person offers you services, ask if payment is expected (and, if so, how much) *before* you accept the services.

KEY TERMS

Contracts
Objective theory of contracts
Unilateral contract
Bilateral contract
Express contracts
Implied contracts
Valid contracts
Void contracts
Voidable contracts
Unenforceable contracts
Executory contracts
Executed contracts
Quasi-contracts

CHAPTER PROBLEMS

1. Maria agrees to go to the movies with Paul, but Paul "breaks" the date. Is this a legally enforceable contract?

2. Marianne stands outside of her burning house. A manuscript for a book she has written is inside the house. She fears the fire will burn the manuscript and screams that she will give a "million dollars" to anyone who saves her manuscript. A bystander hears this, dashes inside the burning house, and saves the manuscript. He then asks Marianne for the "million dollars." Is this a contract?

3. Leon agreed to pay Elmer $1000 to burn his building so he could collect on the fire insurance. Elmer "torched" Leon's building and then asked Leon for the $1000. Leon refused to pay and told Elmer that "contracts" to commit crimes are void. Is Leon correct?

4. Give an example of a contract implied in law.

5. A woman enters a store, picks up a blouse, shows it to the clerk, and hands the clerk the money. The clerk puts the blouse in a bag. Neither party says anything. Does a contract exist in this type of situation? If so, what kind?
6. Is contract law more consistent with a market or planned economy?
7. If two people think they have a contract, does this necessarily mean they do? What is meant by the "objective theory" of contracts?

*8. Contracts contrary to public policy are usually void. Would a contract between an architect and a building owner that provides building plans not conforming to the local building code be contrary to public policy? *Greenhaven Corp. v. Hatchcraft & Associates, Inc.,* 463 N.E.2d 283 (Indiana App. 1984).

*9. Are contracts presumed to be legal and enforceable? That is, does illegality arise as a defense when someone is sued for breach of contract? *National Recovery Systems v. Mazzei,* 475 N.Y.S.2d 208 (N.Y. Sup. 1984).

*10. A life insurance salesperson signed an agreement not to compete with his employer for *one year* after his employment ended. The salesperson quit work and immediately started selling life insurance for his former employer's competitor. The first employer sued the salesperson for breaching the covenant (agreement) not to compete. The salesperson argued that the covenant not to compete was *void* since it barred his working *in any capacity* for another credit life and/or health insurance company for one year after quitting. Was the agreement not to compete *void? Wallace Butts Ins. Agency, Inc., v. Runge,* 314 S.E.2d 293 (N.C. App. 1984).

"I'll make him an offer he can't refuse."

Mario Puzo
The Godfather

Chapter 18

The Agreement: Offer and Acceptance

CHAPTER PREVIEW

- Definition of an offer
- Intent to make an offer
- Ways offers end
- Ways acceptances can occur
- Effect of an acceptance
- Time when acceptances take effect

Lee Calan Imports, a Chicago car dealer, advertised a 1964 Volvo station wagon for sale in the Chicago Sun-Times. *The dealer told the newspaper to advertise the price of the car at $1795. The newspaper made a mistake and, without fault by the car dealer, advertised the car at $1095. A consumer named O'Brien visited the dealer's place of business and said he would buy the car for $1095. The dealer refused, and O'Brien sued for breach of contract. What is the result?*

A contract is a legally enforceable agreement between competent parties. Agreement means mutual assent. Courts usually say that agreements are made up of offers and acceptances. What is an offer? Must an offer be written or can it be oral? How definite must an offer be? How long does it last? What must a person do to accept an offer? This chapter answers all of these questions and many others.

WHAT IS AN OFFER?

The first step in making a contract is for one person to make an **offer** to another. The person making the offer is called the **offeror.** The person to whom the offer is made is called the **offeree.**

What is an offer? An offer is made when the offeror in some way tells the offeree that the offeror wants to enter a contract with the offeree. The offer indicates what the offeror will do and what he or she wants in return from the offeree along with a definite willingness to commit.

Offers can be made *expressly* or by *implication.* For example, an express offer occurs when a person signs a written offer to buy a house. An offer can also be made by implication. If, for example, Barbara Winslow enters K-Mart, sees a blouse she likes, and takes it to the cashier, Winslow has made an offer by implication. The cashier then rings up the sale, puts the blouse in a bag, and hands it to Winslow. During this transaction, no words have been spoken; yet a contract has been made between Winslow and K-Mart.

An easy way to think about making contracts is to remember the formula: offer + acceptance = contract. The remainder of this chapter will examine offers and acceptances.

WEINER v. MCGRAW-HILL, INC.

New York Court of Appeals.
57 N.Y.2d 458, 443 N.E.2d 441 (1982).

FACTS McGraw-Hill, Inc. (M-H), a book publisher, invited Weiner to discuss joining its staff. Weiner then worked for Prentice-Hall (P-H), a competing publisher. After some time, Weiner quit his job at P-H and went to work for M-H. During negotiations, M-H had assured Weiner that company policy prevented firing employees without just cause. Weiner signed a M-H application, which said that employment was subject to the company handbook on personnel policies and procedures. That handbook stated that dismissal would be for just cause only and only after all practical steps toward rehabilitation had been taken and failed. Weiner worked at M-H for eight years, was promoted, given raises, and declined jobs elsewhere. In 1977, Weiner was suddenly fired, which M-H said was for "lack of application." Weiner sued M-H for breach of contract.

ISSUE Did the McGraw-Hill Company manual and application form show the intent of Weiner to enter a contract limiting McGraw's dismissal rights?

DECISION The New York Court of Appeals (New York's highest state court) decided that M-H and Weiner intended to form an employment contract, requiring just cause for dismissal. The court rejected M-H's argument that it did not subjectively intend that its manual and application form would be a contract. The court stressed that the total circumstances showed the parties' contractual intent.

LEGAL TIP
Persons taking jobs with employers should get written contracts that say the employer can fire them only for good cause.

What Intent Is Needed to Make an Offer?

An offer must be made with **objective intent,** which is how something looks to a reasonable person. If a person *appears* to be making an offer, then an offer has been made—even if the offeror does not intend to make an offer. What a person *thinks* he or she has done is called **subjective intent.** It is objective, not subjective, intent that decides if a person has made an offer. The *Weiner v. McGraw-Hill, Inc.* case discusses the issue of intent.

Jokes or excited utterances If an offer is clearly made as a joke or **excited utterance,** it is not a legally enforceable offer at all. So if an offeree accepts an offer that obviously is a joke, there is no contract. Similarly, if in an excited moment a person shouts that a huge reward (which is clearly beyond "reality") will be given, an offer has not been made. A person who "accepts" such an "offer" does not form a contract. The *Lucy v. Zehmer* case is an example of a contract involving an intended joke.

LUCY v. ZEHMER

Supreme Court of Virginia.
196 Va. 493, 84 S.E.2d 516 (1954).

FACTS W. O. Lucy asked Zehmer and his wife if they would sell their farm. Zehmer, thinking Lucy didn't have the money, wrote on the back of a restaurant check: "We hereby agree to sell to W. O. Lucy the Ferguson Farm complete for $50,000, title satisfactory to buyer." Zehmer whispered to his wife so Lucy could not hear that this offer was all a joke. Both Zehmer and his wife signed the paper. Later, when Lucy was ready to turn over the money, the Zehmers refused to give Lucy the deed to the farm. Lucy sued the Zehmers for breach of contract.

ISSUE Had Lucy and the Zehmers intended to contract for the farm?

DECISION Yes. A contract for the farm was made. Therefore, Lucy got the farm from the Zehmers. The Virginia Supreme Court said that a reasonable person looking at the events surrounding the signing of the paper would conclude that the Zehmers and Lucy intended to contract. The court said what the parties *appear* to do, not what they *think* they do, determines their contractual intent.

LEGAL TIP

A contract can be entered even when an individual thinks that none has been made. Do not do anything that could be viewed as making a contract (such as signing a document) unless you actually intend to enter a legally binding agreement.

Social offers **Social offers** to attend events are not legally enforceable offers. For example, if Bill asks Mary to go to a party and then "stands her up" and breaks the date, Mary cannot recover from Bill for breach of contract.

Agreements to agree **Agreements to agree** are not legally binding contracts. Rachael says to Bruce, "I agree that at some future time we shall make a contract to pay you a bonus for coming to work for my company." This is not a legally binding contract because there is no present commitment to an agreement.

Statements showing intent Statements showing intent do not in and of themselves create contracts. The *Pacific Cascade Corp. v. Nimmer* case discusses the issue of present intent in forming a contract.

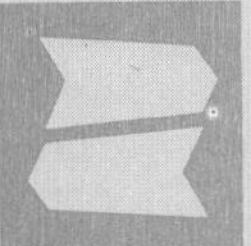

PACIFIC CASCADE CORP. v. NIMMER

Court of Appeals of Washington.
608 P.2d 266 (1980).

FACTS Pacific Cascade Corporation (PCC), a real estate developer, was looking for a site for a new Jafco store. PCC became interested in a plot of Mr. Nimmer's land. During negotiations several lease proposals were exchanged. On September 29, 1977, Mr. Nimmer sent a letter of intent to lease his property to PCC. PCC received this letter and at that point thought it had struck a deal. PCC swung into action to develop the tract hiring surveyors and negotiating construction details and financial arrangements. On October 24, 1977, PCC sent a "draft of a proposed land lease" for Nimmer's review. On December 12, 1977, Nimmer notified PCC he would not lease his land. PCC acquired a replacement site at a much higher price and built its store there. PCC then sued Nimmer, claiming they had a valid lease and Nimmer suffered from "lessor's remorse" (a landlord's feeling that entering a ease was a bad idea).

ISSUE Did PCC and Nimmer have a contract to lease?

DECISION No. The court said parties must show mutual assent to the same bargain at the same time when forming a contract. Mutual assent generally takes the form of an offer and an acceptance. An offer is a promise to do something in exchange for a return promise; but an *intention* to do something is not an actual promise to do it. The court admitted that drawing a line between offers and preliminary negotiations is often difficult. However, the Court of Appeals held that there was substantial evidence to support the trial court's conclusion—that the parties' informal correspondence did not result in a contract.

LEGAL TIP

To form a valid contract, make sure that each party *then* agrees to do something definite. Agreements to agree are not legally binding contracts.

Sham transactions Sometimes people make what appear to be contracts to cheat creditors or the Internal Revenue Service. These transactions that are contracts in form but not in substance are referred to as **sham transactions.** For example, Harvey Slater, about to go bankrupt, contracts to sell his son, Jim, his farm for $5, on the understanding that Jim would return the property to Harvey later. But Harvey's creditors can reclaim the farm from Jim because the "contract" was a sham or fraud on his creditors. No reasonable person viewing this "contract" would say objectively that intent to form a contract existed. Also, Harvey and Jim did not even subjectively intend to contract.

Invitations to negotiate When two people are negotiating, not all of their statements are offers, sometimes not even the first one. Instead, their first remarks are often **invitations to negotiate.** These invitations are not offers and if accepted do not become contracts. They are merely attempts to "feel out" the other party to strike the best deal if an offer and acceptance ever are made. These are often in the form of questions (such as "Would you like to buy my Ford for $1900?"). Ads in newspapers and on television and radio are usually invitations to negotiate if they are general, incomplete, and not addressed to anyone in particular. Thus, it is usually the customer who comes into the store to make an offer, which the merchant may either accept or reject. If the rule were otherwise and merchants' ads were offers, merchants would have to carry huge inventories to avoid contract liability (if many customers accepted the offers in the ads). The *O'Keefe v. Lee Calan Imports, Inc.* case discusses whether a newspaper ad is an offer.

O'KEEFE v. LEE CALAN IMPORTS, INC.

Court of Appeals of Illinois.
128 Ill.App.2d 410, 262 N.E.2d 758 (1970).

FACTS Lee Calan Imports, a Chicago car dealer, advertised a 1964 Volvo station wagon for sale in the *Chicago Sun-Times* newspaper. The dealer told the newspaper to advertise the price of the car at $1795. The newspaper made a mistake and, without fault by the dealer, advertised the car at $1095. A consumer named O'Keefe visited the dealer's place of business and said he would buy the car for $1095. The dealer refused, and O'Keefe sued the dealer for breach of contract.

ISSUE Was the ad in the newspaper incorrectly stating the car's price an offer by the dealer, which was accepted by the customer, thereby forming a binding contract?

DECISION No. The newspaper ad was not an offer; it was an invitation to negotiate. Therefore, when O'Brien said he would buy the car at $1095 he was making an offer to Lee Calan Imports, which it rejected.

LEGAL TIP

Errors in ads do not bind the advertiser if the ad is an invitation to negotiate.

Sometimes media ads are offers. If the ad is definite, complete, certain, and limited to certain specific items, it is more likely an offer than an invitation to negotiate. *Lefkowitz v. Great Minneapolis Surplus Store, Inc.,* is a case where a newspaper ad was an offer.

LEFKOWITZ v. GREAT MINNEAPOLIS SURPLUS STORE, INC.

Supreme Court of Minnesota.
251 Minn. 188, 86 N.W.2d 689 (1957).

FACTS The Great Minneapolis Surplus Store placed an ad in a Minneapolis newspaper stating "Saturday, 9 AM sharp; 3 brand new fur coats worth up to $100; first come, first served; $1 each." Mr. Lefkowitz was the first customer on Saturday, but the store would not sell to him because a "house rule" said that the ads were addressed to women only. A week later the store ran a similar ad for 2 mink scarves for $1 each, which had originally sold for $89.50, as well as one black rabbit stole worth $139.50, for only $1. Lefkowitz appeared first again, but the store turned him down once more saying that this time he knew the house rule. Lefkowitz sued the store for breach of contract.

ISSUE Were the store's newspaper ads offers that Lefkowitz accepted, thereby resulting in contracts?

DECISION The Minnesota Supreme Court decided that the first ad for the minks was too indefinite to be an offer, so Lefkowitz's "acceptance" did *not* result in a contract. However, the store's second ad for the rabbit coat was definite, complete, and certain enough to be an offer, so Lefkowitz's acceptance *did* form a valid contract. The store was liable to Lefkowitz for $138.50 in damages.

LEGAL TIP

Make your newspaper ads vague and incomplete to keep them from being offers.

Certainty

Generally, offers must be certain and definite. This rule helps courts decide the proper remedy if a contract is broken. An acceptance of an indefinite offer generally results in no contract. For example, an offer to lend money as a borrower's needs required was held too uncertain. Another offer stating that hay was to be measured according to government rule when several such rules existed was also held to be too indefinite.

There are several exceptions to the rule that offers (acceptances and the resulting contracts) must be definite. They are as follows:

1. *Trade custom.* Trade custom can clear up an offer's indefiniteness. For example, failure to state a price when it is understood in the trade that market price at the time of delivery was intended will be considered definite.
2. *Previous dealings.* When parties have dealt with one another before and have followed a practice that clears up a vague contract term, courts hold that the offer and contract are not void for lack of definiteness.
3. *Implicit terms.* Some terms in an offer are not expressly stated, but courts nonetheless find them to be implicit. Thus, if a contract fails to state a required performance time, it has been held that performance is to be within a reasonable time.
4. *Open terms in sale of goods contracts.* The UCC allows contract terms such as price or quantity to be valid if there is a commercially reasonable way of filling them later.
5. *Contracts of indefinite length.* Offers for contracts whose performance covers an indefinite period are valid. Courts find the necessary definiteness by allowing either to cancel any time. For example, Sarah is to be Beatrice's cook as long as Beatrice lives, or as long as Sarah performs satisfactorily.
6. *Cost-plus contracts.* In cost-plus contracts, one person agrees to purchase something and pay another's costs plus a fee calculated on some other basis (such as a percentage of the cost). Even though Mike does not know the total cost of building the Empire State Building, his offer to pay Tom his costs plus 10% for the project are definite enough.
7. *Requirements and output contracts.* A requirements contract exists when one person agrees to buy *all* of its requirements from another. Requirements contracts are valid even when a party does not know the exact requirements when the contract is made. Thus, offers to buy all of one's requirements are definite enough.

   Similarly, offers to sell another all that one produces (called output contracts) are definite enough for courts. The indefiniteness arises because no one knows exactly what the production output will be.
8. *Retainer contracts.* The following is an example of a retainer contract: Bob Wilson wants an attorney's services for 1 year. He offers George Blackstone $10,000 to be his attorney. If Blackstone accepts, this contract is valid even though neither Blackstone nor Wilson knows exactly what services Blackstone will perform in the upcoming year. In fact, Blackstone may do nothing, but courts usually require Blackstone to exercise good faith in deciding what actions he should take for Wilson.
9. *Incorporation of another writing.* An offer (and resulting contract) that is too uncertain can be made certain if it refers to another writing. In one case, a building contract lacked crucial terms such as square footage but referred to the building plans and specifications, which cleared up the indefiniteness.

Communication Requirement of Offers

Offers must be communicated before they are effective. For example, Marianne writes out an offer to Mike and puts it in her desk drawer. Mike secretly learns of the letter and calls Marianne to accept the offer. There is no contract in this case because the offer was not communicated to Mike by Marianne or her agent. Assume Marianne has communicated her offer to Mike, the offeree. Mike now has the power to accept and thereby bind Marianne to a contract.

How Offers End

Offers end in a number of ways other than by acceptance, including the following:

1. Time lapse.
2. Revocation.
3. Counter-offer.
4. Rejection.
5. Death or insanity of the offeror or offeree.
6. Destruction of essential subject matter.
7. Intervening or subsequent illegality.

Time lapse Since offers do not last forever, the offeror may state how long the offer will be open. The offer will remain open as long as the offeror states unless it is revoked or ended before that time. When the stated time ends, so does the offer.

If the offer does not say how long it will remain open, the offer lasts for a reasonable time. "Reasonable" takes into account the nature of the subject matter, any trade custom, and similar factors.

Revocation Offerors revoke offers. **Revocation** means recalling or calling back an offer. Offerors generally may revoke an offer any time before acceptance. Revocations need not be in any particular form and take effect when communicated to the offeree. This communication can be indirect. If the offeree accepts before the offer's revocation, a contract exists and the later revocation has no effect on the contract. Public offers are usually revocable if made in a manner similar to the original offer. Revocations need not be communicated to all persons who read the original public offer. Once an offeror revokes an offer, the offeree's later acceptance does not form a contract.

If the offeror promises that the offer will remain open for a stated period of time, may the offeror revoke before that time expires? Yes, assuming no option or firm offer exists.

Options **Options** are offers that stop the offeror from revoking the offer during the stated option period or until a certain date. The option is irrevocable for the option period because the offeree gives the offeror consideration (or something of value). Options are an exception to the general rule that offers are revocable.

For example, if Ken Zeigler offers his farm to Tim Danielson for $100,000 and Danielson is very interested but wants to think about it, an option is the answer. Assume Danielson offers Zeigler $500 if Zeigler will hold open his offer to sell the farm for 30 days and Zeigler agrees. This is an option since Danielson has not yet bought the farm. But he still has time to think about it. If Danielson exercises the option within the 30 days, he must pay Zeigler $100,000 in addition to the option price. (Sometimes the option amount is applied to the purchase price, sometimes not.) If Danielson thinks over the offer during the 30 days and decides not to exercise it, Zeigler keeps the $500 and the farm, and the offer to sell the farm ends.

Two last points: First, just because people call an offer an "option" does not mean it is an irrevocable offer. The offeree must give the offeror consideration (something of value) to turn an ordinarily revocable offer into an irrevocable option contract. Second, options can be given on anything—not just real estate (such as land and buildings).

The *Central Bank & Trust v. Kincaid* case examines a situation involving an option.

CENTRAL BANK & TRUST v. KINCAID

Supreme Court of Kentucky.
Ky, 617 S.W.2d 32 (1981).

FACTS Joan Kincaid sold an option on 90,760 shares of stock she owned in Lexington Finance Company to G. D. Kincaid. The option said that it could not be revoked for 5 years but said nothing about whether it could be exercised by anyone other than G. D. Kincaid. G. D. died before the 5 years had expired, and his executor tried to exercise the option. Joan Kincaid claimed the option expired when G. D. died. G. D.'s estate sued Joan.

ISSUE Could an option given to one person be exercised by another when the option said nothing about this matter?

DECISION An option to buy stock that says nothing about any third party's right to exercise it can only be exercised by the original optionee. An option is a right to exercise a privilege and is not a sale. Common law does not favor restraints on alienation (limits on selling or otherwise disposing of property). Since an option restricts the optionor's right to sell, this restriction is not favored by the law and is given a narrow interpretation.

LEGAL TIP

If you make an option contract, be sure to say whether the option can be exercised only by the people who made the contract or by someone else (such as the estate of the party with the option). If the option contract does not say that someone else can exercise the option, it can *only* be exercised by the person named in the option contract.

Firm offers Firm offers are a second exception to the general rule that offers are revocable at any time. A **firm offer** is a written offer made by a merchant for the sale or purchase of goods, assuring that the offer will be irrevocable for the period of time stated in the offer (up to a three-month maximum, which is renewable). UCC is the law creating firm offers. Every state but Louisiana recognizes UCC firm offers. Note that the firm offer does not exist for realty or services.

Offers to form unilateral contracts Chapter 17 indicated that a unilateral contract is a promise requesting an act in return. If an offeror makes an offer requesting an act and the offeree starts performing the act, can the offeror revoke the offer before the offeree completes the act? Many courts say "No," allowing the offeree reasonable time to complete the requested act. They suspend the offeror's power to revoke during this period.

Rejection A **rejection** is the offeree's unequivocal refusal of an offer that is communicated to the offeror. The legal effect of a rejection is to end the offer. Thus, a rejection followed by an acceptance does not form a contract. The following are rejections in response to offers: "No," "Never," "I don't want that," and words or indications of similar import. On the other hand, the offeree's questions to the offeror concerning the offer are not rejections and do not end the offer. Also, conditional acceptances (such as "I accept *if* you paint the fences) are rejections. Thus, they end offers (and are offers from the original offeree to the original offeror).

Counter-offer **Counter-offers** end offers. Counter-offers are statements by offerees to offerors changing terms in the original offer. Implicitly, a counter-offer amounts to an offeree's saying to an offeror, "I do not want your original offer, but I am making you this offer instead."

A counter-offer could be made even if an offeree tried to accept an offer. Common law says that any addition or change (even a small, unintentional one) of the offeree's acceptance turns an acceptance into a counter-offer. The UCC changes this rule somewhat when goods are involved. (See the section "Acceptance" for further discussion.) The *U.S. v. Roberts* case shows what happens when an offeree conditionally accepts an offer.

U.S. v. ROBERTS

United States District Court, Eastern District of Texas.
436 F.Supp. 553 (1977).

FACTS Mr. Roberts' estate owed the United States Government a disputed amount of back taxes. Mrs. Roberts, the executrix of her husband's estate, offered to pay the United States $13,000 to settle all the estate's tax obligations. The United States accepted the offer with the understanding that the settlement was only of her personal liability as executrix and did not eliminate the United State's tax claims against her husband's estate. The United States then allowed the statute of limitations to expire against tax claims on the husband's estate. This expiration prevented a suit against the estate to recover the taxes. It also meant the only way the United States could recover the disputed taxes was to enforce the settlement agreement.

ISSUE Was there a binding settlement agreement between Mrs. Roberts and the United States?

DECISION There was no binding agreement because her offer was conditionally accepted by the United States. As such, the United States rejected her offer and made a counter-offer, which she never accepted.

LEGAL TIP
When you accept an offer, do not put conditions in your acceptance if you want it to bind the offeror.

Death or insanity of the offeror or offeree If either the offeror or offeree dies or becomes insane after the offer is made but before acceptance, the offer ends automatically.

Intervening or subsequent illegality The following example involves intervening or subsequent illegality. Suppose John Sluck offers Ray Jordan 50 barrels of whiskey for $100 per barrel. If it becomes illegal to make and sell alcoholic beverages before Ray accepts, Sluck's offer would automatically end. If the contract becomes illegal *after* acceptance but before performance, the contract duties end due to illegality.

Summary The preceding sections have discussed the definition of offers, ways offers end, the difference between offers and invitations to negotiate, offers' definiteness requirement, offers' communication requirement, contracts' mutual assent requirement, "mutual assent" means "agreement", and the component of an agreement: an offer and an acceptance.

Acceptance

Once the offeree has an offer, he or she has the power to accept it. Acceptance merges the offer and acceptance into a contract binding both the offeror and offeree.

What is an acceptance? An **acceptance** is an assent by the offeree to the offer's terms. The acceptance can occur by word or act. The offeree must simply communicate the intent to accept to the offeror; he or she does not even have to use the word "accept."

The *Glover v. Jewish War Veterans* case examines the issue of intent to accept.

GLOVER v. JEWISH WAR VETERANS

Municipal Court of Appeals for the District of Columbia.
D.C. Mun., 68 A.2d 233 (1949).

FACTS Maurice Bernstein was murdered. The next day Post 58 of the Jewish War Veterans of the United States put an ad in the newspapers offering a $500 reward for information leading to the conviction of the murderers. Mrs. Glover provided such information to police, but she was unaware of the reward when she did the act the ad requested. She then learned of the reward and asked for it. The Jewish War Veterans refused to pay because Glover did not know of the ad's offer when she did the requested act. She sued to recover the $500.

ISSUE Must an offeree of an ad for a reward by a private organization know of the offer when the act of acceptance is performed?

DECISION Glover lost because she did not know of the offer in the ad when she did the requested act. Therefore, she was not intending to accept when she did the requested act. Assent or intent to accept is an essential element of acceptance.

LEGAL TIP

When someone asks for information, before answering ask if there is a reward or if any pay will be given. This request will help you collect if a reward or any pay has been offered.

The offeree usually has a choice about accepting or rejecting an offer. In a few cases (such as public accommodations—motels and hotels—or restaurants), the federal Civil Rights Act of 1964 requires that hotels and restaurants accept customers' offers to use their facilities. This Act assumes that the customer is able to pay and no public health, safety, or other laws would be broken. Years ago, the Waldorf-Astoria Hotel legally refused to house Fidel Castro because he insisted on bringing live chickens into his room—a clear breach of public health laws.

Also, a merchant's power to accept or reject a customer's offer may be limited by the FTC's regulations forbidding bait-and-switch advertising.

How to accept Acceptance must be done in the way the offeror requests. For example, if the offeror says, "Accept by mail," a telephoned acceptance is invalid and no contract results. If the offeror says, "Accept by return mail," the acceptance must be sent on the same day that the offer was received. If the offeror says, "Paint my house, and I'll pay you $500," a *promise* to paint the house is not acceptance; the offeror asked for painting, not a promise to paint. The *Champagne Chrysler-Plymouth, Inc. v. Giles* case examines the proper form of acceptance.

Who can accept? Only the offeree can accept an offer. The offeree could be directed to one person, a small group of people, or the general public.

What is the effect of an "acceptance" by someone to whom the offer was not directed? The "acceptance" is ineffective, and no contract results. However, the

CHAMPAGNE CHRYSLER-PLYMOUTH, INC. v. GILES

Court of Appeals, Third District.
Fla.App., 388 S.2d 1343 (1980).

FACTS Champagne Chrysler-Plymouth placed a mimeograhed flyer in nearly every Miami bowling alley. It offered a new car to anyone who could bowl a 300-point game on a Miami television show on a particular Saturday. Giles, aware of the general notice, bowled a 300-point game on the television show on February 17, 1978, a different Saturday than the one stipulated. He demanded that Champagne Chrysler-Plymouth give him a car. The car dealer refused. Giles sued for breach of contract.

ISSUE Was the flyer an offer and did Giles comply with it sufficiently to accept and bind the auto dealer to a contract?

DECISION No. The flyer was an offer, but Giles did not comply with it. He did not bowl the 300-point game on the Saturday television show that the dealer (offeror) had designated. Courts require that an acceptance comply strictly with an offeror's demands.

LEGAL TIP

When an offer requests an act to accept, follow the offer's requirements exactly. Acts that are close to but not exactly what the offeror wants usually are not valid as acceptances.

original offeree could treat this "acceptance" as an offer and accept it thereby forming a contract.

Silence as acceptance Silence is generally not acceptance. This prevents an offeror from forcing the offeree to reply to avoid contract liability. For example, suppose a television store with a large inventory of new televisions sends out postcards describing in detail a particular model, offering it for $500, and providing that if the store has not heard from the customer in the next 5 days, it will treat the customer's silence as acceptance. Must the customer send in a postcard rejecting the offer to avoid a contract? No. Silence generally is not acceptance. The *Durick Insurance v. Andrus* case discusses the issue of silence as acceptance.

Two exceptions to the general rule that silence is not acceptance are trade custom and previous dealings. If failure to respond to an offer is regarded as

DURICK INSURANCE v. ANDRUS

Supreme Court of Vermont.
Vt., 424 A.2d 249 (1980).

FACTS Andrus insured his apartment building for $40,000 with Durick Insurance. There was no automatic renewal provision in the policy. Two months before the policy expired, Durick recommended that Andrus increase his coverage to $48,000. Andrus said that he wished to insure only up to $24,000, the balance of the mortgage. Durick then sent Andrus a new policy with $48,000 coverage, containing a provision allowing the insured to cancel the policy by returning it to Durick. Andrus did nothing, and Durick sued for the unpaid premiums on the new policy.

ISSUE Did Andrus' silence result in an acceptance of Durick's offer for higher policy coverage?

DECISION Andrus' silence was not acceptance. The offeror cannot force the offeree to speak or be bound by his acceptance. There was no trade custom or previous dealing exception here to the general rule that silence is not acceptance.

LEGAL TIP

When sending someone an offer, do not interpret silence as acceptance. Ask for written acceptance.

acceptance in a particular trade, then the offeree must reject the offer to avoid contract liability. Previous dealings regarding silence refer to prior contracts that require the offeree to respond to avoid contract liability. For example, in some book and record "clubs" members agree in advance to take the monthly selection unless they send in a stop order (rejection notice).

Unordered goods in the mail Section 3009 of the federal Postal Reorganization Act of 1970 permits people receiving unordered goods in the mail from businesses to keep, use, discard, or dispose of the goods in any manner without any obligation whatsoever to the sender. It is also possible that the senders of unordered merchandise through the mails could be violating laws forbidding use of the mails to defraud and unfair methods of competition under the Federal Trade Commission Act.

Accepting additional rules If the offeror does not specify a way to accept and the offeror mailed or telegraphed the offer, the offeree can use either to accept. The prior rule is common law, which applies to realty and services. In the case of goods, the UCC permits the parties or circumstances clearly to specify a way to accept. If neither the parties or circumstances clearly indicate the medium (e.g., phone, mail, etc.) to use, the UCC permits any reasonable way in the situation.

Acceptances adding to or varying from the offer: Common law exactness rule Is an acceptance effective if it adds to or changes a term in the offer? The answer depends on what was offered. If the offer was for realty, services, or insurance, acceptances must be exact. This is the common law exactness (or mirror image) rule. The acceptance must exactly "mirror" what was offered. The reason is to protect offerors from being forced into contracts they never intended, which would occur if offerees could add to or change the offer and have it bind the offeror.

The following is an example of the common law exactness rule: Tom Simon offers his house to Joe Blanc for $75,000. Blanc says, "I accept. Paint it white." Blanc accepted but added a new term, therefore, there is no contract between Simon and Blanc for Simon's house because Blanc's acceptance was not exact. Putting it another way, Blanc's acceptance was *not* the "mirror image" of Simon's offer. To force Simon to sell a "white house" would force him into a contract his offer never suggested.

Acceptances adding to or varying from the offer: The UCC Rule The common law exactness (or mirror image) rule for acceptances is not followed when goods (distinguished from realty, services, or insurance) are involved. Acceptances of offers to buy (or sell) goods may add to or change the offer and still be acceptances forming contracts. For example, Sellit says to Buyit, "I'll sell you my car for $500." Buyit responds, "I'll take it; put new seat covers on it." Sellit clearly intended to sell the car but nothing in the offer mentions new seat covers. Is there a contract? If so, what are the terms?

The UCC sets out the rules for contracts dealing with goods. Acceptances with added terms are acceptances of the original offer *and* an offer back to the original offeror regarding the added term. In other words, there is a contract regarding what the original offeror offered (e.g., the car in the situation above). The buyer is bound to the original offer only. The buyer's *added term* (e.g., the seat covers) in the acceptance is essentially a new offer made to the original offeror. The original offeror in the example above has sold his or her car and does not have to put seat covers on the car.

When is an acceptance effective? If an offeror says that an acceptance is effective only when received, it is effective only when the *offeror* receives it. If the offeror fails to say anything about an acceptance's effective date, a mailed acceptance is effective on the date it was sent with correct postage and address. This is the **mailbox rule,** meaning that acceptance takes effect when the offeree drops the acceptance in the mailbox (or other appropriate receptacle). This rule applies even if the letter of acceptance never reaches the offeror.

This rule is examined in the *Worms v. Burgess* case.

WORMS v. BURGESS

Court of Appeals of Oklahoma.
Okl.App., 620 P.2d 455 (1980).

FACTS Burgess and Worms entered an option contract. This contract provided that if Worms decided to exercise the option, he should notify Burgess of this fact by registered mail on or before August 21, 1977. Worms decided to exercise the option and sent the registered letter on August 20. Burgess never received the letter and claimed the option had lapsed. Worms sued Burgess.

ISSUE Where an option contract provides for notification on or before a fixed date and the notice is properly mailed on time by the optionee but not timely received by the optionor is the option effective?

DECISION Yes. In this case, the option was effectively exercised. The Oklahoma Court of Appeals relied on the mailbox rule, which says that an acceptance, where mail is an acceptable mode of delivery, is effective when deposited in the mail properly addressed and with sufficient postage on it.

LEGAL TIP

An offer should say that an acceptance is effective *only* when the offeror receives it. This qualification protects the offeror from making an offer and not knowing if the offeree has accepted it.

A telegraphed acceptance is effective when given to the telegraph office official. Again, if the offeror specifies that a telegraphed acceptance is effective only when received, this restriction must be observed.

The telephone can also be used to accept unless the parties involved say otherwise or state law requires a written contract.

Acceptances at an auction Who accepts and who offers at an auction? The auctioneer makes invitations to negotiate, and the audience's bids are offers. The auctioneer accepts these offers when his or her hammer falls to the auction block. Since a bid is an offer, the bidder may withdraw it any time before acceptance. If a bid is accepted, a contract results that binds both the bidder and auctioneer.

If the bids are not high enough to satisfy the auctioneer, must the highest bid be accepted? The answer to that question depends on whether the auction is "with or without reserve." If an auction is "with reserve," the auctioneer may withdraw an item if the bids are too low. If the auction is "without reserve," the highest bidder's offer must be accepted no matter how low it is.

KEY TERMS

Offeror
Offeree
Offer
Objective intent
Subjective intent
Excited utterance
Social offers
Agreement to agree
Sham transactions
Invitations to negotiate
Revocation
Option
Firm offer
Rejection
Counter-offers
Acceptance
Mailbox rule

CHAPTER PROBLEMS

1. Who are the offeror and the offeree?
2. Must an offer be written in all cases?
3. Give an example of a written offer.
4. Does a contract exist if a person offers to sell his or her car for $400 but really does not intend to follow through on the offer, and the offeree accepts?
5. Give an example of an invitation to negotiate.
6. Name some characteristics of offers.
7. Who can accept an offer?
8. If B offers his house to C for $40,000 and C says, "I accept; paint the house before I move in," has C accepted?

*9. A landowner listed certain land with a realtor. When the brokerage listing agreement expired, the broker called the owner to see if the property was still available for sale. The owner replied that the property was still available, but the tenant leasing it had the first option to buy. Shortly after this conversation, the broker secured an offer to buy from a third party. However, the tenant exercised the first option to buy, which prevented the third party from buying. The broker sued the owner for the brokerage commission, arguing that the realtor had satisfied the brokerage contract's terms by producing a ready, able, and willing buyer. Was the landowner's conditional acceptance of the broker's offer accepted by the broker, thereby forming a contract? *Arthur Rubloff & Co. v. Drovers Nat. Bank of Chicago,* 36 Ill. Dec. 194, 400 N.E.2d 614 (1980).

*10. Golestaneh offered to sell his Florida condominium to Mintzberg. The offeror's terms were: selling price $200,000 cash; closing date beginning of October; broker's commission to be split evenly between the parties; price includes light fixtures, carpeting, and major appliances. The prospective buyer, Mintzberg, sent the following letter to the seller: "This will confirm that the October 1, 1979, closing date is acceptable with the understanding that Mr. Mintzberg would prefer an earlier closing date. I would appreciate a more detailed explanation of your advice to my secretary regarding the maintenance charges." Was the buyer's letter an acceptance of the seller's offer? *Mintzberg v. Golestaneh,* 390 So.2d 759 (1980).

"Consideration is the price paid for the promise."

Gordon Schaber and Claude Rohwer

"We know the sound of two hands clapping. But what is the sound of one hand clapping?"

A Zen Koan

Chapter 19

Consideration

CHAPTER PREVIEW

- Meaning of consideration
- Reason for the consideration requirement
- Exceptions to the consideration requirement
- Adequacy of consideration
- Illusory promises
- The past consideration rule
- Moral obligation
- Promissory estoppel
- Promises to pay debts barred by the statute of limitations

"I've been robbed," shouted William Story, Jr. His uncle had promised to pay him $5000 if William would not drink, smoke, swear, or gamble at cards or billiards before becoming 21 years old. William had agreed and his uncle had told William he would hold the money at interest. When his uncle died two years later, William made a claim against his uncle's estate for the $5000 plus interest. The estate argued that William should get nothing since he had given his uncle nothing (no consideration in return for his promise). Therefore, the uncle's promise—it was argued—was unenforceable. Was it?

We have already discussed the parts of a contract which are the offer and acceptance (or some substitutes). This chapter will look again at the agreement to determine if it meets another test: consideration. The chapter will also define consideration and look at some consideration problems. The law has recently increased the number of exceptions to the consideration requirement, which this chapter also covers.

CONSIDERATION DEFINITION

Let's begin by giving a nontechnical and a technical definition of consideration. Nontechnically, **consideration** means that each party making the contract (the offeror and offeree) must bargain for and give up a right in order to make the other's promise or act enforceable.

Technically, consideration is a bargained for benefit to the promisor or a detriment to the promisee.

Benefit to the promisor Consideration can be a benefit to the promisor. For example, B promises to pay A $500 if A promises to paint B's house. B's promise to pay A *benefits* A. B's promise is therefore consideration that supports (makes enforceable) A's promise to paint.

The same is true about A's promise to paint making B's promise to pay enforceable. Figure 19-1 illustrates consideration in a bilateral contract.

The *Sambo's Restaurants v. City of Ann Arbor* case shows how consideration can benefit the promisor.

SAMBO'S RESTAURANTS v. CITY OF ANN ARBOR

U.S. District Court (E.D. Mich.).
473 F.Supp. 41 (1979).

FACTS Sambo's Restaurants (Sambo's) applied to the City of Ann Arbor for site approval for construction of a restaurant in the city. A city councilman (and later the whole council) refused to support the plan because the name "Sambo's" was offensive. Sambo's attorney later wrote on the site plan " 'Sambo's' " will not be used in regard to this restaurant." The city council then approved the site plan on December 4, 1972.

Sambo's built a restaurant in Ann Arbor and operated under the name "Jolly Tiger." The restaurant lost over $18,000 in 1978. Sambo's applied to the local government for a permit to use the name "Sambo's" on a sign outside its restaurant, which was allowed at first. Then the city denied the permit on grounds that the City gave Sambo's the building permit based on Sambo's agreement not to use the name "Sambo's." Sambo's argued this agreement was invalid because the City gave Sambo's no consideration for its promise not to use the name "Sambo's."

ISSUE Had the City of Ann Arbor given Sambo's any consideration for Sambo's promise not to use the name "Sambo's?"

DECISION Yes. Consideration is a right, interest, profit, or benefit to the promisor or some forbearance, detriment, loss, or responsibility given or undertaken by the promisee. In this case, the consideration to Sambo's consisted of the following benefits:

1. Avoiding public discussion and arousing public feeling on a sensitive issue relating to the name "Sambo's."
2. Avoiding an economic boycott (threatened by one city councilman).
3. Receiving speedy site approval to build the restaurant.
4. Avoiding an insult to city council members.

Therefore, the City of Ann Arbor gave Sambo's consideration for its promise. Sambo's promise not to use its name was therefore enforceable.

LEGAL TIP

A promise is enforceable if the promisor receives benefits (or consideration) as a result of the promise.

Figure 19-1 **Example of Consideration in a Bilateral Contract**

A (promisor)	A's promise to paint (consideration) →	B (promisee)
A (promisee)	← B's promise to pay A $500 (consideration)	B (promisor)

Detriment to the promisee A "legal detriment" means giving up a right to something. In the A–B diagram in Figure 19-1 B promises to pay A $500 if A promises to paint B's house.

B's promise to pay A is *both* a benefit to A (since A gets $500) and a detriment to B (since B agrees to give up $500). (A's promise to paint B's house also is a benefit to B and a detriment to A.)

A **detriment to the promisee** is consideration to the promisor if the promisor bargained for it. This detriment occurs even if the promisor gets no benefit when the promisee does what the promisor bargained for. The *Hamer v. Sidway* case illustrates this point.

HAMER v. SIDWAY

Court of Appeals of New York.
27 N.E. 256 (1891).

FACTS William E. Story, Sr. (uncle) had a nephew, William E. Story, Jr. (nephew). At a family dinner, the uncle promised to pay the nephew $5000 if he would not drink, use tobacco, swear, play cards or billiards for money until he became 21 years old.

The nephew followed the uncle's request. Upon reaching age 21, the nephew asked for the $5000. The uncle sent a letter telling how hard he had worked for the money and went on to say he hoped the nephew would not waste it. The uncle also said he was pleased that the nephew had followed his request. The uncle added, "You shall have the $5000, as I promised you. I had the money in the bank the day you were 21 years old. You shall have the money certain. You can consider this money on interest."

The nephew agreed the money should stay with the uncle "on interest" as the letter described.

Two years later, the uncle died without having paid the nephew anything. The nephew sued the uncle's estate for the money. The estate (defendant in this case) argued that the uncle's promise was not binding because the nephew had given the uncle no consideration.

ISSUE Had the nephew given the uncle any consideration for the uncle's promise to pay him $5000?

DECISION Yes. The nephew had given consideration. Consideration can be a benefit to the promisor (the uncle here) or a detriment to the promisee (the nephew here). The uncle's estate argued that the nephew's giving up drinking, smoking, swearing, and gambling (as the uncle had requested) did *not* benefit the uncle (the promisor). However, the estate forgot that consideration does *not* have to benefit the promisor. Consideration exists if the promisor requested something that would be a detriment (cost or burden) to the promisee (the nephew). The nephew gave up his right to drink, smoke, swear, and gamble, which was a detriment to the nephew. Therefore, consideration made the uncle's promise binding.

LEGAL TIP

A promisor's promise is binding if the promisee gives up a right requested by the promisor (even if the promisor receives no benefit).

Forms of consideration Recall that there are bilateral contracts, or agreements, made when the offeror and offeree exchange promises. In bilateral contracts, the consideration is the *two promises.* In other words, making one promise is consideration for the other party's making a return promise.

In unilateral contracts, consideration involves making a promise (the offer) and doing the act the offer requests (the acceptance).

Effect of consideration If consideration exists, each party is bound to a contract, assuming all the other contract requirements (such as offer and acceptance) exist.

Consideration: The difference between contracts and gifts Consideration is the difference between gifts and contracts. When you give something you get nothing in exchange. What is missing (the nothing in exchange) is the consideration. When you make a contract you tell the other person what you will do for him (her) and what you want in return. The "What you want in return" is consideration (that person's consideration going to you). What you will turn over to the other person is your consideration to him or her (what you will do for the other person).

Why require consideration? The reason for requiring consideration is to satisfy the basic natural law idea of fairness. *Both* sides should give something to the other to have a binding agreement.

"Bargained for" part of the consideration definition The "bargained for" part of the consideration definition means that the person receiving the benefit (or requesting the *other* party to suffer a detriment) must have requested or bargained for the benefit (or detriment). The idea is to stop the promisee from giving the promisor something the promisor does not want to make the promisor's promise binding. For example, Bob says that he will pay Davy $500 if Davy promises to paint Bob's house. Instead of promising to paint, Davy promises Bob a coonskin cap. Davy's promising to give Bob the coonskin cap is a benefit to Bob but Bob did not bargain for (or want) the cap. Since Bob has "bargained for" the paint job and *not* the cap, only the paint job is consideration here.

Adequacy of Consideration

Adequacy of consideration means: Did you get a good deal or did you pay too much? Courts (judges) do not usually examine the adequacy of the consideration because of freedom of contract.

Freedom of contract means the parties to the contract, not a judge, decide what and how much consideration each gives the other. Each individual protects his or her own best interest.

For example, suppose Ray Jordan agrees to pay Virginia Mower $10,000 for her clunker of a car. After making the contract, Jordan has second thoughts and refuses to pay. Mower sues him for breach of contract. Jordan defends by claiming that Mower's car is worth $2000, not $10,000. Said another way, Jordan claims Mower's consideration is inadequate. However, this claim is no defense for Jordan. Jordan must bargain for the best price possible *before* entering the contract. If he cannot get a fair price, he should not buy the car. In a free market economy, Ray, *not* a judge, protects Ray's best interest.

Exceptions There are times when courts will say there is inadequate consideration. Generally, the exceptions involve uneven exchanges suggesting duress or undue influence. For example, an uneven exchange of the same currency will cause a court to say the consideration is inadequate (such as Mower exchanging her $5 bill for Jordan's $10 one).

Situations Where There Is No Consideration

There are several instances where something appears to be consideration but actually is not. These situations involve:

1. Past consideration.
2. Illusory promises.
3. Promises involving pre-existing duties.
4. Moral obligations.

Past consideration **Past consideration** is not actual consideration. For example, Marsha House tells Irwin Tankerly, "In consideration of your driving me to work yesterday, I promise to pay you $10. Tankerly cannot enforce House's promise because his consideration to House was *past* consideration (which is not consideration). However, Tankerly can give House present consideration by promising today to drive House to work tomorrow. This present consideration would make her promise enforceable *if* she bargained for it.

Illusory promise An **illusory promise** is not consideration. An illusory promise occurs when someone promises to do something but then maintains control over whether the act will be done. For example, if Ellen Pearse promises to buy Robert Barry's book *if she feels like it,* she has not promised to do anything. She has made an illusory promise because she can do it (or not) as she wishes. Pearse's promise to Barry is not consideration and therefore does not make Barry's promise to her enforceable.

Promise involving pre-existing duties If someone promises to do what he or she already legally has to do, this is *not* consideration. The reason is that the promisor *gives up no right* (he or she gave it up before).

A person could have a pre-existing legal duty because of a previously made contract or statutory duty. For example, a bank offers a $1000 reward for capturing bank robbers. The town sheriff captures the robbers. Since the sheriff had a pre-existing contract duty (and probably statutory duty also) to capture robbers, he or she could not collect the $1000 reward. Similarly, promises not to commit crimes or torts against someone are not consideration; people have a *pre-existing* statutory duty not to commit crimes or torts against others.

The *Libertyville Township v. Woodbury* case shows an unsuccessful attempt to argue pre-existing duty.

Moral obligations A **moral obligation** is not usually consideration. In one case, a wife chased her husband around the neighborhood, swinging an ax and accusing him of marital infidelity. He ran into a neighbor's house, where he tripped and fell. The wife followed him and was about to hit him with the ax, when the neighbor put his hand in front of the ax. The neighbor was struck by the ax instead

LIBERTYVILLE TOWNSHIP v. WOODBURY

Illinois Court of Appeals.
460 N.E.2d 66 (Ill.App. 2 Dist. 1984).

FACTS Patricia Woodbury applied to Libertyville Township for welfare benefits. Before she could get the welfare, she was told to sign a form saying that she promised to repay the township the aid it gave her. She signed the form and received $1090.26 in welfare between February 1, 1980, and March 18, 1981. On or about April 30, 1981, Woodbury sold her house for $42,000. She received $15,705.49 after paying the mortgage. Libertyville Township sued Woodbury for her promise to repay the welfare payments it gave her. Woodbury argued that Libertyville Township had given her no consideration for her promise to repay. She claimed that since the township had a pre-existing legal duty to pay her welfare, its promise to give her welfare was no consideration. Therefore, she said her promise to repay the welfare was unenforceable.

ISSUE Did Libertyville Township give Patricia Woodbury consideration for her promise to repay the welfare she received?

DECISION Yes. Libertyville gave Woodbury consideration. Libertyville did not have a pre-existing legal duty to give her welfare. Therefore, when Libertyville promised to give her welfare, it gave her consideration for her promise to repay—making Woodbury's promise enforceable.

The promise to do what one already is legally obligated to do is not consideration. The Libertyville welfare director had wide discretion in determining welfare recipients. Deciding to give welfare only to those who agreed to repay the money was a valid exercise of this discretion. Libertyville did not owe Patricia Woodbury welfare.

LEGAL TIP

Be sure to give up a right to a person in order to hold that person to his or her promise.

of the husband. The husband's life was saved, but the neighbor's hand was badly injured. The husband later promised to pay the neighbor for his damaged hand. When the husband did not actually pay, the neighbor sued the husband for breach of contract. The husband argued that the neighbor had not given consideration when the husband promised him damages. The neighbor argued that the husband had a moral obligation to pay since the neighbor saved the husband's life. The court rejected the neighbor's argument that moral obligation made the husband's promise enforceable. The neighbor gave no consideration (*at the time of the husband's promise*), so the husband's promise was *unenforceable*.

The *Stone v. Lynch* case illustrates the general rule that moral obligation is not consideration.

Some Consideration Problems

Some types of contracts present consideration problems. Some of these are related to output and requirement contracts, exclusive dealing contracts, debt settlement contracts, novations, and unforeseen difficulties. We discuss these consideration problems in the following subsections.

Output and requirement contracts An **output contract** arises when one business agrees to sell all of its output to another company for a certain time period. This agreement is not illusory. The seller has given up the right to sell elsewhere.

How much output can a business force on a buyer under an output contract? How much can a buyer reduce or increase its requirements under a requirements contract? For goods, the Uniform Commercial Code limits quantities to a good-faith amount based on "normal" output or requirements. In other words, the UCC does not allow large changes in amounts demanded or supplied.

STONE v. LYNCH

Court of Appeals of N.C.
315 S.E.2d 350 (1984).

FACTS The Communications Workers of America (CWA) unionized Rudolph Stone's place of employment in 1979. Several weeks later the newly unionized workers went out on strike. The CWA union gave money to its striking members to live on which it had no legal duty to do. CWA gave Stone living expenses of $1879.95 during the strike. Stone reported this money as nontaxable income on his 1979 North Carolina state income tax return; he claimed the CWA gave him a gift. The State of North Carolina claimed Stone had a moral obligation to repay the money the union gave him. If the money was a gift, Stone owed no state income tax; however, if the money from the union was based on a contract debt, Stone had to pay taxes on the money.

ISSUE Did Stone have a moral obligation to repay the union the strike benefits the union had given him?

DECISION No. The State's argument was that Stone had a moral obligation to repay the union the strike benefits. According to this argument, moral obligation is consideration; therefore, Stone had a contract with the union to repay the strike benefits and, in turn, the benefits became taxable. However, this argument was not accepted. As a general rule, moral obligation is not consideration; therefore, the strike benefits were a gift from the CWA and were not taxable.

LEGAL TIP
Moral obligation is not usually consideration.

Exclusive dealing contracts An **exclusive dealing contract** forces a buyer to purchase only a particular seller's products. The consideration problem with such contracts is that they do not force the buyer to purchase anything. Such contracts have consideration because like requirements contracts, which is what exclusive dealing contracts are, the buyer gives up the right to buy elsewhere. However, it is important to note that certain exclusive dealing contracts violate Section 3 of the Clayton Act.

Debt settlement contracts Partial payment of a debt can cancel the entire debt if the debt amount is disputed. If the debtor and creditor disagree on the amount owed, the debt is unliquidated (uncertain in amount). When the debtor and creditor agree on a certain amount as full payment of an unliquidated debt, they give up the right to sue for some other amount. This agreement is the consideration making settlement of unliquidated debts full payment of the entire debt.

For example, Steven agrees to paint Art's factory for $1000 "over cost." Steve buys paint costing $10 per gallon and gets a 15% discount for paying in cash rather than using a credit card. He pays $850 for the paint but claims that the paint cost $1000. Art argues that Steve's cost is $850—what he actually paid. Rather than suing over this unliquidated debt, Art and Steve agree that Art's paying $900 discharges the entire debt. The consideration making this debt settlement enforceable is the fact that both Art and Steve agreed to give up the right to sue. In this type of situation, there must be a *bona fide* (good faith) disagreement about the amount owed.

Agreements concerning part payment of a liquidated debt (where there is no good-faith dispute about the amount owed) lack consideration. (However, under Section 1-107 of the UCC, certain debt cancellations are valid even if there is no consideration. The subsection in this chapter entitled "Claims that are waived or given up" discusses this point.)

Substituting building contracts: Novations **Novations** are new contracts that replace old, executory contracts. If a contract is partly incomplete on both sides, both parties can agree to end that contract and substitute a new one. The new contract can have different terms.

What would be an example of a novation? Suppose Henry agrees to drill a well for Virginia. Henry assumes the soil is sand, but it turns out to be rock. Therefore, the drilling costs increase twenty times. Henry asks Virginia if they can end their incomplete agreement and substitute a new one that pays Henry more money. If Virginia agrees, the new agreement called a novation will bind both parties. Since both Henry and Virginia gave up the right to complete the old contract, there are no consideration problems.

Unforeseen difficulties To understand the issue of unforeseen difficulties, consider the original Henry-Virginia drilling contract example again. Henry again assumes the soil is sand when it is actually rock. Drilling costs again increase twenty times, but this time Henry does *not* ask for a new contract. Instead, he asks Virginia for twenty times more money, and Virginia agrees. The consideration problem is that Virginia has given up new rights (i.e., *more* money) to Henry, but Henry has given Virginia nothing new. In this type of situation, some courts will say that **unforeseen difficulties** substitute for lack of consideration going from the promisee to the promisor. This decision would make Virginia's promise to pay twenty times more money enforceable.

Promises Enforceable Without Consideration

If a person makes certain promises, they can be enforced even without giving consideration to the promisor. These promises include:

1. Charitable subscriptions.
2. Promissory estoppel.
3. Promises to pay debts barred by bankruptcy.
4. Promises to pay debts barred by the statute of limitations.
5. Firm offers under the UCC.
6. Certain modifications of sale of goods contracts under the UCC.
7. Claims that are waived or given up under the UCC.
8. Some promises made under seal.

The following subsections discuss each of these promises.

Charitable subscriptions Courts enforce written, signed promises to make charitable contributions, which are called **charitable subscriptions.** These contributions must be given even if charities (including churches, hospitals, and schools) give the promisors nothing in exchange. Therefore, those signing charity pledge cards should plan on paying.

Courts give several reasons for enforcing charitable subscriptions:

1. The charity often relies to its detriment on the promise. For example, if Herman Taylor (and others) promise to give $100 to the Episcopal Church for a new building, the church enters contracts with builders. The detrimental reliance in this type of situation is often seen as a consideration substitute.

2. Courts occasionally find consideration to the donor from the other donors' promises to give to a particular project (such as building a new wing on a church).
3. Courts sometimes say the charity promises, through implication, to complete the project.

Promissory estoppel **Promissory estoppel** occurs when a person makes a promise that he or she knows (or should know) will lead a promisee to act (or not to act when they otherwise would have acted). The promisee then acts (or forebears) justifiably relying on the promise. If substantial injustice would occur if the promisor does not perform, courts will force the promisor to keep the promise. The consideration problem here is that the promisor did not receive consideration from the promisee.

An example of promissory estoppel occurred when Red Owl Stores, Inc., talked Mr. Hoffman into selling his grocery store. He did so based on Red Owl's promise that it would give him a franchised Red Owl store. When Red Owl backed out on its promise, the Wisconsin Supreme Court held Red Owl liable for Hoffman's damages. In this case, promissory estoppel applied because Red Owl had promised Hoffman a franchise. Hoffman acted reasonably in reliance on the promise; injustice would be prevented only by holding Red Owl liable.

Promises to pay debts dischargeable in bankruptcy Some promises to pay debts dischargeable in bankruptcy are enforceable even though the promisee gives the promisor (the debtor, here) no consideration. These promises are called **reaffirmation agreements** and are enforceable if:

1. They are written and the debtor signs them.
2. They are made *before* the bankruptcy discharge.
3. The reaffirmation agreement has a clear and conspicuous statement telling the debtor that he or she can escape any time before the discharge or within sixty days after filing it with the bankruptcy court (whichever is later).
4. The reaffirmation agreement is filed with the bankruptcy court and says that the debtor is fully informed and voluntarily signs it; and that the agreement puts no undue hardship on the debtor or a dependent.
5. The debtor does not change his or her mind (remember that debtors may decide not to pay, after agreeing to, any time before discharge or within sixty days after filing the reaffirmation agreement with the bankruptcy court).

The Bankruptcy Amendments of 1984 make it hard to reaffirm agreements because of numerous technicalities. The technicalities protect debtors against unwanted reaffirmations. The idea is that debtors should think twice before agreeing to pay a debt he or she is in bankruptcy trying to get rid of.

Promises to pay debts barred by the statute of limitations If a debtor promises to pay a debt barred by the statute of limitations, that promise is enforceable even if the creditor/promisee gave no consideration for the promise. For example, Virginia owes Tom $100. If Virginia has not paid the debt by tomorrow, Tom can sue Virginia for the $100 since it will be past due then.

The statute of limitations says that a case is automatically lost unless a person *starts* a lawsuit within a certain limited time after his or her rights are violated.

These state laws (with varying time restrictions) encourage people to sue promptly. As an example, assume the statute of limitations for contract debts is six years. If Tom waits seven years before suing Virginia, he will be barred from suing by the statute of limitations. However, if Virginia promises to pay Tom *after* the sixth year, she legally must do so—even if Tom gave Virginia no consideration for her promise. (Technically the statute of limitations period starts all over again.) In some cases, making a debt payment after the statute of limitations expires has been held by courts as an implied promise to pay the *whole* debt.

Firm offers under the UCC A firm offer is enforceable even though the promisee gives the promisor no consideration. The Section 2-205 of the UCC creates this rule.

What is a firm offer? There are several parts to the definition:

a. A **firm offer** is an *offer*
b. to sell or buy *goods* (*not* realty or services)
c. made only by a *merchant* of the kind of goods sold
d. that must be *written* and *signed* by the merchant
e. that assures the offer will be "firm" (not revoked, i.e., withdrawn) for the time stated (up to 3 months, which is renewable) or for a reasonable time if none is specified.

The firm offer is an exception to the consideration requirement because the promisee gives the merchant nothing. Yet the merchant cannot withdraw the offer for the time stated in the offer (which the merchant specifies). Firm offers are like options: the offeror in both may not withdraw the offer during the option period.

Certain modifications of sale of goods contracts under the UCC Section 2-209 of the UCC also eliminates the consideration requirement when parties to an existing sale of goods contract agree to modify the terms to increase the benefits of only one party. This section makes enforceable one party's promise to give consideration to the other, even though the party who receives new benefits does nothing extra (has given *no* consideration). This rule helps business by making it legal to change rights under existing contracts. Remember that this rule only applies to contracts for the sale of goods (*not* realty or services). Also *both* sides to the contract must agree to the modification.

For example, Generous Motors (GM) and Birdseye Windshield Co. (BW) make a contract requiring BW to sell 100,000 windshields to GM. The next day, GM asks BW to make the windshields tinted instead of clear (a more expensive process). BW agrees to this request even though GM gives BW no added consideration. BW's promise is enforceable even though GM gave BW no additional consideration.

Claims that are waived or given up Section 1-107 of the UCC allows a claim or right arising out of an alleged breach to be discharged in whole or part without consideration. This section requires that a written waiver or renunciation be signed and delivered by the aggrieved. Remember that this rule only applies to contracts involving sales of goods (*not* realty or services).

A case[1] when this rule did not apply involved Mr. Foote, a trucker. Mr. Foote bought a truck tractor on an installment contract and missed some payments. The seller, Harris Truck & Trailer Sales (Harris), orally gave Foote a time extension for paying. A Tennessee court said Foote could not enforce Harris' promise of an extension since Harris did not write, sign, and deliver its waiver.

Some promises made under seal In only a few states, promises made "under seal" bind the promisor even if he or she receives no consideration. A promise made "under seal" is a written promise signed with the promisor's personal seal. A seal once was a piece of melted wax stamped on a legal document to show it was binding. Today, where the law recognizes them, seals are any symbol put on legal documents to make them binding. However, most states do not say seals have any effect.

The UCC does not allow seals to be a substitute for consideration. If a person makes a promise "under seal" when selling goods but gets no consideration, the promise is not enforceable.

KEY TERMS

Consideration
Detriment to the promisee
Adequacy of consideration
Freedom of contract
Past consideration
Illusory promise
Moral obligation
Output contract
Exclusive dealing contract
Novations
Unforeseen difficulties
Charitable subscription
Promissory estoppel
Reaffirmation agreements
Firm offer

CHAPTER PROBLEMS

1. Name three instances under the UCC when a promise is enforceable even though the other party (the promisee) gave no bargained for consideration in exchange.
2. What does it mean to say, "Consideration is the price one pays for a promise?"
3. Describe the consideration in a bilateral and a unilateral contract.
4. As a general rule is moral obligation consideration?
5. What is a novation?
6. Can unforeseen difficulties ever be a consideration substitute?

*7. If a promise or act does not have a dollar-and-cents value, can it be "consideration?" *Hyde v. Shapiro,* 346 N.W.2d 241 (Neb. 1984).

*8. Is forebearance to prosecute a disputed claim good consideration? Is forebearance to prosecute a claim *known* to be invalid good consideration? *Salmeron v. U.S.,* 724 F.2d 1357 (9th Cir. 1983).

*9. Failure of consideration is neglect, refusal, or failure of one of the parties to perform or furnish agreed upon consideration. Is protracted (long drawn out) delay in performance failure of consideration? *Goodwin v. Lofton,* 662 S.W.2d 215 (Ark. App. 1984).

[1] *Harris Truck & Trailer Sales v. Foote,* 436 S.W.2d 460 (Tenn. 1968).

*10. A person makes a contract and gives but does not receive any consideration. If that person performs the contract, can he or she later "undo" his or her prior performance because the other person gave no consideration? *Rubenstein v. Sela,* 672 P.2d 492 (Ariz. App. 1983).

Chapter 20

Misconduct or Mistake in Formation

"No rogue should enjoy his ill-gotten plunder for the simple reason that his victim is by chance a fool."

Chamberlin and Currier v. Fuller, 9 A. 832 (1887)

CHAPTER PREVIEW

- Types of mistakes and their uses as contract defenses
- Types of defenses used for misrepresentation and fraud
- Differences between innocent misrepresentation and fraud
- Requirements for duress and types of duress
- Effects of undue influence
- Remedies for the victims of defenses

White submitted a bid for a project and made a $60,000 computation error. White was awarded the project but wants the extra $60,000. Can he get the money?

By now the parties have an agreement. But it may not be a legally enforceable contract if one of the defenses discussed in this chapter applies. If there is mistake, misrepresentation, fraud, duress, undue influence, or unconscionability in the negotiations, the agreement has a legal flaw. The result is that the contract is void, voidable, or subject to reformation. This chapter shows that when the parties agreed to a contract for the wrong reason (by mistake or because of unlawful pressure for example), they may be excused from the contract or have the contract changed or reformed according to their original understandings.

MISTAKE

Some types of errors or **mistakes** made in forming contracts will make the final contract invalid. Mistakes that can invalidate a contract are mistakes of fact and not mistakes in judgment. Contract law does not help those who paid too much for a used car or those who should not have invested their last $1000-savings in a stock deal. These mistakes are personal judgment mistakes, and the contracts are still valid. There are, however, some mistakes of fact that will require the contract to be voidable or at least changed to reflect the parties' true understanding.

Mutual Mistakes

Mutual mistakes are those made by both parties to the contract at the same time about all or part of the contract. There are two types of mutual mistakes: mutual mistakes of fact and mutual mistakes in drafting.

Mutual mistakes of fact If, at the time of contracting, the parties have certain ideas and assumptions about the subject matter of their contract, and then later discover their ideas and assumptions are wrong, they have made a mutual mistake. Their contract then is invalid. For example, if a seller contracts with a buyer to sell the buyer thirty bicycles from the seller's warehouse and both parties later learn that the seller's warehouse has been destroyed by fire, there is no contract; the seller never had the bicycles to sell, and the buyer contracted for existing and available bicycles—and *not* for the bicycles to be manufactured.

A common mistake in real estate contracts is that the acreage figure is incorrect. The size of the land or amount of acreage determines the contract price. The buyer and seller rely on a survey for size. If the survey is wrong, the parties' basic assumptions were incorrect, and the contract is invalid.

Another common mistake is one caused by a change in laws that the parties are unaware of at the time of contracting. For example, suppose Albert contracts to lease Berferd's property for a manufacturing plant. The property has had a zoning change that prohibits use of the property for manufacturing. Neither Albert nor Berferd knows of the change. There has been a mutual mistake and the contract is invalid. In the *Sherwood v. Walker* case, the court discusses the interesting issue of mutual mistake.

If the parties are uncertain about something and enter into a contract anyway, there is no mistake—only conscious ignorance. For example, Annie may quit claim her land title to Babs. The nature of a quit claim deed is one that offers no promises or guarantees that Annie has good title or any title to the property. The whole nature of Annie and Babs' bargain is one of uncertainty. Their contract is not later invalid because Annie did not have good title. If the parties don't know what they

SHERWOOD v. WALKER

Supreme Court of Michigan.
33 N.W. 919 (1887).

FACTS The Walkers were importers and breeders of polled Angus cattle. Sherwood was a banker interested in cattle with distinguished backgrounds. Sherwood viewed the Walkers' selection of cattle and contracted to purchase "Rose 2d of Aberlone" for 5½ cents per pound plus 50 pounds shrinkage or $80. (Rose weighed 1420 pounds) Rose would have been worth ten times or more that amount, but she was barren. After the parties had contracted and before Sherwood picked up Rose, the Walkers discovered Rose was with calf and refused to go through with the contract on the grounds of mutual mistake. Sherwood filed suit.

ISSUE Had the parties made a mutual mistake of fact which made their contract invalid?

DECISION Yes. The parties made the assumption that they were contracting for a barren cow, and the price to be paid was an insignificant sum compared with the cow's value had she been a breeder. The court held that if the thing bargained for is actually different from what is delivered, there is no contract. In this case, the Walkers would never have made the contract if they knew that Rose was a breeder.

LEGAL TIP

Before entering into a contract to buy or sell anything, the subject matter should be thoroughly checked and any assumptions about the subject matter verified.

are contracting for but go ahead and contract anyway, their contract is valid because they assume the unknown. The *Gerard v. Almouli* case is an example of conscious ignorance.

GERARD v. ALMOULI

United States Court of Appeals,
Second Circuit.
747 F.2d 936 (1984).

FACTS Almouli was a resident of Israel and the inventor of the Firejet Extinguisher. Gerard owned and operated Firejet America. Firejet is a small-sized aerosol fire extinguisher, which is portable, easy to use, and already in use throughout the world.

Gerard agreed to buy $300,000-worth of Firejets but only after Almouli had obtained the Underwriters' Laboratory (UL) approval. Most buyers require UL approval in the United States. UL approval takes between three and seven years and is costly. After six years, Almouli still did not have approval, had spent $115,000 more than he had planned, and Gerard refused to take delivery. Almouli claims that there was a mutual mistake of fact on the time and cost for UL approval.

ISSUE Had Gerard and Almouli made a mutual mistake?

DECISION No. They had entered into a contract knowing that UL approval could take six years. They were both willing to take that time risk. They also knew that the longer the testing period, the more the cost. There was no mistake, just an agreement to an unknown.

LEGAL TIP

If a third party is testing contract goods, be sure to get a time limit for their tests in that contract.

Mutual mistakes in drafting Often the parties will reach an oral agreement, but when the contract is put in written form the typist makes an error. If such a drafting mistake has been made, a court may change or reform the writing to reflect the true contract. For example, a landlord and tenant may have made a lease for a seasonal restaurant property with rent to be higher during the tourist season (June, July, and August). The written agreement has a monthly rate that stays the same throughout the year. The landlord may seek reformation if there is enough proof of their tourist-season increase agreement.

Unilateral Mistakes

When only one party to the contract makes a mistake, it is called a **unilateral mistake.** There are three types of unilateral mistakes: unilateral mistakes of fact, unilateral mistakes of computation; and unilateral mistakes of law.

Unilateral mistakes of fact If Clarissa buys a particular type of weed killer thinking that it will kill weeds and not grass, and the weed killer destroys all growing things around her home, the loss is Clarissa's responsibility. The dealer who sold Clarissa the weed killer is not responsible. When one person assumes the product will do a certain thing (kill only weeds), and the other person (dealer) does not know the buyer's assumption, the buyer bears the cost of that mistake. If the dealer knows or should know of Clarissa's incorrect assumption, the dealer must correct her. If the dealer does not correct her, the contract may be invalid under misrepresentation (see discussion below). The general rule is that if one person in a contract makes a mistake, and the other person does not know about the mistake, the contract is valid.

Unilateral mistakes of computation People often make mistakes when providing price estimates or bids for projects. For example, Janet needs 50 copies of a 400-page booklet and calls Bob's printing shop for an estimate. Bob gives Janet an estimate of $1008. The other estimates that Janet gets are between $1700 and $2000. Janet accepts Bob's estimate and has the booklets printed. Bob then discovers a multiplication error, which means that the estimate should have been $1776. Bob wants to charge the added $768. Janet only wants to pay the original $1008 estimate. Bob has made a unilateral mistake. Such mistakes are defenses to contracts if the following requirements are met:

1. The mistake must have been a clerical or computational (such as an adding error). It must not be a misjudgment of cost.
2. Enforcing the contract would be unfair; one party would benefit unjustly.
3. The mistake must be big enough so the other side should have known that there was an error.

In the example, Bob just miscalculated. Janet would benefit by nearly $800 of free services. Considering the range in bids, Janet should have realized that there had been a mistake. If Bob's mistake had been smaller, such as $50, the contract would still be valid. If Bob had just misjudged the time the project would take, the contract would still be valid. In the *White v. Berenda Mesa Water District* case, the court answers the question of whether a unilateral mistake in computation excuses a person from performing a contract.

Unilateral mistakes of law Whether a mistake of law will invalidate a contract depends on the type of law about which the mistake is made. For example, if one or both of the parties makes a mistake about the zoning on a piece of property, it is a mistake of law and a way to invalidate the contract. However, if one party makes a mistake by not understanding that a contract legally binds both parties,

WHITE v. BERENDA MESA WATER DISTRICT

Court of Appeals, Fifth District.
87 Cal.Rptr. 338 (1970).

FACTS White submitted a $427,890 bid to Berenda Mesa Water District for a project involving the regulation of a reservoir. White was the low bidder and was awarded the project. White then discovered that he had made a mistake in computing his bid and appeared before the District Board to withdraw his bid. The bids ranged from White's $427,890 bid to $721,851. The bid nearest White's was $494,320 or $66,430 higher. The District's engineer had estimated the cost of the project at $512,250 or $84,360 above White's bid. White refused to perform. The District sued.

ISSUE Does White's unilateral mistake in computation excuse him from performance of the contract?

DECISION Yes. The range of bids indicated that perhaps a mistake had been made. The District still had time to substitute someone else for the project and remain within their estimate.

LEGAL TIP
Bid figures should always be double-checked. If there is a mistake, and the offeree cannot get another contractor, you will have to perform for the mistaken price. Anyone receiving a bid should question one that is too low.

it is a mistake of law, but the contract is valid. The mistake of law must be related to the subject matter and not a mistake of contract negotiations, formation, or performance.

Figure 20-1 summarizes the types of mistakes and their effects on contract validity.

MISREPRESENTATION

A misrepresentation occurs when one person misleads the other about the nature of the contract or its subject matter. There are two types of misrepresentation: innocent misrepresentation and fraudulent misrepresentation, or fraud.

Innocent Misrepresentation

Innocent misrepresentation occurs when one of the parties is misled, although not intentionally, about the subject matter of the contract. For example, suppose Al wants to have window tinting put on his car windows. In Al's state, there is a statute that regulates how dark that tinting can be. Al has the windows done at Tina's Tinting and Body Shop and is assured by Tina that the darkness complies with the state statute. After the project is completed, Al is driving the car and is stopped and cited for a violation of the statute. Al returns to Tina to have the tinting removed and obtain a refund. In checking the problem, Tina finds her attorney has misread the statute. Tina has unintentionally misled Al and is guilty of innocent misrepresentation. Intent to mislead is not required in innocent misrepresentation. The requirements for proving innocent misrepresentation are covered in the following subsections.

Incorrect statement of fact or law Misrepresentation cannot be based upon an opinion given by a party or claims of excellence or sales puffery. "This house is the best on the block," is an opinion and not a basis for misrepresentation. "This house does not have termites," is an example of a statement of fact, which can

Figure 20-1 **Mistakes in Formation**

	FACT		LAW	
	Unilateral	***Bilateral***	***Unilateral***	***Bilateral***
Example	1. Purchase of wrong weed killer 2. Personal injury	1. Rose 2d 2. Existence of goods	Zoning or validity of controls	Zoning range
Requirements	1. Other Party does not know of mistake 2. Mistake in judgment	1. Parties made basic assumptions 2. Assumptions were incorrect 3. Not conscious ignorame		Must be mistake relating to subject matter
Invalidates Contract	No	Yes	Yes, if law relates to subject matter No, if law relates to formulation validity or performance of contracts	Yes

	DRAFTING		COMPUTATION	
	Unilateral	***Bilateral***	***Unilateral***	***Bilateral***
Example	See computational error	Secretarial typo in final written agreement	Bid is incorrect	See bilateral drafting
Requirements		1. Parties had prior oral agreement 2. Proof of prior oral agreement available	1. Error in computation and not misjudgment of costs 2. Unfair to enforce that price 3. Sizeable mistake	
Invalidates Contract		No, but contract can be reformed to reflect prior agreement	Yes	

be the basis of a misrepresentation action. "This is one of the best used-car buys around," is opinion, but "This car has not been in an accident," is fact. Figure 20-2 provides examples of statements and classifies them as fact or opinion.

Misrepresentation can happen when the "facts" given are not correct. For example, a real estate agent may give a buyer the wrong information about zoning on a piece of land. The agent has misrepresented by not checking information carefully; and therefore the agent is liable for the negligence.

Misrepresentation can happen when relevant facts are not disclosed. If something about the subject matter of the contract should be disclosed, but is not, then there has been an incorrect statement of fact—misrepresentation. For example, if Ralph is trying to sell a car that has been in an accident but does not disclose that, Ralph has misrepresented by nondisclosure.

In some cases, even a promise of future performance is misrepresentation. For example, a promise that a car will last 20,000 miles without a problem would be a basis for misrepresentation. In the *Hollerman v. F. H. Peavey & Co.* case, the court deals with an issue of promise and misrepresentation.

HOLLERMAN v. F. H. PEAVEY & CO.

Supreme Court of Minnesota.
130 N.W.2d 534 (1964).

FACTS Hollerman purchased a chicken-raising franchise from F. H. Peavey based on sales literature promising that a franchise would "return to the careful broiler raiser an income roughly equal to half as much as is obtained from an average-sized farm in the Midwest—and it will do so for about six hours of one person's attention daily." Other statements about the franchise were also overly optimistic. After sixteen-hour days and no income, Hollerman brought suit to have the contract rescinded (set aside) and his money returned on the basis of misrepresentation.

ISSUE Were the promises of good income with limited work statements of fact upon which an action for misrepresentation could be based?

DECISION Yes. The statements were too specific and too direct in their promise to be opinion or sales puffery. Peavey had made definite promises, which could be the basis of a misrepresentation action.

LEGAL TIP

Promises about income, work, and performance should be checked for their sources. Checking with other, earlier buyers is one way to see if promises made are accurate.

The statement is material or is relied upon A **material misrepresentation** is defined as one that would affect the buying decision of a "reasonable person." This second element can also be met by showing that the harmed party relied on a statement and was justified in that reliance. For example, a seller, relying upon a statement from an exterminator, may tell a buyer that a house is termite-free. The fact that a house is termite-free is critical in a property purchase and would be material. A statement that a business can be operated out of the home in that area is not material to the average buyer but may be relied upon by a buyer who runs a home-based business. In the *Fischer v. Division West Chinchilla Ranch* case, the issue of reliance was critical in determining whether there had been misrepresentation.

FISCHER v. DIVISION WEST CHINCHILLA RANCH

United States District Court, District of Minnesota.
310 F.Supp. 424 (1970).

FACTS Division West Chinchilla ranch sold chinchillas and related ranch equipment to Fischer so that he could get started in the chinchilla business. Fischer purchased the items because of Division's statements that chinchilla ranching was "an easy undertaking . . . and . . . no special skills were required to become a successful chinchilla rancher." Fischer had difficulty in operating the ranch, lost money, and brought suit for a refund.

ISSUE Was Fischer justified in relying on Division's statements that chinchilla ranching was an easy undertaking?

DECISION Yes. When one party is as inexperienced as Fischer and the other party is fully knowledgeable, the reliance on the knowledgeable party's representations is justified. Division should have realized Fischer would not have the skills to be successful.

LEGAL TIP

Before entering a new business, check the nature and extent of experience needed.

Intentional Misrepresentation or Fraud

Intentional misrepresentation or contractual fraud is a sufficient basis to set aside a contract. The elements of contractual fraud are:

1. A material misstatement of fact or law.
2. Causation or reliance by the defrauded party.
3. Knowledge of the falsity of the statement—intent to defraud or scienter.

Parties are entitled to rescind contracts based on fraud so that they are not forced to deal with unscrupulous parties. The elements for intentional misrepresentation are discussed in the next three subsections.

Material misstatement The same types of statements that qualified for innocent misrepresentation will qualify for this first element of **fraudulent misrepresentation.** Incorrect statements, omissions, and promises of performance

Figure 20-2 **Fact versus Opinion**

STATEMENT	FACT	OPINION
"This toothpaste has flouride."	X	
"This toothpaste will improve your sex life."		X
"This toothpaste will give you whiter teeth within ten days."	X	
"This toothpaste has been used by more movie stars than any other one."	X	
"This toothpaste has a great taste."		X
"This toothpaste is a gel."	X	
"This toothpaste has a breath freshener in it."	X	
"This toothpaste will give you the sweetest breath ever."		X
"This toothpaste will make you feel fresh all over."		X
"This toothpaste will reduce the number of cavities you have by 20%."	X	

that will not be kept can all be the basis for a **fraud** action. Examples of material misstatements follow:

1. "This printer will interface with any personal computer." (The printer interfaces with only one personal computer which costs $550.)
2. "This neighborhood will have its own pool and clubhouse." (The developer has cancelled the construction contracts for both projects.)
3. "This weed killer will not harm grass and flowers." (The weed killer destroys all living things.)
4. "I have an AA in Chemistry." (Placed on job application for a lab technician when applicant had only a high school chemistry course.)

Causation or reliance Parties who want to have their contracts set aside must establish that the misstatement is responsible for or was a critical factor in their decisions to enter into the contract. In other words, the parties must be deceived by the misstatement and rely upon the misstatement in making the contractual decision. The issue of **reliance** is a question of fact and differs from case to case. If the party hearing the misrepresentation makes an independent investigation, there is no reliance. For example, a used-car dealer may state that the trailer hitch on the back of a small-engine used car is brand new. If a potential buyer checks with the former owner of the car and finds that the hitch was used to tow household goods across the country, there can be no reliance.

Knowledge, intent, or scienter The element of **scienter** is the major difference between innocent misrepresentation and fraudulent misrepresentation. Fraudulent misrepresentation requires proof that the party making the material statement knows that it was false and made the statement with the intent to mislead. Since this element requires proof of a state of mind, it is sometimes difficult to prove. Most of the time, intent is shown by external facts or by circumstances. For example, a car dealer may tell a potential buyer that a used car was a dealer demonstrator and used only for test drives. However, if it can be shown that the car was purchased after an accident and was repaired in the dealer's body shop, the element of intent is established. In the *Dicker v. Smith* case, the court deals with a set of circumstances to determine whether fraudulent misrepresentation occurred.

DURESS

Duress is a wrongful act by one person against another. Persons who are victims of duress enter into a contract that they might not have entered into otherwise. Duress has the following elements:

1. Wrongful act or threat.
2. Party is deprived of a meaningful choice.
3. Party gives up something of economic value.

Wrongful Act or Threat

Physical force or threats of physical force are the most common forms of duress. The statement, "Your signature or your brains on this contract," is an example of

DICKER v. SMITH

Supreme Court of Kansas.
523 P.2d 371 (1974).

FACTS The Smiths were selling their home to the Dickers. As part of the sales contract, the Dickers required the Smiths to provide proof that the house was termite-free. The Smiths hired Hawks Inter-State Exterminators to examine the home, and Hawks found active termites. After discussing the problem with their broker, the Smiths hired United Pest Control to examine their property. United was not told of the Hawks report. United issued a "no-termite" certificate. Shortly after the Dickers moved in, they discovered small insects and, as luck would have it, called Hawks Inter-State Exterminators. Also as luck would have it, the same inspector who found the active termites when the Smiths' hired Hawks came to the Dickers'. When the Dickers were told of Hawks' report by the inspector, they filed suit for fraud.

ISSUE Did the Smiths make a fraudulent misrepresentation to the Dickers?

DECISION Yes. The second examination and the cover- of the Hawks' report indicate intent to defraud.

LEGAL TIP

A real estate sales contract should require the seller to furnish copies of all termite inspection reports for the sale property over the last five years. The buyer might employ an inspector independently and have the seller pay the cost instead of accepting a report furnished by the seller.

a threat of physical force. However, the wrongful act need not be force; it can, for example, be the threat of imprisonment. Suppose Mike is arrested for a rape, but after the arrest it is clear to the police that there has been a mistaken identification. The police then tell Mike that he can be released and the charges dismissed if he will sign a waiver of his rights for false arrest or false imprisonment. Even if Mike signs, the waiver would be invalid because the wrongful act was the threat of continued imprisonment unless the signature was obtained.

A typical wrongful act that does not involve force but is nonetheless unlawful is keeping property to obtain a fee or a contract signature. For example, some towing yard operators will retain towed vehicles until the owners pay or sign for a tremendous fee (in states where it is prohibited). Such conduct, unless the state authorizes towing dealers to do so, is a wrongful act.

Duress can also result from economic pressure. This form of duress is called **economic duress.** For example, suppose general contractor Albie has subcontractor Bert doing work on a major project. Halfway through the project, when Albie is on a tight schedule and cannot find a substitute, Bert refuses to complete the work unless Albie agrees to give the subcontract work to Bert on all future projects. Even if Albie signs such an agreement, it will be invalid because of the duress used by Bert.

A final type of wrongful act occurs when a party threatens to enforce legal rights that are unrelated to the contract subject matter. For example, an employer threatening to fire employees who do not sign over their shares of company stock would be using duress.

In the *Chandler v. Sanger* case, the court deals with the issue of whether a wrongful act sufficient to support a duress action has occurred.

No Meaningful Choice

For duress to exist, it must be shown that the wrongful act or threat deprived the party of a meaningful choice. In the examples of wrongful acts, all the parties had a choice, but an unrealistic choice—not a choice to contract or not contract, but a choice to contract or be kept in jail; a choice to contract or lose a job; a choice

CHANDLER v. SANGER

Supreme Court of Massachusetts.
114 Mass. 364 (1874).

FACTS Chandler had declared bankruptcy and had all of his creditors' claims against him discharged in the bankruptcy proceedings. Sanger, a discharged and disgruntled creditor, obtained a judgment and took Chandler's ice wagon off the street in the pre-dawn hours after it was loaded with ice for deliveries. Sanger refused to give back the wagon until Chandler paid the discharged claim. Chandler paid the claim, got back the wagon, and then sued to get back the amount paid on the discharged claim.

ISSUE Could the claim payment be set aside on the grounds of duress?

DECISION Yes. Chandler had no choice since his ice would have melted. Sanger's act was a wrongful act of trespass and an attempt to enforce a nonenforceable claim.

LEGAL TIP

Once debts are discharged in bankruptcy, they cannot be collected. If a party is forced because of circumstances to pay an amount not due, suit can be brought to recover that amount.

to contract or not complete a construction project. A meaningful choice is one that allows the party to weigh alternatives without jeopardizing everything if the contract is not signed.

Loss of Economic Value

Duress also requires that the victim give up something of economic value. In most cases, this element is easily satisfied—loss of stock, loss of job, payment of an invalid claim, or payment of towing charges. In the *Enslen v. Village of Lombard* case, the issue of duress is the center of the court's decision.

ENSLEN v. VILLAGE OF LOMBARD

Court of Appeal, Second District.
470 N.E.2d 1188 (1984).

FACTS Keith Enslen was employed as a lieutenant in the fire department of the Village of Lombard. Enslen was asked by his Chief, John Corbly, to resign. Corbly told Enslen he was in a no-win situation. Corbly told him that if he did not resign by noon the next day, Corbly would file dismissal proceedings for the following conduct:

1. Inhaling nitrous oxide (laughing gas) on duty.
2. Being an alcoholic.
3. Having the police involved in his marital disputes.

Enslen resigned because he felt that he had no choice. He then brought suit to set aside his resignation on the grounds of duress.

ISSUE Could Enslen have the resignation set aside on the grounds of duress?

DECISION No. The threat was only to bring dismissal proceedings that had some basis. It would be duress only if the chief had threatened other wrongful action such as public disclosure of Enslen's acts or had required more than a resignation (had demanded that Enslen sign away his retirement rights, for example).

LEGAL TIP

Presenting employees with a choice of resigning or facing dismissal proceedings must be handled carefully. It is very easy to cross the line into duress.

UNDUE INFLUENCE

Undue influence is a defense based on unfair persuasion. There are two elements for undue influence:

1. There must be a relationship of trust or confidence between the contracting parties.
2. One party must use the other's trust or confidence to dominate or influence the other party's transactions.

Confidential Relationship

A **confidential relationship** occurs when one party places trust in another party and relies on that party for support, advice, care, etc. Examples include parent/child relationships where the parent is elderly and dependent upon the child; attorney/client relationships where the client relies on the attorney for advice or for business or financial management; and husband/wife relationships where one spouse is dependent upon the other for management of financial affairs. Other relationships that can qualify are physician/patient; trustee/beneficiary; pastor/parishioner and fiancé/fiancée.

Use of the Confidential Relationship to Control

The second element of undue influence requires one party to use the confidential relationship to control or dominate the other party or to influence the other party to make transactions that he or she would not ordinarily make or that might not be in his or her best interest. For example, Adele, a widow, lives with her son Richard and is dependent upon him for shelter, food, and clothing. Richard tells his mother that unless she signs over all her property to him, he will send her to an old folks' home. Richard's actions are undue influence. The *B.A.L. v. Edna Gladney Home* case involves an issue of undue influence.

B.A.L. v. EDNA GLADNEY HOME

Court of Appeals, Second District, Texas.
677 S.W.2d 826 (1984).

FACTS B.A.L. was from New York, nineteen, pregnant, and unmarried. She left New York without telling anyone, including her family, that she was pregnant. She entered the Edna Gladney Home in Forth Worth, Texas, on November 8, 1983. She lived there and had all her prenatal care and expenses covered until her baby girl was born on February 10, 1984. On February 8, 1984, she had told her mother of her pregnancy and talked with her sister on February 9, 1984. Her sister and mother both told her that they would help raise the baby if she decided to keep it.

On February 14, 1984, B.A.L. signed an affidavit relinquishing all her parental rights. There were two witnesses, and Elaine Brown (an employee of the Edna Gladney Home) notarized the signature.

Shortly thereafter, B.A.L. indicated that she wanted her child back, and accused the home of undue influence.

ISSUE Was there undue influence by the home?

DECISION No. B.A.L. was told of her rights. Although the home cared for her, she was permitted to talk with her family before signing and knew of their support. Even though there was a confidential relationship, she also consulted family members before deciding.

LEGAL TIP

Have those in a confidential relationship talk with others before they sign a contract. This gives them independent advice.

REMEDIES FOR MISTAKE OR MISCONDUCT IN FORMATION

When a party discovers that there has been a mistake or misconduct in the contract negotiations or execution, that party has several options and remedies available. First, the party can decide that the contract is still a good deal and adhere to the terms. On the other hand, the party can have the contract rescinded or set aside. If a party chooses rescission, then any monies paid are returned, and the parties involved are returned to the same positions that they were in before the time of contract. It is important that the decision to rescind be made immediately after the defense to the contract is discovered. If the decision takes too long, the right to rescind is lost.

In some cases of misrepresentation, the party may not want the contract rescinded but may want some damages. For example, in the *Dicker v. Smith* case, the Dickers could decide to keep the house and have the Smiths pay the costs of extermination.

These same remedies of honoring the contract or rescission are available in cases of duress and undue influence. Remedies for mistakes were discussed with the types of mistakes (Figure 20-1). Figure 20-3 summarizes the remedies defenses and when they are used.

Figure 20-3 **Remedies for Mistakes and Misconduct in Formation**

NAME OF REMEDY	NATURE OF REMEDY	APPLICATION
Rescission	Contract set aside	Mutual mistake of fact/ innocent and fraudulent misrepresentation Duress Undue influence
Reformation	Mistake corrected	Mutual mistake in drafting
Damages	Money paid to compensate for wrongful conduct	Misrepresentation Duress Undue influence

KEY TERMS

Mutual mistakes
Unilateral mistakes
Mistakes of fact
Mistakes in computation
Mistakes in drafting
Mistakes of law
Innocent misrepresentation
Fraudulent misrepresentation
Fraud
Reliance
Scienter
Duress
Economic duress
Undue influence
Confidential relationship

CHAPTER PROBLEMS

1. Antonio and Rosa Ruggieri were Italian immigrants who owned the Val Rose restaurant and tavern in Malvern, Pennsylvania. Neither spoke English very well, and neither could read English. When they were ready to retire, they decided to have their son, Valentino, take over the business. Valentino brought in a partner (Zampitella) who agreed to pay $40,000. Valentino asked his parents to sign, and they asked to have their attorney to review the contract. Valentino told them that the contract was acceptable and insisted that they sign. The $40,000 was never paid, and Antonio and Rosa brought suit to have Zampitella removed from the business on the grounds of undue influence. Will they win? *Ruggieri v. West Forum Corp.*, 282 A.2d 304 (Pa. 1971)

2. Boynton went to Wood's jewelry store and saw an attractive stone in one of the cases. Boynton asked Wood the price, and Wood told him he didn't know what the stone was. Boynton said it looked like a topaz or a canary egg but that he didn't know what it was either. Wood sold it to Boynton for $1. Boynton then had an expert look at it. The stone was an uncut diamond worth over $1000. Wood brought suit to have the contract rescinded on the grounds of mutual mistake. What is the result? *Wood v. Boynton,* 25 N.W. 42 (Wisconsin 1885).

3. Tri-State Roofing Company was the roofing subcontractor on a job for which Simon was the general contractor. Tri-State was approximately half finished with the work when it informed Simon that it would not complete the work unless Simon signed a release for damages for delays. Simon was unable to get another roofing contractor and signed the release. Tri-State was three weeks late in completing the project and Simon had to pay $21,000 in damages to the project owner. Simon wants to have the release rescinded. Who wins? What is the result? *Tri-State Roofing Co. of Uniontown v. Simon,* 142 A.2d 333 (Pa. 1958).

4. Determine whether each of the following are statements of fact or sales puffery.
   A. "This suit of clothes will wear like iron."
   B. "These bicycles are unsurpassable, having been subjected to severe and practical tests."
   C. "This article will give first-class satisfaction."
   D. "These items sell like hot cakes."

5. Elizaga, a resident of the Phillipines, was offered a job at the Kaiser Foundation Hospital in Oregon. Elizaga accepted the job and moved his family and belongings to Oregon. Shortly after Elizaga arrived in Oregon, the job position he had been offered was eliminated. The administrator was aware that the job was under review for possible elimination, but did not tell Elizaga of the review before Elizaga accepted the position and moved. Elizaga wishes to collect damages—can he? *Elizaga v. Kaiser Foundation Hospitals, Inc.,* 487 P.2d 870 (Oreg. 1971).

6. Mattefs Construction Company submitted a $134,896 bid to Boise Junior College District for a project. The architect's estimate was $150,000. Seven bids were more than $155,000, and three were less than $150,000. Mattefs' bid was the lowest. The next highest bid was $141,048. Mattefs discovered an addition error. Will they have to perform for $134,896? *Boise Junior College District v. Mattefs Const. Co.,* 450 P.2d 870 (Idaho 1971).

7. Odorizzi was employed as an elementary school teacher in the Bloomfield School District. He was arrested on criminal charges of homosexual activity and was asked by the District Board to resign. Because of their request and the negative publicity, Odorizzi resigned. Later the charges were dismissed, and Odorizzi asked to be reinstated. He said that he signed his letter of resignation just after having been arrested, questioned by the police, and not having slept for forty hours. His principal wrote the resignation and brought it to Odorizzi's apartment for his signature. Is the resignation valid? *Odorizzi v. Bloomfield School District,* 54 Cal.Rptr. 533 (1966).

8. Robinson, a young married man, worked as an assistant manager at one of Gallaher's Drug Store outlets. Shortly after he began work, an audit of the store showed that $2000 was missing. After three days of questioning, Robinson signed a note agreeing to be responsible for repaying the $2000. Robinson was told that he could not continue to work for Gallaher unless the note was signed. Is the note valid? *Gallaher Drug Co. v. Robinson,* 232 N.E.2d 668 (Ohio 1965).

9. Give some examples of confidential relationships.

*10. Mrs. Audrey Vokes, was a fifty-one-year-old widow with no remaining family. She went for a free lesson at the Arthur Murray School of Dancing in Davenport.

During her first visit, she was promised a bright future and was sold eight half-hour dance lessons for $14.50. During the next sixteen-month period, she was sold 2302 hours of dance lessons at a total cost of $31,090.45. If she lived to be 120, she would be able to use all the lessons. She was praised for her "skill, poise, grace, and rapid improvement." In reality, Mrs. Vokes could not even discern the beat in music and had no dancing ability. She was also convinced to purchase dancing-level medals—bronze, silver, and gold at a cost of $6000, $12,000, and $18,000, respectively. When one of Mrs. Vokes friends computed all her costs, she convinced Mrs. Vokes to see an attorney and bring suit to have the contracts rescinded. Does she have any defenses? *Vokes v. Arthur Murray,* 212 So.2d 906 (Fla. 1968).

"Youth is a wonderful thing. What a crime to waste it on children."
Bernard Shaw

Chapter 21

Capacity

CHAPTER PREVIEW

- Minors—who they are
- Minors' contract obligations
- Minors' rights to disaffirm contracts
- Contracts for necessaries and their validity
- Requirements for mental capacity
- Ratification—when and how it happens
- Concept of "voidable"

Gary Muniz, age seventeen, purchased a Plymouth dune buggy from Ed Jones on October 18, 1969, for $35. When Gary's father learned of the dune buggy purchase, he ordered Gary to return the dune buggy and get his money back. Two days later, while Gary was on his way to see Ed Jones, he was in an accident and the buggy was totally destroyed. Gary, claiming that he is a minor, still wants to escape the contract, and Ed refuses because there is no longer a dune buggy. Can Gary escape the contract and recover his money?

In the preceding example, Gary and Ed are involved in a contractual relationship that suffers from a major problem—the problem of **capacity.** In order for a valid contract to exist, both parties to the contract must have contractual capacity. Contractual capacity consists of two parts; age capacity and mental capacity. Both parties to the contract must be of the legal age to contract, and both must meet certain mental standards to be classified as having capacity.

If one of the parties to the contract is missing this necessary element of capacity, then the contract is **voidable.** A voidable contract means that the party lacking capacity may choose to back out of or **disaffirm** the contractual deal. What is required for capacity? When can a party disaffirm? How does a party disaffirm? Are there any exceptions to the right to disaffirm? This chapter answers these questions and others about contractual capacity.

AGE CAPACITY

Minimum Age Requirement

Since common law was first recognized in England, there has been a minimum age requirement for a person who wants to enter a contract. Those meeting the age requirement are said to have reached their majority and can execute a valid contract. Those contracting when they are below the age limit are **minors** or infants, and they lack the necessary age to enter a contract.

At common law, the age of majority was reached the day before the twenty-first birthday. Today, each state has a statute that prescribes the age of majority. The most common age since the voting age was decreased is eighteen. Some states still keep the age of twenty-one as the age of majority. Other states hold the age somewhere in between, with nineteen being another popular age of majority.

The Voidable Concept

If a party to a contract does not meet the state's minimum age requirement, the contract is voidable at the option of the minor or infant. Simply stated, this concept means that the minor can choose not to perform under the contract. If the minor so chooses, the adult party is left without remedy for breach of contract.

Of course, if the minor decides to honor the contract, performance is permitted. The law requires the adult party in the contract to perform when the minor chooses to abide by the contractual obligations. The idea of the minimum age and the voidable concept is to protect the minor, who is supposedly not as mature in judgment, education, or knowledge as an adult. However, if the minor chooses to enforce the agreement, the law gives the appropriate contract remedies. The validity of the contract is the minor's decision, but there are certain requirements and limitations, which are discussed below. The *Parrent v. Midway Toyota* case illustrates the minor's absolute right to avoid performance of a contract entered into during minority.

Exceptions to the Voidable Concept

There are certain types of contracts minors enter that the minor cannot avoid. These contracts can be classified into three groups: statutory contracts, contracts for necessaries or necessities, and contracts of emancipated minors.

Statutory contracts Each state has, in addition to a statute setting the minimum age for contracting, several statutory exceptions to the general rule that the contracts of minors are voidable. Common exceptions include student loan agree-

PARRENT v. MIDWAY TOYOTA

Supreme Court of Montana.
626 P.2d 848 (1981).

FACTS On August 15, 1975, Melvin Parrent, then fifteen years old, injured his lower back while lifting heavy objects at his job with Midway Toyota. His injury was diagnosed as a herniated disc, and surgery for fusion of his discs was performed.

Melvin was covered by workers' compensation because the injury occurred on the job; and Tom Mazurek, an adjuster for Midway's insurer, negotiated with Melvin and his mother for a settlement of $63,136.40 in partial disability benefits. Melvin signed a final settlement agreement for that amount. Several years later, when Melvin was working in the oil fields of Montana, he began experiencing back pain and sought to reopen his workers' compensation claim. Based on the signed agreement, Mazurek refused to do so.

ISSUE Does a valid contract exist between Melvin and the insurer?

DECISION No. The contract was voidable since Melvin was only fifteen at the time the contract was entered into and the age of majority in Montana at that time was eighteen. It made no difference that Melvin's mother was present, for she did not sign the contract; Melvin was the only party to the contract and could thus choose to have the contract set aside at a later time. The risk of contracting with a minor is placed on the adult party, and the insurer should have had a guardian sign the contract, if the agreement was to be valid. Melvin was permitted to reopen his claim.

LEGAL TIP

The signature of a minor's guardian is required on all contracts. Age and guardians should be verified before the contract is executed.

ments. Even though the party may be a minor when entering into the loan agreement, some states have a statute providing that such contracts cannot be disaffirmed once the minor has obtained the education for which the funds were borrowed.

Another exception provided by many states is a type of statute that permits the minor to give consent for certain types of medical treatment and then prohibits the minor from withdrawing or disaffirming such consent. Types of medical procedures covered in this statutory exception are treatment for pregnancy, venereal disease, and drug or alcohol addicition.

Contracts entered into by minors with the United States for military service are also not voidable at the minor's option.

Cosigners When an adult, such as a parent, signs a contract as a cosigner/guarantor, he or she is liable for the contract even though the minor is not.

Contracts for necessaries or necessities Minors are responsible, at least in quasi contract, for the value of goods and services that constitute **necessaries.** Whether an item or a service is a necessary will depend upon the minor's living and employment situation. For example, a contract for the lease of an apartment would probably be a necessity for an employed, married minor but would not be a necessity for a minor who is attending high school and living at home.

The issue of medical care as a necessity has arisen many times when a minor has been treated, but the parents do not have the means to pay for medical treatment. If the minor was injured as a result of an accident for which he or she receives compensation, the courts have treated the medical care as a necessary and permitted those providing the care to recover from the tort compensation received by the minor. The *Cidis v. White* case involves the issue of whether a particular contract involved a necessity.

CIDIS v. WHITE

United States District Court, District of New York. 336 N.Y.S.2d 362 (1972).

FACTS Carol Ann White, nineteen, went to Dr. Demetrios Cidis and asked him to furnish her with contact lenses. They agreed on a price of $225, and Carol gave Cidis her personal check for $100. The doctor examined Carol on Thursday evening, ordered the lenses on Friday, and received them on Saturday. On Monday, at the insistence of her father, Carol called and cancelled the contract and stopped payment on the check. At the time, Carol lived at home, had a full-time job, and paid her parents a sum each month for room and board.

Dr. Cidis brought suit, claiming that the lenses were a necessity.

ISSUE Were the contact lenses necessaries for which Carol Ann was liable?

DECISION Yes. The contact lenses, in light of Carol Ann's employment and financial responsibilities, were necessaries for which she was liable in quasi contract for the reasonable value thereof. Dr. Cidis was awarded $150.

LEGAL TIP

What is a necessary depends on the minor's employment and living arrangements.

Those contracts for luxury items are not necessaries and minors can disaffirm the contract. Neither the minor nor the minor's parents are responsible for payment for luxury items. The *Farrar v. Swedish Health Spa* case deals with a situation concerning luxury items.

FARRAR v. SWEDISH HEALTH SPA

United States Court of Appeals, Third Circuit. 337 So.2d 911 (1976).

FACTS Cindy Farrar, seventeen and living at home with her parents, signed a form for a two-year membership at the Oak Park Swedish Health Spa at a price of $324.31. Cindy charged the two-year membership on her father's Master Charge, but she was not an authorized user of the card. Before she used the spa facilities, Cindy called the spa and told them that she was cancelling the contract because she was a minor. The spa still billed the amount on the father's card and maintained Cindy was liable on the grounds that the spa membership was a necessity.

ISSUE Did the Spa membership constitute a necessity for which Cindy was liable?

DECISION No. The spa membership was not a necessity and Cindy was not required to pay for the membership. As for the father's liability, the court held that since Cindy was not an authorized card user, the father was not liable as an adult for the cost of the membership.

LEGAL TIP

Health club memberships are not necessaries. Minors do not have the authority to use their parents' charge cards unless authorized or unless they have their own card. Before a charge card is accepted as payment, signature and buyer should be checked.

Contracts of emancipated minors According to common law, a minor became emancipated when the parents were no longer responsible for furnishing the minor with basic needs. **Emancipation** typically occurred when the minor did any one or a combination of the following: became employed in a full-time job, moved from the parental household, or married. Many states still follow this idea of emancipation, but other states have enacted specific statutes that provide the circumstances under which emancipation occurs.

Once a minor is emancipated, that minor is then liable on contracts entered into, which constitute necessaries. Thus, food, clothing, and shelter contracts would be enforceable against the minor and not subject to the right of disaffirmance.

Minor's Right to Disaffirm

The minor is given the option to perform or avoid contract responsibility on non-necessaries by disaffirming them. The following subsections describe the rules that apply to possible disaffirmance.

When the minor may disaffirm A minor may disaffirm a contract any time during minority and for a reasonable time after reaching majority. What is a reasonable time after majority varies according to the subject matter of the contract and the ability of the minor to review and judge the terms of the agreement.

The minor may disaffirm the contract by giving notice to the adult party to the contract. If such notice is not given during minority or within a reasonable time after reaching majority, the minor loses the right to disaffirm because the minor's conduct implies satisfaction with the agreement. The *Bobby Floars Toyota v. Smith* case deals with the issue of whether a minor had properly disaffirmed a contract within reasonable time limits.

BOBBY FLOARS TOYOTA v. SMITH

Court of Appeals of North Carolina.
269 S.E.2d 320 (1980).

FACTS Charles Edward Smith, Jr., purchased an automobile from Bobby Floars Toyota on August 15, 1978. Smith was then seventeen; the age of majority in North Carolina was eighteen, and Smith reached the age of eighteen on September 25, 1978.

Floars financed the purchase with thirty installment payments. Smith made eleven of the payments (ten after reaching eighteen), and then voluntarily returned the car to Floars and defaulted on the loan. Floars sold the car for less than the amount due on the loan and brought suit to recover the difference from Smith. Smith claimed that he had validly disaffirmed the contract.

ISSUE Did Smith's return of the vehicle constitute a timely disaffirmance of the contract?

DECISION No. Smith's conduct in using, keeping, and paying for the auto for ten months after reaching the age of majority exceeded the reasonable time limit. Smith recognized the contract as binding after reaching majority and waited too long to disaffirm the agreement.

LEGAL TIP

A minor who uses a car (or other purchase) for several months after reaching majority loses the right to disafirm.

Return of consideration When minors disaffirm contracts, they are required to return whatever consideration they may have received under the contract. When a minor disaffirms a contract to purchase a stereo, the stereo is returned to the adult party, and the minor receives back all money paid for the stereo.

Difficulties arise when the minor no longer has the consideration (what was obtained from the other party) received under the contract. In the chapter-opening example, the minor no longer had the dune buggy because of the accident. Can the minor still disaffirm the contract? At common law, the minor still had the right to disaffirm the contract despite the inability to return the consideration. Some courts have determined that this brought hardship to the adult party involved and have required a minor to compensate the adult party by restoring the same position that the adult was in before the contract existed. The payment of rent, depreciation or repair, or replacement costs have been required of the minor by some courts. However, the majority rule is that the minor's right to disaffirm is not conditional on the ability to return the consideration. In the chapter-opening example, the minor can escape (disaffirm) the contract even though the dune buggy is totally destroyed.

Effect of age misrepresentation In many cases where a minor is a party to a contract, the adult did not enter into the contract knowing that a minor was involved but was led to believe by appearance or representation that the minor was, in fact, an adult. An issue that has been presented in many cases is whether the minor's misrepresentation of age should stop the minor from escaping (disaffirming) the contract. Most courts say that misrepresentation will not prevent the minor from disaffirming, since responsibility for age determination is left to the adult party. The adult therefore must determine the other person's age.

Some states have passed statutes dealing with the issue of misrepresentation; those statutes affect the minor's right to disaffirm. In some states, a minor who is guilty of age misrepresentation may disaffirm the agreement but must restore the adult party to the original position—that is, return the consideration or pay damages. Some states give the minor the absolute right to disaffirm despite age misrepresentation but then permit the adult party to recover for the tort of misrepresentation.

The *Halbman v. Lemke* case involves the issues of the return of consideration by the minor and the effect of age misrepresentation upon the minor's right to disaffirm.

HALBMAN v. LEMKE

Supreme Court of Wisconsin.
298 N.W.2d 562 (1980).

FACTS On July 13, 1973, James Halbman, Jr., a minor, entered into a contract with Michael Lemke for the purchase of a 1968 Oldsmobile for the sum of $1250. Halbman paid Lemke $1000 and agreed to pay $25 per week until the balance was paid. Five weeks after the purchase, when Halbman had paid $1100, the connecting rod on the vehicle's engine broke. Lemke offered to help fix the car if Halbman would buy the used engine necessary for repair. Halbman instead took the car to a garage for repair, and the cost was $637.40. Halbman then disaffirmed the contract with Lemke. The garage removed the engine and towed the vehicle to Halbman's home, where it was vandalized and made unsalvageable. Halbman brought suit asking for the return of his $1100. Lemke defended on the grounds that the car could not be returned and that Halbman had misrepresented his age.

ISSUE Could Halbman still disaffirm even though the car was destroyed, and there was age misrepresentation?

DECISION Yes. Upon disaffirming, a minor is under an enforceable duty to return to the adult party, upon disaffirmance, as much of the consideration as remains in his possession. If the minor no longer has the property, the right to disaffirm is not lost. The adult party suffers the loss of contracting with a minor. The issue of age misrepresentation does not affect the right of the minor to disaffirm unless the legislature has passed a statute for such circumstances.

LEGAL TIP

You should always ask for proof of age before entering into a contract with a young person.

Ratification

Contracts of minors can also be treated as valid. This happens if the minor ratifies contracts entered into during minority.

Time of ratification A contract entered into during minority can become valid if the minor, upon reaching the age of majority, ratifies the contract. **Ratification** can take place only when the minor reaches the age of majority. Ratification during minority is totally ineffective. If a contract is ratified after the age of majority, the contract is treated as valid from its inception. In other words, ratification makes the contract as valid as if the minor had capacity at the time the agreement was first signed or negotiated.

Form of ratification Ratification can be express or implied. A minor can expressly ratify a contract by notifying the adult party through a written or oral statement, which indicates the intent to honor the agreement. However, such a formal expression is not necessary for ratification—a minor can also ratify an agreement through conduct. For example, a minor who continues to make payments on a contract after reaching the age of majority implies ratification of that agreement once a reasonable time for disaffirming has passed. Performance after reaching the age of majority is implied ratification.

MENTAL CAPACITY

Test for Mental Capacity

In addition to meeting the requirements of age capacity, both parties to a contract must also meet the standard of having sufficient mental capacity to enter into a binding contract. The following requirements must be met for a contracting party to have sufficient mental capacity:

1. The party must be able to understand the subject matter of the contract.
2. The party must be able to comprehend the nature of contractual obligations.
3. The party must be able to understand the consequences of entering into a valid contractual arrangement.

Basically, each party must understand that the contract is binding and also understand what is being given up under the terms of the contract. Who meets these standards is a question of fact, which must be determined on a case-by-case basis. The *In re Estate of Trahey* case involves the issue of mental capacity.

Right to Disaffirm

If a person lacks sufficient mental capacity to enter into a contract, then the contract is **voidable** at the option of the party lacking capacity (or that party's guardian). The party lacking capacity is required to return to the other party whatever consideration was received under the contract. In cases where the consideration has been destroyed, the competent party must be paid for the lost or damaged consideration. Requiring original restoration to the competent party differs from returning consideration (required of minors). The mentally incompetent have the burden of restitution; however, there is no burden of restitution if the other party to the contract knew about the mental deficiencies of the disaffirming party and entered into the contract anyway.

Liability for Necessaries or Necessities

As with minors, even the mentally incapable are liable in quasi contract when they contract for necessaries. In cases where a guardian has been appointed, recovery for such services can be made from the guardian.

IN RE ESTATE OF TRAHEY

Court of Appeals, First District.
323 N.E.2d 813 (1975).

FACTS On July 7, 1960, Josephine Trahey opened a joint account at Drovers Trust and Savings Bank with her brother and nephew as joint holders entitled to the funds upon her death. On December 7, 1970, Mrs. Trahey transferred the funds (which had grown from $5000 to $30,000) to a joint account with her friend, Mrs. Fitzpatrick.

Shortly thereafter, Mrs. Trahey was declared incompetent and her guardian sought to set aside the 1970 transfer on the grounds that Mrs. Trahey lacked capacity. Evidence indicated that Mrs. Trahey spoke often of a little nun who followed her when there was no nun. She also sat at her window in the evenings watching beautiful light displays, which were headlights of passing autos. She did not recognize friends and relatives and often answered the door for guests who were never there.

ISSUE Did Mrs. Trahey have sufficient mental capacity to make the account transfer in 1970?

DECISION No. Although Mrs. Trahey was not adjudicated an incompetent until after the transfer, the evidence indicated that she did not understand the nature or effect of her actions. Old age and impairment of mental faculties are not conclusive evidence of lack of capacity. But, Mrs. Trahey's failure to recognize her relatives and her sudden decision to leave the money for a friend and not a relative indicated a lack of understanding concerning the nature of the transaction.

LEGAL TIP

After a person is found to be incompetent, any attempt to form a contract will be invalid.

Effect of Declaration of Insanity

The discussion to this point has dealt only with persons who lacked mental capacity at the time of contracting, but who had not been declared insane or incompetent (adjudicated as an incompetent) in any type of judicial proceeding. Contracts of these individuals are voidable. However, once a person has been judged by a court as insane or incompetent and a guardian or conservator has been appointed, then the contracts of that person are void. Neither party can enforce a void agreement, and both sides are excused from performance under the agreement's obligations.

Intoxication and Mental Capacity

It is possible that a person making a contract can lack mental capacity to contract because of a temporary state of intoxication caused by drugs or alcohol, or both. This allows the drugged or drunken person to escape the contract. However, for the contracts of those intoxicated to be voidable, the parties must be able to show that they were lacking the three factors necessary for entering into a valid contract (see page 000). In other words, they must be prepared to establish that they were intoxicated to the extent of mental incapacity.

Ratification

Those who lack mental capacity when they make a contract can ratify the agreement when their mental capacity returns. For example, an individual intoxicated at the time of contracting could ratify the agreement at a later time when he or she is no longer intoxicated. Likewise, persons recovering from a mental disorder can ratify agreements made during the time when they lacked sufficient capacity to contract.

KEY TERMS

Capacity
Voidable
Disaffirm
Minors
Necessaries
Emancipation
Ratification

CHAPTER PROBLEMS

1. On August 5, 1965, Berliner sold Wentzel a 1965 Buick Riviera for a cash price of $5,176.87. At the time of the sale, Wentzel was a minor. One year later, while Wentzel was still a minor, he went to Berliner and offered the vehicle in exchange for his $5,176.87. Berliner refused to return the cash and refused to accept the car. Must he do so? *Wentzel v. Berliner,* 104 So.2d 905 (Fla. 1967).
2. Daubert, nineteen and a minor, was married and an expectant father. He was involved in an auto accident with Mosley. The accident was the result of Mosley's negligence. Daubert and his sixteen-year-old wife signed an agreement with Mosley's insurer for the payment of $1000 for medical expenses and $283.75 for property damages. When other medical bills arose, Daubert asked Mosley's insurer to pay, and the insurer said the signed agreement was a full settlement of all claims. Daubert and his wife disaffirmed the agreement on the basis of their minority. The insurer said the two were emancipated minors and could not disaffirm. What is the result? *Daubert v. Mosley,* 487 P.2d 354 (Okla. 1971).
3. Dennis Harvey, nineteen and a minor, was employed, living away from home, and engaged. He went to Hadfield's Trailer Sales and entered into a contract to purchase a trailer. He told Hadfield that he was a minor. He put $1000 down on the trailer and applied for financing at the bank. The bank refused his loan application because of his minority, and Harvey asked for his $1,000 from Hadfield. Hadfield refused to pay on the grounds that the trailer was a necessary being purchased by an emancipated minor and Harvey could not disaffirm. What is the result? *Harvey v. Hadfield,* 372 P.2d 985 (Utah 1962).
4. Hanks, a widower who was known as the town eccentric, boasted that he had discovered a vitamin to feed to horses to make them taller. The vitamin was produced from old shoe leather and ground brick dust. Hanks contracted for large amounts of coal from McNeil Coal Corporation for the purpose of mass-producing the vitamin. Hanks' relatives brought suit to disaffirm the agreement on the grounds that Hanks lacked mental capacity. What is the result? *Hanks v. McNeil Coal Corp.,* 190 P.2d 44 (Calif. 1946).
5. Snell, an attorney, was hired by a Mrs. Bradshaw to have her appointed as legal guardian for her nephew, who had been orphaned as a result of a tragic car accident involving his parents and grandparents. Snell asked that the court order the payment of attorney's fees from the nephew's estate so that Mrs. Bradshaw would not be required to pay for the services. Snell maintained the appointment of a guardian for the minor nephew was a necessary. What is the result? *Matter of Estate of Bradshaw,* 606 P.2d 578 (Okla. 1980).
6. Vichnes, a minor, purchased a round-trip plane ticket from New York to California. After taking the trip, Vichnes then went to the airplane and sought to disaffirm the agreement and to obtain a return of the funds used in the purchase. What is the result? *Vichnes v. Transcontinental Air,* 18 N.Y.S.2d 603 (1940).
7. Connelly, a minor, registered for several high school classes that required supplementary laboratory materials and manuals. The materials were furnished to the students by International Text Book Company. Connelly used the materials but did not pay for them. When asked to pay before a grade would be awarded in the class, Connelly returned the materials to disaffirm the agreement. International maintained that the materials were necessaries for which Connelly was liable. What is the result? *International Test Book Co. v. Connelly,* 99 N.E. 722 (N.Y. 1912).
8. Robertson, a minor, purchased a rare copy of a program for a movie premiere and paid $55 for it. Shortly thereafter, the program was destroyed in a fire at Robertson's home. Robertson, still a minor, returned to the dealer to disaffirm the contract and recover his $55. The dealer refused since Robertson could not return the program. What is the result?
9. Chestersen is an alcoholic and has just purchased a car. Is this contract voidable because Chestersen is an alcoholic?
10. Robertson, Sr., and his son Robertson, Jr., agreed, while the son was still a minor, that Robertson, Sr., would finance Robertson, Jr.'s way through college and dental school. Robertson, Jr., graduated from dental school, and his father wrote and asked him to begin repayment at the rate of $400 per month. Robertson, Jr., paid $100 per month for three years. Robertson, Jr., then stopped payment, saying that the loan agreement was invalid because he had entered into it while he

was still a minor. Robertson, Sr., says that Robertson, Jr., ratified the agreement after reaching majority by continuing to accept financing for his education and also by making payments for the three-year period. What is the result? *Robertson v. Robertson,* 229 So.2d 642 (Fla. 1969).

"A verbal contract is not worth the paper it is printed on."
Samuel Goldwyn

Chapter 22

The Writing Requirement

CHAPTER PREVIEW

- Types of contracts required to be in writing
- Statute of frauds
- UCC Statute of Frauds
- Merchant's confirmation memorandum
- Exceptions to the statute of frauds
- Required content for a written contract
- Parol Evidence Rule
- Exceptions to the Parol Evidence Rule

Hans Frabel agreed to have Brennan's display his sculptures in their gallery. While several of his sculptures were on display, they were either stolen or destroyed. Frabel and Brennan's written agreement was very simple and had no provision covering the theft or loss of Frabel's sculptures. Frabel thought that Brennan's was responsible because galleries usually assume the risk of loss in displaying sculptures. Brennan's said that there must be a written clause on risk of loss. Who is right?

All contracts should be in writing to protect all parties. However, the law requires only certain types of contracts to be written. If a contract must legally be written but in fact is oral, the contract is unenforceable. This means that the parties have no rights or remedies if the other side does not perform. This chapter answers the following questions: What kinds of contracts must be in writing? What type or form of writing is necessary? How are written contracts interpreted? Can written contract terms ever be changed?

TYPES OF CONTRACTS REQUIRED TO BE WRITTEN

Each state has a statute listing the types of contracts that must be written. These laws are called **statute of frauds.** The term "statute of frauds" originated in England in 1677 when Parliament passed an Act for the Prevention of Fraud and Perjuries. This act had twenty-five different sections. The original purpose of the statute of frauds was to require certain contracts to be written so that people were not encouraged to commit fraud or perjury to get contract benefits. Today each state's version of the statute of frauds will vary, but there are five major categories of contracts covered by most of the state laws. The five groups of contracts are listed and discussed below.

1. A promise to pay the debt of another.
2. A promise to transfer or buy a real property interest.
3. A promise that cannot be performed within one year.
4. A promise to marry.
5. Sales of goods under the UCC.

PROMISES TO PAY THE DEBT OF ANOTHER

Paying someone else's debt is a serious undertaking. Such an undertaking must be given in written form to be enforceable. When someone promises to pay another's debt, there is a three-party relationship. Figure 22-1 illustrates this relationship.

Third Party Promises

When one party agrees to pay the debt of another, that party is acting as a surety or a guarantor. The relationship is called either a "suretyship" or "guaranty" (see Chapter 56 for more details). For example, suppose that a newly formed corporation needs to have goods delivered on credit but does not have a credit history. If the president of the corporation says, "Deliver the goods to the corporation on credit and if it doesn't pay, I will be responsible," the president is offering to act as a surety or guarantor for the debtor corporation. However, for the president's promise to be enforceable, it must be in writing.

Parents are sureties when they cosign for their children's loans. An insurance company that promises to be responsible if a contractor does not perform on a construction project acts as a surety.

Figure 22-1 **Suretyship and the Statute of Frauds**

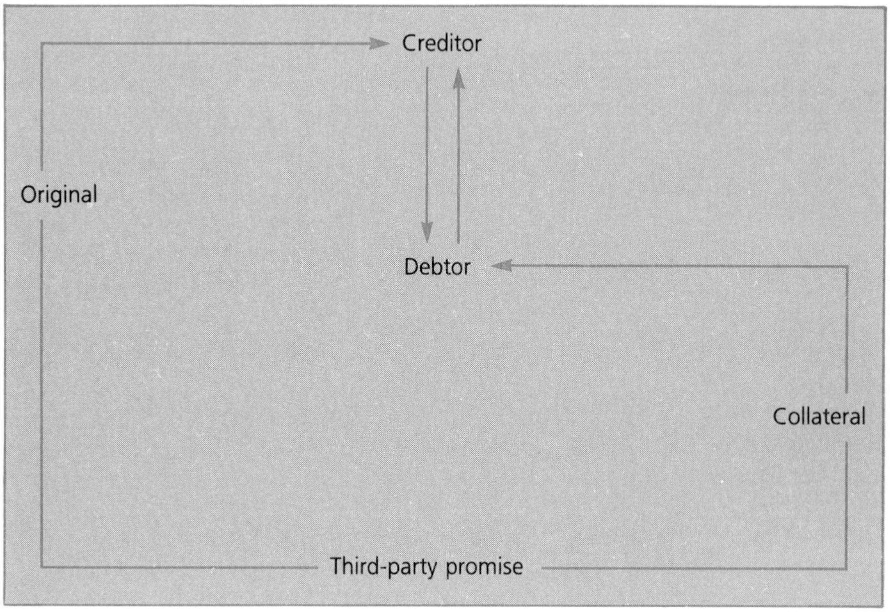

Collateral Versus Original Promises

The promise to pay another's debt is called a **collateral promise.** A promise to get personal benefit is called an **original promise.** The main purpose rule is used to distinguish collateral from original promises. If the main purpose of a promise to pay is one of self-benefit, then the promise is original and need not be in writing. For example, suppose Alfie owes Byron $5000, and Alfie is behind on the payments. Byron is about to repossess some of Alfie's property to satisfy the debt. Clarence is a creditor of Alfie who cannot take property (unsecured) and knows that if Byron takes the property, he will not be paid. Clarence promises Byron that he will pay Alfie's debt if Byron does not take the property and Alfie does not pay. This promise does not have to be written because Clarence's purpose is to benefit himself and not simply to pay the debt of another.

In deciding if a promise is original or collateral, the circumstances creating the promise must be examined. For example, if Cecil says to Burt, "Ship these goods to Alexander, and I'll make sure you are paid," the promise is original. If, on the other hand, Alexander says, "Ship these goods to me on credit," and Clarence agrees to be liable if Alexander does not pay, the promise is collateral and must be in writing to be valid. Figure 22-2 summarizes collateral and original promises.

Figure 22-2 **Collateral and Original Promises and the Statute of Frauds**

EXAMPLE	COLLATERAL/ORIGINAL	WRITING?
"Deliver these goods to my company, and I'll pay you."	Original	No
"Delivery these goods to my company, and if it does not pay, I will."	Collateral	Yes
"Repair the house, and if the estate does not pay you, I will."	Collateral	Yes

In the *Barboza v. Liberty Contractors Co., Inc.* case, the court deals with the issue of collateral versus original promises in a corporate setting.

BARBOZA v. LIBERTY CONTRACTORS CO., INC.

Court of Appeals of Massachusetts.
469 N.E.2d 1303 (1984).

FACTS Liberty was the general contractor on the Fairhaven Housing Authority construction contract. E. G. Mondor was Liberty's subcontractor for excavation and site work. The Barboza brothers delivered gravel to the site to Mondor from February 1974 through June 1974. Mondor had unpaid bills by June 1974 of $13,382.60. As result, the Barbozas cut off shipments and told Liberty. One of Liberty's officers told the Barbozas that they would be paid, and that Liberty should be billed directly for future shipments. The Barbozas were not paid and filed suit against Liberty.

ISSUE Can Barbozas enforce the oral promise of Liberty, or was it a collateral promise required to be in writing under the statute of frauds?

DECISION Yes, on the new shipments; no, on the bills due at the time of the promise. Paying the old bills was a promise to pay someone else's debts. The offer to bill directly after that point was an original contract and enforceable even though oral.

LEGAL TIP

Officers and directors should be cautious about making promises to pay for goods delivered to the corporation. Creditors should always get officers' and directors' promises to pay in writing.

TRANSFERS OF REAL PROPERTY INTERESTS

Promises to transfer land interests must be in writing to be enforceable. Land interests include the following:

1. Homes, buildings, raw land.
2. Mortgages.
3. Liens.
4. Easements.
5. Options.
6. Leases (only of a certain length, which varies from one year to three years in various states).
7. Minerals to be removed by the buyer.
8. Broker listing and commission agreements (in most states).
9. Covenants and restrictions on land use.

More detailed explanations of these land interests can be found in Chapters 47 and 48.

Decisions to Honor an Oral Contract

If both parties to an oral land contract are willing to perform their oral promises, they may do so. Failure to comply with the statute of frauds does not result in a void contract. The oral contract that should be in writing is unenforceable. If one or both parties choose not to perform the promises agreed upon, courts will not require them to do so.

Exceptions for Land Contracts

In some circumstances, unknowing buyers enter into oral agreements for the purchase of land and give the seller a partial payment for the land. Even though the oral contract is unenforceable, the courts will permit an unknowing buyer to recover the money given to the seller.

Still other buyers have gone one step further in the oral purchase agreement and have not only paid money but are living on or developing the property. In such cases, the courts may order the seller to transfer the land to the buyer—a remedy called specific performance. (The seller keeps the money, of course.) This remedy is given under the doctrine of **part performance,** which allows the buyer to obtain the property if several requirements have been met. First, the buyer must have paid all or part of the purchase price. Second, the buyer must have either moved onto the property or have made valuable improvements on the property, such as the grading of the property or the start of building construction on the property. For example, suppose Albert orally contracts to sell Berford a farm for $1,200,000. Berford has paid Albert $500,000, lives on the farm, and has already plowed and planted half the farm when Albert refuses to perform because the contract should have been in writing. If Berford can show that the payment was made, that there is possession, and that the improvements with the crops were made in reliance upon Albert's oral promise, Berford can have specific performance on the contract or have the land conveyed. In the *Williams v. Denham* case, the court was faced with enforcing an oral land contract.

WILLIAMS v. DENHAM

Supreme Court of South Dakota.
162 N.W.2d 285 (1968).

FACTS Mrs. Williams accepted S. J. Denham's oral offer to sell 499 acres of land in Dewey County for $20,000. Mrs. Williams' attorney drew up a contract and sent it to Denham along with a draft for $5000. Denham returned the contract and draft, and said he would not sign the contract nor cash the draft; the deal was off. Mrs. Williams had obtained a title abstract on the property at a cost of $177.50 and brought suit for specific performance.

ISSUE Did Mrs. Williams meet the requirements of part performance so that the oral land contract could be ordered specifically performed?

DECISION No. Attempted payment and a refusal do not satisfy the partial payment requirement. Mrs. Williams was not in possession of the property, and the abstract preparation cost was not an improvement. The abstract could have been prepared if she was just interested in the property, not necessarily because a contract existed.

LEGAL TIP

Before spending any time or money on buying land, a written contract should be signed by both parties.

CONTRACTS NOT TO BE PERFORMED WITHIN A YEAR

Contracts that cannot be performed within one year from the date the contract is made must be in writing to be enforceable. For example, an oral employment contract that is entered into on April 1, 1984, and which is to run from August 1, 1984, through May 15, 1985, must be in writing to be valid; the performance will take longer than a year measured from the April 1 date.

If there is any way the contract promise can be performed within a year, it is not under the statute of frauds and can be a valid oral agreement. For example, suppose Andy promises to pay Bart $1000 when Andy sells a piece of property. The property could be sold in one day or could take three years to sell. The fact that it could be done within a year makes the oral agreement valid. When employees are hired on a permanent basis, the employment is indefinite, and there need not be written agreements for the employment contract to be valid. The job could last one day or twenty years. The fact that it could be less than a year takes it out of the required writing statute of frauds rule. Contracts with uncertain durations can be oral and still be valid. Other examples of contracts with uncertain durations include contracts with cancellation provisions, contracts to perform for a lifetime, and contracts with no performance deadlines. In the *White Lighting Company v. Wolfson* case, the court deals with the one-year issue in an employment contract.

WHITE LIGHTING COMPANY v. WOLFSON

Supreme Court of California.
438 P.2d 345 (1968).

FACTS Wolfson was a salesman for White Lighting Company. He was orally promised an annual commission or bonus based on the total amount of sales that he generated during the year. Wolfson had a good year, but the bonus could not be calculated until after the close of the year when all the sales could be tabulated. White then refused to pay the bonus because there was only an oral agreement and performance took longer than a year. Wolfson brought suit.

ISSUE Was Wolfson's commission or bonus contract required to be in writing under the statute of frauds?

DECISION No. Wolfson performed all the sales within a one-year period. The tabulation was just a technicality necessary for computing the bonus. All that Wolfson was required to do had been completed within a year.

LEGAL TIP

All commission and bonus contracts should be in writing to avoid any question about the employee's rights.

MARRIAGE CONTRACTS

Mutual promises to marry or promises between a man and a woman to marry do not have to be written to be enforceable. The statute of frauds does require a writing when one promises to marry, and the other promises something else. For example, if Max promises to marry Nora, and Nora promises to give Max a farm in return, their agreement must be in writing to be enforceable. If a third party (Nora's father) promises to pay a certain amount to Max and Nora if they marry, this promise must also be written.

CONTRACTS FOR THE SALE OF GOODS

Section 2-201 of the UCC (see Chapters 27 and 28) requires contracts for the sale of goods for a price of $500 or more to be written to be enforceable. This $500 limitation applies only to goods. Other sections of the UCC have different provisions for other items. Under Article VIII, all contracts for the sale of securities must be in writing. Under Article IX, all security agreements must be in writing (see Chapters 56 through 58). There is also a catch-all provision in the Code that requires contracts for the sale of other personal property (patents, trademarks, etc.) at a price of $5000 or more to be in writing.

Section 2-201 also provides several exceptions to the $500 requirement.

Merchant's Confirmation Memorandum Exception

A great deal of business is done over the telephone, since it is fast and economical. But this way of conducting business is also oral. For goods costing $500 or more, oral telephone agreements do not comply with the statute of frauds. To enable business persons to conduct business over the telephone and still comply with the UCC statute of frauds, Section 2-201 provides merchants with the important exception of the **merchant's confirmation memorandum.** This exception applies if:

1. The oral agreement is between two merchants.
2. One merchant sends the other a signed memo confirming the terms of their conversation.
3. The other merchant does not object to the memo within ten days of receiving it.

If all three requirements are met, the parties have an enforceable contract. This result exists even when only one party has signed the writing. The sending merchant must prove mailing, receipt, and the memo's contents. All merchants should review their mail weekly so that inaccurate memos or memos with no basis can be found and corrected. The *J. L. Azevedo v. Minister* case examines whether the requirements for this exception had been met.

J. L. AZEVEDO v. MINISTER
Supreme Court of Nevada.
471 P.2d 661 (1970).

FACTS Azevedo and Minister, through a telephone conversation, reached an agreement for Azevedo to buy 1500 tons of hay from Minister at a price of $28 per ton. The parties agreed that Azevedo would deposit money in an escrow, and the funds would be released as the hay was delivered. Azevedo set up the escrow account, deposited funds, and sent the information about the escrow on his letterhead to Minister. Azevedo then refused to perform the oral contract. Minister brought suit on the basis of his confirmation memorandum.

ISSUE Was the note about the escrow a sufficient memorandum to bring the oral agreement within the merchant's confirmation exception?

DECISION Yes. The letter indicated price and amount, and made reference to their telephone conversation. The letterhead was sufficient for a signature.

LEGAL TIP
Always check and keep all letters and mail coming in because it may eventually be evidence of a contract.

Other UCC Exceptions

Article II also makes exceptions for oral contracts where there is some physical evidence that the parties had a contract. For example, if the goods are being specially manufactured and cannot be used by just anyone, this is some evidence that the parties had an agreement. For example, suppose Alice orders (over the telephone) custom window shutters for her office (total cost of $3000). The shutters are custom-made to fit each window and cannot be used by other buyers. The shutter seller/manufacturer has made the shutters and has only the staining work to complete the job. Alice calls and refuses to perform because the agreement was oral. The shutter seller can enforce the oral agreement against Alice.

Article II also enforces contracts where the parties have already performed (accepted goods or made payment). For example, Bertha orally agrees to buy 3000 tape recorders from Samantha with shipments of 500 each over the next three months. Bertha receives and accepts the first shipment of 500 recorders. She then tells Samantha the contract is oral and invalid. Bertha will be liable for the 500 recorders but not for the remaining 2500.

If a party admits under oath that a contract exists, that contract can then be enforced. The contract can be enforced only for what is admitted.

Figure 22-3 summarizes the statute of frauds' provisions and exceptions.

FORM OF THE WRITING

What Form Is Necessary?

Neither the Restatement nor the UCC requires the parties to execute a formal written agreement to satisfy the statute of frauds. The UCC requires "some writing sufficient to indicate that a contract for sale has been made between the parties and signed by the party against whom enforcement is sought." Under these general rules, courts have held receipts, telegrams, and business records to be sufficient writings.

The writing form can be satisfied if all the terms are on one piece of paper or if the terms can be pieced together from several documents. For example, a contract is written if a letter and company memoranda put together have all the necessary contract terms. The *Gundersen & Son, Inc. v. Cohn* case deals with a problem of grouping papers together to get contract terms.

GUNDERSEN & SON, INC. v. COHN
United States District Court,
Massachusetts.
596 F.Supp. 379 (1984).

FACTS Albert and Sylvia Cohn entered into a contract to have Gundersen & Son build a summer home for them on the island of Martha's Vineyard. In their negotiations, the Cohns said they would agree to a cost-plus contract (they would pay all costs plus a profit to Gundersen). They also said that they put a cap of $90,000 on the project.

The original contract did not have the cap, but the Cohns added it to the bottom. They then wrote a letter reminding Gundersen of the limit. Gundersen wrote back on another matter and mentioned the limit. The total bill came to the Cohns for $112,624.75, and they refused to pay.

ISSUE Was the $90,000 term part of the contract?

DECISION Yes. The three documents together—the contract and two letters—constituted the parties' agreement. Gundersen was bound by the cost cap.

LEGAL TIP
Make sure all terms are in the contract. Although documents can be grouped together, confusion can result.

Figure 22-3 **Statute of Frauds Requirements and Exceptions**

REQUIREMENT	EXAMPLE	EXCEPTIONS
Promise to pay debt of another	"If A doesn't pay you, I will."	Main Purpose Rule
Real property interests	Contract for sale of land; liens	Part performance
Not to be performed within one year	A promises to work for B for four years	Uncertain duration
Marriage	Pre-nuptial agreements	Mutual promise to marry
Contracts		
Sale of goods—$500 or more	Contract for sale of car for $12,000	Merchant's confirmation memorandum; specially manufactured goods; acceptance and receipt or payment; admission

What Content Is Necessary

There are five elements necessary to comply with the statute of frauds in a written agreement. These requirements are discussed in the subsections below.

The writing must indicate a contract has been made Language as simple as "This agreement entered into by ___ and ___ this day of ___, 19 ___." will satisfy this requirement.

The writing must identify the contracting parties Both parties' names can be stated in the contract. Their signature on the contract is enough to identify them.

The writing must describe the subject matter For this requirement under common law, more detail is required—a description of the land or an explanation of the services. Under the UCC, the critical information is the quantity of the goods along with a general description of them (see Chapters 27 and 28).

The writing must contain essential terms Again, under common law more detail is required—the method of payment, the time of performance, delivery dates, etc. Under the UCC, if the parties fail to specify terms, there are code provisions that will govern (see Chapter 28). Thus, a UCC writing need not be as detailed and can still satisfy content requirements in a written agreement.

The writing must be signed by the party to be charged Ideally, both parties should sign the agreement. If only one party signs the agreement (which is required to be in writing under the statute of frauds), the contract is enforceable against the signing party, but not against the nonsigning party. For example, if a seller signs a contract to sell a piece of land, the seller must perform if the buyer wants to perform. But the nonsigning buyer cannot be required to perform if the seller wants to perform. The exception to this rule under the UCC is the merchant's confirmation memorandum.

In applying these rules, the courts demand only reasonable certainty of terms in the writing. The *Marks v. Cowdin* case deals with the issue of whether a written agreement is sufficient.

MARKS v. COWDIN

Supreme Court of New York.
123 N.E. 139 (1919).

FACTS In 1911, Marks was employed by Cowdin for a two-year period as "sales manager." There was a written contract for the two-year employment. When the two years ended, Marks and Cowdin entered into an oral agreement for Marks to continue employment, and Cowdin wrote a memorandum that stated:

> It is understood . . . that the arrangements made for employment of L. Marks in our business on January 1, 1913, for a period of three years from that date at a salary of $15,000 per year plus 5% of the gross profits earned in our business which we agree shall not be less than $5,000 per year—continues in force until January 1, 1916.

Marks was not paid and filed suit on the basis of the memorandum. Cowdin claimed the memo was not a sufficient written agreement because it did not describe the nature of Marks' employment.

ISSUE Did the memorandum contain enough information to satisfy the content requirements for compliance with the statute of frauds?

DECISION Yes. The court said the statute of frauds is not rigid. The only detail missing was the nature of employment, but Marks had worked for Cowdin for two years as a sales manager. Also, the court noted that Cowdin sent out materials to salespersons describing Marks as the sales manager.

LEGAL TIP

Commission and bonus contracts should describe what work will be done to earn the funds paid.

Figure 22-4 summarizes the content requirements under both common law and the UCC.

INTERPRETATION OF WRITTEN CONTRACTS

Once a contract contains acceptable terms that comply with the statute of frauds, the contract is enforceable. However, sometimes the language used in the contract is not as clear as it could be, and the parties may have a dispute over contract interpretation. When interpreting contracts, parties must consider two basic issues:

1. What meaning will be given to the contract terms used.
2. What evidence can be used to determine that meaning.

Figure 22-4 **Content Requirements for the Written Agreement**

CONTENT	COMMON LAW	UCC
Language of agreement	Required	Required
Identity of parties	Required	Required
Subject matter	Full description	Quantity required with reasonable identity
Contract terms	Full details	Code provides sections for price, payment, and delivery
Signature	Party to be charged must sign	One party must sign merchant's confirmation memorandum

Four important rules for interpreting contracts are discussed below.

Plain Meaning Rule

The **Plain Meaning Rule** says that if a contract term is clear and unambiguous, its "plain meaning" must be stated; no other evidence can be used to contradict that plain meaning. For example, if a contract provided for the installation of a "solar water heater," the plain meaning would be a water heater for household uses and not a heater for a swimming pool.

Integration Rule

The **Integration Rule** deals with complete (integrated) contracts. Under it, contract terms are ones with which a "reasonable person," knowing trade customs and the parties' dealings, would agree. Thus, in the solar water heater example, if the parties had talked about heating the swimming pool, the term "solar water heater" would have had a different meaning in their negotiations.

If the contract is not integrated, then all outside or extrinsic evidence may be examined to determine the parties' true intentions. For example, if the contract provided for the installation of solar panels but did not specify the purpose for their installation, the contract would not be integrated. It would require more evidence to determine the extent of the panels, their location, and purpose.

Restatement of Contracts Rule

The Restatement of Contracts Rule says that all evidence can be examined to learn the meaning of contract terms. Courts examine the parties' negotiations, their stated intents, and any trade customs in interpreting the contract. Under this rule, "solar panels" could be interpreted according to the parties' intent or typical installations in the solar panel industry.

UCC Rule

Section 2-202 of the UCC rejects the Plain Meaning Rule and provides that outside or extrinsic evidence can be examined to determine the meaning of a contract—even when there is no ambiguity. The UCC also permits courts to examine industry custom in determining the meaning of contracts. For example, in one case, the parties contracted for the purchase and sale of mohair. There are two types of mohair—adult and kid—and the parties only put "mohair" in their contract. In determining what type of mohair was required to be delivered, the court looked at an industry custom providing that unless specified, "mohair" meant adult mohair. The UCC also permits the court to examine prior dealings (course of dealing) of the parties to determine the contract meanings. If a contract provides for the daily shipment of six dozen eggs but does not specify the type of eggs, the court can take as evidence the fact that for two years the seller has been delivering Grade A large eggs. The courts can also consider the performance of the parties, or the "course of performance," when interpreting a contract. For example, if a buyer has accepted 2″ × 4″ planks for one year in a two-year contract, the contract meaning is clear from the buyer's part performance.

Other Rules of Construction and Interpretation

There are several other rules of contract interpretation. They are:

1. Every part of a contract is to be interpreted so that the general intent of the parties is carried out.
2. Obvious spelling, grammar, and punctuation mistakes are corrected.
3. Contract interpretations go against the drafting party because they had the opportunity to be clear.
4. Written and typed words are adhered to if they conflict with printed words.

5. Contracts are interpreted to make them valid.
6. Greater weight goes to specific rather than to general terms.

In the *Bonner v. Westbound Records, Inc.* case, the court deals with an interpretation problem.

BONNER v. WESTBOUND RECORDS, INC.
Court of Appeals, First District.
394 N.E.2d 1303 (1979).

FACTS Westbound Records makes and sells master recordings to others for production and distribution. Westbound entered into a contract with the group, The Ohio Players. Westbound was given the ownership of two albums and several singles to be recorded by the group for a period of five years. The albums and records were made at Westbound and successfully distributed. One of the records, "Funky Worm," became a gold record with sales in excess of $1,000,000.

After these recordings, the Ohio Players signed an exclusive contract with Mercury Records for distribution rights. Westbound sued to stop performance of the Mercury agreement on the grounds that it had exclusive rights to all Ohio Player records for five years. The Ohio Players claimed that the five years only applied to the already recorded albums and singles. One clause read as follows:

> Company is not obligated to make or sell records manufactured from the master recordings made hereunder or to license such master recordings or to have Artist record the minimum number of record sides referred to in Paragraph 2 (B).

ISSUE Was the contract a five-year agreement for all recordings or a five-year agreement for the already recorded albums?

DECISION The contract was a five-year one for all recordings. The contract did not specify any particular records or albums. The typical contract in the music industry gives the master recorder exclusive rights.

LEGAL TIP
Exclusive rights contracts should list what properties are covered.

CHANGES IN CONTRACT TERMS

In this final section of the chapter, the question of whether the terms of a written contract can ever be changed is discussed. A written agreement can be changed by voluntary action of the parties through modification, novation, or rescission. In a modification, the parties agree to change the contract terms and draw up an addendum or an addition to the contract in order to reflect their changes. The modification must be supported by consideration under common law and must be done in good faith to be valid under the UCC. The parties can also agree to abandon their original contract and execute a new agreement. This process is called a "novation." Finally, the parties can change the existence of a written contract altogether by mutually agreeing to abandon their rights under the contract or by rescinding the contract.

There are times when the terms of a written contract may be changed to more accurately reflect the parties' intentions. Whether the changes will be made is controlled by the Parol Evidence Rule. The effect and purposes of the rule are discussed in the following subsections.

The Parol Evidence Rule

A written contract does not exist suddenly. A formal written contract is the result of much negotiation, many meetings, frequent phone calls, and notes. Sometimes more than two parties are involved in the negotiations—the thoughts, letters, and memos of four parties may be involved if agents are used. The written contract is the final summary of all these negotiations and thoughts; the Parol Evidence Rule operates to ensure that the written agreement remains the final one.

Under the **Parol Evidence Rule,** once a contract is reduced to its final written form, is fully completed, and is intended by the parties to be their final agreement, no evidence of prior conversations, negotiations, memos, letters, or statements can be used to change the terms of the written contract. Parol, or oral evidence, goes beyond the face of the contract, or beyond the letters, memos, conversations, and negotiations. Regardless of how authentic the evidence may be, it is not permitted to be used to change an integrated contract. The rule's purpose is to make the writing important. This rule makes the written contract the only evidence of the contract.

For example, suppose Alice signs a contract to buy a home. At the time of signing, Alice states, "The fence near the garage will be removed." The seller agrees, but the written contract does not state that there will be removal. Assuming that the written contract is complete, the seller is not required to remove the fence. The Parol Evidence Rule prohibits Alice from introducing prior evidence about the seller's oral promise.

Exceptions to the Parol Evidence Rule

There are times when parol evidence is admissible. The exceptions and explanations are here noted and summarized in Figure 22-5.

1. *A nonintegrated contract.* Since the Parol Evidence Rule applies only to integrated contracts, an incomplete agreement could be clarified by extrinsic evidence.
2. *An ambiguous term or terms.* Although a contract may be complete, it may still be ambiguous. Parol evidence is admissible to clarify ambiguities.
3. *Punctuation, typing, spelling, or drafting mistakes.* Parol evidence is admissible to correct mistakes that do not deal with the parties' intents and are only clerical.

Figure 22-5 **Contract Terms and Interpretation**

CIRCUMSTANCES	PAROL EVIDENCE RULE APPLIES?
Fully integrated contract	Yes
Interpretation of fully integrated contract	Yes: Plain meaning rule No: Restatement of contract No: UCC—course of dealing performance, trade usage
Incomplete contract	No
Ambiguous contract	No
Clerical error in contract	No
Evidence of performance	No
Mistake, misrepresentation, fraud, duress, undue influence, illegality, and lack of capacity	No

COFELL'S PLUMBING & HEATING, INC. v. STUMPF

Supreme Court of North Dakota.
290 N.W.2d 230 (1980).

FACTS Cofell's was hired to do the plumbing trench work on Stumpf's construction project. The contract provided that an extra fee would be paid for Cofell's work if the ledge rock in the trenching area could not be removed by "trenching machine or workmen with pick, spade, or shovel." Cofell had to use a backhoe machine for the trenching work and demanded extra payment. Stumpf refused to pay, claiming that a backhoe was a "trenching machine." Cofell brought suit.

ISSUE Is a backhoe a "trenching machine"? Is parol evidence admissible to determine the answer?

DECISION Yes. A backhoe is a "trenching machine," and parol evidence is admissible. The backhoe is the traditional machine used for plumbing trench work. At the time of the contract negotiations, Cofell talked of using a backhoe. Stumpf offered to find a backhoe for Cofell's use at the time of contract negotiations.

LEGAL TIP

Terms that are commonly used in an industry or profession should be used in the contract so that the parties' definitions and intentions are clear.

4. *Interpretation.* As discussed earlier, the various rules on interpretation do permit extrinsic evidence to determine the meaning of terms used in the contract.
5. *Evidence after a contract is written.* Extrinsic evidence after the contract is signed is always allowed. For example, the contract may state, "When $200 is in hand, the debt is paid," and then the $200 check bounces. The evidence of the check bouncing could be used not to contradict the contract but to show nonperformance.
6. *Defenses.* Parol evidence is always admissible to show mistakes, misrepresentation, fraud, duress, undue influence, illegality, or lack of capacity.
7. *Later changes in the contract.* The Parol Evidence Rule allows evidence about modifications, novations, or rescissions.

In the *Cofell's Plumbing & Heating, Inc. v. Stumpf* case, the court deals with the Parol Evidence Rule.

HANS GODO FRABEL, INC. v. BRENNAN'S OF ATLANTA, INC.

Court of Appeals of Georgia.
259 S.E.2d 649 (1979).

FACTS Brennan's agreed to display Hans Frabel's sculptures in its gallery. The contract could be terminated at any time by either party. Several of Frabel's sculptures disappeared from the gallery and several others were broken. Frabel brought suit against Brennan for the loss. Brennan claimed that it was not liable because the contract had no clause on risk of loss.

ISSUE Who is liable for the loss? Is parol evidence admissible?

DECISION Brennan's is liable and parol evidence is admissible. The contract was unclear on risk of loss. There was a letter from Brennan's to Hans stating that Brennan's would assume liability for any losses. The letter was admissible and clarified the parties' intentions.

LEGAL TIP

All terms should be specified in contracts—especially those terms (such as risk of loss) that involve liability.

In some circumstances, the parties have entered into a written contract, but the contract does not cover all issues. When problems arise, courts use the Parol Evidence Rule to interpret incomplete contracts. In the *Hans Godo Frabel, Inc. v. Brennan's of Atlanta, Inc.* case (which deals with the facts presented in the chapter-opening example), the court deals with the problem of an incomplete contract.

KEY TERMS

Statute of frauds
Collateral promise
Part performance
Merchant's confirmation memorandum
Plain Meaning Rule
Integration Rule
Parol Evidence Rule

CHAPTER PROBLEMS

1. Texas and Pacific Railway orally promised Warner that they would maintain a railway switch for as long as Warner needed it. After twenty two years, the Railway refused to maintain the switch and claimed the oral agreement was unenforceable under the statute of frauds? What is the result? *Warner v. Texas and Pacific Railway* 164 U.S. 418 (1896).
2. Fidelity Union Trust orally promised Reeves to employ him for the rest of his life. Three years later, Fidelity terminated Reeves. Reeves brought suit for breach of contract, and Fidelity alleged the statute of frauds as a defense. What is the result? *Fidelity Union Trust Co. v. Reeves,* 129 A. 922 (N.J. 1925).
3. Frigon and his wife received $1500 from Whipple—Frigon's mother-in-law. Two years later, Whipple demanded repayment of the $1500. Frigon alleged the statute of frauds as a defense to the two-year loan. Whipple claims the payback date was indefinite. What is the result? *Frigon v. Whipple,* 360 A.2d 69 (Vt. 1976).
4. Hedda Hopper brought suit to enforce an oral agreement that she had made with Lennen & Mitchell, Inc., for weekly radio appearances for $2000 per week. The oral agreement was entered into on November 12, 1942, and was to run for twenty six weeks commencing on December 27, 1942. The oral agreement also provided a five-year option at the end of the twenty six-week period. Miss Hopper never did the radio appearances as planned, and she filed suit against Lennen & Mitchell for breach of contract. Lennen & Mitchell claim the oral contract is invalid. What is the result? *Hopper v. Lennen & Mitchell, Inc.*, 146 F.2d 364 (9th Cir. 1944).
5. Cohn advertised in the *New York Times* to sell his thirty-foot auxiliary sloop. Fisher phoned Cohn and made an offer of $4650 for the boat, and Cohn accepted. The next day Fisher met Cohn at Cohn's office and gave Cohn a check for $2325 with "Deposit on aux. sloop, D'Arc Wind, full amount $4650." The parties agreed on a closing date, but Fisher stopped payment on the check and failed to show up for the closing. Fisher alleges the statute of frauds as a defense. What is the result? *Cohn v. Fisher,* 287 A.2d 222 (N.J. 1972).
6. Gendzier and Bielecki were both in the rag and waste material business. After a conference, the parties drew up a three-page, handwritten agreement for the sale of various items totaling $6,037.83 in price. The parties initialed the agreement at the end ("A.B." and "S.G."). Bielecki refused to perform and Gendzier brought suit. Bielecki claimed the writing was not sufficient because there were no signatures. What is the result? *Gendzier v. Bielecki,* 97 So.2d 604 (Fla. 1957).
7. * John Anderson was in an auto accident on "Williston Road" just outside Burlington, Vermont and suffered severe injuries. Lawrence was an emergency room physician on duty at the time. John's daughter was there when Lawrence arrived at the accident scene, and she told Lawrence, "do everything you can under the sun to see this man is taken care of." She also

said "whatever the charges . . . I will take care of it." Lawrence arranged for an ambulance and treated Anderson until he died two days later. Lawrence then sent bills to the estate. The estate did not pay and Lawrence brought suit against Anderson's daughter. Anderson's daughter defended on the grounds of the statute of frauds. What is the result? *Lawrence v. Anderson,* 184 A. 689 (Vt. 1936).

* 8 Mr. Dienst (sixty-six years old and Mrs. Dienst (sixty-two years old), both widowed, married after a pen-pal courtship. Mr. Dienst was penniless, but Mrs. Dienst had between $60,000 and $70,000. Before they were married, Mrs. Dienst orally promised Mr. Dienst that she would take care of him, and that she would leave all her property to him in her will. Several months after they were married, Mrs. Dienst filed for divorce on the grounds of extreme cruelty. Mr. Dienst claimed that he was entitled to her property as part of the divorce proceedings. Mrs. Dienst claims the statute of frauds makes her oral promise unenforceable. What is the result? *Dienst v. Dienst,* 141 N.W. 591 (Mich. 1913).

* 9. Shaughnessy leased a home to Eidsmo for $47.50 per month with an option to purchase the house at the end of one year for $4750. At the end of one year, Eidsmo wanted to purchase the house, and Shaughnessy refused on the grounds that their oral agreement was within the statute of frauds and required to be in writing. What result? *Shaughnessy v. Eidsmo,* 23 N.W. 362 (Minn. 1946).

*10. What would happen if a contract for the sale of land had a legal description but the description did not have the county name? *Garner v. Redeaux,* 678 S.W.2d 124 (Tex. 1984).

"Public policy is the unruly horse of the law."
Richardson v. Mellish (1824)

Chapter 23

Illegality and Public Policy

CHAPTER PREVIEW

- Void contracts and their effect
- Types of contracts that are void because they violate statutes
- Usury
- Contracts to commit torts
- Blue laws—effect and constitutionality
- Public policy—what it is; what it does
- Types of contracts that violate public policy

Jones, a skydiver, signed an agreement with an air service, which agreed to provide Jones with a plane for transportation to a jumping site. The contract had a clause stating that the air service was not liable if Jones was hurt in his skydive from one of their planes. Jones is hurt in a skydive and now wants to collect for his damages from the air service. The air service says that the clause protects them from liability. Who is correct?

According to the Restatement of Contracts Rule, a contract is illegal if "either its formation or performance is criminal, tortious, or otherwise opposed to public policy." A contract is illegal if it does one of three things: violates a statute; causes the commission of a tort; or shocks the "public conscience" because its terms or formation are unreasonable. If any of these results occur, public policy says that the contract cannot be enforced. This chapter discusses illegality and what happens when an existing contract is found to be illegal.

AGREEMENTS IN VIOLATION OF STATUTE

If an agreement requires one of the parties to violate a statute, the agreement is void. The following subsections give examples of some agreements that violate statutes.

Agreements to Commit Criminal Wrongs

The phrase "there is a contract on his life," is not really true. An agreement that requires one party to kill another in exchange for payment is actually an agreement to commit a crime—and therefore illegal. The agreement is void, and no contract exists. Any agreement to perform an act that is a crime under state or federal law is illegal and void. Another example of a criminal act that would be void if performed for payment is selling products to a country that the United States has embargoed.

Gambling agreements also are illegal in most states. All states have some legislation on gambling, and most states prohibit the use of courts to collect bets. For example, suppose Alonso bets Betty that the Pittsburgh Pirates will win the World Series. If the Pirates do win and Betty doesn't pay, Alonso cannot collect the bet from Betty.

Some states have statutes prohibiting **commercial bribery.** Commercial bribery exists when money or property is offered to another's agent or employee in order to acquire additional business. For example, if Al gets the movie rights to a story by bribing an employee of the movie rights owner, commercial bribery has occurred. Commercial bribery makes the contract illegal. In the landmark *Sirkin v. Fourteenth Street Store* case, the court deals with the issue of commercial bribery.

Agreements in Violation of Licensing Statutes

Many professionals are required to be licensed before they can work in their field. Failure to obtain a license can make a contract to perform that licensed service illegal and void. Whether a contract will be illegal and void because of a failure to obtain a license will depend on the purpose of the licensing statute. There are two types of licensing statutes: those that license for competency, skill, or moral quality, and those that serve the purpose of raising revenue.

Licenses that are required for competency, skill, or moral quality must be obtained to have contracts for those services validated. Examples of occupations requiring competency licenses are doctors, lawyers, beauticians, and real estate brokers. If an unlicensed lawyer contracts to perform legal services, the agreement is void, and the lawyer cannot be paid. If an unlicensed doctor provides medical care, the recipient has no obligation to pay since the agreement to provide services was void. Any licensing statute that has as its purpose "the protection of the public

SIRKIN v. FOURTEENTH STREET STORE

Supreme Court of New York.
108 N.Y.S. 830 (1908).

FACTS Sirkin sold and delivered hosiery to Fourteenth Street Store. Sirkin had obtained the contract by paying the Store's agent $75 to place the order. Such a payment violated the New York commercial bribery statute, and Sirkin was convicted of a violation. The store refused to pay for the goods, and Sirkin brought suit for payment. Sirkin argued that the criminal penalties were punishment under the statute, and that the contract was still valid.

ISSUE Was the contract, obtained by a bribe, valid?

DECISION No. If the contract were enforced, the statute would be defeated because although a wrongdoer would suffer a fine, he or she would still get the contract. The court held that the contract was void and did not require Fourteenth Store to pay.

LEGAL TIP

Inducements to agents to obtain sales orders may be illegal and can cost the seller the full contract price.

welfare, health and morality against fraud and incompetence," (*Cope v. Rowlands,* 150 Eng.Rep. 707 [1836]) is a protective statute. Performing these services without first obtaining a license is not only illegal but makes the agreement for the services void.

Licensing statutes also may be enacted for the purpose of raising revenue. Unlicensed parties performing services without a revenue-raising license may still recover for the services rendered. For example, in many states contractors' licenses are given upon payment of a fee. In those states where payment of a fee is the only requirement to obtain a license, contractors may recover monies for work done when they were unlicensed.

In some cases, a licensing statute may be a combination of protection and revenue-raising. In those circumstances, the court will determine whether the contract for unlicensed services is void. Many licensing statutes are passed to determine competency levels initially but then become revenue-raising statutes after that initial finding. For example, lawyers are required to take a bar exam and submit proof of good moral character to be licensed initially. However, in many states, once that initial finding of competency is made, the lawyer renews licensing annually simply by paying dues. Thus, providing legal services without ever being licensed would be void; but providing services despite an oversight in paying annual dues would *not* be void. In the *Costello v. Schmidlin* case, the court deals with a technical licensing issue.

Agreements in Violation of Blue Laws

Blue laws or Sunday closing laws are ones that prohibit certain types of businesses from operating on Sunday. In states with such legislation, contracts that violate the closing laws are void. However, the courts tend to permit the enforcement of these agreements if the parties ratify the contract on another day. For example, completing performance of the contract on Monday would be ratifying a Sunday agreement.

The Sunday closing laws are slowly but surely disappearing. Many states have simply repealed the laws. Other states have had their statutes declared unconstitutional; they prevented so few from working, but permitted many more to work and engage in commercial activity. The courts have held the statutes that close only certain businesses unconstitutional.

COSTELLO v. SCHMIDLIN

United States Court of Appeals,
Third District.
404 F.2d 87 (1968).

FACTS Costello was a licensed engineer in New York and several other states. He furnished Schmidlin with $10,000 in engineering services for Schmidlin's project in the state of New Jersey. Costello was not a licensed engineer in the state of New Jersey. Schmidlin refused to pay Costello for the consulting services on the grounds that the agreement was void because Costello was unlicensed.

ISSUE Could an engineer who was unlicensed in one state but licensed in others collect fees for services performed in the state where he is unlicensed?

DECISION Yes. Costello was a competent engineer and was hired for his expertise in the field. The New Jersey statute was intended to protect against unlicensed engineers performing services. Costello was not unlicensed in other states and could have become licensed in New Jersey with some simple paperwork and a fee payment. The agreement for services was valid.

LEGAL TIP

Check licensing statutes when performing consulting work in other states.

Agreements in Violation of Usury Laws

Usury is charging an interest rate greater than the maximum amount permitted by statute. For example, if the state maximum rate for interest is 21% and a lender charges 24% on a loan, the rate is usurious and the loan agreement is void.

The usury rate varies from state to state, frequently according to the type of transaction. For example, in most states, the usury rate for real estate loans is much lower than the rate for credit cards, as well as personal and business loans. Each state's usury statute also explains how the rate of interest charged will be computed. For example, all states include the specified interest charges in computing the rate, but some states also include other charges such as loan processing expenses. A lender must be careful to charge the correct rate and also be sure that loan expenses do not make the interest rate too high.

The penalties for charging a usurious rate vary from state to state. The types of penalties are listed in the next four examples.

1. *Forfeiture of interest:* In many states, the lender can get back the principal amount of the loan but forfeits the right to all interest.
2. *Forfeiture of interest above the maximum:* In some states, the lender can recover the principal amount of the loan and interest to the statutory maximum but forfeits the remaining interest.
3. *Forfeiture of principal and interest:* In a few states, the loan agreement is treated as completely void, and the lender forfeits both principal and interest.
4. *Statutory penalties:* In some states, the lender may be penalized in combination with any of the first three provisions. For example, the lender may recover the principal and interest to the statutory maximum, but the debtor can recover two times the amount of excessive interest charged as a penalty for the lender violating the usury statute.

In the *LaBarr v. Tombstone Terrace Mint et al.* case, the court deals with the issue of usury.

LABARR v. TOMBSTONE TERRACE MINT ET AL.

Supreme Court of Arizona.
582 P.2d 639 (1978).

FACTS Tombstone Terrace (a mining venture) was in need of money for mine operations. After being turned down by the Chase Manhattan Bank for a loan, they were approached by a group of Mexican investors and given a loan for $300,000. The loan was to be repaid in six installments of $50,000 each. In addition, interest in the amount of $30,000 was to be paid in two installments of $15,000, and a financier's fee of $20,000 was to be paid in two installments of $10,000 each. Late payments would be subject to a 2% per month assessment. At the time of the contract negotiations, the usurious rate was 10%.

Tombstone defaulted and refused to pay on the grounds that the loan was usurious and void.

ISSUE Was the loan usurious? Can the investors recover their funds?

DECISION The loan was usurious because there was a $50,000 interest charge. The investors could recover their loan of $300,000 but could not collect any interest.

LEGAL TIP

Add all charges on a loan to make sure the amount of interest, financier's fees, etc., do not exceed the usurious rate.

ILLEGALITY BY COMMISSION OF A TORT

In some contracts, no statute is violated, but a tort will be committed by the performance of the contract. Such agreements are also void. For example, since publication of a libelous statement is a tort, an agreement to publish a libelous statement or work would be void. The tort of interference in business relationships is a frequent subject among business persons. For example, Andrew may promise Bert that if Bert does not extend credit to Carl, he will give more business to Bert. Such an agreement hurts Carl's ability to do business and is a tort. If Bert went ahead and gave credit to Carl, Andrew would not be able to recover damages because the agreement is void.

ILLEGALITY BY VIOLATION OF PUBLIC POLICY

Background on Public Policy

Public policy is not something that can be found in statutes. Public policy often is created with a new set of facts placed before a court. **Public policy** is a general name for a group of reasons that determine a contract's illegality. For example, public policy can be given as a reason for not enforcing a contract that is immoral, unconscionable, unprofessional, or economically unsound. Public policy is used to uphold and protect the general best interests of the public. Public policy is determined by the courts and can change from state to state and from decision to decision. There are, however, several areas in contract subject matters that frequently come before the courts as public policy issues. Those areas are covered in the following subsections.

Contracts for Political Influence

Many times parties enter into contracts that relate to legislatures, courts, or administrative agencies. Such agreements are closely examined by the courts and in many cases are held to be illegal since they violate public policy. Contracts relating to government agencies for purely professional services are perfectly legal. Examples include paying for expert testimony in court or before legislative bodies, and for writing reports used by legislators. Lobbyists can be paid to lobby but not to bribe.

Everyone has the right to work within the system to get legislation passed; others can be hired to help achieve that result. For example, paying someone to talk with his or her political friends about an employer's position on legislation does not violate public policy. However, agreeing to pay legislative members for their votes would violate public policy. More specifically, hiring a salesperson to tell defense department officials about the merits of a product does not violate public policy. However, agreeing to pay those officials if the product is purchased by the defense department, would violate public policy.

Trade Restraints

Contracts that prevent parties from engaging in their trade or profession or from conducting their business violate public policy. The idea of free competition, which is a strong public policy, is violated if business persons and professionals are prevented from competing. However, there are situations when some form of trade restraint is necessary. Those situations exist when a business is sold and in certain types of employment contracts.

Trade restraints in the sale of a business Suppose that Al operates a retail men's clothing store called "Clothing for Accountants." Al's store has been in operation for five years and has done quite well. Al has decided to sell the store to Berferd. Berferd will not only pay for the store, the furnishings, and the inventory but will also pay a large amount for the business "goodwill," or the customer loyalty that Al has built up over a five year period. Since Berferd is paying for the goodwill, the payment and purchase would be defeated if Al were to open another "Clothing for Accountants" in a nearby shopping center three months after the sale.

To give Berferd some protection, public policy does permit a clause in the contract, called a restrictive covenant, which prevents Al from starting a new business for a reasonable period of time in the immediate geographic area. For such a restrictive covenant to be enforceable and not void, several requirements must be met.

First, the covenant must be necessary to protect one of the parties' rights. In this case, the covenant is necessary to protect Berferd from the loss of business that would occur if Al opened another store. Second, the covenant must be reasonable in time and geographic scope. The amount of time for which a covenant will be enforceable varies according to the type of business and the circumstances involved. Five years is a typical time provision since a business can have a new set of clients several years later.

The geographic scope of a covenant must also be reasonable. In determining whether a geographic scope is reasonable, the courts examine the business' nature and economic base. The question being answered in determining geographic reasonableness is, "How many businesses of this type can be supported within the geographic area included in the restrictive covenant?" For example, there is probably only enough of an economic base for one accountant's clothing store in a medium-size town. However, in a larger city, there is enough of a base to have such a store in each suburb. A restrictive covenant preventing Al from starting a business anywhere in the town would be reasonable. In a city, a restrictive covenant for the whole city would be unreasonable, but a restrictive covenant for the suburban area in which the business is located would be reasonable.

In businesses that involve secret processes and formulas, restrictive covenants preventing the start of a business anywhere and anytime by the seller are enforceable; the nature of the business requires protections that are broad in scope. In the *McCart v. H. & R. Block* case, the court deals with the issue of reasonableness in a restrictive covenant.

McCART v. H. & R. BLOCK
Court of Appeals, Third District.
470 N.E.2d 756 (1984).

FACTS Robert and June McCart had been preparing tax returns since 1955. In 1968, they signed a franchise agreement with H & R Block (Block). Robert became a district manager for Block in 1969, and June continued the Block franchise in Rochester, Indiana. In 1981, June wrote to Block and said that because of arthritis, she could no longer operate the business. Shortly afterwards June sent out letters to all of her customers telling them that Block's rates were too high, and that she would help her husband in his tax assistance business which he had started after leaving Block.

Robert had the post office deliver all Block mail to his new office. Through a mix-up in phone numbers, customers who called Block got the McCarts and made appointments with them.

Block brought suit to enforce its restrictive covenant that prevented franchisees from preparing tax returns within a fifty-mile radius of the franchise for two years.

ISSUE Was the two-year/fifty-mile restrictive covenant enforceable?

DECISION Yes. The population base was so small that the fifty-mile radius was necessary. The business was built up over the years, and the McCarts were taking everyone with them. They were also trying to prevent Block from getting new business.

LEGAL TIP

Be certain that a restrictive covenant is long and broad enough to protect a business investment.

Restrictions on employment There are two types of valid restrictive covenants that apply to employment. The first type is a covenant in effect during the course of employment. This type of covenant prohibits an employee from engaging in competitive work either for another party or independently during the course of employment. These types of covenants are valid and enforceable.

The second type of covenant is one that restricts employment after the employee has left that position. These types of covenants are enforceable if they are necessary for the protection of an employer. To determine whether a covenant is necessary, the courts examine an employee's function and look for some quality of uniqueness. This quality of uniqueness is satisfied if the employee had access to trade secrets or had personal traits that resulted in the employer's business success. For example, radio and television personalities have personal traits that attract an audience, and a restrictive covenant may be necessary to prevent personalities from switching to another station, which may lead to viewer confusion.

An employee who has worked on the development of products and projects not yet public or patented is also considered "unique." A computer programmer involved in the development of company software not yet patented or marketed may be restrained for a period of time from working for a competitor so that the employer's efforts are not lost to a competitor.

Some types of jobs do not require restrictive covenants. It would be unreasonable to put a restrictive covenant in a waiter's contract that would prevent him from working for another restaurant. Restaurant employees usually do not carry trade secrets or clients with them when they leave employers.

In addition to the covenant being necessary to protect the employer, the covenant must also be reasonable in time and geographic scope. In the case of radio and television personalities, one year is generally enough time to allow viewers and listeners to forget the personality's work for another station. In the case of the software expert, two years may be necessary to enable the employer to get the product patented and on the market. In the *Central Adjustment Bureau, Inc. v. Ingram* case, the court deals with the issue of validity in an employee's restrictive covenant.

CENTRAL ADJUSTMENT BUREAU, INC. v. INGRAM

Supreme Court of Tennessee.
678 S.W.2d 28 (1984).

FACTS Henry Ingram was hired as a salesman for Central Adjustment Bureau (CAB) in 1970. CAB is a nationwide collection agency. Ingram's contract had a restrictive covenant providing that he would not open a competing business or contact CAB clients after he left the bureau. On January 23, 1979, Ingram filed a corporate charter for Ingram Associates, Inc., (a collection agency). On February 22, 1979, he resigned from CAB. At the time, he was their fifth highest paid employee in the country.

CAB brought suit to enforce Ingram's two-year, nationwide restrictive covenant.

ISSUE Was the CAB restrictive covenant valid?

DECISION The court held the covenant was too long and limited it to one year. The court also held that a nationwide restriction was too broad and limited Ingram's restriction to the state of Tennessee. Finally, the court limited the client contact clause to those who were clients in January 1979.

LEGAL TIP
Indicate narrow time and geographic limitations when drafting restrictive covenants.

Exculpatory Clauses

Exculpatory clauses are clauses in contracts that attempt to protect parties from liability for their negligence. Exculpatory clauses are often found on ticket stubs involving dangerous activities such as riding a ski lift, skating in a roller rink, or watching a hockey game. Exculpatory or "hold harmless" clauses can be found on nearly all parking lot stubs. These stubs usually provide that the lot or garage owner is not responsible for any damages or thefts occurring while the car is parked on the premises. A form of an exculpatory clause can be found on film developing receipts, which state that the developer is not responsible for losses or damages other than the cost of replacing the roll of film.

Exculpatory clauses are generally void and against public policy. However, an exculpatory clause is effective as a warning of risk. For example, an exculpatory clause on a ski lift ticket warns skiers about the dangers involved and holds the ski resort harmless for ordinary skiing injuries.

An exculpatory clause on a hockey ticket warns the viewer about the risks involved in watching that sport. Such a clause would relieve team owners from liability for the inherent dangers of flying pucks. However, the owners would not be relieved from such liability if they failed to put up the proper safety features dictated by code or custom such as nets, walls, and barricades.

Exculpatory clauses, instead of holding one party harmless, can be valid when they simply limit the liability of the party for any negligence that occurs. The film developing receipt is an example of an exculpatory clause coupled with a liability limitation. Limiting liability is valid so long as the liability limitation is reasonable. For example, a parking lot owner could limit liability for theft from vehicles to $50. Those carrying more valuable items in their vehicles would be put on notice. A liability limitation is not a "hold harmless" clause but, rather, is a "hold harmless for any amount in excess of $ clause" and is generally valid. The *Jones v. Dressel* case is an example of a court dealing with an exculpatory clause (see chapter opening).

JONES v. DRESSEL

Supreme Court of Colorado.
623 P.2d 370 (1978).

FACTS Jones, a parachute jumper, signed an agreement with Dressel Air Service to furnish transportation for jumps. The agreement had an exculpatory clause providing that Dressel was not liable for any injuries to Jones occurring while Jones was skydiving. Jones was injured in a jump and brought suit against Dressel for his damages. Dressel claimed no liability because of the clause.

ISSUE Is the exculpatory clause valid?

DECISION Yes. Jones was not forced to skydive but chose to do so. Skydiving has inherent dangers for which Dressel could not be held liable.

LEGAL TIP

No one is liable if you are injured because of the natural dangers involved in an activity.

Unconscionability

An **unconscionable contract** is one that a fair and honest person in his or her right senses would not accept. The term "unconscionable" comes from UCC Section 2-302 (see Chapter 28), which prohibits the enforcement of contracts that are unconscionable in their terms or in their formation.

An example of a contract that is unconscionable in its formation is one in which the terms drawn by the stronger party are forced upon the smaller party on a take-it-or-leave-it basis. The smaller party is not given the right to question or negotiate the terms; if they want the product or service, they must sign the contract. In one case, a buyer who spoke very little English was not given the opportunity to have the contract read or explained to him and was told to sign or forget purchasing the auto (*Jefferson Credit Corp. v. Marcano,* 302 N.Y.S.2d 390 [1969]).

Another type of unconscionable contract is one whose terms force one party (again usually the smaller one) to waive fundamental rights or agree to many assessments and costs (in fine print) that are not shown or explained. Examples in this area include cases where parties have waived their warranty rights, their right to notice of a suit, or their right to claim a breach of contract. In other cases, parties have been subjected to complicated and costly financing arrangements that were not easily found nor understood in the written contract.

In cases of unconscionability in formation of the contract, the entire contract may be declared void. In cases where terms or provisions of a contract are unconscionable, the contract may still be valid but the unconscionable portion will be struck. In the *Discount Fabric House v. Wis. Telephone Co.* case, the court deals with the issue of unconscionability in a contract.

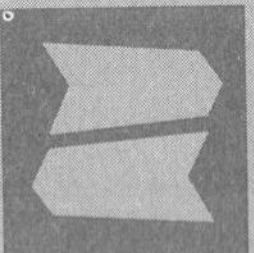

DISCOUNT FABRIC HOUSE v. WIS. TELEPHONE CO.

Supreme Court of Wisconsin.
334 N.W.2d 922 (1983).

FACTS Discount Fabric House of Racine entered into a contract with Wisconsin Telephone Company for three telephone-book listings and two yellow-page ads. A clause in the contract reduced the telephone company's liability for errors to the cost of the ad.

On one of the yellow page ads, the telephone company forgot to list the name Discount Fabric House. When Discount contacted the telephone company about the error, they were given a refund for the cost of the ad. Discount brought suit claiming it had lost $300,000 in business because of this omission.

ISSUE Is the clause limiting the telephone company's liability unconscionable?

DECISION No. The clause is not unconscionable because although the yellow pages are unique in that no other advertising form is the same, businesses do have other advertising means. Further, the liability limitation helps reduce the cost but increase general access to the yellow-page ads.

LEGAL TIP

Ask to proofread all business ads to ensure that they are accurate.

REMEDIES AFTER FINDING ILLEGALITY

Once a court determines that a contract is completely or partially void, there are several remedies for those situations where illegality has been found. The remedies available will depend upon whether the contract is executory or executed, and whether the contract is completely or partially void. An **executed contract** is one that the parties have already performed. An **executory contract** is one where performance has not yet occurred.

Remedies for Executory Contracts

If an executory contract is found to be entirely void, it cannot be enforced. A contract to commit a crime is completely void and unenforceable. A contract for services by an unlicensed professional who is required to be licensed is void and unenforceable.

If a provision in an executory contract is void, the court may strike or remove that provision and enforce the remainder of the contract. For example, suppose Al has contracted to sell his business to Bob, and Al has agreed not to enter into that business anywhere in the world. The restrictive convenant is overly broad and void, but the sales contract still can be enforced.

In some circumstances, one of the parties may choose to enforce an illegal contract. For example, all states have some form of regulating insurance sales. If a party purchased a policy before the insurer's license became effective, the contract would be void. However, licensing was designed to protect insurance purchasers, and, in these circumstances, they can choose to honor the contract. A protected party can choose to waive the effect of illegality.

Executed or Partially Executed Contracts

Where part or all of an illegal contract has been performed, the courts will not help the parties. They will be left in the same position. For example, suppose Anna agrees to pay politician Brewster $5000 for Brewster's favorable vote on some legislation affecting Anna's business. Anna pays the $5000, but Brewster votes the wrong way. Brewster keeps the $5000, and Anna cannot have a court help her. If Brewster votes first and then Anna refuses to pay him, Brewster cannot use a court to get the $5000.

Partially void contracts are an exception to this rule and can be enforced by striking the illegal portion. For example, if a restrictive covenant in the sales agreement of a business is void, the covenant is removed from the contract; the rest of the contract and the sale is still valid.

A second exception is the decision of a protected party to honor a contract. Suppose that Alfredo purchases securities from Buchwald Corporation. The securities were required to be registered prior to sale but were not. Alfredo is a protected party and may decide to keep the securities.

KEY TERMS

Commercial bribery
Blue laws
Usury
Public policy
Exculpatory clauses
Unconscionable contract
Executed contract
Executory contract

CHAPTER PROBLEMS

1. Amesbury Specialty Company wished to construct a building and contracted with Town Planning and Engineering Associates for assistance with the project. Amato was the president of Town Planning but was not a professional, licensed engineer. Amato hired licensed engineers to work on various aspects of the project and then put together all the work for Amesbury.

   In Massachusetts (where both companies were located), it is unlawful for anyone but a licensed engineer to perform engineering services.

   Amesbury decided to terminate its contract with Town Planning on the grounds of illegality since Amato had performed engineering services without a license. What is the result? *Town Planning and Engineering Associates, Inc. v. Amesbury Specialty Co.,* 342 N.E.2d 706 (Mass. 1976).

2. Robert Policky was a licensed veterinarian practicing in Spearfish, Lawrence County, South Dakota. Policky hired Loescher to assist him in his practice on a salary plus commission basis. In the employment contract was a restrictive covenant that prohibited Loescher from practicing veterinary medicine in South Dakota within a twenty-five-mile radius of Spearfish for a period of ten years after leaving Policky's employment for whatever reason. The twenty-five-mile radius covered three counties and several other towns. Loescher left Policky's practice to start his own. Policky sued to enforce the restrictive covenant. Is it valid? *Loescher v. Policky,* 173 N.W.2d 50 (S.D. 1969).

3. The Thomases rented an apartment from the Housing Authority of Bremerton. The apartment was a low-rent, one-bedroom apartment located in a public housing project. Their lease provided as follows:

   LIABILITY The Management shall not be responsible for loss or damage to property, nor injury to persons, occuring (sic) in or about demised premises, by reason of any existing or future condition, defect, matter or thing in said demised premises or the property of which the premises are a part, nor for the acts, omissions or negligence of other persons or Tenants in and about said property. The Tenant agrees to indemnify and save the Management, its representatives and employees harmless from all claims and liability for damages to property or injuries to persons occuring (sic) in or about the premises.

Four months after the Thomases moved into their apartment, their daughter, Carrie (then eighteen months) suffered second- and third-degree burns on the left side of her body when she fell into a basin of water in the bathroom sink. The hot water heater for the complex was twenty-two years old and needed repair in the adjustment mechanism that kept water from boiling. The Thomases had made three requests about the hot water repair prior to the time of the accident. Can the Thomases recover damages or are they bound by the clause? *Thomas v. Housing Authority of Bremerton,* 426 P.2d 836 (Wash. 1967).

4. Is the following clause valid?

Draperies and curtains frequently develop tender areas while hanging as result of heat, sunlight, humidity, and air pollution. Consequently, despite the utmost care exercised in our cleaning process, holes or tears in fabric may occur. Faded areas may not be apparent because of soil coverage. Progressive shrinkage may occur because of the inherent nature of the fabric or because it was not completely preshrunk. For these reasons, we accept your draperies and/or curtains for cleaning subject to your no-fault agreement. I have read the above and agree to hold you blameless in event any of the listed conditions become evident or occur in cleaning my draperies and/or curtains.

5. Southwestern Motors and Mazda Motors of America entered into an agreement to terminate Southwestern's Mazda franchise. Both parties also agreed not to notify the Commissioner of Motor Vehicles about the termination as was required by statute. Later Southwestern decided to reopen the franchise. Mazda filed suit on the basis of the agreement and Southwestern defended on the grounds that the agreement was void. What is the result? *Mazda Motors of America, Inc. v. Southwestern Motors, Inc.,* 250 S.E.2d 250 (N.C. 1978).

6. Rodriguez purchased a home from Gilbertie. A clause in the contract provided that acceptance and delivery of the home was full compliance by the seller with all covenants, conditions, and warranties. Shortly after the home was accepted and Rodriguez moved in, the septic tank overflowed and ruined the floors in the new home. Rodriguez sued and Gilbertie claimed no liability because of the clause. Who wins? *Rodriguez v. Gilbertie,* 363 A.2d 759 (Conn. 1976).

7. Sandas was hired by Gary Van Zeeland Talent agency. In his employment contract was a clause that prohibited him from working for another talent agency if he left Van Zeeland. Sandas left Van Zeeland and went to work for another talent agency. Van Zeeland brought suit seeking an injunction that would prohibit Sandas from working for the other agency. Sandas claims the clause is too broad and void. What is the result? *Gary Van Zeeland Talent, Inc. v. Sandas,* 267 N.W.2d 242 (Wis. 1978).

*8. Bernina Distributors, Inc., entered into a distribution agreement with Bernina Sewing Machine Company for the purchase of Bernina sewing machines. Since Berninas are imported, the sales price in the contract was subject to exchange rate fluctuations for the United States dollar. Because of poor economic conditions, the dollar was devalued, and Bernina Distributors were required to pay a higher price than ever for the machines. They brought suit against the manufacturer seeking to have the exchange rate clause declared unconscionable and void. What is the result? *Bernina Distributors, Inc. v. Bernina Sewing Machine Co.,* 646 F.2d 434 (Utah 1981).

*9. Corti entered into an agreement with several retiring attorneys to take over their clients. The attorneys transferred the files to Corti. Fleisher, a client, objected to the transfer on the grounds that his file was private and could be transferred only upon his request. What is the result? *Corti v. Fleisher,* 417 N.E.2d 764 (Ill. 1981).

*10. Thorpe wishes to sell his land in Montgomery County, Maryland. Frey, a member of an engineering firm that had furnished services to Thorpe, brought Thorpe in contact with Carte, a licensed real estate broker. Thorpe signed a listing agreement with Carte and agreed to pay a 6% commission. The listing contract provided that Carte would pay 35% of the 6% commission to Frey. In the state of Maryland, it is unlawful for any one other than a licensed real estate agent or broker to be paid a commission for the sale of property. After the property was sold, Carte did not pay Frey his 35%, and Frey filed suit. What is the result? *Thorpe v. Carte,* 250 A.2d 618 (Md. 1969).

Chapter 24

Third Party Rights and Duties

"All painters do not paint portraits like Sir Joshua Reynolds, nor landscapes like Claude Lorrainer, nor do all writers write dramas like Shakespeare or fiction like Dickens. Rare genius and extraordinary skill are not transferable, and contracts for their employment are therefore personal, and cannot be assigned. But rare genius and extraordinary talent are not indispensable to the workmanlike digging down of sand hill or the filling up of a depression to a given level, or the construction of brick sewers with manholes and covers, and contracts for such work are not personal, and may be assigned."

Taylor v. Palmer, 31 Cal. 240, 247–248 (1886)

CHAPTER PREVIEW

- Assignments—rights and benefits
- Delegations—rights and benefits
- The parties—their labels and roles
- Differences between delegation and assignment
- Incidental, donee, and creditor beneficiaries
- The FTC Holder-in-Due-Course Rule
- Warranties in assignments
- Roles of promisors and promisees

Pizza of Gaithersburg had a contract with Virginia Coffee Service. Virginia was to furnish and service cold-drink vending machines in six pizza parlors in Montgomery and Prince George Counties in Maryland. Virginia sold its assets to The Macke Company and assigned their contract with Pizza of Gaithersburg to Macke. Pizza of Gaithersburg wanted to stop their contract. They claimed Macke's service would not be of the same high quality as Virginia's. They claimed that Macke did not have the skill, judgment, and experience of Virginia. Can Pizza of Gaithersburg back out?

This chapter adds new "characters" to the study of contracts by dealing with the rights of people who did not even participate in forming the contract. The new characters are called third parties. Third parties are those other than the offeror and offeree (or the promisor and promisee). Third parties are not involved in forming the contract but later have some rights in the performance of the contract. This chapter answers the following questions about these third parties. What types of third parties are there? What is required to have third-party rights? What are third-party rights?

THIRD PARTY TYPE 1: ASSIGNMENT

Creating an Assignment

An **assignment** arises after a contract is formed. An assignment is a transfer of benefits or rights under a contract. For example, suppose that Rob will be buying Cynthia's bicycle for $150. Cynthia wants her younger sister to be paid the $150 because Cynthia owes her sister $150. Cynthia can assign the benefits of payment (the $150) to her sister. Cynthia's sister is the assignee. Figure 24-1 is a picture of what has happened.

Parties to an Assignment

There are three parties to the assignment. The easiest party to identify is the new third party who receives the assignment, or the **assignee.**

The party making the assignment is the **assignor.** However, that party also gives up his or her benefit under the contract. In other words, the role of promisee or beneficiary is given to someone else. Cynthia is the promisee, or obligee, for

Figure 24-1 **Assignment of Benefits**

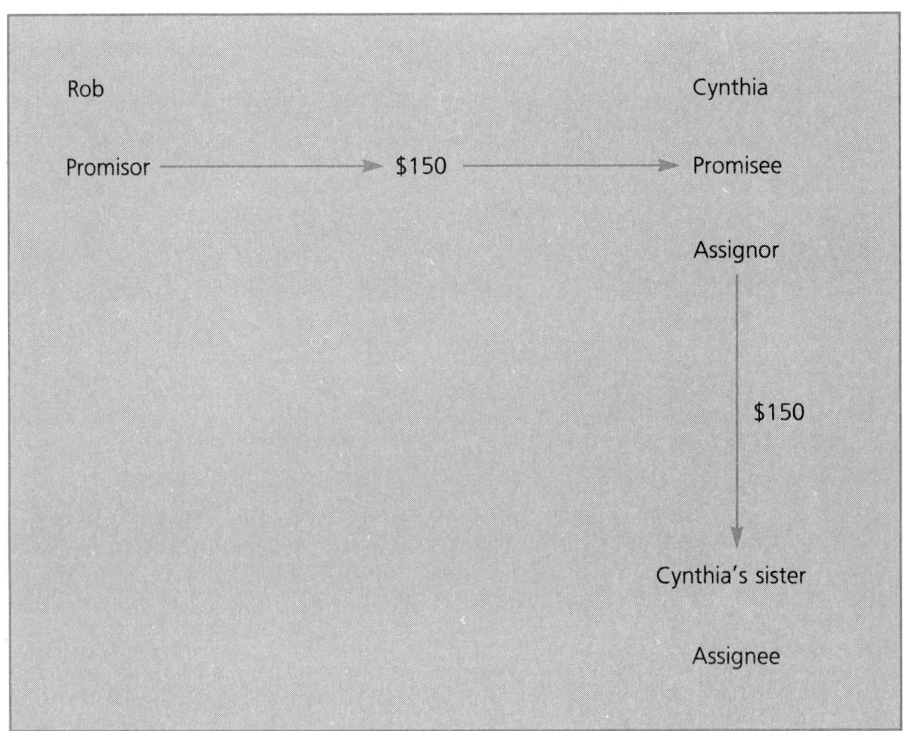

the money, which is her benefit under the contract. The assignor is also called the promisee.

Rob is the party who is paying. His promise under the contract is the payment of $150. He is the promisor, (or obligor), for that money.

Requirements for an Assignment

Intent to assign The basic requirement for an assignment is that the promisee/assignor have the intent to make an assignment. The intent to assign must be shown to the assignee. A promise to make an assignment is not an assignment. There is no assignment until the act is actually done. There are times when the law implies the intent to assign. The *Blagg v. Fred Hunt Co., Inc.* case involves a problem with an assigned warranty.

BLAGG v. FRED HUNT CO., INC.
Supreme Court of Arkansas.
612 S.W.2d 321 (1981).

FACTS Fred Hunt Company, Inc., built a house in the Pleasant Valley addition to Little Rock, Arkansas. The house was sold to the Dentons on October 9, 1978. The Dentons sold the house to American Foundation Life Insurance Company (AFLI). AFLI sold the house to Ted and Kathye Blagg on June 29, 1979.

Shortly after moving in, the Blaggs noticed a strong odor in the house. The Blaggs then noticed fumes that were identified as formaldehyde fumes coming from the carpet. The problem was traced to the carpet pad.

The Blaggs brought suit against Fred Hunt for breach of Arkansas' one-year warranty of habitability on new homes. Fred Hunt claimed that the warranty did not apply to assignees.

ISSUE Can the implied warranty on new house construction be assigned?

DECISION Yes. The implied warranty passes along during that first year. Without assignment rights, the builder could eliminate the warranty just by transferring the property to an insider before selling it.

LEGAL TIP
Before buying a house, check warranty terms.

Is a writing required? Unless it was required that the original contract be written, an assignment need not be. In some assignments, the parties will want the terms written. For example, if there is an assignment of accounts receivable to a creditor, that creditor may want to create and perfect an Article IX security interest (see Chapter 52). Suppose that Bob's Bread Basket owes Fred's Flour Mill $2500 for purchasing flour on credit. Bob does not have the cash to pay but does have $2500 due him from the bread buyers. Bob can assign his right to payment to Fred. This example is diagrammed in Figure 24-2.

Consideration There is no requirement that an assignment be supported by consideration. An assignment can be a gift, which is a gratuitous assignment, and still be valid. The example in Figure 24-1 involves a gratuitous assignment.

Capacity The assignor must have contractual capacity. An assignment made by someone without this capacity is voidable. If a minor assigns rights under a contract, both the contract and the assignment are voidable at the minor's option.

Limitations on Assignments

Material change in promisor's duty Assignments are limited to those types that will not substantially change the promisor's duties under the contract. For example, suppose that Bernard signed a lawn service agreement with Larry's Lawn

Figure 24-2 **Assignment of Accounts Receivable**

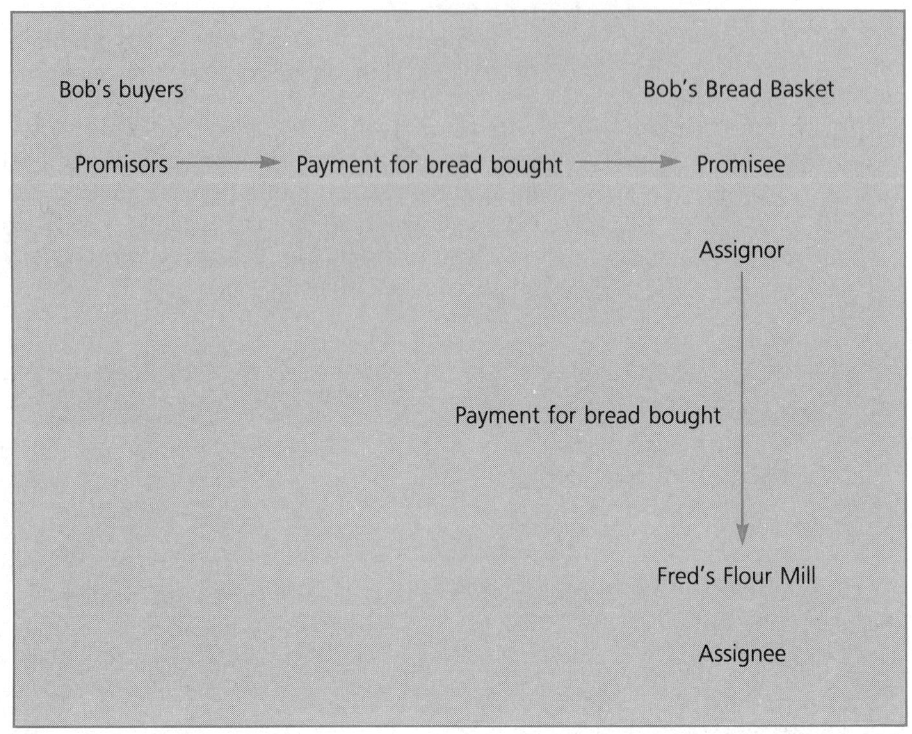

Service. The agreement requires Larry to take care of all the yard work at Bernard's home for $25 per week for twenty weeks. Bernard wants to give the service as a gift to Bif. Bif has a lawn that is three acres larger than Bernard's. Larry's duties would be changed materially. The contract is not assignable.

Material change in the promisor's risk Some contracts are personal and entered into because of the habits and traits of the promisee. Insurance contracts are examples. For instance, suppose that Incidental Insurance has issued Daphney a homeowner's insurance policy. The risk for Incidental and Daphney's premium are affected by the type of person Daphney is. If Daphney sold her home to Bud and assigned the policy to him, it would be ineffective. Bud's habits and personal traits are not the same as Daphney's. Incidental's risk would be different. The *Macke Co. v. Pizza of Gaithersburg, Inc.* case, examines whether a contract is assignable.

Violation of public policy Some contracts are protected from assignment by public policy. For example, attorneys cannot assign their clients' contracts to other attorneys without the clients' consent. A contract with an attorney is personal and cannot be assigned.

Statutory limitations Wage assignments are governed by federal and state laws, which limit the amount of assignments. For example, no more than 50% of

MACKE CO. v. PIZZA OF GAITHERSBURG, INC.

Court of Appeals of Maryland.
270 A.2d 645 (1970).

FACTS Pizza of Gaithersburg had a contract with Virginia Coffee Service. Virginia was to install cold-drink vending machines at the corporation's pizza restaurants.

Shortly after this contract was agreed to, Virginia transferred its assets to the Macke Company. Virginia also assigned its contracts with Pizza of Gaithersburg to Macke.

Pizza of Gaithersburg objected to the assignment claiming that it had relied on Virginia's skill, judgment, and reputation when entering into the contract. They argued that the services were personal and could not be delegated or assigned.

ISSUE Could the contract be assigned?

DECISION Yes. The service was routine and did not require special skill. Macke was involved in the same type of service and could fill in.

LEGAL TIP

Check with suppliers to see if they are negotiating to transfer their firms. Learn about the buyer and his or her reputation.

a spouse's wages can be assigned to pay child support. (See Chapter 54 for a complete review of wage-assignment limitations.)

The Roles of the Three Parties in an Assignment

The promisor The promisor is the party to the original contract, or the one who performs the benefit that has been assigned. Promisors still have the same obligation to perform when an assignment has been made; the only difference is that their performance is given to another party. For example, suppose that Mary has purchased a piano from Milo's Music Company. Mary has signed a time-payment contract and will pay for the piano at a rate of $37 per month for five years. Milo's wants its money now and can assign Mary's contract. Milo's decides to sell the contract to Fig's Finance Company, which Mary will pay. Figure 24-3 is a diagram of this assignment.

When does the promisor pay the assignee? The promisor, Mary, pays the assignee on the same schedule as the assignor/promisee would have been paid. However, the promisor is not obligated to pay the assignee unless the assignee or promisee has been notified of the assignment. For example, suppose that Mary's payments were due on the fifteenth of each month. On November 1, 1984, Milo's transfers the contract to Fig's. Fig's does not notify Mary of the assignment until November 20, 1984, and Mary has already sent her November payment to Milo's. Because she was not notified, she is protected. Fig's will have to collect the November payment from Milo's.

Can the promisor stop paying the assignee? The general rule is that an assignee has no greater contract rights than those of the assignor/promisee. If the promisor has a contract defense against the promisee, that same defense is good against the assignee. For example, suppose that Milo's told Mary that the piano she purchased was a model that would never need tuning. Within three weeks after delivery, Mary is told by an expert that the piano does need tuning. Mary has a defense of misrepresentation against Milo's. But the defense is also good against Fig's, the assignee. Therefore, Mary could stop payment to Fig's until the misrepresentation problem is solved with Milo's.

Figure 24-3 **Roles of the Parties to an Assignment**

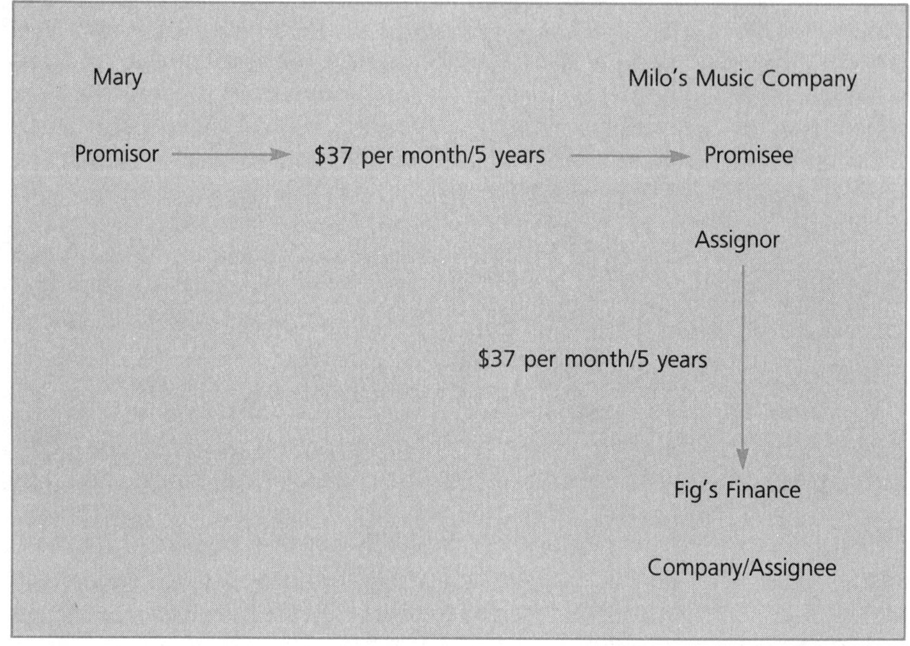

The holder-in-due-course rule and assignees Some special rules apply when an assignee is a holder in due course. Holders in due course are covered in Chapter 52, but a brief explanation is needed here. Very simply, a **holder in due course** is a good-faith assignee who takes a promissory note for value. (see Chapter 51 for a definition of "promissory note"). Under Article III of the UCC, holders in due course enjoy an excellent status. Holders in due course get paid even when promisors have contract defenses against the promisee. In other words, Article III leaves the burden of working out contract problems with the original promisor and promisee.

The Federal Trade Commission (FTC) found that this holder-in-due-course protection sometimes hurt consumers. To prevent this problem, the FTC passed its Holder-in-Due-Course Rule, which eliminates holder-in-due-course protection in consumer credit transactions. A holder in due course in a consumer transaction has the same rights as an assignee and no more.

The FTC doctrine does not apply to commercial transactions.

The promisee/assignor The promisee is the party who was to get the benefits under the contract with the promisor. When an assignment occurs, those benefits have now been transferred to a third party—the assignee. There is a separate contract between the promisee and the assignee. This contract is one for the sale or transfer of contract rights. The contract can have warranties in it on the assignment. Even if no warranties are in the contract or even if no written contract is made, the assignor still makes some implied warranties or promises to the assignee.

Implied warranty not to defeat the assignment. The assignee (in most cases) is paying for the right to get the promisee's contract benefits. The assignee should have some guarantee that the assignor will not destroy the right to get those benefits. This first implied warranty protects the assignee from such a problem.

This warranty promises the assignee that the assignor will not give the rights to someone else. For example, Milo's would breach this warranty if it assigned Mary's contract to Ace Finance Company as well as Fig's. Fig's would have the right to collect any costs that it had in correcting the problem.

Implied warranty of no defenses. This warranty means the assignor promises that the promisor does not have any defenses against the contract. In the example where Cynthia has a defense of misrepresentation, she can stop paying Fig's. However, Fig's will be able to collect their losses on their assignment from Milo's because Milo's breached this warranty.

Implied warranty of title. This warranty has the assignor promise that he or she has good title to the contract benefits. The assignor also promises that he or she has the authority to transfer or assign the benefits. This warranty is a protection for assignees who get contract benefits from those who have no interest in the contract or who have no right to transfer the contract.

No implied warranty of payment. No assignor guarantees payment. No assignor promises that the assignee will be paid in full. The assignee takes the credit risks along with the assignor. There is always the possibility that a promisor will be unable to pay or will become insolvent.

The assignee The assignee is the new party. The assignee now has the right to the promisee's benefits under the contract. The assignee has the protection of the implied warranties. The assignee also has the responsibility of notifying the promisor of the assignment.

The Problems of More Than One Assignment

Assignments often are not single events. Many times there are assignments from assignees to others. Also, some assignors assign the same contract more than once. In both these situations, there are rules for protecting the parties involved.

Assignment by assignee: Subassignments An assignee is free to assign his or her benefits to another party. For example, Fig's could transfer its rights in Cynthia's contract to Wood's World of Finance, which becomes a subassignee. Wood's has the implied warranties from Fig's, but no implied warranties run from Milo's to Wood's. When Cynthia discovers the problem with tuning, she could stop paying Wood's. Wood's would turn to Fig's for breach of warranty, and Fig's could then turn to Milo's. Figure 24-4 is an illustration of this subassignment.

Different assignees, same contract: Successive assignments It often happens that an assignor assigns the same contract benefits to different parties. For example, suppose that Milo's assigned Cynthia's contract to Fig's on November 1, to Wood's on November 2, and to Ace Finance Company on November 3. Figure 24-5 is a diagram of these successive assignments.

Milo's has some serious problems with breach of the implied warranty not to defeat assignments. However, the problem that remains is who gets Cynthia's payments (the benefit) under the contract? There are several rules used to solve this problem.

Figure 24-4 **Subassignments**

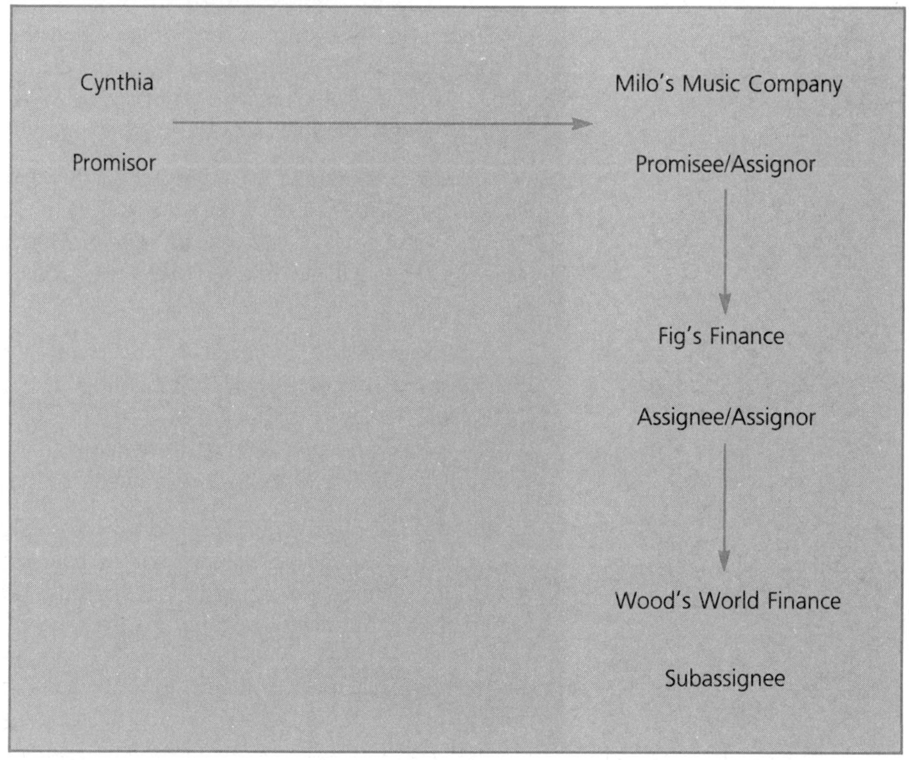

The New York Rule The **New York Rule** or American Rule provides first in time, first in right. This simple solution means that whoever got the assignment first gets the benefits. The other successive assignees are left to breach of warranty actions against the assignor. In the example with Milo's Music Company, the New York Rule would require the benefits to go to Fig's. Wood's and Ace are left to deal with Milo's.

The English Rule The **English Rule** provides first to notify, first in right. This rule means that the first successive assignee to notify the promisor gets the benefits. The assignee must have paid for the assignment and must act on good faith—that is the assignee does not know of any other assignments. Suppose that Wood's notified Cynthia on November 5, 1984, and Fig's and Ace did not notify her until November 10. Under the English Rule, Wood's gets the benefits. Fig's and Ace are left to solve their problems with Milo's under breach of implied warranty.

The Four Horseman Rule The **Four Horseman Rule,** the one used by most of the states, is also called the Restatement of Contracts Rule. This rule is a modified first in time, first in right rule. For instance, Fig's would get the benefits unless Cynthia had already paid someone else—Wood's or Ace. The Four Horseman Rule allows first in time, first in right only until the promisor pays someone. Once payment has been made to one assignee, the rights of the others end. They are left to deal with their assignor.

Figure 24-5 **Successive Assignments**

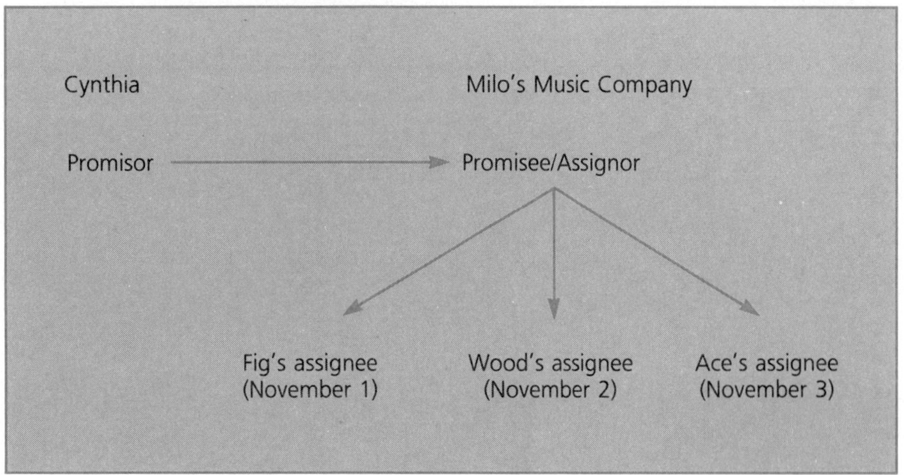

THIRD PARTY TYPE 2: DELEGATION

Assignment deals with the beneficial side of contracts, while **delegation** deals with the detrimental aspect. Benefits are assigned; detriments or duties are delegated. In a delegation, the promisor is appointing someone else to perform the contract. For example, suppose that Larry's Laundry has hired Mary's Messenger Service to handle occasional deliveries of laundry. Mary's has decided to get out of the delivery business. However, they know that Mike's Messenger Service will deliver laundry. Mary's asks Mike's to take over Larry's deliveries. If Mike's agrees, there is a delegation of Mary's responsibilities to Mike. Figure 24-6 is a diagram of this relationship.

Parties in a Delegation

The parties in a delegation are the promisee, the delegant or delegator, and the delegate or delegatee.

1. *Promisee.* The promisee, or obligee, is the party to the original contract who is entitled to the benefits. Since the duties are being transferred, the promisee is the party in the upper-left corner of Figure 24-6.
2. *Delegant/delegator.* The **delegant** is the party to the original contract who has duties and delegates them to a third party.
3. *Delegate/delegatee.* The **delegate** is the new, third party who performs the obligations or duties that originally belonged to the delegator.

Creating a Delegation

Intent The requirements for a delegation are similar to the requirements for an assignment. There must be the intent to make the delegation. A promise of future delegation is not delegation; the transfer of responsibility must be made.

Writing The decision to delegate responsibilities need not be in writing unless the original contract was in writing. However, if the duties that the delegate will perform include signing written contracts, the delegation must be in writing.

Figure 24-6 **Delegation of Duties**

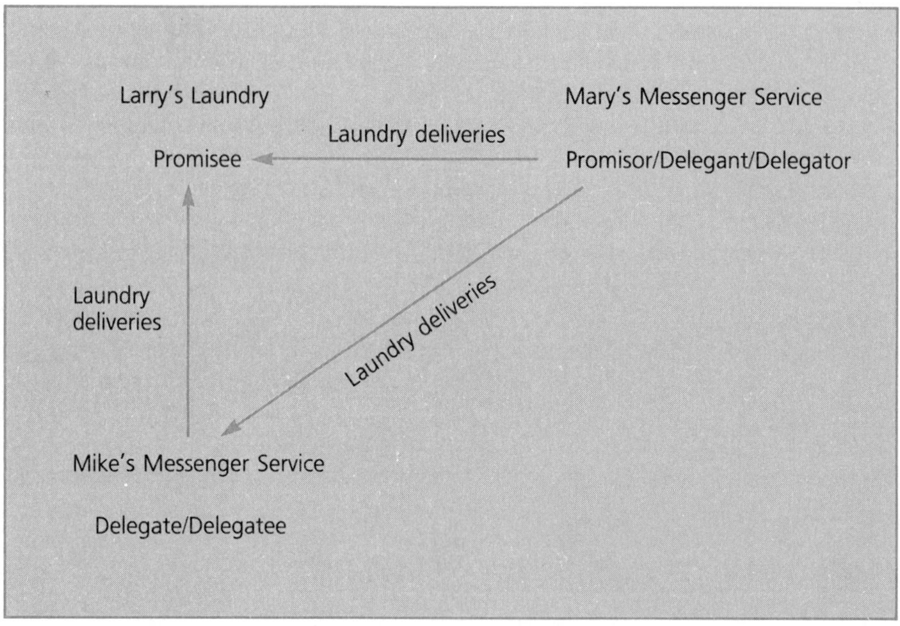

Limitations on Delegation

Some duties can be delegated easily, while others cannot. The types of duties that can be delegated are limited ones.

Contract prohibits delegation If the original parties to the contract add a section that prohibits delegation, delegation is improper. Any attempted delegation of duties under the contract would be voidable.

Unique skills Delegation is prohibited where the promisor has been hired under a contract because of unique skills. For example, if Berferd hires Mr. Neil to do his portrait, that duty cannot be delegated. Mr. Neil was hired for his abilities and reputation. On the other hand, substituting another plumber on a home improvement contract is permissible, since the original plumber was not hired for unique skills.

Trust and confidence When a contract was entered into because the promisee had trust and confidence in the promisor, delegation of the duties would be invalid. For example, suppose that Juanita hired Charles Lauren, her long-time personal accountant, to do the accounting for her newly formed corporation. Since Lauren was hired because of trust and confidence, he could not delegate his responsibilities to another accountant without Juanita's permission. The *Hudgins v. Bacon* case deals with an issue of whether a contract obligation can be delegated.

Does an Assignment Go Along with a Delegation?

There are very few people who are willing to perform the duties of a contract without being paid the benefits. In most cases where there is a delegation, there is an accompanying assignment of benefits. In the Larry's Laundry example, not only is Mary's delegating its responsibilities to Mike's but is also assigning its

HUDGINS v. BACON

Court of Appeals of Georgia.
321 S.E.2d 359 (1984).

FACTS Mr. and Mrs. Hudgins entered into a contract with Bacon and Loomis homes to build and finish a "spec" home. Within a few months after the Hudgins moved in, they discovered that the brick veneer was cracking and falling away from the house; that the walls were cracking; and that the floors (even marble ones) were breaking apart. The Hudgins brought suit for breach of contract. They then discovered that Hudgins had delegated the construction to an independent contractor.

ISSUE Was the delegation proper? Who is liable to the Hudgins?

DECISION The court held that the delegation was improper. The Hudgins had contracted with a well-known and reputable builder. The services sought were personal in nature. Bacon and Loomis were not released from their liability to the Hudgins.

LEGAL TIP

Put a clause in all contracts that prohibits a delegation without your permission.

benefits—the right to be paid. In most delegations, the benefits are assigned along with the delegated duties.

Responsibilities of the Parties

The delegant/delegator The delegant is not excused from liability just because there has been a delegation. The delegant/promisor is still liable to the promisee for adequate performance of the contract. For example, if Mike's does not perform according to the terms of the agreement by making late deliveries or delivering soiled laundry, Mary's will be liable for Larry's damages. The only way that Mary's can be released from this obligation is if Larry's agrees through a novation (or a new contract—see Chapter 25) to hire Mike and release Mary.

The delegate The delegate does not become liable to the promisee by agreeing to a delegation. The delegate will be liable to the delegator/promisor. For example, suppose that Harry hires Case Construction to remodel his home. Case hires Happy Plumbers to do the plumbing work. Happy is a subcontractor, but is also a delegate. Happy performs sloppy work and delays the project three weeks. Harry has to stay in a motel for three weeks for the delay and then for a fourth week for another plumber to fix Happy's errors. Harry's action is against Case. Case would then have the right to recover from Happy for failure to perform properly.

The promisee The promisee has the right to proper performance. If that performance does not come from either the promisor/delegator or the delegate, the promisee has an action for breach of contract. That action for breach of contract is against the promisor.

THIRD PARTY TYPE 3: THIRD PARTY BENEFICIARIES

A third-party beneficiary has no privity with either the promisor or the promisee. A third-party beneficiary is a person on the sidelines who stands to benefit from

Figure 24-7 **Life Insurance Third-Party Beneficiaries**

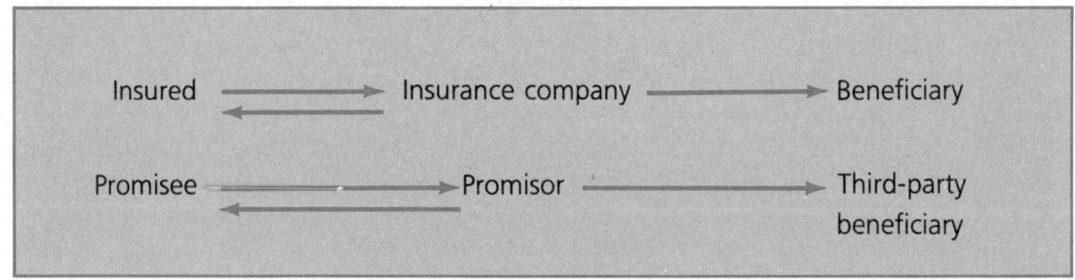

a contract that two other people have agreed to. For example, a person named as a beneficiary in a life insurance policy is not involved in making the contract. There is no privity of contract between the beneficiary and the insurance company. There is also no privity between the insured and the beneficiary. However, the beneficiary is the party who will be paid the benefits when the insured party dies. Figure 24-7 is a diagram of a third-party beneficiary who benefits from an insurance policy.

Types of Beneficiaries

Intended beneficiaries A beneficiary who is set up to benefit from a contract because the parties involved desire it is called an **intended beneficiary.** For example, a life insurance beneficiary is an intended beneficiary. In other words, the contract gives the name of the beneficiary and describes the benefits that the contract will give to the third party.

Creditor beneficiary A **creditor beneficiary** is an intended beneficiary to whom the promisee owes money. For example, a medical insurance policy is used to help pay medical expenses. Those parties (hospitals, doctors, and pharmacies) who will be paid are creditors of the promisee. The insurer (promisor) agrees to pay those debts according to the policy terms. Figure 24-8 shows the relationships among creditor beneficiaries and the contract parties.

Figure 24-8 **Creditor Beneficiaries**

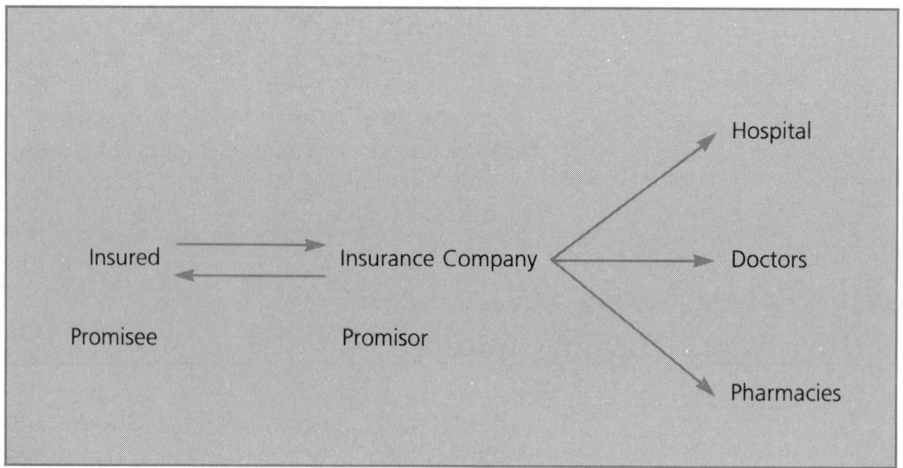

Donee beneficiaries **Donee beneficiaries** are intended beneficiaries who receive a gift because of a contract entered into by the promisee. A life insurance beneficiary is a donee beneficiary. The money is paid as a gift and not as an obligation. The beneficiary is not a creditor but usually a close relative, and the proceeds are a gift. The *Brown v. National Supermarkets, Inc.* case deals with an issue involving a donee beneficiary.

BROWN v. NATIONAL SUPERMARKETS, INC.

Court of Appeals of Montana.
679 S.W.2d 307 (1984).

FACTS Pauline Brown, a shopper at National Supermarket, was shot and seriously injured by an unknown assailant in National's parking lot. Sentry Security Agency had been hired by National to protect customers in the parking lots because there had been 16 firearm robberies, 7 strong arm robberies, and 136 other crimes reported on National's premises.

Mrs. Brown sued both National and Sentry for their failure to provide protection in a known-to-be-dangerous situation. Sentry insisted that it had no liability since they didn't have a contract with Mrs. Brown.

ISSUE Was Mrs. Brown a donee beneficiary of the contract between National and Sentry for patrol of the store parking lot?

DECISION Yes. The clear intent of National was to protect its customers. Sentry owed a duty to National and to its customers. Mrs. Brown could recover for Sentry's failure to protect her in a reasonable manner.

LEGAL TIP
Make sure all contracts indicate who is being protected and who will benefit.

Incidental beneficiaries **Incidental beneficiaries** are third parties who stand to benefit indirectly from a contract. They have no enforceable rights. For example, suppose that Jack wants to sell his house. He tells Gwen that if he sells his house he will buy Gwen's $34,000 Porsche. Gwen would like to see the house sold since she stands to benefit from its sale. But, Gwen's benefit is indirect and incidental. The *Schell v. Knickelbein* case examines the issue of whether a party is an incidental beneficiary.

SCHELL v. KNICKELBEIN

Supreme Court of Wisconsin.
252 N.W.2d 921 (1977).

FACTS Mr. Schell was attacked by the Knickelbein's dog on June 17, 1974. As a result of the injuries from the attack, Mr. Schell died. Mrs. Schell brought a suit against the Knickelbeins for wrongful death in negligence.

Mrs. Schell also sued Security Savings and Loan Association (SS). SS was the mortgagee on the Knickelbeins' home and received a monthly fee, which was to be used to buy homeowner's insurance for the Knickelbeins. SS did not get the insurance because the Knickelbeins did not have homeowners' coverage.

Mrs. Schell claimed that she was a third-party beneficiary (creditor) of the agreement between SS and the Knickelbeins. She claimed that SS's breach of contract resulted in no insurance to pay her for the damages.

ISSUE Is Mrs. Schell a third-party beneficiary of the mortgage contract?

DECISION No. Mrs. Schell would have to show that the contract was directly and primarily for her benefit. The insurance was mostly for the benefit of the Knickelbeins and SS and not for third parties.

LEGAL TIP
Check with mortgage companies occasionally to make sure that insurance and tax payments are up to date.

Creation of a Third Party Beneficiary Contract

The requirements for creating rights in a third party are simple. The third party must be named or identified, as in the case involving doctors and hospitals. The contract must also make clear that these parties are intended beneficiaries. For example, suppose that a builder needed to have government financing available for buyers in his new subdivision. The government agrees to provide financing if a builder agrees to build houses within six months from the time a deposit is received; if the project is not completed at the end of that period, the builder must refund the deposit. The agreement benefits a class of third parties—the buyers. They are donee beneficiaries of the agreement between the builder and the government. The intent of the agreement was protecting these buyers, and they were identified as a group.

The other requirements for creating a third-party beneficiary contract are the same as in other contracts. The parties must follow the statute of frauds and the rules of formation to have a valid contract.

Rights of the Parties

Promisor The promisor is the party required to perform for the promisee and the third-party beneficiary. Life insurers are promisors for the payment of benefits. Medical insurers are the promisors for the payment of covered medical bills. In third-party beneficiary contracts, the promisor just gives the benefits to someone other than the contract promisee.

The promisor can use any defenses against the beneficiary that would be valid against the promisee. For example, if the promisee misrepresented his or her health or prior health problems to get a medical or life policy, those misrepresentations would be a valid defense against beneficiaries claiming payment under the policy. If the promisee was not entitled to the policy, the beneficiaries are not entitled to the benefits.

Promisee The promisee may not be receiving the benefits, but the promisee is still a party to the contract. A party to the contract has the right to sue for nonperformance. If a medical insurer fails to pay proper claims from creditor beneficiaries, the promisee can sue the insurance company for payment.

The promisee also remains obligated to perform under the terms of the contract. The promisee must pay premiums and submit claims properly according to the contract terms.

Beneficiaries Beneficiaries' rights against the promisor and promisee vary according to the type of beneficiary. Incidental beneficiaries have no rights against either the promisor or promisee. Donee beneficiaries have the right to force the promisor to perform according to the contract terms. If a life insurer does not pay properly claimed benefits, the donee beneficiary can sue the insurance company who is the promisor.

However, a donee beneficiary has no rights against the promisee for the promisor's failure to pay. The payment was a gift and does not give the beneficiary contractual rights against the promisee. Creditor beneficiaries can sue a promisor to force performance. If the promisor does not perform, they can always turn to the promisee. Medical bills are an example. If the insurer does not pay, the patient is still required to pay all the bills. Figure 24-9 is a summary of the rights in a third-party beneficiary contract.

Figure 24-9 **Third-Party Beneficiaries: Rights of the Parties to Bring Suit and Recover**

	DONEE BENEFICIARY	
Insured Promisee	***Life Insurance Company: Promisor***	***Named Beneficiary/ Donee Beneficiary***
1. Named beneficiary versus life insurance company Donee beneficiary versus promisor		Yes
2. Named beneficiary versus insured Donee beneficiary versus promisee		No
3. Insured (estate) versus life insurance company Promisee versus promisor		Yes
	CREDITOR BENEFICIARY	
Insured Promisee	***Medical Insurance Company: Promisor***	***Medical Care Creditor Beneficiaries***
1. Medical care providers versus medical insurance company Creditor beneficiaries versus promisor		Yes
2. Medical care providers versus insured Creditor beneficiaries versus promisee		Yes
3. Insured versus medical insurance company Promisee versus promisor		Yes

KEY TERMS

Assignment
Assignee
Assignor
Holder-in-due-course
New York Rule
English Rule
Four Horseman Rule
Delegation
Delegant
Delegate
Intended beneficiary
Creditor beneficiary
Donee beneficiary
Incidental beneficiary

CHAPTER PROBLEMS

1. Carol and Don East were divorced. As part of their property settlement, they agreed to have Charles Aubrey East (at the time two years old) receive forty five acres of land in Clay County, Alabama. When Charles was old enough to hold title to the land, Don did not convey title to him. Charles brought suit against Don as a third-party beneficiary of the property settlement. Is Charles a beneficiary? Can he bring suit? *East v. East,* 395 So.2d 78 (Ala. 1981).
2. Robson and his father entered into an agreement whereby Robson's shares would pass to his father if Robson died. The father agreed to pay Robson's wife $500 per month for five years or until she remarried (whichever came first). When Robson died, his father took the shares but did not pay Robson's wife. Can she collect as a third-party beneficiary? *Robson v. Robson,* 514 F.Supp. 99 (D.C. Ill. 1981).
3. Which of the following contracts would be personal and could not be delegated or assigned?
   A. A contract for credit.
   B. A contract for membership in a health spa.
   C. A contract for the delivery of ice.
   D. A contract for photocopying of a 100-page paper.
   E. A contract for the construction of a swimming pool.

*4. Brehm was a tenant in a building that had a rule requiring him to keep the walk leading to the building free of ice and snow. George, a pedestrian, was injured when he fell on the ice and snow on the walk leading to the building. George sued Brehm for breach of the rule and claimed that he was a third-party beneficiary of the agreement. Was he? *George v. Brehm,* 246 F. Supp. 242 (W.D. Pa. 1965).

*5. Arnold Productions, Inc., owned two motion pictures, "Hangmen Also Die" and "It Happened Tomorrow." Arnold entered into a contract with Favorite Films Inc., which gave Favorite the exclusive right to reproduce, license, lease, exhibit, and rent the films for seven years. Favorite agreed to get as many bookings and as wide a distribution as possible.

The agreement also provided that the contract was "personal" and could not be assigned without Arnold's permission.

Favorite then entered into an agreement with Nationwide Television Corporation for the television distribution of the films. Nationwide then subleased the films to its subsidiary, Film Equities, Inc. Film Equities then subleased to another subsidiary, Unity, Inc.

Arnold brought suit claiming that the personal contract could not be assigned, and that Favorite had breached its contract. Could the contracts be assigned? What if the assignments had the same terms as the original agreement? *Arnold Productions, Inc. v. Favorite Films Corporations,* 298 F.2d 540 (2d Cir. 1962).

*6. McCabe won $100,000 in the New Jersey lottery. He was to be paid the amount in ten equal installments over the next ten years. He assigned his right to the payments to a creditor. The New Jersey Lottery Commission says that the payments could not be assigned. What is the result? *McCabe v. Director of New Jersey Lottery Commission,* 363 A.2d 387 (N.J. 1976).

*7. The Baillys owned a house and three acres in Coker, Alabama. They signed a contract in 1973 with Guaranty Pest Control for termite extermination. They carried a termite treatment bond and had the house treated each year until 1977.

In 1977, the Baillys sold their property to the Rays. Their contract stated that there would be no liability on the Baillys' part for defects or repairs in the property, and that the house was sold "as is." Shortly after moving in, the Rays found great termite damage. The Rays are suing Guaranty Pest Control for their breach of warranty to the Baillys. Guaranty denies liability because the Rays were not parties to the termite contract. Who is correct? *Ray v. Montgomery,* 399 So.2d 230 (Ala. 1980).

*8. Dekalb County, Georgia, had a contract with the Federal Aviation Administration (FAA) to maintain and operate an airport. The county permitted a dump to be put next to the airport. Large numbers of birds gathered in the air above the dump and airport because the birds were attracted to the trash. While trying to land, a plane crashed among all the birds, and everyone aboard the plane was killed.

The relatives of those killed in the crash have filed suit against the county. They are claiming to be third-party beneficiaries of the contract between the FAA and the county. Are they? *Miree v. United States,* 588 F.2d 453 (5th Cir. 1979).

*9. The New York Stock Exchange (NYSE) requires its members to comply with the terms in its exchange manual. One of the terms requires accuracy in press releases. Could a shareholder who sells stock (low) in response to a false news release recover on the basis of breach of contract? *Franklin Life Insurance Company v. Commonwealth Edison Co.,* 451 F.Supp. 602 (D.C. Ill., 1978); affirmed 598 F.2d 1109; cert, den. 444 U.S. 900 (1980).

10. Chevron Oil Company had a contract with the state of New York to provide roadside service to disabled vehicles within thirty minutes after a call is received. Kornblut got a flat tire on a hot day while travelling on the New York state thruway. He called for service. He waited 2½ hours and then tried to change the tire himself. He died of a heart attack from exertion. His survivors sued Chevron as third-party beneficiaries of the contract between New York State and Chevron. Could they recover? *Kornblut v. Chevron Oil Co.,* 407 N.Y.S.2d 498 (1978).

"There is nothing so easy but that it becomes difficult when you do it with reluctance."
Terrence

Chapter 25

Performance and Discharge

CHAPTER PREVIEW

- Conditions and what they do
- Standards for performance
- The use of substantial performance
- When duties are discharged
- Examples of discharges

Kodak Labs had their customers sign an agreement before film could be developed, which covered "sexually explicit" films. If a customer delivered "sexually explicit" film for development, Kodak would not develop or return the film. Penthouse delivered some film that Kodak found to be "sexually explicit." Kodak refused to develop or return the film; Penthouse claimed that there was a breach of contract. Who wins?

Performance is the stage of a contract relationship after there has been an agreement, when no problems with defenses have developed. At this stage, the parties can perform and finish their obligations. However, some problems do come up before, during, and after performance. This chapter covers issues concerning performance and answers several questions: When does performance begin? What is required for performance? Is performance ever excused?

WHEN PERFORMANCE BEGINS: THE PREREQUISITES

Performance comes after the agreement is reached but is not always automatic. Some events may have to occur before the parties are required to perform. Some events result in a release of all contract liabilities. These events or acts are called **conditions.**

Classes of Conditions

Conditions can be put into two large groups. The first group is based on when the condition occurs in relation to the time for performance. This group includes conditions precedent, conditions concurrent, and conditions subsequent. The second group is based on whether the parties agree to a condition or the law provides an automatic condition. This group has express, implied-in-fact, and implied-in-law conditions.

Conditions precedent **Conditions precedent** are acts or events that must happen before the contracting parties are required to perform. If a condition precedent is part of a contract and it never happens, the parties do not have to perform.

An example of a condition precedent is a clause in a home purchase contract that gives the buyer the chance to find financing. The buyer will not have to buy the home if he or she does not qualify for financing. Obtaining financing is a condition precedent to the buyer's performance.

In insurance contracts, the insurer is not required to pay benefits until the policy-holder gives the company proof that a loss occurred. If the insured never makes a claim, the insurer is never required to pay.

Conditions concurrent **Conditions concurrent** are mutual events that give rise to the performance of both parties. For example, when a shopper checks out at a grocery store, there are several conditions going on at the same time. The grocer will not want to give up the food if the shopper does not pay; the shopper does not want to pay if the grocer will not give up the food. The result is that neither would do anything unless their conditions could happen simultaneously. The grocer bags the food, and the buyer gets ready to pay at the same time. Their mutual conditions of the other's performance are met by having them perform at the same time.

A property closing also involves some conditions concurrent. The seller does not want to give title until the buyer pays. The buyer does not want to pay unless the seller can give good title. The buyer may want a title insurance policy, while the seller may want a cashier's check. Their performance conditions are met by having a third party handle all the documents at a set time. All transfers of property and cash are made at the same time.

Conditions subsequent **Conditions subsequent** occur after the duty to perform has already arisen. Conditions subsequent serve to discharge parties of their performance. For example, suppose that an insured has given an insurer a claim for a theft loss. The condition precedent has been met. The time for the insurer's performance (assuming a proper claim) has come. If the insurer does not pay, the insured will have to file suit. That suit must be filed within the policy's time limits or the rights under that claim are lost. If the policy requires suit for a claim within three years, the insured must bring suit within that time. Without a timely suit, the insurer is discharged.

The *Burger King Corp. v. Family Dining, Inc.* case deals with a condition subsequent.

BURGER KING CORP. v. FAMILY DINING, INC.
United States District Court, Eastern District of Pennsylvania.
426 F.Supp. 485 (1977).

FACTS James McLamore and Carl Ferris were school buddies at Cornell in the 1940's. McLamore went on to found Burger King restaurants in Florida. Ferris founded and owned Family Dining located in Bucks and Montgomery Counties, Pennsylvania.

On May 10, 1963, Ferris agreed to buy a Burger King franchise from McLamore. Ferris was given a ninety-year exclusive franchise in Bucks and Montgomery Counties. However, the contract required Ferris to start one restaurant per year for the first ten years and then maintain them for eighty years.

Ferris did fairly well the first few years in starting Burger King restaurants. In 1968, he did not get one started. In 1969, Pillsbury purchased Burger King, and Ferris did not get a restaurant going in that year either. By 1972, Ferris had still not started any new restaurants. His existing restaurants were doing well.

Burger King wanted to end his franchise agreement because he had failed to meet the conditions subsequent of one new restaurant per year.

ISSUE Could Burger King end the franchise agreement for failure of a condition subsequent?

DECISION Yes. Burger King could end the future rights in the franchise. But Ferris was allowed to keep the existing restaurants. Ferris' failure to get a restaurant a year discharged Burger King's obligation to keep the exclusive franchise with him.

LEGAL TIP

Franchise agreements need protections for unforeseen circumstances. For example, economic problems causing a lack of financing should be covered.

Express conditions This first type of condition in the agreed or automatic group includes conditions either stated or written by the contracting parties. For example, the financing condition in the home purchase is an express condition precedent. **Express conditions** can also be part of oral contracts. For example, suppose that Betty agrees to sell her bicycle to Bob for $150. However, Betty tells Bob that she will not give him the bicycle until he pays her $150 in cash. Bob has to comply with the express condition precedent of $150 cash before Betty is required to perform by delivering the bicycle. The *Penthouse International Ltd. v. Eastman Kodak Co.* case deals with the problems surrounding an express condition precedent.

Implied-in-fact conditions There are some contracts that have conditions that are never stated. These conditions exist because of contract circumstances. For example, Susan has hired Jake the plumber to work on her clogged kitchen

PENTHOUSE INTERNATIONAL LTD. v. EASTMAN KODAK CO.

Superior Court of New Jersey.
430 A.2d 971 (1980).

FACTS Kodak Labs adopted a policy in 1978 on developing sexually explicit film. To avoid problems with federal prosecution for the interstate transportation of pornographic materials, Kodak put the following clause in its developing contracts:

> Pictures depicting the following types of conduct will not be developed or returned to customers by Kodak when they are discovered during the work performed in completing a customer order:
>
> (Kodak then listed all sorts and types of lewd conduct including child pornography and masturbation.)

Penthouse signed Kodak's contract for the development of 2000 Kodachrome exposures. Kodak refused to develop or send back 285 of the pictures. Penthouse sued for breach of contract.

ISSUE Was there an express condition of non-pornographic development only? Was Kodak in breach of contract?

DECISION There was an express condition in the contract. The condition precedent required film owners to send only non-pornographic materials. This was a condition for Kodak's performance. Penthouse did not meet the condition and was not entitled to the pictures or the film.

LEGAL TIP

Be aware of all conditions written in contracts and their effects.

sink. Jake cannot perform the work without being able to get into Susan's home. Access to her house is an **implied-in-fact condition** precedent for Jake's performance. If he cannot get in, he does not have to perform.

Implied-in-law conditions Every contract has the **implied-in-law condition** of the other party's performance. If the other side does not perform, the remaining party is not required to perform. The grocery store example shows how implied-in-law conditions work concurrently so that both sides get the expected performance.

WHAT ARE THE REQUIREMENTS FOR PERFORMANCE?

Determining whether a party has performed is sometimes easy. For example, if there is a contract to unload a truck, the truck is either unloaded or not. However, if there is a contract to build a house, there may be some complications. What if the house is not built on schedule? What if the builder substituted materials? What if some mistakes were made? The issues of how much is required for performance is complicated.

Performance of Contract Terms

When performance terms are given in a written contract, the issue of how much is performance is easier to determine. The parties can agree on what has to be done and how much time is allowed for doing it. For example, an office furniture contract could require delivery of the furniture by January 1 and describe all the furniture to be delivered. The contract could also have the price and a date of ninety days from delivery as the final date for payment.

Just having a written contract is no guarantee that performance standards will be easy to determine. Contract terms have to be interpreted. Courts are left with the problems of interpretation and follow the rules covered in Chapter 22. The *Chuy v. Philadelphia Eagles Football Club* case involves the problem of interpreting a contract performance term.

CHUY v. PHILADELPHIA EAGLES FOOTBALL CLUB

United States Court of Appeals, Third District.
595 F.2d 1265 (1979).

FACTS Don Chuy joined the Philadelphia Eagles Football Club in 1969. He was traded by the Los Angeles Rams after serving that club for six years. He was given a three-year contract with the Eagles and was to be paid $30,000 for each season.

His contract provided that in the event of an "injury," he was to be paid "the salary for the term of his contract."

During his first Eagles' season in 1969, Chuy suffered a shoulder injury. He was hospitalized for it. The doctors said that he had a pulmonary embolism—a blood clot in his lung. The Eagles' team physician and Chuy's other doctors agreed that he could no longer play football.

Chuy wanted to collect his remaining two years' salary. The Eagles claimed that the embolism was not an injury but was a disease, and he should not be paid. The Eagles also claimed "the term of his contract" covered only the 1969 season.

ISSUE Is Chuy entitled to performance of the injury clause?

DECISION Yes. Chuy suffered the injury in a game. He could no longer play. His contract was for three seasons and not for one; the term of his contract was the remaining three years.

LEGAL TIP

Be specific on contract performance terms. Use limited terms and not broad ones.

Performance When Satisfaction Is Required

Some parties agree that performance will not be complete unless one party is completely and personally satisfied with the contract services or work. For example, a portrait artist may be hired to paint a portrait to the personal satisfaction of the subject. "Personal satisfaction" is really a condition precedent for the party to pay.

Personal satisfaction standards will be different depending upon the type of contract. Where satisfaction is a matter of taste, the buyer does not have to pay if he or she is not personally satisfied. The portrait contract involves personal-taste standards.

In contracts for satisfaction where personal taste is not involved, the courts use a "reasonably satisfied" standard. For example, an auto mechanic hired to repair a car to the owner's satisfaction will be paid if the repairs meet with the standards of the automobile industry. If other mechanics agree that the performance was done in a reasonable and workmanlike manner, the owner's personal satisfaction is not relevant.

Almost Performance: Substantial Performance

In long and complex contracts, there are many stages of performance. There may be subcontractors and suppliers involved as in the case of a construction contract. What happens when the building is complete but there have been a few substituted materials or a changed color? Does the owner still have to pay? Or does a small breach put the contractor in breach and allow the owner to have a building for free?

Substantial performance provides some protection for builders and others involved in complex service or construction contracts. Even when mistakes or substitutions are made in the course of performance, payment must still be made if certain conditions are met. The standards for substantial performance are listed below:

1. Is the substituted performance (for practical purposes) just as good?
2. Was the breach unintentional? Was it a reasonable substitute?
3. Can the non-breaching party be compensated for the breach?

For example, suppose that Harry has hired Essex Construction to remodel his home. While Essex is doing its work, Harry goes to Europe for an extended vacation. Essex cannot find the imported Italian tile that Harry wants in his kitchen. Essex is able to find some tile that looks like the Italian tile but is slightly cheaper and made in Mexico. When Harry returns and finds there is not Italian but Mexican tile, he claims that there was a breach of contract by Essex and refuses to pay.

Under substantial performance, Essex can still be paid. The tile is for practical purposes just as good. Essex was acting in good faith when finding a substitute and trying to complete the job on time. Harry can be compensated by allowing him to deduct the cost difference in the tiles from the final price. The *Capitol City Drywall v. C. G. Smith Construction Co.* case is one that involves the problem of substantial performance.

CAPITOL CITY DRYWALL v. C. G. SMITH CONSTRUCTION CO.

Supreme Court of Iowa.
270 N.W.2d 608 (1978).

FACTS Smith was the general contractor for the construction of an apartment building. Capitol was hired as a subcontractor to do the drywall in the building. Capitol used regular drywall instead of water-resistant drywall in the bathrooms in the apartments. Capitol also did not put tape between the drywall and the ceramic tile in the bathrooms and used bonding cement instead.

When Smith discovered these problems, it refused to pay for the work. Capitol filed a lien for $39,915 against the building and then brought suit to enforce the lien.

Smith claimed the cost difference between the regular and wet drywall was $5,760. Smith also said that Capitol saved $960 by not taping the ceramic tile. Capitol claimed that there was substantial performance.

ISSUE Was there substantial performance of the drywall subcontract?

DECISION Yes. The bathrooms could still be used and with wall coverings, no one would know what type of drywall had been used. The cost difference could be deducted from the contract price to compensate Smith.

The bonding was actually a better process. The $960 savings could be deducted, but there was still substantial performance.

LEGAL TIP

List the materials to be used in a contract and provide for substitutions.

Performance on Time

Sometimes parties perform a contract and may even perform perfectly. The problem is that the performance is not on time. If a contract states that "time is of the essence," any delay will be a material breach. If the contract does not have a "time is of the essence clause," then reasonable delays are not breaches.

IS PERFORMANCE EVER EXCUSED?

There are times when the parties are excused from their performance; but there are other times when performance is not excused or discharged. This section covers the excuses for non-performance or the ways of discharging the duty to perform.

Discharge by Failure of Conditions

As mentioned above, if the conditions are not met, performance is discharged. However, this discharge happens only if one of the parties has not tried to prevent the condition from happening. For example, suppose Harry has an agreement with his real estate agent. The agreement requires Harry to pay the real estate agent a commission "upon the closing of title." The agent finds a buyer, and before title can close, Harry and the purchaser agree not to go through with the contract. Harry's agent still gets the commission since Harry has prevented the condition from happening. The condition is excused, and the agent is entitled to performance.

Discharge by Full Performance

Once a party has fully performed the duties under a contract, that party is discharged. (See page 310 for a discussion of full performance.) But substantial performance can be treated as full performance and does discharge the performing party.

Discharge by Breach

If one party breaches a contract, the other does not have to perform. For example, suppose a landlord is required to furnish heat and hot water. The tenant, in exchange, is expected to pay rent. If the landlord does not provide the heat and hot water, there is a breach of contract. The tenant is not expected to pay rent for property that was not liveable. When one party breaches, the other is not required to perform.

Discharge by Anticipatory Repudiation

Anticipatory repudiation is a breach, but it is an advance breach. Anticipatory repudiation happens when a party refuses to perform, but the time for performance has not yet arrived. For example, suppose that Manufacturer Ralph is to deliver 1000 cloth dolls to Store Owner Sally by November 1. On October 1, Ralph tells Sally that he will not be able to deliver the dolls. There has been an anticipatory repudiation by Ralph. The result is that Sally can treat Ralph's actions as a breach of contract; she is no longer required to perform. Sally now can go to another manufacturer to get the dolls.

A party who has anticipatorily repudiated can reinstate his or her contract position before performance time. However, reinstatement is possible only if the other party has not taken action to solve the problems of the breach. For example, if Sally ordered new dolls from Manufacturer Mike on October 2, Ralph has lost the right to reinstate. If Sally does nothing, and Ralph discovers he can perform on October 15, he can notify Sally and continue with the contract.

The *Hochester v. De la Tour* case is a landmark case concerning the issue of anticipatory repudiation.

Discharge by Interference with Performance

If one party cannot perform because the other party is interfering, performance is discharged. For example, suppose that Artie's Supply is required to deliver 100 harmonicas to Pop's Pizza Palace by November 5. The price is $10 per harmonica. After Pop signed Artie's contract, he found harmonicas at a price of $8 at another firm. Pop wants to buy the $8 harmonicas but does not want to breach the contract. Pop contacts Artie's supplier and tells him to delay sending the harmonicas. When Artie does not deliver on time, Pop brings suit for damages because of non-delivery. Artie's duties were discharged because of Pop's interference.

HOCHESTER v. DE LA TOUR
2 El. & Bl. 678 (1855).

FACTS In April, 1852, Hochester agreed to work as a courier for De la Tour for three months starting June 1. On May 11, 1852, De la Tour wrote and said that he had changed his mind and no longer required Hochester to work for the three months. On May 22, 1852, Hochester brought suit against De la Tour for breach of contract. De la Tour said there was, as yet, no breach.

ISSUE Was there a breach of contract on May 11, 1852?

DECISION Yes. De la Tour gave his intent not to perform the contract. Hochester had the immediate right to seek his remedies for the breach of the contract.

LEGAL TIP

Provide for damages in employment contracts. Especially provide for what happens if work never begins.

Discharge by Impossibility

If performance is impossible, the parties are discharged. Determining whether performance is impossible is difficult. Courts follow an objective and not a subjective test of **impossibility.** The question is not: can this party perform? The question is: could the contract be performed in some way by somebody else? The standard for or level of impossibility is high.

Additional expense or time do not constitute impossibility. Since unanticipated delays do not involve impossibility, the contract must be truly impossible to perform. For example, suppose that Grace had a contract to sell her lakeside cottage to Bert. The spring waters rise to their highest level ever and the cottage is washed away. Performance is impossible, and Grace has no cottage.

The *Itek Corporation v. First National Bank of Boston* case examines whether there is impossibility.

ITEK CORPORATION v. FIRST NATIONAL BANK OF BOSTON
United States Court of Appeals, First Circuit.
730 F.2d 19 (1984).

FACTS Itek and Iran's Imperial Ministry of War entered into a contract for Itek to sell $22.5 million of optical equipment to the War Ministry. The contract was entered into in 1977, and the War Ministry paid $4.5 million as a down payment. By 1979, Itek was ahead of its production schedule and ready for delivery.

During this time, relations between the United States and Iran were strained. In April 1979, the United States suspended Itek's export license. Itek then applied for a rehearing on the suspension, but before the hearing could be held the Iranians seized the United States Embassy in Teheran. The United States suspended all trade with Iran and denied Itek its rehearing. Itek notified the War Ministry that the contract performance was impossible.

ISSUE Did the political events make the contract impossible to perform?

DECISION Yes. The contract could not be performed so long as there was a trade suspension. That suspension would not be lifted until there was a release of the hostages and the United States Embassy. Itek had no way to perform, and no one else could perform since all trade was forbidden and therefore impossible.

LEGAL TIP

Provide for political events and acts of war in contracts so that all problems are covered.

Discharge by Mutual Agreement

The parties to a contract are always free to release each other. By mutual agreement, contracting parties can discharge their duties to perform. Their mutual agreement can take several forms.

Rescission agreement A **rescission** agreement is one that discharges both parties' duties. The consideration for the agreement is that each is giving up the right to demand the other's performance. For full protection, the rescission agreement should be in writing. The agreement should also provide for monies paid or services already given.

Novation The parties can agree to substitute a new party to perform. For example, suppose that Mr. Frosty has a contract to supply ice to Dolly's Donut and Ice Cream Parlor. Mr. Frosty wants out of the contract and Ice, Inc., is willing to take over. Dolly is willing to make the substitution. All three parties can sign a novation. The **novation** releases Mr. Frosty from all obligations to Dolly or Ice, Inc. In addition, the novation is a contract between Dolly and Ice, Inc., with the same terms as the Dolly/Frosty contract.

Accord and satisfaction An **accord** is an agreement entered into to settle an obligation. **Satisfaction** is performance of the accord. For example, suppose that Springs, Inc., has been supplying Germaine's insurance office with bottled water for six months. Germaine has not been paying. Springs and Germaine agree to end the year-long contract at six months. There is some dispute over how much water was delivered, and Springs' records are not complete. Springs and Germaine can execute an accord that will indicate an amount to be paid. Once that amount is paid or satisfied, the parties' obligations under the original contract and the accord are discharged.

Discharge by Illegality

The subject matter of a contract can become illegal between the time the contract is entered into and when it is performed. If this illegality does arise, the duty to perform is discharged. For example, suppose that a toy manufacturer and distributor have a contract for the manufacturer to deliver 30,000 toy beauty shop sets. After the contract is executed, but before the toys are delivered, the Consumer Product Safety Division recalls the toys and prohibits any further sales because of its danger. The contract for delivery of the toys is now illegal. Therefore, the parties are discharged from their obligations under the contract.

Discharge by Frustration

Some contracts have a specific purpose or objective. When that purpose or objective is clear, it becomes part of the contract. If the objective can no longer be met, the purpose or objective is frustrated. When there is **frustration** of a purpose or objective, performance duties are discharged. For example, suppose that Sally is engaged to be married to Bill. She orders a wedding gown from Bridal Boutique. Before Bridal Boutique begins work, Bill is killed in an auto accident. The purpose or objective for the dress order no longer exists. Frustration will excuse both sides from performing on the dress contract.

Discharge by the Statute of Limitations

The **statute of limitations** is a procedural statute that requires lawsuits to be started within a certain number of years. The number of years depends on the type of lawsuit. If a lawsuit is not brought within the statute of limitations, the right to sue is lost. Contract suits have statutes of limitations. If suit is not brought to

Figure 25-1 **Performance**

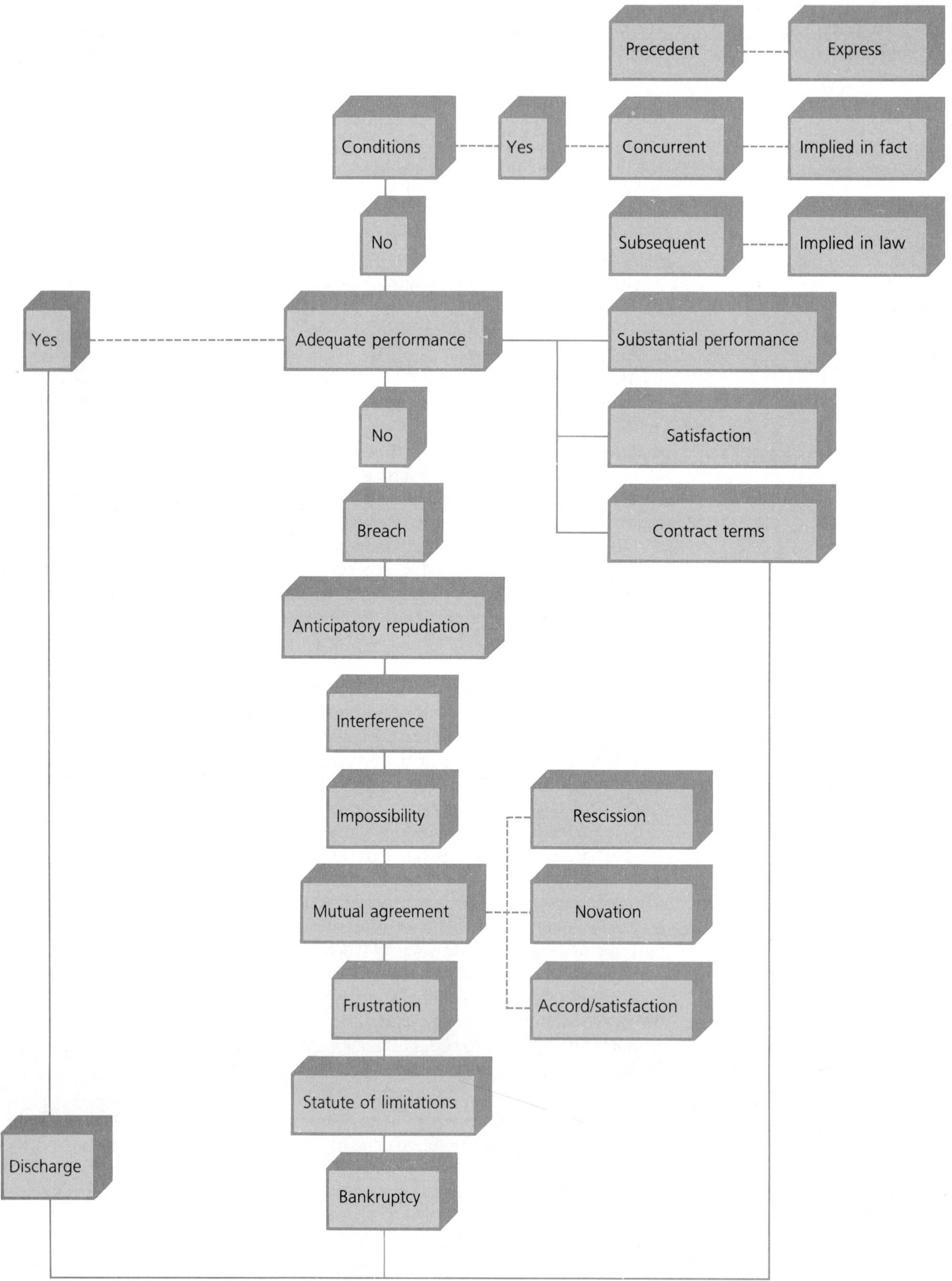

enforce a contract within the time period allowed, the parties are forever discharged on their contract obligations.

Discharge by Bankruptcy

If a party to a contract declares bankruptcy, most of the party's obligations and debts will be discharged. A discharge of a contract in bankruptcy is a discharge of contract duties to perform.

Figure 25-1 is a summary of the performance rights of contracting parties.

KEY TERMS

Conditions
Conditions precedent
Conditions concurrent
Conditions subsequent
Express condition
Implied-in-fact condition
Implied-in-law condition
Substantial performance
Anticipatory repudiation
Impossibility
Rescission
Novation
Accord
Satisfaction
Frustration
Statute of limitations

CHAPTER PROBLEMS

1. Give an example of an implied-in-fact condition precedent.
2. Westinghouse had a bid to manufacture 250 cooling systems for a Garrett federal contract. Garrett and Westinghouse's contract required United States Air Force (USAF) approval before the systems could be manufactured. The USAF would not approve. Westinghouse claimed that there was a breach of contract. Garrett says the condition precedent of approval was not met, and their duty to perform was discharged. Who is correct? *Westinghouse Electric Corporation v. Garrett Corporation,* 601 F.2d 155 (4th Cir. 1977).
3. A. L. Melancon was an exclusive distributor for Dixie Brewing Company. Dixie had noted that Melancon had stale beer on the shelves, did not advertise, did not have adequate retail shelf space, and did not put all Dixie products on the shelf. After ten months of warnings, Dixie ended Melancon's exclusive distributorship. Could they do that? *Fortenberry v. Dixie Brewing Company, Inc.,* 368 So.2d 1240 (La. 1979).
4. Krell advertised his London apartment as available for use in viewing the coronation procession of King Edward VII. Henry responded to the ad and was to have the use of the apartment for two days for several thousand dollars. The king became ill and the coronation was cancelled. Henry wanted his money back. Could he get it back? *Krell v. Henry,* 2 K.B. 740 (1903).
5. Jennie-O Foods, Inc., was to supply processed turkeys to the United States Government. All of Jennie-O's major suppliers were having difficulties with disease. Jennie-O could get the turkeys but only from small sellers and at a 75% cost increase. Is Jennie-O excused on the grounds of impossibility? *Jennie-O Foods, Inc. v. United States,* 580 F.2d 400 (Ct.Cl. 1978).
6. What is the difference between anticipatory repudiation and breach?
7. Bresler's 33 Flavors, Inc., gave 33 Flavors of Greater Delaware a franchise to sell Bresler's ice cream. Greater Delaware failed to use the approved toppings, syrups, and paper goods as required by the franchise agreement. Also, Greater Delaware's performance was consistently low. Bresler's gave them thirty days to improve and comply with the use of approved supplies. Greater Delaware did not comply, and Bresler's terminated the franchise for breach of contract. Could they do so? *33 Flavors of Greater Delaware Valley, Inc. v. Bresler's 33 Flavors, Inc.,* 475 F.Supp. 217 (D.Del. 1979).
8. Merrydale Glass Works installed sixteen panels of cathedral glass in Merriam's home for $614.80. One

of the panels had a crack, and Merriam refused to pay any of the money. Could he so refuse? *Merrydale Glass Works, Inc. v. Merriam,* 349 So.2d 1315 (La. 1977).

* 9. Robert E. McKee, Inc., entered into a construction contract with the city of Atlanta for the construction of a building. Shortly after construction began, McKee discovered bad soil conditions. McKee wanted to be excused from the contract or be allowed to collect additional costs for working with the adverse soil conditions. What is the result? *Robert E. McKee, Inc. v. City of Atlanta,* 414 F.Supp. 957 (D.C. Ga. 1976).

10. Do strikes make performance impossible? *City of New York v. Local 333, Marine Division, International Longshoremen's Association,* 433 N.Y.S.2d 527 (N.Y. 1980).

"Discourage litigation. Persuade your neighbors to compromise whenever you can. Point out to them how the nominal winner is often a real loser—in fees, expenses and waste of time."

Abraham Lincoln
July 1, 1850 Notes for a law lecture

Chapter 26

Remedies for a Breach of Contract

CHAPTER PREVIEW

- Types of damages
- Formulas for computing damages
- When damages can be recovered
- The difference between damages and specific performance

Dierickx hired Vulcan to waterproof the basement of his home. The waterproofing did not work and Dierickx's basement flooded. Dierickx fell in the basement water and spent $2,000 for medical treatment. Dierickx paid $1785 to repair the water damage to the basement walls. He spent $805 to replace tile and paneling damaged by water. His driveway had to be destroyed to repair the walls, and he spent $780.00 to have the driveway replaced. What of these damages can Dierickx collect?

At this stage, there has been a breach of contract. The questions of whether a contract exists and whether there has been a breach are answered. The only question at this point is: What are the remedies for a breach of contract? This chapter answers that question.

WHAT TYPES OF DAMAGES ARE THERE?

Compensatory Damages

These are the damages needed to compensate the non-breaching party for the breach. The idea of **compensatory damages** is to put the non-breaching party in just about the same position that they would have been in if there had not been a breach. For example, suppose that Bif had a contract to purchase Delia's car for $450. Delia changes her mind. Bif could find a similar car, but it would cost him $525. Compensating Bif would require Delia to pay the difference in price—the $75. With these compensatory damages, Delia's breach does not cost Bif extra. He is in the same position that he would have been in if Delia had not breached.

The formulas for compensatory damages are covered later in this chapter.

Punitive Damages

Punitive damages are sometimes called "smart money." Punitive damages are extra damages that "smart" and are paid because the breach was willful or the result of fraud. Recently, punitive damages have been given to insured persons when their insurers failed to pay or delayed paying a good claim. Punitive damages are really a form of civil punishment for an unusually bad contract breach. Punitive damages are not generally used in contract breaches. The *In re General Motors Corporation Engine Interchange Litigation* case is a famous one that involved a recovery of punitive damages.

IN RE GENERAL MOTORS CORPORATION ENGINE INTERCHANGE LITIGATION
United States Court of Appeals, Seventh Circuit. 594 F.2d 1106 (1979).

FACTS In its 1977 models of its Oldsmobile Delta 88's and Coupes, General Motors (GM) used Chevrolet engines. The same engines were used for the less costly Chevrolet cars. GM also used transmissions that were originally designed for use in Chevettes in these same models.

When buyers of these autos were told of these substitutions, they brought a class action for misrepresentation and breach of contract. One of the issues in the litigation was whether the class action litigants could collect punitive damages.

ISSUE Could GM be required to pay punitive damages for the transmission and engine interchanges?

DECISION Yes. The public had been deceived and misled. They thought they were getting an upgraded car model. The cars were advertised as upgraded. Yet their cars had the same equipment as much cheaper models.

LEGAL TIP
Full disclosure of the equipment and parts used in a product is necessary.

Liquidated Damages

Liquidated damages are damages agreed to in advance by the parties. At the time of contracting, the parties agree to a certain amount of damages that will be paid to the non-breaching party if there is a breach. For example, suppose that the seller and buyer of a business agree that the seller will not open a new business for five years within a one-mile radius of the sold business. They can also agree that if the seller breaches this clause, the buyer will get $10,000 in damages.

Liquidated damages clauses are valid if several requirements are met. First, damages for breach of the contract must be hard to determine. In the sale of the business example, the buyer may have no damages or may lose his or her business if the seller breaches the non-competition clause. The figure of $10,000 is reasonable, considering the circumstances and the unknowns.

Second, liquidated damages must be the sole remedy or an alternative remedy. Both liquidated and compensatory damages cannot be collected. For example, the buyer and seller could not require the seller to pay $10,000 in addition to the actual damages that the buyer might have. To try to collect liquidated damages and compensatory damages would be to over-compensate the non-breaching party and penalize the breaching party. Liquidated damages on top of compensatory damages are void as penalties.

Finally, a liquidated damage clause must be a reasonable amount. An amount too large for the losses resulting from a breach will be a penalty and held void by the courts. The *Unified School District No. 315 v. Dewerff* case examines whether a liquidated damage clause is valid.

UNIFIED SCHOOL DISTRICT NO. 315 v. DEWERFF

Supreme Court of Kansas.
626 P.2d 1206 (1981).

FACTS DeWerff was hired as a teacher for the Unified School District. He was given a one-year contract to run for the 1978–1979 school year. He signed the contract in April 1978.

The contract provided that if a teacher cancelled before August 1, the damages would be $400. If a teacher cancelled after August 1, the damages would be the $400 plus $75 for each month after August 1.

On June 28, 1978, DeWerff told the school district that he was cancelling. The school district demanded its $400. DeWerff said the liquidated damage clause was void.

ISSUE Is the liquidated damage clause void?

DECISION No. The clause was set up to encourage performance. The clause gives the school damages for having to find another teacher. The additional damages of $75 per month would be to cover the expenses of a substitute during the school year while a replacement was found. The school district had the unknowns of the costs of finding and rehiring a new teacher. The school district also had the unknown of how many days a substitute would be required. The clause was a valid liquidated damage clause.

LEGAL TIP

Know how much it will cost to end a contract.

Incidental Damages

Incidental damages are the extra expenses or costs of a breach. For example, suppose that Delia has agreed to sell her car to Bif. Bif changes his mind and does not buy the car. Delia now has to run an ad to find a buyer. She has to assume additional time and money costs because of Bif's breach. These additional costs are incidental damages.

Incidental damages include the costs of reselling, the costs of finding replacement goods, the time costs, and the paperwork costs. If a party has to bring legal action to collect damages, the costs of filing the suit, serving process, etc., are incidental damages that can be recovered.

In some states, attorneys' fees are part of incidental damages. The parties can also put a clause in their contract which covers attorneys' fees.

Consequential Damages

Consequential damages are experienced one step away from the actual breach and are a consequence of the breach. For example, suppose that H. Helicopters has a contract with the United States Army to furnish twenty-five jet helicopters by June 1. The contract provides for liquidated damages of $300 per day for each day that H. is late in delivering the contracts. H.'s supplier of blades is given until March 1 to deliver the blades. The supplier is ten days late with the blades. H. works overtime but still does not deliver until June 7. Who pays the $1800 in liquidated damages? Eventually the supplier will pay. H.'s late penalty damages were a consequence of the supplier's breach.

Consequential damages relate to damages resulting from third-party relationships. To be able to recover these consequential damages, certain requirements must be met. First, the problem of consequential damages must be known to the contracting parties. The supplier must be aware of H.'s deadline and the consequences. The deadline can be written in the contract. Or H. can simply tell the supplier of the government contract and the penalty. That time is of the essence must be made clear to the contracting parties.

If the parties do not know of the exact consequential damages but could foresee them, the consequential damages can be recovered. For example, a supplier of flour to a bakery knows that without flour, the baker does not bake. If the baker does not bake, there will be no sales. The loss of sales and resulting lost profits are logical consequential damages that are forseeable to the supplier and recoverable by the buyer.

The *Wynn v. Monterey Clubs* case deals with an interesting issue in consequential damages.

WYNN v. MONTEREY CLUBS

Court of Appeals, Second District.
168 Cal.Rptr. 878 (1980).

FACTS Mrs. Wynn was a compulsive gambler. Mr. Wynn agreed to pay the Monterey Clubs the $1750 (total gambling debts as of December 1976) that Mrs. Wynn owed if the clubs would stop her from cashing checks and playing cards at their clubs.

Gambling debts cannot be the subject of a suit, and Wynn did not have to pay the debt; however, he did pay the full amount of Mrs. Wynn's debts even though the Monterey Clubs did not keep their end of the deal. By May 1977, Mrs. Wynn had debts of over $30,000 at the clubs. She had become so compulsive that their marriage ended in divorce. Mr. Wynn experienced severe emotional distress because of this situation; he sued for breach of contract and wanted to recover for the divorce and emotional distress.

ISSUE Could Wynn recover for the resulting personal problems on the theory that they were consequential damages?

DECISION Yes. Their contract revealed Mrs. Wynn's compulsive nature and showed how much pain and distress her habit had already brought Mr. Wynn. The Clubs were aware of the consequences but failed to keep their end of the agreement.

LEGAL TIP

Check the other party's performance before paying in full.

Nominal Damages

Nominal damages are principle damages. A non-breaching party brings a suit for a breach as a matter of principle. There are no real damages, but the breaching party was wrong to breach. For example, suppose a contract has a clause that prohibits assignments. If the seller assigns the right to payment to someone else, there has been a breach. The buyer is not harmed and just has to send the payment to a different address. The buyer could collect nominal damages. A popular figure is usually $1 for nominal damages.

Specific Performances

In some cases, all the damages in the world cannot put the non-breaching party in as good a position. For example, if a buyer has a contract to buy a piece of land and the seller backs out, there is no other piece of land like that one. The buyer can be given the additional cost of buying the same amount of land elsewhere, but it will not be the same land. In this case, the buyer may have available the remedy of specific performance. Specific performance is an equitable remedy that requires the breaching party to perform according to the contract terms.

Specific performance is court-ordered performance. Because specific performance is a harsh remedy, it is available only in certain circumstances. It is available to buyers when sellers have breached real estate purchase contracts. It is available to buyers who have purchased rare or unique goods from a seller. It is available to buyers who have purchased goods that have sentimental value. For example, buying your old high chair at an auction involves a contract with sentimental value. You do not just want the difference in price required to buy a substitute. You want that high chair for a particular reason. Specific performance can require the seller to transfer the high chair.

Specific performance is not available if the seller has breached because the goods or land have been transferred to third parties. Third parties who buy in good faith are protected. In those cases, buyers will have to claim financial damages. Specific performance is also generally not available in service contracts.

THE DAMAGE FORMULAS

This section gives the formulas for damages in particular contract breaches. The first part of each of the formulas is the compensatory section. The other damages are then added for complete recovery.

Damages in Employment Contracts

Employer breach When an employer breaches an employee contract, the employee has a **duty to mitigate** damages. Mitigate is to minimize damages. An employee mitigates employment contract damages by looking for another job. Employees are required to look for **comparable employment.** They are required to show that they made a good-faith effort to find a comparable job.

A comparable job is one that offers approximately the same pay. It is also one that requires similar qualifications for the same type of work. For example, an accountant is required to take accounting positions but is not required to take a job driving a truck. If an employee cannot find comparable employment, he or she is not required to take a different job or start a new occupation or career. The duty to mitigate is to show a good-faith effort. The *Parker v. Twentieth Century-Fox Film Corp.* case deals with the issue of comparable employment in a unique job-setting.

The damage formula for an employer breach is a logical one. If the employee was able to find comparable employment, the formula for damages is:

Contract salary − comparable employment salary + incidental damages

PARKER v. TWENTIETH CENTURY-FOX FILM CORP.

Supreme Court of California.
474 P.2d 689 (1970).

FACTS Shirley MacLaine Parker signed a contract on August 6, 1965, with Fox Films for the lead part in Fox's production of a Broadway musical called "Bloomer Girl." Parker was to be paid $53,571.42 per week for fourteen weeks for a total of $750,000 for doing the picture.

Parker is a singer/dancer. The production was to be filmed in studios in Hollywood.

In 1966, Fox decided not to do "Bloomer Girl." They notified Parker and told her that she would be doing another film. The other film was "Big Country, Big Man." This film was a dramatic Western that would be filmed in Australia. Her pay was to be the same.

Parker told Fox that she would not do the film. She brought suit for payment of her $750,000. Fox said that she did not mitigate by taking the comparable employment.

ISSUE Did Parker mitigate? Was Parker required to do the Western?

DECISION No. Parker was not required to take a role in a movie that was in no way like a Broadway musical. Her talents were as a singer and dancer. For her to appear in this lower quality movie would be a reflection on her career success.

LEGAL TIP

Unique employees do not have opportunities to mitigate. Make sure that their contracts are negotiated carefully.

If the employee has been unable to find comparable employment despite a reasonable effort, the formula is:

Contract salary + incidental damages

Employee breach If an employee breaches a contract, the employer has the responsibility to mitigate by looking for a substitute employee. If the employer cannot find such an employee, there may be consequential damages that the employee would have to pay. For example, if the employee worked in an ad agency and was responsible for drawing ads, costs of delays in those ads would be consequential damages. The formula for employer damages when an employee breaches is:

Salary of replacement − contract salary + incidental damages + consequential damages

Damages in Construction Contracts

Construction contract damage formulas depend upon which party does the breaching and when they breach. The parties are the contractor and the owner (the party with the land who hired the contractor to build). The times for breach are before, during, and after construction.

Breach by the contractor before construction begins In this situation, the contractor or builder has executed the contract but pulls out. The owner will have to get another contractor to do the job. There will be delays and costs in substituting a contractor. The formula for damages for a breach before construction is:

Cost of new contractor − contract cost + incidental damages + consequential damages

For example, suppose that an owner had hired a contractor to build a home for $250,000. After the contractor pulls out, the owner hires a new contractor. The cost will be $275,000. The $25,000 difference is what is required to compensate the owner.

Consequential damages might result from the owner's loss of financing. Or the owner might be required to pay a premium to extend the financing.

Breach by the contractor during construction Often a contractor has begun a job and then cannot or does not finish. Again, the owner will have to find a substitute builder. Usually the new builder hired to finish the job will cost more. The formula for a breach during construction is as follows:

Cost of completion above contract cost − contract cost + incidentals + consequential damages

Breach by the contractor after construction is complete A breach after completed construction is simply a breach of warranty problem or a problem with improper materials. If the building does not come up to industry standards, the formula for damages is the difference between the value of the building as it is and its value if it were properly constructed. If there is a problem with the materials used or materials substitutions, the doctrine of substantial performance is followed. Is the substitution for practical purposes just as good? Can the owner be compensated? Was it a good-faith substitution? The *Jones v. Honchell* case examines a damage issue for improper completion of a home.

JONES v. HONCHELL
Supreme Court of Ohio.
470 N.E.2d 219 (1984).

FACTS Charles and Bobbie Jones had a contract with William Honchell for Honchell to build a home for them for $57,881. When the house was completed, the Jones were greatly dissatisfied with the brick work—particularly in the chimneys and fireplaces. An expert testified that the only cure was to redo the brick work. The cost of redoing it was about $18,000, and the Jones withheld this amount from their payment to Honchell. A suit resulted.

ISSUE Was there a breach of contract and what are the damages?

DECISION Yes, there was definitely a breach of contract. The expert testified that the work was well below average. The proper amount of damages is the cost of making the structure as it should be—in this case $18,000.

LEGAL TIP
One of the benefits that an owner has is not paying a contractor to get action or paying someone else to fix the construction problem.

Breach by the owner before construction begins Even though a contractor has not spent time or money in actual construction, the contractor has spent time and money in preparing for the project. Also, the contractor has turned down other opportunities to take projects. If the project falls through, the contractor is not working to capacity. For a breach before construction, the contractor is entitled to collect the profits that would have been made by performing the contract. Of course the contractor can collect incidental damages also.

Breach by the owner during construction This breach happens after time and money have been spent on the project. Again, the contractor can collect the lost profits for the project; but the contractor can also collect whatever costs were expended up until the time of the breach. Incidental damages are also part of the contractor's recovery.

Breach by the owner after construction This type of breach involves the problem of no payment. For example, a contractor completes a job but is not paid. The contractor can recover the full contract price plus incidental damages. To collect, the contractor can get a lien on the property and then sue to foreclose on the lien (see Chapter 58 for a complete review of liens).

Damages in Sales Contracts

Buyer breach When the buyer breaches, the seller can try to sell the goods to someone else. For example, suppose that Ralph was to buy Bob's 280ZX for $4500. Ralph backs out of the deal. Bob sells the car to Susan for $4000. This is called resale. Bob's formula for damages is:

Contract price − resale price + incidentals + consequentials

If Bob does not resell, he can collect damages on the basis of market price (the blue book) for the car. The formula is:

Contract price − market price + incidentals + consequentials

Bob's damages would be $500 in the resale case (along with any incidentals that he might have). If the blue book figure for the car was $4600 and he did not resell, his damages would be $600. Further details on damages in sales contracts can be found in Chapter 29.

Seller breach Suppose in the 280ZX example that Ralph still wants the car, but Bob backs out. Ralph has the choice of going out and buying another car or recovering the difference between the market price and the contract price. This difference is called the cover price and has the following formula:

Cover price − contract price + incidentals + consequentials

For example, suppose that Ralph is able to buy another 280ZX for $5000. His damages are $500 plus any incidental and consequential damages.

If Ralph cannot find a car, he can still recover the difference in cost based on market value. The formula is:

Market price − contract price + incidentals + consequentials

For example, if the blue book is $5500, Ralph can recover the $1000 difference.

Inadequate Performance

In some contracts, the parties perform but do not do such a good job. For example, suppose that a company is hired to move your furniture. They move the furniture but lose half the items and severely damage the remaining half. Your damages would be the value of the lost furniture and the loss in value for the damaged furniture.

In some cases, performance is completed but does not meet all the promises and expectations. For example, goods do not live up to their express warranties. The damages in these cases would be the difference in the value of the goods as they are and their value as the contract had promised. The *Dierickx v. Vulcan Industries* case is one that involves novel damage issues.

DIERICKX v. VULCAN INDUSTRIES

Supreme Court of Michigan.
158 N.W.2d 778 (1968).

FACTS Vulcan Industries was in the business of waterproofing basements with the "Nu-Miracle Process." The process forces material into and around the masonry walls and makes a watertight bond. The process can be done without excavating around the basement walls.

In March 1954, Robert Dierickx hired Vulcan to waterproof a certain section of his basement wall. The contract had the following guarantee:

> We guarantee any area where we have applied our Nu-Miracle Process against all seepage through the walls, providing that all areas of the sub-soil masonry is free of defective construction. For a period of five years.

The contract price was $100. Water still leaked after Vulcan used its process. Vulcan made many service calls, but there was still seepage. Vulcan redid the process and charged another $130, but there was still seepage. Dierickx fell in the water-filled basement and was injured; his expenses for the injury were $2000. Also, he had to hire a contractor to fix the basement wall, which cost $1785. That contractor had to destroy his driveway to fix the basement wall; the cost of replacing the driveway was $780. Dierickx also had to replace paneling and tile in the basement at a cost of $805 because of the water damage.

Dierickx brought suit for all of the above damages. The trial court gave him $230—the contract costs. He appealed.

ISSUE Could the water damage costs and repair costs be recovered as consequential damages resulting from the breach of the guarantee?

DECISION Yes. Some of the damages were the direct result of Vulcan not performing properly. The contract called for the basement to be free from water for five years, which did not happen.

LEGAL TIP

Work guarantees are promises that must be kept. Damages resulting from their failure can be recovered as consequential and incidental damages.

KEY TERMS

Compensatory damages
Punitive damages
Liquidated damages
Incidental damages
Consequential damages
Nominal damages
Specific performance
Duty to mitigate
Comparable employment

CHAPTER PROBLEMS

1. Is there a difference between liquidated damages and penalties?
2. Give a formula for compensatory damages for the following circumstances.
   A. Joan has a contract to sell her car to Bill for $3000. Bill backs out, and Joan sells it to Bob for $2500. She has to run an ad that costs $15.
   B. Suppose that Joan backed out, and Bob had to buy a similar car for $4000.
3. Sides Construction Company signed a contract with Scott City to build a swimming pool for $274,000. The contract provided for a $50 penalty for each day the completion of the pool was late. The City said that it would have additional interest and personnel costs for later performance. The City said that it would not know how much the costs would be until and if the delays came. Is the clause a valid liquidated damages clause? *Sides Construction Co. v. City of Scott City,* 581 S.W.2d 443 (Mo. 1979).
5. O'Bannon had a contract to buy property for $85,000. He was required to pay $2000 earnest money. The contract provided that if he did not go through with

the purchase, the $2000 would be given to the seller as damages. Is this legal? *Artz v. C. O'Bannon,* 562 P.2d 674 (Wash. 1977).

6. Harold Lee owned Capitol City Distributorship in Washington, D.C. He sold his assets to Seagrams so that his sons could have their own Seagrams dealership. Although opportunities came up for a new dealership, Seagrams did not give the sons their dealership as they had promised. The sons had no income for fifteen months as result of this breach. They claimed they lost $407,000 in profits. What can they recover? *Lee v. Joseph E. Seagrams & Sons, Inc.,* 552 F.2d 447 (2nd Cir. 1977).

7. Valenti bought a fan from A & P Store Fronts, Inc. The price was $300, and a sign said that installation and electrical connections were included. When A & P refused to install the fan, Valenti had to pay $500 for an electrician to install the fan. Who pays for the electrician? *Valenti v. A & P Store Fronts, Inc.,* 398 N.Y.S.2d 705 (N.Y. 1977).

8. Hadley owned a flour mill and had a large wholesale and retail business. The crank shaft in his mill was broken. He needed to send the crank shaft to the original manufacturers so that it could be remolded. Hadley hired Pickford & Company as the carrier. Hadley told the Company of the need to make the delivery quickly so that business would not be lost. The Company said that they would deliver within a day. They took three days. Could Hadley recover lost profits? *Hadley v. Baxendale,* 9 Exch. 341 (1854).

* 9. Groves was the principal contractor on a United States Government project to build locks in the Ohio River. Groves had hired Burns to do the welding work on the project and was to supply electricity for the welding. Groves did not give power consistently, and Burns was delayed in its work, had to pay overtime, and had to hire extra workers. Burns claimed that Groves should pay its additional costs of $40,313. Who pays? *Burns Bros. Plumbers, Inc. v. Groves Ventures Co.,* 412 F.2d 202 (6th Cir. 1969).

10. In 1974, Muhammed Ali and George Foreman had scheduled a boxing match for the world heavyweight title. The fight was to take place in Zaire, Africa. The fight was to be seen by millions of people on closed-circuit television. The promoters offered closed-circuit viewing to theaters who would pay $60,000 plus $1 for every ticket that was sold for closed-circuit viewing. One theater contacted the promoters about having a closed-circuit showing, but the owner turned down the showing when he was told the price. He then bypassed the block-out and showed the fight without paying any fees. The promoters brought suit and wanted the payment that they wold have received plus punitive damages. What is the result? *Hutchinson v. Brotman-Sherman Theatres, Inc.,* 419 N.E.2d 530 (Ill. 1981).

Part Four

Sales

"Uniformity of commercial law was the impelling goal of those who worked hard and long for the preparation of the Code."

Editorial Board
1964 Draft of the
Uniform Commercial Code

Chapter 27

Introduction to Sales and Formation of Sales Contracts

CHAPTER PREVIEW

- The UCC: Its purpose and history
- The UCC content
- The UCC numbering system
- Contracts governed by the UCC
- Merchants and their UCC role
- UCC Statute of Frauds
- UCC Offer Rules
- Merchant's Firm Offer
- Acceptance timing rules
- The "battle of the forms"

Durpree sent a purchase order to Payco Plastics. In the order, Dupree offered to buy sixty five pounds of No. 2 plastic at $.75 per pound. Payco mailed back its invoice agreeing with the terms. The back of Payco's invoice had a clause that required all contract disputes to be submitted to arbitration. The plastic was sent but a dispute arose and Dupree wants to file suit against Payco. Payco claims that they can't because of the arbitration requirement. Dupree says the arbitration clause isn't valid because they never agreed to it. Who is right?

Commercial transactions such as the one between Dupree and Payco occur every minute. The buyers and sellers may be located in different states or several different states. Because of the different locations of buyers and sellers, the national business network, and the need for legal certainty, many states have adopted the Uniform Commercial Code (the Code or UCC). The Code is a model statute drafted by the National Conference of Commissioners on Uniform Laws.

This chapter discusses the Code and its history and gives an introduction to one part of the Code—Article II on Sales. This chapter also covers the uses of Article II and the formation of contracts under Article II.

INTRODUCTION TO THE UNIFORM COMMERCIAL CODE

History

The National Conference of Commissioners on Uniform State Laws had drafted a number of uniform laws that applied to commercial transactions years before it wrote the Code. Beginning in 1896 with the Uniform Negotiable Instruments Law, many states adopted these uniform laws in an attempt to make the law of commercial transactions uniform and national. There was a Uniform Sales Act that two-thirds of the states adopted in the early 1900's. By the 1930's, our nation became highly industrialized and goods flowed freely from state to state and across the country. The national conference voted to modernize and displace the old uniform laws with one comprehensive code.

The first draft for the Uniform Commercial Code was written between 1944 and 1950. Pennsylvania was the first state to pass the Code in 1953. Other states followed until at the present time, forty nine states, the District of Columbia, and the Virgin Islands have adopted the Code. Louisiana has not adopted the entire Code, but has adopted some provisions.

Set-Up of the Code

The Code has eleven segments (called articles) that are named in the list below:

Article I—General Provisions

Article II—Sales

Article III—Commercial Paper

Article IV—Bank Deposits and Collection

Article V—Letters of Credit

Article VI—Bulk Transfers

Article VII—Warehouse Receipts, Bills of Lading, and Other Documents of Title

Article VIII—Investment Securities

Article IX—Secured Transactions: Sales of Account and Chattel Paper

Article X—Effective Date and Repealer

Article XI—Effective Date and Transmission Provision

Each Article is divided into parts. For example, Article II has seven parts, which deal with specific legal topics. Each part is made up of sections; code section numbers are arranged by their part and section. A code number like 2-207 means that the section is number seven (07) from Part 2 of Article II. The back of this book has portions of the Code reproduced.

INTRODUCTION TO ARTICLE II

Summary of Content

Article II has 104 sections. The article groups the sections into seven parts with the following headings:

Part 1—Short Title, General Construction, and Subject Matter
Part 2—Form, Formation, and Readjustment of Contract
Part 3—General Obligation and Construction of Contract
Part 4—Title, Creditors, and Good-Faith Purchasers
Part 5—Performance
Part 6—Breach, Repudiation, and Excuse
Part 7—Remedies

The seven parts are arranged in the order of a contract's life history. For example, the first part deals with contract formation, and the last part ends by covering remedies for breach. The other parts cover issues such as price, delivery, and passing risk of loss. Article II tries to be a comprehensive statute covering all issues and problems in sales transactions.

When Article II Applies

Sales of goods Article II applies to "transactions in goods." To understand when Article II applies, both words, "transactions" and "goods," must be defined. Section 2-105 of the Code defines **goods** as all items that are movable at the time of contracting (except money). These items include existing goods (buying a car off a lot) or goods to be manufactured in the future (buying a specially made car). Article II also includes as goods the unborn young of animals, minerals that are removed from the land by the seller, timber, and growing crops. Examples of goods are clothing, sporting equipment, cars, bicycles, electronic equipment, and mobile homes.

Article II does not apply to services since common law governs service contracts. For example, Article II does not cover repair contracts with plumbers, gardeners, or electricians. Common law, not Article II, applies to sales of realty. (See Chapters 17 through 26 for a discussion of common law principles, which govern these transactions.) Also, Article VIII, not Article II, covers sales of stocks and other securities.

"Transactions" are defined as sales of goods. Section 2-106 defines sales as "the passing of title from the seller to the buyer for a price." Examples of sales are buying groceries, cars, basketballs, and suits. Title to those items is given when the purchase price is paid. Examples of transactions that would not be covered are gifts of goods, leases of goods, and services. However, some court decisions have followed Article II in lease of goods contracts. For example, in cases where people have rented defective automobiles, some courts have used Article II remedies to make their decisions.

Sales of goods and services Some contracts have both goods and services as their subject matter. A contract for the repair of a car requires the mechanic to supply both parts for the repair and the labor for installing or replacing the parts. In contracts with both services and goods, the question of which law governs—UCC Article II or Common Law—is one of intent. Did the parties want the goods or did they want some service along with the goods? In the case of a car repair, parties want the goods put in the auto; therefore, the contract is one of service. Furniture purchases usually include the service of delivery, but the customer's main purchase and intent is the furniture—not the moving service. In the *Samuel Black Co. v. Burroughs Corp.*, case, the question of UCC versus common law arose.

SAMUEL BLACK CO. v. BURROUGHS CORP.

33 UCC Rep. 954 (Mass. 1981).

FACTS Samuel Black Co. purchased computer software from Burroughs. As part of their contract, Burroughs agreed to provide the services of installation and training for use of the software. Problems arose with the software and Black brought suit. A preliminary issue at trial was whether UCC Article II applied.

ISSUE Does Article II apply to a software contract for both goods and services?

DECISION Yes. Even though it is unclear what the parties wanted, the contract should be governed by Article II. When the intent of the parties is uncertain, Article II should apply by analogy.

LEGAL TIP

In contracts for goods and services, the parties should state whether Article II will apply.

Leases One of the most recent issues concerning the application of Article II has been whether leases of goods are covered under the sale of goods. If the lease is really an installment sale, the contract is under Article II. The *In re Smith Management, Inc.* case deals with the issue of leased goods.

IN RE SMITH MANAGEMENT, INC.

Bankruptcy Court of the United States.
8 B.R. 346 (1980).

FACTS Smith Management leased restaurant equipment for the Westgate Shopping Center. The equipment was valued at $85,000, and Smith would pay $1000 per month for five years and then $2000 per month for one year. Smith originally wanted to purchase the equipment but could not get financing. The total lease payments were $84,000. Smith went bankrupt, and questions arose as to whether Article II applied.

ISSUE Does Article II apply to equipment leases?

DECISION Yes. In this case, since the contract was entered into because there was no financing and the lease payment equaled the price, it was definitely an Article II transaction.

LEGAL TIP

Check terms of leases to find out if you're really paying for the goods. If you have an option to buy, Article II applies.

Merchants versus non-merchants Although Article II applies to all transactions in goods, some sections or parts of sections only apply to a group called "merchants." **Merchants** are defined under Section 2-104 as someone who deals in goods that are the subject matter of the contract or someone who appears to have knowledge or skill with the goods involved. For example, an appliance store is a merchant for televisions, washers, dryers, and refrigerators but not a merchant for running shoes, for athletics wear, or groceries.

The Basics of Sales Contracts

General principles: Good faith The Code gives some general principles that apply to every contract it covers. These principles are found in Article I. The first principle is called the "obligation of good faith" (Section 1-203). The idea of **good faith** is that contracting parties should act reasonably and honestly in performing their duties. For example, sellers who make mistakes and send the wrong goods should be given a chance by buyers to correct their mistakes. Buyers who have damages should be paid for their losses but should not make more money through damages than they would have if the sellers had not breached.

General principles: Following customs The Code also requires that buyers and sellers follow industry and trade customs in carrying out their promises. These customs are called "course of dealing" and "usage of trade" under the Code (Section 1-205). **Course of dealing** is the pattern of conduct between two parties. For example, if Paper Company has always shipped paper to Office Supply store by UPS, that means of shipment is one example of their course of dealing. If Office Supply has always paid within thirty days of shipment during the last ten years, that method of payment is also a course of dealing.

Usage of trade refers to a trade practice or custom, which most people involved in the trade follow. For example, in the lumber industry, it is customary for a shipment to contain some boards that are too long or short. This custom, which allows a margin for error, is honored by lumber buyers and relied on by lumber sellers. The *Nanakuli Paving & Rock Co. v. Shell Oil Co., Inc.* case involves an issue concerning trade practice.

NANAKULI PAVING & ROCK CO. v. SHELL OIL CO., INC.

United States Court of Appeals, Ninth Circuit.
664 F.2d 772 (1981).

FACTS Nanakuli, a contractor, agreed to buy asphalt from Shell Oil. When the time for delivery arrived, Shell tried to raise the price. Nanakuli objected because Oahu custom was for asphalt pavers and suppliers to guarantee their prices. Shell claimed that it did not deal regularly with contractors and therefore did not know the custom.

ISSUE Is a merchant bound to perform according to trade customs?

DECISION Yes. Shell had been in the business long enough to be aware of the price protection custom. Actual knowledge of the custom is not necessary. If a party should be aware of a general business practice, that practice is part of the agreement.

LEGAL TIP

Even new businesses are expected to understand customs. All trade customs should be excluded until experience with business customs shows clear patterns.

FORMING CONTRACTS UNDER ARTICLE II

When Does a Contract Have to Be in Writing?

Contracts for the sale of goods that cost $500 or more must be in writing to be enforceable (Section 2-201). The type of writing is not important as long as the writing is signed, uses contract language, and describes the subject matter. There are some exceptions to this requirement.

Exception one: Merchant's confirmation memorandum There are some exceptions to this $500 rule. One exception that is used quite often in business is called the **merchant's confirmation memorandum.** Suppose that Sam agrees with Bill on the telephone to sell Bill 500 one-pound boxes of his exclusive Swiss chocolate for $5 per box. The parties have reached an agreement over the telephone, but the contract must be in writing. Sam can send a signed letter or memo to Bill confirming their agreement. If Bill receives the memo and does not object within ten days, the one-sided memo satisfies the writing requirement, and Sam can enforce the contract against Bill. The *Cudahy Foods Co. v. Holloway* case deals with a problem involving a merchant's confirmation memorandum.

CUDAHY FOODS CO. v. HOLLOWAY

Supreme Court of North Carolina.
286 S.E. 2d 606 (1982).

FACTS Holloway (a real estate broker) entered into an oral contact for 262 horns of 20-inch mozarella pizza cheese from Cudahy foods for $11,083.63. Cudahy sent a written memo confirming the oral agreement. Holloway refused to take delivery of the cheese, claiming that the contract had to be in writing to be valid. Cudahy said the merchant's confirmation memorandum exception applied.

ISSUE Was the contract between Cudahy and Holloway required to be in writing?

DECISION Yes. Holloway was not a merchant since she did not deal in pizza or cheese. The merchant's confirmation memo must be between two merchants to be valid.

LEGAL TIP

Get written contracts on large orders from buyers who are not regular customers.

Exception two: Special order goods Another exception to the $500 or more rule is for specially manufactured goods. If a seller has put in time and materials and made a good start on special goods that cannot be sold to anyone else, then an oral agreement for manufacturing them is enforceable against the buyer. For example, suppose that a buyer orders 100 rocking horses at a price of $100 each from a seller; and the seller will make the rocking horses according to the buyer's specifications. The seller and buyer reached their agreement over the phone. When the horses are nearly completed, the buyer calls and tells the seller to forget making the horses. The seller can enforce the oral contract because the goods fit this specially manufactured goods exception.

Exception three: Acceptance or payment The third exception for the $500 or more rule is for goods already accepted or payment already made. For example, if a buyer has accepted delivery of 200 cookbooks at $10 each, a contract for those terms is enforceable even if oral. However, if the buyer agreed to purchase 1200 books, the seller is still limited to the 200 actually accepted.

Exception four: "I confess" The final exception applies when parties to a contract admit, under oath, in court proceedings that a contract exists. If a party does admit that the contract exists, it can be enforced.

Step One in Formation: The Offer

As in common law, the offer is the first step in forming a contract. UCC offers require the same things as common law offers. The offer must use language with present intent to contract. The offer must also be communicated to the offeree. However, there are some differences between UCC and common law offers.

How much is necessary for a valid offer? Under common law, an offer needed very specific terms to be valid. The offer had to include the subject matter, performance terms, price, payment, and parties. Under the UCC, not as many details are required since there are Article II sections that protect parties who fail to specify or agree on a contract term (see Chapter 28).

The only requirements needed for a valid offer under Article II are the subject matter (and quantity, if there is more than one subject) and the parties. An offer with language such as, "I'll sell you my 1974 White Ford Torino" would be sufficient under Article II. The *McCarty v. Verson Allsteer Press Co.* case examines whether an offer was made.

McCARTY v. VERSON ALLSTEER PRESS CO.

Court of Appeals, First District.
411 N.E.2d 936 (Ill. 1980).

FACTS Verson sent a price quotation of $325,000 to McCarty for a punch press. Verson said in the quotation that the price would vary according to time and specs. McCarty sent back a purchase order that had language requiring the seller to accept all its terms. Verson began performance and McCarty said there was no contract. Verson said that the purchase order was accepted, and this suit resulted.

ISSUE Is a price quotation an offer?

DECISION No—especially not in this case where the buyer responded by making an offer, and the price was subject to specs.

LEGAL TIP

Specify in negotiations whether a quote is an offer or an invitation for an offer to avoid confusion.

Offers and consideration: The merchant's firm offer Under common law, unless an offer is supported by consideration, the offer can be revoked at any time. If a common law offer is supported by consideration, it is called an option, and the offerer cannot revoke it.

Under the UCC, the **Merchant's Firm Offer** (Section 2-205) is an irrevocable offer but does not require the payment of consideration. A Merchant's Firm Offer is a written offer, given and signed by a merchant, stating that it will be kept open for a certain period of time (a maximum of three months, which is renewable) and signed by a merchant. The offer can be written on anything—a business card, a piece of letterhead, or a special form. Most firm offers will give an expiration date; but if they do not, the offer is good for a reasonable time only up to three months.

Merchants must sign firm offers. A signature is defined under the Code as anything placed with the intent to authenticate. Writing the offer on the back of a business card and initialing it is sufficient. A typical example of a firm offer is a raincheck from a store for sale items that are out of stock. The offer is usually found on a form designed for rainchecks and will be initialed by a clerk or manager.

Step Two in Formation: Acceptance

In acceptance there are three basic issues: how and when does acceptance occur, and what language is necessary for a valid acceptance.

How is acceptance made? Section 2-206 covers the proper methods of acceptance for Article II. There are three situations that can create different means of accepting an offer.

First, the offeror can tell the offeree how acceptance is to be made. If the offeror tells the offeree the method of acceptance, then proper acceptance requires that the offeree use that method. For example, if an offer states that "Express Mail sent to the appropriate address," is required for acceptance then the offeree must use that method to comply with the offer terms. If the offeree does not use the stated method, the offeree's acceptance is treated as a counter-offer and a rejection.

Second, the offeror may not specify any method of acceptance. If the offeror says nothing, then acceptance is made by using a "reasonable" means. "Reasonable" will depend upon the circumstances. If the offeror's situation is urgent, the offeree will use a rapid method of acceptance. A safe rule to follow is for the offeree to use the same or faster method of communication than the one the offeror has used. The same or faster method of communication is "reasonable."

The third type of offer is one that exists only under the Code and is called an offer for prompt shipment. An example would be: "Please ship three crates of your colored oval balloons immediately." If the offer is one for prompt shipment, the offeree can accept by either promptly shipping the goods or by sending a promise to ship the goods promptly. If the offeree accepts by shipping, the goods must be what the offeror ordered. If the wrong goods are sent, the offeree has accepted and breached at the same time. So, in the balloon example, if the seller sent round instead of oval balloons, there would be an acceptance and a breach. This problem of breach can be avoided if the seller notifies the buyer in advance that different goods are being sent.

When does acceptance occur? The timing of an acceptance under the UCC is the same as the timing rules for common law. The **Mailbox Rule** applies if an offeree accepts by using the specified method or by using a reasonable method (when the offerer does not specify one). A proper acceptance takes effect when it is properly mailed or dispatched. If an improper method is used, the acceptance takes effect when the offeror receives it. Figure 27-1 is a summary of the Article II rules on the timing of acceptance.

What language is necessary for an acceptance? An acceptance must have language with an intent to contract. Under common law, an acceptance must be unqualified and unconditional. The common law **Mirror Image Rule** labels an attempted acceptance with conditions or changed terms a rejection and counter-offer. Under the UCC, these acceptance rules have been changed. The rules of acceptance are found in Section 2-207 and are different for merchants and non-merchants.

Acceptance rules for non-merchants. If an offeree makes a statement of acceptance and then adds some terms, there is still a contract under Article II. But, the

Figure 27-1 **UCC Timing Rules for Acceptance**

TYPE OF OFFER	METHOD OF ACCEPTANCE	ACCEPTANCE EFFECTIVE?
No means given	Same or faster method of communication	When properly mailed, dispatched (Mailbox Rule)
No means given	Slower method of communication	When received if offer still open
Specified means	Specified means used	Mailbox Rule
Specified means	Specified means not used	Counter-offer and rejection
Prompt shipment	Proper goods shipped	Upon shipment
Prompt shipment	Improper goods shipped	Breach and acceptance upon shipment

added terms are not part of the contract. For example, suppose the following conversation takes place:

S.—"I'll sell you my 1974 White Ford Torino for $350."
B.—"I'll take it; replace the ashtray."

S. and B. have a contract, but the ashtray term is not included.

Acceptance rules for merchants. When both parties are merchants, the rules are different. If the offeree adds terms to the acceptance, there is still a contract and the additional terms are part of the contract. If S. and B. were used-car dealers in the example, then S. and B. would have a contract and the ashtray would be included. There are three exceptions to this merchant rule. First the additional terms are not part of the contract if they are material. For example, if B. said, "I'll take it. Throw in new tires." S. and B. would have a contract, but the tires would not be included because the cost of the tires would be material.

The second exception applies when the offeror limits the offer only to those terms specified ("accept exactly"). If there is a limited offer and the offeree adds terms in the acceptance, there will be a contract but without the additional terms. If S. added, "This offer is limited to these terms," there would be a contract without the ashtray.

The final exception gives S. an opportunity to object to any terms added by B. If an offeror objects to the added terms within a reasonable time, the parties will have a contract, but without the added terms. In the example, if S. added, "I won't take the ashtray," there would be a contract without the ashtray. Figure 27-2 gives a summary of Section 2-207 rules.

Section 2-207 is often called the **battle of the forms.** This name was given because merchants often send purchase orders and invoices back and forth as their offers and acceptances. The printed terms on these documents would never match, but the parties do agree on their basic terms of subject matter, price, etc. Under Section 2-207, the parties can have a contract and also have rules for determining what fine-print terms are included. The *General Instrument Corp. v. Tie Mfg. Inc.* case involves a Section 2-207 issue.

Step Three in Formation: Consideration

Article II contracts must be supported by consideration. The common law rules of consideration apply to Article II contracts. The one difference deals with the modification of contracts. Both parties can agree to modify a partly unperformed contract, and it will be valid even though there is no consideration for the modification (Section 2-209). So long as the parties agree in good faith to change their performance terms, the change is valid even if no new consideration is given.

Figure 27-2 **UCC Rules for Additional Terms in Acceptance**

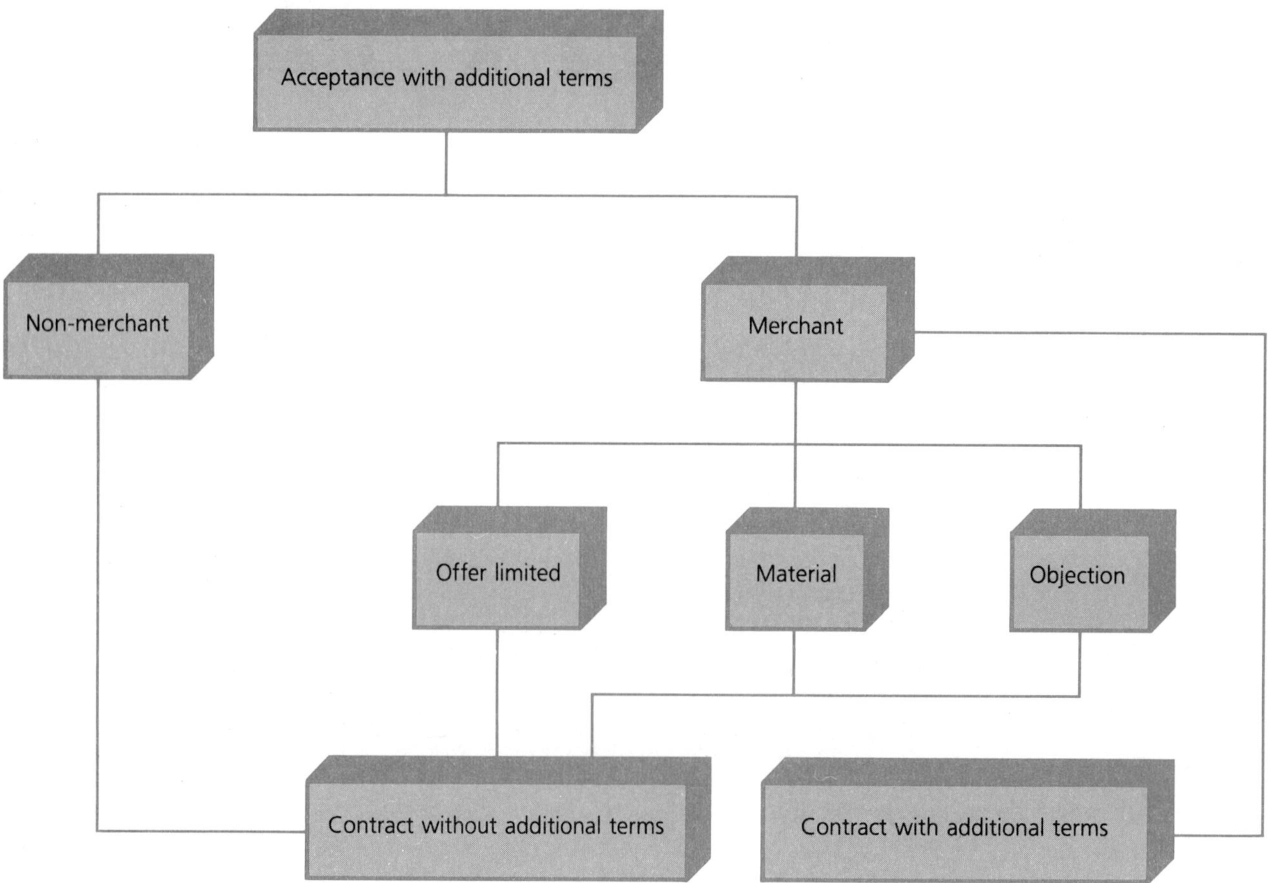

GENERAL INSTRUMENT CORP. v. TIE MFG. INC.

United States District Court, Southern District of New York. 517 F.Supp. 1231 (1981).

FACTS General's invoice to Tie Manufacturing's order for $556,579 in mosfets (small mechanical parts) provided that the parties would submit their disputes to New York courts. Tie did not object. A dispute arose, and General claimed that they were required to go to the New York courts.

ISSUE Was the seller's additional term on courts part of the contract?

DECISION No. The term was material and did not become a part of the contract.

LEGAL TIP

Parties should agree on the state court that will handle disputes in interstate contracts.

Step Four in Formation: No Defenses

All Article II contracts that are formed properly are still subject to the common law defenses of misrepresentation, fraud, lack of capacity, and illegality (see Chapters 20 through 23). These defenses have been incorporated into Article II contract formation (Section 1-103).

Figure 27-3 is a summary of the differences between common law and the UCC on application and formation.

Figure 27-3 **Common Law versus UCC Rules**

AREA	UCC	COMMON LAW
Application	Sale of goods	Services, real estate, and employment contracts
Offers	Need subject matter and quantity; code gives details	Need subject matter, price, terms, and full details agreed upon
Options	Merchant's firm offer; no consideration needed	Need consideration
Acceptance	Can have additional terms	Mirror Image Rule followed
	Mailbox Rule works for reasonable means of acceptance	Must use same method for Mailbox Rule to get Mailbox Rule
Consideration	Required for contracts but not for modification or firm offers	Always required
Defenses	Must be free of all defenses for valid contract	Must be free of all defenses for a valid contract

KEY TERMS

Goods
Merchants
Good faith
Course of dealing
Usage of trade
Merchant's confirmation memorandum
Merchant's firm offer
Mailbox Rule
Mirror Image Rule
Battle of the forms

CHAPTER PROBLEMS

1. McClanahan entered into a contract to purchase an oil refinery. When defects in the refinery arose, McClanahan said the contract was under UCC because the refinery could be broken down into goods. Is he correct? *McClanahan v. American Gilsonite Co.,* 494 F. Supp. 1334 (Colo. 1981).
2. McGlasson entered into a contract to buy 28-foot Chris Craft Cruiser from Peoria Harbor Marina for $20,695. McGlasson would be living on the boat. Is the contract under the UCC? *Peoria Harbor Marina v. McGlasson,* 434 N.E.2d 786 (Ill. 1982).
3. Carr took 10 rolls of thirty six-exposure Ektachrome film to Hoosier Photo for developing. The pictures were of Carr's 1970 tour of Europe. Hoosier lost the film, and Carr wanted the warranty remedies under Article II. Does Article II apply? *Carr v. Hoosier Photo Supplies, Inc.,* 422 N.E.2d 1272 (Ind. 1981).
4. Pierson had on oral contract to buy 500,000 pounds of sunflower seeds from Arnst (a farmer). Pierson sent a memo confirming the sale but Arnst later refused to perform saying the contract should have been in writing under Article II. Who is right? *Pierson v. Arnst,* 33 UCC Rep. 457 (Mont. 1982).
5. Klockner agreed orally to purchase 1800 tons of wire rod from Federal Wire Mill for $658,306.40. Klockner sent a signed, handwritten note confirming the oral agreement. Federal now claims they do not have to perform under the statute of frauds. Who is correct? *Klockner, Inc. v. Federal Wire Mill Corp.,* 663 F.2d 1370 (7th Cir. 1981).
6. * Zahornacky entered into a contract with Edward Chevrolet for the purchase of an "Indy 500" Corvette for $14,628.21. When the car came in, it was selling for about $22,000 to $25,000 because it was a limited edition. Edward refused to sell unless Zahornacky paid $2000 more. Is Edward correct? *Zahornacky v. Edward Chevrolet, Inc.,* 436 A.2d 47 (Conn. 1981).
7. Potter agreed to buy 192,000 turkey poults from Hatter Farms. Is it a UCC transaction? *Potter v. Hatter Farms, Inc.,* 641 P.2d 628 (Oreg. 1982).
8. Interlake sent invoices to Kansas Power & Light for its purchases. The invoices provided for payment of interest on amounts due after thirty days. Kansas did not have an interest provision in its purchase order. Will interest be required on accounts past thirty days? *Interlake v. Kansas Power & Light Co.,* 637 P.2d 464 (Kan. 1981).
9. Lubrication entered into an oral agreement with Union for the purchase of $64,400 of molybendum. Lubrication then sent a signed contract, which Union never signed and returned. Union did not perform and claimed that the contract had to be in writing. Who wins? *Lubrication & Maintenance, Inc. v. Union Resource Co., Inc.,* 522 F.Supp. 1078 (S.D.N.Y. 1981).
10. GNP Commodities decided to become involved in the commodities option market. They chose pork bellies. The value of an option can be affected by the time a hedger inspects the meat (a hedger is a pork bellies buyer). GNP held some options because they believed that the inspection had already occurred and that the meat had passed. In fact, the hedger's inspection had been delayed and when the inspection was done, the bellies were rejected. GNP brought suit for its losses resulting from the delay. The hedger maintains that industry delay (up to two months) is typical. GNP says it was unaware of any industry customs. What is the result? *GNP Commodities, Inc. v. Walsh Heffernan Co.,* 420 N.E. 2d 659 (Ill. 1981).

"I know you think you understood what you thought I said, but I'm not sure you know what I really meant to say."
Gracie Allen

Chapter 28

Terms Under Article II

CHAPTER PREVIEW

- Required terms under a UCC contract
- Terms supplied by the UCC when the parties fail to agree
- Payment under the UCC
- Delivery under the UCC
- Time for performance under the UCC
- Use of industry custom and prior dealings under the UCC
- The UCC Parol Evidence Rule
- Unconscionability and its effects

Buyer B. was buying mohair from Seller S. There are two types of mohair—adult mohair and kid mohair—and their contract didn't specify what type B. was buying. S. delivered adult mohair, and B. wanted kid mohair. Who is right?

One of the reasons for the success of the UCC has been that details not covered in contracts can be filled in with sections of the Code. UCC contracts are valid even though they may not have the details required for common law contracts. Article II also covers the sticky details of insurance, title, and risk of loss so that the parties always know their positions. In this chapter, the term sections of Article II are explained along with the Article II rules for interpreting contracts.

CODE TERMS USED TO PROTECT PARTIES

Sometimes two parties are in such a hurry to contract and perform that they forget to cover important details in their agreement. If the parties intended to contract, then Article II sections can be used to fill in the gaps in their intended agreement. The terms covered by Article II include price, payment, delivery, and time for performing.

How Much? Price Term

Section 2-305 allows parties to contract without reaching an agreement on price. If the parties failed to set a price or left the price open, Section 2-305 provides that a "reasonable price" can be determined at the time of delivery. A "reasonable price" is one that is a market price or a one that a willing buyer would pay a willing seller. This price section can also be used if the parties were supposed to agree on a price after contracting but then cannot agree on that price. For example, a buyer and seller may agree on the sale of a car but may not agree on the price. A good standard for price is the blue book that lists average wholesale and retail prices for used cars. The *Roy Buckner Chevrolet, Inc. v. Cagle* case involves the issue of open price in a car contract.

ROY BUCKNER CHEVROLET, INC. v. CAGLE

Supreme Court of Alabama.
418 So.2d 878 (1982).

FACTS Cagle entered into a contract (form agreement) with Roy Buckner Chevrolet for an "Indy Vette." An "Indy Vette" is a special-edition Corvette car. The agreement provided for the price to be the list price ($16,000). Cagle gave Buckner a $500 deposit.

When the car came in, the market value was much higher than the list price ($22,000), and Buckner attempted to return the deposit on the grounds that a valid contract did not exist. Cagle claimed that the open price term was permitted under the UCC.

ISSUE Was "list price" sufficient?

DECISION Yes. Open price terms are permitted under Article II. It was clear that the parties intended to contract. The open price term requires the parties to assume the risk of the market.

LEGAL TIP

List prices can be less than actual market prices. Be careful when choosing open price terms.

When and How? The Payment Term

The issues of payment are "when" and "how." When must a buyer pay? How or in what form must the payment be made? Under Section 2-310, buyers must pay their sellers at the time and place that they receive their purchases. Of course, the buyer and seller can agree for payment on credit or at a different time.

How the buyer pays is the second question. Under Section 2-304, the buyer and seller can agree to payment by money, goods, or realty. If the buyer and seller agree to payment by money, the buyer can pay by check unless the seller demands cash. However, if the seller demands cash, the buyer must be given time to get cash for payment.

Where? The Delivery Term

Unless the parties agree otherwise, the place of delivery is the seller's place of business (Section 2-308). If the seller is not in business, the place of delivery is the seller's residence. In other words, unless the parties agree, the seller is not required to deliver the goods as part of performance.

Also, unless the parties agree otherwise, all the goods are to be delivered and paid for at one time (Section 2-307). Delivery in lots or installments must be agreed upon in the contract by the buyer and seller.

When? The Performance Term

It is not unusual for parties not to set a date for performing their contract obligations. Under common law, a time for performance is critical. However, the UCC takes care of a performance time if the parties do not provide for a time in their contract. If no time is set, the UCC provides that the time for performance is a "reasonable time." The length of a reasonable time will vary from contract to contract. For example, the time for delivering Christmas trees would be very limited. But the time for delivering a boat or some furniture could be weeks or months. The *Dura-Wood Treating Co. v. Century Fleet Industries, Inc.* case examines whether a contract without all terms is still valid.

DURA-WOOD TREATING CO. v. CENTURY FLEET INDUSTRIES, INC.

United States Court of Appeals, Fifth Circuit.
675 F.2d 745 (1982).

FACTS Dura-Wood and Century are both merchants in the business of treating cross-ties for industrial and commercial use. Dura-Wood's agent called Century's agent, and the two orally agreed that Century would sell Dura-Wood's agent 20,000 cross-ties (8′ × 8″ × 6″) at $8.60 per tie. Dura-Wood's agent sent a confirmation letter. There was no agreement on delivery terms regarding place or time. Century's agent called back and told Dura-Wood to "just let us know." When Dura-Wood called for delivery of the ties, Century denied that a contract existed.

ISSUE Was there a valid contract between Dura-Wood and Century?

DECISION Yes. The Code can supply the time and manner of delivery. The parties clearly intended to contract.

LEGAL TIP

Be sure to confirm all oral agreements in writing. All terms should be listed in the contract to avoid problems.

Limitations on Terms

Although the UCC gives the parties a free hand in negotiating their contracts, there are some restrictions on the types of terms that can be included. One is the good-faith restriction that requires parties to treat each other fairly.

Another restriction is found in Section 2-302 on unconscionable contracts. **Unconscionable contracts** are one-sided and unfair to one of the parties. The unconscionability issue is one for the courts. Examples of unconscionable contracts occur when the buyer gives up rights to damages or waives warranty protection. Other types of unconscionable clauses are those limiting the time for the buyer to make complaints. For example, giving a buyer of a cement truck two days to make any complaints or waive all rights is unfair; it would take more time to use the truck and make sure all the parts worked. The following questions are used to analyze unconscionability issues.

1. Did the seller use a standard printed form? Was "boiler-plate" language (detailed and standard in form) used?
2. Is there a big difference between the actual cost of the goods and the price the buyer is paying?
3. Does the contract deny the buyer basic rights, such as the right to a remedy?
4. Was the buyer given a strong sales pitch?
5. Could the buyer negotiate any terms?

In the *Murphy v. McNamara* case, a court was faced with the problem of unconscionability.

MURPHY v. McNAMARA

Superior Court of Connecticut.
416 A.2d 170 (1979).

FACTS Murphy (a welfare recipient with four children, ages 5 through 16) signed a "rent-to-own" contract for a television set. She was to pay $16 per week for a total of seventy-eight weeks. At the end of that time, she would own the television set. The retail cost of the television was $499. Murphy had the right to terminate the lease at any time. When she had paid $436 in rent, she saw a newspaper story criticizing the rental plan as an unfair violation of the Connecticut Unfair Trade Practices Act. She was threatened by the company when she stopped payments. She then consulted an attorney with Legal Assistance.

ISSUE Were the terms of the television "rent-to-own" contract unconscionable?

DECISION Yes. The contract was a printed form, issued on a take-it-or-leave-it basis. There was no opportunity for negotiation.

LEGAL TIP
Check the terms and the total price in "rent-to-own" contracts.

INTERPRETATION OF TERMS

Even when the parties to a contract have agreed to all the necessary terms, the language used for those terms may need interpretation. Article II provides some interpretation rules for contracts. This section discusses those rules.

Interpretation by Course of Dealing: Have the Parties Dealt with Each Other Before?

Under Section 1-205 of the UCC, courts can look at the "course of dealing" of the parties in interpreting a contract. **Course of dealing** is the way the parties have acted if they have dealt with each other in the past. For example, a contract may provide that the seller is to ship several boxes of envelopes to the buyer. There is no method of shipment given, but the buyer and seller have done business in the past, and the seller has always shipped through the mail. This previously established business custom is applied to interpret the term "shipment by seller" in their contract.

In some cases, the contract may include a price but may only provide that payment is "with terms" or "by usual terms." The meaning of these phrases is determined by finding how the buyer has paid in the past. If the buyer has paid on "net 30" terms for ten years of business with the seller, then "net 30" will be the contract terms.

Under Section 2-208, the parties' "course of performance" can also be used to interpret a contract. The **course of performance** is the way in which the parties began performing an ongoing contract. For example, suppose that S. and B. had a contract in which S. would supply salt-and-pepper packets to B.'s fast-food restaurant. The contract did not include any payment terms, but for the first five months of the contract S. accepted payment forty-five days after delivery. Because S. and B. performed their contract this way and neither one objected, this course of performance would be the payment term in their contract. The *Dunn v. General Equities of Iowa, Ltd.* case shows how the parties' course of performance can change the contract terms.

DUNN v. GENERAL EQUITIES OF IOWA, LTD.

Supreme Court of Iowa.
319 N.W.2d 515 (1982).

FACTS The Dunns purchased some business equipment and signed several promissory notes to General Equities to pay for the equipment. Their notes called for yearly payments (on March 31) of $121,170. The payments were late every year from 1975 to 1979. General Equities still accepted the payments, but in 1979, accelerated the notes when the Dunns' payment was as late as the prior years. Equities called the late payment a default. The Dunns claimed that they were not required to pay on time.

ISSUE Did the seller's acceptance of late payments result in a course of performance allowing late payments?

DECISION Yes. The acceleration clause was not used, and there was no demand for timely payment in the prior years. General Equities could not suddenly demand a timely payment.

LEGAL TIP

If a payment is late, do not accept it. If you accept the late payment, give a written notice that payment on time is expected in the future.

Interpretation by Trade Usage: Are There Any Industry Customs?

Section 1-205 defines **usage of trade** as a regularly observed custom or practice in a trade. Another way of describing this code provision is industry custom. If a term in a contract is unclear, but the industry has certain rules of interpretation for that term, then the industry rule will apply. For example, in contracts for the purchase of poultry, a grade will be specified as Grade A, AA, etc. However, the poultry industry gives the seller a 3% margin of error in filling their contract orders. For example, a Grade A order is met if 97% of the poultry furnished is Grade A. The 3% is the industry custom for error.

In the lumber industry, the seller is given a 10% margin for error in supplying lumber or boards of a certain length. In other words, only 90% of the amount ordered must be of the length ordered by the buyer.

The *Kincheloe v. Geldmeier* case is one in which the court deals with an industry custom in interpreting a contract term.

KINCHELOE v. GELDMEIER

Supreme Court of Texas.
619 S.W.2d 272 (1981).

FACTS Kincheloe purchased cattle to use for breeding (forty Brahma heifers for $15,968) at an auction. The contract did not disclaim any warranties. It was later discovered that the cattle were infected with brucellosis (a chronic, contagious, and incurable disease that localizes in the reproductive organs of female cattle and prevents reproduction). Kincheloe brought suit for breach of the implied warranty of merchantability. Geldmeier claimed that in the cattle auction trade, no warranties are given. Kincheloe claimed that because there was no disclaimer, a warranty was given.

ISSUE Did the cattle trade practice of no warranties apply in the contract?

DECISION Yes. The practice was widely known and used by all members of the industry. Both the buyer and seller were merchants and did know or should have known of the trade custom.

LEGAL TIP

Become familiar with the industry and its customs. Ask questions when you are unsure.

What Other Sources Can Be Used for Interpretation? Parol Evidence

As discussed in Chapter 22, once a contract is in its final written form, other evidence made at or before the contract signing cannot be used to contradict the terms in the written contract. Outside, other, or **extrinsic evidence** is any evidence other than what is written in the contract. However, extrinsic evidence can be used for interpretation. The above evidence of course of dealing, performance, and trade usage are all forms of evidence that are permitted to show the meaning of contract terms.

However, extrinsic evidence cannot be used to contradict a complete form or cannot be used when the contract is complete and unambiguous. The *Illinois Bell Telephone Co. v. Reuben H. Donnelley Corp.* case is an example of the use of the **Parol Evidence Rule.**

ILLINOIS BELL TELEPHONE CO. v. REUBEN H. DONNELLEY CORP.

United States District Court, Northern District of Illinois.
595 F.Supp. 1192 (1984).

FACTS Illinois Bell Telephone (IBT) had a contract with Reuben H. Donnelley Corp. (RHD) for the publication of telephone directories. IBT wanted to end the contract on the date provided in the contract. RHD maintained that even though the contract provided an ending date, they had orally agreed that RHD would continue to publish the directories. A suit resulted and the dispute centered around the ending date of the contract.

ISSUE Could the oral extension be enforced?

DECISION No. The contract was complete and the oral promise could not be introduced as evidence. The contract was clear with no ambiguities and had a definite statement that the contract ended.

LEGAL TIP

Oral promises occurring before or when there is a written contract are unenforceable. Always get the terms in writing.

KEY TERMS

Unconscionable contracts
Course of dealing
Course of performance
Usage of trade
Extrinsic evidence
Parol Evidence Rule

CHAPTER PROBLEMS

1. Frigaliment Importing (a Swiss firm) entered into a contract with B.N.S. International Sales Corporation for the purchase of frozen chickens. There are two types of chickens: young chickens suitable for broiling and frying; and older chickens suitable for stewing. The contract gave the weight of the chickens but did not include the type. Three witnesses (experts in the industry) said that to get broilers the word "broilers" must be written by the term chicken in a contract. B.N.S. says that there is nothing in the contract to indicate "broilers." What is the result? *Frigaliment Importing Co. v. B.N.S. International Sales Corp.,* 190 F.Supp. 116 (N.Y. 1960).
2. Decker Steel entered into a contract for the purchase of "prime Thomas quality 36-inch steel." When the steel was delivered, Decker discovered that it was 37 inches wide. Decker brought suit for breach, and the seller defended with testimony from the American Iron and Steel Institute that allowed a one-inch variance in width. Who wins? *Decker Steel Company v. The Exchange National Bank of Chicago,* 330 F.2d 82 (7th Cir. 1964).
3. Skinner purchased an airplane from Tober Foreign Motors. They had a written agreement that provided for Skinner to make monthly installment payments. After several months, Skinner and Tober orally agreed to reduce the amount of the installments. They continued their agreement with reduced payments. When further troubles developed, suit was brought for Skinner's default. Skinner said their oral agreement applied. What is the result? *Skinner v. Tober Foreign Motors,* 187 N.E.2d 669 (N.Y. 1963).
4. Monsanto manufactured herbicide and sold several cans to Feeders, Inc. The cans had label warnings that there were no implied warranties, that there was a very limited express warranty and that if these terms were unacceptable, the cans were to be returned unopened. Feeders applied the herbicide to 1100 acres of corn, and the crop was lost. Feeders sued for breach of warranty. Feeders claimed that the disclaimers were unconscionable under Section 2-302. Is Feeders correct? *Feeders, Inc. v. Monsanto Co.,* 33 U.C.C. 541 (Minn. 1981).
5. Ciba-Geigy Corporation manufactured a herbicide (Miloguard), which it claimed destroyed the weed, foxtail. Durham used Miloguard but his crop was over-taken by foxtail. Durham sued for breach of express warranty. Ciba-Geigy cited a small provision in its contract that relieved them of all liability for warranties and that stated they would not be responsible for crop damage. Durham claims the clause is unconscionable. What is the result? *Durham v. Ciba-Geigy Corp.,* 315 N.W.2d 696 (S.D. 1982).
6. Robinson delivered 171,154 pounds of peanuts to the Boston Farm Center (Stevens' agent). Their agreement had the amount, time and place of delivery, and other details but no price. At the time of delivery, the market price for the peanuts was $34,805.34. But the Boston Farm Center did not pay immediately, and by the time they paid, the market price was $132,488.56. Is there a contract? What is the price? *Robinson v. Stevens Industries, Inc.,* 290 S.E.2d 336 (Ga. 1982).

*7. Dura-Wood's contract with Century Forest for cross-ties did not specify a place of delivery. The custom in the cross-tie industry was delivery at the buyer's place of business. The Code provides for delivery at the seller's place of business. Which is the place of delivery? *Dura-Wood Treating Co. v. Century Forest Industries, Inc.,* 675 F.2d 745 (5th Cir. 1982).

8. Brooks Shoe Manufacturing Company, a manufacturer of running shoes, sent a $109,511.06 shoe order to Chesapeake Shoe Company, a wholesale distributor. The order did not have all shoe sizes. Chesa-

peake claimed industry custom required all sizes even though the contract did not specify sizes. What is the result? *In re Brooks Shoe Manufacturing Co., Inc.*, 21 B.R. 604 (E.D. Pa. 1982).

9. What happens under the Code when the following terms are left open?

    Price
    Payment
    Delivery
    Performance

10. What factors does a court examine to determine unconscionability?

"There is many a slip between the cup and the lip."
Anonymous

CHAPTER PREVIEW

- Identifying contract goods
- The effect of an insurable interest
- Passage of title
- The importance of passage of title
- Risk of loss—who has it and when
- Sales on approval, sale or return, consignments—the exceptions
- Leaving goods for repair—can they be sold?

Chapter 29

Terms: Identification, Title, and Risk of Loss

Mercanti was an experienced yachtsman and marine engineer. He owned a yacht that lost its mast in a squall. He made an oral agreement with Persson to build him a mast. Mercanti agreed to purchase the necessary materials for the mast. When the mast was nearly completed, a fire swept through Persson's shipyard and destroyed the mast. Persson had been paid $4500 for his labor and refused to build another mast. Mercanti claimed that he was required to build another mast. Who wins?

There is a time in sales transactions between forming and performing the contract that many things can go wrong—the "slips." Goods can be lost in shipment or destroyed in a warehouse fire. In this chapter the slips and rights of the parties in that in-between period are covered. Who has title? When does title pass to the buyer? What are the rights of third parties in the goods? Who bears the risk of loss? Who can carry insurance? All of these questions cover the slips between contract and performance.

INSURING FOR THE SLIP

Both buyer and seller need insurance to protect goods as they flow in transit. Insurance on the goods cannot be obtained until the goods are identified. **Identification** is defined under Section 2-501. Identification occurs at different times and depends upon whether the goods are in existence or will be manufactured.

Existing Goods and Identification

If the buyer and seller are contracting for the sale of goods that already exist, identification takes place at the time the contract is made. For example, if Billy agrees to buy Jimmy's 1974 White Ford Torino, identification occurs when they reach an agreement for the sale and purchase of that car. Billy would then have an insurable interest in that car.

Some goods exist at the time of contracting but are part of a mass of goods and co-exist with everyone else's goods. These are called **fungible goods.** Oil, gas, grains, cases in warehouses, and other fluids are examples of fungible goods. Fungible goods are identified when they are shipped, marked, or otherwise designated for the buyer. For example, if 200 cases of canned corn are set apart from the 5000 cases in the warehouse, there has been identification of a buyer's interest, and the buyer now holds an **insurable interest** in the corn.

Future Goods and Identification

When a buyer purchases goods from a seller who will manufacture them, their contract is one for future goods. For example, if Bessy agrees to buy 100 rocking horses from Sal, and Sal will build them according to Bessy's specifications, there is a contract for future goods. Future goods are identified in the same way as fungible goods—when they are shipped, marked, or otherwise designated for the buyer. Figure 29-1 is a summary of the identification rules.

WHO OWNS THE GOODS? PASSAGE OF TITLE

Once the goods are identified, the title can change hands from buyer to seller. The definition of a sale is the passing of title from the seller to the buyer. This area is one of great importance. The time when title passes will depend upon whether the contract requires delivery (Section 2-401).

No Delivery: Passage of Title

If there is no delivery, the time when title passes will depend upon whether there are documents of title. Documents of title are a familiar concept to most car owners. Referred to as "pink slips" or **titles,** the document given to car owners permitting

Figure 29-1 **Identification Under Article II**

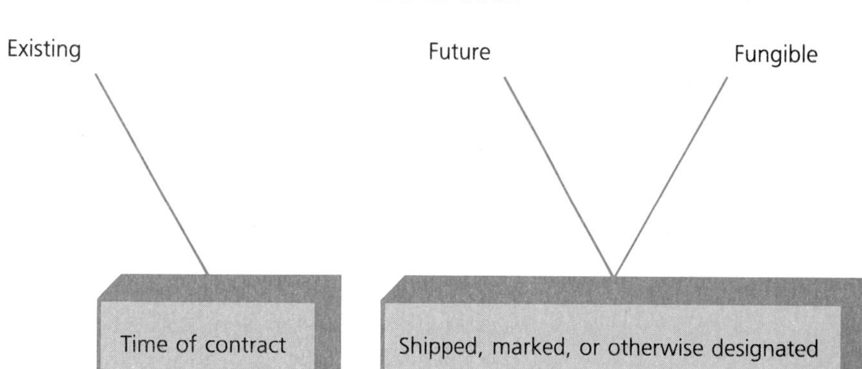

them to sell their cars is a **document of title.** If there is a document of title in a sale, title passes when the document of title is given to the buyer.

If there is no delivery and no document of title, then title passes at the time and place of contracting. For example, when a buyer buys a sofa at a furniture store, there is no document of title. Title to the sofa passes to the buyer when the buyer pays for the sofa or signs a credit agreement.

Key Terms in Delivery and Title

Before discussing passage of title in delivery contracts, some terms must be defined. These terms will be used in nearly all delivery contracts and control not only passage of title but risk of loss.

FOB **FOB** means "free on board." When a term is "FOB place of destination, it means that the seller is responsible for getting the goods to the buyer and must pay for the shipping expense to get them to the buyer. For example, a New York (NY) seller with a Los Angeles (LA) buyer and an "FOB LA" contract must pay to ship the goods to LA.

If the term is "FOB place of shipment," then the seller is required only to get the goods to a carrier. The buyer will pay the cost of shipment. In the example given, a contract with "FOB New York" would mean that the buyer would pay shipment to Los Angeles.

FAS **FAS** means "free alongside." FAS is the FOB term for shipment by boat. "FAS place of shipment" and "FAS" place of destination" have the same meaning as the FOB terms.

COD **COD** means "cash on delivery." This term requires the buyer to pay before the goods can be picked up or received. COD can be used in combination with the FOB or FAS terms.

CIF or CF **CIF** or **CF** means cost of the goods, insurance (to cover the goods while in transit), and freight (shipping charges). In a CIF contract, the seller includes all these charges in the lump sum price of the goods. The seller is required to pay the freight and get insurance to cover the goods. The buyer actually pays them as part of the price for the goods.

Delivery: Passage of Title

Passage of title in delivery contracts depends on the shipping terms in the contract. If the terms are "FOB place of shipment," then title passes to the buyer at the time and place of shipment. If the terms are "FOB place of destination," then title passes to the buyer when the goods are tendered to the buyer at the place of destination. "Tender" means that the buyer knows the goods are available for pick up and has all the papers required.

For example, if Sammy is required to ship goods from his LA firm to Bobby's NY firm and the shipment terms are "FOB LA," title passes to Bobby at the time of shipment in LA. If the terms are "FOB NY," then title passes to Bobby when the goods are tendered in New York. The *In re Turner* case shows the importance of the time of passing title. Figure 29-2 illustrates the rules for passage of title.

IN RE TURNER

32 UCC Rep. 1240 (Bank. Ct. D. Nebr. 1981).

FACTS Turner sold an airplane to Don Glaser for $55,975 in August and was given a down payment of $11,000. Turner was to deliver the airplane but did not deliver it until October. Cessna owned the aircraft, and Turner was not permitted to sell the plane without Cessna's approval. Turner went bankrupt and both Glaser and Cessna claimed title to the plane.

ISSUE Did title pass to Glaser in August with the partial payment?

DECISION No. The title did not pass until delivery. The effect was to make the creditor's interest superior to Glaser. Glaser lost out on the plane.

LEGAL TIP

Title in delivery cases does not pass with payment. Delays in delivery can give the seller's creditors rights to the goods.

Someone Else Is Involved: Third Parties and Title

In many commercial situations, third parties (those other than the buyer or seller) will have goods in their possession. For example, repair businesses have goods in their possession but do not hold title to those goods. However, under Section 2-403, these repair businesses may be able to transfer title to those goods.

Under Section 2-403, there are special provisions for "entrusting" possession of goods to merchants who deal in goods of that kind. For example, leaving your watch with a jeweler for repair is entrusting your watch. If you have entrusted your goods to a merchant who sells those goods to a "buyer in the ordinary course of business," title passes to the buyer. A buyer in the ordinary course of business is a typical customer—someone who would do business at the jewelry store in the example above. If the jeweler sells the watch to another customer, you will be left with a remedy against the jeweler, but the buyer keeps the watch. Wholesaling the watch to another jeweler would not be a sale in the ordinary course of business, and the jeweler would not transfer title.

Figure 29-2 **Passage of Title Under Article II**

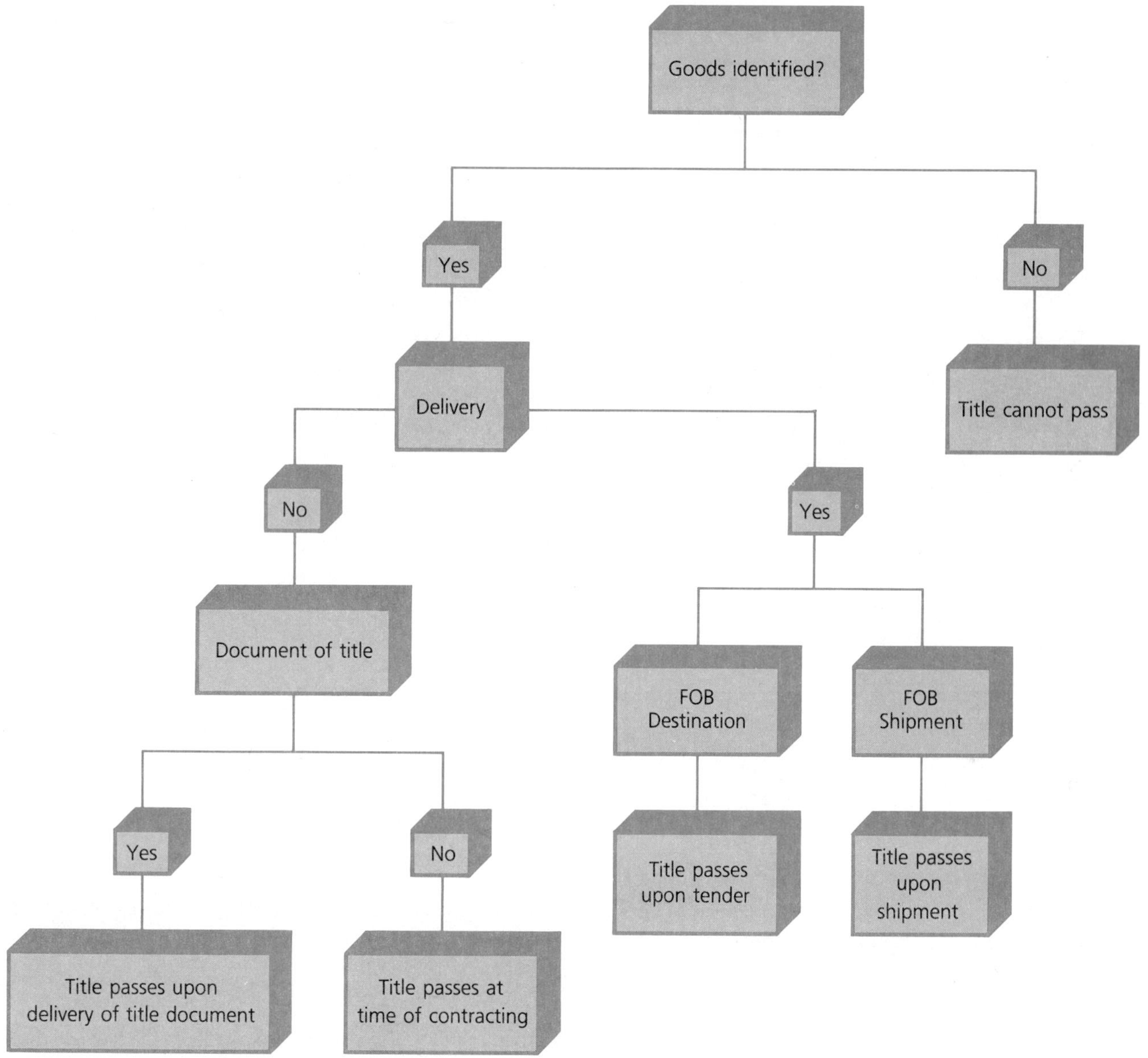

Section 2-403 also covers problems in the passage of title. Even someone with voidable title (ownership that is flawed) can pass good title to a good-faith buyer. For example, suppose Charlie's Used Cars buys a car from sixteen-year-old Ralph for $350. Charlie's shines the car up and puts it on the lot. Cynthia, who is 22 years old, buys the car for $500 and does not know that Charlie's bought the car from a minor. Shortly after Cynthia's purchase, Ralph returns and wants his car back. Cynthia would have good title even though Charlie's had only a voidable title (since Ralph, a minor, could undo the contract). Cynthia would keep the car.

The purpose of Section 2-403 is to protect good-faith buyers, such as "ordinary" consumers. They will get title despite their sellers' flawed title. The *Shacket v. Philko Aviation, Inc.* case deals with a third-party title issue.

SHACKET v. PHILKO AVIATION, INC.

United States Court of Appeals, Seventh Circuit.
681 F.2d 506 (1982).

FACTS Shacket purchased a new airplane (for $126,000) from Smith Aircraft. Smith was a dealer in used aircraft and had been entrusted with the plane by Philko for purposes of selling it. Smith transferred title but did not pay Philko. Philko brought suit to get the plane back from Shacket. Shacket claims that he was a good-faith purchaser and a buyer in the ordinary course of business.

ISSUE Did Shacket take good title?

DECISION Yes. Smith dealt in airplanes. The plane had been entrusted, and he could pass good title to a buyer in the ordinary course of business.

LEGAL TIP

Make sure that agents have the authority to sell and can give good title. Owners should set up a system to make sure that they get paid if an agent is responsible for selling.

THE SLIP: WHO BEARS THE RISK OF LOSS?

When the **risk of loss** passes depends upon whether the goods are being delivered, picked up from the seller, or picked up from a warehouse or third party (Section 2-509). The rules for the passage of risk of loss are determined by the contract delivery terms. The next three subsections discuss delivery terms.

The Slip: Non-Delivery Contracts

Non-delivery contracts are those in which the buyer will be picking up the goods from the seller. When risk of loss passes in non-delivery contracts depends upon whether the seller is a merchant or a non-merchant.

Merchants If the seller is a merchant, the risk of loss passes to the buyer when the buyer actually receives the goods. For example, if Ira buys a refrigerator from Sears, the risk of loss does not pass to Ira until Ira picks up the refrigerator and has it in his truck.

Non-merchants If the seller is a non-merchant, the risk of loss passes to the buyer on tender of delivery. Tender of delivery occurs when the goods are available and ready for the buyer. If Ira bought a refrigerator at a neighborhood garage sale and left to get his truck, the risk of loss has already passed. If, however, the seller said that the refrigerator could not be picked up for three days, tender would not occur and risk of loss would not pass to Ira for three days.

The Slip: Delivery Contracts

The risk of loss in delivery contracts is controlled by the terms of the contract. If the terms of the contract are "FOB place of shipment," then the risk of loss passes to the buyer when the goods are delivered to the carrier. If the delivery terms are "FOB place of destination," the risk of loss passes to the buyer when the goods are tendered at the place of destination.

Using the same example from the title section of this chapter, if the terms are "FOB LA," the risk of loss passes when the goods are given to the carrier in LA. If the terms are "FOB NY," then the risk of loss passes to the buyer when the carrier tenders them to the buyer in New York. The *Rheinberg-Kellerei GMBH v. Vineyard Wine Co.* case involves an issue of lost goods.

RHEINBERG-KELLEREI GMBH v. VINEYARD WINE CO.
Court of Appeals of North Carolina.
281 S.E.2d 425 (1981).

FACTS Rheinberg (a West German wine producer) sent a shipload (1245 cases) of wine to its buyer, Vineyard. The terms were "FAS Charlotte, NC," which was the destination point. The MS Munchen, with all hands and cargo, was lost at sea between December 12 and 22, 1978. Rheinberg sought payment for the lost wine, and Vineyard refused to pay.

ISSUE Who had the risk of loss when the ship was lost?

DECISION Rheinberg. The risk of loss had not passed to Vineyard because the delivery terms were FOB destination.

LEGAL TIP
Get insurance coverage for identified goods so they are covered during the shipment.

The Slip: Non-Delivery, Third-Party Pick-Up Contracts

When the contract goods are held by a third party (someone other than the buyer or seller), the risk of loss rules are slightly different. The time when the risk of loss passes is again dependent on the contract terms. If there is a negotiable instrument (see Chapter 51) involved in the sale, the risk of loss passes to the buyer who is given the negotiable instrument. If there are no negotiable documents, but papers are required to pick up the goods, the risk of loss passes when the buyer has those papers. If there is no paperwork, then the risk of loss passes when the third party acknowledges the buyer's interest in the goods and allows the buyer to pick them up.

Many contracts involve a bill of lading, or a document of title, which is a piece of paper showing who owns the goods. When the buyer receives the bill of lading, the risk of loss passes to the buyer who can then pick up the goods.

Slips: The Exceptions

There are some types of contracts that will not fit under any of the above circumstances. The Code has provided some exceptions to the general rules. The exceptions cover sales on approval, sale or return, and consignments.

Sales on approval **Sales on approval** (Section 2-326) are conditional sales. In these cases, the buyer has the chance to use the goods for a short time before buying them. For example many television offers allow buyers to keep books or recipe cards for ten-day trial periods. The risk of loss rests with the seller until the buyer actually accepts the goods. A buyer accepts the goods by taking any of the following actions:

1. Notifying the seller of acceptance.
2. Keeping the goods longer than the specified trial period.
3. Using the goods instead of sending them back.

Once the buyer has taken any of these actions, the risk of loss has passed. If the buyer does not want the goods, the seller holds the risk of loss during the time that the shipment is returned.

Sale or return A **sale or return** allows a buyer to accept delivery of goods from a seller with the option to return them if they are not wanted. For example, the buyer may be unable to sell the goods at retail level. Marty's Music Store might take thirty pianos on a sale or return basis from Gulbrandsen pianos. If Marty's can sell only twenty of the pianos, the store can return the remaining ten. Risk of loss in a sale or return is the same as risk of loss in a sale. Marty's would have the risk of loss according to the contract delivery terms. If the delivery terms were "FOB Marty's Town," Marty's would have the risk of loss upon tender in the town. Marty's would also have the risk of loss if it returned the goods to Gulbrandsen.

Sale or return goods are subject to the buyer's creditor's claims. The buyer's creditors legally can take sale or return goods as compensation for the buyer's debt. A seller who wishes protection from creditors taking the goods should file an Article IX financing statement (see Chapter 56).

Consignments **Consignments** occur when one person agrees to sell someone else's goods in exchange for a commission or percentage of the sale price. Under the Code (Section 2-326), consignments are treated as sales or returns to protect creditors' rights related to risk of loss. If the party with title wishes to protect its ownership in the goods, there must be a clear indication that there is a consignment arrangement. The business name itself can serve as notice, as in "Judi's Consignment Furniture." Or a sign placed on the goods can indicate that they are on consignment. Figure 29-3 is a summary of Article II rules regarding risk of loss.

KEY TERMS

Identification
Fungible goods
Insurable interest
Titles
Document of title
FOB
FAS
COD
CIF or CF
Risk of loss
Sales on approval
Sale or return
Consignments

Figure 29-3 **Risk of Loss**

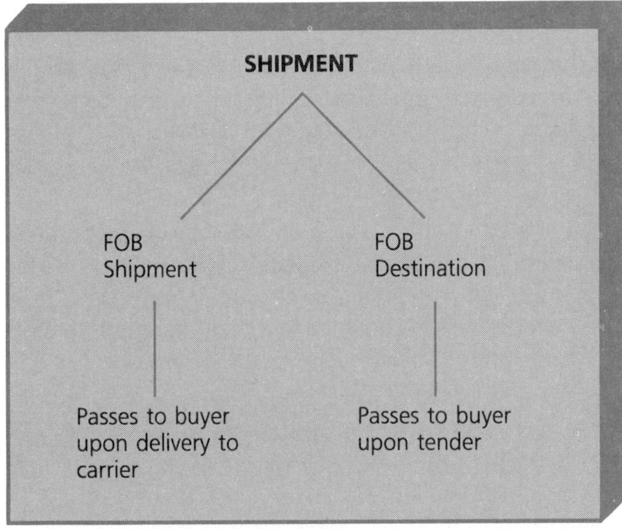

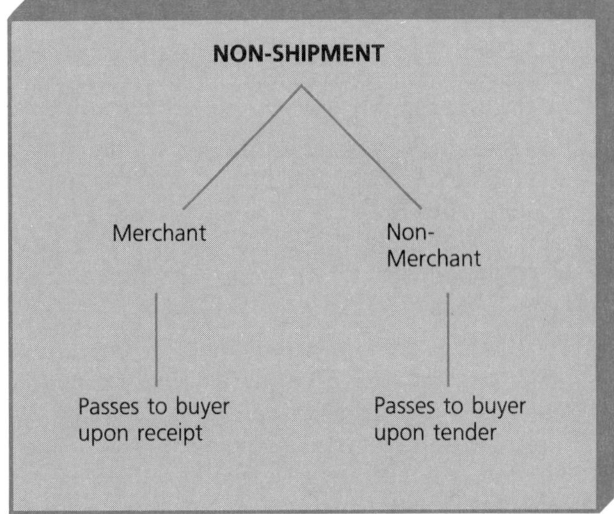

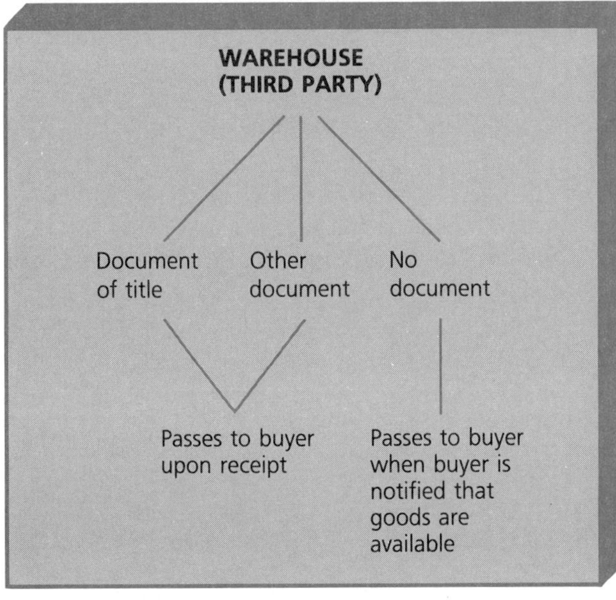

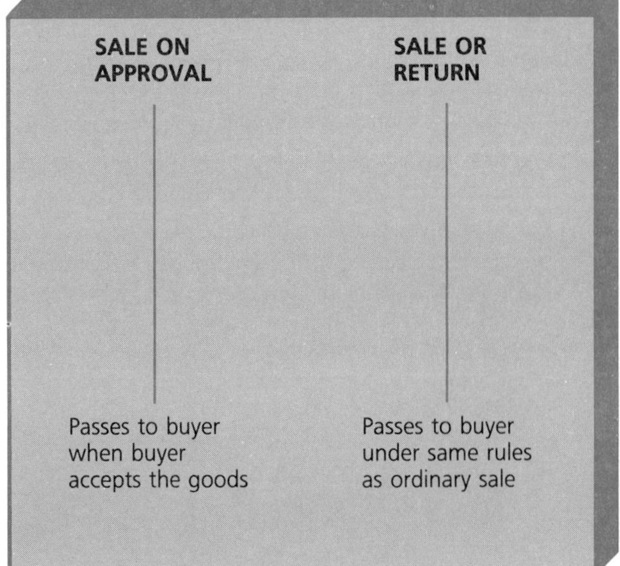

CHAPTER PROBLEMS

1. Helash delivered steel to a United States Air Force Base according to the terms of a contract with the government. The government failed to pay for the steel, and Helash went back to the base and removed the steel. The United States government brought charges against Helash for theft of government property from a military installation. Helash still claimed title to the steel because the Air Force had not paid, insisting that he could not be charged with theft of his own property. What is the result? *Helash v. Ballard,* 638 F.2d 74 (9th Cir. 1980).

2. Jones purchased a fifty-foot yacht. There was no document of title and no delivery; Jones was to pick up

the boat. After the contract was signed, but before Jones picked up the boat, a seller's creditor repossessed the boat, claiming that title had not yet passed to Jones. Jones wants his boat. What is the result? *Jones v. One Fifty-Foot Gulfstar Motor Sailing Yacht,* 625 F.2d 44 (5th Cir. 1980).

3. Petroleum Marketers, Inc., sold oil to the City of Richmond. The City of Richmond was to pick up the oil by sending trucks to a third-party storage tank. An issue of title arose. When does title pass to the city of Richmond? *City of Richmond v. Petroleum Marketers, Inc.,* 269 S.E.2d 389 (Va. 1980).

*4. The Littles entered into an agreement to buy a modular home, which Grizzly Manufacturing of Hamilton, Montana, would manufacture. The house would be constructed in two sections, shipped to the Little's homesite in Butte, Montana, and placed on a foundation there. The units were delivered but were installed improperly. The walls cracked, the windows broke, and the floor tiles were broken. The roof leaked and a bad rain damaged the interior. The price for the house was $38,004, and the Littles refused to pay. Grizzly demanded payment on the grounds that the risk of loss had passed. Who wins? *Little v. Grizzly Manufacturing,* 636 P.2d 839 (Mont. 1981).

5. A cattle auction house sells cattle for owners. The cattle are not present at the auction. In some cases, portions of the owners' herds are sold. When does identification occur? *Ross Cattle Co. v. Lewis,* 415 So.2d 1030 (Miss. 1982).

6. Pullman manufactured 754 subway cars for the city of New York. It tested ten of the cars for final on-line functions and then made them available for the city to pick up. Has title passed? Has the risk of loss passed? *City of New York v. Pullman, Inc.,* 662 F.2d 910 (2nd Cir. 1981).

7. Pillsbury bought 5000 bushels of wheat from Brownsville Grain Company. Pillsbury was to pick up the wheat from Reeves, the farmer holding the wheat. Determine when risk of loss and title would pass in these circumstances. *Reeves v. Pillsbury Co.,* 625 P.2d 440 (Kan. 1981).

8. Ault's contract for the purchase of computers provided for shipment "FOB point of origin." Ault had financial problems, and the goods were taken by an inventory creditor after they arrived. The seller claimed title had not yet passed to Ault. What is the result? *In re Ault,* 6 B.R. 58 (E.D. Tenn. 1981).

9. In a CIF contract, who has the risk of loss during shipment?

10. Xavier Company ran a yacht-repair business. Xavier sold a yacht that had been left for repair. The owner wants the boat back from the buyer. Who has title? *Chartered Bank of London v. Chrysler Corp.,* 171 Cal.Rptr. 748 (1981).

"... fish chowder, as it is served and enjoyed by New Englanders, is a hearty dish, originally designed to satisfy the appetites of our seamen and fishermen. This court knows that we are not talking of some insipid broth as is customarily served to convalescents. No chef should be forced to reduce the pieces of fish in the chowder to miniscule size in an effort to ascertain whether they contained any pieces of bone.

From the brief for the Blue Ship Tea Room in *Webster v. Blue Ship Tea Room*, 198 N.E.2d 309 (Mass. 1964)

CHAPTER PREVIEW

- Theories of product liability: Contract, tort, and strict liability
- Types of warranties under Article II: Express warranty, warranty of title, implied warranty of merchantability, and implied warranty of fitness for a particular purpose
- Warranty disclaimers
- Elements of product or strict tort liability
- Product liability defenses
- Privity requirements in product liability theories
- The Magnuson-Moss Act

Chapter 30

Warranties and Product Liability

Hochberg ordered a vodka martini at O'Donnell's Restaurant in Bethesda, Maryland. While drinking the martini, Hochberg removed the olive and saw that it had a hole cut in it. He placed the olive in his mouth, bit down and then exclaimed that he had broken a tooth on an olive pit. The restaurant manager was shown the olive, the pit, and the part of the tooth. Hochberg sued for his broken tooth.

Everyone has heard of an exploding soda bottle or a dead mouse in a mayonnaise jar. These peculiar experiences are part of product liability law. When products don't operate, malfunction, or contain a foreign substance, they fall short of the seller's or manufacturer's promises. The buyer of these defective products wants to recover.

There are two general branches of product liability: tort and contract. Torts are violations of civil duties. Contract duties come from voluntary agreements. This chapter covers both tort and contract theories, which victims can use to recover for defective products. Figure 30-1 is a summary of the theories of product liability.

UCC/CONTRACT LIABILITY

Sales contracts can contain three types of product warranties: express warranties, the implied warranties of merchantability, and implied warranties of fitness. If a product does not fulfill the promises provided through these warranties, there is a breach of contract. The following subsections discuss these warranties.

Breach of Express Warranties

There are three ways to create express warranties: through language (affirmation of fact), description, or sample or model.

Express warranties by language (affirmation of fact) An **express warranty** is created when sellers use language about goods that buyers rely on to make purchasing decisions. An express warranty can be a statement of fact or a promise about product performance.

The same types of statements used in misrepresentation and fraud cases (see Chapter 20) will satisfy express warranty requirements. The statement must be more than sales puff, or opinion, to be an express warranty. For example, the statement that "This car is the finest car on the road today" is sales puffery. But the remark, "This car has the fastest acceleration rate of any car on the road today" is a statement of fact and, therefore, an express warranty.

A promise concerning product performance is also an express warranty. For example, the statement that "This makeup will not stain clothing" is an express warranty. The statement that "This makeup will make you look better" is an opinion and, therefore, not an express warranty.

Figure 30-1 **Theories of Product Liability**

CONTRACT	TORT
Express warranty	Negligence
Implied warranty of merchantability	Strict tort liability
Implied warranty of fitness	

Express warranty by description A description of a product in a catalogue or ad is a warranty. "These goods are 100% Scottish wool" is a description that is an express warranty. Although the seller may not have intended the description to be a warranty, the description will still be a warranty if the buyer relies on the description. The seller does not have to use words such as "promise," "guarantee," or "warranty" for an express warranty to be created.

Express warranty by sample or model If a seller puts a picture of a product in an ad or displays a sample in the store, that picture or sample will be an express warranty. In addition, some clothing manufacturers send swatches of materials as samples to their buyers; the clothing finally sent to the buyer must be made of the same quality as the swatches.

Recovery for breach of express warranties A buyer can recover for breach of express warranty if the product does not perform as promised. However, the promise of performance, product sample, or description must have been a "basis of the bargain." In other words, the buyer must have given the warranty some importance. For example, selling a water filter and promising that it will remove iron and manganese from water is an express warranty. If the filter does not remove those metals, the buyer involved can recover for breach. The *Lane v. C.A. Swanson and Sons* case is one of the first to deal with the issue of express warranty.

LANE v. C.A. SWANSON AND SONS

Supreme Court of California.
278 P.2d 723 (1955).

FACTS Lane bought a can of Swanson boned chicken from C.A. Swanson Food Company. The words, "boned chicken" were printed in bold on the can label. Swanson had run full-page ads in the *Los Angeles Times* promoting this product. The ads described the product as having "no bones" and "all white and dark meat." Lane broke his tooth on a bone while eating the chicken from the can and sued for breach of express warranty.

ISSUE Did Swanson make an express warranty that the chicken was boned?

DECISION Yes. Swanson claimed that the term "boned chicken" was not intended as a warranty but was just a description of the product's preparation. The ads claimed that the chicken had "no bones," and Lane relied upon them as a buyer. Swanson also claimed that it was impossible to remove all of the bones from a chicken. The court held that Swanson would either have to change their ad claims or improve their processing methods to remove all of the bones.

LEGAL TIP

Since advertisement language can be an express warranty, choose ad language carefully.

Disclaiming express warranties Once an express warranty is given, it is impossible to reclaim or disclaim the statement or promise about product performance by using other language. An express warranty holds for the duration of that warranty.

Breach of Warranty of Title and Infringement

Coverage of the warranty Title means ownership, and the warranty of title is implied. An **implied warranty** exists even when nothing is said about it. The warranty is given in every sale unless the seller specifically disclaims it. The warranty of title implies three promises. First, sellers promise that the title is good. Second, sellers promise that they have the authority to pass that title. Finally, sellers promise that the goods are free of liens and security interests.

The warranty of title also protects against infringement by ensuring that sellers have not "infringed" any copyrights or patents in making or selling the goods. If there were such an infringement, only the seller would be responsible for paying any related expenses.

Disclaimer of the warranty of title The warranty of title can be disclaimed in two ways. First, the seller can disclaim the warranty by including specific language in a written contract stating that there is no warranty. Second, the warranty can be disclaimed by circumstances indicating that there is no warranty. For example, buying goods at a police auction is a clear case where no warranty of title is given.

Breach of the Implied Warranty of Merchantability

The implied warranty of merchantability (Section 2-314) is the most common basis for contract-based product liability suits.

When is the warranty of merchantability given? The **warranty of merchantability** is given in every sale of goods by a merchant, who is someone dealing in the goods involved in a contract (see Chapter 27). For example, this warranty applies to the sale of food and drink in a restaurant.

What are the terms of the warranty of merchantability? When the warranty of merchantability is given, there are several promises made about the goods. The following list summarizes the requirements for merchantability.

1. The goods must meet industry standards.
2. In the case of sales of fungible goods, all of the goods must be of average quality.
3. The goods must be fit to use for ordinary purposes.
4. The goods must be well packaged.
5. The goods must live up to any promises indicated by labeling, packaging, or advertising.

Translated into ordinary terms, these five standards mean that the goods have to work, be adequately packaged, and be of average quality. For example, basketballs must bounce, frozen foods must have leakproof containers, towing chains must be strong, and cigarettes cannot contain foreign items such as toenails. Merchantable does not mean the goods are perfect—only that they are of average quality. The *Cardozo v. True* case involves an interesting issue of merchantability.

Can the warranty of merchantability be disclaimed? The warranty of merchantability can be disclaimed in two different ways. First, the seller can disclaim the warranty by stating that there is no warranty of merchantability; the disclaimer must use the word "merchantability." Second, the seller can disclaim the warranty of merchantability and other implied product warranties by using general **disclaimers** such as "as is," "with all faults," "as they stand," or "there are no warranties associated with the sale of this product." If the disclaimers are written,

CARDOZO v. TRUE

Court of Appeals, Second District.
342 So.2d 1053 (1977).

FACTS Ingrid Cardozo bought a cookbook for tropical fruits and vegetables called *Tradewinds Cookery.* Mrs. Cardozo purchased the recipe book, written by Norma True, from Ellie's Book and Stationery, Inc., retail bookstore in Sarasota, Florida.

Mrs. Cardozo was following a recipe for cooking a dasheen plant, commonly known as "elephant ears." While preparing the roots for cooking, she ate a small slice. Mrs. Cardozo became ill immediately and had to be hospitalized. Mrs. Cardozo sued Mrs. True and the bookstore for failure to adequately test the recipes in the book.

ISSUE Did the book's lack of recipe testing breach the implied warranty of merchantability?

DECISION Yes. True was liable to Mrs. Cardozo for the inadequate testing of the recipes and the failure to warn about plant uses during cooking.

LEGAL TIP

Authors are responsible for accurate content in their books.

they must be written in a different color or bold print so that the disclaimer can be seen easily by the buyer.

The Implied Warranty of Fitness for a Particular Purpose

When the fitness warranty is given The warranty of merchantability is given in all sales by merchants. The **warranty of fitness for a particular purpose** is given only when the merchant makes a particular promise (Section 2-315). In addition to making a particular promise, the following requirements must be met to satisfy this special warranty.

1. The seller must be knowledgeable about the product.
2. The buyer must lack the knowledge and skill necessary to make a wise buying decision.
3. The buyer must rely on the seller's knowledge and experience to make the buying decision.
4. The seller must know that the buyer is relying on the experience and knowledge offered.

An example of an implied warranty of fitness is given in the following situation. Albert plans to go mountain climbing for the first time and needs the right footwear. He goes to Alpine Outdoors Shop and explains his needs to the store owner. The storeowner, who is an experienced mountain climber, recommends a particular pair of boots. The recommended boots cause Albert to slip and fall during his climb, and he is injured. The Alpine Shop made a warranty that the boots would work for Albert's purposes. Since the boots were not suitable, Alpine made and breached the implied warranty of fitness for a particular purpose.

Can the implied warranty of fitness be disclaimed? The warranty of fitness can be disclaimed by the statement, "There is no implied warranty of fitness," which must be in writing. The warranty of fitness can also be disclaimed by the general phrases used to disclaim the warranty of merchantability (see page 364). Figure 30-2 is a summary of Article II warranties.

The *Daniell v. Ford Motor Co., Inc.* case involves several warranty issues.

DANIELL v. FORD MOTOR CO., INC.

United States District Court, Central District of New Mexico.
38 UCC Rep. 464 (1984).

FACTS In 1980, Daniell became locked inside the trunk of her 1973 Ford LTD auto, where she remained for nine days. She entered the trunk, admittedly, to commit suicide. During the nine days, she suffered physically and mentally and was unable to get out until a friend found her.

She brought suit for her damages. She based her suit on the implied warranty of merchantability—that the trunk was not fit for ordinary purposes; and on breach of express warranty—that the trunk was demonstrated as being easily opened and closed. There was no way to open the trunk from the inside.

ISSUE Had Ford breached any warranty by its failure to put an internal latch on the trunk?

DECISION No. No salesperson or literature ever mentioned being inside the trunk. The demonstrations were limited to using the trunk from the outside. There was no express warranty made. The warranty of merchantability was not breached because trunks need only be suitable for holding luggage, carrying items, and opening and closing from the outside. It was clear that Daniell did not rely on an express warranty since she went into the trunk intending to die.

LEGAL TIP

An express warranty cannot exist unless you use it as part of your buying decision.

Figure 30-2 **Warranties**

TYPE	CREATION	RESTRICTIONS	DISCLAIMER
Express	Affirmation of fact or promise of performance (samples, models, descriptions)	Must be part of the basis of the bargain	Cannot make a disclaimer inconsistent with an express warranty
Implied warranty of merchantability	Given in every sale of goods by a merchant ("fit for ordinary purposes")	Only given by merchants	1. Must use *merchantability* or general disclaimer of *as is* or *with all faults* 2. If written, must use bold print 3. Can be oral
Implied warranty of fitness for a particular purpose	Seller knows of buyer's reliance upon product for a particular use (buyer is ignorant)	Seller must have knowledge Buyer must rely	1. Must be written 2. Must be conspicuous 3. Must use disclaimer *as is* or *with all faults*
Title	Given in every sale	Does not apply in circumstances where apparent warranty is not given	1. Must be written 2. Must say "There is no warranty of title"
Magnuson-Moss Act	Only consumer products of $15 or more	None	Full disclosure in writing

Who Is Protected by Warranties? Warranty Beneficiaries

Most contract rights are given only to the parties with privity. **Privity** of contract means that there is a contract between two parties. For example, a buyer and seller have privity of contract.

However, members of the buyer's family, neighbors, and friends may also use a purchased product. Can they recover for breach of the express warranty of secure seat belts (since they are not in privity with the seller or manufacturer)?

Section 2-318 of the UCC governs who recovers for breach of warranty. There are three different versions of Section 2-318, with varying protections, which states can adopt.

Version A—the most frequently adopted version—extends the seller's warranty to the buyer, the buyer's family, and any guests of the buyer who might use the product. A toaster is an example of an appliance that could be used by buyers, their families, and their guests.

Version B affords broader protection than A. Version B allows anyone expected to use the product to recover on a warranty theory. For example, a toaster causing personal injury on a camp-out would be covered under version B, and all those along on the camp-out would have warranty protection. Version B applies only to personal injury loss and not property damage.

Version C is the same as B with one addition. The seller is liable to the same persons but is liable for both personal injuries and property damages.

The most important idea of Section 2-318 is that more persons than the buyer can recover for breach of warranty. Figure 30-3 illustrates warranty beneficiaries under Section 2-318.

The *Ontai v. Straub Clinic and Hospital, Inc.* case shows the warranty coverage of the Code.

ONTAI v. STRAUB CLINIC AND HOSPITAL, INC.

Supreme Court of Hawaii.
659 P.2d 734 (1983).

FACTS Frances Ontai went to Straub for an air contrast barium enema examination of the colon. The x-ray room had General Electric (GE) equipment. Ontai was placed on a table that had to be tilted into a near-vertical position. While he was in this position, the footrest on the table gave out, and he fell to the floor and was injured. He sued Straub and GE for breach of warranty for a particular purpose.

ISSUE Could Ontai recover from GE?

DECISION Yes. The Code protects patients injured on defective equipment since they are the reason for buying the equipment. GE knew who would be using the table and how it would be used.

LEGAL TIP
Test business equipment with weights before using it directly for customers.

NEGLIGENCE AND PRODUCT LIABILITY

Negligence is a second theory for recovery for a defective product. To recover in negligence for a defective product, a party must prove all the elements of negligence discussed in Chapter 5.

Figure 30-3 **Warranty Beneficiaries Under Article II (Section 2-318)**

VERSION	SELLER LIABLE TO	LIABLE FOR
A	Buyer, buyer's family, and guests	Personal injury
B	Buyer, buyer's family, and anyone expected to use product	Personal injury
C	Buyer, buyer's family, and anyone expected to use product	Personal and property injury

The duty and breach of duty elements require plaintiffs to prove that the manufacturers or sellers of a product failed to meet their obligation to make a safe product. For example, if a car's gasoline tank explodes but would not do so if an inexpensive design change was made, the car's manufacturer has been negligent.

STRICT LIABILITY IN TORT

The newest of the theories of product liability is called **strict liability in tort.** Nearly all states have adopted this theory, which can be found in **Section 402A of the Restatement Second of Torts.**

Who Is Liable Under Strict Liability?

Section 402A applies to manufacturers and vendors of products. To be liable in strict liability, the party must be in the business of dealing with the product involved.

Because Section 402A is based in tort, and not in contract, the requirements of privity do not apply. Any party using the defective product has the right to sue for strict liability.

Most courts have held that liability under Section 402A cannot be disclaimed by contract. For example, a clause in a contract providing for no tort liability would not be allowed by most courts.

What Must Be Wrong with the Product?

For a plaintiff to recover under Section 402A, the product must be in a "defective condition unreasonably dangerous." A product can be in a defective condition that is unreasonably dangerous in several different ways. These types of defects are discussed below.

Production or handling defects Sometimes, manufacturers make mistakes on the production line. These mistakes result in a dangerous product. The danger does not come from the design or nature of the product but from a deviation from standard production procedures. For example, a burr in a can of peas is the result of a production defect. A steering wheel on a car that comes loose because a bolt was not properly tightened or inspected is another production mistake.

Defects in product design Under this element, the products are properly manufactured but the design of the product is defective and dangerous. For example, a tractor may be properly assembled; but if the step for mounting and dismounting the machine is located in a place not visible to the driver, there is a design defect. The *Kennedy v. Custom Ice Equipment Co., Inc.* case involves a defective design issue.

KENNEDY v. CUSTOM ICE EQUIPMENT CO., INC.

Supreme Court of South Carolina.
246 S.E.2d 176 (1978).

FACTS Custom Ice designed and installed ice manufacturing equipment. They had manufactured and installed a system at Georgetown Ice Company where Odell Kennedy, 15 years old, was employed.

In the system, ice becomes frozen in the overhead bins in which it is carried. When this freezing occurs, employees are required to climb along a catwalk and push the ice through the bins. The constantly moving conveyor belt is uncovered and located next to the catwalk and bins.

Kennedy was on the catwalk trying to dislodge the ice from the bins when his arm was caught in the conveyor. His left arm was severed, and he had disfiguring scars on his left shoulder. He brought suit against Custom under Section 402A and won a verdict of $208,000. Custom appealed.

ISSUE Was the open conveyor a defective design condition in the ice machinery?

DECISION Yes. Custom could have covered the conveyor to prevent these accidents. Custom was aware of the problem of ice sticking and designed the catwalk to allow removal. The design of the product was unreasonably dangerous.

LEGAL TIP

Employees should not work around open machinery while it is running. Machinery should be covered so that arms and other objects are not caught in motors.

Failure to give proper instructions or warnings A product can be defective because the manufacturer does not explain how it works or give enough information about its dangers. Under Section 402A, sellers are required to give sufficient warnings and instructions "in order to prevent the product from being unreasonably dangerous." For example, the manufacturer of a strong cleaner is required to give instructions on how to mix the product. Lawnmower manufacturers are required to give warnings about keeping hands and feet away from moving mower blades. The *Midgley v. S.S. Kresge Co.* case examines the issue of giving adequate directions.

MIDGLEY v. S.S. KRESGE CO.

Court of Appeals, Third District.
127 Calif. Rptr. 217 (1976).

FACTS Midgley, 13 years old, bought a refracting telescope for sunviewing from S.S. Kresge. A warning on the package stated that the sun should be viewed only with the sun filter on the telescope.

The instructions did not explain how to put on the filter. Midgley put the filter on in such a way that sunlight leaked through and permanently damaged Midgley's eyesight.

ISSUE Were the instructions for the telescope enough?

DECISION No. The instructions gave a warning to use the filter but did not explain adequately how to install the filter. Midgley recovered.

LEGAL TIP

Product instructions sometimes require illustrations along with warnings and instructions.

Defenses to Strict Liability

Although the term "strict liability" seems to mean that a manufacturer is liable no matter what has happened, some defenses do exist. These defenses are discussed in the next three subsections.

When the plaintiff acts foolishly: Misuse Many times an accident with a product occurs because a plaintiff has done something with a product that was beyond the product's intended use. For example, using a lawnmower to trim hedges would be misuse. A plaintiff's **misuse** of a product is a defense to strict liability for the manufacturer/vendor.

In some cases of misuse, the manufacturer will still be liable in strict liability if it can be shown that the misuse was foreseeable. If a manufacturer is aware of a common misuse of its product and does not provide a warning, the manufacturer will be liable.

When the plaintiff changes the product: Alteration For a manufacturer to be liable in strict liability, the product must reach the plaintiff "without substantial change in the condition in which it is sold." An example showing substantial changes is a car that has been redesigned and had body changes. An accident in the altered car would probably not result in liability of the manufacturer.

When the plaintiff makes a mistake: Comparative negligence About two-thirds of the states allow **comparative negligence** as a defense to strict liability. These states view strict liability as a form of negligence per se. This view allows the defendant to introduce evidence of the plaintiff's fault in the injuries. For example, a car may have a defective design that makes it extremely dangerous in a crash. But a plaintiff not wearing a seat belt in that car has contributed to the resulting injuries.

LEGISLATION ON WARRANTIES AND PRODUCT LIABILITY

In addition to the UCC negligence and Restatement product liability protections, there are some legislative protections against defective products.

In 1974, Congress passed the Magnuson-Moss or Federal Consumer Product Warranty Act. The Act was passed because of many problems in consumer product warranties. First, many of the warranties were unclear or extremely limited. Second, many products did not disclose the full warranty terms. Third, many buyers waived warranty protection by not filling out and mailing in warranty registration cards. To eliminate these problems, the act deals with three things: pre-sale disclosures, warranty disclaimers, and warranty enforcement.

Pre-sale disclosures The Magnuson-Moss Act requires sellers to "conspicuously disclose" the provisions of the warranty in language that is easily understood. The warranty must also be labeled as "full" or "limited." The Federal Trade Commission (FTC), which is charged with the responsibility of enforcing the Act, has defined "full" and "limited" warranties. Sellers must meet the FTC standards to be able to label their warranties "full."

Disclaimers This Act overrides much of the UCC on consumer products. If a seller has a written warranty, that warranty cannot disclaim any of the implied warranties of the UCC. This section of the act was included because many written warranties were being given but were very limited; at the same time, these written warranties took away the valuable, or broader, implied warranties.

Warranty enforcement This federal legislation also requires sellers to develop methods for settling consumer warranty disputes. Companies are to set up independent boards or staffs that will arbitrate and attempt to settle warranty problems with consumers. This portion of the act was passed to make it easier for consumers to pursue their rights. The goal is to eliminate the need for court suits concerning problems with small products.

KEY TERMS

Express warranty
Implied warranty
Warranty of merchantability
Disclaimers
Warranty of fitness for a particular purpose
Privity
Negligence
Strict liability in tort
Section 402A of the Restatement Second of Torts
Misuse
Comparative negligence

CHAPTER PROBLEMS

1. List the theories of recovery for product liability and classify them as contract or tort theories.

2. Coeffer purchased a jar of Standard Brands' "Mixed Shelled Nuts." The jar was glass, and the word "shelled" was in prominent print, which was the same size as the words "mixed" and "nuts." When eating nuts from the jar, Coffer bit something hard, and his tooth broke. He later discovered that he had broken his tooth on the shell of an unshelled nut. Coffer brought suit against Standard Brands for breach of express warranty and strict liability. What is the result? *Coffer v. Standard Brands, Inc.,* 226 S.E.2d 534 (N.C. 1976).

*3. Green, a chain-smoker, contracted lung cancer and brought suit against the American Tobacco Company for manufacturing inherently dangerous products that were "unfit and unwholesome for human use." Should Green recover? *Green v. American Tobacco Co.,* 409 F.2d 1166 (5th Cir. 1969).

*4. Federal Pacific Electric Company manufactured electrical switches and the panels for those switches. Federal Pacific warranted that the door to panels containing the switches would not open unless the switch was in the "off" position with all current stopped. Huebert, a repairman, received a severe electrical shock when a panel door opened without all the current stopped. The company's interlock device had been bypassed by lightning damage. Can Huebert recover for his injuries? What are the theories? *Huebert v. Federal Pacific Electric Co., Inc.,* 494 P.2d 1210 (Kan. 1972).

5. Mrs. McCabe bought a coffee maker in a sealed carton from L.K. Liggett Drug Company. When she was making coffee (according to the product's instructions), the coffee maker blew up in her face and caused severe injuries and permanent disfigurement. Mrs. McCabe brought suit and several expert witnesses testified that the explosion occurred because "the area of the notches of the filter was inadequate to provide for the release of the pressure which developed from the boiling water." Should Mrs. McCabe recover? What theory is best? *McCabe v. L.K. Liggett Drug Co.,* 112 N.E.2d 254 (Mass. 1954).

*6. Mrs. D'Arienzo had purchased and used Clairol's hair color product for a period of two years. On every package of the hair color product was this warning, "Before you color, make these two easy tests." Instructions for the testing of skin, hair, and scalp sensitivity were given. After two years of use, Mrs. D'Arienzo applied the product and developed a rash on her face and skin, and her hair fell out. She brought suit against Clairol. She admitted that she did not perform the tests but didn't think she had to after two years of use. Clairol admitted that sensitivities to the product can develop over time. Clairol maintained that their warning was adequate. What is the result? *D'Arienzo v. Clairol, Inc.,* 310 A.2d 106 (N.J. 1973).

7. Mr. Drayton used Jiffee drain cleaner to unclog a bathroom sink. After pouring one-half of a bottle into the drain, he placed the uncapped bottle on the back of the sink and left it in the bathroom along with his preschool-age daughter. Almost immediately he heard screaming and returned to the bathroom to find that his daughter had poured the cleaner all over her and had severe burns.

   Drayton filed suit against Jiffee for strict liability in tort. Jiffee's defense is misuse, claiming that Drayton failed to supervise his daughter. What is the result? *Drayton v. Jiffee Chemical Corporation,* 395 F.Supp. 1081 (N.D. Ohio 1975).

8. California Chemical Company manufactured a product called Triox. Triox was a liquid weed killer sold to consumers for garden use. The warnings on the product told users to avoid breathing the product, avoid contact with eyes, skin or clothing, and to wash after using the product. The warning also said that livestock grazing in treated areas would be poisoned.

   Mrs. Boyl purchased Triox and sprayed her driveway with it. She rinsed out her spray tank applicator and poured out the rinse water in a rough area of grass in her backyard.

   Five days later Mrs. Boyl sunbathed (scantily dressed) in that backyard area. She absorbed Triox into her skin, was hospitalized for three days, and required medical treatment for eighteen months. Mrs. Boyl sued California Chemical for lack of adequate warnings about Triox. What is the result? *Boyl v. California Chemical Co.,* 221 F.Supp. 669 (D. Or. 1963).

9. Vizzini was injured in an accident while driving a Ford automobile. Vizzini has brought suit against Ford in strict liability. Ford's defense is that Vizzini was not wearing a seat belt and his own negligence caused his injuries. What is the result? *Vizzini v. Ford Motor Co.,* 569 F.2d 754 (3rd Cir. 1977).

10. An employee of Cartel Capital Corporation negligently started a fire. Cartel had Fireco extinguishers on its premises. The Fireco extinguishers failed to work. The fire was more damaging than it would have been if the extinguishers had worked. Cartel has sued Fireco for strict liability in tort. What is the result? *Cartel Capital Corporation v. Fireco,* 410 A.2d 674 (N.J. 1980).

"You want it when? ? ?"
Anonymous

CHAPTER PREVIEW

- Buyer's right of inspection
- Time for payment
- Time for rejection
- How to reject
- When acceptance takes place
- Requirements for revocation of acceptance
- What to do with rejected goods
- Demanding assurances
- Anticipatory repudiation
- Commercial impracticability

Chapter 31

Obligations and Performance

Ralph had ordered his usual shipment of Christmas trees for holiday sales, which began around December 1. His seller/supplier sent him the wrong type of trees on November 30. Ralph has four more shipments coming from the same buyer. Ralph has become nervous and wants to buy all the trees from someone else. Can he purchase the trees elsewhere?

Now we assume that the buyer and seller have a contract, but the contract has not yet been performed. Performance occurs when the seller transfers title to the goods, and the buyer pays for them. Performance seems simple enough. But even if the parties have a well-drafted contract, many questions about performance still exist. When does the buyer have to pay? Can the buyer look at the goods before paying? What if a shipment is all wrong? What happens if a seller cannot perform? This chapter answers these questions about performance.

THE OVERALL PERFORMANCE CONTROL: GOOD FAITH

All performances regulated by Article II contracts have one general idea—good faith. Parties involved in these contracts must perform in good faith (Section 1-203). To act in good faith, the parties cannot agree to disregard the obligation.

"Good faith" requires the parties to cooperate with each other. This means not looking for loopholes out of the contract but instead trying to make the contract work. Good faith requires flexibility and commercial courtesy. If performance cannot be worked out, the parties are required to give each other notice of problems and cancellation.

WHAT THE SELLER MUST DO: SELLER'S PERFORMANCE OBLIGATIONS

The seller's basic responsibility is to get the goods to the buyer. This responsibility means delivering the right goods in the right condition at the right time.

Delivering the Right Goods

If the contract is a delivery contract, the seller is required to find a shipper or carrier for the goods (Section 2-504). The carrier chosen by the seller must be a responsible one. Also, the carrier must have the right shipping equipment. For example, if the seller is shipping produce, the seller must choose a refrigerated carrier.

The seller must also notify the buyer of the shipment—when the shipment was made, who the shipper is, and whether the buyer will need to complete any paperwork (a bill of lading, for example) to get the goods from the carrier.

Delivering the Goods at the Right Time

If the contract has a performance date, the seller must deliver at that time. If the contract has no performance date, then the seller must perform within a "reasonable" time (Section 2-309). The definition of "reasonable" depends on the contract circumstances. For example, Christmas trees must be delivered before Christmas. Winter clothing must be delivered to a department store before winter begins. Ice cream for a charity picnic must arrive in time for the picnic.

Delivering the Goods in the Right Condition

The goods must arrive in good condition. The buyer is not required to accept goods that have been damaged by the carrier or goods that don't live up to the seller's warranties. If the seller has made an express warranty that the delivered fabric will not shrink and the buyer's tests show that the material does shrink, the buyer need not take the goods.

If the goods delivered are not in the right condition and the performance date on the contract has not passed, the seller has the right to correct the problems (Section 2-508). This right is called the **right of cure.** As an example of this right, suppose that a seller was required to deliver no-shrink fabric to a buyer by May 1, 1985. The fabric is delivered on April 20, 1985, and the buyer finds that the fabric does shrink. The seller has until May 1 to find a no-shrink fabric. The *Ramirez v. Autosport* case examines the seller's right of cure.

RAMIREZ v. AUTOSPORT

Supreme Court of New Jersey.
440 A.2d 1345 (1982).

FACTS The Ramirezes purchased a van from Autosport on July 20 for $14,100. The van arrived on August 3 with some damage to the exterior. Autosport promised to fix it. When the Ramirezes went to pick up the van on August 14, the windows had been left open, the upholstery was damaged, the hubcaps were missing, and there were no sewer or water hook-ups. The Ramirez family cancelled the contract. Autosport claimed that they could not cancel, and a suit resulted.

ISSUE Can a contract be cancelled if a seller fails to cure defects within the time allowed?

DECISION Yes. The van did not conform in all respects and the seller was given the opportunity to cure. the cure was not timely, and the contract could be cancelled.

LEGAL TIP

Before a seller delivers goods, indicate a time limit for making corrections. Sellers should make corrections within the allowed contract time.

WHAT THE BUYER DOES: THE BUYER'S PERFORMANCE OBLIGATIONS

The buyer is required to pay for the goods. But the buyer will not want to pay unless the goods are in proper condition. The buyer is given the opportunity to check the seller's performance.

Checking on the Seller: Inspection

Unless the parties provide otherwise, every buyer has the right to inspect contract goods before accepting them (Section 2-513). The **inspection** gives the buyer a chance to find out if the goods are the ones ordered.

When does the inspection take place? The buyer has the right to inspect the goods before making payment. One exception to this rule is cash-on-delivery (COD) contracts. Under COD contracts, the buyer pays first and can then inspect. Payment under COD contracts does not mean that the buyer accepts the goods.

The time for inspection is when the goods are tendered or delivered to the buyer. If a buyer is picking up the goods from a carrier, the buyer has the right to inspect the goods when the pick-up is made. If the goods are delivered directly to the buyer, the buyer can inspect them upon arrival.

Where does the inspection take place? If the goods are to be delivered to the buyer, inspection takes place at the buyer's place of business or residence. If the goods are to be picked up by the buyer from a carrier, the inspection occurs at the carrier's place of business. For example, a buyer picking up goods from a railroad would inspect them at the station. If the buyer picks up the goods from the seller or a seller's agent (warehouse), the buyer can inspect them at the seller's place of business or at the warehouse. Finally, the parties can agree to a place of inspection in their contract.

How does the buyer inspect? Inspection is the buyer's way of checking the goods. The buyer can do a number of things to inspect the goods such as opening cartons, boxes, or packages. In the case of large shipments, the buyer can open sample boxes. In single-package deliveries, the buyer can open the package and check the goods.

Second, in certain circumstances, the buyer can test the goods to make sure that they comply with his or her order. In the fabric example, the buyer can test for shrinkage. In the chemicals example, the buyer can test the chemicals. The buyer simply can remove samples of the goods from the carrier or seller and take them to a lab for testing. If the buyer is testing samples, the goods remain with the carrier or seller until the tests are complete. The *Neumiller Farms, Inc. v. Cornett* case deals with a buyer's testing method during inspection.

NEUMILLER FARMS, INC. v. CORNETT

Supreme Court of Alabama.
368 So.2d 272 (1979).

FACTS Cornett ordered twelve loads ($17,500) of chipping potatoes (for potato chips) from Neumiller. When the potatoes were delivered, several of Cornett's chefs began chipping sample potatoes from the shipment. The chefs reported that the potatoes did not chip properly, and the shipment was rejected. Neumiller claimed that the chefs could not inspect in this way.

ISSUE Could Cornett take some samples to chip as part of its inspection?

DECISION Yes. There would be no other way to tell if the potatoes would meet their needs.

LEGAL TIP

Provide for the exact standards and procedures for inspection in the contract so the parties are not surprised.

The buyer must pay for the testing and any other inspection costs. However, if the seller has not sent the right goods and has breached the contract, the buyer can recover the cost of inspection as damages.

What if the Goods Are Wrong or Defective: Rejection

If the buyer's inspection shows that the goods are wrong or have defects, the buyer has the right to reject the goods (Section 2-601).

When can the buyer reject? The standards for **rejection** depend upon whether the contract is a single-delivery contract or an installment delivery contract. In a single-delivery contract, the buyer has the right of rejection if the goods have any defects. (Section 2-601). For example, if a buyer ordered a rocking horse and it arrives without the legs, the buyer can reject the horse. Likewise, if the horse were missing a bow from its neck, the buyer could reject.

Under installment contracts, the standard is slightly different (Section 2-612). An installment contract is one in which the goods will be delivered piecemeal, or in groups. Because more goods are always on the way, the standard for rejection in installment contracts is higher. To reject one installment, the buyer must be able to show the following:

1. The problem with the goods greatly affects the value of the goods.
2. The seller has not promised to correct the defect or remedy the problem.

For example, suppose Bertha ordered napkins for her restaurant that were supposed to be delivered on a weekly basis for one year. After inspection, the first week's installment shows that the napkins have Bertha's name spelled incorrectly; in addition, the trademark on the napkins is one from another restaurant. The misspelled name and incorrect trademark greatly affect the value of the goods. If the seller promises to send double the amount of correctly imprinted napkins next week, then Bertha cannot reject the installment.

In some installment contracts, the delivery of one installment may so greatly affect the value of the installment and contract that the buyer can end the entire contract and not just reject the installment. For example, suppose Azure Airlines has contracted with Harriot's Food Service for Harriot to provide food and drinks for all of Azure's flights. Harriot will service each plane as it arrives at Azure's Cincinnati base. In the first three days of service, Harriot has missed putting food on twenty-three of Azure's thirty flights. In this case, Azure would be justified in cancelling the entire contract. The *McKenzie v. Alla-Ohio Coals, Inc.* case examines the issue of rejection.

McKENZIE v. ALLA-OHIO COALS, INC.

United States Court of Appeals, District Court.
29 UCC Rep. 852 (1979).

FACTS McKenzie, a coal broker, ordered coal from Alla-Ohio Coals and specified that the ash content of the coal was not to exceed 7.5%. The coal was to be used as metallurgical coal, and metallurgical coal must have an ash content no higher than 8%. The delivered coal had an ash content of between 13.5% and 16%. McKenzie refused to take the coal, and Alla-Ohio brought suit.

ISSUE Could McKenzie reject the coal for having too high an ash content?

DECISION Yes. McKenzie had specifically required low-ash coal. The coal did not meet the buyer's needs.

LEGAL TIP

Make sure buyer's specifications are met before goods are shipped.

How the buyer properly rejects goods If the buyer has legitimate grounds for rejection, certain steps must be taken to reject properly. The buyer must notify the seller of rejection within a "seasonable" time. "Seasonable" time varies according to the terms and subject matter of the contract. If the buyer has contracted to buy perishable goods such as vegetables or fruits, then "seasonable" would be immediately after the goods have arrived. If the buyer does not notify the seller, the rejection is ineffective.

The buyer should also give the seller a reason or reasons for the rejection. If the buyer does not explain the problem and the seller could have fixed the defect, the buyer cannot use the reason for rejection in a breach of contract suit by the seller (Section 2-605). For example, suppose Bertha rejected the napkins but did not explain why. If the seller could have printed the correct spelling and trademark on the napkins within three hours, Bertha cannot claim that the seller breached the contract; the seller could have fixed the problem.

The buyer can accept or reject all of the goods, or accept or reject portions of the goods in commercial units. **Commercial units** are usually defined by industry custom, and the reason for rejection in commercial units is convenience. For example, a box of 500 envelopes is a commercial unit for stationery. Returning a box of envelopes is easier than trying to count the number of envelopes returned. Also, with rejection in units, the goods remain in their protective packaging. In the *Abbett v. Thompson* case a complex issue concerning the definition of a commercial unit arose.

ABBETT v. THOMPSON

Court of Appeals of Indiana.
263 N.E.2d 733 (1970).

FACTS Abbett purchased the equipment for an automatic, three-bay car wash from Thompson for $18,950. When the equipment arrived, Abbett discovered that the softeners and heaters in the system were defective. He removed these parts and returned them. Thompson claimed that the system was a commercial unit and that the whole system had to be returned. This suit was a result of Abbett's rejection.

ISSUE Were the parts commercial units or was the whole system a commercial unit?

DECISION Since the whole system was a commercial unit, Abbett could reject only the full system and not just parts.

LEGAL TIP

Since systems, though made up of many parts, are generally considered one commercial unit, the whole system must be rejected.

What does the buyer do with rejected goods? Once the buyer has rejected the goods, the buyer must hold the goods for a reasonable time to allow the seller to pick them up (Section 2-602). If the seller fails to give instructions to the buyer (within a reasonable time) on what to do with the goods, the buyer has three options. First, the buyer can store the goods, and the seller will be required to pay the cost of storage. Second, the buyer can ship the goods back to the seller, with the latter paying the cost of shipment. Third, the buyer can resell the goods for the seller. Any of these actions is proper and does not result in acceptance on the buyer's part (Section 2-604).

Merchant buyers have special obligations for rejected goods. They, too, are required to follow the seller's instructions. If the seller fails to give instructions and the goods are perishable or could lose their value quickly, the buyer is required to resell the goods. The buyer can resell only if the seller does not have an agent or place of business in the buyer's area (Section 2-603). For example, a buyer holding a carload of lettuce could resell if the seller did not provide directions, and the seller did not have a business in the buyer's town.

"I'll Take It": The Buyer's Acceptance

Acceptance means that the buyer will take the goods and pay for them. The statement, "I'll take it" indicates the buyer's acceptance. The issues in acceptance are: When is there acceptance? and What is the effect of acceptance?

When acceptance occurs Acceptance can be express or implied. Express acceptance occurs when the buyer notifies the seller (orally or in writing) that the goods are acceptable. Implied acceptance arises through the buyer's actions. For example, if the buyer fails to reject the goods after a reasonable time, the buyer is deemed to have accepted them. If the buyer rejects the goods, but then uses them anyway, the buyer actually has accepted them. The buyer does not accept goods by storing or selling them under Sections 2-602 and 2-603 as discussed above.

The effects of acceptance Once a buyer accepts goods, they must be paid for according to contract terms. Of course, the buyer may have some remedies for accepted goods, which are defective or for breach of warranty (see Chapter 32). Once a buyer has accepted goods, the right of rejection ends.

"I changed my mind": Revocation of acceptance A buyer can avoid performance, or payment, for accepted goods by indicating a "change of mind." There are four requirements for **revocation of acceptance** (Section 2-608). First, whatever problem has arisen with the goods must "substantially impair" their value. For example, a leaky roof on a mobile home is a substantial impairment of its value.

Second, the buyer must have accepted the goods without knowing or being able to discover the problem, or believing that the problem would be corrected. In the mobile home example, it would be difficult to find out that a roof on a home leaked until the first rain. Buyers often find a problem and want to reject the goods; but sellers encourage buyers to accept the goods with the stipulation that they will be fixed. If the seller does not fix the goods as promised, then this second requirement for revocation is met.

Third, the buyer must revoke acceptance within a "reasonable time." A reasonable time period will vary according to the goods and the circumstances. For example, a restaurant owner who finds bugs in lettuce being chopped will have to revoke acceptance that same day. A manufacturer who finds bubbles in plastic need not act as quickly.

Finally, the buyer must revoke acceptance before there is any major change in the goods, which does not result from the defect. For example, since the water damage to a mobile home is caused by a defect, the buyers could still revoke acceptance. The *Yates v. Clifford Motors, Inc.* case examines proper revocation of acceptance.

Figure 31-1 summarizes the buyer's rights in performance.

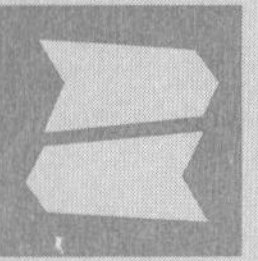

YATES v. CLIFFORD MOTORS, INC.

Superior Court of Pennsylvania.
423 A.2d 1262 (1980).

FACTS Yates purchased a Dodge club-cab truck from Clifford Motors. When Yates got the truck, he discovered many problems with it including windows that would not close, a transmission that would not accelerate above five miles per hour on hills, a radio that fell out, and finally a heater that would not work. Since Clifford Motors assured Yates that they would fix the problems, he continued to drive the truck. After six months, 9000 miles, and unkept promises, Yates took the truck back. Clifford claimed that Yates had kept the truck too long to revoke acceptance. A suit resulted.

ISSUE Could Yates revoke acceptance of the truck after six months and 9000 miles?

DECISION Yes. He kept the truck on the promise that the defects would be fixed. Yates met all the requirements for revocation of acceptance.

LEGAL TIP
Revoke acceptance when promised repairs are not made.

PROBLEMS WITH PERFORMANCE: WILL THE OTHER SIDE COME THROUGH?

Before the buyer and seller get to the points of inspection, rejection, revocation of acceptance, acceptance, and payment, there may be some problems along the way. There are even times when the parties are excused from performance.

"I'm Getting Nervous": The Right to Demand Assurances

When one of the parties appears to be unwilling or unable to perform, the other party has the right to demand assurances (Section 2-609). **Assurance** is evidence that there will be performance such as a written promise, a cash advance, or partial delivery. It would be unfair to force a seller to continue to manufacture special bicycles for a buyer if the buyer cannot pay. The seller would not only risk nonpayment but also losing manufacturing time and other jobs turned down to complete the buyer's work. Likewise, the buyer of the bicycles should not be forced to wait three months for delivery if it is clear the seller cannot finish the bicycles.

In these uncertain circumstances, the buyer or seller could demand assurances. A demand for assurances *must* be in writing, and the demanding party can stop performance until the assurances are given. The party who is given the demand has a reasonable time, which varies according to the contract terms up to 30 days, to give the assurances.

A demand for assurances can just be a request for a promise that the buyer or seller can perform under the contract. In the case of a seller who is nervous about a buyer's payment, the demand for assurances could be money, a promissory note, or full payment. If assurances are not given after there has been a written request and a reasonable time has passed, this failure is treated as a repudiation, or breach, of the contract.

Figure 31-1 **Buyer's Rights Concerning Goods**

BUYER'S RIGHT	WHEN	HOW
Inspection	When goods arrive, before payment (unless COD)	Examination lab tests; samples
Rejection	Single delivery—fail to conform in any respect Installment—substantially impairs value of installment or contract if rejection in full Must reject within reasonable time	Notification Non-use
Acceptance	After inspection	Notification; use; failure to reject in a reasonable time
Revocation of acceptance	After acceptance; must materially impair value and either a non-discoverable defect or a promise of cure	Notification; reshipment or non-use

"I've Changed My Mind": Anticipatory Repudiation

Anticipatory repudiation is a breach of contract before the contract performance date. Anticipatory repudiation occurs when one party indicates clearly by statements or conduct that they will not perform their contract promise (Section 2-610). For example, a seller who closes down his bicycle factory indicates anticipatory repudiation on his bicycle contracts. A buyer who says, "Don't ship the goods, I can't pay," is indicating anticipatory repudiation.

When there is anticipatory repudidation, the non-breaching parties have a couple of choices. First, they can wait for the performance date and hope for performance. Second, they can pursue their remedies for damages immediately. The *Ross Cattle Co. v. Lewis* case examines the combination of assurances and anticipatory repudidation.

"I've Changed My Mind . . . Again": Retraction

Even when a party repudiates an agreement, they may still get back on course (Section 2-611). Any time before performance is due, the repudiator can take back, or retract, the repudiation and reinstate the contract. However, this retraction and **reinstatement** can occur only if the other party has not declared the contract ended and has not pursued remedies or changed his or her position. For example, if the seller of the bicycles reopened the factory before the buyer's bicycles were due, there would be a valid retraction. But if the buyer already has ordered bicycles from another factory, then the retraction is too late.

ROSS CATTLE CO. v. LEWIS

Supreme Court of Mississippi.
415 So.2d 1030 (1982).

FACTS Ross had a contract to sell cattle to Lewis for $47.50 per hundredweight. After the contract was signed, but before delivery of the cattle, Ross heard that Lewis was in poor financial condition, would not be able to pay for the cattle, and planned to take the cattle out of state. Ross refused to deliver the cattle to Lewis and, instead, sold them to a third party. Lewis brought suit. Ross claimed that it made this choice because Lewis had anticipatorily repudiated.

ISSUE Was there anticipatory repudiation on Lewis' part?

DECISION No. Ross should have demanded assurances before taking any action. His failure to deliver and choice to resell were based on rumors and not any actual failure to perform.

LEGAL TIP

Request explanations before pursuing remedies.

"Can I Be Excused?" Failure of Presupposed Conditions

Sometimes the basic assumptions that parties initially make when entering into contracts no longer exist. Section 2-615 allows this change in assumptions to excuse performance if performance is "commercially impracticable." This section is the UCC version of common law impossibility. However, common law impossibility has a higher standard. **Commercial impracticability** is found more easily than common law impossibility. Impossibility requires proof that no one could perform; whereas commercial impracticability requires proof that performing under the contract is commercially impracticable but not impossible. However, this UCC section does *not* excuse parties because of changes in market prices, or market supplies and demands.

Some parties put a "force majeure" clause in their contracts to cover problems such as wars, strikes, and revolutions. The force majeure clause lists the types of acceptable excuses for not performing. The *In re Westinghouse Elec. Corp. Uranium Contracts* case deals with the issue of impracticability.

IN RE WESTINGHOUSE ELEC. CORP. URANIUM CONTRACTS

United States District Court, Eastern District.
517 F.Supp. 440 (1981).

FACTS Westinghouse contracted to supply twenty-two utilities with uranium at prices between $7 and $10 per pound during the late 1960's. By 1973, because of the Arab oil embargo and other energy changes, uranium prices soared to between $45 and $75 a pound—if you could find uranium for sale. Westinghouse sent letters to the utilities saying they would not perform under Section 2-615 of the Code. The utilities brought suit.

ISSUE Did the change in the energy market and the price of uranium excuse Westinghouse's performance?

DECISION No. Price increases alone do not support excused performance under Section 2-615.

LEGAL TIP

Clauses in contracts should cover large price increases in advance.

"Can I Be Excused?" Destruction of the Contract Goods

If the goods are destroyed (without the fault of either party) before the risk of loss has passed from the seller to the buyer, contract performance is excused (Section 2-613). For example, if Paul buys a refrigerator from Sears and will pick it up later in the week, the risk of loss has not yet passed to Paul. If the refrigerator is destroyed in a fire at the store, Paul and Sears are excused from performing on the contract. They could agree to substitute another refrigerator, but their original contract is no longer an obligation.

KEY TERMS

Right of cure
Inspection
Rejection
Commercial units
Acceptance
Revocation of acceptance
Assurance
Anticipatory repudiation
Reinstatement
Commercial impracticability

CHAPTER PROBLEMS

1. T.J. Stevenson & Co. was selling 81,193 bags of flour (100-pound bags) to the Bolivian government. At the time of the contract, both the Bolivian government agents and T.J. Stevenson were in the United States. The agents wanted to defer inspection until the flour reached its destination port of Arica, Chile. T.J. Stevenson said that this inspection was too late. Who is right? *T.J. Stevenson & Co. v. 81,193 Bags of Flour,* 629 F.2d 338 (5th Cir. 1980).
2. Jakowski ordered a Chevrolet from Carole Chevrolet, Inc. The car was to be delivered with a polymer finish and undercoating. When the car arrived, neither of the coatings had been done. Jakowski rejected the car. Carole Chevrolet said the defect was minor, and Jakowski was not entitled to reject. What is the result? *Jakowski v. Carole Chevrolet, Inc.,* 433 A.2d 841 (N.J. 1981).
3. Acme Valve & Fitting ordered a large quantity of valves, fittings, and flanges from Perkins Pipe & Steel. The goods were to be made of steel. When Acme went to pick up their order, they discovered that the items were made of iron and rejected them. Perkins claims that the iron items are just as good. Who wins? *Perkins Pipe & Steel v. Acme Valve & Fitting,* 276 N.E.2d 355 (Ill. 1971).
4. Lynch ordered bags for packaging their candy from Paramount Paper Products. When the bags arrived, most of them were defective. However, there were two boxes of the bags that were fine. Lynch used the two boxes but sent back the remainder. Paramount claims that they can't use some and reject others. Who is right? *Paramount Paper Products v. Lynch,* 128 A.2d 157 (Pa. 1957).
5. Conte purchased a Lincoln from Dwan Lincoln-Mercury. There were problems with the car's engine, and Conte told Dwan he wanted another car. Dwan assured Conte that the problems would be fixed. Fourteen months later, the problems were not fixed and Conte brought the car back. Dwan claimed that it was too late to revoke acceptance. Who is right? *Conte v. Dwan Lincoln-Mercury, Inc.,* 374 A.2d 144 (Conn. 1977).
6. Miron bought a race horse for $32,000 from Yonkers Raceway, Inc. Miron had a vet examine the horse, which seemed fine. The next day the horse was limping and had a swollen leg. Miron sought to reject, but the Raceway claimed that it was too late. What is the result? *Miron v. Yonkers Raceway, Inc.,* 400 F.2d 112 (E.D.N.Y. 1968).
7. Turntables, Inc., was selling a substantial number of turntables to Gestetner for sale in his retail business, called the "The Fifth Avenue Showroom." Gestetner failed to make payment for the first two deliveries of turntables. Turntables, Inc., then discovered from other creditors that Gestetner had a reputation for nonpay-

ment. Turntables, Inc., tried to contact Showroom by telephone and personal visits, but no one was at the place of business. Turntables, Inc., stopped shipping their goods. Gestetner claimed that this action was a breach of contract. Is he right? *Turntables, Inc. v. Gestetner,* 382 N.Y.S.2d 798 (1976).

8. Krouse had a contract to sell Wander Limited 30,000 pounds of Junior Mammoth pecans in June for $1.49 per pound. Krouse notified Wander in November that the pecans would not be available because of a poor growing season. What can Wander do? *Wander Limited v. Krouse,* 368 So.2d 235 (Ga. 1979).

9. Colley contracted to sell 25,000 bushels of wheat to Bi-State, Inc. Because of poor weather conditions, Colley only grew 5000 bushels of wheat. He claimed that he was excused for the remainder of the wheat under Section 2-615. Is he right? *Colley v. Bi-State, Inc.,* 586 P.2d 908 (Utah 1980).

10. Coleman sold soybeans to Jacob Hartz Seed Company. As part of its inspection, Hartz had the Georgia Department of Agriculture test the beans to determine their germination level. The beans tested below the proper level, and Hartz rejected. Coleman objected to the testing. Is he right? *Jacob Hartz Seed Company, Inc. v. Coleman,* 612 S.W.2d 91 (Ga. 1981).

"A pound of that same merchant's flesh is thine. The court awards it, and the law doth give it."

William Shakespeare
The Merchant of Venice
Portia, act IV, scene 1

Chapter 32

Remedies Under Article II

CHAPTER PREVIEW

- Sellers' remedies
- Sellers' right to stop delivery
- Lost profits as damages
- Resale versus market price remedies
- Full contract price as damages
- Recipient of incidental damages
- Buyers' remedies
- Buyers' right to cover
- Specific performance

Howell entered into a contract with Ralston Purina. The terms of the contract required Barry Talbert, Ralston's salesman, to supply all the tonics, disinfectants, and worming medicines that Howell needed to raise his hogs. The hogs were fed only Purina food from October 1 to December 5. At that time, 111 of Howell's 428 pigs became sick and died. Howell changed feeds, and the remaining hogs became healthy and gained weight. Howell has sued Ralston Purina for the lost hogs ($15,000) and for $25,000 in punitive damages. What is the result?

The purpose of the remedies under Article II is to put non-breaching parties in the same positions that they would have been in if the contract had been performed. The remedies are applied liberally. To determine proper remedies, two questions must be answered. The first question is: Who breached? The answer to that question can be found in Chapter 31. The second question is: How can the non-breaching party be compensated? This chapter answers the second question.

SELLERS' REMEDIES

The remedies available to a seller will depend on when the buyer breaches, as well as the type of contract and breach involved. In the following subsections, the remedies are listed along with when they can be used.

Keeping the Goods: Cancellation

When buyers will not perform the contract, the seller can cancel or terminate the contract. When the contract is cancelled, neither party has any obligation to continue performance. The seller can then recover damages. Cancellation works as a remedy when the buyer anticipatorily repudiates, or breaches before the contract is to be performed. Cancellation is also the remedy when a buyer fails to meet a contract obligation on time. For example, if Aldo fails to meet a monthly payment on a contract for the manufacture of a machine, the manufacturer/seller can cancel the contract and stop manufacturing.

Keeping the Goods: Goods in Process and Identification

In some cases, the buyer breaches before the seller has finished manufacturing the goods. Suppose that Sigmund is manufacturing 100 wooden rocking horses for Roy's Toys. Roy's notifies Sigmund that the sale is off when Sigmund has the horses built but unpainted. Under Section 2-704, Sigmund can finish and identify the goods and then seek damages. If Sigmund had only cut out the horses or ordered the wood, then finishing the horses might not be best. However, Sigmund could scrap the materials and sell them as salvage. The seller is required only to use good commercial judgment in making the decision to finish or salvage the goods. Good commercial judgment includes considering the factors that will minimize the damages.

Keeping the Goods: Withholding or Stopping Delivery

Sometimes the goods are complete and may be on their way to the buyer. In this more advanced stage of the contract, the seller needs different remedies. The following are ways to help the seller keep the goods from the buyer.

Withholding delivery If a buyer has not made a required payment and the seller has not shipped the goods, the best remedy is for the seller to withhold shipment. Under this remedy, the seller keeps the goods instead of shipping them to a buyer who has already breached. The seller is not required to send goods to a buyer who is experiencing financial difficulty in paying for the goods (Section 2-703).

Stopping delivery There are times when the seller no longer has the goods, and the buyer has breached or not paid. In these circumstances, Article II provides remedies for the seller, which prevent the goods from ending up in the hands of the buyer (Section 2-703[b]). A seller can stop the delivery of the goods when they are in the hands of a third party, such as a carrier or warehouse.

The rules for stopping delivery depend upon the seller's reason for the stoppage. If the seller is stopping delivery because the buyer is insolvent and would be receiving the goods on credit, then the seller can stop any size shipment (Section 2-705). If the seller stops delivery for reasons other than insolvency, then the right to stop is limited to large shipments. Large shipments are defined as carloads, truckloads, planeloads or other larger shipments. A reason for this distinction in shipment size is that stopping delivery is a burden to carriers and should be as convenient as possible unless there is a problem with the buyer's insolvency.

A carrier who stops delivery according to the seller's instructions is not liable to the buyer for any damages. If the seller has made a mistake in stopping shipment, the buyer's remedies are with the seller and not the carrier. The *Allied Wired Products, Inc. v. Marketing Techniques, Inc.* case is an example of a seller stopping delivery.

ALLIED WIRED PRODUCTS, INC. v. MARKETING TECHNIQUES, INC.

Court of Appeals of Illinois, First District.
424 N.E.2d 1288 (1981).

FACTS Marketing Techniques had a contract with Allied for supplying marketing supplies. Marketing had shipped several television display stands to Allied. Marketing heard rumors about Allied. Although no payment was due and Allied was not insolvent, Marketing instructed the carrier to stop shipment. Allied claimed that Marketing had breached, and this suit resulted.

ISSUE Was Marketing justified in stopping payment under the circumstances?

DECISION No. Since there was no insolvency and no missed payment, the seller was not justified in stopping shipment. The stoppage amounted to a breach by Marketing.

LEGAL TIP

Do not stop shipments because of rumors. Check with the buyer first.

A seller can stop delivery any time prior to the buyer's receipt of the goods or negotiable instruments required to pick up the goods. If the goods are in a warehouse and the warehouse has already acknowledged that the goods belong to the buyer, the seller's right to stop delivery has ended.

Keeping the Goods: Recovering Already Delivered Goods

So far, the seller has been able to cancel or not deliver the goods and stop delivery. In some cases, the seller can actually get back goods that have already been delivered to the buyer (Section 2-702). If a buyer receives goods on credit while insolvent, the seller has the right to reclaim the goods for ten days after the buyer receives them. If the buyer has misrepresented solvency (in writing) within the three months before the delivery of the goods, then the ten-day limitation does not apply. In the case of a written misrepresentation of solvency, the seller could stand ahead of other creditors in bankruptcy proceedings.

For purposes of this section, insolvency can be defined in several different ways. Insolvency is the inability to pay business debts as they become due. Insolvency can also be established according to federal bankruptcy law, which involves a balance-sheet test of assets and liabilities.

Recovering Money from the Buyer: Reselling the Goods

Reselling the goods: Damage formula Instead of keeping the goods, the seller can resell them to another party and recover the difference between the contract and **resale** prices. For example, suppose that Sigmund (after painting the rocking horses) is able to resell them to Irvin's Toys for $60 each. Sigmund's contract price with Roy was $80 per horse. Sigmund can recover the difference between the $80 contract price and the $60 resale price or $2000 ($20 × 100). Sigmund will also be entitled to recover the costs of resale and storage, or the incidental costs of breach. The seller must subtract from the damages any expenses saved through the resale. For example, if Sigmund would have had to pay $75 shipping cost in the contract with Roy, and Irvin's picks up the toys, the $75 is subtracted. The formula for a seller's resale damages is as follows:

Contract price − resale price + incidentals − expenses saved

The *Smith v. Joseph* case involves the resale damage formula.

SMITH v. JOSEPH

District of Columbia Superior Court.
31 UCC Rep. 1560 (D.C. 1981).

FACTS Joseph agreed to buy Smith's car and then later changed her mind. Smith ran another classified ad for three weeks and was able to sell the car for the same price that Joseph had agreed to pay. Joseph claimed that Smith had no damages and a suit resulted.

ISSUE Did Smith have any damages when the resale price was the same as the contract price?

DECISION Yes. Smith had the incidental damages of the cost of running the three-week classified ad.

LEGAL TIP

Keep receipts and records on resale transactions.

Reselling the goods: Terms of the resale The resale must be "commercially reasonable." A commercially reasonable sale is one that is done in a proper place, time, and manner. The sale can be a private or public auction. If a private sale is to be made, the seller must notify the buyer of the intent to resell to a private party. If the sale is public, the seller must notify the buyer of the time and place.

Reselling the goods: Rights of secondary buyers Buyers who buy through resale in good faith are protected even if the seller has made a mistake in the sale. The lack of notice to the breaching buyer does not prevent a resale buyer from taking good title.

Recovering Money from the Buyer: Market Price

Market price: The formula Instead of reselling, the seller can choose to recover from the buyer the difference between the contract price and the **market price** at the time and place of tender (Section 2-708[1]). The seller can also recover any incidental damages caused by the buyer's breach. Again, the seller must subtract any money saved by the breach. The formula for the seller's market price remedy is:

Contract price − market price + incidentals − expenses saved

Sellers are given this choice between resale and market price damages because of the possible fluctuations in market conditions. For example, suppose that each rocking horse has a $70 market value at the time of tender. There is a market shortage by the time a resale occurs, and each rocking horse now has a value of $120. The seller will be able to cover the costs of breach better through resale than through recovering the market price.

Recovering Money from the Buyer: Lost Profits

If the seller cannot recover enough from the market price formula to cover expenses, then **lost profits** can be awarded (Section 2-708[2]). If the market price formula does not put sellers in as good a position as they would have been without the breach, then the lost-profit section applies. This section allows sellers to recover the difference between the selling price and the cost of goods sold. For example, if each rocking horse is sold at $100, and the seller's cost is $65, then lost profits are $35.

Recovering Money from the Buyer: Action for the Price

The seller can recover the contract price from the buyer in several circumstances (Section 2-709). If the goods are lost or destroyed before the buyer receives them but after the risk of loss has passed to the buyer, then the seller can get the contract price. For example, if an LA seller has sold goods to a NY buyer, "FOB LA," and the goods are lost in transit, the buyer must pay the contract price.

An action for the price is also appropriate when the seller cannot sell the goods to anyone else. When goods are specially manufactured, they may be uniquely made for the original buyer. Such goods, which no one else can use, cannot be resold; therefore, they have no market value, and the buyer is forced to take the goods. Figure 32-1 is a summary of sellers' remedies under Article II.

BUYERS' REMEDIES

Buyers' remedies can be placed in three categories. First, there are buyers' remedies when the seller has failed to deliver the goods. Second, there are buyers' remedies when the goods are delivered but rejected by the buyer. Third, there are buyers' remedies when the goods are accepted but develop problems or defects.

Getting the Goods: The Seller's Failure to Deliver, and Specific Performance

In cases where the seller agrees to deliver unique goods and does not, the buyer can require the seller to deliver them. This action of **specific performance** is appropriate only when the goods are heirlooms or priceless objects (Section 2-711). Antiques and limited-edition automobiles are examples of such goods. In addition to getting the goods, the buyer is entitled to incidental damages. The *Schweber v. Rallye Motors, Inc.* case involves specific performance.

Figure 32-1 **Sellers' Remedies Under Article II**

NAME OF REMEDY	Stop delivery	Resale price	Market price	Action for price	Lost profits
SECTION NUMBER	Section 2–702	Sections 2–706 and 2–710	Sections 2–708 and 2–710	Section 2–709	Section 2–708
WHEN AVAILABLE	Insolvency Advance breach by buyer	Buyer fails to take goods	Buyer fails to take goods	Rare, unique goods	Inadequate damages
NATURE OF REMEDY	Stop delivery of any size shipment or recover goods if insolvent; stop delivery of large shipments for other reasons	Contract price – resale price + incidental damages	Contract price – market price + incidental damages	Contract price + incidental damages	Profit margin + incidental damages

Getting the Goods: Replevin

When a buyer has already paid for the goods but the goods have not been delivered, the buyer has some rights to those goods. **Replevin** means that a buyer can get the goods already paid for if the insolvent seller has identified the goods. The buyer's right to get the goods is limited to the ten-day period after the seller

SCHWEBER v. RALLYE MOTORS, INC.

New York Supreme Court.
12 UCC Rep. 1154 (1975).

FACTS Schweber entered into a contract to buy a 1973 Rolls Royce Corniche from Rallye. Schweber gave Rallye a $3500 deposit. When the car came in, Rallye sold it to another party. There are only 100 Rolls Royce Corniches made each year. Rallye offered damages only, and this suit resulted.

ISSUE Was Schweber entitled to specific performance?

DECISION Yes. The car was unique and hard to find.

LEGAL TIP
On unique goods, demand performance.

receives the buyer's payment (Section 2-711(2)). For example, suppose that Alfreda orders a waterbed from Oasis H20. Alfreda will pay $500 down and $1000 upon delivery of the waterbed. After Alfreda has paid the $500 but before the waterbed is delivered, Oasis becomes insolvent and closes its doors. If Alfreda offers to pay the remaining $1000 within ten days from the time Oasis received the $500, Alfreda can have the waterbed.

No Delivery, No Goods: Cover

In some cases the seller has not delivered, but in others the goods were never manufactured or the seller sold them to someone else. In these cases, the buyer has other remedies. The first such remedy is that of **cover.** Cover allows the buyer to purchase substitute goods and then recover the price difference from the seller (Section 2-712). For example, if Atwood School District purchased 500 desks from School Supplies, Inc., for $30 each and School Supplies did not deliver, then Atwood could cover. If Atwood bought substitute desks at a cost of $35 each, then the damages would be $2500 (the difference between the cover price and the contract price) and could also collect **incidental damages.** Any expenses saved are subtracted from the total damages.

Buyers are also entitled to recover **consequential damages** (Section 2-715) when a seller does not deliver the goods. Consequential damages are ones that are caused by a seller's breach. For example, if a factory operates without a machine for a long time, it will lose business. Lost business caused by a seller's failure to deliver a machine on time is a consequential damage. The formula for cover is:

Cover price − contract price + incidentals − expenses saved
+ consequential damages

The *De La Hoya v. Slim's Gun Shop* case illustrates a unique application of consequential damages.

No Delivery, No Goods: Market Price

Instead of cover, the buyer can choose to recover the difference between the market contract prices of the goods (Section 2-713). The market price is the market price when the buyer learned of the seller's breach. For example, in the Atwood example, the market price may have been $40 at the time of the breach. If this

DE LA HOYA v. SLIM'S GUN SHOP

Superior Court of California.
146 Cal. Rptr. 68 (1978).

FACTS De La Hoya bought a used gun for $140 from Slim's. It was later discovered that the gun was stolen. When De La Hoya was at a practice range, he was arrested for possession of a stolen weapon. De La Hoya had to spend $8,001 for an attorney to defend him against a stolen weapon and robbery charge. He brought suit against Slim's for breach of the warranty of title and his resulting consequential damages.

ISSUE Can De La Hoya collect the consequential damages of attorney's fees?

DECISION Yes. The attorney's fees were the result of a breach.

LEGAL TIP

Check goods for title, and demand a bill of sale.

remedy is taken, Atwood recovers the $5000 difference in price plus incidental damages. The formula for the buyer's market price remedy is as follows:

$$\text{Market price} - \text{contract price} + \text{incidentals} - \text{expenses saved} + \text{consequential damages}$$

Delivered but Defective Goods: Warranty Damages

In some cases, the seller delivers the goods and the buyer accepts them, but the acceptance is under protest. Protest means that the goods or some of the goods are defective or not in the condition warranted. In cases where the buyer has defective goods, the buyer can recover as damages the difference between the goods as they are and how they should have been (Section 2-714). The buyer can also recover incidental and consequential damages. For example, if 100 rocking horses are delivered but are missing their bows, the buyer can supply the bows. The damages would be the cost of buying and putting on the bows. If the buyer lost sales or was late in performing other contracts, the resulting damages could be included as consequential damages. In food cases, consequential damages would be the medical expenses resulting from eating or drinking the harmful item. If a bottle of soda has a nail in it and the buyer swallows the nail, any resulting medical bills would be consequential damages.

DAMAGE AGREEMENTS AND LIMITATIONS

Liquidated Damages

Some buyers and sellers agree in their contracts on specific formulas for determining the amounts of possible damages. **Liquidated damages** are ones agreed upon in the contract before the breach. Liquidated damage clauses are valid so long as the following requirements are met:

1. The amount of damages agreed to is reasonable given the harms caused by a breach.
2. The amount of damages would be difficult to prove.
3. Obtaining damages would be too difficult or costly.

Figure 32-2 **Buyers' Remedies Under Article II**

NAME OF REMEDY	Specific performance	Cover	Market price
SECTION NUMBER	Section 2-711	Sections 2-712 and 2-715	Sections 2-713 and 2-715
WHEN AVAILABLE	Rare, unique goods	Seller fails to deliver	Seller fails to deliver
NATURE OF REMEDY	Buyer gets goods	Cover price − Contract price + incidentals + consequential damages	Market price − Contract price + incidentals + consequential damages

For example, the parties in a sugar supply contract could agree that a breach would cost a certain amount per pound. Since the price of sugar as a commodity can vary, this liquidated damage clause would be valid. Figure 32-2 is a summary of buyers' remedies under Article II.

Damage Limitations

In some contracts, the parties agree to limitations on the amount of damages. These limitations are valid so long as they are not unconscionable. For example, limiting personal injury recovery in warranty breach cases is unconscionable.

KEY TERMS

Resale
Market price
Lost profits
Specific performance
Replevin
Cover
Incidental damages
Consequential damages
Liquidated damages

CHAPTER PROBLEMS

*1. Guderian purchased a large quantity of auto parts from Chapman Parts Warehouse. After Chapman had delivered the parts, Guderian sent a check. The check bounced. Chapman demanded the return of the goods. When Guderian refused, Chapman repossessed the goods. It had been less than ten days from the time of delivery when Chapman repossessed. Guderian claimed that Chapman could not repossess. Who is right? *Chapman Parts Warehouse, Inc., v. Guderian,* 609 S.W.2d 317 (Tex. 1980).

2. Pantsmaker, Inc., ordered several hundred yards of fabric from Orbit Manufacturing at a price of $.75 per yard. When Pantsmaker failed to take delivery and pay, Orbit resold the fabric at a price of $.25 per yard and demanded the $.50 difference as damages. Pantsmaker said that the price difference was too great for the resale to be reasonable. Orbit said that the fabric was out of season, and they were lucky to find a substitute buyer. What will the damages be? *Pantsmaker, Inc., v. Orbit Manufg.,* 32 UCC Rep. 103 (N.Y. 1981).

3. Servbest Foods had a contract to buy 200,000 pounds of beef navel trimmings from Emessee Industries for $.70 per pound. Servbest did not perform the contract and Emessee resold the navel trimmings for $.40 per pound. What are Emessee's damages? *Servbest Foods, Inc., v. Emessee Industries, Inc.,* 403 N.E.2d 1 (Ill. 1980).

4. Ford Motor Company had a contract with S.C. Gray for the purchase of a large number of parts. Ford was slow in paying and Gray had to take out several loans to cover expenses while waiting for Ford's payment. Gray claims that Ford should be required to pay the interest on the loans. Is Gray correct? *S.C. Gray, Inc., v. Ford Motor Co.,* 286 N.W.2d 34 (Mich. 1979).

*5. Goodell purchased a conveyor belt from K.T. Enterprises for his pizza freezing business. K.T. did not deliver on time and Goodell purchased another belt, which had more features but was the only type available at the time. K.T. refuses to pay the extra cost of the upgraded belt. Who wins? *Goodell v. K.T. Enterprises, Ltd.,* 394 So.2d 1087 (Fla. 1981).

6. McGinnis purchased a new car from Wentworth Chevrolet. The car, during the first four months after delivery, was in the shop more than it was out. At the end of four months, McGinnis said the contract was off. She rented a car for two weeks while she shopped for another car. The second car cost $500 more than the car from Wentworth. What types of damages can McGinnis recover? *McGinnis v. Wentworth Chevrolet,* 645 P.2d 543 (Oreg. 1982).

7. Perfect Potato Chips bought chipping potatoes from Process Supply. Process was two weeks late in its delivery. Perfect had downtime of ten days because their supply of potatoes lapsed. They want to recover the cost of the downtime from Process. Can they? *Process Supply Co. v. Perfect Potato Chips, Inc.,* 31 UCC Rep. 1622 (Ga. 1981).

8. Wilson ordered a computer from Marquette Electronics. Wilson had ordered a computer with a 10,000 through-put capacity but the one delivered has a 5,000 through-put capacity. The 10,000 capacity could be achieved by adding a $2000 Option 81 to the system. What are Wilson's rights? *Wilson v. Marquette Electronics, Inc.,* 630 F.2d 575 (8th Cir. 1980).

9. Sedmak had a contract to buy the official Indy 500 pace car from Charlie's Chevrolet. After the Indy 500, Charlie's refused to sell the car. What can Sedmak do? *Sedmak v. Charlie's Chevrolet, Inc.,* 622 S.W.2d 694 (Mo. 1981).

10. What is the difference between incidental and consequential damages?

Part Five

Agency and Employment

"A person who acts through another is responsible just as though he or she had acted personally."
Agency principle

Chapter 33

Creation of the Agency Relationship

CHAPTER PREVIEW

- Difference between principal-agent and master-servant relationships
- Reasons for preferring independent contractors over agents
- Respondeat superior
- Express authority
- Ways implied and apparent authority differ
- Ratification

"We'll sue to get it back!" That's what Betty Oliver exclaimed to her boss at MFA Insurance Company. Betty learned that MFA had been paying Social Security taxes on its salespeople. The government said the salespeople were agents, which meant MFA had to pay Social Security taxes on them. Betty thought they were independent contractors, that no taxes were owed, and that taxes already paid could be recovered. Was Betty right?

There are two ways the employer deals with employees: as individuals and through unions. Agency law covers an employer's relationship with employees as individuals. This chapter and the next two deal with agency law. The specific focus of Chapter 38, which covers employer–union law, is labor law.

NATURE OF AGENCY

In the broad sense, people always create agencies by consent. For example, when you pick up a neighbor at the bus station, you are an agent—even though there is no contract. Generally, people create agencies with a contract. For example, when listing houses with realtors, people generally sign contracts. The *Hartke v. Moore-Langen Printing & Pub. Co.* case discusses an agency relationship.

HARTKE v. MOORE-LANGEN PRINTING & PUB. CO.

Court of Appeals of Indiana (4th Dist.).
459 N.E.2d 430 (1984).

FACTS When Vance Hartke ran for re-election to the United States Senate, he appointed Jacques LeRoy as his campaign manager. Hartke also appointed a committee to receive and spend money in his re-election bid. LeRoy ordered Moore-Langen, an Indianapolis printer, to print campaign materials. Hartke approved the material's content and quality. After the campaign, there was no money to pay the printer's $8235.68 bill. Moore-Langen sued Hartke for the bill, and argued that LeRoy was Hartke's agent when he hired Moore-Langen to do the printing.

ISSUE Was there an agency relationship between Hartke and LeRoy?

DECISION Yes. An agency results from one person's consent to act on another's behalf and subject to his or her control and consent by the other to be the principal. Agency arises from the parties' consent. There is often an agency contract between the parties. It is necessary that the agent be subject to the principal's control regarding details of the work. Hartke and LeRoy agreed LeRoy would act on Hartke's behalf during the campaign. Hartke controlled LeRoy and the committee. Hartke approved all proofs the printer submitted. Hartke had veto power over what was used. Hartke allocated the expenditure of campaign funds. The printer's president also said LeRoy identified himself as Hartke's agent. LeRoy asked the printer to deal exclusively through him. Hartke controlled LeRoy. Therefore, LeRoy was Hartke's agent regarding the printing contract.

LEGAL TIP
When a person acts on your behalf at your request, such a person is probably your agent. Select such persons carefully.

What Agency Law Covers

In its broadest meaning, **agency law** covers three relationships: master-servant, agent-principal, and employer-independent contractor. The word "employee" does not have much legal significance.

Master-Servant Relationship

Master-servant sounds like an old-fashioned label. However, the law still uses the term, which describes an employment relationship. In this relationship one person, the **master,** employs another, the **servant,** to do physical work. Servants do not make contracts or enter business deals; they usually do menial work such as gardening or cleaning.

Principal-Agent Relationship

The principal-agent relationship occurs when one person, the **principal,** employs another, the **agent,** to enter business relations (usually contracts) with third persons. The principal-agent relationship differs from the master-servant relationship in one way: the purpose of a principal-agent relationship is to establish legal relations with others. This purpose does not exist in a master-servant relationship.

Employer-Independent Contractor

The employer-independent contractor relationship exists when the employer hires someone, an **independent contractor,** to do a job. The employer leaves the means of doing the work to the independent contractor.

The difference between independent contractors and agents or servants is the employer's lacking a *right to control* the *means* of doing the work in the independent contractor situation. The principal or master in the agent or servant relationship has the right to control *both* the *means* of doing a job as well as the *end,* or *object,* of the work.

Legal Fine Point: Employee as Both Agent and Independent Contractor

An employee could be both an agent (or servant) for one part of a job and an independent contractor for another part. For example, an individual can be an insurance salesperson when selling policies but an independent contractor when driving to the customer's home.

Why Hire an Independent Contractor?

It is possibly more expensive to hire an agent or servant than an independent contractor. There are several reasons: First, employers have greater tort liability (liability for on-the-job wrongs) for agents and servants than independent contractors. Second, many statutes tax or cost employers who hire employees (agents and servants) but *not* employers who hire independent contractors. Social Security tax, unemployment taxes, and workers compensation insurance cover agents and servants but not independent contractors. Also, certain regulatory programs such as Title VII of the Civil Rights Act of 1964 do not cover employers hiring independent contractors.

The *M.F.A. Mutual Insurance Co. v. United States* case illustrates employer Social Security tax liability for agents but not independent contractors.

Borrowed Servant

Suppose master B has a servant. If another person, master C, borrows master B's servant for a short time, C will be liable for the servant's acts while the servant works for C. B will *not* be liable for the servant's acts while the servant is "on loan" to C, assuming B has given up the right to control the servant. This is the **borrowed servant** rule.

The reason the *lending* master is *not* liable is that he/she has given up the right to control the servant while working for another.

Legal Effect of Different Employer-Employee Classifications

Employer-employee classifications are important because the employer has more legal liability when employees are agents or servants than when they are independent contractors. Control is the reason employers have more legal liability for agents and servants than independent contractors. That is, an employer has the right to control agents and servants more than independent contractors. As the right to control increases, so does the extent of liability.

Respondeat superior Vicarious liability means if *one* person does something, *another* is legally responsible. The legal words for vicarious liability are **respon-**

M.F.A. MUTUAL INSURANCE CO. v. United States

U.S. District Court (W.D. Missouri).
314 F.Supp. 590 (1970).

FACTS M.F.A. Mutual Insurance Company (M.F.A.) sued the United States Government to recover Social Security payments. M.F.A. made the payments on its "financed agents" during 1962 through 1965. The Social Security Act covers "employees." Courts in other cases, however, have interpreted "employees" to mean servants or agents but *not* independent contractors. M.F.A.'s contracts with its agents (insurance salespersons) specifically said the agents were "independent contractors." The United States Government argued that the court should look at how M.F.A. treated its employees, not just at what the parties said they were.

ISSUE Were M.F.A's insurance salespeople independent contractors or agents under the Social Security Act?

DECISION The salespeople were agents, not independent contractors. The contract that M.F.A. and the salespeople used to identify their relationship does not control. The *Restatement of the Law* (2d of Agency, section 220) lists ten factors courts consider to decide if someone is an agent or independent contractor. These are:

1. The amount of control the employer exercises over the details of the employees' work. M.F.A. did exercise considerable control in this case. (For example, it required daily salespersons' reports.)
2. The distinction between the employees' work and the employer's business. (In this case, the difference between these two factors was not great since the salespeople sold M.F.A's policies as part of M.F.A.'s business.)
3. The amount of employer supervision of the employees.
4. The requirement of a specialized skill. If this is not required, the employee is more likely to be an agent. (In this case, salespeople were not specialists.)
5. The supplier of business forms, equipment, and "tools" of the trade. (In this case, M.F.A. supplied them.)
6. The control the employer has over the length of employment. If the employer controls this, an agency is indicated. (In this case, M.F.A. could fire someone any time.)
7. The employee's work as a regular part of the employer's business. An agency is likely if this factor exists.
8. The method of payment. Payment by commission suggests independent contractors, while salaries suggest agents. (In this case, M.F.A. gave a guaranteed draw, like a salary.)
9. What label the employment contract gives the employee, such as agent or independent contractor. (In this case, M.F.A. called its salespeople independent contractors.)
10. Whether the employee was part of the employer's business. (In this case, the employees' work was part of the employer's business.)

Because of these factors, M.F.A.'s salespeople were agents. Therefore, M.F.A. did not get a refund of its Social Security payments for its salespeople.

LEGAL TIP

Employers do not have to pay Social Security taxes on independent contractors.

deat superior. When one has the right to control another, one is vicariously responsible for that person's acts.

When respondeat superior applies The respondeat superior rule applies to a principal-agent or master-servant relationship in business and governmental situations.

Respondeat superior does not usually apply to employer-independent contractor relationships. However, there are exceptions. For example, respondeat superior applies to employers when independent contractors perform *nondelegable duties* or take part in ultrahazardous activities for the employer.

NATIONAL SECURITY FIRE & CASUALTY CO. v. BOWEN

Supreme Court of Alabama.
447 So.2d 133 (Ala. 1983).

FACTS In 1976, Stanley Bowen was in the logging business. On two separate occasions Bowen's equipment was damaged. He filed insurance claims with National Security Fire & Casualty Co.'s (National) agent R. D. Johnson. Johnson, suspecting arson, hired private detectives, Bosché and Pearson, to investigate Bowen. During their investigation they would flash a badge. They attempted to bribe or threaten people they interrogated to get them to name Bowen as the arsonist. One time they stuffed $200 in Willie Byrd's pocket, telling him he was counted on to help them. When they tried to get Byrd to sign a statement naming Bowen as arsonist, Byrd refused. They then threatened to have Byrd "locked up." Another time they asked "Frog" Williamson to identify Bowen as the arsonist. When Williamson refused, they threatened to lock him up for selling drugs. Bosché and Pearson finally got Ronnie Worrels and Frog Williamson to sign statements implicating Bowen as an arsonist. Neither "Frog" nor Worrels could read or write.

A grand jury indicted Bowen. Eventually the prosecutor dropped the charges. Even after the indictments, the investigators harassed Bowen. They threatened to kill Bowen's two small children and cut the children's arms off. Bosché and Pearson called Bowen and told him he would look good lying next to his dead brother. The last time Bowen saw Pearson, Pearson and two others pulled a gun and forced Bowen into the woods. They made Bowen lie down. They then placed a gun to his head and threatened to kill him. They snapped the hammer on the gun for 1½ hours. After driving Bowen to a country store, he escaped.

Bowen sued National for the Bosché and Pearson's wrongful acts. Bowen argued they were National's agents. National claimed they were independent contractors.

ISSUE Was there a principal-agent relationship between National and Bosché/Pearson?

DECISION Yes. For an agency to exist, the principal must have the right to control the agent. It is not necessary the *right* be exercised; it is enough that the right exists. Agency is determined by facts, not by the label parties use to identify a relationship. The existence of a principal–agent relationship is a fact question the jury decides. In this case, the jury found a principal-agent relationship existed. Johnson, a National agent, hired Bosché and Pearson. Johnson accompanied them when they offered bribes to two people. Johnson also decided when the investigation would end. The investigators called on Johnson twice during the two-week investigation. There was evidence showing National had the right to control the investigators.

LEGAL TIP

Principals should control how their agents act. Principals are liable for their agents' wrongs within the scope of their employment.

Who May Be Principals, Masters, and Employers?

The general rule is that anyone who can act for himself, herself, or itself may be a principal.[1] Minors may be principals if they can understand the nature and significance of the act done for them. However, they can escape contracts made for them just as they could if they had acted for themselves. Corporations, partnerships, and trusts can also be principals. However, unincorporated associations and legal incompetents, such as persons adjudged insane, may *not* be principals.

Who May Be Agents, Servants, and Independent Contractors?

A person may be an agent, servant or independent contractor if he or she has the mental and physical ability to understand and do the job. Minors can be agents, servants, and independent contractors unless they are too young to meet the job's physical and mental requirements. Corporations, partnerships, and trusts can also be agents, servants, or independent contractors.

[1]Throughout this section, "principal" includes "master" and "employer," in the case of an independent contractor.

Types of Agents

The following subsections describe various types of agents:

General agent The general agent is someone with authority to act for another in many different types of matters. For example, the manager of the Kroger store would be a general agent for the Kroger Company. If a professional athlete appoints a business manager to handle endorsements, exhibitions, media appearances, the books, and tax returns, this person would be a general agent.

Del credere agent A **del credere agent** sells someone else's goods on credit and promises to pay if the buyer does not.

Special agent **Special agents** are hired for a specific assignment (for example, to sell a Model T).

Attorney in fact An **attorney in fact** is someone (not usually a licensed attorney) who acts for another under a document called a "power or letter of attorney." Powers of attorney usually apply only to future matters.

HOW EMPLOYEES GET AUTHORITY

An employee can get authority in any one of four ways: through express, implied, and apparent authority; and through ratification.

Some important questions concerning authority include: What formalities (if any) are needed to create authority? Who creates authority? When does authority begin? When and how does authority end? The sections below answer these questions.

Express Authority

An employer, principal, or master creates **express authority** by orally or in writing telling an employee, agent, servant, or independent contractor to do something.

There are no formal requirements to confer most express authority. One exception involves real estate agents, whose appointments must be written in many states. Also, equal dignity statutes exist in most states. These laws require that principal-agent contracts be written if the statute of frauds requires the contract the agent makes with another on the principal's behalf to be written.

Implied Authority

An agent or servant receives **implied authority** in several ways: by reasonable inference from the express authority, by conduct of the principal and agent, and by emergency or necessity.

Implied authority arising from express authority An example of implied authority arising from express authority would be a principal's telling an agent to "hire a secretary." The principal's command is express authority. Implied authority in this case would include authority to put a want ad in the newspaper, to interview applicants, and to make a reasonable offer. There is no implied authority to hire *two* secretaries or to promise a car to an attractive applicant. No reasonable person would infer that such offers would be necessary to carry out the principal's command.

Implied authority arising from emergencies Implied authority arising from an emergency or necessity occurs when an unexpected event creates a situation in which the agent is unable to contact the principal. Also, the principal has *not* told the agent how to act in the matter. The unexpected event must be an emergency requiring immediate attention to protect property or people.

Apparent Authority

Apparent authority arises when the principal's words or acts lead a third person to believe the agent has authority. Apparent authority can create all or part of the agency. The appearance of authority must come from some act or omission by the principal (*not* of the agent) in which the principal had a duty to act.

For example, Sara Ramirez has no express or implied authority to sell cars. Ken Zeigler, her boss, watches Sara sell a car to a customer. Ken's failure to stop Sara creates the appearance (to the customer) that Sara has apparent authority to sell cars. The *Northington v. Dairyland Insurance Co.* case illustrates an attempt to find apparent authority.

NORTHINGTON v. DAIRYLAND INSURANCE CO.

Supreme Court of Alabama.
445 So.2d 283 (1984).

FACTS In September 1981, Ms. Eunice Northington went to Mr. Leonard Wills to buy auto insurance. Wills owned the Wills Realty and Insurance Company, Inc. and was an independent insurance agent for several companies.

On November 30, 1981, Ms. Northington gave Mr. Wills $80 in cash for auto insurance. He told her she had full auto coverage as of that date. He did not then or later fill out any insurance application for her. Later she contacted Wills several times to ask for her policy. Wills told her she was covered but never gave her the insurer's name.

On December 16, 1981, Ms. Northington had a one-car auto accident. She filed a claim with Wills, who told her to get two estimates of the damage and not to worry. In January 1982, Wills told her Dairyland Insurance Company (Dairyland) insured her car. In February she made a $37.55 premium payment to Wills.

Wills never tried to get insurance for her from Dairyland. He did not send her premium payments to Dairyland or anyone. Nor did he notify Dairyland of her loss. She sued Dairyland, claiming Wills had apparent authority to be its agent.

ISSUE Did Wills have apparent authority to be Dairyland's agent?

DECISION No. In order for a principal to be held liable on apparent authority, the principal must have done something that led the third party to believe the agent had authority to bind the principal. In this case, Dairyland did not tell or do anything that would cause Ms. Northington to believe Wills was its agent. Only Wills told her he was Dairyland's agent. An agent's apparent authority must be based on the principal's—*not* the agent's—conduct. Dairyland did nothing to suggest Wills was its agent, so apparent authority did not exist.

LEGAL TIP

People who deal with agents should check with the principal to make sure the agent has authority to act for the principal.

Ratification

It is possible for an employer, principal, or master to confer authority on a person for an act already done. This process is called **ratification.**

The requirements for ratification are:

1. One person without authority or exceeding his or her authority acts for another.
2. The person the acts were done for could legally do them when they were done *and* when they were ratified. (In other words, the acts were legal—not criminal—and the principal was not insane or drunk when ratification occurred.)

3. The person the acts were done for knew all material facts about the acts done when ratification occurred.
4. Since ratification is usually of contracts, ratification must usually occur while the third person still is in the contract (that is, the third person has not disclaimed the contract).
5. The principal must ratify *all* and not just part of what the purported (fake) agent did.
6. The principal—not the person *doing* the act—must ratify.

The *Hefner v. Estate of Ingvoldson* case illustrates ratification.

HEFNER v. ESTATE OF INGVOLDSON

Minnesota Appellate Court.
346 N.W.2d 204 (1984).

FACTS Myrtle Ingvoldson bought five separate certificates of deposit (CDs) from First National Bank of Fergus Falls. She had these CDs put in joint tenancy between herself and LaVerne Hefner, her daughter. The CDs were automatically renewed over the years. Myrtle also bought six treasury bonds, which she put in joint tenancy with her daughter. Myrtle supplied all the money used to buy the CDs and bonds. Myrtle always kept possession and control of the bonds and certificates.

In 1981, Myrtle executed a power of attorney, which gave Lenhart authority to deposit checks in her checking and savings accounts at Perham National Bank. The power of attorney also let Lenhart write checks and withdraw funds from her savings account to pay her bills. Lenhart cashed in Myrtle's five CDs and received $11,123.01. He deposited the money in Myrtle's checking account. All of the money was used for Myrtle's benefit. Lenhart also sold Myrtle's six savings bonds. He put the money in a money market account in Myrtle's name.

The power of attorney did *not* authorize Lenhart to cash either the CDs or savings bonds. After Myrtle's death her daughter, LaVerne Hefner, sued Lenhart for cashing in the CDs and bonds.

ISSUE Did Lenhart act beyond the scope of his authority when he cashed in the CDs and bonds? Did Myrtle ratify Lenhart's acts?

DECISION Yes. There was neither express or implied authority from the power of attorney to cash the CDs and bonds. However, Myrtle *ratified* Lenhart's acts afterward by signing most of the checks drawn on her account, which contained money from the sale of the CDs.

LEGAL TIP

A principal can authorize an act, through ratification, which was unauthorized when the agent did it.

KEY TERMS

Agency law
Master
Servant
Principal
Agent
Independent contractor
Borrowed servant
Respondeat superior
Del credere agent
Special agent
Attorney in fact
Express authority
Implied authority
Apparent authority
Ratification

CHAPTER PROBLEMS

1. Is consent necessary to create an agency?
2. Must all agencies be based on contracts?
3. Explain the difference between a servant and an agent.
4. What are some reasons an employer would rather hire an agent than an independent contractor?
5. Who is liable for a borrowed servant's wrongs while he or she is under the control of the borrowing master and the lending master has given up the right to control?
6. Does the respondeat superior idea benefit a master or principal?

*7. Several people made down payments on life memberships in a retirement home. The retirement home's name had the word "Lutheran" in its title. The home was a not-for-profit corporation that failed financially. Buyers of life membership who had made down payments to the home sued several Lutheran Churches for the lost down payments. The buyers claimed the corporation operating the retirement home was the agent of the individual churches. To support their claim, the buyers showed that the words "joint agency of the participating congregations" was in the retirement corporation's charter and that the word "Lutheran" was in the home's title—a fact the individual Lutheran churches knew. Did these facts establish an agency by apparent authority? *Hope Lutheran Church v. Chellew,* 460 N.E.2d 1244 (Ind. App. 1984).

*8. As a general rule, may an attorney-in-fact's authority be expressly or impliedly revoked? *Zaubler v. Picone,* 473 N.Y.S.2d 580 (N.Y. Appel. 1984).

*9. If a person enters a contract with someone else, is he or she presumed to be acting on his or her own behalf or as an agent for someone else? *Johnson v. Production Credit Ass'n. of Fargo,* 345 N.W.2d 371 (N.D. 1984).

*10. Is it possible for an agency to exist because of circumstantial evidence instead of express authority? *Hinely v. Barrow,* 313 S.E.2d 739 (Ga. App. 1984).

"No person can serve two masters"

Matthew, VI, 24

CHAPTER PREVIEW

- Meaning of fiduciary duty
- Who owes a fiduciary duty
- Common law duties that masters owe servants
- Common law duties that principals owe agents
- Duties that agents owe principals
- Employment at-will relationships
- Ways an agency can end
- Notice requirements to end an agency

Chapter 34

Rights and Duties Between Employers and Employees

"Lady, you should have watched where you stepped," said Mrs. Overstreet's boss when she filed a damage claim. Mrs. Overstreet suffered injuries when she fell from her employer's truck. She argued that her employer had failed to provide a safe place to work. Her employer claimed that Mrs. Overstreet's own carelessness caused her injuries and kept her from recovering. Who was right?

This chapter examines common law rights employers and employees have against each other as well as the duties employers and employees owe each other. The chapter also discusses rules that end agency and master–servant relationships.

COMMON LAW RIGHTS AND DUTIES

Common Law Duties Masters Owe Servants

Masters (people employing servants) have several duties. These duties arise automatically between the master and servant even if there is no express contract.

Duty to pay Masters generally must pay their servants—even if the employment contract does not specifically mention payment. This requirement assumes the servants' services are ones for which pay is usual and expected. However, it is possible a servant could agree to work for nothing. If so, the master has no duty to pay.

Duty to provide a safe work place Masters have a duty to provide a safe work place, which does not mean a risk-free environment. It is sufficient for a master to provide a relatively safe work place. This duty applies when the employee is actually or constructively doing his (or her) job.

Duty to provide work tools Masters generally have a duty to provide employees with *safe* tools to do their work. However, it is possible for the master and servant to agree that the servant will supply the tools.

The *Overstreet v. Norman* case illustrates the master's duty to provide a safe work place. In this case, the master raises three defenses: the fellow servant rule, contributory negligence, and assumption of risk.

Common Law Duties Principals Owe Agents

This section examines common law duties that principals owe agents.

Duty to pay In a **gratuitous agency,** the agent agrees to work for nothing. Therefore, the principal has no duty to pay.

However, most agencies require the principal to pay. The timing and amount of the payment are usually set by contract. If the parties forget to mention payment in their contract, courts decide if and how much the principal must pay. This amount is based on what a reasonable person would assume the parties intended.

If a person acts on another's behalf *without* authority, the principal has no duty to pay. However, if a principal *ratifies* an unauthorized act, the principal has a duty to pay the agent a reasonable fee.

Excusing the principal's duty to pay Certain acts can excuse the principal's duty to pay. These include:

1. The agent's fraud or conversion against the principal.
2. The agent's waiver of the right to payment.
3. The agent's substantial failure to do the job.
4. The agent's performing a contract known to be illegal (such as a violation of the antitrust laws).

OVERSTREET v. NORMAN

Court of Appeals of Tennessee.
314 S.W.2d 47 (1957).

FACTS Mr. Norman employed Mrs. Overstreet and several other women as bean pickers. Norman took the women from their homes to the bean fields and back on a flatbed truck. The truck bed was 3½ feet or 4 feet above the ground. There was no step to help the women get on and off the truck. When the truck got to the field, the younger women jumped from the truck to the ground. This practice seemed unsafe for the older women, so someone placed a bean hamper with the bottom up for them to step on. Mrs. Overstreet was 51 years old and weighed 197 pounds. When she stepped onto the hamper, it turned, and she fell and injured herself. She sued Norman, her employer, for her injuries. She based her claim on the employer's (master's) negligent failure to provide a safe place to work. Norman defended on grounds that Mrs. Overstreet was contributorily negligent, that a fellow servant injured her, and that she assumed the risk.

ISSUE Did the master breach his common law duty of providing a safe place for his servant to work?

DECISION Yes. Masters owe a duty of care to their servants while the servants are actually or constructively at work. A servant is constructively at work when the master is transporting the servant to or from the job. Therefore, even though Mrs. Overstreet was not picking beans when she was injured, her master owed her a duty of care. Masters owe servants a safe work place and safe appliances.

Reasonable minds could differ as to whether Mrs. Overstreet voluntarily assumed a known risk or was contributorily negligent when she fell. The jury decided that she did not assume a known risk and that she was not contributorily negligent. The fellow servant defense was rejected because the duty to provide a safe work place is nondelegable (meaning that the master legally could not transfer this duty to another employee). So when the fellow servant put the basket down for her to step on, this act did not legally take away the master's duty to provide a safe work place.

LEGAL TIP

Since masters have a duty to provide a safe work place, they should periodically check for work place hazards.

5. The agent's breach of his or her fiduciary duty (discussed below), such as a conflict of interests (representing both parties unknown to both).

Secret commissions Agents representing both parties to a transaction are not entitled to pay from either. However, if both parties are aware of the dual agency and approve of it, the agent has a right to dual payment.

Advances to agents An advance is money an agent gets before making a sale. Agents have no automatic right to advances. Agency contracts can permit advances. A number of cases allow agents to keep advances even if sales commissions are less than the advance.

Duty to reimburse Principals have a duty to reimburse agents for ordinary and necessary expenses incurred while performing agency duties. Principals do not have to reimburse agents for fines or penalties; these are not ordinary or necessary.

Duty to indemnify The principal must indemnify agents for losses and liabilities while performing agency duties. This duty applies only if the agent is not breaching a duty to the principal. For example, if an agent at work negligently drives into a pedestrian who sues and recovers only from the agent, the principal has no duty to indemnify the agent.

Common Law Duties Agents Owe Principals

Agents owe their principals several duties. Such obligations include the duty to account, the duty to communicate, the duty to use care and skill in performing for the principal, the duty to indemnify, the duty to follow instructions, and the fiduciary duty (discussed below).

Duty to account The agent's duty to account requires that the agent keep records of income and expenses. Principals turn over property to their agents to help them perform agency duties. Third persons give agents property (such as money) for their principals. In both cases, agents must account for the property when the principal asks.

Agents must turn over the principal's property when the principal demands. If the agent refuses, he or she commits conversion. Agents must not commingle their property with the principal's.

What satisfies an agent's duty to account? One case held the agent's preparing an income tax return covering the principal's business, which the agent managed, sufficient.

Duty to communicate Agents must tell their principals all information they know that is relevant to the agency. A reason for this rule is that principals are presumed to know what their agents know (that is, regarding agency matters).

Duty to use care and skill Agents owe their principals a duty of care and skill in performing the principal's work. Agents satisfy this duty by using the standard of ordinary care in the occupation. Agents, however, are not insurers of what they do for their principals. Even gratuitous agents are liable for negligence in performing their duties.

Duty to indemnify Agents have a duty of care and skill in doing their jobs. If they are careless and damage the principal, they have a duty to indemnify their principal's losses. For example, if an agent mistakenly erases a principal's valuable computer program, the agent has a duty to pay for it. Principals often waive this indemnification right against their employees to maintain goodwill.

Duty to follow instructions The agent has a duty to follow the principal's instructions. However, agents do *not* have to follow instructions when asked to commit *illegal* acts, such as crimes or torts. If an agent does not obey *legal* instructions, the agent is liable to the principal for damages.

Fiduciary duty The agent's most important duty to his or her principal is the **fiduciary duty.** A fiduciary is one owing great faith, loyalty, and accountability to another.

Some courts include the duties to account and follow instructions under the general term "fiduciary duty." In this book, the definition of "fiduciary duty" includes: the agent's duty to act for only one principal, the agent's duty not to profit at the principal's expense, and the agent's duty not to act adversely to the principal's interests. The fiduciary duty exists even in the case of gratuitous agents.

Some parts of the fiduciary duty last after the agency ends. For example, the agent's duty not to disclose a principal's trade secrets continues after the agent stops working for the principal. This duty does not last forever but for a reasonable time and is limited to a reasonable geographic area.

The *Detroit Lions, Inc., v. Argovitz* case illustrates an agent's fiduciary duty.

DETROIT LIONS, INC. v. ARGOVITZ

U.S. District Court (E.D. Mich.).
580 F.Supp. 542 (1984).

FACTS Billy Sims was a professional football star who played for the Detroit Lions football team. Jerry Argovitz was his agent in negotiating contracts with football teams. Argovitz, while negotiating a new contract for Sims with the Lions, bought 29% interest and became president of the Houston Gamblers, a new, competing professional football team. Argovitz had Lerner, one of the other owners of the Gamblers, offer Sims a contract with the Gamblers. Sims signed a $3.5 million, 5-year contract with the Gamblers July 1, 1983, believing that the Lions would not match these terms. In fact, a Lions representative contacted Argovitz before Sims signed with the Gamblers, but Argovitz would not take his call. Argovitz called the Lions after 5 PM July 1, *after* Sims had signed with the Gamblers. The Lions rep had gone home. Sims later learned of Argovitz's conduct. He signed a contract with the Lions on December 16, 1983. On December 18, 1983, the Lions and Sims sued Argovitz to have the Sims–Gamblers contract invalidated. Sims argued Argovitz violated his fiduciary duty to Sims, making the Sims–Gamblers contract voidable.

ISSUE Did Argovitz breach his fiduciary duty to Sims, justifying invalidation of Sims' contract with the Gamblers?

DECISION Yes. If an agent violated his or her fiduciary duty in negotiating a contract for the principal, the principal can rescind the contract even if it is fair. Argovitz violated his fiduciary duty to Sims in several ways:

1. By self-dealing (representing his ownership in the Gamblers while also representing Sims, who was negotiating with the Gamblers).
2. By not informing the principal of all material facts that are, may be, or might be affecting his principal's rights.
3. By not telling Sims that he (Argovitz) owned 29% interest in the Gamblers and that he received $275,000 per year as the Gamblers' president.
4. By not telling Sims that he (Argovitz) would get 5% of the Gamblers' cash flow.
5. By not giving Sims a contract as good as one the Gamblers gave an unproven rookie of lower potential.
6. By not encouraging a "bidding war" between the Lions and Gamblers over Sims.

LEGAL TIP

Principals can escape contracts their agents make for them if the agent breaks his or her fiduciary duty when negotiating the contract.

Common Law Duties Servants Owe Masters

Servants generally owe masters the same duties agents owe principals. Servants owe masters the following:

1. A fiduciary duty.
2. A duty to follow legal instructions.
3. A duty to use ordinary care and skill.
4. A duty to communicate information.

The scope of the servant's duties is narrower than the agent's because servants lack power to contract for their masters.

Legal fine point A person can be a servant for one part of a job, an agent for another part, and an independent contractor for a third part. Servants cannot make contracts for their masters. However, when the employee shifts out of a servant's role into an agent's role, he or she can contract for the principal.

How Agencies End

This section surveys some of the ways that agencies can end.

Contract ends when job is done Agencies can end when a job is completed or when a date specified by the contract arrives.

Voluntary agreement The principal and agent may agree to end the agency any time. This is so no matter what the agreement says about the termination date.

Other ways agencies can end Other events can end agencies. These include:

1. By death of either the principal or agent.
2. Insanity of either the principal or agent.
3. Bankruptcy of either the principal or agent.
4. Physical or legal incapacitation (such as loss of a real estate license) of the agent.
5. Impossibility to perform due to loss or destruction of an essential subject matter.
6. Illegality of the agency's object.
7. Sudden economic or political changes.

Many of the above events also apply to ending master-servant and employer-independent contractor arrangements.

Notice of the Agency's Ending

There are several types of notice that are possible when agencies end: actual notice, constructive notice, and no notice.

Actual notice When an agency ends, the principal must give actual notice to third persons who have dealt with the principal through the agent. **Actual notice** is a phone call, a personal visit, or a letter. Actual notice is excused if the third person learns from someone else that the agency was ended.

Constructive notice **Constructive notice** is different from actual notice. Principals must give constructive notice of an agency's termination to people who have not actually dealt through the agent. For example, a newspaper or trade journal ad indicating the end of an agency is constructive notice.

No notice No notice of any kind need be given when a special agent completes his or her job.

If an agency ends by the principal's death, the agent's authority ends at that time in most cases. This rule can hurt agents. For example, an agent entering a contract for the principal with a third person may not know the principal has just died. Generally, the agent is liable for the contract—even though the third party understood the agent made the contract for the principal.

A bank is an agent for checking account customers. When such a banking customer dies, the bank's authority to pay checks written before the customer's death does not end immediately. This authority lasts for ten days after the customer's death unless someone with an interest in the account orders payment to stop.

Ending the Employment Relationship: A Disciplinary Tool

Employment at will Many employment relationships are for an indefinite period—an arrangement referred to as an **employment at will.** This type of relationship means that either the employer or employee can end the relationship at any time for any reason.

As a practical matter, employment at will gives employers a strong disciplinary stick against employees since the employer can fire employees any time for any reason. The rule helps employers enforce employees' common law duty to follow instructions. Obedience is important in maintaining production and harmony.

Contracts modifying the at-will rule The employer's common law right to fire an employee can be modified in several ways. First, employees can have employment contracts for a definite period (such as one year). In such a case, the employer's right to fire is limited by a contract. If the contract says nothing about dismissal, the employer can usually fire an employee for "good cause" only. Good cause includes such things as inefficiency, theft of company property, disloyalty, and insubordination.

Statutes modifying the at-will rule A second way the employer's discharge right can be changed in at-will employment is by statute. Many states have passed "dismissal for good cause only" statutes. There is no such federal law.

Modification of the at-will rule: Public policy Some state courts refuse to allow at-will employee terminations if there is a strong public policy against it. In one case, *Petermann v. International Brotherhood of Teamsters,*[1] an employee was subpoenaed to testify before a state legislative committee. The employer told him to give false testimony. The employee disobeyed by telling the truth and was fired. The employee won his claim for wrongful dismissal even though the employment was "at will." The Supreme Court of California reasoned that coercing perjury is "patently contrary to public policy."

The *Mau v. Omaha National Bank* case shows the traditional rule concerning the employer's right to fire an employee in at-will employment.

[1]344 P.2d 25 (1959).

MAU v. OMAHA NATIONAL BANK

Supreme Court of Nebraska.
299 N.W.2d 147 (1980).

FACTS The Omaha National Bank (Bank) had employed Robert Mau for 28 years. On December 3, 1976, the bank fired him for failing to mail 300 pension checks from accounts the Bank administered. When dismissed, Mau was the mailroom supervisor. The incident leading to Mau's dismissal was the employer's receiving many complaints about not receiving pension checks. Mau's supervisor asked him about them. For 3 days, Mau repeatedly told his boss the checks had been sent. Mau finally found the checks in a mailroom drawer, and the Bank fired him.

He sued the Bank for damages, alleging wrongful discharge from his job. Mau had no written employment contract specifying a definite length of time. He argued that conversations with Bank personnel as well as the Bank handbook established an offer for Mau to have a bank career. Mau claimed he accepted the offer by working at the Bank for 28 years.

The Bank defended by claiming Mau was an employee at will. As such, either party could end the employment at any time for any (or no) reason.

ISSUE Did Mau have an employment-at-will arrangement at the Bank?

DECISION Yes. In such a case, the rule is that either the employer or employee can end the employment relationship at any time for any reason. There was no written employment contract between Mau and the Bank. The Bank handbook stated that is was *not* a contract. There was no public policy reason for stopping the Bank from firing Mau. Therefore, he had an indefinite period of employment, which was terminable at the will of either party. The bank *did* have the right to fire Mau.

LEGAL TIP

Employers should be aware that statutes, contracts, and public policy can change the employment-at-will rule. This makes it harder to fire employees.

KEY TERMS

Gratuitous agency
Fiduciary duty
Actual notice
Constructive notice
Employment at will

CHAPTER PROBLEMS

1. Name some common law duties that masters owe servants.
2. Is a principal's common law duty to pay ever excused?
3. What does a principal's duty to indemnify an agent mean?
4. Do agents owe their principals any common law duties? If so, what duties?
5. Does the principal owe the agent a fiduciary duty?
6. Can an employee be both a servant and an independent contractor with respect to a job?
7. What are some ways that agencies can end?

*8. A manufacturer and its agent representative ("rep") ended their relationship. The contract entitled the "rep" to commissions on reorders after the contract was over. Must the principal pay them? *E. F. Higgins, Inc. v. Kuhlman Die Casting Co., Inc.,* 663 S.W.2d 318 (Mo.App. 1983).

*9. Merritt worked on a dairy farm. One day he was herding cows from a holding pen into a smaller holding pen when a cow got its foot caught in a drain. When Merritt tried to help the cow, it fell on him. Merritt sued for $7000 in damages; he claimed the employer was liable because he broke his common law duty to provide a safe place to work. Did Merritt recover? *Merritt v. Carr,* 621 S.W.2d 740 (Tenn. 1981).

*10. An oil company's distribution agent did not tell the oil company that a particular customer had fallen behind in paying its bills. The agent would sometimes pay the delinquent customer's bills from other funds. Did the agent breach a fiduciary duty to the principal by "covering up" for the customer? *In re Blanton Smith Corp.,* 37 B.R. 303 (Bkrtcy. Tenn. 1984).

"All men are liable to error"
John Locke

CHAPTER PREVIEW

- Respondeat superior
- Employers' responsibility for agents', servants', and independent contractors' torts
- Agents', servants', and independent contractors' responsibility for their own torts
- Agents' liability on contracts made for their principals
- Partially disclosed principals
- Corporate employers' criminal liability for their employees' crimes
- Superior agent rule

Chapter 35

Employer and Employee Liability to Third Parties

Jack Hanshaw could not believe it. His corporation was being criminally charged with nineteen counts of knowingly making false entries on a government form in connection with selling guns to foreigners. Hanshaw owned a department store with a sporting goods department that sold guns. He had put Pedro Alvarado in charge of that department. Alvarado broke the federal gun registration law by selling hand guns to foreigners and making false entries on the required government forms (a crime each time it was done). Sometimes customers bribed Alvarado to buy guns; Alvarado was criminally convicted of violating this law. Then federal officials charged Gibson Products Company, Inc., Jack's department store corporation, with the crimes Alvarado had committed. Was the corporation liable?

Agents enter contracts with third persons on behalf of their principals. Agents, servants, and independent contractors commit torts and crimes while at work. This chapter answers two questions: First, what are the employees' liabilities for contracts, torts, and crimes while on the job? Second, is the employer liable for such employee actions at work?

AGENTS' LIABILITY TO THIRD PERSONS: CONTRACTS

Agents could be liable to third persons regarding contracts made for their principal in three ways: on the contract, for the tort of fraud, and for breach of warranty of authority. All three theories may not be available in any one case.

Properly Made Contracts

An agent properly makes a contract for his or her principal with a third person as follows: First, the agent acts within his or her authority; second, the agent discloses the fact of agency and the principal's identity to the third person, third, the agent signs the contract properly so only the principal, not the agent, is bound.

How to sign contracts to bind only the principal A contract that binds only the principal must:

1. Name the principal.
2. Name the agent.
3. Indicate who is principal and who is agent.

The following example fulfills these requirements:

ABC Company
by John Johnson, Agent.

When Agents Are Liable on the Contract

An agent is liable for a contract in three cases. First, the agent is liable if he or she signs for a non-existent principal. This situation can occur when the agent does not know the principal's exact name. For example, the agent mistakenly signs "ABC Corporation" instead of "ABC, Inc." as the principal's name. Courts tend to require the principal's *exact* name, not just a close one. Another situation involves corporate promoters signing preincorporation contracts for non-existent principals.

Secondly, an agent could sign a contract for a **partially disclosed principal** and be liable on the contract. A situation involving a partially disclosed principal is when an agent's name and fact of agency are disclosed to a third person but the principal's identity remains undisclosed. In this type of situation, a third person can hold the agent (or principal but not both) to the contract.

Third, agents are liable on the contract to a third person when there is an **undisclosed principal.** Situations involving undisclosed principals occur when a principal's identity and fact of agency are both unknown to the third person. The third person can hold either the principal or agent (not both) to the contract when the third person learns of the agency and of the principal's identity.

The *American Insurance Co. v. Smith* case is an example involving an undisclosed principal.

AMERICAN INSURANCE CO. v. SMITH

District of Columbia Court of Appeals.
472 A.2d 872 (1984).

FACTS The American Insurance Company (insurer) sued Bob Smith for unpaid insurance premiums. The insurer had issued a policy, which covered Smith's gas station, to "Bob Smith Electronic Tune-Up Center" as the insured. Bob Smith claimed he was merely the agent for his corporation (Bob Smith Electronic Tune-Up Center, *Inc.*) when he bought the policy. The insurer argued that Smith's principal was undisclosed when he bought the policy. Therefore, Smith should be personally liable.

ISSUE If an agent does not disclose the fact of agency and the identity of the principal before or when signing a contract with a third person, is the agent personally liable on the contract?

DECISION Yes. Smith would be personally liable if he did not tell the insurer he was acting for his corporation. Smith must disclose this information before or when buying the policy—*not* afterward. Since Bob omitted the "Inc." in his business' name when buying the policy, he failed to disclose his corporate principal when he bought the policy. He also did not tell the insurer he was an agent when he bought the policy. Agents are personally liable on contracts they make for their principal if they fail to tell the third person the principal's identity and that they are an agent. This disclosure must be *before* or *when* the contract is made.

LEGAL TIP

Agents should disclose the fact of their agency and their principal's identity *before* they make contracts for their principal. This keeps the agent from being personally liable on the contract.

Agent liable to third in contract matter: Breach of warranty of authority Agents sometimes mistakenly believe they have authority when they make contracts for a principal with third parties. An agent can either lack authority to make *any* contract or merely the *type* of contract involved. In such cases, third persons can hold an agent liable for breach of **warranty of authority.** This breach allows third persons to recover against agents who sign contracts properly but who mistakenly believe that principals have authorized the contracts. In such cases, the third person can recover from the agent (*not* the principal) for breach of warranty of authority.

Agent liable to third in contract matter: Fraud Fraud is a third way to hold agents liable to third persons in contract matters. In these situations, agents know they have no authority to contract for the principal. Nonetheless, the agent tells the third person such authority exists. For example, a tall, distinguished-looking man arrives at Mary Skolnik's home and tells Skolnik that he is a Buick salesman for Devoe Buick downtown. He talks Skolnik into taking a test drive in his Buick, which Mary likes. She signs a contract and gives the salesman $500 as a down payment. He promises to deliver the car tomorrow and is never seen again. Skolnik calls Devoe Buick and learns they have no salesman who looks like the man she "bought" the car from. If Skolnik could find the salesman again, she could sue him for fraud. However, Devoe Buick will not be liable to Mary since only the "salesman"—not Devoe—indicated he worked for the company.

AGENTS' LIABILITY TO THIRD PERSONS: TORTS

Agents, servants, and independent contractors are liable for their own torts, or wrongs. This liability occurs whether or not the tort is within or beyond the scope of the job. The reason is that persons should answer for their own wrongs. For example, if an agent commits fraud to get a third person to enter a contract, the agent would be personally liable.

Respondeat Superior Rule

The **respondeat superior rule** makes one person liable for wrongs or acts done by another. This rule applies if the person sued as principal or master has the right to control the actor (wrongdoer).

When the rule applies The respondeat superior rule makes principals liable for agents' acts and makes masters answerable for servants' acts. This rule assumes the agent or servant is acting within the scope of his or her job. However, employers are not liable for employee off the job torts.

When the rule does not apply The respondeat superior rule does not usually apply in employer–independent contractor situations. This restriction means that if an independent contractor commits a wrong while at work, the employer does *not* have to pay. There are two exceptions to the general rule that employers are not liable for independent contractors' on-the-job torts. First, employers are liable if independent contractors injure someone while doing ultrahazardous work (such as dynamiting). Second, employers are liable if they negligently select an independent contractor (who then injures a third person).

Scope of employment The **scope of employment** idea makes a master or principal liable for servants' or agents' on-the-job acts or omissions (meaning the same thing as express, implied, and apparent authority and ratification as discussed in the previous chapter). Authority sets the employee's job boundaries as well as the limits on the employer's liability for the employee's acts.

The *State ex rel. McLeod v. C & L Corp., Inc.* case illustrates a scope of employment issue.

Unacceptable defenses against servants' or agents' torts Determining where an agent's or servant's job starts and stops is difficult. For example, a master hired a servant to deliver packages. The servant negligently drove too fast when there were bad conditions and injured someone. Should the master be held liable? The master will argue that the servant was beyond the scope of the employment. After all, the master hired him or her to deliver packages—not to run into people.

Courts reject such an argument because public policy favors holding employers liable for employees' acts related to their jobs. Courts also reject the defense that employers have told employees to be careful or have trained them to avoid injuries.

LIABILITY FOR CRIMES

Employee liability A person who commits a crime is liable for it. The fact that the criminal is an agent, servant, or independent contractor is no defense.

STATE EX REL. MCLEOD v. C & L CORP., INC.

Court of Appeals of South Carolina.
313 S.E.2d 334 (1984).

FACTS Funderburk and W. L. Cooper formed C & L Corporation (C & L) for the sole purpose of developing and selling a real estate subdivision known as "Green Brier" in rural Lexington County. Wayne Cooper, a licensed realtor, had the idea to develop the project. C & L and W. L. Cooper, Wayne's brother, contracted Wayne Cooper to lay out the subdivision and sell the lots.

Wayne Cooper sold several lots in 1973 in Green Brier. When lots were sold in 1973, this sale violated the county subdivision ordinance. The ordinance required C & L to build roads and drainage to comply with a county-approved preliminary plat. In 1973 county officials several times notified W. L. Cooper in writing that C & L violated the subdivision ordinance. C & L nonetheless continued to sell lots.

Sales agents working for Wayne Cooper made false representations to sell Green Brier lots in 1973. Sales agents told prospective buyers whatever they felt the buyers wanted to hear in order to make a sale. Promises to provide paved roads, drainage, sewage, street lights, city water, access roads, and school bus routes were also given. However, none of these was ever actually provided.

The state Attorney General sued C & L Corporation for the sales agents' misrepresentations. C & L claimed it was not liable because it did not know that the sales agents were making misrepresentations.

ISSUE Is a principal liable for an agent's misrepresentations if the principal does know the agent is making them?

DECISION Yes. Actual knowledge is not necessary to hold a principal liable for an agent's misrepresentations if the agent makes them while within the scope of the agency. The sales people made the misrepresentations while they were selling the lots. The agents clearly were within the scope of their sales authority during this time. C & L Corporation and Wayne Cooper were liable as principals regardless of their knowledge. A principal is liable to third persons for an agent's frauds, deceits, concealments, misrepresentations, negligences, and omissions when the agent is within the scope of the agency. This rule applies even if the principal did not authorize, participate in, or know of the misconduct.

LEGAL TIP

Principals should select agents with care since they must pay for agents' on-the-job torts.

Unacceptable defenses If a boss tells an employee to commit crimes in his or her work, these instructions are no defense for the employee. What if the boss threatens to fire employees who refuse to commit crimes as part of their jobs? Threat of job loss also is not a criminal defense for the employee's crime.

Employer liability If an employer orders an employee to commit a crime, the employer could be criminally liable. For example, H. L. Box, an accountant, tells his assistant, Ken Zeigler, to cheat on a client's income tax return. Zeigler follows instructions, cheats, and is caught. Both Zeigler and Box are criminals. Zeigler is liable because he personally committed the crime (following the boss's orders is no defense). Box is liable based on criminal conspiracy rules.

A **criminal conspiracy** is an agreement with intent to commit an unlawful act or a lawful act illegally. Exactly how the intent must be shown is not always clear. Often a substantial act to carry out the illegal agreement shows the necessary intent. In the tax example, Zeigler's falsifying and filing the tax return shows intent. In this case, both Zeigler and Box would be liable for criminal conspiracy.

Corporate employers Corporate employers are liable for employee crimes on the following occasions: if the respondeat superior rule applies; and sometimes, if strict liability criminal statutes exist.

Respondeat superior rule in corporate criminal matters The respondeat superior rule makes the corporate employer liable for employee crimes committed within the scope of the employee's job and for the employer's benefit. This rule also means employers are not liable for employees' off-duty crimes. Corporations can be liable for employees' on-duty crimes even if the corporation told the employee not to commit the crimes.

The *United States v. Gibson Products Co., Inc.* case shows how the respondeat superior rule was used to hold the corporation liable for its employees' crimes, which were within the scope of the job and for the employer's benefit.

UNITED STATES v. GIBSON PRODUCTS CO., INC.

U.S. District Court (S.D. Texas).
426 F.Supp. 768 (1976).

FACTS Jack Hanshaw was president of Gibson Products Company, Inc. (Gibson). Pedro Alvarado, a long-time employee, was manager of Gibson's sporting goods department and sold hand guns to foreigners. He entered false names on government forms in connection with the sales—acts that were federal crimes. Alvarado put the full retail price of each gun sold in Gibson's cash register.

The United States Government brought a criminal prosecution against Alvarado for knowingly making false entries on federal forms when selling guns to foreigners. Alvarado pled guilty to one count. The federal prosecutors also brought criminal charges against Gibson Products Company, Inc. The government charged Gibson with fourteen counts of knowingly making false entries on federal forms. Gibson defended by arguing: that he specifically told Alvarado to fill out the forms honestly; that Alvarado, not the corporation, committed the crimes; and that Alvarado was beyond the scope of his employment when he committed the crimes.

ISSUE Does the respondeat superior rule apply in criminal matters so that a corporate employer is criminally liable for a corporate employee's crimes?

DECISION Yes. Alvarado's sales benefitted the corporate employer because Alvarado put all money received from the gun sales in Gibson's cash register. The argument that Gibson told Alvarado not to fill in the forms falsely is without merit. Finally, Alvarado was within the scope of his employment when he filled in the forms falsely because his job was to sell guns and fill out forms associated with such sales.

LEGAL TIP

Corporate employers can be criminally liable for employees' acts that benefit the corporation and are within the scope of the employees' jobs.

Corporate criminal liability: Strict liability criminal statutes Some statutes are strict liability criminal laws applying to corporations. A strict liability criminal statute is a law passed by the legislature making an act (or omission) a crime *even though the wrongdoer has no criminal intent.* For example, criminal violations of the Rivers and Harbors Act are strict liability crimes. The act of obstructing navigation is a crime, even if there is *no intent* to do so.

If a corporate employee breaks a strict liability criminal statute at work, the employee is liable. The corporation could also be liable if the statute applies to the corporation (some do).

Limits on corporate criminal liability: Superior agent rule The **superior agent rule** says that corporations are liable only for crimes of high-level employees (superior agents). The reason for the rule is the basic fairness of holding corporations only for crimes by employees close enough to the corporate "inner circle" to say that the corporation knew.

Limits on corporate criminal liability: Beyond the scope of employment A second limit on corporate criminal liability for employee crimes is the requirement that the crime be *within the scope* of the employee's job and *for* the *corporation's benefit.* If an employee crime is *beyond* the scope of the employee's job and *not* for corporate benefit, the corporation is *not* liable.

Consider an extreme example. A small incorporated supermarket has a delivery man. While delivering groceries to a customer, the deliveryman rapes the customer. This act would be beyond the scope of the deliveryman's job and not for the employer's benefit. The deliveryman's corporate employer would not be criminally liable for the rape. The employee's crime must relate directly to the employee's duties before the corporate employer is criminally liable.

Criminal liability of corporate officers Generally, corporate officers (and directors) are *not* criminally liable for employee on-the-job crimes committed on the corporation's behalf. This rule assumes the corporate officers and directors exercise due diligence in overseeing corporate activities and they do not actually know about employee crimes.

Exception: When corporate officers are criminally liable for subordinates' acts Occasionally, courts hold corporate officers criminally liable for corporate employee crimes. This decision occurs when employees break criminal statutes having an extremely important public interest.

An example occurred when a corporation president was unaware his company had shipped contaminated food interstate. This act violated the Pure Food and Drug Law, a strict liability criminal law. Such a shipment by lower corporate employees was a crime. The United States Supreme Court in *United States v. Park* (1975) held the corporate president criminally liable for this illegal shipment. This decision was made even though the corporate president was ignorant of the facts in the matter. The key factor seemed to be the strong public interest in pure food and drugs.

KEY TERMS

Partially disclosed principal
Undisclosed principal
Warranty of authority
Scope of employment
Respondeat superior rule
Criminal conspiracy
Superior agent rule

CHAPTER PROBLEMS

1. Is an agent ever personally liable on a contract made for the principal? If so, when?
2. Who will argue the respondeat superior rule, the principal or the third person suing the principal?
3. What does "scope of employment" mean?
4. Is an employer ever liable for an employee's crimes?
5. Define the superior agent rule.
6. What is a strict liability crime?

*7. Must an agent actually tell a third person that he or she is an agent? Is it possible that facts can put a third person on notice that the agent is representing someone else? *Meisel v. Natal Homes, Inc.*, 447 So.2d 511 (La. App. 1984).

*8. Is an agent liable for a contract executed for a principal if the agent identifies the principal and discloses the agency relationship? *Penick v. Frank E. Basil, Inc., of Delaware,* 579 F.Supp. 160 (D.C. D.C. 1984).

*9. When an agent commits fraud in the course of his or her employment is the principal liable? *Arkel Land Co. v. Cagle,* 445 So.2d 858 (Ala. 1983).

*10. If an agent commits a tort within the scope of his or her employment, is the agent personally liable? *Morteld v. Bernstrauch,* 343 N.W.2d 880 (Neb. 1984).

"The CPAs acknowledge a moral responsibility . . . to be as mindful of the interests of strangers who may rely on their opinion as of the interests of the client who pays their fee. This is at the same time a heavy burden and a proud distinction."

J. Carey

"To err is human, to forgive divine."

Alexander Pope

CHAPTER PREVIEW

- Two general kinds of accountants
- Common law theories for holding accountants civilly liable
- Extent of accountants' civil negligence liability
- Accountants' fraud liability concerning after-acquired information
- Accountants' criminal liability
- Civil liability accountants have under the 1933 Securities Act
- Ways accountants can be liable under the 1934 Securities Exchange Act
- Accountant-client privilege

Chapter 36

Accountants' Legal Liability

Jack Adler was sick. He was a CPA who had just been sued for malpractice. He had been accused of making a mistake while auditing a client, Giant Stores Corporation (Giant). What troubled Adler was that the client who had hired him was not suing him. Rather, the person suing had bought stock in Giant after reading and relying on Giant's financial statements that Adler had audited. The stock later became worthless, and the buyer blamed the problem on Adler's audit and sued him for negligence. Adler remembered something called the "privity rule," which meant accountants are not liable to people who do not hire them. Adler was sure that the privity rule would defeat the malpractice suit. The case went all the way to the New Jersey Supreme Court. Was Adler right?

Accountants have important duties in today's business. Basically, they assemble and guard the accuracy of financial statements (mainly the balance sheet and income statement) and "keep the books." Accountants essentially protect owners, potential owners, creditors, and potential creditors of businesses and other organizations.

This chapter first looks at the kinds of jobs accountants have in our economy. Then the discussion turns to the types of legal liabilities accountants have.

ACCOUNTANTS' JOBS

There are two general ways of looking at accountants' jobs—internally and externally. **Internal accountants** are full-time employees of a business. Legally, such employees are usually either servants or agents. These people perform many functions that are classified under the general heading of "keeping the books."

External accountants are not full-time employees but instead have their own accounting firm. Legally, such persons are usually independent contractors. They are hired occasionally to perform duties that internal accountants do not do (for example, to audit or check up on the internal accountants).

Common Law Civil Liability

There are several law theories to hold accountants liable. These include breach of contract, negligence, and fraud.

Breach of contract Accountants work because they have a contract. A contract tells accountants what jobs they are supposed to do (for example, audit financial statements by April 1 when time is of the essence). If the accountant misses the deadline, he or she is in **breach of contract** and gets no pay. Also, the accountant is liable for damages the client sustains because of the breach—even if the accountant has too much other work. The client has a duty to cooperate so the accountant can complete the work on time.

Accountants are liable for breach of contract to third party beneficiaries of their contracts known by the accountants to be relying on their audit at the time the audit contract was entered. For example, X Company hires K Accountants to audit its books so X can get a loan from B Bank. Assume K knows this. B is the intended beneficiary of the X-K contract and can sue K if it does not do the audit as the contract indicated.

Negligence **Negligence** is a tort theory that holds people liable if they are careless and injure someone. The following elements must exist to find a person liable for negligence:

1. A person must have a duty;
2. that is broken by not living up to the appropriate standard of care;
3. that proximately causes;
4. damages.

Negligence defenses Defenses against negligence include contributory negligence (the victim's carelessness partly caused its loss which totally bars victim's recovery from plaintiff), comparative negligence (a victim's negligence partly caused its loss which reduces the victim's recovery by the amount of the victim's own carelessness), assumption of risk, and the statute of limitations.

Level of care Negligence does not require that accountants do flawless work but generally requires that accountants exercise normal, professional care and skill. Accountants doing auditing work, for example, should use reasonable sampling or testing techniques when examining other accountants' work.

Ways negligence can occur Accountants can commit negligence by doing any part of their job carelessly. For example, negligence occurs if an internal accountant forgets to record business expenses.

Accountants' negligence liability Accountants are liable to their employer for damages and losses caused within the scope of their job. An employer may also fire accountants (internal or external) who negligently perform their duties.

Independent accountants are liable for negligence to people (or organizations) who hire them. If a contract exists between two people, this is called privity of contract. The **privity rule** says that accountants are liable for negligence only to people who hire them (those with whom they have privity of contract).

Modern courts extend accountants' negligence liability further. They hold independent accountants liable to known third persons (persons not in privity with the accountants) and unidentified persons who are members of a class of person (for example, stockholders) that the accountant knows about when the audit is done. Recently, the New Jersey Supreme Court in the *Rosenblum v. Adler* case held independent accountants liable for negligence to all persons the accountant could reasonably foresee as receiving audited statements from the audited business for a proper business purpose to influence a business decision of the user.

Fraud **Fraud** (discussed in Chapter 6) refers to:

1. misrepresentation;
2. of a material fact;
3. by someone who knows of the misrepresentation;
4. who intends to misrepresent;
5. to someone who reasonably relies;
6. and who is damaged because of the misrepresentation.

How fraud occurs An internal accountant could commit fraud by, for example, "padding a payroll" (that is, making payroll checks to a non-existent employee and cashing the check himself or herself). External or independent accountants could commit fraud by "selling their opinions" to clients (that is, issuing a "clean opinion" knowing the client's financial statements are materially wrong). Assume the client uses the audited statements to get a bank loan. If the bank relies on the fraudulently audited statements, makes the loan, and is not repaid, the bank may recover damages for fraud from the accountants. The bank might recover compensatory and punitive damages from the accountants.

For example, suppose an accountant carefully audits a firm's financial statements and believes the statements are correct. Suppose these financial statements become part of reports given to shareholders and are filed under the Securities Exchange

ROSENBLUM v. ADLER

N.J. Supreme Court.
461 A.2d 138 (1983).

FACTS Adler, an independent auditor was hired by Giant Stores Corporation (Giant) to audit its financial statements. Adler failed to catch errors in Giant's financial statements that an auditor would discover using normal care and skill. Rosenblum, a third party, relying on the financial statements Adler audited, bought Giant's stock. The stock later became worthless. Rosenblum sued Adler, claiming he would never have bought Giant stock had Adler's audit been accurate. Adler did not know when the audit was done that Rosenblum or any limited class of persons such as Rosenblum (that is, a stock buyer) would rely on the audited statements.

ISSUE Did the independent auditor owe a duty of care to Rosenblum, a third party who neither as an individual nor as a class member, was foreseen by the auditor as a financial statement user when the audit was done?

DECISION Yes. The New Jersey Supreme Court did not require privity of contract (a contractual relation) for a third party to recover in negligence from the independent auditor. In other words, a third party can recover from an accountant for carelessness (negligence) even though that person did not hire the accountant. Third parties can recover if they receive audited statements from the audited company for a proper company purpose, and rely on the statements to make a business decision, and the statement errors result from the auditor is negligence. In other words, the foreseeable effects of negligent acts determine whether someone may sue an independent accountant. In this case, the court said a corporate client's showing carelessly prepared financial statements (four months after the audit) to third parties, who were thinking of buying the corporation's stock, was foreseeable. The court noted the independent accountant did not limit who the client could show the financial statements to. The court said that the malpracticing accountant was in a better position to bear the loss than certain innocent relying third parties. Malpractice insurance is usually available to accountants.

LEGAL TIP

The trend is to hold independent public accountants liable for negligence to third parties. Such accountants should obtain malpractice insurance covering this risk.

Act of 1934. Suppose the accountant *later* discovers information which shows that information in the Securities Exchange Commission reports is false. Does the accountant have a legal duty to correct a statement if it becomes false based on information acquired later? The *Fischer v. Kletz* case answers this question.

VICARIOUS LIABILITY

The preceding discussion of accountants' liability assumes that the accountant sued broke the contract or committed fraud or negligence. Often, a staff accountant or accounting firm member does something wrong, and the victim sues *other* accountants or firm partners or both. Who is liable in such **vicarious liability** cases?

Accountants who commit wrongs are personally liable for them. The fact that they may be working for someone else as agents, servants, or independent contractors is irrelevant.

If the accountant is an employee of a partnership, the partnership and all partners (but *not* non-partners) are personally liable for an employee's wrongs within the scope of employment. The same is true if a partner commits a wrong. This rule should make accounting firms careful about whom they hire.

Some accounting firms are **professional corporations** (PCs). Accountants working for PCs who commit wrongs within the scope of their jobs bind only the

FISCHER v. KLETZ

U.S. District Court.
266 F.Supp. 180 (1967).

FACTS In 1964 Yale Express System, Inc. (Yale), hired Peat, Marwick, Mitchell & Co. (PMM), an independent external accounting firm, to audit its financial statements. These financial statements became part of the 10-K annual report Yale filed with the Securities and Exchange Commission. The statements also became part of the annual report given to Yale's stockholders. At an unspecified date, probably shortly after PMM completed its audit of Yale, Yale hired PMM to do "special studies." These studies were of Yale's past and current income and expenses. While doing these "special studies" before the end of 1964, PMM discovered that the figures in the annual report were substantially false and misleading. On May 5, 1965, PMM disclosed the falsity of the annual report figures to stock exchanges where Yale stock traded, to the Securities and Exchange Commission, and to the public. PMM did not disclose this information for several months after discovering it. Plaintiffs sued PMM for common law fraud.

ISSUE If accountants make a representation in good faith believing it is correct and later discover it is incorrect, do the accountants have a duty to disclose the after-acquired information if they know people are relying on the earlier statement?

DECISION Yes. Liability for nondisclosure is based upon the duty of good faith and common honesty the law imposes. An accountant who makes a representation believing it to be accurate must correct the information if it becomes false and he or she knows people are relying on it. This rule applies even if the person making the misrepresentation did not personally profit from it when it was made or later. The court did not say how long the duty to disclose after-acquired information lasts.

LEGAL TIP

Avoid common law fraud liability in audits by using information acquired later to correct earlier statements once thought to be true.

PC, not other firm employees or shareholders. However, all the PC's assets may be taken to pay for any wrong a PC employee commits at work.

ACCOUNTANTS' CRIMINAL LIABILITY

Accountants' Common Law Criminal Liability

Accountants can be liable for conspiracy to obtain property under false pretenses if they give a favorable opinion on a firm's financial statements knowing the statements are false.

Accountants can be liable for criminal conspiracy if they agree with another to do a legal act illegally or do an illegal act. For example, if an accountant willfully and knowingly says Vita Corporation has $1 million per year in profits (when it does not) so that Vita can get a bank loan, the accountant could be criminally liable for conspiracy to obtain property under false pretenses.

Accountants' Statutory Criminal Liability

Accountants can commit crimes under the 1933 Securities Act (SA) by willfully making any untrue statement of a material fact or omitting any material fact in a registration statement. Also, any willful violation of any provision of the SA or regulation promulgated under the 1933 SA is a crime. Criminal violations of the 1933 SA are federal felonies. Punishment includes fines of as much as $10,000, 5 years in prison, or both.

Any person commits a federal felony who willfully violates any provision of the 1934 SE Act or any regulation under it if the violation is made unlawful or the observance is required. Similarly, anyone commits a crime who willfully and knowingly makes any statement in any application, report, or document that is required to be filed under 1934 Act or rule. Both violations can result in a $10,000 fine or imprisonment for as much as 5 years.

The *United States v. Simon* case discusses criminal liability under the SEA.

UNITED STATES v. SIMON

U.S. Court of Appeals (2nd Cir.).
425 F.2d 796 (1969).

FACTS Continental Vending Corporation hired Lybrand, Ross Brothers, and Montgomery, an independent public accounting firm, to audit its books. The auditors discovered Roth, Continental's president, was using company money to play the stock market (probably embezzlement). Roth tried to hide his improper use of Continental funds by "laundering" the money (loaning it to Valley, an affiliated company Roth managed, which then loaned it to Roth). Roth's activities raised doubts about Continental's solvency. Lybrand (the auditors) discovered Roth's activities, but Roth threatened them with a malpractice suit (for not detecting his wrongdoing in previous years) unless they gave a favorable opinion on Continental's financial statements in the current year. The auditors gave Continental a "clean" (favorable) opinion on its financial statements but hedged somewhat. The auditor hedged by putting a footnote in the financial statement that incompletely and vaguely pointed out what they knew about Roth. Continental later went bankrupt. The United States Government prosecuted the Lybrand accounting firm partner supervising the audit and two other associates of the auditing firm for criminally violating the 1934 Securities and Exchange Act. The firm defended on grounds that professional auditing standards did not require auditors of Continental to know what Valley did with money borrowed from Continental and loaned to Roth. Several prominent members of the auditing profession corroborated the defendants on this point.

ISSUE Did the independent auditors commit a federal crime by giving favorable opinions on false financial reports filed with the Securities and Exchange Commission?

DECISION Yes. Even though auditing standards did not require auditors of Continental to know that Valley loaned funds it borrowed from Continental to Roth, accountants have a duty to disclose facts they actually know if nondisclosure makes the financial reports materially false. Since the auditors actually knew about Roth's improper activities, failure to disclose this in the SEC financial reports made them materially false and therefore a federal crime.

LEGAL TIP

Auditors' opinions should not hold back information about a client—even if the information is not something auditors have to know.

ACCOUNTANTS' LIABILITY UNDER FEDERAL STATUTES

Two federal statutes that place great potential liability on accountants are the Securities Act of 1933 (SA) and the Securities Exchange Act of 1934 (SEA).

Civil Liability Under the Securities Act of 1933

Section 11 of the SA makes accountants liable for errors or omissions in registration statements. Registration statements are filed with the federal Securities and Exchange Commission. Such statements usually only have to be filed when a *new* security is offered for sale to the public. Therefore, this liability does not cover many sales of securities (since most stocks and bonds traded are "old" or already issued).

Elements of Section 11 case The plaintiffs, or injured persons, in **Section 11 cases** have to prove:

1. They bought the security.
2. The security is covered by a registration statement.
3. A material misstatement or omission was made in the registration statement.
4. They lost money on the security.

Note that investors need not show that they relied on the registration statement.

Defenses against Section 11 lawsuits The following defenses are available to accountants sued under Section 11:

1. *Due diligence.* Due diligence means the accountants sued met the necessary standard of care in preparing their part of the registration statement. An accountant must meet the care that an ordinary, reasonable, prudent accountant would exercise.
2. *Immateriality.* An error or omission in a registration statement is immaterial if it is so small that knowing or not knowing it would not change the average, prudent investor's decision to buy the security. The plaintiff (security buyer) must prove the mistake or omission is material to make a Section 11 case. The defendant (or accountant) can, of course, try to prove the error or omission is so small that it is immaterial.
3. *Buyer knowledge.* Buyer knowledge is a defense if the accountant can prove the security buyer knew of the error or omission when the security was bought.
4. *Other causes of damage.* An accountant can escape liability under Section 11 by showing that the plaintiff's loss was caused by factors *other than* the material error or omission. For example, an economic recession could explain a decline of the stock of all computer firms, quite aside from omissions or errors in the security's registration statement.
5. *No reliance.* Usually a Section 11 defendant is liable even if the plaintiff did not rely on the material error or omission. However, if the issuer released an income statement covering a period of a year or more after the registration statement took effect, and the plaintiff *then* bought the security, the plaintiff would have to show reliance on the error or omission.
6. *Statute of limitations.* A peculiar one-year, three-year statute of limitations exists for SA civil violations. Lawsuits must be started one year after discovering the violation but in no case later than three years after the violation.

Civil Liability Under the Securities Exchange Act of 1934

Accountants can be civilly liable under Section 18 of the SEA. The SEA regulates the secondary market (where "used" or already issued securities are sold). The SEA requires certain persons to file reports with the Securities and Exchange Commission (such as the 10-K or annual report, the 10-Q or quarterly report, and the 8-K or current report).

Elements of Section 18 civil case Any person is civilly liable under Section 18 of the SEA: Who causes a misleading statement; to be made in any report filed with the SEC; under the 1934 SEA; where the plaintiff relies on the misleading statement.

Defenses to Section 18 civil case There are several defenses to a **Section 18** civil charge including:

1. Defendant acted in good faith and had no knowledge that such statement was false or misleading.
2. Plaintiff failed to prove an element of its case. (For example, a plaintiff failed to show there was a misleading statement in an SEC report.)

RULES OF EVIDENCE AFFECTING ACCOUNTANTS

Accountants' Working Papers

Accountants' working papers are the papers (including names, memos, and audit plans) that accountants make while on a job. These belong to the accountant, not the client. Clients may look at the working papers that pertain to them. For example, a client might fear employee theft and therefore want to see the independent accountants' comments on the client's internal controls.

Accountant-Client Privilege

Accountant-client privilege means that communications between the accountant and client may not be discovered or subpoenaed in a lawsuit unless the client agrees. For example, if the client and accountant discuss a legally risky tax deduction, the Internal Revenue Service (IRS) would want to know this information.

Whether the IRS or anyone else can discover what the accountant and client say to each other depends on whether an accountant-client privilege exists. There is no general federal accountant-client privilege applicable to all federal agencies. (Therefore, the SEC or other federal regulator could learn what the accountant and client say to each other.) Some states have an accountant-client privilege, others do not.

However, the United States Supreme Court recently held that independent auditors' notes are not protected by a **work-product privilege** (which allows accountants to refuse to turn over working papers to persons suing the accountants). The *U.S. v. Arthur Young & Co.* case discusses this matter.

U.S. v. ARTHUR YOUNG & CO.

U.S. Supreme Court.
52 U.S.L.W. 4355 (1984).

FACTS Arthur Young (AY) was the independent auditor for Amerada Hess Corporation (AHC). AY audited AHC's financial records (as required by federal securities laws). While doing that AY made notes, called tax accrual work papers, to show how accurately AHC's past income tax reports were made and so AY could tell if AHC had set aside enough money to pay any additional income taxes. The IRS, the United States government's tax collector, did a routine tax audit of AHC. This audit showed AHC had made some questionable deductions in the past. The IRS then began a criminal investigation of AHC's tax returns. The IRS said that federal law allowed it to get AY's tax accrual work papers on AHC. AHC told its independent accountant (AY), not to turn the papers over to the IRS. The IRS sued AY to get the papers. The federal district court told AY to give the papers to the IRS. AY appealed. The United States Court of Appeals said AY did not have to turn over work papers to the IRS. That court said independent auditors' "work papers have a work-product immunity" when made for publicly owned corporations. The IRS appealed to the United States Supreme Court.

ISSUE Are independent accountants' work papers protected from disclosure to the IRS by a "work-product immunity doctrine"?

DECISION No. The United States Supreme Court said that the Internal Revenue Code (tax law) does not give independent accountants a work-product privilege. That court refused to say independent accountants are like lawyers (who do have a work-product privilege that usually lets them refuse to turn over work papers to people suing their clients). The Supreme Court also said the stock markets would not be hurt even though accountants had to turn over their notes about their clients. Independent accountants have a duty to the public to be "watchdogs" of their clients' conduct that outweighs the accountants' duty to their clients.

LEGAL TIP

Accountants should be careful what they write when they make notes for themselves (in work papers) while doing an audit. The IRS might be able to see such notes at a later time.

KEY TERMS

Internal accountants
External accountants
Breach of contract
Negligence
Privity rule
Fraud
Vicarious liability
Professional corporations
Section 11 cases
Section 18 cases
Accountants' working papers
Accountant-client privilege

CHAPTER PROBLEMS

1. Over the past sixty years has the trend of accountants' liability been decreasing or increasing?
2. What are some civil wrongs accountants can be liable for?
3. Can accountants ever be civilly liable for punitive damages?
4. If accountants can be held liable under federal securities laws, what value are common law theories

(for example, negligence, fraud, and breach of contract) now?

5. If an accountant is accused of negligence, must the accountant have *gained* anything from the negligence to the liable?
6. Are all the partners in an accounting firm liable if *one* partner is negligent in performing firm business?
7. Suppose an accounting firm employee (who is not a partner) is negligent in performing partnership business. Are the partners liable for the negligent, on-the-job acts of their employee?

*8. Coopers and Lybrand was hired to do accounting for Minit Man Development Co. (Minit Man) and two limited partnerships, Car Wash Investments No. 1 Ltd. and Car Wash Investments No. 2 Ltd. from 1972 through 1977. Plaintiffs were partners in Hadden View Investment Co., a company whose funds were used to invest as limited partners in the two car washes. Minit Man was the general partner in both car wash limited partnerships. Between 1975 and 1977, Minit Man and both car washes went out of business. Plaintiffs each lost $52,000 (their limited partnership investment). One plaintiff lost $200,000 more on notes she had guaranteed. Plaintiffs sued Coopers and Lybrand, claiming negligence in auditing Minit Man. Coopers and Lybrand defended on grounds that plaintiffs lacked privity with the accountants. Was this defense successful? *Hadden View Investment Co. v. Coopers & Lybrand,* 70 Ohio St.2d 154 (1982).

*9. Arthur Andersen & Co. (AA) is a public accounting firm, which audited Frigitemp Corporation (FC). FC hired Aeronca as a subcontractor to manufacture panels for a large building job FC had. Aeronca had difficulty collecting periodic payments for its work for FC. Aeronca requested FC's financial statements, audited by AA, to see if FC was solvent and worth continuing to work for. Aeronca continued to work for FC and give it credit based on FC's audited financial statements, which showed that FC's finances were healthy. FC filed for bankruptcy and Aeronca was unpaid. Aeronca then sued AA for negligently auditing FC. AA defended saying that it owed no duty of care to Aeronca since it was not in privity with AA. What is the result? *Aeronca, Inc. v. Gorin,* 561 F.Supp. 370 (1983).

*10. Alexander Grant and Company (AG) was a public accounting firm. General Home Products Corporation (GHP) hired AG to prepare an unaudited financial statement for the year 1977. GHP provided AG with the financial information needed to do the audit. When AG finished preparing the unaudited financial statements, GHP showed them to Spherex, another company. Spherex later lost money in its dealings with GHP because of alleged errors in the financial statements AG prepared for GHP. Spherex claimed that it detrimentally relied on the financial statements in extending credit to GHP. Spherex sued AG, claiming that either AG knew the unaudited financial statements were inaccurate or that AG was negligent in preparing the financial statements. AG defended saying that its liability did not extend to a third party (Spherex) not in privity with AG. AG also contended that it was unreasonable as a matter of law for Spherex to rely on unaudited financial statements. Was AG correct? *Spherex, Inc. v. Alexander Grant & Co.,* 451 A.2d 1308 (1982).

Approximately one out of six United States citizens draws some type of Social Security benefit.

United States Department of Health and Human Services

Chapter 37

Employment Law: Some Important Statutes

CHAPTER PREVIEW

- Workers protected by the Fair Labor Standards Act
- Equal Pay Act's coverage
- General duty standard established by the Occupational Safety and Health Act (OSHA)
- Injuries covered by workers' compensation statutes
- Persons entitled to Social Security benefits
- Protection of employee pensions by the Employee Retirement Income Security Act (ERISA)

It looked dangerous. At least that's how it appeared to Virgil Deemer. Virgil had been told by his supervisor at the Whirlpool Corporation to crawl out on a wire mesh screen twenty feet above the factory floor. The purpose was to retrieve parts that had fallen onto the mesh screens from overhead parts conveyors running through the plant. Deemer thought he could be killed or seriously injured if the screen broke and he fell to the concrete floor below. Deemer's boss told him, "Get out onto that screen. Don't be a sissy." Deemer didn't like that last remark. He told his supervisor the job was too dangerous. His boss told him to punch out on the time clock and go home. Virgil told his supervisor that the Occupational Safety and Health Act (OSHA) had a regulation that made it illegal for an employer to dismiss an employee for refusing to do a job the employee thought was dangerous. The supervisor told Deemer that no law—even OSHA—tolerates employee insubordination. What is the rule in this case?

Federal and state statutes have reshaped the entire area of employer–employee relations over the past fifty years. Such statutes address two major employee concerns: job safety and financial security. This chapter divides the statutes into these two major areas. Grouped under the topic of job safety are a *preventive* law (the Occupational Safety and Health Act [OSHA]) and a *compensatory* law (Workers' Compensation). The second topic, workers' financial security, covers ERISA, the Social Security Act, the Fair Labor Standards Act, and Equal Pay Act.

Figure 37-1 presents an historical overview of statutes in the employer-employee area.

JOB SAFETY

This section covers Workers' Compensation and OSHA.

Workers' Compensation

In the early part of the twentieth century, state legislatures started establishing **workers' compensation** systems. These systems have as their objective paying workers (or their dependents) for work-related injuries, diseases, or death. Employers are liable for all such employee harm, even though the employer was not to blame. In other words, employers are insurers of job-related harm to employees.

Early laws tended to cover only hazardous work, and even then they were not always welcomed. For example, Maryland enacted a law in 1902 setting up a cooperative accident fund for miners that was later held unconstitutional. Montana had a similar experience with its 1909 Miners' Compensation Act. Although New York's 1910 Compulsory Workers' Compensation Act covered only a few hazardous jobs, it was likewise declared unconstitutional.

Finally in 1917, the United States Supreme Court held that workers' compensation laws were valid exercises of a state's police power in the *New York Central Railroad v. White* case (243 U.S. 188). The *White* decision broke state resistance to workers' compensation. By 1920, there were only eight states *without* a workers' compensation law. Early statutes tended to cover only hazardous jobs. Today, all

Figure 37-1 **Historical Overview of Some Key Statutes Regulating Employer-Employee Relations**

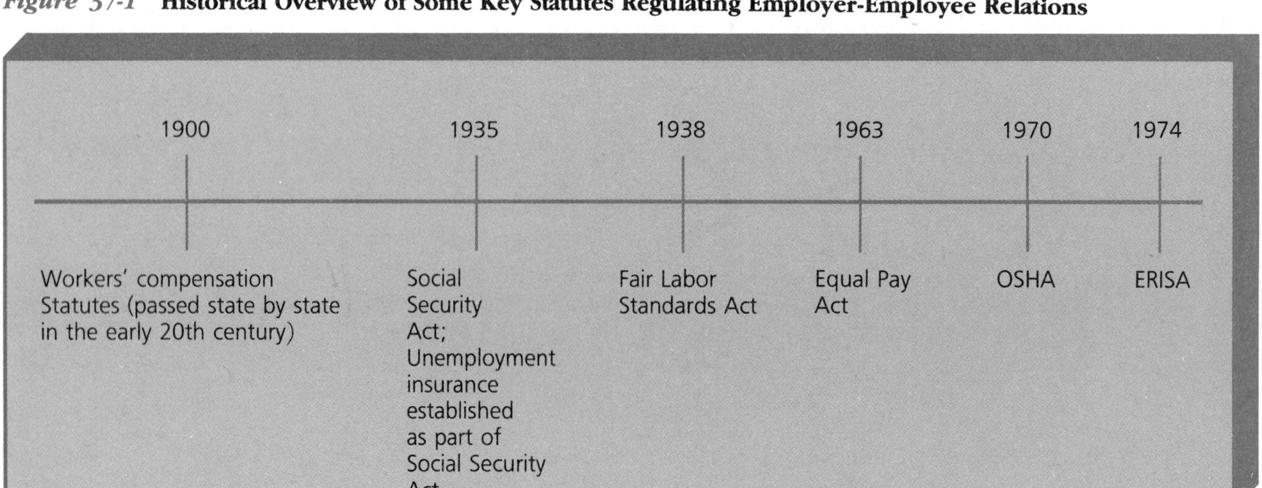

states have workers' compensation laws. Most cover both hazardous and nonhazardous jobs.

Common Law Fault

Before workers' compensation laws, workers injured on the job recovered if they showed employer *fault* (negligence) injured them. This was a common law (judge-made) basis of recovery. Furthermore, even if employer fault were shown, the employer could escape liability by proving any one of the following defenses: the injured employee's **contributory negligence** (that is, the employee's own fault contributed to his or her loss); the worker's **assumption of risk** (that is, the worker voluntarily performed a job knowing of the risk involved and was injured by this risk); or a fellow servant's carelessness injured the worker—called the **fellow servant rule.**

The common law negligence rules just described prevented many injured workers or deceased workers' dependents from recovering for job-related injuries or death. The employers' argument on behalf of common law rules was essentially cost: Common law rules kept worker claims low. Common law rules placed a large part of the cost of industrial injuries on the victims and their families and, indirectly, on society. For example, if an employee broke her back at work due in part to her own carelessness (contributory negligence), she recovered nothing.

Shift to Workers' Compensation

Common law rules were often harsh on injured and diseased workers and their families. Many felt that using negligence's fault idea was too crude to allocate the burden of industrial injury, disease, and death in a complex economy. To such people, these are costs of the goods or service produced and should be borne irrespective of fault by the party in the best position to administer them—the business producing the goods or service. The business in turn will pass this cost on to the consumers of the product or service.

Workers' compensation insurance is the mechanism for imposing these human costs on employers. Workers' compensation abandons common law fault principles in deciding who bears the cost of work-related injuries, diseases, and deaths. Instead, it makes the employer the insurer of these risks.

Key Features of Workers' Compensation Statutes

Workers' compensation statutes (called "workers' comp") are state laws and vary from state to state in terms of types of accidents and diseases covered, beneficiaries, and procedures. However, there are many similarities among these laws as discussed in the following subsections.

Work-related requirements A worker (or dependent) may recover only for injuries, disease, and death occurring on (or related to) his or her job. For example, if an employee carelessly places a ladder against a wall at work, falls, and sustains injuries, workers' comp pays. If that same employee falls from a carelessly placed ladder at home, workers' comp does *not* cover the injuries (since they are not job-related).

Courts tend to construe the work-related requirement liberally. This liberal approach means that if there is a doubt whether an injury occurred on or off the job, courts tend to say it occurred on the job. These rulings allow the insured worker to recover from workers' comp. For example, an accountant working for a large public accounting firm attended a day-long firm outing at a country club. On the way home at midnight, the accountant was killed in an auto accident. A court held this death was work-related, enabling the accountant's family to recover under workers' comp.

Generally, workers' comp statutes do not allow employees to recover for self-inflicted injuries. This rule reduces malingering (pretending one has a covered injury to collect benefits). Suicides present exceptional cases, because malingering is unlikely. The *Delaware Tire Center v. Fox* case indicates that at least one state is willing to regard certain suicides as compensable. According to *Fox,* a suicide is not willful for workers' comp purposes if an industrial accident was the precipitating factor that triggered the worker's suicide.

DELAWARE TIRE CENTER v. FOX

Supreme Court of Delaware.
411 A.2d 606 (1980).

FACTS On April 13, 1973, Earl A. Fox, Jr. had an accident at work and received workers' compensation benefits for his injuries. Due to the resulting pain, he was unable to return to work. In 1977 Dr. LeRoy, Fox's physician, was concerned that mental problems might be contributing to Fox's disability and inability to overcome pain and incapacitation. He sent Fox to Dr. Weintraub, a psychiatrist. Weintraub concluded Fox suffered before and after the accident from depression, anxiety, and a feeling of being incapable of supporting his family. Weintraub also found Fox had a drinking problem and had attempted suicide in 1975. In 1977, Fox committed suicide by a multi-drug overdose. Dr. Weintraub testified that Fox's 1973 injury at work was a cause of the suicide. Fox's widow applied for workers' compensation death benefits. Fox's employer, Delaware Tire Center, challenged the widow's claim. To support this position, the employer pointed to the Delaware Workers' Compensation Act, which denies benefits where death or injury results from an employee's willful intention to injure or kill himself.

ISSUE Was Fox's suicide a willful, intentional act denying his widow worker's compensation death benefits?

DECISION No. Fox's widow recovered workers' compensation death benefits. The Delaware Workers' Compensation Act uses the words "willful intention" to describe employee acts that were not compensable. Death by suicide is sometimes compensable. This occurs if the suicide is caused by severe pain and despair proximately resulting from a compensable accident (here, Fox's 1973 at-work accident). Since the pain and despair is so great that it overrides normal, rational judgment, suicide in such cases is not the result of willful intention, but just intention.

LEGAL TIP

Workers' compensation benefits are not usually given to workers who intentionally injure or kill themselves.

Certain but limited recovery One feature of workers' comp is the certain recovery given to all covered employees. If an employee loses a hand in a press, a loss schedule sets dollar values for all types of losses for all workers. For example, the schedule may allow $5000 for a hand, $7500 for an arm, and $10,000 for an eye. For unscheduled losses, a percentage of disability is determined. This partial (or total) disability recovery is related to an employee's earnings. In either case, employees are handed checks for the amount the workers' comp benefit schedule says they get—no more, no less. Thus, this recovery is certain and does not depend on winning a jury verdict. The common law defenses of contributory negligence, the Fellow Servant Rule, and assumption of risk are not available to employers under workers' comp, because the employer is an insurer (presumed liable provided the worker loss relates to the job). Fault is not an issue as it is in negligence cases.

Exclusivity of remedy Workers' comp statutes eliminate employee common law and statutory claims against their employer. The workers' comp statute is the *only* legal and guaranteed basis for an employee to recover from the employer for job-related injuries, diseases, or death.

If the employee's actual expenses or loss from a work-related accident are more than what workers' comp provides, the injured employee must pay for the difference. This points out that workers' comp statutes are "deals" or bargains between employees and employers. Of course, a harm may be worth more to one person than to another. Even if this premise is true, an employee *cannot* forego the workers' comp recovery and sue on common law principles instead. Employees are *limited* to workers' comp recovery for work-related injuries, diseases, or death—even though a particular employee's real losses may be far greater than what workers' comp allows. This limited, exclusive remedy is a major advantage to employers. Such an advantage is greater in inflationary times because workers' comp benefits usually are not inflation-indexed. Also, workers' comp benefits are often conservative, partly because they try to project mythical "average" employees' losses (in calculating, for example, the value of an arm).

Suits against third parties Workers' comp's exclusive remedy rule applies only to employee lawsuits against their employers. In other words, workers' comp says its recoveries are the only ones available against an employer. However, it does not stop an employee from suing a third party according to common law or other statutory principles for job-related injuries, disease, and death. For example, employees of insulation installers have sued the manufacturer of asbestos fibers. Recently, one such manufacturer, the Manville Corporation, entered bankruptcy allegedly due to such third-party claims.

Nonapplication of independent contractors Most state workers' compensation statutes apply only to employees (agents and servants)—*not* to independent contractors. This rule has great financial consequences for business: Specifically, business would prefer to have independent contractors rather than employees (agents and servants), because it does not directly pay their workers' comp insurance costs. Workers' comp costs are high and rising because of increased medical and hospital costs and the pressures to expand "job relatedness" to include more employee injuries and disease under workers' comp coverage. One Wall Street investment firm's 1976 study on workers' comp showed employers' workers' comp costs increased from $3.9 billion to $6.4 billion in three years.

THE OCCUPATIONAL SAFETY AND HEALTH ACT

The **Occupational Safety and Health Act** (OSHA) is a federal law that was passed in 1970. In the four years before OSHA was passed, more United States workers were killed at work than were killed in the Vietnam War. About two million were disabled each year by work-related accidents. The *President's Report on Occupational Safety and Health* (1972) estimated that 100,000 *deaths* per year are attributable to occupational diseases and illnesses from exposure to chemical and physical hazards. Congress tried to stop this carnage in the work place by passing OSHA. President Nixon signed the Act into law on December 29, 1970; OSHA took effect on April 28, 1971.

OSHA's Objectives

OSHA tries to provide a safe and healthy work place for workers as well as preserve the country's human resources.

How OSHA Works

The Secretary of Labor has promulgated hundreds of regulations to make work safer. For example, some OSHA regulations require a certain amount of lighting, handrails on stairs, and inside toilets.

How do OSHA and workers' comp differ? A key difference is that OSHA is *preventive* (it tries to stop harm before it happens); workers' comp is *compensatory* (it tries to help workers *after* harm occurs).

Employers Covered

When OSHA became law, it covered about four million businesses (both large and small) affecting interstate commerce. This involved about fifty-seven million workers.

Who Administers OSHA?

The Occupational Safety and Health Administration (also confusingly known as "OSHA") administers and enforces OSHA.

State OSHAs (SOSHAs)

The Act lets states develop standards and plans to regulate job safety and health. If a state does this and assures it will regulate as effectively as the federal plan, the state, not the Occupational Safety and Health Administration, regulates workplace safety and health in that state. At least one-half of the states have assumed OSHA administration and enforcement.

In the *Whirlpool Corp. v. Marshall* case, the United States Supreme Court upheld an OSHA regulation that allows employees to refuse to do their work if they reasonably believe death or serious injury would result *and* if the employees believe there is no less drastic way of doing the job.

EMPLOYEE FINANCIAL SECURITY

This section covers the Fair Labor Standards Act, the Equal Pay Act, Social Security, and the Employee Retirement Income Security Act (ERISA).

Fair Labor Standards Act

The **Fair Labor Standards Act (FLSA)** is a federal law that establishes minimum wage rates, overtime pay, equal pay, record keeping, and child labor standards. These rules affect over fifty million full-time and part-time workers. The FLSA does not set minimum wage rates and maximum hours for all jobs.

Covered workers The FLSA covers workers in interstate commerce (such as interstate bus drivers) and workers producing goods for interstate commerce (such as employees in Hastings, Michigan, making piston rings that will be shipped throughout the United States). The following businesses are covered by the FLSA:

1. Laundries or dry cleaners.
2. Construction firms.
3. Hospitals.
4. Schools (including higher education), whether public or private.

WHIRLPOOL CORP. v. MARSHALL

U.S. Supreme Court.
100 S.Ct. 883 (1980).

FACTS The Whirlpool plant had overhead conveyor belts. They carried parts from one area to another. A wire mesh screen suspended about 20 feet above the floor protected employees from parts occasionally falling from the conveyor belts. A foreman ordered two employees to do usual maintenance on the screens. The employees refused, claiming the screens were unsafe. The foreman ordered the employees to punch out without working or being paid for the rest of their shift. The employer put written reprimands into the employees' files. Section 11(e) of the OSHA prohibits an employer from discharging or discriminating against any employee exercising a right under OSHA. Secretary of Labor, Ray Marshall, promulgated a regulation giving employees the right *not* to do assigned work if they reasonably believe death or serious injury will result *and* believe that there is no less drastic way of doing the job. The two discharged employees relied on this OSHA section and regulation in refusing to crawl on the mesh screen. The federal district court held the regulation invalid (and upheld the employee dismissal). The United States Court of Appeals reversed, saying the employees' actions were justified and the regulation was valid. Whirlpool appealed to the United States Supreme Court.

ISSUE Was the OSHA regulation allowing employees to refuse to do assigned work if they have a reasonable fear of death or injury valid?

DECISION Yes. OSHA language gives the Secretary of Labor authority to promulgate regulations to put the Act into effect. This conclusion follows from OSHA's language, structure, and legislative history. The "refusal to work" regulation promotes the Act's purpose of *preventing* occupational deaths and serious injuries. The regulation also promotes the Act's "general duty clause," which requires an employer to furnish each employee employment and a place of employment free from recognized hazards causing or likely to cause death or serious injury. Therefore, the regulation is in harmony with the Act's purpose.

LEGAL TIP

Employees can refuse to do work their employer assigns if they reasonably fear death or serious injury and reasonably believe no less drastic alternative is available.

5. Retail or service businesses with annual gross incomes of at least $362,500 (starting January 1, 1982).
6. Any other business having annual gross sales or business of $250,000 or more.

A business having as its *only* regular employees the owner or members of the owner's immediate family is not covered by the FLSA.

Federal employees are subject to the FLSA's minimum wage, overtime, child labor, and equal pay provisions. The *Garcia* case (53 U.S.L.W. 4135) decided by the U.S. Supreme Court in 1985 held that the FLSA's overtime and minimum wage requirements apply to state and municipal government employees. The *Garcia* case means that state and municipal workers performing traditional government functions such as firefighters must be paid the federal minimum wage. Also federal overtime laws apply to such workers.

Domestic workers such as maids, housekeepers, cooks, chauffeurs, or full-time babysitters are covered if they receive at least $100 cash wages in a calendar year or work eight or more hours per week for one or more employers.

FLSA Wage Standards

Workers covered by the FLSA had a legal right to a minimum wage of $3.35 per hour as of January 1, 1981. Covered workers also have a right to overtime pay at not less than 1½ times the employee's regular rate after 40 hours of work in the work week.

Covered employers may sometimes pay less than the minimum wage. Learners, apprentices, and handicapped workers may, under certain circumstances, be paid less than the minimum wage. Full-time students in retail or service business, agriculture, or higher education institutions may be paid less than the minimum federal wage. (Keep in mind that most states have minimum wage laws that might cover students and others not federally protected.) Special certificates issued by the Department of Labor's Wage and Hour Administrator must be obtained to pay these groups subminimum wages.

FLSA exemptions Despite being employed by a covered firm, some employees are not covered by the FLSA's minimum wage provisions. Others are not protected by the overtime sections. Still others receive no wage or hour protection at all. Certain workers, such as executives, professionals, teachers, outside salespersons, and casual babysitters receive no protection from either the FLSA's minimum wage or overtime provisions. Without this protection such employees can work more than forty hours per week at any wage.

The *Guthrie v. Lady Jane Collieries, Inc.* case examines what workers the FLSA covers.

GUTHRIE v. LADY JANE COLLIERIES, INC.
U.S. Ct. of App. (3rd Cir.).
722 F.2d 1141 (1983).

FACTS Guthrie and other coal mine employees worked as maintenance foremen and senior mine foremen. They sued their coal company employer (Lady Jane Collieries, Inc.) claiming they had been denied overtime pay required by FLSA. The employer defended on grounds that the foremen were "executives" and therefore not protected by the FLSA.

ISSUE Were the coal mine foremen "executives" and therefore *not* protected by the FLSA?

DECISION Yes. The foremen were "executives," and therefore were *not* entitled to overtime pay. Factors the Court of Appeals looked at in deciding whether the foremen were "executives" included: the relative importance of their duties, their discretionary powers, and their freedom from supervision. The foremen here were totally responsible for the health and safety of the men under their command. The foremen assigned jobs and received a salary even if the crew was not working and the mine was closed.

LEGAL TIP
If an employee is an executive, he or she cannot collect overtime pay under the federal FLSA.

FLSA record keeping The FLSA requires employers to keep records on wages and hours. Most of the information is of the kind generally maintained by employers for other laws. These records do not have to be in any particular form, and time clocks need not be used.

FLSA enforcement The United States Department of Labor's Wage and Hour Division administers and enforces the FLSA against business. The Department also enforces the FLSA against state and local governments, federal employees of the Library of Congress, United States Postal Service, Postal Rate Commission, and the Tennessee Valley Authority. The United States Civil Service Commission enforces the FLSA for all other federal employees.

To see that the FLSA is followed, the Department of Labor's Wage and Hour Division has authority to investigate and gather data from an employer on wages, hours, and other employment conditions or practices. The Department can tell an employer to change its way of operating so that it obeys the FLSA.

FLSA Sanctions

Willful violations of the FLSA are crimes carrying fines up to $10,000. Second criminal convictions may result in imprisonment. Civil penalties are possible for violators of the FLSA's child labor provisions. It is also a FLSA violation to fire or in any other manner discriminate against an employee filing a complaint or participating in a FLSA proceeding.

Recovery of Back Wages

One of the FLSA's remedies for workers is the possibility of recovering amounts they were underpaid. Workers can recover unpaid minimum or overtime wages in several ways:

1. The Department of Labor's Wage and Hour Division may supervise such payments.
2. The Secretary of Labor may sue for back wages *and* an equal amount as liquidated damages.
3. An employee may file a private suit for back pay *and* an equal amount as liquidated damages, plus attorney's fees and court costs.
4. The Secretary of Labor may get an injunction to stop anyone from violating the FLSA, including wrongful withholding of the proper minimum wages.

Statute of Limitations

The statute of limitations provides two years for recovery of back pay, except when there is a willful violation, in which case the statute of limitations is three years.

Equal Pay Act

The **Equal Pay Act of 1963** (Act) amends the Fair Labor Standards Act (FLSA) and is part of the FLSA. The Equal Pay Act makes it illegal to pay different wages based on sex to men and women doing substantially the same work. If the jobs require equal skill, effort, and responsibility and working conditions are similar, pay to men and women *must* be equal. Because this requirement is a federal law, it applies in all states to all businesses affecting interstate commerce. Therefore, the Equal Pay Act applies to most businesses (and labor unions as well). The Act also covers federal, state, and local government employees and applies to most employees subject to the FLSA (including executive, administrative, professional, and outside sales personnel).

If a bank has two tellers, one man and one woman, and each has slightly different tasks, the bank must pay them the same wages. Jobs do not have to be identical, but *substantially equal* for the Act to apply. Otherwise, employers could easily defeat the Act's purpose by creating some small difference in their jobs and thereby justify pay differences. If an employer violates the Act, it may not lower an employee's wages to eliminate the differential.

For example, if a wage difference is only partly based on sex, the difference is totally illegal. However, the Act does allow wage differences between men and women if based on factors other than sex. Such things as bona fide seniority systems, merit systems, or systems rewarding productivity do not violate the Act.

The *E.E.O.C. v. Hernando Bank, Inc.* case discusses an alleged violation of the Equal Pay Act.

E.E.O.C. v. HERNANDO BANK, INC.

U.S. Court of Appeals (5th Cir.).
724 F.2d 1188 (1984).

FACTS The Equal Employment Opportunity Commission (EEOC) sued the Hernando Bank, Inc. (Bank) for violating the Equal Pay Act. The EEOC alleged the Bank paid female assistant cashiers less than male assistant cashiers who did "substantially similar" work. The Bank defended with three affidavits by the three female cashiers, who the EEOC claimed were discriminated against. Each affidavit said: "I am not aware of any sex discrimination at Hernando Bank; therefore, I did not request, do not desire, nor have I authorized the EEOC to represent me . . . ." The Federal District Court dismissed the EEOC's case on grounds that there were no facts showing an Equal Pay Act violation. The EEOC appealed. Evidence showed a substantial pay difference between male and female assistant cashiers. No female assistant cashier had ever been paid as much as any male assistant cashier. One male assistant cashier given an unfavorable performance rating was reassigned to a lower job ("courier") but continued to get a higher salary than any female assistant cashier.

ISSUE May the EEOC bring an Equal Pay Act suit against an employer if the alleged victims of the Equal Pay Act violation sign affidavits saying they are unaware they are being discriminated against in pay?

DECISION Yes. The Court of Appeals said that the Equal Pay Act refers to discrimination in terms that may not appear to be discrimination to a layperson. The test for an Act violation (against a women) is whether a woman is paid less for a job "substantially equal" to a man's. This test requires a look at job content rather than job title or description. Matters such as seniority systems, merit systems, quantity or quality productivity schemes, and other differences not based on sex are considered. Therefore, an alleged victim might not be aware a violation is occurring because of the complexity of factors involved. Just because an alleged victim is unaware of a violation of the Act does not mean there is no violation. In this case, the Court of Appeals found a substantial pay difference between male and female assistant cashiers. The Court of Appeals returned the case to the district court for further proceedings.

LEGAL TIP

The EEOC can bring an Equal Pay Act suit against an employer even if the allegedly injured employee does not think there is a violation.

Social Security[1]

The following example discusses the matter of Social Security: Art Wolf had been a tool-and-die worker with American Machine Company for forty-five years. He started work at age twenty after serving three years in the United States Army. Wolf had managed to put his two children through college at State University and had fully paid for his house. He was planning to retire the following year. Both he and his wife were in good health and hoped to move to Florida. Wolf started calculating his retirement, since he knew he would receive a monthly retirement check from the company retirement fund as well as a Social Security check. He was uncertain whether his Social Security income would be taxed. He wondered if his Social Security income would be cut, since he had heard the Social Security system was going bankrupt. Wolf did not know if working part-time would cause him to lose his monthly Social Security income. The following sections examine the answers to these uncertainties.

Background

The Social Security Act (SSA) took effect in 1935 with an original purpose to provide a minimal income for retired workers. In 1939, the SSA increased coverage to pay dependents of a worker who died. The 1935 SSA gave only the worker—

[1]The authors acknowledge the assistance of Social Security Administration brochures in preparing this section.

not dependents—money to live on in retirement. The 1939 amendments gave a *retirement income* to certain dependents of the worker.

The 1935 SSA gave nothing to workers who were totally disabled. It was not until July 1957 that SSA disability insurance benefits were first given to workers who lost income due to total disability.

In 1965, the Social Security program was amended to include Medicare, which assures hospital and medical insurance protection to people age 65 and over. Since 1973, Medicare coverage has been available to certain people under age 65. The 1973 amendments also cover people with permanent kidney failure who need dialysis or kidney transplants.

The *Ellender v. Schweiker* case discusses the SSA.

ELLENDER v. SCHWEIKER

U.S. District Court.
575 F.Supp. 590 (1983).

FACTS The SSA set up two separate programs: SSI (Supplemental Security Income) and OASDI (Old Age, Survivors, and Disability Insurance). SSI gives welfare to the blind, disabled, and poor under 65 years of age. OASDI is an insurance program providing retirement, disability, and survivor benefits to former wage earners who have contributed to OASDI for enough time. Once former wage earners can no longer work due to age, disability, or death, they receive monthly checks. For unexplained reasons, the Social Security Administration made a $1 billion "computational error" between January 1974 and December 1975. As a result, it *overpaid* SSI recipients, such as the plaintiff, Ellender, in this case.

Dorothy Ellender was a 75-year-old widow whose sole present income was a monthly OASDI check for $413.90. She also received $161.85 in monthly benefits under the SSI program between January 1974 and December 1975. On October 5, 1978, she received a Social Security form telling her she had been overpaid $4264.95 in SSI. The form told her she had a right to appeal or seek a waiver. She did neither since in 1978 she no longer got SSI payments and thought the notice was a mistake. She heard nothing else about the matter until 4 years later when she got another notice from the Social Security Administration. This one said she must refund the $4264.95 immediately. She was frightened since she was having a difficult time living on her OASDI widow's check. She could not survive if the check were reduced. She understood her only choice was to repay immediately (impossible since she lacked the money) or authorize the Social Security Administration to reduce her monthly OASDI check until the $4264.95 was paid. Ellender agreed to the withholding but later sued to stop the withholding.

ISSUE Could the Social Security Administration recover overpayments to program beneficiaries in this way?

DECISION No. The court ruled that Ellender had not made a meaningful or voluntary decision when she authorized the reduction in OASDI benefits. Also, the Social Security Administration had no authority to reduce OASDI benefits even if the beneficiary consented. The notices sent to Ellender did not meet constitutional "notice" requirements of procedural due process since they did not fully explain her rights.

LEGAL TIP

When the United States Government tries to recover Social Security overpayments, it must obey the constitution's notice requirements.

Workers covered In 1935, the Social Security program covered only workers in industry and commerce. The 1950s saw the program expand to cover household and farm employees, persons in the United States Armed Forces, members of the clergy, most self-employed workers, and most state and local employees. Today, most workers in the United States (nine out of ten, according to the United States Department of Health and Human Services) are covered by Social Security.

Persons first becoming federal employees as of January 1, 1984, and later are now covered by Social Security. Federal employees before that time continue to be part of a separate federal retirement scheme, which is generally more favorable to federal workers than Social Security.

Administration

The Social Security program is run by the Social Security Administration in the United States Department of Health and Human Services. Employers and self-employed persons send in periodic (monthly or more frequently) Social Security taxes to a Federal Reserve Bank or designated commercial bank.

Employers must keep records for Social Security purposes. Employee names, earnings, Social Security numbers (no two are alike), and other information must be kept for four years after the taxes are due. Government officials may inspect employer Social Security records.

Who gets Social Security benefits? About one out of six persons in the United States gets some form of Social Security benefit.

Types of Social Security benefits Retirement checks are what most people think of when the term Social Security is mentioned. The SSA provides, in addition to retirement benefits, disability and survivors' benefits. A worker becoming severely disabled before age sixty-five can receive disability checks under Social Security. Disability for Social Security purposes exists if a person had a severe physical or mental condition that prevents him or her from working and is expected to last (or has lasted) for at least twelve months, or is expected to last until death. Blindness is one example involving disability benefits. Disability checks start on the sixth full month of a worker's disability and continue as long as the disability lasts. A severely disabled worker (for example, someone totally blinded) can get benefits even if he or she manages to do some work. The size of the disability benefit is currently tied to one's age and work credit.

Some key Social Security features Social Security has a number of significant points:

1. Social Security benefits are not subject to state or municipal income taxes.
2. Beginning January 1, 1984, some Social Security benefits will be subject to federal income tax.
3. Social Security payments may not be garnished by the beneficiary's creditors.
4. Social Security benefits (of *all* types) are covered by a cost of living adjustment (COLA). Before 1983, Social Security's COLA generally increased as the consumer price index (CPI) changed. This change happened without considering how much money Social Security had. In the early 1980s unemployment and recession reduced Social Security's income. At the same time, inflation increased Social Security's outflow to beneficiaries, and Social Security almost went bankrupt. In 1983, when Congress amended the SSA, the COLA also changed. Now, if Social Security's trust fund drops below certain levels, any COLA increases will be based on the lower of the CPI increase or the increase in average national wages. Later, if the trust fund increases to a certain amount, Social Security benefits based on the CPI alone will resume. Also, "catch-up" payments for missed CPI adjustments will be made.
5. The employer *and* employee pay equal Social Security taxes for the employee. (In 1985, both paid 7.05%.)

Regulation of Employee Pensions

The following example concerns an employee's pension: Sara Coleman had contributed 6% of her weekly take-home pay to her employer's retirement plan for the past 5 years. Coleman wondered what was being done with the money. Was it being put in safe or risky investments? Since Coleman was thinking of changing jobs, she wondered whether she would lose all of her pension contributions or whether they would follow her to a new job. Coleman asked her employer for information about the retirement plan. Her employer refused to give her any information. Was Coleman entitled to anything?

Employee Retirement Income Security Act (ERISA)

Many employees, such as Sara Coleman in the above example, pay money into an employer-established retirement plan. Many, like Coleman, wonder what protections the law provides for employee retirement plans. Congress enacted the **Employee Retirement Income Security Act of 1974 (ERISA)** to see that employee retirement plans provide the retirement income they are supposed to *when* they are supposed to.

Fiduciary duties ERISA tries to protect employee retirement plans in several ways. First, it creates fiduciary duties for plan managers and advisers. Second, it requires plan records and reports. Third, it sets plan investment restrictions. Fourth, it creates a federal corporation to insure employee benefits should the plan fail. Fifth, ERISA requires vesting *both* employee and employer contributions. Sixth, it places funding requirements on certain plans. Although ERISA imposes other restrictions on employee retirement plans, the main ones have been listed here.

ERISA's fiduciary duties for plan managers and advisers place the law's highest duty of care and good faith on such persons. Specifically, plan managers and advisers should use the care that prudent people would use in managing their own assets because employee retirement plans must be protected to make sure retirement income is available. Furthermore, plan managers and advisers have millions, sometimes hundreds of millions or even billions, of employee dollars under their control. The temptation to abuse this control is great. Therefore, the deterrent against such abuse must be great. The ERISA fiduciary duty applies to both retirement plan *managers* (those exercising control over the plan) and plan *advisers* who charge for their services.

Records and reports ERISA imposes records and reports requirements. The plan manager must record each individual plan participant's length of employment and the amount of vested benefits. An explanation of the retirement plan must be given to each employee. This explanatory brochure must be simple enough for the average person to understand what the retirement plan is about and might include information concerning loss of plan benefits, claims procedures, and eligibility requirements. Each employee retirement plan must put out an annual report with opinions from both an independent actuary and an independent certified public accountant. Employees and the public have a right to see the retirement plan's annual report. While ERISA imposes disclosure requirements, some suggest they are not as tough as those under the 1933 and 1934 Federal Securities Acts.

Investment restrictions ERISA has investment restrictions that limit what the retirement plan manager can do with the millions or billions of dollars in the plan. Transactions between a plan manager and the plan are illegal. For example, a plan manager's selling his hula-hoop factory to the plan would be a conflict of interest. Loans by the plan to the employer are illegal. The plan can, however, own the employer's securities. For example, Sears employees' retirement plan is the largest stockholder in that company.

ERISA created the **Pension Benefit Guaranty Corporation (PBGC)** to make sure employees get vested retirement benefits if the plan fails. However, the plan *and* the employer are required to repay amounts the PBGC has to pay employees. There are limits on an employer's liability to repay the PBGC.

Vesting One of ERISA's most important reforms is its **vesting requirements.** Vesting basically refers to rights that cannot legally be taken away. For example, workers who have vested pension rights cannot lose them by changing jobs. Often, both employees and employers pay toward an employee retirement plan. Before ERISA, employer contributions often did not vest until just before the worker retired. If a worker changed jobs, was fired, or for some other reason stopped working before vesting, he or she lost the *entire* employer retirement contribution (which might be forty years' accumulation in extreme cases). Before ERISA, if a large number of employees were fired just before vesting at retirement, the employer would get back *all* employer contributions for all such employees. The amounts would be used to pay benefits for other employees who remained until retirement, thus reducing the employer's retirement costs. Most scholars viewed this arrangement as inequitable and assumed that employer contributions were regarded as deferred pay (as opposed to an employer gift or "tip"). Employers argued that late vesting of employer contributions kept down employee retirement costs.

ERISA requires 100% immediate vesting of employee pension contributions. Regarding employer contributions, ERISA requires that employers choose among three vesting options: ten-year full vesting, five-to-fifteen-year graduated vesting, and the rule of forty-five.

All of the ERISA pension reforms aim to do one main thing: insure that employees *will* get the retirement checks they counted on. Remember also that ERISA does not require employers to set up a pension plan. ERISA also does not set retirement benefit levels.

Does ERISA prevent a private employer's retirement plan from reducing retirement benefits by amounts received from other benefit plans? The *Alessi v. Raybestos-Manhattan, Inc.* case provides an answer.

ALESSI v. RAYBESTOS-MANHATTAN, INC.

U.S. Supreme Court.
101 S.Ct. 1895 (1981).

FACTS Retired employees were receiving their pensions and won workers' compensation awards after their retirement. Their former employer's retirement plan reduced a retiree's pension by an amount equal to a workers' compensation award going to a retiree. Private pension plans are subject to ERISA. The retirees claimed the pension offsets (amounts by which workers' compensation awards reduced their pensions) were invalid under ERISA and a New Jersey statute forbidding such offsets. The employees argued that ERISA prevented pension forfeitures except in cases not present here.

ISSUE May an employee's private pension plan reduce a retiree's pension by the amount received from a workers' compensation award?

DECISION Yes. The pension offset was valid. The retirees pensions could be reduced by the after-retirement workers' compensation award. ERISA preempted (invalidated) the New Jersey statute forbidding this reduction. ERISA does have nonforfeiture provisions (meaning ERISA says employee pensions cannot be reduced in certain cases). However this is not such a case. ERISA leaves to the private parties creating the pension plan the question of form and amount of pension benefits. ERISA's "nonforfeitable" pension benefits assures that an employee's claim is legally enforceable but does not guarantee a certain amount or way to calculate benefits. Congress did not prohibit "integration" in figuring employee pension benefits. "Integration" here refers to combining pensions from other government income streams going to retirees. ERISA does not mention "integration" with workers' compensation, but it does allow integration of Social Security and Railroad Retirement benefits. Since such benefits have similar purposes to workers' compensation, the Supreme Court allowed integration here, too.

LEGAL TIP

Employers can keep down pension costs by including offset (integration) provisions in pension plans.

KEY TERMS

Workers' compensation
Contributory negligence
Assumption of risk
Fellow servant rule
Occupational Safety and Health Act (OSHA)
Fair Labor Standards Act (FLSA)
Equal Pay Act of 1963
Employee Retirement Income Security Act of 1974 (ERISA)
Pension Benefit Guaranty Corporation (PBGC)
Vesting requirements

CHAPTER PROBLEMS

1. How could it be argued that the Fair Labor Standards Act causes unemployment among young workers who tend to have low skill levels? Does this result suggest a possible modification in the FLSA? What are some arguments against exempting young workers from the FLSA's protections?
2. Who benefits from the Equal Pay Act? How can it be argued that men benefit from this law?
3. What objectives does OSHA have? In what ways does OSHA achieve them?
4. What is the "integration principle" announced in the *Alessi* case? Does the principle suggest a way to reduce the cost of employer retirement programs?
5. Is it true that the Social Security system *only* benefits senior citizens?

6. When discussing pensions, what does "vesting" refer to?

*7. Workers compensation generally covers only injuries, disease, or death at work. Did the following death occur "at work"? An electric utility company's line foreman supervised correction of a power outage. He corrected the problem at 9 AM but remained on call. He headed home in a company car, did some personal shopping, and stopped at several bars. At 4 PM, while drunk, he got in the company car continuing on his way home and was killed in a two-car accident. Evidence showed the collision occurred when he turned to avoid hitting a pedestrian. His widow and children sued to recover workers' compensation. Was he "at work" when killed? *Oakes v. W.C.A.B.,* 469 A.2d 723 (Pa. 1984).

*8. HPL Ohio, Inc. (HPL) was cited for a serious violation of OSHA regulations requiring handrails on platforms higher than four feet. HPL's platform, used for storage, was seven feet high and did not have handrails. Employees climbed on the platform about every three months. HPL argued the violation was nonserious. Was it? *HPL Ohio, Inc.,* 7 OSHC 2152 (1974).

*9. Employers Temporary Service, Inc. (ETS) was an employment service. A fifteen year old applied for employment, but misrepresented his age as nineteen on the employment application. ETS told the boy he would have to prove his age at his next visit to the hiring hall. No such proof was ever requested or offered. ETS found the boy work at R. A. Young Industries, Inc. (Young). While running a power press there, the boy suffered amputation of two fingers and part of his hand. The boy sued the employers, Young, and ETS for negligence. They defended by arguing the boy's exclusive remedy was under workers' compensation. The boy argued persons illegally employed (here, as child laborers) were not "employees" covered by workers' compensation. (The workers' compensation remedy would probably have been smaller than a judgment in a negligence suit. This would benefit the employers.) Who was right? *Allossey v. Employers Temporary Service, Inc.,* 277 N.W.2d 340 (1979).

*10. Social Security benefits are available for severely disabled workers *under* age sixty-five. In one case a forty-seven-year-old dry-wall finisher suffered from heart disease, hypoglycemia, vertebrovascular insufficiency, mental depression, and possible emphysema. Was this a "slight neurosis, slight impairment of hearing and sight" not entitling him to Social Security disability benefits? *Brady v. Heckler,* 724 F.2d 914 (1974).

"*Employees have as clear a right to organize and select their representatives for lawful purposes as the respondent has to organize its business and select its own officers and agents.*"

Chief Justice Charles Evans Hughes in *NLRB* v. *Jones & Laughlin Steel Corp.* (301 U.S.1, 1937)

Chapter 38

Federal Labor Law: Unionization and Collective Bargaining

CHAPTER PREVIEW

- Unions' effects on wages and the work place
- Four statutes regulating labor
- Two principal jobs of the National Labor Relations Board
- Ways a union can become employees' bargaining agent
- Employers not covered by the National Labor Relations Board
- Employer unfair labor practices
- Union unfair labor practices
- Replacement of strikers

Should a no-strike clause be enforceable? Jack Smith had negotiated a three year collective bargaining contract between the Retail Clerks Union and Men's Markets. The contract included arbitration and no-strike clauses. A dispute arose over the contract, and a strike resulted. Smith sued the union to enforce the no-strike clause. The union then claimed that the Norris-LaGuardia Act prohibited the federal court from issuing an injunction in labor disputes. Could Smith get the injunction to enforce the no-strike clause?

This chapter deals with the federal law of union organization and collective bargaining. It focuses on three federal statutes: the National Labor Relations Act of 1935 (also called the Wagner Act), the Labor-Management Relations Act of 1947 (known as the Taft-Hartley Act), and the Landrum-Griffin Act (or Labor-Management Reporting and Disclosure Act of 1959). Other federal and state laws governing the employment relationship were covered in other chapters.

EFFECTS OF UNIONS

Unions have brought the "labor" sector 10% to 15% higher wages, but employers have also increased their production efficiency. This increased efficiency means there are not as many jobs available for union workers.

A second effect of unions is a leveling of wages, because unions in an industry tend to stop economic declines and increases.

Finally, unions have been responsible for a number of other employee benefits. For example, they have reshaped the employees' economic pie from pure wages to wages, retirement, welfare payments, and various other fringe benefits. Unions have helped set up grievance procedures that reduce arbitrariness in the work place. Unions also help organize blue-collar political efforts.

Development of Labor Law

In the 1800s, the labor organization was treated by state law as a criminal conspiracy, that is a combination of employees who withheld services from their employees. This rule gradually changed by the late 1800s when the legality of union efforts was judged by the ends achieved and not the means used. Throughout the century, the court injunction was used to control unions.

The Sherman Act The year 1890 saw the passage of the Sherman Act, which declared combinations in restraint of trade illegal. The effect of the Sherman Act on unions was soon felt. Court orders stopped picketing and strike activity and killed the strike entirely. During this period and for a considerable time thereafter, judges sympathized with ownership interests and interpreted statutes to curb unions.

Norris-LaGuardia Act After an unsuccessful attempt in the Clayton Act of 1914 to exempt union activity from the antitrust laws, the Norris-LaGuardia Act was passed in 1932. Rather than outlawing the injunction against lawful union activity, the Norris-LaGuardia Act removed federal court power to stop peaceful labor disputes. The effect of this Act was to keep federal courts out of the process of regulating unions. (State courts, it should be noted, *may* issue injunctions in labor disputes.)

Railway Labor Act In 1926, prior to enactment of the Norris-LaGuardia Act, the Railway Labor Act was passed. As the name suggests, the function of this Act was to regulate labor in the railroad industry.

National Labor Relations Act The National Labor Relations Act, also called the **Wagner Act,** became law in 1935. At that time, it had two functions: to provide a way for employees to say if they wanted a union and to set forth a code of unfair labor practices binding employers only, with no prohibitions at all on unions.

Taft-Hartley Act From the management viewpoint, this last feature of the NLRA was a shortcoming, and in 1947 with the conservative trend in the country, the **Taft-Hartley Act** (the Labor-Management Relations Act) was passed. This Act rewrote the original NLRA and provided a new code of unfair labor practices applicable to unions. This Act also outlawed secondary boycotts,[1] enforced collective bargaining agreements, and provided for settling disputes affecting national health and welfare. These procedures were backed up with an eighty-day injunction before a strike could be called, encouraging collective bargaining for the period before the eighty-first day.

Landrum-Griffin Act Further reduction of union power came in 1959 in the **Landrum-Griffin Amendment** to the Labor-Management Relations Act. For the first time, Congress provided for federal regulation of the internal affairs of labor unions. Also, there were further restrictions on secondary boycotts and picketing during organizational campaigns.

THE NATIONAL LABOR RELATIONS ACT

National Labor Relations Board

The National Labor Relations Board (NLRB)[2] was established by the National Labor Relations Act (NLRA). The NLRB is a federal administrative agency whose function is to administer rights and duties arising under the NLRA. The NLRB's two main jobs are to prevent unfair labor practices and to settle representation questions.

The NLRB has jurisdiction to the maximum extent allowable under the United States Constitution's commerce clause. The NLRB does not start labor cases. Anyone except the NLRB may start a labor case.

Two types of proceedings can be started with the NLRB. One is the **complaint case** (C-case), which alleges that an unfair labor practice has been committed. Unfair labor practices can be committed by the company or by the union (and are discussed later). The **representation case** (R-case) is the second type of proceeding brought before the NLRB. Anyone but the NLRB can initiate representation proceedings. In the C-case, a charge can be filed by anyone except the NLRB. The complaint issues from a general counsel's employee. There is no power to review the general counsel's decision not to issue an order.

Unfair Labor Practices

One of the NLRA's main accomplishments was defining **unfair labor practices** (ULPs) as a legal wrong. When passed in 1935, only employers could commit ULPs. In 1947, the Taft-Hartley Act added ULPs that unions could commit. In other words the NLRA, as amended by Taft-Hartley, created several new causes of action based on wrongs that unions or employers could commit.

[1]Secondary boycotts refer to a bargaining technique generally requiring or forcing someone to stop handling another's products or business. In other words, a secondary boycott forces customers or suppliers of an employer the union has a dispute with to stop doing business with that employer. The union is one of the parties involved, and the other party is a customer or supplier of the employer.

[2]The authors acknowledge reliance on government publications in preparing this segment.

Employer ULPs Section 8(a) of the NLRA sets out five specific wrongs or ULPs that employers could commit under the NLRA:

1. Employer interference with restraint or coercion of employees in their rights to form, join, and assist unions [§ 8(a)(1)]
2. Employer dominance or interference with the formation or administration of any labor organization, or giving financial or other support to it [§ 8(a)(2)].
3. Employer discrimination regarding hire or tenure or any term of condition of employment to encourage or discourage union membership [§ 8(a)(3)].
4. Employer discharge or other discrimination against an employee because he or she has filed charges or testified under the NLRA [§ 8(a)(3)].
5. Employer refusal to bargain collectively with employees [§ 8(e)].

The Landrum-Griffin Act amended the Wagner Act and added a sixth employer ULP: an employer's entering any contract or agreement, express or implied, with a union to commit a secondary boycott [§ 8(e)].

The remedies available if an employer commits a ULP include damages and injunctions (court orders telling someone to stop doing something).

Union ULPs The Taft-Hartley Amendments to the NLRA in 1947 added the following union ULPs:

1. Restraining or coercing employees in the exercise of their rights to form, join, or assist unions [§ 8(b)(1)].
2. Causing or attempting to cause an employer to discriminate against an employee in violation of [§ 8(a)(3)] or causing or attempting to cause an employer to discriminate against an employee denied union membership for a reason other than nonpayment of union dues or fees [§ 8(b)(2)].
3. Refusing to bargain with an employer [§ 8(b)(3)].
4. Engaging in a secondary strike or picketing activity [§ 8(b)(4)].
5. Requiring as a condition to union membership a discriminatory or excessive fee [§ 8(b)(5)].
6. Causing or attempting to cause an employer to pay anything of value for services not performed [§ 8(b)(6)] (this is the anti-featherbedding provision).

The 1959 Landrum-Griffin Act added two more union ULPs:

1. Picketing against any employer where an object thereof is forcing an employer to recognize or bargain with an uncertified union [§ 8(b)(7)].
2. Entering an agreement with an employer to engage in a secondary boycott [§ 8(e)].

Generally, state courts handle labor disputes that otherwise would be unfair labor practices but that do not qualify under the NLRB's jurisdictional tests. They do so by applying state common law (to the extent it exists) to resolve the matter. Since the concept of an unfair labor practice as developed under the National

Labor Relations Act is unknown in most states, the primitive law that courts hand out in this complex area of union-management relations is generally unsatisfactory. Also, the state court judges—often with anti-union biases—minister their form of justice in labor disputes.

Non-union Company to Union Company

The following example discusses unions and unfair labor practices: Jack Driver, a former professional golfer who won the Masters and United States Open golf tournaments, made $3 million while on the pro-golf tour. When Jack realized his playing days were numbered, he bought a Cincinnati, Ohio, company that manufactured golf clubs. The company had five clerical employees (two accountants and three secretaries), two full-time sales representatives, one club designer, and twenty-five production and maintenance employees.

Jack had ideas about how golf clubs should be designed. He manufactured clubs incorporating these ideas. He thought there should be one style of club for pros and another for average players. The sales of Jack's company tripled the year after the new club came on the market and company profits tripled. Jack doubled his and the designer's salaries and gave the sales representatives $20,000 bonuses. The clerical, production, and maintenance employees got merit increases of 20% that year. Jack had a Christmas party at his house and gave each employee a Christmas card with a $100 bill inside and a set of golf clubs while they watched video tapes of Jack's Open victory.

Whenever an employee had a problem, he or she used to take it to Jack; however, Jack's accessibility soon diminished as his company expanded. After his success, Jack expanded his plant and doubled the number of production employees. He hired an MBA from State University to handle personnel problems. The next year Jack had too many employees to entertain them at his house. Instead of a party, he put an extra $25 in everyone's Christmas card. There was some employee grumbling about the company's getting too big.

Union organizational efforts One day several of Jack Driver's employees discussed forming a union. Jack regarded this attempt as ingratitude and became very angry. He learned who the pro-union employees were and fired them for their beliefs. This practice is an employer ULP [specifically a Section 8(a)(1) violation], and the fired employees are entitled to reinstatement with back pay and seniority rights.

Company union If Jack were to decide to build up a union financed by the company, he would commit an employer ULP [specifically, Section 8(a)(2)]. Employers may not give financial or other support to labor unions. (Check-off of union dues by an employer is an exception.) An employer may petition the NLRB for a representation election if at least one union claims to represent its employees.

Ways to unionize Jack's employees can unionize in at least three ways:

1. By voting "in" a union at a representation election.
2. By signing authorization cards.
3. By the NLRB's ordering the employer to bargain with a union.

Representation Election

The usual way to unionize is by voting to do so at a **representation election** (R-election) run by the NLRB. The employees vote by secret ballot, and a majority vote is needed for union certification. What prompts the NLRB to hold an R-election for a particular employer's work is a request (called a petition) from the employees, an outside union (who wants to represent such employees), or the employers. Employers cannot make a request for an R-election unless at least one outside union has sought to represent the employees.

Showing of interest Employees or outside unions may not request an election unless there is a showing of interest in a union (at least 30% of the employees must support a vote). Usually the employees' **showing of interest** comes by their signing authorization cards saying they want an R-election or that they want a particular union as their collective bargaining representative. (Employers often complain that unions tell employees that the authorization cards merely request an election when actually the cards authorize a particular union to represent the workers. Workers, employers claim, do not read what they sign. Workers may by authorization card designate a union as a collective bargaining agent, subject to a NLRB check for accuracy and authenticity.)

Pre-election campaign statements Assuming the NLRB orders a representation election (R-election), what may an employer say to its employees to influence the election? The NLRA recognizes that the employer has a free speech right created by the First Amendment of the United States Constitution and implemented by Section 8(c) of the NLRA. This right allows the employer to state its legal position and its views, arguments, or opinions on what unionization will mean, provided that no threats of reprisal or force or promises of benefits are made violating the NLRA's Section 8(a)(1) discussed previously. The idea is that R-elections should be conducted in **"laboratory conditions"**—that is, they should take place in a clinical, dispassionate atmosphere for employee judgments of whether or not to unionize.

Employer ULPs before R-election If an employer commits ULPs in pre-R-election campaign statements, several outcomes are possible. If the union wins the election, probably nothing will happen other than union certification as the employees' collective bargaining agent. If the union loses the election, the election could be rerun. Thus, an employer who has a good chance of winning an R-election should either make no pre-election statements to employees or be cautious about what is said. (If the union loses a close election, it will often claim that the employer statements were ULPs destroying the election "lab conditions.") Another possibility if the employer commits pre-election ULPs is that the NLRB will simply order the employer to bargain with the union. In effect, the NLRB administratively declares the union a winner even though it has not won an R-election. The reason is that the employer has so tainted the election atmosphere that lab conditions are impossible to achieve. This "tainting" is done where a majority of the employees signed cards authorizing the union to be their bargaining agent.

The *NLRB v. Gissel Packing Co.* case is the leading one on NLRB remedies if employer pre-election ULPs taint the R-election.

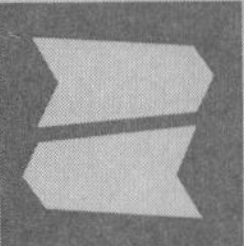

NLRB v. GISSEL PACKING CO.
U.S. Supreme Court.
395 U.S. 575 (1969).

FACTS A union tried to become the collective bargaining agent for Gissel Packing Company's employees. The union got authorization cards from a majority of Gissel's employees. Gissel refused to bargain with the union because it said the employees did not know what they signed. Gissel campaigned against a union for its employees. The National Labor Relations Board held that the union was the employees' bargaining representative because a majority of employees signed authorization cards. Gissel appealed to the courts.

ISSUE If a majority of an employer's employees sign authorization cards, can they make a union their collective bargaining agent?

DECISION Yes. Authorization cards can tell if employees want a union. The NLRB has rules for controlling card authorizations. These rules safeguard against a union's telling employees that signing the cards merely gets a representation election (when actually signing the cards can authorize the union as bargaining agent).

LEGAL TIP
Employees should read what unions ask them to sign. Authorization cards can have as their purpose either deciding whether to have a representation election or naming a union as a collective bargaining representative.

FREQUENCY OF REPRESENTATION ELECTIONS

Election Bar Rule

Suppose an NLRB-run representation election is held, and the union loses. What (if anything) stops the union from getting the required 30% showing of interest (by having employees sign authorization cards) the *next week* and petitioning the NLRB to hold *another* representation election? The answer is the **election bar rule.** The NLRA prevents an R-election if one was held within the previous 12 months and the union was defeated. The NLRB has held that the 12-month bar also applies if the union wins.

There are several reasons for the election bar rule. First, it forces employees to reflect soberly before initially voting for a union. Second, it reduces the disruption of the employer's business that R-elections cause. Third, it reduces the drain on NLRB administrative resources that occurs whenever R-elections are held.

Contract Bar Rule

Once a certified union and employer agree on a collective-bargaining agreement, the NLRB will dismiss any attempt (such as another union's) to have a representation election while the contract is in effect. This is the **contract bar rule.** The reason for this rule is to preserve stable relations between labor and management. In effect, the contract bar rule stops workers from getting rid of or changing unions while a contract exists between an employer and the union certified (by the NLRB) as the employees' collective bargaining agent.

ESCAPING UNIONS

Runaway Shop

The following is an example of a **runaway shop:** Shortly after U-union wins an R-election, Jack decides to shut down his Cincinnati, Ohio, plant and open a newer factory in Sarasota, Florida. This action may or may not be legal under the NLRA. If Jack moves his plant *solely* to get economic advantages of lower taxes and a lower area wage scale in Sarasota, Florida, he does *not* commit a ULP. However, if he moves his plant to escape or discourage unions, he *does* commit a ULP [specifically a Section 8(a)(3) violation]. This distinction creates the problem (or opportunity, depending on one's viewpoint) of employers being able to avoid illegality by simply stating reasons for plant relocation solely on economic grounds.

What sanction is applied if Jack relocates solely to escape a union? The NLRB will *not* order Jack to move his plant back to Cincinnati (the original location from which he fled). However, Cincinnati unionized employees will be offered first opportunity on jobs at the new location in Sarasota and awarded relocation expenses if they take the new jobs.

The Milwaukee Spring Division of Illinois Coil Spring Co. v. NLRB case discusses transferring work from a unionized to an non-unionized plant.

MILWAUKEE SPRING DIVISION OF ILLINOIS COIL SPRING CO. v. NLRB

National Labor Relations Board.
265 N.L.R.B. 28 (1984).

FACTS Illinois Coil Spring Company had plants in three different cities. Its Milwaukee, Wisconsin, plant was unionized. Its McHenry, Illinois, plant was not unionized. The company asked the union to give up a scheduled wage increase and make other contract concessions. When the company lost a major customer, it went to the union and proposed relocating its assembly operations in its non-unionized plant in McHenry. The company admitted its proposed move was to get relief from the higher unionized assembly operations in Milwaukee. (The proposed move was *not* the result of hatred of unions.) The company and union bargained at length over alternatives to relocation. The union then stopped bargaining about the relocation. The company then decided to relocate to its non-unionized plant. The union objected to the company's transferring work from a unionized to a non-unionized plant without the union's consent on the grounds that it was an unfair labor practice.

ISSUE If an employer transfers work from a unionized plant to a non-unionized plant without the union's consent does it commit an unfair labor practice?

DECISION No. The work transfer did not violate the union recognition clause nor the wage-and-benefit provision of the union's collective-bargaining provision (nor any other contract provision). The move would have violated a work-preservation clause if one had been in the contract (but none was). Therefore, the transfer to cut costs was legal since the move was not motivated by anti-union feelings.

LEGAL TIP

Employers can escape costly union contracts by relocating in non-unionized plants.

Bankruptcy to Escape Union Contracts

Bankruptcy is a way for a business to escape union contracts. In 1984 the U.S. Supreme Court allowed a company to file for bankruptcy under Chapter 11 of the Bankruptcy Act to escape union contracts. Such filing could be done without first discussing the matter with the union. Several months later, Congress modified this Supreme Court holding.

Congress amended Chapter 11 of the Bankruptcy Act so that a debtor in possession or a bankruptcy trustee (the person legally running the company after it enters Chapter 11) may not change collective bargaining agreements without first:

1. Making a proposal to the union.
2. Modifying employee benefits and protections needed to reorganize the company in a way that treats all creditors fairly and equitably.
3. Giving the union information to evaluate the proposal.

4. Meeting with the union to confer in good faith an attempt to modify the collective bargaining agreement.

The bankruptcy court may let an employer escape a collective bargaining agreement if:

1. The employer followed the four steps above.
2. The union rejected the proposal without good cause.
3. The balance of the equities favors rejecting the existing union contract.

Going Out of Business

The United States Supreme Court has held that employers may shut down a plant completely (forever) without committing a ULP, provided the employer does not have the intent to discourage unionization elsewhere (at plants in other locations, for instance). Thus, in the Jack Driver example, if the Cincinnati, Ohio, plant unionizes, Jack may legally close the plant permanently if he does not want to deal with a union.

THE COLLECTIVE BARGAINING AGREEMENT

Duty to Bargain

Continuing with this example, U-union is NLRB certified as the collective bargaining representative of Jack Driver's production employees. The U-representative approaches Jack to talk about entering a collective bargaining agreement. Jack says, "I don't believe in unions. I refuse to talk with you. My employees each have individual employment contracts. This arrangement suits me just fine. Get out." Jack has committed a ULP because employers have a duty to bargain (as do unions).

What does "duty to bargain" mean? Could Jack meet once with the union representative, listen to him or her, and leave without saying anything? He may not. The NLRB and courts have added the element of "good faith" to the "duty to bargain" concept. Therefore, Jack must meet and discuss wages, hours, and working conditions with an open mind. However, the parties do not have to agree on anything.

The Supreme Court has also held that employers and unions can bring economic pressures (strikes and lockouts, for example) against each other before, during, and after meeting to bargain and still be bargaining in good faith (and hence not committing ULPs).

Some employers claim they cannot afford union demands Often during bargaining, an employer will claim that it cannot afford a union demand. If the union asks the employer to prove this claim, the employer must document the claim or risk violating the duty to bargain in good faith.

An employer may not *increase* employee wages or employment terms without first bargaining with the union. To do so violates the duty to bargain in good faith, since it undercuts the negotiation process. However, employers may change wages or benefits *after* bargaining with the union about them even if no agreement is reached.

A union negotiates with the employer on the employees' behalf to reach a collective bargaining agreement (CBA). A CBA is a contract that can have any number of terms in it, such as management function clauses, union recognition clauses, arbitration clauses, and no-strike clauses.

In the *Boys Markets, Inc. v. Retail Clerks Union Local 770* case, the United States Supreme Court enforced a no-strike clause in a collective bargaining agreement. The agreement in the *Boys Markets* case had a provision calling for binding arbitration of the dispute that caused the strike. The purpose of binding arbitration is to settle labor disputes by asking a neutral third party (or parties—the arbitrator) to settle the matter without resorting to the court system for remedies. It is important that the parties continue their relationship during the arbitration process. To maintain this working relationship during the arbitration process, an injunction forbidding a union strike at this time is desirable.

BOYS MARKETS, INC. v. RETAIL CLERKS UNION LOCAL 770

U.S. Supreme Court.
398 U.S. 235 (1970).

FACTS Boys Markets, Inc. (Boys) and its employees' union had a collective-bargaining agreement. This agreement had a binding arbitration clause requiring the union and employer to ask a neutral third person to settle any labor disputes before either the employer or the union took the matter to court. The agreement also had a no-strike clause (the union agreed not to strike during the time the agreement was in effect). A labor dispute arose over whether the frozen foods supervisor (a non-union employee) had the right to rearrange packages in the frozen food cases, and a strike resulted. Boys sued the union in state court for an injunction to enforce the no-strike clause. The union removed the case to federal court (which it had the right to do). The union then claimed that the Norris-LaGuardia Act prohibited the federal court from issuing an injunction in labor disputes. Boys argued this prohibition was unfair since Boys would have no remedy when the union broke its no-strike agreement.

ISSUE Can a federal court issue an injunction to enforce a no-strike clause?

DECISION Yes. While the Norris-LaGuardia Act generally stops federal courts from enjoining strikes, this case was different. Here, the collective bargaining agreement had a binding arbitration clause (meaning the contract labor disputes had to go to arbitration). Allowing federal courts to issue injunctions to enforce no-strike clauses *encourages arbitration* (since unions will not want the matter to go to court). Arbitration generally means the employer and union are settling their dispute peacefully without strikes or lawsuits, which is desirable.

LEGAL TIP

If an employer gets a no-strike clause in a contract, it should also get a binding arbitration clause.

Strikes and Lockouts

Strikes and lockouts are devices that unions and employers use to pressure one another to enter collective bargaining agreements with terms favorable to them. **Strikes,** of course, are used by unions. In a **lockout,** the employer temporarily refuses to let employees work. Thus, it is an employer device to pressure employees. With some limits, strikes and lockouts are legal under the NLRA.

Replacing strikers Employers may hire temporary or permanent replacements for employees on economic strikes. Economic strikers are not entitled to full reinstatement after the strike unless and until their replacements leave. However, if employees strike in response to an employer ULP, the employer may only temporarily replace them for the length of the strike. After the ULP strike ends if the strikers unconditionally offer to return to work, the employer must reinstate them fully.

Voting Out the Union: Decertification Elections

Returning to the example in this chapter, suppose Jack Driver's employees have had a union for three years. After assessing their costs (including union dues, meetings, and lost work time for strikes) and benefits (including higher wages and better working conditions), they decide it is not worth having a union. Can they get rid of their union? Yes.

One way employees can eliminate an existing union is by a **decertification election.** One or several employees or another person or union acting for the employees may file a decertification petition with the NLRB. Along with the decertification petition, there should be an indication that at least 30% of the employees want decertification. The NLRB then conducts a decertification election by secret ballot. If a majority of employees vote to decertify the union, it no longer is the collective-bargaining agent.

Employers may *not* file decertification petitions. For example, if Jack Driver learns that some of his employees are unhappy with their union and encourages or helps them to file a decertification petition, he commits an unfair labor practice.

KEY TERMS

Wagner Act
Taft-Hartley Act
Landrum-Griffin Amendment
Complaint case
Representation case
Unfair labor practices
Representation election
Showing of interest
Laboratory conditions
Election bar rule
Contract bar rule
Runaway shop
Strikes
Lockouts
Decertification election

CHAPTER PROBLEMS

1. Explain why the Wagner Act is important.
2. How did the Taft-Hartley Act supplement the Wagner Act to benefit employers?
3. What are the two types of proceedings that can start at the NLRB?
4. Name four union unfair labor practices.
5. Name five employer unfair labor practices.
6. How can a union legally become the employees' collective-bargaining agent?
7. If there is a representation election and the union loses, can the union get another election the next week?
8. Is it possible for an employer to go bankrupt to avoid burdensome union contracts?

*9. Are university faculty members "employees" protected and covered by the NLRA? *NLRB v. Yeshiva University,* 444 U.S. 672 (1980).

*10. Does an employer have the right to replace striking employees? *S. P. Crowers Ass'n. v. Rodriguez,* 552 P.2d 721 (Calif. 1976).

Part Six

Business Organizations

▶ *Chapter 39*

Types of Business Organizations

▶ *Chapter 40*

Partnerships: Forming and Ending Them

▶ *Chapter 41*

Partnership Operation

▶ *Chapter 42*

Nature, Formation, and Termination of Corporations

▶ *Chapter 43*

Management of Corporations

▶ *Chapter 44*

Rights and Responsibilities of Shareholders

"Tis the only comfort of the miserable to have partners in their woes."

Cervantes
Don Quixote

"It (a corporation) is called a body corporate because the persons composing it are made into one body."

Lord Coke

Chapter 39

Types of Business Organizations

CHAPTER PREVIEW

- Reasons for operating as a sole proprietor
- Partnership definition
- Formation of a partnership
- Disadvantages of the partnership form
- Partnership by estoppel
- Advantages of the limited partnership form
- Uses of the business trust
- Definition of a corporation
- Investor advantages of the corporate form
- The Model Business Corporation Act (MBCA)
- Alter ego doctrine

"Eric, I'm not going to pay you," said Dorothy Powell. She had hired Eric's "Stardust Pools" firm to build a pool for her trailer park for $5107.40. He had completed the job, but Dorothy then claimed that he could not collect since he didn't have a swimming pool contractor's license. Eric had not taken the licensing test but had obtained a pool contractor's license jointly with a friend who had such a license. Could Eric recover the $5107.40?

Jake Buffkin was angry. He and his partner, Strickland, had raised tobacco. Their crop had burned while in storage. His partner had insured it for $25,020 in his individual name and refused to share the insurance proceeds with Buffkin. Does Buffkin have any rights to the proceeds?

This chapter has one objective: to survey the legal forms that a business can take. Such forms include the sole proprietorship, business trust, partnership, limited partnership, and corporation.

SOLE PROPRIETORSHIPS

Background

A **sole proprietorship** is simply any person in business to make a profit for himself or herself alone. According to the *Statistical Abstract of the United States* (1985 edition) for the year 1981, there were an estimated 9,585,000 nonfarm businesses in the United States having the legal form "sole proprietorship." The total receipts from sole proprietorships for 1981 were estimated by the same source to be $427.1 billion, with total profits of $53.1 billion.

Legal Form

A sole proprietor owns the business and its property in his or her individual name but may have employees to help in the business. The sole proprietor may operate under an assumed or fictitious (made-up) name. For example, Nancy Wood may own a drug store called "Arrow Pharmacy." States have fictitious name statutes that require registry of assumed names. Generally, the penalties for noncompliance with fictitious name statutes are not severe.

Reasons for Sole Proprietorships

Reasons for having sole proprietorships include simplicity, control, and convenience. Few legal formalities need to be observed to form a sole proprietorship. For instance, if one is a retailer, he or she must obtain a sales tax license and secure an occupational license before doing certain types of work. The state of Illinois, for example, requires licenses for over 180 occupations ranging from florist to insurance broker.[1] The lack of a license by a person engaging in such a profession can mean that contracts entered into by such persons are unenforceable or void.

The *Rushing v. Powell* case shows what can happen when a building contractor does not comply with a state occupational licensing law.

Disadvantages of sole proprietorships Liability exposure is unfavorable for the sole proprietor because sole proprietors are personally liable for all their business' debts. In other words, creditors can take all of the business and personal assets of the sole proprietor to pay business debts. For example, if a proprietor's deliveryman (while at work) runs over and cripples a little girl causing $1 million in damages, the proprietor will be liable.

A second disadvantage of sole proprietorships is that there are no partners to advise, help out in case of injury or illness, or lend their credit or expertise to the business.

Advantages of sole proprietorships The sole proprietor has the advantage of being his or her own boss. Sole proprietorships do have to file federal income tax returns. The return is for the proprietor as an individual and would include all of his or her income information.

[1]A complete list is published in Conard, Alfred et al. *Enterprise Organization,* Foundation Press, 1972, Mineola, N.Y., pp. 10–11.

RUSHING v. POWELL

California Court of Appeal (5th Dist.).
130 Cal.Rptr. 110 (1976).

FACTS Dorothy Powell hired Eric Rushing to build a swimming pool for her trailer park for $5107.40. Eric had an individual California concrete contractor's license. However, he did not have a California swimming pool contractor's license. California law forbids persons from doing work in an area where they are unlicensed.

Junior Ray Anderson had a California swimming pool contractor's license. Eric used Junior to get a swimming pool contractor's license so he could build Dorothy Powell's pool. Eric and Junior got a joint swimming pool contractor's license under the name "Stardust Pools." Since Junior already had such a license, the California licensing officials waived (did not require) Eric from passing the licensing exam or show fitness to be a swimming pool contractor. Eric gave Junior equipment worth $6000 for helping him get the license. Junior never actually did any swimming pool construction with Eric.

Eric built Dorothy Powell's pool, but she refused to pay. She claimed that Eric did not follow the plans. Eric sued Dorothy for breach of contract. Dorothy defended by arguing that Eric had not complied with California's fictitious business name statute or California's contractor licensing law. The trial court awarded Eric $5107.40 (the contract amount) plus $198.73 for extras beyond the contract. Dorothy appealed.

ISSUE May a contractor recover for work if he or she does not have the proper contractor's license and has not complied with the fictitious name statute?

DECISION A contractor may not recover for work if he or she is unlicensed. The contractor's licensing law is intended to protect the public against dishonesty and incompetence and deter would-be violators. The unlicensed contractor may not collect the $5107.40 contract amount. However, the contractor may recover $198.73 for extras since they were not part of the contract.

The contractor (Eric) complied with the fictitious name statute by filing a certificate showing that he was doing business as an individual.

LEGAL TIP

Businesspeople should check to see if work they do requires a license. If an individual does not have a necessary license, he or she will not be paid under the contract.

Unlike a close corporation, which has one or a few shareholders, the sole proprietor does not have to pay an annual franchise fee to a state. Nor does a sole proprietor have to keep minutes of shareholder, director, or executive meetings. However, books of account do have to be kept for federal, state, and municipal income tax purposes and for certain regulatory purposes.

Doing business elsewhere The limits on doing business in other states are not significant for sole proprietorships. Sole proprietors do have to comply with licensing, sales taxes, and other local restrictions applying to intrastate (local) transactions.

PARTNERSHIPS

Background

The 1985 edition of the *Statistical Abstract of the United States* estimates that there are 1,461,000 active partnerships in the United States. Gross receipts are estimated at $262.3 billion operating at a deficit of $2.7 billion for 1981 (the latest year for which figures are available). The strengths of using the partnership as one's legal form of business arise from combining the broader talents and material resources of two or more people. Using the partnership form has other advantages discussed below.

Partnership advantages A **partnership** is easy to form and does not require state approval. Property (real and personal) may be held and transferred by the partnership itself. The partnership may be ignored for federal income tax purposes at the partners' option. In this case, the partnership income is divided among the partners according to the partnership agreement and taxed as part of their personal incomes. This procedure eliminates double taxation.

Partnership disadvantages A major partnership disadvantage is liability exposure, which means that if a partner *or* partnership employee (while at work) harms a third person, the victim can seize all of the partnership's assets as well as all of each individual partner's assets to pay his or her damages. For example, if two doctors are in partnership and one commits malpractice against a patient, the victim can take all of the partnership's assets (as well as each partner's individual assets) to pay the loss.

Second, partners must keep minutes and business records. This requirement is imposed on partners by the **Uniform Partnership Act (UPA).** Also, partnerships selling partnership interests interstate may have to register such interests as securities under the federal securities acts.

Partnership Definition

The UPA is the law in all but two states. The UPA's definition of a partnership is an "association of two or more persons to carry on as co-owners a business for profit."

If two or more persons do not intend to *carry on* the business on a long-term basis, it probably is not a partnership. If two or more persons are in charitable work, the association is not a partnership because it does not do business for profit. The fact that the two or more people do not *actually make* a profit is irrelevant. What is crucial is whether they intend to operate a business for their personal profit. If they do, and they intend to do so over a period of time, they undoubtedly will be partners.

Partnership Existence

There does not have to be any express agreement between two or more people for a partnership to exist. In other words, the law may hold that two or more people are in a partnership even when they do not intend there to be one. Also, the fact that the parties have said their relationship is not a partnership is not conclusive. The courts use an objective, *not* subjective, test to determine the parties' intent to form a partnership.

Example of objective test One example in which two parties are partners (even though they did not intend to be partners) occurs when a corporation is defectively organized. Its shareholders are held to be partners despite clear subjective intent that they desired shareholders' limited liability rather than a general partner's unlimited liability.

Proving partnerships exist The burden of proving that a partnership exists is on the party claiming it exists.

Courts look at a number of factors to determine a partnership's existence. Two of the most important factors are joint right to manage the business and sharing profits.

Profit sharing Section 7 of the UPA declares that a person's sharing the profits of a business with another is prima facie evidence that he or she is a partner in the business. Prima facie evidence means that the evidence is strong enough to allow a judge in a jury trial to let the partnership issue go to the jury, and it can justify (but does not require) a jury's finding that a partnership exists. However, the UPA goes on to say that no prima facie inference that a person is a partner shall be drawn if business profits are received in any of the following ways:

1. As a debt repayment by installments or otherwise.
2. As wages of an employee or rent to a landlord.
3. As an annuity to a widow or representative of a deceased partner.
4. As interest on a loan, although the amount of payment varies with the business' profits.
5. As consideration for the sale of a business' goodwill or other property by installments or otherwise.

The sharing of gross returns (gross income before expenses are deducted to arrive at a profit figure) does not create a prima facie presumption of partnership. Sharing gross returns also does not establish a partnership's existence (whether or not the persons sharing them have a joint interest in property from which the returns are obtained). As these points suggest, the fact that two or more persons jointly own property does not necessarily mean that they are partners. However, joint property ownership does not necessarily *preclude* the joint owners' from being partners. Joint ownership is a neutral fact in determining partnership existence.

Right to manage The right to share in business management is one of the basic perquisites of a partner. However, a partnership agreement may confer the management power on one partner only without destroying the business' legal nature as a partnership. On the other hand, proof that a person has a right to share in partnership management does not establish that he or she is a partner. But when this fact is coupled with the additional one of profit sharing, there is a presumption that a person is a partner.

Partnership as an Entity

The law treats partnerships as legal entities for some purposes but not others. Partnerships are entities for bankruptcy, suing and being sued (in most states), and owning property.

On the other hand, partnerships are not entities for liability purposes. That is, if someone sues the partnership and gets a judgment that uses up all the partnership's assets, individual partners' assets must go toward payment of the debt.

Forming Partnerships

A partnership may be formed between two persons or among three or more persons. Good business practice suggests that the partnership contract be written. If a partnership agreement cannot by its terms be completed within one year, most states' statutes of frauds would require that the partnership agreement be written to be enforceable. For example, if two accountants agree to form a partnership for three years, this partnership agreement cannot be performed within one year and thus would have to be evidenced by a writing signed by the partners to be enforceable. If a partner does not want to honor a partnership agreement, the courts will not force him or her into a partnership. In other words, specific performance will not be awarded for breach of a partnership agreement. Damages, however, will be awarded when appropriate.

The *Buffkin v. Strickland* case shows some problems involved in determining if a partnership exists.

BUFFKIN v. STRICKLAND

Court of Appeals of South Carolina.
312 S.E.2d 579 (1984).

FACTS Buffkin and Strickland orally agreed to a joint farming venture. They agreed to lease some land and tobacco poundage from one Allen Powell. They also agreed to share equally the expenses and profits from the tobacco crop. Strickland paid the rental costs from his personal assets. Buffkin paid most of the other expenses from his funds. Buffkin and Strickland harvested the tobacco crop, which later burned while stored in a warehouse. Strickland received $25,020 in insurance proceeds, which he refused to share with Buffkin. Strickland argued that his providing money to buy the acreage lease and allotment showed the tobacco crop as his sole venture. Also, the insurance policy was in his name.

ISSUE Was there a partnership between Buffkin and Strickland regarding the tobacco crop?

DECISION Yes. A partnership is an association between two or more persons to carry on as co-owners a business for profit. A partnership may be created orally or impliedly. Buffkin did most of the work hiring laborers, getting farm equipment, and supervising the crop planting and harvesting. He also spent over $13,000 of his money for labor, equipment, and fertilizer. The partnership owned the crop. Therefore, when Strickland insured the crop, he did so as agent for the partnership. The insurance proceeds belonged to the partnership.

LEGAL TIP

Write out partnership agreements to eliminate misunderstandings.

Partnership by Estoppel

Partnership by estoppel is a legal theory that plaintiffs will raise against defendants. This theory tries to hold a defendant responsible for obligations of a partnership of which he or she actually is not a member.

Three elements Partnership by estoppel has three elements: reasonable reliance that another is a partnership member, change of position in reliance, and damages. The person claimed to be a partner by estoppel is not, in fact, a partner. Yet, if these three elements of partnership by estoppel can be established, the defendant is estopped (prevented) from saying that he or she is not a partner. In this type of situation, a defendant would be liable to the plaintiff for the partnership debt in question.

Limited Partnerships

A problem Sometimes a person wishes to join another in a business but does not want to take an active role in managing the business. He or she may not want to subject himself or herself to unlimited liability for partnership claims greater than the original capital contribution. Short of incorporating (with attendant double taxation, increased red tape in filing annual state reports, and the problems of qualifying to do intrastate business in other states), what, if anything, can be done to satisfy such a person?

A solution The **limited partnership** is a possible answer. This form is made possible by the Uniform Limited Partnership Act (or the Revised Uniform Limited Partnership Act), which is the law in all states except Louisiana. This Act is also the law in the District of Columbia and the Virgin Islands. Under the *Uniform Limited Partnership Act* (ULPA) there are certain requirements for forming a limited partnership. There must be a filing of the articles of limited partnership (partnership agreement) or a specified information document with a public office prescribed by each state's ULPA. Each state's ULPA will have some variations, one of which will likely be the form and place of filing limited partnership agreements or certificates.

Partners in limited partnerships Any limited partnership must have at least one general partner. This person (or persons) is unlimitedly liable for all the obligations of the limited partnership. The limited partner (or partners) are liable, however, only for the amount of the capital contribution that he or she agreed to make.

Limited partnership registry Ordinary partnerships do not and may not have limited partners; only limited partnerships may do so. The reason for allowing the limited partnership to exist is to help the partnership business attract investors. The limited partnership creditors are protected (from being misled into believing they are extending credit to a partner who has unlimited liability) by the registration of the limited partnership articles in a public office. The creditor or potential creditor should go to such a registry to see if the partnership is listed as limited. In the case of a limited partnership, note should be taken of which partners are limited.

Limited partners are passive The limited partner is supposed to be passive with respect to management of the limited partnership business. The more active a limited partner is in managing the firm's business, the greater the risk that the limited partner will become a general partner. If this situation occurs, the partner has unlimited liability.

Business Trusts

The trust device To understand the business trust, it helps to first examine the trust device. A **trust** involves a settlor, a trustee, a beneficiary, and a res. The settlor has property that is to be the res (the subject matter of the trust). The beneficiaries are the person or persons who are to receive the benefits from the trust. The trustee is the person or institution that manages the trust property. A peculiar feature of a trust is that it has two titles, or owners: a legal title and a beneficial title. The trustee holds the legal title, and the beneficiary has the beneficial title (also called the "equitable title"). A trust arrangement allows one person (the trustee) to manage the trust property and another person (the beneficiary) to receive the trust's benefits. Usually, the beneficiary is unable or unwilling to manage property.

The following subsections turn to business uses and variations of the trust, including the business trust, the Massachusetts trust, and the real estate investment trust (REIT).

Business trust A **business trust** is one in which the managers are trustees and the shareholders are beneficial owners. The basic feature of the business trust is that property is placed in the hands of trustees who manage and deal with it for the use and benefit of the shareholders (who are the beneficiaries). The similarities to the trust are apparent since the guidelines of a conventional trust are applied to a business' organizational form.

Massachusetts trust The *Massachusetts trust* is a business organization wherein property is legally owned by trustees who manage the trust property for the benefit of holders of trust certificates (which are similar to stock certificates). The Massachusetts business trust is an unincorporated association organized under Massachusetts law for investing in real estate in much the same way as a mutual fund invests in corporate securities.

REIT A **real estate investment trust (REIT)** is a financial device in which investors buy shares in a trust, and the trust res is invested in real estate. The REIT has been both in and out of favor as an investment device in the past decade.

CORPORATIONS

Corporations play a major role in our economic and political life. The 1985 edition of the *United States Statistical Abstract* estimates that in 1981 (the latest year for which figures are available) there were 2,812,000 corporations with a total income of $6,224,700,000,000 and profits of $213.6 billion.

Definition of a Corporation

The word **corporation** derives from the Latin word *corpus,* which means "body." Therefore, a corporation is a legal person, body, or entity. It is intangible. True, many of the assets owned by the corporation, such as the corporate office building, are visible and tangible, as are the corporate officers, directors, and shareholders. They are not, however, the legal corporation.

Limited Liability

Another corporate feature helping corporations raise money and encouraging investors to buy corporate stock is "limited liability." "Liability" means having to pay for something. **Limited liability** means a person does not always have to pay or only has to pay up to a certain amount and no more. Generally, shareholders are liable only for the amount they agreed to pay for the stock. There are some exceptions to this rule, but the important point is that one can generally purchase corporate stock and not be liable for any greater amount to the corporation or corporate creditors. If the corporation later goes insolvent, the corporate creditors may not seize the shareholders' individual assets to pay the corporate debt.

Transferable Shares

One other feature making corporate stock attractive is **transferability of corporate shares.** Although it is possible to restrict share ownership, most large corporations do not do so. By allowing share transfer, a corporation lets an investor sell the stock. This transfer protects investors by letting them get money for their stock any time.

Corporations' Constitutional Rights

Corporations are legal persons or entities. They are "persons" for purposes of both the national and state constitutions. A corporation is a "person" entitled to due process protection and equal protection of the laws. Also, corporations have protection against unreasonable searches and seizures.

Despite the above-listed constitutional protections, corporations are not given all the protections possible under the U.S. Constitution. Corporations are not "citizens" within the language of the Constitution conferring on citizens "... all privileges and immunities of citizens of the several states. . . ." This language means that a corporation does not legally exist outside of the state that creates it if intrastate business is done in a second state. Corporations do exist outside the creating state regarding interstate business.

For example, a corporation organized under the laws of California does not exist legally in Nebraska for purposes of doing intrastate business in Nebraska. The persons trying to so operate would legally be a partnership, unless they qualified to do intrastate business as a corporation in Nebraska. This requirement is not exactly the same as reincorporating in Nebraska. Certain documents do have to be filed with Nebraska state officials to enable the California corporation to transact intrastate business in Nebraska.

Law Governing Corporations

Law creating Almost all business corporations are creations of state—not federal—law. There are some federally chartered corporations, such as the Tennessee Valley Authority. There has also been talk of passing a federal corporation statute. As of now, such a proposal is merely talk. From a business standpoint, the advantages of uniformity and being a corporation in all states with one federal incorporation would exist if this proposal were passed as a statute.

Corporate operation The preceding section dealt with what law governs corporate formation. However, even though a corporation is created under one state's corporation law, other states and the national government may have the power to *regulate* that state's corporation. For example, if the corporation sells its securities in in*ter*state commerce, the federal securities laws require registration of the securities. Also, as we just saw, if a corporation is organized in one state and does business in another, it will have to qualify to do in*tra*state business in the other state.

Basic Corporate Definitions

A **domestic corporation** is a corporation organized under the corporation law of the state one is in. For example, a corporation organized under the laws of the state of Michigan is a domestic corporation in the state of Michigan. A domestic corporation is contrasted with a foreign one, which is a corporation organized under the laws of a state *other than* the state one is in. For example, a corporation organized under Indiana law would be a foreign corporation in Michigan. The foreign/domestic distinction is unrelated to the physical location of a corporation's assets. Many corporations are Delaware corporations, even though they have little in the way of physical plants or equipment there.

Governmental corporations refer to organizations, such as the Federal Deposit Insurance Corporation, that have no profit motive but exist for a social goal. Municipal corporations refer to cities and towns that have been given charters by the state to govern a geographic area. **Corporations for profit** are to be contrasted with **corporations not for profit.** Profit corporations are those that may divide profit among shareholders and do not necessarily have to earn a profit to be so classified. Nonprofit corporations are those that may not turn over earnings to their members. (Not-for-profit corporations have no shareholders, merely members.) **Professional corporations** refer to corporations organized by members of certain professions (physicians, accountants, dentists, and attorneys, for example). The professional corporation is relatively new and offers certain tax advantages and fringe benefits to professionals.

Model Business Corporation Act

The Committee on Corporate Laws of the American Bar Association is responsible for drafting the **Model Business Corporation Act** (MBCA). The MBCA is not law until state legislatures pass it. The MBCA gives state legislatures ideas for desirable features their state corporation statutes should have in them. It is up to the state legislatures whether to adopt the MBCA in whole or in part. Thus far, over half of the states have adopted, at least partially, the MBCA.

Why are states adopting the MBCA? In part, to do what Delaware and New Jersey have long done: attract firms from other states to incorporate under their lax laws so that the state can get revenue from corporate franchise taxes. The MBCA often favors management over corporate shareholders and creditors. For example, shareholders have the right to examine corporate books and records but are discouraged from exercising this right because they must have been either a shareholder for at least six months before requesting to see the books or an owner of 5% of all outstanding corporate stock. Further, the shareholder must submit his or her request to see the books in writing and state the reason for the request. The corporation may then grant the shareholder's request at a reasonable time, *if* the shareholder's request is proper (determined in the first instance by corporate officials). Not all provisions of the MBCA place shareholders and corporate creditors at the mercy of the corporate directors (the legal managers of the corporation).

Disregard of Corporateness

Occasionally, someone will follow all the rules for forming a corporation and a court will nonetheless say that a corporation does not exist. The legal theory for this practice is known as **alter ego** (or "piercing the corporate veil" or "disregard of corporateness).

Why would a court say no corporation exists if the rules for forming a corporation have been followed? There are several reasons:

1. The corporation may be used to commit fraud.
2. The corporation may be used contrary to public policy.
3. The people running the corporation may be mingling their business with the corporation's so the corporation actually is not separate.

The *McKibben v. Mohawk Oil Co. Ltd.* case lists eleven factors a court considers in disregarding corporateness.

Comparing Business Forms

Corporations are often compared with sole proprietorships and partnerships. Which is the best legal form for a business? The answer depends on the business and the businesspeople's objectives.

Figure 39-1 shows six factors that are used to develop the advantages and disadvantages of some of the legal forms identified previously: ease of formation,

McKIBBEN v. MOHAWK OIL CO. LTD.

Supreme Court of Alaska.
667 P.2d 1223 (1983).

FACTS McKibben and others had a mine. They leased it to Mohawk, Inc., a wholly owned subsidiary corporation of Mohawk, Ltd. (also a corporation). The lease said that if the mineral content of mined ore reached a specified low level, Mohawk, Inc.'s royalty payment would drop to 10%. McKibben claimed Mohawk, Inc. committed waste and conversion, "unworkmanlike" mining, and intentionally diluted the ore to get the lower royalty rate. McKibben sued Mohawk, Inc. and Mohawk, Ltd. even though *only* Mohawk, Inc. signed the lease. McKibben argued the court should pierce the subsidiary's (Mohawk, Inc.'s) corporate veil and hold the parent corporation (Mohawk, Ltd.) liable for the subsidiary's acts.

ISSUE Is this an appropriate case to pierce the corporate veil?

DECISION Yes. Two theories may be used to justify disregarding the corporate status of a subsidiary: First, a parent corporation may be liable when the parent uses a separate corporation to defeat public convenience, justify wrong, commit fraud, or defend crime. Second, a parent corporation may be liable because the subsidiary is a mere instrumentality of the parent. This means the parent is liable simply because the two corporations are so closely connected they do not deserve to be treated separately. The following eleven factors help decide if a subsidiary is acting merely as a parent's instrumentality (all eleven factors do not have to exist in every case):

1. The parent owns all or most of the subsidiary's stock.
2. The parent and subsidiary corporations have the same officers or directors.
3. The parent corporation finances the subsidiary.
4. The parent subscribes to all the subsidiary's stock or causes its incorporation.
5. The subsidiary has grossly inadequate capital.
6. The parent pays the subsidiary's salaries and other expenses or losses.
7. The subsidiary has substantially no business except with the parent or no assets except those the parent gave it.
8. The parent's papers describe the subsidiary as the parent's department or division or its financial responsibilities are referred to as the parent's own.
9. The parent uses the subsidiary's property as its own.
10. The parent tells the subsidiary's directors and officers what to do.
11. The formal legal requirements are not followed.

The first nine of these eleven factors were present here, so the court pierced Mohawk, Inc.'s corporate veil. Therefore, Mohawk, Ltd. (the parent) was responsible for Mohawk, Inc.'s acts.

LEGAL TIP

Parent corporations should treat subsidiary corporations as separate entities to avoid liability for a subsidiary's acts.

ease of operation (for example, absence of government red tape), attractiveness of the form as an investment vehicle, tax considerations, privacy, and control.

KEY TERMS

Sole proprietorship
Partnership
Uniform Partnership Act (UPA)
Partnership by estoppel
Limited partnership
Trust
Business trust
Real Estate Investment Trust (REIT)
Corporation
Limited liability
Transferability of corporate shares
Corporations
Domestic corporation
Governmental corporation
Corporation for profit
Corporation not for profit
Model Business Corporation Act (MBCA)
Alter ego

Figure 39-1 **Comparing Legal Forms of Business**

BUSINESS ORGANIZA-TIONAL FORM	EASE OF FORMATION	EASE OF OPERATION	LIABILITY EXPOSURE	TAX CONSIDERATIONS	PRIVACY	CONTROL
Sole proprietorship	Ease to form; no agreement required	Simplest form, except for governmental reports.	Unfavorable; unlimited personal liability.	No double taxation, but sole proprietor's income is subject to federal income taxation.	Yes; some reports.	Sole proprietor controls except governmental for regulation.
Partnership	Easy to form; no written agreement required, but one is advisable; two or more carrying on as co-owners a business for profit; could have a partnership and not be aware of it; possible partnership share subject to registration as a security.	Easy to operate, except for governmental reports.	Unfavorable; unlimited personal liability for each partner for all partnership debts; any change in partnership membership dissolves partnership.	No double taxation; partnership income not taxed at partnership level but passes to individual partners, where it is taxed at individual tax rates.	Yes, except possible reports filed with governmental agencies may be public records.	Each partner has equal right to manage irrespective of capital contribution unless contrary agreement.
Corporation	Need state authorization (charter); possible need to register corporate securities before offering to public.	Neutral to poor; many governmental reports possible (see Chapter 7 for government forms required from Gray-Mills Corporation).	Favorable; shareholder liability limited to share subscription or share amount; shareholders not personally liable for corporate debts unless guarantor of them.	Favorable to poor depending on number of shareholders; double taxation (two taxing events) possible when corporate income taxed and shareholder dividend income taxed; Subchapter S corporation avoids double taxation.	Least private business form; corporate charter (articles of incorporation) is public record; various reports filed with federal agencies may be public records.	Management control of proxy system results in shareholder loss of control of board of directors in corporations with large number of shareholders.

CHAPTER PROBLEMS

1. Are there any legal requirements for forming sole proprietorships?
2. What are some disadvantages of being a sole proprietor?
3. Compared to the corporate form, what is a major advantage of the partnership form?
4. Is it possible for two people to have a partnership and not know it?
5. What are some examples of profit sharing that do not give rise to an inference that a partnership exists?
6. Must limited partnerships be registered?
7. Give some key features of corporations.

*8. If a corporation is organized to limit the organizer's liability, is this reason enough to pierce the corporate veil? *Worth Pacific S.S. Co. v. Pyramid Ventures Group, Inc.,* 572 F.Supp. 1436 (D.C.La. 1983).

*9. A limited partnership agreement was signed by all the "partners." However, no one filed a limited partnership certificate with the appropriate public office. Did a limited partnership exist? *Blow v. Shaughnessy,* 313 S.E.2d 868 (N.C.Appel. 1984).

*10. Is use of a person's name in a business with that person's knowledge enough to justify finding the person was "held out" as a partner to establish liability under the doctrine of partnership by estoppel? *Brown v. Gerstein,* 460 N.E.2d 1043 (Mass. App. 558, 1984).

"A partner's fiduciary duty starts when the partnership is a twinkle in a partner's eye and lasts through the partnership's life."

Basic Partnership Rule

Chapter 40

Partnerships: Forming and Ending Them

CHAPTER PREVIEW

- Partnership definition
- Persons qualified to be partners
- Partnership formation
- Reasons for using the partnership form
- Partnership dissolution
- Three steps in ending partnerships
- Order for distributing partnership assets in the winding up process

"Our dreams have died. Now we have to salvage something," said Ted Conventz. He and his wife were in a partnership with the Schymanskis. They planned to build an Alaskan tourist lodge and had agreed that all profits and expenses would be split equally. However, as events occurred the Schymanskis contributed over $100,000 in cash and the Conventzs much less. Now the partnership was being dissolved. Ted claimed that his architectural advice and building supervision was a $50,000 service contribution to the partnership capital. Ted's wife also claimed a $20,000 service contribution to the partnership capital because she had been a cook for one year of the business. The Schymanskis argued that they were being cheated because partners' service contributions are never considered as capital contributions. Were they right?

The previous chapter indicated that a partnership is an association of two or more persons to carry on as co-owners a business for profit. This chapter examines the formation and termination of partnerships. The following chapter discusses partnership operation.

PARTNERSHIP NAME

The law does not force partnerships to have a name. However, most partnerships *do* have a name. If the name is fictitious (such as "E-Z Tax Service"), state laws require registration of such names to let the public know who owns the business.

The *Duris Enterprises v. Moore* case is an example of a fictitious name statute in a partnership matter.

DURIS ENTERPRISES v. MOORE
Ohio Appellate Court.
458 N.E.2d 451 (1983).

FACTS Duris Enterprises (Duris) was a partnership that leased property to Gahanna for one year. Gahanna broke the lease within the year, and Duris sued for breach of contract. Gahanna defended by arguing the partnership had an unregistered fictitious name. This fact, the defendant said, prevented Duris from suing until it registered its name with the state secretary of state.

ISSUE Was "Duris Enterprises" a fictitious name?

DECISION No. If it were fictitious, the partnership could not sue until the name was registered. Here, however, "Duris Enterprises" is *not* fictitious. A "fictitious name" is one that is "assumed, counterfeit, or pretended." "Duris Enterprises" reveals the partners' true surnames. Since the partnership had no other names, the addition of the word "enterprises" did not make the name fictitious. The intent of the fictitious name statute is to give the public a way to find out who the partnership members are. This was done here.

LEGAL TIP
Partnerships using assumed names must register them.

PARTNERSHIP FORMATION

Partnership Agreement

Two or more people carrying on a business for profit could be partners and not realize it. Therefore, it is usually not necessary to have a **partnership agreement** to have a partnership.

Wise partners always have a written partnership agreement (called "articles of partnership"). If the statute of frauds covers the partnership agreement, it *must* be written. For example, an accounting partnership that lasts two years would need a written agreement. (The statute of frauds requires bilateral contracts that cannot be completed in one year to be written.)

Contents of the partnership agreement Partnership agreements can prevent lawsuits by dealing with problems before they arise. The following is a list of *some* matters that the articles of partnership could cover:

1. The partnership's name.
2. The partners' names.

3. The partnership's purpose.
4. The amount and form (such as money, real estate, etc.) of each partner's contribution.
5. The length of the partnership.
6. Procedures to add and eliminate partners.
7. Division of profits and losses.
8. The person (or persons) with management authority.
9. Who, if anyone, is entitled to a salary.
10. The way to handle partnership affairs if a partner dies or is disabled.

The *Giblin v. Schzer* case shows a possible provision in the partnership agreement.

GIBLIN v. SCHZER

New York Supreme Court, App. Division.
468 N.Y.S.2d 719 (1983).

FACTS Giblin and others were members of a partnership. The partnership agreement expressly allowed a majority of partners to expel a partner if they decided his or her continued membership was undesirable. A majority of partners voted to expel Giblin. Giblin argued he had never signed the partnership agreement. Therefore, it did not bind him, he claimed.

ISSUE Is it valid for a partnership agreement to provide for expulsion of a partner by a majority vote for reasons of undesirability?

DECISION Yes. The agreement was valid. Even though plaintiff did not sign the partnership agreement, the partners' course of conduct ratified it.

LEGAL TIP
Partnership agreements can include provisions for getting rid of unwanted individual partners.

Partnership agreements are secret Partnership agreements do not have to be filed in any public office to be valid. Only the partners have a right to see them (unless partnership interests are considered "securities" requiring registration).

Who Can Be a Partner?

Minors Generally any mature, sane adult can be a partner. Minors can also be partners; however, minors can disaffirm their contracts, including their contract setting up the partnership. The partnership itself is still bound to its contracts even if a minor partner withdraws from the partnership. The withdrawing minors can get back what they paid into the partnership *only* if all partnership creditors are paid.

Insane persons A partner who becomes insane can withdraw (avoid) from partnership contracts. Insane persons can be partners if they have *not* been adjudged insane by a court. If a court declares a partner insane, *any* partner can dissolve the partnership.

Corporations Today corporations can be partners. At one time, corporations could not be partners.

How Long Partnerships Last

The partnership agreement can say how long the partnership lasts or can set a particular date for a job to be completed. This type of agreement is called a **partnership for a term.** If a partner breaks the partnership agreement before it ends, he or she is liable for damages.

Partnerships with no ending time are **partnerships at will.** A partner may end it any time with no damage liability.

Partnership Property

Partnership property is all property originally brought into the partnership and includes property bought on the partnership's account. If the partnership uses its money to buy property, it is presumed to be partnership property unless there is a contrary intent.

Partnership as property owner A partnership can own property in its name. Partnership property can also be titled in an individual partner's name, which causes confusion. Individual partners sometimes claim that property used by the partnership and titled in their individual name is their individual property. The best way to deal with this problem is to identify individual pieces of property (e.g., computers) and say who owns the property in the partnership agreement.

Individual Partners' Property Rights in the Partnership

The Uniform Partnership Act names three property rights of individual partners: rights in specific partnership property; partners' rights to an interest in the partnership; and the partners' right to take part in managing the partnership.

Rights in specific partnership property If the partnership owns property, individual partners co-own that property as **tenants in partnership.** Partners, as tenants in partnership, have equal rights to possess partnership property for their non-partnership purposes (unless the other partners agree). For example, a partner in a real estate partnership may not drive the partnership Buick to Disney World for a vacation unless the other partners agree.

Individual partners do not have the right to mortgage, sell, or give by will particular pieces of partnership property.

Partners' rights to an "interest in the partnership" An individual partner's "interest in the partnership" means the right to share in partnership profits and capital. This right can be assigned to third parties (who are not partners). Assigning this right does not dissolve the partnership and does *not* make the assignee a partner. The assignor remains a partner after such an assignment (and remains personally liable for partnership debts).

Partners' rights to manage the partnership Individual partners have the right to manage the partnership. This right can be given to one or a few partners. The next chapter talks more about this right.

Creditors' rights against individual partner's interest Creditors of individual partners cannot seize (attach or execute against) partnership property to pay an individual's debts. However, creditors of individual partners can get a **charging order** against an individual partner's partnership property. Also, a partner may assign his or her "partnership interest" to pay a creditor.

Creditors' rights against the partnership property Partnership creditors may seize partnership property to pay partnership debts.

ENDING THE PARTNERSHIP

There are three steps in ending partnerships: dissolution, winding up, and termination. The following sections discuss these steps.

Ways Dissolution Occurs

There are a number of ways **dissolution** occurs. These include:

1. By the partnership agreement.
2. By a partner's withdrawal.
3. By the entry of new partners.
4. By a partner's death.
5. By a partner's bankruptcy.
6. By illegality of the partnership business.
7. By a partner's being adjudged insane.
8. By a partner's incapacity.
9. By a partner's misconduct.
10. By business impracticality.

The first three types of dissolution occur by the partners' acts, the second three ways are by operation of law, and the last four ways are by court order.

Dissolution by the partnership agreement The partnership agreement can state when the partnership ends. This agreement can indicate a certain date for the completion of a certain job.

Partners can all agree to change the definite time for ending the partnership agreement. If they all agree, they can lengthen or shorten the partnership term.

Partnerships lasting beyond the period in the partnership agreement become partnerships at will. Partnership rights and duties nonetheless stay as they were under the original agreement.

Dissolution by a partner's withdrawal A partner always has the power but not necessarily the right to withdraw. This fact means that courts do not force partners to stay in a partnership they dislike. If a partner withdraws and thereby violates the partnership agreement, the courts let the partner withdraw but hold the withdrawing partner liable for damages.

If a partnership is at will, partners generally have the power and the right to withdraw any time without being liable for damages.

Dissolution by entry of new partners The Uniform Partnership Act says that any change in partnership membership automatically dissolves the partnership. Therefore, adding a partner technically dissolves the old partnership. As a practical matter, partnership agreements almost always allow the partnership to continue operating after "dissolution" by a change in membership. Buy-out provisions (discussed below) deal with adding and dropping partners while the partnership continues.

Dissolution by a partner's death If a partner dies, there is a partnership dissolution by "operation of law," which means dissolution is automatic. **Buy-out**

provisions in partnership agreements allow surviving partners to buy the dead partner's interest. Buy-out provisions let the remaining partners continue in business without winding up.

Dissolution by bankruptcy A partner's bankruptcy dissolves a partnership by operation of law. Also, the partnership's bankruptcy dissolves the firm.

Dissolution by illegality If the partnership business becomes illegal, the partnership dissolves by operation of law. Similarly, a partner's loss of an occupational license (such as a realtor's license in a real estate partnership) dissolves the partnership by operation of law.

Dissolution by a partner's insanity If a partner is adjudged insane or a partner is shown to be of unsound mind, the partnership can be dissolved in court.

Dissolution by a partner's incapacity When a partner is permanently incapacitated (such as by brain damage), which substantially affects his or her job performance, a court can dissolve the partnership.

Dissolution by a partner's misconduct If a partner acts improperly in partnership matters (such as stealing partnership property), a judge can dissolve the partnership. Also, improper behavior that puts the partnership in a bad light (such as use of drugs) is a reason for judicial dissolution.

Finally, continuous, damaging personal feuding among the partners undercutting partnership cooperation is grounds for dissolution.

Dissolution by business impracticality If it is obvious to the partners that only losing money will occur by staying in business, judicial dissolution is possible.

Winding Up

Winding up occurs when the partnership assets are sold, creditors are paid off, and the remaining property is distributed to the partners.

Who does it? The partners do the winding up. If a partner dies, becomes insane, goes bankrupt, or breaks the partnership agreement, he or she does *not* have the right to wind up.

When a court orders a partnership to dissolve, it often appoints a receiver to wind up.

The *Shandell v. Katz* case shows a partner's rights after he voluntarily withdrew from an at-will partnership.

Purpose of winding up The purpose of winding up is to sell the partnership assets for the most money as soon as possible.

Partners' rights during winding up In general, partners' authority to bind the partnership ends with the partnership's dissolution. An exception exists which lets partners make contracts and take actions necessary to wind up the partnership. Also, surviving partners can transfer title to partnership property during winding up.

Partners have apparent authority to bind the partnership to third persons after dissolution. However, if the third person has notice of the dissolution, partners

SHANDELL v. KATZ

New York Supreme Court, App. Div.
464 N.Y.S.2d 177 (1983).

FACTS From 1972 until September 14, 1981, Katz, Shandell, Katz, and Erasmus practiced law as a partnership. The partnership agreements were both oral and written. They specified no definite time for the partnership to last. On September 14, 1981, Shandell notified his partners that he was withdrawing from and dissolving the partnership. Shandell offered to have an orderly winding up, which was rejected. Instead, his former partners changed the office locks and refused to let him see partnership books and records. The partnership bank accounts were closed, and money in old partnership accounts was transferred to a successor firm. Shandell also claimed the new firm changed the attorneys of record on all pending partnership cases. This caused settlement checks to be made out to the successor firm rather than to the old partnership. Also, he alleged his old partners failed to pay the old partnership's taxes, which resulted in a $38,001 judgment against Shandell personally. Shandell estimated his old partners received since dissolution $4.5 million in partnership fees and they deposited them in the new partnership account.

Shandell demanded an accounting and a receiver (a neutral person who receives and holds property while a court decides who owns it) pending litigation.

ISSUE Is a partner who dissolves a partnership at will entitled to an accounting so the partnership can be wound up?

DECISION Yes, in this case. The partnership here could be dissolved at any time by any partner since it was at will and had no definite term. The only way a partnership can be wound up is by an accounting. Shandell is entitled to an accounting now, since a partnership at will can be dissolved on a moment's notice. Shandell was not then entitled to a receiver pendente lite because he did not show that partnership property would be lost, materially injured, destroyed, hidden, or taken from the jurisdiction before the accounting could be done.

LEGAL TIP

Partnerships at will can be dissolved at any time. Partners may want to have a definite term to give more certainty to their relationship.

have no apparent authority. The notice required is *actual* notice (a letter or telephone call) to former partnership creditors. Constructive notice (such as a newspaper ad announcing the dissolution) must be given to persons who formerly dealt with the partnership but who no longer are creditors.

Partners continue to have a fiduciary duty to each other and to any deceased partner's estate after dissolution during the winding up.

Pay during winding up Partners generally are *not* entitled to pay for their winding up services. However, when a partner's death causes dissolution, the surviving partners have the right to be paid for winding up.

"Technical" Dissolution Without Winding Up

As a practical matter, many partnerships continue to operate after a dissolution just as if nothing had happened. "Technical dissolutions" occur when there is any change in partnership membership, yet the partnership agreement says there will be *no* winding up. In such cases, the partnership agreement will have a "buy-out" provision, which lets the remaining partners buy out the departing (or dead) partner's share. It is legal to use life insurance to pay for buy-outs of dead partners' interests. This practice minimizes business disruptions caused by partner personnel changes.

The *Curtin v. Glazier* case asks if there is a buy-out of a partner kicked out of a continuing partnership or simply a partnership dissolution and winding up.

CURTIN v. GLAZIER

New York Supreme Court, App. Div.
464 N.Y.S.2d 899 (1983).

FACTS Glazier, Jackler, & Company were CPAs, who originally organized in 1968. They had articles of partnership (articles) written out. One part of the articles allowed a majority of partners to remove any partner without cause. If this were done, the articles required the partnership to "buy-out" the interest of the partner voted out. The buy-out was to occur according to a formula in the buy-sell part of the articles. The articles had a provision setting a different formula for valuing a partner's interest if the partnership dissolved. The "buy-sell" formula for valuing removed partners was generally more generous to removed partners than the dissolution valuation formula. The articles recognized the possibility the buy-sell formula could be escaped if the partnership dissolved and formed a new partnership without the removed partner. This ploy would be of financial benefit to the remaining partners. Therefore, the articles had a provision prohibiting remaining partners from dissolving and reorganizing without the partner who could have been bought out under the buy-sell provision.

Curtin was a partner in Glazier, Jackler, & Company. That partnership dissolved and formed two different partnerships excluding him. They tried to pay for Curtin's interest in the dissolved partnership using the dissolution valuation formula, which would give Curtin $26,057.65. Curtin argued his old partners had forced him out and his interest should be valued under the buy-sell provision (which would give him $100,638.78 for his interest).

ISSUE Was this a removal of a partner where the buy-sell valuation formula applied, or was this a partnership dissolution with the valuation set by the dissolution formula?

DECISION It was in substance a removal of a partner. Therefore, the buy-sell formula should figure the value of Curtin's share. The articles of partnership clearly prohibited the remaining partners from escaping their obligations by dissolving and forming a new partnership that took over the old partnership's business. This clearly happened in this case. Curtin got $100,638.78 for his partnership interest.

LEGAL TIP

Partnership agreements should clearly provide ways of valuing a partner's interest in the event of removal of a partner or partnership dissolution.

Liability for Existing and New Debts

Old partnership continuing If there is a partnership dissolution but no winding up, what *partnership* liabilities exist? The remaining partnership is liable for all existing and new partnership debts.

Departing partners (or their estates) The departing partners remain personally liable for all partnership debts existing when they leave unless remaining partners and existing creditors excuse them. The departing partners (or their estates) are liable for *new* debts if they have not given third parties proper notice of the dissolution.

New partners New partners joining an existing partnership are personally liable for all debts *after* they join. New partners are also personally liable for "old" debts (those arising *before* they became a partner) *up to the amount* of their partnership capital contribution. Their *personal* assets are not liable for "old" debts.

Winding Up: Distributing Partnership Assets

The end of the winding up process consists of distributing the partnership's assets. Basically there are two possible cases: first, the partnership is solvent; second, the partnership is insolvent.

Distributing assets of a solvent partnership If a partnership is solvent, all creditors will receive full payment first. Second, the partners will be repaid any loans they have made to the partnership. Third, each partner receives back his or her original capital contribution. Fourth, any remaining amounts are paid to the partners according to the partnership agreement.

A common question is, "Must the partnership assets be sold and turned into cash before they are distributed?" Creditors, of course, usually want money. After paying creditors, the partners can distribute the partnership's assets without turning them into cash or can turn them into cash and distribute it. (Of course in distributing cash or noncash assets, the partnership agreement as to amounts must be followed.)

Generally, a partner's services for the firm do *not* count as partnership capital contributions. However, the partnership agreement can allow partners' services to count as capital. The *Schymanski v. Conventz* case shows how the issue of service contributions counting as capital can arise.

SCHYMANSKI v. CONVENTZ

Supreme Court of Alaska.
674 P.2d 281 (1983).

FACTS The Schymanski and Conventz groups entered an oral partnership to build and operate a fishing lodge in Alaska. The partnership was on a fifty-fifty basis between the two groups. Originally the two groups were to contribute equal amounts of cash plus personal services. (The Conventzs were to supervise construction and advertise in Alaska, and the Schymanskis were to handle promotion in Germany.) Later, the partners signed two agreements that Conventz drafted. The writings changed the oral agreement so Conventz gave more service to the partnership and less cash. Construction on the lodge was more expensive than expected. The building's quality was unsatisfactory. The Schymanskis were dissatisfied with Conventz' bookkeeping and refused to provide more money until their records improved. Eventually dissension broke out when the Schymanskis learned the Conventzs claimed Mrs. Conventz made a $20,000 non-cash capital contribution (for her work as a cook) and Mr. Conventz claimed a $50,000 non-cash capital contribution (for his work as architect and building supervisor of the lodge). The Schymanskis asked that the partnership be dissolved and an accounting be made. The Schymanski group had contributed $133,838.06 in cash while the Conventzs made cash contributions of only $39,658.48 plus the disputed $70,000 non-cash labor contribution. A question arose whether to allow Conventzs' $70,000 non-cash (service) capital contributions to the partnership in the dissolution.

ISSUE May personal services be a partnership capital contribution?

DECISION Yes. The general rule is that if there is no agreement covering the matter, a partner contributing *only* personal services is *not* entitled to any share of partnership capital in dissolution. Personal services may be a capital contribution if there is an express or implied agreement allowing it. Since it is unclear if the trial court found an express or implied agreement allowing Conventz' personal services to be a capital contribution, this matter should be returned to the trial court for such a finding.

LEGAL TIP

Articles of partnership should expressly say whether partners' personal services are a capital contribution to the partnership.

Distributing assets for an insolvent partnership Asset distribution for an insolvent partnership follows the same general rules (discussed above) as for solvent partnerships:

1. Pay creditors.
2. Pay loans from partners.

3. Pay partners' capital contributions.
4. Pay any profits remaining to the partners according to the partnership agreement.

The problem in an insolvent partnership is the lack of money to pay even its creditors. The law says fully pay partnership creditors before paying loans from partners or partner capital contributions.

Marshaling of assets **Marshaling of assets** means that partnership assets go to pay partnership creditors and each individual partner's assets go to pay each partner's individual creditors. Any surplus in individual assets goes to pay partnership creditors. Any surplus in partnership assets goes (according to the partnership agreement) to pay individual partners' creditors. This rule treats creditors of individual partners and partnership creditors as separate groups. The marshaling principle only applies in equity courts.

Bankruptcy Reform Act's rejection of marshaling The Bankruptcy Reform Act of 1978 rejects the marshaling idea. This rejection means that if the partnership is bankrupt, the trustee in bankruptcy can take nonbankrupt individual partners' assets to pay partnership debts. The trustee can become a creditor of the individual bankrupt partners (instead of waiting until all the individual creditors are paid *before* getting anything, as happens in marshaling).

Keep in mind that this change in the marshaling principle *only* applies in bankruptcy cases. The marshaling rule still exists in nonbankruptcy partnership matters.

Termination of Partnerships

A partnership is not terminated at the moment it dissolves. **Termination** of a partnership happens at the end of the winding up process. Therefore, when a partnership *dissolves,* but there is no winding up (because the partnership continues), there is *no termination.*

KEY TERMS

Partnership agreement
Partnership for a term
Partnership at will
Tenants in partnership
Charging order
Dissolution
Winding up
Buy-out provision
Marshaling of assets
Termination

CHAPTER PROBLEMS

1. Is it legal for partners to select a name that hides the partners' identities?
2. What would be a reason to have a written partnership agreement?
3. Name five items that would be in a partnership agreement.
4. Are there any dangers in having partners who are minors?
5. Explain the difference between partnerships at will and partnerships for a term.
6. What three property rights does the Uniform Partnership Act confer on individual partners?

*7. Does a partnership remain in existence after dissolution until winding up the partnership's affairs is over? *Nelson v. Warnke,* 461 N.E.2d 523 (Ill. App. 1984).

*8. If one partner dies, are the surviving partners treated as trustees of the legal representative of the dead partner? *Chapman v. Duncan,* 665 S.W.2d 643 (Mo. App. 1984).

*9. A partnership agreement had a provision saying that it could not be amended except in a *writing* that all partners signed. Later, all partners *orally* agreed to amend the partnership agreement. Was this oral amendment valid? *Greenstein v. Simpson,* 660 S.W.2d 155 (Tex. App. 1983).

*10. Ordinarily, if partners use partnership funds to buy property (personally) from a third person, is the property regarded as belonging to the partnership? *Burgess Min. and Const. Corp. v. Lees,* 440 So.2d 321 (Ala. S.Ct. 1983).

"Even in the freest countries our property is subject to the control and disposal of our partners."
Abigail Adams

Chapter 41

Partnership Operation

CHAPTER PREVIEW

- Six duties partners owe each other
- Persons to whom partners owe the fiduciary duty
- Majority rule in partnership management
- Unanimity rule in management of the partnership
- Partners' rights to a salary
- Rights partners have among themselves
- Partnership liability for a partner's contracts
- Times when the partnership is liable for a partner's torts
- Partners' responsibility for co-partners' crimes

"That can't be true," said Fred Hyman. "But it is," said an official of the Boston Insurance Company. "Your co-partner lied when he made a claim under your partnership's fire insurance policy. Since your partnership is bound by this fraud, we are denying your partnership's claim." Fred thought for a minute. Then he said, "But our partnership isn't in business to commit frauds on people. Therefore, if my partner did submit a false insurance claim, it does not bind the partnership because it was beyond the scope of the partnership." Who is right, Fred or the insurer?

This chapter discusses partners' relations to each other and to third persons, and repeats information about agency rules that earlier chapters discuss. Since partners are agents of co-partners regarding matters within the partnership, it is important to have a clear understanding of these rules.

PARTNERS' RELATIONS TO EACH OTHER

The Uniform Partnership Act, court decisions, and the partnership agreement set out the rules covering partners' relations to each other.

Duties Partners Owe Each Other

Partners owe each other the fiduciary duty, the duty to follow instructions, a duty of care, a duty to communicate, a duty to account, and the duty to contribute to partnership losses.

Partner's fiduciary duty **Fiduciary duty** means that each partner must give (and is entitled to receive) the highest level of honesty, trust, and confidence to his or her partners. Partners should not make secret profits at the expense of co-partners. They may make contracts and profit at the partnership's expense only if they fully disclose this information and the other partners agree. While partners owe their co-partners a fiduciary duty, they do *not* owe this duty to third persons such as business customers or partnership employees.

The *Veale v. Rose* case is an example of a case involving the fiduciary duty.

Duty to follow instructions Partners must obey their partnership agreement. Failure to do so makes the disobeying partner liable for any loss.

Duty of care Partners who negligently carry out partnership duties are liable to their partners for any losses. Honest judgment errors by partners are not violations of the **duty of care.**

Duty to communicate Partners have a **duty to communicate** with co-partners about matters they know are relevant to the partnership. This duty supports the agency rule that whatever the agent knows, the principal is also considered to know. Recall that partners are agents of co-partners regarding partnership matters.

Duty to account Partners have a **duty to account** to co-partners for any income or expenses related to partnership business.

Duty to contribute to partnership losses Partners must contribute to partnership losses. The share of the loss each partner must pay is the same as his or her partnership profit share. The partnership agreement can distribute losses in different percentages than the profits. For example, a partner could have a right to 75% of the profits but only 25% of the losses. (This type of distribution assumes all partners are solvent and can pay their share of any loss.)

Partners' Rights

Partners have a number of rights regarding the partnership. These include the right to manage and the right to inspect partnership books. The Uniform Partnership Act also sets out several rights of partners including:

VEALE v. ROSE

Texas Court of Appeals.
657 S.W.2d 834 (1983).

FACTS Larry Rose and four others were CPAs in a partnership offering professional accounting services. Their firm was called Paul G. Veale and Company. The partnership agreement noted that Mr. Veale, Sr. and Rose had outside investments and other business commitments. The agreement allowed all partners to pursue other business activities. It let partners get paid for other business if those activities did not materially interfere with the partner's duties to the partnership or conflict with the partnership's business.

While a partner of Paul G. Veale and Company, Rose did accounting services for Right Away Foods. Rose billed and received payment for such services personally. The Veale partnership did not share in the money from those accounting services. Rose also performed public accounting services *after hours* for Mr. Ed Payne. Rose personally billed Payne and did not share payment with his partners. Rose also used the Veale partnership's secretarial help and computer time to serve his personal clients and did not charge his clients for it.

Rose's partners claimed Rose's actions broke his fiduciary duty to them and caused damages. They claimed these damages should be included in the partnership's winding up and accounting. Rose argued that his former partners knew of his "outside" accounting practices and use of partnership secretaries and computer time, tacitly approved of it, and made personal use of partnership assets.

ISSUE If a partner has clients "on the side" and uses partnership assets for serving such clients, has he or she violated the fiduciary duty owed to co-partners?

DECISION Yes. The partnership agreement had a "will not compete" provision, which Rose violated by offering clients the same services his partnership sold. Additionally, competing with one's partnership, even if "after hours," violates the common law fiduciary duty partners owe co-partners. The fiduciary duty requires the *utmost* good faith and honesty of partners in dealing with one another. Breaches of the duty not to compete are corrected by giving damaged partners their proportionate share of wrongfully acquired profits by a disloyal partner. Misappropriation of partnership property (such as computer time) is constructive fraud. Rose did commit this violation and he (or his personal clients) owed the partnership damages. It was *uncertain* whether Rose's partners knew and approved of his using partnership assets and having clients "on the side." This matter should be sent back to the trial court to get the facts.

LEGAL TIP

Partners who compete with the partnership violate their fiduciary duty unless the other partners know and approve of the outside activity.

1. The right to be repaid his or her capital contribution and share in profits after paying partnership debts.
2. The right to indemnification for expenses incurred in carrying out partnership business.
3. The right to be repaid (with interest) any loans made to the partnership.
4. The right to a full partnership accounting if a partner is wrongfully excluded from the firm, whenever the partnership agreement allows, or whenever an accounting is just and reasonable.

Enforcing partners rights Partners may not sue co-partners to enforce the partnership agreement. The exception to this "no suits against co-partners" rule is the suit for an accounting. The suit against a co-partner for an accounting is the way a partner enforces his or her partnership rights.

Rights discussed here The remaining rights discussed here are the right to manage and the right to inspect the partnership books. (Recall that the previous chapter discussed partners' property rights.)

Right to Manage

Each partner has an equal right in the partnership management. The **right to manage** means each partner has one vote in deciding how to run the firm. This right applies no matter what the size is of the partner's profit share or the amount of a particular partner's capital contribution. The "equal right to share in management" principle may be varied by the partnership agreement. (One partner, for example, could have all the management authority.)

Majority Rule According to this rule, the partners' majority vote decides what action to take in ordinary matters.

Unanimity Rule According to this rule, all partners must agree to any of the following extraordinary partnership actions:

1. Altering the essential nature of the firm's business or altering the capital structure.
2. Entering wholly new businesses or admitting new partners.
3. Assigning partnership property in trust for creditors' benefit.
4. Selling or disposing of the partnership's goodwill.
5. Confessing judgment against the partnership or submitting partnership claims to arbitration.
6. Taking any action that would make further conduct of the business impossible.

Types of authority partners have to bind partnership Partners are agents of co-partners and the partnership regarding matters within the scope of the business. In other words, the respondeat superior idea discussed in the agency chapters applies here, too.

Also, all of the ways principals can give agents authority (express, implied, and apparent authority, and ratification) apply to partnerships. That is, partners get their authority to bind the partnership in the same ways agents get their authority.

Right to Inspect Partnership Books

A partner has the right to inspect the partnership books and records of account. This rule includes the right to make copies of those records. A partner also has the right to have his or her accountant or lawyer inspect the books.

Partners having the right Active and inactive partners have the right to inspect the partnership books. The personal representative of a dead partner also has this right.

Where are the books? The partnership books must be kept at the firm's principal office. All partners must agree if the books are taken elsewhere.

Salaries for Partners

General rule Partners have *no right* to salaries for their partnership work *unless* the partnership agreement allows salaries. This rule seems unbelievable. What are partners supposed to live on? The answer is partnership profits.

Exception An exception to the "no salary for partners" rule occurs when a partner dies. The surviving partners have a right to a salary for the reasonable value of their services in winding up the partnership.

Problem Since partnership agreements often do not say anything about salaries for partners, they may permit "draws." A **draw** is sometimes considered an advance (or early payment) of partnership profits. Other times, draws are considered salaries. The partnership agreement determines if "draws" are salaries or advances against profits. If the agreement allows draws but does not label them, what are they? The *Patecell v. Cook* case gives one possible answer.

PATECELL v. COOK

Court of Appeals of Arizona.
673 P.2d 33 (1983).

FACTS Ron Cook and Rick Patecell had a partnership. Cook contributed $35,395.66 and Patecell $2000 to the partnership capital. The partnership agreement said Patecell could draw $2000 per month and Cook $4000. The partnership agreement did not say if the draws were salaries or were advances against partnership profits. The agreement did say that profits would be divided in proportion to the partners' capital contributions.

Several months later Cook and Patecell agreed to dissolve and wind up the partnership.

Cook sent Patecell an accounting of the business assets, showing for the first time that partner draws were against their partnership equity (and profits) and were not salaries. Patecell argued that the draws were salaries. The dispute arose in the accounting to end the partnership. The partnership equity at dissolution was $100,515.16. If the draws were salary, Patecell's equity was worth $10,461. If the draws were advances against equity, Patecell's equity was worth $4,528.33.

ISSUE Are partners' "draws", "salaries" or "advances against partnership profits"?

DECISION They are salaries in this case. The partnership agreement controls in such questions: If it says "draws" are "advances against profits," that is what they are. In general, partners are *not* entitled to salaries from the partnership *unless* the partnership allows them. Since the partnership agreement was ambiguous in this case, evidence outside of the agreement was considered to determine the partners' intent. At two separate times, these partners had calculated the value of their separate partnership interests without figuring the draws as reducing either partner's equity. In effect, the actions of the parties in not treating the draws as advances of profits reformed the partnership agreement to treat draws as salaries.

LEGAL TIP

The partnership agreement should clearly say if partners are entitled to salaries.

PARTNERS' RELATIONS TO THIRD PARTIES

The first half of this chapter dealt with a partner's relations with other partners. The remainder of the chapter covers partners' relations with others (third parties). We deal with three matters:

1. *Contracts* partners make with third persons.

2. *Torts* partners commit against third persons.
3. *Crimes* partners commit.

Partners' Liability for Contracts

Partners can bind the partnership to contracts if they have authority. There are four ways partners can have authority to bind the partnership to contracts with third persons (see Figure 41-1):

1. Express authority, (which can be oral or written).
2. Implied authority (acts necessary to carry out the express authority but which are not expressly stated), which is reasonably related to express authority.
3. Apparent authority, which includes acts of the partnership reasonably leading third persons to act or forbear in reliance on the partner.
4. Ratification, which means that a partner has no authority to contract for the partnership, does so anyway, and the partners approve of the contract after learning all of the facts.

Joint liability Partners' liability on partnership contracts is joint. **Joint liability** means that if all partners are sued on a contract and one partner is dismissed from the suit (for reasons *other than* infancy, lack of jurisdiction over the partner, or the partner's personal bankruptcy), the suit against *all* the partners is dismissed. Contrast this rule with "joint-and-several liability," where a plaintiff can sue one, a few, or all partners.

Remember that partners' contract liability is joint, but their tort liability is joint and several (see definition below).

The *Farm Bureau Agricultural Credit Corp. v. Dicke* case is an example of a partnership's contract liability.

Partners' Tort Liability

Own torts Partners are liable for their own torts (wrongs) whether they happen on or off the job.

Partner's torts Partners are also liable for any *other* partner's (or employee's) torts if they are within the scope of partnership or within the partner's authority.

Figure 41-1 **Partnership's and Individual Partner's Contract Liability**

	EXPRESS AUTHORITY	IMPLIED AUTHORITY	APPARENT AUTHORITY	RATIFICATION
Partnership's liability*	Yes	Yes	Yes	Yes (after ratification but no before)
Partner's liability*	No	No	Yes	Yes (before ratification but no after)

* Assuming the partnership is solvent.

FARM BUREAU AGRICULTURAL CREDIT CORP. v. DICKE

Court of Appeals of Ohio.
277 N.E.2d 562 (1972).

FACTS Donald Dicke and his wife Virginia had a partnership that owned a farm. Donald signed a cognovit note, which is a confession of judgment note allowing quick enforcement if a payment is missed. Donald signed this note alone and not in the partnership's name. When Donald defaulted on the note, the trial court decided the note was a partnership debt and let the sheriff sell partnership property to pay off the note.

ISSUE Did Virginia Dicke give her husband any authority to sign a cognovit note on the partnership's behalf?

DECISION No. Virginia did not give Donald express or other authority to sign a cognovit note binding their farming partnership. Donald was the sole signer of the note. He did *not* sign in a representative capacity but for himself. A creditor of an individual partner can only seize that partner's property, not the partnership's property. (An individual partner's interest is subject to a charging order to pay his or her personal debts.) A partnership relationship does not imply that the other partner has authority to sign cognovit notes binding the partnership.

LEGAL TIP

All partners must generally agree to sign confession of judgment notes if the other partners or the partnership are to be liable.

The reason is that partners are agents of co-partners on matters within the partnership. The four ways of creating authority apply in these situations. The respondeat superior idea discussed in relation to agency also applies to partnerships.

The respondeat superior idea encourages partners to select intelligent, careful, and competent partners. For example, assume three accountants have a partnership. One partner negligently fills out a customer's tax returns and makes a $10,000 mistake. The partner who committed the negligence in the partnership *and* the other partners who had nothing to do with the partner's error are personally liable.

Type of liability A partner's tort liability for a co-partner's (or employee's) torts within the scope of the partnership is joint and several. **Joint-and-several liability** means the injured victim can sue and collect from any one partner for the entire damage—even if another partner caused the harm. That partner then has a right of contribution against his or her other partners. The partner who caused the harm has a duty to indemnify (a duty to pay) the partnership and any partner who pays.

Joint-and-several liability also means the victim can sue all (or one or a few of) the partners and partnership in one suit. The victim can only get paid by the person(s) sued. This type of liability explains why victims sue all partners and the partnership.

Extent of liability The most shocking feature of a partner's tort liability is its extent. If the victim cannot collect from the partnership property, he or she can seize the property of individual partners (for example, their houses, cars, jewelry, boats, bank accounts) for payment. Of course, the partner who pays (assuming he or she was not the wrongdoer) has a right of indemnification (the right to pro rata payment) from co-partners.

Torts covered A partner's liability for a co-partner's torts extends to those committed within the scope of the partnership or done with the partner's authority. Partners generally are liable for negligence torts committed while on partnership business. Intentional torts such as fraud, defamation, conversion, and trespass can be inside or outside the scope of the partnership. Previous authorization or ratification of unauthorized acts can make partners liable for a co-partner's intentional torts.

The *Zemelman v. Boston Insurance Company* case is an example of a partner's intentional tort (of fraud) *within* the scope of the partnership.

ZEMELMAN v. BOSTON INSURANCE COMPANY

Court of Appeal of California.
84 Cal. Rptr. 206 (1970).

FACTS Co-partners sued six insurance companies (including Boston Insurance Company) to recover on fire insurance policies. The companies had insured partnership property but defended by arguing that the policies were voided since one of the plaintiff-partners (Zemelman) made a false statement in an insurance claim. All partners admitted that Zemelman filed a fraudulent claim on the partnership loss but argued that Zemelman's fraud should not be imputed to them. Therefore, they claimed they should recover under the fire policy.

ISSUE Are all partners bound by one partner's fraud?

DECISION Yes. If a partner acts within the scope of his or her authority, fraudulent acts bind other partners whether or not they were aware of the fraud. In this case, Zemelman's filing an insurance claim was apparently done to carry on partnership business.

LEGAL TIP
When selecting partners, remember that partners can be liable for a co-partner's fraud.

Partners' Liability for Crimes

If a partner commits a crime either inside or outside the scope of the partnership, he or she is *personally* liable.

General rule However, partners generally are not *criminally* liable for a co-partner's crimes. The fact that a co-partner's act is a crime usually takes the matter beyond the partnership's scope.

Exceptions Partners can be criminally liable for a co-partner's crimes if he or she takes part in or assents to them. This crime is called **criminal conspiracy,** which is an agreement to do an unlawful act or to do a lawful act unlawfully.

Partnership's criminal liability In recent years, regulatory statutes and court interpretations of such statutes have made partnerships criminally answerable for such violations. The United States Supreme Court has said that a partnership could be guilty of the crime of violating ICC (Interstate Commerce Commission) regulations. The partnership was fined and partnership assets paid the fine. However, the conviction of the partnership in that case was not used to punish individual partners.

KEY TERMS

Fiduciary duty
Duty to communicate
Duty of care
Duty to account
Right to manage
Draw
Joint liability
Joint-and-several liability
Criminal conspiracy

CHAPTER PROBLEMS

1. What statute sets the general rules covering partnerships?
2. Explain the fiduciary duty.
3. Are partners agents of co-partners for partnership business?
4. Do partners have a duty to keep partnership books?
5. When is a partner *not* liable for a co-partner's torts?
6. Is a partnership ever criminally liable?

*7. Green, during a dinner conversation with Bates, told Bates that Wheeler was not training Bates' horses to the best of Wheeler's ability. Green also told Bates that Wheeler (who worked for Bates) was dishonest. Wheeler sued Wassenburg (Green's partner) for Green's allegedly defamatory remarks. Was Wassenburg bound by his partner's dinner remarks? *Wheeler v. Green,* 593 P.2d 777 (Oreg. 1979).

*8. Can one partner sue another partner at law regarding transactions completed before a full accounting? *Smith v. Hurley,* 589 P.2d 38 (Ariz. 1978).

*9. Can one partner sue another partner about non-partnership matters or matters not involving a partnership accounting? *Smith v. Hurley,* 589 P.2d 38 (Ariz. 1978).

*10. If one partner manages the partnership, does his or her duty to deal fairly, openly, and disclose completely to the other partners increase? *Saballus v. Timke,* 460 N.E.2d 755 (Ill. App. 1983).

"Knights, Gentlemen, Merchants, and other Adventurers of our City of London and elsewhere."

The name of America's first corporation
8 Encyclopedia Americana 14–15

Chapter 42

Nature, Formation, and Termination of Corporations

CHAPTER PREVIEW

- Differences between corporations and other forms of businesses
- Types of corporations
- Laws governing corporations
- Steps for incorporation
- Promoters' roles and liability
- Content of the articles of incorporation
- De jure and de facto corporations
- Ending corporations

Preston was the organizer and promoter of Pan American Motel, Inc. He signed a contract to buy land for the motel for $240,000, made the down payment on the land, and signed a mortgage for the balance of the sales price. After the corporation was formed, he offered to sell the land to the corporation for $350,000. The offer was accepted and the corporation paid him. The directors then found out that Preston had made $110,000 on the deal. Do they have any rights?

Corporations are a way of life for American business. They are only one-tenth of American enterprises but account for 84% of total business receipts and 64% of total business profits (Bureau of the Census, *1982 Statistical Abstract*). This chapter covers the background on corporations and the beginning stages of a corporation. The questions this chapter answers are: What are the features of a corporation? What are the types of corporations? What laws affect corporations? How is a corporation formed? Can a corporation be ended?

THE FEATURES OF A CORPORATION

A corporation has some unique qualities that make them attractive to many businesspeople. Some of these special features are discussed in the following subsections.

Unlimited Duration

Unlike a partnership or sole proprietorship, a corporation does not end when one of its owners dies or withdraws. A corporation can go on forever. When a shareholder dies, the corporation is not affected. The shareholder passes on his or her shares through a will or other means. The only legal step the corporation must take is to change the ownership of the shares on the corporate records.

Limited Liability

The business and personal assets of a sole proprietor or partner are subject to business debts. This unlimited liability is one of the risks of doing business this way. However, shareholders' liability for corporate debts (with some exceptions which are covered later in the chapter) is limited to the value of their shares. Shareholders may lose their investment in the corporation, but their personal assets will be free and clear from corporate creditors' claims.

Free Transferability

The transferring of a sole proprietorship or partnership interest is a complicated transaction. Transfers in these forms of business organizations require paper work, notice, permission, and a host of other legal steps. Shares of a corporation are freely transferable. The only necessary paperwork involves a change of ownership on the corporate level.

Central Management

Management of a partnership depends on the partners, and a sole proprietorship does not operate if something happens to the sole proprietor. Since a corporation is usually managed by a management group, these people continue to run the corporation's daily business—regardless of who owns the stock that day. The group can be changed by the directors, but management does *not* depend on the owners.

Legal Existence

A partnership or sole proprietorship does not have a separate legal existence. Their only legal existence is in the rights of their owners. In contrast, a corporation can sue and be sued in its name. A corporation also pays taxes, has the right to hold title to land, and can enforce a contract in its name. A corporation has a legal existence of its own, and even though called an artificial person, it has all the rights of a natural person.

TYPES OF CORPORATIONS

Profit and Non-Profit Corporations

Business corporations are profit corporations, which operate to make a return on an investment. On the other hand, a non-profit corporation is incorporated for the convenience of having corporate management and limited liability with no profit motivation. A typical non-profit corporation is a charity or service organization.

Public and Private Corporations

The major difference between a public and private corporation is who holds the shares and how those shares are transferred. A **public corporation** is one with at least some of its shares held by the general public. The number of shareholders is usually large in a public corporation. There is a public market for the public corporation's shares. The public market may be through an exchange or among brokers "over the counter." Public corporations are subject to the reporting and disclosure requirements of the federal securities laws (see Chapter 16).

A **private corporation** is one in which the shares are held by a few shareholders. These shareholders are usually active in the management of the business. A private corporation has no public market for its shares and has never issued any of its shares to the public. Most private corporations will have restrictions on the transfer of their shares so that the corporation stays private (see Chapter 44).

Domestic and Foreign Corporations

A corporation is always a **domestic corporation** in the state where it incorporates. It is a **foreign corporation** in every other state. For example, a corporation incorporated in Delaware is a domestic corporation in Delaware and a foreign corporation in the other forty-nine states.

Closely Held Corporations

A **closely held corporation** is a private corporation. Many states have specific requirements for setting up a closely held (or close) corporation. In a close corporation, the shareholders are also likely to be employees. Like the private corporation, there is no public market for close corporation shares. Also like the private corporation, there are restrictions on the transfer of close corporations shares.

Professional Corporations

Many states allow professionals to create a different type of corporation. Professionals may include doctors, lawyers, dentists, architects, and accountants. The idea behind a professional corporation is to give the protection of limited liability while at the same time allow some flexibility in the operation of a professional business.

Subchapter S Corporations

A **Subchapter S corporation** is not a state statutory corporation. It is, instead, a creation of the Internal Revenue Code. A Subchapter S corporation allows businesspeople to form a corporation and have limited liability but to have the direct tax benefits and burdens as if the business were a partnership. In this type of arrangement, there is limited liability but also direct tax responsibility and write-offs. The shareholders in a Subchapter S corporation share the income and losses of the corporation on their individual returns as if they were partners.

THE LAWS AFFECTING CORPORATIONS

State Corporation Statutes

Every state has a statute that governs corporations. Those statutes include the steps for incorporating. The American Bar Association's **Model Business Corporation Act (MBCA)** has been adopted in about one-half of the states in some form. The Delaware Corporation Law has been influential in corporate law. The statutes of New York and California have also been important because of the amount of commercial activity in those states.

Federal Statutes

The Securities Act of 1933 and the Securities Exchange Act of 1934 are two federal statutes that affect corporations. These acts regulate public corporations in issuing and selling their shares of stock (see Chapter 16 for a complete discussion).

Of course there are other statutes that affect corporations. The Internal Revenue Code governs corporate taxation. The environmental statutes regulate corporate activity affecting the environment (see Chapter 12). The Foreign Corrupt Practices Act regulates international corporate ethics and disclosures (see Chapter 16).

FORMING A CORPORATION: STEPS AND ISSUES

Each state has its own procedures for incorporating. The times and names for each step may differ, but the idea of incorporating is the same. This section covers the formation of a corporation.

Where To Begin: Choosing the State of Incorporation

For a small corporation, the business should be incorporated in the state of operation. But for those businesses that are national or regional, there are both legal and practical factors to consider in deciding the state of incorporation.

Many businesses choose to incorporate where the corporation laws are liberal. For example, Delaware is known as one of those states. Many businesses choose Delaware because in addition to its liberal law, it has made many case decisions on corporate issues. Delaware has so many corporations that its judiciary has great expertise concerning corporate issues.

Some states offer various tax advantages that draw corporations to them. For example, the lack of an inventory tax or sales tax can be an important factor for a retailer.

Some states have a lower cost of living or better standard of living. Corporations locate in these states to attract and keep employees.

Who Begins? The Promoter

Promoters match ideas with money. Their basic responsibilities are to get the corporation started through formation and to get the capital necessary to finance the business. In the steps of getting capital and getting the corporation started, the promoter may have some liability.

Promoter liability on contracts: Who pays? A promoter is not an agent of the corporation. An agent must have a principal and without a formed corporation, there is no principal. Yet, the benefits of the contracts will eventually go to the corporation—a factor that presents interesting legal issues of liability.

For preincorporation (before the corporation is formed) contracts, the promoter is primarily liable. This liability occurs even when the promoter enters into the contract in the corporation's name and clearly establishes that the contract will be for the corporation. For example, suppose that Billy Bud is the promoter for a new western-wear business that will be incorporated as Western Gear, Inc. Bud enters into a contract with a clothes manufacturer for that manufacturer to supply the store's first inventory. Bud explains that Western Gear is not incorporated and then signs his name to the contract. If the corporation is never formed, Bud will have to pay.

Exception: The novation Once the corporation is formed, the only way Billy Bud can be relieved of all liability is for Bud, the corporation, and the manufacturer to enter into a novation. In a novation, the corporation is substituted for Bud as the party to the contract. Bud is released from liability, and the corporation now has a contract with the manufacturer. For a novation to work, all three parties must enter into an agreement.

Some relief: Ratification Some newly-formed corporations go through the process of ratifying all the contracts of the promoter. A principal can ratify the conduct of an agent at a later time even if the agent did not have the authority to make the contract at the time it was made. However, ratification requires that the principal must have existed at the time of the contract. With a promoter contract, the corporation did not yet exist. Most states treat a ratification as an act that makes the corporation contractually liable but does not release the promoter from liability on the contract. The benefit of ratification is that the corporation has the right to enforce the contract. The *Malisewski v. Singer* case shows how promoters can be legally liable for contract debts even after the corporation is formed.

MALISEWSKI v. SINGER

Court of Appeals of Arizona.
598 P.2d 1014 (1979).

FACTS Jerry Singer and Gene Hoffman were the promoters for Solahart, Inc. On June 29, 1977, both Singer and Hoffman signed a contract with Josef Malisewski (doing business as "Expert Solar") to be a dealership for Solahart. Both Singer and Hoffamn signed on behalf of Solahart. Solahart was named on the contract as principal.

On August 8, 1977, the Arizona Corporation Commission received Solahart's articles of incorporation. They were filed on August 11, 1977.

In the meantime, the solar water heater business was not going well, and Hoffman and Singer had not paid Expert Solar any money. Malisewski brought suit against both Singer and Hoffman on August 9, 1977. Singer died, but his wife filed a motion for summary judgment asking that her husband be removed as a defendant. She claimed he was not liable for a corporate obligation.

ISSUE Is Singer liable for the corporate (Solahart's) obligation?

DECISION Yes. He was a promoter who contracted before the corporation was formed, and he remains liable for the contract. The corporation did not exist until after the suit had already been filed.

LEGAL TIP

Do not sign contracts as a promoter before the articles of incorporation have at least been filed.

Trustworthy promoters: Fiduciary responsibilities In addition to contract liability, promoters can have liability for not being honest and loyal in their duties. This honesty and loyalty are the promoters' fiduciary responsibilities.

Who are the fiduciaries? Promoters owe their fiduciary duties to co-promoters, the corporation, and the eventual shareholders.

Secret profits One fiduciary duty requires promoters to act for the benefit and best interests of the corporation. This duty prohibits promoters from making personal profits at the expense of the corporation. For example, suppose that Jake is promoting a corporation that will be formed to construct an office complex. Jake buys a piece of land the corporation needs and then sells that land to the corporation (after it is formed) at a profit. Jake has breached his fiduciary duty to the corporation, since the profits from the sale of the land belong to the corporation.

Co-promoters as partners Co-promoters are considered partners for the purpose of forming the corporation. They owe each other the general fiduciary duties partners owe each other. For example, partners also cannot make secret profits at the expense of the other partners.

Promoters pulling out: Duty to future investors Promoters have been known to start a corporation with few assets, issue stock to themselves, and then later sell those shares to the public at a profit. Such conduct is a violation of promoters' fiduciary responsibilities. For example, suppose that Jake contributes the land to the corporation in exchange for all shares of stock of the corporation. Jake overvalues the land and gets more shares than he should. He then sells the shares for more and is out of the corporation altogether. The shareholders are left with no promoter and an overvalued piece of land as a corporate asset.

There are two views of the promoter's liability in these circumstances. One view, called the Federal Rule, is that the shareholders have no rights because they were not shareholders at the time of the transaction. At the time of the transaction, there was full disclosure to all shareholders.

The second view, called the Massachusetts Rule, allows later shareholders to attack the transaction if it was clear at the time of the transaction that later shareholders were contemplated. More states follow the Massachusetts Rule than the Federal Rule. The names for these two rules were developed in the *Bigelow v. Old Dominion Copper Mining & Smelting Co.* case involving promoter liability.

Incorporators: The Signatures at the Bottom Line

Incorporators are the ones who sign the documents needed to meet state incorporation requirements. Usually, the promoters will act as incorporators but they are not required to do so. The number of incorporators required in each state varies. The MBCA requires only one incorporator. An incorporator can be a "natural," or actual, person or a corporation.

The Paperwork: Documents for Incorporation

Incorporating is a transaction that occurs on paper. A corporation comes into existence when complete and accurate paperwork is filed.

Paperwork 1: The articles of incorporation **Articles of incorporation** are the primary paperwork needed for incorporation. This paperwork includes

BIGELOW v. OLD DOMINION COPPER MINING & SMELTING CO.

Court of Chancery of New Jersey.
71 A. 153 (1908).

FACTS Bigelow and Lewisohn were two promoters who organized a syndicate to buy shares of a Baltimore mining company and some other mining property. They formed the Old Dominion Mining & Smelting Company in 1895 for this purpose. They transferred the mining property in exchange for $1,000,000 in shares. They then sold their shares in the corporation for $3,250,000. At the end of all the transactions, the new shareholders discovered they had a company with very few assets for which they had paid over $3,000,000.

The shareholders brought suit against the promoters for breach of fiduciary duty.

ISSUE Could the shareholders recover for breach of the promoters' fiduciary duty?

DECISION Yes and no. The shareholders who brought suit in federal court lost. The federal court said there had been full disclosure of all of the transactions. The court's feeling was that with full disclosure, there was no breach of any fiduciary duty.

The shareholders who were in state court did better. The court found a breach of the fiduciary duty. Their theory was that the duty extended to later shareholders if the intent at the time of the transaction was to bring in those other shareholders. Lewisohn and Bigelow had every intention of selling the shares, and therefore their duty extended to those shareholders.

LEGAL TIP

Investigate the background of corporate promoters. Trace stock transactions for the first years of the corporation to find out if the promoters have made a profit by selling corporate shares.

all the basics of the corporation. Each state may have slight variations in these requirements.

Name The corporation must have a name. Under the MBCA, the name must include one of the following terms or its abbreviation: "corporation," "company," "incorporated," or "limited." The name of the corporation cannot be "deceptively similar" to an existing corporation's name. The idea behind this requirement is to prevent confusion for the public. For example, suppose that Joe has an existing business called "Valley Travel & Tours, Inc." Janice would not be allowed to call her business "Valley Tours & Travel." The names are too similar and would confuse the public.

The MBCA allows parties to reserve a corporate name while they are getting the corporation and paperwork together. The name reservation is filed in the same place as the articles of incorporation. A fee is paid and the name cannot be used by any other incorporator for a period of six months.

Purpose The MBCA requires the incorporators to give a corporate purpose. However, the MBCA allows the purpose to be given as simply "general business" or "business operation."

The benefit of the MBCA general statement is that the corporation will not run into problems with the doctrine of **ultra vires.** The doctrine of ultra vires prohibits a corporation from becoming involved in business outside the scope of its stated purpose. For example, suppose the corporate purpose is "to operate a retail flower shop." With a specific purpose given, the corporation is limited to that business activity unless the articles of incorporation are amended. If this corporation starts a motorcycle shop, the corporation commits an ultra vires act.

Shareholders can stop the corporation from entering into an ultra vires area or contract by suing for an injunction. Shareholders can also collect losses resulting from an ultra vires transaction from the directors who authorized it. But ultra vires contracts are not void once entered into. For example, suppose that the flower shop directors were negotiating to buy a motorcycle dealership. The shareholders could bring suit to get an injunction to stop the deal. But if the contract was already signed, the contract would be valid.

Duration Under the MBCA, the duration (or time that a corporation lasts) is perpetual unless the articles state otherwise. A corporation can be formed for a limited time such as twenty-five years. A corporation can also be formed for a limited purpose such as the completion of a joint venture.

Capital stock authorization This section of the articles of incorporation covers the types, amount, and value of the corporate stock.

Types of stock The stock of a company can be common, preferred, or both. **Common shares** are generally voting shares. Even the **preferred shares** can be various types. For example, **cumulative preferred** shares are shares entitled to a dividend each year. If these shareholders are not paid one year, their dividends cumulate and they must be paid their cumulative amounts before the common shareholders get their dividends.

Amount of stock Authorized shares are the number of shares put in the articles. Issued shares are those that have been sold. Generally, there are more authorized than issued shares. Shares that have been issued are called outstanding shares. Outstanding shares bought back by the corporation are called treasury shares. Shares that are authorized but not issued can be issued at any time with approval by the board of directors.

Value of the stock The true value of the shares will be determined by the market place. However, many states require a **par value** for their shares in the articles of incorporation. Par value has no relation to market value and does not control the price of the shares (except as a minimum—see Chapter 44). The par value times the number of shares issued makes up the company's **stated capital** account. Any amount received over par times the number of shares makes up the company's **capital surplus** account.

Many states and the MBCA allow corporations to issue "no par stock." No par stock has no stated par value. There is no minimum price, and the board of directors is free to set any price. The directors decide on the allocation of the money to the capital accounts. Many states allow a fraction of the amount received to be allocated to capital surplus. The MBCA leaves the allocation to the directors' discretion.

Place of business The main business office address is given for this part of the articles of incorporation. The articles must also name a **statutory agent,** or a person who is entitled to receive legal notices. For example, this statutory or registered agent is the person who would receive notice of a lawsuit (or a service of process).

Directors The initial board of directors must be given in the articles. There must be at least one director under the MBCA.

Incorporation The names and addresses of each incorporator must be given in the articles.

Paperwork 2: Bylaws The **bylaws** are the rules that apply to officers and company operations. The rules for meetings, notices, and procedures are part of the bylaws. Bylaws are usually not required as part of an incorporation filing, but they are necessary to start a corporation.

Paperwork 3: Certificate of disclosure Some states require that the criminal background of the directors, officers, and incorporators be given in a **certificate of disclosure.** In addition, pending litigation and bankruptcy history may also be required.

Paperwork 4: Certificate of incorporation Once the incorporators have met all the requirements and filed their paperwork in the proper place, they will be issued a **certificate of incorporation.** The certificate is proof of a proper filing and incorporation. The certificate also shows when the corporation came into existence.

Paperwork 5: Publication Some states require that the articles of incorporation be published in a general newspaper. The idea behind such publication is to give notice that a corporation has been formed.

Paperwork 6: Minutes of the organizational meeting Many states and the MBCA require the board of directors to hold an **organizational meeting** after the certificate of incorporation is issued. At this meeting, the directors adopt the bylaws and elect officers to run the corporation.

Mistakes in Formation: Not Quite a Corporation

With all the paperwork and requirements for formation, it is not surprising that mistakes are made. Also, sometimes people start acting as a corporation before they actually are one. In either case, some interesting liability questions arise. For instance, when there is corporate business before a corporation exists who is liable?

If the corporation can qualify as a de facto corporation, then the corporate structure provides protection and the corporation is treated as if it really did exist. A **de facto** corporation is one that almost exists legally and has already done business as if it were a corporation. For example, suppose that the incorrect business address was given in the articles of incorporation. The articles are not accepted but the corporation is already operating. The corporation is de facto and it will have an implied existence even though its actual existence is denied. There are three requirements for a de facto corporation:

1. There must be a state incorporation statute.
2. There must have been a good-faith effort to comply with the statute.
3. There must have been operation as a corporation.

Under the MBCA, once the certificate is issued, the corporation is considered **de jure** (meaning properly formed), even though minor mistakes may turn up at a later time. The key is to wait for the certificate to be issued.

POST INCORPORATION: DOES THE CORPORATION EVER END?

Even though a corporation may have perpetual existence, it can be ended. In some cases, the corporation may continue but without limited liability.

Disregarding the Corporation: Piercing the Corporate Veil

There are times when the corporate shell and its protection are disregarded. **Piercing the corporate veil** means that the shareholders and directors will be held personally liable for corporate obligations as if the corporation did not exist. There are several reasons a corporate veil can be pierced.

No money: Undercapitalization Sometimes a corporation is formed but very little or no money is contributed. With this type of undercapitalization, the corporate veil is disregarded and the shareholders are individually liable for corporate debts. For example, suppose that a corporation is formed to lease and operate a swimming pool. The corporation has no assets, but the shareholders want limited liability protection. Because of the operators' negligence, a child drowns in the pool. The shareholders will be liable for damages because the corporation never had assets.

No formalities: Alter ego Many small businesses incorporate for tax and liability benefits. But because they are small businesses with limited shareholders, the formalities of the corporate structure are ignored. For example, there are no meetings, personal and business accounts are mixed, and informal salaries and bonuses are paid. In these types of corporations, the corporate veil is disregarded because the owners want to enjoy all the benefits of a corporation but do not observe formalities. The corporation becomes the **alter ego** of its owner(s) and limited liability is lost. The *U.S. National Bank of Omaha v. Rupe* case deals with the issue of piercing the corporate veil.

U.S. NATIONAL BANK OF OMAHA v. RUPE

Supreme Court of Nebraska.
296 N.W.2d 474 (1980).

FACTS Max Rupe was the sole shareholder of Updike Oil Company. Updike had a contract with Bob & Boots, Inc., for services in the amount of $4114.35. Updike failed to pay. Bob & Boots brought suit against Rupe for the amount.

Bob & Boots wanted to pierce the corporate veil for several reasons. First, Rupe claimed his wife owned 50% of the shares of the corporation, but there was no record of such a transaction. Second, Rupe had conveyed title to corporate property to his wife. Third, the corporation had no records of any meetings, transactions, or finances. Fourth, there was $100 in capital stock in Updike and $56,238 in liabilities. Finally, Rupe owned several corporations and used funds from one corporation's account to pay the debts of other corporations he owned.

ISSUE Could Bob & Boots pierce the corporate veil?

DECISION Yes. Rupe used the corporations as his alter ego. The firm was undercapitalized. In no way was there regard for corporate formalities.

LEGAL TIP

Keep corporate funds separate and keep accurate corporate records.

Confusion: Parent/subsidiary Some corporations form other corporations to eliminate parental liability. These creations are fine so long as the subsidiary has adequate capital and its business does not become commingled with the parent's. The *Bumpers v. International Mill Services, Inc.,* case involves an alter ego/parent subsidiary question.

BUMPERS v. INTERNATIONAL MILL SERVICES, INC.

United States District Court, Eastern District of Pennsylvania.
595 F.Supp. 166 (1984).

FACTS Jay C. Bumpers had worked for Hackett, Inc., since 1954. In 1981, Hackett was acquired as a subsidiary by International Mill Services, Inc. (IMS). Bumpers continued to work in the same $58,000 per year job until he was fired in 1982. He had never been criticized and had excellent performance evaluations. However, Hackett had been told by IMS to fire older, more expensive employees in order to decrease operating costs. Bumpers filed an age discrimination suit against IMS, who said it was not liable.

ISSUE Was the parent IMS liable for a discrimination suit for action taken by a subsidiary?

DECISION Yes. IMS was giving complete operational directions to Hackett. Hackett's management and board was not independent and was not allowed to make independent decisions.

LEGAL TIP

Keep all business organizations separate. Each one should make its own decisions and set its own policies.

Voluntary Dissolution

A corporation can be ended voluntarily. During the incorporation, the corporation can be ended by the incorporators or initial board of directors. They must file a **notice of dissolution** before any corporate business begins.

After the incorporation stage, the corporation can be ended with the unanimous consent of all shareholders if the creditors' rights are covered. Close corporations are usually ended this way.

In larger corporations, unanimous consent may not be possible. In these corporations, dissolution starts with a resolution by the board of directors. The resolution is then voted on by the shareholders. Under the MBCA, a majority of all the shareholders (voting or non-voting) must approve the dissolution.

Involuntary Dissolution

The law automatically terminates a corporation under certain circumstances. For example, in some states, a corporation's certificate is automatically revoked for not filing an annual report. Bankruptcy also ends a corporation's existence. If the state finds the certificate was issued because of fraud, the corporation will be dissolved by the state. The MBCA allows the state to end a corporation if no statutory agent is named.

A corporation can also be dissolved by petition of a shareholder to a court. A shareholder can base a petition on a deadlock. A deadlock occurs when the shareholders are split so that the corporation cannot take any action. A shareholder can also base a petition on the failure of the corporation to earn a profit or at least to do business. The *Gruenberg v. Goldmine Plantation, Inc.,* case deals with an issue of a shareholder's petition for dissolution.

GRUENBERG v. GOLDMINE PLANTATION, INC.

Court of Appeals of Louisiana, Fourth Circuit.
360 So.2d 884 (1978).

FACTS Goldmine Plantation, Inc., had one major asset: a 900-acre tract of land fronting on the right descending bank of the Mississippi River in St. John the Baptist parish.

The corporation had purchased the land in 1941 for $65,000. In 1975, the corporation was offered $2,700,000 for the land by a buyer who wanted to use it for an industrial site. A final offer of $4000 per acre was then made by another buyer. The corporation turned down both offers.

The corporation used the land to grow sugar cane. The company had an average net profit of 1% over the last 10 years. The shareholders earned about $5400 each per year. The farm manager and largest shareholder was paid $12,000 per year plus 20% of everything over $25,000 in sugar cane sales made by the corporation. The manager made an average of $162,000 per year over the last 10 years.

The shareholders brought suit to have the corporation dissolved because of a deadlock and lack of profits.

ISSUE Could the corporation be dissolved for unprofitability?

DECISION No. The corporation was still making money. It was also doing what its corporate charter provided—growing and farming sugar cane. Just because more profit could be made in selling the land, there is not sufficient grounds for dissolution.

LEGAL TIP

Check the terms of corporate salaries and the share ownership among salaried employees.

KEY TERMS

Public corporation
Private corporation
Domestic corporation
Foreign corporation
Closely held corporation
Subchapter S corporation
Model Business Corporation Act (MBCA)
Promoters
Incorporators
Articles of incorporation
Common shares
Preferred shares
Cumulative preferred
Par value
Stated capital
Capital surplus
Statutory agent
Certificate of disclosure
Certificate of incorporation
Organizational meeting
Bylaws
De facto
De jure
Piercing the corporate veil
Notice of dissolution
Alter ego
Ultra vires

CHAPTER PROBLEMS

1. Name four differences between corporations and partnerships.

*2. William and Hazel Patterson together owned fifty-nine of the sixty outstanding shares of Tallegada Nursing Home, Inc. They were also the directors and administrators of the home. St. Paul Insurance Company had issued a comprehensive liability policy for the home.

Otis Cook (who attempted to start another nursing home in the town) sued Tallegada and the Pattersons for wrongful business interference. The Pattersons were successfully prosecuted under a state statute prohibiting wrongful business interference.

St. Paul said the conduct was outside a corporation's legal liability and refused to defend the lawsuit. Who is right? *St. Paul Ins. Companies v. Tallegada Nursing Home, Inc.,* 606 F.2d 631 (11th Cir. 1979).

*3. Arnold Kellos bought his father's interest in Kellos Rental and Sales Company. He also created the companies Kellos-Sims, Inc., and Sims Crane Rental from Kellos Rental. The firms all had offices in different cities, but he supervised all of them.

Sonya Spray brought a Title VII discrimination suit against Kellos. He claimed he was exempt because he did not have fifteen employees in the office where Sonya worked. Sonya said he had more than fifteen employees in all the firms, and he formed the other businesses to avoid Title VII application. Title VII applies only to employers with fifteen or more employees. Who is right? Does Title VII apply? *Spray v. Kellos-Sims Crane Rental, Inc.,* 507 F.Supp. 745 (Ga. 1981).

4. Can the corporate veil be pierced because all the shares are owned by members of the same family? *Kellytown Co. v. Williams,* 426 A.2d 663 (Pa. 1981).

5. Can a corporate veil for a subsidiary be pierced because the parent corporation owns all its shares? *Volkswagenwerk, A. G. v. Klippan,* 611 P.2d 498 (Alaska 1980).

6. Roepke was the president and sole shareholder of a corporation. He was killed in an auto accident while he was driving one of the corporate vans on corporate business. The corporation had insurance for the accident with the corporation as the beneficiary. Could Roepke's family get the insurance proceeds? *Roepke v. Western National Mutual Insurance Co.,* 307 N.W.2d 350 (Minn. 1981).

7. What is the difference between a de facto and a de jure corporation?

8. Toure, Ltd., bought $250,000 of property and equipment in a plastic plant in Mobridge, South Dakota. The $250,000 was to be paid in six installments of $50,000 each. Toure never made the first payment. The seller brought suit and discovered that Toure had only $62.08 in its corporate account. Toure's shareholders were wealthy businesspeople. Could the corporate veil be pierced to sue the shareholders? *Mobridge Community Industries, Inc., v. Toure, Ltd., 273 N.W.2d 128 (S.D. 1978).*

9. Preston was the promoter and organizer of the Pan American Motel, Inc. He entered into a contract to buy land for the motel site for $240,000. He signed the contract before the corporation was formed, and the corporation was never formed. Can the seller recover from Preston? *Frick v. Howard,* 126 N.W.2d 619 (Wis. 1964).

10. Are promoters and incorporators the same people?

"Productivity is as close as you get in economics to a free lunch."

Kenneth Goldstein

Chapter 43

Management of Corporations

CHAPTER PREVIEW

- Powers of corporations and boards
- Electing directors
- Board meetings
- Board committees
- Personal and criminal liability of directors
- Required corporate officers and their duties
- Business judgment rule and the corporate opportunity doctrine

The doctors at the Weiss Medical Group wanted to get rid of their no-competition clause. All the doctors were directors of the Weiss Medical Group Corporation. Some of the doctors had no-competition clauses in their contracts and some did not. Can all of them vote on the issue at the board of directors' meeting?

The formation of a corporation is easy, but the management of a corporation is ongoing. There are long-term direction and policy issues as well as day-to-day operations of the corporation. This chapter discusses how a corporation is managed. The questions answered are: What management powers does a corporation have? Who holds the power? What are the duties, rights, and liabilities of those in power?

CORPORATE POWERS: WHAT ARE THEY?

A corporation has both express and implied powers. The **express powers** come from statutes and the articles of incorporation. The **implied powers** come from custom.

Express Corporate Powers

Express by statute Every state has a statute that lists the general powers of corporations within that state. Under the MBCA, all corporations are given general powers automatically under Section 4. The following list is a summary of the MBCA powers:

1. To sue and be sued in the corporate name.
2. To buy, lease, sell, or mortgage real or personal property.
3. To lend money to its employees.
4. To buy, sell, or pledge its own shares.
5. To borrow and lend money.
6. To start pension plans for its employees.
7. To be a promoter or a partner in a partnership.
8. To make charitable donations.

Express by the articles A corporation can also have express powers given in the articles of incorporation. The articles cannot permit the corporation to do anything illegal. Many articles of incorporation have a general powers clause that allows the corporation to do any lawful act that is necessary to carry on its business. Some articles of incorporation simply give the corporation all the powers provided by statute.

Exceeding express power: Ultra vires If a corporation does something beyond its given powers, the act is **ultra vires** (see Chapter 42 for a complete discussion).

Implied Powers of Corporations

In addition to their express powers, corporations have implied powers, which are determined by custom. For example, a retail store can sponsor marathons, concerts, or pageants. A corporation operating a retail store would have those same powers. Corporations have the power to have their share offerings underwritten by a broker even though the power given in the MBCA is just to buy and sell shares. In other words, the statute and the articles are just the general powers. The implied powers fill in the details. The *Indiana State Board of Embalmers & Funeral Directors v. Keller* case deals with the issue of whether an implied power exists.

INDIANA STATE BOARD OF EMBALMERS & FUNERAL DIRECTORS v. KELLER

Supreme Court of Indiana.
409 N.E.2d 583 (1980).

FACTS Under Indiana law, at least one owner of a funeral home must be a licensed embalmer or funeral director. Donald and Charlene Keller contracted to sell their interest in their funeral home to Flanner & Buchanan, Inc. Flanner & Buchanan is a corporation owning and operating funeral homes in eighteen states. They have a number of employees who are licensed and who operate funeral homes.

The Indiana State Board held the sale illegal and declared that only "natural" as opposed to corporate persons can hold a license. The Kellers sued for a reversal of the Board ruling.

ISSUE Does a corporation have the implied power to hold a license?

DECISION No. The ruling of the Board would hold. An implied power can be taken away by a state law or ruling. The corporation did not meet the requirements for holding a license.

LEGAL TIP

Before selling a business, check all applicable regulations and make sure the sale is legal.

WHO HAS THE POWER? THE BOARD OF DIRECTORS

The **board of directors** is the policy group of the corporation. They do all the long-range planning and goal-setting for the corporation. This section covers the directors and their responsibilities.

How Many Directors?

The traditional number of directors in a corporation required by most states is three. However, the MBCA requires only one. Some states permit one or two directors when there are only one or two shareholders.

The number of directors is included as part of the articles of incorporation or the bylaws, which can be changed in the same way that the articles of incorporation or bylaws are amended for other reasons (see Chapter 42).

Who Are the Directors?

The directors are elected by the shareholders. The time and place for voting for directors is given to shareholders well in advance (see Chapter 42).

Cumulative voting for directors. The bylaws or articles may provide for cumulative voting as the process to be used for electing directors. **Cumulative voting** gives the shareholder more votes. The formula for determining the number of votes given under cumulative voting is:

Number of shares owned × number of directors to be elected

If Jean owns two shares of Amalgamated, Inc., and nine directors are to be elected, Jean will have eighteen votes under a cumulative voting system. The idea of cumulative voting is to help minority shareholders get a voice on the board. Under a cumulative voting system, a certain number of shares, determined by a formula, is required to elect a director. If that director gets those votes, he or she will be elected.

Classes of directors The MBCA allows directors to be elected in classes when there are nine or more board members. The idea is to have staggered terms that overlap so there is not a completely new group of directors every time there is an election.

Vacancies on the board If there is a vacancy before an annual meeting, the remaining members of the board can vote to fill the vacancy. Some states require a shareholder vote unless the articles expressly allow the directors to fill the slot.

Inside/outside directors A corporation can have shareholders as directors (insiders) or non-shareholders as board members (outsiders). The trend today is to increase a board of directors' independence. The idea here is to have a group of people, divorced from top management, who can provide an objective viewpoint. The SEC and other government agencies also take the view that there should be independent voices on the board.

What Powers Do Directors Have?

Directors do not have the authority to act alone. They take action as a group after a vote.

A director could be appointed as an officer or agent of the corporation. If a director takes such a job, the director has the authority to act alone within the scope of powers for that job.

Some actions require a board vote. For example, under the MBCA only the board can declare a dividend. Also, only the board has the power to set the par value and allocate stock sale proceeds to the proper capital accounts. The board is required to make resolutions for major corporate changes such as merger, consolidation (see Chapter 44), and dissolution (see Chapter 42).

How Directors Take Action

The common law rule for directors to take action was that it must be done at a formal meeting. The MBCA allows decisions to be made by conference call. The MBCA also allows action if the directors give unanimous written consent. The formal meeting requirement for action has been relaxed with the MBCA.

For the most part, however, action by the directors is taken at a formal meeting. These meetings need to be held occasionally if for no other reason than to avoid the problems of alter egos and "corporate veils."

Notice of a meeting Regularly scheduled meetings do not require notice. An example of a regularly scheduled meeting would be one held on the third Tuesday of each month. If a special meeting is called, all the directors must be given notice. The amount of notice can be given by statute or bylaws. When there is no time requirement, the directors must be given enough time to consider the topics planned for discussion at the meeting. Directors can waive their right to notice by appearing at a meeting and signing a waiver.

Minimum number: The quorum For the board to take proper action, there must be a **quorum** present at the meeting. The MBCA quorum is a majority of the board of directors. The bylaws of the corporation may require a greater number. For any action to be taken, there must be a majority vote of the quorum number. That majority must be disinterested. If a director stands to benefit from a decision, that director is disqualified from voting. The *Weiss Medical Complex, Ltd., v. Kim* case examines the problems that can arise when a director has an interest in the outcome.

WEISS MEDICAL COMPLEX, LTD., v. KIM

Court of Appeals of Illinois, First District.
408 N.E.2d 959 (1980).

FACTS Weiss is a medical clinic in Harvey, Illinois. Doctors Kim and Chusak had employment contracts with the Weiss corporation. Their contracts had a "no-competition" clause. After they left, they could not practice medicine within a ten-mile radius of the clinic. They also could not serve any of the patients whom they had treated while at the clinic.

There were twelve shareholders in the Weiss corporation; they were all doctors, and seven of them served on the board of directors. The directors felt that the "no-competition" clause was making it difficult to get good doctors for the clinic. The board called a meeting to discuss the problem.

The seven directors attended the meeting. They voted to eliminate the "no-competition" clauses from all of the contracts. Four of the seven directors were doctors at the clinic who had the clauses in their contracts.

Kim and Chusak left the clinic and opened up their own offices a short distance from the clinic. The shareholders brought suit. They claimed that the action taken by the directors was illegal because the four doctors with contract clauses were disqualified.

ISSUE Was the action taken by the board of directors valid?

DECISION No. The four director/doctors with contract clauses had conflicts of interest. They could not impartially decide the question. They were disqualified. There was not a quorum at the meeting. The decision on the clauses would have to be left to the shareholders.

LEGAL TIP

All directors' votes must be disinterested. The action taken should be checked to make sure that there are no conflicts of interest.

Do Directors Get Paid?

Common law does not allow directors to fix their own salaries. The MBCA allows directors to fix their own salaries unless the articles prohibit it. Outside directors are usually paid very small amounts for their service. In non-profit corporations, they serve for free. Inside directors are compensated through the salaried management positions, which they hold in the company.

What Are the Directors' Duties?

The director's duty of care Directors have the duty to manage the corporation and make decisions as prudent people do in managing their own businesses, property, or finances. Directors have the responsibility to stay informed about the business. They also have the responsibility to know background information before any decisions are made. Their duty of care also includes the responsibility of attending board meetings and keeping informed about corporate matters.

Directors can hire outside help to assist them with their work. If they need financial analysis, directors would be required to hire a person competent in that field. For legal advice, they would be permitted to hire a competent attorney. Directors can rely on the advice of these third parties so long as they act reasonably in hiring them in the first place.

Directors can make mistakes and still not be liable to the shareholders or the corporation. The mistake just must be one that anyone in business could make. This protection for directors' mistakes is called the **business judgment rule.** To be liable for an error in business judgment, a director must have acted ignorantly, against all advice, or without common sense. The *Smith v. Van Gorkom* case examines whether a board of directors violated the business judgment rule.

SMITH v. VAN GORKOM

Delaware Supreme Court.
488 A.2d 858 (1985).

FACTS Trans Union Corporation received a takeover offer from Marmon Group, Inc. Trans Union had attractive tax credits from its railcar leasing business and insufficient income for using the credits.

Jerome W. Van Gorkom, the chief executive officer for Trans Union presented the takeover offer to Trans Union's board in a twenty-minute oral presentation at a special meeting.

Based on the oral presentation and oral representations from other officers, the Board approved the merger during that same meeting (which lasted 2 hours).

The Trans Union shareholders brought suit because the offer undervalued their shares and that the quick, unresearched decision of the Board was a violation of the business judgment rule.

ISSUE Could the shareholders recover for violation of the business judgment rule?

DECISION Yes. The action taken was too serious and dramatic for a two-hour meeting with only oral presentations. The Board should have taken time and gathered more information.

LEGAL TIP

Directors must take the time and effort to do their job. They cannot rely on officers for information in all situations.

Loyalty to the corporation and shareholders: Fiduciary responsibilities Directors are responsible for acting in the best interests of the corporation and shareholders. They should not be acting for individual gain. The *Allabastro v. Cummins* case discusses a situation where a director's personal gain is involved.

ALLABASTRO v. CUMMINS

Court of Appeals of Illinois, First District.
413 N.E.2d 86. (Ill. 1980).

FACTS Warren Allabastro and Elmer Anderson entered into a contract with Equity Financial Corporation. Equity was to find them a loan. The contract was signed by Equity's Vice President William Cummins. The terms for the loan were in their contract.

Cummins found a loan for Warren and Elmer with the Southshore National Bank. The terms were higher than those in the written contract. Cummins kept the higher fee difference for himself and did not disclose the extra funds that he received from the loan arrangement. Cummins was sued for breach of his fiduciary duty.

ISSUE Had Cummins breached his fiduciary duty?

DECISION Yes. He was profiting without telling the corporation. He was using the corporation's position to make personal gains.

LEGAL TIP

Check contract terms, compare them with the amount due to a corporation, and determine where any difference in funds is going.

Loyalty to corporate expansion The breach of the **corporate opportunity doctrine** discourages directors from profiting at the expense of the corporation. Under this idea, a director who profits at the expense of the corporation will owe the profits to the corporation. For example, suppose that Fred serves on the board for Forest Products, Inc. Fred has learned of a buy on timberland in South America. The land is cheap, and the costs of labor for the company will be less in South America. Fred buys the land and then has an agent approach the company without telling who owns the land. The corporation buys the land, and Fred makes a huge profit. Any profits that Fred made belong to the company because he seized a corporate opportunity.

The corporate opportunity doctrine applies when a director takes an opportunity that the corporation should ordinarily have. Timberland for a forest products company is one example. Land for a real estate firm is another example.

To avoid problems with this doctrine, the director must first make the opportunity known to the corporation. The corporation must reject the opportunity. Then the director would be free to take the opportunity without the loss of profits. The key to avoiding problems is full disclosure.

Civil and criminal liability of directors Even though directors act as a group, they can be individually liable for any actions taken by the group that are illegal. For example, a director who signs a false securities registration statement is liable for the losses to those who buy the shares. The director may also be prosecuted criminally by the SEC for signing a false registration statement (see Chapter 16). A director can be personally liable for a grossly wrong business judgment. To be able to avoid personal liability if the board is taking incorrect action, the director must take the following steps:

1. Vote against the action at the meeting.
2. File a formal, written dissent with the secretary of the board.

Delegating Board Authority: Committees

In the past decade, boards of directors have taken a new approach to carry out their responsibilities by using committees. These committees save time and in some cases, liability.

The executive committee When a board of directors is large or when the members are scattered throughout the country, it is difficult for the board to meet frequently enough to take care of all corporate business. Under the MBCA and most state acts, boards are authorized to appoint an **executive committee,** which is made up of two or three members of the board. The executive committee is given the same authority as the board with the exceptions of adopting resolutions or taking extraordinary steps in operation. An executive committee cannot declare a dividend, approve a merger, or authorize the issuance of shares.

The audit committee Most public corporations have audit committees. Audit committees are a prerequisite for a company to list its shares on the New York Stock Exchange. The **audit committee** is the watchdog for corporate finances and hires an independent accountant to conduct an audit of the firm and evaluate the firm's internal accounting procedures.

The nominating committee The majority of public corporations have a nominating committee. The general role of the nominating committee is to establish qualifications for directors, make recommendations on where to find directors, review the performance of current directors, and recommend a structure for the board.

Compensation committee This committee reviews the salaries of senior management members. They then make recommendations about salaries, benefits, and profit-sharing plans.

Public policy committees This community relations committee deals with the corporation's involvement in charitable, political, safety, and equality organizations.

Removing Directors

Under the MBCA, directors may be removed with or without cause. A cause would be breach of a fiduciary duty, embezzlement, or failure to attend meetings. Removal requires shareholder approval. In some states, a simple majority will result in removal. In cumulative voting states, a director will not be removed if he or she has enough votes to be elected in a cumulative election. In those states requiring cause, the director is entitled to notice and a hearing before removal.

CORPORATE OFFICERS: THE SERVANTS OF THE BOARD

The **officers** are the agents of the corporation and serve as the board deems appropriate. The officers of a corporation also have duties and liabilities.

Who Are the Officers and How Many Are There?

The MBCA and most state laws give general requirements for officers. The MBCA requires that there be a president, vice president, secretary, and treasurer. The MBCA provides that a person may hold more than one office at the same time except for the offices of secretary and president. The board is free to add other officers in its bylaws.

What Authority Do Officers Have?

The regulations for officers' authority, or express power, can be found in state statutes, the articles of incorporation, the bylaws, and the board resolutions. The job descriptions of the officers can be found in the bylaws. Most of the authority given to officers is general.

President's authority The **president** is usually given the power to supervise and control the business and operation of the corporation. The president has the authority to sign corporate contracts, notes, and stock certificates. His general authority includes much implied authority.

Vice president's authority The **vice president** usually does not have individual power. The power of this office comes from acting in the president's absence, illness, or death. Vice presidents can sign stock certificates and other corporate documents.

Secretary's authority The **secretary** does the clerical work for the officers. The secretary keeps the minutes of shareholder and board meetings. The secretary is also responsible for getting notice about meetings to the shareholders and directors. The secretary keeps shareholders' records and signs the corporation's stock certificates, along with the president or vice president.

Treasurer's authority The **treasurer** is in charge of and has custody of the corporate funds. The treasurer gives receipts, makes deposits, and keeps records of the corporation's finances.

The laws of agency apply to corporate officers. They can have implied and apparent authority to act on behalf of the corporation. Also, even when they exceed their authority, the board can choose to ratify their actions.

Can Officers Be Personally Liable for Their Acts?

Officers who exceed their corporate authority will be personally liable on the contracts. Also, officers who give a personal guaranty for a corporation loan will be personally liable on the loan. Officers may also be required to pay if they do not properly pay taxes or unemployment contributions.

Can Officers Be Criminally Liable for Their Acts?

Officers can be held liable for acts done by the corporation if they were responsible in any way. For example, a corporation owning and operating a restaurant will be required to comply with the health code. Violations of the health code that are brought to officers' attention become the responsibility of that officer. The officer can be prosecuted for failure to follow through even though subordinates are responsible for correcting the problem. The *Landex, Inc. v. State ex rel. List* case examines an officer's criminal liability.

LANDEX, INC., v. STATE EX REL. LIST

Supreme Court of Nevada.
582 P.2d 786 (1978).

FACTS Frank E. Glindmeir was the president of Landex, Inc. Landex was in the business of selling lots of land. The lots were in rural areas and had questionable value.

Glindmeir held a sales meeting and told his employees how to sell the land. He told them to tell prospective buyers that the water was good when there actually was no water; that the land had small rolling hills when there actually were mountains; and that all improvement costs for the land would be tax deductible when they actually were not.

Glindmeir never sold any land himself; the selling was done by company salespeople. The state of Nevada prosecuted Glindmeir for land fraud. The state said that he was responsible for the sales, the salespeople, and the misrepresentations.

ISSUE Could Glindmeir be convicted of land fraud as an officer of the corporation?

DECISION Yes. He could be prosecuted because he was directly responsible. Everything was under his direction. He gave all of the directions to salespeople, and formulated all of the language for sales presentations.

LEGAL TIP

Liability to corporate officers, who give directions to other employees, arises even when others do the dirty work.

Officers can also be held liable for securities act violations (see Chapter 16 for a complete discussion) and violations of antitrust laws (see Chapters 14 through 16). The corporation does not provide a shield for criminal liability. The theory of the courts in imposing liability is that the corporation has no mind or intent but its operators do.

KEY TERMS

Express powers
Implied powers
Ultra vires
Board of directors
Cumulative voting
Quorum
Business judgment rule
Corporate opportunity doctrine
Executive committee
Audit committee
Officers
President
Vice president
Secretary
Treasurer

CHAPTER PROBLEMS

1. Nationwide Leisure Corporation advertised European tours at a low price. Their ads promised high-quality hotels and accommodations. The officers of the corporation had come up with the ads but they booked all the buyers in "unsafe, dirty, and seedy" hotels throughout Europe. The wronged tourists brought suit against the officers when the corporation was unable to refund their money. Is the corporation liable? *DuPack v. Nationwide Leisure Corporation,* 417 N.Y.S.2d 63 (1979).
2. Would a director who woos a takeover of his corporation be breaching a fiduciary duty? *Wellman v. Dickinson,* 475 F.Supp. 783 (D.C., N.Y. 1979).
3. The officers (who were also directors) of Plaque Mines & Oil Sales voted themselves a salary increase from $96,000 to $125,000 over a three-year period. The company was quite profitable during the three years. Was there a breach of any duty in their actions? *Hingle v. Plaque Mines & Oil Sales Corporation,* 399 So.2d 646 (La. 1981).
4. Thurman, a director of Unicure, bought a condominium with corporate funds and took title in his own name. Who owns the condominium? *Unicure, Inc., v. Thurman,* 599 P.2d 925 (Colo. 1979).
5. What is the difference between an election of directors with cumulative votes and one without?
6. A.W. Ham was the attorney for and also a director of Golden Nugget, Inc. The Golden Nugget had been interested for some time in expanding its operations and had tried to buy land around its Las Vegas casino located at 101 W. Fremont. Ham's ex-wife owned the California Club, which was located next to the Golden Nugget. Ham took a ninety-nine-year lease-option on the land from his wife in exchange for $1,000,000. He then offered it to the corporation but did not tell the board that he was the owner. Has Ham done anything wrong? *Golden Nugget, Inc., v. Ham,* 589 P.2d 173 (Nev. 1979).

*7. Myra owns three shares in Xena Corporation. Xena's annual meeting for the election of directors will be held in a month. Twelve directors are to be elected. If the corporation has cumulative voting, how many votes will Myra have? What if the directors were divided into three classes and only one class was up for election, how many votes would Myra have?

*8. Illinois Migrant Council, Inc., was formed for the purposes of educating, improving the health of, and providing vocational programs for migrant farm workers. Members of the council went to a Campbell's Soup mushroom farm to talk to the migrant workers. Campbell said it was trespass. The Council said that its purposes authorized entry. Could the Council legally trespass? *Illinois Migrant Council, Inc., v. Campbell Soup Co.,* 574 F.2d 374 (Ill. 1978).

*9. The Midtown Club was a non-profit corporation formed for the purpose of providing meals to its members. Its bylaws excluded women. Some women who were denied membership sued the club for this ultra vires rule. Is the rule an ultra vires act? *Cross v. Midtown Club, Inc.,* 365 A.2d 1227 (Conn. 1976).

*10. Can directors be held liable for bounced checks? *Super Valu Stores, Inc., v. First National Bank of Columbus, Ga.,* 463 F.Supp. 1183 (Ga. 1979).

"October. This is one of the peculiarly dangerous months to speculate stocks in. The others are July, January, September, April, November, May, March, June, December, August and February."

Mark Twain
Pudd'nhead Wilson, 1898

Chapter 44

Rights and Responsibilities of Shareholders

CHAPTER PREVIEW

- Rights and responsibilities of shareholders
- Personal liability of shareholders
- Paying for and issuing stock
- Requirements for declaring a dividend
- Types of dividends
- Examples of extraordinary corporate transactions
- Voting arrangements and proxies

Dodge was upset. He was a shareholder in a company with lots of earnings and lots of cash. But he and the other shareholders had not been paid a dividend in four years. Dodge has brought suit to ask a court to force the directors to declare a dividend. Can he win?

Shareholders own the corporation. The marvelous thing about their ownership is that they can invest a small or large amount in their business. In a small corporation, a shareholder may own all the shares after having invested a lifetime's savings. In a large corporation, a shareholder may own one share out of a million issued. Regardless of the size of their investment, all shareholders have certain rights and responsibilities. This chapter discusses the rights and responsibilities of all shareholders.

THE NATURE OF SHARE OWNERSHIP: TYPES OF STOCK

Common Stock

Common stock is the voting stock of a corporation. The common stock shareholders are the last in line for dividends. They are also the last to receive their payments if the corporation is liquidated. A corporation may have several classes of common stock. These classes may have different par values. All of the common stock structure must be set up in the articles of incorporation (see Chapter 42).

Preferred Stock

Preferred shareholders are usually non-voting shareholders. However, they are first in the shareholder line for dividends and asset liquidation. A **preferred stock** can be cumulative or non-cumulative. Cumulative means that dividends must be paid every year. If a year is missed, the amount owed to the cumulative preferred shareholders accumulates. These amounts must be paid before the common shareholders would be entitled to a dividend. If the preferred stock is non-cumulative, the shareholders get a dividend only if one is declared.

Restricted Stock

Restricted stock is stock with transfer restrictions on it. These transfer restrictions control when and to whom stock may be transferred.

Why restrictions? Restrictions are used for many different reasons. In a family-owned corporation, the restrictions are designed to keep ownership in the family. In some cases, corporations need to put transfer restrictions on shares to be able to qualify for a securities registration exemption. To keep a "Subchapter S" tax status, a corporation cannot have more than twenty-five shareholders, and restrictions are used to help keep the requirement.

Types of restrictions A restriction can be as simple as a right of first refusal. The shareholder is required to offer the shares first to the corporation or its shareholders before selling them to a third party.

Requirements for a valid restriction A **stock restriction** is a restraint on alienation. The restrictions are closely examined by courts. The first requirement is that there be a valid reason for the restriction. A valid reason would be any of those covered above.

The second requirement is that the restriction be a reasonable one that does not unfairly restrain transfers. An outright prohibition on transfer is illegal and invalid. Restrictions that require a right of refusal or option are reasonable; but a restriction that requires the consent of the board before a sale can be made is probably invalid. Restrictions requiring a shareholder to first offer the shares to a great number of other shareholders are also invalid.

A final requirement for a valid restriction is notice. The restriction must be conspicuous on the face of the stock certificate. Without such notice, the transfer restriction will not apply to third-party buyers unless it can be shown that the buyer had actual knowledge of the restriction. The *In the Matter of the Estate of Spaziani* case deals with a restrictive covenant issue.

IN THE MATTER OF THE ESTATE OF SPAZIANI

Supreme Court of New York.
430 N.Y.S.2d 854 (1984).

FACTS Vincent Spaziana was one of five original shareholders in the Spaziana Bakeries, Inc. His shares had the following restriction:

> No certificate of stock or any interest therein of this corporation shall be transferred to any person, persons, partnership or corporation until it has first been offered for sale in writing by registered mail to this Corporation.

Spaziani died and the remaining four shareholders demanded that his estate give them the shares in exchange for a fair price. The estate claimed that distribution through Spaziani's estate was not a transfer, and that the shares could go to heirs.

ISSUE Did the restriction apply to the estate?

DECISION No. The restriction was not specific enough to include transfers through a shareholder's estate. Such a restriction would control a will and the distribution of property. The restriction would have to be more specific to apply to the estate.

LEGAL TIP

Check stock restrictions before you buy. Find out how hard it will be to sell the shares.

GETTING THE SHARES TO THE SHAREHOLDERS: ISSUING STOCK

Signing Up For the Stock: Subscriptions

A **subscription** is an offer by a shareholder to buy the shares of the corporation. Subscriptions are used to sign up for shares before the shares are actually available. When the board of directors acts to accept the subscriptions, then a formal contract for the purchase and sale of the shares exists.

The MBCA and many states have special rules for subscriptions given before the corporation is formed or before preincorporation certificates are granted. The MBCA provides that subscription agreements are irrevocable for a period of six months. The reason for such a rule is to allow the corporation to get organized with the assurance of capital through the sale of shares. Preincorporation subscriptions must be in writing to be enforceable.

Background Information on the Stock: Federal and State Registration

Before stock is sold, a corporation must satisfy regulations concerning stock registration and the filing of required documents and information. The registration required may be at the federal or state level or both (see Chapter 16).

Who Buys the Stock? Preemptive Rights

Preemptive rights give shareholders the first right to buy newly issued shares. For example, suppose that Lambda Corporation has 100,000 authorized shares. Ralph bought 1,000 of the 50,000 shares that Lambda sold initially. Ralph has a

1/50th interest in the corporation. If Lambda decides to sell the remaining 50,000, Ralph's interest will be reduced to 1/100th. Ralph can be given a first right to buy by the articles of incorporation. Under the MBCA, the articles of incorporation must provide for preemptive rights since they are not automatic rights. There are a wide range of preemptive rights that a corporation can give. Preemptive rights can be limited to only newly authorized shares. Or, as in the Ralph/Lambda example, the rights can be in authorized but unissued shares. Some corporations even give preemptive rights in treasury shares.

Paying for Stock

Form of payment Shares can be paid for with cash or property. The value of the property is set by the board of directors. The board is, of course, permitted to have appraisals conducted. Services already rendered to the corporation can also be used as payment for shares. Many states prohibit corporations from issuing stock in exchange for a promissory note. The MBCA also prohibits issuing stock for a promise of future services. If stock is sold for any of these invalid forms of consideration, the stock issuance can be cancelled. Creditors of the corporation would also be allowed to collect amounts due from these buyers if the corporation was unable to pay.

Amount of payment A buyer must pay at least par value for shares. If par value is not paid, the buyer holds **watered shares.** If a buyer has paid less than par value, the buyer is personally liable to corporation creditors for the difference between the amount paid and the par value of the stock. For example, suppose that Fred transferred a lot worth $18,000 to the corporation in exchange for 1800 shares with a par value of $20 each. Fred's shares are watered; he could be personally liable to corporation creditors for $18,000.

THE SHAREHOLDER'S RIGHT TO A VOICE: VOTING RIGHTS

Shareholders have their input in running the corporation through their voting rights. Shareholders elect the directors and also vote on major corporate transactions and changes (see the discussion on corporate transactions later in the chapter).

When Shareholders Vote

Shareholders vote at the annual meeting of the corporation and at any special meetings called by the board of directors. Annual meetings are required in some states for the corporation to keep its charter or certificate. Under the MBCA, if an annual meeting has not been held in thirteen months, a shareholder can petition a court for an injunction ordering a meeting.

The time and place of the annual meeting may be part of the corporate bylaws. The authority to call a special meeting may also be part of the bylaws. Some bylaws give the president, the board and/or 10% of the shareholders the right to call a special meeting.

How Is Notice of a Meeting Given?

Shareholders are entitled to adequate notice of a meeting. Under the MBCA, shareholders must be given notice at least ten days before the meeting is held but not more than fifty days before. If a special meeting is called, the shareholders must be given a notice that explains the intended purpose.

Who is given notice of a meeting depends upon the record date set by the corporation. A **record date** is one set by the corporation as its cut-off for giving notice. The notice of meetings is sent to whomever is listed as a shareholder on that date. Subsequent buyers will have to rely on their sellers or contact the corporation to find out about meetings. The corporation is justified in setting a cut-off date even though all shareholders will not have notice of the meeting. The reason is that there must be a cut-off. Under the MBCA, the record date can be no less than ten and no more than sixty days before a meeting. Of course subsequent buyers can get proxies (see below) from their sellers that will allow them to vote.

Who Votes at a Shareholder Meeting?

Shareholders as of the record date are entitled to vote at the meeting. However, shareholders can work out several arrangements to have others vote for them or to have a group vote.

Voting for another: The proxy A **proxy** is an authorization by a shareholder to have someone else vote his or her share(s).

Proxies are often used in large corporations where all the shareholders could not possibly attend an annual meeting. They can also be used in small corporations when one of the shareholders cannot personally attend a meeting.

Requirements for a valid proxy A valid proxy must be in writing. A proxy is only good for eleven months. This limitation requires that the proxy be resolicited for every annual meeting. A proxy can be revoked at any time. The exception to this rule occurs when there is a proxy coupled with an interest. A proxy coupled with an interest results when a shareholder pledges shares as collateral for a loan. The lender has an interest in the shares and will have a proxy for the period of the loan that cannot be revoked.

Federal regulation of proxies Under the 1934 Securities Act, soliciting proxies is regulated (see Chapter 16).

Pooling agreements **Pooling agreements** are shareholder voting agreements. Groups of shareholders agree to vote a certain way. For example, Bob could agree to vote for Sue as a director in exchange for Sue's agreement to vote for him.

Most states have no specific requirements for valid pooling agreements. The agreements must simply be entered into as a contract and meet all the requirements for an ordinary contract.

Enforcement of pooling agreements is difficult because the shareholders still own their own shares and are registered as the owners on the corporate books. Some courts have refused to enforce such pooling agreements. Some states have passed statutes that allow courts to declare specific performance of pooling agreements. That is, the parties are ordered to vote their shares according to the terms of the pooling agreements. The *R.H. Sanders Corp. v. Haves* case examines the validity of a pooling agreement.

Voting trusts **Voting trusts** are formal arrangements in which shareholders transfer the title to their shares to a trustee. The trustee is the registered owner of the shares on the corporate records and votes all of the shares in the voting

R.H. SANDERS CORP. v. HAVES
Court of Appeals of Texas, Fifth District.
541 S.W.2d 262 (1976).

FACTS Haves and two others agreed to loan $26,000 to R.H. Sanders Corporation. They also agreed to buy 35% of the corporation's stock. Their contract and loan agreement had the following language: "Each of the three stockholders shall be a director of the corporation and each vote shall be equal." When one of the three failed to vote for the others in a director's election, they brought suit to enforce the clause, which they said was a pooling agreement.

ISSUE Was the clause in their contract a pooling agreement?

DECISION Yes. Because they were making a financial commitment to the corporation, they could expect some say in the government of the corporation. Their intent in the language was clear.

LEGAL TIP

To have a good voting pool agreement, use specific language.

trust. The original shareholders still hold a beneficial interest in the shares since they get the dividends. A voting trust simply has them give up their voting rights. The trustee issues trust certificates to the shareholders as evidence of their beneficial interest in the trust.

The MBCA and most states have specific requirements for setting up a voting trust. Under the MBCA, the trust agreement must be in writing and cannot last for more than ten years. A copy of the agreement must be filed with the main office of the corporation.

Trusts are created for many different reasons. One common reason for shareholders to band together is to maintain control. If they voted separately, they might lose control of the corporation. Sometimes a voting trust is used in bankruptcy to keep a company stable during a reorganization.

How Many Votes Does a Shareholder Get?

The general rule for shareholder votes is one vote per share. However, in the election of directors, some states require—and all states allow—corporations to have cumulative voting (see Chapter 42).

SHAREHOLDER PAYMENT RIGHTS: DIVIDENDS

What Are Dividends?

Dividends are payments to shareholders. These dividends are the shareholders' annual return on their investment in the corporation.

What Are the Types of Dividends?

Dividends can be cash or stock. Cash dividends are simply paid by check to the shareholder; stock dividends are paid by shares to shareholders. Shareholders then own additional shares in the corporation. But since all of the shareholders received the same number of shares, the proportion of ownership is unchanged.

Some corporations will declare a stock split. A stock split means simply that the shareholder will own more shares but each share will be worth less (except in the case of a reverse stock split—see Glossary). A stock split makes it seem as if the shareholder owns more, but the proportion of ownership actually stays the same.

What Are the Requirements for Paying a Dividend?

The states have different requirements for corporations to be able to declare a dividend. Under the MBCA, the corporation must be solvent. Solvent means that the corporation has the ability to pay its debts and obligations as they become due.

A second requirement under the MBCA and in most states is that the corporation have a positive figure in the earned surplus account. The **earned surplus** account is the retained earnings account. The account is a cumulative figure of the corporation's earnings and losses over the years. Some states make an exception to this requirement with a nimble dividends rule. **Nimble dividends** are dividends paid out of earnings for the year, even though the net figure in the earned surplus account may still be negative. The idea behind nimble dividends is to allow a previously losing company to give a return to shareholders without waiting for full recovery in the earned surplus account.

The third requirement is that the dividend be declared by the board of directors.

Under the MBCA, corporations can also make distributions from their capital surplus accounts. These distributions have the same requirements as dividends. Also, the shareholders must be told that they are receiving a **capital surplus distribution** and not a dividend.

When Are Dividends Paid?

Dividends are declared by the board of directors, according to their discretion. Courts avoid deciding when a dividend should or should not be declared; instead, the decision is left to the directors. The landmark *Dodge v. Ford Motor Co.* case examines whether the directors were required to declare a dividend.

DODGE v. FORD MOTOR CO.

Supreme Court of Michigan.
170 N.W. 668 (1919).

FACTS Dodge was a stockholder in the Ford Motor Company. The corporation had been profitable from 1903 through 1916. The capital stock had increased from $150,000 to $2,000,000. A regular dividend of 5% per month had been paid on the stock since 1911. Also, special dividends ranging from $1,000,000 to $10,000,000 had been declared each year. From 1911 through 1915, $41,000,000 in special dividends had been paid.

In 1916, the directors decided to continue the 5% dividend but stop the special dividends. At the time of the decision, the corporation had earned a surplus of $112,000,000; its earnings were $60,000,000 per year. The total liabilities of the corporation were less than $20,000,000, and it had $54,000,000 in its cash account.

Dodge brought suit to force the directors to declare a special dividend.

ISSUE Could the directors be forced to declare a dividend?

DECISION Yes. Although Henry Ford testified that he thought the shareholders made too much money, the duty of the corporation and its board is to its shareholders. The board was not acting in the best interests of the shareholders by not distributing the corporation's earnings when the company was in such excellent condition.

LEGAL TIP

To determine whether dividends are being declared, check the financial statements of corporations each year before investing.

Once a dividend is declared, it becomes a legal obligation of the corporation. The corporation is required to pay a declared dividend unless the corporation is insolvent or the dividend does not meet the requirements covered earlier. When the dividend is declared, the board will also provide for a **payment date.** That date is the final one allowed for payment of this obligation.

Who Gets the Dividends?

As with meeting notices, a record date is set for dividends. When the dividend is declared, the corporation also sets a record date, which is the cut-off date for payment. Everyone who is listed on the books as a shareholder at that time will get the dividend. Those buying shares after that date will have to work out the dividend payment with the seller. The corporation is only obligated to see that the dividends get to record shareholders and not to those who buy into the corporation after that date.

OTHER SHAREHOLDER RIGHTS

Access to Records

Shareholders have the right to see the records of their corporation. Under the MBCA, the shareholder must either own 5% of any class of outstanding shares or have been a shareholder for at least six months. The idea of these requirements is to make sure that the shareholder has an interest in the company and is not using the access right for industrial espionage.

In addition to these minimum requirements, most states require that the shareholder have a good reason or **proper purpose** for wanting to examine the books. An example of a proper purpose is checking expenditures.

Under the MBCA, refusing to allow a shareholder to check the company's books can result in a penalty. The penalty for wrongful refusal of access to the company's books under the MBCA is 10% of the value of the shareholder's shares.

Right to Bring a Derivative Action

A corporation is a legal fiction. The owners of the business are the shareholders. When the business is wronged, it is up to the owners to enforce the business's rights.

Shareholders can enforce the business's rights by bringing a **derivative action** on behalf of the corporation. For example, a director who takes a corporate opportunity has wronged the corporation. A shareholder can bring suit on behalf of the corporation to recover the profits earned by the director. The recovery a shareholder makes in a derivative action belongs to the corporation. In a derivative action, a shareholder is enforcing corporate rights.

Rights in Extraordinary Corporate Transactions

Extraordinary corporate transactions are **mergers, consolidations,** amendments to the articles of incorporation, and liquidation. These unusual transactions give shareholders special rights.

Step one in extraordinary transactions: Resolution Before any of the extraordinary transactions can even be voted on by the shareholders, the board must adopt a resolution that authorizes the transaction. The resolution must be adopted by a majority of the board. The resolution must be scheduled for a shareholder meeting. It could be part of the annual meeting but if a special meeting is scheduled, advance notice must indicate the purpose of the meeting.

Step two in extraordinary transactions: Shareholder vote The shareholders must vote to approve or disapprove the resolution. In the case of a merger or a consolidation, all shareholders are entitled to vote even though they are otherwise non-voting shares. The reason is that all shareholders will be affected by the results. A majority of the shareholders entitled to vote is required to pass a resolution for an extraordinary corporate transaction.

Step three: Dissenters In the case of a merger or consolidation, there will probably be shareholders who do not agree with the resolution. These shareholders are given their appraisal rights by the corporations. This means that they are given the chance to sell their shares to the corporation for fair value. The value of their shares is determined as of the time immediately before the merger. A dissenting shareholder who is not satisfied with the proposed payment can bring suit to have a value determined.

KEY TERMS

Common stock
Preferred stock
Restricted stock
Subscriptions
Preemptive rights
Watered shares
Record date
Proxy
Pooling agreement
Voting trusts
Dividends
Earned surplus
Nimble dividends
Capital surplus distribution
Payment date
Proper purpose
Derivative action
Extraordinary corporate transactions
Merger
Consolidation

CHAPTER PROBLEMS

1. The members of the Sto-Rox Focus on Renewal Neighborhood Corporation wanted the records of the corporation for the following reasons:
   a. To check to see if the membership lists were up to date.
   b. To check for financial irregularities.
   c. To check corporate salaries.
   d. To investigate mismanagement.

   Are these proper purposes for examining books and records? *Sto-Rox Focus on Renewal Neighborhood Corporation v. King,* 398 A.2d 241 (Pa. 1979).
2. When does a dissenting shareholder have a right of appraisal?

*3. Can a competitor who is a stockholder in a corporation have access to its books and records? *Skoglund v. Ormand Industries, Inc.,* 372 A.2d 204 (Del. 1976).

4. Favaro was a shareholder in United Film Corporation. He had paid for his shares by giving the corporation a $40,000 note. McGregor was injured in an accident by a United employee. United was insolvent and McGregor could not recover from the corporation. He sued Favaro because he said Favaro still owed for the shares. Is he right? *McGregor v. United Film Corporation,* 351 So.2d 1224 (La. 1977).
5. Is an oral subscription for stock valid? *Jatoi v. Park Center, Inc.,* 616 S.W.2d 399 (Ark. 1981).

6. Garbe gave equipment worth $395,800 to Excel Mold. Excel agreed to assume the payments on a $244,200 loan balance secured by the equipment. Excel issued Garbe $151,600 in stock to cover the difference. Has Garbe paid for the shares? *Garbe v. Excel Mold, Inc.*, 397 N.E.2d 296 (Ind. 1979).
7. Can a shareholder force the declaration of a dividend?
8. The members of a corporation who were all family voted to put a transfer restriction on their stock. The corporation operated a family farm and the approval on the restriction was unanimous. The vote was not taken until after the shares were issued. Is the restriction valid? *Bloodworth v. Endersville Production Credit Association,* 262 S.E.2d 804 (Ga. 1980).
9. Would a quorum for a meeting on a merger be higher than a quorum for an annual meeting? *Benintendi v. Kenton Hotel Inc.,* 60 N.E.2d 829 (N.Y. 1945).
10. Would a stock restriction in a four-shareholder corporation requiring a shareholder to first offer the shares to the other shareholders before selling be reasonable? *Boss v. Boss,* 200 A.2d 231 (R.I. 1964).

Part Seven

Property

"Finders keepers, losers weepers."
A Child's First Rule of Law

Chapter 45

Personal Property

CHAPTER PREVIEW

- Types and examples of personal property
- Ways to transfer personal property
- Inter vivos gifts—what they are and how to make them
- Gifts causa mortis—their validity and effects
- Accession and confusion
- Patents, trademarks, and copyrights

Morrison served in the army during the Vietnam war. While he was on duty in the Central Highlands, he found nearly $200,000. He claimed that the money belonged to him. The United States Army says that the money belongs to the Army because Morrison was their employee. Who gets the money?

Personal property is movable property. Cars, boats, planes and hair dryers are examples of personal property. Because personal property is movable, it can be transferred, lost, and sometimes destroyed. This chapter discusses the rights of personal property owners in these situations. The questions answered are: What is personal property? How is personal property transferred? How are personal property rights protected?

WHAT IS PERSONAL PROPERTY?

Real property is land or anything permanently attached such as houses, sidewalks, streets, church buildings, factory buildings, and school buildings. Personal property is everything else, including items such as appliances, clothing, vehicles, and food items. "Chattels" is a term sometimes used to describe personal property.

Tangible and Intangible

Personal property can be tangible or intangible. For example, appliances, cars, etc., would be **tangible personal property.** Bank accounts, stock shares, patents, and copyrights would be intangible personal property. **Intangible personal property** is a right usually represented by some document. One actually owns a portion of a company and that is personal property. Evidence of that ownership is the stock certificate.

Fungible Personal Property

Some personal property is tangible but is in a mass. For example, grain and other farm products are tangible personal property. However, those products are **fungible personal property** since they are stored together in grain elevators and warehouses. Fungible goods are part of a mass, and one person's portion cannot be separated from another's portion.

HOW IS PERSONAL PROPERTY TRANSFERRED?

Transfer by Sale

Personal property can be sold. Not much is required for a sale of personal property. There should be a contract for the sale but the contract can be oral or written. The contract can be a simple handwritten one for the sale of a bicycle. Or the contract can be a complex securities document for the transfer of shares.

The requirements for passing title to the property being sold varies for each type of property. For example, with a share of stock, the owner must sign it over to the buyer. The corporation also must have been notified about the transfer.

For some personal property, there is a title that will have to be signed over to pass title. Cars, boats, and planes are examples of personal property requiring a signed title document.

For other types of goods, a bill of sale is the usual means for transferring title. A bill of sale can just be a receipt for the sale. Or there are form bills of sale, which can be completed and used to transfer the title to the personal property. The passing of title for the sale of goods is discussed more completely in Chapter 29.

Transfer by Gift

A gift is a gratuitous transfer (one without consideration) from one party to another. A gift is not a promise to give in the future. A gift is a present action of transfer. Gifts can be made through a will (see Chapter 50 for discussion). There are also inter vivos gifts, which are made during the life of the property owner, and gifts causa mortis, which are gifts made when death is pending. The following sections cover the requirements for such gifts to be valid.

Inter vivos gifts **Inter vivos gifts** are made while the property owner is alive. The party who owns the property and gives the gift is called the donor. The party who receives the gift is the donee. The requirements for a valid inter vivos gift are discussed below.

Capacity of the donor. The donor has to have mental and age capacity to make a gift. The capacity requirements for a gift are the same as the capacity requirements for a contract (see Chapter 20 for a full discussion).

The donor can have mental capacity even if forgetful, eccentric, or senile. The test for capacity is whether the donor knew what property was being given, the nature and value of the property, and to whom the property was being given.

Usually, capacity problems are combined with issues of undue influence. Undue influence happens when someone the donor trusts and relies upon convinces the donor to make a gift to him or her. The trust and reliance forms a confidential relationship between the parties. The donee takes unfair advantage of that relationship and tries to get the donor's property. Gifts made under undue influence are not valid. A court will require the donee to give back the transferred property. The *Estate of Kenneth R. Truckenmiller* case deals with the issues of capacity and undue influence.

Intent to make a gift: Donative intent. A valid gift requires that the donor intended to make a gift. The donor usually does not make a statement of intent. The intent has to be pieced together from related circumstances and actions of the donor. For example, a father may want to give his daughter $25,000 worth of stock. But if he wants it as a reward for her completion of college, he has shown no present donative intent and has not made a gift. The gift is conditional. Engagement rings are examples of conditional gifts; there is the intent to give the gift only if a marriage is intended.

Delivery. **Delivery** is required for a valid gift. The delivery can be actual or constructive.

a. *Actual delivery.* Actual delivery is when the personal property is given to the donee or the donee's agent. This means that the donee now has control of the property. The donee has the right to hold, sell, or pledge the property. If your grandmother tells you that she wants to give you a rocking chair and lets you take it with you, there has been actual delivery. Or, if your grandmother tells you she wants you to have a rocking chair and has it shipped to you, there has been actual delivery.
b. *Constructive delivery.* Constructive delivery occurs when the donee does not have actual possession of the personal property but transfer was clearly intended. Constructive delivery is a combination of a partial turnover of the property and clear intent. For example, suppose that Alfie wants his niece to

ESTATE OF KENNETH R. TRUCKENMILLER

Court of Appeals, Second District.
158 Cal.Rptr. 699 (1979).

FACTS Kenneth R. Truckenmiller was a 68-year-old widower in poor physical health. He lived in a large home with only his housekeeper, Bernice Synagogue. Bernice thought that Truckenmiller was "a strange duck" but not mentally weak.

Truckenmiller had been a horse-racing fan all of his life. During horse-racing season, he would pick up Mrs. Norma Faye Wells at her home and then they would go to the races. They did this several times a week. Mrs. Wells was twenty-three years younger than Mr. Truckenmiller.

Shortly after their racing companionship began, Truckenmiller transferred 300 shares of his Sears, Roebuck & Company stock to himself and Mrs. Wells as joint tenants with right of survivorship (meaning that when he died, she would get the shares). The value of the shares at the time was $30,000.

About a year later, they sold the shares and purchased a $68,000 apartment building. The title was in both their names as joint tenants.

Truckenmiller told several people (including Bernice) that he had transferred the shares and purchased the building because Mr. Wells had caught him in bed with Norma. He said Wells asked for money not to tell anyone about "the indiscretion."

Truckenmiller died shortly thereafter. His will left everything to Bernice. Bernice claimed that the gift of stock shares was invalid. Therefore she claimed that she should get the apartment building. Wells says that it was a valid gift, and they own the apartment building.

ISSUE Was the gift valid? Was there undue influence?

DECISION The gift was not valid. Mr. and Mrs. Wells used undue influence and even duress to get the shares of stock and the apartment building. They took unfair advantage of Truckenmiller.

LEGAL TIP

Property transfers made under pressure can often be invalidated.

have his antique roll-top desk. The desk is in a rented storage facility. Alfie gives his niece the key to the lock of the storage facility as well as the storage contract. He tells her to pay the rental fees and pick the desk up when she is ready. There has been constructive delivery. The *Ross' Estate v. Ross* case deals with the issue of constructive delivery.

Acceptance. Acceptance is generally not a problem. If there is delivery, there is acceptance. The only time there is not acceptance is if the donee refuses the property or gives it back.

Gifts causa mortis A **gift causa mortis** is given when the donor is near death. The requirements for a gift causa mortis are different than the requirements for an inter vivos gift.

Imminent death. The donor must make the gift when contemplating imminent death. A gift from a soldier going off to war does not qualify, nor does a gift from someone considering suicide. However, a gift from someone hospitalized for terminal cancer *does* qualify.

Delivery. This element is the same as the one for an inter vivos gift. Delivery is usually difficult with gifts causa mortis because the donor is incapacitated and cannot get the property to the donee.

Actual death. For a gift causa mortis to be valid, the donor must die. If the donor makes the gift when death is imminent and then does not die, the gift is

ROSS' ESTATE v. ROSS

Supreme Court of Utah.
626 P.2d 489 (1981).

FACTS David Ross was a director, stock transfer agent, and the secretary and treasurer of Equitable Life and Casualty Insurance Company. Rod Ross (David's son) began working for Equitable in 1972. Ross' other two children (David and Betsy) lived out of state and were not interested in working for the company.

David Ross told a number of people that he wanted to reward Rod for his dedication to Equitable. In 1974, he cancelled 2,440.87 shares that he owned and put 2,210.70 in Rod's name and 230.17 in his name. He put the change in ownership on the company ledgers. He put the stock shares in an envelope with Rod's name on it and placed the envelope in his safe deposit box.

When a 25% share dividend was declared in 1977, he gave the 552.67 shares to Rod. He gave the cash dividends in 1976 and 1977 to Rod.

David Ross died on April 19, 1978. David and Betsy challenged the stock transfer to Rod because there had not been delivery.

ISSUE Was there delivery of the stock shares to Rod?

DECISION Yes. There were four reasons that there was constructive delivery. First, the change of ownership was put on company records. Second, the shares were put in a separate envelope and never touched by David once they were in the safe deposit box. Third, David had indicated his clear intent for Rod to have the shares. Fourth, David gave Rod all the dividends (share and cash) once the transfer had been made.

LEGAL TIP

It is best to do more than constructive delivery. Constructive delivery usually results in litigation. Actual delivery is best.

revoked. If the donor makes the gift but dies of another cause, there is no gift and the property goes into the general estate. In addition, the donor can revoke the gift any time prior to death. The *Clark v. O'Neal* case deals with a causa mortis gift.

Statutory changes. Gifts causa mortis were originally created to allow donors their dying wishes. However, many problems resulted. One problem is that the donor is not around to prove that the gift was made. Very often, the donee is the one proving the gift was made, and the donee is hardly a disinterested party. Because of the problems with fraud and perjury by claimed donees, some states have statutes that have changed the common law requirements for gifts causa mortis. Some of these states require the presence of two witnesses for this type of gift to be valid.

Taxes: Gifts in contemplation of death. The Internal Revenue Service has special tax rules that apply to gifts causa mortis. The purpose for these rules is to prevent people from giving away their estates just before death to avoid estate taxes. The taxes on gifts made in contemplation of death are high and cover any gifts made six months or less before the donor's death.

Gifts to minors Many parents and grandparents want to give money and property to their children and grandchildren. Sometimes those children are not adults and do not have capacity to contract or the wisdom to deal with those gifts. There is a statute passed in most states called the Uniform Gifts to Minors Act. This act has procedures for making gifts to minors. The purpose of the statute is to make sure that the property gets to the donees when they are old enough. Another

CLARK v. O'NEAL

Court of Appeals of Missouri.
555 S.W.2d 68 (1977).

FACTS Harold Hawkins was sixty-five years old and a resident of Avalon, Missouri. He had led a tragic life. His father left when he was born and his mother died when he was three years old. He was raised by his grandmother and uncle. He had a half-brother and half-sister whom he never saw.

His only family was Teri O'Neal who was the niece of Hawkins' deceased wife. She was like a daughter to him, and he always had Christmas dinner at her house.

On June 16, 1973, Hawkins was taken to the hospital in Chillicothe. He had suffered a heart attack, was in the intensive care unit, and was weak and struggling to breathe.

Teri came to visit him at the hospital. He sent her back to his house and told her to get some certificates of deposit and a promissory note worth $66,080.00 She went back and picked up the documents. When she came back to the hospital, she showed him the documents in her purse. He said, "Good—keep it." Shortly thereafter, he died.

Hawkins' half-sister, Leeta Clark, challenged the gift causa mortis and claimed that she was entitled to the documents and funds because she was Hawkins' only blood relative.

ISSUE Was there a valid gift causa mortis?

DECISION Yes. Hawkins was in pain but could still describe to Teri where the documents were in his house. There was delivery. Once he saw the documents in her purse, he told her to keep them. Also, Teri's husband was present as a witness. Hawkins died the same day Teri got the documents, so death was imminent.

LEGAL TIP

A gift causa mortis is not the best way to transfer property although witnesses are helpful. A valid will is a better way to transfer property than a gift causa mortis.

purpose is to make sure that the property is protected and invested properly until the minor can take title.

Transfer of Personal Property by Will

Personal property can be transferred by a will. The will needs to be valid and the property described properly. Title passes when the will is probated properly and the administrator or personal representative distributes the gifts (see Chapter 50 for a complete discussion).

Transfer of Personal Property by Accession

Accession is adding labor to personal property so that the personal property is completely changed. For example, someone could mistakenly take $25 worth of lumber and then make the lumber into barrels worth $700. To whom do the barrels belong? The owner of the timber or the barrelmaker? The answer depends on the amount of change and the value.

If the change completely transforms the goods, the courts lean toward giving the property to the laborer. Also, if the laborer has increased greatly the value of the property, the courts lean toward the laborer. In the barrel example, the property goes to the barrelmaker.

However, the original owner of the property does have an action in tort (conversion) against the laborer. The laborer can get the property but will have to pay the original owner the value of the property as it once existed. In the example, the owner gets $25, and the barrelmaker gets the barrels.

Transfer of Personal Property by Confusion

Confusion is mixing together two or more persons' personal property in such a way that the individuals' property cannot be determined. Confusion happens with fungible goods such as gas, oil, grain, minerals, and lumber. For example, farmers may grow a certain amount of grain on their farms. When they deliver it to the grain elevator/broker, their grains are mingled in one grain elevator. It would be impossible to tell who owns what particular grain.

However, the farmers still have title to personal property. Each is entitled to a pro rata share of the total amount. Each farmer is required simply to prove how much was put in to show how much of the grain is his or hers. If the fungible goods were confused without knowing how much each contributed, they all get an equal share and own the goods as tenants in common.

Transfer of Property by Finding Lost Property

Someone who finds **lost personal property** has the right to possess it. The question of who will have title to the lost property is a more difficult one to answer. The answer depends upon where the property was found, who finds it, and why the property is there.

Where is the property: Public versus private When personal property is found in a public place, the finder is entitled to **possession** of the property and can get title if the owner does not claim them. An example of a public place is a department store aisle.

If the property is lost in a private place, the owner of the place is entitled to possession and can get title if the owner does not return. The reason for this difference is that the owner is likely to remember that the property was lost and where it was lost. For example, if you lost or mislaid your wallet on the night of a party at a friend's home, you probably left it at the friend's home. Your friend and not the party guest who found the wallet would have the right to hold the wallet for you.

Who Found the Property?

If an employee finds property while on duty at the employer's place of business, the employer is entitled to possession. For example, if a maid finds property in a hotel room while she is cleaning, the hotel is entitled to possession and not the maid. The *Morrison v. United States* case deals with the problem of employees finding valuable property while on duty.

MORRISON v. UNITED STATES

United States Court of Appeals.
492 F.2d 1219 (Ct.Cl. 1974).

FACTS Morrison was with the United States Army as a ground soldier during the Viet Nam War. He was serving in the Central Highlands in 1968. While on duty, he discovered nearly $200,000 in a cave near an abandoned village. There was $150,000 in United States currency and 550,000 Vietnamese piasters. He wanted to keep the money for himself. The United States Government demanded that he turn it over as his principal. Morrison filed suit for the money.

ISSUE Who is entitled to the found money?

DECISION The United States Government. An agent has a duty to turn property discovered in the course of employment over to the principal.

LEGAL TIP
Finders are not keepers when they are working for someone else.

Why the property is there Property can be found for three reasons: it was lost; it was mislaid; or it was abandoned. **Lost property** should be possessed by its finder since it is property found in a public place. **Mislaid property** should be possessed by the owner of the place where it is found since it is really intentionally placed somewhere but forgotten. **Abandoned property** is property that is intentionally lost or mislaid or property that the owner no longer wants and purposefully leaves for finders.

Some abandoned property is called treasure trove. Treasure trove is gold, silver, or bullion that is buried in the ground. Treasure trove is treated as lost or abandoned property. Unless there is a statute otherwise, treasure trove belongs to its finder. The *Charrier v. Bell* case involves the issue of who gets the treasure trove.

CHARRIER v. BELL

Court of Appeals of Louisiana, First Circuit.
380 So.2d 155 (1979).

FACTS Charrier, an archeologist, discovered a gravesite of the Tunica Indians. He secretly took artifacts from the graves. He sold the artifacts to a university under a contract that didn't have a final price until after appraisal (which turned out to be $175,000).

The state of Louisiana owned the land on which the gravesite was located. The state claimed ownership of the artifacts. Charrier brought an action to quiet title (declare title) in the artifacts.

ISSUE Who is entitled to the discovered buried artifacts?

DECISION Charrier. The treasures were part of a burial ritual. No one intended to come back and get them; they were abandoned property and the finder is entitled to keep them.

LEGAL TIP

Before transferring found property, find out if others have any interest in it.

When does title pass to lost or mislaid property? A majority of the states have statutes that require finders to report their finds to local authorities. There are criminal penalties for not reporting a find. The personal property is deposited with the local authorities (usually the police).

Once the authorities have the property, there is usually a waiting period. The true owner has a certain amount of time to show up and claim the property. If the owner does not appear during the statutory time period, the party entitled to possession becomes the **title** holder of the property. Once the time period is up, the interest of the original owner and any prior possessor is cut off.

Some states also require that notice be published when the property is first turned over to authority. The notice is published in a newspaper with wide circulation. In some states the statutory time period begins running only after publication of notice.

PROTECTION OF PERSONAL PROPERTY

There are some ways to protect personal property. Particularly, these protections cover intangible items. Intangible items are not like cars and blenders that can always be in the owner's possession. Intangible rights exist, and others may know about them and possibly abuse them without protection. Patents, trademarks, and copyrights are forms of intangible personal property that can be protected.

Patents

A **patent** is a publicly given, exclusive right to an idea, product, or process. A patent gives the patentee the exclusive right to use, make, or sell a product for a period of 17 years. A process can be patented for 3½ to 14 years. The length of the protection will depend upon the amount paid. A patent is a legal monopoly of personal property for a given period of time and cannot be renewed.

If someone else uses the patented property, the patentee has the right to sue for infringement. Damages in infringement suits include the profits made by the infringer and any damages suffered by the patentee.

Whether something can be patented is a complex issue. The idea, product, or process cannot have been in public use or sales for more than one year. Others cannot know of the patented item. Also, a patent is no guarantee of protection. If the patent was not properly given, there is no exclusive right and no protection for infringement because it was an exclusive idea to begin with.

Trademarks

A **trademark** is a distinctive name, word, mark, design, or picture used by a company to identify its product. A trademark cannot be a generic term such as "wonderful" or "excellent," and a tradename is subject to the same restrictions. "Steak sandwich" is not a tradename but "Steak-Um" brand steak sandwiches is a tradename.

Trademarks and tradenames can be registered under the Lanham Act (15 USC 1050 through 1127) for twenty-year periods and can be renewed. Once a trademark or tradename is registered, those who use it without permission will be liable for damages. An injunction can also be issued against those who use a registered right without permission.

Copyrights

Copyrights protect literature, music, dramatic works, films, television shows, and pictures. Copyrights can be issued for ads also. A copyright holder has an exclusive right to use, perform, or reproduce the materials. The most recent amendments to the copyright laws allow "fair use." "Fair use" is a general term that is defined by the courts on a case-by-case basis. Generally "fair use" permits teachers to reproduce a chart or limited text from a book for classroom or research use. Copyrighted work can also be fairly used in news reports.

Use of copyrighted material without permission is infringement. The owner of the copyright can bring suit for an infringement and collect whatever damages can be proved. If the damages cannot be proved, the court can award between $250 and $10,000 as damages. No damages can be collected if the work does not have a mark indicating it is copyrighted, which is the symbol ©.

A copyright runs for fifty years past the death of the last author or contributor. A copyright cannot be renewed.

KEY TERMS

Tangible personal property
Intangible personal property
Fungible personal property
Inter vivos gifts
Delivery
Gift causa mortis

Accession
Confusion
Lost property
Mislaid property
Abandoned property
Title
Patent
Trademark
Copyrights
Possession

CHAPTER PROBLEMS

1. Martha Copeland was an eccentric widow who lived alone. She added three names to her checking and savings accounts at Farmers and Merchants Bank. She made the three parties (including Chandler) joint tenants on the accounts, but did not tell any of them what she had done. The accounts were accounts that were payable on death to the survivors. When she died, there was $7700 in the accounts. Her relatives claim that they should get the money. The three joint tenants claim that they should get it. Who gets the money? *Chandler v. Farmers and Merchants Bank,* 355 So.2d 726 (Ala. 1978).
2. Nathan Chandler took one-half of the funds ($15,000) from a joint account, which he held with his wife Brooxie. He put the funds into a joint account with his brother Gordon named as the joint tenant. He then passed away. Brooxie and Gordon both claim the $15,000. Was there a gift to Gordon? *In the Matter of the Estate of Nathan M. Chandler,* 413 N.E.2d 486 (Ill. 1980).
3. In 1977 George Frank suffered a disabling stroke. He was an immigrant who had been in the garbage collection business all of his life. He could not read or write English. After his stroke, his daughter came to take care of him. Shortly thereafter he signed over $15,000 of bonds to her. When he died, the other children said that the gift was invalid because of undue influence. Is the gift valid? *Strain v. Rossman,* 614 P.2d 102 (Oreg. 1980).
4. What differences are there between a gift causa mortis and an inter vivos gift?
5. In 1966, Carrie B. Hare, eccentric widow, was living alone. She had trouble recalling her age, her birth date, and how long she had lived in Daytona Beach, Florida. She was befriended by Joe and Sereata Cripe. Carrie gave them a rent-free apartment in exchange for managing an apartment building that she owned. The Cripes had Carrie sign documents that changed all titles and accounts to joint tenancies. When Carrie died, the money in the joint accounts alone was $90,000. Carrie's relatives claimed there had been undue influence. What is the result? *Atlantic First National Bank of Daytona Beach v. Cripe,* 389 So.2d 224 (Fla. 1980).
6. Several boys were playing together. One of the boys found an old sock. They began playing catch with it. One of the boys opened up the sock and found $800 in it. Who gets the $800? *Keron v. Cashman,* 33 A. 1055 (N.J. 1896).
7. Bessie McEwen Spence was an elderly widow. She lived in Houston with her nearest relatives in San Antonio. When she was ninety-two years old she gave her stockbroker a full and complete power of attorney and told him to do whatever he needed to do to manage her financial affairs. The broker, Joe Dudley Pace, put all of her assets into joint tenancy accounts with himself as the joint surviving tenant. When Bessie died, the relatives sought to have the transfers set aside. Can they win? *Pace v. McEwen,* 574 S.W. 2d 792 (Tex. 1978).
8. What is the difference between lost and abandoned property?
9. White was engaged to marry Finch. Finch gave her a ring. White later discovered that Finch was still married, and she broke off the engagement but kept the ring. Finch wants the ring back since White broke off the engagement. Who gets the ring? *White v. Finch,* 209 A.2d 199 (1964).
10. Can a photo be copyrighted?

"Park your car at your own risk."

Sign outside a parking lot

Chapter 46

Bailments

CHAPTER PREVIEW

- Bailments—types and definitions
- Requirements for a bailment
- Differences between bailments and sales and leases
- Rights and liabilities of the bailor
- Rights and liabilities of a bailee
- Examples of bailments

Rose and Gary Martin took their 1975 BMW 530 automobile to Bellbrook Volkswagen. They signed a consignment agreement with Bellbrook. Bellbrook would sell the car for the Martins. The Martins would get $5,800, and Bellbrook would keep whatever they got above that figure. Bellbrook sold the car to Nager for $7,155. The Martins were never paid, and want their car back. Nager says he did not know anything about the Martins or the consignment. Who gets the car?

Bailment sounds like a complex legal term. But if you ask your friend to hold your books while you stand in a cafeteria line, you have created a bailment. A bailment is the separation of title and possession of personal property for a limited period of time. A bailment is not a transfer of title but a transfer of possession. This chapter deals with the problems and issues related to bailments. This chapter answers the questions: What are the types of bailments? What are the rights of the parties to a bailment? How is a bailment created? What liabilities do the parties to a bailment have?

DEFINITION OF A BAILMENT

A **bailment** is the delivery of an item of personal property from one party to another with the understanding that the property will be returned to the owner. When your car is parked by a valet, you have created a bailment. When you leave your watch at a jeweler's for repairs, you have created a bailment.

PARTIES TO A BAILMENT

The party who owns the property and delivers it to another for possession is the **bailor.** The party who is given possession of the property is the **bailee.** The personal property is called the bailed property.

ELEMENTS OF A BAILMENT

For a valid bailment to exist, three elements must be established: delivery and acceptance of the bailed property; possession for a limited period of time; and express or implied promise that the bailed property will be returned.

Delivery and Acceptance of the Bailed Property

The question for this element is: Did the bailee intend to take possession of the property? Not only must the property be turned over, the bailee must be willing to take possession. Whether the bailee is willing to take possession is usually the critical issue. Whether the bailee does take possession depends upon the circumstances.

Voluntary acceptance of the property There are some circumstances where it is clear that the bailee wanted and intended to take possession of the property. For example, when restaurants and hotels provide valet parking, they intend to take possession of their guest's cars. They have hired employees to be responsible for the cars. When jewelers accept watches for repairs, they voluntarily take possession of the watches. When a nightclub or restaurant provides a place and an employee to check hats and coats, they have taken possession voluntarily.

Leased space versus bailment. On the other hand, someone who owns a lot and lets people park their own cars is not taking possession of the cars. The car owners are simply leasing a space. If you hang up your own coat in a restaurant, there is no bailment. If the restaurant provides a place and a person to hang up your coat for you, there is a bailment. The *Wall v. Fitz-In Auto Parks, Inc.* case examines whether a bailment or a lease was created.

WALL v. FITZ-INN AUTO PARKS, INC.

Supreme Court of Massachusetts.
330 N.E.2d 853 (1975).

FACTS Fitz-Inn owned and operated a parking lot that was 100 × 200 feet in size. It had a chain link fence along its rear boundary to separate it from a facility of the Massachusetts Bay Transportation Authority. There was one entrance to the lot. An attendant was on duty at the lot in the mornings until 10:30 AM or 11:00 AM. The lot was used by commuters, and the attendant was there to collect their fee each morning.

Wall drove in on April 15 and paid the attendant his $.25 parking fee. He parked his car in the space that the attendant indicated. Wall then locked his car and took his keys with him. When he returned after work to get his car, he discovered it had been stolen.

Wall brought suit to recover the value of his car. He claimed that there was a bailment.

ISSUE Was there a bailment with Wall's car?

DECISION No. Fitz-Inn did not have control of the car. Wall parked the car and kept the keys. Fitz-Inn simply leased a space to Wall each day and did not accept possession of his car.

LEGAL TIP

Check the liability of garage and parking lot owners. Find out if there are attendants on duty or other protections.

Limits on property accepted. The voluntary acceptance of the property applies only to what the bailee knows is being accepted. In the coat example, the bailment is for a coat and not for a $10,000 bracelet in the pocket. In the valet parking example, the bailment is for a car and not for a $5000 computer in the trunk of the car. Many bailees warn of their limited acceptances. Parking stubs and coat checks may state: *"Not responsible for valuables left in car (coat)."* This liability limitation is valid because the bailee is just limiting the terms of the bailment and not the liability.

Transfer of possession for a limited period of time This is the requirement that distinguishes a bailment from a gift or a sale. A bailment does not pass title and is not permanent; rather, a bailment is temporary possession of property. For example, allowing your sister to use your bicycle for two weeks is creating a two-week-long bailment. Giving the bicycle to your sister because you have a new one is a gift and a permanent transfer of title.

A consignment is a form of a bailment. Property is given to another with the purpose of finding a buyer. The difference is that the bailment ends when the property is transferred permanently to another party. The bailee in these cases has the right to transfer title to third parties. Third parties who buy in good faith have complete protection. This complete protection exists even when the bailee does not properly pay the bailor. The *Martin v. Nager* case discusses the issue of consignment.

Return of the bailed property The end of the bailment is the return of the bailed property or the transfer of the property to someone else at the bailor's direction. This element also distinguishes bailments from sales and gifts. A bailment

MARTIN v. NAGER

Superior Court of New Jersey.
469 A.2d 519 (1983).

FACTS Bellbrook Volkswagen offered to sell Rose and Gary Martin's 1975 BMW 530 automobile on a consignment basis. The Martins would get $5,800 for the sale and Bellbrook would get whatever amount over that a sale would bring.

Bellbrook sold the car to George Nager for $7155. Bellbrook never paid the Martins. The Martins brought suit to get their car back from Nager.

ISSUE Could Bellbrook transfer good title when they did not honor the terms of the consignment/bailment?

DECISION Yes. So long as Nager had no idea of any problems and bought the car in good faith, Nager gets title. The Martins will have to collect their money from Bellbrook. The case also covered the UCC section on this issue (Section 2-403[2]; see Chapter 29 for a complete discussion).

LEGAL TIP

In a consignment, require the bailee/consignee to get your permission before transferring title. Require the buyer to make out the check to both the owner and the bailee/consignee.

ends with the return of the property. A sale or a gift ends when the property is transferred because there will be no return.

The bailee is required to return the goods in the same condition in which they were accepted. An obvious exception is when the bailment has been for the purpose of repairing or improving the personal property.

The bailee's obligation to return the goods is a strict one. Failure to return bailed property at the end of a bailment is theft as well as the tort of conversion. The bailee will be liable to the bailor for failure to return the property.

THE RIGHTS AND DUTIES OF THE BAILMENT PARTIES

The Rights and Responsibilities of the Bailor

The bailor has the responsibility of delivering the bailed property to the bailee in a nonhazardous condition. The bailor also has the duty to warn the bailee of any defects in the bailed property. Most cases involving the duties of bailors deal with personal property rentals. For example, renting a lawnmower is a lease of personal property, but it is also a bailment. The lawnmower should not be in a condition that will cause injury or damages when it is used. For example, the blade should not fly out when the motor is started.

If there are special problems or instructions for using the mower, the bailor should tell the bailee. For example, instructions on starting the motor, uses of the mower, and ways to stop the motor would be typical instructions given to a bailee. The bailor should warn the user of all the hazards of starting, stopping, and operating a mower.

The bailor also has the responsibility of keeping the mower in good repair. The motor should work, and no parts should be missing. If the motor cover were missing and a bailee was injured because of it, the bailor would be liable for the injuries. The *Craine v. United States* case examines the bailor's duties and responsibilities to the bailee.

CRAINE v. UNITED STATES

United States Court of Appeals, Eleventh Circuit. 722 F.2d 1523 (1984).

FACTS Robert Moore was serving as a sergeant in the United States Army. He was stationed at Fort Benning. Moore rented a 14-foot aluminum boat from the Fort Benning Morale Support Activities Division.

Before the manager of the division turned the boat over to Moore, he inspected the fuel line. He also gave Moore instructions on how to start the motor, steer the boat, stop the boat, and react if the motor stalled.

Moore took the boat out on a lake along with Anthony (another serviceman) and six children. One of the children was the child of Juanita Craine.

Moore was drinking quite heavily while in the boat. The boat motor stalled, and Moore could not get it started. The boat went over the dam. Moore, Anthony, and all of the children except one drowned in the accident.

An autopsy showed Moore's blood alcohol level to be .29%. An expert offered the following opinion about the effect of that much alcohol: "The coordination would be very poor. The decision-making capabilities would be markedly decreased. They would deteriorate appreciably." Juanita Craine sued the Support Activities Division (United States Government) for the wrongful death of her child. She claimed the Division should have warned Moore not to drink.

ISSUE Is the bailor (Division) liable for the injuries to Craine? Did they have a duty to warn of the problems with drinking?

DECISION No. A bailor's duty is to give warnings and instructions concerning the bailed property. The bailor is not required to give common sense advice. Moore had been warned of the dangers of the boat stalling and that there was a dam. The Division had given adequate warning of the boat dangers.

LEGAL TIP

Give thorough instructions when bailed property is transferred. Have the bailee sign and initial a statement with all the instructions and warnings on it.

The Rights and Responsibilities of the Bailee

The duty to return the bailed property As the above sections indicate, the bailee must return bailed property. The bailee does not have title—only possession. Bailees who do not return bailed property when the bailment ends are civilly liable to the bailor and criminally responsible. The *Stifft's Jewelers v. Oliver* case deals with an issue of returning bailment property.

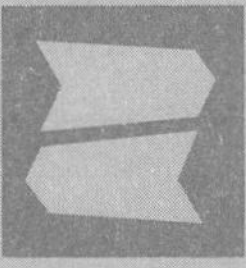

STIFFT'S JEWELERS v. OLIVER

Supreme Court of Arkansas. 678 S.W.2d 372 (1984).

FACTS Charles Oliver delivered a .70 carat diamond ring; a ⅓ carat diamond ring, and a ¼ carat diamond ring to Stifft's jewelers for repair and cleaning. The three rings were valued at a total price of $3800. He also bought a one-carat diamond ring for his wife's anniversary gift while he was delivering the other rings.

Stifft's was to send all four rings to the Olivers' home. When the package arrived, only the new one-carat ring was inside. Stifft's claimed they had sent all and the Olivers sued.

ISSUE Is Stifft's liable for the lost property?

DECISION Yes. There was a mutual benefit bailment. The loss of the rings was during the bailment and Stifft's bears the cost.

LEGAL TIP

It is best to pick up bailed property. Using the mail is risky.

The bailee's duty of care The bailee has to use care in handling and using the bailed property. The amount of care will depend upon the type of bailment. There are three types of bailments: bailments for the sole benefit of the bailor; bailments for the sole benefit of the bailee; and bailments for the benefit of both bailor and bailee, or mutual benefit bailments.

Benefits for the sole benefit of the bailor. This type of bailment is one in which the bailee is doing the bailor a favor. An example would be when you agree to take care of a friend's dog, car, or bicycle while that friend is out of town. You have no benefit; you have the work of watching the property (in one case feeding the dog) and the inconvenience of providing storage space. You have your friend's gratitude but nothing more. This type of bailment is a **gratuitous bailment.**

In a bailment solely for the benefit of the bailor, the bailee is not held to a high duty of care. The bailee has to make sure that nothing is done intentionally to injure the property. The bailee cannot do anything that will obviously result in damaging the property. Leaving keys in a car or locking the dog in a car would obviously be wrong. The bailee is liable for grossly negligent acts. Grossly negligent has sometimes been described as stupid. A bailee is liable in this type of bailment only for damage caused by some obviously wrong act.

Bailments for the sole benefit of the bailee. A benefit for the sole benefit of the bailee is one in which the bailee has all the benefit and the bailor has none. For example, if your friend loans you his or her car for the day, there is a bailment for the sole benefit of the bailee. This is also a gratuitous bailment. Your friend gets nothing other than the reputation of being accommodating and helpful. You, however, have the use of the car.

Because you get something for nothing in this type of gratuitous bailment, the law imposes a high duty of care. The bailee must use utmost care in handling and using the property. Slight negligence allows the bailor to recover damages from the bailee. For example, if you left the car unlocked and it was stolen, you would be liable to the bailor. With a slight negligence standard, if anything goes wrong during the bailment, the bailee will usually be responsible.

Bailments for the benefit of bailor and bailee: Mutual benefit bailments. A **mutual benefit bailment** is one in which both parties receive some benefit either in terms of using the property or receiving payment. For example, when a car is rented from a car rental agency, there is a mutual benefit bailment. The bailee gets the use of the car and the bailor gets rental fees. A watch taken to a jeweler's for repair is a mutual benefit bailment; the bailor gets a fixed watch, and the bailee gets paid for the repairs.

In a mutual benefit bailment, the bailee has an ordinary duty of care. The usual standards for negligence apply; they are not lesser or greater than those in the other two types of bailments. The elements for negligence concerning a reasonable person are applied in mutual benefit bailments. The *Berry Equipment Co. v. Boehck & Gardner Equipment* case involves negligence in a mutual benefit bailment case.

Figure 46-1 is a summary of the duties of care owed in different types of bailments.

Strict liability of bailee. There are times when the bailee will be liable for damage to the bailed property regardless of the type of bailment. Those times are when the bailee uses the property in a way that the bailment prohibits. For example,

BERRY EQUIPMENT CO. v. BOEHCK & GARDNER EQUIPMENT

Court of Appeals of Texas, Fourteenth District.
662 S.W.2d 661 (1983).

FACTS Builders' Supply leased a Caterpillar D-6 Bulldozer from Boehck & Gardner, a broker for Berry. The bulldozer was delivered to Builders' Supply on October 1, 1976. But two weeks after delivery, it was discovered missing and never found. Both Berry and Boehck wanted Builders to pay for the Bulldozer.

ISSUE What type of bailment existed? What duty of care was there? Was the duty of care breached?

DECISION Builders' Supply is liable. They had no fences, night lights, guard dogs, or security people around the construction site. They took no precautions to protect the equipment. There was a mutual benefit bailment and Builders' was required to use ordinary care. They had not exercised ordinary care because they had done nothing.

LEGAL TIP

Leased equipment—regardless of its size—must be guarded carefully against theft.

if a car rental contract prohibits drag-racing with their cars, any violation of that clause resulting in damage to the car would be the bailee's responsibility. If the bailee of leased equipment was told not to run the motor for more than three hours straight but did so and damaged the motor, the bailee would be liable.

Burden of proving liability. It is sometimes difficult for the bailor to know exactly what happened. All they know is that they temporarily turned over their property, and now the property is either damaged or nonexistent. The courts help bailors by allowing them to show that a bailment existed and that the property was delivered to and accepted by the bailee. It then becomes the bailee's responsibility to show that they exercised the proper duty of care. They try to show that the damage or loss occurred despite their care and precautions.

Liability limitations. Some bailees try to limit their liability for their negligence in handling the bailor's property. As Chapter 20 discusses, parties to a contract (a bailment is an express or implied contractual arrangement) cannot hold themselves harmless from their own negligence. However, bailees can limit their liability with

Figure 46-1 **Duty of Care for Bailees' Bailments**

TYPE OF BAILMENT	DEGREE OF NEGLIGENCE	STANDARD OF CARE
Benefit of bailor	Gross	Very slight
Benefit of bailee	Slight	Very high
Mutual benefit	Standard	Ordinary

respect to the bailed property. However, the limitation must be reasonable in light of the value of the goods. For example, airlines have a bailment with your luggage and limit the liability to $1000 per suitcase.

The bailee's right of compensation A bailee who performs services or work on the bailed property is entitled to compensation. This right of compensation exists whether or not there is an express contract. The amount of compensation will be whatever the parties' agreement provides. If there is no compensation figure, the courts will award reasonable compensation.

The bailee is entitled to be paid when the bailor returns for the goods. If the bailor refuses to pay for the work or services, most states give the bailee a lien in the goods for the payment. That lien entitles the bailee to keep the bailed property as security for payment. If there is no payment, the bailee can sell the goods to satisfy the lien. Liens and enforcement of liens are covered in Chapter 56.

APPLICATION OF BAILMENT LAW: SOME EXAMPLES

Bailment may seem to be a foreign term but is part of daily business and personal life. This section covers some specific bailments and the peculiar problems associated with each one.

Trucks, Planes, Boats, and Trains: Common Carrier Bailments

When goods are delivered to a third party to be transported to another party, a bailment is created. The transporter or **common carrier** has possession of the goods for a temporary period and is required to end the bailment by properly delivering the goods. The arrangement is a mutual benefit bailment; the bailor gets the goods moved and the bailee gets paid for doing it. Carriers have the duty to transport the goods in a reasonable manner and get them to the right party. During transit, carriers are liable for lost, damaged, or destroyed goods.

Warehousing

When goods are stored in a warehouse, there is a bailment. The owner of the goods gives the warehouse temporary possession of the goods for storage purposes. The terms of the warehouse agreement will control when the bailment ends. For example, the warehouse may be instructed to turn the goods over to a buyer when the buyer appears with the proper documents. The proper documents usually include a bill of lading. A bill of lading is a document of title. A document of title allows whoever has it to take title to goods regardless of who has the goods in their possession.

Hotels as Bailees: Innkeepers

Common law held **innkeepers** strictly liable for the property of their guests. The common law standard was that if a guest's property disappeared while the guest was at the inn, the inn paid for the property. The common law rule applied to those who were in the business of providing lodging for others.

The old common law rule has been changed in most states today. The changes have been through statutes or case decisions. Most of the statutes and decisions allow the innkeepers to avoid strict liability by taking certain precautions. For example, in many states an innkeeper will not be strictly liable if a safe is provided for valuables and the guests are informed of the safe. The guests may be informed by clerks at registration or by printed notices posted on the back of hotel room doors about these policies. Laws usually allow hotels to limit their liability when property is not placed in the safe. The limitations are usually small figures. These limitations do not apply if the hotel is grossly negligent in the protection of its guests.

KEY TERMS

Bailment
Bailor
Bailee
Gratuitous bailment
Mutual benefit bailment
Common carriers
Innkeepers

CHAPTER PROBLEMS

1. Regent International operated a luxury hotel in New York. They provided a safe-deposit box system for guests' valuables. Their safe-keeping facility consisted of rows of safe deposit boxes that were opened by two keys. The guest was given one key. The boxes were located in a room made of plasterboard. There were two access doors to the room. Both doors were hollow-core wood. One door had a tumbler lock, and the second had no lock at all.

   Regent also had a signature card system for access to the boxes. The signature file was behind the front desk but was visible to the public. The cards showed the signatures and what was in each box. Thieves broke into the boxes and stole most of the guests' valuables. Is the hotel liable? *Concalves v. Regent International Hotels,* Slip. Op. #16 (N.Y. Ct.App. February 17, 1984).
2. Charlotte Voorhis asked a railroad usher (Pereira) to watch her suitcase. While Voorhis was gone, Pereira was called away. When he returned, her suitcase was gone. Voorhis brought suit to recover the value of the suitcase contents. Can she win? *Voorhis v. Consolidated Rail Corporation,* 470 N.Y.S.2d 365 (1983).
3. O'Malley purchased gold krugerrands and put them on deposit with the Putnam Safe Deposit Vaults through its agent, Caten. Caten started using O'Malley's coins to cover deliveries to other customers, who were demanding the return of their coins. He originally put back O'Malley's coins each time he borrowed them, but when the company began having financial troubles, he permanently used most of O'Malley's coins. O'Malley sued for conversion. Can he win? *O'Malley v. Putnam Safe Deposit Vaults,* 458 N.E.2d 752 (Mass. 1983).
4. Loewenstine was on a Delta Airlines flight from Miami to Cincinnati. He was required to give his large camera case to a stewardess for storage during the flight since he could not fit the case under the seat in front of him. The camera equipment and case disappeared during the flight. Delta has a liability limitation for in-flight damage to property of $640. Loewenstine's camera was worth $9000. Can he recover the $9000? *Loewenstine v. Delta Airlines, Inc.,* 455 N.E.2d 3 (Fla. 1983).
5. Indian Head Grain Company was storing sunflower seeds for Big John Company. Grain warehouses are required to periodically check and inspect seeds for biological activity that can cause spontaneous combustion in the seeds. Indian Head did not do regular checks. The seeds were destroyed by a fire. Is Indian Head liable? Is there a bailment? What type? *Big John B. V. v. Indian Head Grain Co.,* 718 F.2d 143 (5th Cir. 1983).
6. Desmond is a mechanic at a garage. He owned his own tools and left them at the garage each night for convenience. They were stolen. The garage was 20 feet above ground level. There was a broken window with plyboard covering it in the garage. Is there a bailment? Is his employer liable? *Desmond v. Wall,* 466 A.2d 803 (Conn. 1983).
7. What are the differences between a gratuitous bailment and a mutual benefit bailment?

8. Dansereau's car was taken from a Classified Parking System's lot after a valet had parked it there. Who will be liable? Who will have to prove negligence? *Classified Parking Systems v. Dansereau,* 535 S.W.2d 14 (Tex. 1976).

9. The Parking Authority of the City of Newark operated several Park'N Lock parking lots. Drivers parked their own cars in the unattended lots. They were instructed to lock their cars and then deposit money in a machine to pay for the space. McGlynn used one of the lots. While his car was parked there, his car tape deck and cassettes were taken. Who is liable? *McGlynn v. Parking Authority of City of Newark,* 432 A.2d 99 (N.J. 1981).

10. What are the differences between bailments and sales? What are the differences between bailments and gifts?

"Cujus Est Solum Ejus est Usque ad Coelum et ed Infernos." (The owner of the soil owns also to the sky and to the depths.)
Blackstone
The Common Law

Chapter 47

Real Property Interests and Regulation

CHAPTER PREVIEW

- Surface, subsurface, air, and water rights
- Fixtures
- Types of real property interests
- Types of easements
- Joint ownership of land
- Covenants
- Nuisances
- Purpose and types of zoning.

Alex lives on property adjacent to a plant that manufactures fertilizer from dead animals and poultry offal. The smells from the plant are so offensive that Alex suffers from nausea day and night. Alex, along with other neighbors, has brought suit seeking to stop the operation of the plant. Will Alex succeed in stopping the operation of the plant?

When people say they own real property, they call what they own "a piece of property," "a lot," or "a piece of land." However, owning real property involves more than owning just the land. Owning realty actually means owning to the middle of the earth and to the heavens. This chapter will answer the following questions: How are land interests created? What is included with a land interest? How are land interests regulated?

THE NATURE OF REAL PROPERTY

The description of real property as a "piece of land" is accurate. Real property ownership includes ownership of the surface or ground. However, real property also includes rights to the air, subsurface, water, and certain attachment rights.

Air Rights

Real property owners own the air space above their property. High rise buildings are examples of property owners using air space to maximize property use. Although landowners' interests extend to the "heavens," their interests are subject to the "right of flight." The right of flight is the right of aircraft (public and private) to use the air space above property for passage without being required to pay and without being liable for trespassing in landowners' air space. These rights are referred to as **air rights.**

Subsurface Rights

Real property owners also own whatever is located below their land. If there are minerals such as oil or gas underground, the surface owner has the right to claim them. **Subsurface rights** can be separated from **surface rights** and sold to others. A landowner can own the surface but sell subsurface rights to someone else. For example, many landowners lease their subsurfaces to companies to extract oil and are given a share of the profits by the companies.

Water Rights

All states have some system of allocating water among landowners. **Water rights** transfer with the land. Real property owners who own property along a stream are called **riparians.** All of these owners have equal rights of use in and access to the stream water. However, they must not reduce the water quality or quantity for other riparians. In those states where water is scarce, water rights are given on a first-come-first-serve or prior appropriation basis. These states give the first landowner to use water in a beneficial way the rights to that water.

Rights in Attachments

Plants, trees, and vegetation Plants, trees, and vegetation that grow naturally on the land are part of real property. These items (called fructus naturales) transfer with title to the property. Plants, trees, and vegetation planted by the landowner are also part of the real property and transfer with title. However, any crops that may come from the vegetation belong to the party responsible for their planting and growth. For example, tenants' leases may end before the time a crop is harvested. Tenants still have the right to remove the crops even after the sale occurs or the lease terminates.

Buildings Homes, offices, and other buildings on land become a part of the real property. Title to the land transfers title to what is on the land.

Personal property attachments: Fixtures **Fixtures** are items that were once personal property but became permanently attached to the real property or buildings located on the property. Once an item becomes a fixture, it is part of the real property.

To decide if an item is a fixture or personal property, four basic questions must be answered (see below). Since the answers to these questions can vary, the determination of whether an item is a fixture can also vary.

1. How firmly is the item attached? The more permanent the attachment, the more likely an item will be considered a fixture. For example, sinks, bathtubs, and kitchen cupboards are personal property items that are permanently attached.
2. What is the relationship of the item to the real property? Some items are uniquely made for the real property and would be useless elsewhere. For example, storm windows are made to fit windows on a particular house and cannot be transferred to other windows. A pipe organ in a church that is part of the decor is an integral part of the real property.
3. Who attached the item to the property? If the owner of the real property attached the item, it is more likely to be considered a fixture. However, if a tenant attaches the item to the property, it is more likely to be considered personal property. The tenant probably does not want the landlord to have his or her property or increase the rental property's value.
4. What are the parties' intentions? The answer to this question decides the matter. Parties can agree to treat certain items as fixtures in their contract. For example, a buyer and seller could include a refrigerator in the sale of a house.

There are some exceptions to these general rules. One exception involves "trade fixtures." **Trade fixtures** are personal property items used in the operation of a business and attached by a commercial tenant. When trade fixtures are attached by a tenant, they remain the personal property of the tenant and do not become true fixtures. For example, even though installing counters in a store seems to create fixtures that are part of the realty, they are actually trade fixtures. In the *Michigan National Bank v. City of Lansing* case, the court decides whether several items used by a business are trade fixtures or real property.

Figure 47-1 summarizes the tests used for determining whether an item is a fixture.

TYPES OF REAL PROPERTY INTERESTS

Property rights in the same piece of land can vary. A tenant can live on leased land but cannot sell it. The landlord who owns the property cannot live on the land during the lease but can sell it. This section of the chapter discusses and defines various types of real property interests.

Fee Simple

The **fee simple** land interest is the type of land interest most property owners have. A fee simple interest gives the property owner full title to the property—

MICHIGAN NATIONAL BANK v. CITY OF LANSING

Court of Appeals of Michigan.
293 N.W.2d 626 (1980).

FACTS The Michigan Tax Tribunal (Tribunal) held that Michigan National Bank's night depository equipment, drive-up window equipment, vault doors, and remote transaction units were part of the Bank's land and buildings. Since these items were fixtures, the Tribunal included them in the valuation of the Bank's real property for tax-assessment purposes. The Bank brought suit challenging the assessment on the grounds that the banking equipment was personal property because all parts were trade fixtures. Therefore, these items were not subject to assessment for real property taxes.

ISSUE Were the bank's various banking machines trade fixtures and personal property or were they real property and subject to taxation?

DECISION All of the items were fixtures and part of the real property. The court noted that all of the items were cemented into place and that the remote transaction units (drive-up windows) were integrated with the bank buildings by pillars and canopies.

The court found the items could not be used outside of the bank buildings. Finally, the court held that the doctrine of trade fixtures applies to a landlord/tenant relationship but not when the owner of real property attaches the trade fixtures.

LEGAL TIP

Property owners should check tax assessment figures to determine what property was included in valuing the real property.

the highest degree of land ownership. While a fee simple holder is alive, he or she can transfer full rights in the property. After the holder's death, these rights can be transferred by a will. A fee simple interest holder can also pledge or mortgage the property. Language creating a fee simple estate can be "To A" or "To A and his (or her) heirs."

Life Estate

A **life estate** is an interest that lets the holders (called life tenants) use the property only as long as they live. When life tenants die, their interests end. A life estate cannot be transferred by will. Language creating a life estate is "To A for life." Estate planners use life estates. For example, many spouses use the life estate as

Figure 47-1 **Fixture versus Personal Property**

TEST	EXAMPLES
1. How firmly is the item attached?	Sinks, bathtubs, and cupboards
2. What is the relationship of the item to the property?	Storm windows and pipe organs
3. Who attached the item to the property?	Shelves by tenant
4. What is the intent of the parties involved?	Washer/dryer in sales contract
5. Is the item a trade fixture?	Counters in store

a way to control the use of their property for their spouse or children. Language such as "To my husband, Jake, for his life, and then to my children," creates a life estate in Jake and a future interest (called a remainder) in the children. Jake may sell his life estate but the sale is good only for his life. The children will get the property upon Jake's death.

Leasehold Interests

Tenants hold **leasehold interests** in real property. A leasehold interest is the right to use the real property of another for a certain period of time. A leasehold is simply a right of use and does not give the tenant any permanent rights in the leased property. A lease may run for a specified period of time or be open-ended and run on a month-to-month basis. Chapter 49 discusses leases in detail.

Easements

Easements are nonpossessory land interests. They give rights in other's real property. An easement is a right to use another's property for some purpose. For example, an owner of a landlocked piece of property will need access and will have to pass over surrounding properties for access. Figure 47-2 illustrates the landlocked circumstances of property owner A. A can get access if B, C, or both give A an easement across their lands. The small roads in red in Figure 47-2 are possible easements that B or C could give. Details on these easements can be found in the following subsections.

Parties in the easement There are always two parties in an easement interest. The party who owns the easement is called the **dominant tenement.** The party with the easement running through his or her land is the **servient tenement.** In Figure 47-2, A holds the dominant tenement interest while B and C hold servient tenements.

Types of easements In Figure 47-2, A's easement is a right-of-way that permits A to cross over property. This type of easement, which benefits a particular piece of land, is called an **easement appurtenant.**

Easements in gross benefit particular people or businesses. For example, utilities have easements in nearly all residential properties so that their service lines can be taken to all homes.

When an easement grants a right of use, it is called an **affirmative easement.** Examples are utility easements and A's easement in Figure 47-2. **Negative easements** stop the servient owner from doing something on the servient land. For example, solar easements prevent the servient landowner from planting trees that would interfere with the dominant tenement's collection of solar rays for the solar panels.

Creation of easements There are several ways to create easements: by expression, by implication and by prescription. When two parties agree that one party shall have an easement in the other's land, there is an express agreement. The formalities for an **express easement** are similar to those for the transfer of land (see Chapter 48).

Often parties do not agree or forget that an easement will be necessary. For example, with reference to Figure 47-2, suppose that B owned A's tract of land and then sold the parcel to A, but no grant of an easement across B's land was made. If A and B cannot agree on an easement, A still needs access. In circumstances

Figure 47-2 **Illustration of an Easement Interest**

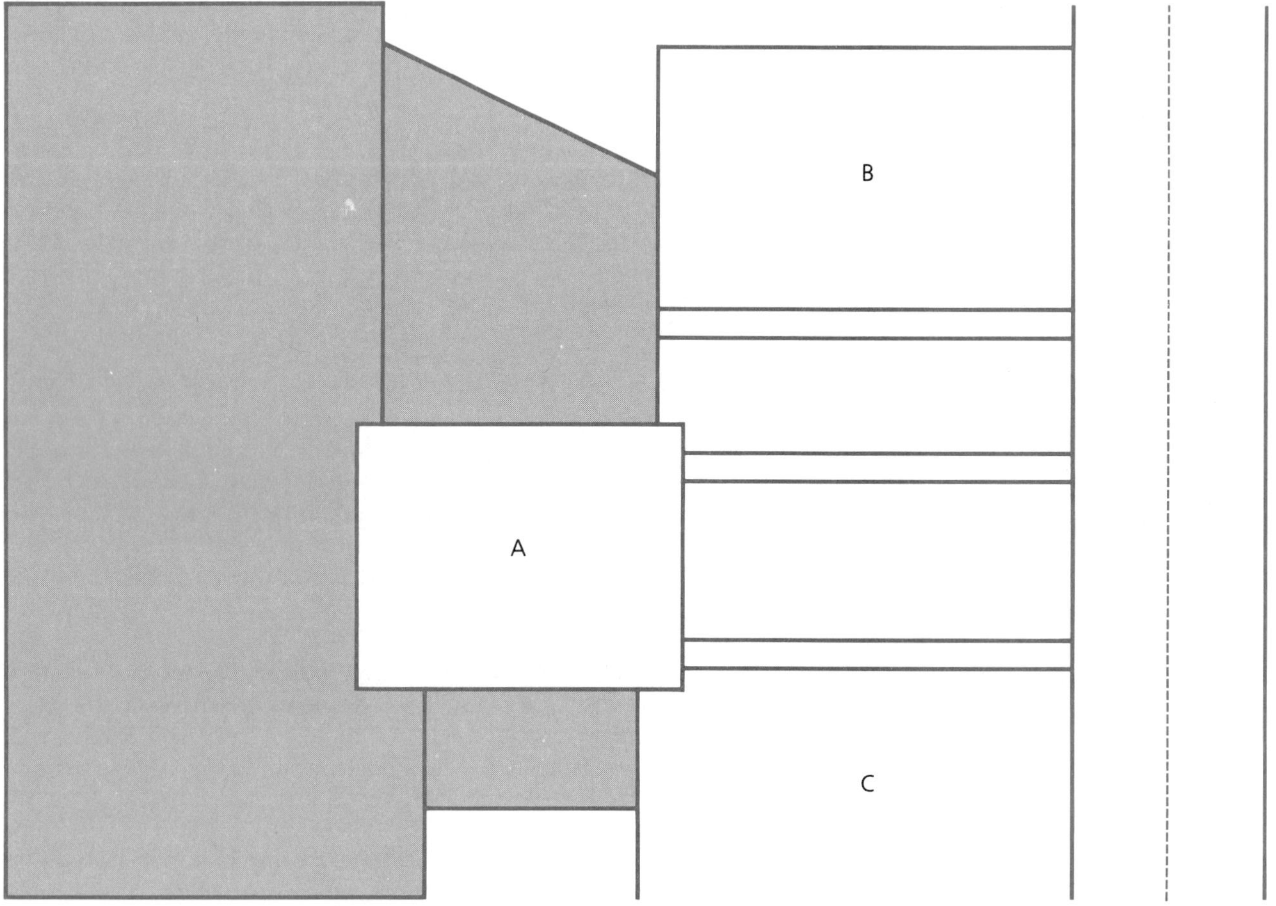

such as these, courts will imply that an easement was meant to be created by the parties.

The *Hunt v. Zimmerman* case decides whether an **easement by implication** exists.

The third way to create an easement is by prescription. An **easement by prescription** results when one party uses another's property for a right of way over a continuous period of time. An easement by prescription is similar to **adverse possession** of property (see Chapter 48).

Transfer and termination of easements Easements are transferrable. Easements appurtenant transfer with the transfer of the dominant tenement. Servient tenements are transferred subject to the easement rights of the dominant tenement. Easements in gross are generally transferrable if they are commercial in nature and if a state statute permits their transfer.

Easements end in various ways. They may end expressly as when the dominant owner transfers the easement to the servient tenement owner. An easement by implication ends if the necessity giving rise to the easement ends. For example, if a public road were built across the top of A's land, an easement by implication through the land of B and C would no longer be necessary and would end.

HUNT v. ZIMMERMAN
Court of Appeals of Indiana.
216 N.E.2d 854 (1966).

FACTS The Hunts and Zimmermans owned adjacent pieces of property. The Zimmermans had access to their property from a public street but had to go through the Hunts' backyard to gain access to their garage. The Hunts objected to the use of their backyard since the prior owners of the Zimmerman property never used the garage. The Zimmermans brought suit when the Hunts blocked access to the garage. The Zimmermans wanted the court to find that they had an easement by implication through the Hunts' property.

ISSUE Did the Zimmermans have an easement by implication in the Hunts' property?

DECISION No. The court stated that there must be some necessity for an easement by implication to exist. The Zimmermans already had access to their land. The court stated that non-use of a particular building on a piece of land is not sufficient necessity to give rise to an easement by implication.

LEGAL TIP
When buying property, check to make sure that driveways and access routes are part of the property or easements benefiting the property.

Profits

Profits are rights to enter the property of others to remove something from that property. A profit can be granted in subsurface minerals, surface topsoil, water, plants, or crops.

License

A **license** is the right to use the property of another. A license differs from an easement in that it is not a real property interest and can be revoked at any time. A license can be oral. For example, when patrons to a movie theater or an amusement park buy admission tickets, they are buying a license that will last for the length of the movie or the operating hours of the park. In the *Bunn v. Offut* case, the important difference between obtaining a license and obtaining an easement is discussed.

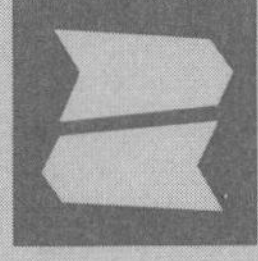

BUNN v. OFFUT
Supreme Court of Virginia.
222 S.E.2d 522 (1976).

FACTS Temco sold a home and lot to Harvey and Rosabelle Wynn. In the purchase contract Temco wrote, "Use of apartment swimming pool to be available to purchaser and his family." Temco owned the nearby apartment complex with the pool. Temco orally promised the Wynns that the purchasers of their home would also be entitled to the use of the swimming pool. In 1969, the Wynns sold their home to the Bunns, and the Bunns were told they could use the apartment pool. However, Temco (through its agent Offut) refused to allow the Bunns to use the pool. The Bunns sued seeking to enforce their swimming easement. The trial court found for Offut and the Bunns appealed.

ISSUE Were the Wynns given a license for pool use or an easement that was transferable to the Bunns?

DECISION The Court held that the Wynns had been given only a license and that a license is personal between the licensor and the licensee, and cannot be assigned or transferred. The language used was limited to the Wynns and was a personal, limited license.

LEGAL TIP
Oral promises should be put in writing. Easements that are not in writing are only licenses.

METHODS FOR HOLDING TITLE TO REAL PROPERTY

Many landowners do not own property individually. Instead, they hold title with one or more other persons. There are several different ways to hold title to real property. This section discusses those methods of co-ownership.

Tenancy in Common

A **tenancy in common** exists when two or more persons hold title to a real property interest. Tenants in common can hold equal or unequal shares. For example, A and B could each own a one-half interest in a parcel of property or A could own one-third and B two-thirds interest. Tenants in common can transfer, pledge, and devise by will their part of the real property.

Joint Tenancy

A **joint tenancy** occurs when two or more own realty, and there is a right of survivorship. To form a joint tenancy, the parties must take equal interests in the property at the same time. In addition, most states require that the deed making A and B joint tenants specify that they are joint tenants. Some states even have specific language that must be used for a joint tenancy to exist.

The survivorship characteristic means the parties cannot transfer their interest by will. Upon the death of one joint tenant, the remaining joint tenant or tenants take the dead tenant's share. Title to the entire property belongs to the last surviving joint tenant.

Joint tenants can convey their interest while alive, but their transferees become tenants in common with the remaining joint tenants. For example, if A, B, and C are joint tenants and A conveys his interest to D, then B and C are joint tenants for two-thirds of the property and D is a tenant in common for one-third of the property.

Tenancy by the Entirety

A **tenancy by the entirety** is a joint tenancy between husband and wife. The same right of survivorship exists in this form of ownership. The surviving spouse has full title to the property. In those states recognizing tenancies by the entirety, there are strict requirements for specifying this method of ownership.

Tenancy in Partnership

When partners own real property, they hold title in the form of a **tenancy in partnership.** The tenancy in partnership has the right of survivorship—when one partner dies or leaves the firm, title to the property goes to the remaining partners (see Chapter 41).

Community Property

In the states of Louisiana, Texas, New Mexico, Arizona, Nevada, California, Idaho, and Washington, a form of marital ownership of property, called **community property,** exists. Community property theory applies only to married couples. The couple shares equally in all property acquired during the time of the marriage. Whether title to real property acquired during marriage is held by one or both of the parties, the spouses have a one-half interest in the property. Neither spouse can pledge or transfer real property, while married, without the signature or consent of the other spouse.

Real Estate Syndications

Real estate investments have become increasingly popular because of the syndication method of owning real estate. **Real estate syndications** are group ownerships of properties. For example, a limited partnership may be formed and real estate investors are sold limited partner interests as a method of acquiring an interest in the partnership's property. Corporations and trusts are also forms of syndications that give investors shares or trust certificates as evidence of their real property ownership. These methods of ownership and issues of transferability are governed by partnership, corporation, and trust law.

Condominiums

Condominiums are multi-unit housing projects where individuals own the space between the walls of each unit. In the case of high-rise condominiums, owners actually purchase a portion of the air rights of the building owner. In addition, condominium owners have an equal interest in all of the common areas (stairs, elevators, pools, etc.) of the building. Although condominium owners have the right to transfer and pledge property, they have additional restrictions on their land ownership. For example, they may be required to pay dues for general maintenance of the building and may be subject to rules and regulations for building operations.

REAL PROPERTY REGULATION

The use of real property has been regulated since the fifteenth century. Private regulation of land use has been accomplished through covenants and nuisance actions. Public regulation of land use exists in zoning laws and ordinances. This section discusses public and private land-use control.

Covenants

Covenants are private restrictions on land use. The most typical types of covenants are those in residential subdivisions. In these subdivisions, the developer will draft and record a set of covenants and restrictions. These covenants may specify use restrictions, architectural restrictions, or both. For example, the covenants may prohibit keeping farm animals such as pigs and chickens in the subdivision. They may also prohibit large antennas or radio towers. The covenants are recorded and noted in each deed transferring title to buyers of homes in the area. Buyers of homes are required to comply with the restrictions. Neighbors can sue a property owner who does not comply with the covenants.

Nuisance

A **nuisance** is an activity that interferes with others' use and enjoyment of their property. Examples of nuisances are cattle-feed lots and their accompanying smells, the operation of noisy machinery during sleeping hours, and the maintenance of a mosquito-infested pool of water. Landowners suffering from nuisance may sue for damages or injunctive relief to stop or limit activity. In determining whether to stop a nuisance, the courts must weigh the benefit of the activity against the harm it causes. For example, a steel mill may produce a great deal of smoke, dust, and noise, but it may also be the economic base of a community. The relief for the nuisances caused by the mill may not be a shut-down. The *Ozark Poultry Products, Inc., v. Garman* case deals with a nuisance remedy.

Zoning

Zoning purposes and plans **Zoning** is the governmental regulation of land use. Zoning is constitutional if it provides for the public health, safety, welfare, and morals of the community. Local governmental agencies create zoning laws after a **master plan** has been developed for the community. Based on the plan, the agency designates certain areas of the city or town for different uses. Some

OZARK POULTRY PRODUCTS, INC. v. GARMAN

Supreme Court of Arkansas.
472 S.W.2d 714 (1971).

FACTS Ozark operated a fertilizer plant using dead animals and poultry offal for the manufacture of the fertilizer. The smell from the plant was so bad that homeowners near the plant experienced nausea day and night. In addition, the water near the plant was polluted by the dead animals and the offal. The neighbors to the plant brought suit for an injunction ordering the closure of the plant.

ISSUE Did the operation of the plant constitute a nuisance?

DECISION Yes. The smells and odors were so bad that the plant prevented people from living in the area. The water supply was being destroyed by the plant's presence.

LEGAL TIP
If manufacturing smells and pollutants are not controlled, the plant can be shut down by a court finding that a nuisance exists.

areas will be residential, others commercial and still others industrial. The areas' classifications (and levels within each category) will control the types of activities permitted there. For example, residential level one, or R1, may be limited to single family dwellings; level two or R2, may be limited to multiple family dwellings; and level three, or R3, may be limited to apartment buildings.

Types of zoning Zoning regulations or ordinances can control the following areas in a community.

1. Land use zoning laws control land use. The residential and commercial divisions for use are examples.
2. Building height and placement.
3. Population density. Zoning laws can restrict the number of persons who can reside in a given area. Such regulations can apply to multi-unit housing or to single-family subdivisions.
4. **Aesthetic control.** This type of zoning controls can regulate public advertising (such as billboards). It can also require uniform building styles. Historical buildings can be maintained by aesthetic zoning.

Variances or special permits **Variances** or **special permits** are exceptions in zoning areas. A hearing and approval is required for a variance.

Nonconforming uses Once a zoning scheme is passed, existing uses not conforming to the area's newly zoned restrictions must be allowed to remain. They are called **non-conforming uses.** For example, an industrial plant in an area now zoned commercial will be permitted to remain.

KEY TERMS

Air rights
Subsurface rights
Surface rights
Water rights
Riparians
Fixtures

Trade fixtures
Fee simple
Life estate
Leasehold interests
Easements
Dominant tenement
Servient tenement
Easement appurtenant
Easements in gross
Affirmative easement
Negative easement
Express easement
Easement by implication
Easement by prescription
Adverse possession
Profits
License
Tenancy in common
Joint tenancy
Tenancy by the entirety
Tenancy in partnership
Community property
Real estate syndications
Condominiums
Covenants
Nuisance
Zoning
Master plan
Aesthetic control
Variances
Special permits
Nonconforming uses

CHAPTER PROBLEMS

1. The Wrights have just purchased lots three, four, five, and six in a subdivision, and the lots are situated next to each other. The lots are pictured in the diagram on page 564. Mrs. Westbrook owns lots seven, eight, nine, and ten and her lots (as pictured) are located next to Gregg Street. The Wrights do not have access to a road from their lots and, in addition, need to hook into the main sewer line, which is located on lot eight. Can the Wrights get an easement? *Westbrook v. Wright,* 477 S.W.2d 663 (Tex. 1972).
2. Carey operated a steak house in a woodframe building, which he rented from Consiglio. When the lease ended, Carey took the following items with him:
   a. A walk-in freezer (purchased by Carey) that could be removed by using an Allen wrench and leaving just the concrete slab.
   b. Two window air conditioners that Carey had purchased and installed.
   c. A dishwasher Carey had purchased from the previous tenant.
   d. A bar that was bolted to the floor, which Carey had installed.

   Consiglio claimed the items were fixtures and should remain. Carey maintains they are trade fixtures. Who is correct? *Consiglio v. Carey,* 421 N.E.2d 1256 (Mass. 1981).
3. Pearl Horton leased a parcel of land from the Willards. The lease provided that all permanent fixtures attached to the property would belong to the Willards. Horton bought a mobile home and put it on cinder blocks on the leased parcel. She also attached a canopy to thc mobile home and laid a concrete slab underneath. Horton passed away and left the mobile home to her niece. The Willards claim the mobile home belongs to them because it was permanently attached. Who gets the mobile home? *In re Estate of Horton,* 606 S.W.2d 792 (Mo. 1980).
4. Hansen's home was located next to a softball field owned by the school district. Hansen was required to be at work at 5 AM each day. During the summer months when league games were held at the field, the noise and lights from the games, which frequently went past 10 PM, disturbed Hansen's sleep. Hansen brought a nuisance suit to stop games on the field. Should Hansen win? *Hansen v. Independent School District No. 1,* 98 P.2d 959 (Idaho 1940).
5. Charles Melms built a large home for himself and his family in 1894 at a cost of $20,000. Upon his death, he left his house to his wife for as long as she lived and then to his children. What type of interests have been created? *Melms v. Pabst Brewing Co.,* 79 N.W. 738 (Wis. 1899).
6. Spur Industries operated a cattle-feed lot near the retirement community of Sun City, Arizona. Spur had 20,000 to 30,000 cattle that produced over a million pounds of manure per day. The manure created an obnoxious odor in the area and attracted flies. The residents of Sun City have brought suit to have the

Diagram for Problem 1

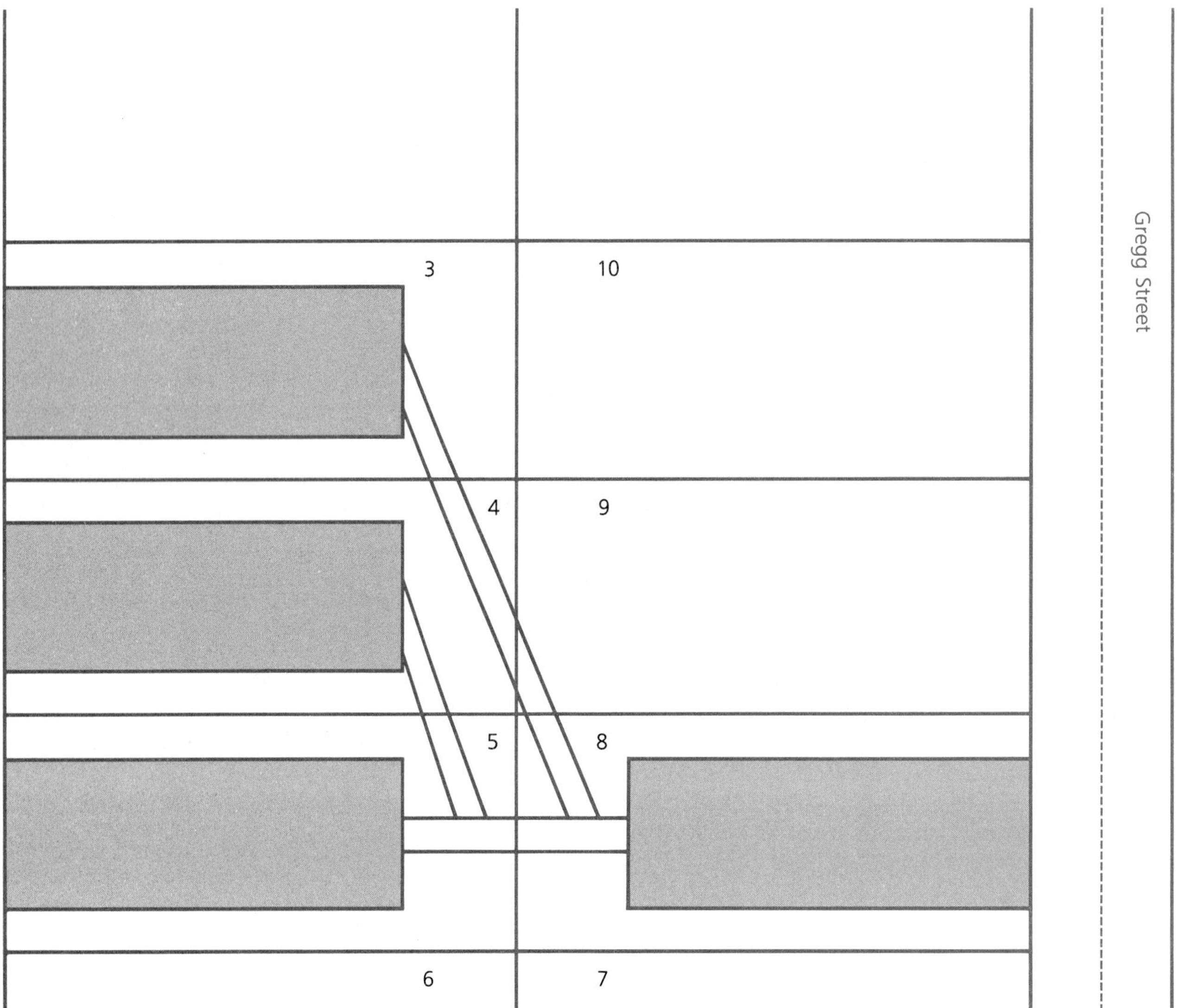

operation stopped. What is the result? *Spur Industries, Inc. v. Del E. Webb Development Co.,* 494 P.2d 700 (Ariz. 1972).

7. Crawford leased some undeveloped land to Gulf Cities Gas Corporation. Gulf Cities erected a masonry building on a concrete slab on the property. When the lease ended, Gulf Cities wished to remove the building as a trade fixture. There was a provision in the lease allowing the landlord to buy permanent fixtures at the end of the lease. Is the building a fixture or a trade fixture? *Crawford v. Gulf Cities Gas Corporation,* 387 So.2d 993 (Fla. 1980).

*8. The Borschowas owned land adjacent to the Haskells. The Borschowas put up a fence on their property and the result was that the Haskells no longer had access to the back of the restaurant located on their property. The Haskells brought suit asking the court to declare an easement for them and have the fence removed. What is the result? *Haskell v. Borschowa,* 532 P.2d 14 (Oreg. 1975).

*9. Baseball Publishing Company entered into an agreement with Bruton to pay him $25 per year for the "exclusive right and privilege to maintain advertising signs" on Bruton's building located at 3003 Washington Street in Boston. Bruton never signed the agreement. After an advertising sign had been on Bruton's building for two months, Bruton took the sign down and told Baseball they could not put up any more signs. Baseball claims it had an easement and Bruton claims he was revoking a license. What is the result? ***Baseball Publishing Co. v. Bruton,*** 18 N.E.2d 362 (Mass. 1938).

*10. The Stoyanoffs applied for a building permit to construct a home in Ladue, Missouri. Their home was to be of ultra-modern design, and they wished to build it in a neighborhood consisting of two-story homes of French, Colonial, or English design. The city of Ladue had an ordinance requiring houses to conform to neighborhood standards. The Stoyanoffs were denied their permit and filed suit objecting to the zoning as invalid. What is the result? ***State of Missouri ex rel. Stoyanoff v. Berkeley,*** 458 S.W.2d 305 (Mo. 1979).

"With this clod of earth, I hereby convey Blackacre."
Typical feudal land transfer language

Chapter 48

Real Property Transfers

CHAPTER PREVIEW

- Steps in selling real property
- Real estate contract basics
- Marketable title
- Interstate Land Sales Full Disclosure Act
- Land financing—mortgages and deeds of trust
- Types of deeds and their warranties
- Requirements for a deed
- Escrows and the Real Estate Settlement Procedures Act
- Adverse possession and its elements
- Foreclosure
- Eminent domain

Murphy and Somon were neighbors and got into an argument one day about where their boundary lines were located. Murphy brought out his deed to show that he was right, but Somon says he now owns part of Murphy's land because he has had it fenced in with his property for twenty years. Murphy has brought suit to get Somon's fence off his property. Will he win?

Real property interests can be transferred to others in several ways. These include transfer by sale, gift, adverse possession, foreclosure, tax sale, and eminent domain. This chapter discusses the steps involved in various transfer methods.

TRANSFER BY SALE

Although a transfer of property from seller to buyer may seem like a simple transaction involving only two parties, there are a great many other people, issues, and steps involved in a **transfer by sale.**

Marketing the Property

The use of brokers Many sellers use real estate **brokers** and salespersons to help them sell their real property interests. Such brokers are generally on a **commission** basis—that is they are paid a certain percentage of the selling price only if they are able to sell the property. This type of arrangement allows the sellers to pay when they have their money and gives brokers incentive to sell.

The listing agreement In many states, the **listing agreement** must be in writing. In all states, the realty broker or salesperson must be licensed to collect a commission. The listing agreement should provide how long the agreement will last, how much the commission will be, when the commission is earned, and what happens when either the buyer or seller backs out of a sale.

In the *Jaudon v. Swink* case, a broker and seller litigated an issue of whether a commission was due.

JAUDON v. SWINK

Court of Appeals of North Carolina.
276 S.E.2d 511 (1981).

FACTS Swink and Jaudon had a listing agreement employing Jaudon as a broker for the Swink property in exchange for a percentage commission. Jaudon brought the Hughes to the property. The Hughes made an offer, which Swink rejected. Immediately after the listing agreement ended, Swink and Hughes contracted for the sale of the property. Jaudon brought suit for his commission.

ISSUE Is Jaudon entitled to his commission for bringing the Hughes to the property even though they bought the property after the listing expired?

DECISION Yes. Swink's and Hughes' conduct was to avoid the commission. Jaudon had done the job of bringing a buyer to Swink. Swink and Hughes entered into the contract the day after the listing ended.

LEGAL TIP

A commission cannot be avoided by waiting until listings expire to contract with buyers brought to the property by the broker.

Negotiations: The Purchase Contract

The basic agreement The agreement between the buyer and seller must be in writing to be enforceable. The minimum requirements for the **purchase contract** include the names and signatures of the parties, a description of the property being sold, the price and the payment terms, and a date for performance. However, many more details should be covered so that the transfer can proceed smoothly. The details should include:

1. Amount the buyer will deposit as "earnest money," or the initial deposit of money made by the buyer to show good faith.
2. Type of land interest being conveyed (such as fee simple, life estate, etc).
3. Date for performance or close of escrow (which is the process whereby the title to the property and the money are exchanged).
4. Type of title the seller must furnish free and clear of all liens and claims.
5. Way the buyer will take title (such as joint title with another party).
6. Repairs the seller must make on the property and condition of the property for transfer.
7. Liability for prepaid insurance and taxes (and any amounts to be prorated along with specified dates).
8. Party responsible for paying the costs of transfer (escrow fees, title insurance policies, financing fees, etc.).
9. Date buyer will move in or take possession.
10. Conditions precedent for performance (such as a buyer qualifying for financing; a seller providing a termite report; or a seller clearing title).

The *Merrit v. Davis* case deals with a problem in conditions precedent.

MERRIT v. DAVIS

Court of Appeals of Florida.
265 So.2d 69 (1972).

FACTS The Merrits agreed to sell their property to the Davises with a condition that the Davises get financing of $76,000 at 7½% interest. The Davises obtained financing of $74,400 and a second amount of $1600 at a higher interest rate. The Davises refused to go through with the transaction, and the Merrits brought suit.

ISSUE Had the financing condition precedent been met, and were the Davises required to go through with the sale?

DECISION No. The condition was specific and was almost met, but almost was not good enough. The buyers were not required to take a second loan at a higher rate.

LEGAL TIP

For sellers, the best financing clause in a purchase contract is a general one which allows the buyer to obtain "reasonable financing."

Marketable title Every seller of land is required to deliver **marketable title** to the buyer. Marketable title is one that is free of liens, title defects, and other encumbrances. For example, if a seller has failed to pay a contractor who has done work on the property, the contractor may have a lien on the seller's property. The seller would have to pay the contractor and have the lien removed to deliver marketable title. If the seller has had an ongoing boundary dispute, it must be resolved to deliver marketable title.

In many cases, the seller can satisfy the requirement of transferring marketable title by furnishing the buyer with a title insurance policy. This policy will provide coverage for the buyer in the event a title defect arises. The title insurer will not issue the policy until the property's title has been checked in the land records.

In some states, the seller will be required to furnish a title abstract as proof of marketable title. A **title abstract** is a summary of the transfers of the property and any liens or encumbrances which might exist. An attorney writes the abstract, which can be used as a basis for obtaining a title insurance policy.

Applicable regulations In some types of land sales, there are federal statutes and regulations governing the sales contracts. The **Interstate Land Sales Full Disclosure Act (ILSFDA)** is an act passed by Congress regulating the sale of undeveloped land. The ILSFDA is administered by the Department of Housing and Urban Development (HUD) and is basically a disclosure act. Sellers under the ILSFDA must provide buyers with certain information and contract forms before the contract is valid. Also, buyers under the act are given a seventy-two-hour period within which to change their minds about purchasing the property.

Financing

Financing the purchase of the property will be covered as part of the payment terms of the contract, but the method of financing and obtaining financing is one of the central issues in every property purchase. Buyers may arrange for their own financing for the purchase, take over payments on the seller's financing, or assume the seller's financing. The seller may act as a lender for part of the purchase price and carry the buyer on a loan. However, whoever finances the purchase will want security for the loan. Mortgages, deeds of trust, and installment contracts provide for that security.

The mortgage The most well-known and frequently used form of security for the lender's funds is the **mortgage.** In a mortgage, the buyer, or mortgagor, pledges the property to the lender, or mortgagee, as security for the loan. The mortgage is a lien on the property and is recorded in the public records so that the mortgagee's interest or lien is protected. Under the mortgage, a buyer who falls behind on payments, or defaults, can lose the property through the lender's foreclosure. Foreclosure allows the lender to acquire full title to the property and sell it to satisfy the buyer's loan.

The deed of trust Another frequently used form of security is the deed of trust. In a **deed of trust,** a third party, or trustee, holds title to the property until the buyer is able to repay the lender, or beneficiary, the amount of the loan. With a deed of trust, a default by the buyer can bring a prompt form of foreclosure—the power of sale—which allows the trustee to sell the property with proper notice but does not require court action.

Installment contracts (land contracts or contracts for deed) **Installment contracts,** or **contracts for deed,** which are **land contracts** are a final method of lender security used when the seller is also the lender. This method of security is popular for buyers in times when money is tight and interest rates high. Under this form of financing, the seller keeps title to the property until the buyer pays the seller the full amount of the loan. If the buyer fails to pay installments as they are due, and the seller already has title, the buyer's interest in the property is forfeited and the seller can take possession of the property.

Transferability of financing Because the financing is obtained personally by a buyer and is based upon the lender's determination of the buyer's ability to pay, the financing arrangement is a personal contract right and may have restrictions on its assignment and transferability. In times when interest rates have increased, many buyers have wanted to simply take over the payments on the seller's existing property loan. Some lending institutions have tried to stop such transactions (called assumptions) by enforcing due-on-sale clauses.

Due-on-sale clauses are provisions in mortgages and deeds of trust making the full amount of the loan due if the property subject to the mortgage or deed of trust is transferred, or sold. Both buyer and seller should learn the lender's position on the transfer of mortgage rights before the sale takes place.

Figure 48-1 summarizes the differences among the three methods of security for real property loans.

Transfer of the Sale Property: Deeds

A **deed** is needed to transfer title to land. Parties should tell what type of deed they will use in the transfer. The types of deeds are the quit-claim deed, the warranty deed, and the special warranty deed. The following subsections discuss these three types of deeds.

Quit-claim deed A **quit-claim deed** is one which transfers any interest the seller has in the property (which could be none). The quit-claim deed carries no warranties or guarantees. This deed conveys what interest the seller has—if the seller has any at all.

Warranty deed A **warranty deed** carries the promises that the seller has good title; that the seller has the authority to transfer title; and that the seller will reimburse the buyer for any costs if a problem with the title on the property arises.

Figure 48-1 **Comparison of Security Methods for Land Financing**

	NUMBER OF PARTIES	FINANCIER	TITLEHOLDER	PROPERTY ENCUMBERENCE	NON-PAYMENT REMEDIES
Mortgages	Two	Lender	Borrower/ buyer*	Lien	Foreclosure
Deeds of Trust	Three	Lender	Third party/ trustee	Deed of trust	Power of sale
Installment Contract	Two	Seller	Seller	Contract	Forfeiture

* In some states (title states) the lender has title.

Special warranty deed A **special warranty deed** carries the same promises as the warranty deed but the promises are limited to the time of the seller's holding of title to the property. Basically, all the seller warrants with a special warranty deed is that no encumbrances or defects have arisen during the time of the seller's ownership. Actions by others are not covered.

Requirements for a valid deed In addition to furnishing the type of deed specified in the contract, the seller and buyer must be sure that the deed meets all formal requirements. For a deed to transfer a real property interest, the following requirements must be met:

1. Language of conveyance must include "grant and convey;" "grant, bargain, and sell;" "or grant and warrant."
2. Consideration need not include sale price. In most deed forms, consideration appears as "for $10 and other good and valuable consideration."
3. Description of real property must be a legal description and identify the land.
4. Type of real property interest must be fee simple or life estate.
5. Signature of the seller is required and usually must be notarized, or acknowledged. The acknowledgment may not be required for the deed itself to be valid; but for the deed to be recorded in public records, the state may require acknowledgment.

In addition to these physical requirements for the deed document, there is one additional step required to make a conveyance by deed valid—the deed must be delivered. Whether proper **delivery** of the deed occurs depends upon two questions:

1. Did the grantor intend to have the deed pass title?
2. Has the grantor completed a physical act which legally involves transfer and delivery?

If a deed is executed and handed to the buyer, or grantee, delivery has occurred. If a deed is executed and then placed in the grantor's safe deposit box to which no one but the grantor has access, delivery has not occurred. In most property sales, the deed is executed and delivered to a third party, or escrow agent, who is instructed to deliver title when the buyer has made payment. Such a transfer to a third party is sufficient delivery on the part of the seller. The *In re Estate of Kennedy* case deals with the issue of delivery of a deed.

Recording the deed Once the deed is executed and delivered, title to the real property has passed. But there is one more step that buyers should take to protect their title. The deed should be recorded in the land records of the state or local agency responsible for the recording of land interests. This **recording** is necessary to assure that the buyer does not lose title to a later purchaser who might buy the property without knowing of the first buyer's interest in the land.

Transferring the Sale Property: Closing

The final step in the transfer of real property by sale is the **closing,** or **escrow.** The purpose of the closing, or escrow, is to have a third party handle all the

IN RE ESTATE OF KENNEDY

Court of Appeals of New York.
318 N.Y.S.2d 759 (1971).

FACTS Kennedy executed a deed conveying title to his property to his sister, Edna Hays. Kennedy showed the deed to Edna and then placed it in his safe deposit box at his bank. Upon Kennedy's death, Edna claimed the property, but the other heirs objected on the grounds that there had been no delivery.

ISSUE Did Kennedy's placement of the deed in the box constitute delivery?

DECISION No. Although Kennedy may have had the intent to convey, he still had control and Edna was not entitled to the property.

LEGAL TIP

Putting deeds in a safe deposit box under your control will not transfer title.

documents and money necessary for the transaction to take place, and to exchange the title and money at the same time. The escrow agent is given the buyer's money and the seller's deed along with a set of escrow instructions (or a contract between the escrow agent and the buyer and seller), which detail what events must occur before title can pass, when title is to pass, who is to be paid what money, and what conditions must be satisfied before the exchange of money and property can take place.

Escrow closings are regulated by a federal statute called the **Real Estate Settlement Procedures Act (RESPA).** This Act was passed by Congress to reduce the cost of closing property transactions; to require that buyers be informed in advance of the cost of closing; to prohibit kickback and referral fees among escrow agents and brokers; and to prohibit brokers and lenders from requiring buyers to use a certain escrow agent.

Under RESPA, all lenders whose loans are federally regulated must furnish buyers with a good-faith estimate of their closing costs and a booklet explaining closing costs and purposes. Lenders are limited in the amount of prepayments they can require of buyers. Prepayments include deposits for monthly loan payments, insurance, and taxes.

RESPA also prohibits brokers and lenders from taking fees or commissions for referring buyers to a particular escrow agent and from requiring buyers to use a certain escrow agent as a requirement for a loan. Violations of these provisions carry criminal penalties.

Figure 48-2 summarizes the steps involved in a real property transfer by sale.

TRANSFER OF PROPERTY BY GIFT

Title to real property can be transferred without an underlying sale; the real property can be conveyed as a gift. The deed is still the form used to transfer title. The key to a valid gift is the delivery of the deed. The same requirements for delivery that were discussed under "Transfer by Sale" apply to a **transfer by gift.** The grantor must also intend the title to pass or the gift to be made. Real property can be transferred as an **inter vivos gift** (made while the grantor is alive) or transferred by will (**testamentary gift**).

Figure 48-2 **Steps in the Transfer of Real Property by Sale**

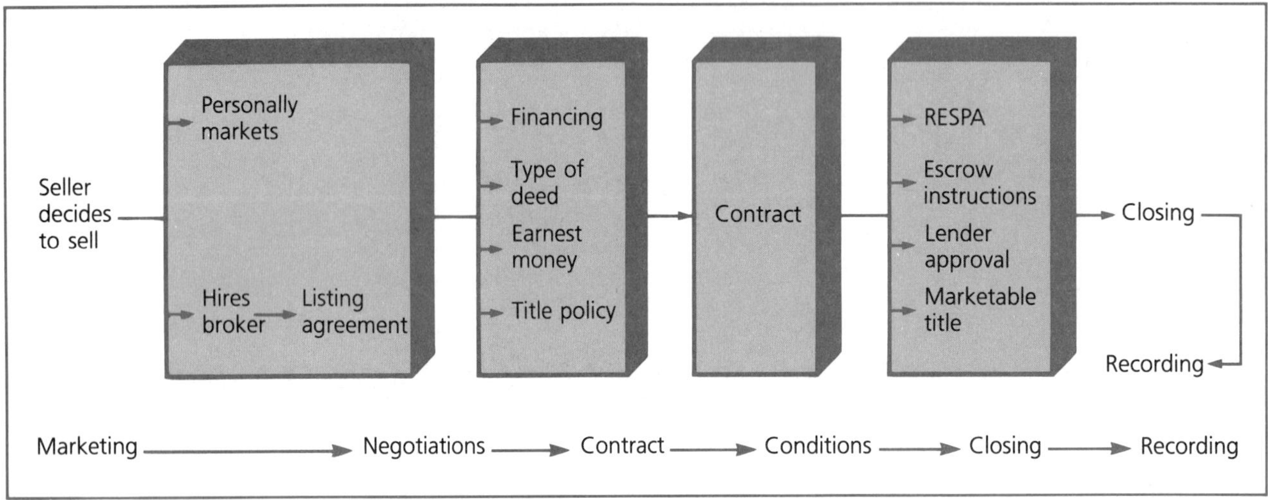

TRANSFER OF PROPERTY BY ADVERSE POSSESSION

Adverse possession is a way to acquire title to real property by using and possessing it. The elements for adverse possession are openness, adverseness, and continuous possession for the statutory period.

Open-and-Notorious Possession of the Property

Under the **open-and-notorious possession requirement,** the adverse possesser must use the property so that an "ordinary" person in the area recognizes that the property is being used as an ordinary landowner would use it.

Continuous-and-Exclusive Possession of the Property

Under the **continuous-and-exclusive possession requirement,** the adverse possesser can claim the property for a certain period of time. Each state has a statute which specifies how long the continuous-and-exclusive possession must be. Different states' time periods range from five to twenty years.

This element does not require the adverse possesser to be on the property at all times, but the property must be used on a regular basis. The definition of "exclusive" is occupation and control by one person and not by others.

Hostile-and-Adverse Possession of the Property

Under the **hostile-and-adverse possession requirement,** the possesser has no permission to be on the property and has no title claim to the property. The adverse possesser need not be angry to satisfy this requirement.

Adverse possession can arise in boundary cases where one neighbor builds a wall on the adjoining neighbor's property. Despite the mistaken placement, most states will find that if the wall remains for the statutory period, the neighbor who built the wall will acquire title to the extra inches of land adversely possessed by the misplacement of the wall. In the *Somon v. Murphy Fabrication & Erection Co.* case, the court deals with the issues of whether the elements of adverse possession have been satisfied. These facts are the same as those presented in the chapter-opening problem.

SOMON v. MURPHY FABRICATION & ERECTION CO.

Supreme Court of West Virginia.
232 S.E.2d 524 (1977).

FACTS Murphy and Somon had an argument over the location of their boundary on their adjacent lands. Murphy's deed indicated he owned the property. Somon claimed he owned the property by adverse possession because his fence had been on Murphy's property for the statutory period.

ISSUE Did Somon acquire title to the strip of land by a mistakenly placed fence?

DECISION Yes. A mistaken belief about a boundary is still a sufficient basis for adverse possession.

LEGAL TIP
Be sure to check boundaries when you or a neighbor puts up a fence or builds a wall on adjacent property.

TRANSFER BY FORECLOSURE

Foreclosure is a form of involuntary transfer of property that occurs after the property owner fails to make payments on a loan for which the property is security. Foreclosure proceedings can be classified into two groups—those requiring court proceedings and those exercised without court proceedings.

Court-ordered Foreclosure

In the first type of foreclosure—the court-proceeding foreclosure and the traditional type of mortgage foreclosure—the mortgagee files a suit in equity seeking the right to sell the property. This type of foreclosure requires that the mortgagor be given the opportunity to respond to the suit brought by the mortgagee. After the mortgagor's response, the court may order the sale of the property; however, even when the property is sold, the mortgagor is still given a period of time to redeem the property by paying the amount due plus costs. This period of time is called the **redemption period,** and those buying property at a foreclosure sale should be aware that their title to the real property is not complete until the redemption period is over.

Private Foreclosure

In the second type of foreclosure proceeding—those in which no court proceedings are required—a power of sale is given in a security document, which is a mortgage or, most typically, a deed of trust. After proper notification and a waiting period, the property is sold. In most states, there is no redemption period after the sale because the debtor has the waiting period during which to redeem the property.

TRANSFER BY TAX SALE

Nearly all local governments have some form of property tax. Under these tax systems, the value of all the land in the area is determined. Then a tax is paid by the landowners based on the value given to their property times the rate. The tax is usually a rate per thousand dollars of valuation. If a tax rate is $4 per thousand, the tax on a piece of property valued at $100,000 would be $400. This tax must be paid by property owners by certain deadlines.

The failure to pay property taxes carries the severe penalty of possible loss of the property. If the tax is not paid, the agency in charge of property taxation can begin proceedings to sell the property to satisfy the taxes. In many states, the steps for a tax sale are streamlined, and court action is not required. The property will be transferred by auction sale unless the property owner is able to pay the taxes and the costs of preparing for the sale before the auction sale is held.

TRANSFER BY EMINENT DOMAIN

Eminent domain is the "taking" of private property by a governmental unit for public purpose. The United States Constitution allows such taking if "just compensation is paid." Appropriate purposes include projects for the public good. The most common projects are highways, government buildings, water projects, and public housing. Just compensation is the fair market value of the property. The *Loretto v. Teleprompter Manhattan CATV Corp., et al.* case shows the taking issue.

LORETTO v. TELEPROMPTER MANHATTAN CATV CORP., ET AL.

Supreme Court of the United States.
458 U.S. 100 (1982).

FACTS CATV was given authority by the city of New York to install cable equipment in apartment buildings in the city. When CATV attempted to install cable equipment in Loretto's building, she filed suit claiming that the installation of the equipment was a taking of her property by eminent domain and demanded compensation. The installation involved a 36′ × ½″ wire and two 4″ × 4″ × 4″ boxes, occupying a total of ⅛th cubic foot of Loretto's property.

ISSUE Did the city's authorization of the placement of cable equipment in private buildings constitute a taking by eminent domain?

DECISION Yes. There was a taking of Loretto's property even though it was minimal. A public purpose was accomplished but Loretto deserved compensation.

LEGAL TIP

Check the authority of utility installers before allowing them to begin a service project.

KEY TERMS

Brokers
Transfer by sale
Commission
Listing agreement
Purchase contract
Marketable title
Title abstract
Interstate Land Sales Full Disclosure Act (ILSFDA)
Mortgage
Deed of trust
Installment contracts
Land contracts
Contracts for deeds

Due-on-sale clauses
Deed
Quit-claim deed
Warranty deed
Special warranty deed
Delivery
Recording
Closing
Escrow
Real Estate Settlement Procedures Act (RESPA)
Transfer by gift
Inter vivos gift
Testamentary gift
Adverse possession
Open-and-notorious possession requirement
Continuous-and-exclusive possession requirement
Hostile-and-adverse possession requirement
Foreclosure
Redemption period
Eminent domain

CHAPTER PROBLEMS

1. The Smiths have applied for a federally insured loan to purchase a home. They have made their application to Western Frontier Mortgage Company. The Smiths are told by a Western loan officer that they will have to use Western Frontier Title Company as the escrow agent for the closing on the property. The Smiths ask the agent about the closing costs and the agent says, "Oh, they will be up there—we'll just have to see." Have any of the Smith's rights been violated?
2. Cain purchased several lots in the downtown area of Topeka, Kansas. Shortly after Cain's purchase, the city of Topeka announced the property would be taken for use in the construction of a civic center. Cain wants to know if this action is legal, and if he is entitled to compensation. *Cain v. City of Topeka,* 603 P.2d 1031 (Kans. 1979).
3. What topics should be covered in a listing agreement?
4. Karrell and West were adjoining landowners. Their property was located in a rural logging area. West did not live on his property and visited there infrequently. Karrell began removing topsoil from West's property and did so for a period of twenty-three years. When West learned of the removal, he filed suit for a court order to stop Karrell's removal of the soil. What is the result? *Karrell v. West,* 616 S.W.2d 692 (Tex. 1981).
5. The Janssens and Joiners were adjoining landowners. Between their properties was a 14-foot strip of property which was described as part of the Janssens' property, but which the Joiners had cared for by planting grass, plants, shrubs, etc. When a dispute arose, the Joiners brought suit seeking a court declaration that they had title by adverse possession. Who wins? *Joiner v. Janssen,* 421 N.E.2d 170 (Ill. 1981).
6. Milton Pesovic had immigrated to the United States and encouraged his son to follow him. In a telephone conversation, Milton promised his son that he would give him a house (which Milton owned in Chicago but was renting to a third party). When his son arrived in the United States, Milton refused to give him the house. His son brought suit seeking to enforce the gift. Will the son win? *Pesovic v. Pesovic,* 295 N.E.2d 261 (Ill. 1973).

*7. Frances Hood executed and recorded a deed conveying her property to her son, Kenneth. When Kenneth learned of the deed, he told his mother to take the property back. Before Mrs. Kennedy could execute another deed, Kenneth died. Mrs. Kennedy claims she still owns the property because Kenneth did not accept the deed. Kenneth's heirs claim they own the property. What is the result? *Hood v. Hood,* 384 A.2d 706 (Maine 1978).

*8. The Juneaus listed their property for sale with Welek Realty, Inc. Welek Realty produced a buyer, and the Juneaus signed a sales agreement. The buyer put $2000 down as earnest money and had obtained financing when the Juneaus said they would not sell the property. Welek still wants its commission. Must the Juneaus pay? *Welek Realty, Inc., v. Juneau,* 596 S.W.2d 495 (Mo. 1980).

*9. The Rosens purchased property from the Luttingers with a condition in the sale contract that the Rosens obtain financing at 8½% on $45,000 for twenty years.

The Rosens applied to the only institution giving loans in that amount and were approved for a loan at 8¾%. The Rosens refused to go through with the purchase, and the Luttingers sued for breach of contract. What is the result? *Luttingers v. Rosen,* 316 A.2d 757 (Conn. 1972).

*10. Ben and Kathleen Pickering owned residential property as joint tenants. They had given a deed of trust to First National Bank in exchange for the advance of funds for the property purchase. Ben then pledged the property to Energy Fuels Corporation as security for a loan from them. Ben defaulted on the loan to Energy Fuels, and they now wish to sell the property. Kathleen thinks they cannot sell the entire property. What is the result? *First National Bank v. Energy Fuels Corp.,* 618 P.2d 1115 (Colo. 1980).

"Can I get my deposit back?"
Typical tenant to typical landlord

Chapter 49

Landlord-Tenant Relationships

CHAPTER PREVIEW

- Four types of common law tenancies
- Requirements for putting leases in writing
- Minimum requirements for a valid lease
- Security deposits
- Rights of tenants under the implied warranty of habitability
- Assignments and subleases
- Rules and regulations
- Ending leases
- Rights and duties of landlords and tenants

Berlinger rented an apartment from Suburban Apartment Management (SAM). His lease had a clause that prohibited tenants from keeping motorcycles on the premises. The clause provided for a fine of $50 for each violation. Berlinger kept a motorcycle on his patio on October 10, 13, and 24 and November 7, 1979. When he moved out, SAM kept $200 for Berlinger's four days of violations of the clause. Berlinger wants to know if the management can do that. Can they?

A landlord-tenant relationship is one in which the tenant is permitted to occupy the landlord's property in exchange for rent. This chapter covers this relationship and answers the following questions: What types of landlord-tenant relationships are there? What is required for a lease agreement? What terms are required for a lease agreement? What terms are permitted in a lease agreement? What terms are advisable for a lease agreement? What happens when the lease agreement is breached or ended?

WHAT TYPES OF LANDLORD-TENANT RELATIONSHIPS ARE THERE?

Common law dealt with the landlord-tenant relationship more than it dealt with fee simple ownership of land. The feudal systems of lords as landowners and serfs as occupants and workers of the land gave us much of our landlord-tenant law today. There are four different types of landlord-tenant relationships under common law, and they are still used today in all the states. These four relationships, called tenancies, are: tenancies for a period or tenancies for years; periodic tenancies; tenancies at will; and tenancies at sufferance.

Tenancy for a Period or Tenancy for Years

A **tenancy for a period,** or **tenancy for years,** is one that runs for a predetermined and definite period of time. Other terms used to describe this type of landlord-tenant relationship are "estate for years" and "estate for a term." Every tenancy for a period has a definite beginning and definite ending date. If you lease an apartment for six months, you have a tenancy for a period.

Periodic Tenancy

A **periodic tenancy** is one without an ending date. A periodic tenancy goes on and on until one of the parties takes the proper steps to end it. A periodic tenancy is sometimes called a tenancy from period to period because it runs from rental period to rental period. For example, a month-to-month tenancy is a periodic tenancy that lasts only through each month. It is possible that the landlord or the tenant could end the tenancy by giving a month's notice.

A periodic tenancy can be created by an express agreement of the parties. However, most periodic tenancies are based on a landlord's conduct in allowing a tenant to remain on a month-to-month basis and a tenant's conduct in paying monthly rent. For example, suppose that Barbara has orally agreed to lease Pat's office building for twenty-four months. In their state, lease agreements over a year are required to be in writing to be valid. Pat and Barbara do not have a valid tenancy for years. But if Barbara moves into the building and pays rent on a monthly basis, they do have a periodic tenancy.

Ending a periodic tenancy is a statutory procedure in most states. Giving notice to the other party is a requirement in all states. The form and time of notice will vary. Common law required six month's notice to terminate a year-to-year lease and a full period's notice to terminate any lease running for a shorter period. For example, a month-to-month tenancy would require a month's notice for termination. Many states have adopted a month's notice for all leases.

Tenancy at Will

A **tenancy at will** is one in which either party can end the lease at any time without advance notice. Parties can agree to a tenancy at will or a tenancy at will can arise because the parties have no lease agreement and no regular pattern to establish a periodic tenancy.

Some states have changed the advance notice requirement and have, in effect, changed a tenancy at will to a periodic tenancy for purposes of termination.

Tenancy at Sufferance

A **tenancy at sufferance** involves a tenant who has no right to be on the landlord's property. A tenant who remains on the landlord's property after the lease expires (holdover tenant) has a tenancy at sufferance. Once the lease agreement is over, the landlord has the right to evict the tenant, since he or she is there only at the sufferance of the landlord. If, however, the landlord begins to accept rent and allows the tenant at sufferance to remain, a tenancy at sufferance turns into a periodic tenancy.

A tenancy at sufferance can result any time someone is in possession of property they are not supposed to have. The *Teston v. Teston* case shows one circumstance in which a tenancy at sufferance arises.

TESTON v. TESTON

Court of Appeals of Georgia.
217 S.E.2d 498 (1975).

FACTS W. R. Teston's will left his house to his sons. Teston had married again after his sons' mother passed away. When he died, the sons were anxious to have the house. When the boys had title turned over to them, they literally threw their stepmother out of the house without warning. They then padlocked the property and told her not to come back. Mrs. Teston protested and filed suit because she was evicted without notice. The boys said no notice was required.

ISSUE Was there a tenancy at sufferance? Was notice required?

DECISION Yes, there was a tenancy at sufferance. Mrs. Teston was wrongfully in possession of the property. She could be evicted at any time. No notice was required because there was no rent and no agreement, and Mrs. Teston had no interest in the property.

LEGAL TIP

When a spouse dies, check property rights so that arrangements can be made and transfers made properly.

WHAT IS REQUIRED FOR A LEASE AGREEMENT?

When Is a Written Agreement Necessary?

As Chapter 22 discussed, the statute of frauds may apply to leases. In most states, the rule that contracts running for longer than a year must be in writing applies to leases. The statute of frauds also requires real estate contracts to be in writing. Many states define a lease as a real estate interest. Others define a lease for six months or more as a real estate interest.

If a lease agreement is required by the statute of frauds to be in writing and it is not, the only rights the parties will have will be those implied by their conduct.

They will probably have a month-to-month tenancy based on the conduct of monthly payment of rent.

Regardless of whether the lease agreement is required to be in writing, it is advisable to have it in writing. The *William Henry Brophy College v. Tovar* case illustrates the problems created by an oral lease agreement.

WILLIAM HENRY BROPHY COLLEGE v. TOVAR

Court of Appeals of Arizona.
619 P.2d 19 (1980).

FACTS Anastasia Nealon owned two parcels of land in the city of Phoenix—lots 2337 and 2339. Nick Mercer (Anastasia's husband) had orally agreed to let the Tovars lease the parcels and operate an adult theater, called "The Empress Theater," and a bookstore on the land.

Anastasia passed away, and her will left the parcels to the Brophy College, a Jesuit preparatory school. Understandably, the College did not want the Tovars operating an adult theater and bookstore on its land. It gave the Tovars notice to leave. The Tovars claimed they had a valid oral lease that had been agreed to in 1977 for a ten-year period. The College claimed the Tovars had a month-to-month tenancy, had been given notice, and must be evicted.

ISSUE Was there a lease agreement? If so, what type of agreement existed?

DECISION A ten-year lease must be in writing to be valid. The best the Tovars had was a month-to-month tenancy that could be terminated at any time by the College, which was required to give only a month's notice. Since the month's notice had been given, the Tovars were required to leave.

LEGAL TIP

Lease agreements should be in writing to avoid questions of whether a valid lease exists.

What Terms Are Required in a Lease Agreement?

The requirements here are basically the same requirements for any valid contract that must be in writing.

The parties In a lease, the landlord and the tenant must be named and their signatures must appear on the contract. If a corporation signs a lease as a tenant, the landlord should make sure the proper corporate authority signs and indicates that the corporation and not just the signing officer is bound to the terms of the agreement.

The property The leased premises should be described. There need not be a legal description for a valid lease; an address is sufficient. If an apartment or suite is involved, the number should be given.

Type of lease The type of lease will most likely be determined by the length of the lease. If it is open-ended lease with monthly rental payments, it is a periodic tenancy. If it is a lease for one year, it is a tenancy for years. The parties also may agree to a tenancy at will.

Rent "Rent" refers to the contract price. Stating the rental figure, due date, and recipient are required for a valid lease to exist.

What Terms Are Advisable for a Lease?

Only minimum requirements are necessary to establish a valid lease. However, minimum requirements do not cover the trouble spots that can arise in lease agreements. Some states have passed statutes that deal with many of these issues. For example, about one-third of the states have adopted the Uniform Residential Landlord Tenant Act (URLTA). The URLTA sections that apply are covered in the following subsections.

Habitability Habitability is a requirement that the leased premises be "livable." Livable means that the property is in a good state of repair and has functioning heat, water, and sewer facilities.

Common law does not require that leased premises be habitable. The tenant takes the property under a form of *caveat emptor,* a term that means let the buyer beware. The effect of this common law rule was that tenants were bound to leases for property in need of services and repair. They were left with the tasks of trying to get landlords to make repairs and provide services.

The URLTA requires that leased property be kept in a habitable condition and gives tenants remedies when the landlord does not meet that standard. Some states have court decisions that impose a **warranty of habitability** on landlords. Most have limited the warranty of habitability to the lease of residential property. *Lemle v. Breeden* was a landmark case in the area of implied warranty of habitability in leases.

LEMLE v. BREEDEN

Supreme Court of Hawaii.
462 P.2d 470 (1969).

FACTS Mrs. Breeden owned a house in the Diamond Head area of Honolulu. She rented the house to Lemle for $800 per month on leases that were to run from September 22, 1964, through March 20, 1965, and from April 17, 1965, through June 17, 1965. Lemle paid $1900 for rent and deposits when the lease was signed.

The house had six bedrooms, six baths, a living room, kitchen, dining room, garage, and salt-water swimming pool. The house was Tahitian style and had a corrugated metal roof. Over the metal roof were woven coconut leaves so that the house had a grass-shack effect.

Lemle and his family moved into the house on September 22, 1964. That evening, the Lemles were kept awake by the sounds of rats running up and down the corrugated metal roof. The next night they noticed rats running throughout the house. They all slept together in the living room—the room with the least amount of rats.

The next day an exterminator was hired and traps were set; however, there was no appreciable decline in the rat population during the next two nights. After these three nights, Lemle and his family moved out and demanded a refund of their $1900. Breeden refused and Lemle sued on a theory of implied warranty of habitability.

ISSUE Is there an implied warranty of habitability in leased residential property? If so, was that warranty breached in this case?

DECISION For the first time in Hawaii, the court held that there was an implied warranty of habitability in the lease of residential property. The court held that concept of *caveat emptor* had no place in an urban society where tenants would be left without the ability to repair dilapidated property.

The court held that the implied warranty had been breached in the case. The fact that the rats were a natural problem and not a repair problem made no difference. The key is habitability, and Lemle and his family could not live in the house.

LEGAL TIP

Put a habitability clause in a lease requiring the landlord to send an exterminator when infestation is discovered by the tenant after moving in.

Deposits Most landlords require some type of deposit when the tenant agrees to a lease. The types of deposits include security deposits, cleaning deposits, and prepaid rent.

Security deposits **Security deposits** are used to protect the landlord. These deposits are taken to cover damage to property or stolen property. They can also cover the landlord's damages if the tenant breaches the lease agreement and moves out before the lease expires.

State regulation of security deposits varies greatly. For example, the URLTA limits the amount of security deposit for which a landlord can ask. Even the limits vary from state to state. Some states regulate what the landlord can do with the security deposit once it is in hand. Common law allows the landlord to use the money as if it were his or her own money. Today, many states require the deposits to be maintained in a separate account. Other states require that the tenant earn a minimum (5%) amount of interest during the time that the landlord has the deposit.

The idea of the security deposit is to have it serve as liquidated damages. The parties agree in advance that if there is a breach, the landlord's damages will be the security deposit.

Some states and the URLTA require the landlord to notify the tenant if the security deposit will be kept. The notice must also explain why the deposit is being kept.

Cleaning deposits Cleaning deposits are used to cover the costs of cleaning anything that needs cleaning because the tenant lived there. These deposits are allowed under the URLTA; if they are nonrefundable, the lease must state that fact in bold print.

Prepaid rent Many landlords require tenants to pay the first and last month's rent before moving in. The landlord is seeking protection to assure rental payments. However, some states limit the amount of prepaid rent the landlord can get. Under the URLTA, prepaid rent and security deposits are limited to a figure not more than 1½ times the monthly rent.

Fixtures Many tenants, particularly commercial tenants, add fixtures to the landlord's property during the lease period. A question that often results is: Who gets the fixtures when the tenant leaves? The lease can spell out the answer or can set a standard for what fixtures will or will not go with the tenant. Without this type of agreement, the landlord and tenant are left with the usual tests for determining whether something is a fixture or personal property. Those tests often produce conflicting results (see Chapter 47).

Rules Every apartment complex has a set of rules for problems such as noise, parking, or laundry. All the states and the URLTA permit landlords to have such rules and treat them as being part of the lease agreement. For the rules to be valid under the URLTA, they must meet the following requirements:

1. The purposes of the rules must be the safety, welfare, or convenience of the tenants.
2. The rules must apply equally to all tenants.

3. The rules must be specific.
4. All tenants must be aware of the rules when they sign a lease.
5. Changes in rules must not be made unless the tenants are given notice of the change.

The *Berlinger v. Suburban Apartment Management* case is one involving problems with both a rule and a security deposit.

BERLINGER v. SUBURBAN APARTMENT MANAGEMENT

Court of Appeals of Ohio.
454 N.E.2d 1367 (1982).

FACTS Berlinger leased an apartment from Suburban Apartment Management (SAM). He was required to pay a security deposit of $420, and his monthly rent was $210. Paragraph 17 of his lease provided as follows: No animals, birds, pets, motorcycles, waterbeds, trucks, jeeps, or vans shall be kept on the premises at any time. The rule also provided for a $50 fine for each violation. Berlinger had a motorcycle on his patio on October 10, 13, and 24 and November 7, 1979.

Berlinger was given notice that he owed $200 for violating the rule. He moved out without paying the fine or his last month's rent. SAM kept his $420 security deposit, claiming Berlinger owed $410 along with $10.50 in interest. Berlinger objected because he said the fine was excessive and the rule arbitrary. He sued to have part of his deposit returned.

ISSUE Was the rule valid? Could SAM keep the security deposit?

DECISION The rule was reasonable. Motorcycles are noisy, and SAM had reason for not wanting them on its premises. In addition, motorcycles often bring other riders as an undesirable element. However, the rule's fine was excessive. A tenant would be liable for $1500 per month for a violation. The court remanded the case to the lower court to determine a reasonable fine for Berlinger's violation of the rule.

LEGAL TIP

Always get apartment rules in writing and find out what violations will cost.

Landlord's right of access The question here is: When can your landlord come into your apartment? The answer is any time with your permission. If you do not give permission, the landlord is required under the URLTA and most states to give the tenant advance notice of entry. For example, if the landlord wants to have all apartments exterminated on one particular day and will need to let the exterminator in, the tenant must be notified.

Under the URLTA, the landlord is required to give two days notice for an exterminator to enter. The URLTA gives exceptions to this two-day requirement. For example, the landlord can go into an apartment if there is an emergency (such as a fire).

The purpose for the access must also be given. The URLTA lists cleaning, painting, repairing, and decorating as valid reasons for entry.

If a law enforcement agency has a warrant to search an apartment, the landlord must let the agents or officers in for the search. If the search was unlawful, the landlord is not liable. The issue of the validity of the search warrant is between an agency and a tenant.

Assignments and subleases Assignments and subleases are alike in that they bring a third party into the landlord-tenant relationship. However, there are some differences between assignments and subleases. An **assignment** is an assignment and delegation of the lease. The assignee agrees to take possession of the property, complete the lease term, and make rental payments to the landlord. As in a contract assignment (see Chapter 24), the original tenant/assignor remains obligated, but the assignee/sublessee is also obligated to the landlord. Likewise, the landlord is still obligated to the assignor/tenant and assignee/sublessee.

In a **sublease,** the tenant transfers the right of possession for only a part of the lease. The tenant may also collect the rent from the sublessee and then pay the landlord. For example, Alberta has a lease for an apartment owned by Management, Inc. The lease runs for one year, and Alberta will be in Europe for two months of that year. If she arranges to have someone live in the apartment and pay rent for those two months, there is a sublease. In a sublease, there is no landlord-tenant relationship between the landlord and the sublessee. The original tenant is the landlord for the sublessee. The sublessee has no right to sue the landlord if the landlord does not honor his obligations. The sublessee would have to sue the tenant and the tenant would sue the landlord. Figure 49-1 is a diagram of the differences between assignment and sublease.

At common law, leases could be assigned and tenants could sublet. This rule is still followed in many states; however, the lease agreement may prohibit an assignment or a sublease. The agreement may also prohibit an assignment or a sublease without the landlord's permission. The *Klager v. Robert Meyer Co.,* case deals with the issues involved in a lease assignment.

KLAGER v. ROBERT MEYER CO.

Court of Appeals of Michigan.
290 N.W.2d 132 (1980).

FACTS Klager leased 10 acres of land to Robert Meyer Company for fifty years at $35,000 per year. Meyer planned to build a shopping center on the land.

The lease was conditional upon Meyer obtaining a zoning change that would allow construction of the shopping center. If the zoning change could not be obtained within a certain period of time, Meyer would be excused from the lease. Meyer was required to give notice of the lack of zoning and his intent to cancel.

The City of Ann Arbor did not approve the zoning. Meyer did not notify Klager but assigned the lease to Packard Plaza, Inc. Packard Plaza was a corporation with about $1000 in equity. Meyer assigned the lease so that he could avoid any liability he might have to Klager. No rent was ever paid and Klager filed suit against Meyer. Meyer said he was no longer liable.

ISSUE Does the assignment of a lease release the original tenant/assignor from liability?

DECISION No. Individuals cannot avoid their liability by assigning their contracts to corporations. Meyer remained liable with the assignment. An assignment does not release the assignor from liability to the landlord.

LEGAL TIP

Get zoning changes before signing a contract. If a contract requires notice in certain areas, be sure to give notice.

Rights and duties of landlords The landlord receives rent from a tenant who uses the property. As part of a lease, a landlord has certain responsibilities. Some of these duties are statutory in some states. But even in those states, it is best to provide a list of rights and duties for each party in the lease agreement.

Figure 49-1 **Assignment versus Sublease**

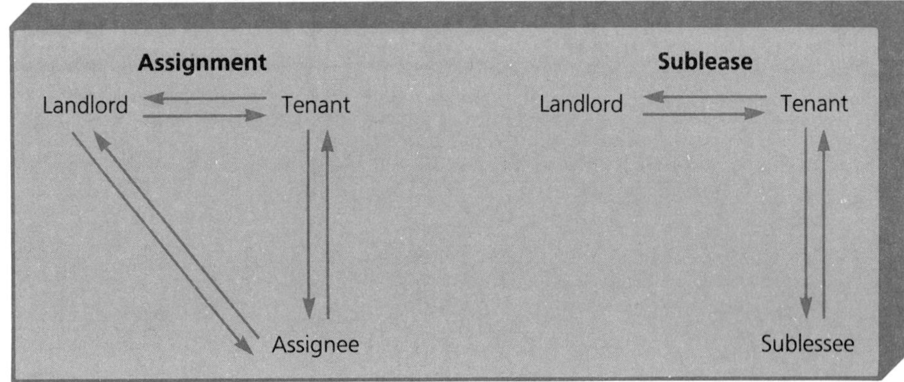

The landlord's duty to maintain Common law did not require a landlord to maintain the property; maintenance was the tenant's responsibility. However, most states and the URLTA have changed this rule. Under the URLTA, the landlord is required to do the following:

1. Comply with all building and safety codes.
2. Make all repairs or do whatever is necessary to keep the leased property habitable.
3. Keep all common areas (such as stairs and hallways) clean and safe.
4. Keep all electrical, plumbing, sanitary, ventilating, and air-conditioning equipment in good and safe working order.
5. Provide places for garbage disposal.
6. Keep heat, air conditioning, and water operable.

The landlord's liability for injuries to tenants—common areas In multiple-unit dwellings (such as apartments, townhouses, etc.) there are areas owned by the landlord that all tenants use. Walkways, stairs, elevators, and hallways are examples. The landlord has the responsibility to make sure that these areas are clean and safe for tenant use. Tenants who are injured because the landlord failed to maintain these areas properly can recover damages from the landlord. For example, a tenant who is injured in the laundry room by plugging his or her iron into a defective socket can recover damages from the landlord. The *Lewis v. W. F. Smith & Co.* case is an example of landlords' duties to maintain common areas.

Right to rent In exchange for upholding these duties, landlords are entitled to receive rent that is paid on time. Nonpayment of rent gives a landlord the right to end the lease and evict the tenant. Under the URLTA, the landlord is required to give written notice that the rent is overdue. If the rent is not received within fourteen days from the time a landlord gives a tenant notice, then the lease is ended in thirty days. Some states have different time limits but follow the same guideline.

Rights and duties of tenants Tenants have rights that correspond to each of the landlord's obligations as well as duties that correspond to each of the landlord's rights.

LEWIS v. W. F. SMITH & CO.

Court of Appeals of Illinois, First District.
390 N.E.2d 39 (1979).

FACTS Mary Lewis fell on the icy stairs of her apartment building in December and broke her leg. Since Lewis was a waitress, she was unable to work for three months.

Lewis filed suit against the building owners (W. F. Smith & Co.). She claimed that they did not clear the stairs of ice and snow, and also did not put up a handrail along the stairs.

ISSUE Is W. F. Smith & Co. liable for Lewis' injuries?

DECISION Yes. The lack of a handrail and the failure to clean the stairs regularly was a failure to maintain common areas. Mary Lewis was awarded $16,832.75.

LEGAL TIP

Landlords should keep stairs and other such common areas clean and free of objects.

Right to habitable property The implied warranty of habitability requires the landlord to deliver the leased property in good condition and repair. The URLTA and state statutes require the landlord to keep the property in good condition. If the landlord fails to meet these obligations, the tenant has several rights against the landlord.

Repair and deduct The URLTA and many other state statutes allow tenants to **repair and deduct.** This term means that tenants may make repairs themselves and then deduct the cost of the repairs from their rent. In most states, the tenant is required to first make a written demand of the landlord for the needed repairs. If within a certain time (fourteen days under the ULTRA), the landlord does not make the repairs, the tenant can attend to them. This right is often called **self-help.** Some states limit the self-help right to minor repairs. Under the URLTA, the limit is $100 or one-half the monthly rent, whichever is greater.

Constructive eviction If the landlord's failure to make repairs makes living circumstances so bad that the tenant cannot live there, the tenant can exercise the right of constructive eviction. **Constructive eviction** allows the tenant to leave the leased property in the middle of a lease without having any liability to the landlord. For constructive eviction to exist, the property must be so bad that no one could be expected to live there. For example, a two-inch layer of water on the floor would give a tenant the right to constructive eviction. No heat in a Minneapolis apartment in February is another example that could involve constructive eviction.

Duty to pay rent The tenant is required to pay rent on time. If the rent is not paid, the landlord can take the steps discussed earlier to end the lease and evict the tenant.

Duty to obey rules If the landlord has valid rules, the tenant is required to follow them. Failure to follow the rules allows the landlord to end the lease and evict the tenant.

What Is Not Allowed in a Lease Agreement?

For the most part, the parties are free to agree on their own lease terms. They can even change the effects of common law and statutes. However, there are two policy restrictions on lease terms.

Unconscionability: The case of an overbearing landlord The test for an unconscionable lease is the same as the test for an unconscionable contract (see Chapters 23 and 28). As applied to landlords and tenants, the questions to be asked are:

1. Did the landlord have an unusually favored bargaining position?
2. Was the lease given on a "take-it-or-leave-it" basis?
3. Are the terms unfair to the tenant?

Examples of unconscionable leases are those charging double rent or requiring an unusually long lease term.

Under the URLTA, it is unconscionable for a landlord to eliminate any of the rights given to tenants under the URLTA. For example, it would be unconscionable for a landlord to eliminate the repair and deduct (self-help) provisions of the URLTA. It is also unconscionable to eliminate the statutory maximums on security deposits.

Exculpatory clauses **Exculpatory clauses** are those protecting a landlord from liability for tenants' injuries or damages during the course of a lease. In effect, these clauses say that landlords are not responsible for any problems that occur. Such clauses are generally not valid in other contracts and are, of course, not valid in leases. Landlords cannot hold themselves harmless for their own negligence. Exculpatory clauses are unconscionable but do not make the entire contract unconscionable. They are simply taken out of the lease agreement.

HOW DOES A LEASE END?

The way a lease ends will determine what obligations and rights the parties have to each other.

The Natural Way: The Lease Ends

The easiest and most liability-proof way for a lease to end is for both parties to fulfill their obligations and end the lease according to the agreement. When this termination occurs, everyone is released from all liability.

The Breach Method: Nonpayment of Rent

If a tenant does not pay rent, the landlord can treat the nonpayment as a breach. As mentioned earlier, the landlord is required under the URLTA to give notice and allow a certain amount of time to pass before the tenant can be evicted. To have the tenant removed from the leased property, the landlord brings a special court action called a **forcible detainer** in most states. The landlord proves that there has not been a rental payment and that the proper amount of time has passed. The court issues an eviction order that is served to the tenant. If the tenant refuses to leave, the sheriff or constable can enforce eviction.

The Breach Method: Uninhabitable Premises

When the landlord has not repaired problems and defects that make the leased property unliveable (uninhabitable), the tenant can claim constructive eviction. The elements for constructive eviction were discussed earlier. If there has been a constructive eviction, the tenant no longer has any obligations under the lease. In addition, the landlord may be liable to the tenant for any damages that have resulted from the constructive eviction. Damages could include the cost of a hotel or motel room used until a new rental property is found. Also included as tenant damages would be the costs of repairing or replacing a tenant's damaged personal property. For example, if two inches of water damaged the tenant's furniture, the landlord would be liable for repair or replacement.

The Breach Method: Tenant Abandonment

Abandonment occurs when a tenant leaves the leased property before the lease expires. The landlord will have suffered damages that can be collected from the tenant. As mentioned earlier, the landlord can keep the security deposit as liquidated damages or can collect actual damages. Actual damages would be the lost rent. If the property goes unleased for the remainder of the lease, the landlord can collect the rent from the tenant even though the tenant was not in possession. The tenant pays the rent for the time required to re-rent the property up until the lease term expires.

The Destruction Method: Loss of the Property

Sometimes the leased property is destroyed by fire, earthquake, tornado, hurricane, or any other "act of God." When any of these problems occur, the landlord and tenant are excused from performance. The destruction of rental property is a defense of impossibility, since the lease cannot be performed if the leased property does not exist.

KEY TERMS

Tenancy for years
Tenancy for a period
Periodic tenancy
Tenancy at will
Tenancy at sufferance
Security deposit
Implied warranty of habitability
Assignment
Sublease
Repair and deduct
Self-help
Constructive eviction
Exculpatory clauses
Forcible detainer

CHAPTER PROBLEMS

1. Park Hill Terrace Associates owned a 100-unit apartment complex in the Borough of Fort Lee, New Jersey. Their form lease agreement for the units provides that even if air conditioning, water, heat, and hot water are not available, the tenants are still expected to pay rent.

   In May 1975, the air conditioning in the building was not working. Glennon and other tenants notified Park Hill, but no repairs were made. In August, Glennon and 52 other tenants withheld 20% of their rent. They withheld 20% because an expert told them that figure is what an apartment like theirs without air conditioning would rent for.

   Park Hill brought an action to have them all evicted for nonpayment of rent. Park Hill said the apartments were still habitable. Glennon and the others said the unusual heat and the close quarters made their apartments unlivable. Who will win? *Park Hill Terrace Associates v. Glennon,* et al. 369 A.2d 938 (N.J. 1977).

2. The following clause appears in a lease. Is it valid?

   The landlord shall not be liable to the tenant for any damage or inconvenience to person, family, or property.

3. Garcia lived in a tenement house in the East Harlem section of Manhattan with his two young children. The paint was peeling off the walls, and Garcia noticed that his children were eating it. The peeling paint contained lead and could be deadly to the children.

   Garcia asked his landlord to repaint the apartment a number of times but was turned down. He bought paint and did the painting himself. He wanted to recover the cost of the paint ($29.53) and his labor ($70). He wanted to deduct the amount from his rent. Can he do it? *Garcia v. Freeland Realty,* 314 N.Y.S.2d 215 (1972).

4. Alice Ireland leased an apartment from Marini. The toilet in the apartment did not work and Alice asked several times to have the toilet repaired. Marini refused, and Alice had the toilet repaired and deducted the cost of repair from her rent. Marini tried to have her evicted for nonpayment of rent. Who wins? *Marini v. Ireland,* 265 A.2d 526 (N.J. 1970).

5. What are the differences between an assignment and a sublease?

6. Name the type of tenancy created in the following examples:
   a. An oral agreement to pay rent every thirty days with no ending date given.
   b. An oral agreement for a three-year lease with rent to be paid every thirty days.
   c. An oral agreement to rent property for as long as the parties wanted. Either party could end the lease at any time.

7. Is an apartment rule that prohibits stereo playing between the hours of 10 P.M. and 6 A.M. valid?

8. What effect will existing building code violations have on the validity of a lease agreement? *Brown v. Southall Realty,* 237 A.2d 834 (D.C. 1968).

*9. Would the shut-down of an elevator in a thirty-five-story apartment complex for retirees involve constructive eviction?

*10. Margaret Skinner owned two adjacent pieces of land. She lived on one and leased the other to Bud Wellington. The Bradys lived on the other side of the land occupied by Wellington. Skinner gave Wellington permission to keep two mules on his property. Arthur Brady, Jr., was kicked by one of the mules and filed suit against landlord Skinner for her failure to maintain safe property. Will he win? *Brady v. Skinner,* 646 P.2d 310 (Ariz. 1982).

Chapter 50

Wills, Estates, and Trusts

CHAPTER PREVIEW

- Ways to transfer property after death
- Intestate succession—who and how much
- Requirements for a valid will
- Probate
- Trusts

John D. Lynch, Jr., died on January 9, 1980. He left a will, a wife (Lillian), two daughters (Virginia Lucille and Mary Louise), and thirteen grandchildren. He left his car, his home, and his personal effects and household goods to Lillian. He left the bulk of his estate to one of his grandchildren. Lillian, Virginia, and Mary are upset about being left out. They want the will set aside. What will happen?

"Bad news, I'm afraid—the fourteen cats are contesting the will."

Death does not end property ownership. When people die, they still own their property. The task left for the courts when someone dies is to award title to the property to other people. The courts can follow the instructions of the deceased person left in a will. If there is no will, the courts follow the directions given by statute in each state for passing along the property.

This chapter covers the three ways property can be transferred at death: by statute (intestate succession), by will, and by trust. All of the requirements for each of these methods are important to understand.

THE MEANING AND LANGUAGE OF PROPERTY TRANSFERS

Words Describing the Property Owner

The property owner is the one who has died. This person can have several names during the transfer process. Frequently used terms are **deceased** and **decedent.** If the decedent died and left a will, the term used is **testator** (for males) and **testatrix** (for females). If the owner died and didn't leave a will, the word **intestate** is sometimes used to describe the owner.

Words Describing the Recipients

The recipients are the ones who get the property. Their names also vary depending upon whether a will exists. Those who take property from an intestate are called **heirs.** The **Uniform Probate Code (UPC)** uses the term issue. **Issue** includes all lineal descendants of the deceased. Lineal descendants are children, grandchildren, and great-grandchildren. Those who receive property under a will are called **devisees, legatees,** or **beneficiaries.** The name used for the recipient will depend upon the type of property involved (see next section).

Words Describing Property

The property being transferred is sometimes called a gift. But there are some specific words for each type of transferred property. For example, a gift of real property is called a **devise.** A gift of money is called a **legacy.** Any gift of personal property is called a **bequest.** Bequest is a general term that includes legacies.

TRANSFER BY STATUTE: INTESTATE SUCCESSION

Property is transferred by statute when the owner has died and made no other arrangements such as a will or trust to transfer the property. Each state has its own scheme for intestate succession. About one-third of the states have adopted the UPC, which has sections covering intestate succession. Even those states that follow the UPC have made some individual changes in the intestate sections. Some states' rules are similar, but very few are identical.

The intestacy statutes divide relatives into groups and give them an order of priority. Property is distributed according to that priority. For example, the UPC has the classes of surviving spouse, issue, parents, issue of parents, grandparents, and issue of grandparents. Some states also base their distributions on the type of property; personal property rules are different than real property rules.

Transferring Property When There Is a Surviving Spouse

The surviving spouse will always receive something under all state intestate statutes. Under the UPC, a spouse with issue gets one-half of the property, and the issue get the other one-half. (Remember that issue means all natural or adopted children of the decedent and their issue. For example, children and grandchildren and great-grandchildren are all issue.) How much the spouse will get depends on what other categories of relatives are alive. For example, if there are a surviving spouse and parents of the decedent, but no issue, the parents may get one-half of the property, and the spouse may get the other one half.

Transferring Property When There Are Issue

If there is no spouse but issue, the intestate distribution of the property changes. For example, under the UPC, if there are issue, the issue take all the property.

Transferring Property When There Are No Issue and No Spouse

The next category in most states and under the UPC will be the parents. If the decedent did not leave a spouse or issue, all the property is given to the parents under the UPC. The UPC also provides that if the parents are not alive but the parents have issue (the brothers and sisters of the decedent), the property will go to the issue. Some states divide the property equally among the parents and the issue.

Transferring Property When There Are No Issue, No Spouse, No Parents, and No Brothers or Sisters

At this point, the states' rules become very different. The UPC gives the property to the grandparents: one-half to the maternal grandparents (mother's parents) and one-half to the paternal grandparents (father's parents). The UPC will give the property to the issue (aunts and uncles) of the grandparents if the grandparents are not alive.

Transferring Property When There Are No Issue, No Spouse, No Parents, No Brothers or Sisters, No Grandparents, No Aunts, No Uncles, and No Cousins: No Heirs

Some states will seek out more distant relatives such as second or third cousins. The UPC provides that the property "escheats," or goes to the state. Other states may go through more distant relatives before escheat, but the ending point in all intestate distributions is escheat. Figure 50-1 is a summary of how intestacy works under the UPC.

Rules Among the Classes of Heirs: Who Gets How Much?

Who is included in each class? Since the terms "heir" and "issue" are general, there are usually specific questions about exactly who is included in these groups. For example, adopted children are treated as heirs and issue of their families. Illegitimate children are treated as members of their mothers' families. They can be treated as members of their fathers' families if their fathers adopt them or are legally declared their fathers.

Other heirs that can raise questions about distributing the decedent's property are **posthumous** (after death) children. These children are conceived before the decedent's death but not born until afterwards. Posthumous children are included as heirs and issue.

The definition of spouse can be another problem for courts. In some states, divorce stops the rights of the ex-spouse but in others the ex-spouse is still included—especially when there are children.

Who is excluded from the classes? Most states and the UPC require heirs to survive the decedent for a period of time to be able to get their share of the property. For example, the UPC requires heirs to survive for 120 hours after the death of the decedent.

Many states have passed the **Uniform Simultaneous Death Act (USDA).** This act takes care of problems resulting from the death of two people at the same time such as in a car or plane crash. For example, if a married couple is killed in the same crash, who will receive their property? The USDA provides that if it is impossible to tell the order of death, the property goes to the next class. For

Figure 50-1 **Intestate Distribution under the UPC**

CONTINGENCY	SPOUSE	ISSUE	PARENTS	PARENTS' ISSUE	GRANDPARENTS AND ISSUE	STATE
1	1/2	NS*	1/2	0†	0	0
2	1/2	1/2	0	0	0	0
3	NS	All	0	0	0	0
4	NS	NS	All	0	0	0
5	NS	NS	NS	All	0	0
6	NS	NS	NS	NS	All‡	0
7	NS	NS	NS	NS	NS	All

*NS = None surviving.
†0 = No intestate share.
‡One-half of the property would go to the maternal grandparents and one-half to the paternal grandparents. If there were only maternal grandparents or vice versa, the surviving grandparents and issue take all of the property.

example, each spouse's property would go to his or her issue. Under the USDA, the property does not have to first go to the other spouse and then to the issue.

Most states exclude those who murder the decedent from the group of heirs or issue. If it were not for this exception, murderers would have great incentive to do away with their relatives.

How is property divided among the heirs? All states and the UPC have rules for dividing up the property among the members of the group entitled to receive it. States follow any one or combination of three ways to distribute property. The first is called per capita, the second is called per stirpes, and the third is the UPC method called representation.

1. Per capita distribution. A **per capita** distribution means that everyone who is entitled to inherit gets an equal share of the property. A per capita distribution does not distinguish between children and grandchildren. All are treated as one class of heirs, and each gets an equal share.
2. Per stirpes. Under the **per stirpes** formula for distribution, the amount heirs receive will depend on their degree of relationship to the decedent. Grandchildren receive less than children. For example, suppose that Agnes has died and has no surviving spouse. She has two children, Althea and Abby, and four grandchildren: Alan (son of Althea); Alfred (son of Abby); and Alice and Anne (daughters of a deceased daughter, Allison). In a per capita distribution, Althea, Abby, Alice, and Anne would get an equal share: one-fourth. In per stirpes, Althea and Abby each get one-third and Alice and Anne will split one-third (that is, each gets one-sixth). See Figure 50-2.

Figure 50-2 **Division of Property According to Per Capita, Per Stirpes, and UPC Representation**

PER CAPITA

Agnes

Abby $4000 — Althea $4000 — Allison

Alfred — Alan — Anne $4000 — Alice $4000

PER STIRPES

Agnes

Abby $8000 — Althea — Allison

Alfred — Alan $8000 — Anne $4000 — Alice $4000

UPC REPRESENTATION

Agnes

Abby $8000 — Althea — Allison

Alfred — Alan $5333.33 — Anne $5333.33 — Alice $5333.33

3. UPC: by representation. The UPC formula for distribution is a combination of per capita and per stirpes. The formula has been called a per capita distribution at each generation formula (each generation gets an equal share). For example, suppose that the situation describing Agnes is the same except that Althea has also died. Under per stirpes, Abby would get one-third of the property, Alan would get one-third, and Alice and Anne would split one-third. Under the UPC, Abby would get one-third of the property, and Alice, Anne, and Alan would share equally the remaining two-thirds. Under the UPC, all three would get one-third of two-thirds. For example, if the estate was $24,000, under per stirpes, Abby and Alan would each get $8000, and Alice and Anne would each get $4000. Under the UPC, Abby would get $8000 and Alan, Alice, and Anne would each get one-third of $16,000 or $5,333.33. Figure 50-2 is a diagram of the problem and the results.

Deductions from gifts: Advancements Common law recognizes advancements. Advancements are gifts made by the deceased while he or she was alive to those who are later designated as heirs. These advancements must be deducted from the heir's share of the property. For example, if Agnes had given Abby a $2000 gift while she was alive, Abby would get $2000 less of the property when Agnes died. The UPC does not recognize advancements but some states do.

LEAVING INSTRUCTIONS FOR TRANSFERRING PROPERTY AT DEATH: WILLS

Wills are instructions for transferring property. They must be developed before death. Wills can take different forms and have different requirements. But they have the same purpose of indicating who will receive the deceased's property.

Types of Wills

There are three types of wills: **nuncupative** (or oral) wills, **holographic** (or handwritten) wills, and **written** (or formal) wills.

Nuncupative (or oral) wills Oral wills are only recognized in some states and are not valid under the UPC. Even in the states in which they are valid, these wills can create problems. Relying on memory to determine what the decedent wanted is difficult. In states allowing nuncupative wills, witnesses are usually required. Some states limit the types of property that can be transferred through a nuncupative will.

Holographic (or handwritten) wills The UPC and many states recognize holographic wills as valid. The UPC requires that the will be written in the testator's handwriting and that it be signed by the testator. Some states require witnesses for a valid holographic will but the UPC does not.

Written (or formal) wills These are the wills usually drafted by attorneys and formally signed in a ceremony with witnesses. These wills are the safest way to transfer property.

Requirements for a Valid Formal Will

Writing Valid formal wills must be in writing. This requirement goes back to the 1540 Statute of Wills that was passed to prevent unjustified claims for deceased persons' property. All states require that there be a signature of the testator as part of the writing. The signature can even be an "X." Under the UPC and in most states, a testator who is unable to sign because of disease or hospital equipment can have someone else sign. This proxy signature is valid so long as the testator directed the signature. The *In re Estate of Hobelsberger* case is one in which there was a question concerning a signature on a will.

IN RE ESTATE OF HOBELSBERGER

Supreme Court of South Dakota.
181 N.W.2d 455 (1970).

FACTS John Hobelsberger suffered a heart attack and was recovering in a nursing home. He was unable to move, and had an IV and several other tubes hooked to his arm and mouth. He asked his attorney to come to the home. He told his attorney to draw up a will and gave instructions on how he wanted his property distributed.

Hobelsberger had twenty-seven nieces and nephews and seven grandnieces and nephews. He did not leave property to all of them—only to the ones he was close to.

His attorney returned with his secretary and read the will to Hobelsberger. Hobelsberger said this final will was what he wanted. He could not move and had trouble signing. The attorney's secretary (at Hobelsberger's request) held Hobelsberger's hand and helped him move the pen across the will.

Hobelsberger died shortly thereafter. Nine nieces and nephews contested the will as invalid because the signature was improper. The trial court held the signature was valid, and the nieces and nephews appealed.

ISSUE Was the signature proper?

DECISION Yes. It was clear Hobelsberger wanted the will as stated. It was also clear that he was physically incapable of signing it. The secretary helped only at his request. He had also had trouble signing his checks and had asked for help on those from others.

LEGAL TIP
A will should be executed before illness and physical disability become a problem.

Capacity Capacity means that the testator has reached the age of majority. Under the UPC, the age is eighteen. It also means that the testator has mental capacity. Many wills begin by stating that the testator is of "sound mind." Sound mind and mental capacity do not mean that the testator must be intelligent, logical, or reasonable or leave property only to relatives. Old age and eccentric behavior do not necessarily mean the absence of mental capacity. Mental capacity means the testator meets these requirements:

1. The testator knows the nature and extent of his or her property—including the property's extent and value.
2. The testator knows his or her family members and who would usually get the property.
3. The testator understands whom he or she is giving the property to.
4. The testator can give the property away in an orderly distribution.

Every testamentary capacity case has a different set of colorful facts. The *In re Estate of Morton* case is only one of the many interesting examples.

IN RE ESTATE OF MORTON

Supreme Court of Wyoming.
428 P.2d 725 (Wyo. 1967).

FACTS Robert Morton's wife died in 1956. They had no children, and Morton went to live at the Pioneer Hotel. He was suffering from diabetes and arteriosclerosis and took medication for both.

Melvin Condron, the owner of the Pioneer Hotel, said that Morton would often come back from walks with his pants soiled because he had voided in public. Condron would send the pants to the cleaners, and Morton would call the police to report his pants had been stolen. During his time at the hotel, Morton slowly forgot how to play checkers. He insisted that he had money problems. He often forgot to pay his rent or would offer to pay it again when he had already paid.

Walter Jensen, the manager of the Cheyenne Credit Bureau, said that Morton often lost money to con men. He also said that Morton changed his mind about matters from day to day.

In 1960, Morton executed a will that left his property to a friend, Emilio, and to the First Presbyterian Church. He was 85 when he executed the will.

Morton died in 1965, and the will was offered for probate. He had an estate of $55,000. Morton's only heirs—two nephews—challenged the will on the grounds that Morton did not have mental capacity. Morton had given each of them $1000 in the will. The trial court held he did have capacity. The disinherited nephews appealed.

ISSUE Did Morton have mental capacity at the time he made the will?

DECISION Yes. Morton was unclean, untidy, forgetful, aging, and seriously ill. However, Emilio had been a lifelong friend, and Morton's wife had been active in the First Presbyterian Church. He understood who was getting his property and had reason to give it to them. The nephews had barely paid attention to Morton while he was alive. He acknowledged them by giving them a token amount, so he knew he had family.

LEGAL TIP

A will is a lifelong need. Do not wait until old age to make one.

Witnesses All states require that a will be witnessed. The number of witnesses required and who can be a witness varies from state to state. The number of witnesses required is two or three, depending on the state. The UPC requires two witnesses. Some states, but not the UPC, require that the witnesses be disinterested parties. "Disinterested" means that they are not beneficiaries under the will.

Using a notary: The self-proving will The UPC allows testators to execute a self-proving will. A self-proving will is one where the signatures of the testator and the witnesses are notarized. This process is sometimes called an acknowledgement. If a will is acknowledged, the UPC gives a presumption that it is valid. The presumption means that the signatures are genuine and that it is, in fact, the testator's will. The presumption can be challenged but much proof is required.

Changing or Getting Rid of a Will: Revocation

A will is not carved in stone. Testators can change their wills or revoke them any time while they are alive so long as they still have capacity.

Changes by codicil A **codicil** is an addition to a will. It must be executed properly—as if it were a will. Codicils are used to change minor sections of a will such as giving a gift to someone else because the originally named party died.

Changes by destruction: Revocation When a testator physically destroys a will and indicates an intent to abandon it, there is a **revocation** of the will. A will can be destroyed by cutting, tearing, burning or writing "cancelled" or "void" across the will. The *In re Estate of Bancker* case is an example of the effects of destruction.

IN RE ESTATE OF BANCKER

Court of Appeals of Florida.
232 So.2d 431 (1970).

FACTS Adrian C. Bancker executed a will in 1962 and then amended it with a 1965 codicil. In 1966, Bancker executed a new will. Six months after executing the new will, he decided he did not like it. He called the attorney who had drafted the 1962 will and asked him what to do. The attorney told him to destroy the 1966 will to reinstate the 1962 will.

Bancker was bedridden, but he told his wife and stepdaughter to take the will from the safe in the den and burn it. Bancker never saw them do it, but the 1966 will was never found.

Bancker died in 1967 and his wife offered the 1962 will for probate. The will was found invalid for several reasons. She then tried to offer a copy of the 1966 will for probate. The trial court held the will had been revoked. Mrs. Bancker appealed.

ISSUE Was the 1966 will revoked?

DECISION No. The 1966 will was destroyed but Bancker had it destroyed assuming the 1962 will was valid. His intent to destroy was conditioned upon that assumption. If the 1962 will was not valid, Bancker wanted some will to exist. Without the intent to revoke, the physical destruction does not control.

LEGAL TIP

It is risky to have several wills and no clear intent. There should always be just one valid will.

Revocation by a new will As the Banker case shows, an old will is revoked by a new will. It is a good idea to destroy the old will when a new valid will is executed. The new will should also state that all old wills and codicils are revoked.

Revocation by changes in circumstances: Operation of law The law has some rules that change the effect of wills. For example, many states provide that divorce revokes any gifts to the ex-spouse in either spouse's will. Most states have protections for pretermitted children in their revocation sections. **Pretermitted children** are children born after a will is executed. Most states require that these children receive the same portion of the estate as the other children or that they be given their intestate share. Most states also prohibit testators from disinheriting certain family members. Spouses and children are entitled to a certain share of the estate in all states. A will that gives everything away to others is at least partially revoked to give the spouse and children their shares.

THE ADMINISTRATION OF WILLS AND ESTATES: PROBATE

Probate is made up of all the legal proceedings required to transfer a decedent's property. Probate does everything from determining whether there was a valid will to distributing the property.

Putting Someone in Charge of Probate

Every probate has someone who is put in charge. This person appears in court for all hearings, does all the paperwork for the estate, and acts as the estate's representative. There are many names for this person. If there was a will, the person in charge is the **executor** (male) or **executrix** (female). If there was no will, the person in charge is the **administrator** (male) or **administratrix** (female). Under the UPC, the person in charge is always called the **personal representative (PR).**

Who will be appointed to the PR position depends upon whether there was a will. If there was a will, the person named by the decedent is the PR. If there was no will, each state has a statute that lists who is entitled to be PR. The first on the list is the surviving spouse.

Admitting the Will to Probate

Probate begins with determining whether there was a will and whether the will is valid. Any interested party can file a petition or application to open a probate. All interested parties are notified of the petition or application. Anyone can challenge the will because of an invalid signature, lack of the testator's capacity, or undue influence.

Undue influence for challenging wills is the same as undue influence for challenging contracts. The testator has a confidential relationship with a close friend, relative, or advisor and then that person has the will drafted and executed. The *In re Estate of Malnar* case is one that involves a problem with undue influence.

IN RE ESTATE OF MALNAR

Supreme Court of Wisconsin.
243 N.W.2d 435 (1976).

FACTS Frances Malnar was a 74-year-old widow who was suffering from advanced liver disease. Frances could speak very little English and could write only her name. She had no children but had a sister in Yugoslavia, and several nieces and nephews in the United States. She kept in touch with them.

In 1971 she executed a will that left everything to her nieces and nephews and a $100 gift to a Catholic church.

She became quite ill in 1972 and was in and out of the hospital. Genevieve Malnar, the wife of one of Frances' husband's nephews, began to help her. Genevieve took her to the doctor, got her groceries for her, visited her 2 to 3 times per month, and phoned her daily.

In July 1972, Frances gave Genevieve a power of attorney. Genevieve used it to open a checking account and paid Frances' bills.

In June 1973, Frances was hospitalized. She remained there until her death. In July 1973, Genevieve brought her mother's attorney to the hospital. Frances had used a different attorney for the 1971 will. The new attorney drafted a will with Genevieve as the sole beneficiary.

When the will was executed, Frances was too ill to sign, so Genevieve helped her make an "X" for a signature.

When Frances died, Genevieve offered the will for probate. The nieces and nephews challenged the will on the basis of undue influence.

ISSUE Was there undue influence?

DECISION Yes. Genevieve had gained a position of trust. She forced the execution of the will. She brought the attorney to the hospital, had the will drafted, and even helped with the signature. She had gained so much control that Frances, in her weak condition, could not have objected.

LEGAL TIP

Check on elderly and ill relatives to make sure no one is taking advantage of their dependent positions.

Getting the Property Together

Once the PR is appointed, he or she begins the job of gathering all the property in the estate. The PR is required to develop an inventory. The PR must also collect any debts owed to the decedent and finalize any business transactions.

Distributing the Property to Creditors and Beneficiaries

During the time the inventory is being done, the creditors are given notice, and notice of the probate is published. The creditors are required to submit their claims to the PR. The PR reviews all the claims and decides which ones are proper and will be paid and which will be disallowed.

Once the creditors are paid, the PR has the job of distributing the property. If there is a will, the property is distributed according to those instructions. If there is no will, the rules of intestate distribution are followed. Under the UPC and in most states, the PR is required to submit to the court a proposal for distribution before the distribution is made. This gives the parties a chance to object to any errors the PR might have made.

TRANSFERRING PROPERTY BY TRUST

A trust is a three-party relationship. The party who sets up the trust and transfers the property to the trust is called the settlor/trustor. The party who benefits from the trust is the beneficiary. The third party who is put in charge of the property is the trustee. Trusts are a way to transfer funds and properties to others after death in a controlled way. For example, trusts are set up as college funds or income funds for spouses. In a college trust fund, the child does not get $50,000 immediately for college. But a trust can provide $50,000 of income over the four years it takes to earn the degree.

The Elements Required for a Trust

There are five elements required to create a trust. Reduced to a minimum they are: transfer, res, settlor, trustee, and beneficiary.

The transfer A transfer of property to a trust can be while the owner is alive or can be done by will. But the property ownership must be transferred to the trustee. If the trust is set up as a gift, all the requirements for a gift must be met—including delivery. The property must be delivered to the trustee with the intent to give it to the trustee.

Trust res or corpus The trust must have some property in it. The property can be cash or real, personal, tangible, or intangible personal property. This property is called the trust **res** or **corpus.** The res or corpus must be some present interest in income or property. An expectation of profits given to set up a trust has no res or corpus and would not be valid. Transferring an orchard to a trust for one year is a trust res. Transferring the profits from the sales from the orchard for the next year is not a trust res.

The settlor The **settlor** must own the property, have the right to transfer it to the trust res, and have the capacity to do so. Once the property is transferred to the trustee, the settlor is really no longer involved.

The trustee A third party to handle the property must be appointed. This third party is a **trustee** who will hold legal title to the property. The trustee can be any natural person or legal entity with capacity. A corporation can be a trustee. The trustee can also be the settlor or the beneficiary. The settlor decides who plays the role of trustee.

Beneficiaries The ideas of a trust is to benefit someone. A trust must have beneficiaries. The beneficiaries must be named or at least be determinable from the trust document. Some trusts name groups as beneficiaries. This type of trust is valid so long as the courts can determine who goes in the group. For example, a trust "for my employees" is definite, but a trust created "for my friends" is too indefinite.

Most of the cases involving a problem with this element deal with **charitable trusts.** In these cases, people often have good intentions but are not definite enough. The courts do try to find beneficiaries for trusts set up for the good of the community. A trust formed "for charity" or "for the relief of poverty" will still be enforced. The court will be left with the task of giving out the funds. Figure 50-3 is a diagram of the elements of a trust and the relationships of the parties.

Types of Trusts

Totten trust A **Totten trust** is one that is known to many people but probably not known by name. A payable-on-death (POD) account at a bank is a form of a Totten trust. The settlor starts an account that is joint and will be paid to the joint payee when the settlor dies. But the settlor has the right while he or she is alive to deposit and withdraw from the account. This type of trust is typically used by parents with their children named as the joint account holder.

Charitable trusts A charitable trust is any trust set up to benefit the human race in some way. The trust must name beneficiaries but, as was discussed earlier, the beneficiary group can be broad.

Spendthrift trusts Spendthrift trusts are trusts for beneficiaries who have trouble handling money. A spendthrift trust prohibits creditors of the beneficiary from

Figure 50-3 **The Trust Relationship**

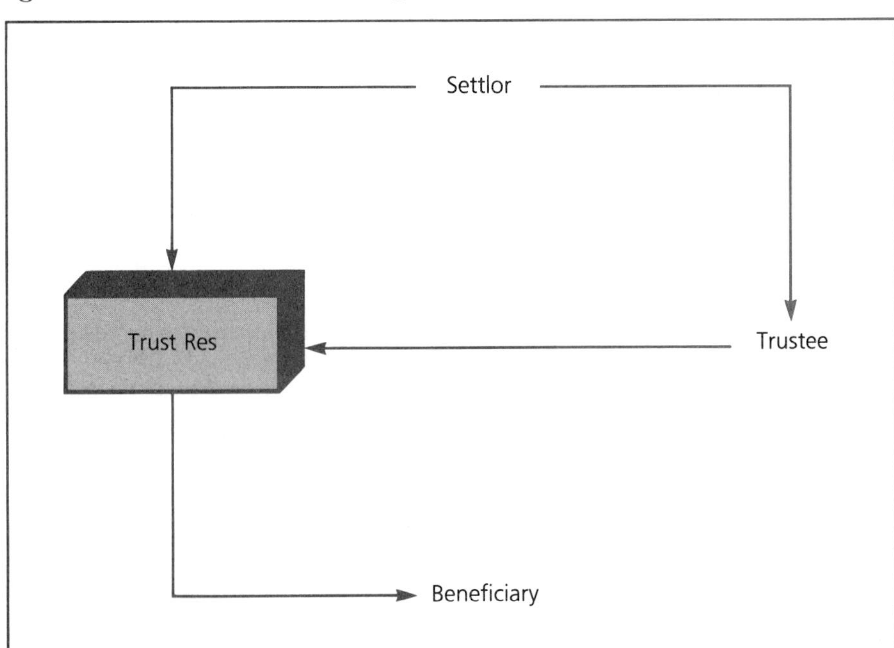

getting to the trust funds. A spendthrift trust also prevents a beneficiary from signing away his or her rights to receive income from the trust or the res.

Express trusts Express trusts are those created by express language of the settlor. A trust created in a will is an example of an express trust.

Implied trust An implied trust is a creature of the courts. In the best interests of the parties, courts sometimes create trusts to protect those interests. When a corporate director breaches the corporate opportunity doctrine, a constructive (or implied) trust is imposed on the profits earned (see Chapter 43 for a complete discussion of the corporate opportunity doctrine).

Management of the Trust

Once the trust res is transferred, the trustee has the responsibility of managing the property. The trustee has a fiduciary relationship to the beneficiaries. **Fiduciary** means that the trustee is in a position of trust and responsibility. The trustee is required to act in the beneficiaries' best interests.

The trustee has the duty to act as a reasonable person would in managing his or her own financial affairs. The reasonable person standard is also imposed. The trustee can hire help so long as the help is chosen prudently.

The trustee's duty is to the beneficiaries. The trustee cannot be involved in self-enrichment at the expense of the trust or the beneficiaries.

Ending a Trust

Once a trust is begun, it generally cannot be revoked. A trust ends at the time the trust documents specify. A trust without an ending date ends when the purpose is accomplished. For example, a college trust may not have an ending date, since it could take longer then four years to graduate. But the trust will end when the beneficiary graduates from college.

KEY TERMS

Deceased
Decedent
Testator
Testatrix
Intestate
Heirs
Uniform Probate Code (UPC)
Issue
Devisees
Legatees
Beneficiaries
Devise
Legacy
Bequest
Posthumous
Uniform Simultaneous Death Act (USDA)
Per capita
Per stirpes
Nuncupative wills
Holographic wills
Written wills
Codicil
Revocation
Pretermitted children
Probate
Executor
Executrix
Administrator
Administratrix
Personal representative (PR)
Res
Corpus
Settlor
Trustee
Charitable trusts
Totten trust
Fiduciary

CHAPTER PROBLEMS

1. Ralph has died a widower. He has left behind three sons: Richard, Robert, and Ronald. He has also left behind four grandchildren: Ricky (the son of Richard); Ryan (the son of Robert); and Rollins and Rory (sons of a deceased son Roger). Ralph did not leave a will. How would his property be distributed on a per capita basis? On a per stirpes basis? Under the UPC?
2. Suppose the same facts exist as in the above problem, except that Richard also died before Ralph. Determine the property distribution under all three systems.
3. Maude Perkins executed a will in 1965 that left her property to the Christian Church of Holton, Kansas. This will revoked an earlier will that had left all her property to her nephew. At the time she executed the will, she had trouble recognizing people and could not remember names. When she went to see her doctor, she would often forget why she had come and would just return home. She could not remember which bank had her money or how much she had. She suffered from cerebral arteriosclerosis.

   When the will was offered for probate, the nephew challenged it by saying his aunt did not have capacity. Is he right? *In re Estate of Perkins,* 504 P.2d 564 (Kans. 1972).
4. Grace Supplee executed a will on July 29, 1965. The will left everything to her brother, her niece, and her stepdaughter. The will was executed after Grace had several heart attacks and after the court had appointed a guardian for her. Grace told all her neighbors that her stepdaughter was to get all the property. She also told the stepdaughter. When the will was offered for probate, Grace's stepdaughter challenged it. Will she win? *In re Estate of Supplee,* 247 So.2d 488 (Fla. 1971).
5. Maye Elizabeth Ramage Davis wrote an unsigned holographic will that left everything to the Texarkana Historical Society and Museum. The only words at the end of the will were, "I am in my sane mind today." Is the will valid? *Nelson v. Texarkana Historical Society and Museum,* 516 S.W.2d 882 (Ark. 1974).
6. Treitinger was eighty-five years old and nearly blind when he had his will drawn up. A nurse helped him make an "X" on the signature line. The will was witnessed. Is it valid?
7. The partners of attorney Joseph Berzin served as witnesses on the will of Olive Meskimen. The will left 10% of the property to Berzin. When the will was offered for probate, Olive's husband challenged it on the grounds that the witnesses were not disinterested. What is the result? *In re Estate of Meskimen,* 228 N.E.2d 255 (Ill. 1967).
8. George Baxter Gordon executed a will in which he left all of his property to the Church of Christ of New Boston, Texas. Two church members witnessed the will. Is the will valid? *In re Estate of Gordon,* 519 S.W.2d 902 (Tex. 1975).

*9. Speelman transferred 5% of his share of the profits from the stage and movie production of "My Fair Lady." Speelman had purchased the rights, but the play and movie had not yet been produced. The transfer was made to a trustee and these rights were the sole asset of the trust. Is there a res? *Speelman v. Pascal,* 178 N.E.2d 723 (N.Y. 1961).

*10. Can the settlor also be the trustee? Who is the trustee in a Totten trust?

Part Eight

Commercial Paper

"What we need are couriers without luggage."
Karl Llewlyn discussing commercial paper

Chapter 51

Commercial Paper: The Basic Concepts

CHAPTER PREVIEW

- Importance of commercial paper
- Types of commercial paper
- Differences between order and bearer paper
- Differences between promises to pay and orders to pay
- Requirements for negotiability
- Requirements affecting negotiability
- Agents' liability on negotiable instruments

On demand, Queensmarble, Inc. promises to pay to the order of David B. Johnson, John G. Mutschler, Arthur Bunker, and Fred H. Metcalf ten thousand dollars and no cents, payable at Minneapolis, Minnesota, value received with interest before and after maturity at the rate of 6½% per annum.

Queensmarble, Inc.
/s/ Edward J. O'Donnell
/s/ Kent A. Larson
/s/ Byron W. Sams

Commercial paper is a general term used to describe **checks, drafts,** and **promissory notes.** Commercial paper is a creation of the business world. Commercial paper provides a simple method of payment and allows business to operate without cash payment. Commercial paper allows business to involve others in financing a transaction. In this chapter, the following questions are answered: What laws govern commercial paper? What are the purposes of commercial paper? What types of commercial paper exist? What is negotiable commercial paper? How is negotiable commercial paper created?

INTRODUCTION AND HISTORY

Commercial paper makes business easier. Because of this benefit, commercial paper has been around about as long as business. In 1300, English merchants used commercial paper to simplify their transactions with foreign businesses. Notes were in use in English business transactions as early as 1600. By the 1700's, English courts had developed a great deal of law to deal with commercial paper issues. In the United States, the first national law—the Uniform Negotiable Instruments Law—was drafted in 1898. By 1924, all the states had adopted it as law. Uniform laws for commercial paper existed before uniform laws for sales.

When the Uniform Commercial Code (UCC) was drafted, Articles III and IV were devoted to the topics of commercial paper. These Articles of the Code have been adopted in all states (even Louisiana, which has avoided Article II).

THE LAWS OF COMMERCIAL PAPER: ARTICLES III AND IV

Article III governs the issues surrounding "commercial paper," which includes drafts, notes, and checks. No rules indicate when Article III applies, but there are rules for when Article III does not apply. Under Section 3-103, Article III does not apply to money, documents of title, or investment securities.

Article IV is the bank article and governs checks and their collection. Article IV also governs the relationship between banks and their customers. Banks are also subject to the Article III sections that deal with checks and drafts.

COMMERCIAL PAPER: REASONS AND ADVANTAGES

There are four basic reasons for the rise and continued use of commercial paper. These four reasons can be found in the next four subsections.

A Cash Substitute: Float, Safety, and Financing

Commercial paper is a substitute for cash. For example, instead of paying $100 in ten $10 bills, the buyer writes one check for $100. Cash is easily stolen and passed along. Stolen commercial paper can be traced, so there is a safety factor in its use. Checks provide record-keeping systems for businesses and individuals, whereas cash purchases are difficult to record and document.

Commercial paper also gives buyers the benefit of "floating funds." If a cash payment is made, the money is gone. If a payment is made by check, the money is not actually gone until the bank debits the buyer's account. The buyer may have several days to work with funds not yet withdrawn from the account.

The note and time draft forms of commercial paper also give the buyer an easy form of financing for a transaction. The financing is between two parties and the problems of loan approval are avoided. Times for repayment can be set up by the parties. Using commercial paper for financing a transaction gives the parties flexibility.

Control over the Goods: Bills of Lading

Combining commercial paper with bills of lading gives sellers a way to ensure payment and control delivery of goods. A bill of lading is a document that is given by a shipper. The shipper gives the seller the bill of lading and keeps a copy. No one can pick up the goods unless they have the bill of lading from the seller.

The seller can use the bill of lading along with a draft to make sure the buyer pays before getting the goods. The seller can send the bill of lading and draft to the buyer's bank. The buyer's bank will not turn over the bill of lading until the buyer has paid the amount of the draft.

The Ease of Transferability of Commercial Paper

Commercial paper moves quickly and easily through the streams of commerce. This movability can help get cash when needed. For example, the buyer may give the seller a note or time draft to pay for the purchased goods. The seller can wait the thirty, sixty, or ninety days for the buyer to pay, or can pass the note or draft along and get cash immediately. The note or draft can be sold or transferred to a bank or other party. The seller receives the present value of the draft or note, and the other party can await payment. These transfers allow buyers to buy on credit but do not require sellers to wait for payment.

Protection for a Holder in Due Course

The final benefit of using commercial paper is the protection it offers owners. A negotiable note can give its transferees much greater rights than a transferred contract. A transferee or assignee of a contract takes the risk of problems developing or already existing with the contract. But if the transferee of a negotiable instrument is a holder in due course, the risks or problems of a contract are not an issue. A holder in due course is free of these risks and problems (see Chapter 52). Negotiable instruments make it possible for financial transactions to be passed along without the risks of contract problems.

TYPES OF COMMERCIAL PAPER

There are two basic groups of commercial paper: orders to pay and promises to pay.

Orders to Pay

Orders to pay are instruments that direct a third party to pay a certain amount. Checks and drafts are orders to pay. In fact, a check is a draft that is drawn on a bank.

Orders to pay involve three roles. The three parties are the drawer, the drawee, and the payee. For example, suppose that Fisher writes a check to Jennings in the amount of $2000, and Fisher's checking account is with the First National Bank of

Tennessee. Fisher is the **drawer** of the check, or the one who makes up the draft or check and directs who will make payment and to whom. Jennings is the **payee,** or the one who is entitled to the money. The **drawee** is the one who will pay the check—in this case, First National Bank of Tennessee. Figure 51-1 is a sample check.

A draft that is not a check is usually drawn up by the seller. The seller decides who the parties will be. For example, the seller or the seller's bank may be the payee. The buyer will be the drawee—the one who pays. The seller could be both the drawer and the payee, but there are still three roles being played. A seller generally draws a draft so the buyer can pay for the goods. Figure 51-2 is an example of a draft.

Promises to Pay

Promises to pay are two-party arrangements in which one party agrees to pay the other a certain amount. Promissory notes are promises to pay and are usually signed when a bank or other lender gives a loan. Certificates of deposit (CDs) are promises from banks to customers. When customers deposit certain amounts with the bank for a definite period of time, banks promise to pay that amount plus interest.

Promises to pay involve two parties: a maker and a payee. The **payee** is the lender and the **maker** is the borrower, or the one promising to repay the funds. For example, if Western Mortgage Company loans Albie $40,000 to buy a condominium, Albie will be the maker of the $40,000 note and Western will be the payee. Figure 51-3 is an example of a promissory note.

The Odd Pieces of Commercial Paper

There are some instruments that do not fit into the two Article III categories of orders and promises to pay. The courts have dealt with these instruments on a case-by-case basis.

Travelers' checks Travelers' checks are treated as Article III commercial paper, or orders to pay.

Figure 51-1 **Sample Check**

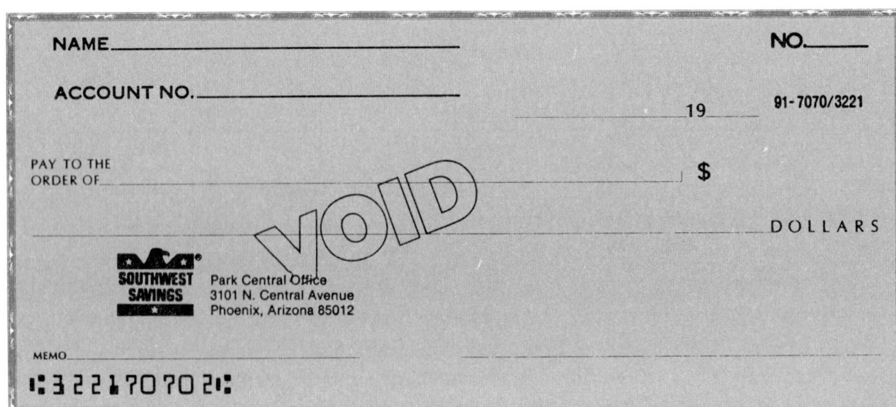

Check appears courtesy of Southwest Savings, Phoenix, Arizona

Figure 51-2 **Sample Draft**

The Sixth National Bank

_______________, New York

No. ____

DATED at _______ this _______ day of _______, 19__. _______ days after sight subject to approval of title. Attachments: ______________________

Pay to the order of ______________ $_______ _______ _______ Dollars.

To ____________

____

THROUGH The Sixth National Bank

_______________, New York

____

Cashier's check These are checks that have a bank (the same bank) as the drawer and the drawee. In other words, the bank writes a check on itself. These checks are governed by Article III.

Money orders Money orders are treated as if they are personal checks under Article III.

Negotiable orders of withdrawal (NOW's) **Negotiable Orders of Withdrawal (NOW's)** are instruments used to withdraw funds from savings accounts. The savings accounts can be in banks, savings and loans, or any other Federal-Reserve-regulated institution. Not all NOWs are checks because not all of them are drawn on banks. Also, those institutions using NOWs can require customers to give fourteen days notice for withdrawal and the NOWs are not payable immediately like a check. Some courts have held that NOW's are not part of Article III. (An example of this type of case is *Pennsylvania Bankers' Assn. v. Secretary of Banking,* 392 A.2d 1319 [Pa. 1978]).

Credit union share drafts **Share drafts** are instruments used to withdraw funds from a credit union account. They look like checks but are not because they are not drawn on a bank. Some courts have also excluded these documents from Article III.

REQUIREMENTS FOR NEGOTIABILITY

To be entitled to the status of a holder in due course, the party with commercial paper must have more than just commercial paper. The commercial paper must be negotiable; a piece of negotiable commercial paper is called a **negotiable**

Figure 51-3 Example of a Promissory Note

SOUTHWEST SAVINGS

NOTE

, Arizona

U.S. $ (Date)

1. FOR VALUE RECEIVED, the undersigned ("Borrower") promise(s) to pay SOUTHWEST SAVINGS AND LOAN ASSOCIATION, a state chartered association, 2933 North Central Avenue, Phoenix, Arizona, or order, the principal sum of

U.S. DOLLARS,

($), with interest on the unpaid principal balance from the date of this Note, until paid, at the rate of percent per annum. Principal and interest shall be payable at 2933 North Central Avenue, Phoenix, Arizona 85012, or such other place as the Note holder may designate, in consecutive monthly installments of

U.S. DOLLARS

($), on the day of each month beginning , 19 . Such monthly installments shall continue until the entire indebtedness evidenced by this Note is fully paid, except that any remaining indebtedness, if not sooner paid, shall be due and payable on ,

2. If any monthly installment under this Note is not paid when due and remains unpaid after a date specified by a notice to Borrower, the entire principal amount outstanding and accrued interest thereon shall at once become due and payable at the option of the Note holder. The date specified shall not be less than thirty days from the date such notice is mailed. The Note holder may exercise this option to accelerate during any default by Borrower regardless of any prior forbearance. If suit is brought to collect this Note, the Note holder shall be entitled to collect all reasonable costs and expenses of suit, including, but not limited to, reasonable attorneys' fees.

3. Borrower shall pay to the Note holder a late charge of percent of any monthly installment not received by the Note holder within days after the installment is due.

4. Borrower may prepay the principal amount outstanding in whole or in part. The Note holder may require that any partial prepayments (i) be made on the date monthly installments are due and (ii) be in the amount of that part of one or more monthly installments which would be applicable to principal. Any partial prepayment shall be applied against the principal amount outstanding and shall not postpone the due date of any subsequent monthly installments or change the amount of such installments, unless the Note holder shall otherwise agree in writing.

5. Presentment, notice of dishonor, and protest are hereby waived by all makers, sureties, guarantors and endorsers hereof. This Note shall be the joint and several obligation of all makers, sureties, guarantors and endorsers, and shall be binding upon them and their successors and assigns.

6. Any notice to Borrower provided for in this Note shall be given by mailing such notice by certified mail addressed to Borrower at the property address stated below, or to such other address as Borrower may designate by notice to the Note holder. Any notice to the Note holder shall be given by mailing such notice by certified mail, return receipt requested, to the Note holder at the address stated in the first paragraph of this Note, or at such other address as may have been designated by notice to Borrower.

7. The indebtedness evidenced by this Note is secured by a Deed of Trust, dated , 19 , and reference is made to the Deed of Trust for rights as to acceleration of the indebtedness evidenced by this Note.

Property Address:

(Street) ______________________

(City, State and Zip Code) ______________________

____

____

Loan Number

ARIZONA — 1 to 4 Family — 6/75 — FNMA/FHLMC UNIFORM INSTRUMENT

Note appears courtesy of Southwest Savings, Phoenix, Arizona

instrument. For commercial paper to be negotiable, six requirements must be met. The six requirements are discussed in the following subsections.

The Writing Requirement of Negotiability

For an instrument to be negotiable, it must be in writing. The form of the writing is not important, so long as there is something physical to represent the instrument. Of course, most banks require customers to use forms (provided by or ordered through the bank) when using their checking accounts. The banks can require these forms but can choose to honor checks written in other forms.

The Signature Requirement of Negotiability

To be negotiable, all instruments must be signed by the maker or drawer (Section 3-104 [1] [a]). Under the UCC, a **signature** is anything put on a document with the intent to "authenticate it" (Section 1-201 [39]). A signature can be handwritten, stamped, or printed. The complete signature is not necessary; initials are enough. The signature does not have to be on any particular part of the instrument.

One interesting problem which relates to signatures is the agency matter. Who is liable when an agent signs an instrument for a principal? Section 3-403 provides the proper method for an agent to sign on behalf of a principal. Agents must sign their principals' names, followed by their signature, followed by their title or role. For example, "Xcore Corporation by John Filbert, VP" is a proper signature for Xcore to be liable on the negotiable instrument. If John Filbert signs any other way, there is the risk that he may be held liable on the instrument. For example, if he signs "John Filbert," then he will be liable. If he signs "John Filbert, VP," then he will be liable but can offer evidence to show his principal is obligated. If he signs "Xcore Corporation, John Filbert," he is liable but, again, can offer evidence to show the corporation's liability. Figure 51-4 summarizes the rules for the liability of agents and principals.

The *Colonial Baking Co. of Des Moines v. Dowie* case involves an issue of signature liability.

The Unconditional Promise or Order to Pay

When Karl Llewlyn indicated that he wanted "couriers without luggage," he was referring to the idea that negotiable instruments should float through commerce alone. Negotiable instruments should not have the "luggage" of additional documents or reference books. All necessary information about the instrument should be written on the instrument.

Other documents A promise or order is conditional if it includes another document's terms. For example, if a note states, "This note is subject to and includes the terms of the mortgage executed this same date," the note is conditioned upon

Figure 51-4 **Liability of Agents and Principals Under Article III**

SIGNATURE	PARTY LIABLE	ADDITIONAL EVIDENCE
"A. Agent"	Agent	No
"A. Agent, VP"	Agent	Yes
"P. Prince, A. Agent"	Agent	Yes
"P. Prince by A. Agent, VP"	Principal	No
"P. Prince"	Principal	No

COLONIAL BAKING CO. OF DES MOINES v. DOWIE

Supreme Court of Iowa.
330 N.W.2d 279 (1983).

FACTS Fred Dowie was the president and sole stockholder of Fred Dowie Enterprises, Inc., a catering business. He ordered 325,000 hot dog buns for expected use at concession stands that were to be operated in Des Moines during the 1979 visit of the Pope. Dowie paid for the buns with a postdated check in the amount of $28,640. The check had the name of the corporation and its address in the upper left-hand corner. The check was signed, "Frederick J. Dowie." Unfortunately, dreams turned to dust and only 300 hot dogs were sold. Dowie stopped payment on the check and refused to pay for the buns.

ISSUE Who is liable on the $28,640 check?

DECISION The court held Dowie liable because Dowie did not sign in a representative capacity. The imprint of the corporate name on the check was not enough to relieve Dowie of his personal liability.

LEGAL TIP

Officers and directors of corporations should give their titles when signing to show they are acting as representatives and not signing in a personal capacity.

the mortgage terms and is not negotiable. However, if the note only refers to the mortgage, the note is still negotiable. For example, if the note states, "This note is secured by a mortgage," it is not conditioned on the mortgage and is still negotiable.

Payment from an account If a note provides that an instrument must be paid from a certain account, it is non-negotiable. The payment of the note has been made conditional upon the existence of the account. But government agency checks and drafts can list certain accounts, require payment from them, and still have negotiable instruments. Private checks and drafts can reference an account for bookkeeping purposes and still be negotiable. The *Holsonback v. First State Bank of Albertsville* case deals with an issue of conditional language.

HOLSONBACK v. FIRST STATE BANK OF ALBERTSVILLE

Court of Appeals of Alabama.
394 So.2d 381 (Ala. 1980).

FACTS Holsonback issued a draft ($8115) to Higgins as payment for a Corvette car. On the draft were the words, "Enclosed—Title on 77 Chev. Vette Free of all Liens and Encumbrances." The bank would not accept the draft, claiming it was conditional and non-negotiable.

ISSUE Does the reference to the title on the draft make it conditional and non-negotiable?

DECISION No. The draft just referenced a document involved in the transaction. The draft language did not require delivery of the document or condition payment on its existence.

LEGAL TIP

Write messages on documents other than checks and notes. Keep checks and notes as simple and clean as possible.

The Requirement of Payable on Demand or Definite Time

On demand means that the instruments will be paid when the party holding the instrument demands payment. For example, checks and sight drafts are payable on demand. If an instrument does not provide a time for payment, it is payable on demand (Section 3-108).

Payable at a **definite time** means the instrument has a due date. For example, a promissory note may have a due date of "90 days from date of execution." The note can also give a specific date: "Due June 2, 1986."

Acceleration clauses Notes and drafts are still payable at definite times even when there are acceleration clauses. **Acceleration clauses** make the full amount of the note due early if the maker defaults, or fails to pay one installment on time.

Extensions for payment Extensions are just extra time for the borrower to pay. Extensions do not affect an instrument's negotiability.

Unknown events A draft or note is not payable at a definite time if the payment date is tied to some unknown event. For example, a note payable "when the war ends" is non-negotiable. This non-negotiability applies even after the war has ended.

Sum Certain in Money Requirement

This requirement actually has two requirements: that there be a sum certain and that the instrument be payable in money.

Money: dollars, pesos, or pounds? Money is defined as anything which is recognized by some nation as its currency or medium of exchange (Section 3-107). A note made in the United States by two United States citizens but payable in francs is still negotiable. The reason for this liberal definition is the need for international flexibility in trade. The *Lakeway Co. v. Bravo* case involves an issue of currency.

LAKEWAY CO. v. BRAVO

Court of Appeals of Texas, Fourteenth District.
576 S.W.2d 926 (1979).

FACTS On July 31, 1976, Bravo bought a piece of land (located in Travis County, Texas) from Lakeway Company (a Texas firm). Bravo made partial payment with a check drawn on a Mexican Bank and payable in pesos (260,250 pesos or $20,820). The value of the peso dropped sharply between the time the check was delivered and when it was presented for payment. The peso was devalued on August 30, 1976, and the result was that the check amount was now about $12,631.55 in value. Lakeway wanted to use the exchange rate at the time of the payment. Bravo and the bank wanted to use the exchange rate at the time the check was delivered. Lakeway brought suit.

ISSUE If a foreign currency is used for a negotiable instrument, when and how is the exchange rate determined?

DECISION The exchange rate is determined at the time the check is presented to the bank for payment and not at the time the check is issued.

LEGAL TIP

Exchange rates fluctuate. When using a foreign currency, use caution and consider adjusting the price for possible fluctuations.

Sum certain: How much is due? The **sum certain** requirement means that the amount due on the instrument must always be computable from the face of the instrument (Section 3-106). Requiring the parties to use outside information to compute what is due adds "luggage" and makes the note non-negotiable. For example, a note "payable with interest at market rates" is non-negotiable. Market rates would have to be determined from an outside source before the amount due could be computed. A note "payable with interest at prime" is also non-negotiable.

A note can change interest rates and still be negotiable so long as all the rates are written in the note. A note can be payable in installments and still be negotiable—so long as the interest rate is stated.

Notes can provide for the payment of attorneys' fees and collection costs and still be negotiable even though these amounts are now known.

Words of Negotiability Requirement

The idea behind this requirement is to have some language that shows the instrument was intended to be transferable. Either order language or bearer language will satisfy this requirement.

A negotiable instrument must either have order language or be payable to bearer (Sections 3-110 and 3-111). Checks have "Pay to the order of" language so the instrument will be paid according to the payee's directions. Any instrument with "Pay to the order of" on its face meets the words of negotiability requirement.

An instrument can still be negotiable without order language. For example, an instrument with "Pay to Bearer" on its face is still negotiable. This type of instrument does not specify a particular person; therefore, anyone holding the instrument is a bearer.

When an instrument is made to the order of a particular person, it is called **order paper.** Instruments made payable to bearers are called **bearer paper.** For example, if a check uses the language "Pay to the order of John Jones," it is order paper. If a check uses the language "Pay to the order of Bearer," "Pay to the order of John Jones or Bearer," or "Pay to Bearer," it is bearer paper. A check which is made to the order of cash is also bearer paper. The difference between bearer and order paper becomes more important in the next chapter's discussion of negotiation.

PROBLEMS NOT AFFECTING NEGOTIABILITY

Some problems in drafting instruments do not affect negotiability. For example, postdating a check does not make a check nonnegotiable; the check simply cannot be negotiated until that date arrives (Section 3-114). If an instrument is not dated, the date can be filled in and it will be negotiable. If an instrument is incomplete, it can be completed and be negotiable (Section 3-115).

INTERPRETATION OF NEGOTIABLE INSTRUMENTS (SECTION 3-118)

Sometimes instruments have some inconsistencies on their faces. For example, the numbers may have a different amount than the written words on a check. There are several general rules for interpreting instruments.

Words over Figures

In case of a problem, words control over numbers. For example, "$1000" may appear in the upper right blank of a check, but the words may say "one hundred dollars." The check will be for $100.

The *Yates v. Commercial Bank & Trust Co.* case involves an issue of number versus figure interpretation.

YATES v. COMMERCIAL BANK & TRUST CO.

Court of Appeals of Florida, Third District.
432 So.2d 725 (1982).

FACTS Emmett E. McDonald, the personal representative for an estate, wrote a check from the estate's account and drawn on Commercial Bank & Trust and payable to him. The language from the check was, "Pay to the order of Emmett E. McDonald 10,075.00 ten hundred seventy five ______________Dollars." Commercial Bank & Trust paid $10,075.00 to Emmett. Emmett left (absconded) with the funds. The estate beneficiaries and Yates (the new personal representative) filed suit against Commercial.

ISSUE Did the bank pay the proper amount on the check?

DECISION No. The court held that the amount in the words was controlling, and it was improper for the bank to pay the $9,000 difference.

LEGAL TIP

Personal representatives, executors, or administrators of estates need supervision or a bond for protection of the estate's assets. Use caution in writing checks to avoid ambiguities.

Handwritten Terms over Printed or Typed Terms

In determining the correct amount of an instrument, courts look to find the parties' intent. Handwritten terms will better indicate intent than printed or typed terms; handwritten terms will control interpretation. Likewise, typed terms will control over printed since the printed terms are part of a form, but the typed terms were entered personally.

KEY TERMS

Checks
Promissory notes
Drafts
Orders to pay
Drawer
Payee
Drawee
Promises to pay
Payee
Maker
Negotiable orders of withdrawal (NOWs)
Share drafts
Negotiable instrument
Signature
On demand
Definite time
Acceleration clauses
Sum certain
Order paper
Bearer paper

CHAPTER PROBLEMS

1. Classify the following as promises or orders to pay: check, share draft, CD, and note.
2. Petit signed a check made out to Sterling Press, which had the printed name "Investor's Publishing Company" in the upper left-hand corner of the check. Investor's Publishing Company was a newly formed subsidiary of Investor's National Corporation. The publishing subsidiary had been formed to publish a magazine called *The Utah Equestrian.* Petit did not indicate his office or capacity on the check. Investor's Publishing had not been incorporated properly. Sterling now wants to collect Investor's Publishing Company's bill from Petit. Can they? *Sterling Press v. Petit,* 580 P.2d 599 (Utah 1978).
3. Robins Federal Credit Union loaned money to Anderson to purchase a mobile home. Robins made a check jointly payable to Anderson and Larry's Mobile Homes. The check had language that made its payment conditional on Larry's putting a notice of Robin's security interest in the mobile home on the title. Anderson's president (Fortney) cashed the check and forgot to note the security interest on the title. Anderson defaulted, and Robins then discovered it had no lien and could not repossess the home. Robins has sued Fortney. Who wins? *Larry's Mobile Homes v. Robins Fed. Credit Union,* 288 S.E.2d 800 (Ga. 1982).

*4. Miller (a tax protestor) stamped his checks with the following notice: "No copy permitted without signed permission of signer(s). Offense punishable by up to a $10,000 fine and 10 years in prison. U.S. Criminal Code, Title 18, Section 241–242." Are Miller's checks negotiable? *State ex rel. Dorgan v. Union State Bank,* 267 N.W.2d 777 (N.D. 1978).

5. George Robinson purchased a money market certificate naming his stepdaughter, Loretta Wygant, as a "pay-on-death" beneficiary. Robinson then married Hope and asked the bank to change the beneficiary to his new wife. Six months later, Robinson died. In the fight between his stepdaughter and widow, the issue of whether the instrument is negotiable has arisen. Is the certificate negotiable? *West Greeley Nat. Bank v. Wygant,* 650 P.2d 1339 (Colo. 1982).
6. All checks have a printed number in the upper right hand corner to help drawers and drawees keep track of checks, account balances, and transactions. Do these numbers affect negotiability? *Dailey v. State,* 374 So.2d 414 (Ala. 1979).
7. St. Paul Fire & Marine drew a check on a check imprinter for $100,478.23. The imprinter printed this amount in red. The amount in the figure space was typed in as $478.23. The figures amount was then changed (in crude handwriting) to $100,478.23. The drawee, the State Bank of Salem, paid $100,478.23. St. Paul claimed the proper amount was $478.23. Who is right? *St. Paul Fire & Marine Insurance Company v. State Bank of Salem,* 412 N.E.2d 103 (Ind. 1980).
8. J. M. Cook, the treasurer of Arizona Auto Auction, Inc., signed three checks without giving his capacity. The checks were made payable to Central Motors Company—an auto dealer. On the upper left-hand corner of the check "Arizona Auto Auction, Inc.," appeared along with an address and phone number. Who is liable? *Valley National Bank v. Cook,* 665 P.2d 576 (Ariz. App. 1983).
9. Susan Dawson won a federal oil and gas lease (in a United States Government drawing). She was required to submit the first year's rental of $1281. She sent a check with $1281 written in the figure portion and "one thousand eighty-one and 00/100" in words. The bank would only cash the check for $1081. Since the money had to be in by a certain date and the bank's interpretation made her $200 low on her deposit, Dawson lost her very valuable lease. Dawson brought suit. What is the proper amount of the check? *Dawson v. Andrus,* 612 F.2d 1280 (10th Cir. 1980).

*10. A note provided a time of payment as follows: "This note is promised payment for ownership in Casper project when option is exercised for second half." Is the note (proper in all other respects) negotiable? *Northwestern Nat. Bank of Minneapolis v. Shuster,* 307 N.W.2d 767 (Minn. 1981).

"All that glisters is not gold."
Prince of Morocco
The Merchant of Venice
Act II, Scene VII

Chapter 52

Commercial Paper: Transfer and Negotiation

CHAPTER PREVIEW

- Process of negotiation
- Bearer versus order negotiation
- Types of indorsements
- Rights of holders in due course
- Requirements concerning holders in due course
- Real versus personal defenses
- FTC rule on holders in due course

The First National Bank of Akron cashed a check that was made payable to Cincinnati Insurance Company and Smith, with only Smith's signature. Cincinnati has filed suit claiming the transfer of the check to the First National Bank was improper. Who wins?

One of the features of commercial paper is its ease of transfer. Negotiable instruments flow easily through commerce if the rules for transfer or negotiation are followed. This chapter answers these questions: How are instruments transferred or negotiated? What are the rights of the transferees of the instruments? What kinds of transferees are there?

THE BASICS OF NEGOTIATION

Negotiation is the transfer of an instrument so that the transferee becomes a holder (Section 3-202). A **holder** is someone who is in possession of an instrument that "runs to" him or her. An instrument runs to someone if it is made payable or is indorsed to the recipient, or is bearer paper. For example, if Bruce Fisher writes a check to Marianne Jennings, then that check runs to Marianne Jennings. If Marianne Jennings indorsed that check to Sarah Jennings, then the check would run to Sarah Jennings.

THE REQUIREMENTS: HOW TO NEGOTIATE

Negotiation depends upon the type of instrument involved. Bearer paper and order paper are negotiated in different ways. Bearer paper is negotiated by delivery, whereas order paper is negotiated by indorsement and delivery.

Delivery: What Is It?

If a check is made payable to bearer, anyone can become a holder of that check by having it delivered. **Delivery** occurs when an instrument is actually or constructively given to another person. For example, if Fisher gives Jennings a bearer note, there is delivery. Constructive delivery is not actual but is still delivery. For example, a bearer note is constructively delivered when it is put in the mail. The *Scherer v. Hyland* case involves an issue of delivery.

Indorsements: What Are They?

An **indorsement** is a signature of a payee on an instrument. For example, if the check from Bruce Fisher is made "Pay to the order of Marianne Jennings," then Marianne Jennings must indorse the check to negotiate it. If there are two payees, then both payees must indorse the instrument to negotiate it. In the chapter-opening example, a bank cashed a check without one of the payee's signature. This transfer would not be a negotiation. If an instrument is made payable to alternate payees, then one signature will negotiate the instrument. For example, if a royalty check is made payable to Bruce Fisher or Marianne Jennings, then either one can sign and negotiate the instrument.

Indorsements: How To

An indorsement can appear anywhere on an instrument and be valid. Most banks require indorsements for checks to be written on the back of the check.

Occasionally, customers of banks forget to indorse checks when depositing them. A section in Article IV (Section 4-205) allows a depositary bank to provide an indorsement of its customer when the customer deposits a check without indorsement. For example, if Bella deposits a $250 salary check in her account at First Federal and forgets to indorse it, First Federal can provide the indorsement. The *Callahan v. C & S State Bank* case involves an issue of joint signatures.

SCHERER v. HYLAND

Supreme Court of New Jersey.
380 A.2d 698 (1977).

FACTS Catherine Wagner received a check for $17,400 in settlement for injuries (facial wounds and broken hips), which she had suffered in a car accident. She indorsed the check in blank (making it bearer paper). She then put it on the kitchen table in the apartment she had shared with her lover, Robert Scherer, for fifteen years. Scherer had rented the apartment in his name.

Wagner then wrote two suicide notes to Scherer. One asked his forgiveness for "taking the easy way out." The other left everything she owned to him including "the check," which she specified in the note. She left the apartment, locked the door, went to the roof of the building and jumped to her death.

When the police arrived, they took possession of the check. Hyland (one of Scherer's relatives) was appointed administrator of Wagner's estate and claims the check is part of the estate. Scherer claims the check was bearer paper, was delivered, and is his.

ISSUE Had the check been delivered?

DECISION There was constructive delivery. Only Scherer had another key to the apartment. It was his apartment, and Wagner had locked the door. No one else had access to the apartment. The check was a gift causa mortis because she had shown her clear intent to leave the premises and this life.

LEGAL TIP

Suicide leaves behind a trail of legal problems.

Indorsements: The Problem Areas

There are some problems that arise when indorsements are needed to further negotiate instruments. For example, a check may be made payable to "Mary Ann Jennings" when the spelling should have been "Marianne Jennings." Marianne Jennings can still indorse and negotiate the check. She can sign either "Mary Ann Jennings" or "Marianne Jennings." Whoever is taking or cashing the check can require her to indorse or sign with both spellings (Section 3-203).

When minors are the payees on checks or notes, the minor's signature along with the signature of a parent or guardian is required for a valid indorsement. Without the adult's signature, the minor's indorsement would be voidable.

CALLAHAN v. C & S STATE BANK

Court of Appeals of Georgia.
256 S.E.2d 666 (1979).

FACTS Mr. and Mrs. Callahan received a check from their stockbroker as payment for the sale of some of their stock holdings. The check was made payable to both of them and was in the amount of $61,201.56. Mr. Callahan indorsed it and deposited it into their joint account. He then drew a check in the same amount on that account, and the bank gave him the cash. The Callahans had a divorce pending at this time. Mrs. Callahan sued the bank for cashing the check without her signature.

ISSUE Was Mrs. Callahan's signature required for negotiation?

DECISION No—not when the check was deposited in their joint account. A bank can supply its customer's indorsement for purposes of a deposit. Banks are not liable for pending divorces.

LEGAL TIP

When a divorce is pending, give special instructions to the bank on joint accounts, or close the joint accounts and open separate ones.

Indorsements: The Types

There are four types of indorsements under Article III: blank, special, restrictive, and qualified.

Blank indorsements (Section 3-204) **Blank indorsements** are simply signatures. If the check made payable to Marianne Jennings is indorsed on the back as "Marianne Jennings," there is a blank indorsement. A blank indorsement turns an order instrument into a bearer instrument. Once Marianne Jenning's signature is on the back of the check, the check becomes bearer paper and can be negotiated to someone else just by delivery. A check that has been indorsed in blank can be stolen and then validly transferred to another party.

Special indorsements (Section 3-204) **Special indorsements** are indorsements made to a specific person or entity. For example, suppose Marianne Jennings is the payee of a check in the amount of $100. She owes Bruce Fisher $100. She can indorse the check to Bruce by writing on the back: "Pay to Bruce Fisher /s/ (signed) Marianne Jennings." The check continues to be order paper and will require Bruce's signature for further negotiation.

The special indorsement does not require words of negotiability. The "Pay to" language is sufficient. This limitation works only for indorsements, and words of negotiability are still required on the front of the instrument. The *Casarez v. Garcia* case deals with the issue of special indorsements.

CASAREZ v. GARCIA

Supreme Court of New Mexico.
660 P.2d 598 (1983).

FACTS Blas Cecil Garcia and Oakley Guillory were hired by Arthur and Lucy Casarez to construct a home for them. Although they had claimed to be, neither Garcia nor Guillory were licensed contractors. Their project was "red-tagged"—halted by state building inspectors. In addition, Garcia took a check from the kitchen table in the Casarez home.

The check was for $25,000 and represented a construction loan to the Casarezes from Rio Grande Valley Bank. The check had been made payable to Cecil Garcia. When the project was redtagged, Lucy asked Cecil to indorse the check. She then indorsed the check to another contractor working on their home. The back of the check looked like this:

Pay to the order of Lucy N. Casarez, /s/ Cecil Garcia

Pay to the order of Albuquerque Fence Co. /s/ Lucy N. Casarez

Garcia took the check and the Bank cashed it. The Casarezes filed suit claiming the check was order paper, and the bank should not have cashed it. The bank claimed the check was bearer paper and that Garcia was a bearer and could cash it.

ISSUE Was the check bearer or order paper?

DECISION The check was order paper because of the special indorsements on the back. The first indorsement made the check order paper to Lucy N. Casarez. The second indorsement made the check order paper to Albuquerque Fence. Albuquerque's indorsement was needed for negotiation.

LEGAL TIP

Check the backgrounds and licenses of contractors before hiring them.

Restrictive indorsements A **restrictive indorsement** is an indorsement with instructions. For example, the words "For Deposit Only" written above a signature will result in a restrictive indorsement. The words "Pay Any Bank" followed by a signature will also be a restrictive indorsement. A restrictive indorsement is also called a **conditional indorsement.** An example of a conditional indorsement would be "Pay to Billy Bowdin when he delivers the title to the oil well."

A restrictive indorsement does not prevent further transfer of the instrument. The only requirement of a restrictive indorsement is that the first transferee after the indorsement comply with the restrictions. If a check is indorsed, "For Deposit Only /s/ Marianne Jennings," and First Federal is the first transferee of the check after Jennings, then they must credit Jennings' account. Transferees after First Federal are not affected by the restriction.

Qualified indorsements A **qualified indorsement** is one that limits the warranty liability of the indorser. The language used for a qualified indorsement is "Without Recourse." When this language appears above a signature, the indorser limits his or her warranty liability. The warranty that is eliminated is the warranty that no defense of any party is good against the indorser (Section 3-147 [2] [d]). Warranty liability is discussed in Chapter 53.

Figure 52-1 is an example of a series of indorsements on the back of an instrument. For each lined area, the type of indorsement is noted along with whether the instrument is bearer or order paper.

SUPER TRANSFER AND NEGOTIATION: THE HOLDER IN DUE COURSE

Negotiation gets the transferee the status of holder but can bring holders the even higher status of **holder in due course.** There are many advantages to being a holder in due course. The basic advantage is that a holder in due course enjoys more protection than a holder and more than an assignee of a contract (more

Figure 52-1 **Sample Series of Indorsements**

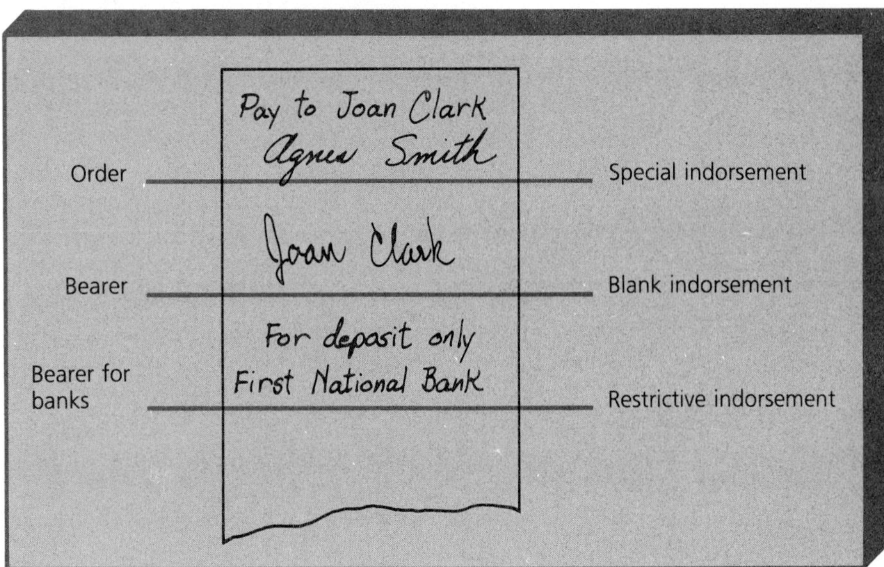

details on the advantages of being a holder in due course can be found in Chapter 53). Not all holders are holders in due course. The requirements are that a holder must take an instrument for value, in good faith, and without notice of defenses, dishonor, or lateness.

The Value Requirement

In very simple terms, **value** means that a holder paid something to get the instrument. Value is basically the same as consideration. But, for holders in due course, the consideration must have actually passed (or been paid) to the other party. For example, suppose Fred agrees to paint Berford's house for $500. Berford signs a promissory note for $500 plus interest to pay Fred. There is consideration, but Fred could not take the note for value until he actually performed the painting.

Past consideration Another distinction between consideration and value is that value can be based on past consideration. For example, suppose Ada has supplied Ralph's Roost with cocktail napkins for 3 months. Their contract requires Ralph to pay Ada $30 per month. If Ralph signs a promissory note for that amount at the end of 3 months, Ada has given value—the napkins. Thus, value was given even though Ada had simply performed her obligation under an existing agreement.

Depositary banks Depositary banks can be holders in due course. They are holders in due course to the extent they let the depositing customer draw on or use the deposited funds. For example, suppose that Beulah has $200 in her checking account. She receives a gift of $500 from an uncle and deposits the amount in her checking account. Beulah's bank will be a holder in due course of that check if they let Beulah draw on the $500. The customer must use up whatever balance was in the account before the check was deposited—a first-in-first-out method of accounting for value.

The Good-Faith Requirement

Good faith is defined under the UCC as "honesty in fact in the conduct or transaction concerned" (Section 1-201 [19]). Good faith has been said to require a "pure heart and an empty head." The good-faith requirement does not require a holder to act prudently or be diligent—only that no suspicions existed at the time the instrument was taken for value.

The No-Notice Requirement

The "no-notice" requirement means that the holder takes the instrument without any knowledge that there is anything wrong with the instrument, the parties to it, or the underlying transaction. No notice includes no knowledge and no reason to know anything is wrong. If all the facts and circumstances surrounding the instrument would have led a reasonable person to conclude something was wrong—the no notice requirement is not met. Whether a holder knew or should have known is the issue in notice.

There are actually three parts to the no-notice requirement: no notice of defenses; no notice of dishonor; no notice that the instrument is overdue.

No notice of defenses The first form of notice is no notice of defenses. Defenses (as used in Article III) include the contract defenses. A holder in due course cannot know of any problems underlying the original parties' agreement. For example, if Ace Solar Heaters used misrepresentation to induce Doug to sign a note for a $2000 solar panel system, Doug has a defense to the note. If Ace transfers that note to Fred's Finance Company and says Doug is "bellyaching" about the system, then Fred has notice that there is a defense or at least a problem with the contract.

Many finance companies work closely with sales companies and buy all the notes the companies have their customers sign. If the finance company begins to see a pattern of upset customers, it can no longer acquire future notes as a holder in due course because they have reason to believe there are defenses to the notes.

Notice of defenses can also come from an inspection of the note or check. If the note or check is incomplete and missing major portions, there is notice of a defense. If there is evidence that the instrument has been altered, there is notice of a defense. If the instrument appears to carry a forged signature, there is notice of a defense.

There are several types of problems that can appear on an instrument, which do not result in notice of a defense. For example, an instrument can be signed in different handwriting than the remainder of the document—as when a check is signed in different writing than that used in the payee and amount sections. An instrument can be postdated and still not indicate a defense. The instrument need not be perfect—only complete and without any obvious changes.

Finally, notice of defenses can come from the circumstances surrounding its transfer. If the transferee is able to get the instrument for a great discount, there is notice of a problem. For example, if Alfie buys a $1000 promissory note on March 30, which is due April 1 for a price of $800, the discount is great enough to indicate a problem. A race track cashing checks for a church treasurer when the checks are written on the church account is notice of a defense. The *McCarthy v. Kasperak* case involves an issue of defenses.

McCARTHY v. KASPERAK

Court of Appeals of Ohio.
444 N.E.2d 472 (1981).

FACTS Frank O'Leary purchased a $10,000 bearer treasury bill on January 16, 1975. The bill had a due date of July 17, 1975. A month later, O'Leary was found dead in his home but the bill was never found.

On April 13, 1975, Mel Weinstein (an accountant) approached a woman named Irene Kasperak in her tavern and offered to sell her O'Leary's bearer treasury bill for $9500. Weinstein told Kasperak he was acting for someone else. Kasperak bought the bill and then cashed it.

McCarthy, the personal representative for O'Leary's estate brought suit challenging Kasperak's ownership of the bill.

ISSUE Was Kasperak a holder in due course?

DECISION No. There were too many suspicious circumstances. She ignored facts that would have suggested problems: the substantial discount, the sale in a bar, and the accountant's acting for someone else. There were enough strange circumstances to alert a buyer of problems.

LEGAL TIP

Buying commercial paper under odd circumstances is risky. Traditional sources for purchase are safer and less costly in the long run.

Notice of dishonor The second form of notice is one indicating that an instrument was refused payment. If an instrument is not going to be paid, transferees are not holders in due course and are foolish to take such a risk.

For example, suppose that Fisher wrote a check to Jennings. Jennings took the check to Fisher's bank to cash it, and the bank refused. Jennings then tells Smith the story and asks Smith to take the check for a discount. Smith is hoping to be able to return to Fisher's bank and cash the check at a time when there are funds in the account. Smith cannot be a holder in due course because he had knowledge of the bank dishonoring Fisher's check. The *Money Mart Check Cashing Center v. Epicycle* case deals with an issue of dishonor.

MONEY MART CHECK CASHING CENTER v. EPICYCLE

Supreme Court of Colorado.
667 P.2d 1372 (1983).

FACTS John Cronin was an employee of Epicycle. He had borrowed money from Epicycle, and repayments were taken from his paycheck. When Cronin was fired and given his last paycheck, the bookkeeper forgot to take out the amount of money he still owed on the various loans. Epicycle stopped payment on the check. After the stop payment order had been issued, Money Mart cashed Cronin's check. Epicycle's bank returned the check to Money Mart because of the stop payment order. Money Mart sued Epicycle to recover as a holder in due course.

ISSUE Was Money Mart a holder in due course?

DECISION Yes. Money Mart is in the business of cashing paychecks. They checked Cronin's identification and had no knowledge of the stop payment order. There was nothing on the check to indicate a problem. Money Mart is not required to call to see if stop payments have been issued before they can take a check as a holder in due course.

LEGAL TIP

Be sure check amounts are correct. If those checks are transferred, the transferees will be holders in due course who will be required to pay the amount indicated.

Notice that an instrument is overdue An overdue notice states that time for payment has passed and payment has not been received.

If the instrument is a note, it is overdue if the due date on the instrument has passed. A holder taking an instrument after the due date cannot be a holder in due course. An instrument is overdue if there has been default in the payment of the principal. An instrument is also overdue if the lender has accelerated the note and made the full amount due.

If the instrument is a check or sight draft, it is overdue if it is more than thirty days after the instrument was issued. Anyone who takes a check after thirty days cannot be a holder in due course.

SUPER STATUS: RIGHTS OF THE HOLDER IN DUE COURSE

In this section, all the reasons and justifications for becoming a holder in due course are given. A holder of an instrument will still have the basic contractual rights. But a holder in due course enjoys protection from most defenses and freedom from the problems of contractual assignees. A holder in due course takes an instrument free from all personal defenses but is subject to all the real defenses.

Freedom from Personal Defenses

Personal defenses cannot be used against a holder in due course. **Personal defenses** include misrepresentation, mistake, lack of consideration, breach of contract or breach of warranty, and lack of authority of the signing party (see Chapter 51).

Real Defenses

Section 3-305 lists real defenses. **Real defenses** include infancy (or minority), duress, illegality, fraud in factum, insolvency discharge, forgery, and material alteration.

Infancy or minority Minority is a defense to a holder in due course in the same way it is a defense in contracts. A minor's obligation on commercial paper is voidable at the minor's option. Of course, the exceptions to the minor's right to disaffirm also apply to commercial paper (see Chapter 21). The defenses of insanity and intoxication also apply to commercial paper and to holders in due course.

Duress Duress is a valid defense against a holder in due course if the conduct labeled duress is illegal. For example, a note signed under threat of a lawsuit would not be a defense against a holder in due course. But, a note signed with a gun to one's head would be a defense against a holder in due course.

Illegality Commercial paper issued to pay for illegal contract obligations is void. Illegality is a valid defense against a holder in due course. For example, a note issued to pay for an illegal gambling debt is void and a holder in due course is subject to the defense of illegality. The *Sea Air Support, Inc., v. Herrman* case illustrates the effect of illegality on checks.

SEA AIR SUPPORT, INC., v. HERRMAN

Supreme Court of Nevada.
613 P.2d 413 (1980).

FACTS Nevada allows gambling but does not allow its courts to enforce checks and notes issued for payment of gambling debts. Herrman wrote a check for $10,000 to the Ormsby House Hotel and Casino in Carson City, Nevada. He was issued $10,000 worth of gambling chips for the check. The check was dishonored, and Ormsby House assigned the check to Sea Air (a collection agency) for collection. The collection agency could not collect and brought suit as a holder in due course.

ISSUE Was Sea Air a holder in due course? Did the underlying gambling debt make the check void?

DECISION Sea Air knew of the underlying gambling debt. The check was void, and Sea Air would not have the rights of a holder in due course. Sea Air had notice of a defense on the check (the illegal gambling debt). With such notice Sea Air could not be a holder in due course. A holder with this knowledge of all the facts could not collect the money without notice or in good faith.

LEGAL TIP

Make sure the transaction underlying a check or note is legal.

Fraud There are two types of fraud. The first type (discussed in Chapter 20) is called **fraud in the inducement,** which exists when false statements induce a party to enter into a contract. Such fraud is not a defense against a holder in due course.

The second type of fraud is called **fraud in factum,** which occurs when one party induces another to sign a document by misleading them as to the nature of the document. For example, suppose that the Vincents have had a demonstration of a solar heater in their home. They tell the salesman from Gentle Alternatives, Inc., that they are not interested. The salesman then asks if he can leave the equipment overnight so that he can return for neighborhood demonstrations. The Vincents agree and are asked to sign a document, which they are told is a receipt for the equipment. They later learn the document was a note to pay for a solar system. The salesman has committed fraud in factum. This type of fraud is a defense against a holder in due course. The *Riviera Motors, Inc., v. Higbee* case deals with the issue of fraud.

RIVIERA MOTORS, INC. v. HIGBEE

Supreme Court of Oregon.
609 P.2d 369 (1980).

FACTS Riviera Motors, Inc., a retail Volkswagen (VW) dealer, advertised a VW overhaul special for $368.56. Higbee took his car in for the advertised overhaul. Riviera made unauthorized repairs and when Higbee arrived to pick up his car, he was presented with a bill for $583.76. Riviera refused to release Higbee's car until he paid the amount due. Higbee wrote a personal check for the amount and took his car. The next day he stopped payment on the check and sent a new check for $368.55—the amount of the advertised special.

Riviera brought suit as a holder in due course of the original check. Higbee raised the defense of fraudulent advertising and unauthorized repairs.

ISSUE Would the false advertising and unauthorized repairs be real or personal defenses?

DECISION Both are personal defenses. The advertising is fraud in the inducement. The unauthorized repairs relate to the contract performance terms. Higbee could bring an action in contract to recover for his problems, but Riviera is a holder in due course. A holder in due course is not affected by personal defenses.

LEGAL TIP

Give clear instructions when leaving your car for repair. Have the service personnel write down the specific repairs required and the related charges. Write "Do Not Do Additional Work without Permission" on the service form. Check state statutes for any requirements and rights concerning car repairs and related bills.

Insolvency Although holders in due course have many protections against defenses, they still do not have a guarantee of payment. Holders in due course are still subject to the risks of insolvency or bankruptcy of the maker or drawer of an instrument. There is never a promise to holders in due course that they will be paid.

Forgery A holder in due course has no protection on a forged instrument. If a maker's or a drawer's signature had been forged, the maker or drawer is not required to pay even a holder in due course who ends up with the instrument (Section 3-401). For example, suppose that Berferd stole a check from Fisher and then forged Fisher's signature. Berferd made the check payable to "Cash" and then transferred it to Jennings. Jennings then took the check to her bank and cashed it. When Jennings' bank tried to collect the amount of the check from Fisher's bank, they were turned down because the instrument was forged. Jennings' bank (even though they may be a holder in due course) will not be paid by the bank because the signature was forged (for a discussion of who takes the final loss see Chapter 53).

There are some exceptions to this forgery rule. If Jennings' bank can show Fisher was negligent—that he left his checks laying around for thieves—they can still collect the amount of the check. A second exception is the imposter rule (Section 3-405). This exception makes a distinction between a thief who forges and someone who poses as another and then forges. For example, suppose Tyler has a rent refund of $200 due to him. Ross knows that Tyler has the refund due. Ross goes to the apartment management, poses as Tyler and has a check made out to Tyler for $200. Ross then forges Tyler's signature on the back and cashes the check at his bank. A second bank ends up with the check and demands payment from the apartment management's bank. The management has since learned of the mistake and instructs its bank not to cash the check. The second bank (as a holder in due course) can demand that the check be cashed. A holder in due course is not subject to the defense of an imposter's forgery. The management firm is ultimately liable for not checking identification more carefully. Figure 52-2 provides a summary of the forgery rules for holders in due course.

Material alteration A holder in due course who receives an instrument after it has been altered cannot enforce the altered amount of the instrument. Ordinarily, all the parties are discharged when there is an alteration. However, a holder in due course can demand payment of the instrument's original amount. For example, suppose Fisher writes a check to Jennings for $50. Jennings raises the amount of the check to $500 and transfers it to Berferd (a holder in due course). Berferd can still get the $50. If it can be shown that Fisher was negligent in making out the check and accepted the alteration, then Berferd could collect the full $500. If Berferd collects only $50, he will have to pursue Jennings for the remainder.

For these rules to apply, the instrument must have been altered according to the definition of material alteration in Article III (Section 3-407). **Material alteration** is alteration by a holder that is fraudulent and that changes the contract of any party to the instrument. The example given above meets all of these requirements. The *Ray v. Farmers State Bank* case deals with a problem in material alteration.

Exceptions to the Holder in Due Course Super Status

Consider the following example. Alice needs a new roof on her house. She hires a contractor who requires her to sign a note for the full cost of the work—$2000. Alice signs the note and never hears from, sees, or finds the contractor again. However, she soon discovers that the contractor sold the note to Credit Finance.

Figure 52-2 **Forgeries and the Holder in Due Course (HDC)**

TYPE OF FORGERY	HDC PAID	LIABILITY
Non-negligent	No	Initial party who could check for identification (see Chapter 53)
Negligent	Yes	Drawer or maker who was negligent
Imposter forgery	Yes	Party who issued check to imposter

RAY v. FARMERS STATE BANK

Supreme Court of Texas.
576 S.W.2d 607 (1979).

FACTS On May 7, 1975, Mrs. Nora Ray (80 years old) was wakened from a nap by pounding on her door. When she answered the door, she discovered a man in a uniform who was later identified as Robert Freeman. He told Mrs. Ray he was from the utility company and was there to check her power. He examined some outlets around the house and looked at her meter. He then told her she would be required to pay a $1.50 service charge.

Mrs. Ray refused to pay so Freeman got her purse and forced her to sign a check for $1.50. Freeman was not from the utility company, but was a con artist. He took the check, left, raised the amount of the check to $1851.50, and cashed it at Farmers States Bank.

Mrs. Ray tried to phone to stop payment when Freeman left, but he had cut her phone wires. By the time she got to the bank, the check had been cashed. Mrs. Ray brought suit against the bank for cashing the altered check.

ISSUE Who is liable for the altered check?

DECISION The bank will be liable and not Mrs. Ray. The instrument was altered by a holder and the alteration was material. Mrs. Ray is not liable for the altered amount—only the $1.50. When there is an alteration, any party whose obligation is changed is discharged. Mrs. Ray was discharged when the amount of the check was changed.

LEGAL TIP

Check identification of service personnel. Write checks carefully and do not leave room for alteration.

Credit Finance now wants the payments on the note. Alice tells her story of fraud, but Credit claims it is a holder in due course and not subject to the defense of fraudulent misrepresentation. Alice, the poor consumer, is stuck paying for a new roof while living under the old one.

Many government agencies did not like the results and effects of the Article III protections for holders in due course—particularly in consumer transactions. As a result, the federal government and some states have passed legislation or regulation eliminating the status of holders in due course in consumer transactions.

Uniform Consumer Credit Code (UCCC) Many states have adopted the Uniform Consumer Credit Code (UCCC) or some version of it. The UCCC allows various methods for eliminating the holder in due course protections in consumer transactions. Most of the states that have adopted the UCCC define consumer transactions as those in which goods or services are purchased for personal, family, or household use. Some states have held simply that holder in due course status in consumer notes is unconscionable.

Federal Trade Commission (FTC) Rule In 1975, the Federal Trade Commission (FTC) stepped in to protect consumers because all of the states had not taken action concerning holders in due course. The FTC adopted its Holder in Due Course Rule to apply to consumer transactions. Consumer transactions under this federal regulation are defined as *credit transactions* for the purchase of goods or services for family, personal, or household use. The effect of the FTC Rule is to eliminate holder in due course status for those acquiring notes from consumer transactions. The result is that holders of consumer notes are like assignees in contracts—they are subject to all defenses.

The FTC Rule requires all consumer credit contracts to contain a notice regarding the effect of the rule. The notice must be printed in bold (at least 10-point) type and reads as follows:

NOTICE

Any holder of this consumer credit contract is subject to all claims and defenses which the debtor could assert against the seller of goods or services obtained pursuant hereto or with the proceeds hereof. Recovery hereunder by the debtor shall not exceed amounts paid by the debtor hereunder.

The rule shifts the burden of finding and dealing with those parties who have created a defense or breached a contract and eliminates the blind protection for the holder in due course.

KEY TERMS

Negotiation
Holder
Delivery
Indorsement
Blank indorsement
Special indorsement
Restrictive indorsement
Conditional indorsement
Qualified indorsement
Holder in due course
Personal defenses
Real defenses
Fraud in the inducement
Fraud in factum
Material alteration
Value

CHAPTER PROBLEMS

1. A check was made payable to "Grater Mesilla Valley Sanitation District." The government agency indorsed the check with its correct name: "Greater Mesilla Valley Sanitation District." Can the check be negotiated? *Western Casualty & Surety Co. v. Citizens Bank of Las Cruces,* 676 F.2d 1344 (10th Cir. 1982).

*2. A check was made payable (by computer) to two payees whose names were separated by a diagonal (/) (i.e., Jack Harper/Plymart). Does the slash mean alternate or joint payees? *Ryland Group, Inc., v. Gwinnett County Bank,* 259 S.E.2d 152 (Ga. 1979).

3. The United States Government issued a check for $12,000 to "Alamance Builders, Inc., and Glen Slaughter." Glen Slaughter indorsed the check and deposited it in his account at Central Carolina Bank and Trust without an indorsement on behalf of Alamance. Alamance wants it share of the check amount back from Central Carolina because of the lack of indorsement. Can Alamance win? *Alamance Builders, Inc., v. Central Carolina Bank & Trust Co.,* 262 S.E.2d 338 (N.C. 1980).

4. A check was payable as follows:
   Moram Agencies
   FAS Agency—Public Ledger Bldg.
   Phila., PA 19106

   The check was indorsed:
   FOR DEPOSIT ONLY
   Dunnington Arnold of Phila., Inc.

   Can the check be negotiated? *Moram Agencies, Inc., v. Farrell Transportation Co.,* 35 UCC Rep. 1236 (D.C. Pa. 1982).

5. The Joffes entered into an Investment Agreement with Continental Financial Systems for the purchase of property in Calabasas. They were to deposit $25,000 in the Continential Financial System's escrow account at Wells Fargo Bank. A check was made payable to "Continental Financial Systems—Wells Fargo Escrow Trust Account." Continental Financial Systems stamped the back of the check: "Pay to the Order of Bank of America. For Deposit Only /s/ CFS." The check was deposited in Continental's account at Bank of America. Has the check been properly negotiated? *Joffe v.*

United Bank of California, 190 Cal. Rptr. 443 (Calif. 1983).

*6. Robinson (a Colorado resident) wanted to buy a 1978 Subaru car from Tomball Motor Company (a Houston, Texas, dealer) for $4600. Robinson arranged to borrow the money for the car purchase from Poudre Valley Federal Credit Union. Poudre Valley issued a check for $4600 made payable to both Robinson and the car dealer. Robinson wrote the following and then signed the check: "Payment conditioned upon delivery of title to the following described vehicle to the Credit Union." A Texas bank cashed the check. Robinson never got the car. Poudre never got the title. Who made the mistake? *Robinson v. Poudre Valley Credit Union,* 654 P.2d 861 (Colo. 1982).

7. Bank of the Southwest cashed a savings-and-loan check, which had typewriter correction fluid in the payee space and a new payee named typed over the fluid. Before cashing the check, the teller telephoned someone at the savings and loan bank to verify the check's validity. She talked to someone whose name had been given to her by the party trying to cash the check. Is bank of the Southwest a holder in due course? *New Hampshire Insurance Co. v. Bank of the Southwest,* 584 S.W.2d 560 (Tex. 1979).

*8. Roger D. Pownell, an accountant, worked for the Greeley Street clinic, was questioned by them about $64,000 in shortages, and was accused of embezzlement. Pownell borrowed $77,875 from another client, Dr. Robert Wohlrabe. Pownell had Wohlrabe get the money in the form of a cashier's check made payable to the clinic. Dr. Wohlrabe later had problems and wanted his money back. The clinic claimed it was a holder in due course. Was it? *Wohlrabe v. Pownell,* 307 N.W.2d 478 (Minn. 1978).

*9. Oh Boy!, a wholesale grocer, filled an order for South East, a small grocery and liquor store. The delivery boy for Oh Boy! was to deliver the $7500 in groceries and then get a certified check. A dispute arose over what and how much was delivered. The police were called to settle the dispute. A police sergeant told South East's manager, "You have to give him the check now." The officer waited for the manager to sign the check, give the check to the delivery boy, and made him leave. South East claims the check is void because of duress. Who wins? *Oh Boy! Grocers v. South East Food & Liquor, Inc.,* 398 N.E.2d 269 (Ill. 1979).

10. Moody Manufacturing Company sold products to Venturi Construction Company on credit. Venturi signed $33,725.57 in drafts to pay for the goods. Venturia had only purchased about $10,000 in goods. Venturia had signed drafts for more because Moody asked it to sign new drafts, claimed the old drafts had been torn up, and that the reason for the new drafts was bookkeeping convenience. Moody sold the drafts to Illinois Valley Acceptance Corporation. Illinois Valley went bankrupt and the trustee in bankruptcy, Christinson, claimed to be a holder in due course and wanted to collect the amount of the drafts from Venturi. Venturi uses fraud in factum as a defense. Who is right? *Christinson v. Venturi Construction Co.,* 440 N.E.2d 226 (Ill. 1982).

"Your check bounced."
The three words most dreaded by checking account holders, banks, sellers, creditors, and students

Chapter 53

Commercial Paper: Liability of the Parties

CHAPTER PREVIEW

- Primary and secondary parties
- Obligations of primary and secondary parties
- Role of accommodation parties
- Requirements for presentment
- Dishonor
- Time limits for presentment, dishonor, and notice of dishonor.
- Imposters and fictitious payees
- Warranty liability
- Discharge from liability

Michael Martin hired a new legal secretary, Carol Tozzer. She handled all the money he earned in his law practice. She made all the deposits and withdrawals from his accounts. Over a 5-month period, Tozzer was able to embezzle $11,200 from Martin. He did not check his bank statements during that five-month period and was not aware of any problems. He now wants to recover from the bank for the Tozzer forgeries. Can he?

When everything goes right, there is nothing simpler than the flow of commercial paper. But when something goes wrong, there is nothing more complicated. This chapter answers the following questions: Who pays when all is right with commercial paper? Who pays when something is wrong?

POSSIBLE PARTIES IN THE COMMERCIAL PAPER SCHEME

Although the parties to negotiable instruments were listed in Chapter 51, their roles in the liability scheme and the order of their liability has not been covered yet. These topics concerning primary, secondary and accommodation parties are discussed in the following sections.

Primary Parties

Primary parties are the people first in line to pay on a commercial instrument. Primary parties are the makers of notes and the drawees/acceptors of drafts (Section 3-102). Primary parties are the first ones who are expected to pay a negotiable instrument. The maker of a note promises to pay the note according to its "tenor at the time of his engagement." A drawee is liable in the same way on a draft as soon as the drawee accepts the draft. A drawee accepts a draft by signing it. A drawee has no liability for the draft until there has been a signature.

A bank is the primary party on a check. But the bank usually pays a check on provisional credit. Provisional credit means the bank has the right to return the check to the depositor or presenter if the check bounces.

Secondary Parties

Drawers and indorsers are **secondary parties,** who back up primary parties. If the primary parties do not pay, then secondary parties are expected to pay.

The drawer is the party who issues the draft. When a drawer writes a check, the drawer is telling the payee to take the check to the bank first and "if the bank does not pay, then come back to me." The drawer does not agree to pay first (that is, the drawer is not primarily liable). The *Esecson v. Bushnell* case illustrates the relationship between primary and secondary parties.

The indorser also gives a promise of secondary liability. Indorsers are liable in the order in which they indorsed the instrument. If a holder is not paid, they can go back to those who transferred the instrument—the indorsers.

Accommodation Parties

Accommodation parties are those who sign instruments to lend their names to some other party to the instrument. An accommodation party can sign as a maker, drawer, drawee, or indorser. However, the accommodation party signs in the capacity of the role they are playing. For example, if accommodation parties sign as co-signers on a note, they are makers and liable as primary parties. The accommodation party is not liable to the accommodated party in any way; the accommodation party is liable only to the other parties to the instrument.

If an accommodation party is required to pay, then the accommodation party acquires the rights of the holder. These rights mean that accommodation parties can recover what they have paid for the accommodated parties who failed to pay. This right to collect from the accommodated parties is called **subrogation.**

ESECSON v. BUSHNELL
Supreme Court of Colorado.
663 P.2d 258 (1983).

FACTS Stanton Esecson contracted to sell Donna Bushnell his condominium. Bushnell gave Esecson a $5000 personal check for the earnest money. The contract was entered into on March 13, 1981. The check was dated March 24, 1981. When Esecson went to cash the check, the bank refused to pay because Bushnell had stopped payment. Esecson went to Bushnell for payment, and she claimed she was not liable.

ISSUE Is Bushnell liable for the $5000 check?

DECISION Yes. Even though Bushnell changed her mind about buying the condominium, she was still liable as a secondary party to the check. Esecson had been refused payment by the primary party and could turn to the secondary party—Bushnell.

LEGAL TIP
Taking personal checks for large sums is risky. Require cashier's checks to avoid any problems.

CONTRACTUAL LIABILITY OF THE PARTIES

Unless otherwise agreed, primary and secondary parties make certain implied contractual promises under Article III. These promises require them to go through some steps to collect on negotiable instruments.

Presentment

Presentment is the formal name for asking the primary party to pay an instrument (Section 3-504). For presentment to occur, the following requirements must be met (Section 3-505):

1. The instrument must be shown.
2. The person presenting the instrument must have reasonable identification.
3. If an agent presents the instrument, the agent must have evidence of his or her authority.
4. The person presenting must be willing to surrender the instrument.

An example of presentment is when someone goes to a bank to cash a check, takes some identification, turns the check over to the bank, and is given cash in return.

When is presentment made? There are two issues concerning the question of when presentment is made. The first issue is the time of day. Under Section 3-503, presentment must be made during a business day and at a reasonable hour. If presentment is to a bank, the presentment must be during banking hours.

The second question concerning presentment is how long does a holder have to present an instrument? On dated notes and drafts, the answer is simple. Presentment must be made on or before the due date. In the case of an ordinary check, thirty days after the date of the check's issue is the generally accepted time. The thirty-day requirement is imposed to attach the liability of the drawer. If an indorser's liability is to be preserved, then presentment must be made within seven days of indorsement. If these time limits are not honored, then the indorser and drawer are discharged from their positions of secondary liability.

To understand these time limits, consider the following example. Fisher writes a check to Jennings for $500. The check is drawn on Fisher's Tennessee bank and is dated April 1, 1985. Jennings takes the check to her Arizona bank, indorses it, and deposits it. Jennings' Arizona bank then indorses the check and sends it to a Federal Reserve Bank. The Federal Reserve Bank indorses the check and sends it to Fisher's Tennessee bank. The roles of the parties are summarized in Figure 53-1.

For Fisher to be liable, Jennings must get the check to the Tennessee bank in thirty days. For the Arizona bank to be able to go back to Jennings, they must get the check to the Tennessee bank within seven days from the time of Jennings' indorsement. For the Federal Reserve Bank to be able to go back to the Arizona bank, they must get the check to the Tennessee bank within seven days of the time of the Arizona bank's indorsement.

Dishonor

What is dishonor? **Dishonor** follows presentment. Dishonor is the refusal to pay or accept an instrument when it is presented (Section 3-507).

How does dishonor occur? Dishonor occurs when the primary party states that the instrument will not be paid or accepted. For example, if a bank says the drawer has insufficient funds, there has been dishonor. If a bank requires more than is necessary for presentment, there is dishonor. For example, if a bank requires the holder to pledge assets to honor a check, there has been dishonor.

Notice of Dishonor

Notice of dishonor is required in order for a holder to turn to secondary parties to collect on the instrument. The procedures for notice of dishonor can be complicated. If notice is not given properly, it is as if the instrument was never presented for payment.

How notice is given Under Section 3-508, notice of dishonor can be given in "any reasonable manner." Notice by telephone, mail, telegraph, or through a clearing house (a banking institution where checks are exchanged among banks and returned to the drawee banks for payment) is appropriate. In giving notice, the primary party should remember that the dishonoring party has the burden of proving notice. Therefore, most parties choose to give some written form of notice

Figure 53-1 **Parties' Roles in Presentment Example**

Drawer	Drawee	Indorser	Payee	Primary
Fisher	Tennessee bank	Jennings Arizona bank Federal Reserve	Jennings	Tennessee bank

so that there is adequate proof. Even if oral notice is given, it should be followed by a written confirmation. If notice is mailed, the Code applies the Mailbox Rule. The notice is effective when sent. The mailed notice must be properly addressed, stamped, and placed in the hands of any box, chute, receptacle, or agent of the post office.

Who gets notice? Notice should be given to anyone who may be liable for the instrument, including all secondary parties. If there are joint parties involved (co-payees), then both must be notified. Most parties give notice to their immediate transferors. This notice limitation is reasonable because they have dealt only with that party, and they are recovering from the parties in the order the Code intended.

Time allowed for giving notice Non-bank parties have a **midnight deadline** of the third business day after they receive notice of dishonor to notify their prior transferor. Banks have until midnight of the next banking day to notify (Section 4-104). For instance, recall the circumstances in the example above with Fisher, Jennings, and the three banks. But this time, suppose that the Tennessee bank has dishonored Fisher's check. Figure 53-2 shows the notice requirements and the time frames.

The *Memphis Aero Corp. v. First American National Bank* case involves an issue of timely notice.

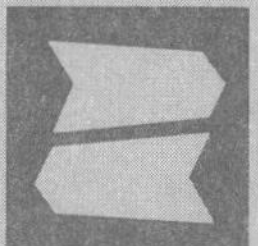

MEMPHIS AERO CORP. v. FIRST AMERICAN NATIONAL BANK

Supreme Court of Tennessee. 647 S.W.2d 219 (1983).

FACTS Mid-South purchased a Piper aircraft from Memphis Aero Corporation. A draft was drawn with Mid-South as the drawee. Mid-South did not have enough funds to pay the draft. Comin, an officer of the First American, notified Mid-South on November 14, 1981, that the draft would not be paid.

On November 26, 1981, Comin notified Memphis Aero of the problem and also explained that Mid-South would try to get a loan from someone to cover the draft. First American then dishonored the draft and notified Memphis Aero of the complete dishonor on December 20, 1981. Memphis-Aero claims they were not notified in time of the dishonor.

ISSUE Was there adequate notice of dishonor?

DECISION No. Comin did not actually dishonor on November 26, 1981; there was still a promise of a loan. First American will be liable to Memphis Aero for failure to provide notice of dishonor.

LEGAL TIP

Commercial paper requires fast and clear action. Holding on to checks and drafts is dangerous. Waiting for possible payment on an oral promise is also dangerous.

THE WARRANTY LIABILITIES OF THE PARTIES

In addition to all the contractual promises the parties make under Article III, they make some implied promises in the form of warranties. **Warranty liability** can exist even though a party has not signed an instrument. Even transferors of bearer

Figure 53-2 **Time Allowed for Notice of Dishonor**

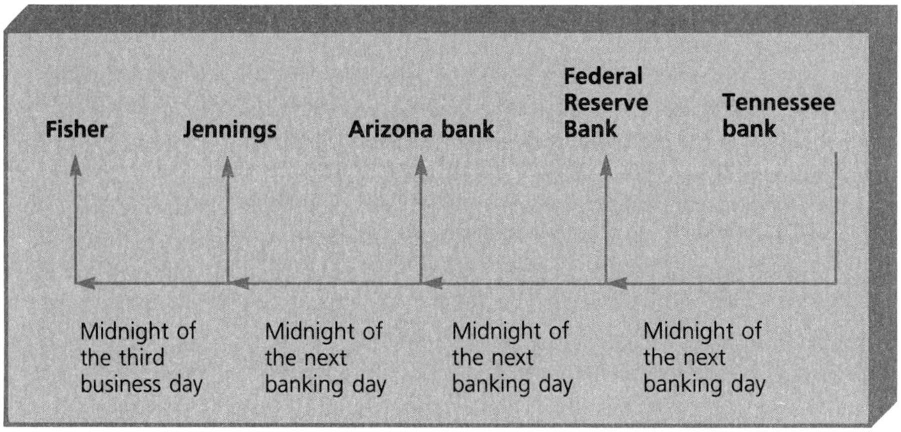

paper make certain warranties under the Code. The types of warranties given will depend upon the party's involvement with the commercial paper. There are transferor's warranties and presenter's warranties.

Transferor's Warranties

Who gives transferor's warranties? A transferor is anyone who negotiated the instrument—either by indorsing and delivering or by just delivering (in the case of bearer paper). In the example given in the prior section, Jennings, the Arizona bank, and the Federal Reserve Bank are all transferors.

Who benefits from transferor's warranties? The transferor's warranties are given not only to the immediate transferee but also to any subsequent holders who take the instrument in good faith. Jennings makes her warranties to the Federal Reserve Bank, the Arizona bank, and the Tennessee bank.

The actual warranties Transferors give five warranties (Sections 3-417 [2] and 4-207 [2] for bank transferors). The first is the warranty of title. Under this warranty, transferors promise that they have good title or that they are acting as an agent for someone with good title. They also warrant that they have the authority to transfer the instrument. Generally, this warranty is breached when a signature is forged somewhere along the line in the execution or transfer of the instrument.

The second transferor warranty is the warranty that all the signatures on the instrument are genuine or authorized. If there is a forgery, then both this warranty and the warranty of title have been broken.

The third transferor warranty is the promise that the instrument has not been altered materially. If such an alteration occurs, a transferor could end up paying a holder in due course. For example, suppose that Berferd writes a check for $50 to Alfred. Alfred transfers the check to Bonzo who raises the amount to $500. Bonzo then transfers the check to Charlie and Charlie transfers the check to Berferd's bank. Berferd's bank (through some checking) discovers the alteration and will only pay $50 on the check. Charlie can turn to Bonzo to collect the remaining $450 because Bonzo's warranty of no alterations has been breached.

The fourth transferor warranty is the warranty that there are no defenses to the instrument. This warranty covers the problems with fraud, breach, and other contractual defenses arising on the instrument. This is the warranty that the indorser escapes by signing "without recourse." A without recourse indorsement means the indorser gives only four of the five transferor warranties.

The final warranty of a transferor is no knowledge of any insolvency proceedings. The transferor does not warrant that the parties to the instrument are solvent or that they are good credit risks. The limited scope of the warranty is that none of the parties is in bankruptcy.

Presenters' Warranties

Who gives presenters' warranties? Those parties who obtain payment from the primary party or in the case of a draft obtain the acceptance of the primary party give presenters' warranties (Section 3-417 [1]). In the Fisher example, the Federal Reserve Bank is the presenter.

Who benefits? The primary parties are the beneficiaries of the presenters' warranties. If the primary party pays the wrong person, then the primary party will have a breach of warranty action against the presenter.

The actual warranties Presenters give three warranties. The first warranty is the same as the warranty for transferors—the warranty of title. Presenters' warranties of title consist of the same promises.

The second presenters' warranty differs slightly from the transferor's second warranty. This warranty provides that the presenter has no knowledge that the signature of the maker or drawer is unauthorized. This warranty is not an absolute promise that the signatures are authorized—only a promise of no knowledge of any problem warranty. Further, the warranty applies to only the signatures of the maker or drawer.

The final presenters' warranty is the same as one for transferors—that the instrument has not been materially altered. The *Morgan Guaranty Trust Co. of New York v. Chase Manhattan Bank, NA* case examines the issue of warranty liability.

THE BOTTOM LINE: WHO ACTUALLY PAYS?

When everything goes right, when the primary party is solvent, when there are no forgeries or alterations when the primary party pays and everyone (including presenters, transferors, holders in due course, makers, drawers, and indorsers) is satisfied. However, the purpose of this chapter has been to discuss the promises, rights, and responsibilities of the parties when something goes wrong. Their contractual and warranty promises have been covered but as yet, the scenario is not complete. This section covers the interrelationship between all of the rules as well as bottom-line liability.

Cast of Characters

Consider the following example. Berferd bought 200 wooden rocking horses from Sally's Toy Town for $20,000 and gave Sally a check for that amount. A thief stole the check from Sally (through no negligence on her part). The thief (or wrongdoer) forged Sally's signature and cashed the check (for a discount) at Charlie's Check Cashing Center (CCCC). Charlie deposited the check at his bank (Bank 1). Bank

MORGAN GUARANTY TRUST CO. OF NEW YORK v. CHASE MANHATTAN BANK, NA
36 UCC 584 (N.Y. 1983).

FACTS Kingsley is the beneficial owner of some shares of stock in Royal Dutch Petroleum Company. Morgan Guaranty holds the shares for Kingsley. Kingsley was entitled to a dividend on the shares and a check was issued by Royal Dutch, but Kingsley never received the check. The check eventually was cashed by Chase Manhattan (the drawee).

The words "or Mr. Peter Tyson" had been added to the front of the check in the payee section. Tyson had indorsed the check to cash it. The history of the check is as follows:

Drawer—Royal Dutch
↓
Sent to Morgan Guaranty
↓
Tyson
↓
Brooklyn Savings
↓
Manufacturers Hanover
↓
Chase

Morgan paid Kingsley and then sued to collect from Chase for breach of the warranty of title and material alteration.

ISSUE Is Chase liable under breach of warranty?

DECISION Yes. Chase did not have title to the instrument and the instrument had been materially altered. The instrument had been paid on a forgery.

LEGAL TIP
When a broker is handling property or stocks, check annual payments and dividends. Registered mail is a good way to avoid theft.

1 sends the check to Federal Reserve Bank, and Federal Reserve Bank sends the check to Berferd's bank (Bank 2) for payment. Berferd bank refuses to pay the check because they have been notified about the theft and the forgery. In diagram form, the cast of characters looks like Figure 53-3.

Liability

The primary party (Bank 2) has dishonored the instrument. Bank 2 must give notice to the Federal Reserve Bank of the dishonor by midnight of the next banking day. The Federal Reserve Bank can then turn to a secondary party (an indorser) or Bank 1 for recovery. The Federal Reserve Bank will have to give notice of dishonor to Bank 1 by midnight of the next banking day (after notice is given). The Federal Reserve Bank will be able to recover what is paid for the check from Bank 1 because Bank 1 has breached the transferor's warranties of title and genuine signatures.

Bank 1 will have until midnight of the next banking day (after it gets notice) to notify Charlie of the dishonor. Bank 1 can recover because Charlie has breached the transferor's warranties of signatures and title.

Charlie will then have until midnight of the third business day to notify the thief of the problem of dishonor. In most cases, the thief will be long gone and Charlie is left holding the bag. However, there is wisdom in the Code's result. Charlie was the first one to take the check from the thief. Charlie had the opportunity to get identification and verify signatures. The result of the liability sections of the Code is to assign the liability to the party who had contact with the thief.

Exceptions

There are some exceptions to the results in the Berferd case. For example, if it could be shown that Sally was negligent and the check was stolen because of her negligence, she would end up paying the check regardless of the thief. The issue of negligence is covered in the *Florida Federal Savings & Loan Ass'n. v. Martin* case.

FLORIDA FEDERAL SAVINGS & LOAN ASS'N. v. MARTIN

Court of Appeals of Florida, Second District.
400 So.2d 151 (1981).

FACTS Attorney Michael Martin hired Carol Tozzer to do general legal secretarial work. Martin had a password account—an account for which there is a secret password that must be used before any money can be withdrawn from the account. Tozzer handled all the finances for Martin's practice.

Over a 5-month period, Tozzer was able to forge checks and withdrawal slips and divert $11,200 of Martin's funds to herself. When Martin discovered the embezzlement, he fired Tozzer and sued Florida Federal for paying forged instruments.

ISSUE Is Florida Federal liable for paying forged instruments?

DECISION No. Martin gave Tozzer his password. Martin did not check his account statements for 5 months. Martin gave Tozzer too much control and no supervision.

LEGAL TIP

Employee supervision and review is necessary. A monthly review of bank statements is a must. Expenses and deposits should be cross-checked with the statement.

Returning to the Berford example given earlier, if the check was issued to an **imposter,** the theft rules do not apply and the check could be properly honored and paid by Bank 2. The *Federal Insurance Company v. First National Bank* case discusses an imposter issue.

FEDERAL INSURANCE COMPANY v. FIRST NATIONAL BANK

United States Court of Appeals, First Circuit.
633 F.2d 978 (1980).

FACTS Federal Insurance Company (FICO) insured Investment Companies Service Corporation (ISCO). ISCO received a forged request for redemption of shares, which was represented as being from a Florida shareholder—Helen Whitaker. Helen Whitaker owned 3172.307 shares held by ISCO.

A check was drawn and made payable to First National Bank and Helen Whitaker. The check amount was $40,288.30. The check was delivered to the desk of a First National Bank officer while he was away from the desk. He opened an account in Helen Whitaker's name and deposited the check.

Later, a young woman who claimed to be Helen Whitaker's niece appeared at the bank. She had signature cards for the account and withdrew $40,000 from the account. She was never seen nor found again.

In the meantime, the real Helen Whitaker became concerned when she did not receive her statement from ISCO. When all the facts came to light, Helen filed suit against First National.

ISSUE Is the bank liable or does the Imposter Rule apply?

DECISION The Imposter Rule applies, and the bank is not liable. Someone was posing as an imposter, which is more than a forgery.

LEGAL TIP

Carefully check identification and develop procedures for dealing with mail withdrawal requests.

Figure 53-3 **Schematic of Liability**

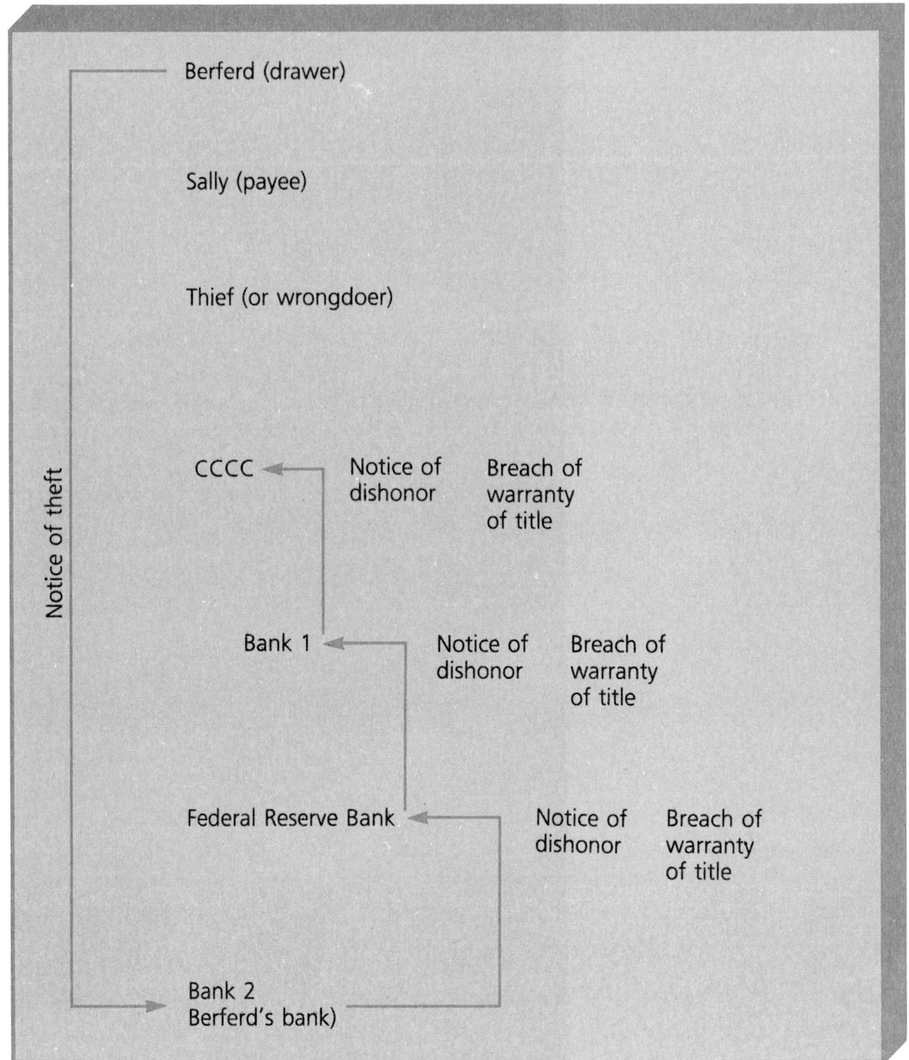

A third exception to the general rules of liability is the **fictitious payee** exception. Under this exception, the traditional setting is a company employee making payroll checks out to a fictitious name; a dead, fired, or transferred employee; or a real employee who does not know about the check. These checks are then cashed by the payroll employee. The company bears the cost of such schemes since they should maintain internal control to avoid them. The *Clinton Weilbacher Builder, Inc., v. Kirby State Bank* case deals with the employer control problem.

CLINTON WEILBACHER BUILDER, INC. v. KIRBY STATE BANK

Court of Appeals of Texas, Fourth District.
643 S.W.2d 473 (1982).

FACTS Norma Wilson was the bookkeeper for Clinton Weilbacher. She prepared the checks for Weilbacher's signature. She made out 5 checks totaling $22,738 to payees not entitled to receive them. Wilson forged the signatures and then cashed the checks at Kirby State Bank. When Weilbacher discovered the scheme, he sued Kirby for paying on a forged instrument.

ISSUE Was the bank guilty of paying on a forged instrument or the victim of a fictitious payee scheme?

DECISION The bank was a victim of a fictitious payee scheme. Weilbacher was held responsible because of inadequate supervision and the failure to check bank statements.

LEGAL TIP

Supervision and cross-checks of employees are necessary. Verify checks—to whom, what for, and how much.

TERMINATION OF LIABILITY: DISCHARGE

There are certain events that relieve the parties to an instrument of their liability. This section discusses methods for the termination of liability, which include: payment, reacquisition, alteration, and impairment of collateral.

Payment

The easiest and the most common method for discharging liability is to pay. Once a proper person has paid an instrument, all the parties to the instrument are discharged. The payment must be made to a proper person such as a holder. Of course, if a person is not a holder or there is a forgery in the chain of title, everyone is not discharged. The liability in that case will be determined according to the rules concerning forgeries (discussed earlier).

Reacquisition

When a primary party reacquires an instrument, all the intervening parties are discharged. For example, suppose that Fisher issues Jennings a $500 note, and Jennings sells it to Xavier who sells it to Zeke who then sells it to Fisher. In this situation, Jennings, Xavier and Zeke would all be discharged.

Material Alteration

If there has been **material alteration** of an instrument by a holder, any party whose promise is changed is discharged. For example, suppose Fisher executed a bearer $500 note to Jennings. Jennings transfers it to Xavier. Xavier raises the amount to $5000 and transfers it to Zeke—a holder in due course. Jennings is totally discharged. However, Fisher will still be liable to the holder in due course for original $500. If Zeke can show that Fisher made the alteration easy, then Fisher will be liable for the full $5000.

Impairment of Collateral

One of the principles of suretyship is that if a creditor releases the debtor without telling the surety, the surety is discharged. This same principle applies in commercial paper. For example, suppose that Fisher executed a promissory note for $5000 to Jennings and pledged his car as collateral. Jennings transferred the note to Xavier who transferred it to Yolanda who then transferred it to Zeke. Zeke allowed Fisher to sell his car. Zeke has impaired the security or collateral for the loan. Jennings, Xavier, and Yolanda are discharged.

KEY TERMS

Primary parties
Secondary parties
Accommodation parties
Subrogation
Presentment
Dishonor
Notice of dishonor
Midnight deadline
Warranty liability
Imposters
Fictitious payees
Termination of liability
Material alteration

CHAPTER PROBLEMS

1. What are the differences between transferor's and presenter's warranties?
2. An employee of Merrill Lynch, Pierce, Fenner & Smith, Inc., made up false invoices and issued 13 checks (totaling $115,180.10) to the firms on the invoices (the firms existed but the debts did not). The employee then forged the signatures for the companies and deposited the checks in an out-of-state account. Through a Federal Reserve Bank the checks went back to Merrill Lynch's bank—Chemical Bank—and they were honored. Merrill Lynch brought suit against Chemical for cashing the checks based on bogus invoices. Who will win? *Merrill Lynch, Pierce, Fenner & Smith, Inc., v. Chemical Bank of New York v. Federal Reserve Bank of New York,* 440 N.Y.S.2d 643 (1981).
3. Gish was in the process of selling his grocery store to Kenneth Smith and Barry Gill. Gill and Smith were to build two homes for Gish as payment. Smith and Gill would work in the store to train until the houses were complete. Gill and Smith opened an account under the name "Gish's General Store." By using Gish's rubber stamp, they were able to indorse checks and deposit them in their account. When Gish discovered the events, he sued the bank. The bank claimed it was not liable because Gish was negligent. Who is correct? *Springhill Bank & Trust Co. v. Gish,* 403 So.2d 819 (N.C. 1981).
4. Reuben R. Graff Company operates a scrap yard and processes scrap metals and sells it to mills. Available Iron & Metal had a rent-free office in Graff's yard, and Graff picked up scrap from Available's customers. Graff paid Available by check for the scrap that Available brought in itself.

   Graff began having financial problems. When Available tried to cash three checks at First National Bank, a teller sent the agent to a vice president. The vice president told Available's agent, "There's no money now, but we can work it out." The vice president took the checks and gave the agent a receipt. Available called continually to see if the checks could be cashed and was reassured by the bank.

   Graff went bankrupt and Available wants to collect from First National for their failure to give timely notice. Will Available win? *Available Iron & Metal Co. v. First National Bank of Blue Island,* 371 N.E.2d 1032 (Ill. 1977).

*5. Can a bank dishonor its own cashier's checks? *Rezapolvi v. First National Bank of Maryland,* 459 A.2d 183 (Md. 1983).

*6. Santos obtained a $15,514.46 cashier's check from First National State Bank of New Jersey and mailed it to Puerto Rico. The check was made payable to Santos. Eleven days later Santos told the bank the check had been lost and asked for a new one. Should the bank be concerned about whether Santos had indorsed the check? Why, or why not? *Santos v. First National State Bank of New Jersey,* 451 A.2d 401 (N.J. 1982).

*7. Kaiser-Georgetown Community Health Plan turned over a $100,000 cashier's check to a financial consultant with no restrictions on its use. The financial consultant had been instructed to purchase a certificate of deposit for Kaiser. The financial consultant cashed the check and left. Kaiser-Georgetown sued the bank that cashed the check—Banker's Trust of Albany. Could they recover? *Kaiser-Georgetown Community Health Plan, Inc., v. Bankers Trust Co. of Albany New York,* 442 N.Y.S.2d 48 (1981).

*8. First Arlington National Bank had a note that had been signed by three couples. Several weeks before the note was due, the bank sent notices of demand to the couples in care of the husbands' business addresses. Has there been presentment? *First Arlington National Bank v. Stathis,* 413 N.E.2d 1288 (Va. 1980).

*9. Does death discharge a party's obligations and liabilities on a negotiable instrument? *Estate of Harbaugh,* 639 P.2d 495 (Mont. 1982).

*10. Kinney received his annual bonus in the form of a note payable to him. His employer, Columbus Temperature Control, was experiencing financial difficulties and asked Kinney to waive his bonus. At first Kinney refused and then he marked the note void and put it in the desk of the chairman of the board. Kinney changed his mind again and wanted his bonus. Columbus claims they are discharged because Kinney returned the note to the maker. Are they correct? *Kinney v. Columbus Temp. Control Co.,* 34 UCC Rep. 1636 (Ohio 1982).

"Bank Wins."
David Epstein's Basic Law of Commercial Paper

Chapter 54

Banks and Commercial Paper

CHAPTER PREVIEW

- Dishonor and checks
- Overdrafts
- Stop payment orders
- Customers' bank statements
- Types of banks
- Electronic funds transfer (EFT) transactions and regulations

Mrs. Schuler needs to stop payment on a check but she did not write down and cannot remember the amount. Can she issue a valid stop payment order?

A study of Article III is not complete without a study of Article IV. Article IV is a discussion of commercial paper as it applies to banks. Article IV also covers banks and their relationships with customers. This chapter deals with these topics.

CUSTOMER RELATIONS: THE BANK AND THE DRAWER

A bank that handles a checking account is an agent for its customer. The bank handles the customer's funds and agrees to pay the amounts in the checks written by the customer.

Paying the Checks: The Bank's Duties

A bank is required to pay all "proper" items. Any check that has been completed by a customer and is correct in form is a "proper" item and must be honored by the bank. Of course, a bank is not required to pay if a customer does not have funds. But if the check is proper and a customer has the funds, the bank is liable if it dishonors the check (Section 4-402).

If a customer's check is dishonored wrongfully, the customer can recover the actual damages of the dishonor. For example, if the bank dishonored (or bounced) a check that you wrote to the grocery store and the store charged you $10 for the bounced check, the bank would be required to pay that amount. If you were arrested for writing a bad check (which was really a good check), the bank would be responsible for the damages resulting from your arrest. In some cases, the drawer can recover consequential damages for wrongful dishonor. For example,, if you wrote a check as a down-payment on a house, the bank dishonored it, and you lost your contract, the bank might have to pay the consequential damages of any additional cost in signing for another house. The *Elizarraras v. Bank of El Paso* case deals with the issue of damages for **wrongful dishonor.**

ELIZARRARAS v. BANK OF EL PASO

United States Court of Appeals, Fifth Circuit.
631 F.2d 366 (1980).

FACTS Francisco Elizarraras wrote checks drawn on Bank of El Paso for $64,000 to Financiera Del Norte, SA (a Mexican bank). The checks were for Elizarraras' loan payments. The Bank of El Paso dishonored the checks and returned them stamped "Insufficient Funds." As a result, Elizarraras had to pay a $12,800 penalty for late payment and an additional $2000 in interest. It was later discovered that the bank had made a mistake and wrongfully dishonored the checks. Elizarraras brought suit to collect the extra charges and also for damages to his credit reputation.

ISSUE Is Elizarraras entitled to damages for wrongful dishonor? What damages should he receive?

DECISION Yes. Elizarraras is entitled to damages because the bank had made a clear error. In this case, the court awarded the $12,800 penalty, the $2000 in interest, and $75,000 for damages to his credit reputation.

LEGAL TIP

For large sum payment, use cashier's checks to avoid the problems of dishonor.

When does the bank pay? A bank is not required to pay a check that is over six months old (Section 4-404). The bank could honor the check if it chose to but would have to do so in good faith. Good faith means showing that the customer wanted the check cashed despite the fact that six months had passed.

Can the bank be stopped? A bank customer still has the right to issue a **stop payment order** after a check is written (Section 4-403). Although most banks require the stop payment order to be in writing, the Code allows an oral stop payment order to be valid for fourteen days. After fourteen days, a written notice is required to keep a stop payment order valid.

The stop payment order must describe the item with certainty and specificity. To describe the item "with certainty" means naming at least the payee and the amount. Most banks require more information such as the date and check number. The *Capital Bank v. Schuler* case involves an issue of whether a stop payment order had enough information.

CAPITAL BANK v. SCHULER
Court of Appeals of Florida, Third District.
421 So.2d 633 (1982).

FACTS Mrs. Schuler wrote a check to Charles Mouyas. She had paid Mouyas $1450—part in cash and part in check. The breakdown was $750 and $700 but she could not remember which amount was cash and which was the check. She issued a stop payment order for a $750 check, but the check was for $700. Capital Bank honored the $700 check and Mrs. Schuler brought suit for the bank's failure to honor her stop payment order.

ISSUE Was the stop payment order sufficient?

DECISION No. The amount is critical because the bank is liable if they wrongfully dishonor the wrong instrument. The bank was correct here.

LEGAL TIP
Keep accurate check registers—when, to whom, how much and for what should be recorded.

Once the bank receives a stop payment order, the check that is stopped can no longer be cashed and the bank would be liable for checks cashed over a stop payment order. However, the bank must be given a reasonable amount of time to get the notice of a stop payment to its tellers and branches. From the *Dunbar v. First National Bank of Sotia,* case, it seems that an hour is enough time.

A stop payment order is an absolute. The bank must honor it and is required to honor it for a period of six months. The right to stop payment is a customer's right and cannot be challenged on the grounds that a bad check was intentionally written. The *Hardeman v. State* case involves an interesting question concerning the use of a stop payment order.

The Bank's Duty of Care: Reasonable Commercial Practices

Under Article IV, banks have several obligations. First they must exercise good faith in carrying out all their responsibilities. Second, they must use ordinary care in all areas of their operations. This ordinary care principle applies to posting, presenting, and dishonoring checks. In other words, the bank must verify the

DUNBAR v. FIRST NATIONAL BANK OF SOTIA

Court of Appeals of New York, Third Department.
404 N.Y.S.2d 722 (1978).

FACTS Dunbar placed a stop payment order on a $1000 check at First National's main office at 9:05 AM. Sometime before 10:15 AM, the same office cashed the check presented by Dunbar's wife. A bank officer's approval was required and was given. The stop payment order was not circulated until 11:55 AM. The teller who cashed the check got notice of the stop payment at 12:30 PM. Dunbar sued the bank for its failure to follow the stop payment order.

ISSUE Did the bank have sufficient time to circulate the stop payment order before the check was cashed?

DECISION Yes. The stop payment and presentment for check were at the same branch. A bank officer's approval was required so the check should have caught someone's attention.

LEGAL TIP

Be sure to have proof of when you issue a stop payment order.

HARDEMAN v. STATE

Court of Appeals of Georgia.
268 S.E.2d 415 (1980).

FACTS Cheryl Hardeman had front-end alignment work done on her car at Firestone Tire & Rubber Company. She picked up her car and wrote a check for $40.20 for the work. After she drove the car, she discovered that the Firestone outlet had not corrected her car's problem of pulling to the right. She stopped payment on the check to Firestone.

Firestone reported Hardeman, and she was prosecuted for writing a bad check. She had sufficient funds in her account to cover the check but had a dispute with Firestone over the adequacy of the repairs.

ISSUE Is stopping payment after writing a check considered to be the crime of writing an insufficient funds check?

DECISION No. She had a bona fide dispute and had the right to stop payment on the check. She had no intent at the time she wrote the check to write a bad check.

LEGAL TIP

Check out car repairs before paying and before driving away. Let the mechanic take a test ride with you.

identity of those presenting checks, be cautious in their bookkeeping procedures, and verify accounts before dishonoring a check.

Charging the Customer's Account

Overdraft A bank can pay an instrument even when payment will cause an **overdraft** in the customer's account (Section 4-401). The bank can charge a fee for covering the amount of the overdraft. Likewise, the bank can refuse to pay an instrument that will cause an overdraft; the decision is left to the bank. Some banks have policies on overdrafts, and some even have accounts with overdraft protection. Overdraft protection allows customers to use a credit line to cover checks when they go over the amount in their checking account. The *Clairmont v. State Bank of Burleigh County* case examines an overdraft problem.

CLAIRMONT v. STATE BANK OF BURLEIGH COUNTY

Supreme Court of North Dakota.
295 N.W.2d 154 (1980).

FACTS Clairmont operated a car dealership called Classic Automobiles of Bismarck, Ltd. He agreed to sell a custom patterned Excalibur on consignment for Dr. Neville Jones and his son, Barrie. Clairmont's bank, State Bank, agreed to loan John Igoe money to buy the car.

The bank deposited the loan amount in Clairmont's account. The bank then discovered that Igoe was in severe financial trouble and had falsified his application for the loan. The bank called the loans and took the funds from Clairmont's account.

Clairmont, in the meantime, had drawn a check to pay the Joneses. The check was returned to the Joneses marked, "Refer to Maker." Clairmont sued the bank for wrongful dishonor.

ISSUE Did the bank wrongfully dishonor the check?

DECISION No. The funds were not there, and the bank can cover the check or dishonor it. Here they could not get the funds and properly chose to dishonor.

LEGAL TIP

Verify loan applications. Use cashier's checks for large amounts. Be sure to have bank notification when deductions are made from an account.

Death of customer The bank is the agent for a checking account customer. One of the rules of agency is that if a principal (in this case a customer) dies, then the agency ends; the agent no longer has any authority. However, Section 4-405 provides a statutory exception to this rule, allowing a bank to continue paying presented checks until actual death (or incompetence) of a customer is determined.

Checks flow into a bank on a continual basis. The bank cannot be expected to stop payment of checks at the moment of death when they might not know of the death for days. In fact, Section 4-405 allows the bank to go even further in exercising its agency. Even after the bank has knowledge of death, it may continue to pay checks for a period of ten days, unless someone claiming an interest in the account asks the bank to stop. Someone claiming an interest would be an heir or creditor of the deceased. The reason for this extension is to allow the last debts and payments of the deceased to be settled.

Forgeries: Who Pays If the Bank Pays?

Suppose that a bank honors a check believed to belong to one of its customers and which, in fact, is a forgery. Who pays for the forgery? Ultimately the forger should pay, but forgers are usually not the types of individuals from whom funds can be recovered. The bank, who had a chance to check signatures and identification, will be responsible for paying. However, the customer has the responsibility for finding a forgery and notifying the bank. The customer learns of forgeries by checking the monthly statements and/or cancelled checks sent by the bank.

Once a customer has received a monthly statement, he or she has fourteen days (from receipt) to notify the bank of a forgery (Section 4-406). If a customer does not check the statement and notify the bank within fourteen calendar days, the customer would be liable for any forged checks cashed after that time; the bank is no longer held responsible. The *K & K Mfg., Inc., v. Union Bank* case illustrates how liability can result from lack of attention to bank statements.

K & K MFG., INC. v. UNION BANK

Court of Appeals of Arizona.
628 P.2d 44 (1981).

FACTS K & K Manufacturing had two employees: Bill J. Knight, the president, and Eleanor Garza, a bookkeeper. Garza kept the records for both K & K's account and for Knight's personal account.

Between March 1977 and January 1978, she forged 66 checks on both accounts. The forgeries totaled $49,859.31 from the corporate account and $11,350 from Knight's personal account. She was able to "doctor" the books to conceal the forgeries. Knight did not check the records or the bank statements even though his personal account had been overdrawn 12 times during the period of the forgery and even though he testified that he was aware Garza was "inaccurate and tardy." Knight brought suit for the bank's payment of forged instruments. Union Bank claims Knight is responsible.

ISSUE Is the Bank liable for cashing the forged instruments?

DECISION No. There were only a few checks cashed before the 14 days had expired. The remainder were cashed after he had an opportunity to examine the statements. Knight failed to supervise his employee and check his bank statements.

LEGAL TIP

Employees need to be supervised and have their work checked. Never neglect bank balances for longer than 14 days.

THE BANK COLLECTION PROCESS

Taking care of a check is more than just writing and cashing it. There will usually be two or three banks and many code sections involved in a simple check transaction. This section covers the types of banks involved in check collection as well as their rights, responsibilities, and liabilities.

Types of Banks

Depositary bank A **depositary bank** is the first bank to which a check is taken for collection (Section 4-105). For example, suppose that Fisher writes a check to Jennings on his Tennessee bank checking account. Jennings takes the check to her Arizona bank for depositing or cashing. Jennings' Arizona bank is a depositary bank. If Jennings happened to be in Tennessee and took the check to Tennessee bank for cashing, the Tennessee bank would be the depositary bank (even though it also happens to be the drawee).

Payor bank The **payor bank** is the drawee. In the Jennings/Fisher example above, the Tennessee bank is the payor bank.

Intermediary bank An **intermediary bank** is any bank other than the depositary or payor bank. If the Jennings/Fisher example is expanded to include a Federal Reserve 1 and Federal Reserve 2 Bank between the two state banks, these Federal banks would both be intermediary banks.

Collection bank A **collection bank** is any bank other than the payor bank. In the example above, the Arizona bank, Federal Reserve 1, and Federal Reserve 2 are collection banks.

Presenting bank A **presenting bank** is any bank (other than the payor bank) that presents a check for payment. Federal Reserve 2 in the Jennings/Fisher example is a presenting bank.

Remitting bank A **remitting bank** is a payor or intermediary bank—in other words, any bank but the depositary bank.

Figure 54-1 illustrates the Fisher/Jennings example and labels all the parties according to their Article IV titles.

The Collection Process

Step one: The depositary bank Jennings' first step is to take the check for deposit to her bank. The bank will give Jennings provisional credit. If the Fisher check is dishonored, the funds are removed from Jennings' account. Some banks deposit the check but put a hold on the amount of the check in the account. The depositary bank's action is a way of preserving rights and way of noting that the transaction is not over yet—presentment has not yet been made.

Step two: The intermediary or collecting banks These banks are simple links in the chain. These banks are the way checks get across the country. They indorse the items and pass them along. They also give provisional credit to the bank preceding them. Provisional credit means the check is taken on the condition that it is valid. It is important to remember that all the banks make certain transferor's warranties as they move the check along (see Chapter 53 and Section 4-207). With provisional credit, if the check is dishonored, the banks can turn to their transferors to recover (Sections 4-211 and 4-212).

Figure 54-1 **The Bank Collection Process**

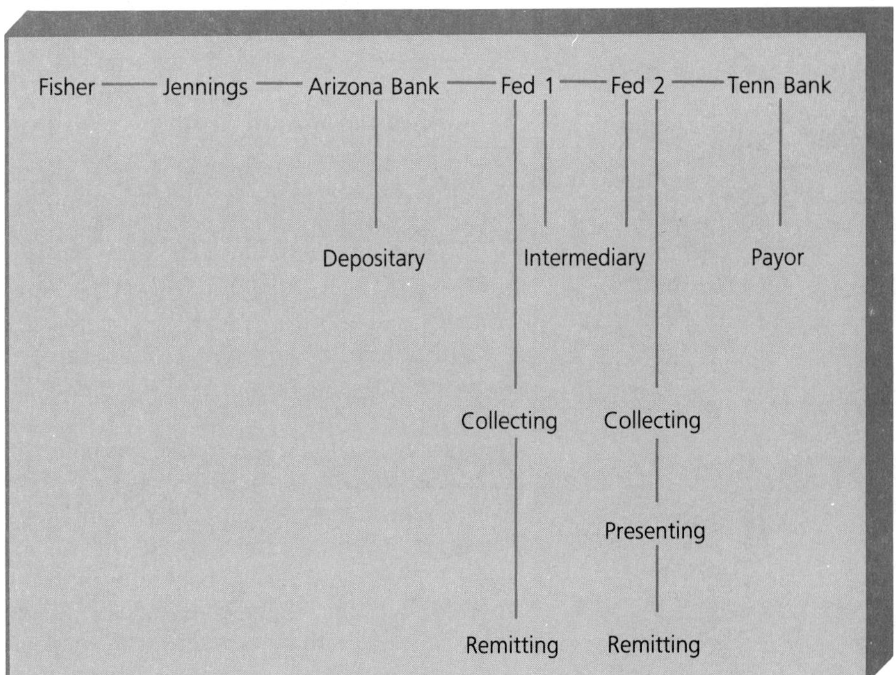

Step three: Presentment and the payor bank The buck (in this case the check) stops here. The payor bank goes through the process of posting (Section 4-109). Posting includes verifying the signature, determining whether funds are available for payment, stamping the check paid, and charging the customer's account. When the process of posting is complete, the bank pays the presenting bank and the provisional credit arrangements made by the banks all the way back to Jennings are made final. At this point, the transaction is permanent and complete.

When problems arise (such as forgeries or alterations) and the check is not paid, the rules for liability apply (discussed in Chapter 53).

ELECTRONIC FUNDS TRANSFER

What Is Electronic Funds Transfer?

One of the drawbacks of commercial paper is the paperwork involved. Negotiable instruments require paperwork, including posting, signatures, transfers, and delays. In this age of computer technology, commercial paper is progressing. **Electronic funds transfers (EFT)** are ways of making payments and depositing funds without physical transfers of a negotiable instrument. The following list gives some examples of EFT transactions:

1. Automatic deposit of paychecks, social security checks, and pension checks are EFT transactions. Instead of sending checks to the payees for them to indorse and deposit, the amounts of the checks are transferred by computer. The payees' accounts are simply credited with the amount of the check on a certain day or days of the month.
2. Automatic bill paying services involve deducting bill and savings deposit amounts from paycheck balances before checks are issued to payees. These bills are paid automatically each month or each paycheck.
3. Machine banking is an EFT transaction in which deposits and cash withdrawals can be made at automated teller machines. A customer has a card and a **personal identification number (PIN)** for access to the machines.
4. Point of sale transfer is an EFT service that automatically deducts the amount of a purchase at the time the account holder buys the goods. The merchant's funds are set aside.

How Is EFT Regulated?

The Electronic Funds Transfer Act (EFT Act) was passed by Congress as part of the Financial Institutions Regulatory and Interest Rate Act of 1978. This act, along with the regulations passed by the Federal Reserve's Board of Governors, provides the basic regulatory scheme.

The EFT Act applies to banks, savings and loans institutions, and credit unions. Its application is limited to EFT accounts held by consumers. Transfers by electronic terminal, instrument, or magnetic tape are covered. Transactions covered include point of sales transfers, automated teller transactions, direct deposits and withdrawals, and telephone transactions.

The EFT Act requires the bank to provide the consumer with an easily understandable contract explaining the system and their rights and liabilities. Consumers must be given monthly statements with summaries of their EFT transactions. They have sixty days after receiving the statement to report errors. The bank has ten days after they receive an error report to investigate. If an error is found, the bank has one day to correct it. Instead of using the ten-day limit, the bank can elect to temporarily credit the customer's account and then take forty-five days to investigate.

The EFT Act also has liability limitations. Consumers are liable for a maximum of $50 for unauthorized transfers. They are liable for that $50 maximum only if the transfers are made before they notify the bank. Consumers can be liable for up to $500 if they do not notify the bank within 2 business days after they discover that their EFT card is lost. If notice is not given within 60 days, the consumer has unlimited liability.

The *Judd v. Citibank* case deals with EFT liability.

JUDD v. CITIBANK

Supreme Court of New York.
435 N.Y.S.2d 210 (1980).

FACTS Judd was issued an EFT transfer card for use in Citibank's automatic teller machines. She was given a personal identification code for access. When she received her monthly statement, she discovered that 2 withdrawals totaling $800 had been made on her account. She had not made them.

One withdrawal was on February 26, 1980, between 2:13 and 2:14 PM. The second was on March 28, 1980, between 2:30 PM and 2:32 PM. Judd offered her testimony and that of her employer's to support that she was at work at those times. Citibank claims no one else could have had access to her account and that she was liable for the $800.

ISSUE Is Judd liable for the $800?

DECISION No. The court held that the EFT Act relieves account holders from liability unless the bank can prove that the account holder was negligent or that they contributed to the unauthorized use.

LEGAL TIP

When using EFT machines, keep records of where and when withdrawals and deposits are made. Carefully guard EFT cards and PINs.

KEY TERMS

Stop payment orders
Overdraft
Wrongful dishonor
Depositary bank
Payor bank
Intermediary bank
Collection bank
Presenting bank
Remitting bank
Electronic funds transfers (EFT)
Personal identification number (PIN)
Provisional credit

CHAPTER PROBLEMS

1. Thomas wrote a check at 12:00 AM on January 9, 1978. Thomas then telephoned a stop payment order to the Bank of Springfield on the check between 7:00 AM and 8:00 AM on that same day. The bank paid

the check shortly after opening for business. Who will be liable for the check? *Thomas v. Bank of Springfield,* 631 S.W.2d 346 (Mo. 1982).

2. Sherrill issued a stop payment order on a check he had written to purchase a Buick Skyhawk through a fleet plan. The check was written to "Frank Morris Buick" on June 2, 1976, and was for $4860.61. Sherrill's stop payment order said the check was dated June 3, 1976, and was written to "Walter Morris Buick." The amount on the stop payment order was correct. Is the stop payment order sufficient? *Sherrill v. Frank Morris Pontiac-Buick-GMC, Inc.,* 366 So.2d 251 (Ala. 1978).
3. Poulier wrote a check to Nacua Motors for $4247.65. Poulier issued a stop payment order for the check with the amount given as $4287.65. The bank did not stop payment when the check came through. The bank claimed its computer could not check for the $40 difference. Is the bank liable? *Poulier v. Nacua Motors, Inc.,* 439 N.Y.S.2d 85 (1982).
4. Can a customer stop payment on a cashier's check? *Santos v. First National State Bank of New Jersey,* 451 A.2d 401 (N.J. 1982).
5. Dorothy Edgerly, a bookkeeper, was able to forge her employer's signature on 99 checks during a 1-year period without detection for a total embezzlement of $19,711.90. Her employer, Ossip Harris has brought suit against its banks to collect for cashing the forged checks. Who will win? *Ossip Harris Insurance v. Barnett Bank of So. Florida,* 428 So.2d 363 (Fla. 1983).
6. What is the difference between provisional credit and final payment?
7. Identify the types of banks in the following diagram

Bob's Banana Boutique (buyer)
↓
Sally's Fruits and Nuts (Seller and payee)
↓
Sally deposits check at
First National Bank
↓
First Federal
↓
First Western
↓
Drawee for Bob's check—First
American Bank

8. Ferguson opened a drugstore in Krum, Texas, He obtained several loans from Merchants State Bank to open and operate the store. The loans were secured by interests in the store's inventory and fixtures. Ferguson had his personal and business accounts at Merchants.

   Things did not go well with the business. With the bank's permission, Ferguson began selling off the inventory and fixtures. The bank then froze Ferguson's accounts but did not tell him. He deposited all the sale proceeds in his accounts. When he tried to draw a salary, his check bounced. He borrowed $2000 to get him through this period and sued the bank for wrongful dishonor. He claimed the following damages: $3000 for loss of credit reputation; $25,000 for mental anguish; $5000 for loss of time; $345.56 for cost of loan; and $1500 for late penalties. Can he collect these damages? *Farmers' & Merchants State Bank v. Ferguson,* 617 S.W.2d 918 (Tex. 1981).

*9. Charles R. Shaw was a joint tenant in some accounts with Emma B. Nauman at Union Bank and Trust. Emma died on May 9, 1978, and Charles asked for the account balances. The bank refused to give them to Charles until he had a tax release. On May 31, 1978, Charles went to the bank with the release and was still refused payment. Shaw hired an attorney at a cost of $1000. The estate was probated even though it was exempt from probate and on June 30, 1978, the bank released the funds. Shaw brought suit for wrongful dishonor and asked for the $1000 attorney's fee, $56.26 in interest on the funds, and $25,000 for pain and suffering. Can he win? *Shaw v. Union Bank and Trust Co.,* 640 P.2d 953 (Okla. 1981).

*10. Merchants Bank of New York sold personal money orders for American Express. Merchants was not involved in the transfer, negotiation or payment of the money orders. Merchants issued three $1000 money orders to Sony at Lewis' request. The money orders were stolen by Brian Taylor who cashed two of them at National Bank of North America and one at Morgan Guaranty and Trust Company. Sony brought suit against Merchants. Is Merchants liable? *Sony Corp. of America v. American Express Co.,* 455 N.Y.S.2d 227 (1982).

Part Nine

Creditor/Debtor Relationships

"Neither a borrower nor a lender be, for loan oft loses both itself and friend."

William Shakespeare
Polonius to Laertes
Act I, Scene III
Hamlet

Chapter 55

Consumer Protection for Credit Transactions

CHAPTER PREVIEW

- Truth in Lending Act: requirements and disclosures
- Rights of credit card holders
- Effects of Fair Credit Reporting Act
- Consumer leasing protections
- Equal credit rights

Berferd had a swimming pool salesperson come to his home. Before he knew it, Berferd had signed up for a $15,000 pool. The pool would be financed by First Bank and Berferd's payments would be $183 per month for 15 years. Two days have passed since Berferd signed the contract, and he wants out. Is it too late?

The United States is a credit society. There is a "buy now, pay later" philosophy that everyone seems to follow. Because credit is used so often by so many, the legislatures and courts have been very active in making sure creditors and debtors are protected. This chapter covers the basics of credit transactions and answers the following questions: How is a credit transaction set up? What statutes affect the contract?

SETTING UP THE CREDIT TRANSACTION: CONTRACT TERMS

A credit contract is like any other contract. The contract should be in writing and the terms should be clear for complete protection. The following items should be included in the credit contract:

1. The amount the debtor owes.
2. The amount of interest the debtor will pay.
3. The length of time the debtor has to repay the debt.
4. Payment dates and amounts.
5. Penalties for late payments.
6. Security or collateral (if any) for the creditor.
7. Any statutory language required (discussed below).

SETTING UP THE CREDIT TRANSACTION: WHAT STATUTES APPLY?

A creditor is subject to a number of laws affecting credit contracts. Before drafting a contract or enforcing payment on a credit contract, the creditor must be aware of all the statutes and their requirements. The statutes most frequently involved are:

1. Usury laws (state laws).
2. The Equal Credit Opportunity Act.
3. Truth-in-Lending Act.
4. Fair Credit Billing Act.
5. Fair Credit Reporting Act.
6. Consumer Leasing Act.
7. Fair Debt Collections Practices Act.

Usury Laws

Usury is charging an interest rate higher than the rate permitted by law. A creditor cannot charge a rate higher than the maximum rate (for more details on usury see Chapter 23).

Equal Credit Opportunity Act

The **Equal Credit Opportunity Act** (ECOA) prohibits consumer creditors from considering certain factors in determining whether they extend credit. The factors that cannot be considered in determining whether a debtor is a good credit risk are:

1. Applicant's sex.
2. Applicant's marital status.
3. Whether the applicant receives public assistance income (welfare).
4. Whether the applicant receives alimony or child support.
5. Applicant's plans to have children.
6. Applicant's race, color, religion, national origin, or age (these questions can be asked because lenders must keep records for government statistics, but the information cannot be used as a basis for the credit decision).

In addition to making it illegal to use the above information in deciding whether to extend credit, the ECOA allows married persons certain individual credit rights. Married persons have the right to apply for individual credit accounts. They must be told that they do not have to disclose their spouse's income or support payments in their applications unless they are relying on that income to qualify for credit. In community property states, some types of credit transactions (such as real property loans) require information and consent from both spouses.

If joint accounts are held, married persons can require the creditor to report the credit rating in both spouses' names. The credit history of the account belongs to both spouses, and it is illegal for a creditor to refuse to consider the history of both individuals.

Individuals whose rights are violated under the ECOA can sue the creditor for damages. The individual can collect actual damages for embarrassment and mental distress and also up to $10,000 in punitive damages (civil penalties for violations). If several individuals bring a class action suit against a creditor, they can collect their damages plus up to the lesser of $500,000 or 1% of the creditor's net worth as punitive damages. The ECOA allows individuals to collect the punitive amounts even when they have no actual damages. The *Miller v. American Express Co.* case is one interpreting the ECOA.

Truth-in-Lending Act (TILA)

In 1968, Congress passed the Consumer Credit Protection Act (15 USC §1601). The **Truth-in-Lending Act** is part of the statute. These acts were the first (on a national level) to require creditors to deal with their debtors more fairly. The purpose of the acts was to promote informed use of consumer credit. The key term in the acts is "disclosure." In addition to the acts, the Federal Reserve Board (placed in charge of enforcement) has passed regulations to provide details for required disclosure. These regulations are part of Regulation Z (12 CFR §226).

When TILA applies. The TILA applies to all **consumer credit transactions.** Consumer credit transactions are those for goods and services to be used personally or in the home. The TILA applies to both closed-end and open-end credit transactions. **Open-end** credit transactions are credit card transactions or open account charges. **Closed-end** transactions are single-amount transactions in which the amount of the debt is fixed and a definite payment schedule is adopted. For

MILLER v. AMERICAN EXPRESS CO.

United States Court of Appeals, Ninth Circuit.
688 F.2d 1235 (1982).

FACTS Maurice Miller received an American Express Credit card in 1966 and his wife, Virginia, was given a supplementary card. Her application was signed by both Miller and his wife. Her card had a different number, was issued in her name, and had a separate fee.

They used their cards until May 1979 when Mr. Miller died. Two months later Virginia attempted to use her card but was told by a store clerk that her account had been cancelled. This was her first notice. When she contacted American Express, they explained their policy of cancelling the supplementary card when the basic card holder died. They invited her to apply for a new card. She sued for violation of the ECOA.

ISSUE Does American Express' policy of cancelling a spouse's card upon the death of the other spouse violate the ECOA?

DECISION Yes. American Express could not automatically terminate on the basis of a change in marital status. They had no proof that Virginia was unable to pay her obligations. Further, her credit rights were interrupted and one of the purposes of the ECOA was to prevent such credit interruptions because of a death or divorce.

LEGAL TIP

Check on credit status upon death or divorce of a spouse.

example, when a car is purchased on credit, the credit arrangement is a closed-end transaction.

Open-end disclosures When a debtor first opens a charge account, the creditor must disclose certain information. The information required is:

1. Finance charges: amount and computation methods.
2. Creditor's possession of a lien (or security interest) in the goods bought on credit.
3. Billing information: time period for sending bills; debtor's rights to question bills; and time limits for objecting to bills.

The creditor is required to send a periodic statement. This monthly bill must list the following information:

1. The account balance from last statement and the current balance.
2. A list of transactions (purchases bought with the credit card during statement period).
3. Finance charge rate.
4. Computation method for finance charges.
5. Amount of the finance charges for the period.
6. Closing date for the bill.
7. "Free-ride" period: time for paying the bill before there are finance charges.
8. Address for sending questions about bills.

If the creditor changes any terms in the credit arrangement, the credit card holder must be told of the changes. Notice of any changes must be given at least one period in advance of the effective date. The *Peterson v. Wells Fargo Bank* case was a landmark one decided at the height of the economic crisis of 1980 to 1981.

PETERSON v. WELLS FARGO BANK

United States District Court, Northern District of California.
556 F.Supp. 1100 (1980).

FACTS Patricia Peterson held a VISA and Master Charge card through Wells Fargo Bank. In May 1980, she received a notice with her cards that the finance charge would increase from 18% to 20%. The notice stated that the rate would go into effect automatically if the cardholder used the card after July 15, 1980. Peterson brought a class action suit alleging that the notice and increased rates violated the Truth-in-Lending Act.

ISSUE Could the creditor increase the finance charge? Was the notice adequate?

DECISION Yes. The bank could increase the finance charge. The notice was sent out at least one period in advance. The notice had been printed in large thick letters and was adequate.

LEGAL TIP

Check billing inserts. Some changes and critical terms may be included.

Figure 55-1 is a sample open-end disclosure statement.

Closed-end transaction disclosures The creditor must disclose the following in closed-end transactions:

1. Identity of the creditor.
2. Amount the debtor is financing.
3. Finance charge—amount the credit will cost the debtor.
4. Annual percentage rate—the finance charge in a percentage figure (for example, 18%, 21%).
5. A payment schedule—the amount of the payments and dates they are due.
6. Total of payments—the amount that will have been paid when all the payments are made.
7. Existence of any prepayment penalties.
8. Charges for late payments.
9. Creditor's possession of a security interest (lien or collateral in any property).
10. Debtor's payment for credit insurance and charges for that insurance.

All of the terms used in the disclosure statement are defined in Regulation Z. Regulation Z also has formulas for computing finance charges, annual percentage rates, and prepayment penalties. The basic idea behind all of these requirements is to make sure that the debtor knows how much it costs to "buy on time." For example, a car may have a contract price of $8000, but the total cost to the debtor (to be able to borrow the $8000) may be $12,000 including the interest on the loan. The *Mars v. Spartanburg Chrysler Plymouth, Inc.* case shows how strictly the courts apply these requirements.

Figure 55-1 **Retail Installment Credit Agreement**

Schedule of **FINANCE CHARGE** Rates

State	Monthly Periodic Rates	ANNUAL PERCENTAGE RATE
AZ, CO, DE, GA, ID, IL, KY, MS, MT, NV, NH, NJ, NM, NY, OK, OR, UT, WY, AND NON U.S. RESIDENTS	1.65%	19.8%
AL, CT, DC, FL, HI, IN, KS, LA, ME, MA, MI, MN, MO, NE, NC, ND, OH, RI, SC, SD, TN, TX, VA, WA, WI, WV	1.5%	18%
CA	1.6% on First $1,000 1% on excess	19.2% 12%
AK, MD	1.5% on First $700 1% on excess	18% 12%
IA, VT	1.5% on First $500 1.25% on excess	18% 15%
PA	1.25%	15%
AR	.833%	10%

YOUR BILLING RIGHTS — KEEP THIS NOTICE FOR FUTURE USE

This notice contains important information about your rights and our responsibilities under the Fair Credit Billing Act.

NOTIFY US IN CASE OF ERRORS OR QUESTIONS ABOUT YOUR BILL

If you think your bill is wrong, or if you need more information about a transaction on your bill, write us (on a separate sheet) at P.O. Box 64788, Dallas, Texas 75206. Write to us as soon as possible. We must hear from you no later than 60 days after we sent you the first bill on which the error or problem appeared. You can telephone us, but doing so will not preserve your rights.

In your letter, give us the following information:

— Your name and account number.
— The dollar amount of the suspected error.
— Describe the error and explain, if you can, why you believe there is an error. If you need more information, describe the item you are not sure about.

If you have authorized us to pay your credit card bill automatically from your savings or checking account, you can stop the payment on any amount you think is wrong. To stop payment your letter must reach us three business days before the automatic payment is scheduled to occur.

YOUR RIGHTS AND OUR RESPONSIBILITIES AFTER WE RECEIVE YOUR WRITTEN NOTICE

We must acknowledge your letter within 30 days, unless we have corrected the error by then. Within 90 days, we must either correct the error or explain why we believe the bill was correct.

After we receive your letter, we cannot try to collect any amount you question, or report you as delinquent. We can continue to bill you for the amount you question, including finance charges, and we can apply any unpaid amount against your credit limit. You do not have to pay any questioned amount while we are investigating, but you are still obligated to pay the parts of your bill that are not in question.

If we find that we made a mistake on your bill, you will not have to pay any finance charges related to any questioned amount. If we didn't make a mistake, you may have to pay finance charges, and you will have to make up any missed payments on the questioned amount. In either case, we will send you a statement of the amount you owe and the date that it is due.

If you fail to pay the amount that we think you owe, we may report you as delinquent. However, if our explanation does not satisfy you and you write to us within ten days telling us that you still refuse to pay, we must tell anyone we report you to that you have a question about your bill. And, we must tell you the name of anyone we reported you to. We must tell anyone we report you to that the matter has been settled between us when it finally is.

If we don't follow these rules, we can't collect the first $50 of the questioned amount, even if your bill was correct.

SPECIAL RULE FOR CREDIT CARD PURCHASES

If you have a problem with the quality of property or services that you purchased with a credit card, and you have tried in good faith to correct the problem with the merchant, you may have the right not to pay the remaining amount due on the property or services.

RETAIL INSTALLMENT CREDIT AGREEMENT

NEIMAN-MARCUS as Seller and the applicant as Buyer agree that all purchases charged to Buyer's account shall be governed by the following terms, subject to the right of NEIMAN-MARCUS to change such terms upon notice given in accordance with applicable laws. (1) The closing balance shown on the monthly statement is to be paid at Dallas, Texas, within 30 days from the closing date on such statement, in which case no **FINANCE CHARGE** will be added, or at Buyer's option may be paid in monthly installments of 1/5 or more of the closing balance (but not less than $25). (2) A **FINANCE CHARGE** is added upon any statement showing a previous balance, unless payments and credits during the cycle equal or exceed such previous balance. The **FINANCE CHARGE** is computed by applying to the average daily balance during the billing cycle periodic rates based upon Buyer's state of residence as shown on the schedule below, subject to a minimum monthly **FINANCE CHARGE** of 50¢ where permitted by law. The average daily balance is determined by totalling the balances outstanding for each day in the billing cycle, including all purchases and payments and other charges and credits made on or prior to such day, and dividing that total by the number of days in the billing cycle, except that purchases made since the last billing date are not included in the daily balances for residents of Maine, Massachusetts, Minnesota, Mississippi, Montana, Nebraska, New Mexico and Rhode Island. If you change your state of residence, the **FINANCE CHARGE** will be calculated in accordance with the terms applicable to your new state of residence. (3) If Buyer fails to pay any installment when due, Seller may declare the entire balance due and payable at once and Buyer agrees to pay the maximum attorneys' fees and court costs as may be permitted by law. (4) Buyer authorizes Seller to investigate Buyer's credit references and credit history, to issue a charge card to Buyer, to establish in Seller's sole discretion a maximum amount of credit which may be extended on this account and to report to appropriate persons or agencies with respect to Buyer's performance under this agreement. Buyer agrees to surrender, upon demand, any charge card issued hereunder. In order to properly process your application, or in the event of any update, renewal or extension thereof, Seller may request a consumer report. Upon your request, you will be informed whether or not a consumer report was requested, and if so, the name and address of the consumer reporting agency that furnished the report. (5) Seller retains a security interest under the Uniform Commercial Code in merchandise purchased under this agreement until such merchandise is paid in full. **(6) NOTICE—ANY HOLDER OF THIS CONSUMER CREDIT CONTRACT IS SUBJECT TO ALL CLAIMS AND DEFENSES WHICH THE DEBTOR COULD ASSERT AGAINST THE SELLER OF GOODS OR SERVICES OBTAINED PURSUANT HERETO OR WITH THE PROCEEDS HEREOF. RECOVERY HEREUNDER BY THE DEBTOR SHALL NOT EXCEED AMOUNTS PAID BY THE DEBTOR HEREUNDER. (7) NOTICE TO BUYER—DO NOT SIGN THIS AGREEMENT BEFORE YOU READ IT OR IF IT CONTAINS BLANK SPACES. YOU ARE ENTITLED TO A COMPLETELY FILLED IN COPY OF THIS AGREEMENT, WHICH YOU SHOULD KEEP TO PROTECT YOUR LEGAL RIGHTS. YOU MAY AT ANY TIME PAY THE TOTAL INDEBTEDNESS. BUYER ACKNOWLEDGES RECEIPT OF A COPY OF THIS AGREEMENT.**

NEIMAN-MARCUS MAIN AT ERVAY STREETS DALLAS, TEXAS By L. A. Jenkins
VICE PRESIDENT

YOUR NEIMAN-MARCUS CREDIT CARD IS EXCLUSIVE, IT WILL BE HONORED AT ALL OF THE FOLLOWING STORE LOCATIONS.

- **DALLAS, DOWNTOWN**
Main at Ervay, Dallas, Texas 75201
Phone (214) 741-6911
- **DALLAS, NORTHPARK CENTER**
400 NorthPark Center, Dallas, Texas 75225
Phone (214) 363-8311
- **DALLAS, PRESTONWOOD TOWN CENTER**
5285 Belt Line Rd., Dallas, Texas 75240
Phone (214) 233-1100
- **FT. WORTH, RIDGMAR MALL**
2100 Green Oaks Rd., Ft. Worth, Texas 76116
Phone (817) 738-3581
- **HOUSTON, GALLERIA**
2600 South Post Oak Rd., Houston, Texas 77056
Phone (713) 621-7100
- **HOUSTON, TOWN AND COUNTRY MALL**
10615 Town & Country Way, Houston, Texas 77024
Phone (713) 984-2100
- **BAL HARBOUR**
9700 Collins Ave., Bal Harbour, Florida 33154
Phone (305) 865-6161
- **FORT LAUDERDALE, GALLERIA**
2442 East Sunrise Blvd., Ft. Lauderdale, Florida 33304
Phone (305) 566-6666
- **ATLANTA, LENOX SQUARE**
3393 Peachtree Rd., N.E., Atlanta, Georgia 30326
Phone (404) 266-8200
- **ST. LOUIS, PLAZA FRONTENAC**
100 Plaza Frontenac, St. Louis, Missouri 63131
Phone (314) 567-9811
- **WASHINGTON, D.C. MAZZA GALLERIE**
5300 Wisconsin Ave., N.W. Washington, D.C. 20015
Phone (202) 966-9700
- **CHICAGO, NORTHBROOK**
5000 Northbrook Court, Northbrook, Illinois 60062
Phone (312) 564-0300
- **CHICAGO, OAKBROOK CENTER**
6 Oakbrook Center, Oak Brook, Illinois 60521
Phone (312) 789-1500
- **CHICAGO, MICHIGAN AVE.**
737 North Michigan Ave., Chicago, Illinois 60611
Phone (312) 642-5900
- **BEVERLY HILLS**
9700 Wilshire Blvd., Beverly Hills, California 90212
Phone (213) 550-5900
- **NEWPORT BEACH, FASHION ISLAND**
49 Fashion Island, Newport Beach, California 92660
Phone (714) 759-1900
- **SAN DIEGO, FASHION VALLEY**
280 Fashion Valley Rd., San Diego, California 92108
Phone (619) 692-9100
- **SAN FRANCISCO, UNION SQUARE**
150 Stockton St., San Francisco, California 94108
Phone (415) 362-3900
- **WHITE PLAINS**
Maple and Paulding Ave., White Plains, New York 10601
Phone (914) 428-2000
- **LAS VEGAS, THE FASHION SHOW**
3200 Las Vegas Blvd. S., Las Vegas, Nevada 89109
Phone (702) 731-3636
- **BOSTON, COPLEY PLACE**
5 Copley Place, Boston, Massachusetts 02116
Phone (617) 536-3660

- **MAIL ORDER** P.O. Box 2968, Dallas, Texas 75221 Phone (214) 823-7939 TOLL FREE 1-800-NEIMANS

Appears courtesy of Neiman-Marcus

Figure 55-2 shows the required closed-end disclosures.

Creditors who advertise closed-end credit to help buyers must also disclose certain information in their ads. Ads can only give the annual percentage rate as the cost of credit. If the ad gives a monthly payment figure, then the creditor's ad must also give the amount of the down payment, the annual percentage rate, and the repayment terms. Figure 55-3 is an example of a credit ad with the right disclosures.

MARS v. SPARTANBURG CHRYSLER PLYMOUTH, INC.

United States Court of Appeals,
Fourth Circuit.
713 F.2d 65 (1983).

FACTS Carrie Mars bought an auto from Spartanburg Chrysler Plymouth. She financed the car through a closed-end transaction. Spartanburg's closed-end disclosure statement had the following violations:

1. Used the term "Amount financed" instead of the proper "Unpaid balance."
2. Paragraph titles "Late Payment" and "Prepayment" were only printed in 8-point type instead of the required 10-point type.

Mars brought suit for violation of the Truth-in-Lending Act. She admitted that these technical violations did not affect her credit decision. She insisted that any violation allowed her to recover.

ISSUE Can a debtor recover for technical violation of the Truth-in-Lending Act when there are no actual damages?

DECISION Yes. The debtor's right to suit and recover is the way the act is enforced. The damages are automatic for violations even though the debtor is not affected. Mars was awarded her total finance charge of $1174 as damages along with $1000 in attorney's fees.

LEGAL TIP
Carefully draft and print credit forms.

The right to cancel: Regulation Z's three-day cooling-off period and the right of rescission Regulation Z is famous for its buyers' "cold feet" protection. The cold feet protection is a three-day period during which the buyer can back out (or rescind) the credit agreement.

The right to rescind applies to credit transactions when the creditor takes a security interest (or lien) in the debtor's residence, which is called the "principal dwelling." For example, if Berferd signs a contract to install a swimming pool, Berferd's lender for the pool cost will take a security interest in Berferd's house. Berferd has the three-day period to change his mind.

The three days runs from the signing of the contract until midnight of the third business day. If Berferd signs the contract on Thursday, he has until the following Tuesday to rescind.

Creditors are required to give the debtor notice of the right to rescind. The notice must explain the right, tell the debtor how to rescind, and explain how long the debtor has to to it. Figure 55-4 is an example of notice language from a credit contract.

Credit card rights Credit cards make using credit easy. They are small and can be used without filling out a contract for every purchase. However, the benefits of using credit cards also make them targets for misuse. Credit card theft is one problem. Regulation Z has built-in protections for credit card holders. These protections must also be part of the creditor's notice to the debtor.

Credit cards cannot be issued to a debtor unless the debtor requested them or the card is a renewal card. This rule exists because unsolicited credit cards would be easy targets for theft. The intended debtor would never know to report such a loss.

Even if a credit card is stolen, the debtor has some protection. The maximum amount of liability for the unauthorized use of a credit card is $50. If the debtor promptly notifies the creditor of the stolen card, there will be no liability. The creditor must give the debtor information needed for calling or writing about a lost or stolen credit card.

Figure 55-2 **Federal Truth in Lending Act Disclosures**

CONSUMER GOODS OR TITLED VEHICLES

FEDERAL TRUTH IN LENDING ACT DISCLOSURES

The Valley National Bank of Arizona Mesa Main Street Office.

You have the right to receive at this time an itemization of the Amount Financed.

☐ I want an itemization. ☒ I do not want an itemization.

ANNUAL PERCENTAGE RATE
The cost of your credit as a yearly rate.
16.00 %

FINANCE CHARGE
The dollar amount the credit will cost you.
$ 269.80

Amount Financed
The amount of credit provided to you or on your behalf.
$ 2,000.00

Total of Payments
The amount you will have paid after you have made all payments as scheduled
$ 2,269.80

e means an estimate

Your payment schedule will be

Number of Payments	Amount of Payments	When Payments Are Due
18	126.10	Monthly, beginning on July 15, 1983

Insurance Credit life insurance and credit disability insurance are not required to obtain credit, and will not be provided unless you sign and agree to pay the additional cost.

Type	Premium	Signature
Credit Life	N/A	I want credit life insurance SIGNATURE
Credit Life and Disability	N/A	I want credit life and disability insurance SIGNATURE
Joint Credit Life	N/A	I want joint credit life insurance SIGNATURE
Joint Credit Life and Disability	N/A	I want joint credit life and disability insurance SIGNATURE

You may obtain property insurance from anyone you want that is acceptable to The Valley National Bank of Arizona. If you get the insurance through The Valley National Bank of Arizona, you will pay $ N/A for N/A months of coverage.

Security You are giving a security interest in

☒ the goods or property being purchased

☐ ______ (brief description of other property)

Filing Fees N/A

Late Charge If a payment is late, you will be charged $10 or 5% of the payment, whichever is less.

Prepayment If you pay off early, you will not have to pay a penalty.

See your contract documents for any additional information about nonpayment, default, and any required repayment in full before the scheduled date.

CONSUMER GOODS OR TITLED VEHICLES
MONTHLY INSTALMENT NOTE AND SECURITY AGREEMENT

For value received, the undersigned jointly and severally promise to pay in lawful money of the United States of America, to The Valley National Bank of Arizona ("Bank"), or order, at the Bank's office indicated below, the principal balance shown in "Amount Financed" above, plus interest calculated and charged on a daily basis on the unpaid principal balance of the debt. The agreed interest rate, stated above as "Annual Percentage Rate", is shown below. This loan is payable in consecutive monthly payments as shown in Payment Schedule above, with monthly payments credited first to interest earned and then to principal balance outstanding. Any delay in payment could cause the "Finance Charge" and Total of Payments to be greater than disclosed, resulting in a larger final payment; early payments could cause those amounts to be less than disclosed, resulting in a smaller final payment. Any scheduled payment not paid in full within 10 days of its due date will result in a late charge in the amount of 5% of the payment, or $10, whichever is less (which is not in lieu of interest accrued or accruing). In the event of default in the payment of any instalment, the makers, endorsers, and guarantors hereof jointly and severally promise to pay on demand, in addition to all other amounts payable hereunder, reasonable collection costs, fees, and attorney's fees. If any amount owed is not paid when due, then at the option of the Holder this Note shall become immediately due and payable without notice or demand upon the makers, endorsers or guarantors or any of them. The makers, endorsers and guarantors jointly and severally waive presentment hereof for payment, protest and notice of nonpayment and of protest.

THE INTEREST RATE ON THIS LOAN IS 16.00 % PER ANNUM.

The undersigned, the Debtor(s) hereunder, for value received, hereby grant(s) to Bank, the Secured Party hereunder, a security interest in the Goods (described under "Security Interest" below and any security agreement addendum attached) and all physical damage loss insurance policy coverage on such Goods and any unearned premium refunds from such insurance policies, and all proceeds thereof (however, this does not mean that Bank consents to any sale of such Goods), herein collectively referred to as "Collateral", to secure performance of the covenants and agreements set forth herein and on the reverse hereof and payment of all indebtedness and liabilities of Debtor(s) to Bank as evidenced by this Monthly Instalment Note and Security Agreement. This Note and Security Agreement is not secured by any other security interest held by Bank.

	YEAR	MAKE	MODEL	SERIAL NUMBER
SECURITY INTEREST	1975	Toyota	Station Wagon	FJ40203505

IMPORTANT – THIS MONTHLY INSTALMENT NOTE AND SECURITY AGREEMENT IS SUBJECT TO THE ADDITIONAL PROVISIONS ON THE BACK, WHICH ARE INCORPORATED HEREIN.

Executed at Mesa, Arizona, this 8th day of June, 19 83.

Secured Party
The Valley National Bank of Arizona

Mesa Main Street Office
Address 66 W. Main Street
Mesa (City or Town) Arizona 85201 (Zip Code)
By [signature]
Its Assistant Manager

Debtor(s)
(Type or Print)

(X) ______ (Debtor's Signature)
(X) ______ (Debtor's Signature)
228 E. Gary Circle (Number and Street)
Mesa (City or Town) AZ (State) 85201 (Zip Code)

0-105-0511

VNS NOTE FILE

PAID
OCT 24 1983
MESA DIRECT LOAN CENTER
VALLEY NATIONAL BANK, MESA

Figure 55-2 **Continued**

TERMS AND CONDITIONS GOVERNING SECURITY INTERESTS GRANTED BANK

1. Debtor acknowledges express intent to hereby waive and abandon all personal property exemptions granted by law upon the property which is the subject of the Agreement. NOTICE: BY SIGNING THIS AGREEMENT, DEBTOR WAIVES ALL RIGHTS PROVIDED BY LAW TO CLAIM SUCH PROPERTY EXEMPT FROM PROCESS.

2. DEBTOR'S REPRESENTATIONS, WARRANTIES AND AGREEMENTS: Debtor represents, warrants and agrees: Any true and correct carbon, photographic or other reproductive copy of this Collateral Agreement may be filed or recorded as a Financing Statement. The Collateral will be principally stored at Debtor's address on the face hereof.

Debtor will permit the Holder of this Agreement to examine the Collateral at any time, will maintain the Collateral in good condition and repair; will not permit the Collateral to be permanently removed from the State of Arizona without the prior written consent of the Holder; will not permit the Collateral to be removed from Debtor's possession; will not permit the Collateral to be attached or other process to be levied thereon nor create nor permit to be created any lien or encumbrance or adverse claim of any character whatsoever, whether for storage, repairs, or otherwise, justified or unjustified; will not sell, transfer, assign or attempt to assign Debtor's right, title or interest in the Collateral or this Agreement in contravention of security interests granted herewith; will pay all taxes and assessments of every character levied or assessed against the Collateral, this Agreement and the indebtedness represented hereby.

Time is of the essence of this Agreement. The acceptance by Bank of partial payments shall not be construed as a waiver of any subsequent defaults on Debtor's part nor shall it waive the "time is of the essence" provision. This Agreement is not assignable by Debtor except with the prior written consent of Bank. Debtor agrees that it will not use nor permit the Collateral to be used for any unlawful purpose, nor to be used for hire, nor will Debtor allow any person to operate or use the Collateral who is not allowed under the terms of the insurance policies herein provided to so operate or use the Collateral.

Any written notice required to be given Debtor if mailed by ordinary mail, postage prepaid, to Debtor's mailing address given herein or to Debtor's most recent address as shown by a "notice of change of address" on file with Bank shall be deemed reasonable notification.

3. INSURANCE: Debtor agrees to keep the Collateral insured at its own expense against loss by fire, theft, transportation, collision and such other risks as Bank shall designate; such insurance shall be for an amount not less than the balance due under this Agreement and shall be in force so long as any part thereof remains unpaid; such insurance is to be placed in insurance companies acceptable to Bank and loss thereon is to be paid to Bank and Debtor as their interests may appear. Debtor hereby requests and authorizes Bank, at Bank's option and without obligation to do so, to pay the premiums for such insurance or similar insurance protecting Bank only, adding same to the principal balance then owing, or by an advance which constitutes additional indebtedness and is secured hereunder and payable in additional instalments at the time and in addition to the payments due on this Agreement. The policies therefor shall be held by Bank until this Agreement is fully performed. Such action by Bank shall not cure any default, or waive any rights or remedies of Bank because of Debtor's failure to do so. This provision does not apply to life insurance nor to public liability and property damage insurance.

If Bank retakes possession of the Collateral, the insurance policies thereon shall become the sole property of Bank and Debtor shall have no further interest therein. Debtor hereby assigns to Bank the proceeds of all such insurance to the extent of the unpaid balances hereunder and directs any insurer to make payments directly to Bank. In the event of any default hereunder, Bank is authorized to cancel any insurance and credit any premium refund against said unpaid balances.

Debtor authorizes Bank, at its option and without obligation to do so, to discharge taxes, liens, security interests or other encumbrances at any time levied or placed on the Collateral, to place and pay for insurance on the property upon the failure by Debtor, after having been requested so to do. Debtor hereby agrees, if such insurance is placed and paid for by Bank, to reimburse Bank on demand or on the basis of a designated payment schedule (as communicated to Debtor by Bank or Insurance carrier) for any payment made for insurance or any expense incurred by Bank pursuant to this authorization, plus interest on all sums so expended until paid at an interest rate not to exceed the Annual Percentage Rate contracted for and disclosed on the front side of this loan document.

4. EVENTS OF DEFAULT:

(A) Any one of the following shall constitute an event of default:

(1) Failure of Debtor to pay when due any indebtedness secured hereby;

(2) If any warranty, representation, or statement made herein or furnished to Bank by or on behalf of Debtor in connection with this Agreement proves to have been false in any material respect when made or furnished;

(3) The commencement of any bankruptcy, arrangement, reorganization, insolvency, receivership or similar proceedings by or against Debtor or any guarantor or surety for Debtor;

(4) If the Collateral is sold or disposed of or a security interest is created with respect thereto.

(5) The occurrence of any adverse change in the financial condition of Debtor deemed material by Bank, or if, in the judgment of Bank, the Collateral becomes unsatisfactory in character or value, or if Bank shall deem itself insecure.

(6) If Debtor defaults in performing any of its obligations, promises, covenants or agreements contained herein or in any agreements, paper or document given by Debtor to Bank;

(7) If Debtor uses the Collateral in violation of any law or governmental regulation.

(8) If Debtor fails to keep and maintain exclusive possession of, and title to, the Collateral.

(9) If Debtor fails to pay promptly when due all taxes, liens, fees, charges and assessments upon the Collateral or fails to keep the Collateral in good condition and repair or fails to keep the Collateral properly insured at all times with an insurance company or companies acceptable to Bank and with loss payable to Bank as its interest may appear, against fire (with extended coverage), theft, physical damage and such other risks, and in such amounts for all risks as Bank shall require.

(B) Any one of the following shall constitute an event of default if, in Bank's opinion, such occurrence itself, or such occurrence together with surrounding circumstances, materially increases Bank's risk with regard to repayment of the indebtedness due it:

(1) Death or incompetence of Debtor;

(2) If the Collateral is levied upon or seized under any levy, attachment, garnishment, written or other legal process, or if any lien is attached thereto.

(3) If the Collateral is lost, stolen or suffers substantial damage or destruction.

5. RIGHTS AND REMEDIES. Upon the happening of any of the foregoing events of default and at any time thereafter, Bank may, at its option and without notice to Debtor, declare all of the indebtedness of Debtor to Bank to be immediately due and payable and Bank shall have the rights, options, duties and remedies of a secured party, and Debtor shall have the rights and duties of a debtor under the Uniform Commercial Code as adopted in the State of Arizona, and, without limitation thereto, Bank shall have the following specific rights:

(A) To terminate any commitment to make loans or otherwise extend credit to Debtor,

(B) To take immediate possession of the Collateral without notice or resort to legal process and for such purpose to enter upon any premises on which the Collateral or any part thereof may be situated and remove the same therefrom or, at its option, to render the Collateral unusable.

(C) To make or have made any repairs deemed necessary or desirable, the cost of which is to be charged to Debtor.

(D) To apply the proceeds realized from disposition of the Collateral according to law and to payment of reasonable attorney's fees and legal expenses incurred by Bank whether or not suit be filed:

(E) If the proceeds realized from disposition of the Collateral shall fail to satisfy all of the obligations of Debtor to Bank, Debtor shall pay any deficiency balance to Bank.

6. SET-OFF. Any indebtedness owing from Bank to Debtor may be set-off and applied by Bank on the indebtedness or liability of Debtor to Bank at any time and from time to time, either before or after maturity, and without demand upon or notice to anyone.

7. GENERAL. This Agreement shall be governed by the laws of the State of Arizona. All terms used herein which are defined in the Uniform Commercial Code of Arizona have the same meaning herein as in the Code. Any provisions found to be invalid shall not invalidate the remainder hereof. Waiver of any default shall not constitute waiver of any subsequent default. If this instrument is signed by more than one Debtor, the singular word "Debtor" shall include the plural, and the obligations of all such Debtors shall be joint and several. All words used herein shall be construed to be of such gender and number as the circumstances require and all references herein to Debtor shall include all other persons primarily or secondarily liable hereunder. This instrument shall be binding upon the heirs, personal representatives, successors and assigns of Debtor and inure to the benefit of Bank, its successors and assigns. THIS AGREEMENT CONSTITUTES THE ENTIRE AGREEMENT BETWEEN THE PARTIES AND MAY NOT BE ALTERED OR AMENDED EXCEPT BY A WRITING SIGNED BY THE DEBTOR AND BANK.

Appears courtesy of Valley National Bank

Figure 55-3 **Credit Ad**

ABC DATSUN

ONLY $\$88^{00}$ DOWN

BUYS:

1979 DATSUN B210	1980 PONTIAC PHOENIX	1981 PLYMOUTH RELIANT K	1982 PONTIAC J2000
2-door, air, Stock #9337–8	2-door, auto, P/S, air, Stock #1290	4-door, auto, air, P/S, Stock #1297	2-door P/S Air
Amount financed $2725.00	Amount financed $3048.00	Amount financed $4225.00	
Deferred payment price $3552.00	Deferred payment price $4026.00	Deferred payment price $5782.00	
Annual percentage rate 16.75%	Annual percentage rate 16.49%	Annual percentage rate 16.25%	
Sales price $2813.00	Sales price $3213.00	Sales price $4313.00	
24 PAYMENTS OF	24 PAYMENTS OF	36 PAYMENTS OF	
$\$134^{40}$	$\$149^{99}$	$\$149^{06}$	$\$126^{91}$
PER MONTH plus tax & license O.A.C.	PER MONTH plus tax & license O.A.C.	PER MONTH plus tax & license O.A.C.	PER MONTH plus tax & license O.A.C.

ASK US ABOUT OTHER SPECIAL BUYS

1300 EAST CAMELBACK **264–2332**

Appears courtesy of ABC Datsun

Penalties for violations of TILA If a creditor does not give the debtor the required information or violates some other requirement of Regulation Z, the creditor may be civilly liable to the debtor. A violating creditor is liable for twice the amount of the finance charge in the transaction or no less then $100 and no more than $1000 plus costs and attorneys' fees. If there is a class action suit by a group of debtors, the liability is the lesser of $500,000 or 1% of the creditor's net worth.

Fair Credit Billing Act (FCBA)

The **Fair Credit Billing Act** (FCBA) gives debtors the right to challenge monthly bills. Regulation Z also provides details on this Act. All of the procedures of the Act must be given as part of the monthly statement sent to the debtor. These notices, rights, and procedures will be found under a section saying, "Notify Us in Case of Errors or Questions about Your Bill." (see Figure 55-1).

Debtors are required to comply with certain procedures to be able to get their remedies under the Fair Credit Billing Act (FCBA). If a debtor receives a statement with an error, the debtor has sixty days from the date of receipt to protest the error. A proper protest is in writing, lists the account number, and gives a brief explanation of the error.

After receiving this written protest, the creditor has thirty days to send the debtor a notice acknowledging that the protest has been received. The creditor has ninety days from receipt of the protest to take action by either correcting the bill or continuing to demand payment.

Figure 55-4 **Notice of Cancellation**

NOTICE OF CANCELLATION

____
Date

You may cancel this transaction, without any penalty or obligation, within three business days from the above date.

If you cancel, any property traded in, any payments made by you under the contract or sale, and negotiable instrument executed by you will be returned within 10 business days following receipt by the seller of your cancellation notice, and any security interest arising out of the transaction will be cancelled.

If you cancel, you must make available to the seller at your residence, in substantially as good condition as when received, any goods delivered to you under this contract or sale: or you may if you wish, comply with the instructions of the seller regarding the return shipment of the goods at the seller's expense and risk.

If you do make the goods available to the seller and the seller does not pick them up within 20 days of the date of your notice of cancellation, you may retain or dispose of the goods without any further obligation. If you fail to make the goods available to the seller, or if you agree to return the goods to the seller and fail to do so, then you remain liable for performance of all obligations under the contract.

To cancel this transaction, mail or deliver a signed and dated copy of this cancellation notice or any other written notice, or send a telegram, to Cristoria Pools, [illegible] Rd., Mesa, Arizona, 85203, not later than

1629 E. University Dr.

midnight of ____________________.
(Date)

I HEREBY CANCEL THIS TRANSACTION

VOID

__________ **(Date)** __________ **(Buyer's Signature)**

Buyers acknowledge they have received two (2) copies of this Notice attached, but easily detachable, to Contract, and have been orally informed of their Right To Cancel this transaction.

__________ **(Date)** __________ **(Buyer's Signature)**

__________ **(Buyer's Signature)**

Appears courtesy of Cristoria Pools, Mesa, AZ

During the time when the debtor and creditor are resolving the billing question, the debtor does not have to pay the disputed amount (including any finance charges). If the error is corrected, finance charges for the dispute period must also be corrected. If the creditor says there was no error, the creditor must give documentation and the debtor will owe the amount along with finance charges accruing during the dispute period.

It is important to follow the requirements for disputing a bill. Although some errors could be taken care of over the telephone, these oral protests will not give the full protection under the FCBA. If a creditor does not comply with the requirements of notice and time limits, the debtor's remedy is to be excused from the obligation—whether the debtor actually owed it or not.

Fair Credit Reporting Act

The **Fair Credit Reporting Act** (FCRA) is one that gives rights and protections for debtors' credit histories. Debtors have the right to see their credit histories as they are kept by credit reporting agencies. They also have the right to challenge the information included in the credit report.

Application of FCRA The FCRA applies to "consumer reporting agencies." **Consumer reporting agencies** are those agencies that compile, evaluate, and sell credit information to third parties. The rights given in the Act are for consumer and not commercial transactions. For example, if Ralph applies for a loan to purchase inventory for his stereo business, FCRA does not apply to the agency giving the report to the lender. But if Ralph applied for a loan to purchase a car, the agency would be under the FCRA.

Who gets the information? These agencies are limited in their disclosures. They can disclose the information to a creditor who has the debtor's application

Figure 55-5 **Sample Credit Report Disclosure Statement**

The Federal Equal Credit Opportunity Act prohibits creditors from discriminating against credit applicants on the basis of sex or marital status. The Federal agency which administers compliance with this law concerning this bank, is Comptroller of the Currency, Consumer Affairs Division, Washington, D.C. 20219.

Office ________
Address ________
P.O. Box ________
City ________
State ________

Re: ________

Thank you for your recent credit request, submitted by the above named seller. After serious consideration, we have determined not to approve your request as presented because of the following reason(s) indicated:

☐ 1. As you can appreciate, whether to extend credit involves certain judgment decisions. For example, length of time at present employment, credit history and background (or lack), length of time in the area, amount and burden of other obligations, amount and continuity of income are factors considered and our loan policies require that certain standards be met on these factors.

We have evaluated these factors and, in making our credit judgment, we have declined your credit request as presented. We also obtained a consumer credit report from ________

(name and address of consumer reporting agency)

which was considered in our decision but which does not, in our opinion, contain derogatory information.

☐ 2. Information contained in a consumer credit report obtained from ________

(name and address of consumer reporting agency)

☐ 3. Information obtained from an outside source, other than a consumer reporting agency. If you wish, you may obtain the nature of such information by directing to the address above a written request within sixty (60) days from receipt of this letter.

☐ (If checked) Your credit request was not approved as originally submitted; however, the credit request was approved subject to the following condition(s)

____

This formal means of notification is in compliance with the Fair Credit Reporting Act.

Credit circumstances often change. Even though credit was not granted, we hope to retain your good will and would appreciate an opportunity to receive your future credit requests. Should you have any questions, or desire to discuss this matter further, please call.

Sincerely,
The Valley National Bank of Arizona
by ________

Obtained from the Valley National Bank of Arizona April 21, 1980

Reference to Chapter 44 Equal Credit Opportunity Act

for credit, a debtor who asks (in writing) for a copy of the report, a court, or an employer. Consumers have the right to know who furnished the credit report to a creditor. Figure 55-5 is a sample credit report disclosure statement.

What information can be in a credit report? The credit report must have old information removed periodically. For example, bankruptcies that occurred more than 14 years ago must be removed. Lawsuits that were finalized more than 7 years ago must be removed. Criminal convictions and arrests that have been disposed of for more than 7 years must also be removed. If the report is for a loan of more than $50,000 or a job with an annual salary of more then $20,000, these old items can still be disclosed.

Debtor's right to check and correct The FCRA gives debtors opportunities to check their credit reports. They can make a written demand to see a copy of the report and then challenge the information given in the report. To challenge information, a debtor must notify the credit reporting agency of the alleged mistake or error. The agency is then required to investigate the debtor's complaint. If an error is found, it must be corrected. Also, the debtor can require the agency to notify those who have received a report in the last two years of the error.

If the agency still maintains the information is correct, the debtor may have a statement inserted in the credit file to explain his or her position. The length of the statement is limited to 100 words. The agency must send a copy or summary of the statement with every credit report. The *Thompson v. San Antonio Retail Merchants Ass'n* case show how important it is to correct inaccurate credit reports.

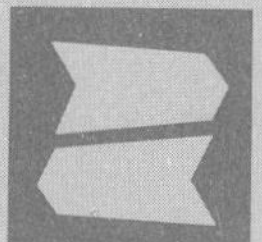

THOMPSON v. SAN ANTONIO RETAIL MERCHANTS ASS'N

United States Court of Appeals, Fifth Circuit.
682 F.2d 509 (1982).

FACTS In November 1974, William Daniel Thompson, Jr., opened a credit account with Gordon's Jewelers. Thompson was single and worked as a truck loader. He used the credit account and failed to pay off a $77.25 balance. Gordon wrote the amount off as a bad debt and gave the information to the San Antonio Retail Merchants Association computerized credit reporting agency (SARMA). There was no social security number with the report. Thompson was given a derogatory credit rating as a result of this report.

In 1978, William Douglas Thompson III applied for a Gulf and Ward's credit card. This Thompson was married and worked as a grounds keeper. SARMA mixed up the credit files and based on William Daniel Thompson, Jr.'s record, William Douglas Thompson III was denied the credit cards.

He was denied several times again when he applied for other forms of credit in 1978 and 1979. He assumed the denials were because of his 5-year probation for a felony burglary conviction.

In 1979, he was told he was denied credit because of his delinquent account. He went to SARMA and told them he had never had an account with Gordon's. SARMA told him the information would be corrected. He applied for a Ward's credit card and was denied again on the basis of the Gordon's account. He filed suit against SARMA for violation of the FCRA.

ISSUE Did SARMA's conduct violate the FCRA?

DECISION Yes. They did not have a social security number with the record. They were negligent in how they handled their files and records. They were also negligent in failing to correct the record once they were aware of the mistake.

William Douglas Thompson III was awarded $10,000 in actual damages and $4485 in attorney's fees.

LEGAL TIP
Check your credit rating periodically. Make sure it is accurate and follow through on corrections.

Consumer Leasing Act

The **Consumer Leasing Act** is part of the Truth-in-Lending Act and carries the same penalties for violation. This Act was passed to require those who lease goods to consumers to give complete information. The consumers must be told how much they will be paying during the lease. They must also be told whether they will have any liability at the end of the lease, whether the lease can be transferred, and whether the lease can be terminated.

KEY TERMS

Usury
Equal Credit Opportunity Act
Consumer credit transactions
Truth-in-Lending Act
Open-end transactions
Closed-end transactions
Fair Credit Billing Act
Fair Credit Reporting Act
Consumer Leasing Act

CHAPTER PROBLEMS

1. Patsy Anderson applied for a loan with United Finance Corporation. Before she could get the loan, United required her to get her husband's signature. Is this a violation of ECOA? *Anderson v. United Finance Co.,* 666 F.2d 1274 (9th Cir. 1982).

2. Opal Huff bought furniture from Stewart-Gwinn Furniture company on a closed-end credit deal. The form used by Stewart-Gwinn gave all the necessary information except a total cost with the finance charges. Has Stewart-Gwinn violated TILA? *Huff V. Stewart-Gwinn Furn. Co.,* 713 F.2d 67 (9th Cir. 1983).

3. Christine Jarrett signed a promissory note to Trustees Loan and Discount. The note contained the following:

   > Schedule of Monthly Payments: The first one of \$36.00 and 143 (sic) of \$36.00. First payment due date 8/27/81. Final payment 10/27/82.

   She filed suit for violation of TILA because she was not sure how many payments she was making. Is there a violation? *Trustees Loan & Discount Co. v. Jarrett,* 426 So.2d 857 (Ala. 1983).

4. When does the \$50 limit on credit card liability apply?

5. Juan Molina purchased a 1977 ¾ ton pick-up truck from Wayne Strand Pontiac-GMC. Through a miscalculation of his loan terms, he was overcharged \$5.53 in finance charges. Molina has brought suit for a violation of TILA. Will he win? *Wayne Strand Pontiac-GMC v. Molina,* 653 S.W.2d 45 (Tex. 1983).

*6. Robert Martin loaned his American Express card to E. L. McBride for business purposes. He told McBride he could charge up to \$500, but McBride charged \$5300. Martin claimed he was liable for only \$50 because there had been an unauthorized use of his card. Is Martin liable? *Martin v. American Express,* 361 So.2d 597 (Ala. 1978).

*7. Carroll applied for a credit card from Exxon. She was denied credit. When she asked for a reason, Exxon told her the credit bureau did not have enough information but then refused to give her the name of the credit bureau. Has any law been violated? *Carroll v. Exxon,* 434 F.Supp. 557 (La. 1977).

*8. Loraine Schreve declared bankruptcy in 1978. In 1979, she married Joe T. Morris. When he applied for credit over the next two years, he was denied. When he examined his credit report he discovered that Loraine's bankruptcy was on his report. Does Morris have any remedies? *Morris v. Credit Bureau of Cincinnati, Inc.,* 563 F.Supp. 962 (S.D. Ohio 1983).

*9. Curtis Thorn took out a second mortgage on his house to invest in a real estate limited partnership. Is the loan a consumer transaction? *Thorn v. Sundance Properties,* 562 F.Supp. 882 (Nev. 1983).

*10. Patricia Alexander and James Okubo tried to rent an apartment. They were denied the apartment after the landlord said their credit report was bad. Their credit reports indicated they had not paid rent and had bounced checks. Alexander and Okubo say all this happened because of their former roommates.Is there anything they can do to clear up their credit reports? *Alexander v. Moore & Associates, Inc.,* 553 F.Supp. 948 (Haw. 1982).

"But we are borrowers . . ."
Mary Norton

Chapter 56

Introduction to Secured Credit Transactions

CHAPTER PREVIEW

- Types of liens
- Roles of sureties
- Article IX security interests
- Applications of Article IX
- Requirements for a security agreement
- Effect of attachment of a security interest

Barbara rented a stall in Pilgrim Self-Service Storage. Her contract gave Pilgrim a lien on her goods for unpaid rent. Barbara missed her rent payment two months in a row. Pilgrim sold her goods to recover the rent. Barbara says they are thieves. Is she right?

Credit contracts must be repaid. Often getting the money repaid is not easy. However, getting the money becomes easier if the creditor has more than a signed contract. The creditor can get security for repayment of the debt. The creditor can ask for a back-up debtor, which is a co-signer or a surety. The creditor can take a lien or security interest in some of the debtor's property. These methods of security are the focus of this chapter.

THE BACK-UP DEBTOR

The idea of getting someone else involved in a credit transaction is to have more than one person responsible for a debt. If one debtor fails to pay, there is another to fall back on. A back-up debtor can be as simple as the co-signer on a loan or as complex as a surety in a construction project. The idea is that there is a secondary party to whom the creditor can turn when the primary party fails to pay.

Co-signer

Someone who co-signs a loan simply lends his or her credit worthiness to a credit agreement. But co-signers also promise that if the original debtor does not pay, they will. For example, if a father co-signs for his son's new car and the son falls behind on the payments, the father is also responsible for the payments. While the father and son work out an arrangement between themselves, the creditor gets paid.

Surety/Guarantor

A **surety** is the legal name for a co-signer. A surety can be a voluntary party—as in the case of the father signing for the son. However, a surety can also be paid. For example, disability or death credit insurance that pays off a debt is a paid-for surety. The insurance company agrees to pay debts if certain events occur, and they are paid a fee for standing second in the liability line.

In construction, contractors are often required to pay sureties to back up their performance and payment. If the contractor does not perform or pay suppliers and subcontractors, a surety will be required to pay as the secondary party.

Once a surety pays off a debt, he or she assumes the creditor's role. The surety has the right to collect the amount paid from the original debtor. For example, the father who pays off the son's car loan has the right to collect the amount from the son. The creditor is assured payment by one or both of the two. Their liability to each other is left for them to determine.

SECURITY THROUGH LIENS

Liens are statutory property rights given to creditors. A lien means that if the creditor is not paid, the creditor has the right to sell the property to pay the debt. There are several types of liens. The most commonly known type is the mechanics' lien. All states have some form of mechanics' liens. Contractors who work on real property and improve it can get mechanics' liens. For example, if Jake is hired to re-roof Sam's house and Sam doesn't pay Jake, Jake has a lien on Sam's property for the cost of doing the roof. That lien allows Jake to force a sale of the property to pay the debt.

Another common type of lien is the artisan's lien. States vary on what is included in their artisan's lien statutes, but the idea is the same. The idea is to give those who do work or make improvements on personal property the right to a lien on that property. For example, many states give auto mechanics a lien on the vehicles they repair. They can keep the vehicle until the debt for the work is paid. If the debt is not paid, they can sell the car to pay the debt.

Liens give creditors some rights in property. Those rights include the right of sale. If the debtor does not pay, the creditor can use the property to pay the debt. The *Guthrie v. Pilgrim Realty Co.* case discusses a type of lien given in one state.

GUTHRIE v. PILGRIM REALTY CO.

Court of Appeals of Georgia.
275 S.E.2d 686 (1980).

FACTS Barbara Guthrie rented a stall in a mini-warehouse operated by Pilgrim Realty d/b/a Pilgrim Self-Service Storage. She missed her rental payments on the stall two months in a row.

The contract between Guthrie and Pilgrim provided that Pilgrim "shall at all times have a valid, contractual lien for all rentals or other sums due hereunder from tenant upon items situated upon the premises, without liability for trespass or conversion."

Pilgrim sold Guthrie's goods to recover the rent. Guthrie brought suit, claiming the sale was illegal.

ISSUE Did Pilgrim have a valid lien on the goods and could they sell them?

DECISION Yes. The lien was agreed to in the contract. There was a seven-day notice provision, and Guthrie was given notice. The lien was used to satisfy a debt and was valid.

LEGAL TIP

Check storage contracts for terms. Be sure to give any notice of change of address so that bills and notices can get to you.

SECURITY UNDER ARTICLE IX

Article IX is the UCC's section on creditor's security. Article IX allows creditors to have security in goods and fixtures. A **security interest** is defined as an "interest in personal property or fixtures which secures performance or payment of an obligation" (Section 1-201 [37]). Article IX gives the rights and responsibilities of both the debtor and creditor when they create a security interest.

What Is Covered? The Scope of Article IX

Article IX covers security interests in goods and fixtures. Consumer, business, and agricultural financings are all covered by Article IX. Article IX gives three categories of items, which can be used for security interests. The categories are tangibles, intangibles, and proceeds.

Tangible security: Goods (Section 9-109) This first category includes the types of items most familiar as security for a debt.

Consumer goods. Consumer goods are those used or bought primarily for personal, family, or household use. For example, a sofa for the family room is a consumer good, but a sofa for a dentist's waiting room is not one.

Equipment. Equipment consists of goods used or bought primarily for a business. For example, a dentist's sofa or a copy machine for a copy center are considered equipment.

Farm products. Crops, livestock, and supplies used or produced in farming operations are included in this group. In addition, the products of the crops and livestock are covered. For example, maple syrup, eggs, milk, and cotton are farm products.

Inventory. Goods held for sale or lease are inventory. Raw materials to be used in manufacturing inventory are also covered in this group. For example, a copy machine to a copy machine manufacturer is inventory. A sofa to a furniture manufacturer is inventory.

Intangible security: Documents (Section 9-106) These items are called **intangibles** because although they exist, the only evidence of their existence is on a piece of paper. The paper represents a right to something more.

1. *Accounts.* The term "accounts" is used here to mean accounts receivable. An account is a right to payment for good sold or for services rendered. To be classified as an account, there cannot be a note or other payment document involved. In other words, accounts are the day-to-day receivables of a firm.
2. *Instruments.* All the types of instruments covered under Article III are included in this group of intangibles. Checks, notes, and drafts are all covered.
3. *Documents.* Documents of title such as bills of lading are included here.
4. *General intangibles.* This group includes anything that does not fit into the other three categories. For example, goodwill, literary rights, patents, and copyrights are all intangible items, which can be used for Article IX security interests.

Proceeds (Section 9-306) **Proceeds** include whatever is received when collateral is sold or otherwise disposed of. For example, if the dentist has given a security interest in the sofa and then sells it, the money received would be proceeds. Most creditors who have a security interest in inventory also include a security interest in proceeds. That way, when the inventory is sold, they still have security in the funds paid. For example, if First Bank has a security interest in Don's Golf Shop's inventory and Don sells off the inventory, First Bank will have a right to the sales money put in the bank if they have a security interest in the proceeds.

If the property subject to a security interest is stolen or destroyed and the debtor is paid by an insurer, the funds paid are proceeds. Proceeds cover cash, checks, and funds deposited in bank accounts.

Terminology (Section 9-105)

Article IX parties have their own labels. The party who owes the money and who has pledged property is the debtor. The pledge of property is called a security interest. A security interest is created by a **security agreement.** The creditor is the party who has advanced money, who holds the security interest, and who is referred to as the **secured party. Collateral** is the property subject to the security interest.

A **purchase money security interest** (Section 9-107) is a special type of security interest limited to certain creditors. A seller who takes a security interest in property being sold has a purchase money security interest. For example, if

Fred's Furniture sells a sofa to Alice on credit and takes a security interest, Fred's has a purchase money security interest. Third parties who make advances to a debtor for a purchase and then take a security interest in that purchase also have a purchase money security interest. If First Bank loaned Alice the money to buy the sofa and took a security interest in it, they would also have a purchase money security interest.

How Is a Security Interest Created? (Section 9-203)

A security interest requires a written agreement, value, and an interest in the collateral. When all three requirements are met, the creditor's security interest becomes a lien on the collateral, or attaches.

The written agreement: Content and form A security interest must be in writing to be valid and must be signed by the debtor. The same signature requirements discussed for Articles II and III apply here, but no party is responsible unless he or she signs a security agreement. The *Clark Jewelers v. Satterthwaite* case involves an interesting issue of a missing signature.

CLARK JEWELERS v. SATTERTHWAITE

Supreme Court of Appeals of Kansas. 662 P.2d 1301 (1983).

FACTS Clark Jewelers sold a bridal set to Don Satterthwaite for $14,420. He paid $5000 down with the balance due in 90 days. His fiancé, Arlene Grabber, was with him when he bought the rings so that they could be fitted. Don executed a security agreement and gave the rings to Arlene as an engagement gift.

Arlene and Don broke up, and Don failed to pay the final $3654.94 due on the ring. Arlene kept the ring, which Clark wants to repossess. Arlene claims they cannot since she was not a party to the security agreement.

ISSUE Can a secured party repossess goods from third parties who have received them as gifts and who did not sign a security agreement?

DECISION No. Since Arlene did not sign the agreement and took the ring in good faith, she is protected. The jewelers are left to collect from Don.

LEGAL TIP

Pay for an engagement ring or do not break off the engagement.

There must be an adequate description of collateral in a security agreement. "Adequate" means that there is enough of a description to reasonably identify the goods. General descriptions are valid so long as the collateral is clear. For example, "all my inventory" is valid so long as the debtor's name, the name of the business, or both are on the agreement. The description "my red car" is not enough. A car description requires the model, year, and serial number. The description "all my farm equipment" is also not sufficient, since it is not clear what would actually be farm equipment.

Most businesses have some type of form to use for a security agreement. Figure 56-1 is an example of a typical security agreement. Agreements used may be titled security agreement, chattel mortgage or purchase money security agreement. The title is not important so long as the requirements are met. There are no specific language requirements under Article IX. However, the parties must indicate the

Figure 56-1 **Security Agreement**

(Loan Officer Note: Use only when Pledgor is Obligor)

VALLEY NATIONAL BANK

Valley National Bank of Arizona

SECURITY AGREEMENT

(Pledge of Savings and PSP Accounts, C.D.'s, Growth Bonds and Savings and Loan Accounts)

In consideration of one or more loans or credit accommodations granted to undersigned (Debtor) by THE VALLEY NATIONAL BANK OF ARIZONA, a national banking association (Bank), Debtor hereby pledges and assigns to Bank, and grants to Bank a security interest in, the following:
(Describe by name of Institution and branch if Valley National Bank or name of Institution if other than Valley National Bank, type, number, names under which account carried.)

together with all moneys and claims for moneys due or to become due or payable thereon or with respect therefor, all shares, deposits, investments and interest of every kind of the undersigned evidenced by any of the foregoing, and all proceeds thereof (all of which are hereinafter sometimes referred to as "Collateral")

☐ to secure the performance of the covenants and agreements herein set forth and payment of any and all indebtedness or liability of any one or more of the undersigned to Bank, now existing or hereafter arising, due or to become due, and however evidenced or acquired, whether direct or indirect, absolute or contingent, and whether several, joint, or joint and several, and any and all revisions, extensions or renewals thereof in whole or in part.

☐ to secure performance of the covenants and agreements herein set forth and payment of Debtor's note dated____________, 19____,
in the sum of ____ ($__________)
and interest as specified therein and any and all extensions or renewals thereof in whole or in part.

Debtor Promises and Agrees:

1. Upon request, to execute and/or deliver all such instruments, documents and other papers as may be requested by Bank in order to cause any and all payments and notices provided under the terms of the Collateral to be made and given directly to Bank.

2. To pay to Bank on demand all costs and expenses, including reasonable attorneys' fees, incurred by Bank in the preservation, realization, enforcement and exercise of the rights, powers and remedies of Bank and the obligations of Debtor hereunder whether suit be filed or not.

3. Any amounts received by Bank may be applied on such indebtednesses hereby secured, whether due or not due, and in such order as Bank, in its sole discretion, may determine.

4. Any of the following shall constitute an event of default:
(a) Failure of Debtor to pay, when due, any indebtedness secured hereby.
(b) The commencement of any bankruptcy, arrangement, reorganization, insolvency, receivership or similar proceedings by or against Debtor or against any guarantor or surety for Debtor.
(c) Death or incompetence of Debtor, dissolution, termination or merger of corporate or partnership existence.
(d) If the Collateral is levied on or seized under any levy, attachment, garnishment, writ or other legal process or if any liens shall attach thereto, or if a security interest is created with respect thereto.
(e) The occurrence of any adverse change in the financial condition of Debtor deemed material by Bank, or if in the judgment of Bank the Collateral shall become unsatisfactory in character or value, or if Bank shall deem itself Insecure.

5. Upon the happening of any of the foregoing events of default, Bank may, at its option, and without notice to any party, declare all the indebtedness hereby secured to be immediately due and payable, and Bank shall have the rights, options, duties and remedies afforded a secured party under the laws of the State of Arizona. Without limitation thereto, Bank shall have the following specific rights:
(a) To terminate any commitments to make loans or otherwise extend credit to Debtor;
(b) To apply the Collateral in payment of the indebtedness secured, and to payment of reasonable attorneys' fees and legal expense incurred by Bank, whether or not suit be filed;
(c) If the proceeds realized from the Collateral shall fail to satisfy all of the obligations of the Debtor to Bank, Debtor shall forthwith pay any deficiency balance to Bank.

6. It is understood and agreed that Bank does not assume and will not be subject to any obligation or liability of Debtor under any Collateral in which Bank is granted a security interest.

7. This security agreement/assignment is not taken in payment of the obligation except to the extent that Bank actually recovers payment hereunder.

8. Debtor hereby irrevocably authorizes and empowers Bank at any time, in its own name or in the name of Debtor, to demand, apply for, withdraw, receipt and give acquittance for any and all of the Collateral and to exercise any and all rights and privileges and receive all benefits accorded by said Collateral, and to execute any and all instruments required therefor. Any obligor under the terms of said Collateral is specifically authorized and directed, on demand of Bank, to pay and deliver all Collateral to said Bank.

9. *DEBTOR ACKNOWLEDGES EXPRESS INTENT TO HEREBY WAIVE AND ABANDON ALL PERSONAL PROPERTY EXEMPTIONS GRANTED BY LAW UPON THE COLLATERAL WHICH IS THE SUBJECT OF THIS AGREEMENT.* **NOTICE: By signing this Agreement, Debtor waives all rights provided by law to claim Collateral exempt from process.**

10. This Agreement shall be governed by the laws of the State of Arizona. Any provisions found to be invalid shall not invalidate the remainder hereof. Waiver of any default shall not constitute waiver of any subsequent default. Any true and correct carbon, photographic or other reproductive copy of this Agreement may be filed or recorded as a financing statement. If this instrument is signed by more than one Debtor the singular word "Debtor" shall include the plural, and the obligations of all such Debtors shall be joint and several. All words used herein shall be construed to be of such gender and number as the circumstances require, and all references herein to Debtor shall include all other persons primarily or secondarily liable hereunder. This instrument shall be binding upon the heirs, personal representatives, successors and assigns of Debtor, and inure to the benefit of Bank, its successors and assigns. **THIS AGREEMENT CONSTITUTES THE ENTIRE AGREEMENT BETWEEN THE PARTIES, AND MAY NOT BE ALTERED OR AMENDED EXCEPT BY A WRITING SIGNED BY ALL PARTIES.**

Figure 56-1 Continued

Executed this ______________ day of ______________, 19___

SECURED PARTY:

THE VALLEY NATIONAL BANK OF ARIZONA

By ______________

Its ______________

Address ______________ (Number and Street)

______________ (City or Town) (State) (Zip Code)

DEBTOR:

______________ (Debtor — type or print)

______________ (Debtor's signature)

______________ (Debtor — type or print)

______________ (Debtor's signature)

Address: ______________ (number and street)

______________ (City or Town) (State) (Zip Code)

RECEIPT

Receipt is acknowledged of the foregoing. We have no notice of any prior interest in the Collateral; we shall hold, subject to your rights any of the Collateral in or coming into our hands, which is described above; and we shall make payment of same to you, except as noted hereafter: ______________

____

Date: ______________

____

______________ (Signature)

Appears courtesy of Valley National Bank

intent to give the creditor some rights or interest in the property described. The agreement must be more than a loan agreement and must include some right to the property described. In addition to meeting the minimum requirements for the security agreement, the parties may want to put some other clauses in for their protection.

1. *After-acquired property clause.* Many security agreements not only cover specific property but also cover property the debtor acquires in the future. For example, a security interest in inventory will not last long, since inventory is always being sold. An **after-acquired property clause** gives the secured party what used to be called a floating lien and is now called a security interest. This floating lien means that the security interest continues in the inventory so long as the debt exists. The security interest is in the inventory regardless of what is included in the inventory and how many times it changes hands.

   An after-acquired clause can also be used in fixture security interests. For example, a seller may sell an air conditioning unit to a homeowner who will attach it to his or her home. The seller can take a security interest in the air conditioner and any other air conditioner that is attached until the debt is satisfied. The *Cargill, Inc. v. Perlich* case involves an issue of description and the validity of an after-acquired clause.

2. *Sale of collateral.* As will be discussed in Chapter 57, the sale of the collateral can create some complications for the creditor's rights. A clause in the security agreement should establish the right of resale (if any), the procedures for resale, and any penalties for violation of the resale clause. The sale clause should also cover the debtor's rights to pledge the same collateral to another debtor.

3. *Terms of repayment.* The security agreement is often the lending agreement. The payments, time for payment, and penalties for late payments should be part

CARGILL, INC. v. PERLICH

Court of Appeals of Indiana.
418 N.E.2d 274 (1981).

FACTS Wayne Perlich entered into a security agreement with the Shipshewana State Bank. The security agreement was to secure a loan from the bank with Perlich's hogs. The security agreement described the collateral as "the hogs on Perlich's farm together with the young, product and produce thereof."

Perlich operates a hog farm and hogs are purchased, fattened, and sold every six months. Cargill had sold Perlich some hogs on credit and when Perlich did not pay, he wanted his hogs back. The bank claimed they had a security interest. Cargill said that since the security agreement was signed in 1973 and he sold the hogs in 1974, the bank's interest no longer applied.

ISSUE Did the bank describe the hogs adequately? Was there an after-acquired clause or was the bank limited to the first set of hogs?

DECISION There was a sufficient description of the hogs. The language used was adequate for an after-acquired clause. The court added that it is also a trade custom to include future hog purchases as collateral.

LEGAL TIP
Use precise language in security agreements.

of the agreement. In addition, the secured party should define default. Default gives the secured party the right to repossess collateral (see Chapter 58 for a complete discussion). The default section should cover what would be a default and how long it takes for a default to occur.

4. *Insurance.* If the goods are stolen or destroyed, the secured party has very little security. The secured party can require (as part of the security agreement) the debtor to maintain current insurance on the property.

Value must be given The second requirement for a security interest to attach is that the secured party must give **value.** Giving value can be simply giving consideration in a contract. If a seller agrees to sell the buyer a good on credit and take a security interest, value has been given. The buyer gets the goods on credit—the seller has given that consideration as value.

In addition, a seller can give value through a pre-existing obligation. For example, suppose that Ralph owes Joan $3000, and Ralph has not paid Joan. Joan is nervous about Ralph's ability to pay. Ralph agrees to a new payment schedule and gives Joan a security interest in his motorcycle. Joan has given value even though she loaned the money some time ago. The requirement of value is basically that the debtor owes the creditor some obligation. The purpose of value is to prevent general pledges of goods without some benefit.

Debtor's interest in the collateral A security agreement will be completely ineffective if the debtor has no right or title in the goods being pledged. For example, a tenant cannot pledge the furniture in his or her apartment if the landlord owns the furniture. A seller cannot pledge goods that are at his or her business for repair. The debtor must own the goods now or in the future.

When a creditor takes a purchase money security interest, the buyer/debtor will have a security interest at the time the title to the goods passes to the buyer. The parties can execute their security agreement in advance of the title passing. But the security interest will not attach until the buyer has the title to the goods.

Effect of attachment Once a security interest attaches, the secured party has certain rights. The most important right is the right to repossess the goods in the event the buyer does not pay or defaults (see Chapter 58 for details on repossession). The secured party also has a superior position or priority over creditors who have no security (see Chapter 57 for a discussion of priorities).

KEY TERMS

Surety
Liens
Security interest
Intangibles
Proceeds
Security agreement
Secured party
Collateral
Purchase money security interest
After-acquired property clause
Value

CHAPTER PROBLEMS

1. Black & Decker manufactures hand-held saws. What form of collateral are the saws in Black & Decker's possession? If Black & Decker sells the saws to retail stores, what form of collateral are the saws in the possession of the retail stores? If a consumer buys a saw on credit, what is the form of collateral to that consumer?

2. Mr. and Mrs. Rex have purchased a mobile home to be delivered to them in Yuma, Arizona. The Phoenix, Arizona, seller has taken a security interest in the mobile home since the Rexes are buying on credit. When does the seller's security interest attach? *Rex v. Mobile America Corp.,* Rex Financial Corp., 580 P.2d 8 (Ariz. 1978).

3. Classify each of the following into types of collateral:
   A. Trucks used in a delivery service company.
   B. Trucks at the Ford factory.
   C. A truck used by a business person for commuting.

4. Is the description "all my inventory" adequate for a valid security interest?

5. What is a floating lien?

*6. Does a surety's promise have to be in writing to be valid?

*7. A clamming license is required in the state of Pennsylvania to dig commercially for clams. Licenses are limited and quite valuable. Wildwood Clam Company has pledged their license as security to First Pennsylvania Bank for a term loan of $600,000. Can there be a valid security interest in the clamming license? *First Pennsylvania Bank, N.A. v. Wildwood Clam Co., Inc.,* 535 F.Supp. 266 (E.D. Pa. 1982).

*8. On February 9, 1979, Donna and Emma Haus signed a sales contract for the purchase of a gas range from Cole-McLaurin Company, Inc. They paid $200, which left a balance of $183.84. On March 2, 1979, they paid $183.76, leaving a balance of $.08. On that same day, they purchased a washer, a dryer, and a color television from Cole-McLaurin. The contracts on both purchases provided that the seller retained title to the goods until the price was paid in full. Payment in full could be within 30 days before there were any finance charges. The Hauses went bankrupt and Cole-McLaurin claimed it was a secured party. The contracts were signed by both Donna and Emma and described all the items purchased by model, description, and serial number. Does Cole-McLaurin have a security interest? *Haus v. Barclays American Corporation,* 33 UCC Rep. 694 (Bankruptcy Court, 1982, Conn.).

*9. Nuzum pledged his accounts receivable to Daly. Later when Nuzum got new accounts, he sold them to Shrimplin. Daly claimed all the accounts. Who holds the accounts? *Daly v. Shrimplin,* 610 P.2d 397 (Wyo. 1980).

*10. Could a liquor license be subject to an Article IX security interest? *Tomb v. Lavalle,* 444 A.2d 666 (Pa. 1981).

"First in Time, First in Right"
White and Summers
The First Rule of Priorities

Chapter 57

Priorities of Creditors in Secured Credit Transactions

CHAPTER PREVIEW

- Methods of perfection
- Places for filing for perfection
- Automatic perfection
- General priority rules
- Exceptions to the general rules
- Buyers' rights in perfected goods

Mitch's Music Store has an inventory of thirty-five baby grand pianos. The pianos were sold to Mitch on credit by Grandville Piano Company. Grandville has a security interest in the pianos. Mitch sells one of the pianos to Melissa Sue Jones. Mitch then fails to pay Grandville. Can Grandville get the piano back from Melissa Sue?

Although having a security interest gives a creditor extra protection, there can still be problems with other creditors. The key to a creditor's protection is to get priority or a superior position over other creditors. This chapter answers several questions on priorities. How can a creditor get priority? What are the general priority rules? Are there exceptions to the general rules?

PRIORITIES AMONG SECURITY INTERESTS

Although a security interest is not the best protection, it does give the secured creditor priority over some other creditors (Section 9-301). For example, a secured party has priority over unsecured creditors.

Secured parties enjoy their priority according to the time their security interest attached. If First Bank takes a security interest in Sal's car on August 13 and Second Bank takes a security interest in the same car on September 1, First Bank has priority.

Lien creditors can also become involved with the collateral used for a security interest. The rule for priority between lien creditors and secured parties is first in time, first in right. If the security interest attaches before the lien, the security interest has priority. If the security interest attaches after the lien, the lien has priority.

THE ROAD TO PRIORITY: PERFECTION

An interest must be perfected to give the secured party priority over later and in some cases earlier creditors. **Perfection** can eliminate the first in time, first in right rule. Once a perfected secured party is involved, the perfection becomes more important than when the security interest attached. Perfection can occur by filing, by possession, or by attachment, and in some circumstances by automatic perfection.

The Road to Perfection: Filing (Section 9-302)

Perfection by **filing** requires the secured party to file a document called a financing statement in the proper public place. The idea of this filing is to give public notice that a security interest exists. With public notice, the secured party has a better priority position (see discussion below).

What is filed: The financing statement (Section 9-402) The financing statement is generally a standard form used routinely by a creditor. The financing statement must include the following:

1. Names of the debtor and secured party.
2. Signature of the debtor.
3. Address of the secured party (so that interested parties can get information about the collateral).
4. Mailing address of the debtor.
5. Description of the collateral.

If the security agreement has all of the above information, it can be used as a financing statement. Figure 57-1 is a sample of a financing statement.

Although the content of the financing statement seems clear, some problems do arise. The first concerns the debtor's name. The secured party must be careful to use the debtor's correct business name. If the debtor is a corporation, the proper corporate name must be used. If the debtor is a sole proprietorship, the secured party must use the debtor's name along with any d/b/a. Some states do not allow the use of trade names for public records. The secured party must be certain of the debtor's business status (that is, corporation, partnership, or sole proprietorship) and the proper name. The *In re Mcbee* case involves a problem with a name on a financing statement.

IN RE McBEE

United States Bankruptcy Court, Western District Texas, Austin Division.
20 B.R. 361 (1982).

FACTS Cynthia McBee, a partner in the Oak Hill Gun Shop, signed a security interest agreement and financing statement for some inventory on January 8, 1979. Union National Bank was giving the shop the loan for the inventory and taking the security interest in it as collateral. Both documents named Oak Hill Gun Shop as the debtor.

On April 22, 1980, McBee signed another security agreement and financing statement for Wholesale Supply. Wholesale's documents gave them a security interest in the "equipment, inventory and furniture" of the business. These documents named the debtor as "Joe B. Colley d/b/a Oak Hill Gun Shop."

The Oak Hill Gun Shop went bankrupt and the issue of priority between Union and Wholesale arose. Union claims priority as first in time, first in right. Wholesale claims the financing statement of Union is ineffective because it does not properly name the debtor.

ISSUE Was the debtor named properly? If not, what is the effect on priority?

DECISION No. "Oak Hill Gun Shop" was a trade name. A trade name does not properly name the debtor. The proper name was the d/b/a used by Wholesale. The effect is that Union financing statement is defective, and the court cannot give it priority.

LEGAL TIP

Check to see who owns a business. Find out whether a corporation, partnership, or sole proprietorship is involved. Use the right name and status on the financing statement.

The second problem area in financing statements is the description. Since the public will have to determine what collateral has been pledged from the financing statement, the description should be as thorough and as accurate as possible. The *In re Bob Schwermer & Associates, Inc.* case deals with the problem of a financing statement description.

Where to file (Section 9-401) Article IX provides for two filing places: central and local. The central location for filing in most states is with the state's Secretary of State. The local location for filing is the office responsible for keeping the real property records. County recorders' offices or Offices of the Recorder are the usual local filing places. In local filings, states have different rules for which county office is used. In some cases, it is the county where the debtor lives. In the case of fixtures, the county is usually the one where the property is located.

Section 9-401 provides three alternatives for states to adopt in setting up their filing system. Figure 57-2 gives a summary of Code alternatives.

Figure 57–1 **Uniform Commercial Code Financing Statement**

INSTRUCTIONS: Use this form to perfect a security interest. Use form F-UCC-2 for any changes to this financing statement. Use form F-UCC-3 to request information or copies of another party's presently effective financing statements or statement of assignment.

This instrument was recorded at request of:

The recording official is directed to return this instrument or a copy to the above person.

Space Reserved For Recording Information

UNIFORM
COMMERCIAL CODE
FINANCING STATEMENT
F-UCC-1 © LawForms 6-72, 9-81

Effective Date	County and State of Transaction
DEBTOR (Name, Address and Zip Code)	SECURED PARTY (Name, Address and Zip Code)
Assignee of Secured Party (Name, Address and Zip Code)	Record Owner of Real Property, If Not Debtor (Name, Address and Zip Code)
Counties Where Collateral is Located	☐ Products of Collateral are also covered. ☐ Proceeds of Collateral are also covered.

Financing Statement covers the following types or items of property:

If collateral is timber to be cut, crops growing or to be grown, minerals or the like, accounts to be financed at the wellhead or minehead of the well or mine, or goods which are or are to become fixtures, the real property to which these are affixed or concerned is legally described:

☐ This financing statement is to be filed in the office where a mortgage on the real property would be recorded.

This Financing Statement is filed or recorded without Debtor's signature to perfect a security interest in collateral which:

- ☐ Is already subject to a security interest in another jurisdiction when it was brought into the state or which Debtor changed location to this State;
- ☐ Are proceeds of the original collateral described above in which a security interest was perfected;
- ☐ Is no longer effective due to lapse of the original filing;
- ☐ Was acquired four months or less after Debtor has changed its name, identity or corporate structure.

Signatures of Debtor or Assignor	Signatures of Secured Party or Assignee

Appears courtesy of Law Forms Phoenix, AZ

Filing in the proper place is critical in all states. If a secured party files in the wrong place, the perfection is not completely effective. If a filing was made locally and it was supposed to be central, the filing is not perfected except against those who actually know of the financing statement and the filing. For example, suppose secured party Crandall files a financing statement for fixtures centrally. In Crandall's

IN RE BOB SCHWERMER & ASSOCIATES, INC.

United States Bankruptcy Court, Northern District of Illinois.
27 B.R. 304 (1983).

FACTS First National Bank and Trust Company of Evanston took a security interest in 8 horses to secure an $842,134.66 loan. First National filed a financing statement with the number "16" typed in the description section. Attached to the financing statement was a copy of the security agreement, which had the names of the 8 horses along with the location of the foal certificates. When Schwermer went bankrupt, other creditors claimed the financing statement was not valid because of the description.

ISSUE Was the financing statement valid?

DECISION Yes. Since an adequate description of all of the documents were filed together, the collateral description was adequate.

LEGAL TIP

If documents are going to be attached to the financing statement, put a note and reference them on the financing statement. Note that there are attachments for the description.

state, fixture financing statements must be filed locally. Crandall's perfection is good only against those who actually know of the financing statement. Proper filing is notice to all. Improper filing is not notice unless others actually know of the filing.

Some states have a separate filing place for motor vehicles. The Department of Motor Vehicles or Department of Transportation may be the exclusive filing place for security interests in motor vehicles. In addition, the notice of the security interest may be put on the title to the vehicle for actual notice.

How long is a filing valid? (Section 9-403) Under Article IX, a financing statement is effective for five years from the date of filing. Some states have variations on this length of time.

The filing can be renewed any time during the last six months of its effective period. If the financing statement is renewed during that six month period, it will be good for another five years. The renewal is done by filing a continuation statement. The continuation statement must be signed by the secured party, identify the original financing statement by its file number, and state that the original financing statement is still in effect.

A financing statement's effect can be ended voluntarily. A voluntary ending occurs when the secured party files a termination statement (Section 9-404). The termination statement is filed in the same place and must include a statement that the secured party is no longer owed an obligation. With consumer goods, the

Figure 57-2 **Location of Filing Alternatives**

ALTERNATIVE	LOCAL	CENTRAL
1	Timber, mineral, and fixture accounts	All other
2	Farming equipment and products, consumer goods, timber, minerals, fixtures	All other
3	Farming equipment and products, consumer goods, timber, minerals. All others in county of residence	None

consumer has a right to make a written demand that a termination statement be filed. After receiving such a written demand, the secured party has 10 days to file a termination statement. If the secured party does not file within 10 days from the time of the written request, the debtor can collect $100 plus any other damages suffered from the failure to file.

When is filing required? (Section 9-302) There are some types of transactions in which filing is required for perfection. Article IX lists the times when a filing is not required for perfection. Filing is not required for perfection when:

1. The secured party has the collateral in its possession.
2. There is temporary perfection provided under Article IX (discussed below).
3. There is a purchase money security interest in consumer goods (see below).

In other words, filing is not required when the secured party has perfection by some other means.

The Road to Perfection: Perfection by Possession

Possession may not be nine points of the law, but it is Article IX perfection in some circumstances. Security interests in money or instruments can be perfected by possession (Section 9-304). Security interests in letters of credit, goods, and negotiable documents can also be perfected by possession (Section 9-305).

Perfection by possession lasts only as long as the goods are in the possession of the secured party. Perfection is lost the moment possession stops. The only way to continue the perfection is by filing. Field warehousing where the seller keeps the goods until the buyer pays is one example of perfection by possession.

The Road to Perfection: Automatic Perfection

In some cases, Article IX gives the secured party a bonus. Their interest is given **automatic perfection.** The circumstances are limited to negotiable instruments, purchase money security interests in consumer goods, and proceeds.

Automatic perfection in negotiable instruments (Section 9-304) A security interest in negotiable instruments is automatically perfected for a period of twenty-one days after attachment of the security interest. This perfection occurs without possession or filing.

Automatic perfection in consumer purchase money security interests (Section 9-302) When a seller sells consumer goods on credit and takes a security interest, that interest is perfected automatically. This perfection occurs without filing and without possession. The secured party must be either the seller of the goods or a lender who has financed the purchase and takes the purchased item as collateral.

There is an exception to this automatic perfection rule, which involves fixtures. Consumer and non-consumer fixture security interests always require filing for perfection. For example, if Harry buys a solar water heating system to install on his home, it is a consumer transaction. But the solar system will become a fixture and a filing is required for perfection.

Automatic perfection in sales proceeds (Section 9-306) Proceeds are whatever a seller receives upon the sale of collateral subject to a security agreement.

Money, checks, and deposits in accounts are proceeds. If the secured party had a perfected security interest in the collateral sold, that perfected interest continues in the proceeds from the sale. However, the automatic perfection in the proceeds lasts only ten days. Also, the automatic perfection applies only if the proceeds are identifiable. Proceeds are identifiable when they can be traced as the funds from the sale. For example, a buyer's check deposited in the seller's 0- balance account is identifiable.

To be able to continue their priority and perfected status, secured parties must file a financing statement covering the proceeds. They also must have had a filed financing statement covering the collateral originally. In other words, the automatic perfection for proceeds is only temporary. The secured party must decide what to do within ten days to maintain perfection. The *In re Turner* case shows how the automatic perfection in proceeds works.

IN RE TURNER

United States Bankruptcy Court of Nebraska.
13 B.R. 15 (1981).

FACTS Millard Aviation, Inc., owned by Charles Turner, was a dealer for Cessna Aircraft. Cessna retained a security interest, which was perfected by filing, in all the planes shipped to Millard. Millard was required to obtain Cessna's approval before selling a plane. Upon sale, Millard was required to deposit sale proceeds in a separate and special account.

Millard sold a plane, and Turner deposited the proceeds in his account. He withdrew some of the funds and then filed bankruptcy. Cessna claimed they had a perfected security interest in the funds in the account.

ISSUE Did Cessna have a perfected interest in the proceeds deposited in Turner's account?

DECISION Yes. There was automatic perfection. Cessna had filed a financing statement covering the collateral. The proceeds (although deposited in the wrong account) could be traced. Even with the withdrawal, funds remained and Cessna had a perfected interest in them.

The court used a first in-first out method in determining how much of the account was Cessna's. They assumed that Turner's withdrawal was of funds already in the account before the deposit.

LEGAL TIP

The secured party should require a signature on the title before a transfer. With this requirement, secured parties can get their proceeds before a problem with priorities arises.

RULES OF PRIORITIES

The rules of **priorities** among perfected secured creditors are a bit more complex than the rules among secured and other creditors. There are general rules and exceptions. This section of the chapter covers the priorities among the perfected secured creditors.

The Basics: General Rules

Perfected secured party versus secured party (Section 9-312) The rule applied between these two parties is that the perfected secured party wins. This rule applies even if the perfected secured party's security interest attached after the secured party's interest attached.

Perfected secured party versus perfected secured party (Section 9-312) When two parties have perfected secured interests in the same collateral, the first in time, first in right rule applies. The first party to perfect has the superior interest.

Perfected secured party versus lien creditor A lien creditor is someone who has a lien in the same property that is the subject of the perfected security interest. For example, the lien could result from a mechanics' work, a judgment, or any other statutory lien. The priority rule here is also first in time, first in right. The priority goes to the party who is either first to file the financing statement or the first to file the lien (regardless of the type of lien). For example, suppose that Fred gives Sam a security interest in his 1984 Bronco II auto on May 5. On May 10, Jerry wins a judgment against Fred for Fred's breach of a contract. Jerry files a judgment lien on May 30. Sam files a financing statement on May 31. Jerry will have priority since he filed his lien before Sam perfected his security interest by filing. The *United States v. Waterford No. 2 Office Ctr.* case deals with a priority issue between a perfected secured party and a judgment creditor.

UNITED STATES v. WATERFORD NO. 2 OFFICE CTR.

Supreme Court of Georgia.
271 S.E.2d 790 (1980).

FACTS United States Electronics (US) leased its office space in the Waterford No. 2 Center. US borrowed money from a Missouri bank and gave the bank a security interest in all of its equipment and machinery at its Atlanta place of business. The Small Business Administration (SBA) guaranteed the loan.

The Missouri bank filed its financing statement in the wrong place (unperfected). US defaulted, and the SBA claimed a security interest in all the equipment and machinery.

In March 1979, Waterford got a judgment for $7000 due in back rent. They filed their judgment lien that day. The court has been able to sell the equipment and machinery for $3000. The parties dispute who has priority.

ISSUE Who has priority in the $3000?

DECISION Waterford. The judgment was obtained and the lien filed before a perfection by any party. The faulty filing made the bank and the SBA's failure to file made them unperfected secured parties.

LEGAL TIP

Make sure financing statements are filed in the correct location. Without proper filing, there can be no perfection and no priority.

The Exceptions: Complex Priorities or First in Time, Second in Right

For every priority rule, there is an exception. Under Article IX, there are more exceptions than rules. This section covers priority exceptions.

Perfected secured party versus buyer (Section 9-307) Buyers in the ordinary course of business buy the goods free and clear of any security interest. This is true even though the security interest is perfected and even though the buyer knows of the secured party's interest.

A buyer in the ordinary course of business is someone buying goods from a seller who deals in those goods. The buyer is acting in good faith. A buyer from a pawnbroker cannot be a buyer in the ordinary course of business (Section 1-201 [9]). If a buyer is not in the ordinary course of business, he or she will be subject to the security interest.

The *Keystone Data Systems, Inc., v. James F. Wild, Inc.* case deals with the issue of priority when a buyer purchases the collateral.

KEYSTONE DATA SYSTEMS, INC. v. JAMES F. WILD, INC.

United States District Court, Eastern District of Pennsylvania.
549 F.Supp. 790 (1982).

FACTS Keystone sold a computer and ancillary equipment to Video Systems Corporation for $64,000. Keystone had a security agreement executed. Two months after the sale and seven months before Keystone filed a financing statement, Video sold the computer and equipment to James Wild for $59,000. The reason for the sale to Wild was for a partial settlement of a dispute between the two parties. Video has not paid Keystone, and Keystone wants its computer back from Video.

ISSUE Did Wild buy the computer and equipment free and clear of the security interest?

DECISION Yes. This buyer did not know of the security interest. There had been no perfection and even if there were perfection, Wild (as a buyer in ordinary course) made a purchase free and clear of the security interest. The fact that Video has a poor reputation in the community does not cause Wild to lose his status as a buyer in ordinary course.

LEGAL TIP

Do not wait to file a financing statement. Maintain control over sales so that funds can be transferred.

In *In re Teel* case examines the problem of someone who is not a buyer in the ordinary course of business.

IN RE TEEL

United States Bankruptcy Court.
33 UCC Rep. 1658 (1981).

FACTS In 1978, Teel purchased 22 Kimball organs. Teel financed the purchase through Borg-Warner Acceptance Corporation. Borg-Warner took a floating lien in the inventory. Borg had a filed perfected security interest in the inventory and an after-acquired clause covering future inventory.

Teel transferred the 22 organs to his Video School of Music on Seymour Highway in Wichita Falls. Morgan Leasing then bought the organs for $19,690. Teel leased them back for 36 months at $622.41 per month. Teel closed the school and filed bankruptcy. The issue of the priority of Borg-Warner and Morgan was raised by those two parties.

ISSUE Was Morgan a buyer in the ordinary course and entitled to priority?

DECISION No. Morgan was definitely not a buyer in the ordinary course. Morgan was setting up a mutually beneficial transaction with the debtor. Borg-Warner would have priority.

LEGAL TIP

Check financing arrangements for large purchases. Require notification for bulk transfers of inventory.

PMSI in consumer goods versus buyer (Section 9-307 [2]) A PMSI (Purchase Money Security Interest) in consumer goods gives the secured party automatic perfection. For example, if Sears sells a refrigerator to Bill on credit and takes a security interest in the refrigerator, they have an automatically perfected security interest.

Suppose that Bill sells his refrigerator in a garage sale to his neighbor, Betty. Betty will take the refrigerator free and clear of the security interest if she is buying the refrigerator for her own use and if she does not know of Sears' security interest. However, if Sears files a financing statement anyway—regardless of the automatic perfection—Betty will not buy the refrigerator free and clear of Sears' security interest. Although expensive, filing the financing statement for consumer collateral does give the creditor more protection.

PMSI in inventory versus perfected secured party (Section 9-312) This exception helps sellers who ship inventory on credit. If it were not for this exception, many businesses would be unable to get inventory on credit. Under this exception, a PMSI creditor in inventory has priority over prior perfected security interests if the PMSI perfects before the inventory is delivered. Other creditors must be notified *before* delivery is made.

For example, suppose that First Bank loans Joan's Kitchen $10,000 for the purchase of inventory for her gourmet cook's store. The bank takes a security interest in the inventory, perfects, and has an after-acquired property clause in the agreement. Joan sells most of the original inventory and will now receive $10,000 more in inventory on credit from Gourmet Platters, Inc. If Gourmet takes a security interest in the inventory, files its financing statement, and notifies First Bank before delivery, it will have priority even though they were second in time to perfect. The same would be true if a third creditor came along after Gourmet and followed the requirements.

PMSI in equipment versus perfected secured party (Section 9-312) A PMSI creditor in equipment can get the same type of benefits as a PMSI inventory creditor. A PMSI creditor who is later in time will have priority over prior perfected creditors if he or she files a financing statement covering the equipment within ten days after the equipment is delivered.

For example, suppose that First National Bank took a security interest in equipment from Karen's Salad Bar. First files a financing statement covering the equipment. As business improves, Karen orders a new ice machine on credit from Mr. Ice. If Mr. Ice files its financing statement within ten days from delivering the machine to Karen, it will have priority over First National in that equipment. This priority is true even if First had an after-acquired property clause in its agreement with Karen.

The reason for this exception is to allow the replacement of equipment without having to pay off prior debts or without having to pay cash for all later purchases.

PMSI in fixtures versus perfected secured party A PMSI fixture creditor can have priority over prior perfected parties if the PMSI creditor files a financing statement before the fixtures are attached or within ten days of their attachment. This exception allows property owners to replace items and repair defects in their homes and buildings on a continual basis.

For example, suppose that Ralph has purchased an air conditioner from Mr. Cool. Mr. Cool takes a security interest and files the appropriate financing statement. Later Ralph purchases a water heater on credit from Aloe Water Heaters. If Aloe files a financing statement before the water heater is attached or within ten days after, Aloe will have priority over Mr. Cool even though they were later in filing. The *AMFAC Mortgage Corp. v. Arizona Mall of Tempe* case deals with the issue of priorities among fixture creditors.

AMFAC MORTGAGE CORP. v. ARIZONA MALL OF TEMPE

Court of Appeals of Arizona.
618 P.2d 240 (1980).

FACTS The Arizona Mall Project entered into a contract with Watson to construct the mall. AMFAC served as the construction lender for the $22.5 million project. AMFAC took a security interest "in all building materials, fixtures and equipment to be incorporated into the improvements for which the construction loan secured hereby is being made . . .."

Reppel furnished structural steel. He delivered 850 tons to the site and they were never put in the building because the Project went bankrupt. AMFAC and Reppel both claim priority in the steel.

ISSUE Who has priority?

DECISION AMFAC has priority because Reppel never filed a financing statement. Since the steel was never attached, it never became a fixture. Reppel also did not file within the 10-day provision.

LEGAL TIP

Get payment before or at the time materials are delivered to a construction site.

Figure 57-3 is a summary of the priority rules under Article IX.

Figure 57-3 **Priority of Secured Interests Under Article IX**

CONFLICT	PRIORITY
Secured party versus secured party	Party whose security interest attached first
Unsecured party versus secured party	Secured party
Perfected secured party versus secured party	Perfected secured party
Perfected secured party versus perfected secured party	Party who is first to perfect
Perfected secured party versus party with a lien	Party who filed (financing statement or lien) first (Section 9-307[2])
Exceptions	
PMSI in fixtures versus perfected secured party	PMSI creditor if perfected before attachment or within 10 days after attachment (PMSI will have priority even over prior perfected secured party) (Sections 9-313 and 9-314)
PMSI in equipment versus perfected secured party	PMSI if perfected within 10 days after delivery (Sections 9-301[2] and 9-312[4])
PMSI in inventory versus perfected secured party	PMSI if perfected before delivery and if prior perfected secured party given notice before delivery (Section 9-312[3])
PMSI in consumer goods versus buyer	Buyer unless perfection is by filing before purchase (Section 9-302[1][d])
Perfected secured party versus buyer	Buyers (in good faith) of consumer goods have priority (Section 9-306[2])

KEY TERMS

Perfection
Filing
Automatic perfection
Possession
Priorities

CHAPTER PROBLEMS

1. Charlie Moore operated a mining and welding business and the business had been known under the following names: Charlie Moore d/b/a/ Moore's Welding and Mining Co.; Charlie Moore Co.; Moore's Mining Co.; Moore's Welding Co.; Moore's Mining & Welding Co.; Charlie Moore; Moore's Welding; and MHS Investment. There was also more than one address used for the business. How should a creditor file a financing statement? *In re Moore,* 33 UCC Rep. 773 (E.D. Tenn. 1982).

2. First National Bank took a security interest in Chemical Products' Equipment and filed financing statements with both the Secretary of State and the Recorder of Deeds. Under the description of collateral section of the forms, was written "See Attached List." No list was attached. Is the filing effective? *First National Bank of St. Charles v. Chemical Products, Inc.,* 34 UCC Rep. 300 (Mo. 1982).

3. Would a financing statement (proper in other respects) describing collateral as "hog equipment" and "farm machinery" be adequate? *In re Grey,* 36 UCC Rep. 724 (Kans. 1983).

4. Ford Motor Company sold some farm equipment to Wil-Win Farms, Inc., on credit and took a security interest in the equipment. Ford filed its financing statement in Clay County, Florida. Wil-Win had its mailing in Clay County but its place of business was in St. John's county. Is Ford's interest perfected? *In re Wil-Win Farms,* 34 UCC Rep. 349 (Fla. 1982).

5. A financing statement describes a debtor as "American Supply Company" rather than "AMSCO, Inc." "AMSCO, Inc." is the debtor's true corporate name. Is there perfection? *In re AMSCO, Inc.,* 35 UCC Rep. 640 (Conn. 1982).

6. The Keidels purchased a mobile home on May 17, 1977, and gave First National Bank of Wood River a security interest in it. They also signed a financing statement that was not properly filed until December 7, 1977. The Keidels filed bankruptcy on November 7, 1977. The bankruptcy trustee claims priority over First National. Is he right? *In re Keidel,* 613 F.2d 172 (7th Cir. 1980).

7. Hilfiker bought a restaurant at a foreclosure sale. Zecher had perfected security interests (by filing) in the restaurant equipment. Is Hilfiker subject to the security interests? *Bankers Trust Co. of Western New York v. Zecher v. Hilfiker,* 426 N.Y.S.2d 960 (1980).

*8. Would a bank's security interest in 114 shares of stock cover the 144 shares resulting from a stock split by the corporation? *In re Mathews,* 29 UCC Rep. 684 (4th Cir. 1980).

9. Masson Cheese sold cheese on credit to Valley Lea Dairies, Inc. Masson had a floating lien on Valley's inventory. Valley sold all of its inventory to Blue Valley Cheese but did not pay Masson. Masson wants the cheese back. Who has priority? *Masson Cheese Corp. v. Valley Lea Dairies,* 411 N.E.2d 716 (Ind. 1980).

10. Who has priority between two unperfected but secured creditors?

"The check is in the mail."
One of the Great Lies of Our Time

Chapter 58

Enforcement and Collection of Credit Transactions

CHAPTER PREVIEW

- Common law torts and collection
- The Fair Debt Collections Practices Act
- When a debtor defaults
- Creditor's right to repossession under Article IX
- Article IX repossession limitations
- Article IX resale requirements
- Creditors' and debtors' rights in sale of collateral
- Garnishment procedures and limitations

Freida owes Wake Funeral Home $2000 for her husband's funeral. Freida has good intentions and wants to pay, but she is a financially distressed widow. Wake has turned over the account to Ace Collection Agency. Ace calls Freida at least seven times each day to remind her of the debt. Ace has called her employer to tell him of Freida's debt. Ace has just written a letter, which includes the following language: "If you don't pay up by March 10, 1984, we will obtain a court order to dig up your husband's grave and repossess the casket." Freida has taken the letter to the local Legal Aid Society. Does Freida have any rights the Legal Aid Society can protect?

Although many people enter into credit transactions, not all of them complete their obligations under those transactions. Because of the loss of a job, medical bills, or over-extended finances, some debtors do not repay their credit obligations. This chapter deals with the problem of the non-paying debtor. What can a creditor do to collect from a debtor? What is default? What are creditors' rights upon default? What other ways can be used to collect a debt?

STEP ONE: THE NON-PAYMENT/ COLLECTION STAGE

In this stage, the creditor simply needs to take some action to encourage payment. During this stage the creditor can make calls, write letters, and personally contact the debtor to encourage payment. There are some restrictions on the actions a creditor can take to collect the debt. The next sections cover these restrictions.

Torts in the Collection Stage

Creditors can be energetic and creative in their collection process within certain limitations. Some of those limitations come from the common law of torts. Creditors cannot commit a tort in their efforts to collect a debt. For example, a creditor who makes false statements about a debtor can be sued for defamation. Suppose that Charlie wrote the following to Dan's employer: "Dan is not an honorable individual. He gets credit and doesn't pay. He doesn't meet his obligations and is untrustworthy." In this letter, Charlie has strayed from the facts. He has made statements beyond his experience that may or may not be true. The letter is likely to be the subject of a defamation suit if Dan can show the general statements to be false.

Creditors who publish lists of non-paying debtors or post debtors' names at their places of business commit the tort of public disclosure of private facts. Notifying others is not a protected collection activity.

The creditor can approach the debtor at his or her home and in a public place. But contact with a debtor in the hospital or a restroom is the tort of intrusion upon private affairs.

If the creditor is outrageous in his or her collection tactics, the tort of intentional infliction of emotional distress will apply. The conduct must be offensive, bizarre, and outrageous. The *Everett v. Community Credit Company* case illustrates the type of outrageous conduct required before the debtor can recover.

The Fair Debt Collections Practices Act

In 1977, Congress became involved in the regulation of debt collection. The **Fair Debt Collection Practices Act (FDCPA)** became effective in 1978 and regulates the collection of certain consumer debts.

When does the FDCPA apply? The FDCPA applies only to consumer debts. It also only applies to "debt collectors." "Debt collectors" are defined as third-party collectors. For example, if Bert's Department Store refers an account for collection to Ace Collection Agency, Ace is covered by the FDCPA. However, Bert's would not be governed by the FDCPA in collecting its own debts.

The FDCPA would apply if Bert's collected its own debts under a different name. It does not apply to banks, attorneys, or the Internal Revenue Service. It also does not apply to the collection of commercial credit accounts.

EVERETT v. COMMUNITY CREDIT COMPANY

Court of Appeals of Louisiana.
224 So.2d 145 (1969).

FACTS Mrs. Everett was past due on her payments on a loan. Community Credit was hired to collect the amount due. Mrs. Everett had a heart condition and was confined to bed.

Community sent one of its representatives to Mrs. Everett's home to question her about the debt. Mrs. Everett protested and asked that the Community representative not talk about the debt in front of her twelve-year-old son. The representative proceeded and dwelled on questions about her husband's desertion in front of the boy.

The day after the Community representative visited, Mrs. Everett had to be hospitalized. She died shortly thereafter of an aggravated heart condition.

ISSUE Did Community commit any torts in their collection process?

DECISION Yes. There was intentional infliction of emotional distress and intrusion on private affairs. Considering Mrs. Everett's condition, the conduct was bizarre and outrageous.

LEGAL TIP

Collection from ill people is outrageous. Do not use collection "tactics" when seriously ill people are involved.

About two-thirds of the states have adopted their own collection practices acts. If the state law provides the same or greater protection than the FDCPA and the state enforces its law, then the state law and not the FDCPA will apply to collectors in that state. If there is no state law, the collectors in that state are subject to the FDCPA.

What is required under the FDCPA? Debt collectors must provide written verification of debts if the debtor asks. Within five days after contacting the debtor, the verification must be sent. The verification must include the following:

1. The amount of the debt.
2. The name of the creditor.
3. A notice that the debtor may dispute the debt and how to proceed.

If the debtor disputes the debt, the collector has thirty days to verify the existence of the debt between the creditor and the debtor.

What is prohibited under the FDCPA?

Contact with the debtor. The FDCPA limits the times during which a debtor can be contacted. The hours for contacting debtors are from 8 AM to 9 PM. The time range is measured by the debtor's time zone. If a debtor works a shift different from a day shift, the collector cannot contact him or her during what would be sleeping time. For example, if someone works a shift from 11 PM to 7 AM, it would be a violation to call him or her during the day.

Collectors are also prohibited from contacting debtors at inconvenient places. Home contact is fine, but contact at a parent/teacher meeting or a church meeting would be a violation of the FDCPA. Collectors can approach debtors at their places of employment. However, if the employer objects or has a policy against it, the collector must abide by the employer's wishes.

Debtors represented by attorneys cannot be contacted by collectors. However, if the attorney authorizes it, the collector may contact the debtor. Also, if the attorney fails to respond to the collector, the collector may again contact the debtor.

Debtors can give written notice to collectors that they refuse to pay the debt or do not want to be contacted again. If such notice is given, the collector must stop all contact. The collector will have to try legal action (discussed later in the chapter). The collector can then have contact to inform the debtor of the legal action.

Any contact a collector has with a debtor cannot harass, oppress, or abuse the debtor. The collector cannot use abusive language or intimidation in collecting. Collectors cannot pose as government officials or use false stationery to give the appearance of court or police action on the debt.

Collectors cannot mislead debtors about the former's powers. They cannot threaten debtors with prison or legal action for which there is no authority. For example, threatening to get a court order to dig up a grave is a threat without legal authority and therefore a violation of the FDCPA. Posing as a police officer would also be a violation of the FDCPA. The *Wright v. Credit Bureau of Georgia, Inc.* case involves an issue regarding a collector's contact with a debtor.

WRIGHT v. CREDIT BUREAU OF GEORGIA, INC.

United States District Court, Northern District of Georgia.
548 F.Supp. 591 (1982).

FACTS The Credit Bureau of Georgia (CBI) was given the account of Juanita Wright for collection by Peoples Furniture Company. The amount due on the account was $173.74. CBI sent the following notice to Wright:

> Your account, as indicated above, has not been paid and has now been placed with this company for collection. Payment in full must be received within five days. Otherwise further action will be taken. To insure proper credit, it is necessary to return this notice with your payment in the enclosed envelope. . . .

Mrs. Wright then received four telephone calls from CBI between October 1980 and May 1981. Wright agreed to pay $12 per month to pay off the debt. She sent three payments and then stopped. CBI sent the following notice to her:

> Your broken promises have convinced us that you deserve no further consideration in the above matter.
>
> Therefore, five (5) days from this date, if the above account is not paid in full, we will recommend to our client that they refer to their attorney for immediate action.

Mrs. Wright did not pay and she was sent the following:

> This is our final notice to you before recommending that our client give the account to their attorney for legal action. Although it may cause you embarrassment, inconvenience and further expense, we will do so if the entire balance is not in this office within the next five days.
>
> To insure proper credit, please return this notice with your payment in the envelope enclosed.
>
> Attend to it NOW—This is a FINAL NOTICE!

Mrs. Wright brought suit for violation of the FDCPA.

ISSUE Did CBI violate the FDCPA?

DECISION No. Their letters gave adequate disclosures about the debt. There was no harassment—only timed letters. Mrs. Wright did not protest at any time receiving the letters.

LEGAL TIP
To stop personal contact from a collection agency, notify the agency in writing or hire an attorney for the collector to contact directly.

Contacts with third parties. The FDCPA covers the common law tort areas of privacy violations through third-party contacts. The FDCPA prohibits collectors from contacting anyone other than the debtor, the debtor's spouse, or parents. Others may be contacted for information on locating the debtor. Such information is limited to address, telephone number, and place of employment.

If a third party is contacted, the collector cannot tell why the debtor's location is needed. They cannot give any indication that they are a collection agency unless the third party asks. They cannot disclose that the debtor owes a debt at any time.

Collectors are also required to be careful not to disclose information through their correspondence. For example, collectors cannot use post cards to contact debtors when the amount of the debt and the fact that it is past due are revealed on the post card. Collectors cannot use envelopes with return addresses that would indicate they are collecting a delinquent account.

Penalties for violating the FDCPA. The Federal Trade Commission (FTC) has been given the responsibility of enforcing the FDCPA. The FTC can issue cease-and-desist orders against collectors who are violating the FDCPA. The FTC can also assess penalties against collectors for violations.

Debtors have a private right of action under the FDCPA. They can recover for actual injuries and mental distress suffered from a collector's actions. The FDCPA also provides for damages of up to $1000 in addition to actual damages when the collector's actions were outrageous, repeated, malicious, or extreme. Debtors who successfully recover damages can also get their attorneys' fees.

STEP TWO: DEFAULT STAGE

When Does Default Occur?

Article IX has no definition of **default**—nor does any other section of the Code. The security agreement can list the events that will result in default. The usual reason for default is non-payment of an installment when it is due. Other defaults include sale without permission, removal of the collateral, or bankruptcy of the debtor. The *Williams v. Ford Motor Credit Co.* case deals with the issue of whether a default has occurred.

WILLIAMS v. FORD MOTOR CREDIT CO.

Supreme Court of Alabama.
435 So.2d 66 (1983).

FACTS Curtis Williams bought a 1974 Oldsmobile from Joe Meyers Ford in Houston, Texas, on November 1, 1976. Ford Motor Credit Company financed the transaction. Curtis was to make 30 payments of $136.40 beginning December 7, 1976. Curtis missed the February 7, 1977, payment. On March 4, 1977, Curtis sent a check for $151.40 for the February payment plus late charges. That same day Curtis mailed a check for $136.40 for the March payment. Ford treated Curtis as having defaulted on March 5 and repossessed the car. Ford did not receive either payment until March 7.

ISSUE Was Curtis in default on March 5?

DECISION Yes. Curtis was in default when he missed the February payment. The fact that Ford took action after the checks were mailed is irrelevant. Ford could declare default when the February payment was missed.

LEGAL TIP

Late payments are defaults.

STEP THREE: POST DEFAULT AND POST COLLECTION

Once collection efforts become hopeless, the creditor can exercise Article IX rights. An Article IX security interest is an interest in collateral that gives the creditor payment assurance. When a debtor defaults, the creditor has certain rights that can be pursued.

Repossession (Section 9-503)

Repossession is a term familiar to most consumers. Article IX security interests allow secured creditors to repossess the collateral of defaulting debtors. This right to repossession does not require judicial procedure. Creditors can proceed on their own to repossess the collateral. The only restriction on creditors' repossession is that they cannot "breach the peace." **Breach of the peace** does not necessarily require a scuffle and covers a violation of the law—either statute or tort. For example, removing collateral from private property is a breach of the peace. Taking collateral from private property is the tort of trespass. Using a gun to repossess property is a criminal offense and the tort of assault and, of course, a breach of the peace. The *Big Three Motors, Inc. v. Rutherford* case deals with the issue of breach of the peace.

BIG THREE MOTORS, INC. v. RUTHERFORD

Supreme Court of Alabama.
432 So.2d 483 (1983).

FACTS Christine Rutherford bought a 1974 Cadillac Sedan de Ville from Big Three Motors. She had missed several monthly payments on the car. While driving the car along Interstate 65 in Mobile County, Alabama, Rutherford was forced off the road by a truck. The truck was driven by Roan and another man who were both employees of Big Three. They had been told to repossess the car.

After Rutherford pulled off the road, she and Roan exchanged harsh words. Rutherford tried to leave, but Roan used the truck to block her access to the highway. Roan then got in and drove the Cadillac back to Big Three. Roan locked the car and took the keys. Rutherford protested at the dealership office but received no response. She went home in a taxi. She brought suit for breach of the peace.

ISSUE Was there a breach of the peace in this repossession?

DECISION Yes. Roan was probably guilty of traffic violations, kidnapping, and assault. Rutherford was awarded $15,000 in damages.

LEGAL TIP
Repossessions done with force are a breach of the peace.

Court Action (Section 9-501)

In addition to the non-judicial right of repossession, Article IX creditors also have the full rights to bring court actions to collect from a debtor. The creditor simply files a suit and proves that a contract exists and that the debtor has not paid. If creditors meet their burdens of proof, they are awarded a **judgment** for the amount of the debt plus interest and costs. This judgment is the requirement for a debtor to pay. If debtors do not pay a judgment, the judgment can be used to levy or attach their money or property to satisfy the debt. Post judgment procedures are covered later in the chapter.

Foreclosure (Section 9-501)

Instead of repossessing the collateral, a creditor can bring an action to have the court foreclose on the property. This process avoids the problems of private repossession. This process also gives the court the job of getting the property and holding a sale of the property. Most creditors do not resort to judicial foreclosure, but judicial foreclosure allows creditors to buy the property at the sale. With private repossession, they do not have this right of purchase.

STEP FOUR: POST REPOSSESSION AND POST JUDGMENT

Under Article IX, creditors have more than the right of repossession—they have the right to sell the collateral. In the case of a judgment, creditors have methods for collecting the amount of that judgment. This section covers these two final steps in the creditor's relationship with the debtor.

Rights of the Creditor in Repossessed Collateral (Section 9-504)

Secured parties who have repossessed collateral may sell, lease, or otherwise dispose of the collateral. The only restriction on secured parties is that they must act in a commercially reasonable fashion. The *Cordova v. Lee Galles Oldsmobile, Inc.,* case deals with the issue of whether a creditor acted reasonably in using repossessed collateral.

CORDOVA v. LEE GALLES OLDSMOBILE, INC.

Court of Appeals of New Mexico.
668 P.2d 320 (1983).

FACTS Cordova bought a 1979 Oldsmobile from Lee Galles in February 1980. He financed part of the purchase price through General Motors Acceptance Corporation (GMAC). By 1981, Cordova could no longer make the payments. He surrendered the car to Lee Galles on July 8, 1981. He told them he would try to come up with the money to pay for the car to get it back.

Cordova received notice from GMAC on July 10, 1981, that he would have until July 23, 1981, to pay for the car to get it back.

Sometime during that 15-day period, an employee of Lee Galles loaned the car to the Albuquerque Police Department for use in their vice-squad operations.

During the vice-squad use, the car was damaged. It took $110 in repairs to fix the car.

Cordova did not want to redeem the car because it had been damaged. He also claimed that use of the car by the vice squad would harm him. His car had unique color combinations and would now be recognized as a vice squad car. He claimed his clients at the County Rehabilitation Services would no longer trust him. Cordova brought suit for Lee Galles' improper use of collateral.

ISSUE Did Lee Galles improperly use the collateral?

DECISION No. Creditors have the right to loan or lease collateral after repossession. The unique nature of Cordova's job did not affect this right.

LEGAL TIP

Check the terms of repossession and how the collateral will be used during repossession.

Type of sale (Section 9-504 (3) A creditor's sale of collateral can be a **private or public sale.** The creditor is required to give the debtor reasonable notice of the sale. This right of notice can be waived by the debtor in writing after the goods are repossessed. The sale, whether private or public, must be commercially reasonable. To be commercially reasonable, a public sale should be advertised. The collateral should be properly displayed. The *Smith v. Daniels* case deals with the question of whether a sale was commercially reasonable.

SMITH v. DANIELS

Supreme Court of Tennessee.
634 S.W.2d 276 (1982).

FACTS Smith and Daniels were partners (until 1978) in the Tramel Amusement Company in Pigeon Forge, Tennessee. They were in the business of renting coin-operated amusement equipment.

In 1978, Daniels sold his interest in the partnership to Smith. Daniels loaned Smith $54,000 for the purchase. The loan was secured by the amusement equipment. Daniels had filed the proper financing statement.

Smith defaulted on his loan payments and Daniels repossessed the equipment. Daniels hired Action Auction Company to resell the equipment. The equipment was sold for $12,500. Smith brought suit challenging the sale as unreasonable based on the following:

1. No list of the equipment being sold was ever given to bidders or in ads.
2. The sale was advertised only twice and only in local papers.
3. Bidders were not allowed to test the equipment.
4. There was no electricity available for testing the equipment at the sale place.
5. The machines were sold in bulk instead of individually.

ISSUE Was the sale commercially reasonable?

DECISION No. The sale should have been advertised in trade papers and statewide. Testing should have been available. The equipment should have been sold individually to bring a better price. Buyers should have been told what machines were available to bring higher bids.

LEGAL TIP
Debtors should check creditors' sale procedures. Creditors should take steps to get the best price for collateral.

When is a sale required? (Section 9-505). There are some circumstances in which Article IX requires the creditor to sell the collateral. If a consumer has paid 60% of the cash price on a purchase money security interest or 60% of the amount of the loan secured by an interest in consumer goods, the creditor must sell the collateral.

If a creditor has a debtor in this position and does not sell within 90 days of repossession, the debtor has several alternatives (Section 9-507). First, the debtor can sue for conversion. Second, the debtor can bring suit to require the sale. Third, the debtor can bring suit to recover any loss that may have resulted from the creditor's failure to sell.

If consumer goods are involved and the 60% minimums have not been met or are in non-consumer security interests, the requirements are slightly different. If the creditor intends to keep the collateral, written notice must be sent to the debtor. If the debtor does not object within 21 days after receiving the notice, the creditor can go ahead and keep the collateral. If a debtor wishes to object, the objection must be in writing and be made within 21 days.

Can a debtor stop the sale? (Section 9-506) Any time before the collateral is sold, the debtor can **redeem** the collateral. To redeem the collateral, the debtor must pay the full amount due along with the expenses of repossession, storage fees, sales preparation costs, and attorneys' fees. The full amount due may be the full amount of the credit or loan balance since a default can accelerate the full amount of the debt.

How is the money from the sale used? (Section 9-504) The sale proceeds are applied to the following expenses in the following order:

1. The expenses of repossessing, storing, holding, and preparing for sale of the collateral along with any legal expenses and attorneys' fees.
2. The amount of the debt.
3. The amounts of any debts owed to secured parties or lien holders with lesser priority.

If the sale does not bring enough money to pay the amount of the debt, the secured party may bring a deficiency action. A **deficiency action** is a suit to recover the difference between what was owed and what the sale brought. The secured party is seeking a judgment. Once that judgment is obtained, it can be used in the same way to collect on other property as any other judgment.

Are buyers protected? (Section 9-504) Buyers of repossessed property buy the property free and clear of the creditors' security interests. This rule is true so long as the buyer buys in good faith at a private sale.

What if the creditor errs? (Section 9-507) If the creditor makes a mistake and does not follow the Article IX sale procedures, the debtor has rights. If consumer goods are involved, the debtor can bring suit and recover the interest or finance charge along with 10% of the principal amount of the loan or purchase.

In other cases, the debtors can recover any actual damages resulting from the creditor's mistake. For example, if a creditor conducted a sale improperly and brought in only $10,000 for property valued at $20,000, the difference would be the debtor's damages.

Rights of the Post Judgment Creditor

A judgment is the court's way of saying the creditor is correct and is entitled to collect, but judgment is only the beginning. Post judgment actions are the steps used to collect the amount of the judgment. The creditor can collect or execute a judgment by attachment or garnishment.

Attachment Attachment is the process of getting a lien for the judgment (or judgment lien) on some property that belongs to the debtor. Judgment liens can attach to real or personal property. For real property, the judgment must be recorded with the land records. For personal property, many states give an automatic lien.

Attachment is just the first part of judgment enforcement. The creditor must now do something with the judgment lien. Some states require the creditor to bring a foreclosure action to have the court sell the attached property. In other states the creditor can get a writ of execution. A **writ of execution** is an order obtained by the creditor that requires the property to be sold. Writ of execution proceedings are handled by the creditor. Copies of documents are sent to the debtor for objection. However, if the judgment is proper, there is little defense the debtor can have against a writ of execution.

Most states limit the time that a judgment can be attached before it is foreclosed on or executed. A typical time limitation is five years. The creditor can reattach at the end of the time period (five years) for another five years.

Finding a debtor's assets for attachment can be a problem. Most states have a proceeding for what was once called a creditor's bill and is now called a **supplemental proceeding.** In this proceeding, the creditor simply asks the court to require the debtor to turn over all assets. The assets can then be sold to pay the judgment.

Garnishment Attachment is the execution of a judgment on property and **garnishment** is the execution of judgment on funds. Bank accounts, wages, and accounts receivable can be garnished. A garnishment proceeding is more like a full lawsuit. The creditor actually brings the garnishment action against whomever holds the funds—the debtor's bank, the debtor's employer, or the debtor's customer. Creditors must give these parties a summons and a chance to answer the garnishment suit.

Once the third party (or garnishee) is served with the garnishment, the creditor has a lien on the funds. The garnishee must answer the summons within a certain time period. The answer must list all the funds held that belong to the debtor. The garnishee can admit the debt, and the court will order payment of the amount held by the garnishee. The third party or the debtor could also challenge the garnishment. A challenge could be based on the fact that the creditor has been paid.

Garnishments are limited on wages. Federal law (Consumer Credit Protection Act—15 U.S.C., 1673) prohibits the garnishment of more than 25% of the net wages. Garnishment for child support payments can be up to 50% of net wages.

KEY TERMS

Fair Debt Collections Practices Act (FDCPA)
Default
Repossession
Breach of the peace
Redeem
Deficiency action
Judgment
Garnishment
Private or public sale
Writ of execution
Supplemental proceeding

CHAPTER PROBLEMS

1. William was a commodities broker for Shearson Loeb Rhodes for 16 years. He was making $45,000 per year. His wife filed for a divorce, and he reported his income as $15,000 per year. The court awarded his wife $1740 per month in alimony and child support. The court ordered a wage assignment for that amount. William appealed the decision claiming that the assignment of his wages for that amount exceeded the federal 50% limit. Is he correct? *Carol v. William,* 464 N.Y.S.2d 635 (1983).

2. Lucas defaulted on his Allegro mobile home payments. Citicorp repossessed the Allegro and gave notice of a public sale with a minimum price of $31,725.64.

There were no offers at the sale. Citicorp advertised the home and displayed it at recreational vehicle dealers' lots in Ohio for 10 months. Finally, the home sold for $20,853—the "black book" wholesale value for the home. Lucas says the sale was commercially unreasonable. Is he right? *In re Lucas,* 35 UCC 1688 (Ohio 1982).

3. Decide whether either of the following situations are violations of the FDCPA.

   a. A debt collector threatens (in the presence of a neighbor at a debtor's home) to have an arrest warrant issued if the debtor does not pay.

   b. A debt collector contacts the grandparents of a 21-year-old debtor and reveals the past due debt to them. *West v. Costen,* 558 F.Supp. 564 (W.D. Va. 1983).

4. Jordan was behind in his car payments. While he was out driving the car, he was pursued by a tow truck in a high speed chase. The tow truck and its driver had been hired by the secured creditor to repossess the car. Jordan was able to lose the truck and arrived home at 11 PM. He parked the car in front of his house with the keys in it. The tow truck arrived and repossessed the car. Was there a breach of the peace? *Jordan v. Citizens & Southern National Bank of South Carolina,* 298 S.E.2d 213 (S.C. 1982).

5. Idonia Brown defaulted on the payments for her 1978 Ford Pinto. The car had extensive damage when Lakeshore Motor Company repossessed it. The damage included the grill, the roof, and the doors. Lakeshore repaired the car in its body shop before selling it. Can Lakeshore recover the cost of repairing the car as well as the other Article IX costs? *Brown v. Ford Motor Credit,* 36 UCC Rep. 1819 (Ark. 1983).

6. Diamond Timber bought $222,173.80 of equipment from Cascade. Diamond failed to pay. Cascade sold the equipment at a well-advertised public sale for $62,700. Diamond says the sale was commercially unreasonable because of the low price. Is Diamond right? *Leasing Service Corporation v. Diamond Timber, Inc.,* 559 F.Supp. 972 (N.Y. 1983).

7. Rhodes gave Oaklawn Bank a promissory note and a security interest in his restaurant equipment and prefabricated aluminum building. Rhodes defaulted, and the bank put up a "For Sale" sign on the property. Rhodes lived 100 feet from the building and the sign. Was this notice of sale? *Rhodes v. Oaklawn Bank,* 648 S.W.2d 470 (Ark. 1983).

8. Baldwin bought a 1972 Ford from Bondy's in 1973. Ford Motor Credit financed the transaction. Baldwin lived next door to the Warrens and used their address to receive his mail. After he bought the car, Warren was transferred overseas (he was in the army). He gave the auto to the Warrens if they agreed to make the payments. In January 1976, there was fire damage to the car and Ford Motor Credit repossessed the car.

   The Warrens had been frequently late on their payments. Ford decided to sell the car. The notice of sale was sent to Baldwin. The Warrens objected to the sale because they were not given notice. Were they entitled to notice? *Warren v. Ford Motor Credit Co.,* 693 F.2d 1373 (11th Cir. 1982).

9. Chesire worked for the United States Postal Service and earned $508 in net income every 2 weeks. After his divorce, an amount of $214 was taken from every paycheck for child support. He owed Long Island Trust Company $607.50. They got a judgment and wanted to garnish 25% of Chesire's wages. Chesire said he already exceeded the limitation on garnishment and that Long Island Trust could not garnish. Who is right? *Long Island Trust Co. v. United States Postal Service,* 647 F.2d 336 (2nd Cir. 1981).

10. What is the difference between attachment and garnishment?

"And forgive us our debts, as we forgive our debtors."

Matthew 6:12
The Holy Bible

Chapter 59

Bankruptcy

CHAPTER PREVIEW

- Objectives of the Bankruptcy Code
- Straight bankruptcy
- Bankruptcy trustee's duties
- Steps in filing for Chapter Seven bankruptcies
- Order of creditor claims in straight bankruptcies
- Frequency of Chapter Seven bankruptcies
- Chapter Thirteen bankruptcy plans

Lee Hurd told a creditor that he (Lee) and his wife were filing for bankruptcy. The Hurds had gone through straight bankruptcy just five years earlier. The creditor said that "straight" bankruptcy discharges were available only once every six years. Lee nodded in agreement. But he said that another part of the bankruptcy law lets individuals with regular income get their debts adjusted, and the six-year limit does not apply to this adjustment. Is Lee right?

GENERAL BANKRUPTCY OBJECTIVES

Two general objectives of the Bankruptcy Act are to provide an honest debtor with a fresh start from hopeless indebtedness and to provide an equitable distribution of the debtor's assets to the creditors.

Overview of the Bankruptcy Act

The present Bankruptcy Act went into effect on October 1, 1979. It covers straight bankruptcies in Chapter Seven; adjustment of debts of individuals with a regular income (formerly known as "wage-earner plans") in Chapter Thirteen; reorganizations (mainly of businesses) in Chapter Eleven; and municipal debt adjustments in Chapter Nine. The word "chapter" should not confuse you. It is often used in law to describe large parts of lengthy statutes called codes. In other words, one major part of the bankruptcy statute is devoted to straight bankruptcies. This division of the Bankruptcy Act indicates there are different ways of going bankrupt. Not all types are available to all debtors. Municipalities, for example, cannot go through straight bankruptcy. This chapter of the book will look at straight bankruptcy and Chapter Thirteen, formerly called wage-earner plans. The text only mentions reorganizations briefly and does not discuss municipal debt adjustments.

Brief History of Bankruptcy in the United States

As an English-American concept, bankruptcy dates to 1542 when the first English Bankruptcy Act was passed. It was originally designed to excuse only merchants from paying their debts since they were often unable to pay because their customers did not pay them. In other words, the basic idea of bankruptcy—excusal from legally owing a debt—was originally applied only to the limited class of merchants, not everyone.

"I hereby pronounce you bankrupt. Congratulations."

The United States' present Constitution recognizes the bankruptcy concept by giving Congress the power to pass bankruptcy laws. During the period roughly between 1800 and 1900, Congress changed its position several times on whether bankruptcy should or should not be allowed. No doubt bankruptcy is controversial because someone is allowed to escape an otherwise legal debt. Also, the fluctuating position on bankruptcy reflects the pattern of economic panics in the United States; bankruptcy laws were often passed by the popularly elected Congress after an economic depression.

In 1800 Congress passed the first federal bankruptcy act and, like the English law, it applied to merchants only. However, in 1803 Congress repealed that law and bankruptcy was not allowed again until 1841, when Congress passed a second federal bankruptcy act. This law, too, did not last long and was repealed in 1843. Again, a gap of years passed when no bankruptcy law existed. In 1867, shortly after the Civil War, a third federal bankruptcy act was passed. This law lasted a bit longer than its predecessors but was repealed in 1878. Again, a period followed during which no federal bankruptcy law existed. This lasted until 1898 when a long-lived federal bankruptcy statute was passed that, although amended by the Chandler Act in 1938, lasted until the Bankruptcy Reform Act of 1978 took effect on October 1, 1979.

The Bankruptcy Reform Act of 1978 established a federal bankruptcy code. In 1984 Congress amended the 1978 Act (or code). The remainder of this chapter will discuss that code. Included in this discussion will be the types of bankruptcies and the steps in filing for a straight bankruptcy.

CHAPTER SEVEN: STRAIGHT BANKRUPTCY

Chapter Seven of the Bankruptcy Act lays out the rules for **straight bankruptcies.** "Straight" is not a technical word but a substitute word to describe what most people think of when "bankruptcy" is mentioned: the debtor's turning over all assets to the bankruptcy court, which distributes them fairly to creditors and cancels (or discharges) debts. This procedure is easier said than done. There are many rules governing who can go bankrupt, how often one can go bankrupt, and what debts are and are not discharged by bankruptcy.

Who Can Be a Voluntary Bankrupt?

There are two types of straight bankruptcy: voluntary and involuntary. A voluntary bankrupt is someone who wants to go bankrupt. A person must be a debtor but does not have to be insolvent to be a voluntary bankrupt. Anyone (including a partnership or corporation) can be a voluntary straight bankrupt *except* a railroad, insurance company, bank, savings and loan association or building and loan association, credit union, or municipality.

Who Can Be an Involuntary Bankrupt?

Involuntary bankrupts are people or businesses who are put into bankruptcy by their creditors. This type of bankruptcy occurs to prevent the debtor's favoring some creditors over others. Anyone can be an involuntary bankrupt except a farmer, a railroad, a noncommercial corporation (e.g., a charitable corporation), a bank, a building and loan or savings and loan association, a credit union, or a municipality.

The steps in a straight voluntary bankruptcy are indicated in Figure 59-1.

A person can only get a straight bankruptcy discharge once every six years. This rule applies to both voluntary and involuntary petitions under Chapter Seven.

Steps in a Voluntary Bankruptcy

A **voluntary bankruptcy** under Chapter Seven is started by the debtor's filing a petition with the bankruptcy court. This process amounts to the debtor's asking to be declared a bankrupt. A voluntary bankruptcy petition is an **order for relief.**

An involuntary bankruptcy under Chapter Seven is started by creditors filing a petition with the bankruptcy court asking it to declare the debtor bankrupt. If the debtor has 12 or more total creditors, it takes 3 creditors with total claims of $5000 more than their security to file an involuntary petition. If there are fewer than 12 total creditors, 1 creditor with $5000 in claims beyond his or her security (such as a mortgage or UCC Article 9 security interest) may file an involuntary petition to put the debtor into bankruptcy. If an involuntary petition has been filed against a business debtor, the debtor may continue to operate, use, and dispose of property as though no petition had been filed until the bankruptcy court enters an order for relief. However, any time after the start of an involuntary case the bankruptcy court may appoint an interim trustee to take possession of the debtor's property and operate the debtor's business to preserve the estate's property. This is done to prevent the debtor from preferring some creditors by selling assets to them for ridiculously low amounts or otherwise squandering the business' assets.

Parties Involved in a Bankruptcy

There are a number of functional groups involved in bankruptcies. First, of course, is the debtor who is going bankrupt. This person used to be called a bankrupt but is now called a **debtor.** Among the debtor's duties are to file a list of creditors, a schedule of assets and liabilities, and a statement of the debtor's financial affairs.

Figure 59-1 **Steps in Voluntary Straight Bankruptcies**

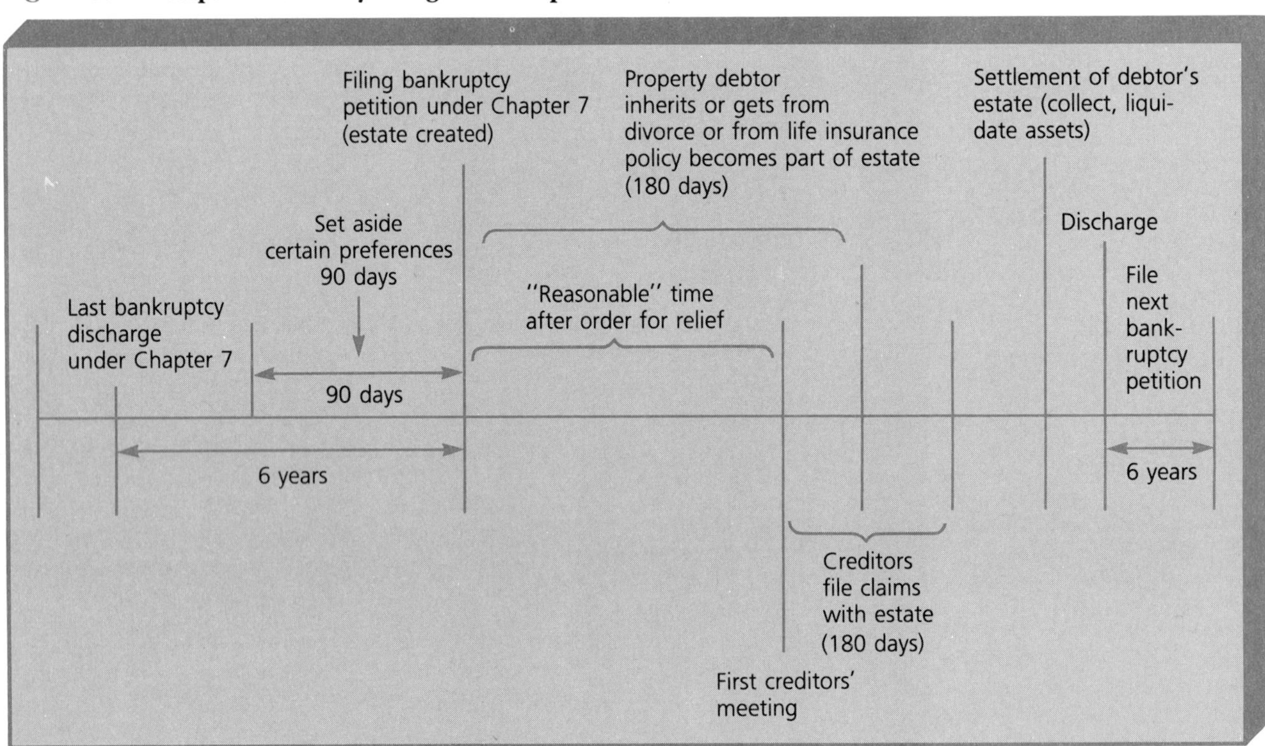

The debtor must cooperate with the bankruptcy trustee including turning over the debtor's estate to the trustee and appearing at the discharge hearing. A second group in bankruptcy are creditors or people to whom the debtor owes money. There are secured creditors (people who by security interest, liens of various types, or mortgages have claims on specific property of the debtor) and unsecured creditors (persons who have only a general claim on the creditor but not on specific property, such as a department store where the debtor has a charge account).

Bankruptcy officials Additionally, there are federal bankruptcy officials: the **bankruptcy judge** and **bankruptcy trustee.** The bankruptcy judge is appointed for a fourteen-year term by the United States president with Senate approval. There are two kinds of trustees that could be involved in bankruptcies. One is the United States trustee appointed by the United States Attorney General in an experimental program in a few United States cities. This is a public official who oversees administration of bankruptcies under Chapters Seven, Eleven, and Thirteen.

Trustee The other type of trustee in bankruptcy is a private person (not a permanent government employee) elected with court approval by the bankrupt's creditors at the first creditors' meeting. This person is simply called a trustee in bankruptcy and should not be confused with United States trustees. Since this person is the usual "trustee" thought of in bankruptcies, the remainder of the discussion will focus on this trustee.

Trustee's duties There is one trustee in a straight bankruptcy. Each *unsecured* creditor holding an allowable, fixed, undisputed, and liquidated claim may cast one vote for the trustee. The trustee, as noted above, is elected at the first creditors' meeting. The trustee's duties include:

1. Collecting and reducing to money the debtor's property and distributing this property as quickly as is compatible with the best interests of all parties.
2. Accounting for all property received.
3. Ensuring the debtor performs its, his, or her duties regarding retentions, surrenders, claimed exemptions, redemptions, or reaffirmations.
4. Investigating the debtor's finances.
5. Examining creditors' claims to see if they are allowable.
6. Providing information requested by creditors or other interested parties.
7. Filing government reports and paying taxes if the debtor's business continues in operation.
8. Opposing the debtor's discharge if it is advisable.
9. Making a final report and filing a final account of the case.

Creditors' Meeting

Within a reasonable time after the order for relief, a **creditors' meeting** must be held. The bankruptcy judge may not preside at or attend this meeting.

What happens at the creditors' meeting? The debtor must appear at the creditors' meeting to answer questions from the creditors and trustee. Common questions asked are whether the debtor is hiding property and whether all of the claims submitted are legitimate. Before the creditors' meeting, the debtor must submit a list of assets and debts to the bankruptcy court. This list is available as a basis for creditors' and trustees' questions to the debtor.

Automatic Stay

One effect of filing a petition in bankruptcy is that it stops most types of lawsuits and legal proceedings against the debtor. This result is called an **automatic stay.** Included in matters stopped are most lawsuits and other legal claims that were or could have been started before filing the bankruptcy petition. Also stayed are acts to possess the debtor's property, to get liens on such property, or to set-off debts if any of the aforementioned arose before the bankruptcy petition was filed. A particular creditor can obtain relief from the stay upon showing that either the creditor's interest is inadequately protected or the debtor has no equity in the property in question and the property is unnecessary for reorganization. This relief would allow a creditor to take property from the debtor's estate that otherwise could not be seized. The automatic stay does not apply to (does not stop) criminal suits or regulatory matters (such as enforcement of health code violations) against the debtor or collection of alimony or support from third parties.

Debtor's Estate

One of the most important aspects of straight bankruptcy concerns the amount of the debtor's property available to pay the creditors. This property is called the **debtor's estate.** Technically, the term is not the debtor's estate but the debtor's *former* estate. The estate is created by filing a voluntary or involuntary bankruptcy petition.

The estate consists of the following property *wherever* it is located:

1. All the debtor's property (legal or equitable) that exists when the case starts.
2. All community property of the debtor and debtor's spouse partly or entirely under the debtor's control when the case starts.
3. Any property the trustee recovers from third parties (banks and partnerships, for example) owing the debtor.
4. Any property the debtor inherits, gets from a divorce, or from a life insurance policy within 180 days after the bankruptcy petition is filed.
5. Profits, products, or offspring from estate property (e.g., crops, cattle, dividend income) after the bankruptcy petition is filed (*not* including earnings from the debtor's services).
6. Any property the estate acquires after the case starts (e.g., someone owing the debtor money pays it off).

One final point about the bankruptcy estate: **bankruptcy clauses** put, for example, in leases are not valid against the trustee. In the past, these clauses were used to end the debtor's interest in property if the debtor filed for bankruptcy.

The *In re Malloy* case discusses a bankruptcy estate.

Exemptions

May all of the debtor's property described above be sold to pay creditors' claims? Most, but not all. The Bankruptcy Act allows the debtor to keep certain property—called **exempt property**—necessary or useful for the debtor's survival. Each state has laws exempting certain property and the Bankruptcy Act exempts certain property. Debtors may select either their state exemption *or* the federal bankruptcy exemption packages in bankruptcy cases unless the debtor's particular state allows

IN RE MALLOY
2 B.R. 674 (1980) (Fla.).

FACTS Peter Malloy (debtor) was an insurance sales agent paid by commission. When he sold a policy he received part of the commission immediately. The remainder was held back and would be paid to him over a number of years provided the policyholder renewed the policy. The debtor argued the renewal commissions were future wages and not part of the bankruptcy estate going to the creditors.

ISSUE Were the renewal commissions property of the bankruptcy estate or future wages belonging to the debtor?

DECISION The renewal commissions were 80% property of the estate and 20% future wages. The court said that if income is already earned but has not yet been paid when a bankruptcy petition is filed, that earned, but as yet unpaid income is property of the estate. With respect to that part of future commissions which are earned by future servicing of policies already sold, the court said they are future wages and may not be transferred to the bankruptcy estate as property.

LEGAL TIP

A debtor's estate for bankruptcy purposes includes renewal commissions which are received in future years, if they are paid for services earned before bankruptcy.

only state exemptions in bankruptcy. Over thirty states allow only state exemptions. Each state's exemption laws differ from those of other states; but generally, most states exempt at least the debtor's home, car, tools of the debtor's trade, clothing, and household goods.

Federal or state exemptions The major point to make about exemption laws, whether they are federal or from a particular state, is that they differ. They differ in the *extent* to which they exempt particular property. For example, while most states exempt a debtor's home, they usually exempt only a small part of its value—typically $5000. (Most garages cost at least this much!) Of course, remember the *equity* (ownership without debt) of most homeowners is much less than the house's value. Similarly, cars are often exempt up to only $1000. Try to find an operating car for this amount. Some states have more generous exemptions than others. The federal exemptions are also more generous than most states' exemptions. A frequent answer given to the charge of exemption law stinginess is that debtors who use them are "debt dodgers"—people trying to evade legal obligations. Should the law help deadbeats? Of course some debtors using exemption laws are unlucky people who are victims of health, accident, or job loss problems beyond their control who must go bankrupt and use exemption laws. Others go bankrupt and use exemption laws to beat (and abuse) their creditors. Therefore, exemption laws (and the amounts) represent a compromise between helping the unfortunate and the irresponsible. This discussion also explains why all types of property are not exempt—just the essential ones.

Federal exemptions The federal bankruptcy exemption package provides up to $7500 for a homestead. This can be in realty (a house) or personalty (house trailer) that the debtor uses as a residence. Another federal exemption allows as much as $1200 for one motor vehicle. The debtor's interest in household furnishings, household goods, clothes, appliances, books, animals, crops, or musical instruments held for the personal use of the debtor or debtor's family is limited to a $4000 total amount, with a $200 per item limit.

In addition to housing, clothing, and a car, federal bankruptcy law exempts $500 in jewelry of the debtor or debtor's family and $400 in any property (including cash). Also up to $3750 of any unused part of the $7500 homestead exemption may exempt *any* property of the debtor. This rule is especially helpful to debtors who rent residential property and have no homestead. Professional implements or tools of the debtor's trade are exempt up to $750. Unmatured life insurance contracts owned by the debtor are exempt (except credit life insurance) and so is up to $4000 in loan value of any unmatured life insurance contract owned by the debtor.

To protect the debtor's health, the bankruptcy law exempts all professionally prescribed health aids for the debtor or debtor's dependents. The debtor's security is protected by exempting amounts from various public and private retirement and other benefit programs. Included are:

1. Social Security benefits.
2. Unemployment compensation.
3. Local public assistance benefits.
4. Veterans' benefits.
5. Disability, illness, or unemployment benefits.
6. Alimony, support, or separate maintenance if needed to support the debtor and any dependents.
7. Payments under stock bonus, pension, profit sharing, annuity or similar plan if made on account of illness, death, age, or length of service and needed for the debtor's support (within certain limits).
8. A property award under a crime victim's reparation law.
9. Payment on account of the wrongful death of someone the debtor is a dependent of.
10. Personal injury payments not to exceed $7500 (excluding pain and suffering).
11. Payments for loss of future earnings of the debtor or someone the debtor is a dependent of if needed for support.

The above list of federal exemptions is comprehensive. A few other points should be noted. First, this federal exemption scheme is available *only* in bankruptcy situations (not, for example, in other non-bankruptcy situations where a creditor tries to collect a debt). Second, each of the federal exemption amounts may be *doubled* when spouses file a joint bankruptcy petition. Third, the federal Bankruptcy Act lets states eliminate the federal exemption package, leaving the debtor only with the state exemption package; over thirty states have eliminated this package. Fourth, debtors are protected from waiving their exemptions by the Bankruptcy Act's nullifying such waivers for nonpurchase money loans.

Claims

Creditors want to be paid. In bankruptcy only creditors with **provable claims** are entitled to share in the estate (the debtor's former property) if they file their claims within six months after the first creditors' meeting. Examples of provable debts include overdue notes, open accounts (e.g., amounts owed to a department store), rent claims of up to one year (including unexpired leases), and judgments in lawsuits.

Non-Provable

Some creditors have secured claims. Examples are building and loan associations with mortgages on the debtor's home and GMAC (General Motors Acceptance Corporation) with a perfected security interest in the debtor's car. These claims entitle creditors holding them to use the security item to pay that **creditor's claim.** The building and loan association would have first claim to the house and GMAC would have first claim to the car. Any money left following sale of the security item and paying that secured creditor is available for other creditors' claims.

Even if a creditor's claim is provable, it may not be allowable. An **allowable claim** is one to which the debtor does not have a defense. The trustee in bankruptcy steps into the debtor's defenses against creditors' claims. If the debtor has a defense (such as fraud by the creditor), the claim is not allowable. An allowable creditor's claim may be reduced as in the case, for example, where a debtor buys a television on credit but has a warranty claim against the creditor.

Priority of Claims

Suppose the bankruptcy trustee has collected all of the debtor's property, identified all the creditors, and now wants to distribute the property to the creditors. Remember, the debtor's total assets are much smaller than the creditors' total claims. This fact means creditors are going to be paid less than all of their claims and perhaps nothing; they also have no further claims against the debtor. In other words, creditors will likely lose something. How does the Bankruptcy Act determine who loses? It sets up **priorities of claims** among creditors. Some creditors are paid *fully* before others get one cent.

The Bankruptcy Act priorities are as follows:

1. Secured claims, while not technically a priority, are recognized first (examples are valid mortgages and valid perfected security interests; a bank with a mortgage on the debtor's house will have first claim on the house to pay what the debtor owes the bank).
2. Bankruptcy administrative expenses are given "top" priority.
3. Claims arising in the ordinary course of the debtor's business after an involuntary case starts but before either an order for relief or trustee's appointment.
4. Wage claims up to $2000 per employee (vacation pay included) for services within 90 days before filing the petition.
5. Payments to employee benefit plans up to $2000 per employee for services performed within 180 days before the petition is filed.
6. Unsecured claims of grain farmers against owners or operators of grain elevators for grain or grain proceeds. Also unsecured claims of $2000 or less per individual of United States fishermen against debtor/fish storage or processing plants acquiring fish from United States fishermen.
7. Consumer claims of up to $900 each (this could be for down payments or payments on goods or services to a debtor who goes bankrupt before shipping or performing).
8. Taxes to federal, state, or local government.

There are a couple of observations that should be made about priorities. First, all claims within a priority category are paid fully *before* the next lower priority category gets anything. Second, general creditors (those with no mortgage or security interest from the debtor such as Master Charge) are at the end of the creditor line. They receive nothing until *all* claims in priority categories are paid fully.

A Bankruptcy Scenario

Just before debtors file for bankruptcy or are put into bankruptcy, they often become creative with their finances. For example, Mary Fisher, a bank teller, owes $5000 on her Visa credit card, $4000 to a department store for carpeting, $1100 to her cousin James, $3000 to Ace Auto Sales, and $10,000 to others. Mary plans to file for bankruptcy in 1 month since she is presently unable to keep up her debt payments. She first decides to take her life savings of $2100 from her bank account and pay the $1100 debt to James. She tells Ace Auto Sales of her impending bankruptcy. Ace promptly obtains a perfected security interest in the car. Mary "gives" $1,000 to her mother on the understanding that her mother will return it after Mary's bankruptcy. She also "sells" her $2000 stereo to her brother for $20. Mary then files for bankruptcy.

Preferences

A **preference** in bankruptcy is any transfer of money or other property for a preexisting debt within ninety days before filing a bankruptcy petition; the transfer is made by an insolvent debtor to a creditor so the creditor will obtain a larger share of debt repayment than other similarly situated creditors. One of the main objectives of bankruptcy is equal treatment of creditors of the same class. The debtor should not be able to "play favorites" by preferring some creditors over others. If the debtor does so within ninety days before filing for bankruptcy, the trustee in bankruptcy has the power to retrieve the property (or void the preference) from the preferred creditor for the estate. This power to set aside preferences exists in both voluntary and involuntary straight bankruptcies. Debtors are presumed to be insolvent within ninety days before filing the bankruptcy petition. The trustee may recover property from "inside" creditors for the period between ninety days and one year before the bankruptcy petition is filed if the creditor was an insider when the transfer was made.

The *New York Credit Men's Adjustment Bureau, Inc. v. Adler* case examines the issue of transferring funds before a bankruptcy.

In the above scenario, Mary made a preferential transfer of $1100 to her cousin James within ninety days of filing a bankruptcy petition. She is presumed to be insolvent during this period. This payment can be reclaimed by the trustee for the bankruptcy state.

A voidable preference can also take the form of a lien or mortgage if it comes within the ninety days before the bankruptcy petition is filed, is for an antecedent (or prior) debt, and enables the particular creditor to get a greater return of what is owed than other creditors of the same type. Consider in the example above that Ace Auto Sales obtains a perfected security interest on Mary's car to protect Ace's claim on the car it had sold earlier on unsecured credit to Mary. Since it was an already existing (or antecedent) debt and the perfected security interest was obtained during the ninety days before Mary filed her bankruptcy petition (when Mary is presumed to be insolvent), the perfected security interest is a voidable preference that can be set aside by the bankruptcy trustee. The theory behind setting aside such preferential liens is the same as the reason for voiding other preferences: to prevent creditors from getting more than their fair share of the debtor's estate.

NEW YORK CREDIT MEN'S ADJUSTMENT BUREAU, INC. v. ADLER

2 B.R. 752 (1980) (NY).

FACTS There were transfers of money from a corporate debtor to its president, accountant, and accountant's wife. These transfers occurred within one year before the filing of the corporate debtor's bankruptcy petition. No consideration was received by the corporation for these transfers. At the time of the transfers, the corporation was insolvent and constantly behind in paying its bills.

ISSUE Were the transfers from the corporate debtor fraudulent and voidable by the bankruptcy trustee?

DECISION Yes. Since the transfers were to insiders, the transfers could be recovered for up to one year before filing of the debtor's bankruptcy petition, provided the insiders had actual intent to hinder, delay, or defraud existing or future creditors. The court said the insiders here had this intent.

LEGAL TIP

Preferences to certain insiders of debtors going bankrupt can be set aside for one year before the debtor files for bankruptcy.

Fraudulent Transfers

In the situation above Mary made a "gift" to her mother and "sale" to her brother. The trustee in bankruptcy can reclaim the gift and sale for the bankruptcy estate because they are fraudulent transfers. These include any transfers of property interests or any debts incurred by the debtor within one year of filing the bankruptcy petition if made with *intent* to hinder, delay, or defraud creditors. The rules concerning a fraudulent transfer also apply if the debtor received less than reasonably equivalent value in exchange for the property. The trustee in bankruptcy may avoid (or cancel) such transfers. The $1000 gift to Mary's mother is not actually a present, since it is understood that the mother will eventually return the money. The "gift" was made with intent to hinder, delay, or defraud creditors; therefore, the trustee can recover the $1000 "gift" for the estate. The $2000 "sale" of the stereo to Mary's brother for $20 is also a fraudulent transfer, since Mary received less than reasonable value for it. Therefore, the trustee may recover the stereo for the bankruptcy estate.

The *In re Oesterle* case discusses a fraudulent transfer by a debtor.

Discharge

The objective of a debtor's going through a Chapter Seven "straight" bankruptcy is to obtain a **discharge.** A discharge bars a creditor from enforcing the debt, unless the debtor waives the discharge or reaffirms the debt (see below for a discussion of both). Only individuals, not partnerships or corporations, may obtain a Chapter Seven discharge.

To obtain a discharge, an individual must be an "honest debtor." An individual debtor is not considered honest and is denied a discharge if he or she does any one of the following:

1. Conceals, removes, or mutilates assets within one year before the bankruptcy petition is filed with the intent to hinder, delay, or defraud creditors (also applies to estate property after the bankruptcy petition is filed).
2. Fails to keep books or financial records.

IN RE OESTERLE
2 B.R. 122 (1979) (Fla.).

FACTS The debtor had deeded real property to his mother in 1973 without receiving anything in return. The deed covering this transfer was not recorded until two days *after* the debtor's bankruptcy petition was filed in 1978. Under Georgia state law, which determines the timing of property transfers in bankruptcy, the transfer was not effective until it had been recorded.

ISSUE Was this a fraudulent transfer by the debtor, which could be set aside by the bankruptcy court?

DECISION Yes. State law determines when property is transferred in bankruptcy. Under Georgia law (where the property was located), the transfer was not perfected. If a transfer by the debtor has not occurred before filing the bankruptcy petition, it is deemed to have occurred just prior to filing the bankruptcy petition. Since the debtor had received nothing from his mother, the transfer to her was fraudulent and therefore void. The trustee could rightfully claim the realty as part of the bankruptcy estate.

LEGAL TIP

State law is used in bankruptcy cases to help determine what property belongs to the debtor.

3. Knowingly and fraudulently makes a false oath or claim.
4. Fails to explain any loss or disappearance of the debtor's property.
5. Refuses to obey court orders.

A creditor or the bankruptcy trustee may raise any of these questions.

The *In re Mausser* case discussers discharge.

IN RE MAUSSER
4 B.R. 728 (1980) (Fla.)

FACTS Mrs. Evelyn Mausser borrowed money from Southern Discount Company (Southern) to refinance her existing loan. To obtain this refinancing loan, she submitted a financial statement to Southern that failed to list all her debts to third persons. Southern relied on the false statement and loaned Mrs. Mausser the money. Later when Mrs. Mausser filed for bankruptcy, Southern objected to discharge of its loan on grounds that Mrs. Mausser had made false statements to obtain it.

ISSUE Should Mrs. Mausser be considered a dishonest debtor and be barred from discharge of her debt?

DECISION No. In her case, the failure to state certain obligations on her financial statement was inadvertent, not intentional. She omitted accounts opened in her name for her daughter and on which her daughter made payments because she believed it was unnecessary to list such debts. Several of her other debts were omitted because of an oversight. In this case, the court believed the debtor made a good-faith effort to supply the creditor's requested information. Therefore, the debtor did not submit the materially false financial statement with intent to deceive. The court allowed the debt to be discharged.

LEGAL TIP

If a debtor lies to get a particular loan before bankruptcy, that loan is not a dischargeable debt.

Frequency

Individuals must wait six years following their last discharge before filing for another straight bankruptcy. If there were no limit on how many times a person could go bankrupt, a debtor could escape all debts by constantly filing for bankruptcy.

One device creditors use to get around bankruptcy discharges is the reaffirmation agreement. Debtors who have gone bankrupt are often the sort of people who need to borrow money after the bankruptcy has ended and after they have discharged their previous debts. These former bankrupt debtors are often forced by circumstances (such as having borrowed from everyone in a small town) to return to old creditors for new loans. As a condition to granting new loans, former creditors require the debtor to agree to pay the debts discharged in bankruptcy. This process is called a **reaffirmation of a debt.** It is now legal for a creditor to obtain debt reaffirmations only if:

1. The reaffirmation hearing occurs *before* discharging a debt.
2. The debtor has not rescinded (changed his or her mind) within sixty days after reaffirming.
3. The bankruptcy judge makes the debtor aware that a reaffirmation is not required and what will happen if the debtor reaffirms and later defaults.
4. The reaffirmed debt is a consumer debt not secured by realty, which the bankruptcy court must approve.

Unless reaffirmations comply with the procedures outlined above, they are invalid. Reaffirmations nullify a bankruptcy's effect regarding the reaffirmed debt. Since the debtor went bankrupt to discharge a debt, it seems foolish for the debtor to then say, "I want to pay that debt." Some people have concluded that debtors do not understand what they are doing where they reaffirm. Hence, these protections are provided so debtors cannot later claim they did not realize what reaffirmations were.

Nondischargeable Debts

Bankruptcy does not stop *all* debts being enforced against the debtor. Obviously debts arising *after* the discharge bind the debtor (at least for six years, unless the debtor enters Chapter Thirteen proceedings). However, there are some debts that arose *before* discharge, which bankruptcy does not affect. **Nondischargeable debts** include:

1. Taxes or customs duties.
2. Loans obtained by false pretenses or fraud.
3. Debts not put on the list given to the court.
4. Debts arising from defalcation or fraud as a fiduciary or embezzlement or larceny.
5. Alimony, child support, or separation agreement debts.
6. Debts for willful and malicious injury to another's person or property.
7. Fines or penalties to governmental units.
8. Educational loans due less than five years before filing for bankruptcy.
9. Debts where the discharge was waived or denied.

Debts falling into any one of the above categories are *not* discharged or reduced in amount by going bankrupt. Even though a debt is nondischargeable, the creditor holding that debt may still prove it and share in the estate. Following discharge, the *unpaid part* of the nondischargeable debt remains to be paid.

CHAPTER ELEVEN: REORGANIZATIONS

When a business is broken up and sold to pay creditor claims, the assets' value often shrinks greatly. A going concern is usually able to pay off its debts better than a dead business. Chapter Eleven is a complex area of bankruptcy law permitting rehabilitation of "dying" businesses by reorganizations. Sole proprietorships are entitled to its protections, too. Either the debtor or creditors may petition for **reorganization.**

General Approach of Chapter Eleven

Basically what occurs in a Chapter Eleven bankruptcy case is that various creditors can be grouped into classes and then rights of the creditors within a class may be modified by a plan to help rehabilitate the debtor. Examples of plan modifications include extensions of maturities, reduction of interest rates, curing or waiving any default, and merging the debtor with another entity. There are limited protections given to creditors who disagree with these adjustments. To approve a reorganization plan, two-thirds in amount of claims and one-half in number of creditors of each creditor class must agree. This rule is nontechnically referred to as a **"cramdown" provision,** meaning dissenting shareholders have the plan crammed down their throats, like it or not. In order to get approval of the plan, solicitations sent to creditors are exempt from federal securities laws requirements if certain conditions are met.

Confirmation

A reorganization plan must be approved (confirmed) by the bankruptcy judge. The debtor or any entity the plan calls for must carry out the plan. Reorganization plans may be modified after they are approved.

1984 Amendments

In 1984 the United States Supreme Court allowed debtor/employers to escape collective bargaining agreements by merely filing for Chapter Eleven bankruptcy. The 1984 Bankruptcy Amendments modified this case by requiring the the debtor to make a proposal with "necessary" modifications that treats all affected parties fairly and equitably. The debtor/employer must give the union information necessary to evaluate the proposal. The existing collective bargaining agreement may be rejected if the debtor presents a fair and equitable plan, and the union rejects it without good cause.

CHAPTER THIRTEEN: ADJUSTMENT OF DEBTS OF AN INDIVIDUAL WITH REGULAR INCOME

There is a stigma to being a bankrupt. Many people want to avoid the stigma and yet get some relief from their debts. Chapter Thirteen of the Bankruptcy Code lets an individual with a regular income submit a plan to adjust his or her debts.

Chapter Thirteen Eligibility

An individual must have regular income and owe less than $100,000 in liquidated, unsecured debts and less than $350,000 in liquidated, secured debts to qualify for Chapter Thirteen. Furthermore, a sole proprietor may file a plan but a partnership, limited partnership, or corporation may not use Chapter Thirteen to adjust their debts. Individuals joined by their spouses may also file such a plan. Stockbrokers and commodity brokers may *not* file Chapter Thirteen plans. Only the debtor, not the creditors, may put a debtor into Chapter Thirteen.

What exactly do we mean by "debt adjustment"? Examples include lengthening the time to pay off installment debts and reducing payment amounts.

Starting a Chapter Thirteen Case

How does one go about getting debts adjusted under Chapter Thirteen? A person files a proposed plan with the bankruptcy court.

A debtor voluntarily decides to file a Chapter Thirteen plan. Unlike straight bankruptcy, his or her creditors may not force the debtor into Chapter Thirteen.

Mandatory plan contents What must a Chapter Thirteen plan contain? It must provide for turning over to a trustee all or as much of the debtor's future earnings or income as is needed to execute the plan. (The trustee is a person appointed by the court to supervise the carrying out of the plan. The trustee's duties under Chapter Thirteen are similar to those under straight bankruptcies.) The plan must also provide for paying off in full all debts entitled to priority treatment unless the creditor agrees to another arrangement. Finally, if the plan classifies claims it must treat all class members alike.

Optional plan contents There are also some things a plan *may* contain. Creditors may be grouped into different classes. Rights of secured creditors may be modified except for a claim secured by a security interest in the debtor's principal residence. Rights of *unsecured* creditors may be modified. Defaults may be cured or waived. Payments to unsecured creditors may be made concurrently with those of any secured or unsecured claims. This rule allows unsecured creditors to get something as soon as the plan goes into effect. The plan may allow partial or total payment of the debt owed to a creditor. Unperformed contracts or unexpired leases may also be accepted or rejected by the plan. Similarly, the plan may let the debtor pay all or part of any claim. The plan may vest the debtor with ownership of the estate's property or make any provision the Bankruptcy Code allows. The plan must contain the three items noted above and *could* contain many others.

Considering what a debtor can include in the plan, creditors may suffer substantial losses. For example, part payment of a debt can be considered full payment. The debtor also may retain ownership of all the property even if he or she has not paid for it. Payment times, interest rates, or payment amounts may be changed to help the debtor and hurt the creditors. In effect, the debtor can rewrite his or her contracts.

Secured creditor veto What can the creditor do? Remember the debtor merely submits a proposed debt adjustment plan. The creditors must confirm (agree to) the plan before it takes effect. The bankruptcy court holds a confirmation hearing. The court (bankruptcy judge) is the one who confirms or refuses confirmation. The court confirms a plan if 1) it is made in good faith; 2) lets *unsecured* creditors get as much of their claims paid as they would have if the debtor had gone through straight bankruptcy; 3) *secured* creditors accept the plan, retain their liens, and the value of what a secured creditor is to get is not less than such claim or the secured creditor surrenders the property to the debtor; and 4) the debtor will be able to comply with the plan (e.g., keep up with the payments). Secured creditors have a veto power over the plan. The court will not confirm a plan unless all secured creditors agree to it.

Unsecured creditor veto The 1984 Bankruptcy Amendments give unsecured creditors a *conditional* veto of Chapter Thirteen plans. An unsecured creditor with an allowed claim can veto a plan if: the plan calls for less than full payment of the claim *or* less than all of the debtor's disposable income for the three years after the plan's confirmation goes to pay the plan. ("Disposable income" here means income *not* reasonably necessary to maintain and support the debtor and his or her dependents; or if the debtor is in business, income *not* needed to continue and preserve the business' operation.)

Plan confirmation What happens when the bankruptcy judge confirms a plan? The plan binds the debtor and *all* creditors even if the plan pays the creditors nothing. Confirmation results in the debtor's becoming the owner of all the property free and clear of any creditor's claim except those provided for in the plan.

The plan may *not* provide for payments by the debtor over a period longer than three years unless the bankruptcy court has cause to approve a longer period, which cannot be longer than five years.

May the plan be modified if the debtor's circumstances change after the plan has been confirmed but not completed? Yes. Some examples of modifications would be increasing or decreasing the payment size of a particular class of claims, or extending or reducing the time for payments. (But extensions may not be for more than three years beyond the first payment of the original plan unless the court has cause to extend it to five years.)

May a plan once confirmed ever be cancelled? Yes. This procedure is called **revocation.** If within 180 days of a plan's confirmation the bankruptcy court may revoke a confirmation obtained by fraud. An example of such fraud would be a debtor's concealment of assets or income.

Assuming the debtor makes all payments under the Chapter Thirteen plan, his or her debts covered by the plan are discharged. This is a happy day for the debtor (and creditors, too)! Even if the debtor does not make all payments under the plan, he or she may still get all plan debts discharged if failure to pay is due to circumstances beyond the debtor's control, plan modification is not practicable, and the creditors received as much as they would have had the debtor gone through straight bankruptcy. If the debtor falls behind in payments under a Chapter Thirteen plan or fails to submit a plan agreeable to creditors and the court, straight bankruptcy is a possible solution.

Chapter Seven or Chapter Thirteen?

Why would a debtor select Chapter Thirteen instead of Chapter Seven? After all, Chapter Seven discharges a person's debts, while Chapter Thirteen results in paying off one's debts.

First, straight bankruptcy does not end *all* a person's debts entirely. A few debts including alimony, child support, tax liability, loans obtained by fraud, educational loans less than five years overdue, and judgments for having committed an intentional tort are *not* discharged in Chapter Seven. Second, a Chapter Thirteen proceeding enables persons to be responsible by honoring their obligations while getting some breathing room from creditors' claims. Remember, creditors may not sue a debtor for a debt covered by a Chapter Thirteen plan while the plan is in effect. Third, creditors benefit from Chapter Thirteen because they get as much and often more than they would have gotten had the debtor gone through straight bankruptcy.

The *In re Hurd* case discusses Chapter Thirteen.

IN RE HURD

4 B.R. 551 (1980) (Mich.).

FACTS Lee and Mary Hurd filed a joint, voluntary bankruptcy petition under Chapter Thirteen. Lee had filed for a straight (Chapter Seven) bankruptcy in 1975 and had received a discharge. The couple's Chapter Thirteen plan proposed that the Hurds pay $330 monthly to all their creditors. The plan proposed that $23,000 owed to unsecured creditors be cancelled by payment of $1150.

ISSUE Was the Hurds' Chapter Thirteen plan calling for a 5% payment of unsecured debts filed in good faith?

DECISION No. The court determined that a 5% plan could be meaningful only under exceptional circumstances. The court said exceptional circumstances were not present in the Hurds' case and refused to approve the proposed plan and suggested amending it. The court noted that each Chapter Thirteen case is unique and that the court would consider many factors in its decision to confirm or deny a plan. Factors cited included meaningfulness of payments to unsecured creditors, ability of the debtor to pay, prior bankruptcy petitions, extent and nature of debts, inability to obtain a Chapter Seven straight bankruptcy discharge, and the relationship of attorney's fees and administration expenses to the amount to be paid to unsecured creditors. The court refused to limit bankruptcy relief to once every six years, which is done under straight bankruptcies. The court refused to deny Chapter Thirteen bankruptcy relief if a Chapter Seven bankruptcy had occurred within the previous six years.

LEGAL TIP

Bankruptcy judges have great power to approve or reject Chapter Thirteen plans. The six-year limit on bankruptcy discharges under Chapter Seven does not apply to Chapter Thirteen.

KEY TERMS

Straight bankruptcies
Voluntary bankruptcy
Order for relief
Involuntary bankruptcy
Debtor
Bankruptcy judge
Bankruptcy trustee
Chapter Seven
Chapter Thirteen
Creditors' meeting
Automatic stay
Debtor's estate
Bankruptcy clauses
Exempt property
Provable claim
Creditors' claims
Allowable claim
Priorities of claims
Preference
Discharge
Reaffirmation of a debt
Nondischargeable debts
Reorganization
"Cramdown" provision
Revocation

CHAPTER PROBLEMS

1. What are the reasons the Bankruptcy Act exists?
2. How can the Bankruptcy Act (any part, or chapter, of it) benefit creditors and debtors?
3. Who can file for a voluntary straight bankruptcy?
4. Which of the following *cannot* be put into *involuntary* straight bankruptcy?
   A. Municipalities
   B. Railroads
   C. Insurance companies
   D. Banks
   E. Building and loan associations
   F. Credit unions
   G. Farmers
   H. Foreign banks
5. A wage-earner plan may be which of the following lengths?
   A. One year
   B. Two years
   C. Three years
   D. Four years with bankruptcy court approval
   E. Five years with bankruptcy court approval
   F. Six years with bankruptcy court approval
6. When should a secured creditor object if he or she disagrees with a debtor's Chapter Thirteen plan?
7. May debts covered by a plan ever be discharged even though the debtor has not completed all payments?

*8. Allen Caggiano filed a Chapter Seven petition for straight bankruptcy. Among his debts were 15 unpaid parking tickets totalling $360. Each was originally $15. Due to late charges, 12 were increased to $20 each, and 3 were increased to $40 each. Fines payable to governmental units are not dischargeable in bankruptcy unless they relate to pecuniary loss. (That is, this amount is dischargeable if part of the "fine" is actually an expense to the government for administering the program). Were the parking tickets or any part of them dischargeable? *In re Caggiano,* 34 B.R. 449 (Massachusetts 1983).

*9. Before 1979, Charles Drewett bought for himself a $1500 diamond ring. The diamond was slightly more than 1 carat and was set in a man's ring. On February 3, 1979, 3 days before he married his wife, Marsha, he told her that the diamond was hers. She accepted the ring, but Charles continued to wear it until after their marriage when they could reset the diamond in a woman's ring. On February 6, 1979, Charles married Marsha. Nineteen months later on September 16, 1980, Charles filed a voluntary Chapter Seven bankruptcy petition. On that date he still wore the diamond ring but did not list it as his property in the bankruptcy schedules. In late October 1980, Marsha left Charles because of marital problems. She took the diamond ring with her and had it reset in a woman's ring in January 1981. In late January 1981, Charles and Marsha resumed living together. Marsha has worn the diamond as an engagement ring ever since their reunion. The bankruptcy trustee claimed the diamond ring was actually Charles' asset and should be part of his bankruptcy estate and available for payment of his debts. Who was right? *In re Drewett,* 34 B.R. 316 (Pennsylvania 1983).

*10. David J. Weiss, a debtor, filed a Chapter Thirteen petition asking for an adjustment of his debts. Weiss' plan to pay off his debts called for unsecured creditors to get a 5% payment as complete payment. The Bankruptcy Code requires Chapter Thirteen plans to be made in good faith, before a bankruptcy judge will confirm them. One of Weiss' creditors claimed Weiss' Chapter Thirteen plan was not filed in good faith, since it called for such a low payment to unsecured creditors. What is the result? *In re Weiss,* 34 B.R. 346 (Pennsylvania 1983).

"Take calculated risks. That is quite different from being rash."

General George S. Patton (1944)

"It is only by risking our persons from one hour to another that we live at all."

William James (1897)

Chapter 60

Insurance

CHAPTER PREVIEW

- Definition of insurance
- Difference between insurance and gambling
- Effect of lying on a policy application
- Insurable interest
- Difference between co-insurance clauses and pro rata clauses
- Traditional auto insurance versus no-fault insurance
- Homeowners insurance

It was common knowledge in Rosholt, South Dakota, that Bob Braaten had a drinking problem. When he died, the insurance company refused to pay Bob's widow his $20,000 life insurance coverage. The company claimed Bob misrepresented his drinking problem by not disclosing it on the policy application. Bob's widow sued claiming his nondisclosure was not fraud, since everyone in town knew about Bob's problem. Did she recover?

There are many reasons why people sue others. Persons can lose thousands of dollars and perhaps all of their possessions in lawsuits. To guard against these risks, a person can buy insurance. A famous comic even insured his large nose.

This chapter defines insurance, discusses some basic insurance terms, and looks at four kinds of insurance: life, fire, auto, and homeowners.

INSURANCE

Insurance is a contract in which the insurer agrees to pay value (usually money) to someone else (the insured or beneficiary) if some future uncertain event happens.

Pooling Risks

Insurance helps people cope with risk, which is the chance of loss. Insurance companies pool (group or gather together) many risks of the same kind. The law of large numbers helps us predict that when many similar risks are pooled, the risk of loss will occur to a certain small number of the total risk pool. However, the particular persons in the pool who will suffer loss are not known. But **pooling risks** help predict with reasonable certainty how many will suffer loss in the pool. Each pool member pays a small amount called a **premium** to cover these losses. These amounts add up to the *total* losses everyone in the pool will have over a certain time period. Pooling, in other words, socializes risk by using the group to bear the cost. Pooling makes insurance a clever idea.

How Gambling and Insurance Differ

Insurance takes existing risks (those previously uninsured) and socializes them by pooling. **Gambling,** on the other hand, *creates* a risk that did not exist before the bet. For example, if Sally bets Jim $5 that she can swim 100 yards and Jim agrees, this bet is gambling, not insurance.

If Sally insures her house against fire loss, is she gambling that her house will burn? And is the insurer gambling that it will *not* burn? No. This type of situation is not a gamble because the risk the house would burn existed *before* Sally bought the insurance. When Sally bought the insurance she *did not create* any new risk. She merely transferred it to the insurer.

In other words, if someone will lose financially if the insured item is damaged, that person has an insurable interest in the item. For example, Walter Mondale has an insurable interest in his house but not in the White House. Therefore, Mr. Mondale may not buy fire insurance on the White House.

Insurance Is a Contract

General Contracts create insurance. Therefore, the basic contract requirements we talked about in earlier chapters apply. For example, there must usually be an offer, acceptance, consideration, and legality. The policy application is the offer, and the insurer's issuance of the policy is the acceptance. Statutes often let minors enter enforceable insurance contracts (that is, such statutes remove the incapacity of minority).

Writings The statute of frauds (requiring that certain contracts be written) does not apply to most insurance contracts. Other state statutes do require that insurance contracts be written.

Misrepresentations If the insured misrepresents something material (big), this often enables the insurer to cancel the policy. For example, if the insured is unmarried and insures his "wife," the insurer may cancel the policy. On the other hand, if the insured has a wife and insures her life and represents that she has blue eyes when they really are hazel, this error is immaterial. The insurer may not cancel the policy in this type of situation.

Misrepresentation takes place in the policy application, not in the policy itself. The *Braaten v. Minnesota Mutual Life Ins. Co.* case discusses misrepresentation.

BRAATEN v. MINNESOTA MUTUAL LIFE INS. CO.

S. Dakota S.Ct.
302 N.W.2d 48 (1981).

FACTS Robert Braaten died July 17, 1976, solely as a result of medical problems associated with his alcohol addiction. Fifteen months before his death, Braaten had purchased $20,000 of credit life insurance in connection with a bank loan. The insurance application asked Braaten if he had had any diseases and the name of the treating physician. Braaten disclosed only two medical problems—pneumonia treated by Dr. Kass and cataract surgery by Dr. Ness. He failed to mention hospitalization March 12 through 18, 1974, and April 19 through 28, 1974, for alcohol addiction. The bank officer who sold Braaten the policy knew Braaten "drank." Various bank officers who sold credit life insurance also knew Braaten had a severe drinking problem. When Braaten died solely of liver disease related to alcoholism, his wife tried to collect on the $20,000 life insurance policy. The insurer denied liability claiming Braaten misrepresented or concealed facts material to the risk.

ISSUE Did the insured (Braaten) misrepresent by concealing his alcoholism on his life insurance application? Was this material to the insurer's risk?

DECISION Yes (to both questions). The South Dakota Supreme Court held that Braaten's failure to disclose the doctors' names who had treated him for alcoholism were misrepresentations and concealments of fact that were fraudulent.

LEGAL TIP

Be sure to answer honestly and completely questions asked on an insurance policy application in order to collect when the insured event happens.

Breach of warranty **Breaches of warranty** are misrepresentations by the insured put in the policy itself (not the application) and are presumed material. The insured makes them. If breaches of warranty occur, the insurer is not liable. Recall the example about the color of the wife's eyes. If her eyes are hazel and eye color is a warranty and the policy misrepresents her eyes as blue, the common law rule said the husband could not collect the policy face when the wife dies. If the policy is unclear, state statutes soften this tough rule by making the insured's statements in the policy representations, not warranties.

Basic Insurance Terms

Below are some key words used in insurance law:

Policy **Policy** refers to the insurance contract.

Premium The **premium** is the money the insured periodically pays the insurer to keep the policy in effect.

Insured event An **insured event** is the event insured against (such as death in the case of life insurance or fire in the case of fire insurance).

Policy face The **policy face** is the maximum amount of insurance coverage under an insurance policy. For example, a life insurance policy with a $20,000 face amount means the policy pays $20,000 when the insured dies.

Insured The person who buys and owns the insurance policy is called the **insured.** This term also refers to the person whose life is insured in life insurance.

Insurer The **insurer** issues the policy and must pay when the insured event occurs.

Beneficiary The **beneficiary** receives the policy benefits when the insured event occurs.

Insurable Interest

Insurable interest refers to the idea that a person can only insure something if he or she would suffer financially or legally if the insured item or person were damaged, destroyed, injured, or killed.

Why require an insurable interest? There are two reasons for requiring that the insured have an insurable interest. First, the insurable interest requirement distinguishes insurance from gambling. For example, if Betty takes out fire insurance on her house for one year, is she gambling the house will burn during the year? And is the insurer gambling that it will not burn? No, because Betty will lose her house if it burns *whether or not it is insured.* The insurance merely indemnifies (or restores) her. Gambling also creates a risk that formerly did not exist. (For example, Joe promises to pay Margie $5 if the Yankees win the World Series.) Insurance merely helps deal with a pre-existing risk.

Second, the insurable risk requirement removes immoral temptations. For example, if Don could buy fire insurance on Dwight's house, Don would be tempted to commit arson (since he would not lose anything if someone else's house burns). Likewise, people must have an insurable interest in a life before they can insure it. This requirement removes the temptation to insure a stranger, murder him, and pocket the life insurance benefits. However, a beneficiary of a life insurance contract does not need an insurable interest in the insured's life (only the person buying the policy has to). Therefore, Imogene Posey can insure her own life and name the Baptist Church (which has no insurable interest) as a beneficiary.

Examples of persons having insurable interests Examples of persons with insurable interests include: a person in his or her own life, spouses in their spouse's life, parents in their minor (not adult) children's lives, homeowners in their home, a business in a key employee, and tenants in the leased property. There are many other examples.

Kinds of insurance requiring insurable interest All kinds of insurance require that the insured have an insurable interest. Life insurance and property insurance, for example, require such an interest.

When insurable interests must exist Both life and property insurance require an insurable interest. However, the time this interest must exist differs. In life insurance, the insurable interest must exist when the policy is bought. It need not exist when the loss occurs. For example, if Joe Dimaggio and Marilyn Monroe marry, Joe may buy life insurance on Marilyn's life. If Marilyn and Joe later divorce, Joe may keep this life insurance and collect if Marilyn *then* dies. Joe may not buy life insurance on Marilyn *after* they divorce because he no longer has an insurable interest in her life.

In property insurance, the insurable interest must exist when the loss occurs, not when the insurance is bought. (Of course, insurers will not sell in the first place to persons not having an insurable interest.) So if Erik insures his house against fire loss, sells it to Steven, and then the house burns, Erik may not collect even if he continued to pay premiums after selling the house.

The *Castle Cars, Inc. v. U.S. Fire Insurance Co.* is a case example of insurable interest.

CASTLE CARS INC. v. U.S. FIRE INS. CO.

Supreme Court of Virginia.
273 S.E.2d 793 (1981).

FACTS A used car dealer (Castle Cars, Inc.) bought a used car for $2600. The seller signed the car's title document over to the dealer. The car was then stolen from the dealer's lot. The dealer filed a claim under its theft insurance policy (a garage keeper's liability insurance policy) against the U.S. Fire Insurance Co. (its insurer). The insurer paid the dealer. The dealer, in turn, signed the title certificate over to the insurance company in accordance with the insurance policy's subrogation provision (recall that once the insurer pays a claim it is subrogated—steps into the insured's shoes or takes over the insured's interest in the insured property). The insurance company's later investigation showed that the person who sold the car to the dealer was a thief, who did not own the car. The thief had replaced the stolen car's identification number with identification from a wrecked car of similar description. The stolen car's true owner was never found. The insurer then sued the dealer for the money it had paid the dealer. The insurer argued that since the dealer bought a stolen car, it had no insurable interest in it and therefore could not collect on its insurance when the car was stolen from it.

ISSUE Did the used car dealer have an insurable interest in the car it bought in good faith for value from a thief?

DECISION Yes. The court admitted that a property insurance policy is void unless the insured has an insurable interest in the insured property. The court also indicated that different states do not agree on the answer to this question. Some states require that an insured must have legal or equitable title (that is, "own" the insured property) before it can recover on property insurance if the property is destroyed or stolen. The court rejected this rule in this case. Instead, the court noted that courts have broadened the "title" definition of insurable interest. In this case, the court said reasons for requiring insurable interests in property (preventing gambling and discouraging destruction of property a person does not have an interest in) continue to exist if the definition is broadened a bit. The court concluded by saying a person has an insurable interest in property if the "insured's interest is such that he will be benefitted by its continued existence or suffer a direct pecuniary injury by its loss." Thus, a person may have an insurable interest in property even if he or she has no legal or equitable title to it. The dealer here paid the thief value in good faith. Even though the dealer did not get "title" in the traditional sense, it got an "economic, substantial, and lawful" interest that was insurable.

LEGAL TIP

The definition of insurable interest is changing. In some states the definition is limited to legal or equitable interests. In other states insurable interest also includes interests which will benefit the insured if they continue or damage the insured if they end.

Subrogation

Subrogation means the insurer steps into the insured's shoes against any third parties once it pays the insured's claim. For example, Wayne Morse negligently drives his car into Charles Horngren and injures him. Charles collects from *his* insurer who then takes Charles' claim and sues Wayne.

The subrogation idea applies to auto, fire, and accident policies but *not* to life insurance.

If the insured releases the person causing the injury by signing a contract excusing the wrongdoer, the insurer is also released. This is because the release destroys the insurer's subrogation right against the wrongdoer.

Insurance Regulation

Insurance is one of the most heavily regulated businesses, in large part, because it is so affected with public interest. If an insurance company fails, many people, who may have depended on insurance protection, are hurt. Therefore, both policy terms and insurer finances are closely watched by government.

In 1868, the United States Supreme Court decided that issuing an insurance policy is not "commerce." This decision meant that the United States Government may not regulate insurance but that individual states *could* regulate it. However, in 1944 the law changed. The Supreme Court decided that an insurance company doing business across state lines *was* commerce. This decision had the effect of reversing the 1868 case. The national government could now regulate insurance interstate. Lobbying by the insurance business resulted in passage of the McCarran-Ferguson Act having a 1945 effective date. Basically, that Act let state regulation of the insurance business continue provided that no federal law did so. The Act also exempted insurance from federal antitrust laws if states regulated the insurance business. In effect, the McCarran-Ferguson Act is a club the national government can threaten to use if state insurance regulation becomes too lax.

Life Insurance

There are several kinds of life insurance: term, whole life, limited pay life, and endowment.

Term life insurance **Term insurance** gives life insurance for a fixed, limited time; premiums are paid for the term. If the insured dies during the term, the beneficiary gets the policy face amount. If the insured does not die during this term, the beneficiary gets nothing.

Term insurance is "pure" insurance. That is, the policy has no investment element. There are no possible policy loans and no cash surrender value. Term insurance is the cheapest form of pure life insurance protection.

Term insurance is flexible since it can be tailored to fit many needs. For example, homeowners often buy term insurance whose face amount decreases over the term (called decreasing term life insurance). In case the homeowner dies during the term, the amount of insurance is set so it pays off the homeowner's mortgage (which also usually decreases in time).

Whole life (or ordinary life) insurance **Whole life insurance** is the most common type. The insured pays premiums for as long as he or she lives. The insurer pays the policy's face amount (minus any unpaid policy loans) to the beneficiary when the insured dies. It combines both insurance and an investment element. The investment part is called the cash surrender value, which earns untaxed interest (called dividends) while the policy is in force. The insured can also borrow from the cash surrender value during the life of the policy. The cash surrender value is less than the face of the policy.

Limited pay life insurance One of the main problems with whole life insurance is the requirement that the insured pay premiums during all of his or her life. People often live past retirement when they have reduced income. It is often difficult to pay premiums during such periods. A solution to this problem are **limited pay life insurance** policies. Under these policies, the insured pays premiums only for a fixed number of years (usually working years) when income is high. Premiums are larger than in ordinary whole life policies. Coverage, however, lasts for the insured's entire life. Other features (such as the investment element and the insured's right to borrow against it) are the same as ordinary life coverage.

Endowment policies Under **endowment insurance** policies, the insured pays premiums for a fixed number of years. A set amount is paid if the insured dies during the fixed period. If the insured survives this period, this set amount is paid to the insured.

Endowment policies have the highest investment element. Premiums are also the highest of any of the life insurance policies.

The advantage of endowment insurance is its "forced savings feature." Endowment insurance forces a person to save and provides a large amount of money at a definite future time. This money can be used to buy a house or educate a child. No matter what kind of life insurance one buys (term, whole life, etc.), the following are some common features:

Some Common Features of Life Insurance Policies

Grace periods **Grace periods** are included in many life insurance policies. They permit payment of premiums after the due date, if within the grace period, without causing the policy to lapse. The grace period is often thirty days. If an insured does not pay within the grace period, the policy usually lapses and protection ends.

Reinstatement provisions Even if the insured fails to pay premiums within the grace period, it is possible to reinstate the policy. **Reinstatement provisions** (when they exist) let the insured pay back missed premiums and interest. At this time, the old policy springs back into existence as though it had never lapsed.

Incontestibility clauses If the insured lies or conceals material information when applying for life insurance, this ordinarily would be grounds for the insurer to deny liability. However, it is generally thought to be unfair to let years go by and then allow the insurer to raise the insured's earlier misrepresentations and concealments. There are two wrongs in this situation: the insured's initial concealment or misrepresentation and the insurer's lulling the insurer into thinking that life insurance exists. The **incontestibility clause** lets the insurer raise certain defenses such as fraud in the application *for a limited time* (often two years) after the policy starts. This limited period gives the insurer time to do follow-up investigations to check on claims occurring soon after the policy took effect. However, after the contestibility period expires, the insurer loses these defenses.

Even if the contestibility period has passed, the insurer can still raise certain defenses. These include: death is not proven; the policy owner (but *not* beneficiary) had no insurable interest in the insured's life; the policy had lapsed (because premiums had not been paid); and the policy did not cover the risk.

Suicide clauses **Suicide clauses** prevent recovery under a life insurance policy if the insured intentionally takes his or her own life within a certain period after buying the policy. The period is often two or three years. If the insured commits suicide *after* the suicide period, the policy pays the full face amount.

The *Rome v. Life & Casualty Ins. Co. of Tenn.* case below indicates that there is a presumption against suicide in life insurance cases.

ROME v. LIFE & CASUALTY INS. CO. OF TENN.

Court of Appeal of La. 1st Cir.
336 So.2d 275 (1976).

FACTS Mr. Lovincy A. Rome, Jr., and his wife had been separated for 3 months. Three weeks earlier Mrs. Rome had filed a lawsuit seeking legal separation. Mr. Rome wanted to save his marriage. His relationship between him and his wife improved after the separation. Then something happened. At about 5:30 AM one morning, Mr. Rome, intoxicated, went to his wife's home. He went directly to her bedroom, took a pistol she had under her pillow, and left the house. As he went out he shouted, "Take care of the baby." He got in his car, drove 210 feet, almost to an intersection, and stopped next to some woods. Two shots were heard. Soon after, a neighbor found Mr. Rome slumped in his seat dead from a bullet wound in his temple. The car's engine was running and its lights were on. The car's transmission was in first gear and Rome's foot depressed the clutch. The glove compartment was open. Rome had a cigarette in his left hand. Rome had a life insurance policy with a clause limiting the insurer's liability to the return of premiums if death was by suicide within 2 years of taking out the policy. The policy had been taken out 18 months before his death. The insurer paid Mrs. Rome $267.60, the amount of premiums paid. She sued the insurer for $27,860, the amount of accidental death insurance under the policy. The trial court held for the insurer, saying the cause of death was suicide. Mrs. Rome appealed.

ISSUE Did the physical facts surrounding the death exclude with reasonable certainty any possibility of accident? Does the evidence show a suicide motive sufficient to overcome the presumption against suicide?

DECISION No (to both questions). The appellate court reversed the original decision. Mrs. Rome recovered $27,860 plus interest, less the amount already paid. The circumstances of Mr. Rome's death indicate he killed himself but left doubt whether it was accidental or suicide. The possibility of accidental death was created by the fact that the car was running and the transmission was in first gear. Only Mr. Rome's foot on the clutch kept the car from moving. Also, the cigarette in his left hand and the open glove compartment suggest he was trying to put the gun in the glove compartment. Where alcohol, cars, and guns are mixed, an accident is very possible.

As to motive, the court said that Mr. Rome was in good physical and financial health. Therefore, the facts did not overcome the presumption against suicide. This burden fell on the insurer, who failed to meet it.

LEGAL TIP

Life insurance allows recovery if there are doubts about whether a death was accidental or suicide. Doubts are resolved against suicide.

Rights to life insurance proceeds The life insurance beneficiary has the right to receive the policy benefits when the insured dies. The beneficiary's creditors usually can get this insurance money. Some states do not let creditors get life insurance benefits if they go to the insured's spouse.

Insured persons sometimes make life insurance proceeds payable to their estates or reserve the right to change beneficiaries. This decision is unwise because the insured's creditors can get the proceeds in either case.

Age misrepresentations If a person misrepresents his or her age in buying life insurance (usually by understating it), the policy is not usually invalidated. Instead, either the premiums or benefits are adjusted to the proper age.

Change of beneficiary The policy owner can usually change beneficiaries before the insured dies. Where the beneficiary is irrevocably named (has vested rights or property), no change of beneficiary is possible.

How life insurance policies end Life insurance policies can end in several ways: by payment of benefits when the insured dies; by nonpayment of premiums (in which case the policy lapses); by cashing in the policy and taking the cash surrender value; and by expiration of the policy (as when the term expires in term insurance).

The insurer may not cancel life insurance policies at any time. Otherwise, life insurers would collect premiums for years and then cancel policies as insured persons got older and nearer death.

Settlement options Most life insurance policies give beneficiaries several **settlement options** to take policy benefits. The beneficiary may receive one large sum or periodic installments. Installments often can be guaranteed in amount for a fixed number of years. Installments can also be received as an annuity for the rest of the beneficiary's life.

Fire Insurance

Coverage Fire insurance protects against loss caused by hostile fires. Direct fire damage plus damage from smoke, water, and other materials used to stop the fire are also covered.

Hostile and friendly fires **Hostile fires** are unwanted and unintended fires. A burning rug in the middle of the living room is an example. Hostile fire damage is covered by fire insurance. Friendly fire damage is not. **Friendly fires** are intended and desired, such as a fire in a fireplace. A friendly fire could become hostile if it leaves its intended burning place. An example would be a burning log that rolls from the fireplace onto the living room rug.

Kinds of policies There are two general kinds of fire insurance policies: valued and blanket. **Valued policies** set the value of specific insured property *before* the loss. This amount is the maximum recovery, or face amount. In open, or unvalued, policies the value of the insured item is set shortly *after* the loss occurs. Usually there is a maximum recoverable amount under open policies.

Blanket policies cover general kinds (but not specific items) of property. Inventory, which constantly changes, is an example of what could be covered by a blanket policy.

Amount of recovery Under a valued policy, the insured recovers the face amount if there is a total loss. The actual damage is recovered if there is only a partial loss.

Under open policies, the amount of the recovery is the fair market value of the property lost in the fire. The fair market value is what the property was worth just before the fire.

The insured's general creditors may usually seize the fire insurance proceeds to pay any of the insured's debts. Secured creditors (for example, mortgagees) have no first claim on insurance proceeds unless they are named as policy beneficiaries or some other contract right gives them this protection. Secured creditors have insurable interests in the property used as security. They can, therefore, buy fire insurance on the secured property up to the amount of their insurable interest.

Pro rata clauses **Pro rata clauses** deal with the problem of two or more fire policies covering the same loss. Pro rata clauses let the insured recover from each insurer the part of the loss its insurance is of the *total* insurance on the property. For example, if a fire loss is $21,000, insurer B insured the property for $10,000, and insurer C insured it for $20,000, insurer B will pay $7000 (one third of the total insurance so it pays one third of the loss) and C will pay $14,000 (two thirds of the total insurance and therefore two thirds of the $21,000 loss).

Coinsurance clauses Since most fires do not completely destroy the insured property, many people shrewdly decide to underinsure and save money. For example, if a building is worth $50,000, the owner might buy only $25,000 in fire insurance (hoping the fire department puts out the fire before more than half of the property is destroyed).

To deal with this underinsurance problem, insurance companies have developed the **coinsurance clause.** Coinsurance clauses require the insured to buy insurance covering a specific percentage of the property's value. For example, it is common for fire insurance policies to have an 80% coinsurance clause. This clause means that the insured must carry fire insurance in an amount equal to 80% of the property's value. If the insured does not buy the required amount of insurance, the insurer will only pay *part* of the loss (even if the loss is less than the policy's face amount).

An example shows how coinsurance clauses work. Assume a house is worth $50,000 and is insured for $25,000. Assume also there is an 80% coinsurance clause and a $25,000 fire loss. Will the insured recover $25,000? No, even though the policy provides $25,000 in insurance. This answer follows because there was an 80% coinsurance clause but the insured only carried insurance equal to 50% of the property's value. How much will the insured recover? The formula is shown in Figure 60-1.

Assignability **Assignability** refers to the idea that after two people make a contract, one of them can transfer his or her rights to a third person. Fire insurance policies generally are not assignable because the third person may be a higher risk for the insurer than the original insured. The idea is that the insurer sets premiums based on the risk of a particular person (the insured). If the insured changes, so does the risk.

For example, suppose that Brad Schweiger owns an office building and has fire insurance. His premiums are low because he has never had a fire. He sells the building to Jim Dietrich whose business has a history of fires whenever his

Figure 60-1 **How Coinsurance Clauses Work**

$$\text{Amount recovered} = \frac{\text{Total insurance}}{\text{Co-insurance percentage required} \times \text{Value of insured property}} \times \text{Amount of loss}$$

In the example above this is

$$\$15,625 = \left(\frac{\$25,000}{80\% \times \$50,000}\right) \times \$25,000$$

goods do not sell. Since Jim is a greater risk than Brad, Brad may not assign his fire insurance policy to Jim. However, Jim can get insurance if he can buy it directly from an insurer (probably at a high premium reflecting his risk).

Proving a fire loss Once a fire occurs, the insured must file a claim, which describes the cause, amount, and other details, with the insurer. This claim must be filed within a certain time (such as sixty to ninety days after the loss). The insurer does not have to pay the claim if the insured fails to file within the claim period. The reason is to allow the insurer to investigate the loss while evidence is fresh. Some events, such as the insured's death, can excuse filing claims late.

Automobile Insurance

Traditional Remember the discussion of the tort of negligence (carelessness) in an earlier chapter. People are liable if they drive cars negligently and injure or kill others or damage their property. Auto insurance protects car owners from this risk. It also usually protects against theft, fire, and storm loss. There is frequently a deductible amount (such as $100) from the coverage. The *Almadova v. State Farm Mutual Automobile Insurance Co.* case presents a problem of theft coverage in auto insurance.

No-fault auto insurance Several states have passed **no-fault** auto insurance laws. Traditional auto insurance is based on "fault," which means that an individual must pay for injuring someone else or damaging his or her property *only* when carelessness caused the loss.

Under no-fault auto insurance, each car owner buys auto insurance covering his or her car. If the car is in an accident, each owner's insurer pays *its* insured—not the other driver's—no matter who caused the accident. No-fault auto insurance is intended to lower legal costs, reduce court crowding, and decrease delays in getting accident recovery. People driving cars involved in auto accidents may not sue the person causing the accident except for large personal injuries exceeding fixed amounts. A disadvantage of no-fault auto insurance is that it reduces the incentive to be careful (since careless people driving cars do not have to pay for their victim's losses). No-fault states still let non-motorists (such as pedestrians) sue careless auto drivers who injure them. The *Heard v. State Farm Mutual Auto Insurance Co.* case shows how difficult it is to tell if someone is a motorist or a

ALMADOVA v. STATE FARM MUTUAL AUTOMOBILE INSURANCE CO.

Supreme Court of Arizona.
649 P.2d 284 (1982).

FACTS State Farm insured Almadova's 1976 Porsche through an auto policy with theft coverage. On September 11, 1979, Almadova agreed to sell the car to Fairchild Car Company (which operated a Phoenix used-car lot). Almadova turned over the car and signed the car's title over to David Raines, president of Fairchild. Raines then gave Almadova a $14,000 check for the car. Almadova presented the check for payment the next day. It was dishonored for lack of sufficient funds. Almadova then confronted Raines with the dishonored check. Raines said he was aware it would be dishonored. He then gave Almadova another $14,000 check drawn on another checking account. This check also "bounced." Some time later Almadova unsuccessfully tried to get the car back from Raines. Fairchild went out of business and Almadova could not find the car. Almadova then filed a claim under the theft coverage of his auto insurance. His auto insurance policy said the following about theft coverage: "We will pay for the loss to your car . . . in excess of the deductible amount, . . . caused by . . . theft, larceny . . . . There is no coverage for . . . loss to any vehicle due to . . . conversion, embezzlement or secretion by any person who has the vehicle due to any lien, rental or sales agreement." The trial court decided in favor of Almadova. State Farm appealed.

ISSUE Does "theft" occur within the car insurance theft coverage when an auto loss happens as a result of the insured's voluntary transfer of title and possession to a buyer who gives a "bad check" for the purchase price?

If the loss is covered by the policy's theft coverage, does the policy exclusion nonetheless prevent the insured's recovery?

DECISION The Arizona Supreme Court said neither question could be answered based on the record before them. It reversed the result and sent the matter back to trial. The Arizona Supreme Court did conclude that if the dealer took the car and at that time intended not to pay for it, the loss would be a theft within the policy coverage. As to the exclusion, the court said that no theft coverage existed when the person buying the car takes lawful possession but *later* forms a dishonest criminal intent. Therefore, if Raines got the car due to a preconceived fraudulent plan (never intended to give a "good" check when he "paid" for the car), Almadova is covered and the exclusion does not apply. If, however, Raines did not have a fraudulent intent when he bought the car but only formed this intent later, the policy does not cover the loss.

LEGAL TIP

Theft coverage in auto policies often does not cover embezzlement of an auto. Therefore, be careful about entrusting your car.

pedestrian injured by another driver. Remember that motorists generally may not sue other motorists in no-fault states but pedestrians may.

Homeowners Insurance

You invite several friends at work over to your house for a backyard picnic on your new deck. Suddenly it collapses, breaking the legs of several guests. What can a homeowner do about this risk?

The answer is: buy homeowners insurance. This type of policy provides homeowners with liability and loss (which usually covers collapsing decks, fire, and theft) coverages. Usually there is a deductible amount for each loss. Therefore, if a thief breaks in and steals a $500 television, a $200 deductible policy means the insurer pays the homeowner $300 (the $500 loss minus the $200 deductible). The larger the deductible, the cheaper the insurance.

Homeowners insurance does not usually cover business carried on in the home. Is babysitting in the home a business? The *Camden Fire Insurance Ass'n. v. Johnson* case answers this question.

HEARD v. STATE FARM MUTUAL AUTO INSURANCE CO.

Supreme Court of Michigan.
324 N.W.2d 1 (1982).

FACTS Heard was pumping gasoline into his car at a self-service station. His car was uninsured. Suddenly another car crashed into Heard's car pinning him between the two cars. Heard sued the driver for his injuries. The other driver's insurer argued that it should not be liable since the accident occurred in Michigan, a no-fault state. Michigan's no-fault statute required that vehicle owners insure their own cars and themselves from property damage and personal injury. They generally have no right to sue other vehicle owners involved with them in auto accidents. Heard argued that since his car was standing still and he was not even in his car when the other car struck him, he was a pedestrian, who can recover for injuries from a negligent driver under Michigan's no-fault law.

ISSUE May an uninsured driver injured by another car while filling his car at a gas station recover for personal injuries from the other driver in a no-fault state?

DECISION Yes. Even though the Michigan no-fault statute does not generally allow uninsured motorists to recover under it (from another motorist), there are exceptions. One occurs where the uninsured vehicle is not involved in the accident giving rise to the motorist's injuries. For example, where the injured person's injuries occur in a motor vehicle accident while he or she is a pedestrian, bicyclist, motorcyclist, or passenger (not driver) of another vehicle, he or she may recover from the other driver if that person is at fault. The problem in the case of the motorist injured while filling his car with gas is in deciding whether he is more like a motorist (who usually can only recover from his own insurer) or a pedestrian (who can recover from the negligent driver). The Michigan Supreme Court said the person standing near his or her vehicle is more like a pedestrian than a motorist and can therefore sue the driver at fault, even though Michigan is a no-fault state.

LEGAL TIP

No-fault auto insurance stops motorists from suing other motorists if they are both involved in the same auto accident. However, pedestrians hit by a car may sue the motorist at fault.

CAMDEN FIRE INSURANCE ASS'N v. JOHNSON

Supr. Ct. of W. Va.
294 S.E.2d 116 (1982).

FACTS An auto struck James and Sadie Johnson's grandson while Sadie was babysitting with him at her house. Stella Hubbard, the boy's mother, paid Sadie $80 per month to babysit while Stella worked. Stella sued Sadie for the boy's injuries due to negligent babysitting. At the time of the accident, the Camden Fire Insurance Association insured the Johnsons against personal liability for accidental injuries under a homeowners insurance policy. The policy excluded from coverage "bodily injury . . . arising from business pursuits of any insured except activities ordinarily incident to non-business pursuits." The policy also required that the insurer defend the Johnsons in any suit covered by the policy. The insurer claimed babysitting was a business not covered, and therefore it did not have to provide free legal defense for the Johnsons.

ISSUE Was babysitting excluded from coverage under a homeowners policy, which did not cover business in the insured's home?

DECISION Babysitting was covered even though Sadie was paid for doing it in her home. The court said the "business pursuits exclusion" in the homeowner's policy referred to a continuous or regular activity engaged in by the insured to earn a profit. In other words, the court looked at the babysitter's motive. To figure out motive, the court examined whether the babysitting was done to help a friend or relative, whether the babysitter was licensed, whether the babysitter advertised, and whether the babysitter charged for this service.

LEGAL TIP

Check homeowners insurance policies to see if they cover liabilities from the risk of doing business at home. Many homeowners policies often do not cover this risk.

KEY TERMS

Insurance
Pooling risks
Premium
Gambling
Misrepresentation
Breach of warranty
Policy
Premium
Insured event
Policy face
Insured
Insurer
Beneficiary
Insurable interest
Subrogation
Term life insurance
Whole life insurance
Limited pay life insurance
Endowment insurance
Term insurance
Grace period
Reinstatement provisions
Incontestibility clause
Suicide clauses
Settlement options
Hostile fires
Friendly fires
Valued policies
Blanket policies
Pro rata clauses
Co-insurance clause
Assignability
No-fault auto insurance

CHAPTER PROBLEMS

1. Max bets Ann $2 that Washtenaw Community College will defeat State Tech in the next basketball game. Max has taken out car insurance covering his property and medical expenses if he has an accident with his car. Are both the basketball bet and the car insurance policy examples of gambling?
2. Louise Lacey buys car insurance covering personal liability property damage and medical expenses. Louise drives too fast on an icy road and demolishes her car in a one-car accident. She sustains $12,000 in property damages and $8600 in medical bills. What is the result when her insurer refuses to pay, claiming that insurance does not cover her negligence?
3. What type of insurance policy usually has a co-insurance clause?
4. What kinds of insurance policies require an insurable interest?
5. Mike Harrison bought a life insurance policy after stating on the application that he was thirty years old. Mike was actually 32 years old. Three years later, the insurance company discovered this error. As yet there are no claims against the policy. What is the insurer likely to do?
6. Many kinds of insurance policies are indemnity policies. However, life insurance is not one. Why?
7. What is the purpose of a pro rata clause in a fire insurance policy?
8. What did the McCarran-Ferguson Act do to the regulation of insurance?
9. What is meant by the face amount of an insurance policy?

*10. Frederic Wheeler was a truck driver for 19 years. His job caused him back problems, disabling him completely by late 1979. Wheeler tried to recover personal protection insurance benefits under Michigan's No-Fault Insurance Act. Wheeler claimed that his back problems, resulting from years of truck driving, were an "accidental bodily injury" and entitled him to personal protection under no-fault insurance benefits. What is the result? *Wheeler v. Tucker Freight Lines Co., Inc.* 336 N.W.2d 14 (Mich. 1983).

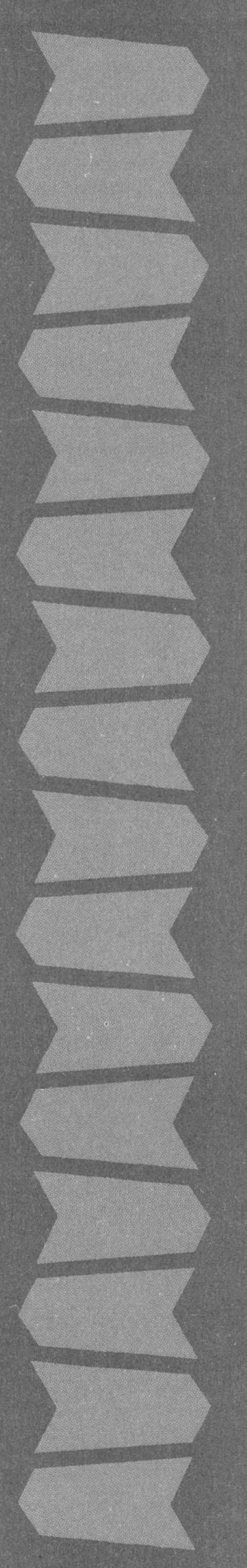

Part Ten

International Law

Chapter 61

Law in International Business

"The world is your oyster."
Shakespeare

Chapter 61

Law in International Business

CHAPTER PREVIEW

- Bills of lading
- Letters of credit
- Reasons bills of lading and letters of credit exist in international business
- Mechanics of bills of lading and letters of credit
- Repatriation's effects on United States business abroad
- The Foreign Corrupt Practices Act and bribery
- Act of state doctrine
- Legal disputes involving international contracts

Art opened an oriental rug shop in Atlanta, Georgia. He had never dealt in international trade before. Now, here he was, arranging a $20,000 letter of credit with the local bank to pay for oriental rugs he was buying from Ali's Rug Store in Ankara, Turkey. The Atlanta bank would issue a letter of credit to Ali through a Turkish bank. Art knew the letter of credit would be paid when Ali turned a bill of lading for the rugs over to the Ankara Bank. But what if Ali sent different rugs than Art ordered? Could Ralph stop payment on the letter of credit?

Business is becoming international and includes even small businesses, such as Art's Oriental Rug Shop in the example above. Because of this trend, the average person must know some laws affecting international business. This chapter will explain how an international contract works using a letter of credit and a bill of lading. Then we examine the Foreign Corrupt Practices Act to learn about bribes in foreign business. Finally, the chapter explores what business legally can do if there are contract problems.

INTERNATIONAL BUSINESS DEALS

This section discusses an international business deal. The facts show a transaction. Then we see possible problems with the deal and solutions to those problems.

How an International Business Deal Works

Possible international business deal (foreign seller, U.S. buyer) As a possible international business deal, suppose, for example, that Art is an Atlanta rug dealer. He makes a contract to buy fifty 8′ × 10′ red, Turkish, handwoven rugs for $20,000 from Ali, a rug maker in Ankara, Turkey.

Possible problems with international business deals The contract between Art and Ali in the example above presents many practical problems including:

1. How can Ali be sure that he will be paid *after* shipping the rugs?
2. How can Art be certain that he will get the rugs after paying for them?
3. Can Art stop the deal if Ali sends different rugs?

Why Art does not pay Ali directly You might look at the above facts and say, "What's the problem?" Art should simply mail Ali a check for $20,000, and Ali can send Art the rugs when the check clears (is paid). But what if Art is unsure Ali will send the rugs once the check clears? What if Ali does not know if Art will pay?

Art wants to keep the money until he gets the rugs. Ali wants to keep the rugs until he gets paid. Since Art and Ali mistrust each other, the deal might never occur.

A solution: A letter of credit and bill of lading Art and Ali's mistrust problem is solved by a letter of credit (letter) and bill of lading (bill). Basically, both the bill and letter use third parties (banks in the letter and transport companies in the bill of lading) in these situations. Assume Art and Ali trust banks and transport companies more than they trust each other.

Definition of a letter of credit A **letter of credit** is a bank's commitment to pay a definite amount of money (or extend a certain amount of credit) to a third person, called a **beneficiary.** The bank extends credit to the beneficiary because a customer, called the **account party,** pays the bank to do so. The bank extends credit to pay the beneficiary (Ali) when he gives the bank certain pieces of paper (often, bills of lading).

Definition of a bill of lading A **bill of lading** is a piece of paper a transport company gives to someone. It shows three things: a receipt for goods; a contract to transport the goods; and title to (ownership of) the goods.

Using a letter of credit and bill of lading First, Art and Ali enter a contract for the rugs. (Recall that Art is an Atlanta buyer. Ali is an Ankara, Turkey, seller.) Then, Art arranges with his Atlanta bank to issue a letter of credit to Ali, which is how Art pays Ali (see Figure 61-1).

Often the bank issuing the letter of credit arranges for another bank, called a **correspondent bank,** in the seller's city to physically issue the letter of credit to the seller. The letter of credit will set out certain conditions the foreign seller (Ali) must meet before it can "draw on the credit." **Drawing on the credit** is how the seller is paid and happens when the seller writes a draft (or a check) on the letter of credit. This term can be understood by comparing a letter of credit to a checking account that one person sets up for another. When an account is set up, an individual can write checks using someone else's money. The same thing is true for the letter of credit the buyer of goods has set up for the foreign seller.

Next, Ali delivers the rugs to a transport company in Ankara, Turkey. The transport company gives Ali a bill of lading for the rugs. Recall that the bill of lading is three things: a receipt (showing Ali actually turned something over to the shipper; a contract (showing the shipper agreed to transport the rugs to Art); and a title (showing that whoever has the bill of lading owns the goods). Ali turns the bill of lading over to either Art's Atlanta bank or (more likely) the Atlanta bank's correspondent bank in Ankara. (Remember that a correspondent bank is a

Figure 61-1 **Anatomy of an International Business Deal Using Letter of Credit (LOC) and Bill of Lading (BOL)***

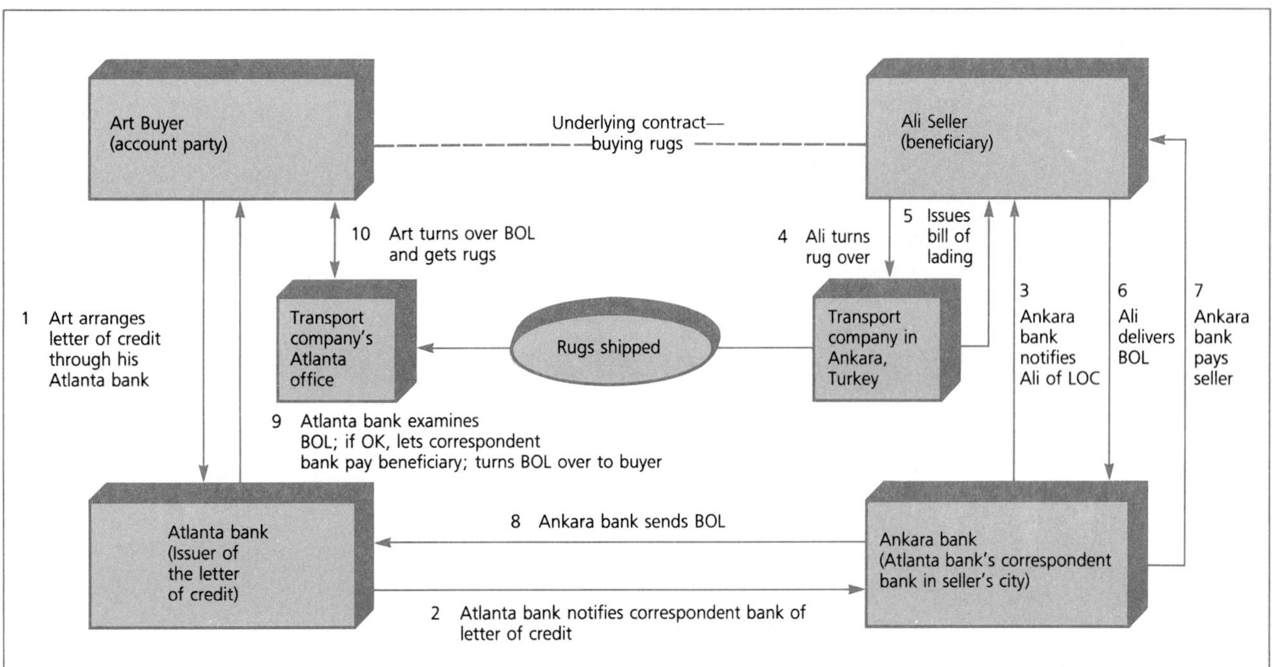

Note: LOC = letter of credit
BOL = bill of lading

bank doing business with another bank in another city. Assume that the Atlanta bank has a correspondent bank in Ankara.)

When Ali turns the bill of lading over to the Ankara bank, it pays Ali or it can wait until the Atlanta bank determines that the bill of lading meets the letter of credit's requirements. The Ankara bank sends the bill of lading to Art's Atlanta bank. The Atlanta bank checks the bill of lading to see that it meets the letter of credit's terms (for example, is not forged).

Notice that Art's Atlanta bank will *not* check the *rugs,* just the bill of lading for the rugs. The contract for the rugs is *independent from* the letter of credit and the bill of lading. If the bill of lading meets the letter of credit's requirements, Art's Atlanta bank credits the Ankara bank's account. (The Ankara bank would be wise to wait until the Atlanta bank approves the bill of lading before paying Ali.)

Art's Atlanta bank charges Art for the letter of credit. It then gives Art the bill of lading. Art takes the bill of lading to the transport company's local office and gets the rugs. The deal is complete. Ali has his money, and Art has his rugs.

Letters of credit: The independence principle The general rule is that letters of credit are independent of (separate from) the underlying contract (to buy rugs in the example above). This rules means that if Ali sends blue instead of red rugs, the issuing bank must honor the letter of credit. The beneficiary (Ali) must present the documents, which the letter of credit requires (often a bill of lading). This rule also assumes that Ali (the seller) substitutes nonconforming goods (blue instead of red rugs) in good faith.

The *GATX Leasing Corp. v. DBM Drilling Corp.* case illustrates the independence principle.

GATX LEASING CORP. v. DBM DRILLING CORP.

Tex. App. 4th Dist.
657 S.W.2d 178 (1983).

FACTS DBM Drilling Corporation (DBM) was the account party of an irrevocable letter of credit. DBM arranged with Frost National Bank to issue an irrevocable letter of credit to GATX Leasing Corporation (GATX) to pay for a drilling rig. GATX presented documents to Frost National Bank as the letter of credit required. DBM, however, claimed that the oil rig itself did not live up to the contract DBM had with GATX. DBM sued to enjoin (stop) the Frost Bank from honoring (paying) under the letter of credit.

ISSUE May the account party on a letter of credit stop the issuing bank from paying the letter of credit when the goods do not conform to the underlying contract, but the documents conform to the letter of credit?

DECISION No. The account party may not stop the issuing bank from paying an irrevocable letter of credit if there is merely a breach of the underlying contract. This situation was not a case involving fraud or forgery by the beneficiary. Instead, the beneficiary and account party merely disagreed about whether the oil rig was being sold or leased.

LEGAL TIP

It pays to deal with a reliable seller when you (the buyer) pay using an irrevocable letter of credit. A buyer may not stop its bank from honoring an irrevocable letter of credit, assuming the seller acts in good faith when shipping nonconforming goods and presents documents the letter of credit requires.

Stopping payment on letters of credit: Forgery Assume a letter of credit requires the seller (beneficiary) to submit a bill of lading to get paid. If the seller submits a forged bill of lading and knows it, the buyer (account party) can stop payment on the letter of credit. The *Prutscher v. Fidelity International Bank* case examines this rule.

PRUTSCHER v. FIDELITY INTERNATIONAL BANK

U.S. District Court (S. Dist. N.Y.).
502 F. Supp. 535 (1980).

FACTS Prutscher, a limited partnership, was located in Vienna, Austria. It entered a contract to sell furniture to Eid Trading Agency (Eid). Payment was to take place as follows: Eid asked its local bank, Banque Med (located in Beirut, Lebanon), to issue to Prutscher a letter of credit for 10,915,859 Austrian shillings. Banque Med issued this letter in favor of Prutscher. Fidelity International Bank (Fidelity) confirmed this letter of credit, enabling Prutscher to draw credit from Fidelity. The letter of credit required that the goods all be shipped in one lot. Also, the letter set July 6, 1974, as the latest date to ship the furniture. The furniture was actually sent on 3 separate ships on July 4, 6, and 12, 1974. Prutscher presented a bill of lading to Banque Med, claiming it satisfied the letter of credit. Since Banque Med issued the letter of credit, and Fidelity confirmed it, Prutscher tried to get money on it. Fidelity defended by saying the bill of lading was fraudulent.

ISSUE Does a bank (Fidelity), which confirms a letter of credit, have to honor it (that is, let the holder draw cash or credit on it) if the letter of credit requires a bill of lading before credit is extended and the bill of lading is fraudulent?

DECISION No, for Fidelity Bank. The UCC Section 5-114 sets the rules for refusing to honor or stop a letter of credit. A bank that has confirmed a letter of credit is not required to honor a draft drawn on it if the bank receives information that a bill of lading the letter requires is forged or fraudulent and that the presenter took part in the fraud. The court thought the evidence proved Prutscher (the seller) knew the bill of lading was fraudulent.

LEGAL TIP

If a letter of credit requires a bill of lading and the seller submits a forged bill of lading, payment can be stopped.

Stopping payment on irrevocable letters of credit: Fraud The buyer (account party) can stop the issuer from paying a letter of credit if the beneficiary commits fraud in the underlying contract. The *Sztejn v. J. Henry Schroder Banking Corp.* case presents this issue.

Bribing to Get Foreign Business

In 1977 Congress passed the **Foreign Corrupt Practices Act.** This Act prohibits foreign corrupt practices by domestic concerns.

Foreign corrupt practices Foreign corrupt practices are bribes. The Act prohibits bribes to foreign officials (government employees) to influence official acts. For example, a United States company violates the Act if it bribes an Iranian official to get oil drilling rights.

Businesses covered The Foreign Corrupt Practices Act does not cover all businesses. The Act only covers businesses required to register their securities (called "issuers") under the 1934 Securities Exchange Act. Covered businesses (issuers) can be corporations, partnerships, limited partnerships, business trusts, and unincorporated organizations.

SZTEJN v. J. HENRY SCHRODER BANKING CORP.

31 N.Y.S. 2d 631 (1941).

FACTS Sztejn, a United States businessman contracted to buy bristles from Transea Traders, Ltd. (Transea), located in India. Sztejn arranged for a letter of credit to pay for the goods. Transea fraudulently sent fifty crates with cowhair and other rubbish instead of the bristles agreed upon. Transea presented documents conforming to those the letter of credit required. The buyer tried to stop the issuing bank from paying Transea's drafts drawn on the letter of credit. Transea argued that the letter of credit was independent of the bristle contract. Therefore, Transea claimed the buyer could not stop payment of the letter of credit. Instead it should sue Transea for breach of contract (a costly, slow, and uncertain process).

ISSUE Can a buyer stop payment under an irrevocable letter of credit when the seller fraudulently ships nonconforming goods but presents documents (bills of lading, etc.) conforming to the letter of credit?

DECISION Yes. The letter of credit ordinarily is independent of the underlying contract. Therefore, if the seller presents documents (pieces of paper) that conform to what the letter of credit requires, a court will not enjoin payment on the letter of credit. In this case, the seller's fraud was called to the issuing bank's attention *before* presentation of the drafts and documents for payment. In such a case, the idea that the letter of credit is independent of the underlying contract should not be extended to protect a fraudulent seller.

The court noted the seller would have won if the buyer had notified the bank of the seller's fraud *after* the bank had paid the letter of credit.

LEGAL TIP

Payment under an irrevocable letter of credit can be stopped if the beneficiary (seller) fraudulently ships nonconforming goods to the buyer. The buyer must notify the issuing bank of the fraud before the bank honors (pays) the letter of credit.

People covered Persons covered by the Foreign Corrupt Practices Act include an issuer's shareholders, officers, and directors bribing to help the issuer.

Penalties Violations of the Foreign Corrupt Practices Act are federal felonies. Punishments for individual persons include 5 years in prison and/or a $10,000 fine.

Covered business issuers violating the Act can be fined up to $1 million.

Loopholes The Act does not apply to:

1. Small bribes (called grease payments) to foreign officials.
2. Bribes to private (non-governmental) foreigners.
3. Extortion payments (given by the issuer when a foreign official first asks for a bribe).

Act of State Doctrine

The **"act of state" doctrine** says that United States courts should accept foreign governments' official acts at face value. For example, if Japan gives two people a marriage license, the United States should not question its validity. This doctrine generally applies to a government's official acts within its territory.

Reason for the act of state doctrine The act of state doctrine keeps United States courts out of foreign affairs. Under the United States Constitution, the Senate and the president—not the courts—run foreign affairs.

Business example Suppose, for example, that the government of South Africa owns all the country's diamond mines. Suppose also that no company can mine diamonds unless it has a government permit. If the South African government gives deBoors Company such a permit, the United States courts cannot say the permit is illegal. This activity is South Africa's business, not the United States courts'.

What to Do if Problems Occur in an International Business Deal

Settle it yourselves There are several solutions to problems with international business deals. First, the parties can work out their problems themselves. This solution is the cheap, quick way to settle contract disputes. The parties should be reasonable and flexible to do this. They should avoid the legal system if possible. International litigation is filled with uncertainty and is expensive. Most importantly, it destroys a business' good will.

Arbitration Second, the parties can put an arbitration provision in their contract. An arbitration provision names a neutral third person to settle contract disputes. This solution is slower and costs more than the parties' settling their problem themselves. However, arbitration is faster and cheaper than suing in a court.

Lawsuits Third, the parties can sue each other in court, which is expensive and slow. It is also difficult to find a court that will handle international business disputes. The International Court of Justice in the Hague, Netherlands, is not available for private lawsuits. Only governments can sue governments there.

It is possible for one business to sue another in a country's courts, assuming that the suing business can "find" the business sued in a country where jurisdiction exists. The parties can put in the contract what country's rules will settle contract disputes.

Two Remaining Legal Problems: Expropriation and Repatriation

Expropriation **Expropriation** refers to a foreign government's seizing a United States business' assets in that country and giving less than fair value (sometimes nothing) in return. This result often occurs following a foreign political revolution. The Iranian revolution in 1979 is an example. Millions (perhaps billions) of dollars of United States' firms' assets were seized and inadequately paid for by the new Iranian government. Expropriation arises only if a United States company has a plant or property in a foreign country. Therefore, companies in the United States do not have to worry about foreign expropriation.

Repatriation **Repatriation** means bringing back to the United States income and investments which United States businesses have earned or made in foreign countries. Many foreign countries lure United States businesses into deals with them by promising high profits. Sometimes they "forget" to reveal the limits on getting those profits back to the United States. However, United States businesses should be sure to ask if a foreign country restricts taking profits back to the United States.

KEY TERMS

Letters of credit
Beneficiary account party
Bill of lading
Correspondent bank
Drawing on the credit
Foreign Corrupt Practices Act
Expropriation
"Act of state" doctrine
Repatriation

CHAPTER PROBLEMS

1. What is a bill of lading?
2. Name the parties to a letter of credit.
3. Why would someone use a letter of credit instead of a personal check in an international business deal?
4. Suppose Art, the rug dealer, gets into a legal dispute with Ali, the Turkish rug seller. Why would Ali and Art not take the case to the International Court of Justice (in the Hague, Netherlands)?
5. What is the "act of state" doctrine?
6. What effect does the independence principle have on letters of credit?
7. If a seller submits a forged bill of lading and knows it, can the buyer stop payment on the letter of credit?
8. Is it possible to stop payment on an irrevocable letter of credit when there is fraud in the underlying contract?

*9. Did Congress intend to do away with the "act of state" doctrine in private lawsuits when someone says there are violations of the Foreign Corrupt Practices Act? In one case, Clayco Petroleum Corporation (Clayco) sued Occidental Petroleum Corporation (Oxy) claiming that Oxy's agents bribed a government official of the country of Umm Al Qaywayn to get unlawfully an offshore oil concession. (An oil concession gives an oil company the exclusive right to drill for oil in part of another country and is a valuable right.) Clayco claimed that in September 1969 Sheikh Amed (the ruler) told Clayco it would get the oil concession. But in November 1969 Amed gave Oxy the concession. Clayco claimed this happened because Oxy bribed Amed. The Foreign Corrupt Practices Act prohibits corporations covered by the 1934 Securities Exchange Act (or their agents) from bribing foreign officials to get or keep business. Should Shiekh Amed's action in giving Oxy the oil concession be presumed legal as the "act of state" doctrine would require? Or does the Foreign Corrupt Practices Act allow a United States court to examine the motives of a foreign government's giving the oil concession to Oxy? *Clayco Petroleum Corp. v. Occidental Petroleum Corp.*, 712 F.2d 404 (1983).

*10. If a beneficiary of a letter of credit presents fraudulent documents to the confirming bank to get money on the letter, an account party is entitled to get a court to stop payment under the letter of credit. Consider the case in which a letter of credit covered shipments of sugar. The letter provided that drafts were to be drawn under it only when invoices (bills) and warehouse receipts showed the sugar's "net landed weight." The invoices and receipts were presented to the bank and credit was requested. The sugar was not actually weighed until four days *after* the request for credit. The buyer sued to enjoin the bank from issuing credit under the letter of credit. The seller of the sugar under the letter of credit claimed the bank had to honor the letter of credit because the seller presented the bank with the documents required. The buyer of the sugar, on the other hand, argued that there was fraud because the letter of credit required that the seller weigh the sugar and present a weight certificate to the bank before credit would be given. Since the seller presented the weight certificate to the bank four days *before* the sugar was officially weighed, the buyer claimed this action clearly was fraud justifying a court in enjoining the confirming bank from giving credit under the bill of lading. Who was correct, the buyer or seller? *Old Colony Trust Co. v. Lawyer's Title and Trust Co.*, 297 F. 152 (2nd Cir. 1924).

Appendix Contents

Appendix I

The Constitution of the United States of America

We the People of the United States, in Order to form a more perfect Union, establish Justice, insure domestic Tranquility, provide for the common defence, promote the general Welfare, and secure the Blessings of Liberty to ourselves and our Posterity, do ordain and establish this Constitution for the United States of America.

ARTICLE I

Section 1

All legislative Powers herein granted shall be vested in a Congress of the United States, which shall consist of a Senate and House of Representatives.

Section 2

The House of Representatives shall be composed of Members chosen every second Year by the People of the several States, and the Electors in each State shall have the Qualifications requisite for Electors of the most numerous Branch of the State Legislature.

No Person shall be a Representative who shall not have attained to the Age of twenty five Years, and been seven Years a Citizen of the United States, and who shall not, when elected, be an Inhabitant of that State in which he shall be chosen.

Representatives and direct Taxes shall be apportioned among the several States which may be included within this Union, according to their respective Numbers, which shall be determined by adding to the whole Number of free Persons, including those bound to Service for a Term of Years, and excluding Indians not taxed, three fifths of all other Persons. The actual Enumeration shall be made within three Years after the first Meeting of the Congress of the United States, and within every subsequent Term of ten Years, in such Manner as they shall by Law direct. The Number of Representatives shall not exceed one for every thirty Thousand, but each State shall have at Least one Representative; and until such enumeration shall be made, the State of New Hampshire shall be entitled to chuse three, Massachusetts eight, Rhode Island and Providence Plantations one, Connecticut five, New York six, New Jersey four, Pennsylvania eight, Delaware one, Maryland six, Virginia ten, North Carolina five, South Carolina five, and Georgia three.

When vacancies happen in the Representation from any State, the Executive Authority thereof shall issue Writs of Election to fill such Vacancies.

The House of Representatives shall chuse their Speaker and other Officers; and shall have the sole Power of Impeachment.

Section 3

The Senate of the United States shall be composed of two Senators from each State, chosen by the Legislature thereof, for six Years; and each Senator shall have one Vote.

Immediately after they shall be assembled in Consequence of the first Election, they shall be divided as equally as may be into three Classes. The Seats of the Senators of the first Class shall be vacated at the Expiration of the second Year, of the second Class at the Expiration of the fourth Year, and of the third Class at the Expiration of the sixth Year, so that one third may be chosen every second Year; and if Vacancies happen by Resignation, or otherwise, during the Recess of the Legislature of any State, the Executive thereof may make temporary Appointments until the next Meeting of the Legislature, which shall then fill such Vacancies.

No Person shall be a Senator who shall not have attained to the Age of thirty Years, and been nine Years a Citizen of the United States, and who shall not, when elected, be an Inhabitant of that State for which he shall be chosen.

The Vice President of the United States shall be President of the Senate, but shall have no Vote, unless they be equally divided.

The Senate shall chuse their other Officers, and also President pro tempore, in the Absence of the Vice President, or when he shall exercise the Office of President of the United States.

The Senate shall have the sole Power to try all Impeachments. When sitting for that Purpose, they shall be on Oath or Affirmation. When the President of the United States is tried the Chief Justice shall preside: And no Person shall be convicted without the Concurrence of two thirds of the Members present.

Judgment in Cases of Impeachment shall not extend further than to removal from Office, and disqualification to hold and enjoy any Office of honor, Trust or Profit under the United States: but the Party convicted shall nevertheless be liable and subject to Indictment, Trial, Judgment and Punishment, according to Law.

Section 4

The Times, Places and Manner of holding Elections for Senators and Representatives, shall be prescribed in each State by the Legislature thereof; but the Congress may at any time by Law make or alter such Regulations, except as to the Places of chusing Senators.

The Congress shall assemble at least once in every Year, and such Meeting shall be on the first Monday in December, unless they shall by Law appoint a different Day.

Section 5

Each House shall be the Judge of the Elections, Returns and Qualifications of its own Members, and a Majority of each shall constitute a Quorum to do Business; but a smaller Number may adjourn from day to day, and may be authorized to compel the Attendance of absent Members, in such Manner, and under such Penalties as each House may provide.

Each House may determine the Rules of its Proceedings, punish its Members for disorderly Behaviour, and, with the Concurrence of two thirds, expel a Member.

Each House shall keep a Journal of its Proceedings, and from time to time publish the same, excepting such Parts as may in their Judgment require Secrecy; and the Yeas and Nays of the Members of either House on any question shall, at the Desire of one fifth of those Present, be entered on the Journal.

Neither House, during the Session of Congress, shall, without the Consent of the other, adjourn for more than three days, nor to any other Place than that in which the two Houses shall be sitting.

Section 6

The Senators and Representatives shall receive a Compensation for their Services, to be ascertained by Law, and paid out of the Treasury of the United States. They shall in all Cases, except Treason, Felony and Breach of the Peace, be privileged from Arrest during their Attendance at the Session of their respective Houses, and in going to and returning from the same; and for any Speech or Debate in either House, they shall not be questioned in any other Place.

No Senator or Representative shall, during the Time for which he was elected, be appointed to any civil Office under the Authority of the United States, which shall have been created, or the Emoluments whereof shall have been increased during such time; and no Person holding any Office under the United States, shall be a Member of either House during his Continuance in Office.

Section 7

All Bills for raising Revenue shall originate in the House of Representatives; but the Senate may propose or concur with amendments as on other Bills.

Every Bill which shall have passed the House of Representatives and the Senate, shall, before it become a Law, be presented to the President of the United States; If he approve he shall sign it, but if not he shall return it, with his Objections to that House in which it shall have originated, who shall enter the Objections at large on their Journal, and proceed to reconsider it. If after such Reconsideration two thirds of that House shall agree to pass the Bill, it shall be sent, together with the Objections, to the other House, by which it shall likewise be reconsidered, and if approved by two thirds of that House, it shall become a Law. But in all such Cases the Votes of both Houses shall be determined by Yeas and Nays, and the Names of the Persons voting for and against the Bill shall be entered on the Journal of each House respectively. If any Bill shall not be returned by the President within ten Days (Sunday excepted) after it shall have been presented to him, the Same shall be a Law, in like Manner as if he had signed it, unless the Congress by their Adjournment prevent its Return, in which Case it shall not be a Law.

Every Order, Resolution, or Vote to which the Concurrence of the Senate and House of Representatives may be necessary (except on a question of Adjournment) shall be presented to the President of the United States; and before the Same shall take Effect, shall be approved by him, or being dissapproved by him, shall be repassed by two thirds of the Senate and House of Representatives, according to the Rules and Limitations prescribed in the Case of a Bill.

Section 8

The Congress shall have Power To lay and collect Taxes, Duties, Imposts and Excises, to pay the Debts and provide for the common Defence and general Welfare of the United States; but all Duties, Imposts and Excises shall be uniform throughout the United States;

To borrow Money on the credit of the United States;

To regulate Commerce with foreign Nations, and among the several States, and with the Indian Tribes;

To establish an uniform Rule of Naturalization, and uniform Laws on the subject of Bankruptcies throughout the United States;

To coin Money, regulate the Value thereof, and of foreign Coin, and fix the Standard of Weights and Measures;

To provide for the Punishment of counterfeiting the Securities and current Coin of the United States;

To establish Post Offices and post Roads;

To promote the Progress of Science and useful Arts, by securing for limited Times to Authors and Inventors the exclusive Right to their respective Writings and Discoveries;

To constitute Tribunals inferior to the supreme Court;

To define and punish Piracies and Felonies committed on the high Seas, and Offences against the Law of Nations;

To declare War, grant Letters of Marque and Reprisal, and make Rules concerning Captures on Land and Water;

To raise and support Armies, but no Appropriation of Money to that Use shall be for a longer Term than two Years;

To provide and maintain a Navy;

To make Rules for the Government and Regulation of the land and naval Forces;

To provide for calling forth the Militia to execute the Laws of the Union, suppress Insurrections and repel Invasions;

To provide for organizing, arming, and disciplining, the Militia, and for governing such Part of them as may be employed in the Service of the United States, reserving to the States respectively, the Appointment of the Officers, and the Authority of training the Militia according to the discipline prescribed by Congress;

To exercise exclusive Legislation in all Cases whatsoever, over such District (not exceeding ten Miles square) as may, be Cession of particular States, and the Acceptance of Congress, become the Seat of the Government of the United States, and to exercise like Authority over all Places purchased by the Consent of the Legislature of the State in which the Same shall be, for the Erection of Forts, Magazines, Arsenals, dock-Yards, and other needful Buildings;—And

To make all Laws which shall be necessary and proper for carrying into Execution the foregoing Powers, and all other Powers vested by this Constitution in the Government of the United States, or in any Department or Officer thereof.

Section 9

The Migration or Importation of such Persons as any of the States now existing shall think proper to admit, shall not be prohibited by the Congress prior to the Year one thousand eight hundred and eight, but a Tax or duty may be imposed on such Importation, not exceeding ten dollars for each Person.

The Privilege of the Writ of Habeas Corpus shall not be suspended, unless when in Cases of Rebellion or Invasion the public Safety may require it.

No Bill of Attainder or ex post facto Law shall be passed.

No Capitation, or other direct, Tax shall be laid, unless in Proportion to the Census or Enumeration herein before directed to be taken.

No Tax or Duty shall be laid on Articles exported from any State.

No Preference shall be given by any Regulation of Commerce or Revenue to the Ports of one State over those of another; nor shall Vessels bound to, or from, one State, be obliged to enter, clear or pay Duties in another.

No Money shall be drawn from the Treasury, but in Consequence of Appropriations made by Law; and a regular Statement and Account of the Receipts and Expenditures of all public Money shall be published from time to time.

No Title of Nobility shall be granted by the United States: And no Person holding any Office of Profit or Trust under them, shall, without the Consent of the Congress, accept of any present, Emolument, Office, or Title, of any kind whatever, from any King, Prince or foreign State.

Section 10

No State shall enter into any Treaty, Alliance, or Confederation; grant Letters of Marque and Reprisal; coin Money; emit Bills of Credit; make any Thing but gold and silver Coin a Tender in Payment of Debts; pass any Bill of Attainder, ex post facto Law, or Law impairing the Obligation of Contracts, or grant any Title of Nobility.

No State shall, without the Consent of the Congress, lay any Imposts or Duties in Imports or Exports, except what may be absolutely necessary for executing its inspection Laws: and the net Produce of all Duties and Imposts, laid by any State on Imports or Exports, shall be for the Use of the Treasury of the United States; and all such Laws shall be subject to the Revision and Controul of the Congress.

No State shall, without the Consent of Congress, lay any Duty of Tonnage, keep Troops, or Ships of War in time of Peace, enter into any Agreement or Compact with another State, or with a foreign Power, or engage in War, unless actually invaded, or in such imminent Danger as will not admit of delay.

ARTICLE II

Section 1

The executive Power shall be vested in a President of the United States of America. He shall hold his Office during the Term of four Years, and, together with the Vice President, chosen for the same Term, be elected, as follows

Each State shall appoint, in such Manner as the Legislature thereof may direct, a Number of Electors, equal to the whole Number of Senators and Representatives to which the State may be entitled in the Congress: but no Senator or Representative, or Person holding an office of Trust or Profit under the United States, shall be appointed an Elector.

The Electors shall meet in their respective States, and vote by Ballot for two Persons, of whom one at least shall not be an Inhabitant of the same State with themselves. And they shall make a List of all the Persons voted for, and of the Number of Votes for each; which List they shall sign and certify, and transmit sealed to the Seat of the Government of the United States, directed to the President of the Senate. The President of the Senate shall, in the Presence of the Senate and House of Representatives, open all the Certificates, and the Votes shall then be counted. The Person having the greatest Number of Votes shall be the President, if such Number be a Majority of the whole Number of Electors appointed; and if there be more than one who have such Majority, and have an equal Number of Votes, then the House of Representatives shall immediately chuse by Ballot one of them for President; and if no Person have a Majority, then from the five highest on the List the said House shall in like Manner chuse the President. But in chusing the President, the Votes shall be taken by States, the Representation from each State having one Vote; a quorum for this Purpose shall consist of a Member or Members from two thirds of the States, and a Majority of all the States shall be necessary to a Choice. In every Case, after the Choice of the President, the Person having the greatest Number of Votes of the Electors shall be the Vice President. But if there should remain two or more who have equal Votes, the Senate shall chuse from them by Ballot the Vice President.

The Congress may determine the Time of chusing the Electors, and the Day on which they shall give their Votes; which Day shall be the same throughout the United States.

No Person except a natural born Citizen, or a Citizen of the United States, at the time of the Adoption of this Constitution, shall be eligible to the Office of President; neither shall any Person be eligible to that Office who shall not have attained to the Age of thirty five Years, and been fourteen years a Resident within the United States.

In Case of the Removal of the President from Office, or of his Death, Resignation, or Inability to discharge the Powers and Duties of the said Office, the Same shall devolve on the Vice President, and the Congress may by Law provide for the Case of Removal, Death, Resignation or Inability, both of the President and Vice President, declaring what Officer shall then act as President, and such Officer shall act accordingly, until the Disability be removed, or a President shall be elected.

The President shall, at stated Times, receive for his Services, a Compensation, which shall neither be increased nor diminished during the Period for which he shall have been elected, and he shall not receive within that Period any other Emolument from the United States, or any of them.

Before he enter on the Execution of his Office, he shall take the following Oath or Affirmation:—"I do solemnly swear (or affirm) that I will faithfully execute the Office of President of the United States, and will to the best of my Ability, preserve, protect and defend the Constitution of the United States."

Section 2

The President shall be Commander in Chief of the Army and Navy of the United States, and of the Militia of the several States, when called into the actual Service of the United States; he may require the Opinion, in writing, of the principal Officer in each of the executive Departments, upon any Subject relating to the Duties of their respective Offices, and he shall have Power to grant Reprieves and Pardons for Offenses against the United States, except in Cases of Impeachment.

He shall have Power, by and with the Advice and Consent of the Senate, to make Treaties, provided two thirds of the Senators present concur; and he shall nominate, and by and with the Advice and Consent of the Senate, shall appoint Ambassadors, other public Ministers and Consuls, Judges of the supreme Court, and all other Officers of the United States, whose Appointments are not herein otherwise provided for, and which shall be established by Law: but the Congress may by Law vest the Appointment of such inferior Officers, as they think proper, in the President alone, in the Courts of Law, or in the Heads of Departments.

The President shall have Power to fill up all Vacancies that may happen during the Recess of the Senate, by granting Commissions which shall expire at the End of their next Session.

Section 3

He shall from time to time give to the Congress Information of the State of the Union, and recommend to their Consideration such Measures as he shall judge necessary and expedient; he may, on extraordinary Occasions, convene both Houses, or either of them, and in Case of Disagreement between them, with Respect to the Time of Adjournment, he may adjourn them to such Time as he shall think proper; he shall receive Ambassadors and other public Ministers; he shall take Care that the Laws be faithfully executed, and shall Commission all the Officers of the United States.

Section 4

The President, Vice President and all Civil Officers of the United States, shall be removed from Office on Impeachment for, and Conviction of, Treason, Bribery, or other high Crimes and Misdemeanors.

ARTICLE III

Section 1

The judicial Power of the United States, shall be vested in one supreme Court, and in such inferior Courts as the Congress may from time to time ordain and establish. The Judges, both of the supreme and inferior Courts, shall hold their Offices during good Behaviour, and shall, at stated Times, receive for their Services, a Compensation, which shall not be diminished during their Continuance in Office.

Section 2

The judicial Power shall extend to all Cases, in Law and Equity, arising under this Constitution, the Laws of the United States, and Treaties made, or which shall be made, under their Authority;—to all Cases affecting Ambassadors, other public Ministers and Consuls;—to all Cases of admiralty and maritime Jurisdiction;—to Controversies to which the United States shall be a Party;—to Controversies between two or more States;—between a State and Citizens of another State;—between Citizens of different States;—between Citizens of the same State claiming Lands under Grants of different States, and between a State, or the Citizens thereof, and foreign States, Citizens or Subjects.

In all Cases affecting Ambassadors, other public Ministers and Consuls, and those in which a State shall be Party, the supreme Court shall have original Jurisdiction. In all the other Cases before mentioned, the supreme Court shall have appellate Jurisdiction, both as to Law and Fact, with such Exceptions, and under such Regulations as the Congress shall make.

The Trial of all Crimes, except in Cases of Impeachment, shall be by Jury; and such Trial shall be held in the State where the said Crimes shall have been committed; but when not committed within any State, the Trial shall be at such Place or Places as the Congress may by Law have directed.

Section 3

Treason against the United States, shall consist only in levying War against them, or in adhering to their Enemies, giving them Aid and Comfort. No Person shall be convicted of Treason unless on the Testimony of two Witnesses to the same overt Act, or on Confession in open Court.

The Congress shall have Power to declare the Punishment of Treason, but no Attainder of Treason shall work Corruption of Blood, or Forfeiture except during the Life of the Person attainted.

ARTICLE IV

Section 1

Full Faith and Credit shall be given in each State to the public Acts, Records, and judicial Proceedings of every other State. And the Congress may by general Laws prescribe the Manner in which such Acts, Records and Proceedings shall be proved, and the Effect thereof.

Section 2

The Citizens of each State shall be entitled to all Privileges and Immunities of Citizens in the several States.

A Person charged in any State with Treason, Felony, or other Crime, who shall flee from Justice, and be found in another State, shall on Demand of the executive Authority of the State from which he fled, be delivered up, to be removed to the State having Jurisdiction of the Crime.

No Person held to Service or Labour in one State, under the Laws thereof, escaping into another, shall, in Consequence of any Law or Regulation therein, be discharged from such Service or Labour, but shall be delivered up on Claim of the Party to whom such Service or Labour may be due.

Section 3

New States may be admitted by the Congress into this Union; but no new State shall be formed or erected within the Jurisdiction of any other State; nor any State be formed by the Junction of two or more States, or Parts of States, without the Consent of the Legislatures of the States concerned as well as of the Congress.

The Congress shall have Power to dispose of and make all needful Rules and Regulations respecting the Territory or other Property belonging to the United States; and nothing in this Constitution shall be so construed as to Prejudice any Claims of the United States, or of any particular State.

Section 4

The United States shall guarantee to every State in this Union a Republican Form of Government, and shall protect each of them against Invasion; and on Application of the Legislature, or of the Executive (when the Legislature cannot be convened) against domestic Violence.

ARTICLE V

The Congress, whenever two thirds of both Houses shall deem it necessary, shall propose Amendments to this Constitution, or, on the Application of the Legislatures of two thirds of the several States, shall call a Convention for proposing Amendments, which, in either Case, shall be valid to all Intents and Purposes, as Part of this Constitution, when ratified by the Legislatures of three fourths of the several States, or by Conventions in three fourths thereof, as the one or the other Mode of Ratification may be proposed by the Congress; Provided that no Amendment which may be made prior to the Year One thousand eight hundred and eight shall in any Manner affect the first and fourth Clauses in the Ninth Section of the first Article; and that no State, without its Consent, shall be deprived of its equal Suffrage in the Senate.

ARTICLE VI

All Debts contracted and Engagements entered into, before the Adoption of this Constitution, shall be as valid against the United States under this Constitution, as under the Confederation.

This Constitution, and the Laws of the United States which shall be made in Pursuance thereof; and all Treaties made, or which shall be made, under the Authority of the United States, shall be the supreme Law of the Land; and the judges in every State shall be bound thereby, any Thing in the Constitution or Laws of any State to the Contrary notwithstanding.

The Senators and Representatives before mentioned, and the Members of the several State Legislatures, and all executive and judicial Officers, both of the United States and of the several States, shall be bound by Oath or Affirmation, to support this Constitution; but no religious Test shall ever be required as a Qualification to any Office or public Trust under the United States.

ARTICLE VII

The Ratification of the Conventions of nine States, shall be sufficient for the Establishment of this Constitution between the States so ratifying the Same.

AMENDMENT I [1791]

Congress shall make no law respecting an establishment of religion, or prohibiting the free exercise thereof; or abridging the freedom of speech, or of the press; or the right of the people peaceably to assemble, and to petition the Government for a redress of grievances.

AMENDMENT II [1791]

A well regulated Militia, being necessary to the security of a free State, the right of the people to keep and bear Arms, shall not be infringed.

AMENDMENT III [1791]

No Soldier shall, in time of peace be quartered in any house, without the consent of the Owner, nor in time of war, but in a manner to be prescribed by law.

AMENDMENT IV [1791]

The right of the people to be secure in their persons, houses, papers, and effects, against unreasonable searches and seizures, shall not be violated, and no Warrants shall issue, but upon probable cause, supported by Oath or affirmation, and particularly describing the place to be searched, and the persons or things to be seized.

AMENDMENT V [1791]

No person shall be held to answer for a capital, or otherwise infamous crime, unless on a presentment or indictment of a Grand Jury, except in cases arising in the land or naval forces, or in the Militia, when in actual service in time of War or public danger; nor shall any person be subject for the same offence to be twice put in jeopardy of life or limb; nor shall be compelled in any criminal case to be a witness against himself, nor be deprived of life, liberty, or property, without due process of law; nor shall private property be taken for public use, without just compensation.

AMENDMENT VI [1791]

In all criminal prosecutions, the accused shall enjoy the right to a speedy and public trial, by an impartial jury of the State and district wherein the crime shall have been committed, which district shall have been previously ascertained by law, and to be informed of the nature and cause of the accusation; to be confronted with the witnesses against him; to have compulsory process for obtaining Witnesses in his favor, and to have the Assistance of Counsel for his defence.

AMENDMENT VII [1791]

In Suits at common law, where the value in controversy shall exceed twenty dollars, the right of trial by jury shall be preserved, and no fact tried by a jury, shall be otherwise re-examined in any Court of the United States, than according to the rules of the common law.

AMENDMENT VIII [1791]

Excessive bail shall not be required nor excessive fines imposed, nor cruel and unusual punishments inflicted.

AMENDMENT IX [1791]

The enumeration in the Constitution, of certain rights, shall not be construed to deny or disparage others retained by the people.

AMENDMENT X [1791]

The powers not delegated to the United States by the Constitution, nor prohibited by it to the States, are reserved to the States respectively, or to the people.

AMENDMENT XI [1798]

The Judicial power of the United States shall not be construed to extend to any suit in law or equity, commenced or prosecuted against one of the United States by Citizens of another State, or by Citizens or Subjects of any Foreign State.

AMENDMENT XII [1804]

The Electors shall meet in their respective states and vote by ballot for President and Vice-President, one of whom, at least, shall not be an inhabitant of the same state with themselves; they shall name in their ballots the person voted for as President, and in distinct ballots the person voted for as Vice-President, and they shall make distinct lists of all persons voted for as President, and of all persons voted for as Vice-President, and of the number of votes for each, which lists they shall sign and certify, and transmit sealed to the seat of the government of the United States, directed to the President of the Senate;—The

President of the Senate shall, in the presence of the Senate and House of Representatives, open all the certificates and the votes shall then be counted;—The person having the greatest number of votes for President, shall be the President, if such number be a majority of the whole number of Electors appointed; and if no person have such majority, then from the persons having the highest numbers not exceeding three on the list of those voted for as President, the House of Representatives shall choose immediately, by ballot, the President. But in choosing the President, the votes shall be taken by states, the representation from each state having one vote; a quorum for this purpose shall consist of a member or members from two-thirds of the states, and a majority of all the states shall be necessary to a choice. And if the House of Representatives shall not choose a President whenever the right of choice shall devolve upon them, before the fourth day of March next following, then the Vice-President shall act as President, as in the case of the death or other constitutional disability of the President—The person having the greatest number of votes as Vice-President, shall be the Vice-President, if such number be a majority of the whole number of Electors appointed, and if no person have a majority, then from the two highest numbers on the list, the Senate shall choose the Vice-President; a quorum for the purpose shall consist of two-thirds of the whole number of Senators, and a majority of the whole number shall be necessary to a choice. But no person constitutionally ineligible to the office of President shall be eligible to that of Vice-President of the United States.

AMENDMENT XIII [1865]

Section 1

Neither slavery nor involuntary servitude, except as a punishment for crime whereof the party shall have been duly convicted, shall exist within the United States, or any place subject to their jurisdiction.

Section 2

Congress shall have power to enforce this article by appropriate legislation.

AMENDMENT XIV [1868]

Section 1

All persons born or naturalized in the United States and subject to the jurisdiction thereof, are citizens of the United States and of the State wherein they reside. No State shall make or enforce any law which shall abridge the privileges or immunities of citizens of the United States; nor shall any State deprive any person of life, liberty, or property, without due process of law; nor deny to any person within its jurisdiction the equal protection of the laws.

Section 2

Representatives shall be apportioned among the several States according to their respective numbers, counting the whole number of persons in each State, excluding Indians not taxed. But when the right to vote at any election for the choice of electors for President and Vice President of the United States, Representatives in Congress, the Executive and Judicial officers of a State, or the members of the Legislature thereof, is denied to any of the male inhabitants of such State, being twenty-one years of age, and citizens of the United States, or in any way abridged, except for participation in rebellion, or other crime, the basis of representation therein shall be reduced in the proportion which the number of such male citizens shall bear to the whole number of male citizens twenty-one years of age in such State.

Section 3

No person shall be a Senator or Representative in Congress, or elector of President and Vice President, or hold any office, civil or military, under the United States, or under any State, who, having previously taken an oath, as a member of Congress, or as an officer of the United States, or as a member of any State legislature, or as an executive or judicial officer of any State, to support the Constitution of the United States, shall have engaged in insurrection or rebellion against the same, or given aid or comfort to the enemies thereof. But Congress may by a vote of two-thirds of each House, remove such disability.

Section 4

The validity of the public debt of the United States, authorized by law, including debts incurred for payment of pensions and bounties for services in suppressing insurrection or rebellion, shall not be questioned. But neither the United States nor any State shall assume or pay any debt or obligation incurred in aid of insurrection or rebellion against the United States, or any claim for the loss or emancipation of any slave; but all such debts, obligations and claims shall be held illegal and void.

Section 5

The Congress shall have power to enforce, by appropriate legislation, the provisions of this article.

AMENDMENT XV [1870].

Section 1

The right of citizens of the United States to vote shall not be denied or abridged by the United States or by any State on account of race, color, or previous condition of servitude.

Section 2

The Congress shall have power to enforce this article by appropriate legislation.

AMENDMENT XVI [1913]

The Congress shall have power to lay and collect taxes on incomes, from whatever source derived, without apportionment among the several States, and without regard to any census or enumeration.

AMENDMENT XVII [1913]

The Senate of the United States shall be composed of two Senators from each State, elected by the people thereof, for six years; and each Senator shall have one vote. The electors in each State shall have the qualifications requisite for electors of the most numerous branch of the State legislatures.

When vacancies happen in the representation of any State in the Senate, the executive authority of such State shall issue writs of election to fill such vacancies: *Provided,* That the legislature of any State may empower the executive thereof to make temporary appointments until the people fill the vacancies by election as the legislature may direct.

This amendment shall not be so construed as to affect the election or term of any Senator chosen before it becomes valid as part of the Constitution.

AMENDMENT XVIII [1919]

Section 1

After one year from the ratification of this article the manufacture, sale, or transportation of intoxicating liquors within, the importation thereof into, or the exportation thereof from the United States and all territory subject to the jurisdiction thereof for beverage purposes is hereby prohibited.

Section 2

The Congress and the several States shall have concurrent power to enforce this article by appropriate legislation.

Section 3

This article shall be inoperative unless it shall have been ratified as an amendment to the Constitution by the legislatures of the several States, as provided in the Constitution, within seven years from the date of the submission hereof to the States by the Congress.

AMENDMENT XIX [1920]

The right of citizens of the United States to vote shall not be denied or abridged by the United States or by any State on account of sex.

Congress shall have power to enforce this article by appropriate legislation.

AMENDMENT XX [1933]

Section 1

The terms of the President and Vice President shall end at noon on the 20th day of January, and the terms of Senators and Representatives at noon on the 3d day of January, of the years in which such terms would have ended if this article had not been ratified; and the terms of their successors shall then begin.

Section 2

The Congress shall assemble at least once in every year, and such meeting shall begin at noon on the 3d day of January, unless they shall by law appoint a different day.

Section 3

If, at the time fixed for the beginning of the term of the President, the President elect shall have died, the Vice President elect shall become President. If a President shall not have been chosen before the time fixed for the beginning of his term, or if the President elect shall have failed to qualify, then the Vice President elect shall act as President until a President shall have qualified; and the Congress may by law provide for the case wherein neither a President elect nor a Vice President elect shall have qualified, declaring who shall then act as President, or the manner in which one who is to act shall be selected, and such person shall act accordingly until a President or Vice President shall have qualified.

Section 4

The Congress may by law provide for the case of the death of any of the persons from whom the House of Representatives may choose a President whenever the right of choice shall have developed upon them, and for the case of the death of any of the persons from whom the Senate may choose a Vice President whenever the right of choice shall have devolved upon them.

Section 5

Sections 1 and 2 shall take effect on the 15th day of October following the ratification of this article.

Section 6

This article shall be inoperative unless it shall have been ratified as an amendment to the Constitution by the legislatures of three-fourths of the several States within seven years from the date of its submission.

AMENDMENT XXI [1933]

Section 1

The eighteenth article of amendment to the Constitution of the United States is hereby repealed.

Section 2

The transportation or importation into any State, Territory, or possession of the United States for delivery or use therein of intoxicating liquors, in violation of the laws thereof, is hereby prohibited.

Section 3

This article shall be inoperative unless it shall have been ratified as an amendment to the Constitution by conventions in the several States, as provided in the Constitution, within seven years from the date of the submission hereof to the States by the Congress.

AMENDMENT XXII [1951]

Section 2

No person shall be elected to the office of the President more than twice, and no person who has held the office of President, or acted as President, for more than two years of a term to which some other person was elected President shall be elected to the office of the President more than once. But this Article shall not apply to any person holding the office of President when this Article was proposed by the Congress, and shall not prevent any person who may be holding the office of President, or acting as President, during the term within which this Article becomes operative from holding the office of President or acting as President during the remainder of such term.

Section 2

This article shall be inoperative unless it shall have been ratified as an amendment to the Constitution by the legislatures of three-fourths of the several States within seven years from the date of its submission to the States by the Congress.

AMENDMENT XXIII [1961]

Section 1

The District constituting the seat of Government of the United States shall appoint in such manner as the Congress may direct:

A number of electors of President and Vice President equal to the whole number of Senators and Representatives in Congress to which the District would be entitled if it were a State, but in no event more than the least populous State; they shall be in addition to those appointed by the States, but they shall be considered, for the purposes of the election of President and Vice President, to be electors appointed by a State; and they shall meet in the District and perform such duties as provided by the twelfth article of amendment.

Section 2

The Congress shall have power to enforce this article by appropriate legislation.

AMENDMENT XXIV [1964]

Section 1

The right of citizens of the United States to vote in any primary or other election for President or Vice President, for electors for President or Vice President, or for Senator or Representative in Congress, shall not be denied or abridged by the United States or any State by reason of failure to pay any poll tax or other tax.

Section 2

The Congress shall have power to enforce this article by appropriate legislation.

AMENDMENT XXV [1967]

Section 1

In case of the removal of the President from office or of his death or resignation, the Vice President shall become President.

Section 2

Whenever there is a vacancy in the office of the Vice President, the President shall nominate a Vice President who shall take office upon confirmation by a majority vote of both Houses of Congress.

Section 3

Whenever the President transmits to the President pro tempore of the Senate and the Speaker of the House of Representatives his written declaration that he is unable to discharge the powers and duties of his office, and until he transmits to them a written declaration to the contrary, such powers and duties shall be discharged by the Vice President as Acting President.

Section 4

Whenever the Vice President and a majority of either the principal officers of the executive departments or of such other body as Congress may by law provide, transmit to the President pro tempore of the Senate and the Speaker of the House of

Representatives their written declaration that the President is unable to discharge the powers and duties of his office, the Vice President shall immediately assume the powers and duties of the office as Acting President.

Thereafter, when the President transmits to the President pro tempore of the Senate and the Speaker of the House of Representatives his written declaration that no inability exists, he shall resume the powers and duties of his office unless the Vice President and a majority of either the principal officers of the executive department or of such other body as Congress may by law provide, transmit within four days to the President pro tempore of the Senate and the Speaker of the House of Representatives their written declaration that the President is unable to discharge the powers and duties of his office. Thereupon Congress shall decide the issue, assembling within forty-eight hours for that purpose if not in session. If the Congress, within twenty-one days after receipt of the latter written declaration, or, if Congress is not in session, within twenty-one days after Congress is required to assemble, determines by two-thirds vote of both Houses that the President is unable to discharge the powers and duties of his office, the Vice President shall continue to discharge the same as Acting President; otherwise, the President shall resume the powers and duties of his office.

AMENDMENT XXVI [1971]

Section 1

The right of citizens of the United States, who are eighteen years of age or older, to vote shall not be denied or abridged by the United States or by any State on account of age.

Section 2

The Congress shall have power to enforce this article by appropriate legislation.

Appendix II

Administrative Procedure Act

(Excerpts include Freedom of Information Act, Federal Privacy Act of 1974, and Open Meeting Law.)

Section 551. DEFINITIONS

For the purpose of this subchapter—

(1) "agency" means each authority of the Government of the United States, whether or not it is within or subject to review by another agency, but does not include—

(A) the Congress;

(B) the courts of the United States;

(C) the governments of the territories or possessions of the United States;

(D) the government of the District of Columbia;

or except as to the requirements of section 552 of this title—

(E) agencies composed of representatives of the parties or of representatives of organizations of the parties to the disputes determined by them;

(F) courts martial and military commissions;

(G) military authority exercised in the field in time of war or in occupied territory; or

(H) functions conferred by sections 1738, 1739, 1743, and 1744 of title 12; chapter 2 of title 41; or sections 1622, 1884, 1891–1902, and former section 1641(b)(2), of title 50, appendix;

(2) "person" includes an individual, partnership, corporation, association, or public or private organization other than an agency;

(3) "party" includes a person or agency named or admitted as a party, or properly seeking and entitled as of right to be admitted as a party, in an agency proceeding, and a person or agency admitted by an agency as a party for limited purposes;

(4) "rule" means the whole or a part of an agency statement of general or particular applicability and future effect designed to implement, interpret, or prescribe law or policy or describing the organization, procedure, or practice requirements of an agency and includes the approval or prescription for the future of rates, wages, corporate or financial structures or reorganizations thereof, prices, facilities, appliances, services or allowances therefor or of valuations, costs, or accounting, or practices bearing on any of the foregoing;

(5) "rule making" means agency process for formulating, amending, or repealing a rule;

(6) "order" means the whole or a part of a final disposition, whether affirmative, negative, injunctive, or declaratory in form, of an agency in a matter other than rule making but including licensing;

(7) "adjudication" means agency process for the formulation of an order;

(8) "license" includes the whole or a part of an agency permit, certificate, approval, registration, charter, membership, statutory exemption or other form of permission;

(9) "licensing" includes agency process respecting the grant, renewal, denial revocation, suspension, annulment, withdrawal, limitation, amendment, modification, or conditioning of a license;

(10) "sanction" includes the whole or a part of an agency—

(A) prohibition, requirement, limitation, or other condition affecting the freedom of a person;

(B) withholding of relief;

(C) imposition of penalty or fine;

(D) destruction, taking, seizure, or withholding of property;

(E) assessment of damages, reimbursement, restitution, compensation, costs, charges, or fees;

(F) requirement, revocation, or suspension of a license; or

(G) taking other compulsory or restrictive action;

(11) "relief" includes the whole or a part of an agency—

(A) grant of money, assistance, license, authority, exemption, exception, privilege, or remedy;

(B) recognition of a claim, right, immunity, privilege, exemption, or exception; or

(C) taking of other action on the application or petition of, and beneficial to, a person;

(12) "agency proceeding" means an agency process as defined by paragraphs (5), (7), and (9) of this section;

(13) "agency action" includes the whole or a part of an agency rule, order, license, sanction, relief, or the equivalent or denial thereof, or failure to act; and

(14) "ex parte communication" means an oral or written communication not on the public record with respect to which reasonable prior notice to all parties is not given, but it shall not include requests for status reports on any matter or proceeding covered by this subchapter.

Section 552. PUBLIC INFORMATION; AGENCY RULES, OPINIONS, ORDERS, RECORDS, AND PROCEEDINGS (THE FREEDOM OF INFORMATION ACT)

(a) Each agency shall make available to the public information as follows:

(1) Each agency shall separately state and currently publish in the *Federal Register* for the guidance of the public—

(A) descriptions of its central and field organization and the established places at which, the employees (and in the case of a uniformed service, the members) from whom, and the methods whereby, the public may obtain information, make submittals or requests, or obtain decisions;

(B) statements of the general course and method by which its functions are channeled and determined, including the nature and requirements of all formal and informal procedures available;

(C) rules of procedure, descriptions of forms available or the places at which forms may be obtained, and instructions as to the scope and contents of all papers, reports, or examinations;

(D) substantive rules of general applicability adopted as authorized by law, and statements of general policy or interpretations of general applicability formulated and adopted by the agency; and

(E) each amendment, revision, or repeal of the foregoing.

Except to the extent that a person has actual and timely notice of the terms thereof, a person may not in any manner be required to resort to, or be adversely affected by, a matter required to be published in the *Federal Register* and not so published. For the purpose of this paragraph, matter reasonably available to the class of persons affected thereby is deemed published in the *Federal Register* when incorporated by reference therein with the approval of the Director of the *Federal Register*.

(2) Each agency, in accordance with published rules, shall make available for public inspection and copying—

(A) final opinions, including concurring and dissenting opinions, as well as orders made in the adjudication of cases;

(B) those statements of policy and interpretations which have been adopted by the agency and are not published in the *Federal Register;* and

(C) administrative staff manuals and instructions to staff that affect a member of the public;

unless the materials are promptly published and copies offered for sale. To the extent required to prevent a clearly unwarranted invasion of personal privacy, an agency may delete identifying details when it makes available or publishes an opinion, statement of policy, interpretation, or staff manual or instruction. However, in each case the justification for the deletion shall be explained fully in writing. Each agency shall also maintain and make available for public inspection and copying current indexes providing identifying information for the public as to any matter issued, adopted, or promulgated after July 4, 1967, and required by this paragraph to be made available or published. Each agency shall promptly publish, quarterly or more frequently, and distribute (by sale or otherwise) copies of each index or supplements thereto unless it determines by order published in the *Federal Register* that the publication would be unnecessary and impracticable, in which case the agency shall nonetheless provide copies of such index on request at a cost not to exceed the direct cost of duplication. A final order, opinion, statement of policy, interpretation, or staff manual or instruction that affects a member of the public may be relied on, used, or cited as precedent by an agency against a party other than an agency only if—

(i) it has been indexed and either made available or published as provided by this paragraph; or

(ii) the party has actual and timely notice of the terms thereof.

(3) Except with respect to the records made available under paragraphs (1) and (2) of this subsection, each agency, upon any request for records which (A) reasonably describes such records and (B) is made in accordance with published rules stating the time, place, fees (if any), and procedures to be followed, shall make the records promptly available to any person.

(4)(A) In order to carry out the provisions of this section, each agency shall promulgate regulations, pursuant to notice and receipt of public comment, specifying a uniform schedule of fees applicable to all constituent units of such agency. Such fees shall be limited to reasonable standard charges for document search and duplication and provide for recovery of only the direct costs of such search and duplication. Documents shall be furnished without charge or at a reduced charge where the agency determines that waiver or reduction of the fee is in the public interest because furnishing the information can be considered as primarily benefiting the general public.

(B) On complaint, the district court of the United States in the district in which the complainant resides, or has his principal place of business, or in which the agency records are situated, or in the District of Columbia, has jurisdiction to enjoin the agency from withholding agency records and to order the production of any agency records improperly withheld from the complainant. In such a case the court shall determine the matter de novo, and may examine the contents of such agency records in camera to determine whether such records or any part thereof shall be withheld under any of the exemptions set forth in subsection (b) of this section, and the burden is on the agency to sustain its action.

(C) Notwithstanding any other provision of law, the defendant shall serve an answer or otherwise plead to any complaint made under this subsection within thirty days after service upon the defendant of the pleading in which such complaint is made, unless the court otherwise directs for good cause shown.

(D) Except as to cases the court considers of greater importance, proceedings before the district court, as authorized by this subsection, and appeals therefrom, take precedence on the docket over all cases and shall be assigned for hearing and trial or for argument at the earliest practicable date and expedited in every way.

(E) The court may assess against the United States reasonable attorney fees and other litigation costs reasonably incurred in any case under this section in which the complainant has substantially prevailed.

(F) Whenever the court orders the production of any agency records improperly withheld from the complainant and assesses against the United States reasonable attorney fees and other litigation costs, and the court additionally issues a written finding that the circumstances surrounding the withholding raise questions whether agency personnel acted arbitrarily or capriciously with respect to the withholding, the Special Counsel shall promptly initiate a proceeding to determine whether disciplinary action is warranted against the officer or employee who was primarily responsible for the withholding. The Special Counsel, after investigation and consideration of the evidence submitted, shall submit his findings and recommendations to the administrative authority of the agency concerned and shall send copies of the findings and recommendations to the officer or employee or his representative. The administrative authority shall take the corrective action that the Special Counsel recommends.

(G) In the event of noncompliance with the order of the court, the district court may punish for contempt the responsible employee, and in the case of a uniformed service, the responsible member.

(5) Each agency having more than one member shall maintain and make available for public inspection a record of the final votes of each member in every agency proceeding.

(6)(A) Each agency, upon any request for records made under paragraph (1), (2), or (3) of this subsection, shall—

(i) determine within ten days (excepting Saturdays, Sundays, and legal public holidays) after the receipt of any such request whether to comply with such request and shall immediately notify the person making such request of such determination and the reasons therefor, and of the right of such person to appeal to the head of the agency any adverse determination; and

(ii) make a determination with respect to any appeal within twenty days (excepting Saturdays, Sundays, and legal public holidays) after the receipt of such appeal. If on appeal the denial of the request for records is in whole or in part upheld the agency shall notify the person making such request of the provisions for judicial review of that determination under paragraph (4) of this subsection.

(B) In unusual circumstances as specified in this subparagraph, the time limits prescribed in either clause (i) or clause (ii) of subparagraph (A) may be extended by written notice to the person making such request setting forth the reasons for such extension and the date on which a determination is expected to be dispatched. No such notice shall specify a date that would result in an extension for more than ten working days. As used in this subparagraph, "unusual circumstances" means, but only to the extent reasonably necessary to the proper processing of the particular request—

(i) the need to search for and collect the requested records from field facilities or other establishments that are separate from the office processing the request;

(ii) the need to search for, collect, and appropriately examine a voluminous amount of separate and distinct records which are demanded in a single request; or

(iii) the need for consultation, which shall be conducted with all practicable speed, with another agency having a substantial interest in the determination of the request or among two or more components of the agency having substantial subject-matter interest therein.

(C) Any person making a request to any agency for records under paragraph (1), (2) or (3) of this subsection shall be deemed to have exhausted his administrative remedies with respect to such request if the agency fails to comply with the applicable time limit provisions of this paragraph. If the Government can show exceptional circumstances exist and that the agency is exercising due diligence in responding to the request, the court may retain jurisdiction and allow the agency additional time to complete its review of the records. Upon any determination by an agency to comply with a request for records, the records shall be made promptly available to such person making such request. Any notification of denial of any request for records under this subsection shall set forth the names and titles or positions of each person responsible for the denial of such request.

(B) This section does not apply to matters that are—

(1)(a) specifically authorized under criteria established by an Executive order to be kept secret in the interest of national defense or foreign policy and (B) are in fact properly classified pursuant to such Executive order;

(2) related solely to the internal personnel rules and practices of an agency;

(3) specifically exempted from disclosure by statute (other than section 552b of this title), provided that such statute (A) requires that the matters be withheld from the public in such a manner as to leave no discretion on the issue, or (B) establishes particular criteria for withholding or refers to particular types of matters to be withheld;

(4) trade secrets and commercial or financial information obtained from a person and privileged or confidential;

(5) inter-agency or intra-agency memorandums or letters which would not be available by law to a party other than an agency in litigation with the agency;

(6) personnel and medical files and similar files the disclosure of which would constitute a clearly unwarranted invasion of personal privacy;

(7) investigatory records compiled for law enforcement purposes, but only to the extent that the production of such records would (a) interfere with enforcement proceedings, (b) deprive a person of a right to a fair trial or an impartial adjudication, (c) constitute an unwarranted invasion of personal privacy, (d) disclose the identity of a confidential source and, in the case of a record compiled by a criminal law enforcement authority in the course of a criminal investigation, or by an agency conducting a lawful national security intelligence investigation, confidential information furnished only by the confidential source, (e) disclose investigative techniques and procedures, or (f) endanger the life or physical safety of law enforcement personnel;

(8) contained in or related to examination, operating, or condition reports prepared by, on behalf of, or for the use of an agency responsible for the regulation or supervision of financial institutions; or

(9) geological and geophysical information and data, including maps, concerning wells.

Any reasonably segregable portion of a record shall be provided to any person requesting such record after deletion of the portions which are exempt under this subsection.

(c) This section does not authorize withholding of information or limit the availability of records to the public, except as specifically stated in this section. This section is not authority to withhold information from Congress.

(d) On or before March 1 of each calendar year, each agency shall submit a report covering the preceding calendar year to the Speaker of the House of Representatives and President of the Senate for referral to the appropriate committees of the Congress. The report shall include—

(1) the number of determinations made by such agency not to comply with requests for records made to such agency under subsection (a) and the reasons for each such determination;

(2) the number of appeals made by persons under subsection (a)(6), the result of such appeals, and the reason for the action upon each appeal that results in a denial of information;

(3) the names and titles or positions of each person responsible for the denial of records requested under this section, and the number of instances of participation for each;

(4) the results of each proceeding conducted pursuant to subsection (a)(4)(F), including a report of the disciplinary action taken against the officer or employee who was primarily responsible for improperly withholding records or an explanation of why disciplinary action was not taken;

(5) a copy of every rule made by such agency regarding this section;

(6) a copy of the fee schedule and the total amount of fees collected by the agency for making records available under this section; and

(7) such other information as indicates efforts to administer fully this section.

The Attorney General shall submit an annual report on or before March 1 of each calendar year which shall include for the prior calendar year a listing of the number of cases arising under this section, the exemption involved in each case, the disposition of such case, and the cost, fees, and penalties assessed under subsections (A)(4)(e), (f), and (g). Such report shall also include a description of the efforts undertaken by the Department of Justice to encourage agency compliance with this section.

(e) For purposes of this section, the term "agency" as defined in section 551(1) of this title includes any executive department, military department, Government corporation, Government controlled corporation, or other establishment in the executive branch of the Government (including the Executive Office of the President), or any independent regulatory agency.

Section 552b. OPEN MEETINGS ("SUNSHINE" LAW)

(a) For purpose of this section—

(1) the term "agency" means any agency, as defined in section 552(e) of this title, headed by a collegial body composed of two or more individual members, a majority of whom are appointed to such position by the President with the advice and consent of the Senate, and any subdivision thereof authorized to act on behalf of the agency;

(2) the term "meeting" means the deliberations of at least the number of individual agency members required to take action on behalf of the agency where such deliberations determine or result in the joint conduct or disposition of official agency business, but does not include deliberations required or permitted by subsection (d) or (e); and

(3) the term "member" means an individual who belongs to a collegial body heading an agency.

(b) Members shall not jointly conduct or dispose of agency business other than in accordance with this section. Except as provided in subsection (c), every portion of every meeting of an agency shall be open to public observation.

(c) Except in a case where the agency finds that the public interest requires otherwise, the second sentence of subsection (b) shall not apply to any portion of an agency meeting, and the requirements of subsections (d) and (e) shall not apply to any information pertaining to such meeting otherwise required by this section to be disclosed to the public, where the agency properly determines that such portion or portions of its meeting or the disclosure of such information is likely to—

(1) disclose matters that are (A) specifically authorized under criteria established by an Executive order to be kept secret in the interests of national defense or foreign policy and (B) in fact properly classified pursuant to such Executive order;

(2) relate solely to the internal personnel rules and practices of an agency;

(3) disclose matters specifically exempted from disclosure by statute (other than section 552 of this title), provided that such statute (A) requires that the matters be withheld from the public in such a manner as to leave no discretion on the issue, or (B) establishes particular criteria for withholding or refers to particular types of matters to be withheld;

(4) disclose trade secrets and commercial or financial information obtained from a person and privileged or confidential;

(5) involve accusing any person of a crime, or formally censuring any person;

(6) disclose information of a personal nature where disclosure would constitute a clearly unwarranted invasion of personal privacy;

(7) disclose investigatory records compiled for law enforcement purposes, or information which if written would be contained in such records, but only to the extent that the production of such records or information would (A) interfere with enforcement proceedings, (B) deprive a person of a right to a fair trial or an impartial adjudication, (C) constitute an unwarranted invasion of personal privacy, (D) disclose the identity of a confidential source and, in the case of a record compiled by a criminal law enforcement authority in the course of a criminal investigation, or by an agency conducting a lawful national security intelligence investigation, confidential information furnished only by the confidential source, (E) disclose investigative techniques and procedures, or (F) endanger the life or physical safety of law enforcement personnel;

(8) disclose information contained in or related to examination, operating, or condition reports prepared by, on behalf of, or for the use of an agency responsible for the regulation or supervision of financial institutions;

(9) disclose information the premature disclosure of which would—

(A) in the case of an agency which regulates currencies, securities, commodities, or financial institutions, be likely to (i) lead to significant financial speculation in currencies, securities, or commodities, or (ii) significantly endanger the stability of any financial institution; or

(B) in the case of any agency, be likely to significantly frustrate implementation of a proposed agency action.

except that subparagraph (B) shall not apply in any instance where the agency has already disclosed to the public the content or nature of its proposed action, or where the agency is required by law to make such disclosure on its own initiative prior to taking final agency action on such proposal; or

(10) specifically concern the agency's issuance of a subpena, or the agency's participation in a civil action or proceeding, an action in a foreign court or international tribunal, or an arbitration, or the initiation, conduct, or disposition by the agency of a particular case of formal agency adjudication pursuant to the procedures in section 554 of this title or otherwise involving a determination on the record after opportunity for a hearing.

(d)(1) Action under subsection (c) shall be taken only when a majority of the entire membership of the agency (as defined in subsection (a)(1)) votes to take such action. A separate vote of the agency members shall be taken with respect to each agency meeting a portion or portions of which are proposed to be closed to the public pursuant to subsection (c), or with respect to any information which is proposed to be withheld under subsection (c). A single vote may be taken with respect to a series of meetings, a portion or portions of which are proposed to be closed to the public, or with respect to any information concerning such series of meetings, so long as each meeting in such series involves the same particular matters and is scheduled to be held no more than thirty days after the initial meeting in such series. The vote of each agency member participating in such vote shall be recorded an no proxies shall be allowed.

(2) Whenever any person whose interests may be directly affected by a portion of a meeting requests that the agency close such portion to the public for any of the reasons referred to in paragraph (5), (6), or (7) of subsection (c), the agency, upon request of any one of its members, shall vote by recorded vote whether to close such meeting.

(3) Within one day of any vote taken pursuant to paragraph (1) or (2), the agency shall make publicly available a written copy of such vote reflecting the vote of each

member on the question. If a portion of a meeting is to be closed to the public, the agency shall, within one day of the vote taken pursuant to paragraph (1) or (2) of this subsection, make publicly available a full written explanation of its action closing the portion together with a list of all persons expected to attend the meeting and their affiliation.

(4) Any agency, a majority of whose meetings may properly be closed to the public pursuant to paragraph (4), (8), (9)(a), or (10) of subsection (c), or any combination thereof, may provide by regulation for the closing of such meetings or portions thereof in the event that a majority of the members of the agency votes by recorded vote at the beginning of such meeting, or portion thereof, to close the exempt portion or portions of the meeting, and a copy of such vote, reflecting the vote of each member on the question, is made available to the public. The provisions of paragraphs (1), (2), and (3) of this subsection and subsection (e) shall not apply to any portion of a meeting to which such regulations apply: *Provided,* That the agency shall, except to the extent that such information is exempt from disclosure under the provisions of subsection (c), provide the public with public announcement of the time, place, and subject matter of the meeting and of each portion thereof at the earliest practicable time.

(e)(1) In the case of each meeting, the agency shall make public announcement, at least one week before the meeting, of the time, place, and subject matter of the meeting, whether it is to be open or closed to the public, and the name and phone number of the official designated by the agency to respond to requests for information about the meeting. Such announcement shall be made unless a majority of the members of the agency determines by a recorded vote that agency business requires that such meeting be called at an earlier date, in which case the agency shall make public announcement of the time, place, and subject matter of such meeting, and whether open or closed to the public, at the earliest practicable time.

(2) The time or place of a meeting may be changed following the public announcement required by paragraph (1) only if the agency publicly announces such change at the earliest practicable time. The subject matter of a meeting, or the determination of the agency to open or close a meeting, or portion of a meeting, to the public, may be changed following the public announcement required by this subsection only if (A) a majority of the entire membership of the agency determines by a recorded vote that agency business so requires and that no earlier announcement of the change was possible, and (B) the agency publicly announces such change and the vote of each member upon such change at the earliest practicable time.

(3) Immediately following each public announcement required by this subsection, notice of the time, place, and subject matter of a meeting, whether the meeting is open or closed, any change in one of the preceding, and the name and phone number of the official designated by the agency to respond to requests for information about the meeting, shall also be submitted for publication in the *Federal Register.*

(f)(1) For every meeting closed pursuant to paragraphs (1) through (10) of subsection (c), the General Counsel or chief legal officer of the agency shall publicly certify that, in his or her opinion, the meeting may be closed to the public and shall state each relevant exemptive provision. A copy of such certification, together with a statement from the presiding officer of the meeting setting forth the time and place of the meeting, and the persons present, shall be retained by the agency. The agency shall maintain a complete transcript or electronic recording adequate to record fully the proceedings of each meeting, or portion of a meeting, closed to the public, except that in the case of a meeting, or portion of a meeting, closed to the public pursuant to paragraph (8), (9)(a), or (10) of subsection (c), the agency shall maintain either such a transcript or recording, or a set of minutes. Such minutes shall fully and clearly describe all matters discussed and shall provide a full and accurate summary of any actions taken, and the reasons therefor, including a description of each of the views expressed on any item and the record of any rollcall vote (reflecting the vote of each member on the question). All documents considered in connection with any action shall be identified in such minutes.

(2) The agency shall make promptly available to the public, in a place easily accessible to the public, the transcript, electronic recording, or minutes (as required by paragraph (1)) of the discussion of any item on the agenda, or of any item of the testimony of any witness received at the meeting, except for such item or items of such discussion or testimony as the agency determines to contain information which may be withheld under subsection (c). Copies of such transcript, or minutes, or a transcription of such recording disclosing the identity of each speaker, shall be furnished to any person at the actual cost of duplication or transcription. The agency shall maintain a complete verbatim copy of the transcript, a complete copy of the minutes, or a complete electronic recording of each meeting, or portion of a meeting, closed to the public, for a period of at least two years after such meeting, or until one year after the conclusion of any agency proceeding with respect to which the meeting or portion was held, whichever occurs later.

Section 553. RULE MAKING

(a) This section applies, according to the provisions thereof, except to the extent that there is involved—

(1) a military or foreign affairs function of the United States; or

(2) a matter relating to agency management or personnel or to public property, loans, grants, benefits, or contracts.

(B) General notice of proposed rule making shall be published in the *Federal Register,* unless persons subject thereto are named and either personally served or otherwise have actual notice thereof in accordance with law. The notice shall include—

(1) a statement of the time, place, and nature of public rule making proceedings;

(2) reference to the legal authority under which the rule is proposed; and

(3) either the terms or substance of the proposed rule or a description of the subjects and issues involved.

Except when notice or hearing is required by statute, this subsection does not apply—

(A) to interpretative rules, general statements of policy, or rules of agency organization, procedure, or practice; or

(B) when the agency for good cause finds (and incorporates the finding and a brief statement of reasons therefor in the rules issued) that notice and public procedure thereon are impracticable, unnecessary, or contrary to the public interest.

(c) After notice required by this section, the agency shall give interested persons an opportunity to participate in the rule making through submission of written data, views, or arguments with or without opportunity for oral presentation. After consideration of the relevant matter presented, the agency shall incorporate in the rules adopted a concise general statement of their basis and purpose. When rules are required by statute to be made on the record after opportunity for an agency hearing, sections 556 and 557 of this title apply instead of this subsection.

(d) The required publication or service of a substantive rule shall be made not less than 30 days before its effective date, except—

(1) a substantive rule which grants or recognizes an exemption or relieves a restriction;

(2) interpretative rules and statements of policy; or

(3) as otherwise provided by the agency for good cause found and published with the rule.

(e) Each agency shall give an interest person the right to petition for the issuance, amendment, or repeal of a rule.

Section 554. ADJUDICATIONS

(a) This section applies, according to the provisions thereof, in every case of adjudication required by statute to be determined on the record after opportunity for an agency hearing, except to the extent that there is involved—

(1) a matter subject to a subsequent trial of the law and the facts de novo in a court;

(2) the selection or tenure of an employee, except an administrative law judge appointed under section 3105 of this title;

(3) proceedings in which decisions rest solely on inspections, tests, or elections;

(4) the conduct of military or foreign affairs functions;

(5) cases in which an agency is acting as an agent for a court; or

(6) the certification of worker representatives.

(b) Persons entitled to notice of an agency hearing shall be timely informed of—

(1) the time, place, and nature of the hearing;

(2) the legal authority and jurisdiction under which the hearing is to be held; and

(3) the matters of fact and law asserted.

When private persons are the moving parties, other parties to the proceeding shall give prompt notice of issues controverted in fact or law; and in other instances agencies may by rule require responsive pleading. In fixing the time and place for hearings, due regard shall be had for the convenience and necessity of the parties or their representatives.

(c) The agency shall give all interested parties opportunity for—

(1) the submission and consideration of facts, arguments, offers of settlement, or proposals of adjustment when time, the nature of the proceeding, and the public interest permit; and

(2) to the extent that the parties are unable so to determine a controversy by consent, hearing and decision on notice and in accordance with sections 556 and 557 of this title.

(d) The employee who presides at the reception of evidence pursuant to section 556 of this title shall make the recommended decision or initial decision required by section 557 of this title, unless he becomes unavailable to the agency. Except to the extent required for the disposition of ex parte matters as authorized by law, such an employee may not—

(1) consult a person or party on a fact in issue, unless on notice and opportunity for all parties to participate; or

(2) be responsible to or subject to the supervision or direction of an employee or agent engaged in the performance of investigative or prosecuting functions for an agency.

An employee or agent engaged in the performance of investigative or prosecuting functions for an agency in a case may not, in that or a factually related case, participate or advise in the decision, recommended decision, or agency review pursuant to section 557 of this title, except as witness or counsel in public proceedings. This subsection does not apply—

(A) in determining applications for initial licenses;

(B) to proceedings involving the validity or application of rates, facilities, or practices of public utilities or carriers; or

(C) to the agency or a member or members of the body comprising the agency.

(e) The agency, with like effect as in the case of other orders, and in its sound discretion, may issue a declaratory order to terminate a controversy or remove uncertainty.

Section 556. HEARINGS; PRESIDING EMPLOYEES; POWERS AND DUTIES; BURDEN OF PROOF; EVIDENCE; RECORD AS BASIS OF DECISION

(a) This section applies, according the provisions thereof, to hearings required by section 553 or 554 of this title to be conducted in accordance with this section.

(b) There shall preside at the taking of evidence—

(1) the agency;

(2) one or more members of the body which comprises the agency; or

(3) one or more administrative law judges appointed under section 3105 of this title.

This subchapter does not supersede the conduct of specified classes of proceedings, in whole or in part, by or before boards or other employees specially provided for by or designated under statute. The functions of presiding employees and of employees participating in decisions in accordance with section 557 of this title shall be conducted in an impartial manner. A presiding or participating employee may at any time disqualify himself. On the filing in good faith of a timely and sufficient affidavit of personal bias or other disqualification of a presiding or participating employee, the agency shall determine the matter as a part of the record and decision in the case.

(c) Subject to published rules of the agency and within its powers, employees presiding at hearings may—

(1) administer oaths and affirmations;

(2) issue subpenas authorized by law;

(3) rule on offers of proof and receive relevant evidence;

(4) take depositions or have depositions taken when the ends of justice would be served;

(5) regulate the course of the hearing;

(6) hold conferences for the settlement or simplification of the issues by consent of the parties;

(7) dispose of procedural requests or similar matters;

(8) make or recommend decisions in accordance with section 557 of this title; and

(9) take other action authorized by agency rule consistent with this subchapter.

(d) Except as otherwise provided by statute, the proponent of a rule or order has the burden of proof. Any oral or documentary evidence may be received, but the agency as a matter of policy shall provide for the exclusion of irrelevant, immaterial, or unduly repetitious evidence. A sanction may not be imposed or rule or order issued except on consideration of the whole record or those parts thereof cited by a party and supported by and in accordance with the reliable, probative, and substantial evidence. The agency may, to the extent consistent with the interests of justice and the policy of the underlying statutes administered by the agency, consider a violation of section 557(d) of this title sufficient grounds for a decision adverse to a party who has knowingly committed such violation or knowingly caused such violation to occur. A party is entitled to present his case or defense by oral or documentary evidence, to submit rebuttal evidence, and to conduct such cross-examination as may be required for a full and true disclosure of the facts. In rule making or determining claims for money or benefits or applications for initial licenses an agency may, when a party will not be prejudiced thereby, adopt procedures for the submission of all or part of the evidence in written form.

(E) The transcript of testimony and exhibits, together with all papers and requests filed in the proceeding, constitutes the exclusive record for decision in accordance with section 557 of this title and, on payment of lawfully prescribed costs, shall be made available to the parties. When an agency decision rests on official notice of a material fact not appearing in the evidence in the record, a party is entitled, on timely request, to an opportunity to show the contrary.

Section 601. DEFINITIONS

For purposes of this chapter—

(1) the term "agency" means an agency as defined in section 551(1) of this title;

(2) the term "rule" means any rule for which the agency publishes a general notice of proposed rulemaking pursuant to section 553(b) of this title, or any other law, including any rule of general applicability governing Federal grants to State and local governments for which the agency provides an opportunity for notice and public comment, except that the term "rule" does not include a rule of particular applicability relating to rates, wages, corporate or financial structures or reorganizations thereof, prices, facilities, appliances, services, or allowances therefor or to valuations, costs or accounting, or practices relating to such rates, wages, structures, prices, appliances, services, or allowances;

(3) the term "small business" has the same meaning as the term "small business concern" under section 3 of the Small Business Act, unless an agency, after consultation with the Office of Advocacy of the Small Business Administration and after opportunity for public comment, establishes one or more definitions of such term which are appropriate to the activities of the agency and publishes such definition(s) in the *Federal Register*;

(4) the term "small organization" means any not-for-profit enterprise which is independently owned and operated and is not dominant in its field, unless an agency establishes, after opportunity for public comment, one or more definitions of such term which are appropriate to the activities of the agency and publishes such definition(s) in the *Federal Register*;

(5) the term "small governmental jurisdiction" means governments of cities, counties, towns, townships, villages, school districts, or special districts, with a population of less than fifty thousand, unless an agency establishes, after opportunity for public comment, one or more definitions of such term which are appropriate to the activities of the agency and which are based on such factors as location in rural or sparsely populated areas or limited revenues due to the population of such jurisdiction, and publishes such definition(s) in the *Federal Register*; and
(6) the term "small entity" shall have the same meaning as the terms "small business," "small organization" and "small governmental jurisdiction" defined in paragraphs (3), (4) and (5) of this section.

Section 602. **REGULATORY AGENDA**

(a) During the months of October and April of each year, each agency shall publish in the *Federal Register* a regulatory flexibility agenda which shall contain—

(1) a brief description of the subject area of any rule which the agency expects to propose or promulgate which is likely to have a significant economic impact on a substantial number of small entities;
(2) a summary of the nature of any such rule under consideration for each subject area listed in the agenda pursuant to paragraph (1), the objectives and legal basis for the issuance of the rule, and an approximate schedule for completing action on any rule for which the agency has issued a general notice of proposed rulemaking, and
(3) the name and telephone number of an agency official knowledgeable concerning the items listed in paragraph (1).

(b) Each regulatory flexibility agenda shall be transmitted to the Chief Counsel for Advocacy of the Small Business Administration for comment, if any.
(c) Each agency shall endeavor to provide notice of each regulatory flexibility agenda to small entities or their representatives through direct notification or publication of the agenda in publications likely to be obtained by such small entities and shall invite comments upon each subject area on the agenda.
(d) Nothing in this section precludes an agency from considering or acting on any matter not included in a regulatory flexibility agenda, or requires an agency to consider or act on any matter listed in such agenda.

Section 603. **INITIAL REGULATORY FLEXIBILITY ANALYSIS**

(a) Whenever an agency is required by section 553 of this title, or any other law, to publish general notice of proposed rulemaking for any proposed rule, the agency shall prepare and make available for public comment an initial regulatory flexibility analysis. Such analysis shall describe the impact of the proposed rule on small entities. The initial regulatory flexibility analysis or a summary shall be published in the *Federal Register* at the time of the publication of general notice of proposed rulemaking for the rule. The agency shall transmit a copy of the initial regulatory flexibility analysis to the Chief Counsel for Advocacy of the Small Business Administration.
(b) Each initial regulatory analysis required under this section shall contain—

(1) a description of the reasons why action by the agency is being considered;
(2) a succinct statement of the objectives of, and legal basis for, the proposed rule;
(3) a description of and, where feasible, an estimate of the number of small entities to which the proposed rule will apply;
(4) a description of the projected reporting, recordkeeping and other compliance requirements of the proposed rule, including an estimate of the classes of small entitles which will be subject to the requirement and the type of professional skills necessary for preparation of the report or record;
(5) an identification, to the extent practicable, of all relevant Federal rules which may duplicate, overlap or conflict with the proposed rule.

(c) Each initial regulatory flexibility analysis shall also contain a description of any significant alternatives to the proposed rule which accomplish the stated objectives of applicable statutes and which minimize any significant economic impact of the proposed rule on small entities. Consistent with the stated objectives of applicable statutes, the analysis shall discuss significant alternatives such as—

(1) the establishment of differing compliance or reporting requirements or timetables that take into account the resources available to small entities;
(2) the clarification, consolidation, or simplification of compliance and reporting requirements under the rule for such small entities;
(3) the use of performance rather than design standards; and
(4) an exemption from coverage of the rule, or any part thereof, for such small entities.

Section 604. **FINAL REGULATORY FLEXIBILITY ANALYSIS**

(a) When an agency promulgates a final rule under section 553 of this title, after being required by that section or any other law to publish a general notice of proposed rulemaking, the agency shall prepare a final regulatory flexibility analysis. Each final regulatory flexibility analysis shall contain—

(1) a succinct statement of the need for, and the objectives of, the rule;

(2) a summary of the issues raised by the public comments in response to the initial regulatory flexibility analysis, a summary of the assessment of the agency of such issues, and a statement of any changes made in the proposed rule as a result of such comments; and

(3) a description of each of the significant alternatives to the rule consistent with the stated objectives of applicable statutes and designed to minimize any significant economic impact of the rule on small entities which was considered by the agency, and a statement of the reasons why each one of such alternatives was rejected.

(b) The agency shall make copies of the final regulatory flexibility analysis available to members of the public and shall publish in the *Federal Register* at the time of publication of the final rule under section 553 of this title a statement describing how the public may obtain such copies.

Section 605. AVOIDANCE OF DUPLICATIVE OR UNNECESSARY ANALYSES

(a) Any Federal agency may perform the analyses required by sections 602, 603, and 604 of this title in conjunction with or as a part of any other agenda or analysis required by any other law if such other analysis satisfies the provisions of such sections.

(b) Sections 603 and 604 of this title shall not apply to any proposed or final rule if the head of the agency certifies that the rule will not, if promulgated, have a significant economic impact on a substantial number of small entities. If the head of the agency makes a certification under the preceding sentence, the agency shall publish such certification in the *Federal Register,* at the time of publication of general notice of proposed rulemaking for the rule or at the time of publication of the final rule, along with a succinct statement explaining the reasons for such certification, and provide such certification and statement to the Chief Counsel for Advocacy of the Small Business Administration.

(c) In order to avoid duplicative action, an agency may consider a series of closely related rules as one rule for the purposes of sections 602, 603, 604 and 610 of this title.

Section 610. PERIODIC REVIEW OF RULES

(a) Within one hundred and eighty days after the effective date of this chapter, each agency shall publish in the *Federal Register* a plan for the periodic review of the rules issued by the agency which have or will have a significant economic impact upon a substantial number of small entities. Such plan may be amended by the agency at any time by publishing the revision in the *Federal Register.* The purpose of the review shall be to determine whether such rules should be continued without change, or should be amended or rescinded, consistent with the stated objectives of applicable statutes, to minimize any significant economic impact of the rules upon a substantial number of such small entities. The plan shall provide for the review of all such agency rules existing on the effective date of this chapter within ten years of that date and for the review of such rules adopted after the effective date of this chapter within ten years of the publication of such rules as the final rule. If the head of the agency determines that completion of the review of existing rules is not feasible by the established date, he shall so certify in a statement published in the *Federal Register* and may extend the completion date by one year at a time for a total of not more than five years.

(b) In reviewing rules to minimize any significant economic impact of the rule on a substantial number of small entities in a manner consistent with the state objectives of applicable statutes, the agency shall consider the following factors—

(1) the continued need for the rule;

(2) the nature of complaints or comments received concerning the rule from the public;

(3) the complexity of the rule;

(4) the extent to which the rule overlaps, duplicates or conflicts with other Federal rules, and, to the extent feasible, with State and local governmental rules; and

(5) the length of time since the rule has been evaluated or the degree to which technology, economic conditions, or other factors have changed in the area affected by the rule.

(c) Each year, each agency shall publish in the *Federal Register* a list of the rules which have a significant economic impact on a substantial number of small entities, which are to be reviewed pursuant to this section during the succeeding twelve months. The list shall include a brief description of each rule and the need for and legal basis of such rule and shall invite public comment upon the rule.

Section 702. RIGHT OF REVIEW

A person suffering legal wrong because of agency action, or adversely affected or aggrieved by agency action within the meaning of a relevant statute, is entitled to judicial review thereof. An action in a court of the United States seeking relief other than money damages and stating a claim that an agency or an officer or employee thereof acted or failed to act in an official capacity or under color of legal authority shall not be dismissed nor relief therein be denied on the ground that it is against the United States or that the United States is an indispensable party. The United States may be named as a defendant in any such action, and a judgment or decree may be entered against the United States: *Provided,* That any mandatory or injunctive decree shall specify the Federal officer or officers (by name or by title), and their successors in office, personally responsible for compliance. Nothing herein (1) affects other limitations on judicial review or the power or duty of the court to dismiss any action or deny relief on any other appropriate legal or equitable ground; or (2) confers authority to grant relief if any other statute that grants consent to suit expressly or impliedly forbids the relief which is sought.

Section 704. ACTIONS REVIEWABLE

Agency action made reviewable by statute and final agency action for which there is no other adequate remedy in a court are subject to judicial review. A preliminary, procedural, or intermediate agency action or ruling not directly reviewable is subject to review on the review of the final agency action. Except as otherwise expressly required by statute, agency action otherwise final is final for the purposes of this section whether or not there has been presented or determined an application for a declaratory order, for any form of reconsideration, or, unless the agency otherwise requires by rule and provides that the action meanwhile is inoperative, for an appeal to superior agency authority.

Section 705. RELIEF PENDING REVIEW

When an agency finds that justice so requires, it may postpone the effective date of action taken by it, pending judicial review. On such conditions as may be required and to the extent necessary to prevent irreparable injury, the reviewing court, including the court to which a case may be taken on appeal from or on application for certiorari or other writ to a reviewing court, may issue all necessary and appropriate process to postpone the effective date of an agency action or to preserve status or rights pending conclusion of the review proceedings.

Section 706. SCOPE OF REVIEW

To the extent necessary to decision and when presented, the reviewing court shall decide all relevant questions of law, interpret constitutional and statutory provisions, and determine the meaning or applicability of the terms of an agency action. The reviewing court shall—

(1) compel agency action unlawfully withheld or unreasonably delayed; and

(2) hold unlawful and set aside agency action, findings, and conclusions found to be–

(A) arbitrary, capricious, an abuse of discretion, or otherwise not in accordance with law;

(B) contrary to constitutional right, power, privilege, or immunity;

(C) in excess of statutory jurisdiction, authority, or limitations, or short of statutory right;

(D) without observance of procedure required by law;

(E) unsupported by substantial evidence in a case subject to sections 556 and 557 of this title or otherwise reviewed on the record of an agency hearing provided by statute; or

(F) unwarranted by the facts to the extent that the facts are subject to trial de novo by the reviewing court.

In making the foregoing determinations, the court shall review the whole record or those parts of it cited by a party, and due account shall be taken of the rule of prejudicial error.

Appendix III

The Sherman Act
(Excerpts)

Section 1. TRUSTS, ETC., IN RESTRAINT OF TRADE ILLEGAL; PENALTY

Every contract, combination in the form of trust or otherwise, or conspiracy, in restraint of trade or commerce among the several States, or with foreign nations, is declared to be illegal. Every person who shall make any contract or engage in any combination or conspiracy hereby declared to be illegal shall be deemed guilty of a felony, and, on conviction thereof, shall be punished by fine not exceeding one million dollars if a corporation, or, if any other person, one hundred thousand dollars or by imprisonment not exceeding three years, or by both said punishments, in the discretion of the court.

Section 2. MONOPOLIZING TRADE A FELONY; PENALTY

Every person who shall monopolize, or attempt to monopolize, or combine or conspire with any other person or persons, to monopolize any part of the trade or commerce among the several States, or with foreign nations, shall be deemed guilty of a felony, and, on conviction thereof, shall be punished by fine not exceeding one million dollars if a corporation, or, if any other person, one hundred thousand dollars or by imprisonment not exceeding three years, or by both said punishments, in the discretion of the court.

Appendix IV

The Clayton Act
(Excerpts)

Section 3. LEASE, SALE, ETC. ON CONDITION NOT TO USE COMPETITOR'S GOODS

It shall be unlawful for any person engaged in commerce, in the course of such commerce, to lease or make a sale or contract for sale of goods, wares, merchandise, machinery, supplies, or other commodities, whether patented or unpatented, for use, consumption, or resale within the United States or any Territory thereof or the District of Columbia or any insular possession or other place under the jurisdiction of the United States, or fix a price charged therefor, or discount from, or rebate upon, such price, on the condition, agreement, or understanding that the lessee or purchaser thereof shall not use or deal in the goods, wares, merchandise, machinery, supplies, or other commodities of a competitor or competitors of the lessor or seller, where the effect of such lease, sale, or contract for sale or such condition, agreement, or understanding may be to substantially lessen competition or tend to create a monopoly in any line of commerce.

Section 4. SUITS BY PERSONS INJURED; AMOUNT OF RECOVERY; PREJUDGMENT INTEREST

Any person who shall be injured in his business or property by reason of anything forbidden in the antitrust laws may sue therefor in any district court of the United States in the district in which the defendant resides or is found or has an agent, without respect to the amount in controversy, and shall recover threefold the damages by him sustained, and the cost of suit, including a reasonable attorney's fee. The court may award under this section, pursuant to a motion by such person promptly made, simple interest on actual damages for the period beginning on the date of service of such person's pleading setting forth a claim under the antitrust laws and ending on the date of judgment, or for any shorter period therein, if the court finds that the award of such interest for such period is just in the circumstances. In determining whether an award of interest under this section for any period is just in the circumstances, the court shall consider only—

(1) whether such person or the opposing party, or either party's representative, made motions or asserted claims or defenses so lacking in merit as to show that such party or representative acted intentionally for delay, or otherwise acted in bad faith;

(2) whether, in the course of the action involved, such person or the opposing party, or either party's representative, violated any applicable rule, statute, or court order providing for sanctions for dilatory behavior or otherwise providing for expeditious proceedings; and

(3) whether such person or the opposing party, or either party's representative, engaged in conduct primarily for the purpose of delaying the litigation or increasing the cost thereof.

Section 4B. LIMITATION OF ACTIONS

Any action to enforce any cause of action under sections 4 or 4A (omitted) of this title shall be forever barred unless commenced within four years after the cause of action accrued. No cause of action barred under existing law on the effective date of this section and sections 15a and 16 of this title shall be revived by said sections.

Section 4C. ACTIONS BY STATE ATTORNEYS GENERAL—PARENS PATRIAE; MONETARY RELIEF; DAMAGES; PREJUDGMENT INTEREST

(2)(1) Any attorney general of a State may bring a civil action in the name of such State, as parens patriae on behalf of natural persons residing in such State, in any district court of the United States having jurisdiction of the defendant, to secure monetary relief as provided in this section for injury sustained by such natural persons to their property by reason of any violation of Sections 1 to 7 of this title. The court shall exclude from the amount of monetary relief awarded in such action any amount of monetary relief (a) which duplicates amounts which have been awarded for the same injury, or (b) which is properly allocable to (i) natural persons who have excluded their claims pursuant to subsection (B)(2) of this section, and (ii) any business entity.

(2) The court shall award the State as monetary relief threefold the total damage sustained as described in paragraph (1) of this subsection, and the cost of suit, including a reasonable attorney's fee. The court may award under this paragraph, pursuant to motion by such State promptly made, simple interest on the total damage for the period beginning on the date of service of such State's pleading setting forth a claim under the antitrust laws and ending on the date of judgment, or for any shorter period therein, if the court finds that the award of such interest for such period is just in the circumstances. In determining whether an award of interest under this paragraph for any period is just in the circumstances, the court shall consider only—

(A) whether such State or the opposing party, or either party's representative, made motions or asserted claims or defenses so lacking in merit as to show that such party or representative acted intentionally for delay or otherwise acted in bad faith;

(B) whether, in the course of the action involved, such State or the opposing party, or either party's representative, violated any applicable rule, statute, or court order providing for sanctions for dilatory behavior or otherwise providing for expeditious proceedings; and

(C) whether such State or the opposing party, or either party's representative, engaged in conduct primarily for the purpose of delaying the litigation or increasing the cost thereof.

Notice; Exclusion Election; Final Judgment

(b)(1) In any action brought under subsection (A)(1) of this section, the State attorney general shall, at such times, in such manner, and with such content as the court may direct, cause notice thereof to be given by publication. If the court finds that notice given solely by publication would deny due process of law to any person or persons, the court may direct further notice to such person or persons according to the circumstances of the case.

(2) Any person on whose behalf an action is brought under subsection (A)(1) of this section may elect to exclude from adjudication the portion of the State claim for monetary relief attributable to him by filing notice of such election with the court within such time as specified in the notice given pursuant to paragraph (1) of this subjection.

(3) The final judgment in an action under subsection (A)(1) of this section shall be res judicata as to any claim under section 5 of this title by any person on behalf of whom such action was brought and who fails to give such notice within the period specified in the notice given pursuant to paragraph (1) of this subsection.

Dismissal or Compromise of Action

(c) An action under subsection (A)(1) of this section shall not be dismissed or compromised without the approval of the court, and notice of any proposed dismissal or compromise shall be given in such manner as the court directs.

Attorney's Fees

(d) In any action under subsection (A) of this section—

(1) the amount of the plaintiffs' attorney's fee, if any, shall be determined by the court; and

(2) the court may, in its discretion, award a reasonable attorney's fee to a prevailing defendant upon a finding that the State attorney general has acted in bad faith, vexatiously, wantonly, or for oppressive reasons.

Section 5. JUDGMENT IN FAVOR OF GOVERNMENT AS EVIDENCE; SUSPENSION OF LIMITATIONS

(a) A final judgment or decree heretofore or hereafter rendered in any civil or criminal proceeding brought by or on behalf of the United States under the antitrust laws to the effect that a defendant has violated said laws shall be prima facie evidence against such defendant in any action or proceeding brought by any other party against such defendant under said laws or by the United States under section 15a of this title, as to all matters respecting which said judgment or decree would be an estoppel as between the parties thereto: *Provided,* That this section shall not apply to consent judgments or decrees entered before any testimony has been taken or to judgments or decrees entered in actions under section 15a of this title.

(b) Whenever any civil or criminal proceeding is instituted by the United States to prevent, restrain, or punish violations of any of the antitrust laws, but not including an action under section 15a of this title, the running of the statute of limitations in respect of every private right of action arising under said laws and based in whole or in part on any matter complained of in said proceeding shall be suspended during the pendency thereof and for one year thereafter: *Provided, however,* That whenever the running of the statute of limitations in respect of a cause of action arising under section 15 of this title is suspended hereunder, any action to enforce such cause of action shall be forever barred unless commenced either within the period of suspension or within four years after the cause of action accrued.

Section 6. ANTITRUST LAWS NOT APPLICABLE TO LABOR ORGANIZATIONS

That the labor of a human being is not a commodity or article of commerce. Nothing contained in the antitrust laws shall be construed to forbid the existence and operation of labor, agricultural or horticultural organizations, instituted for the purposes of mutual help, and not having capital stock or conducted for profit, or to forbid or restrain individual members of such organizations from lawfully carrying out the legitimate objects thereof; nor shall such organizations, or the members thereof, be held or construed to be illegal combinations or conspiracies in restraint of trade, under the antitrust laws.

Section 7. ACQUISITION BY ONE CORPORATION OF STOCK OF ANOTHER

No corporation engaged in commerce shall acquire, directly or indirectly, the whole or any part of the stock or other share capital and no corporation subject to the jurisdiction of the Federal Trade Commission shall acquire the whole or any part of the assets of another corporation in any section of the country, the effect of such acquisition may be substantially to lessen competition, or to tend to create a monopoly.

No corporation shall acquire, directly or indirectly, the whole or any part of the stock or other share capital and no corporation subject to the jurisdiction of the Federal Trade Commission shall acquire the whole or any part of the assets of one or more corporations engaged in commerce, where in any line of commerce in any section of the country, the effect of such acquisition, of such stocks or assets, or of the use of such stock by the voting or granting of proxies or otherwise, may be substantially to lessen competition, or to tend to create a monopoly.

This section shall not apply to corporations purchasing such stock solely for investment and not using the same by voting or otherwise to bring about, or in attempting to bring about, the substantial lessening of competition. Nor shall anything contained in this section prevent a corporation engaged in commerce from causing the formation of subsidiary corporations for the actual carrying on of their immediate lawful business, or the natural and legitimate branches or extensions thereof, or from owning and holding all or a part of the stock of such subsidiary corporations, when the effect of such formation is not to substantially lessen competition.

Nor shall anything herein contained be construed to prohibit any common carrier subject to the laws to regulate commerce from aiding in the construction of branches or short lines so located as to become feeders to the main line of the company so aiding in such construction or from acquiring or owning all or any part of the stock of such branch lines, nor to prevent any such common carrier from acquiring and owning all or any part of the stock of a branch or short line constructed by an independent company where there is no substantial competition between the company owning the branch line so constructed and the company owning the main line acquiring the property or an interest therein, nor to prevent such common carrier from extending any of its lines through the medium of the acquisition of stock or otherwise of any other common carrier where there is no substantial competition between the company extending its lines and the company whose stock, property, or an interest therein is so acquired.

Nothing contained in this section shall be held to affect or impair any right heretofore legally acquired: *Provided,* That nothing in this section shall be held or construed to authorize or make lawful anything heretofore prohibited or made illegal by the antitrust laws, nor to exempt any person from the penal provisions thereof or the civil remedies therein provided.

Nothing contained in this section shall apply to transactions duly consummated pursuant to authority given by the Civil Aeronautics Board, Federal Communications Commission, Federal Power Commission, Interstate Commerce Commission, the Securities and Exchange Commission in the exercise of its jurisdiction under section 79j of this title, the United States Maritime Commission, or the Secretary of Agriculture under any statutory provision vesting such power in such Commission, Secretary, or Board.

Section 8. INTERLOCKING DIRECTORATES AND OFFICERS

No private banker or director, officer, or employee of any member bank of the Federal Reserve System or any branch thereof shall be at the same time a director, officer, or employee of any other bank, banking association, savings bank, or trust company organized under the National Bank Act or organized under the laws of any State or of the District of Columbia, or any branch thereof, except that the Board of Governors of the Federal Reserve System may by regulation permit such service as a director, officer, or employee of not more than one other such institution or branch thereof; but the foregoing prohibition shall not apply in the case of any one or more of the following or any branch thereof:

(1) A bank, banking association, savings bank, or trust company, more than 90 per centum of the stock of which is owned directly or indirectly by the United States or by any corporation of which the United States directly or indirectly owns more than 90 per centum of the stock.

(2) A bank, banking association, savings bank, or trust company which has been placed formally in liquidation or which is in the hands of a receiver, conservator, or other official exercising similar functions.

(3) A corporation, principally engaged in international or foreign banking or banking in a dependency or insular possession of the United States which has entered into an agreement with the Board of Governors of the Federal Reserve System pursuant to sections 601 to 604a of Title 12.

(4) A bank, banking association, savings bank, or trust company, more 50 per centum of the common stock of which is owned directly or indirectly by persons who own directly or indirectly more than 50 per centum of the common stock of such member bank.

(5) A bank, banking association, savings bank, or trust company not located and having no branch in the same city, town, or village as that in which such member bank or any branch thereof is located, or in any city, town, or village contiguous or adjacent thereto.

(6) A bank, banking association, savings bank, or trust company not engaged in a class or classes of business in which such member bank is engaged.

(7) A mutual savings bank having no capital stock.

Until February 1, 1939, nothing in this section shall prohibit any director, officer, or employee of any member bank of the Federal Reserve System, or any branch thereof, who is lawfully serving at the same time as a private banker or as a director, officer, or employee of any other bank, banking association, savings bank, or trust company, or any branch thereof, on August 23, 1935, from continuing such service.

The Board of Governors of the Federal Reserve System is authorized and directed to enforce compliance with this section, and to prescribe such rules and regulations as it deems necessary for that purpose.

No person at the same time shall be a director in any two or more corporations, any one of which has capital, surplus, and undivided profits aggregating more than $1,000,000, engaged in whole or in part in commerce, other than banks, banking associations, trust companies, and common carriers subject to the Act to regulate commerce, approved February fourth, eighteen hundred and eighty-seven, if such corporations are or shall have been theretofore, by virtue of their business and location of operation, competitors, so that the elimination of competition by agreement between them would constitute a violation of any of the provisions of any of the antitrust laws. The eligibility of a director under the foregoing provision shall be determined by the aggregate amount of the capital, surplus, and undivided profits, exclusive of dividends declared but not paid to stockholders, at the end of the fiscal year of said corporation next preceding the election of directors, and when a director has been elected in accordance with the provisions of this Act it shall be lawful for him to continue as such for one year thereafter.

When any person elected or chosen as a director or officer or selected as an employee of any bank or other corporation subject to the provisions of this Act is eligible at the time of his election or selection to act for such bank or other corporation in such capacity his eligibility to act in such capacity shall not be affected and he shall not become or be deemed amenable to any of the provisions hereof by reason of any change in the affairs of such bank or other corporation from whatsoever cause, whether specifically excepted by any of the provisions hereof or not, until the expiration of one year from the date of his election or employment.

Appendix V

The Robinson-Patman Act
(Excerpts)

Section 2. DISCRIMINATION IN PRICE, SERVICES, OR FACILITIES—PRICE; SELECTION OF CUSTOMERS

(a) It shall be unlawful for any person engaged in commerce, in the course of such commerce, either directly or indirectly, to discriminate in price between different purchasers of commodities of like grade and quality, where either or any of the purchases involved in such discrimination are in commerce, where such commodities are sold for use, consumption, or resale within the United States or any Territory thereof or the District of Columbia or any insular possession or other place under the jurisdiction of the United States, and where the effect of such discrimination may be substantially to lessen competition or tend to create a monopoly in any line of commerce, or to injure, destroy, or prevent competition with any person who either grants or knowingly receives the benefit of such discrimination, or with customers of either of them; *Provided,* That nothing herein contained shall prevent differentials which make only due allowance for differences in the cost of manufacture, sale, or delivery resulting from the differing methods or quantities in which such commodities are to such purchasers sold or delivered: *Provided, however,* That the Federal Trade Commission may, after due investigation and hearing to all interested parties, fix and establish quantity limits, and revise the same as it finds necessary, as to particular commodities or classes of commodities, where it finds that available purchasers in greater quantities are so few as to render differentials on account thereof unjustly discriminatory or promotive of monopoly in any line of commerce; and the foregoing shall then not be construed to permit differentials based on differences in quantities greater than those so fixed and established: *And provided further,* That nothing herein contained shall prevent persons engaged in selling goods, wares, or merchandise in commerce from selecting their own customers in bona fide transactions and not in restraint of trade: *And provided further,* That nothing herein contained shall prevent price changes from time to time where in response to changing conditions affecting the market for or the marketability of the goods concerned, such as but not limited to actual or imminent deterioration of perishable goods, obsolescence of seasonal goods, distress sales under court process, or sales in good faith in discontinuance of business in the goods concerned.

Burden of Rebutting Prima-Facie Case of Discrimination

(b) Upon proof being made, at any hearing on a complaint under this section, that there has been discrimination in price or services or facilities furnished, the burden of rebutting the prima-facie case thus made by showing justification shall be upon the person charged with a violation of this section, and unless justification shall be affirmatively shown, the Commission is authorized to issue an order terminating the discrimination: *Provided, however,* That nothing herein contained shall prevent a seller rebutting the prima-facie case thus made by showing that his lower price or the furnishing of services or facilities to any purchaser or purchasers was made in good faith to meet an equally low price of a competitor, or the services or facilities furnished by a competitor.

Payment or Acceptance of Commission, Brokerage or Other Compensation

(c) It shall be unlawful for any person engaged in commerce, in the course of such commerce, to pay or grant, or to receive or accept, anything of value as a commission, brokerage, or other compensation, or any allowance or discount in lieu thereof, except for services rendered in connection with the sale or purchase of goods, wares, or merchandise, either to the other party to such transaction or to an agent, representative, or other intermediary therein where such intermediary is acting in fact for or in behalf, or is subject to the direct or indirect control, of any party to such transaction other than the person by whom such compensation is so granted or paid.

Payment for Services or Facilities for Processing or Sale

(d) It shall be unlawful for any person engaged in commerce to pay or contract for the payment of anything of value to or for the benefit of a customer of such person in the course of such commerce as compensation or in consideration for any services or facilities furnished by or through such customer in connection with the processing, handling, sale, or offering for sale of any products or commodities manufactured, sold, or offered for sale by such person, unless such payment or consideration is available on proportionally equal terms to all other customers competing in the distribution of such products or commodities.

Furnishing Services or Facilities for Processing, Handling, etc.

(e) It shall be unlawful for any person to discriminate in favor of one purchaser against another purchaser or purchasers of a commodity bought for resale, with or without processing, by contracting to furnish or furnishing, or by contributing to the furnishing of, any services or facilities connected with the processing, handling, sale, or offering for sale of such commodity so purchased upon terms not accorded to all purchasers on proportionally equal terms.

Knowingly Inducing or Receiving Discriminatory Price

(f) It shall be unlawful for any person engaged in commerce, in the course of such commerce, knowingly to induce or receive a discrimination in price which is prohibited by this section.

Section 3. DISCRIMINATION IN REBATES, DISCOUNTS, OR ADVERTISING SERVICE CHARGES; UNDERSELLING IN PARTICULAR LOCALITIES; PENALTIES

It shall be unlawful for any person engaged in commerce, in the course of such commerce, to be a party to, or assist in, any transaction of sale, or contract to sell, which discriminates to his knowledge against competitors of the purchaser, in that, any discount, rebate, allowance, or advertising service charge is granted to the purchaser over and above any discount, rebate, allowance, or advertising service charge available at the time of such transaction to said competitors in respect of a sale of goods of like grade, quality, and quantity; to sell, or contract to sell, goods in any part of the United States at prices lower than those exacted by said person elsewhere in the United States for the purpose of destroying competition, or eliminating a competitor in such part of the United States; or, to sell, or contract to sell, goods at unreasonably low prices for the purpose of destroying competition or eliminating a competitor.

Any person violating any of the provisions of this section shall, upon conviction thereof, be fined not more than $5,000 or imprisoned not more than one year, or both.

Appendix VI

The Federal Trade Commission Act

(Excerpts)

Section 5. UNFAIR METHODS OF COMPETITION UNLAWFUL; PREVENTION BY COMMISSION—DECLARATION OF UNLAWFULNESS; POWER TO PROHIBIT UNFAIR PRACTICES

(a)(1) Unfair methods of competition in or affecting commerce, and unfair or deceptive acts or practices in or affecting commerce, are declared unlawful.

Penalty for Violation of Order; Injunctions and Other Appropriate Equitable Relief

(l) Any person, partnership, or corporation who violates an order of the Commission after it has become final, and while such order is in effect, shall forfeit and pay to the United States a civil penalty of not more than $10,000 for each violation, which shall accrue to the United States and may be recovered in a civil action brought by the Attorney General of the United States. Each separate violation of such an order shall be a separate offense, except that in the case of a violation through continuing failure to obey or neglect to obey a final order of the Commission, each day of continuance of such failure or neglect shall be deemed a separate offense. In such actions, the United States district courts are empowered to grant mandatory injunctions and such other and further equitable relief as they deem appropriate in the enforcement of such final orders of the Commission.

Appendix VII

The Uniform Commerical Code

(Excerpts)
General Provisions

ARTICLE I

Part 1

Short Title

Section 1—102. PURPOSES; RULES OF CONSTRUCTION; VARIATION BY AGREEMENT

(1) This Act shall be liberally construed and applied to promote its underlying purposes and policies.

(2) Underlying purposes and policies of this Act are

(a) to simplify, clarify and modernize the law governing commercial transactions;

(b) to permit the continued expansion of commercial practices through custom, usage and agreement of the parties;

(c) to make uniform the law among the various jurisdictions.

(3) The effect of provisions of this Act may be varied by agreement, except as otherwise provided in this Act and except that the obligations of good faith, diligence, reasonableness and care prescribed by this Act may not be disclaimed by agreement but the parties may by agreement determine the standards by which the performance of such obligations is to be measured if such standards are not manifestly unreasonable.

(4) The presence in certain provisions of this Act of the words "unless otherwise agreed" or words of similar import does not imply that the effect of other provisions may not be varied by agreement under subsection (3).

(5) In this Act unless the context otherwise requires

(a) words in the singular number include the plural, and in the plural include the singular;

(b) words of the masculine gender include the feminine and the neuter, and when the sense so indicates words of the neuter gender may refer to any gender.

Section 1—106. REMEDIES TO BE LIBERALLY ADMINISTERED

(1) The remedies provided by this Act shall be liberally administered to the end that the aggrieved party may be put in as good a position as if the other party had fully performed but neither consequential or special nor penal damages may be had except as specifically provided in this Act or by other rule of law.

(2) Any right or obligation declared by this Act is enforceable by action unless the provision declaring it specifies a different and limited effect.

Part 2

General Definitions and Principles of Interpretation

Section 1—201. GENERAL DEFINITIONS

Subject to additional definitions contained in the subsequent Articles of this Act which are applicable to specific Articles or Parts thereof, and unless the context otherwise requires, in this Act:

(1) "Action" in the sense of a judicial proceeding includes recoupment, counterclaim, set-off, suit in equity and any other proceedings in which rights are determined.

(2) "Aggrieved party" means a party entitled to resort to a remedy.

(3) "Agreement" means the bargain of the parties in fact as found in their language or by implication from other circumstances including course of dealing or usage of trade or course of performance as provided in this Act (Sections 1—205 and 2—208). Whether an agreement has legal consequences is determined by the provisions of this Act, if applicable; otherwise by the law of contracts (Section 1—103). (Compare "Contract".)

(4) "Bank" means any person engaged in the business of banking.

(5) "Bearer" means the person in possession of an instrument, document of title, or certificated security payable to bearer or indorsed in blank.

(6) "Bill of lading" means a document evidencing the receipt of goods for shipment issued by a person engaged in the business of transporting or forwarding goods, and includes an airbill. "Airbill" means a document serving for air transportation as a bill of lading does for marine or rail

transportation, and includes an air consignment note or air waybill.
(7) "Branch" includes a separately incorporated foreign branch of a bank.
(8) "Burden of establishing" a fact means the burden of persuading the triers of fact that the existence of the fact is more probable than its non-existence.
(9) "Buyer in ordinary course of business" means a person who in good faith and without knowledge that the sale to him is in violation of the ownership rights or security interest of a third party in the goods buys in ordinary course from a person in the business of selling goods of that kind but does not include a pawnbroker. All persons who sell minerals or the like (including oil and gas) at wellhead or minehead shall be deemed to be persons in the business of selling goods of that kind. "Buying" may be for cash or by exchange of other property or on secured or unsecured credit and includes receiving goods or documents of title under a pre-existing contract for sale but does not include a transfer in bulk or as security for or in total or partial satisfaction of a money debt.
(10) "Conspicuous": A term or clause is conspicuous when it is so written that a reasonable person against whom it is to operate ought to have noticed it. A printed heading in capitals (as: NON-NEGOTIABLE BILL OF LADING) is conspicuous. Language in the body of a form is "conspicuous" if it is in larger or other contrasting type or color. But in a telegram any stated term is "conspicuous". Whether a term or clause is "conspicuous" or not is for decision by the court.
(11) "Contract" means the total legal obligation which results from the parties' agreement as affected by this Act and any other applicable rules of law. (Compare "Agreement".)
(12) "Creditor" includes a general creditor, a secured creditor, a lien creditor and any representative of creditors, including an assignee for the benefit of creditors, a trustee in bankruptcy, a receiver in equity and an executor or administrator of an insolvent debtor's or assignor's estate.
(13) "Defendant" includes a person in the position of defendant in a cross-action or counterclaim.
(14) "Delivery" with respect to instruments, documents of title, chattel paper, or certificated securities means voluntary transfer of possession.
(15) "Document of title" includes bill of lading, dock warrant, dock receipt, warehouse receipt or order for the delivery of goods, and also any other document which in the regular course of business or financing is treated as adequately evidencing that the person in possession of it is entitled to receive, hold and dispose of the document and the goods it covers. To be a document of title a document must purport to be issued by or addressed to a bailee and purport to cover goods in the bailee's possession which are either identified or are fungible portions of an identified mass.
(16) "Fault" means wrongful act, omission or breach.
(17) "Fungible" with respect to goods or securities means goods or securities of which any unit is, by nature or usage of trade, the equivalent of any other like unit. Goods which are not fungible shall be deemed fungible for the purposes of this Act to the extent that under a particular agreement or document unlike units are treated as equivalents.
(18) "Genuine" means free of forgery or counterfeiting.
(19) "Good faith" means honesty in fact in the conduct or transaction concerned.
(20) "Holder" means a person who is in possession of a document of title or an instrument or a certificated investment security drawn, issued, or indorsed to him or his order or to bearer or in blank.
(21) To "honor" is to pay or to accept and pay, or where a credit so engages to purchase or discount a draft complying with the terms of the credit.
(22) "Insolvency proceedings" includes any assignment for the benefit of creditors or other proceedings intended to liquidate or rehabilitate the estate of the person involved.
(23) A person is "insolvent" who either has ceased to pay his debts in the ordinary course of business or cannot pay his debts as they become due or is insolvent within the meaning of the federal bankruptcy law.
(24) "Money" means a medium of exchange authorized or adopted by a domestic or foreign government as a part of its currency.
(25) A person has "notice" of a fact when
  (a) he has actual knowledge of it; or
  (b) he has received a notice or notification of it; or
  (c) from all the facts and circumstances known to him at the time in question he has reason to know that it exists.

A person "knows" or has "knowledge" of a fact when he has actual knowledge of it. "Discover" or "learn" or a word or phrase of similar import refers to knowledge rather than to reason to know. The time and circumstances under which a notice or notification may cease to be effective are not determined by this Act.
(26) A person "notifies" or "gives" a notice or notification to another by taking such steps as may be reasonably required to inform the other in ordinary course whether or not such other actually comes to know of it. A person "receives" a notice or notification when
  (a) it comes to his attention; or
  (b) it is duly delivered at the place of business through which the contract was made or at any other place held out by him as the place for receipt of such communications.

(27) Notice, knowledge or a notice or notification received by an organization is effective for a particular transaction from the time when it is brought to the attention of the individual conducting that transaction, and in any event from the time when it would have been brought to his attention if the organization had exercised due diligence. An orga-

nization exercises due diligence if it maintains reasonable routines for communicating significant information to the person conducting the transaction and there is reasonable compliance with the routines. Due diligence does not require an individual acting for the organization to communicate information unless such communication is part of his regular duties or unless he has reason to know of the transaction and that the transaction would be materially affected by the information.

(28) "Organization" includes a corporation, government or governmental subdivision or agency, business trust, estate, trust, partnership or association, two or more persons having a joint or common interest, or any other legal or commercial entity.

(29) "Party," as distinct from "third party," means a person who has engaged in a transaction or made an agreement within this Act.

(30) "Person" includes an individual or an organization (See Section 1—102).

(31) "Presumption" or "presumed" means that the trier of fact must find the existence of the fact presumed unless and until evidence is introduced which would support a finding of its non-existence.

(32) "Purchase" includes taking by sale, discount, negotiation, mortgage, pledge, lien, issue or re-issue, gift or any other voluntary transaction creating an interest in property.

(33) "Purchaser" means a person who takes by purchase.

(34) "Remedy" means any remedial right to which an aggrieved party is entitled with or without resort to a tribunal.

(35) "Representative" includes an agent, an officer of a corporation or association, and a trustee, executor or administrator of an estate, or any other person empowered to act for another.

(36) "Rights" includes remedies.

(37) "Security interest" means an interest in personal property or fixtures which secures payment or performance of an obligation. The retention or reservation of title by a seller of goods notwithstanding shipment or delivery to the buyer (Section 2—401) is limited in effect to a reservation of a "security interest." The term also includes any interest of a buyer of accounts or chattel paper which is subject to Article 9. The special property interest of a buyer of goods on identification of such goods to a contract for sale under Section 2—401 is not a "security interest", but a buyer may also acquire a "security interest" by complying with Article 9. Unless a lease or consignment is intended as security, reservation of title thereunder is not a "security interest" but a consignment is in any event subject to the provisions on consignment sales (Section 2—326). Whether a lease is intended as security is to be determined by the facts of each case; however, (a) the inclusion of an option to purchase does not of itself make the lease one intended for security, and (b) an agreement that upon compliance with the terms of the lease the lessee shall become or has the option to become the owner of the property for no additional consideration or for a nominal consideration does make the lease one intended for security.

(38) "Send" in connection with any writing or notice means to deposit in the mail or deliver for transmission by any other usual means of communication with postage or cost of transmission provided for and properly addressed and in the case of an instrument to an address specified thereon or otherwise agreed, or if there be none to any address reasonable under the circumstances. The receipt of any writing or notice within the time at which it would have arrived if properly sent has the effect of a proper sending.

(39) "Signed" includes any symbol executed or adopted by a party with present intention to authenticate a writing.

(40) "Surety" includes guarantor.

(41) "Telegram" includes a message transmitted by radio, teletype, cable, any mechanical method of transmission, or the like.

(42) "Term" means that portion of an agreement which relates to a particular matter.

(43) "Unauthorized" signature or indorsement means one made without actual, implied or apparent authority and includes a forgery.

(44) "Value." Except as otherwise provided with respect to negotiable instruments and bank collections (Sections 3—303, 4—208 and 4—209) a person gives "value" for rights if he acquires them

(a) in return for a binding commitment to extend credit or for the extension of immediately available credit whether or not drawn upon and whether or not a chargeback is provided for in the event of difficulties in collection; or

(b) as security for or in total or partial satisfaction of a pre-existing claim; or

(c) by accepting delivery pursuant to a pre-existing contract for purchase; or

(d) generally, in return for any consideration sufficient to support a simple contract.

(45) "Warehouse receipt" means a receipt issued by a person engaged in the business of storing goods for hire.

(46) "Written" or "writing" includes printing, typewriting or any other intentional reduction to tangible form. Amended in 1962, 1972 and 1977.

Section 1—203. **OBLIGATION OF GOOD FAITH**

Every contract or duty within this Act imposes an obligation of good faith in its performance or enforcement.

Section 1—204. **TIME; REASONABLE TIME; "SEASONABLY"**

(1) Whenever this Act requires any action to be taken within a reasonable time, any time which is not manifestly unreasonable may be fixed by agreement.

(2) What is a reasonable time for taking any action depends on the nature, purpose and circumstances of such action.
(3) An action is taken "seasonably" when it is taken at or within the time agreed or if no time is agreed at or within a reasonable time.

Section 1—205. COURSE OF DEALING AND USAGE OF TRADE

(1) A course of dealing is a sequence of previous conduct between the parties to a particular transaction which is fairly to be regarded as establishing a common basis of understanding for interpreting their expressions and other conduct.
(2) A usage of trade is any practice or method of dealing having such regularity of observance in a place, vocation or trade as to justify an expectation that it will be observed with respect to the transaction in question. The existence and scope of such a usage are to be proved as facts. If it is established that such a usage is embodied in a written trade code or similar writing the interpretation of the writing is for the court.
(3) A course of dealing between parties and any usage of trade in the vocation or trade in which they are engaged or of which they are or should be aware give particular meaning to and supplement or qualify terms of an agreement.
(4) The express terms of an agreement and an applicable course of dealing or usage of trade shall be construed wherever reasonable as consistent with each other; but when such construction is unreasonable express terms control both course of dealing and usage of trade and course of dealing controls usage of trade.
(5) An applicable usage of trade in the place where any part of performance is to occur shall be used in interpreting the agreement as to that part of the performance.
(6) Evidence of a relevant usage of trade offered by one party is not admissible unless and until he has given the other party such notice as the court finds sufficient to prevent unfair surprise to the latter.

Section 1—206. STATUTE OF FRAUDS FOR KINDS OF PERSONAL PROPERTY NOT OTHERWISE COVERED

(1) Except in the cases described in subsection (2) of this section a contract for the sale of personal property is not enforceable by way of action or defense beyond five thousand dollars in amount or value of remedy unless there is some writing which indicates that a contract for sale has been made between the parties at a defined or stated price, reasonably identifies the subject matter, and is signed by the party against whom enforcement is sought or by his authorized agent.
(2) Subsection (1) of this section does not apply to contracts for the sale of goods (Section 2—201) nor of securities (Section 8—319) nor to security agreements (Section 9—203).

ARTICLE II

Sales

Part 1

Short Title, General Construction and Subject Matter

Section 2—102. SCOPE; CERTAIN SECURITY AND OTHER TRANSACTIONS EXCLUDED FROM THIS ARTICLE

Unless the context otherwise requires, this Article applies to transactions in goods; it does not apply to any transaction which although in the form of an unconditional contract to sell or present sale is intended to operate only as a security transaction nor does this Article impair or repeal any statute regulating sales to consumers, farmers or other specified classes of buyers.

Section 2—103. DEFINITIONS AND INDEX OF DEFINITIONS

(1) In this Article unless the context otherwise requires
(a) "Buyer" means a person who buys or contracts to buy goods.
(b) "Good faith" in the case of a merchant means honesty in fact and the observance of reasonable commercial standards of fair dealing in the trade.
(c) "Receipt" of goods means taking physical possession of them.
(d) "Seller" means a person who sells or contracts to sell goods.
(2) Other definitions applying to this Article or to specified Parts thereof, and the sections in which they appear are:
"Acceptance". Section 2—606.
"Banker's credit". Section 2—325.
"Between merchants". Section 2—104.
"Cancellation". Section 2—106(4).
"Commercial unit". Section 2—105.
"Confirmed credit". Section 2—325.
"Conforming to contract". Section 2—106.
"Contract for sale". Section 2—106.
"Cover". Section 2—712.
"Entrusting". Section 2—403.
"Financing agency". Section 2—104.
"Future goods". Section 2—105.
"Goods". Section 2—105.
"Identification". Section 2—501.
"Installment contract". Section 2—612.
"Letter of Credit". Section 2—325.
"Lot". Section 2—105.

"Merchant". Section 2—104.
"Overseas". Section 2—323.
"Person in position of seller". Section 2—707.
"Present sale". Section 2—106.
"Sale". Section 2—106.
"Sale on approval". Section 2—326.
"Sale or return". Section 2—326.
"Termination". Section 2—106.

(3) The following definitions in other Articles apply to this Article:

"Check". Section 3—104.
"Consignee". Section 7—102.
"Consignor". Section 7—102.
"Consumer goods". Section 9—109.
"Dishonor". Sections 3—507.
"Draft". Section 3—104.

(4) In addition Article 1 contains general definitions and principles of construction and interpretation applicable throughout this Article.

Section 2—104. DEFINITIONS: "MERCHANT"; "BETWEEN MERCHANTS"; "FINANCING AGENCY"

(1) "Merchant" means a person who deals in goods of the kind or otherwise by his occupation holds himself out as having knowledge or skill peculiar to the practices or goods involved in the transaction or to whom such knowledge or skill may be attributed by his employment of an agent or broker or other intermediary who by his occupation holds himself out as having such knowledge or skill.

(2) "Financing agency" means a bank, finance company or other person who in the ordinary course of business makes advances against goods or documents of title or who by arrangement with either the seller or the buyer intervenes in ordinary course to make or collect payment due or claimed under the contract for sale, as by purchasing or paying the seller's draft or making advances against it or by merely taking it for collection whether or not documents of title accompany the draft. "Financing agency" includes also a bank or other person who similarly intervenes between persons who are in the position of seller and buyer in respect to the goods (Section 2—707).

(3) "Between merchants" means in any transaction with respect to which both parties are chargeable with the knowledge or skill of merchants.

Section 2—105. DEFINITIONS: TRANSFERABILITY; "GOODS"; "FUTURE" GOODS; "LOT"; "COMMERCIAL UNIT"

(1) "Goods" means all things (including specially manufactured goods) which are movable at the time of identification to the contract for sale other than the money in which the price is to be paid, investment securities (Article 8) and things in action. "Goods" also includes the unborn young of animals and growing crops and other identified things attached to realty as described in the section on goods to be severed from realty (Section 2—107).

(2) Goods must be both existing and identified before any interest in them can pass. Goods which are not both existing and identified are "future" goods. A purported present sale of future goods or of any interest therein operates as a contract to sell.

(3) There may be a sale of a part interest in existing identified goods.

(4) An undivided share in an identified bulk of fungible goods is sufficiently identified to be sold although the quantity of the bulk is not determined. Any agreed proportion of such a bulk or any quantity thereof agreed upon by number, weight or other measure may to the extent of the seller's interest in the bulk be sold to the buyer who then becomes an owner in common.

(5) "Lot" means a parcel or a single article which is the subject matter of a separate sale or delivery, whether or not it is sufficient to perform the contract.

(6) "Commercial unit" means such a unit of goods as by commercial usage is a single whole for purposes of sale and division of which materially impairs its character or value on the market or in use. A commercial unit may be a single article (as a machine) or a set of articles (as a suite of furniture or an assortment of sizes) or a quantity (as a bale, gross, or carload) or any other unit treated in use or in the relevant market as a single whole.

U.L.A.-U.C.C. 9th Ed. '78 Pamph.—3

Section 2—106. DEFINITIONS: "CONTRACT"; "AGREEMENT"; "CONTRACT FOR SALE"; "SALE"; "PRESENT SALE"; "CONFORMING" TO CONTRACT; "TERMINATION"; "CANCELLATION"

(1) In this Article unless the context otherwise requires "contract" and "agreement" are limited to those relating to the present or future sale of goods. "Contrat for sale" includes both a present sale of goods and a contract to sell goods at a future time. A "sale" consists in the passing of title from the seller to the buyer for a price (Section 2—401). A "present sale" means a sale which is accomplished by the making of the contract.

(2) Goods or conduct including any part of a performance are "conforming" or conform to the contract when they are in accordance with the obligations under the contract.

(3) "Termination" occurs when either party pursuant to a power created by agreement or law puts an end to the contract otherwise than for its breach. On "termination" all obligations which are still executory on both sides are discharged but any right based on prior breach or performance survives.

(4) "Cancellation" occurs when either party puts an end to the contract for breach by the other and its effect is the same as that of "termination" except that the cancelling party also retains any remedy for breach of the whole contract or any unperformed balance.

Section 2—107. GOODS TO BE SEVERED FROM REALTY; RECORDING

(1) A contract for the sale of minerals or the like (including oil and gas) or a structure or its materials to be removed from realty is a contract for the sale of goods within this Article if they are to be severed by the seller but until severance a purported present sale thereof which is not effective as a transfer of an interest in land is effective only as a contract to sell.
(2) A contract for the sale apart from the land of growing crops or other things attached to realty and capable of severance without material harm thereto but not described in subsection (1) or of timber to be cut is a contract for the sale of goods within this Article whether the subject matter is to be severed by the buyer or by the seller even though it forms part of the realty at the time of contracting, and the parties can by identification effect a present sale before severance.
(3) The provisions of this section are subject to any third party rights provided by the law relating to realty records, and the contract for sale may be executed and recorded as a document transferring an interest in land and shall then constitute notice to third parties of the buyer's rights under the contract for sale. As amended 1972.

Part 2
Form, Formation and Readjustment of Contract

Section 2—201. FORMAL REQUIREMENTS; STATUTE OF FRAUDS

(1) Except as otherwise provided in this section a contract for the sale of goods for the price of $500 or more is not enforceable by way of action or defense unless there is some writing sufficient to indicate that a contract for sale has been made between the parties and signed by the party against whom enforcement is sought or by his authorized agent or broker. A writing is not insufficient because it omits or incorrectly states a term agreed upon but the contract is not enforceable under this paragraph beyond the quantity of goods shown in such writing.
(2) Between merchants if within a reasonable time a writing in confirmation of the contract and sufficient against the sender is received and the party receiving it has reason to know its contents, it satisfies the requirements of subsection (1) against such party unless written notice of objection to its contents is given within 10 days after it is received.
(3) A contract which does not satisfy the requirements of subsection (1) but which is valid in other respects is enforceable

(a) if the goods are to be specially manufactured for the buyer and are not suitable for sale to others in the ordinary course of the seller's business and the seller, before notice of repudiation is received and under circumstances which reasonably indicate that the goods are for the buyer, has made either a substantial beginning of their manufacture or commitments for their procurement; or
(b) if the party against whom enforcement is sought admits in his pleading, testimony or otherwise in court that a contract for sale was made, but the contract is not enforceable under this provision beyond the quantity of goods admitted; or
(c) with respect to goods for which payment has been made and accepted or which have been received and accepted (Sec. 2—606).

Section 2—202. FINAL WRITTEN EXPRESSION: PAROL OR EXTRINSIC EVIDENCE

Terms with respect to which the confirmatory memoranda of the parties agree or which are otherwise set forth in a writing intended by the parties as a final expression of their agreement with respect to such terms as are included therein may not be contradicted by evidence of any prior agreement or of a contemporaneous oral agreement but may be explained or supplemented

(a) by course of dealing or usage of trade (Section 1—205) or by course of performance (Section 2—208); and
(b) by evidence of consistent additional terms unless the court finds the writing to have been intended also as a complete and exclusive statement of the terms of the agreement.

Section 2—204. FORMATION IN GENERAL

(1) A contract for sale of goods may be made in any manner sufficient to show agreement, including conduct by both parties which recognizes the existence of such a contract.
(2) An agreement sufficient to constitute a contract for sale may be found even though the moment of its making is undetermined.
(3) Even though one or more terms are left open a contract for sale does not fail for indefiniteness if the parties have intended to make a contract and there is a reasonably certain basis for giving an appropriate remedy.

Section 2—205. FIRM OFFERS

An offer by a merchant to buy or sell goods in a signed writing which by its terms gives assurance that it will be held open is not revocable, for lack of consideration, during the time stated or if no time is stated for a reasonable time, but in no event may such period of irrevocability exceed three months; but any such term of assurance on a form supplied by the offeree must be separately signed by the offeror.

Section 2—206. OFFER AND ACCEPTANCE IN FORMATION OF CONTRACT

(1) Unless otherwise unambiguously indicated by the language or circumstances

(a) an offer to make a contract shall be construed as inviting acceptance in any manner and by any medium reasonable in the circumstances;

(b) an order or other offer to buy goods for prompt or current shipment shall be construed as inviting acceptance either by a prompt promise to ship or by the prompt or current shipment of conforming or non-conforming goods, but such a shipment of non-conforming goods does not constitute an acceptance if the seller seasonably notifies the buyer that the shipment is offered only as an accommodation to the buyer.

(2) Where the beginning of a requested performance is a reasonable mode of acceptance an offeror who is not notified of acceptance within a reasonable time may treat the offer as having lapsed before acceptance.

Section 2—207. ADDITIONAL TERMS IN ACCEPTANCE OR CONFIRMATION

(1) A definite and seasonable expression of acceptance or a written confirmation which is sent within a reasonable time operates as an acceptance even though it states terms additional to or different from those offered or agreed upon, unless acceptance is expressly made conditional on assent to the additional or different terms.

(2) The additional terms are to be construed as proposals for addition to the contract. Between merchants such terms become part of the contract unless:

(a) the offer expressly limits acceptance to the terms of the offer;

(b) they materially alter it; or

(c) notification of objection to them has already been given or is given within a reasonable time after notice of them is received.

(3) Conduct by both parties which recognizes the existence of a contract is sufficient to establish a contract for sale although the writings of the parties do not otherwise establish a contract. In such case the terms of the particular contract consist of those terms on which the writings of the parties agree, together with any supplementary terms incorporated under any other provisions of this Act.

Section 2—208. COURSE OF PERFORMANCE OR PRACTICAL CONSTRUCTION

(1) Where the contract for sale involves repeated occasions for performance by either party with knowledge of the nature of the performance and opportunity for objection to it by the other, any course of performance accepted or acquiesced in without objection shall be relevant to determine the meaning of the agreement.

(2) The express terms of the agreement and any such course of performance, as well as any course of dealing and usage of trade, shall be construed whenever reasonable as consistent with each other; but when such construction is unreasonable, express terms shall control course of performance and course of performance shall control both course of dealing and usage of trade (Section 1—205).

(3) Subject to the provisions of the next section on modification and waiver, such course of performance shall be relevant to show a waiver or modification of any term inconsistent with such course of performance.

Section 2—209. MODIFICATION, RESCISSION AND WAIVER

(1) An agreement modifying a contract within this Article needs no consideration to be binding.

(2) A signed agreement which excludes modification or rescission except by a signed writing cannot be otherwise modified or rescinded, but except as between merchants such a requirement on a form supplied by the merchant must be separately signed by the other party.

(3) The requirements of the statute of frauds section of this Article (Section 2—201) must be satisfied if the contract as modified is within its provisions.

(4) Although an attempt at modification or rescission does not satisfy the requirements of subsection (2) or (3) it can operate as a waiver.

(5) A party who has made a waiver affecting an executory portion of the contract may retract the waiver by reasonable notification received by the other party that strict performance will be required of any term waived, unless the retraction would be unjust in view of a material change of position in reliance on the waiver.

Part 3

General Obligation and Construction of Contract

Section 2—302. UNCONSCIONABLE CONTRACT OR CLAUSE

(1) If the court as a matter of law finds the contract or any clause of the contract to have been unconscionable at the time it was made the court may refuse to enforce the contract, or it may enforce the remainder of the contract without the unconscionable clause, or it may so limit the application

of any unconscionable clause as to avoid any unconscionable result.

(2) When it is claimed or appears to the court that the contract or any clause thereof may be unconscionable the parties shall be afforded a reasonable opportunity to present evidence as to its commercial setting, purpose and effect to aid the court in making the determination.

Section 2—304. PRICE PAYABLE IN MONEY, GOODS, REALTY, OR OTHERWISE

(1) The price can be made payable in money or otherwise. If it is payable in whole or in part in goods each party is a seller of the goods which he is to transfer.

(2) Even though all or part of the price is payable in an interest in realty the transfer of the goods and the seller's obligations with reference to them are subject to this Article, but not the transfer of the interest in realty or the transferor's obligations in connection therewith.

Section 2—305. OPEN PRICE TERM

(1) The parties if they so intend can conclude a contract for sale even though the price is not settled. In such a case the price is a reasonable price at the time for delivery if

(a) nothing is said as to price; or

(b) the price is left to be agreed by the parties and they fail to agree; or

(c) the price is to be fixed in terms of some agreed market or other standard as set or recorded by a third person or agency and it is not so set or recorded.

(2) A price to be fixed by the seller or by the buyer means a price for him to fix in good faith.

(3) When a price left to be fixed otherwise than by agreement of the parties fails to be fixed through fault of one party the other may at his option treat the contract as cancelled or himself fix a reasonable price.

(4) Where, however, the parties intend not to be bound unless the price be fixed or agreed and it is not fixed or agreed there is no contract. In such a case the buyer must return any goods already received or if unable so to do must pay their reasonable value at the time of delivery and the seller must return any portion of the price paid on account.

Section 2—307. DELIVERY IN SINGLE LOT OR SEVERAL LOTS

Unless otherwise agreed all goods called for by a contract for sale must be tendered in a single delivery and payment is due only on such tender but where the circumstances give either party the right to make or demand delivery in lots the price if it can be apportioned may be demanded for each lot.

Section 2—308. ABSENCE OF SPECIFIED PLACE FOR DELIVERY

Unless otherwise agreed

(a) the place for delivery of goods is the seller's place of business or if he has none his residence; but

(b) in a contract for sale of identified goods which to the knowledge of the parties at the time of contracting are in some other place, that place is the place for their delivery; and

(c) documents of title may be delivered through customary banking channels.

Section 2—310. OPEN TIME FOR PAYMENT OR RUNNING OF CREDIT; AUTHORITY TO SHIP UNDER RESERVATION

Unless otherwise agreed

(a) payment is due at the time and place at which the buyer is to receive the goods even though the place of shipment is the place of delivery; and

(b) if the seller is authorized to send the goods he may ship them under reservation, and may tender the documents of title, but the buyer may inspect the goods after their arrival before payment is due unless such inspection is inconsistent with the terms of the contract (Section 2—513); and

(c) if delivery is authorized and made by way of documents of title otherwise than by subsection (b) then payment is due at the time and place at which the buyer is to receive the documents regardless of where the goods are to be received; and

(d) where the seller is required or authorized to ship the goods on credit the credit period runs from the time of shipment but post-dating the invoice or delaying its dispatch will correspondingly delay the starting of the credit period.

Section 2—312. WARRANTY OF TITLE AND AGAINST INFRINGEMENT; BUYER'S OBLIGATION AGAINST INFRINGEMENT

(1) Subject to subsection (2) there is in a contract for sale a warranty by the seller that

(a) the title conveyed shall be good, and its transfer rightful; and

(b) the goods shall be delivered free from any security interest or other lien or encumbrance of which the buyer at the time of contracting has no knowledge.

(2) A warranty under subsection (1) will be excluded or modified only by specific language or by circumstances which give the buyer reason to know that the person selling does not claim title in himself or that he is purporting to sell only such right or title as he or a third person may have.

(3) Unless otherwise agreed a seller who is a merchant regularly dealing in goods of the kind warrants that the goods shall be delivered free of the rightful claim of any third person by way of infringement or the like but a buyer who furnishes specifications to the seller must hold the seller harmless against any such claim which arises out of compliance with the specifications.

Section 2—313. EXPRESS WARRANTIES BY AFFIRMATION, PROMISE, DESCRIPTION, SAMPLE

(1) Express warranties by the seller are created as follows:

(a) Any affirmation of fact or promise made by the seller to the buyer which relates to the goods and becomes part of the basis of the bargain creates an express warranty that the goods shall conform to the affirmation or promise.

(b) Any description of the goods which is made part of the basis of the bargain creates an express warranty that the goods shall conform to the description.

(c) Any sample or model which is made part of the basis of the bargain creates an express warranty that the whole of the goods shall conform to the sample or model.

(2) It is not necessary to the creation of an express warranty that the seller use formal words such as "warrant" or "guarantee" or that he have a specific intention to make a warranty, but an affirmation merely of the value of the goods or a statement purporting to be merely the seller's opinion or commendation of the goods does not create a warranty.

Section 2—314. IMPLIED WARRANTY: MERCHANTABILITY; USAGE OF TRADE

(1) Unless excluded or modified (Section 2—316), a warranty that the goods shall be merchantable is implied in a contract for their sale if the seller is a merchant with respect to goods of that kind. Under this section the serving for value of food or drink to be consumed either on the premises or elsewhere is a sale.

(2) Goods to be merchantable must be at least such as

(a) pass without objection in the trade under the contract description; and

(b) in the case of fungible goods, are of fair average quality within the description; and

(c) are fit for the ordinary purposes for which such goods are used; and

(d) run, within the variations permitted by the agreement, of even kind, quality and quantity within each unit and among all units involved; and

(e) are adequately contained, packaged, and labeled as the agreement may require; and

(f) conform to the promises or affirmations of fact made on the container or label if any.

(3) Unless excluded or modified (Section 2—316) other implied warranties may arise from course of dealing or usage of trade.

Section 2—315. IMPLIED WARRANTY: FITNESS FOR PARTICULAR PURPOSE

Where the seller at the time of contracting has reason to know any particular purpose for which the goods are required and that the buyer is relying on the seller's skill or judgment to select or furnish suitable goods, there is unless excluded or modified under the next section an implied warranty that the goods shall be fit for such purpose.

Section 2—316. EXCLUSION OR MODIFICATION OF WARRANTIES

(1) Words or conduct relevant to the creation of an express warranty and words or conduct tending to negate or limit warranty shall be construed wherever reasonable as consistent with each other; but subject to the provisions of this Article on parol or extrinsic evidence (Section 2—202) negation or limitation is inoperative to the extent that such construction is unreasonable.

(2) Subject to subsection (3), to exclude or modify the implied warranty of merchantability or any part of it the language must mention merchantability and in case of a writing must be conspicuous, and to exclude or modify any implied warranty of fitness the exclusion must be by a writing and conspicuous. Language to exclude all implied warranties of fitness is sufficient if it states, for example, that "There are no warranties which extend beyond the description on the face hereof."

(3) Notwithstanding subsection (2)

(a) unless the circumstances indicate otherwise, all implied warranties are excluded by expressions like "as is," "with all faults" or other language which in common understanding calls the buyer's attention to the exclusion of warranties and makes plain that there is no implied warranty; and

(b) when the buyer before entering into the contract has examined the goods or the sample or model as fully as he desired or has refused to examine the goods there is no implied warranty with regard to defects which an examination ought in the circumstances to have revealed to him; and

(c) an implied warranty can also be excluded or modified by course of dealing or course of performance or usage of trade.

(4) Remedies for breach of warranty can be limited in accordance with the provisions of this Article on liquidation

or limitation of damages and on contractual modification of remedy (Sections 2—718 and 2—719).

Section 2—317. CUMULATION AND CONFLICT OF WARRANTIES EXPRESS OR IMPLIED

Warranties whether express or implied shall be construed as consistent with each other and as cumulative, but if such construction is unreasonable the intention of the parties shall determine which warranty is dominant. In ascertaining that intention the following rules apply:

(a) Exact or technical specifications displace an inconsistent sample or model or general language of description.

(b) A sample from an existing bulk displaces inconsistent general language of description.

(c) Express warranties displace inconsistent implied warranties other than an implied warranty of fitness for a particular purpose.

Section 2—318. THIRD PARTY BENEFICIARIES OF WARRANTIES EXPRESS OR IMPLIED

Alternative A

A seller's warranty whether express or implied extends to any natural person who is in the family or household of his buyer or who is a guest in his home if it is reasonable to expect that such person may use, consume or be affected by the goods and who is injured in person by breach of the warranty. A seller may not exclude or limit the operation of this section.

Alternative B

A seller's warranty whether express or implied extends to any natural person who may reasonably be expected to use, consume or be affected by the goods and who is injured in person by breach of the warranty. A seller may not exclude or limit the operation of this section.

Alternative C

A seller's warranty whether express or implied extends to any person who may reasonably be expected to use, consume or be affected by the goods and who is injured by breach of the warranty. A seller may not exclude or limit the operation of this section with respect to injury to the person of an individual to whom the warranty extends. As amended 1966.

Section 2—319. F.O.B. AND F.A.S. TERMS

(1) Unless otherwise agreed the term F.O.B. (which means "free on board") at a named place, even though used only in connection with the stated price, is a delivery term under which

(a) when the term is F.O.B. the place of shipment, the seller must at that place ship the goods in the manner provided in this Article (Section 2—504) and bear the expense and risk of putting them into the possession of the carrier; or

(b) when the term is F.O.B. the place of destination, the seller must at his own expense and risk transport the goods to that place and there tender delivery of them in the manner provided in this Article (Section 2—503);

(c) when under either (a) or (b) the term is also F.O.B. vessel, car or other vehicle, the seller must in addition at his own expense and risk load the goods on board. If the term is F.O.B. vessel the buyer must name the vessel and in an appropriate case the seller must comply with the provisions of this Article on the form of bill of lading (Section 2—323).

(2) Unless otherwise agreed the term F.A.S. vessel (which means "free alongside") at a named port, even though used only in connection with the stated price, is a delivery term under which the seller must

(a) at his own expense and risk deliver the goods alongside the vessel in the manner usual in that port or on a dock designated and provided by the buyer; and

(b) obtain and tender a receipt for the goods in exchange for which the carrier is under a duty to issue a bill of lading.

(3) Unless otherwise agreed in any case falling within subsection (1) (a) or (c) or subsection (2) the buyer must seasonably give any needed instructions for making delivery, including when the term is F.A.S. or F.O.B. the loading berth of the vessel and in an appropriate case its name and sailing date. The seller may treat the failure of needed instructions as a failure of cooperation under this Article (Section 2—311). He may also at his option move the goods in any reasonable manner preparatory to delivery or shipment.

(4) Under the term F.O.B. vessel or F.A.S. unless otherwise agreed the buyer must make payment against tender of the required documents and the seller may not tender nor the buyer demand delivery of the goods in substitution for the documents.

Section 2—320. C.I.F. AND C. & F. TERMS

(1) The term C.I.F. means that the price includes in a lump sum the cost of the goods and the insurance and freight to the named destination. The term C. & F. or C.F. means that the price so includes cost and freight to the named destination.

(2) Unless otherwise agreed and even though used only in connection with the stated price and destination, the term C.I.F. destination or its equivalent requires the seller at his own expense and risk to

(a) put the goods into the possession of a carrier at the port for shipment and obtain a negotiable bill or bills of lading covering the entire transportation to the named destination; and
(b) load the goods and obtain a receipt from the carrier (which may be contained in the bill of lading) showing that the freight has been paid or provided for; and
(c) obtain a policy or certificate of insurance, including any war risk insurance, of a kind and on terms then current at the port of shipment in the usual amount, in the currency of the contract, shown to cover the same goods covered by the bill of lading and providing for payment of loss to the order of the buyer or for the account of whom it may concern; but the seller may add to the price the amount of the premium for any such war risk insurance; and
(d) prepare an invoice of the goods and procure any other documents required to effect shipment or to comply with the contract; and
(e) forward and tender with commercial promptness all the documents in due form and with any indorsement necessary to perfect the buyer's rights.

(3) Unless otherwise agreed the term C. & F. or its equivalent has the same effect and imposes upon the seller the same obligations and risks as a C.I.F. term except the obligation as to insurance.

(4) Under the term C.I.F. or C. & F. unless otherwise agreed the buyer must make payment against tender of the required documents and the seller may not tender nor the buyer demand delivery of the goods in substitution for the documents.

Section 2—326. SALE ON APPROVAL AND SALE OR RETURN; CONSIGNMENT SALES AND RIGHTS OF CREDITORS

(1) Unless otherwise agreed, if delivered goods may be returned by the buyer even though they conform to the contract, the transaction is
(a) a "sale on approval" if the goods are delivered primarily for use, and
(b) a "sale or return" if the goods are delivered primarily for resale.

(2) Except as provided in subsection (3), goods held on approval are not subject to the claims of the buyer's creditors until acceptance; goods held on sale or return are subject to such claims while in the buyer's possession.

(3) Where goods are delivered to a person for sale and such person maintains a place of business at which he deals in goods of the kind involved, under a name other than the name of the person making delivery, then with respect to claims of creditors of the person conducting the business the goods are deemed to be on sale or return. The provisions of this subsection are applicable even though an agreement purports to reserve title to the person making delivery until payment or resale or uses such words as "on consignment" or "on memorandum". However, this subsection is not applicable if the person making delivery
(a) complies with an applicable law providing for a consignor's interest or the like to be evidenced by a sign, or
(b) establishes that the person conducting the business is generally known by his creditors to be substantially engaged in selling the goods of others, or
(c) complies with the filing provisions of the Article on Secured Transactions (Article 9).

(4) Any "or return" term of a contract for sale is to be treated as a separate contract for sale within the statute of frauds section of this Article (Section 2—201) and as contradicting the sale aspect of the contract within the provisions of this Article on parol or extrinsic evidence (Section 2—202).

Section 2—327. SPECIAL INCIDENTS OF SALE ON APPROVAL AND SALE OR RETURN

(1) Under a sale on approval unless otherwise agreed
(a) although the goods are identified to the contract the risk of loss and the title do not pass to the buyer until acceptance; and
(b) use of the goods consistent with the purpose of trial is not acceptance but failure seasonably to notify the seller of election to return the goods is acceptance, and if the goods conform to the contract acceptance of any part is acceptance of the whole; and
(c) after due notification of election to return, the return is at the seller's risk and expense but a merchant buyer must follow any reasonable instructions.

(2) Under a sale or return unless otherwise agreed
(a) the option to return extends to the whole or any commercial unit of the goods while in substantially their original condition, but must be exercised seasonably; and
(b) the return is at the buyer's risk and expense.

Part 4
Title, Creditors and Good Faith Purchasers

Section 2—401. PASSING OF TITLE; RESERVATION FOR SECURITY; LIMITED APPLICATION OF THIS SECTION

Each provision of this Article with regard to the rights, obligations and remedies of the seller, the buyer, purchasers or other third parties applies irrespective of title to the goods except where the provision refers to such title. Insofar as situations are not covered by the other provisions of this Article and matters concerning title become material the following rules apply:

(1) Title to goods cannot pass under a contract for sale prior to their identification to the contract (Section 2—501), and unless otherwise explicitly agreed the buyer acquires by their identification a special property as limited by this Act. Any retention or reservation by the seller of the title (property) in goods shipped or delivered to the buyer is limited in effect to a reservation of a security interest. Subject to these provisions and to the provisions of the Article on Secured Transactions (Article 9), title to goods passes from the seller to the buyer in any manner and on any conditions explicitly agreed on by the parties.

(2) Unless otherwise explicitly agreed title passes to the buyer at the time and place at which the seller completes his performance with reference to the physical delivery of the goods, despite any reservation of a security interest and even though a document of title is to be delivered at a different time or place; and in particular and despite any reservation of a security interest by the bill of lading

(a) if the contract requires or authorizes the seller to send the goods to the buyer but does not require him to deliver them at destination, title passes to the buyer at the time and place of shipment; but

(b) if the contract requires delivery at destination, title passes on tender there.

(3) Unless otherwise explicitly agreed where delivery is to be made without moving the goods,

(a) if the seller is to deliver a document of title, title passes at the time when and the place where he delivers such documents; or

(b) if the goods are at the time of contracting already identified and no documents are to be delivered, title passes at the time and place of contracting.

(4) A rejection or other refusal by the buyer to receive or retain the goods, whether or not justified, or a justified revocation of acceptance revests title to the goods in the seller. Such revesting occurs by operation of law and is not a "sale".

Section 2—402. RIGHTS OF SELLER'S CREDITORS AGAINST SOLD GOODS

(1) Except as provided in subsections (2) and (3), rights of unsecured creditors of the seller with respect to goods which have been identified to a contract for sale are subject to the buyer's rights to recover the goods under this Article (Sections 2—502 and 2—716).

(2) A creditor of the seller may treat a sale or an identification of goods to a contract for sale as void if as against him a retention of possession by the seller is fraudulent under any rule of law of the state where the goods are situated, except that retention of possession in good faith and current course of trade by a merchant-seller for a commercially reasonable time after a sale or identification is not fraudulent.

(3) Nothing in this Article shall be deemed to impair the rights of creditors of the seller

(a) under the provisions of the Article on Secured Transactions (Article 9); or

(b) where identification to the contract or delivery is made not in current course of trade but in satisfaction of or as security for a pre-existing claim for money, security or the like and is made under circumstances which under any rule of law of the state where the goods are situated would apart from this Article constitute the transaction a fraudulent transfer or voidable preference.

Section 2—403. POWER TO TRANSFER; GOOD FAITH PURCHASE OF GOODS; "ENTRUSTING"

(1) A purchaser of goods acquires all title which his transferor had or had power to transfer except that a purchaser of a limited interest acquires rights only to the extent of the interest purchased. A person with voidable title has power to transfer a good title to a good faith purchaser for value. When goods have been delivered under a transaction of purchase the purchaser has such power even though

(a) the transferor was deceived as to the identity of the purchaser, or

(b) the delivery was in exchange for a check which is later dishonored, or

(c) it was agreed that the transaction was to be a "cash sale", or

(d) the delivery was procured through fraud punishable as larcenous under the criminal law.

(2) Any entrusting of possession of goods to a merchant who deals in goods of that kind gives him power to transfer all rights of the entruster to a buyer in ordinary course of business.

(3) "Entrusting" includes any delivery and any acquiescence in retention of possession regardless of any condition expressed between the parties to the delivery or acquiescence and regardless of whether the procurement of the entrusting or the possessor's disposition of the goods have been such as to be larcenous under the criminal law.

(4) The rights of other purchasers of goods and of lien creditors are governed by the Articles on Secured Transactions (Article 9), Bulk Transfers (Article 6) and Documents of Title (Article 7).

Part 5

Performance

Section 2—501. INSURABLE INTEREST IN GOODS; MANNER OF IDENTIFICATION OF GOODS

(1) The buyer obtains a special property and an insurable interest in goods by identification of existing goods as goods to which the contract refers even though the goods so iden-

tified are non-conforming and he has an option to return or reject them. Such identification can be made at any time and in any manner explicitly agreed to by the parties. In the absence of explicit agreement identification occurs

(a) when the contract is made if it is for the sale of goods already existing and identified;

(b) if the contract is for the sale of future goods other than those described in paragraph (c), when goods are shipped, marked or otherwise designated by the seller as goods to which the contract refers;

(c) when the crops are planted or otherwise become growing crops or the young are conceived if the contract is for the sale of unborn young to be born within twelve months after contracting or for the sale of crops to be harvested within twelve months or the next normal harvest season after contracting whichever is longer.

(2) The seller retains an insurable interest in goods so long as title to or any security interest in the goods remains in him and where the identification is by the seller alone he may until default or insolvency or notification to the buyer that the identification is final substitute other goods for those identified.

(3) Nothing in this section impairs any insurable interest recognized under any other statute or rule of law.

Section 2—502. BUYER'S RIGHT TO GOODS ON SELLER'S INSOLVENCY

(1) Subject to subsection (2) and even though the goods have not been shipped a buyer who has paid a part or all of the price of goods in which he has a special property under the provisions of the immediately preceding section may on making and keeping good a tender of any unpaid portion of their price recover them from the seller if the seller becomes insolvent within ten days after receipt of the first installment on their price.

(2) If the identification creating his special property has been made by the buyer he acquires the right to recover the goods only if they conform to the contract for sale.

Section 2—503. MANNER OF SELLER'S TENDER OF DELIVERY

(1) Tender of delivery requires that the seller put and hold conforming goods at the buyer's disposition and give the buyer any notification reasonably necessary to enable him to take delivery. The manner, time and place for tender are determined by the agreement and this Article, and in particular

(a) tender must be at a reasonable hour, and if it is of goods they must be kept available for the period reasonably necessary to enable the buyer to take possession; but

(b) unless otherwise agreed the buyer must furnish facilities reasonably suited to the receipt of the goods.

(2) Where the case is within the next section respecting shipment tender requires that the seller comply with its provisions.

(3) Where the seller is required to deliver at a particular destination tender requires that he comply with subsection (1) and also in any appropriate case tender documents as described in subsections (4) and (5) of this section.

(4) Where goods are in the possession of a bailee and are to be delivered without being moved

(a) tender requires that the seller either tender a negotiable document of title covering such goods or procure acknowledgment by the bailee of the buyer's right to possession of the goods; but

(b) tender to the buyer of a non-negotiable document of title or of a written direction to the bailee to deliver is sufficient tender unless the buyer seasonably objects, and receipt by the bailee of notification of the buyer's rights fixes those rights as against the bailee and all third persons; but risk of loss of the goods and of any failure by the bailee to honor the non-negotiable document of title or to obey the direction remains on the seller until the buyer has had a reasonable time to present the document or direction, and a refusal by the bailee to honor the document or to obey the direction defeats the tender.

(5) Where the contract requires the seller to deliver documents

(a) he must tender all such documents in correct form, except as provided in this Article with respect to bills of lading in a set (subsection (2) of Section 2—323); and

(b) tender through customary banking channels is sufficient and dishonor of a draft accompanying the documents constitutes non-acceptance or rejection.

Section 2—508. CURE BY SELLER OF IMPROPER TENDER OR DELIVERY; REPLACEMENT

(1) Where any tender or delivery by the seller is rejected because non-conforming and the time for performance has not yet expired, the seller may seasonably notify the buyer of his intention to cure and may then within the contract time make a conforming delivery.

(2) Where the buyer rejects a non-conforming tender which the seller had reasonable grounds to believe would be acceptable with or without money allowance the seller may if he seasonably notifies the buyer have a further reasonable time to substitute a conforming tender.

Section 2—509. RISK OF LOSS IN THE ABSENCE OF BREACH

(1) Where the contract requires or authorizes the seller to ship the goods by carrier

(a) if it does not require him to deliver them at a particular destination, the risk of loss passes to the buyer when the goods are duly delivered to the carrier even though the shipment is under reservation (Section 2—505); but

(b) if it does require him to deliver them at a particular destination and the goods are there duly tendered while in the possession of the carrier, the risk of loss passes to the buyer when the goods are there duly so tendered as to enable the buyer to take delivery.

(2) Where the goods are held by a bailee to be delivered without being moved, the risk of loss passes to the buyer

(a) on his receipt of a negotiable document of title covering the goods; or

(b) on acknowledgment by the bailee of the buyer's right to possession of the goods; or

(c) after his receipt of a non-negotiable document of title or other written direction to deliver, as provided in subsection (4) (b) of Section 2—503.

(3) In any case not within subsection (1) or (2), the risk of loss passes to the buyer on his receipt of the goods if the seller is a merchant; otherwise the risk passes to the buyer on tender of delivery.

(4) The provisions of this section are subject to contrary agreement of the parties and to the provisions of this Article on sale on approval (Section 2—327) and on effect of breach on risk of loss (Section 2—510).

Section 2—512. PAYMENT BY BUYER BEFORE INSPECTION

(1) Where the contract requires payment before inspection non-conformity of the goods does not excuse the buyer from so making payment unless

(a) the non-conformity appears without inspection; or

(b) despite tender of the required documents the circumstances would justify injunction against honor under the provisions of this Act (Section 5—114).

(2) Payment pursuant to subsection (1) does not constitute an acceptance of goods or impair the buyer's right to inspect or any if his remedies.

Section 2—513. BUYER'S RIGHT TO INSPECTION OF GOODS

(1) Unless otherwise agreed and subject to subsection (3), where goods are tendered or delivered or identified to the contract for sale, the buyer has a right before payment or acceptance to inspect them at any reasonable place and time and in any reasonable manner. When the seller is required or authorized to send the goods to the buyer, the inspection may be after their arrival.

(2) Expenses of inspection must be borne by the buyer but may be recovered from the seller if the goods do not conform and are rejected.

(3) Unless otherwise agreed and subject to the provisions of this Article on C.I.F. contracts (subsection (3) of Section 2—321), the buyer is not entitled to inspect the goods before payment of the price when the contract provides

(a) for delivery "C.O.D." or on other like terms; or

(b) for payment against documents of title, except where such payment is due only after the goods are to become available for inspection.

(4) A place or method of inspection fixed by the parties is presumed to be exclusive but unless otherwise expressly agreed it does not postpone identification or shift the place for delivery or for passing the risk of loss. If compliance becomes impossible, inspection shall be as provided in this section unless the place or method fixed was clearly intended as an indispensable condition failure of which avoids the contract.

Part 6

Breach, Repudiation and Excuse

Section 2–601. BUYER'S RIGHTS ON IMPROPER DELIVERY

Subject to the provisions of this Article on breach in installment contracts (Section 2—612) and unless otherwise agreed under the sections on contractual limitations of remedy (Sections 2—718 and 2—719), if the goods or the tender of delivery fail in any respect to conform to the contract, the buyer may

(a) reject the whole; or

(b) accept the whole; or

(c) accept any commercial unit or units and reject the rest.

Section 2—602. MANNER AND EFFECT OF RIGHTFUL REJECTION

(1) Rejection of goods must be within a reasonable time after their delivery or tender. It is ineffective unless the buyer seasonably notifies the seller.

(2) Subject to the provisions of the two following sections on rejected goods (Sections 2—603 and 2—604),

(a) after rejection any exercise of ownership by the buyer with respect to any commercial unit is wrongful as against the seller; and

(b) if the buyer has before rejection taken physical possession of goods in which he does not have a security interest under the provisions of this Article (subsection (3) of Section 2—711), he is under a duty after rejection to hold them with reasonable care at the seller's disposition for a time sufficient to permit the seller to remove them; but

(c) the buyer has no further obligations with regard to goods rightfully rejected

(3) The seller's rights with respect to goods wrongfully rejected are governed by the provisions of this Article on Seller's remedies in general (Section 2—703).

Section 2—603. MERCHANT BUYER'S DUTIES AS TO RIGHTFULLY REJECTED GOODS

(1) Subject to any security interest in the buyer (subsection (3) of Section 2—711), when the seller has no agent or place of business at the market of rejection a merchant buyer is under a duty after rejection of goods in his possession or control to follow any reasonable instructions received from the seller with respect to the goods and in the absence of such instructions to make reasonable efforts to sell them for the seller's account if they are perishable or threaten to decline in value speedily. Instructions are not reasonable if on demand indemnity for expenses is not forthcoming.

(2) When the buyer sells goods under subsection (1), he is entitled to reimbursement from the seller or out of the proceeds for reasonable expenses of caring for and selling them, and if the expenses include no selling commission then to such commission as is usual in the trade or if there is none to a reasonable sum not exceeding ten per cent on the gross proceeds.

(3) In complying with this section the buyer is held only to good faith and good faith conduct hereunder is neither acceptance nor conversion nor the basis of an action for damages.

U.L.A.-U.C.C. 9th Ed. '78 Pamph.—5

Section 2—604. BUYER'S OPTIONS AS TO SALVAGE OF RIGHTFULLY REJECTED GOODS

Subject to the provisions of the immediately preceding section on perishables if the seller gives no instructions within a reasonable time after notification of rejection the buyer may store the rejected goods for the seller's account or reship them to him or resell them for the seller's account with reimbursement as provided in the preceding section. Such action is not acceptance or conversion.

Section 2—605. WAIVER OF BUYER'S OBJECTIONS BY FAILURE TO PARTICULARIZE

(1) The buyer's failure to state in connection with rejection a particular defect which is ascertainable by reasonable inspection precludes him from relying on the unstated defect to justify rejection or to establish breach

(a) where the seller could have cured it if stated seasonably; or

(b) between merchants when the seller has after rejection made a request in writing for a full and final written statement of all defects on which the buyer proposes to rely.

(2) Payment against documents made without reservation of rights precludes recovery of the payment for defects apparent on the face of the documents.

Section 2—606. WHAT CONSTITUTES ACCEPTANCE OF GOODS

(1) Acceptance of goods occurs when the buyer

(a) after a reasonable opportunity to inspect the goods signifies to the seller that the goods are conforming or that he will take or retain them in spite of their nonconformity; or

(b) fails to make an effective rejection (subsection (1) of Section 2—602), but such acceptance does not occur until the buyer has had a reasonable opportunity to inspect them; or

(c) does any act inconsistent with the seller's ownership; but if such act is wrongful as against the seller it is an acceptance only if ratified by him.

(2) Acceptance of a part of any commercial unit is acceptance of that entire unit.

Section 2—607. EFFECT OF ACCEPTANCE; NOTICE OF BREACH; BURDEN OF ESTABLISHING BREACH AFTER ACCEPTANCE; NOTICE OF CLAIM OR LITIGATION TO PERSON ANSWERABLE OVER

(1) The buyer must pay at the contract rate for any goods accepted.

(2) Acceptance of goods by the buyer precludes rejection of the goods accepted and if made with knowledge of a nonconformity cannot be revoked because of it unless the acceptance was on the reasonable assumption that the nonconformity would be seasonably cured but acceptance does not of itself impair any other remedy provided by this Article for non-conformity.

(3) Where a tender has been accepted

(a) the buyer must within a reasonable time after he discovers or should have discovered any breach notify the seller of breach or be barred from any remedy; and

(b) if the claim is one for infringement or the like (subsection (3) of Section 2—312) and the buyer is sued as a result of such a breach he must so notify the seller within a reasonable time after he receives notice of the litigation or be barred from any remedy over for liability established by the litigation.

(4) The burden is on the buyer to establish any breach with respect to the goods accepted.

(5) Where the buyer is sued for breach of a warranty or other obligation for which his seller is answerable over

(a) he may give his seller written notice of the litigation. If the notice states that the seller may come in and defend and that if the seller does not do so he will be bound in any action against him by his buyer by any determination of fact common to the two litigations, then unless the seller after seasonable receipt of the notice does come in and defend he is so bound.

(b) if the claim is one for infringement or the like (subsection (3) of Section 2—312) the original seller may demand in writing that his buyer turn over to him control of the litigation including settlement or else be barred from any remedy over and if he also agrees to bear all expense and to satisfy any adverse judgment, then unless the buyer after seasonable receipt of the demand does turn over control the buyer is so barred.

(6) The provisions of subsections (3), (4) and (5) apply to any obligation of a buyer to hold the seller harmless against infringement or the like (subsection (3) of Section 2—312).

Section 2—608. REVOCATION OF ACCEPTANCE IN WHOLE OR IN PART

(1) The buyer may revoke his acceptance of a lot or commercial unit whose non-conformity substantially impairs its value to him if he has accepted it

(a) on the reasonable assumption that its non-conformity would be cured and it has not been seasonably cured; or

(b) without discovery of such non-conformity if his acceptance was reasonably induced either by the difficulty of discovery before acceptance or by the seller's assurances.

(2) Revocation of acceptance must occur within a reasonable time after the buyer discovers or should have discovered the ground for it and before any substantial change in condition of the goods which is not caused by their own defects. It is not effective until the buyer notifies the seller of it.

(3) A buyer who so revokes the same rights and duties with regard to the goods involved as if he had rejected them.

Section 2—609. RIGHT TO ADEQUATE ASSURANCE OF PERFORMANCE

(1) A contract for sale imposes an obligation on each party that the other's expectation of receiving due performance will not be impaired. When reasonable grounds for insecurity arise with respect to the performance of either party the other may in writing demand adequate assurance of due performance and until he receives such assurance may if commercially reasonable suspend any performance for which he has not already received the agreed return.

(2) Between merchants the reasonableness of grounds for insecurity and the adequacy of any assurance offered shall be determined according to commercial standards.

(3) Acceptance of any improper delivery or payment does not prejudice the aggrieved party's right to demand adequate assurance of future performance.

(4) After receipt of a justified demand failure to provide within a reasonable time not exceeding thirty days such assurance of due performance as is adequate under the circumstances of the particular case is a repudiation of the contract.

Section 2—610. ANTICIPATORY REPUDIATION

When either party repudiates the contract with respect to a performance not yet due the loss of which will substantially impair the value of the contract to the other, the aggrieved party may

(a) for a commercially reasonable time await performance by the repudiating party; or

(b) resort to any remedy for breach (Section 2—703 or Section 2—711), even though he has notified the repudiating party that he would await the latter's performance and has urged retraction; and

(c) in either case suspend his own performance or proceed in accordance with the provisions of this Article on the seller's right to identify goods to the contract notwithstanding breach or to salvage unfinished goods (Section 2—704).

Section 2—611. RETRACTION OF ANTICIPATORY REPUDIATION

(1) Until the repudiating party's next performance is due he can retract his repudiation unless the aggrieved party has since the repudiation cancelled or materially changed his position or otherwise indicated that he considers the repudiation final.

(2) Retraction may be by any method which clearly indicates to the aggrieved party that the repudiating party intends to perform, but must include any assurance justifiably demanded under the provisions of this Article (Section 2—609).

(3) Retraction reinstates the repudiating party's rights, under the contract with due excuse and allowance to the aggrieved party for any delay occasioned by the repudiation.

Section 2—612. "INSTALLMENT CONTRACT"; BREACH

(1) An "installment contract" is one which requires or authorizes the delivery of goods in separate lots to be separately accepted, even though the contract contains a clause "each delivery is a separate contract" or its equivalent.

(2) The buyer may reject any installment which is non-conforming if the non-conformity substantially impairs the value of that installment and cannot be cured or if the non-conformity is a defect in the required documents; but if the non-conformity does not fall within subsection (3) and the seller gives adequate assurance of its cure the buyer must accept that installment.

(3) Whenever non-conformity or default with respect to one or more installments substantially impairs the value of the whole contract there is a breach of the whole. But the aggrieved party reinstates the contract if he accepts a non-conforming installment without seasonably notifying of can-

cellation or if he brings an action with respect only to past installments or demands performance as to future installments.

Section 2—613. CASUALTY TO IDENTIFIED GOODS

Where the contract requires for its performance goods identified when the contract is made, and the goods suffer casualty without fault of either party before the risk of loss passes to the buyer, or in a proper case under a "no arrival, no sale" term (Section 2—324) then

(a) if the loss is total the contract is avoided; and

(b) if the loss is partial or the goods have so deteriorated as no longer to conform to the contract the buyer may nevertheless demand inspection and at his option either treat the contract as avoided or accept the goods with due allowance from the contract price for the deterioration or the deficiency in quantity but without further right against the seller.

Section 2—615. EXCUSE BY FAILURE OF PRESUPPOSED CONDITIONS

Except so far as a seller may have assumed a greater obligation and subject to the preceding section on substituted performance:

(a) Delay in delivery or non-delivery in whole or in part by a seller who complies with paragraphs (b) and (c) is not a breach of his duty under a contract for sale if performance as agreed has been made impracticable by the occurrence of a contingency the non-occurrence of which was a basic assumption on which the contract was made or by compliance in good faith with any applicable foreign or domestic governmental regulation or order whether or not it later proves to be invalid.

(b) Where the causes mentioned in paragraph (a) affect only a part of the seller's capacity to perform, he must allocate production and deliveries among his customers but may at his option include regular customers not then under contract as well as his own requirements for further manufacture. He may so allocate in any manner which is fair and reasonable.

(c) The seller must notify the buyer seasonably that there will be delay or non-delivery and, when allocation is required under paragraph (b), of the estimated quota thus made available for the buyer.

Part 7

Remedies

Section 2—702. SELLER'S REMEDIES ON DISCOVERY OF BUYER'S INSOLVENCY

(1) Where the seller discovers the buyer to be insolvent he may refuse delivery except for cash including payment for all goods theretofore delivered under the contract, and stop delivery under this Article (Section 2—705).

(2) Where the seller discovers that the buyer has received goods on credit while insolvent he may reclaim the goods upon demand made within ten days after the receipt, but if misrepresentation of solvency has been made to the particular seller in writing within three months before delivery the ten day limitation does not apply. Except as provided in this subsection the seller may not base a right to reclaim goods on the buyer's fraudulent or innocent misrepresentation of solvency or of intent to pay.

(3) The seller's right to reclaim under subsection (2) is subject to the rights of a buyer in ordinary course or other good faith purchaser under this Article (Section 2—403). Successful reclamation of goods excludes all other remedies with respect to them. As amended 1966.

Section 2—703. SELLER'S REMEDIES IN GENERAL

Where the buyer wrongfully rejects or revokes acceptance of goods or fails to make a payment due on or before delivery or repudiates with respect to a part or the whole, then with respect to any goods directly affected and, if the breach is of the whole contract (Section 2—612), then also with respect to the whole undelivered balance, the aggrieved seller may

(a) withhold delivery of such goods;

(b) stop delivery by any bailee as hereafter provided (Section 2—705);

(c) proceed under the next section respecting goods still unidentified to the contract;

(d) resell and recover damages as hereafter provided (Section 2—706);

(e) recover damages for non-acceptance (Section 2—708) or in a proper case the price (Section 2—709);

(f) cancel.

Section 2—704. SELLER'S RIGHT TO IDENTIFY GOODS TO THE CONTRACT NOTWITHSTANDING BREACH OR TO SALVAGE UNFINISHED GOODS

(1) An aggrieved seller under the preceding section may

(a) identify to the contract conforming goods not already identified if at the time he learned of the breach they are in his possession or control;

(b) treat as the subject of resale goods which have demonstrably been intended for the particular contract even though those goods are unfinished.

(2) Where the goods are unfinished an aggrieved seller may in the exercise of reasonable commercial judgment for the purposes of avoiding loss and of effective realization either complete the manufacture and wholly identify the goods to the contract or cease manufacture and resell for scrap or salvage value or proceed in any other reasonable manner.

Section 2—705. SELLER'S STOPPAGE OF DELIVERY IN TRANSIT OR OTHERWISE

(1) The seller may stop delivery of goods in the possession of a carrier or other bailee when he discovers the buyer to be insolvent (Section 2—702) and may stop delivery of carload, truckload, planeload or larger shipments of express or freight when the buyer repudiates or fails to make a payment due before delivery or if for any other reason the seller has a right to withhold or reclaim the goods.

(2) As against such buyer the seller may stop delivery until

(a) receipt of the goods by the buyer; or

(b) acknowledgment to the buyer by any bailee of the goods except a carrier that the bailee holds the goods for the buyer; or

(c) such acknowledgment to the buyer by a carrier by reshipment or as warehouseman; or

(d) negotiation to the buyer of any negotiable document of title covering the goods.

(3)(a) To stop delivery the seller must so notify as to enable the bailee by reasonable diligence to prevent delivery of the goods.

(b) After such notification the bailee must hold and deliver the goods according to the directions of the seller but the seller is liable to the bailee for any ensuing charges or damages.

(c) If a negotiable document of title has been issued for goods the bailee is not obliged to obey a notification to stop until surrender of the document.

(d) A carrier who has issued a non-negotiable 'bill of lading is not obliged to obey a notification to stop received from a person other than the consignor.

Section 2—706. SELLER'S RESALE INCLUDING CONTRACT FOR RESALE

(1) Under the conditions stated in Section 2—703 on seller's remedies, the seller may resell the goods concerned or the undelivered balance thereof. Where the resale is made in good faith and in a commercially reasonable manner the seller may recover the difference between the resale price and the contract price together with any incidental damages allowed under the provisions of this Article (Section 2—710), but less expenses saved in consequence of the buyer's breach.

(2) Except as otherwise provided in subsection (3) or unless otherwise agreed resale may be at public or private sale including sale by way of one or more contracts to sell or of identification to an existing contract of the seller. Sale may be as a unit or in parcels and at any time and place and on any terms but every aspect of the sale including the method, manner, time, place and terms must be commercially reasonable. The resale must be reasonably identified as referring to the broken contract, but it is not necessary that the goods be in existence or that any or all of them have been identified to the contract before the breach.

(3) Where the resale is at private sale the seller must give the buyer reasonable notification of his intention to resell.

(4) Where the resale is at public sale

(a) only identified goods can be sold except where there is a recognized market for a public sale of futures in goods of the kind; and

(b) it must be made at a usual place or market for public sale if one is reasonably available and except in the case of goods which are perishable or threaten to decline in value speedily the seller must give the buyer reasonable notice of the time and place of the resale; and

(c) if the goods are not to be within the view of those attending the sale the notification of sale must state the place where the goods are located and provide for their reasonable inspection by prospective bidders; and

(d) the seller may buy.

(5) A purchaser who buys in good faith at a resale takes the goods free of any rights of the original buyer even though the seller fails to comply with one or more of the requirements of this section.

(6) The seller is not accountable to the buyer for *any profit made on any* resale. A person in the position of a seller (Section 2—707) or a buyer who has rightfully rejected or justifiably revoked acceptance must account for any excess over the amount of his security interest, as hereinafter defined (subsection (3) of Section 2—711).

Section 2—708. SELLER'S DAMAGES FOR NON-ACCEPTANCE OR REPUDIATION

(1) Subject to subsection (2) and to the provisions of this Article with respect to proof of market price (Section 2—723), the measure of damages for non-acceptance or repudiation by the buyer is the difference between the market price at the time and place for tender and the unpaid contract price together with any incidental damages provided in this Article (Section 2—710), but less expenses saved in consequence of the buyer's breach.

(2) If the measure of damages provided in subsection (1) is inadequate to put the seller in as good a position as performance would have done then the measure of damages is the profit (including reasonable overhead) which the seller would have made from full performance by the buyer, together with any incidental damages provided in this Article (Section 2—710), due allowance for costs reasonably incurred and due credit for payments or proceeds of resale.

Section 2—709. ACTION FOR THE PRICE

(1) When the buyer fails to pay the price as it becomes due the seller may recover, together with any incidental damages under the next section, the price

(a) of goods accepted or of conforming goods lost or damaged within a commercially reasonable time after risk of their loss has passed to the buyer; and
(b) of goods identified to the contract if the seller is unable after reasonable effort to resell them at a reasonable price or the circumstances reasonably indicate that such effort will be unavailing.

(2) Where the seller sues for the price he must hold for the buyer any goods which have been identified to the contract and are still in his control except that if resale becomes possible he may resell them at any time prior to the collection of the judgment. The net proceeds of any such resale must be credited to the buyer and payment of the judgment entitles him to any goods not resold.

(3) After the buyer has wrongfully rejected or revoked acceptance of the goods or has failed to make a payment due or has repudiated (Section 2—610), a seller who is held not entitled to the price under this section shall nevertheless be awarded damages for non-acceptance under the preceding section.

Section 2—710. SELLER'S INCIDENTAL DAMAGES

Incidental damages to an aggrieved seller include any commercially reasonable charges, expenses or commissions incurred in stopping delivery, in the transportation, care and custody of goods after the buyer's breach, in connection with return or resale of the goods or otherwise resulting from the breach.

Section 2—711. BUYER'S REMEDIES IN GENERAL; BUYER'S SECURITY INTEREST IN REJECTED GOODS

(1) Where the seller fails to make delivery or repudiates or the buyer rightfully rejects or justifiably revokes acceptance then with respect to any goods involved, and with respect to the whole if the breach goes to the whole contract (Section 2—612), the buyer may cancel and whether or not he has done so may in addition to recovering so much of the price as has been paid
(a) "cover" and have damages under the next section as to all the goods affected whether or not they have been identified to the contract; or
(b) recover damages for non-delivery as provided in this Article (Section 2—713).

(2) Where the seller fails to deliver or repudiates the buyer may also
(a) if the goods have been identified recover them as provided in this Article (Section 2—502); or
(b) in a proper case obtain specific performance or replevy the goods as provided in this Article (Section 2—716).

(3) On rightful rejection or justifiable revocation of acceptance a buyer has a security interest in goods in his possession or control for any payments made on their price and any expenses reasonably incurred in their inspection, receipt, transportation, care and custody and may hold such goods and resell them in like manner as an aggrieved seller (Section 2—706).

Section 2—712. "COVER"; BUYER'S PROCUREMENT OF SUBSTITUTE GOODS

(1) After a breach within the preceding section the buyer may "cover" by making in good faith and without unreasonable delay any reasonable purchase of or contract to purchase goods in substitution for those due from the seller.

(2) The buyer may recover from the seller as damages the difference between the cost of cover and the contract price together with any incidental or consequential damages as hereinafter defined (Section 2—715), but less expenses saved in consequence of the seller's breach.

(3) Failure of the buyer to effect cover within this section does not bar him from any other remedy.

Section 2—713. BUYER'S DAMAGES FOR NON-DELIVERY OR REPUDIATION

(1) Subject to the provisions of this Article with respect to proof of market price (Section 2—723), the measure of damages for non-delivery or repudiation by the seller is the difference between the market price at the time when the buyer learned of the breach and the contract price together with any incidental and consequential damages provided in this Article (Section 2—715), but less expenses saved in consequence of the seller's breach.

(2) Market price is to be determined as of the place for tender or, in cases of rejection after arrival or revocation of acceptance, as of the place of arrival.

Section 2—714. BUYER'S DAMAGES FOR BREACH IN REGARD TO ACCEPTED GOODS

(1) Where the buyer has accepted goods and given notification (subsection (3) of Section 2—607) he may recover as damages for any non-conformity of tender the loss resulting in the ordinary course of events from the seller's breach as determined in any manner which is reasonable.

(2) The measure of damages for breach of warranty is the difference at the time and place of acceptance between the value of the goods accepted and the value they would have had if they had been as warranted, unless special circumstances show proximate damages of a different amount.

(3) In a proper case any incidental and consequential damages under the next section may also be recovered.

Section 2—715. BUYER'S INCIDENTAL AND CONSEQUENTIAL DAMAGES

(1) Incidental damages resulting from the seller's breach include expenses reasonably incurred in inspection, receipt, transportation and care and custody of goods rightfully rejected, any commercially reasonable charges, expenses or commissions in connection with effecting cover and any other reasonable expense incident to the delay or other breach.

(2) Consequential damages resulting from the seller's breach include

(a) any loss resulting from general or particular requirements and needs of which the seller at the time of contracting had reason to know and which could not reasonably be prevented by cover or otherwise; and

(b) injury to person or property proximately resulting from any breach of warranty.

Section 2—716. BUYER'S RIGHT TO SPECIFIC PERFORMANCE OR REPLEVIN

(1) Specific performance may be decreed where the goods are unique or in other proper circumstances.

(2) The decree for specific performance may include such terms and conditions as to payment of the price, damages, or other relief as the court may deem just.

(3) The buyer has a right of replevin for goods identified to the contract if after reasonable effort he is unable to effect cover for such goods or the circumstances reasonably indicate that such effort will be unavailing or if the goods have been shipped under reservation and satisfaction of the security interest in them has been made or tendered.

Section 2—723. PROOF OF MARKET PRICE: TIME AND PLACE

(1) If an action based on anticipatory repudiation comes to trial before the time for performance with respect to some or all of the goods, any damages based on market price (Section 2—708 or Section 2—713) shall be determined according to the price of such goods prevailing at the time when the aggrieved party learned of the repudiation.

(2) If evidence of a price prevailing at the times or places described in this Article is not readily available the price prevailing within any reasonable time before or after the time described or at any other place which in commercial judgment or under usage of trade would serve as a reasonable substitute for the one described may be used, making any proper allowance for the cost of transporting the goods to or from such other place.

(3) Evidence of a relevant price prevailing at a time or place other than the one described in this Article offered by one party is not admissible unless and until he has given the other party such notice as the court finds sufficient to prevent unfair surprise.

Article III

Commercial Paper

Section 3—102. DEFINITIONS AND INDEX OF DEFINITIONS

(1) In this Article unless the context otherwise requires

(a) "Issue" means the first delivery of an instrument to a holder or a remitter.

(b) An "order" is a direction to pay and must be more than an authorization or request. It must identify the person to pay with reasonable certainty. It may be addressed to one or more such persons jointly or in the alternative but not in succession.

(c) A "promise" is an undertaking to pay and must be more than an acknowledgment of an obligation.

(d) "Secondary party" means a drawer or endorser.

(e) "Instrument" means a negotiable instrument.

(2) Other definitions applying to this Article and the sections in which they appear are:

"Acceptance". Section 3—410.
"Accommodation party". Section 3—415.
"Alteration". Section 3—407.
"Certificate of deposit". Section 3—104.
"Certification". Section 3—411.
"Check". Section 3—104.
"Definite time". Section 3—109.
"Dishonor". Section 3—507.
"Draft". Section 3—104.
"Holder in due course". Section 3—302.
"Negotiation". Section 3—202.
"Note". Section 3—104.
"Notice of dishonor". Section 3—508.
"On demand". Section 3—108.
"Presentment". Section 3—504.
"Protest". Section 3—509.
"Restrictive Indorsement". Section 3—205.
"Signature". Section 3—401.

(3) The following definitions in other Articles apply to this Article:

"Account". Section 4—104.
"Banking Day". Section 4—104.
"Clearing house". Section 4—104.
"Collecting bank". Section 4—105.
"Customer". Section 4—104.
"Depositary Bank". Section 4—105.
"Documentary Draft". Section 4—104.
"Intermediary Bank". Section 4—105.
"Item". Section 4—104.
"Midnight deadline". Section 4—104.
"Payor bank". Section 4—105.

(4) In addition Article 1 contains general definitions and principles of construction and interpretation applicable throughout this Article.

Section 3—103. LIMITATIONS ON SCOPE OF ARTICLE

(1) This Article does not apply to money, documents of title or investment securities.
(2) The provisions of this Article are subject to the provisions of the Article on Bank Deposits and Collections (Article 4) and Secured Transactions (Article 9).

Section 3—104. FORM OF NEGOTIABLE INSTRUMENTS; "DRAFT"; "CHECK"; "CERTIFICATE OF DEPOSIT"; "NOTE"

(1) Any writing to be a negotiable instrument within this Article must
(a) be signed by the maker or drawer; and
(b) contain an unconditional promise or order to pay a sum certain in money and no other promise, order, obligation or power given by the maker or drawer except as authorized by this Article; and
(c) be payable on demand or at a definite time; and
(d) be payable to order or to bearer.
(2) A writing which complies with the requirements of this section is
(a) a "draft" ("bill of exchange") if it is an order;
(b) a "check" if it is a draft drawn on a bank and payable on demand;
(c) a "certificate of deposit" if it is an acknowledgment by a bank of receipt of money with an engagement to repay it;
(d) a "note" if it is a promise other than a certificate of deposit.
(3) As used in other Articles of this Act, and as the context may require, the terms "draft", "check", "certificate of deposit" and "note" may refer to instruments which are not negotiable within this Article as well as to instruments which are so negotiable.

Section 3—105. WHEN PROMISE OR ORDER UNCONDITIONAL

(1) A promise or order otherwise unconditional is not made conditional by the fact that the instrument
(a) is subject to implied or constructive conditions; or
(b) states its consideration, whether performed or promised, or the transaction which gave rise to the instrument, or that the promise or order is made or the instrument matures in accordance with or "as per" such transaction; or
(c) refers to or states that it arises out of a separate agreement or refers to a separate agreement for rights as to prepayment or acceleration; or
(d) states that it is drawn under a letter of credit; or
(e) states that it is secured, whether by mortgage, reservation of title or otherwise; or
(f) indicates a particular account to be debited of any other fund or source from which reimbursement is expected; or
(g) is limited to payment out of a particular fund or the proceeds of a particular source, if the instrument is issued by a government or governmental agency or unit; or
(h) is limited to payment out of the entire assets of a partnership, unincorporated association, trust or estate by or on behalf of which the instrument is issued.
(2) A promise or order is not unconditional if the instrument
(a) states that it is subject to or governed by any other agreement; or
(b) states that it is to be paid only out of a particular fund or source except as provided in this section. As amended 1962.

Section 3—106. SUM CERTAIN

(1) The sum payable is a sum certain even though it is to be paid
(a) with stated interest or by stated installments; or
(b) with stated different rates of interest before and after default or a specified date; or
(c) with a stated discount or addition if paid before or after the date fixed for payment; or
(d) with exchange or less exchange, whether at a fixed rate or at the current rate; or
(e) with costs of collection or an attorney's fee or both upon default.
(2) Nothing in this section shall validate any term which is otherwise illegal.

Section 3—107. MONEY

(1) An instrument is payable in money if the medium of exchange in which it is payable is money at the time the instrument is made. An instrument payable in "currency" or "current funds" is payable in money.
(2) A promise or order to pay a sum stated in a foreign currency is for a sum certain in money and, unless a different medium of payment is specified in the instrument, may be satisfied by payment of that number of dollars which the stated foreign currency will purchase at the buying site rate for that currency on the day on which the instrument is payable or, if payable on demand, on the day of demand. If such an instrument specifies a foreign currency as the medium of payment the instrument is payable in that currency.

Section 3—108. PAYABLE ON DEMAND

Instruments payable on demand include those payable at sight or on presentation and those in which no time for payment is stated.

Section 3—109. DEFINITE TIME

(1) An instrument is payable at a definite time if by its terms it is payable

(a) on or before a stated date or at a fixed period after a stated date; or

(b) at a fixed period after sight; or

(c) at a definite time subject to any acceleration; or

(d) at a definite time subject to extension at the option of the holder, or to extension to a further definite time at the option of the maker or acceptor or automatically upon or after a specified act or event.

(2) An instrument which by its terms is otherwise payable only upon an act or event uncertain as to time of occurrence is not payable at a definite time even though the act or event has occurred.

Section 3—110. PAYABLE TO ORDER

(1) An instrument is payable to order when by its terms it is payable to the order or assigns of any person therein specified with reasonable certainty, or to him or his order, or when it is conspicuously designated on its face as "exchange" or the like and names a payee. It may be payable to the order of

(a) the maker or drawer; or

(b) the drawee; or

(c) a payee who is not maker, drawer or drawee; or

(d) two or more payees together or in the alternative; or

(e) an estate, trust or fund, in which case it is payable to the order of the representative of such estate, trust or fund or his successors; or

(f) an office, or an officer by his title as such in which case it is payable to the principal but the incumbent of the office or his successors may act as if he or they were the holder; or

(g) a partnership or unincorporated association, in which case it is payable to the partnership or association and may be indorsed or transferred by any person thereto authorized.

(2) An instrument not payable to order is not made so payable by such words as "payable upon return of this instrument properly indorsed."

(3) An instrument made payable both to order and to bearer is payable to order unless the bearer words are handwritten or typewritten.

Section 3—111. PAYABLE TO BEARER

An instrument is payable to bearer when by its terms it is payable to

(a) bearer or the order of bearer; or

(b) a specified person or bearer; or

(c) "cash" or the order of "cash", or any other indication which does not purport to designate a specific payee.

Section 3—112. TERMS AND OMISSIONS NOT AFFECTING NEGOTIABILITY

(1) The negotiability of an instrument is not affected by

(a) the omission of a statement of any consideration or of the place where the instrument is drawn or payable; or

(b) a statement that collateral has been given to secure obligations either on the instrument or otherwise of an obligor on the instrument or that in case of default on those obligations the holder may realize on or dispose of the collateral; or

(c) a promise or power to maintain or protect collateral or to give additional collateral; or

(d) a term authorizing a confession of judgment on the instrument if it is not paid when due; or

(e) a term purporting to waive the benefit of any law intended for the advantage or protection of any obligor; or

(f) a term in a draft providing that the payee by indorsing or cashing it acknowledges full satisfaction of an obligation of the drawer; or

(g) A statement in a draft drawn in a set of parts (Section 3—801) to the effect that the order is effective only if no other part has been honored.

(2) Nothing in this section shall validate any term which is otherwise illegal. As amended 1962.

Section 3—114. DATE, ANTEDATING, POSTDATING

(1) The negotiability of an instrument is not affected by the fact that it is undated, antedated or postdated.

(2) Where an instrument is antedated or postdated the time when it is payable is determined by the stated date if the instrument is payable on demand or at a fixed period after date.

(3) Where the instrument or any signature thereon is dated, the date is presumed to be correct.

Section 3—115. INCOMPLETE INSTRUMENTS

(1) When a paper whose contents at the time of signing show that it is intended to become an instrument is signed while still incomplete in any necessary respect it cannot be enforced until completed, but when it is completed in accordance with authority given it is effective as completed.

(2) If the completion is unauthorized the rules as to material alteration apply (Section 3—407), even though the payer was not delivered by the maker or drawer; but the burden of establishing that any completion is unauthorized is on the party so asserting.

Section 3—116. INSTRUMENTS PAYABLE TO TWO OR MORE PERSONS

An instrument payable to the order of two or more persons

(a) if in the alternative is payable to any one of them and may be negotiated, discharged or enforced by any of them who has possession of it;

(b) if not in the alternative is payable to all of them and may be negotiated, discharged or enforced only by all of them.

Section 3—118. AMBIGUOUS TERMS AND RULES OF CONSTRUCTION

The following rules apply to every instrument:

(a) Where there is doubt whether the instrument is a draft or a note the holder may treat it as either. A draft drawn on the drawer is effective as a note.

(b) Handwritten terms control typewritten and printed terms, and typewritten control printed.

(c) Words control figures except that if the words are ambiguous figures control.

(d) Unless otherwise specified a provision for interest means interest at the judgment rate at the place of payment from the date of the instrument, or if it is undated from the date of issue.

(e) Unless the instrument otherwise specifies two or more persons who sign as maker, acceptor or drawer or indorser and as a part of the same transaction are jointly and severally liable even though the instrument contains such words as "I promise to pay."

(f) Unless otherwise specified consent to extension authorizes a single extension for not longer than the original period. A consent to extension, expressed in the instrument, is binding on secondary parties and accommodation makers. A holder may not exercise his option to extend an instrument over the objection of a maker or acceptor or other party who in accordance with Section 3—604 tenders full payment when the instrument is due.

Part 2

Transfer and Negotiation

Section 3—201. TRANSFER: RIGHT TO INDORSEMENT

(1) Transfer of an instrument vests in the transferee such rights as the transferor has therein, except that a transferee who has himself been a party to any fraud or illegality affecting the instrument or who as a prior holder had notice of a defense or claim against it cannot improve his position by taking from a later holder in due course.

(2) A transfer of a security interest in an instrument vests the foregoing rights in the transferee to the extent of the interest transferred.

(3) Unless otherwise agreed any transfer for value of an instrument not then payable to bearer gives the transferee the specifically enforceable right to have the unqualified indorsement of the transferor. Negotiation takes effect only when the indorsement is made and until that time there is no presumption that the transferee is the owner.

U.L.A.-U.C.C. 9th Ed. '78 Pamph.—7

Section 3—202. NEGOTIATION

(1) Negotiation is the transfer of an instrument in such form that the transferee becomes a holder. If the instrument is payable to order it is negotiated by delivery with any necessary indorsement; if payable to bearer it is negotiated by delivery.

(2) An indorsement must be written by or on behalf of the holder and on the instrument or on a paper so firmly affixed thereto as to become a part thereof.

(3) An indorsement is effective for negotiation only when it conveys the entire instrument or any unpaid residue. If it purports to be of less it operates only as a partial assignment.

(4) Words of assignment, condition, waiver, guaranty, limitation or disclaimer of liability and the like accompanying an indorsement do not affect its character as an indorsement.

Section 3—203. WRONG OR MISSPELLED NAME

Where an instrument is made payable to a person under a misspelled name or one other than his own he may indorse in that name or his own or both; but signature in both names may be required by a person paying or giving value for the instrument.

Section 3—204. SPECIAL INDORSEMENT; BLANK INDORSEMENT

(1) A special indorsement specifies the person to whom or to whose order it makes the instrument payable. Any instrument specially indorsed becomes payable to the order of the special indorsee and may be further negotiated only by his indorsement.

(2) An indorsement in blank specifies no particular indorsee and may consist of a mere signature. An instrument payable to order and indorsed in blank becomes payable to bearer and may be negotiated by delivery alone until specially indorsed.

(3) The holder may convert a blank indorsement into a special indorsement by writing over the signature of the indorser in blank any contract consistent with the character of the indorsement.

Section 3—205. RESTRICTIVE INDORSEMENTS

An indorsement is restrictive which either

(a) is conditional; or

(b) purports to prohibit further transfer of the instrument; or
(c) includes the words "for collection", "for deposit", "pay any bank", or like terms signifying a purpose of deposit or collection; or
(d) otherwise states that it is for the benefit or use of the indorser or of another person.

Section 3—206. EFFECT OF RESTRICTIVE INDORSEMENT

(1) No restrictive indorsement prevents further transfer or negotiation of the instrument.
(2) An intermediary bank, or a payor bank which is not the depositary bank, is neither given notice nor otherwise affected by a restrictive indorsement of any person except the bank's immediate transferor or the person presenting for payment.
(3) Except for an intermediary bank, any transferee under an indorsement which is conditional or includes the words "for collection", "for deposit", "pay any bank", or like terms (subparagraphs (a) and (c) of Section 3—205) must pay or apply any value given by him for or on the security of the instrument consistently with the indorsement and to the extent that he does so he becomes a holder for value. In addition such transferee is a holder in due course if he otherwise complies with the requirements of Section 3—302 on what constitutes a holder in due course.
(4) The first taker under an indorsement for the benefit of the indorser or another person (subparagraph (d) of Section 3—205) must pay or apply any value given by him for or on the security of the instrument consistently with the indorsement and to the extent that he does so he becomes a holder for value. In addition such taker is a holder in due course if he otherwise complies with the requirements of Section 3—302 on what constitutes a holder in due course. A later holder for value is neither given notice nor otherwise affected by such restrictive indorsement unless he has knowledge that a fiduciary or other person has negotiated the instrument in any transaction for his own benefit or otherwise in breach of duty (subsection (2) of Section 3—304).

Section 3—208. REACQUISITION

Where an instrument is returned to or reacquired by a prior party he may cancel any indorsement which is not necessary to his title and reissue or further negotiate the instrument, but any intervening party is discharged as against the reacquiring party and subsequent holders not in due course and if his indorsement has been cancelled is discharged as against subsequent holders in due course as well.

Part 3
Rights of a Holder

Section 3—301. RIGHTS OF A HOLDER

The holder of an instrument whether or not he is the owner may transfer or negotiate it and, except as otherwise provided in Section 3—603 on payment or satisfaction, discharge it or enforce payment in his own name.

Section 3—302. HOLDER IN DUE COURSE

(1) A holder in due course is a holder who takes the instrument
(a) for value; and
(b) in good faith; and
(c) without notice that it is overdue or has been dishonored or of any defense against or claim to it on the part of any person.
(2) A payee may be a holder in due course.
(3) A holder does not become a holder in due course of an instrument:
(a) by purchase of it at judicial sale or by taking it under legal process; or
(b) by acquiring it in taking over an estate; or
(c) by purchasing it as part of a bulk transaction not in regular course of business of the transferor.
(4) A purchaser of a limited interest can be a holder in due course only to the extent of the interest purchased.

Section 3—303. TAKING FOR VALUE

A holder takes the instrument for value
(a) to the extent that the agreed consideration has been performed or that he acquires a security interest in or a lien on the instrument otherwise than by legal process; or
(b) when he takes the instrument in payment of or as security for an antecedent claim against any person whether or not the claim is due; or
(c) when he gives a negotiable instrument for it or makes an irrevocable commitment to a third person.

Section 3—304. NOTICE TO PURCHASER

(1) The purchaser has notice of a claim or defense if
(a) the instrument is so incomplete, bears such visible evidence of forgery or alteration, or is otherwise so irregular as to call into question its validity, terms or ownership or to create an ambiguity as to the party to pay; or
(b) the purchaser has notice that the obligation of any party is voidable in whole or in part, or that all parties have been discharged.
(2) The purchaser has notice of a claim against the instrument when he has knowledge that a fiduciary has negotiated

the instrument in payment of or as security for his own debt or in any transaction for his own benefit or otherwise in breach of duty.

(3) The purchaser has notice that an instrument is overdue if he has reason to know

(a) that any part of the principal amount is overdue or that there is an uncured default in payment of another instrument of the same series; or

(b) that acceleration of the instrument has been made; or

(c) that he is taking a demand instrument after demand has been made or more than a reasonable length of time after its issue. A reasonable time for a check drawn and payable within the states and territories of the United States and the District of Columbia is presumed to be thirty days.

(4) Knowledge of the following facts does not of itself give the purchaser notice of a defense or claim

(a) that the instrument is antedated or postdated;

(b) that it was issued or negotiated in return for an executory promise or accompanied by a separate agreement, unless the purchaser has notice that defense or claim has arisen from the terms thereof;

(c) that any party has signed for accommodation;

(d) that an incomplete instrument has been completed, unless the purchaser has notice of any improper completion;

(e) that any person negotiating the instrument is or was a fiduciary;

(f) that there has been default in payment of interest on the instrument or in payment of any other instrument, except one of the same series.

(5) The filing or recording of a document does not of itself constitute notice within the provisions of this Article to a person who would otherwise be a holder in due course.

(6) To be effective notice must be received at such time and in such manner as to give a reasonable opportunity to act on it.

Section 3—305. RIGHTS OF A HOLDER IN DUE COURSE

To the extent that a holder is a holder in due course he takes the instrument free from

(1) all claims to it on the part of any person; and

(2) all defenses of any party to the instrument with whom the holder has not dealt except

(a) infancy, to the extent that it is a defense to a simple contract; and

(b) such other incapacity, or duress, or illegality of the transaction, as renders the obligation of the party a nullity; and

(c) such misrepresentation as has induced the party to sign the instrument with neither knowledge nor reasonable opportunity to obtain knowledge of its character or its essential terms; and

(d) discharge in insolvency proceedings; and

(e) any other discharge of which the holder has notice when he takes the instrument.

Section 3—307. BURDEN OF ESTABLISHING SIGNATURES, DEFENSES AND DUE COURSE

(1) Unless specifically denied in the pleadings each signature on an instrument is admitted. When the effectiveness of a signature is put in issue

(a) the burden of establishing it is on the party claiming under the signature; but

(b) the signature is presumed to be genuine or authorized except where the action is to enforce the obligation of a purported signer who has died or become incompetent before proof is required.

(2) When signatures are admitted or established, production of the instrument entitles a holder to recover on it unless the defendant establishes a defense.

(3) After it is shown that a defense exists a person claiming the rights of a holder in due course has the burden of establishing that he or some person under whom he claims is in all respects a holder in due course.

Part 4
Liability of Parties

Section 3—401. SIGNATURE

(1) No person is liable on an instrument unless his signature appears thereon.

(2) A signature is made by use of any name, including any trade or assumed name, upon an instrument, or by any word or mark used in lieu of a written signature.

Section 3—403. SIGNATURE BY AUTHORIZED REPRESENTATIVE

(1) A signature may be made by an agent or other representative, and his authority to make it may be established as in other cases of representation. No particular form of appointment is necessary to establish such authority.

(2) An authorized representative who signs his own name to an instrument

(a) is personally obligated if the instrument neither names the person represented nor shows that the representative signed in a representative capacity;

(b) except as otherwise established between the immediate parties, is personally obligated if the instrument names the person represented but does not show that the representative signed in a representative capacity, or if the instrument does not name the person represented but does show that the representative signed in a representative capacity.

(3) Except as otherwise established the name of an organization preceded or followed by the name and office of an authorized individual is a signature made in a representative capacity.

Section 3—405. IMPOSTORS; SIGNATURE IN NAME OF PAYEE

(1) An indorsement by any person in the name of a named payee is effective if

(a) an impostor by use of the mails or otherwise has induced the maker or drawer to issue the instrument to him or his confederate in the name of the payee; or

(b) a person signing as or on behalf of a maker or drawer intends the payee to have no interest in the instrument; or

(c) an agent or employee of the maker or drawer has supplied him with the name of the payee intending the latter to have no such interest.

(2) Nothing in this section shall affect the criminal or civil liability of the person so indorsing.

Section 3—406. NEGLIGENCE CONTRIBUTING TO ALTERATION OR UNAUTHORIZED SIGNATURE

Any person who by his negligence substantially contributes to a material alteration of the instrument or to the making of an unauthorized signature is precluded from asserting the alteration or lack of authority against a holder in due course or against a drawee or other payor who pays the instrument in good faith and in accordance with the reasonable commercial standards of the drawee's or payor's business.

Section 3—407. ALTERATION

(1) Any alteration of an instrument is material which changes the contract of any party thereto in any respect, including any such change in

(a) the number or relations of the parties; or

(b) an incomplete instrument, by completing it otherwise than as authorized; or

(c) the writing as signed, by adding to it or by removing any part of it.

(2) As against any person other than a subsequent holder in due course.

(a) alteration by the holder which is both fraudulent and material discharges any party whose contract is thereby changed unless that party assents or is precluded from asserting the defense;

(b) no other alteration discharges any party and the instrument may be enforced according to its original tenor, or as to incomplete instruments according to the authority given.

(3) A subsequent holder in due course may in all cases enforce the instrument according to its original tenor, and when an incomplete instrument has been completed, he may enforce it as completed.

Section 3—413. CONTRACT OF MAKER, DRAWER AND ACCEPTOR

(1) The maker or acceptor engages that he will pay the instrument according to its tenor at the time of his engagement or as completed pursuant to Section 3—115 on incomplete instruments.

(2) The drawer engages that upon dishonor of the draft and any necessary notice of dishonor or protest he will pay the amount of the draft to the holder or to any indorser who takes it up. The drawer may disclaim this liability by drawing without recourse.

(3) By making, drawing or accepting the party admits as against all subsequent parties including the drawee the existence of the payee and his then capacity to indorse.

Section 3—414. CONTRACT OF INDORSER; ORDER OF LIABILITY

(1) Unless the indorsement otherwise specifies (as by such words as "without recourse") every indorser engages that upon dishonor and any necessary notice of dishonor and protest he will pay the instrument according to its tenor at the time of his indorsement to the holder or to any subsequent indorser who takes it up, even though the indorser who takes it up was not obligated to do so.

(2) Unless they otherwise agree indorsers are liable to one another in the order in which they indorse, which is presumed to be the order in which their signatures appear on the instrument.

Section 3—415. CONTRACT OF ACCOMMODATION PARTY

(1) An accommodation party is one who signs the instrument in any capacity for the purpose of lending his name to another party to it.

(2) When the instrument has been taken for value before it is due the accommodation party is liable in the capacity in which he has signed even though the taker knows of the accommodation.

(3) As against a holder in due course and without notice of the accommodation oral proof of the accommodation is not admissible to give the accommodation party the benefit of discharges dependent on his character as such. In other cases the accommodation character may be shown by oral proof.

(4) An indorsement which shows that it is not in the chain of title is notice of its accommodation character.

(5) An accommodation party is not liable to the party accommodated, and if he pays the instrument has a right of recourse on the instrument against such party.

Section 3—417. WARRANTIES ON PRESENTMENT AND TRANSFER

(1) Any person who obtains payment or acceptance and any prior transferor warrants to a person who in good faith pays or accepts that

(a) he has a good title to the instrument or is authorized to obtain payment or acceptance on behalf of one who has a good title; and

(b) he has no knowledge that the signature of the maker or drawer is unauthorized, except that this warranty is not given by a holder in due course acting in good faith

(i) to maker with respect to the maker's own signature; or

(ii) to a drawer with respect to the drawer's own signature, whether or not the drawer is also the drawee; or

(iii) to an acceptor of a draft if the holder in due course took the draft after the acceptance or obtained the acceptance without knowledge that the drawer's signature was unauthorized; and

(c) the instrument has not been materially altered, except that this warranty is not given by a holder in due course acting in good faith

(i) to the maker of a note; or

(ii) to the drawer of a draft whether or not the drawer is also the drawee; or

(iii) to the acceptor of a draft with respect to an alteration made prior to the acceptance if the holder in due course took the draft after the acceptance, even though the acceptance provided "payable as originally drawn" or equivalent terms; or

(iv) to the acceptor of a draft with respect to an alteration made after the acceptance.

(2) Any person who transfers an instrument and receives consideration warrants to his transferee and if the transfer is by indorsement to any subsequent holder who takes the instrument in good faith that

(a) he has a good title to the instrument or is authorized to obtain payment or acceptance on behalf of one who has a good title and the transfer is otherwise rightful; and

(b) all signatures are genuine or authorized; and

(c) the instrument has not been materially altered; and

(d) no defense of any party is good against him; and

(e) he has no knowledge of any insolvency proceeding instituted with respect to the maker or acceptor or the drawer of an unaccepted instrument.

(3) By transferring "without recourse" the transferor limits the obligation stated in subsection (2) (d) to a warranty that he has no knowledge of such a defense.

(4) A selling agent or broker who does not disclose the fact that he is acting only as such gives the warranties provided in this section, but if he makes such disclosure warrants only his good faith and authority.

Section 3—419. CONVERSION OF INSTRUMENT; INNOCENT REPRESENTATIVE

(1) An instrument is converted when

(a) a drawee to whom it is delivered for acceptance refuses to return it on demand; or

(b) any person to whom it is delivered for payment refuses on demand either to pay or to return it; or

(c) it is paid on a forged indorsement.

(2) In an action against a drawee under subsection (1) the measure of the drawee's liability is the face amount of the instrument. In any other action under subsection (1) the measure of liability is presumed to be the face amount of the instrument.

(3) Subject to the provisions of this Act concerning restrictive indorsements a representative, including a depositary or collecting bank, who has in good faith and in accordance with the reasonable commercial standards applicable to the business of such representative dealt with an instrument or its proceeds on behalf of one who was not the true owner is not liable in conversion or otherwise to the true owner beyond the amount of any proceeds remaining in his hands.

(4) An intermediary bank or payor bank which is not a depositary bank is not liable in conversion solely by reason of the fact that proceeds of an item indorsed restrictively (Sections 3—205 and 3—206) are not paid or applied consistently with the restrictive indorsement of an indorser other than its immediate transferor.

Part 5

Presentment, Notice of Dishonor and Protest

Section 3—501. WHEN PRESENTMENT, NOTICE OF DISHONOR, AND PROTEST NECESSARY OR PERMISSIBLE

(1) Unless excused (Section 3—511) presentment is necessary to charge secondary parties as follows:

(a) presentment for acceptance is necessary to charge the drawer and indorsers of a draft where the draft so provides, or is payable elsewhere than at the residence or place of business of the drawee, or its date of payment depends upon such presentment. The holder may at his option present for acceptance any other draft payable at a stated date;

(b) presentment for payment is necessary to charge any indorser;

(c) in the case of any drawer, the acceptor of a draft payable at a bank or the maker of a note payable at a bank, presentment for payment is necessary, but failure to make presentment discharges such drawer, acceptor or maker only as stated in Section 3—502(1)(b).

(2) Unless excused (Section 3—511)

(a) notice of any dishonor is necessary to charge any indorser;

(b) in the case of any drawer, the acceptor of a draft payable at a bank or the maker of a note payable at a bank, notice of any dishonor is necessary, but failure to give such notice discharges such drawer, acceptor or maker only as stated in Section 3—502(1)(b).

(3) Unless excused (Section 3—511) protest of any dishonor is necessary to charge the drawer and indorsers of any draft which on its face appears to be drawn or payable outside of the states, territories, dependencies and possessions of the United States, the District of Columbia and the Commonwealth of Puerto Rico. The holder may at his option make protest of any dishonor of any other instrument and in the case of a foreign draft may on insolvency of the acceptor before maturity make protest for better security.

(4) Notwithstanding any provision of this section, neither presentment nor notice of dishonor nor protest is necessary to charge an indorser who has indorsed an instrument after maturity. As amended 1966.

Section 3—503. TIME OF PRESENTMENT

(1) Unless a different time is expressed in the instrument the time for any presentment is determined as follows:

(a) where an instrument is payable at or a fixed period after a stated date any presentment for acceptance must be made on or before the date it is payable;

(b) where an instrument is payable after sight it must either be presented for acceptance or negotiated within a reasonable time after date or issue whichever is later;

(c) where an instrument shows the date on which it is payable presentment for payment is due on that date;

(d) where an instrument is accelerated presentment for payment is due within a reasonable time after the acceleration;

(e) with respect to the liability of any secondary party presentment for acceptance or payment of any other instrument is due within a reasonable time after such party becomes liable thereon.

(2) A reasonable time for presentment is determined by the nature of the instrument, any usage of banking or trade and the facts of the particular case. In the case of an uncertified check which is drawn and payable within the United States and which is not a draft drawn by a bank the following are presumed to be reasonable periods within which to present for payment or to initiate bank collection:

(a) with respect to the liability of the drawer, thirty days after date or issue whichever is later; and

(b) with respect to the liability of an indorser, seven days after his indorsement.

(3) Where any presentment is due on a day which is not a full business day for either the person making presentment or the party to pay or accept, presentment is due on the next following day which is a full business day for both parties.

(4) Presentment to be sufficient must be made at a reasonable hour, and if at a bank during its banking day.

Section 3—504. HOW PRESENTMENT MADE

(1) Presentment is a demand for acceptance or payment made upon the maker, acceptor, drawee or other payor by or on behalf of the holder.

(2) Presentment may be made

(a) by mail, in which event the time of presentment is determined by the time of receipt of the mail; or

(b) through a clearing house; or

(c) at the place of acceptance or payment specified in the instrument or if there be none at the place of business or residence of the party to accept or pay. If neither the party to accept or pay nor anyone authorized to act for him is present or accessible at such place presentment is excused.

(3) It may be made

(a) to any one or two or more makers, acceptors, drawees or other payors; or

(b) to any person who has authority to make or refuse the acceptance or payment.

(4) A draft accepted or a note made payable at a bank in the United States must be presented at such bank.

(5) In the cases described in Section 4—210 presentment may be made in the manner and with the result stated in that section. As amended 1962.

Section 3—507. DISHONOR; HOLDER'S RIGHT OF RECOURSE; TERM ALLOWING RE-PRESENTMENT

(1) An instrument is dishonored when

(a) a necessary or optional presentment is duly made and due acceptance or payment is refused or cannot be obtained within the prescribed time or in case of bank collections the instrument is seasonably returned by the midnight deadline (Section 4—301); or

(b) presentment is excused and the instrument is not duly accepted or paid.

(2) Subject to any necessary notice of dishonor and protest, the holder has upon dishonor an immediate right of recourse against the drawers and indorsers.

(3) Return of an instrument for lack of proper indorsement is not dishonor.

(4) A term in a draft or an indorsement thereof allowing a stated time for re-presentment in the event of any dishonor of the draft by nonacceptance if a time draft or by nonpay-

ment if a sight draft gives the holder as against any secondary party bound by the term an option to waive the dishonor without affecting the liability of the secondary party and he may present again up to the end of the stated time.

Section 3—508. NOTICE OF DISHONOR

(1) Notice of dishonor may be given to any person who may be liable on the instrument by or on behalf of the holder or any party who has himself received notice, or any other party who can be compelled to pay the instrument. In addition an agent or bank in whose hands the instrument is dishonored may give notice to his principal or customer or to another agent or bank from which the instrument was received.

(2) Any necessary notice must be given by a bank before its midnight deadline and by any other person before midnight of the third business day after dishonor or receipt of notice of dishonor.

(3) Notice may be given in any reasonable manner. It may be oral or written and in any terms which identify the instrument and state that it has been dishonored. A misdescription which does not mislead the party notified does not vitiate the notice. Sending the instrument bearing a stamp, ticket or writing stating that acceptance or payment has been refused or sending a notice of debit with respect to the instrument is sufficient.

(4) Written notice is given when sent although it is not received.

(5) Notice to one partner is notice to each although the firm has been dissolved.

(6) When any party is in insolvency proceedings instituted after the issue of the instrument notice may be given either to the party or to the representative of his estate.

(7) When any party is dead or incompetent notice may be sent to his last known address or given to his personal representative.

(8) Notice operates for the benefit of all parties who have rights on the instrument against the party notified.

U.L.A.-U.C.C. 9th Ed. '78 Pamph.—9

Part 6

Discharge

Section 3—601. DISCHARGE OF PARTIES

(1) The extent of the discharge of any party from liability on an instrument is governed by the sections on

(a) payment or satisfaction (Section 3—603); or

(b) tender of payment (Section 3—604); or

(c) cancellation or renunciation (Section 3—605); or

(d) impairment of right of recourse or of collateral (Section 3—606); or

(e) reacquisition of the instrument by a prior party (Section 3—208); or

(f) fraudulent and material alteration (Section 3—407); or

(g) certification of a check (Section 3—411); or

(h) acceptance varying a draft (Section 3—412); or

(i) unexcused delay in presentment or notice of dishonor or protest (Section 3—502).

(2) Any party is also discharged from his liability on an instrument to another party by any other act or agreement with such party which would discharge his simple contract for the payment of money.

Section 3—804. LOST, DESTROYED, OR STOLEN INSTRUMENTS

The owner of an instrument which is lost, whether by destruction, theft or otherwise, may maintain an action in his own name and recover from any party liable thereon upon due proof of his ownership, the facts which prevent his production of the instrument and its terms. The court may require security indemnifying the defendant against loss by reason of further claims on the instrument.

ARTICLE IV

Bank Deposits and Collections

Part One

General Provisions and Definitions

Section 4—104. DEFINITIONS AND INDEX OF DEFINITIONS

(1) In this Article unless the context otherwise requires

(a) "Account" means any account with a bank and includes a checking, time, interest or savings account;

(b) "Afternoon" means the period of a day between noon and midnight;

(c) "Banking day" means that part of any day on which a bank is open to the public for carrying on substantially all of its banking functions;

(d) "Clearing house" means any association of banks or other payors regularly clearing items;

(e) "Customer" means any person having an account with a bank or for whom a bank has agreed to collect items and includes a bank carrying an account with another bank;

(f) "Documentary draft" means any negotiable or nonnegotiable draft with accompanying documents, securities or other papers to be delivered against honor of the draft;

(g) "Item" means any instrument for the payment of money even though it is not negotiable but does not include money;

(h) "Midnight deadline" with respect to a bank is midnight on its next banking day following the banking day on which it receives the relevant item or notice or from which the time for taking action commences to run, whichever is later;

(i) "Properly payable" includes the availability of funds for payment at the time of decision to pay or dishonor;

(j) "Settle" means to pay in cash, by clearing house settlement, in a charge or credit or by remittance, or otherwise as instructed. A settlement may be either provisional or final;

(k) "Suspends payments" with respect to a bank means that it has been closed by order of the supervisory authorities, that a public officer has been appointed to take it over or that it ceases or refuses to make payments in the ordinary course of business.

(2) Other definitions applying to this Article and the sections in which they appear are:

"Collecting bank"	Section 4—105.
"Depositary bank"	Section 4—105.
"Intermediary bank"	Section 4—105.
"Payor bank"	Section 4—105.
"Presenting bank"	Section 4—105.
"Remitting bank"	Section 4—105.

(3) The following definitions in other Articles apply to this Article:

"Acceptance"	Section 3—410.
"Certificate of deposit"	Section 3—104.
"Certification"	Section 3—411.
"Check"	Section 3—104.
"Draft"	Section 3—104.
"Holder in due course"	Section 3—302.
"Notice of dishonor"	Section 3—508.
"Presentment"	Section 3—504.
"Protest"	Section 3—509.
"Secondary party"	Section 3—102.

(4) In addition Article 1 contains general definitions and principles of construction and interpretation applicable throughout this Article.

Section 4—105. "DEPOSITARY BANK"; "INTERMEDIARY BANK"; "COLLECTING BANK"; "PAYOR BANK"; "PRESENTING BANK"; "REMITTING BANK"

In this Article unless the context otherwise requires:

(a) "Depositary bank" means the first bank to which an item is transferred for collection even though it is also the payor bank;

(b) "Payor bank" means a bank by which an item is payable as drawn or accepted;

(c) "Intermediary bank" means any bank to which an item is transferred in course of collection except the depositary or payor bank;

(d) "Collecting bank" means any bank handling the item for collection except the payor bank;

(e) "Presenting bank" means any bank presenting an item except a payor bank;

(f) "Remitting bank" means any payor or intermediary bank remitting for an item.

Part Two

Collection of Items; Depositary and Collecting Banks

Section 4—205. SUPPLYING MISSING INDORSEMENT; NO NOTICE FROM PRIOR INDORSEMENT

(1) A depositary bank which has taken an item for collection may supply any indorsement of the customer which is necessary to title unless the item contains the words "payee's indorsement required" or the like. In the absence of such a requirement a statement placed on the item by the depositary bank to the effect that the item was deposited by a customer or credited to his account is effective as the customer's indorsement.

(2) An intermediary bank, or payor bank which is not a depositary bank, is neither given notice nor otherwise affected by a restrictive indorsement of any person except the bank's immediate transferor.

Section 4—207. WARRANTIES OF CUSTOMER AND COLLECTING BANK ON TRANSFER OR PRESENTMENT OF ITEMS; TIME FOR CLAIMS

(1) Each customer or collecting bank who obtains payment or acceptance of an item and each prior customer and collecting bank warrants to the payor bank or other payor who in good faith pays or accepts the item that

(a) he has a good title to the item or is authorized to obtain payment or acceptance on behalf of one who has a good title; and

(b) he has no knowledge that the signature of the maker or drawer is unauthorized, except that this warranty is not given by any customer or collecting bank that is a holder in due course and acts in good faith

(i) to a maker with respect to the maker's own signature; or

(ii) to a drawer with respect to the drawer's own signature, whether or not the drawer is also the drawee; or

(iii) to an acceptor of an item if the holder in due course took the item after the acceptance or obtained the acceptance without knowledge that the drawer's signature was unauthorized; and

(c) the item has not been materially altered, except that this warranty is not given by any customer or collecting bank that is a holder in due course and acts in good faith

(i) to the maker of a note; or

(ii) to the drawer of a draft whether or not the drawer is also the drawee; or

(iii) to the acceptor of an item with respect to an alteration made prior to the acceptance if the holder in due course took the item after the acceptance, even though the acceptance provided "payable as originally drawn" or equivalent terms; or

(iv) to the acceptor of an item with respect to an alteration made after the acceptance.

(2) Each customer and collecting bank who transfers an item and receives a settlement or other consideration for its warrants to his transferee and to any subsequent collecting bank who takes the item in good faith that

(a) he has a good title to the item or is authorized to obtain payment or acceptance on behalf of one who has a good title and the transfer is otherwise rightful; and

(b) all signatures are genuine or authorized; and

(c) the item has not been materially altered; and

(d) no defense of any party is good against him; and

(e) he has no knowledge of any insolvency proceeding instituted with respect to the maker or acceptor or the drawer of an unaccepted item.

In addition each customer and collecting bank so transferring an item and receiving a settlement or other consideration engages that upon dishonor and any necessary notice of dishonor and protest he will take up the item.

(3) The warranties and the engagement to honor set forth in the two preceding subsections arise notwithstanding the absence of indorsement or words of guaranty or warranty in the transfer or presentment and a collecting bank remains liable for their breach despite remittance to its transferor. Damages for breach of such warranties or engagement to honor shall not exceed the consideration received by the customer or collecting bank responsible plus finance charges and expenses related to the item, if any.

(4) Unless a claim for breach of warranty under this section is made within a reasonable time after the person claiming learns of the breach, the person liable is discharged to the extent of any loss caused by the delay in making claim.

Section 4—209. WHEN BANK GIVES VALUE FOR PURPOSES OF HOLDER IN DUE COURSE

For purposes of determining its status as a holder in due course, the bank has given value to the extent that it has a security interest in an item provided that the bank otherwise complies with the requirements of Section 3—302 on what constitutes a holder in due course.

Section 4—212. RIGHT OF CHARGE-BACK OR REFUND

(1) If a collecting bank has made provisional settlement with its customer for an item and itself fails by reason of dishonor, suspension of payments by a bank or otherwise to receive a settlement for the item which is or becomes final, the bank may revoke the settlement given by it, charge bank the amount of any credit given for the item to its customer's account or obtain refund from its customer whether or not it is able to return the items if by its midnight deadline or within a longer reasonable time after it learns the facts it returns the item or sends notification of the facts. These rights to revoke, charge-back and obtain refund terminate if and when a settlement for the item received by the bank is or becomes final (subsection (3) of Section 4—211 and subsections (2) and (3) of Section 4—213).

[(2) Within the time and manner prescribed by this section and Section 4—301, an intermediary or payor bank, as the case may be, may return an unpaid item directly to the depositary bank and may send for collection a draft on the depositary bank and obtain reimbursement. In such case, if the depositary bank has received provisional settlement for the item, it must reimburse the bank drawing the draft and any provisional credits for the item between banks shall become and remain final.]

Note: *Direct returns is recognized as an innovation that is not yet established bank practice, and therefore, Paragraph 2 has been bracketed. Some lawyers have doubts whether it should be included in legislation or left to development by agreement.*

(3) A depositary bank which is also the payor may charge-back the amount of an item to its customer's account or obtain refund in accordance with the section governing return of an item received by a payor bank for credit on its books. (Section 4—301).

(4) The right to charge-back is not affected by

(a) prior use of the credit given for the item; or

(b) failure by any bank to exercise ordinary care with respect to the item but any bank so failing remains liable.

(5) A failure to charge-back or claim refund does not affect other rights of the bank against the customer or any other party.

(6) If credit is given in dollars as the equivalent of the value of an item payable in a foreign currency the dollar amount of any charge-back or refund shall be calculated on the basis of the buying sight rate for the foreign currency prevailing on the day when the person entitled to the charge-back or

refund learns that it will not receive payment in ordinary course.

Part 4

Relationship Between Payor Bank and Its Customer

Section 4—401. WHEN BANK MAY CHARGE CUSTOMER'S ACCOUNT

(1) As against its customer, a bank may charge against his account any item which is otherwise properly payable from that account even though the charge creates an overdraft.
(2) A bank which in good faith makes payment to a holder may charge the indicated account of its customer according to

(a) the original tenor of his altered item; or
(b) the tenor of his completed item, even though the bank knows the item has been completed unless the bank has notice that the completion was improper.

Section 4—402. BANK'S LIABILITY TO CUSTOMER FOR WRONGFUL DISHONOR

A payor bank is liable to its customer for damages proximately caused by the wrongful dishonor of an item. When the dishonor occurs through mistake liability is limited to actual damages proved. If so proximately caused and proved damages may include damages for an arrest or prosecution of the customer or other consequential damages. Whether any consequential damages are proximately caused by the wrongful dishonor is a question of fact to be determined in each case.

Section 4—403. CUSTOMER'S RIGHT TO STOP PAYMENT; BURDEN OF PROOF OF LOSS

(1) A customer may by order to his bank stop payment of any item payable for his account but the order must be received at such time and in such manner as to afford the bank a reasonable opportunity to act on it prior to any action by the bank with respect to the item described in Section 4—303.
(2) An oral order is binding upon the bank only for fourteen calendar days unless confirmed in writing within that period. A written order is effective for only six months unless renewed in writing.
(3) The burden of establishing the fact and amount of loss resulting from the payment of an item contrary to a binding stop payment order is on the customer.

Section 4—404. BANK NOT OBLIGATED TO PAY CHECK MORE THAN SIX MONTHS OLD

A bank is under no obligation to a customer having a checking account to pay a check, other than a certified check, which is presented more than six months after its date, but it may charge its customer's account for a payment made thereafter in good faith.

Section 4—405. DEATH OR INCOMPETENCE OF CUSTOMER

(1) A payor or collecting bank's authority to accept, pay or collect an item or to account for proceeds of its collection if otherwise effective is not rendered ineffective by incompetence of a customer of either bank existing at the time the item is issued or its collection is undertaken if the bank does not know of an adjudication of incompetence. Neither death nor incompetence of a customer revokes such authority to accept, pay, collect or account until the bank knows of the fact of death or of an adjudication of incompetence and has reasonable opportunity to act on it.
(2) Even with knowledge a bank may for 10 days after the date of death pay or certify checks drawn on or prior to that date unless ordered to stop payment by a person claiming an interest in the account.

Section 4—405. DEATH OR INCOMPETENCE OF CUSTOMER

(1) A payor or collecting bank's authority to accept, pay or collect an item or to account for proceeds of its collection if otherwise effective is not rendered ineffective by incompetence of a customer of either bank existing at the time the item is issued or its collection is undertaken if the bank does not know of an adjudication of incompetence. Neither death nor incompetence of a customer revokes such authority to accept, pay, collect or account until the bank knows of the fact of death or of an adjudication of incompetence and has reasonable opportunity to act on it.
(2) Even with knowledge a bank may for 10 days after the date of death pay or certify checks drawn on or prior to that date unless ordered to stop payment by a person claiming an interest in the account.

Section 4—406. CUSTOMER'S DUTY TO DISCOVER AND REPORT UNAUTHORIZED SIGNATURE OR ALTERATION

(1) When a bank sends to its customer a statement of account accompanied by items paid in good faith in support of the debit entries or holds the statement and items pur-

suant to a request for instructions of its customer or otherwise in a reasonable manner makes the statement and items available to the customer, the customer must exercise reasonable care and promptness to examine the statement and items to discover his unauthorized signature or any alteration on an item and must notify the bank promptly after discovery thereof.

(2) If the bank establishes that the customer failed with respect to an item to comply with the duties imposed on the customer by subsection (1) the customer is precluded from asserting against the bank

(a) his unauthorized signature or any alteration on the item if the bank also establishes that it suffered a loss by reason of such failure; and

(b) an unauthorized signature or alteration by the same wrongdoer on any other item paid in good faith by the bank after the first item and statement was available to the customer for a reasonable period not exceeding fourteen calendar days and before the bank receives notification from the customer of any such unauthorized signature or alteration.

(3) The preclusion under subsection (2) does not apply if the customer establishes lack of ordinary care on the part of the bank in paying the item(s).

(4) Without regard to care or lack of care of either the customer or the bank a customer who does not within one year from the time the statement and items are made available to the customer (subsection (1)) discover and report his unauthorized signature or any alteration on the face or back of the item or does not within 3 years from that time discover and report any unauthorized indorsement is precluded from asserting against the bank such unauthorized signature or indorsement or such alteration.

(5) If under this section a payor bank has a valid defense against a claim of a customer upon or resulting from payment of an item and waives or fails upon request to assert the defense the bank may not assert against any collecting bank or other prior party presenting or transferring the item a claim based upon the unauthorized signature or alteration giving rise to the customer's claim.

ARTICLE IX

Secured Transactions
Part One
Short Title, Applicability and Definitions

Section 9—105. DEFINITIONS AND INDEX OF DEFINITIONS

(1) In this Article unless the context otherwise requires:

(a) "Account debtor" means the person who is obligated on an account, chattel paper or general intangible;

(b) "Chattel paper" means a writing or writings which evidence both a monetary obligation and a security interest in or a lease of specific goods, but a charter or other contract involving the use or hire of a vessel is not chattel paper. When a transaction is evidenced both by such a security agreement or a lease and by an instrument or a series of instruments, the group of writings taken together constitutes chattel paper;

(c) "Collateral" means the property subject to a security interest, and includes accounts and chattel paper which have been sold;

(d) "Debtor" means the person who owes payment or other performance of the obligation secured, whether or not he owns or has rights in the collateral, and includes the seller of accounts or chattel paper. Where the debtor and the owner of the collateral are not the same person, the term "debtor" means the owner of the collateral in any provision of the Article dealing with the collateral, the obligor in any provision dealing with the obligation, and may include both where the context so requires;

(e) "Deposit account" means a demand, time, savings, passbook or like account maintained with a bank, savings and loan association, credit union or like organization, other than an account evidenced by a certificate of deposit;

(f) "Document" means document of title as defined in the general definitions of Article 1 (Section 1—201), and a receipt of the kind described in subsection (2) of Section 7—201;

(g) "Encumbrance" includes real estate mortgages and other liens on real estate and all other rights in real estate that are not ownership interests;

(h) "Goods" includes all things which are movable at the time the security interest attaches or which are fixtures (Section 9—313), but does not include money, documents, instruments, accounts, chattel paper, general intangibles, or minerals or the like (including oil and gas) before extraction. "Goods" also includes standing timber which is to be cut and removed under a conveyance or contract for sale, the unborn young of animals, and growing crops;

(i) "Instrument" means a negotiable instrument (defined in Section 3—104), or a certificated security (defined in Section 8—102) or any other writing which evidences a right to the payment of money and it is not itself a security agreement or lease and is of a type which is in ordinary course of business transferred by delivery with any necessary indorsement or assignment;

(j) "Mortgage" means a consensual interest created by a real estate mortgage, a trust deed on real estate, or the like;

(k) An advance is made "pursuant to commitment" if the secured party has bound himself to make it, whether or not a subsequent event of default or other event not within his control has relieved or may relieve him from his obligation;

(l) "Security agreement" means an agreement which creates or provides for a security interest;

(m) "Secured party" means a lender, seller or other person in whose favor there is a security interest, including a person to whom accounts or chattel paper have been sold. When the holders of obligations issued under an indenture of trust, equipment trust agreement or the like are represented by a trustee or other person, the representative is the secured party;

(n) "Transmitting utility" means any person primarily engaged in the railroad, street railway or trolley bus business, the electric or electronics communications transmission business, the transmission of goods by pipeline, or the transmission or the production and transmission of electricity, steam, gas or water, or the provision of sewer service.

(2) Other definitions applying to this Article and the sections in which they appear are:

"Account".	Section 9—106.
"Attach".	Section 9—203.
"Construction mortgage".	Section 9—313(1).
"Consumer goods".	Section 9—109(1).
"Equipment".	Section 9—109(2).
"Farm products".	Section 9—109(3).
"Fixture".	Section 9—313(1).
"Fixture filing".	Section 9—313(1).
"General intangibles".	Section 9—106.
"Inventory".	Section 9—109(4).
"Lien creditor".	Section 9—301(3).
"Proceeds".	Section 9—306(1).
"Purchase money security interest".	Section 9—107.
"United States".	Section 9—103.

(3) The following definitions in other Articles apply to this Article:

"Check".	Section 3—104.
"Contract for sale".	Section 2—106.
"Holder in due course".	Section 3—302.
"Note".	Section 3—104.
"Sale".	Section 2—106.

(4) In addition Article 1 contains general definitions, and principles of construction and interpretation applicable throughout this Article.

Amended in 1966, 1972 and 1977.

Section 9—106. DEFINITIONS: "ACCOUNT"; "GENERAL INTANGIBLES"

"Account" means any right to payment for goods sold or leased or for services rendered which is not evidenced by an instrument or chattel paper, whether or not it has been earned by performance. "General intangibles" means any personal property (including things in action) other than goods, accounts, chattel paper, documents, instruments, and money. All rights to payment earned or unearned under a charter or other contract involving the use or hire of a vessel and all rights incident to the charter or contract are accounts. Amended in 1966, 1972.

Section 9—107. DEFINITIONS: "PURCHASE MONEY SECURITY INTEREST"

A security interest is a "purchase money security interest" to the extent that it is

(a) taken or retained by the seller of the collateral to secure all or part of its price; or

(b) taken by a person who by making advances or incurring an obligation gives value to enable the debtor to acquire rights in or the use of collateral if such value is in fact so used.

Section 9—109. CLASSIFICATION OF GOODS; "CONSUMER GOODS"; "EQUIPMENT"; "FARM PRODUCTS"; INVENTORY"

Goods are

(1) "consumer goods" if they are used or bought for use primarily for personal, family or household purposes;

(2) "equipment" if they are used or bought for use primarily in business (including farming or a profession) or by a debtor who is a non-profit organization or a governmental subdivision or agency or if the goods are not included in the definitions of inventory, farm products or consumer goods;

(3) "farm products" if they are crops or livestock or supplies used or produced in farming operations or if they are products of crops or livestock in their unmanufactured states (such as ginned cotton, wool-clip, maple syrup, milk and eggs), and if they are in the possession of a debtor engaged in raising, fattening, grazing or other farming operations. If goods are farm products they are neither equipment nor inventory;

(4) "inventory" if they are held by a person who holds them for sale or lease or to be furnished under contracts of service or if he has so furnished them, or if they are raw materials, work in process or materials used or consumed in a business. Inventory of a person is not to be classified as his equipment.

Section 9—110. SUFFICIENCY OF DESCRIPTION

For the purposes of this Article any description of personal property or real estate is sufficient whether or not it is specific if it reasonably identifies what is described.

Section 9—112. WHERE COLLATERAL IS NOT OWNED BY DEBTOR

Unless otherwise agreed, when a secured party knows that collateral is owned by a person who is not the debtor, the owner of the collateral is entitled to receive from the secured party any surplus under Section 9—502(2) or under Section 9—504(1), and is not liable for the debt or for any deficiency after resale, and he has the same right as the debtor

(a) to receive statements under Section 9—208;

(b) to receive notice of and to object to a secured party's proposal to retain the collateral in satisfaction of the indebtedness under Section 9—505;

(c) to redeem the collateral under Section 9—506;

(d) to obtain injunctive or other relief under Section 9—507(1); and

(e) to recover losses caused to him under Section 9—208(2).

Part 2

Validity of Security Agreement and Rights of Parties Thereto

Section 9—201. GENERAL VALIDITY OF SECURITY AGREEMENT

Except as otherwise provided by this Act a security agreement is effective according to its terms between the parties, against purchasers of the collateral and against creditors. Nothing in this Article validates any charge or practice illegal under any statute or regulation thereunder governing usury, small loans, retail installment sales, or the like, or extends the application of any such statute or regulation to any transaction not otherwise subject thereto.

Section 9—203. ATTACHMENT AND ENFORCEABILITY OF SECURITY INTEREST; PROCEEDS; FORMAL REQUISITES

(1) Subject to the provisions of Section 4—208 on the security interest of a collecting bank, Section 8—321 on security interests in securities and Section 9—113 on a security interest arising under the Article on Sales, a security interest is not enforceable against the debtor or third parties with respect to the collateral and does not attach unless:

(a) the collateral is in the possession of the secured party pursuant to agreement, or the debtor has signed a security agreement which contains a description of the collateral and in addition, when the security interest covers crops growing or to be grown or timber to be cut, a description of the land concerned;

(b) value has been given; and

(c) the debtor has rights in the collateral.

(2) A security interest attaches when it becomes enforceable against the debtor with respect to the collateral. Attachment occurs as soon as all of the events specified in subsection (1) have taken place unless explicit agreement postpones the time of attaching.

(3) Unless otherwise agreed a security agreement gives the secured party the rights to proceeds provided by Section 9—306.

(4) A transaction, although subject to this Article, is also subject to ....*, and in the case of conflict between the provisions of this Article and any such statute, the provisions of such statute control. Failure to comply with any applicable statute has only the effect which is specified therein. Amended in 1972 and 1977.

Section 9—204. AFTER-ACQUIRED PROPERTY; FUTURE ADVANCES

(1) Except as provided in subsection (2), a security agreement may provide that any or all obligations covered by the security agreement are to be secured by after-acquired collateral.

(2) No security interest attaches under an after-acquired property clause to consumer goods other than accessions (Section 9—314) when given as additional security unless the debtor acquires rights in them within ten days after the secured party gives value.

(3) Obligations covered by a security agreement may include future advances or other value whether or not the advances or value are given pursuant to commitment (subsection (1) of Section 9—105). Amended in 1972.

Section 9—207. RIGHTS AND DUTIES WHEN COLLATERAL IS IN SECURED PARTY'S POSSESSION

(1) A secured party must use reasonable care in the custody and preservation of collateral in his possession. In the case of an instrument or chattel paper reasonable care includes taking necessary steps to preserve rights against prior parties unless otherwise agreed.

(2) Unless otherwise agreed, when collateral is in the secured party's possession

(a) reasonable expenses (including the cost of any insurance and payment of taxes or other charges) incurred in the custody, preservation, use or operation of the collateral are chargeable to the debtor and are secured by the collateral;

(b) the risk of accidental loss or damage is on the debtor to the extent of any deficiency in any effective insurance coverage;

(c) the secured party may hold as additional security any increase or profits (except money) received from the collateral, but money so received, unless remitted to the debtor; shall be applied in reduction of the secured obligation;

(d) the secured party must keep the collateral identifiable but fungible collateral may be commingled;

(e) the secured party may repledge the collateral upon terms which do not impair the debtor's right to redeem it.

(3) A secured party is liable for any loss caused by his failure to meet any obligation imposed by the preceding subsections but does not lose his security interest.

(4) A secured party may use or operate the collateral for the purpose of preserving the collateral or its value or pursuant to the order of a court of appropriate jurisdiction or, except in the case of consumer goods, in the manner and to the extent provided in the security agreement.

Part 3

Rights of Third Parties; Perfected and Unperfected Security Interests; Rules of Priority

Section 9—301. PERSONS WHO TAKE PRIORITY OVER UNPERFECTED SECURITY INTERESTS; RIGHTS OF "LIEN CREDITOR"

(1) Except as otherwise provided in subsection (2), an unperfected security interest is subordinate to the rights of

(a) persons entitled to priority under Section 9—312;

(b) a person who becomes a lien creditor before the security interest is perfected;

(c) in the case of goods, instruments, documents, and chattel paper, a person who is not a secured party and who is a transferee in bulk or other buyer not in ordinary course of business or is a buyer of farm products in ordinary course of business, to the extent that he gives value and receives delivery of the collateral without knowledge of the security interest and before it is perfected;

(d) in the case of accounts and general intangibles, a person who is not a secured party and who is a transferee to the extent that he gives value without knowledge of the security interest and before it is perfected.

(2) If the secured party files with respect to a purchase money security interest before or within ten days after the debtor receives possession of the collateral, he takes priority over the rights of a transferee in bulk or of a lien creditor which arise between the time the security interest attaches and the time of filing.

(3) A "lien creditor" means a creditor who has acquired a lien on the property involved by attachment, levy or the like and includes an assignee for benefit of creditors from the time of assignment, and a trustee in bankruptcy from the date of the filing of the petition or a receiver in equity from the time of appointment.

(4) A person who becomes a lien creditor while a security interest is perfected takes subject to the security interest only to the extent that it secures advances made before he becomes a lien creditor or within 45 days thereafter or made without knowledge of the lien or pursuant to a commitment entered into without knowledge of the lien. Amended in 1972.

Section 9—302. WHEN FILING IS REQUIRED TO PERFECT SECURITY INTEREST; SECURITY INTERESTS TO WHICH FILING PROVISIONS OF THIS ARTICLE DO NOT APPLY

(1) A financing statement must be filed to perfect all security interests except the following:

(a) a security interest in collateral in possession of the secured party under Section 9—305;

(b) a security interest temporarily perfected in instruments or documents without delivery under Section 9—304 or in proceeds for a 10 day period under Section 9—306;

(c) a security interest created by an assignment of a beneficial interest in a trust or a decedent's estate;

(d) a purchase money security interest in consumer goods; but filing is required for a motor vehicle required to be registered; and fixture filing is required for priority over conflicting interests in fixtures to the extent provided in Section 9—313;

(e) an assignment of accounts which does not alone or in conjunction with other assignments to the same assignee transfer a significant part of the outstanding accounts of the assignor;

(f) a security interest of a collecting bank (Section 4—208) or in securities (Section 8—321) or arising under the Article on Sales (see Section 9—113) or covered in subsection (3) of this section;

(g) an assignment for the benefit of all the creditors of the transferor, and subsequent transfers by the assignee thereunder.

(2) If a secured party assigns a perfected security interest, no filing under this Article is required in order to continue the perfected status of the security interest against creditors of and transferees from the original debtor.

(3) The filing of a financing statement otherwise required by this Article is not necessary or effective to perfect a security interest in property subject to

(a) a statute or treaty of the United States which provides for a national or international registration or a national or international certificate of title or which specifies a place of filing different from that specified in this Article for filing of the security interest; or

(b) the following statutes of this state; [list any certificate of title statute covering automobiles, trailers, mobile homes, boats, farm tractors, or the like, and any central filing statute.]; but during any period in which collateral is inventory held for sale by a person who is in the business of selling goods of that kind, the filing provisions of this Article (Part 4) apply to a security interest in that collateral created by him as debtor; or

(c) a certificate of title statute of another jurisdiction under the law of which indication of a security interest on the certificate is required as a condition of perfection (subjection (2) of Section 9—103).

(4) Compliance with a statute or treaty described in subsection (3) is equivalent to the filing of a financing statement under this Article, and a security interest in property subject to the statute or treaty can be perfected only by compliance therewith except as provided in Section 9—103 on multiple state transactions. Duration and renewal of perfection of a security interest perfected by compliance with the statute or treaty are governed by the provisions of the statute or treaty; in other respects the security interest is subject to this Article. Amended in 1972 and 1977.

Section 9—303. WHEN SECURITY INTEREST IS PERFECTED; CONTINUITY OF PERFECTION

(1) A security interest is perfected when it has attached and when all of the applicable steps required for perfection have been taken. Such steps are specified in Sections 9—302, 9—304, 9—305 and 9—306. If such steps are taken before the security interest attaches, it is perfected at the time when it attaches.

(2) If a security interest is originally perfected in any way permitted under this Article and is subsequently perfected in some other way under this Article, without an intermediate period when it was unperfected, the security interest shall be deemed to be perfected continuously for the purposes of this Article.

Section 9—304. PERFECTION OF SECURITY INTEREST IN INSTRUMENTS, DOCUMENTS, AND GOODS COVERED BY DOCUMENTS; PERFECTION BY PERMISSIVE FILING; TEMPORARY PERFECTION WITHOUT FILING OR TRANSFER OF POSSESSION

(1) A security interest in chattel paper or negotiable documents may be perfected by filing. A security interest in money or instruments (other than certificated securities or instruments which constitute part of chattel paper) can be perfected only by the secured party's taking possession, except as provided in subsections (4) and (5) of this section and subsections (2) and (3) of Section 9—306 on proceeds.

(2) During the period that goods are in the possession of the issuer of a negotiable document therefor, a security interest in the goods is perfected by perfecting a security interest in the document, and any security interest in the goods otherwise perfected during such period is subject thereto.

(3) A security interest in goods in the possession of a bailee other than one who has issued a negotiable document therefor is perfected by issuance of a document in the name of the secured party or by the bailee's receipt of notification of the secured party's interest or by filing as to the goods.

(4) A security interest in instruments (other than certificated securities) or negotiable documents is perfected without filing or the taking of possession for a period of 21 days from the time it attaches to the extent that it arises for new value given under a written security agreement.

(5) A security interest remains perfected for a period of 21 days without filing where a secured party having a perfected security interest in an instrument (other than a certificated security), a negotiable document or goods in possession of a bailee other than one who has issued a negotiable document therefor

(a) makes available to the debtor the goods or documents representing the goods for the purpose of ultimate sale or exchange or for the purpose of loading, unloading, storing, shipping, transshipping, manufacturing, processing or otherwise dealing with them in a manner preliminary to their sale or exchange, but priority between conflicting security interests in the goods is subject to subsection (3) of Section 9—312; or

(b) delivers the instrument to the debtor for the purpose of ultimate sale or exchange or of presentation, collection, renewal or registration of transfer.

(6) After the 21 day period in subsections (4) and (5) perfection depends upon compliance with applicable provisions of this Article.

Amended in 1972 and 1977.

Section 9—305. WHEN POSSESSION BY SECURED PARTY PERFECTS SECURITY INTEREST WITHOUT FILING

A security interest in letters of credit and advices of credit (subsection (2)(a) of Section 5—116), goods, instruments (other than certificated securities), money, negotiable documents, or chattel paper may be perfected by the secured party's taking possession of the collateral. If such collateral other than goods covered by a negotiable document is held by a bailee, the secured party is deemed to have possession from the time the bailee receives notification of the secured party's interest. A security interest is perfected by possession from the time possession is taken without relation back and continues only so long as possession is retained, unless otherwise specified in this Article. The security interest may be otherwise perfected as provided in this Article before or after the period of possession by the secured party.

Amended in 1972 and 1977.

Section 9—307. PROTECTION OF BUYERS OF GOODS

(1) A buyer in ordinary course of business (subsection (9) of Section 1—201) other than a person buying farm products from a person engaged in farming operations takes free of a security interest created by his seller even though the security interest is perfected and even though the buyer knows of its existence.

(2) In the case of consumer goods, a buyer takes free of a security interest even though perfected if he buys without knowledge of the security interest, for value and for his own personal, family or household purposes unless prior to the purchase the secured party has filed a financing statement covering such goods.

(3) A buyer other than a buyer in ordinary course of business (subsection (1) of this section) takes free of a security interest to the extent that it secures future advances made after the secured party acquires knowledge of the purchase, or more than 45 days after the purchase, whichever first occurs, unless made pursuant to a commitment entered into without knowledge of the purchase and before the expiration of the 45 day period. Amended in 1972.

Section 9—310. PRIORITY OF CERTAIN LIENS ARISING BY OPERATION OF LAW

When a person in the ordinary course of his business furnishes services or materials with respect to goods subject to a security interest, a lien upon goods in the possession of such person given by statute or rule of law for such materials or services takes priority over a perfected security interest unless the lien is statutory and the statute expressly provides otherwise.

Section 9—312. PRIORITIES AMONG CONFLICTING SECURITY INTERESTS IN THE SAME COLLATERAL

(1) The rules of priority stated in other sections of this Part and in the following sections shall govern when applicable: Section 4—208 with respect to the security interests of collecting banks in items being collected, accompanying documents and proceeds; Section 9—103 on security interests related to other jurisdictions; Section 9—114 on consignments.

(2) A perfected security interest in crops for new value given to enable the debtor to produce the crops during the production season and given not more than three months before the crops become growing crops by planting or otherwise takes priority over an earlier perfected security interest to the extent that such earlier interest secures obligations due more than six months before the crops become growing crops by planting or otherwise, even though the person giving new value had knowledge of the earlier security interest.

(3) A perfected purchase money security interest in inventory has priority over a conflicting security interest in the same inventory and also has priority in identifiable cash proceeds received on or before the delivery of the inventory to a buyer if

(a) the purchase money security interest is perfected at the time the debtor receives possession of the inventory; and

(b) the purchase money secured party gives notification in writing to the holder of the conflicting security interest if the holder had filed a financing statement covering the same types of inventory (i) before the date of the filing made by the purchase money secured party, or (ii) before the beginning of the 21 day period where the purchase money security interest is temporarily perfected without filing or possession (subsection (5) of Section 9—304); and

(c) the holder of the conflicting security interest receives the notification within five years before the debtor receives possession of the inventory; and

(d) the notification states that the person giving the notice has or expects to acquire a purchase money security interest in inventory of the debtor, describing such inventory by item or type.

(4) A purchase money security interest in collateral other than inventory has priority over a conflicting security interest in the same collateral or its proceeds if the purchase money security interest is perfected at the time the debtor receives possession of the collateral or within ten days thereafter.

(5) In all cases not governed by other rules stated in this section (including cases of purchase money security interests which do not qualify for the special priorities set forth in subsections (3) and (4) of this section), priority between conflicting security interests in the same collateral shall be determined according to the following rules:

(a) Conflicting security interests rank according to priority in time of filing or perfection. Priority dates from the time a filing is first made covering the collateral or the time the security interest is first perfected, whichever is earlier, provided that there is no period thereafter when there is neither filing nor perfection.

(b) So long as conflicting security interests are unperfected, the first to attach has priority.

(6) For the purposes of subsection (5) a date of filing or perfection as to collateral is also a date of filing or perfection as to proceeds.

(7) If future advances are made while a security interest is perfected by filing, the taking of possession, or under Section 8—321 on securities, the security interest has the same prior-

ity for the purposes of subsection (5) with respect to the future advances as it does with respect to the first advance. If a commitment is made before or while the security interest is so perfected, the security interest has the same priority with respect to advances made pursuant thereto. In other cases a perfected security interest has priority from the date the advance is made.

Amended in 1972 and 1977.

Section 9—313. PRIORITY OF SECURITY INTERESTS IN FIXTURES

(1) In this section and in the provisions of Part 4 of this Article referring to fixture filing, unless the context otherwise requires

(a) goods are "fixtures" when they become so related to particular real estate that an interest in them arises under real estate law

(b) a "fixture filing" is the filing in the office where a mortgage on the real estate would be filed or recorded of a financing statement covering goods which are or are to become fixtures and conforming to the requirements of subsection (5) of Section 9—402

(c) a mortgage is a "construction mortgage" to the extent that it secures an obligation incurred for the construction of an improvement on land including the acquisition cost of the land, if the recorded writing so indicates.

(2) A security interest under this Article may be created in goods which are fixtures or may continue in goods which become fixtures, but no security interest exists under this Article in ordinary building materials incorporated into an improvement on land.

(3) This Article does not prevent creation of an encumbrance upon fixtures pursuant to real estate law.

(4) A perfected security interest in fixtures has priority over the conflicting interest of an encumbrancer or owner of the real estate where

(a) the security interest is a purchase money security interest, the interest of the encumbrancer or owner arises before the goods become fixtures, the security interest is perfected by a fixture filing before the goods become fixtures or within ten days thereafter, and the debtor has an interest of record in the real estate or is in possession of the real estate; or

(b) the security interest is perfected by a fixture filing before the interest of the encumbrancer or owner is of record, the security interest has priority over any conflicting interest of a predecessor in title of the encumbrancer or owner, and the debtor has an interest of record in the real estate or is in possession of the real estate; or

(c) the fixtures are readily removable factory or office machines or readily removable replacements of domestic appliances which are consumer goods, and before the goods become fixtures the security interest is perfected by any method permitted by this Article; or

(d) the conflicting interest is a lien on the real estate obtained by legal or equitable proceedings after the security interest was perfected by any method permitted by this Article.

(5) A security interest in fixtures, whether or not perfected, has priority over the conflicting interest of an encumbrancer or owner of the real estate where

(a) the encumbrancer or owner has consented in writing to the security interest or has disclaimed an interest in the goods as fixtures; or

(b) the debtor has a right to remove the goods as against the encumbrancer or owner. If the debtor's right terminates, the priority of the security interest continues for a reasonable time.

(6) Notwithstanding paragraph (a) of subsection (4) but otherwise subject to subsections (4) and (5), a security interest in fixtures is subordinate to a construction mortgage recorded before the goods become fixtures if the goods become fixtures before the completion of the construction. To the extent that it is given to refinance a construction mortgage, a mortgage has this priority to the same extent as the construction mortgage.

(7) In cases not within the preceding subsections, a security interest in fixtures is subordinate to the conflicting interest of an encumbrancer or owner of the related real estate who is not the debtor.

(8) When the secured party has priority over all owners and encumbrancers of the real estate, he may, on default, subject to the provisions of Part 5, remove his collateral from the real estate but he must reimburse any encumbrancer or owner of the real estate who is not the debtor and who has not otherwise agreed for the cost of repair of any physical injury, but not for any diminution in value of the real estate caused by the absence of the goods removed or by any necessity of replacing them. A person entitled to reimbursement may refuse permission to remove until the secured party gives adequate security for the performance of this obligation. Amended in 1972.

Part 4
Filing

Section 9—401. PLACE OF FILING; ERRONEOUS FILING; REMOVAL OF COLLATERAL

First Alternative Subsection (1)

(1) The proper place to file in order to perfect a security interest is as follows:

(a) when the collateral is timber to be cut or is minerals or the like (including oil and gas) or accounts subject to subsection (5) of Section 9—103, or when the financing

statement is filed as a fixture filing (Section 9—313) and the collateral is goods which are or are to become fixtures, then in the office where a mortgage on the real estate would be filed or recorded;
(b) in all other cases, in the office of the [Secretary of State].

Second Alternative Subsection (1)

(1) The proper place to file in order to perfect a security interest is as follows:
(a) when the collateral is equipment used in farming operations, or farm products, or accounts or general intangibles arising from or relating to the sale of farm products by a farmer, or consumer goods, then in the office of the .... in the county of the debtor's residence or if the debtor is not a resident of this state then in the office of the .... in the county where the goods are kept, and in addition when the collateral is crops growing or to be grown in the office of the .... in the county where the land is located;
(b) when the collateral is timber to be cut or is minerals or the like (including oil and gas) or accounts subject to subsection (5) of Section 9—103, or when the financing statement is filed as a fixture filing (Section 9—313) and the collateral is goods which are or are to become fixtures, then in the office where a mortgage on the real estate would be filed or recorded;
(c) in all other cases, in the office of the [Secretary of State].

Third Alternative Subsection (1)

(1) The proper place to file in order to perfect a security interest is as follows:
(a) when the collateral is equipment used in farming operations, or farm products, or accounts or general intangibles arising from or relating to the sale of farm products by a farmer, or consumer goods, then in the office of the ...... in the county of the debtor's residence or if the debtor is not a resident of this state then in the office of the .... in the county where the goods are kept, and in addition when the collateral is crops growing or to be grown in the office of the ...... in the county where the land is located;
(b) when the collateral is timber to be cut or is minerals or the like (including oil and gas) or accounts subject to subsection (5) of Section 9—103, or when the financing statement is filed as a fixture filing (Section 9—313) and the collateral is goods which are or are to become fixtures, then in the office where a mortgage on the real estate would be filed or recorded;
(c) in all other cases, in the office of the [Secretary of State] and in addition, if the debtor has a place of business in only one county of this state, also in the office of ...... of such county, or, if the debtor has no place of business in this state, but resides in the state, also in the office of ...... of the county in which he resides.

Note: One of the three alternatives should be selected as subsection (1).

(2) A filing which is made in good faith in an improper place or not in all of the places required by this section is nevertheless effective with regard to any collateral as to which the filing complied with the requirements of this Article and is also effective with regard to collateral covered by the financing statement against any person who has knowledge of the contents of such financing statement.
(3) A filing which is made in the proper place in this state continues effective even though the debtor's residence or place of business or the location of the collateral or its use, whichever controlled the original filing, is thereafter changed.

Alternative Subsection (3)

[(3) A filing which is made in the proper county continues effective for four months after a change to another county of the debtor's residence or place of business or the location of the collateral, whichever controlled the original filing. It becomes ineffective thereafter unless a copy of the financing statement signed by the secured party is filed in the new county within said period. The security interest may also be perfected in the new county after the expiration of the four-month period; in such case perfection dates from the time of perfection in the new county. A change in the use of the collateral does not impair the effectiveness of the original filing.]
(4) The rules stated in Section 9—103 determine whether filing is necessary in this state.
(5) Notwithstanding the preceding subsections, and subject to subsection (3) of Section 9—302, the proper place to file in order to perfect a security interest in collateral, including fixtures, of a transmitting utility is the office of the [Secretary of State]. This filing constitutes a fixture filing (Section 9—313) as to the collateral described therein which is or is to become fixtures.
(6) For the purposes of this section, the residence of an organization is its place of business if it has one or its chief executive office if it has more than one place of business.
Amended in 1962 and 1972.

Section 9—402. FORMAL REQUISITES OF FINANCING STATEMENT; AMENDMENTS; MORTGAGE AS FINANCING STATEMENT

(1) A financing statement is sufficient if it gives the names of the debtor and the secured party, is signed by the debtor, gives an address of the secured party from which information concerning the security interest may be obtained, gives a mailing address of the debtor and contains a statement in-

dicating the types, or describing the items, of collateral. A financing statement may be filed before a security agreement is made or a security interest otherwise attaches. When the financing statement covers crops growing or to be grown, the statement must also contain a description of the real estate concerned. When the financing statement covers timber to be cut or covers minerals or the like (including oil and gas) or accounts subject to subsection (5) of Section 9—103, or when the financing statement is filed as a fixture filing (Section 9—313) and the collateral is goods which are or are to become fixtures, the statement must also comply with subsection (5). A copy of the security agreement is sufficient as a financing statement if it contains the above information and is signed by the debtor. A carbon, photographic or other reproduction of a security agreement or a financing statement is sufficient as a financing statement if the security agreement so provides or if the original has been filed in this state.

(2) A financing statement which otherwise complies with subsection (1) is sufficient when it is signed by the secured party instead of the debtor if it is filed to perfect a security interest in

(a) collateral already subject to a security interest in another jurisdiction when it is brought into this state, or when the debtor's location is changed to this state. Such a financing statement must state that the collateral was brought into this state or that the debtor's location was changed to this state under such circumstances; or

(b) proceeds under Section 9—306 if the security interest in the original collateral was perfected. Such a financing statement must describe the original collateral; or

(c) collateral as to which the filing has lapsed; or

(d) collateral acquired after a change of name, identity or corporate structure of the debtor (subsection (7)).

(3) A form substantially as follows is sufficient to comply with subsection (1):

Name of debtor (or assignor) ____________________
Address ____________________
Name of secured party (or assignee) ____________________
Address ____________________

1. This financing statement covers the following types (or items) of property:
   (Describe) ____________________
2. (If collateral is crops) The above described crops are growing or are to be grown on:
   (Describe Real Estate) ____________________
3. (If applicable) The above goods are to become fixtures on*
   (Describe Real Estate) ____________ and this financing statement is to be filed [for record] in the real estate records. (If the debtor does not have an interest of record) The name of a record owner is ____________________
4. (If products of collateral are claimed) Products of the collateral are also covered.

(use whichever is applicable)	____________________ Signature of Debtor (or Assignor) ____________________ Signature of Secured Party (or Assignee)

(4) A financing statement may be amended by filing a writing signed by both the debtor and the secured party. An amendment does not extend the period of effectiveness of a financing statement. If any amendment adds collateral, it is effective as to the added collateral only from the filing date of the amendment. In this Article, unless the context otherwise requires, the term "financing statement" means the original financing statement and any amendments.

(5) A financing statement covering timber to be cut or covering minerals or the like (including oil and gas) or accounts subject to subsection (5) of Section 9—103, or a financing statement filed as a fixture filing (Section 9—313) where the debtor is not a transmitting utility, must show that it covers this type of collateral, must recite that it is to be filed [for record] in the real estate records, and the financing statement must contain a description of the real estate [sufficient if it were contained in a mortgage of the real estate to give constructive notice of the mortgage under the law of this state]. If the debtor does not have an interest of record in the real estate, the financing statement must show the name of a record owner.

(6) A mortgage is effective as a financing statement filed as a fixture filing from the date of its recording if

(a) the goods are described in the mortgage by item or type; and

(b) the goods are or are to become fixtures related to the real estate described in the mortgage; and

(c) the mortgage complies with the requirements for a financing statement in this section other than a recital that it is to be filed in the real estate records; and

(d) the mortgage is duly recorded.

No fee with reference to the financing statement is required other than the regular recording and satisfaction fees with respect to the mortgage.

(7) A financing statement sufficiently shows the name of the debtor if it gives the individual, partnership or corporate name of the debtor, whether or not it adds other trade names or names of partners. Where the debtor so changes his name or in the case of an organization its name, identity or corporate structure that a filed financing statement becomes seriously misleading, the filing is not effective to perfect a security interest in collateral acquired by the debtor more than four months after the change, unless a new appropriate financing statement is filed before the expiration of that time. A filed financing statement remains effective with respect to collateral transferred by the debtor even though the secured party knows of or consents to the transfer.

(8) A financing statement substantially complying with the requirements of this section is effective even though it contains minor errors which are not seriously misleading. Amended in 1972.

*Where appropriate substitute either "The above timber is standing on . . . ." or "The above minerals or the like (including oil and gas) or accounts will be financed at the wellhead or minehead of the well or mine located on . . . ."

Section 9—403. WHAT CONSTITUTES FILING; DURATION OF FILING; EFFECT OF LAPSED FILING; DUTIES OF FILING OFFICER

(1) Presentation for filing of a financing statement and tender of the filing fee or acceptance of the statement by the filing officer constitutes filing under this Article.

(2) Except as provided in subsection (6) a filed financing statement is effective for a period of five years from the date of filing. The effectiveness of a filed financing statement lapses on the expiration of the five year period unless a continuation statement is filed prior to the lapse. If a security interest perfected by filing exists at the time insolvency proceedings are commenced by or against the debtor, the security interest remains perfected until termination of the insolvency proceedings and thereafter for a period of sixty days or until expiration of the five year period, whichever occurs later. Upon lapse the security interest becomes unperfected, unless it is perfected without filing. If the security interest becomes unperfected upon lapse, it is deemed to have been unperfected as against a person who became a purchaser or lien creditor before lapse.

(3) A continuation statement may be filed by the secured party within six months prior to the expiration of the five year period specified in subsection (2). Any such continuation statement must be signed by the secured party, identify the original statement by file number and state that the original statement is still effective. A continuation statement signed by a person other than the secured party of record must be accompanied by a separate written statement of assignment signed by the secured party of record and complying with subsection (2) of Section 9—405, including payment of the required fee. Upon timely filing of the continuation statement, the effectiveness of the original statement is continued for five years after the last date to which the filing was effective whereupon it lapses in the same manner as provided in subsection (2) unless another continuation statement is filed prior to such lapse. Succeeding continuation statements may be filed in the same manner to continue the effectiveness of the original statement. Unless a statute on disposition of public records provides otherwise, the filing officer may remove a lapsed statement from the files and destroy it immediately if he has retained a microfilm or other photographic record, or in other cases after one year after the lapse. The filing officer shall so arrange matters by physical annexation of financing statements to continuation statements or other related filings, or by other means, that if he physically destroys the financing statements of a period more than five years past, those which have been continued by a continuation statement or which are still effective under subsection (6) shall be retained.

(4) Except as provided in subsection (7) a filing officer shall mark each statement with a file number and with the date and hour of filing and shall hold the statement or a microfilm or other photographic copy thereof for public inspection. In addition the filing officer shall index the statement according to the name of the debtor and shall note in the index the file number and the address of the debtor given in the statement.

(5) The uniform fee for filing and indexing and for stamping a copy furnished by the secured party to show the date and place of filing for an original financing statement or for a continuation statement shall be $.......... if the statement is in the standard form prescribed by the [Secretary of State] and otherwise shall be $.........., plus in each case, if the financing statement is subject to subsection (5) of Section 9—402, $....... The uniform fee for each name more than one required to be indexed shall be $........... The secured party may at his option show a trade name for any person and an extra uniform indexing fee of $.......... shall be paid with respect thereto.

(6) If the debtor is a transmitting utility (subsection (5) of Section 9—401) and a filed financing statement so states, it is effective until a termination statement is filed. A real estate mortgage which is effective as a fixture filing under subsection (6) of Section 9—402 remains effective as a fixture filing until the mortgage is released or satisfied of record or its effectiveness otherwise terminates as to the real estate.

(7) When a financing statement covers timber to be cut or covers minerals or the like (including oil and gas) or accounts subject to subsection (5) of Section 9—103, or is filed as a fixture filing, [it shall be filed for record and] the filing officer shall index it under the names of the debtor and any owner of record shown on the financing statement in the same fashion as if they were the mortgagors in a mortgage of the real estate described, and, to the extent that the law of this state provides for indexing of mortgages under the name of the mortgagee, under the name of the secured party as if he were the mortgagee thereunder, or where indexing is by description in the same fashion as if the financing statement were a mortgage of the real estate described. Amended in 1972.

Part 5

Default

Section 9—501. DEFAULT; PROCEDURE WHEN SECURITY AGREEMENT COVERS BOTH REAL AND PERSONAL PROPERTY

(1) When a debtor is in default under a security agreement, a secured party has the rights and remedies provided in this Part and except as limited by subsection (3) those provided in the security agreement. He may reduce his claim to judgment, foreclose or otherwise enforce the security interest by any available judicial procedure. If the collateral is documents the secured party may proceed either as to the doc-

uments or as to the goods covered thereby. A secured party in possession has the rights, remedies and duties provided in Section 9—207. The rights and remedies referred to in this subsection are cumulative.

(2) After default, the debtor has the rights and remedies provided in this Part, those provided in the security agreement and those provided in Section 9—207.

(3) To the extent that they give rights to the debtor and impose duties on the secured party, the rules stated in the subsections referred to below may not be waived or varied except as provided with respect to compulsory disposition of collateral (subsection (3) of Section 9—504 and Section 9—505) and with respect to redemption of collateral (Section 9—506) but the parties may by agreement determine the standards by which the fulfillment of these rights and duties is to be measured if such standards are not manifestly unreasonable:

(a) subsection (2) of Section 9—502 and subsection (2) of Section 9—504 insofar as they require accounting for surplus proceeds of collateral;

(b) subsection (3) of Section 9—504 and subsection (1) of Section 9—505 which deal with disposition of collateral;

(c) subsection (2) of Section 9—505 which deals with acceptance of collateral as discharge of obligation;

(d) Section 9—506 which deals with redemption of collateral; and

(e) subsection (1) of Section 9—507 which deals with the secured party's liability for failure to comply with this Part.

(4) If the security agreement covers both real and personal property, the secured party may proceed under this Part as to the personal property or he may proceed as to both the real and the personal property in accordance with his rights and remedies in respect of the real property in which case the provisions of this Part do not apply.

(5) When a secured party has reduced his claim to judgment the lien of any levy which may be made upon his collateral by virtue of any execution based upon the judgment shall relate back to the date of the perfection of the security interest in such collateral. A judicial sale, pursuant to such execution, is a foreclosure of the security interest by judicial procedure within the meaning of this section, and the secured party may purchase at the sale and thereafter hold the collateral free of any other requirements of this Article. Amended in 1972.

Section 9—503. SECURED PARTY'S RIGHT TO TAKE POSSESSION AFTER DEFAULT

Unless otherwise agreed a secured party has on default the right to take possession of the collateral. In taking possession a secured party may proceed without judicial process if this can be done without breach of the peace or may proceed by action. If the security agreement so provides the secured party may require the debtor to assemble the collateral and make it available to the secured party at a place to be designated by the secured party which is reasonably convenient to both parties. Without removal a secured party may render equipment unusable, and may dispose of collateral on the debtor's premises under Section 9—504.

Section 9—504. SECURED PARTY'S RIGHT TO DISPOSE OF COLLATERAL AFTER DEFAULT; EFFECT OF DISPOSITION

(1) A secured party after default may sell, lease or otherwise dispose of any or all of the collateral in its then condition or following any commercially reasonable preparation or processing. Any sale of goods is subject to the Article on Sales (Article 2). The proceeds of disposition shall be applied in the order following to

(a) the reasonable expenses of retaking, holding, preparing for sale or lease, selling, leasing and the like and, to the extent provided for in the agreement and not prohibited by law, the reasonable attorneys' fees and legal expenses incurred by the secured party;

(b) the satisfaction of indebtedness secured by the security interest under which the disposition is made;

(c) the satisfaction of indebtedness secured by any subordinate security interest in the collateral if written notification of demand therefor is received before distribution of the proceeds is completed. If requested by the secured party, the holder of a subordinate security interest must seasonably furnish reasonable proof of his interest, and unless he does so, the secured party need not comply with his demand.

(2) If the security interest secures an indebtedness, the secured party must account to the debtor for any surplus, unless otherwise agreed, the debtor is liable for any deficiency. But if the underlying transaction was a sale of accounts or chattel paper, the debtor is entitled to any surplus or is liable for any deficiency only if the security agreement so provides.

(3) Disposition of the collateral may be by public or private proceedings and may be made by way of one or more contracts. Sale or other disposition may be as a unit or in parcels and at any time and place and on any terms but every aspect of the disposition including the method, manner, time, place and terms must be commercially reasonable. Unless collateral is perishable or threatens to decline speedily in value or is of a type customarily sold on a recognized market, reasonable notification of the time and place of any public sale or reasonable notification of the time after which any private sale or other intended disposition is to be made shall be sent by the secured party to the debtor, if he has not signed after default a statement renouncing or modifying his right to notification of sale. In the case of consumer

goods no other notification need be sent. In other cases notification shall be sent to any other secured party from whom the secured party has received (before sending his notification to the debtor or before the debtor's renunciation of his rights) written notice of a claim of an interest in the collateral. The secured party may buy at any public sale and if the collateral is of a type customarily sold in a recognized market or is of a type which is the subject of widely distributed standard price quotations he may buy at private sale.

(4) When collateral is disposed of by a secured party after default, the disposition transfers to a purchaser for value all of the debtor's rights therein, discharges the security interest under which it is made and any security interest or lien subordinate thereto. The purchaser takes free of all such rights and interests even though the secured party fails to comply with the requirements of this Part or of any judicial proceedings

(a) in the case of a public sale, if the purchaser has no knowledge of any defects in the sale and if he does not buy in collusion with the secured party, other bidders or the person conducting the sale; or

(b) in any other case, if the purchaser acts in good faith.

(5) A person who is liable to a secured party under a guaranty, indorsement, repurchase agreement or the like and who receives a transfer of collateral from the secured party or is subrogated to his rights has thereafter the rights and duties of the secured party. Such a transfer of collateral is not a sale or disposition of the collateral under this Article. Amended in 1972.

Section 9—505. COMPULSORY DISPOSITION OF COLLATERAL; ACCEPTANCE OF THE COLLATERAL AS DISCHARGE OF OBLIGATION

(1) If the debtor has paid sixty per cent of the cash price in the case of a purchase money security interest in consumer goods or sixty per cent of the loan in the case of another security interest in consumer goods, and has not signed after default a statement renouncing or modifying his rights under this Part a secured party who has taken possession of collateral must dispose of it under Section 9—504 and if he fails to do so within ninety days after he takes possession the debtor at his option may recover in conversion or under Section 9—507(1) on secured party's liability.

(2) In any other case involving consumer goods or any other collateral a secured party in possession may, after default, propose to retain the collateral in satisfaction of the obligation. Written notice of such proposal shall be sent to the debtor if he has not signed after default a statement renouncing or modifying his rights under this subsection. In the case of consumer goods no other notice need be given. In other cases notice shall be sent to any other secured party from whom the secured party has received (before sending his notice to the debtor or before the debtor's renunciation of his rights) written notice of a claim of an interest in the collateral. If the secured party receives objection in writing from a person entitled to receive notification within twenty-one days after the notice was sent, the secured party must dispose of the collateral under Section 9—504. In the absence of such written objection the secured party may retain the collateral in satisfaction of the debtor's obligation. Amended in 1972.

Section 9—506. DEBTOR'S RIGHT TO REDEEM COLLATERAL

At any time before the secured party has disposed of collateral or entered into a contract for its disposition under Section 9—504 or before the obligation has been discharged under Section 9—505(2) the debtor or any other secured party may unless otherwise agreed in writing after default redeem the collateral by tendering fulfillment of all obligations secured by the collateral as well as the expenses reasonably incurred by the secured party in retaking, holding and preparing the collateral for disposition, in arranging for the sale, and to the extent provided in the agreement and not prohibited by law, his reasonable attorneys' fees and legal expenses.

Section 9—507. SECURED PARTY'S LIABILITY FOR FAILURE TO COMPLY WITH THIS PART

(1) If it is established that the secured party is not proceeding in accordance with the provisions of this Part disposition may be ordered or restrained on appropriate terms and conditions. If the disposition has occurred the debtor or any person entitled to notification or whose security interest has been made known to the secured party prior to the disposition has a right to recover from the secured party any loss caused by a failure to comply with the provisions of this Part. If the collateral is consumer goods, the debtor has a right to recover in any event an amount not less than the credit service charge plus ten per cent of the principal amount of the debt or the time price differential plus 10 per cent of the cash price.

(2) The fact that a better price could have been obtained by a sale at a different time or in a different method from that selected by the secured party is not of itself sufficient to establish that the sale was not made in a commercially reasonable manner. If the secured party either sells the collateral in the usual manner in any recognized market therefor or if he sells at the price current in such market at the time of his sale or if he has otherwise sold in conformity with reasonable commercial practices among dealers in the type of property sold he has sold in a commercially reasonable manner. The principles stated in the two preceding

sentences with respect to sales also apply as may be appropriate to other types of disposition. A disposition which has been approved in any judicial proceeding or by any bona fide creditors' committee or representative of creditors shall conclusively be deemed to be commercially reasonable, but this sentence does not indicate that any such approval must be obtained in any case nor does it indicate that any disposition not so approved is not commercially reasonable.

U.L.A.-U.C.C. 9th Ed. '78 Pamph.—18

Appendix VIII

The National Labor Relations Act (Excerpts)

DEFINITIONS

Section 2

When used in this Act—

(1) The term "person" includes one or more individuals, labor organizations, partnerships, associations, corporations, legal representatives, trustees, trustees in bankruptcy, or receivers.

(2) The term "employer" includes any person acting as an agent of an employer, directly or indirectly, but shall not include the United States or any wholly owned Government corporation, or any Federal Reserve Bank, or any State or political subdivision thereof, or any person subject to the Railway Labor Act, as amended from time to time, or any labor organization (other than when acting as an employer), or anyone acting in the capacity of officer or agent of such labor organization.

(3) The term "employee" shall include any employee, and shall not be limited to the employees of a particular employer, unless the Act explicitly states otherwise, and shall include any individual whose work has ceased as a consequence of, or in connection with, any current labor dispute or because of any unfair labor practice, and who has not obtained any other regular and substantially equivalent employment, but shall not include any individual employed as an agricultural laborer, or in the domestic service of any family or person at his home, or any individual employed by his parent or spouse, or any individual having the status of an independent contractor, or any individual employed as a supervisor, or any individual employed by an employer subject to the Railway Labor Act, as amended from time to time, or by any other person who is not employer as herein defined.

(4) The term "representatives" includes any individual or labor organization.

(5) The term "labor organization" means any organization of any kind, or any agency or employee representation committee or plan, in which employees participate and which exists for the purpose, in whole or in part, of dealing with employers concerning grievances, labor disputes, wages, rates of pay, hours of employment, or conditions of work.

(11) The term "supervisor" means any individual having authority, in the interest of the employer, to hire, transfer, suspend, lay off, recall, promote, discharge, assign, reward, or discipline other employees, or responsibly to direct them, or to adjust their grievances, or effectively to recommend such action, if in connection with the foregoing the exercise of such authority is not of a merely routine or clerical nature, but requires the use of independent judgment.

(12) The term "professional employee" means—

(A) any employee engaged in work (i) predominantly intellectual and varied in character as opposed to routine mental, manual, mechanical, or physical work; (ii) involving the consistent exercise of discretion and judgment in its performance; (iii) of such a character that the output produced or the result accomplished cannot be standardized in relation to a given period of time; (iv) requiring knowledge of an advanced type in a field of science or learning customarily acquired by a prolonged course of specialized intellectual instruction and study in an institution of higher learning or a hospital, as distinguished from a general academic education or from an apprenticeship or from training in the performance of routine mental, manual, or physical processes; or

(B) any employee, who (i) has completed the courses of specialized intellectual instruction and study described in clause (iv) of paragraph (A), and (ii) is performing related work under the supervision of a professional person to qualify himself to become a professional employee as defined in paragraph (A).

(13) In determining whether any person is acting as an "agent" of another person so as to make such other person responsible for his acts, the question of whether the specific acts performed were actually authorized or subsequently ratified shall not be controlling.

(14) The term "health care institution" shall include any hospital, convalescent hospital, health maintenance organi-

zation, health clinic, nursing home, extended care facility, or other institution devoted to the care of sick, infirm, or aged person.

NATIONAL LABOR RELATIONS BOARD

Section 3

(A) The National Labor Relations Board (hereinafter called the "Board") created by this Act prior to its amendment by the Labor Management Relations Act 1947 is hereby continued as an agency of the United States, except that the Board shall consist of five instead of three members, appointed by the President by and with the advice and consent of the Senate. Of the two additional members so provided for, one shall be appointed for a term of five years and the other for a term of two years. Their successors, and the successors of the other members, shall be appointed for terms of five years each, excepting that any individual chosen to fill a vacancy shall be appointed only for the unexpired term of the member whom he shall succeed. The President shall designate one member to serve as Chairman of the Board. Any member of the Board may be removed by the President, upon notice and hearing, for neglect of duty or malfeasance in office, but for no other cause.

Section 6

The Board shall have authority from time to time to make, amend, and rescind, in the manner prescribed by the Administrative Procedure Act, such rules and regulations as may be necessary to carry out the provisions of this Act.

RIGHTS OF EMPLOYEES

Section 7

Employees shall have the right to self-organization, to form, join, or assist labor organizations, to bargain collectively through representatives of their own choosing, and to engage in other concerted activities for the purpose of collective bargaining or other mutual aid or protection, and shall also have the right to refrain from any or all of such activities except to the extent that such right may be affected by an agreement requiring membership in a labor organization as a condition of employment as authorized in section 9(A)(3).

UNFAIR LABOR PRACTICES

Section 8

(A) It shall be an unfair labor practice for an employer—

(1) to interfere with, restrain, or coerce employees in the exercise of the rights guaranteed in section 7;

(2) to dominate or interfere with the formation or administration of any labor organization or contribute financial or other support to it: *Provided,* That subject to rules and regulations made and published by the Board pursuant to section 6, an employer shall not be prohibited from permitting employees to confer with him during working hours without loss of time or pay;

(3) by discrimination in regard to hire or tenure of employment or any term or condition of employment to encourage or discourage membership in any labor organization: *Provided,* That nothing in this Act, or in any other statute of the United States, shall preclude an employer from making an agreement with a labor organization (not established, maintained, or assisted by any action defined in section 8(A) of this Act as an unfair labor practice) to require as a condition of employment membership therein on or after the thirtieth day following the beginning of such employment or the effective date of such agreement, whichever is the later, (i) if such labor organization is the representative of the employees as provided in section 9(A), in the appropriate collective-bargaining unit covered by such agreement when made, and (ii) unless following an election held as provided in section 9(E) within one year preceding the effective date of such agreement, the Board shall have certified that at least a majority of the employees eligible to vote in such election have voted to rescind the authority of such labor organization to make such an agreement: *Provided further,* That no employer shall justify any discrimination against an employee for nonmembership in a labor organization (a) if he has reasonable grounds for believing that such membership was not available to the employee on the same terms and conditions generally applicable to other members, or (b) if he has reasonable grounds for believing that membership was denied or terminated for reasons other than the failure of the employee to tender the periodic dues and the initiation fees uniformly required as a condition of acquiring or retaining membership;

(4) to discharge or otherwise discriminate against any employee because he has filed charges or given testimony under this Act;

(5) to refuse to bargain collectively with the representatives of his employees, subject to the provisions of section 9(A).

(B) It shall be an unfair labor practice for a labor organization or its agents—

(1) to restrain or coerce (a) employees in the exercise of the rights guaranteed in section 7: *Provided,* That this paragraph shall not impair the right of a labor organization to prescribe its own rules with respect to the acquisition or retention of membership therein; or (b) an employer in the selection of his representatives for the purposes of collective bargaining or the adjustment of grievances;

(2) to cause or attempt to cause an employer to discriminate against an employee in violation of subsection (A)(3) or to

discriminate against an employee with respect to whom membership in such organization has been denied or terminated on some ground other than his failure to tender the periodic dues and the initiation fees uniformly required as a condition of acquiring or retaining membership;

(3) to refuse to bargain collectively with am employer, provided it is the representative of his employees subject to the provisions of section 9(A);

(4)(i) to engage in, or to induce or encourage any individual employed by any person engaged in commerce or in an industry affecting commerce to engage in, a strike or a refusal in the course of his employment to use, manufacture, process, transport, or otherwise handle or work on any goods, articles, materials, or commodities or to perform any services; or (ii) to threaten, coerce, or restrain any person engaged in commerce or in an industry affecting commerce, where in either case an object thereof is:

(a) forcing or requiring any employer or self-employed person to join any labor or employer organization or to enter into any agreement which is prohibited by section 8(E);

(b) forcing or requiring any person to cease using, selling, handling, transporting, or otherwise dealing in the product of any other producer, processor, or manufacturer, or to cease doing business with any other person, or forcing or requiring any other employer to recognize or bargain with a labor organization as the representative of his employees unless such labor organization has been certified as the representative of such employees under the provisions of section 9: *Provided,* That nothing contained in this clause (b) shall be construed to make unlawful, where not otherwise unlawful, any primary strike or primary picketing;

(c) forcing or requiring any employer to recognize or bargain with a particular labor organization as the representative of his employees if another labor organization has been certified as the representative of such employees under the provisions of section 9;

(d) forcing or requiring any employer to assign particular work to employees in a particular labor organization or in a particular trade, craft, or class rather than to employees in another labor organization or in another trade, craft, or class, unless such employer is failing to conform to an order or certification of the Board determining the bargaining representative for employees performing such work:

Provided, That nothing contained in this subsection (B) shall be construed to make unlawful a refusal by any person to enter upon the premises of any employer (other than his own employer), if the employees of such employer are engaged in a strike ratified or approved by a representative of such employees whom such employer is required to recognize under this Act: *Provided further,* That for the purposes of this paragraph (4) only, nothing contained in such paragraph shall be construed to prohibit publicity, other than picketing, for the purpose of truthfully advising the public, including consumers and members of a labor organization, that a product or products are produced by an employer with whom the labor organization has a primary dispute and are distributed by another employer, as long as such publicity does not have an effect of inducing any individual employed by any person other than the primary employer in the course of his employment to refuse to pick up, deliver, or transport any goods, or not to perform any services, at the establishment of the employer engaged in such distribution;

(5) to require of employees covered by an agreement authorized under subsection (A)(3) the payment, as a condition precedent to becoming a member of such organization, of a fee in an amount which the Board finds excessive or discriminatory under all the circumstances. In making such a finding, the Board shall consider, among other relevant factors, the practices and customs of labor organizations in the particular industry, and the wages currently paid to the employees affected;

(6) to cause or attempt to cause an employer to pay or deliver or agree to pay or deliver any money or other thing of value, in the nature of an exaction, for services which are not performed or not to be performed; and

(7) to picket or cause to be picketed, or threaten to picket or cause to be picketed, any employer where an object thereof is forcing or requiring an employer to recognize or bargain with a labor organization as the representative of his employees, or forcing or requiring the employees of an employer to accept or select such labor organization as their collective bargaining representative, unless such labor organization is currently certified as the representative of such employees:

(a) where the employer has lawfully recognized in accordance with this Act any other labor organization and a question concerning representation may not appropriately be raised under section 9(C) of this Act,

(b) where within the preceding twelve months a valid election under section 9(C) of this Act has been conducted, or

(c) where such picketing has been conducted without a petition under section 9(C) being filed within a reasonable period of time not to exceed thirty days from the commencement of such picketing; *Provided,* That when such a petition has been filed the Board shall forthwith, without regard to the provisions of section 9(C)(1) or the absence of a showing of a substantial interest on the part of the labor organization, direct an election in such unit as the Board finds to be appropriate and shall certify the results thereof: *Provided further,* That nothing in this subparagraph (c) shall be construed to prohibit any picketing or other publicity for the purpose of truthfully advising the public (including consumers) that an employer does not employ members of, or have a contract with, a labor organization, unless an effect of such picketing is to induce any individual employed by any other person in the course of his employment, not to pick up, deliver or transport any goods or not to perform any services.

Nothing in this paragraph (7) shall be construed to permit any act which would otherwise be an unfair labor practice under this section 8(B).

(C) The expressing of any views, argument, or opinion, or the dissemination thereof, whether in written, printed, graphic, or visual form, shall not constitute or be evidence of an unfair labor practice under any of the provisions of this Act, if such expression contains no threat of reprisal or force or promise of benefit.

(D) For the purposes of this section, to bargain collectively is the performance of the mutual obligation of the employer and the representative of the employees to meet at reasonable times and confer in good faith with respect to wages, hours, and other terms and conditions of employment, or the negotiation of an agreement, or any question arising thereunder, and the execution of a written contract incorporating any agreement reached if requested by either party, but such obligation does not compel either party to agree to a proposal or require the making of a concession: *Provided,* That where there is in effect a collective-bargaining contract covering employees in an industry affecting commerce, the duty to bargain collectively shall also mean that no party to such contract shall terminate or modify such contract, unless the party desiring such termination or modification—

(1) serves a written notice upon the other party to the contract of the proposed termination or modification sixty days prior to the expiration date thereof, or in the event such contract contains no expiration date, sixty days prior to the time it is proposed to make such termination or modification;

(2) offers to meet and confer with the other party for the purpose of negotiating a new contract or a contract containing the proposed modifications;

(3) notifies the Federal Mediation and Conciliation Service within thirty days after such notice of the existence of a dispute, and simultaneously therewith notifies any State or Territorial agency established to mediate and conciliate disputes within the State or Territory where the dispute occurred, provided no agreement has been reached by that time; and

(4) continues in full force and effect, without resorting to strike or lockout, all the terms and conditions of the existing contract for a period of sixty days after such notice is given or until the expiration date of such contract, whichever occurs later:

The duties imposed upon employers, employees, and labor organizations by paragraphs (2), (3), and (4) shall become inapplicable upon an intervening certification of the Board, under which the labor organization or individual, which is a party to the contract, has been superseded as or ceased to be the representative of the employees subject to the provisions of section 9(A), and the duties so imposed shall not be construed as requiring either party to discuss or agree to any modification of the terms and conditions contained in a contract for a fixed period, if such modification is to become effective before such terms and conditions can be reopened under the provisions of the contract. Any employee who engages in any strike within the appropriate period specified in subsection (G) of this section shall lose his status as an employee of the employer engaged in the particular labor dispute, for the purposes of sections 8, 9, and 10 of this Act, as amended, but such loss of status for such employee shall terminate if and when he is reemployed by such employer. Whenever the collective bargaining involves employees of a health care institution, the provisions of this section 8(D) shall be modified as follows:

(a) The notice of section 8(D)(1) shall be ninety days; the notice of section 8(D)(3) shall be sixty days; and the contract period of section 8(D)(4) shall be ninety days;

(b) Where the bargaining is for an initial agreement following certification or recognition, at least thirty days' notice of the existence of a dispute shall be given by the labor organization to the agencies set forth in section 8(D)(3).

(c) After notice is given to the Federal Mediation and Conciliation Service under either clause (a) or (b) of this sentence, the Service shall promptly communicate with the parties and use its best efforts, by mediation and conciliation, to bring them to agreement. The parties shall participate fully and promptly in such meetings as may be undertaken by the Service for the purpose of aiding in a settlement of the dispute.

(E) It shall be an unfair labor practice for any labor organization and any employer to enter into any contract or agreement, express or implied, whereby such employer ceases or refrains or agrees to cease or refrain from handling, using, selling, transporting or otherwise dealing in any of the products of any other employer, or to cease doing business with any other person, and any contract or agreement entered into heretofore or hereafter containing such an agreement shall be to such extent unenforceable and void: *Provided,* That nothing in this subsection (E) shall apply to an agreement between a labor organization and an employer in the construction industry relating to the contracting or subcontracting of work to be done at the site of the construction, alteration, painting, or repair of a building, structure, or other work: *Provided further,* That for the purposes of this subsection (E) and section 8(D)(4)(b) the terms "any employer," "any person engaged in commerce or in industry affecting commerce", and "any person" when used in relation to the terms "any other producer, processor, or manufacturer", "any other employer", or "any other person" shall not include persons in the relation of a jobber, manufacturer, contractor, or subcontractor working on the goods or premises of the jobber or manufacturer or performing parts of an integrated process of production in the apparel and clothing industry: *Provided further,* That nothing in this Act shall prohibit the enforcement of any agreement which is within the foregoing exception.

(F) It shall not be an unfair labor practice under subsections (A) and (B) of this section for an employer engaged primarily in the building and construction industry to make an agreement covering employees engaged (or who, upon their employment, will be engaged) in the building and construction industry with a labor organization of which building and construction employees are members (not established, maintained, or assisted by any action defined in section 8(A) of this Act as an unfair labor practice) because (1) the majority status of such labor organization has not been established under the provisions of section 9 of this Act prior to the making of such agreement, or (2) such agreement requires as a condition of employment, membership in such labor organization after the seventh day following the beginning of such employment or the effective date of the agreement, whichever is later, or (3) such agreement requires the employer to notify such labor organization of opportunities for employment with such employer, or gives such labor organization an opportunity to refer qualified applicants for such employment, or (4) such agreement specifies minimum training or experience qualifications for employment or provides for priority in opportunities for employment based upon length of service with such employer, in the industry or in the particular geographical area: *Provided,* That nothing in this subsection shall set aside the final proviso to section 8(A)(3) of this Act: *Provided further,* That any agreement which would be invalid, but for cause (1) of this subsection, shall not be a bar to a petition filed pursuant to section 9(C) or 9(3).

(G) A labor organization before engaging in any strike, picketing, or other concerted refusal to work at any health care institution shall, not less than ten days prior to such action, notify the institution in writing and the Federal Mediation and Conciliation Service of that intention, except that in the case of bargaining for an initial agreement following certification or recognition the notice required by this subsection shall not be given until the expiration of the period specified in clause (b) of the last sentence of section 8(D) of this Act. The notice shall state the date and time that such action will commence. The notice, once given, may be extended by the written agreement of both parties.

REPRESENTATIVES AND ELECTIONS

Section 9

(A) Representatives designated or selected for the purposes of collective bargaining by the majority of the employees in a unit appropriate for such purposes, shall be the exclusive representatives of all the employees in such unit for the purposes of collective bargaining in respect to rates of pay, wages, hours of employment, or other conditions of employment: *Provided,* That any individual employee or a group of employees shall have the right at any time to present grievances to their employer and to have such grievances adjusted, without the intervention of the bargaining representative, as long as the adjustment is not inconsistent with the terms of a collective-bargaining contract or agreement then in effect: *Provided further,* That the bargaining representative has been given opportunity to be present at such adjustment.

(B) The Board shall decide in each case whether, in order to assure to employees the fullest freedom in exercising the rights guaranteed by this Act, the unit appropriate for the purposes of collective bargaining shall be the employer unit, craft unit, plant unit, or subdivision thereof: *Provided,* That the Board shall not (1) decide that any unit is appropriate for such purposes if such unit includes both professional employees and employees vote for inclusion in such unit; or (2) decide that any craft unit is inappropriate for such purposes on the ground that a different unit has been established by a prior Board determination, unless a majority of the employees in the proposed craft unit vote against separate representation or (3) decide that any unit is appropriate for such purposes if it includes, together with other employees, any individual employed as a guard to enforce against employees and other persons rules to protect property of the employer or to protect the safety of persons on the employer's premises; but no labor organization shall be certified as the representative of employees in a bargaining unit of guards if such organization admits to membership, or is affiliated directly or indirectly with an organization which admits to membership, employees other than guards.

(C)(1) Wherever a petition shall have been filed, in accordance with such regulations as may be prescribed by the Board—

(a) by an employee or group of employees or any individual or labor organization acting in their behalf alleging that a substantial number of employees (i) wish to be represented for collective bargaining and that their employer declines to recognize their representative as the representative defined in section 9(A), or (ii) assert that the individual or labor organization, which has been certified or is being currently recognized by their employer as the bargaining representative, is no longer a representative as defined in section 9(A); or

(b) by an employer, alleging that one or more individuals or labor organizations have presented to him a claim to be recognized as the representative defined in section 9(A);

the Board shall investigate such petition and if it has reasonable cause to believe that a question of representation affecting commerce exists shall provide for an appropriate hearing upon due notice. Such hearing may be conducted by an officer or employee of the regional office, who shall not make any recommendations with respect thereto. If the Board finds upon the record of such hearing that such a question of representation exists, it shall direct an election by secret ballot and shall certify the results thereof.

(2) In determining whether or not a question of representation affecting commerce exists, the same regulations and rules of decision shall apply irrespective of the identity of the persons filing the petition or the kind of relief sought and in no case shall the Board deny a labor organization a place on the ballot by reason of an order with respect to such labor organization or its predecessor not issued in conformity with section 10(C).

(3) No election shall be directed in any bargaining unit or any subdivision within which, in the preceding twelve-month period, a valid election shall have been held. Employees engaged in an economic strike who are not entitled to reinstatement shall be eligible to vote under such regulations as the Board shall find are consistent with the purposes and provisions of this Act in any election conducted within twelve months after the commencement of the strike. In any election where none of the choices on the ballot receives a majority, a run-off shall be conducted, the ballot providing for a selection between the two choices receiving the largest and second largest number of valid votes cast in the election.

(4) Nothing in this section shall be construed to prohibit the waiving of hearings by stipulation for the purpose of a consent in conformity with regulations and rules of decision of the Board.

(5) In determining whether a unit is appropriate for the purposes specified in subsection (b) the extent to which the employees have organized shall not be controlling.

(D) Whenever an order of the Board made pursuant to section 10(c) is based in whole or in part upon facts certified following an investigation pursuant to subsection (c) of this section and there is a petition for the enforcement or review of such order, such certification and the record of such investigation shall be included in the transcript of the entire record required to be filed under section 10(E) or 10(F), and thereupon the decree of the court enforcing, modifying, or setting aside in whole or in part the order of the Board shall be made and entered upon the pleadings, testimony, and proceedings set forth in such transcript.

(E)(1) Upon the filing with the Board, by 30 per centum or more of the employees in a bargaining unit covered by an agreement between their employer and a labor organization made pursuant to section 8(A)(3), of a petition alleging they desire that such authority be rescinded, the Board shall take a secret ballot of the employees in such unit and certify the results thereof to such labor organization and to the employer.

(2) No election shall be conducted pursuant to this subsection in any bargaining unit or any subdivision within which, in the preceding twelve-month period, a valid election shall have been held.

Appendix IX

The Uniform Partnership Act

(Adopted in 48 States, all except Georgia and Louisiana; the District of Columbia, the Virgin Islands, and Guam. The adoptions by Alabama and Nebraska do not follow the official text in every respect, but are substantially similar, with local variations.)

The Act consists of 7 Parts as follows:

I. Preliminary Provisions

II. Nature of Partnership

III. Relations of Partners to Persons Dealing with the Partnership

IV. Relations of Partners to One Another

V. Property Rights of a Partner

VI. Dissolution and Winding Up

VII. Miscellaneous Provisions

An Act to make uniform the Law of Partnerships Be it enacted, etc.:

Part I

Preliminary Provisions

Section 1. NAME OF ACT.

This act may be cited as Uniform Partnership Act.

Section 2. DEFINITION OF TERMS.

In this act, "Court" includes every court and judge having jurisdiction in the case.

"Business" includes every trade, occupation, or profession.

"Person" includes individuals, partnerships, corporations, and other associations.

"Bankrupt" includes bankrupt under the Federal Bankruptcy Act or insolvent under any state insolvent act.

"Conveyance" includes every assignment, lease, mortgage, or encumbrance.

"Real property" includes land and any interest or estate in land.

Section 3. INTERPRETATION OF KNOWLEDGE AND NOTICE.

(1) A person has "knowledge" of a fact within the meaning of this act not only when he has actual knowledge thereof, but also when he has knowledge of such other facts as in the circumstances shows bad faith.

(2) A person has "notice" of a fact within the meaning of this act when the person who claims the benefit of the notice.

(a) States the fact to such person, or

(b) Delivers through the mail, or by other means of communication, a written statement of the fact to such person or to a proper person at his place of business or residence.

Section 4. RULES OF CONSTRUCTION.

(1) The rule that statutes in derogation of the common law are to be strictly construed shall have no application to this act.

(2) The law of estoppel shall apply under this act.

(3) The law of agency shall apply under this act.

(4) This act shall be so interpreted and construed as to effect its general purpose to make uniform the law of those states which enact it.

(5) This act shall not be construed so as to impair the obligations of any contract existing when the act goes into effect, nor to affect any action or proceedings begun or right accrued before this act takes effect.

Section 5. RULES FOR CASES NOT PROVIDED FOR IN THIS ACT.

In any case not provided for in this act the rules of law and equity, including the law merchant, shall govern.

Part II
Nature of Partnership

Section 6. PARTNERSHIP DEFINED.

(1) A partnership is an association of two or more persons to carry on as co-owners a business for profit.
(2) But any association formed under any other statute of this state, or any statute adopted by authority, other than the authority of this state, is not a partnership under this act, unless such association would have been a partnership in this state prior to the adoption of this act; but this act shall apply to limited partnerships except in so far as the statutes relating to such partnerships are inconsistent herewith.

Section 7. RULES FOR DETERMINING THE EXISTENCE OF A PARTNERSHIP.

In determining whether a partnership exists, these rules shall apply:

(1) Except as provided by Section 16 persons who are not partners as to each other are not partners as to third persons.
(2) Joint tenancy, tenancy in common, tenancy by the entireties, joint property, common property, or part ownership does not of itself establish a partnership, whether such co-owners do or do not share any profits made by the use of the property.
(3) The sharing of gross returns does not of itself establish a partnership, whether or not the persons sharing them have a joint or common right or interest in any property from which the returns are derived.
(4) The receipt by a person of a share of the profits of a business is prima facie evidence that he is a partner in the business, but no such inference shall be drawn if such profits were received in payment:

(A) As a debt by installments or otherwise,
(B) As wages of an employee or rent to a landlord,
(C) As an annuity to a widow or representative of a deceased partner,
(D) As interest on a loan, though the amount of payment vary with the profits of the business.
(E) As the consideration for the sale of a good-will of a business or other property by installments or otherwise.

Section 8. PARTNERSHIP PROPERTY.

(1) All property originally brought into the partnership stock or subsequently acquired by purchase or otherwise, on account of the partnership, is partnership property.
(2) Unless the contrary intention appears, property acquired with partnership funds is partnership property.
(3) Any estate in real property may be acquired in the partnership name. Title so acquired can be conveyed only in the partnership name.
(4) A conveyance to a partnership in the partnership name, though without words of inheritance, passes the entire estate of the grantor unless a contrary intent appears.

Part III
Relations of Partners to Persons Dealing with the Partnership

Section 9. PARTNER AGENT OF PARTNERSHIP AS TO PARTNERSHIP BUSINESS.

(1) Every partner is an agent of the partnership for the purpose of its business, and the act of every partner, including the execution in the partnership name of any instrument, for apparently carrying on in the usual way the business of the partnership of which he is a member binds the partnership, unless the partner so acting has in fact no authority to act for the partnership in the particular matter, and the person with whom he is dealing has knowledge of the fact that he has no such authority.
(2) An act of a partner which is not apparently for the carrying on of the business of the partnership in the usual way does not bind the partnership unless authorized by the other partners.
(3) Unless authorized by the other partners or unless they have abandoned the business, one or more but less than all the partners have no authority to:

(A) Assign the partnership property in trust for creditors or on the assignee's promise to pay the debts of the partnership,
(B) Dispose of the good-will of the business,
(C) Do any other act which would make it impossible to carry on the ordinary business of a partnership,
(D) Confess a judgment,
(E) Submit a partnership claim or liability to arbitration or reference.

(4) No act of a partner in contravention of a restriction on authority shall bind the partnership to persons having knowledge of the restriction.

Section 10. CONVEYANCE OF REAL PROPERTY OF THE PARTNERSHIP.

(1) Where title to real property is in the partnership name, any partner may convey title to such property by a conveyance executed in the partnership name; but the partnership may recover such property unless the partner's act binds the partnership under the provisions of paragraph (1) of section 9 or unless such property has been conveyed by the grantee or a person claiming through such grantee to a holder for value without knowledge that the partner, in making the conveyance, has exceeded his authority.

(2) Where title to real property is in the name of the partnership, a conveyance executed by a partner, in his own name, passes the equitable interest of the partnership, provided the act is one within the authority of the partner under the provisions of paragraph (1) of section 9.

(3) Where title to real property is in the name of one or more but not all the partners, and the record does not disclose the right of the partnership, the partners in whose name the title stands may convey title to such property, but the partnership may recover such property if the partners' act does not bind the partnership under the provisions of paragraph (1) of section 9, unless the purchaser or his assignee, is a holder for value, without knowledge.

(4) Where the title to real property is in the name of one or more or all the partners, or in a third person in trust for the partnership, a conveyance executed by a partner in the partnership name, or in his own name, passes the equitable interest of the partnership, provided the act is one within the authority of the partner under the provisions of paragraph (1) of section 9.

(5) Where the title to real property is in the names of all the partners a conveyance executed by all the partners passes all their rights in such property.

Section 11. PARTNERSHIP BOUND BY ADMISSION OF PARTNER.

An admission or representation made by any partner concerning partnership affairs within the scope of his authority as conferred by this act is evidence against the partnership.

Section 12. PARTNERSHIP CHARGED WITH KNOWLEDGE OF OR NOTICE TO PARTNER.

Notice to any partner of any matter relating to partnership affairs, and the knowledge of the partner acting in the particular matter, acquired while a partner or then present to his mind, and the knowledge of any other partner who reasonably could and should have communicated it to the acting partner, operate as notice to or knowledge of the partnership, except in the case of a fraud on the partnership committed by or with the consent of that partner.

Section 13. PARTNERSHIP BOUND BY PARTNER'S WRONGFUL ACT.

Where, by any wrongful act or omission of any partner acting in the ordinary course of the business of the partnership or with the authority of his co-partners, loss or injury is caused to any person, not being a partner in the partnership, or any penalty is incurred, the partnership is liable therefor to the same extent as the partner so acting or omitting to act.

Section 14. PARTNERSHIP BOUND BY PARTNER'S BREACH OF TRUST.

The partnership is bound to make good the loss:

(A) Where one partner acting within the scope of his apparent authority receives money or property of a third person and misapplies it; and

(B) Where the partnership in the course of its business receives money or property of a third person and the money or property so received is misapplied by any partner while it is in the custody of the partnership.

Section 15. NATURE OF PARTNER'S LIABILITY.

All partners are liable

(A) Jointly and severally for everything chargeable to the partnership under sections 13 and 14.

(B) Jointly for all other debts and obligations of the partnership; but any partner may enter into a separate obligation to perform a partnership contract.

Section 16. PARTNER BY ESTOPPEL.

(1) When a person, by words spoken or written or by conduct, represents himself, or consents to another representing him to any one, as a partner in an existing partnership or with one or more persons not actual partners, he is liable to any such person to whom such representation has been made, who has, on the faith of such representation, given credit to the actual or apparent partnership, and if he has made such representation or consented to its being made in a public manner he is liable to such person, whether the representation has or has not been made or communicated to such person so giving credit by or with the knowledge of the apparent partner making the representation or consenting to its being made.

(A) When a partnership liability results, he is liable as though he were an actual member of the partnership.

(B) When no partnership liability results, he is liable jointly with the other persons, if any, so consenting to the contract or representation as to incur liability, otherwise separately.

(2) When a person has been thus represented to be a partner in an existing partnership, or with one or more persons not actual partners, he is an agent of the persons consenting to such representation to bind them to the same extent and in the same manner as though he were a partner in fact, with respect to persons who rely upon the representation. Where all the members of the existing partnership consent to the representation, a partnership act or obligation results; but in all other cases it is the joint act or obligation of the person acting and the persons consenting to the representation.

Section 17. LIABILITY OF INCOMING PARTNER.

A person admitted as a partner into an existing partnership is liable for all the obligations of the partnership arising before his admission as though he had been a partner when such obligations were incurred, except that this liability shall be satisfied only out of partnership property.

Part IV

Relations of Partners to One Another

Section 18. RULES DETERMINING RIGHTS AND DUTIES OF PARTNERS.

The rights and duties of the partners in relation to the partnership shall be determined, subject to any agreement between them, by the following rules:

(A) Each partner shall be repaid his contributions, whether by way of capital or advances to the partnership property and share equally in the profits and surplus remaining after all liabilities, including those to partners, are satisfied; and must contribute towards the losses, whether of capital or otherwise, sustained by the partnership according to his share in the profits.

(B) The partnership must indemnify every partner in respect of payments made and personal liabilities reasonably incurred by him in the ordinary and proper conduct of its business, or for the preservation of its business or property.

(C) A partner, who in aid of the partnership makes any payment or advance beyond the amount of capital which he agreed to contribute, shall be paid interest from the date of the payment or advance.

(D) A partner shall receive interest on the capital contributed by him only from the date when repayment should be made.

(E) All partners have equal rights in the management and conduct of the partnership business.

(F) No partner is entitled to remuneration for acting in the partnership business, except that a surviving partner is entitled to reasonable compensation for his services in winding up the partnership affairs.

(G) No person can become a member of a partnership without the consent of all the partners.

(H) Any difference arising as to ordinary matters connected with the partnership business may be decided by a majority of the partners; but no act in contravention of any agreement between the partners may be done rightfully without the consent of all the partners.

Section 19. PARTNERSHIP BOOKS.

The partnership books shall be kept, subject to any agreement between the partners, at the principal place of business of the partnership, and every partner shall at all times have access to and may inspect and copy any of them.

Section 20. DUTY OF PARTNERS TO RENDER INFORMATION.

Partners shall render on demand true and full information of all things affecting the partnership to any partner or the legal representative of any deceased partner or partner under legal disability.

Section 21. PARTNER ACCOUNTABLE AS A FIDUCIARY.

(1) Every partner must account to the partnership for any benefit, and hold as trustee for it any profits derived by him without the consent of the other partners from any transaction connected with the formation, conduct, or liquidation of the partnership or from any use by him of its property.

(2) This section applies also to the representatives of a deceased partner engaged in the liquidation of the affairs of the partnership as the personal representatives of the last surviving partner.

Section 22. RIGHT TO AN ACCOUNT.

Any partner shall have the right to a formal account as to partnership affairs:

(A) If he is wrongfully excluded from the partnership business or possession of its property by his copartners,

(B) If the right exists under the terms of any agreement,

(C) As provided by section 21,

(D) Whenever other circumstances render it just and reasonable.

Section 23. CONTINUATION OF PARTNERSHIP BEYOND FIXED TERM.

(1) When a partnership for a fixed term or particular undertaking is continued after the termination of such term or particular undertaking without any express agreement, the rights and duties of the partners remain the same as they were at such termination, so far as is consistent with a partnership at will.

(2) A continuation of the business by the partners or such of them as habitually acted therein during the term, without any settlement or liquidation of the partnership affairs, is prima facie evidence of a continuation of the partnership.

Part V

Property Rights of a Partner

Section 24. EXTENT OF PROPERTY RIGHTS OF A PARTNER.

The property rights of a partner are (1) his rights in specific partnership property, (2) his interest in the partnership, and (3) his right to participate in the management.

Section 25. NATURE OF A PARTNER'S RIGHT IN SPECIFIC PARTNERSHIP PROPERTY.

(1) A partner is co-owner with his partners of specific partnership property holding as a tenant in partnership.

(2) The incidents of this tenancy are such that:

(A) A partner, subject to the provisions of this act and to any agreement between the partners, has an equal right with his partners to possess specific partnership property for partnership purposes; but he has no right to possess such property for any other purpose without the consent of his partners.

(B) A partner's right in specific partnership property is not assignable except in connection with the assignment of rights of all the partners in the same property.

(C) A partner's right in specific partnership property is not subject to attachment or execution, except on a claim against the partnership. When partnership property is attached for a partnership debt the partners, or any of them, or the representatives of a deceased partner, cannot claim any right under the homestead or exemption laws.

(D) On the death of a partner his right in specific partnership property vests in the surviving partner or partners, except where the deceased was the last surviving partner, when his right in such property vests in his legal representative. Such surviving partner or partners, or the legal representative of the last surviving partner, has no right to possess the partnership property for any but a partnership purpose.

(E) A partner's right in specific partnership property is not subject to dower, courtesy, or allowances to widows, heirs, or next of kin.

Section 26. NATURE OF PARTNER'S INTEREST IN THE PARTNERSHIP.

A partner's interest in the partnership is his share of the profits and surplus, and the same is personal property.

Section 27. ASSIGNMENT OF PARTNER'S INTEREST.

(1) A conveyance by a partner of his interest in the partnership does not of itself dissolve the partnership, nor, as against the other partners in the absence of agreement, entitle the assignee, during the continuance of the partnership to interfere in the management or administration of the partnership business or affairs, or to require any information or account of partnership transactions, or to inspect the partnership books; but it merely entitles the assignee to receive in accordance with his contract the profits to which the assigning partner would otherwise be entitled.

(2) In case of a dissolution of the partnership, the assignee is entitled to receive his assignor's interest and may require an account from the date only of the last account agreed to by all the partners.

Section 28. PARTNER'S INTEREST SUBJECT TO CHARGING ORDER.

(1) On due application to a competent court by any judgment creditor of a partner, the court which entered the judgment, order, or decree, or any other court, may charge the interest of the debtor partner with payment of the unsatisfied amount of such judgment debt with interest thereon; and may then or later appoint a receiver of his share of the profits, and of any other money due or to fall due to him in respect of the partnership, and make all other orders, directions, accounts and inquiries which the debtor partner might have made, or which the circumstances of the case may require.

(2) The interest charged may be redeemed at any time before foreclosure, or in case of a sale being directed by the court may be purchased without thereby causing a dissolution:

(A) With separate property, by any one or more of the partners, or

(B) With partnership property, by any one or more of the partners with the consent of all the partners whose interests are not so charged or sold.

(3) Nothing in this act shall be held to deprive a partner of his right, if any, under the exemption laws, as regards his interest in the partnership.

Part VI
Dissolution and Winding Up

Section 29. DISSOLUTION DEFINED.

The dissolution of a partnership is the change in the relation of the partners caused by any partner ceasing to be associated in the carrying on as distinguished from the winding up of the business.

Section 30. PARTNERSHIP NOT TERMINATED BY DISSOLUTION.

On dissolution the partnership is not terminated, but continues until the winding up of partnership affairs is completed.

Section 31. CAUSES OF DISSOLUTION.

Dissolution is caused:

(1) Without violation of the agreement between the partners,

(A) By the termination of the definite term or particular undertaking specified in the agreement,

(B) By the express will of any partner when no definite term or particular undertaking is specified,

(C) By the express will of all the partners who have not assigned their interests or suffered them to be charged

for their separate debts, either before or after the termination of any specified term or particular undertaking.
(D) By the explusion of any partner from the business bona fide in accordance with such a power conferred by the agreement between the partners;
(2) In contravention of the agreement between the partners, where the circumstances do not permit a dissolution under any other provision of this section, by the express will of any partner at any time;
(3) By any event which makes it unlawful for the business of the partnership to be carried on or for the members to carry it on in partnership;
(4) By the death of any partner;
(5) By the bankruptcy of any partner or the partnership;
(6) By decree of court under section 32.

Section 32. DISSOLUTION BY DECREE OF COURT.

(1) On application by or for a partner the court shall decree a dissolution whenever:
(A) A partner has been declared a lunatic in any judicial proceeding or is shown to be of unsound mind,
(B) A partner becomes in any other way incapable of performing his part of the partnership contract,
(C) A partner has been guilty of such conduct as tends to affect prejudicially the carrying on of the business,
(D) A partner wilfully or persistently commits a breach of the partnership agreement, or otherwise so conducts himself in matters relating to the partnership business that it is not reasonably practicable to carry on the business in partnership with him,
(E) The business of the partnership can only be carried on at a loss,
(F) Other circumstances render a dissolution equitable.
(2) On the application of the purchaser of a partner's interest under sections 27 or 28:
(A) After the termination of the specified term or particular undertaking,
(B) At any time if the partnership was a partnership at will when the interest was assigned or when the charging order was issued.

Section 33. GENERAL EFFECT OF DISSOLUTION ON AUTHORITY OF PARTNER.

Except so far as may be necessary to wind up partnership affairs or to complete transactions begun but not then finished, dissolution terminates all authority of any partner to act for the partnership,
(1) With respect to the partners,
(A) When the dissolution is not by the act, bankruptcy or death of a partner; or
(B) When the dissolution is by such act, bankruptcy or death of a partner, in cases where section 34 so requires.
(2) With respect to persons not partners, as declared in section 35.

Section 34. RIGHT OF PARTNER TO CONTRIBUTION FROM COPARTNERS AFTER DISSOLUTION.

Where the dissolution is caused by the act, death or bankruptcy of a partner, each partner is liable to his copartners for his share of any liability created by any partner acting for the partnership as if the partnership had not been dissolved unless
(A) The dissolution being by act of any partner, the partner acting for the partnership had knowledge of the dissolution, or
(B) The dissolution being by the death or bankruptcy of a partner, the partner acting for the partnership had knowledge or notice of the death or bankruptcy.

Section 35. POWER OF PARTNER TO BIND PARTNERSHIP TO THIRD PERSONS AFTER DISSOLUTION.

(1) After dissolution a partner can bind the partnership except as provided in Paragraph (3)
(A) By any act appropriate for winding up partnership affairs or completing transactions unfinished at dissolution;
(B) By any transaction which would bind the partnership if dissolution had not taken place, provided the other party to the transaction
(I) Had extended credit to the partnership prior to dissolution and had no knowledge or notice of the dissolution; or
(II) Though he had not so extended credit, had nevertheless known of the partnership prior to dissolution, and, having no knowledge or notice of dissolution, the fact of dissolution had not been advertised in a newspaper of general circulation in the place (or in each place if more than one) at which the partnership business was regularly carried on.
(2) The liability of a partner under paragraph (1b) shall be satisfied out of partnership assets alone when such partner had been prior to dissolution
(A) Unknown as a partner to the person with whom the contract is made; and
(B) So far unknown and inactive in partnership affairs that the business reputation of the partnership could not be said to have been in any degree due to his connection with it.
(3) The partnership is in no case bound by any act of a partner after dissolution
(A) Where the partnership is dissolved because it is unlawful to carry on the business, unless the act is appropriate for winding up partnership affairs; or
(B) Where the partner has become bankrupt; or

(C) Where the partner has no authority to wind up partnership affairs; except by a transaction with one who

(I) Had extended credit to the partnership prior to dissolution and had no knowledge or notice of his want of authority; or

(II) Had not extended credit to the partnership prior to dissolution, and, having no knowledge or notice of his want of authority, the fact of his want of authority has not been advertised in the manner provided for advertising the fact of dissolution in paragraph (1bII).

(4) Nothing in this section shall affect the liability under section 16 of any person who after dissolution represents himself or consents to another representing him as a partner in a partnership engaged in carrying on business.

Section 36. EFFECT OF DISSOLUTION ON PARTNER'S EXISTING LIABILITY.

(1) The dissolution of the partnership does not of itself discharge the existing liability of any partner.

(2) A partner is discharged from any existing liability upon dissolution of the partnership by an agreement to that effect between himself, the partnership creditor and the person or partnership continuing the business; and such agreement may be inferred from the course of dealing between the creditor having knowledge of the dissolution and the person or partnership continuing the business.

(3) Where a person agrees to assume the existing obligations of a dissolved partnership, the partners whose obligations have been assumed shall be discharged from any liability to any creditor of the partnership who, knowing of the agreement, consents to a material alteration in the nature or time of payment of such obligations.

(4) The individual property of a deceased partner shall be liable for all obligations of the partnership incurred while he was a partner but subject to the prior payment of his separate debts.

Section 37. RIGHT TO WIND UP.

Unless otherwise agreed the partners who have not wrongfully dissolved the partnership or the legal representative of the last surviving partner, not bankrupt, has the right to wind up the partnership affairs; provided, however, that any partner, his legal representative or his assignee, upon cause shown, may obtain winding up by the court.

Section 38. RIGHTS OF PARTNERS TO APPLICATION OF PARTNERSHIP PROPERTY.

(1) When dissolution is caused in any way, except in contravention of the partnership agreement, each partner as against his co-partners and all persons claiming through them in respect of their interests in the partnership, unless otherwise agreed, may have the partnership property applied to discharge its liabilities, and the surplus applied to pay in cash the net amount owing to the respective partners. But if dissolution is caused by expulsion of a partner, bona fide under the partnership agreement and if the expelled partner is discharged from all partnership liabilities, either by payment or agreement under section 36(2), he shall receive in cash only the net amount due him from the partnership.

(2) When dissolution is caused in contravention of the partnership agreement the rights of the partners shall be as follows:

(A) Each partner who has not caused dissolution wrongfully shall have,

(I) All the rights specified in paragraph (1) of this section, and

(II) The right, as against each partner who has caused the dissolution wrongfully, to damages for breach of the agreement.

(B) The partners who have not caused the dissolution wrongfully, if they all desire to continue the business in the same name, either by themselves or jointly with others, may do so, during the agreed term for the partnership and for that purpose may possess the partnership property, provided they secure the payment by bond approved by the court, or pay to any partner who has caused the dissolution wrongfully, the value of his interest in the partnership at the dissolution, less any damages recoverable under clause (2AII) of the section, and in like manner indemnify him against all present or future partnership liabilities.

(C) A partner who has caused the dissolution wrongfully shall have:

(I) If the business is not continued under the provisions of paragraph (2B) all the rights of a partner under paragraph (I), subject to clause (2AII), of this section,

(II) If the business is continued under paragraph (2B) of this section the right as against his co-partners and all claiming through them in respect of their interests in the partnership, to have the value of his interest in the partnership, less any damages caused to his co-partners by the dissolution, ascertained and paid to him in cash, or the payment secured by bond approved by the court, and to be released from all existing liabilities of the partnership; but in ascertaining the value of the partner's interest the value of the good-will of the business shall not be considered.

Section 39. RIGHTS WHERE PARTNERSHIP IS DISSOLVED FOR FRAUD OR MISREPRESENTATION.

Where a partnership contract is rescinded on the ground of the fraud or misrepresentation of one of the parties thereto, the party entitled to rescind is, without prejudice to any other right, entitled,

(A) To a lien on, or right of retention of, the surplus of the partnership property after satisfying the partnership liabilities to third persons for any sum of money paid by him for the purchase of an interest in the partnership and for any capital or advances contributed by him; and

(B) To stand, after all liabilities to third persons have been satisfied, in the place of the creditors of the partnership for any payments made by him in respect of the partnership liabilities; and

(C) To be indemnified by the person guilty of the fraud or making the representation against all debts and liabilities of the partnership.

Section 40. RULES FOR DISTRIBUTION.

In settling accounts between the partners after dissolution, the following rules shall be observed, subject to any agreement to the contrary:

(A) The assets of the partnership are:

(I) The partnership property,

(II) The contributions of the partners necessary for the payment of all the liabilities specified in clause (B) of this paragraph.

(B) The liabilities of the partnership shall rank in order of payment, as follows:

(I) Those owing to creditors other than partners,

(II) Those owing to partners other than for capital and profits,

(III) Those owing to partners in respect of capital,

(IV) Those owing to partners in respect of profits.

(C) The assets shall be applied in the order of their declaration in clause (A) of this paragraph to the satisfaction of the liabilities.

(D) The partners shall contribute, as provided by section 18(A) the amount necessary to satisfy the liabilities; but if any, but not all, of the partners are insolvent, or, not being subject to process, refuse to contribute, the other parties shall contribute their share of the liabilities, and, in the relative proportions in which they share the profits, the additional amount necessary to pay the liabilities.

(E) An assignee for the benefit of creditors or any person appointed by the court shall have the right to enforce the contributions specified in clause (D) of this paragraph.

(F) Any partner or his legal representative shall have the right to enforce the contributions specified in clause (D) of this paragraph, to the extent of the amount which he has paid in excess of his share of the liability.

(G) The individual property of a deceased partner shall be liable for the contributions specified in clause (d) of this paragraph.

(H) When partnership property and the individual properties of the partners are in possession of a court for distribution, partnership creditors shall have priority on partnership property and separate creditors on individual property, saving the rights of lien or secured creditors as heretofore.

(I) Where a partner has become bankrupt or his estate is insolvent the claims against his separate property shall rank in the following order:

(I) Those owing to separate creditors,

(II) Those owing to partnership creditors,

(III) Those owing to partners by way of contribution.

Section 41. LIABILITY OF PERSONS CONTINUING THE BUSINESS IN CERTAIN CASES.

(1) When any new partner is admitted into an existing partnership, or when any partner retires and assigns (or the representative of the deceased partner assigns) his rights in partnership property to two or more of the partners, or to one or more of the partners and one or more third persons, if the business is continued without liquidation of the partnership affairs, creditors of the first or dissolved partnership are also creditors of the partnership so continuing the business.

(2) When all but one partner retire and assign (or the representative of a deceased partner assigns) their rights in partnership property to the remaining partner, who continues the business without liquidation of partnership affairs, either alone or with others, creditors of the dissolved partnership are also creditors of the person or partnership so continuing the business.

(3) When any partner retires or dies and the business of the dissolved partnership is continued as set forth in paragraphs (1) and (2) of this section, with the consent of the retired partners or the representative of the deceased partner, but without any assignment of his right in partnership property, rights of creditors of the dissolved partnership and of the creditors of the person or partnership continuing the business shall be as if such assignment had been made.

(4) When all the partners or their representatives assign their rights in partnership property to one or more third persons who promise to pay the debts and who continue the business of the dissolved partnership, creditors of the dissolved partnership are also creditors of the person or partnership continuing the business.

(5) When any partner wrongfully causes a dissolution and the remaining partners continue the business under the provisions of section 38(2B), either alone or with others, and without liquidation of the partnership affairs, creditors of the dissolved partnership are also creditors of the person or partnership continuing the business.

(6) When a partner is expelled and the remaining partners continue the business either alone or with others, without liquidation of the partnership affairs, creditors of the dissolved partnership are also creditors of the person or partnership continuing the business.

(7) The liability of a third person becoming a partner in the partnership continuing the business, under this section,

to the creditors of the dissolved partnership shall be satisfied out of partnership property only.

(8) When the business of a partnership after dissolution is continued under any conditions set forth in this section the creditors of the dissolved partnership, as against the separate creditors of the retiring or deceased partner or the representative of the deceased partner, have a prior right to any claim of the retired partner or the representative of the deceased partner against the person or partnership continuing the business, on account of the retired or deceased partner's interest in the dissolved partnership or on account of any consideration promised for such interest or for his right in partnership property.

(9) Nothing in this section shall be held to modify any right of creditors to set aside any assignment on the ground of fraud.

(10) The use by the person or partnership continuing the business of the partnership name, or the name of a deceased partner as part thereof, shall not of itself make the individual property of the deceased partner liable for any debts contracted by such person or partnership.

Section 42. RIGHTS OF RETIRING OR ESTATE OF DECEASED PARTNER WHEN THE BUSINESS IS CONTINUED.

When any partner retires or dies, and the business is continued under any of the conditions set forth in section 41 (1, 2, 3, 5, 6), or section 38(2B), without any settlement of accounts as between him or his estate and the person or partnership continuing the business, unless otherwise agreed, he or his legal representative as against such persons or partnership may have the value of his interest at the date of dissolution ascertained, and shall receive as an ordinary creditor an amount equal to the value of his interest in the dissolved partnership with interest, or, at his option or at the option of his legal representative, in lieu of interest, the profits attributable to the use of his right in the property of the dissolved partnership; provided that the creditors of the dissolved partnership as against the separate creditors, or the representative of the retired or deceased partner, shall have priority on any claim arising under this section, as provided by section 41(8) of this act.

Section 43. ACCRUAL OF ACTIONS.

The right to an account of his interest shall accrue to any partner, or his legal representative, as against the winding up partners or the surviving partners or the person or partnership continuing the business, at the date of dissolution, in the absence of any agreement to the contrary.

Part VII

Miscellaneous Provisions

Section 44. WHEN ACT TAKES EFFECT.

This act shall take effect on the _____ day of _____ one thousand nine hundred and _____ .

Section 45. LEGISLATION REPEALED.

All acts or parts of acts inconsistent with this act are hereby repealed.

Appendix X

Model Business Corporation Act
(Selected Sections)

Section 2. DEFINITIONS

As used in this Act, unless the context otherwise requires, the term:

(a) "Corporation" or "domestic corporation" means a corporation for profit subject to the provisions of this Act, except a foreign corporation.

(b) "Foreign corporation" means a corporation for profit organized under laws other than the laws of this State for a purpose or purposes for which a corporation may be organized under this Act.

(c) "Articles of incorporation" means the original or restated articles of incorporation or articles of consolidation and all amendments thereto including articles of merger.

(d) "Shares" means the units into which the proprietary interests in a corporation are divided.

(e) "Subscriber" means one who subscribes for shares in a corporation, whether before or after incorporation.

(f) "Shareholder" means one who is a holder of record of shares in a corporation. If the articles of incorporation or the by-laws so provide, the board of directors may adopt by resolution a procedure whereby a shareholder of the corporation may certify in writing to the corporation that all or a portion of the shares registered in the name of such shareholder are held for the account of a specified person or persons. The resolution shall set forth (1) the classification of shareholder who may certify, (2) the purpose or purposes for which the certification may be made, (3) the form of certification and information to be contained therein, (4) if the certification is with respect to a record date or closing of the stock transfer books within which the certification must be received by the corporation and (5) such other provisions with respect to the procedure as are deemed necessary or desirable. Upon receipt by the corporation of a certification complying with the procedure, the persons specified in the certification shall be deemed, for the purpose or purposes set forth in the certification, to be the holders of record of the number of shares specified in place of the shareholder making the certification.

(g) "Authorized shares" means the shares of all classes which the corporation is authorized to issue.

(h) "Employee" includes officers but not directors. A director may accept duties which make him also an employee.

(i) "Distribution" means a direct or indirect transfer of money or other property (except its own shares) or incurrence of indebtedness, by a corporation to or for the benefit of any of its shareholders in respect of any of its shares, whether by dividend or by purchase, redemption or other acquisition of its shares, or otherwise.

Section 3. PURPOSES

Corporations may be organized under this Act for any lawful purpose or purposes, except for the purpose of banking or insurance.

Section 4. GENERAL POWERS

Each corporation shall have power:

(a) To have perpetual succession by its corporate name unless a limited period of duration is stated in its articles of incorporation.

(b) To sue and be sued, complain and defend, in its corporate name.

(c) To have a corporate seal which may be altered at pleasure, and to use the same by causing it, or a facsimile thereof, to be impressed or affixed or in any other manner reproduced.

(d) To purchase, take, receive, lease, or otherwise acquire, own, hold, improve, use and otherwise deal in and with, real or personal property, or any interest therein, wherever situated.

(e) To sell, convey, mortgage, pledge, lease, exchange, transfer and otherwise dispose of all or any part of its property and assets.

(f) To lend money and use its credit to assist its employees.

(g) To purchase, take, receive, subscribe for, or otherwise acquire, own, hold, vote, use, employ, sell, mortgage, lend, pledge, or otherwise dispose of, and otherwise use and deal in and with, shares or other interests in, or obligations of, other domestic or foreign corporations, associations, partnerships or individuals, or direct or indirect obligations of the United States or of any other government, state, territory, governmental district or municipality or of any instrumentality thereof.

(h) To make contracts and guarantees and incur liabilities, borrow money at such rates of interest as the corporation may determine, issue its notes, bonds, and other obligations, and secure any of its obligations by mortgage or pledge of all or any of its property, franchises and income.

(i) To lend money for its corporate purposes, invest and reinvest its funds, and take and hold real and personal property as security for the payment of funds so loaned or invested.

(j) To conduct its business, carry on its operations and have offices and exercise the powers granted by this Act, within or without this State.

(k) To elect or appoint officers and agents of the corporation, and define their duties and fix their compensation.

(l) To make and alter by-laws, not inconsistent with its articles of incorporation or with the laws of this State, for the administration and regulation of the affairs of the corporation.

(m) To make donations for the public welfare or for charitable, scientific or educational purposes.

(n) To transact any lawful business which the board of directors shall find will be in aid of governmental policy.

(o) To pay pensions and establish pension plans, pension trusts, profit sharing plans, stock bonus plans, stock option plans and other incentive plans for any or all of its directors, officers and employees.

(p) To be a promoter, partner, member, associate, or manager of any partnership, joint venture, trust or other enterprise.

(q) To have and exercise all powers necessary or convenient to effect its purposes.

Section 6. POWER OF CORPORATION TO ACQUIRE ITS OWN SHARES

A corporation shall have the power to acquire its own shares. All of its own shares acquired by a corporation shall, upon acquisition, constitute authorized but unissued shares, unless the articles of incorporation provide that they shall not be reissued, in which case the authorized shares shall be reduced by the number of shares acquired.

If the number of authorized shares is reduced by an acquisition, the corporation shall, not later than the time it files its next annual report under this Act with the Secretary of State, file a statement of cancellation showing the reduction in the authorized shares. The statement of cancellation shall be executed in duplicate by the corporation by its president or a vice president and by its secretary or an assistant secretary, and verified by one of the officers signing such statement, and shall set forth:

(a) The name of the corporation.

(b) The number of acquired shares cancelled, itemized by classes and series.

(c) The aggregate number of authorized shares, itemized by classes and series, after giving effect to such cancellation.

Duplicate originals of such statement shall be delivered to the Secretary of State. If the Secretary of State finds that such statement conforms to law, he shall, when all fees and franchise taxes have been paid as in this Act prescribed:

(1) Endorse on each of such duplicate originals the word "Filed", and the month, day and year of the filing thereof.

(2) File one of such duplicate originals in his office.

(3) Return on the other duplicate original to the corporation or its representative.

Section 7. DEFENSE OF ULTRA VIRES

No act of a corporation and no conveyance or transfer of real or personal property to or by a corporation shall be invalid by reason of the fact that the corporation was without capacity or power to do such act or to make or receive such conveyance or transfer, but such lack of capacity or power may be asserted:

(a) In a proceeding by a shareholder against the corporation to enjoin the doing of any act or the transfer of real or personal property by or to the corporation. If the unauthorized act or transfer sought to be enjoined is being, or is to be, performed or made pursuant to a contract to which the corporation is a party, the court may, if all of the parties to the contract are parties to the proceeding and if it deems the same to be equitable, set aside and enjoin the performance of such contract, and in so doing may allow to the corporation or to the other parties to the contract, as the case may be, compensation for the loss or damage sustained by either of them which may result from the action of the court in setting aside and enjoining the performance of such contract, but anticipated profits to be derived from the performance of the contract shall not be awarded by the court as a loss or damage sustained.

(b) In a proceeding by the corporation, whether acting directly or through a receiver, trustee, or other legal representative, or through shareholders in a representative suit, against the incumbent or former officers or directors of the corporation.

(c) In a proceeding by the Attorney General, as provided in this Act, to dissolve the corporation, or in a proceeding by the Attorney General to enjoin the corporation from the transaction of unauthorized business.

Section 8. CORPORATE NAME

The corporate name:

(a) Shall contain the word "corporation," "company," "incorporated" or "limited," or shall contain an abbreviation of one of such words.

(b) Shall not contain any word or phrase which indicates or implies that it is organized for any purpose other than one or more of the purposes contained in its articles of incorporation.

(c) Shall not be the same as, or deceptively similar to, the name of any domestic corporation existing under the laws of this State or any foreign corporation authorized to transact business in this State, or a name the exclusive right to which is, at the time, reserved in the manner provided in this Act, or the name of a corporation which has in effect a registration of its corporate name as provided in this Act, except that this provision shall not apply if the applicant files with the Secretary of State either of the following: (1) the written consent of such other corporation or holder of a reserved or registered name to use the same or deceptively similar name and one or more words are added to make such name distinguishable from such other name, or (2) a certified copy of a final decree of a court of competent jurisdiction establishing the prior right of the applicant to the use of such name in this State.

A corporation with which another corporation, domestic or foreign, is merged, or which is formed by the reorganization or consolidation of one or more domestic or foreign corporations or upon a sale, lease or other disposition to or exchange with, a domestic corporation of all or substantially all the assets of another corporation, domestic or foreign, including its name, may have the same name as that used in this State by any of such corporations if such other corporation was organized under the laws of, or is authorized to transact business in, this State.

Section 9. RESERVED NAME

The exclusive right to the use of a corporate name may be reserved by:

(a) Any person intending to organize a corporation under this Act.

(b) Any domestic corporation intending to change its name.

(c) Any foreign corporation intending to make application for a certificate of authority to transact business in this State.

(d) Any foreign corporation authorized to transact business in this State and intending to change its name.

(e) Any person intending to organize a foreign corporation and intending to have such corporation make application for a certificate of authority to transact business in this State.

The reservation shall be made by filing with the Secretary of State an application to reserve a specified corporate name, executed by the applicant. If the Secretary of State finds that the name is available for corporate use, he shall reserve the same for the exclusive use of the applicant for a period of one hundred and twenty days.

The right to the exclusive use of a specified corporate name so reserved may be transferred to any other person or corporation by filing in the office of the Secretary of State a notice of such transfer, executed by the applicant for whom the name was reserved, and specifying the name and address of the transferee.

Section 10. REGISTERED NAME

Any corporation organized and existing under the laws of any state or territory of the United States may register its corporate name under this Act, provided its corporate name is not the same as, or deceptively similar to, the name of any domestic corporation existing under the laws of this State, or the name of any foreign corporation authorized to transact business in this State, or any corporate name reserved or registered under this Act.

Such registration shall be made by:

(a) Filing with the Secretary of State (1) an application for registration executed by the corporation by an officer thereof, setting forth the name of the corporation, the state or territory under the laws of which it is incorporated, the date of its incorporation, a statement that it is carrying on or doing business, and a brief statement of the business in which it is engaged, and (2) a certificate setting forth that such corporation is in good standing under the laws of the state or territory wherein it is organized, executed by the Secretary of State of such state or territory or by such other official as may have custody of the records pertaining to corporations, and

(b) Paying to the Secretary of State a registration fee in the amount of . . . . for each month, or fraction thereof, between the date of filing such application and December 31st of the calendar year in which such application is filed.

Such registration shall be effective until the close of the calendar year in which the application for registration is filed.

Section 12. REGISTERED OFFICE AND REGISTERED AGENT

Each corporation shall have and continuously maintain in this State:

(a) A registered office which may be, but need not be, the same as its place of business.

(b) A registered agent, which agent may be either an individual resident in this State whose business office is identical with such registered office, or a domestic corporation, or a foreign corporation authorized to transact business in this State, having a business office identical with such registered office.

Section 14. SERVICE OF PROCESS ON CORPORATION

The registered agent so appointed by a corporation shall be an agent of such corporation upon whom any process, notice or demand required or permitted by law to be served upon the corporation may be served.

Whenever a corporation shall fail to appoint or maintain a registered agent in this State, or whenever its registered agent cannot with reasonable diligence be found at the registered office, then the Secretary of State shall be an agent of such corporation upon whom any such process, notice, or demand may be served. Service on the Secretary of State of any such process, notice, or demand shall be made by delivering to and leaving with him, or with any clerk having charge of the corporation department of his office, duplicate copies of such process, notice or demand. In the event any such process, notice or demand is served on the Secretary of State, he shall immediately cause one of the copies thereof to be forwarded by registered mail, addressed to the corporation at its registered office. Any service so had on the Secretary of State shall be returnable in not less than thirty days.

The Secretary of State shall keep a record of all processes, notices and demands served upon him under this section, and shall record therein the time of such service and his action with reference thereto.

Nothing herein contained shall limit or affect the right to serve any process, notice or demand required or permitted by law to be served upon a corporation in any other manner now or hereafter permitted by law.

Section 15. AUTHORIZED SHARES

Each corporation shall have power to create and issue the number of shares stated in its articles of incorporation. Such shares may be divided into one or more classes with such designations, preferences, limitations, and relative rights as shall be stated in the articles of incorporation. The articles of incorporation may limit or deny the voting rights of or provide special voting rights for the shares of any class to the extent not inconsistent with the provisions of this Act.

Without limiting the authority herein contained, a corporation, when so provided in its articles of incorporation, may issue shares of preferred or special classes:

(a) Subject to the right of the corporation to redeem any of such shares at the price fixed by the articles of incorporation for the redemption thereof.

(b) Entitling the holders thereof to cumulative, noncumulative or partially cumulative dividends.

(c) Having preference over any other class or classes of shares as to the payment of dividends.

(d) Having preference in the assets of the corporation over any other class or classes of shares upon the voluntary or involuntary liquidation of the corporation.

(e) Convertible into shares of any other class or into shares of any series of the same or any other class, except a class having prior or superior rights and preferences as to dividends or distribution of assets upon liquidation.

Section 16. ISSUANCE OF SHARES OF PREFERRED OR SPECIAL CLASSES IN SERIES

If the articles of incorporation so provide, the shares of any preferred or special class may be divided into and issued in series. If the shares of any such class are to be issued in series, then each series shall be so designated as to distinguish the shares thereof from the shares of all other series and classes. Any or all of the series of any such class and the variations in the relative rights and preferences as between different series may be fixed and determined by the articles of incorporation, but all shares of the same class shall be identical except as to the following relative rights and preferences, as to which there may be variations between different series:

(a) The rate of dividend.

(b) Whether shares may be redeemed and, if so, the redemption price and the terms and conditions of redemption.

(c) The amount payable upon shares in the event of voluntary and involuntary liquidation.

(d) Sinking fund provisions, if any, for the redemption or purchase of shares.

(e) The terms and conditions, if any, on which shares may be converted.

(f) Voting rights, if any.

Section 17. SUBSCRIPTIONS FOR SHARES

A subscription for shares of a corporation to be organized shall be irrevocable for a period of six months, unless otherwise provided by the terms of the subscription agreement or unless all of the subscribers consent to the revocation of such subscription.

Unless otherwise provided in the subscription agreement, subscriptions for shares, whether made before or after the organization of a corporation, shall be paid in full at such time, or in such installments and at such times, as shall be determined by the board of directors. Any call made by the board of directors for payment on subscriptions shall be uniform as to all shares of the same class or as to all shares of the same series, as the case may be. In case of default in the payment of any installment or call when such payment is due, the corporation may proceed to collect the amount due in the same manner as any debt due the corporation. The by-laws may prescribe other penalties for failure to pay installments or calls that may become due, but no penalty working a forfeiture of a subscription, or of the amounts paid thereon, shall be declared as against any subscriber unless the amount due thereon shall remain unpaid for a period of twenty days after written demand has been made therefor. If mailed, such written demand shall be deemed to be made when deposited in the United States mail in a sealed envelope addressed to the subscriber at his last post-office address known to the corporation, with postage thereon prepaid. In the event of the sale of any shares by reason of any forfeiture, the excess of proceeds realized over the amount due and unpaid on such shares shall be paid to the delinquent subscriber or to his legal representative.

Section 18. ISSUANCE OF SHARES

Subject to any restrictions in the articles of incorporation:

(a) Shares may be issued for such consideration as shall be authorized by the board of directors establishing a price (in money or other consideration) or a minimum price or general formula or method by which the price will be determined; and

(b) Upon authorization by the board of directors, the corporation may issue its own shares in exchange for or in conversion of its outstanding shares, or distribute its own shares, pro rata to its shareholders or the shareholders of one or more classes or series, to effectuate stock dividends or splits, and any such transaction shall not require consideration; provided, that no such issuance of shares of any class or series shall be made to the holders of shares of any other class or series unless it is either expressly provided for in the articles of incorporation, or is authorized by an affirmative vote or the written consent of the holders of at least a majority of the outstanding shares of the class or series in which the distribution is to be made.

Section 19. PAYMENT FOR SHARES

The consideration for the issuance of shares may be paid, in whole or in part, in money, in other property, tangible or intangible, or in labor or services actually performed for the corporation. When payment of the consideration for which shares are to be issued shall have been received by the corporation, such shares shall be non-assessable.

Neither promissory notes nor future services shall constitute payment or part payment for the issuance of shares of a corporation.

In the absence of fraud in the transaction, the judgment of the board of directors or the shareholders, as the case may be, as to the value of the consideration received for shares shall be conclusive.

Section 25. LIABILITY OF SUBSCRIBERS AND SHAREHOLDERS

A holder of or subscriber to shares of a corporation shall be under no obligation to the corporation or its creditors with respect to such shares other than the obligation to pay to the corporation the full consideration for which such shares were issued or to be issued.

Any person becoming an assignee or transferee of shares or of a subscription for shares in good faith and without knowledge or notice that the full consideration therefor has not been paid shall not be personally liable to the corporation or its creditors for any unpaid portion of such consideration.

An executor, administrator, conservator, guardian, trustee, assignee for the benefit of creditors, or receiver shall not be personally liable to the corporation as a holder of or subscriber to shares of a corporation but the estate and funds in his hands shall be so liable.

No pledgee or other holder of shares as collateral security shall be personally liable as a shareholder.

Section 26. SHAREHOLDERS' PREEMPTIVE RIGHTS

The shareholders of a corporation shall have no preemptive right to acquire unissued shares of the corporation, or securities of the corporation convertible into or carrying a right to subscribe to or acquire shares, except to the extent, if any, that such right is provided in the articles of incorporation.

Section 27. BY-LAWS

The initial by-laws of a corporation shall be adopted by its board of directors. The power to alter, amend or repeal the by-laws or adopt new by-laws, subject to repeal or change by action of the shareholders, shall be vested in the board of directors unless reserved to the shareholders by the articles of incorporation. The by-laws may contain any provisions for the regulation and management of the affairs of the corporation not inconsistent with law or the articles of incorporation.

Section 28. MEETINGS OF SHAREHOLDERS

Meetings of shareholders may be held at such place within or without this State as may be stated in or fixed in accordance with the by-laws. If no other place is stated or so fixed, meetings shall be held at the registered office of the corporation.

An annual meeting of the shareholders shall be held at such time as may be stated in or fixed in accordance with the by-laws. If the annual meeting is not held within any thirteen-month period the Court of ....may, on the application of any shareholder, summarily, order a meeting to be held.

Special meetings of the shareholders may be called by the board of directors, the holders of not less than one-tenth of all the shares entitled to vote at the meeting, or such other persons as may be authorized in the articles of incorporation or the by-laws.

Section 29. NOTICE OF SHAREHOLDERS' MEETINGS

Written notice stating the place, day and hour of the meeting and, in case of a special meeting, the purpose or purposes for which the meeting is called, shall be delivered not less than ten nor more than fifty days before the date of the meeting, either personally or by mail, by or at the direction of the president, the secretary, or the officer of persons calling the meeting, to each shareholder of record entitled to vote at such meeting. If mailed, such notice shall be deemed to be delivered when deposited in the United States mail addressed to the shareholder at his address as it appears on the stock transfer books of the corporation, with postage thereon prepaid.

Section 30. CLOSING OF TRANSFER BOOKS AND FIXING RECORD DATE

For the purpose of determining shareholders entitled to notice of or to vote at any meeting of shareholders or any adjournment thereof, or entitled to receive payment of any dividend, or in order to make a determination of shareholders for any other proper purpose, the board of directors of a corporation may provide that the stock transfer books shall be closed for a stated period but not to exceed, in any case, fifty days. If the stock transfer books shall be closed for the purpose of determining shareholders entitled to notice of or to vote at a meeting of shareholders, such books shall be closed for at least ten days immediately preceding such meeting. In lieu of closing the stock transfer books, the by-laws, or in the absence of an applicable by-law the board of directors, may fix in advance a date as the record date for any such determination of shareholders, such date in any case to be not more than fifty days and, in case of a meeting of shareholders, not less than ten days prior to the date on which the particular action, requiring such determination of shareholders, is to be taken. If the stock transfer books are not closed and no record date is fixed for the determination of shareholders entitled to notice of or to vote at a meeting of shareholders, or shareholders entitled to receive payment of a dividend, the date on which notice of the meeting is mailed or the date on which the resolution of the board of directors declaring such dividend is adopted, as the case may be, shall be the record date for such determination of shareholders. When a determination of shareholders entitled to vote at any meeting of shareholders has been made as provided in this section, such determination shall apply to any adjournment thereof.

Section 31. VOTING RECORD

The officer or agent having charge of the stock transfer books for shares of a corporation shall make a complete record of the shareholders entitled to vote at such meeting or any adjournment thereof, arranged in alphabetical order, with the address of and the number of shares held by each. Such record shall be produced and kept open at the time and place of the meeting and shall be subject to the inspection of any shareholder during the whole time of the meeting for the purposes thereof.

Failure to comply with the requirements of this section shall not affect the validity of any action taken at such meeting.

An officer or agent having charge of the stock transfer books who shall fail to prepare the record of the shareholders, or produce and keep it open for inspection at the meeting, as provided in this section, shall be liable to any shareholder suffering damage on account of such failure, to the extent of such damage.

Section 32. QUORUM OF SHAREHOLDERS

Unless otherwise provided in the articles of incorporation, a majority of the shares entitled to vote, represented in person or by proxy, shall constitute a quorum at a meeting of shareholders, but in no event shall a quorum consist of less than one-third of the shares entitled to vote at the meeting. If a quorum is present, the affirmative vote of the majority of the shares represented at the meeting and entitled to vote on the subject matter shall be the act of the shareholders, unless the vote of a greater number or voting by classes is required by this Act or the articles of incorporation or by-laws.

Section 33. VOTING OF SHARES

Each outstanding share, regardless of class, shall be entitled to one vote on each matter submitted to a vote at a meeting of shareholders, except as may be otherwise provided in the articles of incorporation. If the articles of incorporation provide for more or less than one vote for any share, on any matter, every reference in this Act to a majority or other proportion of shares shall refer to such a majority or other proportion of votes entitled to be cast.

Shares held by another corporation if a majority of the shares entitled to vote for the election of directors of such other corporation is held by the corporation, shall not be voted at any meeting or counted in determining the total number of outstanding shares at any given time.

A shareholder may vote either in person or by proxy executed in writing by the shareholder or by his duly authorized attorney-in-fact. No proxy shall be valid after eleven months from the date of its execution, unless otherwise provided in the proxy.

[Either of the following prefatory phrases may be inserted here: "The articles of incorporation may provide that" or "Unless the articles of incorporation otherwise provide"] . . . at each election for directors every shareholder entitled to vote at such election shall have the right to vote, in person or by proxy, the number of shares owned by him for as many persons as there are directors to be elected and for whose election he has a right to vote, or to cumulate his votes by giving one candidate as many votes as the number of such directors multiplied by the number of his shares shall equal, or by distributing such votes on the same principle among any number of such candidates.

Shares standing in the name of another corporation, domestic or foreign, may be voted by such officer, agent or proxy as the by-laws of such other corporation may prescribe, or, in the absence of such provision, as the board of directors of such other corporation may determine.

Shares held by an administrator, executor, guardian or conservator may be voted by him, either in person or by proxy, without a transfer of such shares into his name. Shares standing in the name of a trustee may be voted by him, either in person or by proxy, but no trustee shall be entitled to vote shares held by him without a transfer of such shares into his name.

Shares standing in the name of a receiver may be voted by such receiver, and shares held by or under the control of a receiver may be voted by such receiver without the transfer thereof into his name if authority so to do be contained in an appropriate order of the court by which such receiver was appointed.

A shareholder whose shares are pledged shall be entitled to vote such shares until the shares have been transferred into the name of the pledgee, and thereafter the pledgee shall be entitled to vote the shares so transferred.

On and after the date on which written notice of redemption of redeemable shares has been mailed to the holders thereof and a sum sufficient to redeem such shares has been deposited with a bank or trust company with irrevocable instruction and authority to pay the redemption price to the holders thereof upon surrender of certificates therefor, such shares shall not be entitled to vote on any matter and shall not be deemed to be outstanding shares.

Section 34. **VOTING TRUSTS AND AGREEMENTS AMONG SHAREHOLDERS**

Any number of shareholders of a corporation may create a voting trust for the purpose of conferring upon a trustee or trustees the right to vote or otherwise represent their shares, for a period of not to exceed ten years, by entering into a written voting trust agreement specifying the terms and conditions of the voting trust, by depositing a counterpart of the agreement with the corporation at its registered office, and by transferring their shares to such trustee or trustees for the purposes of the agreement. Such trustee or trustees shall keep a record of the holders of voting trust certificates evidencing a beneficial interest in the voting trust, giving the names and addresses of all such holders and the number and class of the shares in respect of which the voting trust certificates held by each are issued, and shall deposit a copy of such record with the corporation at its registered office. The counterpart of the voting trust agreement and the copy of such record so deposited with the corporation shall be subject to the same right of examination by a shareholder of the corporation, in person or by agent or attorney, as are the books and record of the corporation, and such counterpart and such copy of such record shall be subject to examination by any holder of record of voting trust certificates, either in person or by agent or attorney, at any reasonable time for any proper purpose.

Agreements among shareholders regarding the voting of their shares shall be valid and enforceable in accordance with their terms. Such agreements shall not be subject to the provisions of this section regarding voting trusts.

Section 35. **BOARD OF DIRECTORS**

All corporate powers shall be exercised by or under authority of, and the business and affairs of a corporation shall be managed under the direction of, a board of directors except as may be otherwise provided in this Act or the articles of incorporation. If any such provision is made in the articles of incorporation, the powers and duties conferred or imposed upon the board of directors by this Act shall be exercised or performed to such extent and by such person or persons as shall be provided in the articles of incorporation. Directors need not be residents of this State or shareholders of the corporation unless the articles of incorporation or by-laws so require. The articles of incorporation or by-laws may prescribe other qualifications for directors. The board of directors shall have authority to fix the compensation of directors unless otherwise provided in the articles of incorporation.

A director shall perform his duties as a director, including his duties as a member of any committee of the board upon which he may serve, in good faith, in a manner he reasonably believes to be in the best interests of the corporation, and with such care as an ordinarily prudent person in a like position would use under similar circumstances. In performing his duties, a director shall be entitled to rely on information, opinions, reports or statements, including financial statements and other financial data, in each case prepared or presented by:

(A) one or more officers or employees of the corporation whom the director reasonably believes to be reliable and competent in the matters presented,

(B) counsel, public accountants or other persons as to matters which the director reasonably believes to be within such person's professional or expert competence, or

(C) a committee of the board upon which he does not serve, duly designated in accordance with a provision of the articles of incorporation or the by-laws, as to matters within its designated authority, which committee the director reasonably believes to merit confidence,

but he shall not be considered to be acting in good faith if he has knowledge concerning the matter in question that would cause such reliance to be unwarranted. A person who so performs his duties shall have no liability by reason of being or having been a director of the corporation.

A director of a corporation who is present at a meeting of its board of directors at which action on any corporate matter is taken shall be presumed to have assented to the action taken unless his dissent shall be entered in the minutes of the meeting or unless he shall file his written dissent to such action with the secretary of the meeting before the adjournment thereof or shall forward such dissent by registered mail to the secretary of the corporation immediately after the adjournment of the meeting. Such right to dissent shall not apply to a director who voted in favor of such action.

Section 36. NUMBER AND ELECTION OF DIRECTORS

The board of directors of a corporation shall consist of one or more members. The number of directors shall be fixed by, or in the manner provided in, the articles of incorporation or by the by-laws, except as to the number constituting the initial board of directors, which number shall be fixed by the articles of incorporation. The number of directors may be increased or decreased from time to time by amendment to, or in the manner provided in, the articles of incorporation or the by-laws, but no decrease shall have the effect of shortening the term of any incumbent director. In the absence of a by-law providing for the number of directors, the number shall be the same as that provided for in the articles of incorporation. The names and addresses of the members of the first board of directors shall be stated in the articles of incorporation. Such persons shall hold office until the first annual meeting of shareholders, and until their successors shall have been elected and qualified. At the first annual meeting of shareholders and at each annual meeting thereafter the shareholders shall elect directors to hold office until the next succeeding annual meeting, except in case of the classification of directors as permitted by this Act. Each director shall hold office for the term for which he is elected and until his successor shall have been elected and qualified.

Section 37. CLASSIFICATION OF DIRECTORS

When the board of directors shall consist of nine or more members, in lieu of electing the whole number of directors annually, the articles of incorporation may provide that the directors be divided into either two or three classes, each class to be as nearly equal in number as possible, the term of office of directors of the first class to expire at the first annual meeting of shareholders after their election, that of the second class to expire at the second annual meeting after their election, and that of the third class, if any, to expire at the third annual meeting after their election. At each annual meeting after such classification the number of directors equal to the number of the class whose term expires at the time of such meeting shall be elected to hold office until the second succeeding annual meeting, if there be two classes, or until the third succeeding annual meeting, if there be three classes. No classification of directors shall be effective prior to the first annual meeting of shareholders.

Section 38. VACANCIES

Any vacancy occurring in the board of directors may be filled by the affirmative vote of a majority of the remaining directors though less than a quorum of the board of directors. A director elected to fill a vacancy shall be elected for the unexpired term of his predecessor in office. Any directorship to be filled by reason of an increase in the number of directors may be filled by the board of directors for a term of office continuing only until the next election of directors by the shareholders.

Section 39. REMOVAL OF DIRECTORS

At a meeting of shareholders called expressly for that purpose, directors may be removed in the manner provided in this section. Any director or the entire board of directors may be removed, with or without cause, by a vote of the holders of a majority of the shares then entitled to vote at an election of directors.

In the case of a corporation having cumulative voting, if less than the entire board is to be removed, no one of the directors may be removed if the votes cast against his removal would be sufficient to elect him if then cumulatively voted at an election of the entire board of directors, or, if there be classes of directors, at an election of the class of directors of which he is a part.

Whenever the holders of the shares of any class are entitled to elect one or more directors by the provisions of the articles of incorporation, the provisions of this section shall apply, in respect to the removal of a director or directors so elected, to the vote of the holders of the outstanding shares of that class and not to the vote of the outstanding shares as a whole.

Section 40. QUORUM OF DIRECTORS

A majority of the number of directors fixed by or in the manner provided in the by-laws or in the absence of a by-law fixing or providing for the number of directors, then of the number stated in the articles of incorporation, shall constitute a quorum for the transaction of business—unless a greater number is required by the articles of incorporation or the by-laws. The act of the majority of the directors present at a meeting at which a quorum is present shall be the act of the board of directors, unless the act of a greater number is required by the articles of incorporation or the by-laws.

Section 41. DIRECTOR CONFLICTS OF INTEREST

No contract or other transaction between a corporation and one or more of its directors or any other corporation, firm, association or entity in which one or more of its directors are directors or officers or are financially interested, shall be either void or voidable because of such relationship or interest or because such director or directors are present at the meeting of the board of directors or a committee thereof which authorizes, approves or ratifies such contract or transaction or because his or their votes are counted for such purpose, if:

(A) the fact of such relationship or interest is disclosed or known to the board of directors or committee which authorizes, approves or ratifies the contract or transaction by a vote or consent sufficient for the purpose without counting the votes or consents of such interested directors; or

(B) the fact of such relationship or interest is disclosed or known the shareholders entitled to vote and they authorize, approve or ratify such contract or transaction by vote or written consent; or

(C) the contract or transaction is fair and reasonable to the corporation.

Common or interested directors may be counted in determining the presence of a quorum at a meeting of the board of directors or a committee thereof which authorizes, approves or ratifies such contract or transaction.

Section 42. EXECUTIVE AND OTHER COMMITTEES

If the articles of incorporation or the by-laws so provide, the board of directors, by resolution adopted by a majority of the full board of directors, may designate from among its members an executive committee and one or more other committees each of which, to the extent provided in such resolution or in the articles of incorporation or the by-laws of the corporation, shall have and may exercise all the authority of the board of directors, except that no such committee shall have authority to (i) authorize distributions, (ii) approve or recommend to shareholders actions or proposals required by this Act to be approved by shareholders, (iii) designate candidates for the office of director, for purposes of proxy solicitation or otherwise, or fill vacancies on the board of directors or any committee thereof, (iv) amend the by-laws, (v) approve a plan of merger not requiring shareholder approval, (vi) authorize or approve the reacquisition of shares unless pursuant to a general formula or method specified by the board of directors, or (vii) authorize or approve the issuance or sale of, or any contract to issue or sell, shares or designate the terms of a series of a class of shares, provided that the board of directors, having acted regarding general authorization for the issuance or sale of shares, or any contract therefor, and, in the case of a series, the designation thereof, may, pursuant to a general formula or method specified by the board by resolution or by adoption of a stock option or other plan, authorize a committee to fix the terms of any contract for the sale of the shares and to fix the terms upon which such shares may be issued or sold, including, without limitation, the price, the dividend rate, provisions for redemption, sinking fund, conversion, voting or preferential rights, and provisions for other features of a class of shares, or a series of a class of shares, with full power in such committee to adopt any final resolution setting forth all the terms thereof and to authorize the statement of the terms of a series for filing with the Secretary of State under this Act.

Neither the designation of any such committee, the delegation thereto of authority, nor action by such committee pursuant to such authority shall alone constitute compliance by any member of the board of directors, not a member of the committee in question, with his responsibility to act in good faith, in a manner he reasonably believes to be in the best interests of the corporation, and with such care as an ordinarily prudent person in a like position would use under similar circumstances.

Section 45. DISTRIBUTIONS TO SHAREHOLDERS

Subject to any restrictions in the articles of incorporation, the board of directors may authorize and the corporation may make distributions, except that no distribution may be made if, after giving effect thereto, either:

(a) the corporation would be unable to pay its debts as they become due in the usual course of its business; or

(b) the corporation's total assets would be less than the sum of its total liabilities and (unless the articles of incorporation otherwise permit) the maximum amount that then would be payable, in any liquidation, in respect of all outstanding shares having preferential rights in liquidation.

Determinations under subparagraph (B) may be based upon (i) financial statements prepared on the basis of accounting practices and principles that are reasonable in the circumstances, or (ii) a fair valuation or other method that is reasonable in the circumstances.

In the case of a purchase, redemption or other acquisition of a corporation's shares, the effect of a distribution shall be measured as of the date money or other property is transferred or debt is incurred by the corporation, or as of the date the shareholder ceases to be a shareholder of the corporation with respect to such shares, whichever is earlier. In all other cases, the effect of a distribution shall be measured as of the date of its authorization if payment occurs 120 days or less following the date of authorization, or as of the date of payment if payment occurs more than 120 days following the date of authorization.

Indebtedness of a corporation incurred or issued to a shareholder in a distribution in accordance with this Section shall be on a parity with the indebtedness of the corporation to its general unsecured creditors except to the extent subordinated by agreement.

Section 48. LIABILITY OF DIRECTORS IN CERTAIN CASES

In addition to any other liabilities, a director who votes for or assents to any distribution contrary to the provisions of this Act or contrary to any restrictions contained in the articles of incorporation, shall, unless he complies with the standard provided in this Act for the performance of the duties of directors, be liable to the corporation, jointly and severally with all other directors so voting or assenting, for the amount of such dividend which is paid or the value of such distribution in excess of the amount of such distribution which could have been made without a violation of the provisions of this Act or the restrictions in the articles of incorporation.

Any director against whom a claim shall be asserted under or pursuant to this section for the making of a distribution and who shall be held liable thereon, shall be entitled to contribution from the shareholders who accepted or received any such distribution, knowing such distribution to have been made in violation of this Act, in proportion to the amounts received by them.

Any director against whom a claim shall be asserted under or pursuant to this section shall be entitled to contribution from any other director who voted for or assented to the action upon which the claim is asserted and who did not comply with the standard provided in this Act for the performance of the duties of directors.

Section 50. OFFICERS

The officers of a corporation shall consist of a president, one or more vice presidents as may be prescribed by the by-laws, a secretary, and a treasurer, each of whom shall be elected by the board of directors at such time and in such manner as may be prescribed by the by-laws. Such other officers and assistant officers and agents as may be deemed necessary may be elected or appointed by the board of directors or chosen in such other manner as may be prescribed by the by-laws. Any two or more offices may be held by the same person, except the offices of president and secretary.

All officers and agents of the corporation, as between themselves and the corporation, shall have such authority and perform such duties in the management of the corporation as may be provided in the by-laws, or as may be determined by resolution of the board of directors not inconsistent with the by-laws.

Section 51. REMOVAL OF OFFICERS

Any officer or agent may be removed by the board of directors whenever in its judgment the best interests of the corporation will be served thereby, but such removal shall be without prejudice to the contract rights, if any, of the person so removed. Election or appointment of an officer or agent shall not of itself create contract rights.

Section 52. BOOKS AND RECORDS: FINANCIAL REPORTS TO SHAREHOLDERS; EXAMINATION OF RECORDS

Each corporation shall keep correct and complete books and records of account and shall keep minutes of the proceedings of its shareholders and board of directors and shall keep at its registered office or principal place of business, or at the office of its transfer agent or registrar, a record of its shareholders, giving the names and addresses of all shareholders and the number and class of the shares held by each. Any books, records and minutes may be in written form or in any form capable of being converted into written form within a reasonable time.

Any person who shall have been a holder of record of shares or of voting trust certificates therefor at least six months immediately preceding his demand or shall be the holder of record of, or the holder of record of voting trust certificates for, at least five percent of all the outstanding shares of the corporation, upon written demand stating the purpose thereof, shall have the right to examine, in person, or by agent or attorney, at any reasonable time or times, for any proper purpose its relevant books and records of account, minutes, and record of shareholders and to make extracts therefrom.

Any officer or agent who, or a corporation which, shall refuse to allow any such shareholder or holder of voting trust certificates, or his agent or attorney, so to examine and make extracts from its books and records of account, minutes, and record of shareholders, for any proper purpose, shall be liable to such shareholder or holder of voting trust certificates in a penalty of ten per cent of the value of the shares owned by such shareholder, or in respect of which such voting trust certificates are issued, in addition to any other damages or remedy afforded him by law. It shall be a defense to any action for penalties under this section that the person suing therefor has within two years sold or offered for sale any list of shareholders or of holders of voting trust certificates for shares of such corporation or any other corporation or has aided or abetted any person in procuring any list of shareholders or of holders of voting trust certificates for any such purpose, or has improperly used any information secured through any prior examination of the books and records of account, or minutes, or record of shareholders or of holders of voting trust certificates for shares of such corporation or any other corporation, or was not acting in good faith or for a proper purpose in making his demand.

Nothing herein contained shall impair the power of any court of competent jurisdiction, upon proof by a shareholder or holder of voting trust certificates of proper purpose, irrespective of the period of time during which such shareholder or holder of voting trust certificates shall have been a shareholder of record or a holder of record of voting trust certificates, and irrespective of the number of shares held by him or represented by voting trust certificates held by him, to compel the production for examination by such shareholder or holder of voting trust certificates of the books and records of account, minutes and record of shareholders of a corporation.

Upon the written request of any shareholder or holder of voting trust certificates for shares of a corporation, the corporation shall mail to such shareholder or holder of voting trust certificates its most recent financial statements showing in reasonable detail its assets and liabilities and the results of its operations.

Each corporation shall furnish to its shareholders annual financial statements, including at least a balance sheet as of the end of each fiscal year and a statement of income for such fiscal year, which shall be prepared on the basis of generally accepted accounting principles, if the corporation prepares financial statements for such fiscal year on that basis for any purpose, and may be consolidated statements of the corporation and one or more of its subsidiaries. The financial statements shall be mailed by the corporation to each of its shareholders within 120 days after the close of each fiscal year and, after such mailing and upon written request, shall be mailed by the corporation to any shareholder (or holder of a voting trust certificate for its shares) to whom a copy of the most recent annual financial statements has not previously been mailed. In the case of statements audited by a public account, each copy shall be accompanied by a report setting forth his opinion thereon; in other cases, each copy shall be accompanied by a statement of the president or the person in charge of the corporation's financial accounting records (1) stating his reasonable belief as to whether or not the financial statements were prepared in accordance with generally accepted accounting principles and, if not, describing the basis of presentation, and (2) describing any respects in which the financial statements were not prepared on a basis consistent with those prepared for the previous year.

Section 53. INCORPORATORS

One or more persons, or a domestic or foreign corporation, may act as incorporator or incorporators of a corporation by signing and delivering in duplicate to the Secretary of State articles of incorporation for such corporation.

Section 54. ARTICLES OF INCORPORATION

The articles of incorporation shall set forth:

(a) The name of the corporation.

(b) The period of duration, which may be perpetual.

(c) The purpose or purposes for which the corporation is organized which may be stated to be, or to include, the transaction of any or all lawful business for which corporations may be incorporated under this Act.

(d) The aggregate number of shares which the corporation shall have authority to issue and, if such shares are to be divided into classes, the number of shares of each class.

(e) If the shares are to be divided into classes, the designation of each class and a statement of the preferences, limitations and relative rights in respect of the shares of each class.

(f) If the corporation is to issue the shares of any preferred or special class in series, then the designation of each series and a statement of the variations in the relative rights and preferences as between series insofar as the same are to be fixed in the articles of incorporation, and a statement of any authority to be vested in the board of directors to establish series and fix and determine the variations in the relative rights and preferences as between series.

(g) If any preemptive right is to be granted to shareholders, the provisions therefor.

(h) The address of its initial registered office, and the name of its initial registered agent at such address.

(i) The number of directors constituting the initial board of directors and the names and addresses of the persons who are to serve as directors until the first annual meeting of shareholders or until their successors be elected and qualify.

(j) The name and address of each incorporator.

In addition to provisions required therein, the articles of incorporation may also contain provisions not inconsistent with law regarding:

(1) the direction of the management of the business and the regulation of the affairs of the corporation;

(2) the definition, limitation and regulation of the powers of the corporation, the directors, and the shareholders, or any class of the shareholders, including restrictions on the transfer of shares;

(3) the par value of any authorized shares or class of shares;

(4) any provision which under this Act is required or permitted to be set forth in the by-laws.

It shall not be necessary to set forth in the articles of incorporation any of the corporate powers enumerated in this Act.

Section 55. FILING OF ARTICLES OF INCORPORATION

Duplicate originals of the articles of incorporation shall be delivered to the Secretary of State. If the Secretary of State finds that the articles of incorporation conform to law, he shall, when all fees have been paid as in this Act prescribed:

(a) Endorse on each of such duplicate originals the word "Filed," and the month, day and year of the filing thereof.

(b) File one of such duplicate originals in his office.

(c) Issue a certificate of incorporation to which he shall affix the other duplicate original.

The certificate of incorporation, together with the duplicate original of the articles of incorporation affixed thereto by the Secretary of State, shall be returned to the incorporators or their representative.

Section 56. EFFECT OF ISSUANCE OF CERTIFICATE OF INCORPORATION

Upon the issuance of the certificate of incorporation, the corporate existence shall begin, and such certificate of incorporation shall be conclusive evidence that all conditions precedent required to be performed by the incorporators have been complied with and that the corporation has been incorporated under this Act, except as against this State in a proceeding to cancel or revoke the certificate of incorporation or for involuntary dissolution of the corporation.

Section 57. ORGANIZATION MEETING OF DIRECTORS

After the issuance of the certificate of incorporation an organization meeting of the board of directors named in the articles of incorporation shall be held, either within or without this State, at the call of a majority of the directors named in the articles of incorporation, for the purpose of adopting by-laws, electing officers and transacting such other business as may come before the meeting. The directors calling the meeting shall give at least three days' notice thereof by mail to each director so named, stating the time and place of the meeting.

Section 59. PROCEDURE TO AMEND ARTICLES OF INCORPORATION

Amendments to the articles of incorporation shall be made in the following manner:

(a) The board of directors shall adopt a resolution setting forth the proposed amendment and, if shares have been issued, directing that it be submitted to a vote at a meeting of shareholders, which may be either the annual or a special meeting. If no shares have been issued, the amendment shall be adopted by resolution of the board of directors and the provisions for adoption by shareholders shall not apply. If the corporation has only one class of shares outstanding, an amendment solely to change the number of authorized shares to effectuate a split of, or stock dividend in, the corporation's own shares, or solely to do so and to change the number of authorized shares in proportion thereto, may be adopted by the board of directors; and the provisions for adoption by shareholders shall not apply, unless otherwise provided by the articles of incorporation. The resolution may incorporate the proposed amendment in restated articles of incorporation which contain a statement that except for the designated amendment the restated articles of incorporation correctly set forth without change the corresponding provisions of the articles of incorporation as therefore amended, and that the restated articles of incorporation together with the designated amendment supersede the original articles of incorporation and all amendments thereto.

(b) Written notice setting forth the proposed amendment or a summary of the changes to be effected thereby shall be given to each shareholder of record entitled to vote thereon within the time and in the manner provided in this Act for the giving of notice of meetings of shareholders. If the meeting be an annual meeting, the proposed amendment of such summary may be included in the notice of such annual meeting.

(c) At such meeting a vote of the shareholders entitled to vote thereon shall be taken on the proposed amendment. The proposed amendment shall be adopted upon receiving the affirmative vote of the holders of a majority of the shares entitled to vote thereon, unless any class of shares is entitled to vote thereon as a class, in which event the proposed amendment shall be adopted upon receiving the affirmative vote of the holders of a majority of the shares of each class of shares entitled to vote thereon as a class and of the total shares entitled to voter thereon.

Any number of amendments may be submitted to the shareholders, and voted upon by them, at one meeting.

Section 71. PROCEDURE FOR MERGER

Any two or more domestic corporations may merge into one of such corporations pursuant to a plan of merger approved in the manner provided in this Act.

The board of directors of each corporation shall, by resolution adopted by each such board, approve a plan of merger setting forth:

(a) The names of the corporations proposing to merge, and the name of the corporation into which they propose to merge, which is hereinafter designated as the surviving corporation.

(b) The terms and conditions of the proposed merger.

(c) The manner and basis of converting the shares of each corporation into shares, obligations or other securities of the surviving corporation or of any other corporation or, in whole or in part, into cash or other property.

(d) A statement of any changes in the articles of incorporation of the surviving corporation to be effected by such merger.

(e) Such other provisions with respect to the proposed merger as are deemed necessary or desirable.

Section 72. PROCEDURE FOR CONSOLIDATION

Any two or more domestic corporations may consolidate into a new corporation pursuant to a plan of consolidation approved in the manner provided in this Act.

The board of directors of each corporation shall, by a resolution adopted by each such board, approve a plan of consolidation setting forth:

(a) The names of the corporations proposing to consolidate, and the name of the new corporation into which they propose to consolidate, which is hereinafter designated as the new corporation.

(b) The terms and conditions of the proposed consolidation.

(c) The manner and basis of converting the shares of each corporation into shares, obligations or other securities of the new corporation or of any other corporation or, in whole or in part, into cash or other property.

(d) With respect to the new corporation, all of the statements required to be set forth in articles of incorporation for corporations organized under this Act.

(e) Such other provisions with respect to the proposed consolidation as are deemed necessary or desirable.

Section 80. RIGHT OF SHAREHOLDERS TO DISSENT AND OBTAIN PAYMENT FOR SHARES

(a) Any shareholder of a corporation shall have the right to dissent from, and to obtain payment for his shares in the event of, any of the following corporate actions:

(1) Any plan of merger or consolidation to which the corporation is a party, except as provided in subsection (C);

(2) Any sale or exchange of all or substantially all of the property and assets of the corporation not made in the usual or regular course of its business, including a sale in dissolution, but not including a sale pursuant to an order of a court having jurisdiction in the premises or a sale for cash on terms requiring that all or substantially all of the net proceeds of sale be distributed to the shareholders in accordance with their respective interests within one year after the date of sale;

(3) Any plan of exchange to which the corporation is a party as the corporation the shares of which are to be acquired;

(4) Any amendment of the articles of incorporation which materially and adversely affects the rights appurtenant to the shares of the dissenting shareholder in that it:

(i) alters or abolishes a preferential right of such shares;

(ii) creates, alters or abolishes a right in respect of the redemption of such shares, including a provision respecting a sinking fund for the redemption or repurchase of such shares;

(iii) alters or abolishes a preemptive right of the holder of such shares to acquire shares or other securities;

(iv) excludes or limits the right of the holder of such shares to vote on any matter, or to cumulate his votes, except as such right may be limited by dilution through the issuance of shares or other securities with similar voting rights; or

(5) Any other corporate action taken pursuant to a shareholder vote with respect to which the articles of incorporation, the bylaws, or a resolution of the board of directors directs that dissenting shareholders shall have a right to obtain payment for their shares.

(b) (1) A record holder of shares may assert dissenters' rights as to less than all of the shares registered in his name only if he dissents with respect to all the shares beneficially owned by any one person, and discloses the name and address of the person or persons on whose behalf he dissents. In that event, his rights shall be determined as if the shares as to which he has dissented and his other shares were registered in the names of different shareholders.

(2) A beneficial owner of shares who is not the record holder may assert dissenters' rights with respect to shares held on his behalf, and shall be treated as a dissenting shareholder under the terms of this section and section 31 if he submits to the corporation at the time of or before the assertion of these rights a written consent of the record holder.

(c) The right to obtain payment under this section shall not apply to the shareholders of the surviving corporation in a merger if a vote of the shareholders of such corporation is not necessary to authorize such merger.

(d) A shareholder of a corporation who has a right under this section to obtain payment for his shares shall have no right at law or in equity to attack the validity of the corporate action that gives rise to his right to obtain payment, nor to have the action set aside or rescinded, except when the corporate action is unlawful or fraudulent with regard to the complaining shareholder or to the corporation.

Section 81. PROCEDURES FOR PROTECTION OF DISSENTERS' RIGHTS

(a) As used in this section:

(1) "Dissenter" means a shareholder or beneficial owner who is entitled to and does assert dissenters' rights under section 80, and who has performed every act required up to the time involved for the assertion of such rights.

(2) "Corporation" means the issuer of the shares held by the dissenter before the corporate action, or the successor by merger or consolidation of that issuer.

(3) "Fair value" of shares means their value immediately before the effectuation of the corporate action to which the dissenter objects, excluding any appreciation or depreciation in anticipation of such corporate action unless such exclusion would be inequitable.

(4) "Interest" means interest from the effective date of the corporate action until the date of payment, at the average rate currently paid by the corporation on its principal bank loans, or, if none, at such rate as is fair and equitable under all the circumstances.

(b) If a proposed corporate action which would give rise to dissenters' rights under section 80(a) is submitted to a vote at a meeting of shareholders, the notice of a meeting shall notify all shareholders that they have or may have a right to dissent and obtain payment for their shares by complying with the terms of this section, and shall be accompanied by a copy of sections 80 and 81 of this Act.

(c) If the proposed corporate action is submitted to a vote at a meeting of shareholders, any shareholder who wishes to dissent and obtain payment for his shares must file with the corporation, prior to the vote, a written notice of intention to demand that he be paid fair compensation for his shares if the proposed action is effectuated, and shall refrain from voting his shares in approval of such action. A shareholder who fails in either respect shall acquire no right to payment for his shares under this section or section 80.

(d) If the proposed corporate action is approved by the

required vote at a meeting of shareholders, the corporation shall mail a further notice to all shareholders who gave due notice of intention to demand payment and who refrained from voting in favor of the proposed action. If the proposed corporate action is to be taken without a vote of shareholders, the corporation shall send to all shareholders who are entitled to dissent and demand payment for their shares a notice of the adoption of the plan of corporate action. The notice shall (1) state where and when a demand for payment must be sent and certificates of certificated shares must be deposited in order to obtain payment, (2) inform holders of uncertificated shares to what extent transfer of shares will be restricted from the time that demand for payment is received, (3) supply a form for demanding payment which includes a request for certification of the date on which the shareholder, or the person on whose behalf the shareholder dissents, acquired beneficial ownership of the shares, and (4) be accompanied by a copy of sections 80 and 81 of this Act. The time set for the demand and deposit shall be not less than 30 days from the mailing of the notice.

(e) A shareholder who fails to demand payment, or fails (in the case of certificated shares) to deposit certificates, as required by a notice pursuant to subsection (D) shall have no right under this section or section 80 to receive payment for his shares. If the shares are not represented by certificates, the corporation may restrict their transfer from the time of receipt of demand for payment until effectuation of the proposed corporate action, or the release of restrictions under the terms of subsection (F). The dissenter shall retain all other rights of a shareholder until these rights are modified by effectuation of the proposed corporate action.

(f) (1) Within 60 days after the date set for demanding payment and depositing certificates, if the corporation has not effectuated the proposed corporate action and remitted payment for shares pursuant to paragraph (3), it shall return any certificates that have been deposited, and release uncertificated shares from any transfer restrictions imposed by reason of the demand for payment.

(2) When uncertificated shares have been released from transfer restrictions, and deposited certificates have been returned, the corporation may at any later time send a new notice conforming to the requirements of subsection (D), with like effect.

(3) Immediately upon effectuation of the proposed corporate action, or upon receipt of demand for payment if the corporate action has already been effectuated, the corporation shall remit to dissenters who have made demand and (if their shares are certificated) have deposited their certificates the amount which the corporation estimates to be the fair value of the shares, with interest if any has accrued. The remittance shall be accompanied by:

(i) The corporation's closing balance sheet and statement of income for a fiscal year ending not more than 16 months before the date of remittance, together with the latest available interim financial statements;

(ii) a statement of the corporation's estimate of fair value of the shares; and

(iii) a notice of the dissenter's right to demand supplemental payment, accompanied by a copy of sections 80 and 81 of this Act.

(g) (1) If the corporation fails to remit as required by subsection (f), or if the dissenter believes that the amount remitted is less than the fair value of his shares, or that the interest is not correctly determined, he may send the corporation his own estimate of the value of the shares or of the interest, and demand payment of the deficiency.

(2) If the dissenter does not file such an estimate within 30 days after the corporation's mailing of its remittance, he shall be entitled to no more than the amount remitted.

(h) (1) Within 60 days after receiving a demand for payment pursuant to subsection (G), if any such demands for payment remain unsettled, the corporation shall file in an appropriate court a petition requesting that the fair value of the shares and interest thereon be determined by the court.

(2) An appropriate court shall be a court of competent jurisdiction in the county of this state where the registered office of the corporation is located. If, in the case of a merger or consolidation or exchange of shares, the corporation is a foreign corporation without a registered office in this state, the petition shall be filed in the county where the registered office of the domestic corporation was last located.

(3) All dissenters, wherever residing, whose demands have not been settled shall be made parties to the proceeding as in an action against their shares. A copy of the petition shall be served on each such dissenter; if a dissenter is a nonresident, the copy may be served on him by registered or certified mail or by publication as provided by law.

(4) The jurisdiction of the court shall be plenary and exclusive. The court may appoint one or more persons as appraisers to receive evidence and recommend a decision on the question of fair value. The appraisers shall have such power and authority as shall be specified in the order of their appointment or in any amendment thereof. The dissenters shall be entitled to discovery in the same manner as parties in other civil suits.

(5) All dissenters who are made parties shall be entitled to judgment for the amount by which the fair value of their shares is found to exceed the amount previously remitted, with interest.

(6) If the corporation fails to file a petition as provided in paragraph (1) of this subsection, each dissenter who made a demand and who has not already settled his claim against the corporation shall be paid by the corporation the amount demanded by him, with interest, and may sue therefor in an appropriate court.

(i) (1) The costs and expenses of any proceeding under subsection (H), including the reasonable compensation and expenses of appraisers appointed by the court, shall be determined by the court and assessed against the corporation, except that any part of the costs and expenses may be apportioned and assessed as the court may deem equitable against all or some of the dissenters who are parties and whose action in demanding supplemental payment the court finds to be arbitrary, vexatious, or not in good faith.

(2) Fees and expenses of counsel and of experts for the respective parties may be assessed as the court may deem equitable against the corporation and in favor of any or all dissenters if the corporation failed to comply substantially with the requirements of this section, and may be assessed against either the corporation or a dissenter, in favor of any other party, if the court finds that the party against whom the fees and expenses are assessed acted arbitrarily, vexatiously, or not in good faith in respect to the rights provided by this Section and Section 80.

(3) If the court finds that the services of counsel for any dissenter were of substantial benefit to other dissenters similarly situated, and should not be assessed against the corporation, it may award to these counsel reasonable fees to be paid out of the amounts awarded to the dissenters who were benefitted.

(j)(1) Notwithstanding the foregoing provisions of this section, the corporation may elect to withhold the remittance required by subsection (F) from any dissenter with respect to shares of which the dissenter (or the person on whose behalf the dissenter acts) was not the beneficial owner on the date of the first announcement to news media or to shareholders of the terms of the proposed corporate action. With respect to such shares, the corporation shall, upon effectuating the corporate action, state to each dissenter its estimate of the fair value of the shares, state the rate of interest to be used (explaining the basis thereof), and offer to pay the resulting amounts on receiving the dissenters' agreement to accept them in full satisfaction.

(2) If the dissenter believes that the amount offered is less than the fair value of the shares and interest determined according to this section, he may within 30 days after the date of mailing of the corporation's offer, mail the corporation his own estimate of fair value and interest, and demand their payment. If the dissenter fails to do so, he shall be entitled to no more than the corporation's offer.

(3) If the dissenter makes a demand as provided in paragraph (2), the provisions of subsections (H) and (I) shall apply to further proceedings on the dissenter's demand.

Section 83. VOLUNTARY DISSOLUTION BY CONSENT OF SHAREHOLDERS

A corporation may be voluntarily dissolved by the written consent of all of its shareholders.

Upon the execution of such written consent, a statement of intent to dissolve shall be executed in duplicate by the corporation by its president or a vice president and by its secretary or an assistant secretary, and verified by one of the officers signing such statement, which statement shall set forth:

(a) The name of the corporation.

(b) The names and respective addresses of its officers.

(c) The names and respective addresses of its directors.

(d) A copy of the written consent signed by all shareholders of the corporation.

(e) A statement that such written consent has been signed by all shareholders of the corporation or signed in their names by their attorneys thereunto duly authorized.

Section 106. ADMISSION OF FOREIGN CORPORATION

No foreign corporation shall have the right to transact business in this State until it shall have procured a certificate of authority so to do from the Secretary of State. No foreign corporation shall be entitled to procure a certificate of authority under this Act to transact in this State any business which a corporation organized under this Act is not permitted to transact. A foreign corporation shall not be denied a certificate of authority by reason of the fact that the laws of the state or country under which such corporation is organized governing its organization and internal affairs differ from the laws of this State, and nothing in this Act contained shall be construed to authorize this State to regulate the organization or the internal affairs of such corporation.

Without excluding other activities which may not constitute transacting business in this State, a foreign corporation shall not be considered to be transacting business in this State, for the purposes of this Act, by reason of carrying on in this State any one or more of the following activities:

(a) Maintaining or defending any action or suit or any administrative or arbitration proceeding, or effecting the settlement thereof or the settlement of claims or disputes.

(b) Holding meetings of its directors or shareholders or carrying on other activities concerning its internal affairs.

(c) Maintaining bank accounts.

(d) Maintaining offices or agencies for the transfer, exchange and registration of its securities, or appointing and maintaining trustees or depositaries with relation to its securities.

(e) Effecting sales through independent contractors.

(f) Soliciting or procuring orders, whether by mail or through employees or agents or otherwise, where such orders require acceptance without this State before becoming binding contracts.

(g) Creating as borrower or lender, or acquiring, indebtedness or mortgages or other security interests in real or personal property.

(h) Securing or collecting debts or enforcing any rights in property securing the same.

(i) Transacting any business in interstate commerce.

(j) Conducting an isolated transaction completed within a period of thirty days and not in the course of a number of repeated transactions of like nature.

Section 107. POWERS OF FOREIGN CORPORATION

A foreign corporation which shall have received a certificate of authority under this Act shall, until a certificate of revocation or of withdrawal shall have been issued as provided in this Act, enjoy the same, but no greater, rights and privileges as a domestic corporation organized for the purposes set forth in the application pursuant to which such certificate of authority is issued; and, except as in this Act otherwise provided, shall be subject to the same duties, restrictions, penalties and liabilities now or hereafter imposed upon a domestic corporation of like character.

Section 108. CORPORATE NAME OF FOREIGN CORPORATION

No certificate of authority shall be issued to a foreign corporation unless the corporate name of such corporation:

(a) Shall contain the word "corporation," "company," "incorporated," or "limited," or shall contain an abbreviation of one of such words, or such corporation shall, for use in this State, add at the end of its name one of such words or an abbreviation thereof.

(b) Shall not contain any word or phrase which indicates or implies that it is organized for any purpose other than one or more of the purposes contained in its articles of incorporation or that it is authorized or empowered to conduct the business of banking or insurance.

(c) Shall not be the same as, or deceptively similar to, the name of any domestic corporation existing under the laws of this State or any foreign corporation authorized to transact business in this State, or a name the exclusive right to which is, at the time, reserved in the manner provided in this Act, or the name of a corporation which has in effect a registration of its name as provided in this Act except that this provision shall not apply if the foreign corporation applying for a certificate of authority files with the Secretary of State any one of the following:

(1) a resolution of its board of directors adopting a fictitious name for use in transacting business in this State which fictitious name is not deceptively similar to the name of any domestic corporation or of any foreign corporation authorized to transact business in this State or to any name reserved or registered as provided in this Act, or

(2) the written consent of such other corporation or holder of a reserved or registered name to use the same or deceptively similar name and one or more words are added to make such name distinguishable from such other name, or

(3) a certified copy of a final decree of a court of competent jurisdiction establishing the prior right of such foreign corporation to the use of such name in this State.

Section 115. SERVICE OF PROCESS ON FOREIGN CORPORATION

The registered agent so appointed by a foreign corporation authorized to transact business in this State shall be an agent of such corporation upon whom any process, notice or demand required or permitted by law to be served upon the corporation may be served.

Whenever a foreign corporation authorized to transact business in this State shall fail to appoint or maintain a registered agent in this State, or whenever any such registered agent cannot with reasonable diligence be found at the registered office, or whenever the certificate of authority of a foreign corporation shall be suspended or revoked, then the Secretary of State shall be an agent of such corporation upon whom any such process, notice, or demand may be served. Service on the Secretary of State of any such process, notice or demand shall be made by delivering to and leaving with him, or with any clerk having charge of the corporation department of his office, duplicate copies of such process, notice or demand. In the event any such process, notice or demand is served on the Secretary of State, he shall immediately cause one of such copies thereof to be forwarded by registered mail, addressed to the corporation at its principal office in the state or country under the laws of which it is incorporated. Any service so had on the Secretary of State shall returnable in not less than thirty days.

The Secretary of State shall keep a record of all processes, notices and demands served upon him under this section, and shall record therein the time of such service and his action with reference thereto.

Nothing herein contained shall limit or affect the right to serve any process, notice or demand, required or permitted by law to be served upon a foreign corporation in any other manner now or hereafter permitted by law.

Section 125. ANNUAL REPORT OF DOMESTIC AND FOREIGN CORPORATIONS

Each domestic corporation, and each foreign corporation authorized to transact business in this State, shall file, within the time prescribed by this Act, an annual report setting forth:

(a) Th name of the corporation and the state or country under ıe laws of which it is incorporated.

(b) The address of the registered office of the corporation in this State, and the name of its registered agent in this State at such address, and, in case of a foreign corporation, the address of its principal office in the state or country under the laws of which it is incorporated.

(c) A brief statement of the character of the business in which the corporation is actually engaged in this State.

(d) The names and respective addresses of the directors and officers of the corporation.

(e) A statement of the aggregate number of shares which the corporation has authority to issue, itemized by class and series, if any, within each class.

(f) A statement of the aggregate number of issued shares, itemized by class and series, if any, within each class.

(g) A statement, expressed in dollars, of the value of all the property owned by the corporation, wherever located, and the value of the property of the corporation located within this State, and a statement, expressed in dollars, of the gross amount of business transacted by the corporation for the twelve months ended on the thirty-first day of December preceding the date herein provided for the filing of such report and the gross amount thereof transacted by the corporation at or from places of business in this State. If, on the thirty-first day of December preceding the time herein provided for the filing of such report, the corporation had not been in existence for a period of twelve months, or in the case of a foreign corporation had not been authorized to transact business in this State for a period of twelve months, the statement with respect to business transacted shall be furnished for the period between the date of incorporation or the date of its authorization to transact business in this State, as the case may be, and such thirty-first day of December. If all the property of the corporation is located in this State and all of its business is transacted at or from places of business in this State, then the information required by this subparagraph need not be set forth in such report.

(h) Such additional information as may be necessary or appropriate in order to enable the Secretary of State to determine and assess the proper amount of franchise taxes payable by such corporation.

Such annual report shall be made on forms prescribed and furnished by the Secretary of State, and the information therein contained shall be given as of the date of the execution of the report, except as to the information required by subparagraphs (G) and (H) which shall be given as of the close of business on the thirty-first day of December next preceding the date herein provided for the filing of such report. It shall be executed by the corporation by its president, a vice president, secretary, an assistant secretary, or treasurer, and verified by the officer executing the report, or, if the corporation is in the hands of a receiver or trustee, it shall be executed on behalf of the corporation and verified by such receiver or trustee.

Section 126. FILING OF ANNUAL REPORT OF DOMESTIC AND FOREIGN CORPORATIONS

Such annual report of a domestic or foreign corporation shall be delivered to the Secretary of State between the first day of January and the first day of March of each year, except that the first annual report of a domestic or foreign corporation shall be filed between the first day of January and the first day of March of the year next succeeding the calendar year in which its certificate of incorporation or its certificate of authority, as the case may be, was issued by the Secretary of State. Proof to the satisfaction of the Secretary of State that prior to the first day of March such report was deposited in the United States mail in a sealed envelope, properly addressed, with postage prepaid, shall be deemed a compliance with this requirement. If the Secretary of State finds that such report conforms to the requirements of this Act, he shall file the same. If he finds that it does not so conform, he shall promptly return the same to the corporation for any necessary corrections, in which event the penalties hereinafter prescribed for failure to file such report within the time hereinabove provided shall not apply, if such report is corrected to conform to the requirements of this Act and returned to the Secretary of State within thirty days from the date on which it was mailed to the corporation by the Secretary of State.

Glossary

Abandoned property Property intentionally left
Abuse of process Misuse of criminal or civil proceedings against another
Acceleration clauses Clauses in loan agreements that make the full amount of the loan due in the event of default, transfer etc.
Acceptance Unconditional assent to all terms of the offer which results in contract between offeror and offeree
Accession Process of improving personal property or changing its character; gives the party who does the changing or improvement title
Accommodation party Party who signs his/her name to a document to enable transfer
Accord and satisfaction Agreement to pay debt and full payment according to that agreement
Account party In a letter of credit the person who pays a bank to extend credit or pay money to a third person called the account party
Accountant-client privilege Communications privilege between accountant and client that protects from judicial disclosure
Actual notice Notice in fact; personal notice
Adjudication Hearing before an administrative law judge
Administrative Procedure Act Statute which sets out rules on how federal administrative agencies are supposed to operate
Administrative agency A nonlegislative, nonjudicial lawmaker
Administrative law All law governing administrative agencies
Administrative searches Searches by agencies to see if laws are being violated
Administrator/Administratrix Person in charge of a probate where there is no will
Adverse possession Means of acquiring title to real property by use of another's land without right or permission
Advisory opinion An FTC opinion on proposed business conduct and whether there would be a Section 5 violation
Aesthetic control Zoning that controls public appearance; e.g., billboard regulations
After-acquired property clause Clause in security agreement or mortgage that gives creditor rights in future property
Agency law Law governing employer-employee relations
Agent Principal's employee who has authority to enter into contracts on principal's behalf
Air rights Right of landowners in the air above their properties
Allowable claim Amount of a bankruptcy claim for which the debtor has no defense
Alter ego Legal doctrine that allows courts to pierce the corporate veil and impose liability when a corporation is not operated as a separate entity
Answer Formal written response of a defendant in a lawsuit
Anticipatory repudiation A breach in advance of the date performance is due
Antimerger provision Part of the Clayton Act that prohibits mergers
Antitrust Law that aims to prevent anticompetitive restraints of trade
Apparent authority Authority arising from the principal's conduct that leads a third party to believe the principal has given authority to another
Appellate courts Courts "above" the trial level in the state and federal systems
Arbitrary, capricious, and unreasonable test Test to decide if there is enough evidence to justify the agency's regulation
Arbitration Means of settling disputes that involves the decision of a third party on what should be done
Arbitrator Person who decides a dispute
Area-wide waste treatment programs A way to deal with water pollution caused by runoff
Articles of incorporation The creation document of a corporation; sets up the board, the shares, etc.
Asset mergers Merger of two companies by one buying the other company's assets
Assignee Party who receives the contract rights from another
Assignment The transfer of benefits under a contract to a third party who was not involved originally in the contract
Assignor Party who assigns contract rights
Assumption of risk Plaintiff victim in a negligence case voluntarily took risk in acting as he/she did
Assurance Statement by one party to another in a contract that performance will be completed
Attorney in fact Agent with written authority in the form of a power of attorney
Audit committee Watchdog financial committee of the Board
Automatic perfection Perfection without filing
Automatic stay Order issued by bankruptcy judge to halt most legal actions against the bankrupt

Bailee Party in temporary possession of another's property

Bailment Temporary possession of the goods of another
Bailor Party who creates a bailment
Bait and switch Form of advertising prohibited by FTC that lures customers in on low-price goods and then directs them to high-price goods
Bankruptcy clauses Contract clauses that cancel the contract in the event of a bankruptcy of the debtor
Bankruptcy trustee Person who manages the day-to-day mechanics of a debtor's bankruptcy
Battle of the forms Lay term for additional terms in acceptance
Bearer paper Commercial paper with no specific payee
Beneficiary A third party who is not the promisor or promisee to a contract but will receive benefits upon the contract's performance; also a beneficiary under a will (recipient of property under a will)
Bequest Any gift of personal property at death
Bilateral contract Contract in which both parties promise to perform
Bill A proposed statute
Blackmail Use of threats to have another give up property
Blank indorsements Signature of payee on order paper; makes it bearer paper
Blue laws State laws controlling the types of businesses and transactions that can be conducted on Sundays
Breach of the peace Breaking the law in the course of repossession
Broker Real estate salesperson
Business judgment rule Standard of liability for directors; allows directors to make business judgments that are wrong but well-reasoned without having liability
Business trust Business organization where property is transferred to a trustee for management
Buy-out provision Provision in partnership agreement that allows partners to buy out a departing partner
Bylaws Rules for corporation officers and operations

CIF Cost, insurance and freight; a shipping term
COD Cash on delivery; a shipping term
Capital surplus Number of shares times the amount paid over par is the amount in this corporate account
Capital surplus distribution A form of "dividend" taken from capital surplus account
Cause of action A legal wrong
Certificate of disclosure Document required to be filed in some states that gives criminal history of those involved in the corporation
Chancery courts Equity courts
Charging order Order obtained by a creditor of an individual partner that allows creditor to get the partner's share of profits
Charitable subscription Promise to a charity or such organization to make a contribution; generally enforceable even though charity gives nothing in return
Check A draft drawn on a bank
Cite Abbreviated form of telling where a case was decided and by what court and when
Civil law Law governing rights and duties between private parties
Clayton Act Federal antitrust statute passed in 1914
Clean Air Act Federal law to control air pollution
Clean Water Act Federal law designed to promote cleaner water
Closed end Credit with a fixed repayment amount and time
Closely held corporation Privately owned corporation; created by state statute
Code of Federal Regulations Set of books containing federal regulations in effect
Codicil An addition to an existing will
Collateral Property pledged as security for a debt
Collateral promise A promise to pay another's debt; e.g. an officer agreeing to be personally liable for a corporate debt
Collection bank Any bank other than payor bank
Commerce clause Part of the U.S. Constitution that gives the federal government power over interstate commerce
Commercial impracticability Basic contractual assumptions of the parties have changed
Commercial paper Orders to pay and promises to pay; checks, drafts, notes, CDs
Commercial speech Advertising
Commission Percentage of sales price as a fee in broker/agent relationships
Commercial units Division of goods in easy to handle numbers; a box of envelopes is a commercial unit
Common carrier Public transportation provider
Common law Judge-made law
Community property Marital property rights and ownership followed in some states
Comparative negligence Defense to negligence that allows proof of who was more responsible for the injury
Compensatory damages Damages paid to put the party in the same position as if there were no breach
Computation mistakes Mistakes in figuring bids or offers
Concealment Fraud occurring by defendant's intentional non-disclosure of a material fact
Concurrent jurisdiction Two or more courts with the power to deal with the same case
Condition precedent Condition that must happen before there is an obligation of performance
Condominiums Type of real property interest that gives owner the right to the space between four walls
Confidential relationship Requirement for undue influence; relationship of trust and dependency e.g. attorney/client; child/elderly parent
Confusion Process of commingling fungible personal property so that individual's portions are no longer known
Conglomerate mergers Mergers between corporations in different businesses
Consequential damages Damages with third parties as a result of a breach; e.g. late penalties on construction contracts
Consideration Voluntary giving up of a known right that

is bargained for in exchange for another's consideration
Consignment Delivering possession of goods to another for the purpose of using them as an agent to sell the goods
Constitution Basic outline for a legal and political system; tells who has the power to make, interpret and enforce laws
Constructive eviction Doctrine that permits tenant to leave rental property that is uninhabitable
Constructive notice Notice in a newspaper, trade journal or public filing
Consumer Leasing Act Federal statute regulating the disclosures in the lease of consumer goods
Consumer reporting agency Credit evaluation service that does reports on those applying for consumer credit
Contract An agreement between competent parties that is enforceable in court
Contract for deed A security arrangement in which the seller holds title to the property until the buyer repays the purchase amount
Contributory negligence Plaintiff victim's negligence that contributes to his/her loss
Conversion Unauthorized, unjustified interference with the dominion and control of another's personal property
Cooling-off period FTC regulation that allows those who sign contracts in their homes three days to change their minds and rescind
Copyrights Federal protection for writings, photographs, painting
Corporate opportunity doctrine Rule that prevents directors from profiting from an opportunity that should have gone to the corporation
Corporation A fictional person (entity) owned by a group of shareholders
Corporation not for profit a corporation organized for governmental or charitable purposes
Corpus Trust property
Corrective advertising Advertising required to correct mistaken consumer beliefs about a product
Correspondent bank In letters of credit, a bank in another city that will issue or honor letters of credit for a bank in another city
Counteroffer An offer with different terms back to the original offeror; ends the original offer
Course of dealing Two contracting parties' previous methods of doing business
Court of original jurisdiction Court where a case can start
Covenants Obligations in a contract
Cover Buyer's remedy of buying substitute goods
Creditor beneficiary Third party entitled to collect from the promisor or promisee in a contract
Creditor's claim Amount bankrupt owes creditor before bankruptcy
Creditors' meeting First of several meetings where the creditors ask questions of the debtor about the amount and location of property
Crime Mens rea (guilty mind) plus actus reus (prohibited act)
Criminal conspiracy Agreement to do an illegal act
Criminal law Law designed to protect society
Cumulative preferred shares Type of stock entitled to a dividend every year; if not paid one year amount carries over
Cumulative voting Process used to elect directors to give minority shareholders representation—each shareholder gets his/her number of shares X the number of directors to be elected as a vote

De facto corporation A corporation formed in good faith compliance with statutes that is missing some legal step or paperwork
De jure corporation A corporation properly formed under the law
Decertification election Election to determine whether employees still want a union to represent them
Deed Document used to transfer title to real property
Deed of trust A three-party financing arrangement whereby third party holds title to pledged property until borrower repays the lender
Defamation Statement by one person about another that holds the person spoken about up to ridicule, contempt or scorn
Default judgment Judgment awarded to plaintiff when the defendant fails to answer the complaint filed within proper time periods
Deficiency action Suit brought by creditor after foreclosure or repossession to obtain any amount the sale of the property did not bring but is still part of the debt
Del credere agent Agent who sells goods on credit and guarantees the buyer's credit
Delegant Party who delegates contract duties
Delegate Party who undertakes contract duties
Delegation Transfer of the responsibilities under a contract to a third party not originally involved in the contract
Depositary bank First bank to which check is taken for collection
Derivative action Suit by a shareholder on behalf of the corporation
Detriment A form of consideration; value or forebearance
Devise Gift of real property by will
Direct emission standards A method of air pollution control that limits stationary pollution (building emissions)
Directed verdict Verdict by judge given when one side has not met its burden of proof
Disaffirm Renounce a contract one has no obligation to perform
Discharge A release from debt given to a bankrupt once the bankruptcy has been completed
Disclaimer Removing warranty liability
Dishonor Primary party's refusal to honor negotiable instrument
Dissenting shareholder One who objects to a merger or consolidation and is paid fair value for his/her shares
Dissolution Any change in partnership membership

Divestiture Forcing sale of part of a business to eliminate an antitrust violation
Dividends Shareholders' return on their investment in a corporation
Domestic corporation A corporation organized under the laws of the state one is in
Domestic relations court Court handling family law
Dominant tenement Owner of an easement
Donee beneficiary A beneficiary in a life insurance policy
Draft A three party instrument where the parties agree to pay certain sums other than through a bank
Draw A salary or advance of profits to a partner
Drawee The bank in a check; the buyer in a draft
Drawer The signer of the check; the person whose account the check is drawn on
Due process Idea that people are owed a fair procedure in civil and criminal legal issues
Due-on-sale clauses Clauses in loans that permit lenders to demand full payment if the borrower sells or transfers the land pledged as security for the loan
Duress Wrongful force used to obtain a contract
Duty of care Level of care owed by one party to another
Duty to account Duty agent owes to principal to keep track of income and expenses

Earned surplus MBCA term for retained earnings
Easement The right to use another's property or restrict the use of another's property
Election bar rule Rule that prohibits a union election at a particular employer's business more than once each year
Electronic funds transfer Computerized methods for transferring funds without the usual commercial paper—e.g: automatic tellers; automatic bill paying services
Emancipation State of a minor in which he/she is responsible for his support and works to provide that support.
Embezzlement Fraudulent conversion of another's property by someone who lawfully possesses it
Eminent domain The taking of private land by a governmental entity for a public purpose
Emission standards Limits on discharges of impurities into the air
Employee Retirement Income Security Act (ERISA) Federal statute that regulates employee pension plans
Employment at will Employment arrangement where employee or employer can end relationship at any time
Enabling statute Law by which legislature gives administrative agency the power to make regulations
Endorsements Honest belief, opinion or experience of someone other than the sponsoring advertiser
Endowment insurance Life insurance with a heavy investment element which is paid for over a period of time
English Rule Rule of priority for successive assignments
Enumerated powers Lawmaking powers listed in the U.S. Constitution
Environmental impact statements (EIS) Documents prepared by federal agencies telling the environmental impact of action about to be taken by the agency
Equal Credit Opportunity Act (ECOA) Federal law that prohibits discrimination in the credit decision
Equal Pay Act of 1963 Federal statute making it illegal to pay different wages based on sex to men and women doing the same jobs
Equal protection Constitutional idea that the law should not discriminate between or among people
Equity courts Courts where judge is a chancellor who uses fairness ideas to decide cases
Escrow Process of formally transferring title of property to buyer and funds to seller
Ethics Moral principles; values
Excited utterances Apparent offer which is not legally an offer because it was made while the offeror was excited
Exclusive dealing Marketing arrangment where a seller requires a buyer to deal only in the seller's line of products
Exculpatory clauses "Hold harmless" clauses; clauses that attempt to relieve a party of liability for negligence; generally against public policy
Executive committee Committee of a board of directors that takes care of day-to-day business so that the number of board meetings is reduced
Executor/Executrix Person in charge of a probate in which there is a will
Executory A contract that has been entered into but not yet performed
Exempt property Property that cannot be seized by a judgment creditor
Exemptions Categories of securities not required to be formally registered with the SEC
Exhaustion doctrine Idea that a person must go through "agency channels" before asking a court to correct an agency wrong
Express authority Oral or written authority given by principal or master
Express contracts Contracts either orally stated or written
Express warranty Warranty given in writing or stated
Expropriation A foreign government's seizing another government's or private business' property
External accountants Accountants who are independent contractors who only periodically check the work of a firm's accountants
Extortion Blackmail
Extraordinary corporate transactions Mergers, consolidations, articles amendments, dissolution

FAS Free along side; a shipping term
FOB Free on board; a shipping term
FTC holder in due course rule Rule that eliminates holder in due course status in consumer credit transactions
Failing company defense Defense to a Clayton Act merger charge; acquisition of a failing company does not affect competition
Fair Credit Billing Act Federal statute that requires certain disclosures on monthly credit card bills
Fair Credit Reporting Act (FCRA) Federal law that regulates the use of credit information
Fair Debt Collections Practices Act (FDCPA) Federal statute that regulates the type of collection tactics collection agencies can use

Fair Labor Standards Act (FLSA) Federal minimum wage statute
False imprisonment Tort of unlawful detainment of another
False pretenses Crime of defrauding another of property
Federal Consumer Product Warranty Law Federal statute on warranty disclosures and coverage
Federal Privacy Act Federal law regulating the disclosure of information about private persons to third parties
Federal Register Newspaper-like publication containing proposed and promulgated regulations plus other agency announcements
Federal Register System System that organizes federal administrative law
Federal Tort Claims Act Federal statute allowing those injured by federal agents' tort to recover from the federal government
Federal Trade Commission (FTC) Federal agency charged with preserving competition and protecting consumers
Federal district court The trial court of the federal system
Federalism Dual sovereigns; government of a country divided so that the national government is supreme in some areas and states are supreme in others
Fee simple Full title to real property; can transfer, pledge and will the property
Fellow servant rule Rule that employers are not liable for employees' injuries or illness caused by acts of other employees
Felony Serious crime with greater penalties
Fictitious payee Scheme for embezzlement where payroll checks are made out to non-existent employees
Fiduciary A person in a position of responsibility and trust
Financing statement Document signed by debtor and filed by creditor to obtain perfection
First Amendment First amendment to U.S. Constitution that preserves freedom of speech, press, religion and assembly
Floating lien An after acquired clause in a security interest for inventory that allows the interest to continue even though the inventory is turned over
Forcible detainer Equitable action to have tenant ordered to move for non-payment of rent
Foreclosure Judicial process of repossessing and selling land that has been pledged as security for repayment of a debt
Foreign Corrupt Practices Act (FCPA) Federal statute regulating bribes to foreign governments
Forgery Crime of signing another's name to obtain money or property
Formal rulemaking Making regulation "on the record"
Four Horseman Rule Rule of priority for successive assignments
Fraud Intentional as opposed to negligent or accidental misrepresentation
Fraud in factum Deceiving as to the nature of the document being signed
Freedom of Information Act Federal law governing how a person can get information from federal agencies
Friendly fires Fires that are wanted and intended
Frustration Purpose for entering into a contract no longer exists
Fungible goods Goods indistinguishable when together; e.g.—oil, grain, canned goods

Garnishment Taking of funds to pay a judgment
Gifts causa mortis Gifts in contemplation of death
Good faith Performance obligation; good intentions and no knowledge of problems
Government Manual Book of organization of the federal government
Government in the Sunshine Act Federal law requiring that meetings of top agency officials be open to the public
Governmental corporation A corporation organized to perform a governmental function
Grace period Period that lets an insured pay premiums late; often 30 days after premium is due
Gratuitous agency Agency in which agent is not paid
Gratuitous bailment Bailment for the sole benefit of the bailor
Group boycotts Per se antitrust violation where several competitors refuse to deal with certain person (price cutters)

Hazardous waste control programs Ways to control hazardous waste
Heirs Those who inherit property from decedents
Holder Someone in possession of an instrument that is to his order or is endorsed in blank
Holder in due course A good faith purchaser of negotiable instrument for value
Holographic will A will in the handwriting of the testator
Homestead exemption Residence of a judgment debtor that cannot be taken by judgment creditor
Horizontal market division Competitor agreement to divide up their market
Horizontal mergers Mergers between competitors
Horizontal price fixing Price fixing by competitors
Hostile fires Fires that are unwanted or unattended
Howey test Supreme court definition of a security; see security
Hybrid rulemaking A type of rulemaking that is a cross between formal and informal rulemaking

Identification When goods are shipped, marked or otherwise designated for the buyer; time when buyer has an insurable interest in the goods purchased from the seller
Illusory promise A promise that does not relinguish any rights at present; sole discretion of promisor as to whether there will be a relinqishment
Implied authority Authority not stated but reasonably implied by custom, nature of the job, etc.
Implied contracts Contracts which arise from the facts or circumstances even though nothing is said
Implied warranty of fitness for a particular purpose Warranty given to a buyer that goods will meet buyer's needs
Implied warranty of merchantability Warranty of average quality given in all sales of goods by merchants
Impossibility Objective inability to perform a contract
Imposter One who poses as another to obtain benefits under a negotiable instrument
In pari delicto Both arc equally guilty

In personam jurisdiction Power of a court over people
Incidental damages Nonbreaching parties costs to recover from breach
Incontestability clause Provisions in life insurance contracts that limit the time to raise defenses such as fraud
Incorporators Those who complete the paperwork for a corporation and sign the articles of incorporation
Independent contractor Employee who has the right to control means but not end or object of employer's assigned job
Indorsement Signature of a payee on a negotiable instrument
Informal rulemaking Rulemaking by Federal Register notice where there is no public hearing
Innocent misrepresentation Misrepresentation of a material fact where there is no knowledge or intent to misrepresent
Inspection Right of buyer under UCC to check goods before accepting them
Installment contract A contract for deed; seller retains title to land until buyer pays full purchase price
Insurable interest Interest that can be insured; some interest in the property or person
Insurance Contract that shifts a pre-existing risk in the future from the insured to an insurer in exchange for money (premium)
Insured Person who buys and owns an insurance policy
Insurer The institute issuing an insurance policy
Intangibles Personal property evidenced by documents: stocks; patents; etc.
Intentional infliction of emotional distress Intentional injury of another through bizarre or outrageous conduct
Intentional torts Breaches of noncontractual duties; some intent to do act although not necessarily the intent to do harm
Interbrand competition Competition between competing brands
Interlocking directorates Same director(s) of firms where one has a net worth of at least $1,000,000 and they are competitors
Intermediary bank Any bank other than depositary and payor
Internal bank accountants Accountants who are full-time employees for their employer
Interpretive regulations Regulations without the force and effect of law
Interstate Land Sales Full Disclosure Act A federal law that regulates the sale of unimproved lots
Intervivos gift Gift while the donor is alive
Intrabrand competition Competition among those who sell the same product
Invasion of privacy Public disclosure of private facts; intrusion on another's solitude; unauthorized appropriation of name or likeness
Involuntary bankruptcy Bankruptcy started by a debtor's creditors filing of a petition

JP Court Justice of the peace court; a low level court
Joint and several liability Liability is as a group of partners but each partner is also individually liable
Joint liability Liability of partners on partnership contracts
Joint tenancy Co-ownership of land where co-owners hold equal shares and survivors retain title
Judgment Court decree that the defendant is or is not liable to the plaintiff
Judgment creditor Winner in a lawsuit
Judgment debtor Loser in lawsuit who owes money
Judgment notwithstanding the verdict (NOV) Judgment of a court entered after the jury verdict by the judge

Laissez-faire An economic theory that believes in little regulation of business
Landrum-Griffin Amendment Federal statute regulating internal affairs of the union
Lawyers Professionals who represent others in legal matters
Leasehold interests A temporary interest in real property; a lease
Legacy Gift of money at death
Letter of credit Bank's promise to pay a definite amount of money to a third party
Libel Written defamation
Liens Statutory rights in property given to creditors
Life estate A land interest good for the life of the grantee
Limited partnership Form of partnership where general partners have unlimited liability and limited partners have liability only to the extent of their investment
Limited pay life insurance Life insurance lasting for a person's entire life but which is paid for over a limited number of years
Liquidated damages Damages agreed to in the contract in advance of any breach
Listing agreement Contract used to hire a real estate agent or broker
Lockouts Employer economic weapon in bargaining process wherein employer locks up its plant and refuses to let workers in
Long arm statutes Statutes that let one state's courts get in personam jurisdiction over non-residents of the state
Lost profits Form of UCC damages that allows seller to collect profit that would have been made on sale if buyer had not breached
Lost property Property unintentionally left behind

MBCA Model Business Corporation Act; model act patterned after Delaware's law that has been adopted in about one-third of the states. Contains general provisions governing all areas of corporations
Magnuson-Moss Warranty Law The Federal Consumer Product Warranty Law
Mail fraud Federal felony of fraud through the use of the mails
Mailbox rule Timing of acceptance rule
Maker The borrower who signs the promissory note
Manifest system System that keeps track of hazardous wastes under RCRA

Market price What a willing buyer would pay a willing seller; standard for recovery of damages under UCC
Marketable title A title free of defects
Marshaling of assets Doctrine that gives partnership creditors first rights in partnership property
Master Employer
Master plan Governmental entity plan for land-use restrictions; the zoning plan
Material alteration Material change in instrument by a holder
Mediation Process of settling a dispute through the use of a third party
Merchant Someone in the business of selling a particular good
Merchant's Confirmation Memorandum Under UCC 2-201, a writing confirming an oral agreement between merchants for the sale of goods for $500 or more.
Merchant's firm offer Written offer by a merchant that states it will remain open
Merchantability Goods are of average quality, properly packaged and with adequate instructions
Midnight deadline Banking deadline for processing checks—midnight of the next banking day
Miller-Tydings Act Federal law that allows vertical price fixing if states allow resale price maintenance
Minor A person below the legal contractual age—generally the age of 18 is the contract age.
Mirror image rule Rule that acceptance must be the mirror image of the offer to be valid
Misdemeanors Minor crimes
Mislaid property Property accidentally left behind
Misrepresentation Statement of fact or promise of performance that is the basis of a contract bargain and later is discovered false.
Mistake An error in the contract or facts underlying the contract
Misuse A defense to product liability because injured plaintiff was injured because of misuse of the product
Mitigate Obligation to keep damages as little as possible
Mobile sources Air pollution sources that move (cars)
Moral consideration Idea that "moral" debts should be enforceable but there is not generally consideration
Mortgage A two-party security arrangement whereby the borrower pledges real property to the lender as security for a loan
Mutual benefit bailment Bailment where both sides receive consideration
Mutual mistake Mistake by both parties to a contract

National Environmental Policy Act (NEPA) Federal law that created the Council on Environmental Quality and requires the preparation of EISs.
National Labor Relations Act (NLRA) The Wagner Act
National Pollutant Discharge Elimination System Federal permit system requiring all dischargers to have a permit
Natural law Fairness; what a person thinks is "right"
Necessaries Food, clothing and shelter; a term used to describe the types of items minors are responsible for through contract even if they disaffirm.
Negligence Conduct below the normal—accidental conduct causing injury
Negligent infliction of emotional distress A cause of action for negligently caused emotional distress
Negotiable An instrument that meets certain UCC Article III requirements; high level of transferabilty
Negotiable orders of withdrawal (NOWs) Form of commercial paper used to withdraw funds from saving accounts
New York Rule Rule of priority for successive assignments
Nimble dividends Payment of dividends after two years of earnings even though the earned surplus account figure remains negative
No-fault insurance Type of auto insurance where each car owner insures his/her own vehicle from another's negligence
Nondeterioration standards Standards for air quality in areas without pollution
Noerr doctrine Exemption to antitrust laws that permits competitors to work together to petition government agencies and representatives
Nolo contendre Plea in a criminal case that neither admits nor denies quilt
Nominal damages Damages paid for a breach where there was no real injury; figure is usually $1.00
Nonconforming use A prior use of land that is permitted to continue after zoning laws are put into effect
Nondischargeable debt Bankruptcy debts that remain with the debtor and for which the debtor is liable even after bankruptcy; e.g.: alimony and taxes
Novation A new agreement between two parties already bound by an existing contract
Nuisance Any activity or land use that interferes with another's use and enjoyment of property
Nuncupative An oral will; not valid in some states

Occupational Saftety and Health Act (OSHA) Federal statute with the purposes of providing a safe and healthy workplace and preserving the nation's human resources
Offer An indication of an intent to contract and on what terms
Offeree Person to whom offer is directed
Offeror Person who makes offer
Ombudspersons Employees of administrative agencies who are to make certain that the agency operates properly
Open end Credit card credit
Option A contract where the subject matter is an offer and the bargain is to hold the offer open for a certain period in exchange for consideration
Order paper Commercial paper with a specific payee
Ordinances Laws made by cities and municipalities
Organic act Statute creating an administrative agency
Organizational meeting First meeting of a newly formed corporation
Orphan's court Probate court
Output contract A promise to sell all of one's output to another
Overdraft An overdrawn account

Par value Minimum amount to be paid for shares for shareholder to avoid liability
Parker doctrine Exemption from federal antitrust laws for conduct controlled or required by a state
Parol evidence Evidence other than what is in a written contract; extrinsic evidence; outside evidence
Parsitic damage rule Rule designed to prevent recovery for mental harm unless there are also physical harms
Partially disclosed principal Agency in which third party knows principal exists but does not know identity
Partnership Association of two or more persons carrying on a business for profit
Partnership by estoppel Partnership impliedly created because a third party has relied on representations
Past consideration Relinquishment of a past right in exchange for a present promise
Patent Federal protection for a process, machine, idea
Payee Person entitled to payment of a piece of commercial paper
Payor bank Drawee
Pension Benefit Guaranty Corporation Federal corporation providing insurance for failed pension plans
Per capita Method of estate distribution; equal shares
Per se offense Antitrust violation with no defenses
Per stirpes Method of estate distribution; equal amounts dropped down lines; those of lesser degree relationship get less
Perfection Process of obtaining superior rights in secured property
Periodic tenancy A lease with no definite ending period that runs on a month-to-month basis generally
Personal defenses Defenses in contract not good against a holder in due course; e.g. mistake; misrepresentation
Personal identification number (PIN) Access number for EFT systems
Personal property Tangible and intangible movable property; e.g. cars, boats, planes, patents
Personal representative Name for both executors and administrators under the UPC
Piercing the corporation veil Setting aside the shield of limited corporate liability
Point sources Discrete discharge points where water leaves land and runs into streams, rivers, etc.
Policy An insurance contract
Policy face the maximum amount of coverage under an insurance policy
Political speech Speech which advocates or takes positions on matters of public policy
Pollutant Anything foreign to water in its natural state
Pooling Insurance concept where similar risks are grouped together to forecast future, uncertain losses
Pooling agreement Contract to vote shares a certain way
Posthumous Children conceived before but born after testator dies
Preemptive rights Right of current shareholders to first refusal of new corporate stock offerings
Preference In bankruptcy a debt that has more paid than would be legally authorized in bankruptcy
Preferred stock Type of stock with dividend priority; generally non-voting
Premanufacture notice A requirement under TOSCA that tries to control toxic chemical manufacturing with a preapproval requirement
Premium Amount an insured pays for insurance against future loss
Prescription Adverse possession term for easements
Presenter Party who presents negotiable instrument to primary party for payment
Presenting bank Bank that presents instrument to drawee for payment
Presentment Process of asking primary party for payment of negotiable instrument
Pretermitted children Children born after a testator makes a will
Pretreat Treatment of sewage before put into the public sewers
Primary line injury Type of injury under Robinson-Patman price discrimination statute
Primary market Security issued and sold for the first time
Primary party Party with first liability on a negotiable instruments: makers and drawees
Principal Person who employs agents
Priorities Rules of who goes first in collecting from debtors
Privilege A defense to defamation that allows exceptions for freedom of expression
Privity Direct contractual relationship; some rules of liability require privity
Pro rata clauses Clauses in fire insurance policies that allocate a loss among several insurers
Pro se Latin "through oneself"; acting as one's own lawyer
Probate Legal proceedings required to distribute the estate of a decedent
Probate court Court handling wills and estates matters
Procedural due process Notice and fair hearing
Procedural law Laws governing legal administration
Proceeds Money from the sale of property subject to a security interest
Professional corporations Corporations whose stockholders are all members of a particular profession (lawyers; CPAs)
Profits Right to remove a substance (oil; water) from another's property
Promissory estoppel A promise that leads to another's actions or forebearance; if there is substantial action or forebearance, promise is enforceable
Promissory note A two-party instrument where one loans money and the other promises to pay back
Promoter Initiator of a corporation; party who brings ideas and financing together
Promulgate To put into effect
Prosecutor Lawyer representing society in a criminal case
Prospectus Part of the registration statement given to potential investors to inform them about the issuer and the possible success of the security
Provable claims Claims in bankruptcy entitling the claim-

holder to share in the debtor's estate
Proximate cause Close cause of an accident
Proxy Authorization to have another cast a shareholder's vote
Public Policy Body of legal thought that provides protection against grossly unfair contracts
Puffing Exaggerated statements of opinion designed to make what one is selling attractive
Punitive damages Extra damages for a particularly bad breach
Purchase money security interest (PMSI) Security interest held by creditor who loaned money for the purchase of the collateral or extended credit for the purchase of the collateral

Qualified indorsement One that limits the warranty liability of the giver
Quasi-contracts Contracts implied in law to prevent unjust enrichment
Quit claim deed Type of deed that offers no warranties; grantor conveys whatever title held but grantor does not promise actual title is held
Quorum The necessary number needed to be present at a meeting for a group to take action

Racketeer Influenced Corrupt Organizations Act (RICO) Federal statute attacking complicated criminal activity
Ratification Act of agreeing to or honoring an agreement one is not required to keep.
Rational basis test Test applied in equal protection cases
Reaffirmation of debt Debtor's promise to pay a debt discharged in bankruptcy
Real Estate Settlement Procedures Act (RESPA) Federal law that regulates the cost of disclosures of escrow
Real defenses The defenses good against a holder in due course; insolvency; fraud in factum
Real estate investment trust (REIT) Form of business organization that owns and operates real estate through a trust
Redemption period Time after foreclosure sale during which defaulting borrower can pay amount due and reclaim land sold in foreclosure
Reformation A redrafting of a contract to reflect the parties intentions or correct a mistake
Registration statement Document of disclosure filed with the SEC regarding an upcoming sale of securites
Regulation Z The Federal Reserve Board's regulations drafted with the authority given under TILA
Regulatory Flexibility Act Federal law designed to improve federal rulemaking
Reinstatement provision Clause in life insurance policy that lets insured pay missed premiums and interest to get the policy effective again
Rejection Offeree refusal of offer; UCC—refusal of delivered goods for breach
Remitting bank Payor or intermediary bank
Reorganization In bankruptcy, Chapter 11 proceeding which allows businesses to rehabilitate through rewriting stock, debt, bond contracts
Repatriation Bringing back from a foreign country income and investments made there
Replevin Right of buyer to get paid-for goods from an insolvent seller
Repossession Article IX remedy for default
Requirements contracts Contract forcing a business to buy all its requirements from a seller
Res Property of a trust
Res ipsa loquitur "The thing speaks for itself"; specialized form of negligence
Res judicata Rule that person has the right to have a civil case tried only once
Resale Seller's remedy of selling breaching buyer's goods to another
Resale price maintenance Vertical price fixing limiting amount retailers can charge
Rescission A termination of contract obligations
Resource Conservation and Recovery Act Federal law requiring records on hazardous waste and controlling amounts of garbage
Respondeat superior "Let the master answer"; doctrine that holds employers liable for the actions of employees
Restricted stock Stock that is subject to transfer restrictions
Restrictive indorsement "For Deposit Only"; a restriction on the use of the instrument
Revocation In contracts, taking back an offer; UCC performance—returning goods after use because of latent defect
Right of cure Seller's right to send substitute goods
Riparian A landowner along a stream; system of water allocation
Ripeness Idea that an administrative agency's actions may not be developed enough before court can examine them
Risk of loss Term meaning liability for loss or destruction of goods
Robinson-Patman Act Federal antitrust law passed in 1936 to amend the Clayton Act
Rule of reason A rule of federal antitrust law that determines the legality of some types of trade restraints
Rulemaking Process by which an administrative agency makes regulations
Runaway shop Employer who moves its physical location to escape a unionized work force

SEC Securities and Exchange Commission; federal agency charged with regulating securities
Sale on approval Sale in which goods are delivered for a trial period and there is no acceptance until after approval period
Sale or return Goods are shipped to retailer with option of returning them if they are not sold
Scienter Mental intent to defraud

Scope of employment Amount of authority agent or servant has been given by the principal
Secondary line injury Type of injury under Robinson-Patman price discrimination antitrust statute
Secondary market Market where securities already issued and sold are resold
Secondary party Party second in liability on a negotiable instrument: drawers and indorsers
Section 10b-5 The antifraud section of the 1934 Act
Section 11 Civil liability section of the 1933 Act for failure to disclose information or making a misstatement in the registration statement
Section 16b The short-swing profit section of the 1934 Act
Securities Act of 1933 Federal law regulating the sale of new securities
Securities Exchange Act of 1934 Federal statute regulating the securities markets
Security Investment in a common enterprise with profits to come from the efforts of others
Security agreement Written document that creates a security interest
Security deposit Tenant's deposit given to landlord to cover property damage or secure payment of rent
Security interest Interest in personal property or fixtures which secures performance or payment of an obligation
Self-help URLTA remedy that allows tenants to repair property if landlord refuses
Separation of powers Idea that one level of government should have authority split among several branches
Servant Person who does menial tasks for a master
Servient tenement Owner of land through which easement runs
Settlement options Different ways of getting proceeds under a life insurance policy
Settlor Creator of a trust; contibutor of res
Sham transactions Transactions which appear to be contracts but are not and exist only to deceive creditors or the government
Share draft Instrument used to withdraw funds from a credit union
Sherman Act Major federal antitrust statute
Slander Oral defamation
Slander per se Slander of person with regard to their profession, business, chastity, criminal conduct or horrendous disease
Social offers Invitations to "go out"; not legally enforceable
Sole proprietorship A business owned by one person
Sovereign immunity Idea that a government may not be sued for its wrongs
Special agent Agent hired to do a specific task; has no general authority
Special indorsement An indorsement making the instrument payable to a specific person or company
Special permits Exceptions to zoning area uses approved by a board or agency
Special warranty deed Warranty deed given only for the time period during which the grantor held title
Specific performance Contract remedy for the actual performance of an agreement (used instead of damages in antique and real estate cases)
State implementation plans (SIPs) Collection of state and municipal laws that together make the state's air pollution control plan
State police power Authority of state to pass statutes regulating the health, safety, morals and general welfare of the people
Stated capital Number of shares times the par value is amount in this corporation account
Statute of Frauds Generic name for statute requiring contracts to be in writing
Statute of limitations Maximum time length for bringing suit
Statutes Laws made by legislatures
Statutory agent Corporate agent entitled to receive suits and other legal notices for the corporation
Stock mergers Merger brought about by one company buying the other's stock
Stop payment order Document signed by drawer that orders drawee bank not to pay a particular check
Straight bankruptcy Chapter 7 bankruptcies where debtor turns over assets to creditors in exchange for a discharge
Strict scrutiny Test applied in equal protection cases; tougher standard than rational basis
Strict tort liability Product liability; absolute liability for defective products with few defenses
Strikes Economic weapons of unions used as leverage in bargaining power
Subchapter S corporation Type of corporation created for special tax advantages
Subject matter jurisdiction Power of a court to decide a particular type of case
Sublease Transfer by tenant to another of part of the tenant's lease
Subrogration Insurer steps into insured's shoes for claims against third persons who caused the loss once the insured has been paid
Substantial performance Performance that is not perfect or exactly according to contract terms but is for practical purposes just as good
Substantive due process Law should be fair in what it does
Substantive law Laws governing how people relate or act to one another in their daily lives
Substantive regulations Regulations enforceable as law
Subsurface rights Rights of landowners in the minerals and water below their properties
Suicide clauses Clauses put in life insurance policies that deny recovery if the insured commits suicide
Sunset laws Law designed to kill administrative agencies
Superior courts Basic trial level courts; also called circuit courts
Supplemental proceeding Court orders debtor to present property for collection of a judgment
Surety One who signs to guarantee a project, note or contract
Surrogate's court Probate court

Syndications Partnership, corporation or trust ownership of real estate

Taft-Hartley Act Federal labor statute that amended National Labor Relations Act by adding unfair labor practices by unions
Tenancy at sufferance A holdover tenant; one who has no right to remain on the landlord's property
Tenancy at will Lease of property in which either the landlord or tenant is free to end the lease at anytime
Tenancy by the entirety A joint tenancy between husband and wife
Tenancy for a period A lease for a predetermined period
Tenancy in common Form of co-ownership that permits more than one person to hold title to real property
Tenancy in partnership Form of partners' land ownership; has characteristics of a joint tenancy
Term life insurance Life insurance with no investment element; lasts for a definite time period
Termination End of partnership's winding up process
Testamentary gift Gift made by will
Testator/Testatrix Label for decedent with a will
Testimonial Ad designed to make consumers think it is the belief of someone other than the advertiser
Tied product The unneeded product in a tying arrangement
Title Ownership with full right to transfer, pledge, mortgage
Title abstract Summary of title to a piece of real property
Tort Breach of a non-contractual civil duty
Totten trust A trust that pays to the named beneficiary upon death of the settlor
Toxic Substances Control Act (TSCA) Federal law that tries to control toxic chemicals for their entire life cycle
Trade fixture A fixture used in a trade or business that is treated as personal property
Trademark A name specifically used and associated with a particular product
Treason Overthrow of government by unlawful and violent means
Treble damages Triple damages
Trustee A fiduciary who handles property for others' benefits
Truth in Lending Act (TILA) Federal statute that was the foundation of the federal regulation of credit
Tying arrangements Marketing arrangement that requires a party to buy an unwanted product to get the product needed
Tying product The desired product in a tying arrangement

U.S. Claims Court Federal court for suits involving the collection of funds from the U.S. Government
U.S. Court of Appeals Appellate court of the federal system
U.S. Supreme Court Highest federal court; located in Washington, D.C.
UCC Uniform Commercial Code; a uniform law for commercial transactions adopted in nearly all states
Ultra vires Beyond the scope of authority; applies to administrative agencies and corporations
Unconscionable A contract that is so unfair that it shocks the conscience
Undisclosed principal Agency relationship where third party does not know there is a principal involved
Undue influence Improper control over another's contractual rights
Unenforceable contract Oral contract that cannot be enforced because it was not written as required by the statute of frauds
Unfair labor practices Conduct prohibited by the NLRA to ensure fairness in the union process and election and in strikes and other economic weapons
Uniform Consumer Credit Code (UCCC) Uniform law adopted in some states that governs consumer credit transactions
Uniform Partnership Act (UPA) A "model act" enacted in nearly all states that governs partners' relations in the absence of an agreement otherwise
Uniform Probate Code (UPC) Uniform law on property distribution at death and wills adopted in some states
Uniform Residential Landlord Tenant Act (URLTA) A uniform statute on landlord/tenant relationships adopted in some of the states
Uniform Simultaneous Death Act (USDA) Uniform law that helps distribute property directly when two people who have willed to each other die at the same time
Unilateral contract Contract where offeror requests offeree to perform an act in exchange for a promise
Unilateral mistake Mistake by only one party to a contract
Usage of trade Industry custom; used to interpret UCC contracts
Usury Charging an interest rate in excess of the statutory maximum
Utilitarian ethic That greatest good for the greatest number

Valid contract Legally flawless contract
Value Something given in exchange
Variances Exceptions to zoning restrictions approved by a board or agency
Vertical mergers Mergers between companies at different levels in the distribution chain
Vertical price fixing Price fixing by those in the chain of distribution
Vesting requirements Requirements that employees have immediate property interest in their contributions to pension plans and future predetermined rights to employer's contributions
Vicarious liability Liability through another
Void contract Legal nullity; no contract at all
Voidable A contract one party has the right to disaffirm.
Voting trust Trust in which trustee has voting rights on shares placed in trust

Wagner Act Federal law that sets up the NLRB and code of unfair labor practices

Warrantless searches Searches by government officials where there is no search warrant (generally illegal)
Warranty Promise as to the quality or ability of a good
Warranty deed Deed in which grantor makes promises that the title is good
Warranty of habitability Implied promise that leased residential property is in habitable condition
Warranty of title Under the UCC, promise that seller has good title and there are no liens on the goods
Watered shares Shares for which the buyer has not paid at least par
Whole life insurance Life insurance with an investment as well as insurance element
Will Legal document transferring property after death
Winding up Process of ending a partnership by gathering property, paying debts and distributing assets
Workers' compensation A system for compensating employees sustaining job-related injuries, illness or death
Working papers Notes an accountant makes while working on books for an employer or client
Writ of execution Order obtained by creditor that requires property to be sold
Wrongful dishonor Error by primary party in refusing to pay a negotiable instrument upon presentment
Wrongful interference with business Tort of a competitor; trying to destroy another's business by attracting customers for sake of destroying
Wrongful interference with contractual relations Interference with a contract between two other parties by encouraging one to breach or not perform

Zoning Regulatory process that restricts forms of land use according to a master plan developed by a governmental entity

Index